1 MONTH OF
FREE
READING

at

www.ForgottenBooks.com

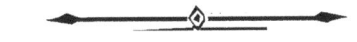

By purchasing this book you are
eligible for one month membership to
ForgottenBooks.com, giving you
unlimited access to our entire
collection of over 1,000,000 titles via
our web site and mobile apps.

To claim your free month visit:

www.forgottenbooks.com/free927680

ISBN 978-0-260-09630-2
PIBN 10927680

DOCUMENTS

OF THE

SENATE

OF THE

STATE OF NEW YORK

ONE HUNDRED AND FORTIETH SESSION

1917

VOL. XXX.—Nos. 61 TO 66, INCLUSIVE

ALBANY
J. B. LYON COMPANY, PRINTERS
1917

STATE OF NEW YORK

No. 61.

IN SENATE

APRIL 23, 1917.

Statement of Financial Condition of the Cities of the State, Prepared by Elon R. Brown, Temporary President of the Senate

To THE SENATE:

The annexed tabular statement showing the financial condition of the cities of the State has been prepared on information acquired from the Mayors and Officers of the several cities, and from the State Tax Commission. The Commission also kindly assigned Mr. Bidwell, statistician of that Department, to aid in verifying the statistics and to tabulate them.

It is believed that the information contained in the statement should have an important bearing upon legislation affecting cities as a class and separately.

ELON R. BROWN,
Temporary President.

April 20, 1917.

TABLE SHOWING ASSESSMENT VALUES, RATIOS, RATES, ETC.

CITIES	1916 assessed value of real estate	Ratio to full value at which real estate is assessed as determined by State Tax Department	Full value real estate	Ten per cent debt limit of assessed real estate	Potential debt limit if property were assessed at full value	Non-exempt indebtedness	Margin of debt incurring capacity	Potential margin of debt incurring capacity	Tax rate	Tax rate if property were assessed at full value
Albany†	$104,701,690	85	$123,178,458	$10,470,169	$12,317,846	$7,133,660	$3,336,509	$5,184,186	.0256	.0217
Amsterdam	14,315,845	50	28,631,690	1,438,584	2,863,169	1,161,850	276,734	1,701,319	.03818	.01909
Auburn	21,339,627	75	28,452,836	2,133,912	2,845,294	1,052,141	1,081,821	1,763,143	.03241	.0243
Batavia	11,454,045	83	13,800,054	1,145,404	1,380,006	530,000	615,404	850,005	.01816	.01507
Beacon	6,556,389	75	8,741,852	655,639	874,185	484,612	171,027	389,573	.02512	.01884
Binghamton†	38,980,940	70	57,115,628	3,898,094	5,771,563	2,132,536	1,765,558	3,579,027	.02967	.02076
Buffalo	376,419,650	86	437,697,267	37,641,965	43,769,727	34,871,844	2,770,121	8,897,883	.03317	.02852
Canandaigua	4,692,018	70	6,702,882	469,201	670,288	137,000	332,201	533,288	.02498	.01748
Cohoes†	12,233,558	75	16,311,410	1,223,356	1,631,141	694,854	528,502	936,287	.0296	.01695
Corning*	8,938,951	81	11,035,741	893,895	1,103,574	240,000	653,895	863,574	.027	.02187
Cortland*	8,429,527	70	12,042,181	842,952	1,204,218	447,715	395,237	756,503	.02008	.01447
Dunkirk†	9,734,180	60	16,223,633	973,418	1,622,363	457,970	515,448	1,164,393	.02851	.0171
Elmira	31,579,009	82	38,511,084	3,157,907	3,851,108	1,284,000	1,873,907	2,567,108	.02572	.02109
Fulton†	6,226,080	70	8,894,400	622,608	889,440	462,281	160,327	427,159	.03442	.024
Geneva	9,477,666	70	13,538,522	947,767	1,353,852	417,683	530,084	936,269	.02039	.0142
Glens Falls	9,186,910	60	15,311,516	918,691	1,531,153	267,850	650,841	1,263,302	.0321	.01926
Gloversville	8,940,245	55	16,254,990	894,024	1,625,499	656,500	237,524	968,999	.0348	.01914
Hornell†	7,150,300	75	9,533,733	715,030	953,373	317,350	397,680	636,023	.03098	.0232
Hudson†	5,155,839	80	6,874,452	515,584	687,445	444,512	71,072	242,933	.03479	.02909
Ithaca	10,919,280	66	19,853,236	1,091,928	1,985,324	1,198,920		786,404	.03188	.01753
Jamestown	17,773,117	60	29,621,861	1,777,312	2,962,186	1,365,007	412,305	1,597,179	.3883	.0232
Johnstown	3,537,050	55	6,976,454	398,705	697,646	254,185	129,520	443,460	.0444	.02442
Kingston	15,506,342	75	20,620,789	1,550,634	2,062,079	1,126,500	424,134	935,579	.02957	.02217
Lackawanna†	10,682,880	50	21,165,760	1,068,288	2,116,576	527,591	530,697	1,588,985	.0245	.01225
Little Falls†	7,051,097	70	10,072,995	703,110	1,097,299	417,750	287,360	589,549	.02089	.01462
Lockport†	11,189,197	65	17,520,303	1,118,820	1,752,030	906,673	212,147	815,357	.02813	.01528

City									
Mechanicville	2,874,790	90	4,791,316	287,470	479,132	250,299	37,210	228,863	.0427	.02562
Middletown†	8,514,969	45	18,922,153	851,497	1,982,215	373,586	477,911	1,518,629	.0342	.01639
Mount Vernon†	41,393,250	70	59,180,928	4,138,325	5,918,063	4,006,800	132,525	1,911,393	.029955	.02094
Newburg	13,639,941	55	24,799,892	1,363,995	2,470,989	1,127,686	225,309	1,352,303	.0322	.01771
New Rochelle†	62,273,066	75	89,104,422	6,297,309	8,910,442	3,022,687	3,214,622	5,887,755	.0417	.01906
New York, Greater	8,207,822,361	93	8,825,615,442	820,783,236	882,561,144	769,280,484	51,501,752	5,887,755	.0205	.01247
Niagara Falls	37,437,389	45	83,194,197	3,743,739	8,319,420	2,213,719	1,630,020	113,281,060	.027716	.01453
North Tonawanda†	9,555,920	60	15,926,533	955,592	1,592,653	632,450	383,142	6,105,701	.0472	.02308
Norwich*†	3,174,280	60	5,290,466	317,428	529,047	183,866	133,586		.03848	.0165
Ogdensburg	5,619,410	60	8,027,728			246,750	315,191	556,023	.02575	.0165
Olean†	9,952,806	70	14,218,294	995,281	1,421,839	538,399	456,882	983,430	.02588	.01978
Oneida†	4,706,386	75	6,277,848	470,639	627,785	104,960	365,879	525	.03473	.02904
Oneonta	5,477,030	60	9,128,383	547,703	912,838	277,460	270,243		.031668	.019
Oswego	12,595,978	77	16,358,412	1,259,598	1,635,841	830,455	429,143		.0359	.0276
Plattsburg	3,627,150	50	7,254,300	362,715	725,430	344,500	18,215	380,530	.04065	.020475
Poughkeepsie†	26,266,725	80	32,833,406	2,626,672	3,283,341	2,070,677	556,095	1,212,764	.02507	.02077
Port Jervis†	2,544,200	25	10,176,800	254,420	1,017,680	159,800	94,620	867,880	.0437	.0159
Rensselaer	5,894,116	75	7,858,820	589,411	785,882	416,404	369,478	369,478	.03366	.02449
Rochester	231,565,084	83	278,994,077	23,55,508	27,899,408	21,193,034	1,963,473	6,706,374	.02397	.01989
Rome†	10,240,025	75	17,066,708	1,024,002	1,706,671	784,177	239,525	922,494	.037	.022
Salamanca	4,736,483	76	6,316,310	473,648	6531	348,515	125,133	283,016	.094	.018
Saratoga Springs†	9,211,207	65	14,171,087	921,121	1,417,109	433,000	438,121	934,109	.03638	.02494
Schenectady†	57,802,083	72	80,280,670	5,780,208	8,028,087	4,690,450	1,089,758	3,337,077	.0236	.01699
Syracuse	144,940,472	80	181,173,090	14,493,847	18,117,309	10,821,986	1,672,181	7,295,443	.02452	.0196
Tonawanda†	5,443,342	70	7,776,202	544,334	777,620	377,325	167,009	400,395	.02724	.0 904
Troy	58,907,689	80	65,452,987	5,880,769	6,545,299	3,652,241	2,288,525	2,923,058	.027548	.02470
Utica	49,361,080	90	82,268,466	908	8,226,847	2,769,780	2,166,328	5,457,067	.03417	.0239
Watertown†	15,426,860	65	23,733,680	1,542,686	2,373,363	1,164,235	378,451	1,209,128	.03046	.01979
Watervliet†	5,828,025	90	6,475,583	582,802	647,558	384,244	198,558	263,314	.03562	.032
White Plains	23,361,055	90	38,935,091	2,336,105	3,893,509	2,671,999		1,221,540	.03011	.01906
Yonkers	123,227,440	85	144,973,458	12,322,744	14,497,346	10,077,728	2,245,016	4,419,618	.0286	.0242

* Nothing to show whether the nonexempt indebtedness reported by the cities of Corning, Cortland, Fulton and Norwich include water bonds issued prior to January 1, 1910.

† The ratio to full value at which real estate is assessed as determined by State Tax Department for the cities of Albany, Binghamton, Cohoes, Dunkirk, Fulton, Hudson, Lackawanna, Lockport, Middletown, Mount Vernon, New Rochelle, North Tonawanda, Norwich, Olean, Oneida, Port Jervis, Rome, Saratoga Springs, Schenectady, Watertown and Watervliet are the ratios adopted in 1916, those for 1917 not having been adopted as yet. The ratios for all the other cities are those adopted in 1917.

THE TRAINING OF GIRLS

THIRTEENTH ANNUAL REPORT

OF THE

Board of Managers

OF THE

New York State
Training School for Girls

AT

HUDSON, N. Y.

For the Nine Months Ending June 30, 1916

TRANSMITTED TO THE LEGISLATURE APRIL 3, 1917

ALBANY
J. B. LYON COMPANY, PRINTERS
1917

STATE OF NEW YORK

No. 62

IN SENATE

APRIL 3, 1917.

Thirteenth Annual Report of the Board of Managers of the New York State Training School for Girls, at Hudson, N. Y.

HUDSON, N. Y., *July* 1. 1916.

To the Legislature of the State of New York:

The board of managers of the New York State Training School for Girls, as required by law, respectfully submits its report for the nine months ending June 30, 1916.

There were two changes in the membership of the board during that period. The board has met regularly at the School each month, besides holding necessary committee meetings. At regular meetings a quorum of members has always been present. One member has not been absent from any meetings.

The retirement of one member from the board must be especially noted. Dr. Thomas Wilson had served the Institution as manager or consultant from July, 1899, five years before it became a Training School. He had been on the board all but five of these sixteen years. He still continues his service as consulting physician. In all this time he has been of unfailing value to the School.

Since there has been little change at the School since last year, no account need be given of the outfit, the pupils, the methods, etc. Persons interested will find all such information substantially up to date in last year's report, and all new facts are in the tables which follow.

[3]

Only one point needs to be especially emphasized:

If a girl, after being committed to the School, proves mentally incapable of being benefited by the instruction of the School, the board of managers is required to return her to the sheriff of the county from which she came. The sheriff is then required to take her to the court from which she was committed and the court, if possible, commits her to some other institution. (The reading of the law is: "to be by such magistrate resentenced for the offense for which she was committed to such institution and dealt with in all respects as though she had not been so committed.") But if there is no suitable institution, the court has no choice but to discharge her. This is a serious evil, since it means that feeble-minded or mentally unbalanced girls (psychopathic but not technically adjudged insane) are thus from time to time returned to a vicious life in the community. It thus becomes clear that this State needs to make special provision for the custodial care of feeble-minded delinquent girls and for the hospital care of incipient cases of mental derangement in girls who are not yet technically insane. The numbers of both these types among delinquents seem to have increased with the growing complexity of modern life.

The board respectfully urges the appropriation by this Legislature of sums sufficient to cover the following items:

APPROPRIATIONS DESIRED AT THE 1917 SESSION OF THE LEGISLATURE BY THE NEW YORK STATE TRAINING SCHOOL FOR GIRLS, AT HUDSON, N. Y.

For personal service......................		$77,922 50
For maintenance and operation...............		87,070 00
Food	$30,000 00	
Fuel, light, power and water....	13,800 00	
Printing and advertising........	350 00	
Equipment	6,500 00	
Supplies	7,500 00	
Materials	4,900 00	
Communication	1,650 00	
Traveling expenses	9,000 00	
Fixed charges and contributions.	8,470 00	
Rent	....	
General plant service..........	4,000 00	
Contingencies	900 00	
		$164,992 50

DEFICIENCY APPROPRIATION FOR 1916-17

For personal service................	$110 00
For supplies	625 00
For fixed charges and contributions..	2,314 00
	$3,049 50

Total	$168,041 50

Average inmate population nine months ending June 30, 1916	348.74
Per capita cost nine months ending June 30, 1916......	$313 19
Population estimated for year beginning July 1, 1917..	400

SPECIAL BILLS

1. Protective fence, entrance gate house and guards' room. $25,000

We have pleaded for more than ten years past for suitable fencing. A protective fence which will compel respect for State property and be suited to the character of the institution should be erected. Because of the location, a fence is a necessity for this institution, the School property lying close to an undesirable section of Hudson and being bounded by railroad tracks and much travelled public roads. It is the policy of the institution to give the girls as much freedom as is compatible with their safety. While the present dilapidated wooden fence suggests a penal institution, it is no deterrent to those who wish to get on or off the grounds. For the sides of the property bounded by public roads, there should be a suitable iron fence (about 200 rods). For the line boundaries, there should be an unclimbable wire fence (about 400 rods). An entrance gate house, containing at least a room for the guard and a waiting room, is a necessity at the main entrance to the property. The old gate house stands within the grounds and has been condemned as a fire trap.

2. Repairs, necessary improvements, etc., to buildings and
land, McIntyre property, to keep from deterioration. $10,000

Such as,—patching plaster, (badly cracked and falling), repairs to windows, patching roof, repairs to chimney, repairs to barn floor, repairs to house near Worth Ave. for employees' use, rough road and repairs to roads, and with the addition of $4,000, or whatever balance remains in appropriation for repairs, chapter 646, Laws of 1916, part 3, to put house near the railroad in good repair for the use of farmer or engineer.

3. Storehouse, refrigerating plant, equipment and outside
   connections $40,000

Appropriations granted in 1913 proved too small to cover low bids
for this work, even after two sets of advertisements. The Legislature of 1915 reappropriated this fund, together with funds for
hospitals, also too small, thus permitting the construction and furnishing of a general and a contagious hospital, both of which are
now completed. The present storehouse is far too small for present
population, has no equipment for handling heavy supplies, and is
inadequate for cold storage. The ice-house cannot store enough ice
for half the summer. Storehouse work is part of the training given
the pupils.

4. Extraordinary repairs, etc. $6,650

For repairs to roads.	$1,500
For painting interior of cottages.	3,000
For painting exterior of buildings, tin roofs, gutters, trim	1,500
For repairs to roofs and gutters.	200
For furniture for officers' rooms.	350
For repairs to water mains.	100

5. To finish work in older cottages. $22,500

For electric annunciator system for 10 cottages	$8,000
For new floors in cottages 1 and 3, finishing floors in cottages 2 and 4, and electric lights in cottages 5, 6, 7 and 10, cupboards and shelves in cottages 1 to 7 and cottage 10. . . .	5,000
For seven porches for old cottages.	7,000
For improvements to Lowell Cottage.	2,500

Repeated returns to cottages by outside workmen for small
improvements and repairs, which could more economically be
accomplished at one time were there sufficient funds, is reason for
grouping needs of old cottages in the hope of avoiding serious
recurring interruptions. In ten cottages the pupils are still locked
in their rooms at night because annunciators are not provided. In
four cottages pupils have no lights in their bedrooms. Light is
necessary for proper personal attention. Two cottages have urgent
need of new floors, and the floors in two other cottages should be
finished; eight cottages need book-cases, cabinets and shelves to
bring them up to a fair comparison with the six newer cottages.
Pupils' clothing now hangs on nails driven in the doors. Books

and fancy work, games, etc., used in living rooms should have cases and drawers to hold them when not in use. Two-story porches on seven old cottages would give very important recreation centers. In institution life, as many variations as possible in routine, such as out-door eating, sleeping, singing, resting, which porches help procure, are necessary. Lowell cottage was poorly built and is unsatisfactory in details for household duties. It must be wholly replastered, doors renewed; pantry, storage and linen rooms altered.

6. Curb, walk and grading on Worth Avenue........... $1,300
    840 ft. unless this is otherwise provided for.

    Curb.................................. $419 55
    Walk.................................. 630 00
    Grading.............................. 250 45
                        =======

The curb has already been constructed by the city of Hudson and bill of $419.55 presented for same. An estimate for laying the walk was obtained from the city of Hudson last June. Amount of estimate is $630.00. We estimate the grading will cost the balance.

7. Improvements to grounds......................... $5,000
    Labor and material for
    (1) Removal of brush, undergrowth and noxious growths, such as poison ivy.
    (2) Transplanting trees and shrubs and reforestration.
    (3) Grading and seeding.

The labor allowed in maintenance is entirely needed for the productive work on the farm and gardens. To clear away the undergrowth of many years, a special fund for labor should be allowed. Not only are the borders of the School property unsightly, but the growth affords most undesirable hiding places. Taken in connection with the dilapidated fence, this condition of the grounds exposes the School to constant and unnecessary nervous strain.

Respectfully submitted,

ANNIE WINSOR ALLEN,
President.
NATHANIEL H. LEVI,
Vice-President.
HELEN ESSELSTYN,
Secretary.
JOHN F. BRENNEN,
Treasurer.
MARY HINKLEY,
LOUIS VAN HOESEN.

SUPERINTENDENT'S REPORT

Movement of Population

Received October 1, 1915, to July 1, 1916

By commitment and return from conditional discharge......	168
In School temporarily for visit........................	2
Infants...	18
Total..	188

Detail

By commitment.......................................	114
By recall for ill health..............................	1
By recall for change of place.........................	12
By recall for incompetence...........................	2
By recall for unsatisfactory conduct..................	3
By recall for unsatisfactory work and conduct...........	9
By recall for improper associations...................	2
By recall for improper associations and unsatisfactory conduct..	4
By recall for improper associations and running away.....	1
By recall for immorality.............................	2
By recall for immorality and running away.............	1
By recall for stealing and running away................	.
By recall for immorality, stealing and running away......	1
Returned from general hospital.......................	15
In School for visit over June 30th, 1916...............	2
Infants...	18
Total..	188

Discharged

Girls..	177
Infants...	18
Total..	195

DETAIL

Discharged to relatives or guardians.......................... 45
Discharged to service...................................... 56
Discharged to general hospital 15
Discharged to custodial institutions 5
Discharged to state hospital............................. 1
Discharged and returned to county authorities as improper commitments...................................... 50
Discharged by order of court............................. 2
Discharged under State Charities Law, Chapter 57, Section 206, relating to mothers.............................. 1
Out after visit over September 30, 1915................. 1
Died.. 1
Discharged to other institutions (infants)................ 7
Discharged with mothers (infants)....................... 11

Total.. 195

Total absolute discharges................................ 64
Total conditional discharges............................. 112
Died.. 1
Infants... 18

Total.. 195

SUMMARY

Population October 1, 1915............................... 341
Received October 1, 1915 to July 1, 1916................ 188

Total.. 529

Discharged October 1, 1915 to July 1, 1916.............. 195

Population July 1, 1916.................................. 334
Girls committed 326
Infants... 8

Committed since June 1, 1904........................... 1337

AGE OF ADMISSION

11 years (improper commitment)......................... 1
12 years 10
13 years 17

14 years 38
15 years 47
16 years (improper commitment)........................ 1

    Total.. 114

Nativity

American 106
    Georgia 2
    New Jersey 3
    New York 99
    Pennsylvania 2
Foreign.. 8
    Austria 3
    Canada 3
    England 1
    Russia 1

    Total.. 114

Parentage

American 63
Austrian 7
Canadian 3
English 2
German 3
Italian 1
Mixed.. 13
Russian 2
Unknown 20

    Total.. 114

Number of Girls from Each County

Cattaraugus 2
Chautauqua 3
Chemung 1
Clinton 1
Columbia 3
Cortland 1
Delaware 1
Dutchess 4
Erie 3

Essex   2
Greene   1
Herkimer   1
Jefferson   1
Kings   26
Lewis   1
Monroe   1
Nassau   1
New York   11
Niagara   5
Onondaga   3
Oneida   2
Ontario   2
Orange   5
Oswego   2
Queens   4
Richmond   2
Rockland   2
Saratoga   1
Schenectady   4
Steuben   4
Suffolk   2
Tioga   1
Ulster   2
Washington   1
Wayne   1
Westchester   3
Yates   4

                                                                        114

Biographical

EDUCATION

Preparatory A   19
Preparatory B   8
First year   37
Second year   37
Third year   3
Fourth year   7
No record   3

                                                                        114

See Schools for explanation of above grading.

Occupation

Clerk	2
Factory girl	3
Farm work	1
Housework	22
Mill work	2
Millinery	1
None	19
Nurse girl	3
School girl	57
Seamstress	1
Waitress	3
	114

Religion

Catholic	12
Jewish	7
Protestant	95
	114

Race

Colored	23
White	91
	114

PAROLE STATISTICS — 1916

Number on parole October 1, 1915:

From year ending September 30, 1910	1
From year ending September 30, 1911	2
From year ending September 30, 1912	1
From year ending September 30, 1913	12
From year ending September 30, 1914	26
From year ending September 30, 1915	64
Total	105

Paroled from October 1, 1915 to July 1, 1916:

First time	61
Second time	15
Third time	11

Fourth time 6
Fifth time 3

Total 96

Detail for years ending September 30:

	1910	1911	1912	1913	1914	1915	1916
Honorably discharged	..	..	..	3	1	4	4
Dishonorably discharged	..	..	..	2	2	3	..
Discharged by marriage	..	..	..	1	2	3	2.
Returned for incompetence and returned to county as mentally incapable	..	..	..	..	..	..	1
Returned for change of place and discharged to relatives	..	..	..	..	..	1	..
Returned for change of place and reparoled	..	..	..	..	1	5	5
Returned for ill health and reparoled	..	..	..	..	..	1	..
Returned for unsatisfactory conduct and reparoled	..	..	..	..	1	2	..
Returned for unsatisfactory work and conduct and reparoled	..	..	..	..	..	3	1
Returned for improper associations and reparoled	..	..	..	..	..	1	1
Returned for improper associations and running away and reparoled	..	..	..	..	..	1	..
Returned for immorality and running away and reparoled	..	..	..	..	..	1	..
Returned for incompetence and not yet reparoled	..	..	..	..	..	..	1
Returned for unsatisfactory work and conduct and not yet reparoled	..	..	..	..	..	1	4
Returned for unsatisfactory conduct and improper associations and not yet reparoled	..	..	..	..	..	..	4
Returned for immorality and not yet reparoled	..	..	..	..	..	1	1
Returned for stealing, running away and not yet reparoled	..	..	..	..	..	1	..
Returned for immorality, stealing and running away and not yet reparoled	..	..	..	..	..	..	1
In other institutions	..	..	..	..	1	1	..

	1910	1911	1912	1913	1914	1915	1916
Not reporting	..	1	..	2	6	2	4
Maintaining regular correspondence	1	..	1	4	12	33	67
	1	1	1	12	26	64	96

Changes of place without return to School for year ending
June 30, 1916.................................. 18

		Delinquent	In other institutions
On parole from year ending September 30, 1910........	1	..	..
On parole from year ending September 30, 1911........	1		
On parole from year ending September 30, 1912........	1		
On parole from year ending September 30, 1913........	6	2	
On parole from year ending September 30, 1914........	19	6	
On parole from year ending September 30, 1915........	36	2	
On parole from year ending June 30, 1916............	71	4	..
Total number on parole July 1, 1916	135	15	2

	Less than 1 year	1-2 years	2-3 years	3-4 years	4-5 years	5-6 years
Period of training in School previous to first parole....	2	2	35	12	8	2
Period of training in School previous to final discharge.	23	9	13	11	12	14

SCHOOLS
Book Schools
Number of teachers employed............................. 15

Friday afternoon is given to classes in religious instruction; thus
morning sections report five days per week, afternoon sections four
days.
Preparatory B (Morning) :
Number of pupils enrolled............................. 25
Number of days taught................................. 143

Preparatory A (Afternoon):
Number of pupils enrolled........................... 41
Number of days taught.............................. 116
First Year, Section 1 (Morning):
Number of pupils enrolled........................... 44
Number of days taught.............................. 145
First Year, Section 2 (Afternoon)
Number of pupils enrolled........................... 41
Number of days taught.............................. 130
First Year, Section 3 (Morning):
Number of pupils enrolled........................... 35
Number of days taught.............................. 155
Second Year, Section 1 (Morning):
Number of pupils enrolled........................... 25
Number of days taught.............................. 176
Second Year, Section 2 (Afternoon):
Number of pupils enrolled........................... 28
Number of days taught.............................. 134
Second Year, Section 3 (Morning):
Number of pupils enrolled........................... 33
Number of days taught.............................. 173
Third Year (Afternoon):
Number of pupils enrolled........................... 31
Number of days taught.............................. 140
Fourth Year (Afternoon):
Number of pupils enrolled........................... 28
Number of days taught.............................. 123
Advanced (Morning):
Number of pupils enrolled........................... 17
Number of days taught.............................. 175
Special Class:
Number of pupils enrolled........................... 20
Number of days taught.............................. 103

SEWING SCHOOL

Sewing 1, Section 1 (Morning):
Number of pupils enrolled..................... 49
Number of days taught.............................. 171
Sewing 1, Section 2 (Afternoon):
Number of pupils enrolled........................... 46
Number of days taught.............................. 137

Sewing 2, Section 1 (Morning):
Number of pupils enrolled........................ 50
Number of days taught............................ 179
Sewing 2, Section 2 (Afternoon):
Number of pupils enrolled........................ 47
Number of days taught............................ 142
Sewing 3, Section 1 (Morning):
Number of pupils enrolled........................ 44
Number of days taught............................ 182
Sewing 3, Section 2 (Afternoon):
Number of pupils enrolled........................ 48
Number of days taught............................ 144
Sewing 4, Section 1 (Morning):
Number of pupils enrolled........................ 39
Number of days taught............................ 191
Sewing 4, Section 2 (Afternoon):
Number of pupils enrolled........................ 46
Number of days taught............................ 152

Special Class from October, 1915, to January, 1916

Sewing 1, Section 1 (Morning):
Number of pupils enrolled........................ 17
Number of days taught............................ 54
Sewing 1, Section 2 (Afternoon):
Number of pupils enrolled........................ 17
Number of days taught............................ 44

COOKING SCHOOL

Morning Class:
Number of pupils enrolled........................ 48
Number of days taught............................ 150
Afternoon Class:
Number of pupils enrolled........................ 48
Number of days taught............................ 122
Evening Class for Cottage Cooks:
Number of pupils enrolled........................ 30
Number of days taught............................ 6
Class organized January, 1916.

LAUNDRY SCHOOL

Hand Laundry, Section 1 (Morning):
Number of pupils enrolled........................ 188
Number of days taught............................ 198

Hand Laundry, Section 2 (Afternoon):
   Number of pupils enrolled........................... 185
   Number of days taught............................. 148
Steam Laundry, Section 1 (Morning):
   Number of pupils enrolled........................... 23
   Number of days taught............................. 193
Steam Laundry, Section 2 (Afternoon):
   Number of pupils enrolled........................... 19
   Number of days taught............................. 151
Evening Class for Cottage Laundresses:
   Number of pupils enrolled........................... 22
   Number of evenings taught......................... 2
Class organized April, 1916.

HANDICRAFT SCHOOL

Handicraft, Section 1:
   Number of pupils enrolled........................... 32
   Number of days taught............................. 127
Handicraft, Section 2:
   Number of pupils enrolled........................... 33
   Number of days taught............................. 132

PHYSICAL CULTURE

Number of classes each week......................... 20
Number of pupils enrolled............................ 482
Average daily attendance............................ 64
Number of days taught............................... 108

MUSIC SCHOOL

Tuesday Class:
   Number of days taught............................. 35
   Average attendance 123
Wednesday Class:
   Number of days taught............................. 33
   Average attendance 58
Thursday Class:
   Number of days taught............................. 32
   Average attendance 48
Friday Class:
   Number of days taught............................. 34
   Average attendance 240

RELIGIOUS SERVICE

Catholic Service:
  Number of pupils enrolled........................... 80
  Number of days taught............................... 38
Jewish Service:
  Number of pupils enrolled........................... 47
  Number of days taught............................... 40
Protestant Service:
  Number of days taught............................... 33
  Average attendance 155
Episcopal Service:
  Number of pupils enrolled........................... 56
  Number of days taught............................... 44

CHILDREN OF THE REPUBLIC

Number of chapters organized.......................... 10
Number enrolled 164
Number of chapter meetings............................ 59
Number of general meetings............................ 6

DRILL CORPS OF CHILDREN OF THE REPUBLIC

Number of pupils enrolled............................. 84
Number of days taught................................. 23

CHAMBERMAIDS' SCHOOL

Main Building Class:
  Number of pupils enrolled........................... 22
  Number of days taught............................... 172
  Record of attendance began January, 1916.
Old Hospital Class:
  Number of pupils enrolled........................... 14
  Number of days taught............................... 171
  Record of attendance began January, 1916.
Evening Class for Chambermaids:
  Number of pupils enrolled........................... 20
  Number of evenings taught........................... 4
  Class organized January, 1916.

STOREHOUSE

Morning Class:
  Number of pupils enrolled........................... 6
  Number of days taught............................... 101

Afternoon Class:
    Number of pupils enrolled............................   2
    Number of days taught..............................   96
    Record of attendance began January, 1916.

GARDEN

Morning Class:
    Number of pupils enrolled............................   80
    Number of days taught..............................   169
Afternoon Class:
    Number of pupils enrolled............................   80
    Number of days taught..............................   111

Farm and Garden Produce from October 1, 1915, to July 1, 1916

Apples, bus.	99	Lettuce, lbs.	507
Asparagus, lbs.	2,161	Manure, dbl. loads....	36
Beans, lima, lbs.......	547	Onions, green, lbs.....	585
Beans, string, lbs.....	1,046	Parsnips, bus.	126
Beets, bus.	340	Pears, bus.	43
Beet greens, lbs......	497	Peppers, green, lbs....	793
Cabbage, lbs.	12,132	Pork, fresh, lbs.......	5,219
Carrots, bus.	150	Pork, salt, lbs........	2,090
Cauliflower, lbs.	1,481	Radishes, lbs.	2,023
Celery, lbs.	162	Rhubarb, lbs.	1,304
Cherries, qts.	60	Salsify, lbs.	1,539
Chicken, lbs.	794	Spinach, lbs.	182
Chickory, lbs.	226	Squash, summer, lbs..	5,167
Eggs, doz.	875	Squash, winter, lbs....	5,400
Egg plant, lbs.	1,522	Strawberries, qts.	678
Endive, lbs.	428	Swiss Chard, lbs......	2,281
Ham, lbs.	264	Tomatoes, lbs.	3,056
Hay, lbs.	4,010	Turnips, lbs.	5,960
Lard, lbs.	345		

Articles Made in Sewing, Dressmaking and Handicraft Departments from October 1, 1915, to July 1, 1916

Aprons, gingham band..	621	Bands, sanitary	235
Aprons, gingham pina-		Bags, canvas, mail......	2
fore	16	Baskets, reed	9
Aprons, white pinafore..	2	Bonnets, infants	17
Aprons, waitress	14	Caps, crocheted	16
Aprons, white band.....	420	Cloths, bread	31

Cloth, table, linen.......	1	Napkins, checked	598
Cloths, tray	3	Napkins, sanitary	1,134
Coats, gray	102	Nightgowns, brown	323
Coats, infants	17	Nightgowns, infants	6
Coats, separate	25	Nightgowns, white	142
Corset covers, brown....	287	Outfits, baby	39
Corset covers, white....	143	Outfit, burial	1
Covers, dresser	42	Pillow slips, brown.....	149
Covers, mangle	2	Pillow slips, white......	64
Covers, mattress	131	Rugs, rag	7
Covers, piano	2	Sheets, brown, 6/4......	173
Covers, sleeve board....	30	Sheets, ironing	112
Curtains, long, muslin...	32	Sheets, white, 6/4......	25
Curtains, sash, muslin...	62	Sheets, white, 8/4......	64
Curtains, long, scrim....	37	Shirtwaists	73
Curtains, sash, scrim....	17	Skirts, colored	187
Curtains, shelf, muslin...	179	Skirts, infants	4
Drawers, brown, pr.....	158	Skirts, white	73
Drawers, infants, pr.....	2	Skirts, wool dress......	7
Drawers, white, pr......	82	Suits, gymnasium	45
Dresses, calico	140	Suits, wool	64
Dresses, cottage	738	Trays, reed	4
Dresses, infants	4	Towels, dish	306
Dresses, wool	1	Towels, hand	292
Doilies, 12-in.	148	Towels, huck	245
Handkerchiefs	887	Towels, huck, individual.	30
Kimonos	4	Towels, Turkish, girls...	20

PHYSICIAN'S REPORT

During the nine months ending June 30, 1916, the following cases were treated:

Abscess of breast.........	1	New cases	14
Acne	4	Cured	9
Adenitis (cervical)	14	Discharged (not	
Adenitis (auxiliary)	2	cured)	3
Alopecia	2	Now under treat-	
Amenorrhoea	13	ment	15
Appendicitis	4	Heart	3
Broncho-pneumonia	1	Aortic murmur	2
Burns	56	Irregular..........	1
Bursitis	5	Herpes zoster	2
Chorea	1	Hordeolum	26
Clavus	24	Hyperidrosis	1
Cocaine poisoning	1	Hysteria	3
Confinements	13	Indigestion, acute	1
Conjunctivitis	4	Ingrowing toe nails.......	14
Constipation	7	La grippe	63
Coryza	57	Menorrhagia	6
Dermatitis (poison ivy)...	1	Nephritis	1
Diabetes mellitus (fatal)..	1	Onychia	7
Diarrhoea	3	Otitis media	10
Diphtheria carriers	9	Pediculosis.............	7
Dysmenorrhoea	38	Pes planus	5
Dysurea	2	Psoriasis..............	3
Eczema	1	Pleurisy	3
Enuresis	14	Pneumonia	1
Epilepsy	2	Rheumatism	2
Epistaxis	7	Sprain	4
Erysipelas	1	Synovitis	4
Foreign bodies, ext. of....	59	Syphilis	8
Furunculosis	36	Oct. 1, 1915, under	
Goitre	10	treatment	5
Gonorrhoea	27	New cases	3
Oct. 1, 1915, under		Discharged	1
treatment ....:	13	Cured	3

Syphilis now under treatment	4	
Tonsilitis	41	
Trachoma	9	
Oct. 1, 1915, under treatment	4	
Admitted with disease	4	
Recurrence — June 12.	1	

Cured	7
Now under treatment	2
Tuberculosis	4
Vaccinations	142
Verruca	12
Wounds, contused........	7
Wounds, incised	27
Wounds, infected	31
Wasserman tests, blood for.	16

Daily average at sick call................................ 17

Gonorrhoea cases:

Slides examined for gonococci........................ 220
Douches given in cottage............................. 1,384
Douches given at hospital............................ 1,703

There has been one death during the nine months, from diabetes mellitus.

SURGICAL REPORTS

Opening breast abscess................................ 1
Operation for webbed fingers, a result of an old burn..... 1
Operation for imperforate hymen 1
Operation for chronic appendicitis, at Hudson City Hospital. 1
Operation for tubercular glands of neck, at Hudson City Hospital.. 1
Operation for femoral hernia, at Hudson City Hospital.... 1

OCULIST'S AND LARYNGOLOGIST'S REPORTS

Refractions 75
Eyes, ears, nose and throats examined.................. 110
Ears only 9
Nose only 1
Throat only 7
Trachoma inspections and treatments................... 100
Trachoma, girls inspected.............................. 22
Trachoma, officers inspected........................... 1
Eyes inspected by Resident Physician.................. 4,633

DENTISTRY

Extractions	189
Teeth filled	347
Teeth treated	210
Teeth cleaned	114
Crowns removed	2
Crown replaced	1

STEWARD'S REPORT

This institution was originally the House of Refuge for Women and was opened for that purpose April 15, 1887. By an act of the Legislature, in 1904, it was changed to the New York State Training School for Girls, date of opening being June 1, 1904.

Total acreage of ground and buildings.............. 171 acres

Value of real estate............................. $793,122 00
Value of personal property....................... 65,520 66

Total value of property..................... $858,642 66

Disbursements during the year for maintenance and daily per capita cost:

Salaries of officers and employees........	$48,286 60	$0.5053
Provisions............................	17,075 46	.1786
General supplies	2,329 97	.0243
Farm and garden......................	1,947 16	.0203
Clothing..............................	4,835 12	.0505
Furniture and furnishings..............	1,392 29	.0145
Transportation of inmates..............	4,816 81	.0504
Fuel and light........................	8,986 74	.0940
Ordinary repairs and shops..............	4,203 08	.0439
Medical supplies	474 52	.0049
Miscellaneous.........................	10,883 29	.1138
Lawns, roads and grounds..............	3,991 26	.0417
	$109,222 30	$1.1430

Total weekly per capita cost.................... $8.0305

Total disbursements during the year for extraordinary
   improvements................................ $87,109 43
Total expenditures 196,331 73
Estimated value of farm and garden products........ 2,794 83
Estimated value of articles made or manufactured
   during the year................................ 2,768 41
Average number of inmates (including 12 infants)... 348 74
Number of girls and infants for whom 221 5/7 weeks'
   board was paid outside of the School, girls 17,
   infants 11 28

TREASURER'S REPORT

HUDSON, N. Y., *June* 30, 1916.

The annual statement of the Treasurer of the New York State Training School for Girls, at Hudson, N. Y., for the nine months ending June 30, 1916:

RECEIPTS

Bank balance October 1, 1915, maintenance.......................	$4,952 71	
From general appropriations.........	105,969 23	
From special appropriations..........	87,109 43	
Miscellaneous.....	193 82	
		$198,225 19

DISBURSEMENTS

From general fund..................	$109,222 30	
From special fund..................	87,109 43	
Returned to State Treasurer..........	193 82	
		196,525 55

Bank balance July 1, 1916...................	$1,699 64

CLASSIFIED DISBURSEMENTS

Salaries of officers and wages of employees	$48,286 60	
Provisions	17,075 46	
General supplies	2,329 97	
Farm and garden...................	1,947 16	
Clothing	4,835 12	
Furniture and furnishings...........	1,392 29	
Transportation of inmates...........	4,816 81	
Fuel and light.....................	8,986 74	
Ordinary repairs and shops..........	4,203 08	
Medical supplies	474 52	
Miscellaneous	10,883 29	
Lawns, roads and grounds...........	3,991 26	
Return to State Treasurer............	193 82	
		$109,416 12

Chapter 531, Laws of 1914:   .
Retaining wall $472 78
Outside lighting 73 57
Locking Devices 1,220 00
Repairs to Administration Building....   931 06
                                        ————— $2,697 41

Chapter 727, Laws of 1915:
Equipment, new school house........ $2,146 22
Purchase of land and buildings........   15,000 00
Extra repairs and equipment..........   1,596 66
                                        —————   18,742 88

Chapter 728, Laws of 1915:
Conduits and outside connections...... $555 00
Laundry equipment 2,700 00
Boilers and equipment................   287 90
Feeder cables 139 00
Enlargement of laundry..............   1,232 14
Guard house repairs.................   1,209 70
                                        —————   6,123 74

Chapter 334, Laws of 1915:
Buildings, construction, equipment, repairs..........   59,545 40
                                                       —————————
                                                       $196,525 55

Balance in the hands of the Comptroller July 1, 1916, is as follows:

Chapter 646, Laws of 1916:
Repairs $5,000 00
Stokers for boiler. 2,500 00
Fire apparatus and additional fire protection. 2,500 00
Re-razing Stuyvesant hospital and old ice house. 1,491 50
Chapter 727, Laws of 1915:
Telephone clocks, etc. 1,500 00
Equipment, new school house. 2,509 58
Extraordinary repairs and equipment. 746 67
Chapter 728, Laws of 1915:
Conduits and outside connections. 5,779 38
Feeder cables 1,047 49
Chapter 334, Laws of 1915:
Buildings, construction, equipment, repairs. 38,662 93
                                                                 —————————
                                                                 $61,737 55

Special appropriation showing an available balance same as cash balance:

Chapter 646, Laws of 1916:

Repairs ,	$5,000 00
Stokers for boilers	2,500 00
Fire apparatus and additional fire protection	2,500 00
Re-razing Stuyvesant hospital and old ice house	1,491 50

Special appropriation showing an available balance less than the cash balance:

Chapter 727, Laws of 1915:

Equipment, new school house	1,097 95

Chapter 728, Laws of 1915:

Conduits and outside connections	2,226 03

Chapter 334, Laws of 1915:

Buildings, construction, equipment, repairs	14,506 34

Special appropriations showing no available balance:

Chapter 727, Laws of 1915:

Telephone clocks, etc.

Extraordinary repairs and equipment.

Chapter 728, Laws of 1915:

Feeder cables.

Respectfully submitted, `

JOHN F. BRENNEN,

Treasurer.

NEW YORK STATE TRAINING SCHOOL FOR GIRLS FOR YEAR ENDING JUNE 30, 1916

Population

	Male	Female	Total
Number of inmates present at beginning of fiscal year, including 8 infants............	2	339	341
Number received during the year, including 18 infants	12	176	188
Number discharged during the year, including 18 infants	9	186	195
Number at end of fiscal year, including 8 infants................................	5	229	334
Daily average attendance (i. e., number of inmates actually present during the year)..	..	..	348.74
Average number of officers and employees during the year.......................	28	79	107

Expenditures

Current expenses:

1. Salaries and wages.........................	$48,286 60
2. Clothing....................................	4,835 12
3. Subsistence.................................	17,075 46
4. Ordinary repairs	4,378 61
5. Office, domestic and outdoor expenses...........	41,377 29
	$115,953 08

Extraordinary expenses:

1. New buildings, land, etc....................	78,154 02
2. Permanent improvements to existing buildings....	2,224 63
Grand total	$196,331 73

HORTENSE V. BRUCE,
Superintendent.

APPENDIX

The Book School work is divided into:
1. Preparatory School.
2. Departmental School.
3. Advanced School.
4. Special School.

1. *The Preparatory School* covers the work of the first three grades of a public school. There are three classes of pupils:

Preparatory C, for those beginning to read.
Preparatory B
Preparatory A

In these classes the work given is that necessary to prepare the pupil to enter the Departmental School.

Syllabus

Arithmetic. English literature and language. Nature study. Human physiology and hygiene.

Arithmetic.— Simple combinations and drill upon addition, subtraction, multiplication and short division.

English Literature and Language:

Preparatory C:
Robert Louis Stevenson — A Child's Garden of Verse.
Poems from Stevenson to memorize and illustrate.
Supplementary reading and drill work from readers.

Preparatory B:
Eugene Field — Selections from poetic works.
A Little Book of Profitable Tales, and A Second Book of Tales.
Supplementary work in second readers.
Memory selections from Field.
Reproduction of stories — oral.

Preparatory A:

Hans Andersen and Hawthorne — Fairy Tales.
Wonder Book.
Tanglewood Tales.
Grandfather's Chair.
Memory work from third readers.
Reproduction of stories and writing short sentences.

Nature Study.— Special attention to all specimens of interest in nature, according to their season. Items from periodicals, Cornell leaflets, etc.

Special reading.— Introduction to Leaves from Nature's Story Book — Kelly; Leaves from Nature's Story Book, Vol. 1 — Kelly. Special topics: Birds, insects, flowers, trees, stars, weather.

Human Physiology and Hygiene.—At least one lesson each week on simple principles of body care. Special Text: Good Health — The Gulick Hygiene Series, Book I.

2. *Departmental School* is divided into four departments or courses:

Department of History and Geography.
Department of English and Literature.
Department of Arithmetic.
Department of Nature Study.

The work of these departments is to extend over four years. The classes are therefore to be called:

First Year.
Second Year.
Third Year.
Fourth Year.

These courses in geography and history, English and literature, arithmetic and nature study aim to include all given in those subjects under Regents system for fourth, fifth, sixth, seventh and eighth grades, and also give some work not there included.

SYLLABUS

History and Geography

First Year:

Geog. 1. New York State.
Geog. 2. The United States.
Geog. 3. North America.
Geog. 4. Europe.

Second Year:
    Geog. 5. Other Continents.
    Geog. 6. Topical Survey.
    Hist. 1. Biographical Study of U. S. History — to the Revolution.
    Hist. 2. Biographical Study of later U. S. History.

Third Year:
    Hist. 3. History of New York State.
    Hist. 4. The homes of our Ancestors and Colonial governments.
    Hist. 5. The Revolution (causes and results).
    Hist. 6. The Civil War (causes and results).

Fourth Year:
    Hist. 7. Industrial development.
    Hist. 8. Study of development in form of government, and present government.
    Hist. 9. General History.
    Hist. 10. Special Topics in Review.

English Literature and Language

First Year:
    English 1:
        Lewis Carroll —Alice in Wonderland.
        Through the Looking Glass.
        Memory selections from Longfellow.
        Abbreviations, contractions, quotations, capitals, letter-writing. .

    English 2:
        Longfellow — Miles Standish and Evangeline.
        Memory selections from Longfellow.
        Indirect quotations.
        Paragraphs.
        Number of nouns.
        Changing poetry to prose.

    English 3:
        Longfellow — Hiawatha and shorter poems.
        Supplementary; The Odyssey for Boys and Girls.
        Memory selections from Longfellow.
        Possessives.
        Writing facts obtained from poetry.

English 4:
> Charles Lamb — Tales from Shakespeare and selections.
> Memory selections from Holmes.
> Nouns; kinds, gender, person, case, possessive nouns
> changed to phrases.

Second Year:
> English 5:
>> Whittier and Lowell — Memory selections from these
>> authors.
>> Apposition, describing nouns, personal pronouns, gender,
>> number and case of.
>> Writing parodies.
>
> English 6:
>> George Eliot — Silas Marner and selections.
>> Patriotic memory selections.
>> Punctuation, colon, semicolon.
>> Words used with nouns.
>> Predicate noun and adjective.
>
> English 7:
>> Stories of King Arthur.
>> Memory selections from Byron and Burns.
>> Adverbs, articles, parts of speech, pronoun and antecedent.
>
> English 8:
>> Charles Dickens — Nicholas Nickleby.
>> Home reading from Dickens.
>> Miscellaneous memory selections.
>> Interrogative pronouns; kinds and comparison of adjec-
>> tives and adverbs; adjective phrases.

Third Year:
> English 9:
>> Scott — The Lady of the Lake.
>> Home reading from Scott.
>> Memory selections from Bryant.
>> Diaries and Journals.
>> Verbs; kinds, modes, tenses, person and number.
>
> English 10:
>> Irving — The Sketch Book, and selections.
>> Home reading from Irving.

Miscellaneous memory selections.

The verb " be " progressive form, voice.

Auxiliary verbs, interrogative sentences.

English 11 :

Cooper — The Deerslayer.

Home reading from Cooper.

Memory selections from famous orations.

Imperative mode, verbs alike in sound and agreement, participles.

English 12:

Tennyson — The Princess, and other poems.

Memory selections and dramatizations from Tennyson.

Subject, predicate, modifiers, complements, plain and figurative language.

Fourth Year:

English 13:

Browning — Saul and other poems.

Memory work and dramatizations from Browning.

Infinitives, prepositions, phrases and words expanded, clauses and phrases contracted.

Complex sentences.

English 14:

Shakespeare —As You Like It.

Memory selections from plays.

Home reading from Shakespeare.

Kinds of phrases, conjunctions, similes and metaphors.

English 15:

Shakespeare — Julius Caesar — Memory selections from plays.

Home reading from Shakespeare.

Compound sentences, principle parts of irregular verbs, analysis of words, figures of rhetoric.

English 16:

Shakespeare — Macbeth and Merchant of Venice.

Memory selections from plays.

Review of English.

Throughout the course there will be both written and oral work to put in practice the principles studied ; reading to the class by the teacher, especially of famous orations.

Arithmetic

First Year:

   Arithmetic 1:

      Review addition, subtraction, multiplication, and short division. Drill on long division. Simple work in money and measurements.

   Arithmetic 2:

      Factoring, cancellation, etc., developing the idea of fractions.

   Arithmetic 3:

      Addition, subtraction, multiplication and division of fractions.

   Arithmetic 4:

      Drill in mixed numbers.

Second Year:

   Arithmetic 5:

      Decimals. Review and drill in use of money and measurements.

   Arithmetic 6:

      Reduction. Fractions to decimals and decimals to fractions.

   Arithmetic 7:

      Tables in money, U. S. and other countries. Tables of measures. Relations of one table to another. Explanation of terms and practical illustrations.

   Arithmetic 8:

      Review problems in all previous processes and tables.

Third Year:

   Arithmetic 9:

      Principles of percentage.

   Arithmetic 10:

      Interest, commission, discount and profit and loss.

   Arithmetic 11:

      Bills, accounts, a bank account, review money and exchange.

   Arithmetic 12:

      Establish the principle of ratio, proportion, power, root.

Fourth Year:
  Arithmetic 13:
    Review of general principles for accuracy and rapidity.

  Arithmetic 14:
    Household arithmetic. Cost of food, clothing, fuel, light-
      ing, papering, building, etc. Development of taste and
      economy in choice.

  Arithmetic 15:
    Agricultural arithmetic. Land productivity, live stock, etc.

  Arithmetic 16:
    Business arithmetic. Insurance, taxes, interest, banking,
      personal bookkeeping, investments, etc., as applied to
      personal use.

Nature Study

First Year:
  Nature Study 1 — October to December.
    Plants: Fruitage and change to winter condition.
    Animals: Changes for winter protection.

  Nature Study 2 — January to March.
    Trees: Recognition in winter condition.
    Birds: Study of birds found in winter.
    Stars: To locate and name special stars and constellations.
    Winds: Atmosphere, forms of rain, snow, ice, fog, etc.

  Nature Study 3 — April to June.
    Seeds: growth of seedlings; recognition of spring flowers.
    Birds: recognition; flight; nesting.
    Insects: recognition; forms; habits.

  Nature Study 4 — July to September.
    Recognition of summer birds.
    Flowers; insects.
    Study of plants found growing in water and marshy places.

  Special Reading:
    Leaves from Nature's Story Book, Vol. I.
    Leaves from Nature's Story Book, Vol. II.
    Selections from graded readers.

Human Physiology and Hygiene. One lesson each week throughout the year. Emergencies — The Gulick Hygiene Series, Book 2.

Second Year:

Botany 1 — October to December.
Fruits: Collection of various forms; arrangement of like forms together.

Botany 2 — January to March.
Growth of different forms of ferns and mosses in a hot-box. Study of life, history, fruitage, etc.

Botany 3 —April to June.
Germinate the different classes of seeds. Study food, form, method of growth, and conditions for growth. Plant physiology.

Botany 4— July to September.
Special study of flowers. Pollination, etc.

Special Readings:
Nature on the farm — Keffer.
Selections from graded readers, and pamphlets.

Human Physiology and Hygiene No. 2 — One lesson each week throughout the year. Sanitation; Town and City; The Gulick Hygiene Series. Book 3.

Third Year:

Zoology 1 — October to December.
Frog, crayfish, brief study of reptiles and turtles.

Zoology 2 — January to March.
Mammalia: Guinea pig; rabbit; readings on habits of mammalia.

Zoology 3 — April to June.
Special study of birds. Recognition; flight; nesting.

Zoology 4 — July to September.
Insects: Butterfly; grasshopper; bee or ant.

Special Texts:
The First Book of Birds — Miller.
Stories of Insect Life, Vols. I and II.

Human Physiology and Hygiene No. 3. One lesson each week throughout the year. The Body at Work — Gulick Hygiene Series. Book 4.

Fourth Year:
Biology 1 — October to December.
Lower forms of plant and animal life. Microscopic study where necessary.

Biology 2 — January to March.
Simple study of microscopic structure of plants, ferns, mosses, flowers, fruits, stems, leaves, etc. Function; Repairs; Growth, etc.

Biology 3 —April to June.
Study of microscopic structure of animals: Cells, organs. Function; care; repair; growth, etc.

Biology 4.
Special topics applied to all life.
Adaptation of structure to function.
Cause and effect. Laws of development and growth.
Laws of animal or plant body as applied to habit, mental states, etc. Study of mind.
Study of control of mind over matter. Subjects of habit, attention, ideals, etc., developed from study of natural laws.

Supplementary Reading:
Madam How and Lady Why.— Kingsley.
How the World is Fed.— Carpenter.

Human Physiology and Hygiene, No. 4. One lesson each week throughout the year. Control of Body and Mind. The Gulick Series, Book 5.

3. *Advanced School.*— Follow the syllabus prescribed for first year high school work under the Board of Regents for the two subjects: English Literature and Language; Biology.

4. *Special School.*— Designed for (a) girls who enter school after the beginning of the quarter; (b) girls who have been absent and so are not ready for work in regular classes; (c) those unable to follow courses prescribed for other classes, because of peculiar temperament or needs. The work of this school varies greatly in subject and scope according to the pupils.

Sewing School Syllabus

Sewing 1:
Plain hemming. Work on (a) sanitary cloth; (b) dish towels;

(c) hand towels; (d) ironing sheets; (e) checked handkerchiefs. These five materials are chosen in this order to give
work of gradually increasing difficulty.

Table linen hemming. On table napkins.

Hemstitching. (a) Huck toweling; (b) plain handkerchiefs;
(c) scrim curtains.

Embroidery. (a) Huck toweling, edge; (b) damask doilies for
tables, edge; (c) collars, cuffs, etc., for girls' dresses; (d)
bags, pincushions, etc., for Christmas work.

Crochet work. (a) Borders for huck towels; (b) edge on
bath towels; (c) girls' winter caps; (d) coin purses and
other bags for Christmas; (e) fine edge on Christmas handkerchiefs.

Feather stitching, cross stitching and other fancy stitches. (a)
On flannel pieces for infant outfits; (b) guest towels; (c)
Christmas articles.

Machine stitching. (a) Brown muslin strips for button hole
practice; (b) sanitary bands; (c) girls' sheets; (d) girls'
pillowslips.

Gathering. (a) Gingham band aprons.

Overhanding. (a) On selvedge of girls' pillowslips.

Buttonholes. Practice on buttonhole strips until able to make
good buttonholes.

Carpet rags. Cutting to certain measurements, width and
length for various combinations in rugs for bath rooms and
girls' rooms, sewing by hand and on machine.

Advanced work. Bags and other fancy articles for Christmas.
Cutting and making garments in infants' outfits.

Sewing 2:

*Cutting, joining, sewing and special finishing of all personal
garments for pupils.* (a) Gingham band aprons; (b) white
band aprons; (c) petticoats; (d) drawers; (e) nightgowns;
(f) corset covers; (g) gingham and white pinafores; (h)
work dresses.

Making more difficult articles for household use. (a) Mattress
covers; (b) bed pads; (c) special requirements.

Sewing 3:

Drill in more careful construction and finer workmanship on
above articles for parole outfits; officers' sheets and pillow-
cases.

Selection of materials and styles for school dresses and chapel dresses, with as much variety as possible.

Cutting, fitting, and further methods of trimming.

Special articles required from time to time such as plain bureau spreads, etc., dressing gowns and other articles required for hospital.

Sewing 4:

Tailoring. Cutting, fitting and finishing parole suits and shirt waists, heavy winter coats for pupils of the school, and infants' coats.

Ability to use patterns.

Shrinking and pressing materials for suits and coats.

Cooking School Syllabus

1. Introduction to kitchen work and kitchen utensils.

2. Food Types:

   Protein; Carbohydrates (starch and sugar); fats; water and mineral matter.

   (1) Starchy food; potato; study of contents; baked potato; Cereal: growth; method of cooking; food value.

   (2) Starch as thickening agent.

       (a) Creamed vegetables; cooking of strong and sweet flavored vegetables.

       (b) Cream of tomato soup.

3. Protein food.

   (1) Study of egg; composition and structure; methods of cooking.

   (2) Egg as thickening agent applied to steamed custard.

   (3) Study of meat; composition; structure; food value.

       (a) Pan broiled steak.

       (b) Roast.

       (c) Stews and soups.

       (d) Use of left-overs; hash and cottage pie.

   (4) Study of legumes.

   Beans and peas.

4. Study of milk.

   Perfect food.

5. Study of fat — Food values.

   (a) Deep fat frying.

6. Cheese — Food value.

7. Study of Flour and Flour mixtures.
   (1) 1. Pour batters.
       2. Drop batters.
       3. Soft dough.
       4. Stiff dough.
   (2) Leavening agents.
       (a) Soda.
       (b) Baking powder.
       (c) Yeast.
       (d) Egg.
   (3) Making bread.
       Study of bread and pastry flour.
   (4) Pastry.

8. Salads — Food value.

9. Lessons in candy making.

10. Deserts.
    Hot.
    Cold.

11. Canning, preserving and pickling.

12. Invalid cooking.

13. Serving.

14. Practical review.
    Planning and cooking of menus.

15. Arrangement of table.
    Serving.

Laundry

Hand Laundry:

From three to six months of training is given to girls in hand laundry work. Emphasis is laid upon neatness in performance of work, care of room and equipment, and a high grade of work is required.

The girls begin with ironing sheets, gingham band aprons, white aprons. Afterward they work through all articles of an ordinary laundry, which require careful ironing. Only the finer work, such as can be furnished by the officers' selected garments are reserved for these classes.

The student is required to be proficient in care of room and fire, in all operations pertaining to washing; in the ironing of fine embroidery, heavy tailored garments, silk waists, etc., before completing this course with honor.

Steam Laundry:

About two months is required to familiarize the students with the details of steam laundry work required. They are taught to sort and arrange the clothing and transfer from one part of machinery to another. They become proficient in putting garments through the flat piece ironer with speed and accuracy.

Handicraft School

The following lines of work have been organized in this department:

Chair caning; Reed basketry, including staining and finishing; ruffia weaving for baskets, bags, etc.; lace making; linen weaving; rug weaving; wood-work, simple subjects, such as coathangers, bird houses and other small articles.

Art Department

A special class has instruction in:

(a) Water color work on post cards, Christmas cards, etc.
(b) Selection of color schemes, cutting and mounting pictures.
(c) Making calendars.
(d) Some hand drawing, pen and ink work and lettering.

CHILDREN OF THE REPUBLIC

When our school was visited by Mrs. Simon Baruch, Regent of Knickerbocker Chapter, D. A. R., of New York, May 6, 1915, the suggestion was made that this would be a fine field of labor for organizations of Children of the Republic Clubs among the cottages. Since that time clubs have been organized in eight cottages with membership aggregating one hundred girls. Each candidate for membership must have at least one month's good record before being admitted. One cottage club meeting is held each month, and one general meeting. Mrs. Charles Benson, Regent of Hudson, D. A. R., is the Directress, Mary D. Dusinberre, First Assistant, Lois Dean, Second Assistant, and Mary Harrigan, Third Assistant. In connection with this work Miss Harrigan has organized a Ribbon Girl Military Club, which meets for drill in marching once each week. The work of the Children of the Republic is to foster patriotism and teach the rudiments of parliamentary usage. A literary program forms a part of each meeting and it is designed to have volunteer speakers at several public meetings during the coming year.

STATE CHARITIES LAW

§ 204. Commitments; papers furnished by committing magistrates. 1. Whenever any female not over the age of sixteen years shall be brought before any court or committing magistrate, and it shall appear to the satisfaction of such court or magistrate by the confession of such female, or by competent testimony, that such female frequents reputed houses of prostitution or assignation, or frequents the company of thieves or prostitutes, or is found associating with vicious and dissolute persons or is wilfully disobedient to parent or guardian, and is in danger of becoming morally depraved; or is of intemperate habits, or is a vagrant or is guilty of any criminal offense, and who is not insane nor mentally or physically incapable of being substantially benefited by the training and discipline of such institution, she may be sentenced and committed to the New York State Training School for Girls, or placed in charge of the board of managers thereof, to be there confined under the provisions of law relating to such institution, but no person under the age of twelve years shall be committed to such institution for any crime or offense less than a felony, and no commitment made under this section which shall recite the facts upon which it is based, shall be deemed or held to be invalid by reason of any imperfection or defect in form. No person shall be committed to such institution nor placed in the charge of the board of managers thereof for a definite term, but any such person may be paroled or discharged at any time after her commitment, by the board of managers of such institution. Any such female under the age of fifteen years when so committed or placed in charge of the board of managers of said school, shall not be retained therein for a longer period than until she becomes of the age of eighteen; and such females, fifteen years of age or over, when so committed, shall not be detained for a period longer than three years from the time of such commitment. Every such female shall continue to be a ward of such institution until she becomes of the age of twenty-one years, notwithstanding her parole or discharge therefrom, and it shall be the duty of said board of managers to continue to exercise over her such control as may be necessary for her welfare during her said minority as a ward of said institution; and if deemed by said board of managers necessary for her welfare or for her protection from evil associations or companionship, said board may return her temporarily to said institution at any time during her said minority. If any such female shall marry during her said minority such wardship shall thereupon terminate.

2. The board of managers of such institution shall furnish the several county clerks of the state with suitable blanks for the commitment of females thereto. Such county clerks shall immediately notify the magistrates of their respective counties of the reception of such blanks and that upon application they will be furnished to them.

3. The magistrate committing a female, pursuant to this section, shall immediately notify the superintendent of the institution to which the commitment is made of the conviction of such female, and shall cause a record to be kept of the name, age, birthplace, occupation, previous commitments, if any, and for what offenses; the last place of residence of such female, and the particulars of the offense for which she is committed. The magistrate shall also execute a warrant of commitment, which shall recite the facts upon which it is based, and the name, age, birthplace, occupation, previous commitments, if any, and for what offenses, and the last place of residence of such female. This warrant of commitment shall be delivered to a person authorized by law to accompany such female to the institution, and shall be delivered by such person to the superintendent of such institution, who shall cause the facts stated therein, and such other facts as may be directed by the board of managers, to be entered in a book of record. This warrant of commitment shall constitute the only paper requisite to a commitment to this institution.

4. Such magistrate shall, before committing any such female, inquire into and determine the age of such female at the time of commitment, and her age as so determined shall be stated in the warrant. The statement of the age of such female in such warrant shall be conclusive evidence as to such age, in any action to recover damages for her detention or imprisonment under such warrant, and shall be presumptive evidence thereof in any other inquiry, action or proceeding relating to such detention or imprisonment. If the court or magistrate shall omit to insert in the warrant of commitment the age of any delinquent committed to such school, the managers, shall as soon as may be after such delinquent shall be received by them, ascertain her age by the best

means in their power, and cause the same to be entered in a book
to be designated by them for that purpose, and the age of such
delinquent thus ascertained shall be deemed and taken to be the
true age of such delinquent. (*As amended by chapter* 340 *of the
Laws of* 1909, *and chapter* 449 *of the Laws of* 1910, *and chapter*
486 *of the Laws of* 1911.)

§ 205. **Return of females improperly committed.** Whenever it
shall appear to the satisfaction of the board of managers of such
institution, that any person committed thereto is not of proper age
to be so committed or is not properly committed, or is insane or
mentally incapable of being materially benefited by the discipline
of such institution, such board of managers shall cause the return
of such female to the county from which she was so committed.
Such female shall be so returned in the custody of one of the
persons employed by such board of managers to convey to such
institution females committed thereto, who shall deliver her into
the custody of the sheriff of the county from which she was committed. Such sheriff shall take such female before the magistrate
making the commitment, or some other magistrate having equal
jurisdiction in such county, to be by such magistrate resentenced
for the offense for which she was committed to such institution
and dealt with in all respects as though she had not been so committed. The cost and expenses of the return of such female, necessarily incurred and paid by such board of managers, shall be a
charge against the county from which such female was committed, to be paid by such county to such board of managers in the
same manner as other county charges are collected.

§ 206. **Disposition of children of females so committed and of
the mothers of such children.** If any female committed to such
institution, at the time of such commitment, is a mother of a
nursing child in her care under one year of age, or is pregnant
with child which shall be born after such commitment, such child
may accompany its mother to and remain in such institution until
it is two years of age and must then be removed therefrom. The
board of managers of such institution may cause such child to be
placed in any asylum for children in this state, or may place such
child under the care and custody of a proper person willing to
assume such care, and pay for the care and maintenance of such
child at a reasonable rate, until the mother of such child shall
have been discharged from the institution, and may make such

change from time to time in the care and custody of such child as the board may deem advisable. If such female, at the time of such commitment, shall be the mother of and have under her exclusive care a child more than one year of age, which might otherwise be left without proper care or guardianship, the magistrate committing such female shall cause such child to be committed to such asylum as may be provided by the law for such purposes, or to the care and custody of some relative or proper person willing to assume such care. If a female, when committed, is pregnant with child, the board of managers may, at any time after commitment, place such female in any maternity hospital, or with any proper person or family in this state, and pay at a reasonable rate for the care and maintenance of such female and such child, if any, until such child becomes two years of age, when the mother must be returned to such institution and the child disposed of as hereinabove provided in the case of a child who remains in the institution until it is two years of age. If a female, when committed, is the mother of a nursing child in her care under one year of age, the board of managers may also cause such mother and child to be placed in the care and custody of a proper person willing to assume such care, and pay therefor a reasonable rate for maintenance and care until the child becomes two years of age, when the mother must be returned to such institution and the child disposed of as hereinabove provided, in the case of a child who remains in the institution until it is two years of age. Said board shall cause the return to the institution of said mother, in either case hereinbefore provided for, before the child becomes two years of age, whenever, in the opinion of said board, the best interests of said mother and child will justify the separation. (*As amended by chapter* 555 *of the Laws of* 1911, *and chapter* 158 *of the Laws of* 1915.)

§ 208. **Conveyance of females committed.** The board of managers of such institution shall employ suitable female persons to be known as marshals, to convey from the place of conviction to such institution all females legally committed thereto, and such marshals shall have the power and authority of deputy sheriffs in respect thereto. All expenses necessarily incurred in making such conveyance shall be paid by the treasurer of the board of managers.

§ 209. **Detentions and rearrests in cases of escape.** The board of managers of such institution may detain therein, under the rules and regulations adopted by them, any female legally committed thereto, according to the terms of the sentence and commitment, and conditionally discharge such female at any time prior to the expiration of the term of commitment. If an inmate escape or be conditionally discharged from such institution, the board of managers may cause her to be rearrested and returned to such institution, to be detained therein for the unexpired portion of her term, dating from the time of her escape or conditional discharge. A person employed by the board of managers of such institution to convey to such institution females committed thereto, may arrest, without a warrant, an escaped inmate in any county in this state, and shall forthwith convey her to the institution from which she escaped; and a magistrate may cause an escaped inmate to be arrested and held in custody, until she can be removed to such institution, as in the case of her first commitment thereto. A person conditionally discharged from such institution may ·be arrested and returned thereto, upon a warrant issued by its president and secretary. Such warrant shall briefly state the reason for such arrest and return, and shall be directed and delivered to a person employed by such board of managers to convey to such institution females committed thereto, and may be executed by such person in any county of this state.

§ 210. **Employment of inmates.** The board of managers of such institution shall determine the kind of employment for females committed thereto and shall provide for the necessary custody and superintendence. The provisions for the safe keeping and employment of such females shall be made for the purpose of teaching such females a useful trade or profession and improving their mental and moral condition. Such board of managers may credit such females with a reasonable compensation for the labor performed by them, and may charge them with the necessary expenses of their maintenance and discipline, not exceeding the sum of two dollars per week. If any balance shall be found to be due such females at the expiration of their terms of commitment, such balance may be paid to them at the time of their discharge. To secure the safe keeping, obedience and good order of the females committed to such institution, the superintendent thereof has the same powers as to such females as keepers of jails and penitentiaries possess as to persons committed to their custody.

§ 211. **Clothing and money to be furnished discharged inmates.** The board of managers of such institution may, in their discretion, furnish to each inmate of such institution who shall be discharged therefrom, necessary clothing not exceeding twelve dollars in value, or if discharged between the first day of November and the first day of April to the value of not exceeding eighteen dollars, and ten dollars in money, and a ticket for the transportation of one person from such institution to the place of conviction of such inmate, or to such other place as such inmate may designate, at no greater distance from such institution than the place of conviction.

§ 212. **Freedom of worship.** Nothing herein contained shall interfere with the right of freedom of worship of ·any inmate confined within said institution, as provided by the constitution of the state of New York.

§ 213. **Confinement of female juvenile delinquents under sentences by the courts of the United States.** The superintendent of the New York state training school for girls, at Hudson, shall receive and safely keep in such institution, subject to the regulations and discipline thereof, and the provisions of this article, any female not over the age of sixteen years convicted of any offense against the United States, and sentenced to imprisonment by any court of the United States, sitting within this state, until such sentences be executed, or until such delinquent shall be discharged by due course of law, conditioned upon the United States supporting such delinquent and paying the expenses attendant upon the execution of such sentence. (*As amended by chapter 449 of the Laws of* 1910.)

PENAL LAW

§ 486. **Prohibited acts; destitute children.** Any child actually or apparently under the age of sixteen years who is found:

1. Begging or receiving or soliciting alms, in any manner or under any pretense; or gathering or picking rags, or collecting cigar stumps, bones or refuse from markets; or,

2. Not having any home or other place of abode or proper guardianship; or who has been abandoned or improperly exposed or neglected, by its parents or other person or persons having it in charge, or being in a state of want or suffering; or,

3. Living or having lived with or in custody of a parent or guardian who has been sentenced to imprisonment for crime, or who has been convicted of a crime against the person of such child,

or has been adjudged an habitual criminal; or, (*As amended by chapter 480 of the Laws of* 1915.)

4. Frequenting or being in the company of reputed thieves or prostitutes, or in a reputed house of prostitution or assignation, or living in such a house either with or without its parent or guardian, or being in concert saloons, dance houses, theatres, museums or other places of entertainment, or places where wines, malt or spirituous liquors are sold, without being in charge of its parent or guardian; or playing any game of chance or skill in any place wherein or adjacent to which any beer, ale, wine or liquor is sold or given away, or being in any such place; or,

5. Coming within any of the descriptions of children mentioned in section four hundred and eighty-five.

Must be arrested and brought before a proper court or magistrate, who may commit the child to any incorporated charitable reformatory, or other institution, and when practicable, to such as is governed by persons of the same religious faith as the parents of the child, or may make any disposition of the child such as now is, or hereafter may be authorized in the cases of vagrants, truants, paupers or disorderly persons, but such commitment shall, so far as practicable, be made to such charitable or reformatory institutions.

Whenever any child shall be committed to an institution under this chapter, and the warrant or commitment shall so state, and it shall appear therefrom that either parent, or any guardian or custodian of such child, was present at the examination before such court or magistrate, or had such notice thereof as was by such court or magistrate deemed and adjudged sufficient, no further or other notice required by any local or special statute, in regard to the committal of children to such institution, shall be necessary, and such commitment shall in all respects be sufficient to authorize such institutions to receive and retain such child in its custody as therein directed.

Whenever any commitment of a child shall for any reason be adjudged or found defective, a new commitment of the child may be made or directed by the court or magistrate, as the welfare of the child may require. And no commitment of a child which shall recite therein the facts upon which it is based shall be deemed invalid by reason of any omission of the court or magistrate by whom such commitment is made to file any documents, papers or proceedings relating thereto, or by reason of any limitation as to the age of the child committed, contained in the act or articles of incorporation of the institution to which it may have been committed.

*   *   *   *   *   *   *   *   *   *   *   *

7. All children actually or apparently under the age of sixteen who desert their homes, without good or sufficient cause, or keep company with dissolute, immoral or vicious persons, shall be deemed disorderly children. Those actually or apparently under the like age who are not susceptible of proper restraint or control by their parents, guardians, or lawful custodians, or who are habitually disobedient to their reasonable and lawful commands, shall be deemed ungovernable children. A disorderly or ungovernable child may be dealt with as provided in the fifth subdivision of this section.

8.   *   *   *   *   *   *   *   *   *   *   *

No child under restraint or conviction, actually or apparently under the age of sixteen years, shall be placed in any prison or place of confinement, or in any court-room, or in any vehicle for transportation in company with adults charged with or convicted of crime.

9. Whenever any child is brought before any court or magistrate, to be dealt with under any of the subdivisions of this section, instead of committing such child to confinement in any institution, the court or magistrate may place such child under the custody of a probation or parole officer, and at any time within one year thereafter such court or magistrate, may issue a warrant for such child, and after giving such child an opportunity to be heard, may make the commitment which could have been made in the first instance as aforesaid. The foregoing provision shall not apply to a children's court created by special enactment in cities of the first class, but this exception shall not be construed as taking away or limiting any jurisdiction now possessed by such children's courts. If at any time during the proceedings it shall seem to the magistrate that any child brought before him under any of the subdivisions of this section, appears to be feeble-minded, he may cause the child to be examined by two physicians of at least five years' experience in the treatment of mental disease, and on the written statement of the two examining physicians that in their opinion the child is feeble-minded, he may commit him to a public institution for the feeble-minded, and such child shall be detained therein

until duly discharged by direction of the board of managers thereof.
(*As amended by chapter 480 of the Laws of* 1915.)

*   *   *   *   *   *   *   *   *   *   *   *

§ 2184. Sentence to * * * New York State Training
School for Girls.

*   *   *   *   *   *   *   *   *   *   *   *

Where a female person not over the age of twelve years is convicted of a crime amounting to felony, or where a female person
of the age of twelve years and not over the age of sixteen years
is convicted of a crime, the trial court may, instead of sentencing her
to imprisonment in a state prison or in a penitentiary, direct her to
be confined in the New York State Training School for Girls, under
the provisions of the statute relating thereto, but nothing in this
section shall affect any of the provisions contained in section
twenty-one hundred and ninety-four. (*As amended by chapter* 607
of the Laws of 1913.)

*   *   *   *   *   *   *   *   *   *   *   *

§ 2186. Sentence of minors to imprisonment. * * * A
child of more than seven and less than sixteen years of age, who
shall commit any act or omission which, if committed by an adult,
would be a crime not punishable by death or life imprisonment,
shall not be deemed guilty of any crime, but of juvenile delinquency
only, but any other person concerned therein, whether as principal
or accessory, who otherwise would be punishable as a principal
or accessory shall be punishable as a principal or accessory in the
same manner as if such child were over sixteen years of age at
the time the crime was committed. Any child charged with any
act or omission which may render him guilty of juvenile delinquency
shall be dealt with in the same manner as now is or may hereafter
be provided in the case of adults charged with the same act or
omission except as specially provided heretofore in the case of
children under the age of sixteen years. (*As amended by chapter*
478 *of the Laws of* 1909.)

§ 2194. Sentence of minor under sixteen years of age. When
a person under the age of sixteen is convicted of a crime, he may,
in the discretion of the court, instead of being sentenced to fine
or imprisonment, be placed in charge of any suitable person or
institution willing to receive him, and be thereafter, until majority
or for a shorter term, subjected to such discipline and control of
the person or institution receiving him as a parent or guardian may
lawfully exercise over a minor. A child under sixteen years of age

committed for misdemeanor, under any provision of this chapter, must be committed to some reformatory, charitable or other institution authorized by law to receive and take charge of minors. And when any such child is committed to an institution it shall, when practicable, be committed to an institution governed by persons of the same religious faith as the parents of such child.

*   *   *   *   *   *   *   *   *   *   *   *

CODE OF CRIMINAL PROCEDURE.

§ 887. A vagrant child is a child between the age of five and fourteen, having sufficient bodily health and mental capacity to attend the public schools, found wandering in the streets or lanes of any town or city. or incorporated village, a truant, without any lawful occupation.

STATE OF NEW YORK

REPORT

OF THE

Joint Legislative Committee

ON THE

Simplification of Civil Practice

TRANSMITTED TO THE LEGISLATURE APRIL 25, 1917

ALBANY
J. B. LYON COMPANY, PRINTERS
1917

No. 63

IN SENATE

APRIL 25, 1917.

REPORT OF THE JOINT LEGISLATIVE COMMITTEE ON THE SIMPLIFICATION OF CIVIL PRACTICE

To the Legislature:

The Joint Committee of the Legislature on the Simplification of Civil Practice in the courts of the State was appointed pursuant to joint resolution adopted April 22, 1915, and continued by joint resolution, adopted March 6, 1916. The resolution directed the committee " to investigate and inquire into the report of the board of statutory consolidation on the simplification of the civil practice in the courts of the State, and to investigate and inquire into all matters pertaining thereto." The powers of the committee it will be observed are not confined to an investigation of the report of the board of statutory consolidation, but extend to an inquiry into all matters pertaining to the simplification of the civil practice. The investigation of the committee has involved a study of the history and development of procedure, as well as an examination of systems in other jurisdictions.

Procedure for the enforcement of rights has of necessity existed since the recognition of rights and the establishment by organized society of tribunals and courts for their enforcement. The report of the commission of code revision made to the Legislature of 1896, constituting Assembly Document No. 42, contains an interesting sketch of the development of procedure from the earliest

times and a synopsis of the systems of practice then in force in
other states and countries. The commission states that its object
is " to place before the public information, perhaps not otherwise
easily accessible, showing the striking similarity in all ages in the
main features of procedure and that the general principles of our
practice are firmly established as a part of our institutions." The
common law procedure of England, as the same had been modified
by the Legislature of the colony of New York, became the procedure in this State under the Constitution of 1777, subject to
such alterations and additions as the Legislature might from time
to time enact with reference thereto. The Legislature very early
commenced to enact alterations and additions.

Early Statutes

From the organization of the State in 1777 to the year 1800,
inclusive, there were 78 general statutes relating to practice; in
1801 there were 37 of the same character. The Legislature of
1801 passed chapter 90, " for the amendment of the law and the
better administration of justice." This act constituted a revision
of many prior laws on the subject of practice. The same Legislature revised the laws concerning costs and fees. From 1801 to
1812, inclusive, there were 33 general practice acts. In 1813
there was a general revision of the law and the subject of practice
was embraced in 26 statutes. This was a revision of special subjects but not a general codification. From 1814 to 1827, inclusive,
there were 47 general practice acts. The foregoing data in relation to the early statutes is contained in the report of the code
revision commission of 1896, referred to above.

Revised Statutes

The first legislative attempt at an extensive and comprehensive
statement of the jurisdiction and powers of the courts of the State
as well as regulating the proceedings therein was made by the
Revised Statutes of 1828, Part III of which contained 10 chapters, entitled "An act concerning courts and ministers of justice
and regulating proceedings in civil cases." This part of the
Revised Statutes was intended, as stated in its preamble, to be a

consolidation and rearrangement of existing statutes, a simplification of their language and a supplying of omissions and other defects. A very large number of the sections were new in form.

Parts II and III of the Revised Statutes contained 3,294 sections relating to courts, actions and proceedings, while the Code of Civil Procedure of 1876, as added to in 1880, contained 3,356 sections. In making this comparison it is apparent that the Code of Civil Procedure, numerous as are its sections, is not much greater in bulk of sections than the provisions on related subjects in the Revised Statutes of 1828. The provisions of the Revised Statutes formed the basis for many of the provisions of the Code of Procedure of 1848, and for the greater part of the Code of Civil Procedure.

Code of Procedure of 1848

Pursuant to a direction contained in the Constitution of 1846 commissioners were shortly thereafter selected whose duty was "to reduce into a written and systematic code the whole body of the law of this State, or so much and such parts thereof as to the said commissioners shall seem practicable and expedient." The commissioners proceeded diligently with their task and a part of the results of their labors is found in the Code of Procedure enacted in 1848. This Code, commonly known as the "Field Code," was not intended by the commissioners to be a complete enactment. It was but a fragment of the whole work later submitted to the Legislature but not adopted; in fact, it was once referred to by David Dudley Field, its real author, as "the fragment of 1848."

The Field Code as originally enacted consisted of 391 sections, and of 473 sections, as amended in 1849. There were, however, sections making provisions of other statutes applicable without reincorporating the same, for example, § 421 (382) applying about 12 sections of the Revised Statutes relating to referees; § 448 relating to partition, applying about 95 sections of the Revised Statutes; § 456 relating to actions for waste, applying about 29 sections of the Revised Statutes; § 455 relating to real property actions generally, applying about 24 sections of the

Revised Statutes. The Code as amended in 1849, with these sections included by reference, embraced 633 sections.

Only statutory provisions inconsistent were repealed. All others were left standing. Provisions in the Revised Statutes concerning mandamus and prohibition (12 sections) were expressly preserved, except where plainly inconsistent; also appeals from Surrogate's Courts (about 30 sections); also special statutory remedies not theretofore obtained by action (about 375 sections); also proceedings provided for by chapter 5 of Part II of the Revised Statutes (87 sections); also the sixth and eighth titles of chapter 5 of Part II (24 sections); also chapter 8 of Part III (560 sections); also chapter 9, title 1, Part III (86 sections).

If the amended Code of 1849 had been enacted with all of the provisions actually forming a part of the same, both sections of the Code itself and the sections of the Revised Statutes expressly included by reference, it would have contained a total of 1807 sections.

The Code of 1848, as amended in 1849, included but 13 sections and 15 rules relating to Justice Courts and the practice therein, and repealed in terms but 11 sections of the Revised Statutes relating to these courts, so that about 270 sections were left in existence governing Justice Court Practice.

The Surrogate Court practice in the Revised Statutes (about 390 sections) was left practically untouched by the 1848 Code.

The Field Code, as amended in 1849, with sections of the Revised Statutes included by reference and those relating to Justice and Surrogate Courts makes an actual bulk of 2,467 sections. In addition to these sections, existing statutory provisions relating to actions not inconsistent with the Code and in substance applicable to actions therein provided were expressly preserved, this clause saving from repeal a large number of sections.

It is thus evident that the Field Code of 1848, contrary to a popular idea of many of the present members of the profession, was not and did not purport to be a complete statement of the statutes relating to courts and the practice and procedure therein. As a matter of fact the Field Code provisions, with the unrepealed provisions of the Revised Statutes and other enactments passed between 1828 and 1848, if brought together into one volume of statute instead of being left scattered, would make a bulk of statutory regulation quite as formidable as the present Code of Civil Procedure.

Much of the Field Code was new enactment making changes in the common law practice and stating settled principles not theretofore incorporated in our statutes. The language of the Code sections was comparatively simple in form and the style was generally commended. The work simplified the practice so far as it went, abolished many of the perplexing technicalities of the old practice, and thus became the model for the Codes of many other States of the Union. Practice in the courts, however, had not yet reached the happy state where litigation had become easy and justice immediate. The courts were at once called upon to construe provisions of the Field Code and numerous questions continued to arise over various provisions of the Revised Statutes. The court decisions upon questions of practice after the adoption of this Code filled many volumes of reports. The Field Code was published in handy form no larger than the modern vest pocket diary but the bar soon found that it contained but a small portion of the provisions governing court practice.

Code of Civil Procedure

Before many years a new agitation began for another commission to revise and consolidate the statutes relating to courts and procedure and in 1870 a commission was created for this purpose by the Legislature. In 1876 the labors of this commission bore fruit in a Code of 1,496 sections, and in 1880 the second instalment of its work followed with an addition of more than 1,800 sections. These two enactments were called the Code of Civil Procedure, for many years referred to as the Throop Code. The Throop Code, with amendements and additions, is our present Code of Civil Procedure.

This Code met with great opposition at the time it was proposed for enactment and the objections to it have continued with varying vigor since that time. The grounds given for the criticism of the Throop Code are many. It is claimed that it is too minute;

that it attempts to regulate too many details of practice which
should not be the subject of statutory regulation; that it is too
cumbrous and too verbose.

Whatever the faults of the Troop Code, its chief claim to favor
was that it brought together into one volume all of the outstanding
statutory enactments relating to courts, practice and procedure,
including the Revised Statutes, the Field Code of 1848 and independent acts. In addition to the restatement of existing law the
Throop Code embraced many new statements based on court
decisions and suggestions received from members of the bar.

Size of the Code

The Throop Code upon the enactment of the chapters adopted
in 1880 contained 3,356 sections and it was subsequently
increased by inclusion of the Condemnation Law, the Mechanic's
Lien Law and other acts to 3,441 sections. Opponents of the
Code lay special stress upon its vast bulk as one of the chief
reasons for its repeal. The statement that the Code contains 3,441
sections is misleading. Many sections have been repealed from
time to time without re-enactment; many have been repealed and
transferred to the consolidated laws. As a matter of fact there are
now in the Code a total of 2,742 sections and neither by transfer
to rules or to consolidated laws can actual volume be materially
reduced. In this connection it is interesting to note that while
the board of statutory consolidation recommended many code
provisions for repeal, the whole number of sections of statute law
and rules proposed by the Board is 2681, including practice acts,
rules and amendments and additions to the Consolidated Laws.
An analysis of the Code discloses a comparatively small number
of sections, 767 sections actually relating to procedure in the
course of an ordinary civil action. Exclude from the total number
of sections relating to Justices' Courts, Surrogates' Courts, the
Court of Claims, the New York City Court and condemnation,
and there remain 1,975 sections to be considered. Exclude
268 sections which the committee deems may be properly transferred to the Consolidated Laws, and there remain 1,707 sections.
Exclude 523 sections relating to particular actions (partition,

foreclosure, matrimonial actions, etc.) and there remain 1,184 sections. Exclude 309 sections relating to limitation of actions, evidence, costs and fees, and exemption from execution and there remain 875 sections, which may be properly considered as relating to the procedure in an ordinary civil action. While the number of sections excluded may be somewhat reduced by revision, they will continue to constitute part of the statute law of the State governing practice and procedure as those terms are generally understood by the profession. If we exclude them from the Code or from the practice act it will simply mean that they will be compiled by editors, as has been done in England, and the bulk of the practice law will not be diminished.

The compilation of the rules and statutes relating to practice in England published under the title of " The Annual Practice," is a volume of 2,415 finely printed pages, with an index of 382 pages, and contains the citation of 11,400 decisions interpreting the meaning of the English practice acts and rules. The practice acts themselves, independently of the rules and orders, contain approximately 3,500 sections. While the committee has not made an examination of the volume of practice law in the State of New Jersey, wherein a short practice act and system of rules prevail, it has been informed by attorneys practicing in that State that the actual volume of the practice law is not materially less than in the State of New York.

These suggestions are made simply for the purpose of indicating that the expedient of adopting a short practice act and a system of rules will not result in reducing the general practice provisions, as the same are ordinarily understood, to a single brief legislative practice act and rules.

Code Amendments

One of the chief complaints against the Code is its frequent amendment by the Legislature, by reason whereof the practice is kept in an unsettled condition. While it is true that numerous amendments to the Code are annually proposed, and some of these probably for the purpose of affecting particular law suits, nevertheless it is also true that the Legislature proceeds very cautiously in adopting amendments to the portions of the Code affecting the well established procedure in the course of an action. Amendments affecting these portions of the Code are as a rule only considered when referred to the Legislature by responsible bodies, such as the New York State Bar Association or the Bar Association of the City of New York. The adoption of a short practice act or a system of rules will not prevent the proposal of amendments to the general practice law of the State. A careful examination of the amendments which have been made from time to time since the Code of 1877, reveals the fact that with the exception of important amendments which have been proposed by responsible authorities, the actual working portions of the Code remain almost unchanged since its adoption. Exclusive of amendments made for correction in 1877 and for changes required by the new Constitution of 1895, of 843 sections covering the general provisions of the Code relating to the procedure in an ordinary civil action, but 159 have been amended by the Legislature during the forty years since its adoption. These suggestions are made in view of the claim that the Legislature is constantly tinkering with the Code.

Subsequent Reports

Since the enactment of the Code of Civil Procedure several commissions and committees have been appointed and charged with an examination of the Code, and each has made a report as to the best method to be adopted for simplifying the practice in civil courts. The Code Revision Commission was appointed in 1895, pursuant to chapter 1036 of the Laws of that year, which directed the Commission to " examine the Code of Procedure of this State and the codes of procedure and practice acts in force in other states and countries, and report to the next Legislature the result of their investigations." The Commission made a preliminary report to the Legislature of 1896, constituting Assembly Document No. 42 of that year. It subsequently reported to the Legislature a rearrangement and partial revision of the Code of Civil Procedure, including in its plan a separate Surrogates' Code and a separate Justices' Code. None of its work was approved by the Legislature.

The last commission to report was the Board of Statutory Consolidation created in 1904. The work of this Board from its establishment until 1909 consisted mainly in the preparation of the Consolidated Laws which have been enacted. The Legislature in 1912 directed this Board "to report to the next Legislature a plan for the classification, consolidation, and simplification of the civil practice in the courts of this State." The Board presented to the Legislature of 1913 a plan in pursuance of the 1912 act and were then "authorized and directed to prepare and present to the Legislature as herein provided, a practice act, rules of court and short forms as recommended by said Board in its report to the Legislature of 1913."

Report of Board of Statutory Consolidation

The Board of Statutory Consolidation presented its complete report, contained in four volumes, to the Legislature of 1915. Volume I contained a short practice act of 71 sections, and 401 rules of court; volume II, the practice in Surrogates' Courts, Justices' Courts, and certain inferior local courts; volume III, provisions of the Code distributed to various consolidated laws; and volume IV, source tables and tables of distribution of Code sections. Each volume contained the notes of the Board referring to the various provisions contained therein.

The report was transmitted to the Legislature by the Governor on April 21, 1915, with a suggestion that a joint committee of the Legislature be appointed to act with other committees in consideration of the subject; and on the following day a joint resolution was adopted creating the committee here reporting.

Preliminary Work of Committee

In pursuance of the authority received from the Legislature the Joint Committee at the outset, realizing to some extent the stupendous task with which it was confronted, had prepared a number of necessary indexes, tables and other working tools to enable it to begin its work understandingly and make the minute and detailed studies and comparisons required before a report of any value could be made. In this connection it is well to remember that the Board of Statutory Consolidation presented a report which if adopted and enacted would repeal the present Code of Civil Procedure, substitute a short practice act and transfer to the courts the power to regulate practice and procedure. Whatever the objections to the Code might be, it had been in existence in one form or another for nearly a century, and the committee, regardless of the demand from many quarters for its repeal, felt that the questions involved were of vast importance and merited the most deliberate and careful examination and research.

In the first place a pamphlet was prepared and distributed containing a comprehensive index of the practice act and rules reported by the Board, as no index accompanied the Board's report. This pamphlet also outlined the Code provisions assigned by the Board to the various Consolidated Laws.

The Code of Civil Procedure was pasted on large sheets, section by section, and opposite each section was pasted the parts of the practice act and rules or Consolidated Laws into which the Code section was distributed or the section of the act or rules which the Board said superseded or covered the Code section. A sample sheet from this volume, reduced in size, is shown in Figure I.

The practice act and rules were pasted on large sheets, section by section, and opposite each section was pasted the note of the Board referring to such section or rule. Each section of the practice act and each rule were then marked by bracketing and underscoring to indicate whether the section was all new, or if not all new, what portion was new and what portion was derived from the Code, and the change in language, if any. A sample sheet from this volume, reduced in size, is shown in Figure II.

The Code of Civil Procedure was marked to correspond with the disposition of the various sections and parts of sections by the Board, and a series of abbreviated references was adopted and marked on the margin of the Code sections, and from this marked Code a number of "Key" Codes were marked for use by the

committee and its assistants and for distribution to various bar
association committees. A sample page from one of these marked
Codes is shown in Figure III.

A series of large cards was prepared and printed with a different color for sections of the practice act, the rules, the special
court practice, and the Consolidated Law amendments. A
separate color was also used for cards to contain the sections in the
form finally adopted by the Committee.

New Practice Recommended by the Board

The idea underlying the new system of practice recommended
by the Board of Statutory Consolidation may be summarized in
the language of the Board as follows:

"(1) The preparation of a short practice act to be adopted by
the Legislature which would direct the changes necessary to
simplify procedure and adapt it to present conditions;

(2) The preparation of rules of court by the courts which would
regulate the important matters of practice and which would be
under the control of the courts;

(3) The preparation of such changes in the practice as would
simplify and modernize it so as to secure a prompt determination
of legal controversies according to the substantive rights of the
parties."

The changes proposed by the Board may be separated into two
main divisions, as follows:

(a) A complete change in the method of regulating civil practice
from a statutory code enacted by the Legislature to court rules
adopted by the courts, and (b) radical and far reaching changes
in the practice itself, involving extensive revision and condensa-
tion of the present practice provisions.

The absolute repeal of the Code of Civil Procedure is contemplated under the first division (Civil Practice Act, § 70) to be
replaced by a brief practice act of seventy-one sections containing
a statement of principles of practice to bind the courts in formulating rules to the extent specified in the act. Hereafter all
matters of practice would be regulated by rules of court which
would be under the control of the courts, except so far as limited

by the short practice act. (Civil Practice Act, §§ 5, 6.) A convention of appellate division justices is given plenary power to make and amend rules of practice and procedure from time to time. (Civil Practice Act, § 6.) Where no provision is made by the act or rules the proceedings shall be regulated by the court or judge before whom the action is pending. (Civil Practice Act, § 5.)

The second division mentioned deals with the actual rewriting of our civil practice and procedure and includes the various changes suggested by the board in practice provisions from the commencement of an action to its complete determination and satisfaction.

In order to review the different portions of the work of the Board, the Committee will take up separately: (1) The proposed short practice act. (2) The proposed rules of court. (3) The special court practice acts. (4) The distribution of Code matters not contained in either of the foregoing divisions, and (5) Specific changes in practice recommended by the Board.

Proposed Short Practice Act

The short practice act proposed by the Board consists of 71 sections, 13 sections of which are sections concerning the construction of the act, saving and repealing clauses, leaving 56 sections relating strictly to practice and procedure in the courts. Reference is made by the Board to the fact that the English Judicature Act of 1873 contains 100 sections and the New Jersey Practice Act, 34 sections.

The theory of the practice act is that it should define merely the fundamental principles which should direct, govern, and restrict the courts in the formulation of rules of practice. The Board says: " It leaves the working out of the details of practice to the court rules, thus placing the responsibility for legal procedure upon the courts where it belongs." The Board further states: " The plan herein proposed is not that of the English system under which so much of the details of practice is left to the decisions of the courts, but one under which the ground work or fundamentals of procedure are defined by the Legislature and the superstructure or details are regulated by stated written rules of court binding upon the courts and litigants alike, but modifiable in the interest of justice whenever necessary."

In examining the report of the board it will be seen that the suggested new system of practice is not modeled entirely upon any system existing in any other jurisdiction but that it has been prepared so as to retain a large part of our present practice system as well as including features adapted from other States and from England.

The first eighteen sections of the practice act contain general provisions relating to the construction of the act, general powers of courts and judges as to rules of practice, mistakes and defects, amendments, consolidation and severance, terms of court, orders, costs, classification of causes, classification of practice in rules, filing and docketing of papers.

Sections 19–28 contain provisions relating to the commencement of actions, as joinder of causes and parties, pleadings and rules for service; §§ 29–32 cover preparations for trial; §§ 33–41 cover matters relating to the trial of actions; §§ 41–46 relate to judgments; §§ 47–54 to appeals; § 55 to execution; §§ 56–71 cover certain miscellaneous matters and also provisions laying down rules for the construction of the act, the effect on other acts, repealed provisions, saving clauses, the repeal of the Code of Civil Procedure and the time when the act takes effect.

Of the 58 sections of the act relating to practice and procedure, 38 state principles of practice and the other 20 relate to the construction and application of the act, the method of formulating rules by the courts and directions to the courts as to certain features which the rules must contain. Many of the matters stated in the act have been practically duplicated in the rules.

A civil action in our courts to-day is brought to obtain the enforcement of a right or to secure the redress or prevention of a wrong. In the very nature of things, there are certain principles underlying various procedural matters in the course of an action which are recognized as fundamental and which are purely matters of strict right and so substantive in character that they should be a part of our statutory system. Many of these fundamental statements were included by the Board in the practice act. Other provisions, similar in character, which the Board hesitated to place within the power of the courts to alter, were distributed to various existing Consolidated Laws and to certain proposed new laws. A careful examination of the proposed rules discloses other provisions which in the judgment of your committee are of a similar nature and which should, therefore, be eliminated from the rules. They pertain to jurisdiction; to due process of law, or confer rights and privileges, which should not be entrusted to the judgment of any court.

Rules of Court

The Board reports a set of court rules to accompany the Short Practice Act to be known as the " Civil Practice Rules," which shall be the rules governing practice and procedure in the courts until general rules of practice shall be made in accordance with the provisions of the Practice Act.

The convention of justices assigned to the Appellate Division shall have plenary power to make, alter and amend rules of practice and procedure from time to time, not inconsistent with law, binding upon all courts of the State and the judge and justices thereof, except the Court of Appeals, unless otherwise expressly stated, and the court for the trial of impeachments.

In addition to such rules the courts of record might make such rules necessary to carry into effect the powers and jurisdiction possessed by them, not inconsistent with the foregoing rules, as they might deem necessary.

Non-compliance with any of the civil practice rules, or with any rule of practice for the time being in force, shall not render any proceedings void unless the court or a judge shall so direct, but such proceedings may be set aside either wholly or in part as irregular, or amended, or otherwise dealt with in such manner and upon such terms as the court or judge shall think fit.

The rules submitted by the Board, 401 in number, are logically arranged according to the steps in an action. They are intended to be broad and liberal in terms, omitting minute details, containing as few exceptions as possible and leaving a wide discretion in the courts.

The rules are divided into eight divisions called " Orders," as follows:

Order   I. General provisions. (Rules 1–75.)
Order   II. Commencement of action. (Rules 76–223.)
Order   III. Preparation for trial. (Rules 224–252.)
Order   IV. Trial. (Rules 253–290.)
Order   V. Judgment. (Rules 291–328.)
Order   VI. Appeal. (Rules 329–377.)
Order   VII. Execution. (Rules 378–399.)
Order   VIII. Construction. (Rules 400–401.)

The Code of Civil Procedure provisions have been largely taken as the basis for many of the suggested rules. Other rules are adopted from the English rules and from the New Jersey practice. The present General Rules of Practice are also included, such portions as are not classified elsewhere in the new arrangement being omitted.

This committee is of the opinion that the rules prepared by the Board contain many provisions which should be statutory. The committee feels that the existing General Rules of Practice should be thoroughly revised and that many provisions now in the Code might well be relegated to Rules of Court. The committee is not prepared to recommend the enlargement of the rules to the extent recommended by the Board. This question is probably the most important one involved in the suggested changes in practice. Opinions of those members of the profession who have given the subject most careful thought differ widely as to the proper course to be followed. Whatever is done in this matter should have the most deliberate consideration because the success or failure of the revised system of practice will depend almost entirely upon the correct solution of this problem and the proper execution of the mechanical details incident to such change as may be adopted.

Flexibility is the chief argument advanced for the rule system of practice as opposed to the statutory code system. The Board says " These rules being subject to modification by the courts and not hard and fast statutory enactments will discourage litigation over procedural matters and place the responsibility for the efficiency of judicial administration upon the courts where it belongs rather than upon the Legislature."

The Committee favors a liberalizing of practice in the courts together with such extension of the powers of the courts as may be required to enable them to deal with pending actions in accordance with the merits of the questions involved rather than with the form in which the matters are presented. The best way to accomplish these results has perplexed the minds of all who have studied the subject.

When the Board prepared its proposed Rules of Court it contemplated that there should be submitted with the practice act and rules, a set of forms, the legislative direction to the Board being to prepare and present to the Legislature " a practice act, rules of court and short forms." The Board in its report states " short forms of pleading and other legal papers will be prepared as a guide to the profession and as a means of avoiding the technical and cumbersome forms which so generally prevail." The Board did not prepare such forms and none have been submitted to the Legislature. It would be impracticable to repeal the Code and substitute the recommendations contained in the report of the Board without such a set of official forms.

Special Court Practice Acts

The Board of Statutory Consolidation proposed as a part of its report a separate Surrogates' Act, a separate Justices' Court Act and a separate New York City Court Act, transferring to those acts the sections of the Code applying specially to such courts. The Board also recommended, at least as to the Surrogates' Court Act and the Justices' Court Act, that provisions of the general practice affecting such courts should be re-enacted in terms, instead of being applied by reference. The Board also proposed to transfer to the State Boards and Commissions Law the provisions of the Code relating to the Court of Claims. Your Committee has made an examination of this portion of the report of the Board of Statutory Consolidation, and in the main approves its recommendations. It, therefore, separately submits herewith for your consideration a proposed Surrogates' Court Act, Justices' Court Act and New York City Court Act, substantially as proposed by the Board of Statutory Consolidation; a Court of Claims Act, and a Condemnation Law. So far as practicable each of these acts is complete in itself without cross references to general practice provisions. Each proposed bill repeals the sections of the Code of Civil Procedure, which are re-enacted by it.

Distribution of Other Code Matter

The idea of the Board of Statutory Consolidation in the preparation of a short practice act seems to have been to include as few sections as possible in this act transferring elsewhere a great many sections of the Code which in its opinion should not be left to the courts to cover by rules. This theory has required the distribution of a large number of provisions ordinarily considered practice provisions to an extent which the committee believes is unwise and impracticable. For example, the provisions of the Code relating to judgments are distributed in the rules and in 10 different statutes, as follows: Civil Practice Act; General Construction Law; Lien Law; Costs, Fees, Disbursements and Interest Law; Judiciary Law; County Law; Real Property Law; New York City Court Act; Debtor and Creditor Law, and Civil Rights Law. The sections relating to summary proceedings to recover the possession of real property have been distributed into rules and 8 Consolidated Laws; the provisions relating to proceedings supplementary to execution into rules and 7 Consolidated Laws; the provisions relation to partition into rules and 7 Consolidated Laws; and the provisions relating to attachment into rules and 7 Consolidated Laws.

Looking from the matter from the standpoint of a strictly scientific classification of related matters it may be admitted that if we have a Debtor and Creditor Law, all matters relating to " judgments " should be embraced within such law, and if we have a Lien Law, all matters relating to the lien of an execution should be embraced in that law. So also if we have a Civil Rights Law, all matters relating to the rights of an individual should be contained in such law. The Committee believes, however, that in dealing with the subject of the statutory regulation of the prosecution of the rights of citizens in the courts, science in strict analysis and classification should yield somewhat to convenience and practicability in reference. As was said by David Dudley Field, "There are two aspects of a Code; one as a scientific treatise, the other as a work useful and convenient for daily use. In the one view the Code should be arranged and expressed according to the most scientific theory of legal rights and duties, and the dependence of the different parts upon one another; in the other view it should be arranged and expressed in the way easiest for reference and easiest to understand."

This feature of the Board's work has been generally condemned by bar associations and individuals who have given close study to the subject, and, in the main, is disapproved by your committee.

As an alternative plan the special committee of the New York State Bar Association recommends the preparation of a Practice Manual, which shall contain in one book the practice act, parts of the Consolidated Laws containing provisions removed from the Code and the proposed new Consolidated Laws such as " Evidence Law " and " Costs, Fees, Disbursements and Interest Law."

Your Committee is not impressed with the sanctity of a short practice act merely because it contains a small number of sections. If we must have in statute form several hundred sections containing similar provisions now in the Code of Civil Procedure, as nearly all admit, the committee recommends that all of such provisions be contained, properly classified and logically arranged, in the practice act or Code or whatever the statute may be termed. We would except such provisions as clearly should be transferred to the Consolidated Laws as substantive law.

In view of the fact that the original theory of the Throop Code to combine in a single act all the provisions of statute law affecting the organization of courts and practice and procedure therein has been abandoned by the Legislature in the enactment of the Judiciary Law, the Decedent Estate Law, and other provisions of the Consolidated Law, we would also except and transfer to the Consolidated Laws certain special proceedings which are only of occasional use or application.

Your Committee has prepared a number of bills amending the Consolidated Laws accordingly, which it separately reports herewith.

Specific Changes in Practice

The proposed short practice act and rules contain a number of fundamental changes in our practice. In the fall of 1916 the Committee prepared a pamphlet summarizing the more important changes in civil practice recommended by the Board and distributed 10,000 copies to the lawyers of the State, with the request that each person receiving the pamphlet fill out and return to the Committee an enclosed blank giving the personal views of the writer on the subjects mentioned. The Committee did not attempt to include all proposed changes in practice, but merely the main features to which the Board had given attention in its report. The Committee requested an opinion as to the desirability of such changes in practice, without regard to whether they might be accomplished by statute or rules. Some of these changes seemed to meet with very general approval, but as to a few of the more vital changes the opposition was very emphatic.

Among the proposed changes which met with general approval were the following: That the distinction in form between court orders and judge's orders be abolished; that in general a mistake in count, venue, remedy or procedure shall not defeat an action or proceeding; that all parties in interest may be joined; that no action shall be defeated by non-joinder or misjoinder of parties; that there shall be simplification and facility in obtaining evidence before trial; that pleadings should be required to be more definite so as to define the issues; that substituted service shall be simplified; that all questions of fact involved be disposed of at one trial; that exceptions to rulings on trial be abolished; that an appeal from a judgment shall present all questions of fact and law in the case, including questions involved in intermediate orders; that the order on appeal should state the exact ruling of the appellate court; that the procedure for provisional remedies should be made uniform.

Among the proposed changes which met with almost uniform general disapproval are the following: That a new or different

cause of action may be set up by amendment at the trial; that
all preliminary questions must be determined by one motion for
directions within fourteen days after issue joined; that a jury
trial be deemed waived unless expressly demanded in writing
within ten days after the cause is at issue; that a jury may not
render a special verdict unless so directed; that interlocutory
judgments be abolished; that an appellate court may take
additional proof; that a retrial shall only be had of questions
with respect to which an error was committed; that on reversal
because damages are excessive or inadequate the issues on retrial
shall be confined to the amount of damages; that the allowance or
disallowance of statutory costs shall be in the discretion of the
court or judge; that the meaning of a statute, ordinance or written
instrument may be determined by the court before it becomes the
subject of an actual law suit.

Certain other proposed changes while not generally disapproved
met with considerable criticism. Among these are the following:
That all special proceedings and state writs be abolished and
civil actions substituted; that orders to show cause be abolished
and short notice of motion permitted by the judge be substituted;
that short summons to appear be permitted in commercial actions;
that all kinds of causes of action or counterclaims may be joined,
subject to a direction by the court for a separate trial of any issue;
that practically all evidence before trial be taken by written inter-
rogatories only; that original pleadings subsequent to the reply
may be ordered; that an early trial may be ordered where it
appears that the determination of a motion will involve an examination of the whole merits; that the case on appeal shall present in
question and answer form only so much of the evidence as shall be
necessary to present the questions raised; that no action or defense
shall fail because the party has an adequate remedy at law.

These proposed changes were also the subject of consideration
at many public meetings of the Committee held throughout the
State at which similar diversity of opinion was expressed by the
lawyers in attendance.

The Committee has carefully considered the proposed changes
and has determined that while some of them are most desirable,

others are too radical to meet its approval. It is thus apparent that the Committee cannot approve these changes as a whole. If only a part of the proposed changes be recommended it will practically involve the creation of an original plan for simplifying the practice, instead of a mere readjustment of the plan proposed by the board.

Our system of practice has been an evolution. Notwithstanding the insistent demands from certain sources important changes should be made only after careful study and mature consideration. Nor does the Committee feel that the bar of the state, as a whole, has sufficiently informed itself as to the nature of all of these changes. While it is claimed that all or nearly all of them have been successfully tried in other jurisdictions, the organization of our courts, the congestion of population, the volume of litigation, or other local conditions, may render them unsuitable in this State.

The Committee feels that it is not now prepared to pass final judgment upon all of the changes proposed by the Board.

Practice Index

One of the most frequent complaints made at the hearings held by the Committee was the lack of an adequate index of the practice law. The indexes of the various editions of the Code of Civil Procedure do not contain references to the civil practice provisions contained in the rules or in the Consolidated Laws. Since the transfer in recent years to the Consolidated Laws of so many provisions of the Code of Civil Procedure the need of a comprehensive index to include all practice provisions, whether contained in the Code of Civil Procedure, the Consolidated Laws or in rules of court, is especially felt. Whatever revision of the practice is adopted by the Legislature, the Committee recommends the preparation of such an official index.

Summary

Your Committee has been engaged in an analytical study of the Civil Practice Act, Civil Practice Rules and additions and amendments to the Consolidated Laws reported to the Legislature by the

Board of Statutory Consolidation. We have compared these proposals with the existing Code of Civil Procedure and General Rules of Practice. We have held numerous hearings before bar associations in many cities of the State, and have invited and sought the suggestions and advice of judges and lawyers throughout the entire State.

The Committee discovered that outside of a few bar association committees and comparatively few individual members of the bar no actual study was being given to the work, certainly not the study and close examination which a subject of so great importance demanded. The Committee endeavored to arouse the bench and bar generally to a study of the report and of the whole question of simplification in civil practice and procedure. The efforts of the committee along this line were very largely rewarded and many excellent ideas and valuable constructive suggestions were obtained.

The Committee found that while there are many who do not hesitate to recommend the most far reaching and drastic changes in court procedure, there are also a large number of judges and lawyers engaged in the actual and every day practice and trial of actions who hold exactly the opposite view and who urge practically no change whatsoever.

The Committee has studied the whole subject of simplification from every reasonable view point. Some material changes in the system of practice must be made without delay. The right of every man, whatever may be his station in life, to have his day in court and to have justice administered in as quick and inexpensive a manner as practicable, must be assured, and any change in the practice must have that end in view. Statutory technicalities tend to defeat justice by increasing the delays of litigation and in numerous cases the cost to the honest litigant; on the other hand, the uncertainty resulting from too few statutory requirements and too elastic a system of practice works just as great hardship in the individual case.

The practice should be made less rigid in some respects but the greatest care must be taken in so doing. When the rigidity is

removed the system must not be so loose and elastic that the litigant may be worse off than he was under the former plan. To
draw the dividing line between offensive technicality and proper
elasticity is a task requiring the greatest skill and care and intelligent discrimination.

The committee has been impressed by the great work performed by the board of statutory consolidation, and desires to
express its appreciation of the skill, research and labor of the
board. Whatever criticism may attach to the details or plan of
its report, the legislature and the people are greatly indebted to
the members of the board for its presentation in tangible form
of a plan for simplified practice. Its classifications and
arrangements, its compilations of co-related topics, its comparisons of our procedure with the procedure of other jurisdictions,
its eliminations of obsolete and conflicting provisions and its
comprehensive notes, explanations and tables will be invaluable
in devising any plan for a simplified practice that may be ultimately adopted in this state.

The authority of the committee was limited to an investigation of the report of the board and of matters pertaining to simplification of the practice. There was no direction to the committee to prepare *a plan* for simplification of the practice. Even
had there been such direction the time of the committee has been
so fully occupied in study of the report of the board, in the examination of the systems of practice in other jurisdictions, in making other necessary investigations and in endeavoring to ascertain
the sentiment of the bench and bar of the state, that it would
have been impossible for it to prepare for presentation at this
session of the legislature final recommendations in complete and
concrete form for consideration. Nor was it possible to reach
the conclusion that a new plan was desired until the committee
had finished the investigation already made.

The committee believes that the time taken by its examination
of the board's report and its investigations made throughout the
State has been well spent and that a vast amount of information
and data has been collected which will be invaluable in the preparation of constructive recommendations and of acts embodying

the same. Practically all of the necessary equipment has now been acquired to enable the committee to proceed with such work.

If it be the will of the legislature to continue the committee it should be authorized to prepare and submit a plan of simplification proposed legislative bills therefor. This would not mean that the committee should discard the results of the labors of the board; on the contrary the committee would utilize the valuable matter contained in its report.

Dated, April 23, 1917.

Respectfully submitted,

J. HENRY WALTERS, *Chairman.*
CHARLES D. NEWTON,
WILLIAM B. CARSWELL,
JOHN KNIGHT,
AUGUST C. FLAMMAN,
ABRAM ELLENBOGEN,
FRANK ARANOW,

Joint Legislative Committee on the Simplification of Civil Practice.

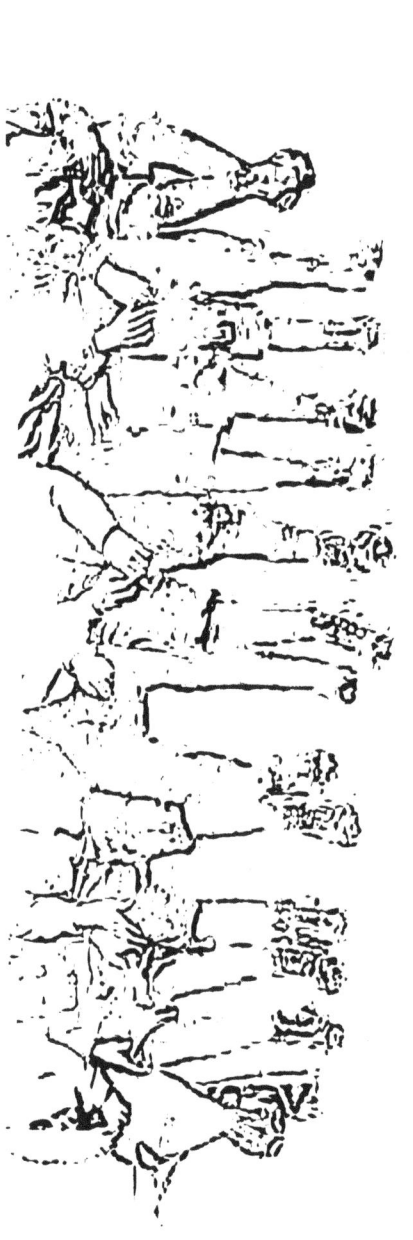

A GROUP OF HUMANE SOCIETY BOYS.

The Humane Society receives in its two principal shelters for children, nearly 600 of this type each year. Most of them are delinquents, some of them guilty of serious misdeeds. Under the old system of handling youthful culprits, most of them would have become confirmed criminals, holpers or _____, in other words social perverts. Under the splendid, persuasion

THIRTIETH ANNUAL REPORT

OF

The Mohawk and Hudson River Humane Society

(INCORPORATED)

FOR THE YEAR 1916

PRINCIPAL OFFICES:

ALBANY OFFICE:
Humane Bldg., cor. Eagle & Howard Sts.
Telephone: Bell 61 Main

TROY OFFICE:
Humane Building, 77 and 79 Fourth St.
Telephone: Bell 1753

SCHENECTADY OFFICE: 304 Clinton St.
Telephone: Bell 707

HUDSON OFFICE:
Police Headquarters

SARATOGA SPRINGS OFFICE:
G. A. R. Hall

GLENS FALLS OFFICE:
10 Sherman Ave.

JOHNSTOWN OFFICE:
Recorder's Office

GLOVERSVILLE OFFICE:
41 West Fulton St.

PLATTSBURGH OFFICE:
109 Cornelia St.

HOOSICK FALLS OFFICE:
" The Pines "

COBLESKILL OFFICE:
Farmers and Merchants' Bank

CATSKILL OFFICE:
370 Main St.

THE ACTIVE WORK OF THIS SOCIETY IS SUPPORTED MAINLY BY
VOLUNTARY CONTRIBUTIONS

STATE OF NEW YORK

ALBANY
J. B. LYON COMPANY, PRINTERS
1917

MOHAWK AND HUDSON RIVER HUMANE SOCIETY

(Incorporated under original title in 1887 for children only; animal society incorporated in 1892; the two consolidated in 1894; subject to subsequent consolidations.)

ORGANIZATION FOR 1916

President:

Dr. WILLIAM OLIN STILLMAN, Albany.

Vice-Presidents:

Mr. HARVEY S. McLEOD, Troy.
Mr. SAMUEL BROWN, Albany.
Mr. FRED N. STEVENS, Hoosick Falls.
Mr. ALBERT L. ROHRER, Schenectady.
Mr. GEORGE H. PAGE, Cohoes.
*Mr. JAMES McNEILL, Hudson.

Mr. VERNON M. BELLINGER, Cobleskill.
Mr. IRVING I. GOLDSMITH, Saratoga Springs.
Mr. D. L. ROBERTSON, Glens Falls.
Mr. WILLIAM M. GRANT, Johnstown.
Mr. ELMER F. BOTSFORD, Plattsburgh.

Honorary Vice-Presidents:

Hon. MARTIN H. GLYNN, Albany.
Mr. ROBERT C. PRUYN, Albany.
Mrs. GEORGE P. HILTON, Albany.
Mrs. F. J. ROWE, Hartford, N. Y.
Mr. J. J. CHILDS, Troy.
Dr. THOMAS H. FOULDS, Glens Falls.
Hon. JAMES L. SCOTT, Saratoga Spa.
Mr. WALTER McEWAN, Albany.
Mr. SEYMOUR VAN SANTVOORD, Troy.

Mr. J. TOWNSEND LANSING, Albany.
Rt. Rev. JOHN WALSH, Troy.
Mrs. JOSEPH C. PLATT, Waterford.
Mr. J. K. P. PINE, Troy.
Hon. HENRY A. STRONG, Cohoes.
Mr. J. WRIGHT GARDNER, Troy.
Miss S. MARGARET WELLS, Johnstown.
Mr. JOHN PAINE, Troy.
Mr. R. C. REYNOLDS, Troy.

Mr. G. E. EMMONS, Schenectady.

Secretary:

Mr. NATHANIEL J. WALKER, Troy.

Treasurer:

Miss M. C. JERMAIN, Troy Road, Albany.

Treasurer of the Kennel Department:

Mr. EDMUND W. CORRIE, Albany.

Members of the Board of Directors:

For Albany: Miss M. C. Jermain, Dr. W. O. Stillman, Rev. Max Schlesinger, Mr. Harold Alexander, Mr. Samuel Brown, Hon. James F. Tracey, Mr. Robert Olcott, Miss Margaret Tucker, Miss Emma A. Hagaman.

For Troy: Mr. H. S. McLeod, Mr. Paul Cook, Mr. W. H. Shields, Mr. Harry S. Ludlow, Mr. H. F. Boardman, Mrs. Harvey D. Cowee.

For Schenectady: Mr. Albert L. Rohrer, *Rev. E. C. Lawrence, Ph.D., Miss Katharine A. Furman.

For Cohoes: Mr. George H. Page, Mr. Egbert P. Lansing.

---

* Deceased.

Wanted: An endowment to safeguard the future of the work

[3]

Wanted: An endowment to safeguard the future of the work

Miss Nora Parks. Inspector, Troy, Mr. Patrick McGrath; Agent. Schenectady, Mr. Berton J. Beebe; Inspector, Cohoes, Mr. William C. Mesick; Inspector, Hoosick Falls, Mr. John Marshall.

CHILDREN'S SHELTER STAFF, TROY:

Matron, Mrs. Barbara Strain; Matron's Assistant, Mrs. Anna Rosenstine; Housekeeper, Mrs. Mary Hollingsworth; Janitor, Mr. William LaRose.

CHILDREN'S SHELTER STAFF, ALBANY:

Matron, Miss Grace Dare; Matron's Assistants, Mrs. Mary Clark, Mrs. Sophia Havens; Housekeeper, Mrs. Ellen Cullen; Janitor, Mr. Charles F. Hempstead.

KENNEL DEPARTMENTS:

Albany: Poundmaster, Mr. William C. Burns; Inspectors, Mr. Robert L. Ste. Fleure, Mr. Wilfred D. MacGiffert.
Troy: Poundmaster, Mr. William C. LaRose; Inspector, Mr. Joseph Lyons.
Schenectady: Poundmaster, Mr. Harry Hartley.
Cohoes and Watervliet: Poundmaster, Mr. William C. LaRose.
Plattsburgh: In charge of Superintendent William A. Hennessy.
Hudson: In charge of Acting Superintendent William C. Mesick.
Saratoga: Poundmaster, Mr. Moses R. Capen.

PRINCIPAL OFFICES:

Albany office, corner Eagle and Howard streets; Bell telephone, Main 61.
Troy office, 79 Fourth street; Bell telephone, Troy 1753.
•Schenectady office, 304 Clinton street; Bell telephone No. 797.
Hudson office, Police Headquarters.
Saratoga Springs office, G. A. R. Hall.
Glens Falls office, 10 Sherman avenue; Bell Telephone No. 3-W.
Hoosick Falls office, " The Pines " and 90 High street.
Plattsburgh office, 109 Cornelia street; Home telephone No. 315.
Johnstown office, Recorder's office.
Gloversville office, 41 West Fulton street.
Cobleskill office, Farmers and Merchants' Bank.
Catskill office, 370 Main street.

SPECIAL AGENTS OF SOCIETY DURING 1916

FOR ALBANY COUNTY:

Albany: Mr. B. W. Burdick, Mr. E. J. Flood, Mr. Gustave Hannock, Dr. William H. Kelly, Mr. J. Norman Northrup, Mr. Foster Pruyn, Mr. Gilbert M. Tucker, Dr. Harold D. Cochrane, Mr. Charles N. Morgan, Mr. Sidney H. Coleman, Mr. Daniel Lantz, Jr., Mr. J. A. Delehanty, Mr. Clayton E. Marsters.
Cohoes: Mr. William T. Ford, Mr. George H. Page, Mr. Caleb J. Slade, Mr. Charles V. Gould.
Ravena: Mr. Samuel Winnie.
Guilderland: Mr. William J. Capron.
Rensselaerville: Henry F. C. Muller, M. D.
Westerlo: Hon. John M. Peck.
Watervliet: Mr. Clifford H. Frake.

FOR RENSSELAER COUNTY:

Troy: Mr. H. F. Boardman, Dr. Charles F. Archambeault, Dr. Irwin Johnson, T. A. Connolly, D. V. S.
Hoosick Falls: Mr. John Marshall, Mr. Richmond L. Perry.
Schaghticoke: Mr. Richard E. Ralston.
North Hoosick: Dr. William E. Fox.
Valley Falls: Mr. Arthur G. Atwood.
Johnsonville: Mr. George H. Warren.
East Nassau: Mr. L. Frank Vincent.
North Petersburgh: Mr. John R. Tifft.
Berlin: Mr. James Wadsworth.

FOR COLUMBIA COUNTY:

Stockport: Mr. William Fitzgerald.

FOR WASHINGTON COUNTY:

Greenwich: Mr. Joseph M. Battie.
Fort Edward: Mr. David H. King, Mr. James J. Kennedy.
White Creek: Mr. B. W. Niles.
Hartford: Mr. William W. Norton.

FOR SARATOGA COUNTY:

Saratoga Springs: Mr. Irving I. Goldsmith.
Waterford: Mr. Charles E. Catlin.
Mechanicville: Mr. Franz H. Moak.
Corinth: Mr. Charles E. Salisbury.
Ballston: Mr. James J. O'Brien.
Schuylerville: Dr. Frank F. Gow.

Wanted: An endowment to safeguard the future of the work

Wanted: An endowment to safeguard the future of the work

IN SENATE

MAY 3, 1917.

REMARKS INTRODUCTORY TO THE THIRTIETH ANNUAL REPORT OF THE MOHAWK AND HUDSON RIVER HUMANE SOCIETY FOR THE YEAR ENDING DECEMBER 31, 1916

By President WILLIAM O. STILLMAN, A. M., M. D., Albany, N. Y.

Any one reviewing the work of this Society, as set forth in the enclosed statistical report, will find that a very large amount of benevolent, practical and thoroughly useful work has been accomplished. The work of this Society during 1916 involved 9,606 children. A careful study of the details of cases shows that large numbers of children were rescued from conditions prejudicial to life and health, as well as morals. The serious character of many of these cases is proved by the hundreds of prosecutions and convictions which were conducted by the Society's officers in connection with its child-saving work. It may well be noted by the patrons of this work that $23,504.79 were collected, under orders of courts, almost entirely, in prosecutions instituted by the Society, from delinquent parents in support of their families, or, of children sent to institutions. A large part of this money is paid at

Wanted: An endowment to safeguard the future of the work

the offices of the Society and transmitted by its officers to the
beneficiaries.

It is also worthy of notice that the three large shelters for children maintained by the Society, cared for 1,099 children during
1916 for a total of 8,880 days. Any child, turned adrift on the
streets, homeless or vagrant, can apply to the Society's shelters at
any hour of the day or night, and obtain admittance without red
tape. We believe that the quality of mercy is not strained, and
that a work of this kind, undertaken to give relief for the weak
and helpless, should accomplish results with as little delay and
bureaucracy as possible. We commend the report of the officers
of the Society who are doing probation work. Hundreds of children are being saved for better citizenship. The possibilities of
protection and child-saving in Humane Society work are almost
unlimited in the opportunities for doing good which are presented.

The animal work of the Society has gone forward without interruption. A much larger number of animals have been cared for
during 1916 than during any previous year of the Society's history. For the details of this important work, embracing many
thousands of animals, you are referred to the statistical report for
the Department contained in this pamphlet. There is no nobler
work than that of caring for the weak and helpless, especially
those who cannot speak for themselves. Animals particularly appeal to the humane instinct, for they stand so largely alone and
friendless in the face of the formidable neglect and abuse which
have been so frequently their part in the past. Through the efforts
of humane societies public sentiment has enormously changed. It
is recognized that even animals have rights, and that when man
abuses an animal he degrades his own nature and becomes a less
desirable member of the community.

In addition to the regular field work of the Society in caring
for animals, it has conducted for some time past, in connection
with its central department, a humane farm and shelter for animals, where large numbers of dogs and cats, largely voluntarily
surrendered by their owners, have been received. When homes
could not be found for them they have been humanely put to death.
The enormous number of 2,786 dogs have been destroyed at the
Society's kennels during the past year, and 12,649 cats. The cats

Wanted: An endowment to safeguard the future of the work

are practically, in all cases, voluntarily surrendered and have been collected by the Society without charge in order to reduce the amount of suffering and relieve society of the menace of thousands of homeless and infected animals, which would otherwise come more or less in contact with children and others upon the streets. The Society has also conducted a careful inspection of dumping grounds, excavations, freight-yards, poultry markets, sales-stables, horses on the streets, hack-stands, wharves, etc. The net result of all these labors has been a great change in the treatment of animals within the jurisdiction of the Society.

Our work has not been, by any means, as complete and extensive as the Society would like to have it. More officers are urgently needed upon the streets to look after the numerous complaints which reach the offices of the Society and to do patrol work in search of violations of law. Especially in the country districts does the Society need to have roaming agents who can look after complaints promptly in remote and inaccessible places. To do this work satisfactorily an automobile is needed and, if possible, one or two motor cycles. There is the greatest necessity for this motor equipment and additional agents to look after cases which are absolutely beyond the reach of the Society at the present time, except after undue delay, owing to the large amount of work and the few agents which we have.

FINANCES

This Society, as in the past, is largely dependent upon voluntary subscriptions to carry on this great work of mercy and reform. We need hundreds of new subscribers. Particularly, the Society needs testamentary endowments on the part of the wealthy, who, by leaving a few hundred, or thousand, dollars to the Society can guarantee its safety for the future. A society wholly dependent upon yearly contributions is subject to fluctuations in its annual income, due to the variation in the condition of the times, which constantly imperil its work. Many persons have been generous to the Society by remembering it in their wills. An endowment is the only way by which the future of the Society can be safeguarded. We all of us wish to do something to make the world

Wanted: An endowment to safeguard the future of the work

better while we are living. Why not let this influence continue
after you are gone by making a contribution, in your will, to the
endowment of the Society so that an income may be assured in
this way and your influence for good will then be continued long
after you are passed away. It is the universal experience of every
large anti-cruelty society in this country that three-fourths of its
income must necessarily be derived from an endowment or else an
equal proportion of its work would remain undone. Our power
for doing good is only limited by the amount of our income, for
the field stretches out, demanding relief, in far more directions
than we are able to reach.

In particular, I would call to the attention of all friends of this
work of humanity that we need some special liberal contributions
in order to extinguish a debt of $15,000 on the Humane Society
Farm, and special gifts with which to purchase a suitable ambulance for large animals. Most of the larger cities in the middle
and eastern states, and in many of the western states, have excellent veterinary ambulances. Our local Humane Society, with several considerable cities within its jurisdiction, is entirely destitute
of suitable facilities for removing animals which may be injured
on the streets, by falling, or accident, or which have been suddenly
taken sick. Our officers have been deeply chagrined to be called
to cases where valuable horses have fallen on icy streets during
the past winter and were left obliged to lie on the snow and ice
for several hours, poorly protected by means of blankets and hay,
for want of an ambulance, such as cities like Rochester and Syracuse have long had. We feel that the friends of this work must
realize the great necessity which exists for this relief. An additional building at the Humane Society Farm to afford a home or
asylum for old horses or family pets, and animals which have been
pensioned out, is sorely needed.

The work which this Society has accomplished and its needs for
the future are earnestly submitted to our friends and patrons for
their approval and careful consideration. Those who have made
this work of humanity possible are cordially thanked by the Society. The gifts and support of our members and contributors is
more than gratefully appreciated, as is also the splendid service

Wanted: An endowment to safeguard the future of the work

which has been given the Society by magistrates and the police, by special agents, by physicians, and our committees of ladies and gentlemen, who have looked after important details of this work. This report is respectfully submitted in the hope that greater opportunities for good will be vouchsafed to us and that the necessary support and co-operation will be given us by our friends in the future as in the past.

Wanted: An endowment to safeguard the future of the work

GENERAL STATISTICAL REPORT FOR ENTIRE JURISDICTION OF SOCIETY

CHILDREN'S DEPARTMENT
FROM JANUARY 1, 1916, TO JANUARY 1, 1917

Number of complaints received 6,376
Number of children involved 9,606

ORIGIN OF COMPLAINTS

Central Department 3,480
Schenectady County Department............................... 1,420
Columbia County Department................................... 232
Saratoga County Department.................................... 77
Warren County Department (Warren and Washington counties)..... 23
Hoosick Falls Branch 4
Clinton County Department..................................... 703
Fulton County Department...................................... 415
Schoharie County Department................................... 13
Greene County Department....................................... 5
Other places 4

CHARGES

Neglect by father............	835	Selling firearms to child......	1
Neglect by mother...........	68	Feeble-minded children	20
Desertion by father.........	68	Admitting to theatre without	
Desertion by mother.........	16	parent	29
Improper guardianship	967	Admitting to pool rooms......	19
Abandonment of child.......	28	Burglary	129
Assault, first and second de-		Grand larceny	23
gree...................	11	Petit larceny	452
Assault, third degree........	158	Intoxication	27
Violation Education Law.....	86	Riding on freight trains......	17
Endangering morals	158	Begging or peddling.........	11
Endangering life or limb.....	73	Vagrancy	178
Sending for liquor...........	16	Truancy	229
Selling liquor	8	Disorderly children	935
Selling tobacco	25	Lost or strayed child.........	59
Kidnapping	1	Rape and attempted rape.....	31
Abduction	8	Destitute	183
Seduction	1	Permitted to appear in thea-	
Bastardy	10	tricals	13
Application to place in asylum	61	Not permitted to appear in	
Application to take from asy-		theatricals	17
lum	95	Without homes	90
Admitting to saloons........	4	Violation city ordinance......	77
Carrying firearms	21	Children gambling	21
Violation Labor Law........	172	Action to compel parent to pay	
Receiving stolen property.....	15	asylum	7
Sodomy	11	Held as witness.............	11
Violation parole	75	Using tobacco	67
Incest	2	Employing child to beg.......	1
Child used as acrobat........	1	Runaway	69
Employment of children in		Employed in street trades....	135
street trade	4	Child in disorderly house.....	1
Child used for exhibition.....	3	Malicious mischief	36

Miscellaneous 487

Wanted: An endowment to safeguard the future of the work

DISPOSITIONS

Complaints sustained	4,718	Imprisonment imposed, 19 years, 11 months and 3 days.	
Complaints unsustained	247		
Action undesirable	117	Pending settlement	57
Not found	30	Sentence suspended	1,172
Advised and warned	2,802	Summoned to court	406
Prosecutions (adults)	545	Warned by court	470
Convictions (adults)	515	Compelled to pay by court	86
Prosecutions (minors)	1,114	Compelled to furnish bond	6
Convictions (minors)	1,077	Not in jurisdiction	54
Fines imposed	$949	Referred to public officers	133
Receiving hospital treatment	30	Placed in families	45
Placed in institutions	300	Returned to homes	307
Transferred to other societies.	21	Bailed to grand jury	19
Court order to pay asylum	1	Relieved in other ways	218

Paid by order of court for maintenance of children in families and asylums $23,504 79

PLACED IN INSTITUTIONS — 300 CHILDREN

Albany Orphan Asylum	20	Hawley Home, Saratoga	4
House of Good Shepherd, Albany	7	St. John's Asylum, Rensselaer.	7
		Troy Orphan Asylum	26
Fairview Home, Watervliet	5	St. Vincent's Male Orphan Asylum, Albany	26
Troy Catholic Male Orphan Asylum	7	St. Vincent's Female Orphan Asylum, Albany	10
Training School, Hudson	14		
St. Coleman's Home, Colonie	18	St. Vincent's Female Orphan Asylum, Troy	3
House of Refuge, Randall's Island	14	St. Joseph's Asylum, Troy	5
Maternity Hospital and Infants' Home, Albany	20	State Industrial and Agricultural School	41
House of Good Shepherd, Troy	7	Child's Hospital, Albany	2
		St. Margaret's House, Albany.	7
Reformatory for Women, Bedford	1	New York Catholic Protectory.	3
		Other institutions	53

Wanted: An endowment to safeguard the future of the work

REPORT OF PROBATION OFFICERS FOR CENTRAL DEPARTMENT ONLY

Includes minors placed on probation in Children's Courts of Albany, Troy, Cohoes, Watervliet, Rensselaer, Green Island and Colonie.

FROM JANUARY 1, 1916, TO JANUARY 1, 1917

	Albany	Troy	Cohoes	Water-vliet	Colonie and Green Island
Continued under probationary over-sight from 1915.................	42	44	7	3	......
Boys on probation from January 1, 1916, to January 1, 1917........	60	63	20	......	10
	102	107	27	3	10

NATURE OF CHARGES*

	Albany	Troy	Cohoes	Water-vliet	Colonie and Green Island
Arson...........................	2	......	......	......	......
Burglary and larceny.............	11	1	......	......	......
Burglary third and petit larceny...	15	......	......	......	......
Petit larceny	54	35	5	2	10
Disorderly children	4	2	2	......	......
Truancy	3	40˙	2	......	......
Violation city ordinance...........	3	......	......	......	......
Malicious destruction property.....	....	16	......	......	......
Disorderly conduct	....	......	......	1	......
Assault, second degree.............	1	......	......	......	......
Assault, third degree..............	2	......	......	......	......
Burglary.........................	....	......	18	......	......
Jumping trains	1	......	......	......	......
Extortion	1	......	......	......	......
Intoxication	4	......	......	......	......
Operating auto without a license...	1	......	......	......	......
Attempted burglary	....	3	......	......	......
Insubordination in school..........	....	9	......	......	......
Violation Section 484, Penal Law...	....	1	......	......	......
	102	107	27	3	10

* Most of the cases cited above are children under sixteen years of age who were charged with juvenile delinquency only. The actual charge is used in the above report for statistical purposes.

Wanted: An endowment to safeguard the future of the work

TERMS OF PROBATION

	Albany	Troy	Cohoes	Water-vliet	Colonie and Green Island
One month	3	3	......	......	1
Two months	4	2	......	......	......
Three months	1	5	......	......	......
Four months	3	7	......	......	......
Five months	2	11	......	......	......
Six months	3	7	8	......	......
Seven months	1	13	......	1	......
Eight months	6	9	......	1	......
Nine months	2	3	......	......	......
Ten months	3	4	......	......	......
Eleven months	3	1	......	1	......
Twelve months	4	2	18	......	......
Thirteen months	3	1	......	......	......
Fourteen months	2	1	......	......	......
Fifteen months	1	1	......	......	......
Sixteen months	1	......	......	......	......
Eighteen months	2	......	......	......	......
Nineteen months	4	......	......	......	......
Twenty-one months	2	......	......	......	......
Twenty-two months	1	......	......	......	......
Twenty-four months	1	......	......	......	......
Twenty-seven months	1	......	......	......	......
Still on probation	49	36	1	......	9
	102	107	27	3	10

NUMBER TIMES ON PROBATION

	Albany	Troy	Cohoes	Water-vliet	Colonie and Green Island
First time	88	80	21	2	10
Second time	12	23	5	1	......
Third time	2	4	1	......	......
	102	107	27	3	10

DISPOSITION OF CASES

	Albany	Troy	Cohoes	Water-vliet	Colonie and Green Island
Discharged with improvement	30	59	23	3	......
Discharged without improvement	3	1	1	......	......
Rearrested and committed	14	......	2	......	1
Sent to asylum by Charity Department	1	8	......	......	......
Discharged because of illness	1	......	......	......	......
Enlisted	3	......	......	......	......
Absconded	1	2	......	......	......
Discharged to work in asylum	....	1	......	......	......
Still on probation	49	36	1	......	9
	102	107	27	3	10

AGES

	Albany	Troy	Cohoes	Water-vliet	Colonie and Green Island
Eight years	1	1	......	......	......
Nine years	1	3	1	......	1
Ten years	5	5	3	......	2

Wanted: An endowment to safeguard the future of the work

	Albany	Troy	Cohoes	Water-vliet	Colonie and Green Island
Eleven years	8	12	8	......	......
Twelve years	15	21	7	1	2
Thirteen years	20	23	5	......	1
Fourteen years	15	19	2	1	2
Fifteen years	20	17	1	1	2
Sixteen years	8	5	......	......	......
Seventeen years	1	1	......	......	......
Eighteen years	1	......	......	......	......
Nineteen years	6	......	......	......	......
Twenty years	1	......	......	......	......
	102	107	27	8	10

NATIVITY OF CHILD

	Albany	Troy	Cohoes	Water-vliet	Colonie and Green Island
American	93	102	21	3	8
Italian	6	3	......	......	2
Russian	....	1	......	......	......
Polish	1	......	5	......	......
Armenian	....	1	......	......	......
Austrian	1	......	......	......	......
English	1	......	......	......	......
Canadian	1	......	1	......	......
	102	107	27	3	10

COLOR

	Albany	Troy	Cohoes	Water-vliet	Colonie and Green Island
White	101	106	27	3	10
Black	1	1	......	......	......
	102	107	27	3	10

RELIGION

	Albany	Troy	Cohoes	Water-vliet	Colonie and Green Island
Catholic	74	84	27	2	8
Protestant	22	19	......	1	2
Jewish	6	4	......	......	......
	102	107	27	3	10

AS REGARDS PARENTS

	Albany	Troy	Cohoes	Water-vliet	Colonie and Green Island
Both parents living	81	77	22	2	10
Father dead	11	13	3	1	......
Mother dead	9	13	2	......	......
Both parents dead	1	3	......	......	......
Parents separated	....	1	......	......	......
	102	107	27	3	10

NATHANIEL J. WALKER,
THOMAS J. KEATING,
WILLIAM C. MESICK,

Probation Officers.

Other probation work is included in department reports.

Wanted: An endowment to safeguard the future of the work

REPORT OF PROBATION OFFICERS FOR ALBANY AND RENSSELAER COUNTY COURTS FROM JANUARY 1, 1916, TO JANUARY 1, 1917

	Albany	Rensselaer
Continued under probationary oversight from 1915......	46	9
Men placed on probation during 1916..................	34	26
	80	35

NATURE OF CHARGES

	Albany	Rensselaer
Petit larceny	1	....
Receiving stolen property..............................	6	....
Grand larceny, first and second degrees.................	16	2
Burglary, third degree, and petit larceny................	27	....
Attempted burglary	3	....
Desertion..	1	....
Rape...	1	....
Burglary, third degree, and grand larceny, second degree.	11	1
Selling cocaine	1	....
Assault, first degree	......	1
Assault, second degree	6	4
Carrying concealed weapon.............................	5	1
Abandonment..	2	1
Burglary, third degree.................................	......	18
Burglary and larceny..................................	......	1
Forgery, second degree.................................	......	1
Robbery, second degree.................................	......	2
Violation Section 1991, Penal Law......................	......	3
	80	35

TERMS OF PROBATION

	Albany	Rensselaer
Two months	2	....
Three months	2	1
Five months	1	....
Six months	2	....
Eight months	1	....
Nine months	1	....
Ten months	1	....
Eleven months	2	....
Twelve months	11	4
Thirteen months	2	1
Fourteen months	1	1
Fifteen months	2	....
Sixteen months	1	1
Seventeen months	2	....
Eighteen months	5	....
Nineteen months	1	....
Twenty-one months	1	....
Twenty-nine months	1	....
Thirty months	1	....
Still on probation.....................................	40	27
	80	35

Wanted: An endowment to safeguard the future of the work

DISPOSITION OF CASES

	Albany	Rensselaer
Discharged with improvement	23	8
Discharged without improvement	2	....
Absconded	3	....
Transferred to other officers	1	....
Discharged because of illness	1	....
Rearrested and committed	8	....
Enlisted	2	....
Still on probation	40	27
	80	35

NUMBER OF TIMES ON PROBATION

First time	78	34
Second time	2	1
	80	35

AGES

Sixteen years	3	....
Seventeen years	6	1
Eighteen years	6	4
Nineteen years	6	3
Twenty years	9	....
Twenty-one years	6	....
Twenty-two years	5	5
Twenty-three years	7	....
Twenty-four years	4	1
Twenty-five years	2	1
Twenty-six years	2	3
Twenty-seven years	3	2
Twenty-eight years	1	2
Twenty-nine years	3	2
Thirty years	3	3
Thirty-one years	3	1
Thirty-two years	5	1
Thirty-four years	......	2
Thirty-five years	1	1
Thirty-six years	......	1
Forty years	4	....
Forty-two years	......	1
Forty-five years	1	....
Forty-six years	......	1
	80	35

NATIVITY

American	73	28
Italian	2	5
German	2	....
Irish	2	1
Bulgarian	1	....
Canadian	......	1
	80	35

Wanted: An endowment to safeguard the future of the work

COLOR

	Albany	Rensselaer
White	79	33
Black	1	2
	80	35

RELIGION

	Albany	Rensselaer
Catholic	64	23
Protestant	14	12
Jewish	2	....
	80	35

NATHANIEL J. WALKER,
THOMAS J. KEATING,
Probation Officers.

Wanted: An endowment to safeguard the future of the work

REPORT OF PROBATION OFFICER FOR ADULTS FOR ALBANY POLICE COURT FROM JANUARY 1, 1916, TO JANUARY 1, 1917

Continued on probation from 1915 1

Placed on, January 1, 1916, to January 1, 1917............. 18

NATURE OF CHARGES

Public intoxication 12
Obtaining money under false pretense 2

Petit larceny 2
Disorderly conduct 3

AGES

Twenty-one years.............. 1
Twenty-three years............ 1
Twenty-four years............. 1
Twenty-five years............. 2
Twenty-six years.............. 2
Twenty-seven years............ 1

Thirty years 1
Thirty-two years.............. 3
Thirty-seven years............ 2
Forty-two years............... 2
Forty-four years.............. 1
Forty-seven years............. 1

NATIVITY

American 17

French 1

RELIGION

Catholic 13

Protestant 5

DISPOSITIONS

Discharged with improvement... 9
Enlisted with permission of court 1

Rearrested and committed...... 3
Still on probation............. 5

THOMAS J. KEATING,
Probation Officer.

Wanted: An endowment to safeguard the future of the work

ALBANY, TROY AND SCHENECTADY BUILDINGS

NUMBER OF INMATES

January 1, 1916, to January 1, 1917

	Albany	Troy	Schenectady
Boys	376	213	221
Girls	114	93	82
	490	306	303

Nativity of Those Received

	Albany	Troy	Schenectady
American	412	279	266
Canadian	1	2	......
Italian	20	5	19
Russian	10	......	6
English	3	2	1
Polish	6	3	6
German	3	......	......
Austrian	9	5	3
French	1	1	......
Armenian	....	3	......
Arabian	....	1	......
Danish	2	......	......
Greek	4	1	......
Irish	2	1	1
Scottish	1	......	1
Dutch	1	......	......
Bohemian	1	......	......
Finnish	1	......	......
Syrian	....	1	......
Swedish	....	1	......
Not known	4	2	......
	490	306	303

Religion of Those Received

	Albany	Troy	Schenectady
Catholic	326	200	228
Protestant	141	97	58
Jewish	23	......	17
	490	306	303

Color of Those Received

	Albany	Troy	Schenectady
White	477	299	301
Black	13	7	2
	490	306	303

Total Number of Days

Number days — Albany Shelter	3,847
Number days — Troy Shelter	2,859
Number days — Schenectady Shelter	2,174

Note — The Schenectady Shelter was opened March 10, 1916.

Wanted: An endowment to safeguard the future of the work

GENERAL STATISTICAL REPORT FOR ENTIRE JURISDICTION OF SOCIETY

ANIMAL DEPARTMENT

JANUARY 1, 1916, TO JANUARY 1, 1917

Number of complaints received...................................	5,209
Number animals involved:	
In office complaints...	7,402
In kennel work:	
Dogs..	3,106
Cats..	12,746
Total animals involved............................	23,254
Humanely killed at kennel:	
Dogs...	2,786
Cats...	12,649
Total animals humanely destroyed at kennels..........	15,435

ORIGIN OF COMPLAINTS

Central Department	3,452
Schenectady County Department.................................	543
Columbia County Department...................................	88
Saratoga County Department....................................	69
Warren County Department (Warren and Washington Counties)....	3
Clinton County Department.....................................	567
Fulton County Department......................................	474
Schoharie County Department...................................	11
Greene County Department......................................	1
Hoosick Falls Branch...	1
	5,209

NATURE OF CASES AND RELIEF AFFORDED

Horses worked when sick.....	23	Abandoned animals	26
Horses worked when lame.....	158	Overloading	78
Horses worked without shoes..	41	Dog fighting	1
Horses worked with sores.....	129	Cock fighting	17
Unblanketed in winter........	372	Poisoning animals	14
Suffering from exposure......	28	Malicious torturing	51
Overdriven	116	General neglect and cruelty...	187
Disabled animals	349	Vicious animals	215
Starved and neglected........	44	Carried in cruel way.........	44
Sick and suffering............	2,124	Crates of fowl overcrowded...	17
Loose blinders	200	Beating and abusing.........	200
Lost and strayed.............	263	Homeless animals	147
Checked too high.............	2	Cats rescued from trees......	46
Overcrowded in cars..........	1	Miscellaneous	316

Wanted: An endowment to safeguard the future of the work

DISPOSITIONS

Complaints sustained	4,687	Disabled horses killed	135
Complaints unsustained	119	Other animals killed	2,660
Action not needed	95	Suspended from labor	87
Compelled to furnish food	19	Homes found	43
Compelled to repair stable	12	Sent to kennels	2,050
Returned to owners	110	Sent to blacksmith	23
Referred to other societies	13	Relieved in other ways	83
Not found	199	Warned by court	37
Advised and warned	1,810	Veterinarians called	50
Prosecutions	65	Sentence suspended	27
Convictions	60	Relieved by padding	25
Fines imposed	$339	Dog fights stopped	8
Imprisonment imposed	20 days	Cock fights stopped	5
Discharged	12	Referred to public officers	15

Wanted: An endowment to safeguard the future of the work

ALBANY, TROY, COHOES AND WATERVLIET KENNEL REPORT

JANUARY 1, 1916, TO JANUARY 1, 1917

Dog Department:	Albany	Troy	Cohoes	Water-vliet
Dogs in kennel, January 1, 1916...........	3	8	6	2
Dogs voluntarily surrendered	792	363	81	86
Dogs seized during period.................	165	391	116	98
Dogs brought in	8	......	......	......
	968	762	203	186
Homes found for dogs.....................	55	20	5	7
Dogs redeemed and released...............	43	58	6	......
Dogs humanely put to death..............	867	682	192	178
Dogs in kennels January 1, 1917...........	3	2	......	1
	968	762	203	186
Cat Department:				
Cats voluntarily surrendered..............	4,904	4,553	917	636
Homes found for cats.....................	34	13	......	......
Cats humanely put to death..............	4,870	4,540	917	636
	4,904	4,553	917	636

NOTE — See also kennel reports in other departments.

Wanted: An endowment to safeguard the future of the work

INSPECTION OF DUMPING GROUNDS, FREIGHT YARDS, WHARFS, EXCAVATIONS, POULTRY MARKETS, SALES STABLES, HORSES ON STREET, HACK STANDS, ETC.

During the year just closed our agents have paid 224 visits to dumping grounds in the various cities within the jurisdiction of the Society; 316 visits to freight yards; 297 visits to wharves and docks; 276 visits to excavations and building operations; 297 visits to poultry markets; 52 visits to sales stables; 36 inspections at West Albany yards, and 5,000 horses examined on streets. A total of 6,498 inspections.

This system of inspection resulted in relieving many animals from suffering and neglect and was also the means of helping many children whose parents were impressed with the danger of permitting the children to frequent dumping grounds, freight yards, etc.

Wanted: An endowment to safeguard the future of the work

ANNUAL REPORT OF THE TREASURER OF THE MOHAWK AND HUDSON RIVER HUMANE SOCIETY FOR THE YEAR ENDING JANUARY 1, 1917

FOR CENTRAL DEPARTMENT

NOTE — This report does not include other departments or kennels.

RECEIPTS

Regular Department

Cash on hand..		$1,439 09
Regular memberships	$50 00	
Sustaining memberships	340 00	
Donations	2,843 00	
Fines	223 80	
Hudson Society	179 08	
Lawyers' Mortgage Co., interest...................	213 75	
Mechanics' & Farmers' Savings Bank, interest.......	5 14	
Chicago, Milwaukee & St. Paul coupons...........	50 00	
Northern Pacific & Great Northern coupons........	120 00	
Loan to Endowment Fund........................	200 00	
Atchison, Topeka & Santa Fe coupons..............	20 00	
Lake Shore & Michigan Southern coupons...........	200 00	
Albany county	1,500 00	
Rensselaer county	1,500 00	
Pennsylvania R. R. Co. coupons...................	67 50	
Sundries	32 23	
		7,544 50

Albany Building

Rentals...	$3,701 70	
Albany county	1,545 50	
Columbia county	38 07	
Essex county	36 21	
Greene county	39 92	
Schoharie county	130 00	
Schenectady county	637 00	
Washington county	5 52	
Sundries.......................................	155 86	
		6,269 78

Troy Building

Rentals...	$1,391 64	
N. Y. Central & H. R. R. R. Co., interest...........	110 00	
New York City bonds, interest.....................	80 00	
Bond & Mortgage Guarantee Co., Sparago mortgage..	125 00	
Albany County bond, interest.....................	212 50	
Union National Bank of Troy, interest..............	36 00	
Albany Savings Bank, interest.....................	6 40	
Chesapeake & Ohio coupons.......................	337 50	
Lake Shore & Michigan Southern coupons..........	200 00	
New York, Chicago & St. Louis coupons...........	200 00	
Southern Pacific R. R. coupons...................	200 00	
Rensselaer county	1,000 00	
Sundries.......................................	19 11	
		3,918 15
		$19,171 52

Wanted: An endowment to safeguard the future of the work

DISBURSEMENTS

Regular Department

Salaries and expenses	$6,613 50	
Stationery and printing	129 30	
Telephone	81 21	
Office expenses	400 50	
Contribution, American Humane Association	10 00	
Contribution, N. Y. State Convention of Anti-Cruelty Societies	10 00	
Accrued interest on bonds	58 67	
Supplies	39 70	
Sundries	119 59	
		$7,742 47

Albany Building

Salaries and expenses	$1,694 69	
Light and fuel	1,041 57	
Food	1,420 85	
Insurance	179 64	
Telephone	6 00	
Dry goods	15 83	
Drugs	35 94	
Repairs	447 62	
Supplies	243 30	
Sundries	85 01	
Taxes and assessments	761 29	
		5,931 74

Troy Building

Salaries and expenses	$913 46	
Light and fuel	559 37	
Taxes and assessments	357 36	
Food	683 68	
Insurance	310 26	
Telephone	57 18	
Dry goods	25 90	
Drugs	17 09	
Repairs	303 99	
Supplies	28 96	
Sundries	9 56	
		3,266 81
To cash on hand December 31, 1916		2,530 50
		$19,171 52

Treasurer of Columbia county $13.46 ent. for coll. due March 1, 1917.
Treasurer of Essex county   5.11 ent. for coll. due March 1, 1917.
Treasurer of Schoharie county   29.25 ent. for coll. due February 1, 1917.
Treasurer of Washington county 97.97 ent. for coll. due February 15, 1917.

MISS M. C. JERMAIN,
Treasurer.

Wanted: An endowment to safeguard the future of the work

STATEMENT OF ENDOWMENT FUND

FOR GENERAL ACCOUNT

RECEIPTS

Legacies and donations previous to year 1900	$650	00
1902 — Donation of H. B. Silliman, Cohoes	5,000	00
1909 — Legacy of Andrew B. Jones, Albany	492	35
1909 — Gift from Estate of Miss Mary A. Leach	1,174	30
1912 — Legacy of Elizabeth W. Sheldon	950	00
1013 — Legacy of Miss Anna Ten Eyck, Albany	2,905	00
1915 — Legacy of Mrs. James Kidd, Albany	590	00
1915 — Legacy of Bradford R. Wood, Albany	500	00
1915 — Legacy of Philander Deming, Albany	1,000	00
1915 — Mortgage Bond Certificate with interest	250	16
1915 — Accrued interest on bonds repaid	83	17
1915 — Borrowed from Current Account	200	00
	$13,704	**98**

INVESTMENTS

Mortgage given by Lawyers' Mtg. Co. on Brooklyn real estate.. (Paid on account of price of this mortgage $250 re-invested in certificate of Mortgage Bond Co.)	$5,000	00
$3,000 Chicago, Burlington & Quincy Joint 4 per cent. bonds, with accrued interest and costs	2,905	00
$1,000 Chicago, Milwaukee & St. Paul Cons. 5 per cent. bonds, with accrued interest and costs	1,052	75
$5,000 Lake Shore & Michigan Southern 4 per cent. bonds, with accrued interest and costs	4,607	67
	$13,565	**42**
Balance on hand	139	56
	$13,704	**98**

Wanted: An endowment to safeguard the future of the work

STATEMENT OF ENDOWMENT FUND

FOR TROY BUILDING

RECEIPTS

1902 — Legacy of Miss Mary O. Hall........................	$2,000 00
1911 — Legacy of Mrs. Hannah S. Earl.....................	20,000 00
1914 — Legacy of Georgianna S. Conkey:	
Cash $6,699 42	
22 shares N. Y. Central stock at 80........ 1,760 00	
12 shares of stock of Union National Bank	
of Troy at 55...................... 660 00	
	9,119 42
	$31,110 42
Accrued interest on bonds repaid..........................	217 91
	$31,337 33

INVESTMENTS

$5,000 Lake Shore & Michigan Southern 4's, with accrued interest and costs......................................	$4,718 75
$5,000 Chesapeake & Ohio 4½'s (interest and costs)..........	5,083 75
$5,000 New York, Chicago & St. Louis Debenture 4's (accrued interest and costs)...............................	4,600 00
$5,000 Southern Pacific Refunding 4's (accrued interest and costs)..	4,787 50
Commissions	25 00
Corporate stock of New York City.........................	2,000 00
Accrued interest on bonds repaid..........................	217 91
$5,000 Albany County Registered 4¼ per cent. bonds and costs..	4,820 16
Certificate for 22 shares stock of New York Central R. R. at 80..	1,760 00
Certificate for 12 shares stock of Union National Bank at Troy at 55	660 00
Bond & Mortgage Guarantee Co, for mortgage on Brooklyn property (Sparago)	2,500 00
Interest paid, Mechanics & Farmers' Bank....................	3 27
Cash in Albany Savings Bank.............................	160 99
	$31,337 33

MISS M. C. JERMAIN.
Treasurer.

Wanted: An endowment to safeguard the future of the work

KENNEL ACCOUNTS

ANNUAL REPORT FOR ALBANY, TROY, COHOES AND WATER-
VLIET KENNEL DEPARTMENTS IN CONNECTION WITH
HUMANE SOCIETY FARM FOR THE PERIOD FROM JANUARY
15, 1916, TO JANUARY 1, 1917

RECEIPTS

Cash on hand, January 15, 1916....................	$784 10
Received from City of Albany......................	3,134 17
Received from rentals, Albany	365 00
Received from City of Troy	1,963 75
Received from City of Cohoes	679 85
Received from City of Watervliet	567 00
Received from City of Rensselaer.................	76 55
Received from J. Montgomery, New York, share of draining......................................	8 00
Received from O. F. Burkhart.....................	50
Received from Mrs. J. T. Chapman.................	4 00
Received from Mrs. E. Sill	1 00
Received from Mrs. Louise Clark	5 00
Received from Mr. F. G. Koutz....................	1 00
Received from Mrs. Mary V. Spielman.............	1 00

$7,590 96

DISBURSEMENTS

Salaries, Albany	$1,639 45
Salaries, Troy	1,002 33
Salaries, Cohoes — Watervliet	818 30
Salaries, Rensselaer	33 09
Salaries, Farm	701 65
Care of horses, shoeing, etc., Farm and Kennel......	118 77
Feed for horses, Farm, Kennels, etc................	263 09
Gas and oil for Troy, Cohoes and Watervliet automobile...	222 63
New tires, repairs and incidentals for maintaining Troy, Cohoes and Watervliet automobile..........	291 44
Taxes, water rent, 226 First street.................	69 21
Insurance, 226 First street........................	61 25
Insurance, Farm	32 50
New York Telephone, Farm........................	73 30
Feed for dogs and cats............................	60 47
Lumber, etc., Farm...............................	90 14
Coal and electric lights, Farm.....................	68 01
Taxes at Farm....................................	5 70
Repairs, 226 First street..........................	78 08
Gas for destroying cats............................	37 50
Miscellaneous expenses, Farm......................	41 84
Bridge tickets to Rensselaer and return............	3 00
Mechanics & Farmers' Bank, interest..............	450 00

Wanted: An endowment to safeguard the future of the work

National Commercial Bank, interest................ 322 29
W. C. LaRose, reward for finding Reicherter dog....   5 00
Sundry expenses, Farm.........................   28 64
                                                              6,517 68

   Balance on hand................. .... $1,073 24

Due Mechanics and Farmers' Bank for Farm Loan............ $9,000 00
Due New York State National Bank, for Kennel Building loan... 6,450 00

Respectfully submitted,
THOMAS J. KEATING,
Acting Treasurer Kennel Department.

NOTE.— The expense of the Humane Farm is divided between the different kennel departments in proportion to the size of the various cities.

Wanted: An endowment to safeguard the future of the work

LIST OF MEMBERS AND CONTRIBUTORS

PATRONS

(Patrons are those giving $500 or more at one payment to the Society.)
Prior to January, 1902, patrons were those giving $100 or more in one payment to the Society.

*Brady, Anthony N., Albany.
*Cluett, J. W. A., Troy.
*Cluett, George B., Troy.
*Conkey, Mrs. G. S., Troy.
*Doughty, William Howard, Troy.
*Earl, William S., Troy.
*Earl, Mrs. William S., Troy.
*Gazeley, James, Albany.
Gerry, Elbridge T., New York.
*Gurley, Lewis E., Troy.
*Hart, Mrs. William Howard, Troy.
Hascy, Oscar L., Albany.
Jermain, Miss M. C., Albany.

*Kennedy, William, Troy.
Kennedy & Murphy, Troy.
*Lansing, Mrs. Abby Townsend, Albany.
*Ludlow, H. G., Troy.
*MacCartee, Mrs. Robert, Lakewood, N. J.
McLeod, Harvey S., Troy.
*Miller, Justus, Troy.
*Silliman, H. B., Cohoes.
Stillman, Dr. W. O., Albany.
*Warren, J. M., Troy.

LIFE MEMBERS

(Life members are those giving $100 or more at one payment to the Society.)
Prior to January, 1902, life members were those giving $25 or more in one payment to the Society.

Arnold, Benjamin W., Albany; Apollo Commandery No. 15, Troy; Barker, S. W., Troy; Berry, Mrs. George T., Troy; Boardman, Mrs. H. F., Troy; Boardman, H. F., Troy; Brooks, Miss Julia Newton, Albany (by Mrs. Samuel Patton); Burden, Mrs. Joseph W., New York; Child, James J., Upper Troy; Cleminshaw, Charles, Troy; Cluett, Robert, Troy; Cluett, Walter H., Troy; Cluett, Mrs. George B., Troy; Cook, Paul, Troy; Coon, D. W., Troy; Covell, Mrs. A., Albany; Dietz, Lewis, Poughkeepsie; Eddy, James A., Troy; Fifth Avenue M. E. Church, Troy; Fuller, Miss Mary, Troy; Geer, William C., Troy; Gurley, Miss Edith B., Troy; Herrick, Mrs. Charlotte J., Albany; Hun, Dr. Henry, Albany; Hun, Marcus T., Albany; King's Sons' Circle, Albany; Laidlow, Rev. Walter, New York; Lansing, Mrs. Gerritt Y., Albany; Lansing, Gerritt Y., Albany; Lansing, Mrs. Catherine Gansevoort, Albany; Lansing, J. Townsend, Albany; Leggett, J. A., Troy; Leggett, John & Sons, Troy; Ludlow, H. S., Troy; Ludlow, Mrs. H. S., Troy; McDonald, William, Albany; McDowell, George H., Cohoes; McCarthy, Peter, Troy; Olcott, Dudley, Albany; O'Neil, James, Troy; Page, Harlan, Germantown, Pa.; Page, George H., Cohoes; Paine, John, Troy; Pine, J. K. P., Troy; Platt, Mrs. J. C., Waterford; Pruyn, Robert C., Albany; Rice, William G., Albany; Robbins, Very Rev. W. L., Albany; Ross Brothers, Troy; Sage, William H., Albany; Sard, Grange, Albany; Selden, Mrs. Edward W., Albany; Shields, H. C., Troy; Sleicher, William, Jr., Troy; Sleicher, Mrs. William, Jr., Troy; Starks, R. Edson, Troy; Stewart, Charles A., Waterford; Sumner, Miss Emily D., Albany; Talcott, Miss Anna M., Albany; Thurman, Miss Sarah, Troy; Tibbits, Dudley, Troy; Vail, Mrs. S. M., Troy; Vail, Miss F. H., Troy; Vander Veer, Dr. Albert, Albany; Van Santvoord, Seymour, Troy; Walsh, Rt. Rev. John, Troy; Whitney, William M., & Co., Albany; Young, Horace G., Albany.

---

* Deceased.

Wanted: An endowment to safeguard the future of the work

LIST OF MEMBERS AND CONTRIBUTORS FOR 1910

Ackroyd, James, Albany......$10 00
Alexander, C. B., Troy....... 10 00
Alexander, Harold D., Albany. 25 00
Andrews, Horace, Albany..... 6 00
Arnold, B. W., Albany....... 50 00
Babcock, Rev. Edw. W., Troy. 2 00
Baldwin, Mrs. George C., Troy. 1 00
Baldwin, William H., New
  Baltimore 5 00
Bamer & McDowell, Albany.. 5 00
Banfill, Mr. and Mrs. Arthur,
  Albany 10 00
Banfill, Bradford B., Albany.. 5 00
Bascom, Mrs. Ellen F., Lans-
  ingburgh 5 00
Batchelder, Howard, Albany... 2 00
Bayer & McConihe, Troy...... 5 00
Benedict, Mrs. C. M., Albany. 5 00
Betts, Mrs. Edgar Hayes, Troy 5 00
Boardman, Henry F., Troy.... 50 00
Bolton's Sons, S., Lansing-
  burgh 25 00
Brady, Mrs. A. N., Albany.... 25 00
Brandow, Rev. John H., Al-
  bany 1 00
Bronk, Mrs. Henry, Albany.. 5 00
Broughton, Misses C. M. and
  E. L., Troy............... 25 00
Brown, Mr. and Mrs. Samuel
  W., Albany 50 00
Brown, William K., Lansing-
  burgh 2 00
Buell, Mrs. Frederick F., Troy. 2 00
Bullions, Mr. and Mrs. S. S.,
  Albany 5 00
Burden, Miss Mary S., Troy. 5 00
Burnap, Miss Ida C., Albany. 1 00
Burns, James A., Albany..... 5 00
Bush, Miss Julia H., Troy.... 25 00
Button, Charles R., Waterford. 3 00
Byington, Mrs. W. W., Albany. 1 00
Carland, W. C., Albany...... 2 00
Chapman, Mrs. John T., Al-
  bany 5 00
Christie, John T., Troy...... 10 00
Cluett, Mrs. A. E., Troy...... 5 00
Cluett, Mrs. Edmund, Troy... 15 00
Cluett, Mrs. George B., Troy..100 00
Cluett, Miss Nellie A., Troy... 25 00
Cluett, Robert, Troy.......... 50 00
Cluett, Walter H., Troy...... 15 00
Cogswell, Ledyard, Albany.... 5 00
Colwell, Mrs. Thomas, Troy... 25 00

Coons, F. W., Troy.......... 5 00
Cooper, Mrs. James Fenimore,
  Albany 35 00
Corning, Mrs. Douglas, Troy.. 5 00
Cowee, Mrs. Harvey D., Troy.. 80 00
Cox, James W., Jr., Albany... 5 00
Cramell, Miss Sarah, Albany. 2 00
Culver, Mrs. C. M., Albany.. 2 00
Cuyler, Mrs. E. C., Albany.... 2 00
Darling, Edwin R., & Co., Troy 5 00
Davidson, George G., Albany.. 5 00
Day, Richard E., Albany..... 2 00
Dederick, A. M., Albany...... 10 00
Delehanty, John A., Albany... 5 00
Dennis, William A., Waterford 2 00
DeWitt, Miss Sarah W., Al-
  bany 5 00
Dexter, Miss Catherine C., Al-
  bany 5 00
Dey Ermand, William, Co., Al-
  bany 10 00
Docherty, Andrew, Troy...... 3 00
Don, John, Troy............. 25 00
Egerton, Mrs. W. S., Albany.. 3 00
Fearey, W. S., Albany........ 10 00
Ford, Charles R., Cohoes..... 2 00
Foster, C. H., Troy.......... 2 00
Frear, Edwin H., Troy........ 70 00
Freeman, Miss Ellen A., Troy. 1 00
Freeman, Miss Sarah M., Troy. 5 00
Freer, Mrs. Harris A., North
  Hackensack, N. J.......... 1 00
Gale, Mrs. E. Courtland, Troy. 10 00
Gazeley, Mrs. Mary A., Albany 5 00
Gips, Mrs. Hyman, New York
  City 1 00
Glavin, Rev. John F., Rens-
  selaer 5 00
Glover, William L., Troy..... 5 00
Graham, Hugh, Cohoes....... 5 00
Graser, C. B., Troy.......... 2 00
Greene, Mrs. David M., Troy.. 2 00
Hagaman, Charles A., Albany. 15 00
Hagaman, Miss Emma A., Al-
  bany 15 00
Hall, William L., Troy....... 10 00
Hallenbeck, Chas. W., Albany. 2 00
Hannock, Gustave, Albany.... 2 00
Hascy, O. L., Albany.........100 00
Hawley, George C., Albany.... 25 00
Headley, Mrs. Russell, Albany. 2 00
Henry, L. C., Troy........... 5 00
Herrick, Mrs. Charlotte J., Al-
  bany 10 00

Wanted: An endowment to safeguard the future of the work

2

Hoffman, Mrs. John, Albany..	5 00
Hopkins, Rev. William Herman, Albany	2 00
Hun, Mrs. E. R., Albany	5 00
Hun, Marcus T., Albany	25 00
Hun, Mrs. Henry, Albany....	5 00
Hussey, Edward J., Albany...	10 00
Huyck, Mrs. Emily N., Albany.	25 00
Hyatt, Charles M., Albany....	5 00
Ide, A. Harris, Troy	10 00
Ide, Mrs. George P., Troy	5 00
Ide, Mrs. James M., Troy	15 00
Jermain, Miss M. C., Albany..	500 00
Judson, Mrs. A. L., New York City	5 00
Kennedy, R. Oakley, Troy....	2 00
Killip, Mrs. J. B., Albany....	10 00
Knight, Joseph H., Troy	1 00
Kurtz, Jacob, Albany	5 00
Lansing, A. W., Cohoes	10 00
Lansing, J. Townsend, Albany.	20 00
Learned, Mrs. W. L., Albany..	5 00
Leonard, Daniel, Albany	5 00
Leonard, Gardner C., Albany.	10 00
Leonard, Miss Mary L., Albany	5 00
Limerick, Charles H., Troy...	5 00
Ludlow, Harry S., Troy	100 00
Lyon, Mrs. T. Lyttleton, Albany	5 00
McDonald, William, Albany...	50 00
McDowell, G. H., Cohoes	25 00
McEwan, Walter S., Albany..	10 00
McKinney, Edward N., Albany.	10 00
McLeod, Harvey S., Troy	50 00
Madden, William B., Troy....	5 00
Mann, Benjamin A., Albany...	2 00
Mann, Mrs. David S., Albany..	2 00
Manny, John L., Troy	5 00
Martin, Mrs. W. E., Troy....	5 00
Marvin, Rev. Frederic R., Albany	5 00
Meneely, Mr. and Mrs. Clinton H., Troy	20 00
Meneely, Miss Eleanor, Albany	5 00
Meneely, Mrs. G. R., Albany..	5 00
Meyrowitz Bros., Albany	5 00
*Miller, Miss Mary C., Yonkers	3 00
Mix, Frederic L., Albany	5 00
Mount, Mrs. Amelia, Albany..	2 00
Munson, S. L., Albany	5 00
Murray, Edward F., Troy	25 00
Northrup, James N., Albany..	1 00
Ogden, Mrs. Kenneth C., Loudonville	2 00
Olcott, Dudley, Albany	50 00
Olcott, Robert, Albany	15 00
Page, George H., Cohoes	25 00
Paine, John, Troy	50 00

Palmer, Mr. and Mrs. Walter L., Albany	10 00
Parker, Amasa J., Albany....	10 00
Paterson, John S., Albany....	15 00
*Patten, Mrs. Samuel, Albany.	10 00
Patterson, Mrs. John H.; Albany	20 00
Pattison, George B., Troy	2 00
Peltz, Mrs. W. L. L., Albany..	2 00
Perle, Joseph, Albany	3 00
Perry, Edward Rodman, Albany	10 00
Peterson, Mrs. Sarah M., Troy.	10 00
Phillips, Mrs. J. K., Menands.	2 00
Potter, Mrs. Amelia C., Albany	5 00
Pruyn, Mr. and Mrs. Robert C., Albany	25 00
Rathbone, Sard & Co., Albany.	10 00
Reynolds, Mrs. Cuyler, Albany.	1 00
Reynolds, Cuyler, Albany	2 00
Reynolds, Marcus T., Albany..	10 00
Reynolds, R. C., Troy	25 00
Righter & Son Coal Co., Albany	5 00
Robinson, John, Albany	5 00
Root Mfg. Co., Cohoes	25 00
Rosendale, Mrs. Simon W., Albany	10 00
Ross, William, Troy	5 00
Rowe, Mr. and Mrs. Ellis L., Lansingburgh	25 00
Sage, William H., Menands...	50 00
Sampson, Mrs. A. A., Troy...	5 00
Schlesinger, Rev. Max, Albany.	5 00
Schoonmaker, Miss Elizabeth S., Troy	4 00
Schwartz, Samuel, Albany....	4 00
Selden, Mrs. Edward G., Albany	10 00
Shafer, Mrs. John F., Selkirk.	2 00
Sherman, William H., Troy...	2 00
Sherry, A. G., Troy	5 00
Shields, William L., Troy	10 00
Shields, W. H., Troy	10 00
Shirley, John B., Troy	2 00
Sim, F. W., Troy	10 00
Sleicher, William, Troy	25 00
Smith, A. Page, Albany	25 00
Smith, Ben V., Albany	5 00
Smith, Oscar, Albany	5 00
Smith, Mrs. W. Stone, Saratoga Springs	5 00
Spicer, Miss Sarah J., Troy...	2 00
Sporborg, Mrs. Henry J., Albany	5 00
Squires, John, Troy	5 00
Stephens, James & Son, Albany	10 00
Stow, Miss Stella, Troy	5 00

* Deceased.

Wanted: An endowment to safeguard the future of the work

Streibert, Henry, Albany	5 00	Van Rensselaer, Mrs. William	
Sumner, Miss Emily D., Albany	50 00	Bayard, Albany	10 00
Taylor, Mrs. David A., Albany.	1 00	Van Santvoord, Seymour, Troy	25 00
Ten Eyck, Miss Caroline, Albany	2 00	Van Slyke, Mrs. Mary E., Albany	5 00
Thacher, Mrs. John Boyd, Albany	10 00	Von Salis, E., Ph.D., Albany..	5 00
Thompson, Hobart W., Troy..	5 00	Vosburgh, Miss Mary McD., Albany	2 00
Thurman, Miss Sarah, Troy...	25 00	Waldman, Louis J., Albany...	10 00
Tibbits, Dudley, Troy.........	50 00	Walker, John M., Albany.....	10 00
Tibbits, Miss Sarah B., Troy..	10 00	Walsh, Rt. Rev. John, Troy..	10 00
Tillinghast, Mrs. J. W., Albany	25 00	Ward, Mrs. R. H., Troy......	5 00
Tolhurst, Mrs. Helen T., Troy.	10 00	Warren, Prof. Henry P., Albany	2 00
Townsend, Mrs. Theodore, Albany	5 00	Warren, Mrs. Walter P., Troy.	25 00
Tucker, Miss Margaret C., Albany	5 00	Wend, Mrs. George, Albany...	1 00
Tucker, Mrs. Henry O'R., Troy.	2 00	W. J. S., Troy...............	10 00
Tucker, Dr. Willis G., Albany.	2 00	Wilcox, Mrs. Margaret, Albany	1 00
Uhlman, Ernest, Albany......	5 00	Willing Hands Circle of the King's Daughters of the Emmanuel Baptist Church, Albany	5 00
Vail, Mrs. S. M.. Troy........	20 00		
Van Antwerp, Thomas I., Albany	10 00		
Vanderpool, Mrs. Isaac, Albany	2 00	Willing Ten Circle, King's Daughters of Madison Avenue Reformed Church, Albany	5 00
Vander Veer, Dr. Albert, Albany	5 00	Winne. Dr. C. K., Albany.....	5 00
Van Loon, Dr. and Mrs. A. B., Albany	5 00	Woman's Aid Society of St. Paul's Church, Troy........	15 00
		Woodworth, Miss Florence, Albany	2 00

List of deceased members of the Central and other departments will be found on page 39.

Wanted: An endowment to safeguard the future of the work

MISCELLANEOUS GENERAL DONATIONS

Sampson, Murdock & Company, Albany and Troy directories.
The Argus Company, daily paper.
The Albany Evening Journal, daily paper.
The Times-Union, daily paper.
Miss Mary Warren, Youth's Companion for one year for Troy Shelter.
Christian Science Monitor.
Samuel Bolton's Sons and Stoll Brewing Company, spring water for Troy Shelter.
A. Sansoucy and Company, shoeing horses and repairs.

The Society desires to thank the following photographers for their kindness in photographing children at the Albany and Troy buildings:
Emery I. Wendell, 15 North Pearl street, Albany, N. Y.
Albert Lloyd, 44 Third street, Troy, N. Y.

The Society desires to thank Dr. Charles F. Archambeault of Troy, N. Y., and Mr. Matthew A. DeFreest, Albany, for their kindness in furnishing automobiles and teams during the past year, whereby the Society has been enabled to investigate cases in the country that otherwise might not have been reached.

Wanted: An endowment to safeguard the future of the work

MISCELLANEOUS DONATIONS TO ALBANY BUILDING
FOR 1916

Mrs. Chapman, 16 Ten Broeck place, fruit, vegetables, bread, butter, canned goods, eggs, honey, pineapple, canned soup. Mrs. Gomph, 354 Madison avenue, clothing. Mrs. Dr. Moore, Hudson avenue, clothing. Mrs. Mary D. Bender, 57 Lancaster street, magazines. Mrs. Robert K. Quayle, Jr., 198 Western avenue, clothing. Mrs. Edmond Roy, 484 Washington avenue, clothing and toys. Mrs. Guy V. Sweet, Ramsay street, clothing. Mrs. Edith I. Sill, 94 Morris street, clothing, shoes, stockings, hats, nuts, candy, cookies, crackers, apples and bananas. Coxsackie Branch of Needlework Guild of America, 12 stockings, 4 muslin drawers, 6 knit drawers, 2 shirts, 6 coats and 2 pairs shoes. Miss Bertha Bond, 370 Hamilton street, coat. Mrs. Grace Willis, 21 High street, boy's clothing. Mrs. J. C. E. Scott, 68 Chestnut street, girl's and boy's clothing. Mrs. Ansel Pomeroy, 175 Jay street, clothing and toys. Mr. Robert L. Ste. Fleure, shirts, coat and ties. Mrs. Marion Ste. Fleure, waists, skirt and shoes. W. B. Robinson, Loudonville, boy's suits, shirts and stockings. King's Daughters of the Emanuel Baptist Church, 8 boy's shirts. Albany Branch of Needlework Guild of America, 1 dozen handkerchiefs, 4 caps, 4 scarfs, 9 outing skirts, 7 pairs stockings, 6 pairs mittens, 8 suits underwear, 16 towels and 12 pairs mittens. James Butler, 75 Beaver street, cakes, nuts, figs, oranges grapes and apples. Christian Endeavor Society, Calvary Methodist Church, 16 loaves bread. Miss M. C. Jermain, Troy road, chickens, celery and cranberries. S. S. Hoff, 29 Lancaster street, candy. Miss Mae Cunningham, $1.00 for children. Burkhardt, baker, Delmar, 100 biscuits. Kindergarten Class, First Congregational Church, bananas, oranges, dates, preserves and canned soup. King's Daughters, First Congregational Church, $3 for children. Mrs. H. Rextrew, 294 Morton avenue, 4 glasses jelly. Mrs. F. Tyler, 526 Mercer street, $1 for children. Mrs. Caroline Pladwell, 50 Chestnut street, turkey, celery, bread, biscuits, oranges and bananas. Mrs. J. A. MacArthur, 1 Leonard place, 1 turkey. Mrs. E. V. Huyck, 387 State street, 2 turkeys. Edward J. Flood, 183 Hamilton street, gallon ice cream. Delmar Reformed Church, 6 half-pound boxes candy. Mrs. E. G. Mitchell, 7 High street, 2 dozen popcorn balls, cards and books. Mrs. Joseph Killip, 706 Madison avenue, 3 pounds candy and Christmas toys. Mrs. E. Touceda, 38 North Pine avenue, candy, nuts, dolls and other toys. Mrs. Jessie Merwitz, Lake Placid, N. Y., 1 boy's suit, 2 extra pants, 2 sweaters, 2 caps, raincoat, 2 overcoats, 7 boy's waists, 1 pair stockings and 3 pairs woolen gloves. Mrs. William Allen, 4 Judson street, underwear and stockings. Mrs. George Gorham, 214 State street, suit clothes, coat and vest, books, perfume, writing paper and toys. Mrs. C. Smith, 24 Hulbert street, 1 box sewing cards, 1 set furs, children's dresses, gloves, ties and books. Misses A. E. Butler, Spiegle and Dressler, 167 Bradford street, 6 half-pound boxes candy, 3 pounds candy and 1½ dozen popcorn balls. Miss Mary H. Beardsley, 898 Myrtle avenue, 2½ dozen popcorn balls. Anonymous, boy's corduroy suit, stockings, waists, overcoat and pencil box. Special donations of cash at Christmas time were also received from Mrs. Helen M. Watkins, Probation Officer, received $10 from Lincoln League and turned it over to the Society; Miss Laura Townsend, 39 Elk street, $2; Miss Louise Townsend, 39 Elk street, $2; Employees of A. Hagaman Company, $2.15; Mrs. L. Marshall, 278 Western avenue, $2; Mrs. J. T. Chapman, 16 Ten Broeck place, $1; Mrs. T. Wend, 70 South Swan street, $1; Miss Mabel Utterback, $2; Anonymous, $1.

Wanted: An endowment to safeguard the future of the work

MISCELLANEOUS DONATIONS TO TROY BUILDING
FOR 1916

Miss Anne Shields, Congress street, 2 games, punching bag.
Mrs. Harvey D. Cowee, $12 to pay for Physical Instructor, ice
cream, cake. Mrs. Kallenburg, Grand street, boy's clothing. Mrs.
W. E. Martin, 193 Eighth street, clothing. Mrs. Bailey, 138
Second street, magazines. Mr. B. Burdick, Fourth street, magazines, clothing. Mrs. H. F. Boardman, Washington Park, box
assorted worsted shoes, 8 bushels apples, games, sea shells, magazines, pears. Miss Mary Lane, $2. Mrs. F. B. Jillson, pair boy's
shoes, bunnies and candy, 4 pairs boys' stockings (new), boys'
clothing. Mrs. Edgar Betts, Easter cards. Miss Rhoda Nichols,
raffia. Mrs. Cowee received $5 from Mr. H. S. McLeod toward
salary of Physical Instructor for children. Seven dollars from
Ladies' Committee for Physical Instructor. Mrs. Angus Gil-
lespie, clothing. Sunshine Society, Mrs. Atkins, leader, crate
strawberries and 14 pounds sugar. Miss E. L. Remele, Fourth
street, hats. Mrs. Morehouse, Peru, Clinton county, clothing.
Mrs. G. Bell, 561 River street, clothing. Mr. Timothy Hayes,
magazines. Miss Alice Ward, $2. Mrs. F. B. Jillson, check
for $1. Mrs. R. C. Reynolds, games, toys, dolls. Mrs. William
B. Frear, 2 mufflers, 2 caps, 2 sets underwear, 2 pairs bed slippers,
3 toy stockings for Christmas tree. Mrs. J. P. Curley, 154 Second
street, Christmas tree. Mrs. H. D. Cowee, $3 cash for Christmas.
Mrs. Madden, 741 Third avenue, north, ice cream and cake. Mrs.
Rockwell, 147 Fifth avenue, north, clothing. Mr. Bushnell, suit
of clothes for boy. Mrs. H. F. Boardman, bushel pears, games,
tennis ball. Hugh Taggart, fruit for children. Mrs. Chester
Warren, Washington Park, children's clothing. Mrs. Kallenberg,
502 Grand street, boys' clothing.

Wanted: An endowment to safeguard the future of the work

IN MEMORIAM

The Society mourns the loss of the following members, whose deaths have been reported to it during the year 1916:   ·

Albany County

Mrs. Samuel Patten,   Mr. Jesse W. Potts.

Rensselaer County

Mr. Esek Bussey, Sr..   Mr. S. W. Barker.

Schenectady County

Mrs. T. W. Wright,   Mrs. O. S. Luffman,
Mrs. Emma Shuler,   Mr. W. F. Hanrahan,
Miss Jerusha Strong,   Prof. J. Bert Curley,
Miss Eliza Bonney,   Rev. C. B. Magill,
          Rev. E. C. Lawrence, Ph.D.

Columbia County

Mrs. Emma Kissellburgh,   Mrs. Helen Miller.
          Mr. James McNeill.

Fulton County

Mr. L. P. Streeter.   Mr. J. S. G. Edwards.

Clinton County

Mr. James Burns,   Mr. C. N. Hopkins,
Hon. John B. Riley,   Mr. F. P. Lobdell,
Mr. Ferd Chase,   Mr. A. Alpert,
Mr. Fred E. Pierce,   Mr. Marcus Miller.

Saratoga County

Mr. Charles F. Wells.

Wanted: An endowment to safeguard the future of the work

REPORT OF THE LADIES' VISITING COMMITTEE OF THE TROY SHELTER FOR CHILDREN FOR YEAR 1916

The House Committee of the Troy Shelter has held regular monthly meetings during the past year. There have been two resignations and one of the places has been filled. One hundred and sixty-two visitors have inspected the building.

Although the attendance at our meetings has been small much interest has been felt and each committee has faithfully attended to the work of its department. Owing to the excellent management of the Matron, Mrs. Strain, the building is always in perfect condition. The well-planned menus for the month, read at each meeting, show careful attention to diet and a variety greater than would be expected from the amount of money expended. Very little sewing is accomplished as few of the girls detained at the Shelter are old enough to sew.

Miss Rousseau, the teacher furnished by the Board of Education, comes daily for two hours and her work with the children is highly satisfactory. Both Miss Boyd and Miss English have made frequent visits for the purpose of giving religious instruction. Miss Boyd keeps in close touch with the older girls after they are discharged from the Shelter.

On Thanksgiving Day, as has been her custom for several years, a generous friend of the Shelter gave the children, seven in number, a sumptuous dinner.

Christmas was duly celebrated and proved a very happy day. Good friends contributed a gaily decorated tree with toys and candy for each child, followed by a bountiful dinner of turkey and ice-cream which was hugely enjoyed.

I can finish my report in no more fitting manner than in the words of the Secretary of the House Committee in closing her annual report: " In looking backward, should we not feel a sense of gratification? Will not the thoughtfully planned system evolved

Wanted: An endowment to safeguard the future of the work

from years of earnest interest result in inspiring the children who come under its influence with an ambition to do better, and to mould their future in the way of right and regular living?"

MRS. L. B. CLUETT COWEE,
Chairman Ladies' Visiting Committee.

Wanted: An endowment to safeguard the future of the work

PHYSICIAN'S REPORT FOR ALBANY AND TROY
SHELTERS FOR CHILDREN FOR YEAR 1916

ALBANY SHELTER

The health of the children and young people at the Albany Shelter during 1916 has been above the average, largely due to the efficient care of Miss Grace Dare, the matron, and her corps of assistants.

Dr. George B. Randall gave generously of his time during my absence from the city from June to November. Jointly we desire to express our appreciation of the kindly co-operation upon the part of all the staff at the Shelter in making our professional duties agreeable and satisfactory.

HAROLD DUNCAN COCHRANE. M. D.

TROY SHELTER

During 1916 I made nineteen visits to the Troy Shelter of the Humane Society attending children suffering from various minor ills and a few cases of serious illness.

H. L. WALDO, M. D.

We wish to express our appreciation for the assistance received from Dr. LeRoy S. Blatner and the Albany Dental Association for the dental care given to the children at our Albany Shelter.

Wanted: An endowment to safeguard the future of the work

THE SCHENECTADY COUNTY DEPARTMENT

OF THE

MOHAWK AND HUDSON RIVER HUMANE SOCIETY

———

REPORT FOR 1916

[43]

THE SCHENECTADY COUNTY DEPARTMENT

OF THE

MOHAWK AND HUDSON RIVER HUMANE SOCIETY

Office, 304 Clinton Street, Schenectady.   Telephone, Bell 797.

ORGANIZATION AND REPORT FOR 1916

President

MR. ALBERT L. ROHRER.

Vice-President

DR. HERBERT L. TOWNE.

Secretary

MR. CHARLES L. PRINCE.

Treasurer

* REV. E. C. LAWRENCE, Ph. D.

Board of Managers

Rev. F. W. Adams, D. D., Mr. Joseph H. Clements, Jr., Mr. William Dalton, Hon. Alvah Fairlee, Dr. Louis Faust, Miss Katharine Furman, Dr. E. V. R. Gillette, Mr. Willis T. Hanson, Jr., Mrs. Elliott Hyser, *Rev. E. C. Lawrence, Ph. D., Mr. John R. Parker, Mr. Charles L. Prince, Rt. Rev. Mgr. J. L. Reilly, Pres. C. A. Richmond, D. D., Mr. Albert L. Rohrer. Mrs. A. L. Rohrer, Mr. Joseph Smitley, Dr. Herbert L. Towne, Prof. E. R. Whitney, M. A., Rabbi Pizer W. Jacobs, Rev. C. B. Magill.

Executive Committee

Mr. Albert L. Rohrer, Dr. Herbert L. Towne, Mr. C. L. Prince, *Rev. E. C. Lawrence, Ph. D., Mr. Joseph H. Clements, Jr., Miss Katharine Furman, Dr. E. V. R. Gillette, Mrs. A. L. Rohrer.

Executive Staff

Mr. W. H. McGinn, Superintendent and Probation Officer; Mr. B. J. Beebe, Special Officer; Miss N. A. Parks, Stenographer; Mr. Harry Hartley, Inspector.

Kennel Department Staff

Mr. Harry Hartley, Poundmaster.

Counsel

Mr. John R. Parker, Mr. James Cooper, Hon. Everett Smith, Hon. E. D. Cutler, Hon. J. Teller Schoolcraft, Mr. Alexander T. Blessing, Hon. Alvah Fairlee, Mr. John E. Kelly, Mr. George H. Smith.

Physicians and Surgeons

Dr. E. V. R. Gillette, Dr. W. L. Fodder, Dr. Louis Faust, Dr. John J. O'Brien, Dr. Frank Vander Bogart.

Veterinary Surgeons

J. Shults, D. V. S.; A. G. Wicks, D. V. S.

* Deceased.

Wanted: An endowment to safeguard the future of the work

SCHENECTADY COUNTY DEPARTMENT

PREFATORY REMARKS BY PRESIDENT A. L. ROHRER

The year 1916 was the most active in the history of our department. The principal event was the opening of our Shelter, which occurred on March 10th; and from that day until the close of the year, 303 children (82 girls and 221 boys) were cared for. Several times during this period the capacity of the Shelter was taxed; the largest number cared for at any time was 15.

Mr. McGinn, our Superintendent, still continues to serve the city of Schenectady as Probation Officer without pay, and this court work is one of our important activities. The total number placed on probation during the year was 341. Mr. McGinn's work with delinquent fathers grows larger each year. Six thousand nine hundred and eighty-one dollars and seventeen cents was collected from these men and paid to their families through this office. The amount collected for the year 1915 was $3,512. All of this work, as indicated above, has served to call the attention of our citizens to this important work with and for children.

During the year we were able to make several small payments against the debt on our Shelter. The statistical report that accompanies this will serve to give a measure of all the work done during the year.

Wanted: An endowment to safeguard the future of the work

SCHENECTADY COUNTY DEPARTMENT

CHILDREN'S STATISTICS

January 1, 1916, to January 1, 1917

Number of complaints received.................................. 1,420
Number of children involved...................................... 2,068
Number of boys.. 1,409
Number of girls... 659
Number of white children... 2,054
Number of colored children....................................... 14

Nature of Charges

Neglect by father............	170	Held as witness..............	1
Endangering morals..........	35	Neglect by mother............	15
Disorderly and unruly........	273	Improper guardianship	181
Vagrancy	19	Petit larceny	180
Application to take from asylum	31	Runaway	31
		Application to place in asylum.	2
Assault	57	Destitute	47
Violation city ordinance......	28	Burglary and larceny.........	21
Children begging.............	2	Lost and strayed children.....	38
Rape and attempted rape.....	2	Violation parole	48
Truancy	19	Riding on freight trains......	6
Abandonment of child........	6	Carrying firearms	1
Permitted to appear in theatricals	1	Not permitted to appear......	2
		Endangering life and limb....	6
Grand larceny..............	6	Allowed in pool room........	1
Selling tobacco..............	2	Children gambling...........	4
Abduction	1	Malicious mischief...........	36

Miscellaneous 147

Disposition of Cases

Complaints sustained........	1,291	Referred to other societies....	3
Action undesirable...........	24	Unsustained	60
Referred to public officers.....	21	Not found	21
Prosecutions (adults)	183	Advised and warned..........	684
Prosecutions (children)	386	Convictions (adults)	173
Imprisonment imposed, 2 yrs., 7 mos., 18 days.		Convictions (children)	362
		Sentence suspended	341
Fines imposed	$738	Returned to homes...........	136
Pending settlement	17	Held for grand jury..........	1
Placed in institutions........	51	Relieved in other ways.......	28

Placed in Institutions

State Industrial School......	21	St. Vincent's Female Orphan Asylum	3
Albany Orphan Asylum......	7		
Schenectady Children's Home..	4	St. Vincent's Male Orphan Asylum	6
Hudson Training School......	5		
House of Good Shepherd......	2	Other institutions	3

Amount of money paid through Society's office by order of court, $6,981.17.

Wanted: An endowment to safeguard the future of the work

SCHENECTADY COUNTY DEPARTMENT

PROBATION REPORT

JANUARY 1, 1916, TO JANUARY 1, 1917

Continued on probationary oversight from 1915...................... 118
Placed on probation 159

Total number on probation.................................. 277

NATURE OF CHARGES

Disorderly and unruly........	24	Burglary and robbery........	11
Truancy	4	Assault	8
Petit larceny	77	Intoxication	4
Train riding	5	Endangering morals	1
Violation city ordinance......	13	Vagrancy	1
Miscellaneous	6	Malicious mischief	5

DISPOSITION OF CASES

Discharged with improvement. 128   Removed with permission..... 3
Discharged without improve-   Re-arrested and committed.... 28
ment 4   Absconded 9
Total number discharged.. 172
Men reported as on probation for non-support on December 30, 1916.... 35
Total number reported as being on probation....................... 140
Number of men who paid at office by order of court during 1916...... 67

TERMS OF PROBATION

One month	16	Six months	35
Three months	21	Eight months	7
Four months	2	One year	78

NUMBER OF TIMES ON PROBATION

First time	113	Third time	14
Second time	32		

AGES

9 years	7	18 years	4
10 years	15	19 years	6
11 years	7	20 years	3
12 years	14	21 years	1
13 years	19	22 years	1
14 years	27	23 years	3
15 years	29	24 years	1
16 years	9	28 years	1
17 years	10	29 years	2

NATIVITY OF CHILD

American	128	Irish	1
Austrian	2	English	3
Hungarian	2	Polish	6
Italian	16	Russian	1

Wanted: An endowment to safeguard the future of the work

Religion

Catholic	129	Jewish	4
Protestant	26		

As Regards Parents

Both father and mother living.	119	Mother dead	12
Both father and mother dead..	8	Father dead	20

Nativity of Parents

Father		Mother	
French	2	French	2
Scotch	1	Scotch	1
American	49	American	50
Italian	55	Italian	55
Polish	27	Polish	26
Irish	2	Irish	2
Russian	5	Russian	7
Austrian	4	Austrian	5
Hungarian	3	Hungarian	3
English	3	English	3
German	2	German	5

Wanted: An endowment to safeguard the future of the work

SCHENECTADY COUNTY DEPARTMENT

ANIMAL STATISTICS

JANUARY 1, 1916, TO JANUARY 1, 1917

Number complaints received 543

Number animals involved:

In office complaints	794	
In Kennel work, dogs..................................	697	
In Kennel work, cats..................................	1,108	
	———	2,599

Asphyxiated at kennels: Dogs, 594; cats, 1,069.................... 1,663

NATURE OF CHARGES

Horses worked when lame....	27	Horses worked with sores.....	12
Horses worked when sick.....	3	Disabled animals	75
General neglect and cruelty...	44	Vicious animals	44
Sick and suffering...........	146	Lost and strayed.............	3
Beating and abusing.........	34	Unblanketed in winter.......	52
Maliciously torturing	6	Overloaded	7
Miscellaneous	71	Abandoned animals	10
Starved and neglected........	1	Rescued from trees...........	5
Chickens overcrowded	2	Overcrowded in cars..........	1

DISPOSITION OF CHARGES

Complaints sustained	471	Complaints unsustained	19
Not found	45	Advised and warned.........	206
Prosecutions	13	Convicted	13
Amount of fines.............	$102	Sentence suspended	5
Suspended from labor........	20	Referred to public officer.....	6
Disabled horses killed........	23	Other animals killed.........	165
Relieved in other ways.......	35	Action not needed...........	1
	Referred to other societies....	1	

KENNEL REPORT

Dogs in kennels on January 1, 1916..............................	0
Dogs seized	134
Dogs asphyxiated	594
Dogs sold...	21
Dogs redeemed	22
Dogs on orders	563
Dogs returned to owners......................................	60
Dogs in kennels, January 1, 1917...............................	0
Cats in kennels on January 1, 1916.............................	0
Cats received at the kennels...................................	1,108
Homes found	39
Cats asphyxiated	1,069
Cats in the kennel on January 1, 1917..........................	0

Wanted: An endowment to safeguard the future of the work

SCHENECTADY COUNTY DEPARTMENT

REPORT OF TREASURER

JANUARY 1, 1916, TO JANUARY 1, 1917

RECEIPTS

Cash on hand January 1, 1916...............................		$1,970 43
Contributions	$1,036 55	
Dog contract	2,217 89	
Schenectady county	1,000 00	
Court fines	443 00	
Removal of cats..................................	64 82	
Rent from garage.................................	44 00	
Refunds	53 87	
Interest	22 45	
		4,882 58
		$6,853 01

DISBURSEMENTS

Salaries and expenses..............................	$3,421 18	
Shelter equipment	937 99	
Operating Shelter	1,170 50	
Upkeep of Kennels, including auto supplies..........	434 39	
Office supplies	171 92	
Payments on building and interest.................	429 82	
		6,565 80
Cash on hand January 1, 1917.........................		$287 21

JOHN R. PARKER.
Acting Treasurer.

Wanted: An endowment to safeguard the future of the work

CONTRIBUTIONS TO THE SCHENECTADY COUNTY DEPARTMENT FOR 1916

LIFE MEMBERS

Hyser, Mrs. Annie DeGroot.   Perkins, Mrs. A. D.

MEMBERS AND CONTRIBUTORS FOR 1916

Abbe, A. Wolcott	$1 00	Carl Company	1 00
Aitken, J. C.	5 00	Carr, James O.	5 00
Aitkin, James H.\	5 00	Case, Miss Anna	5 00
Alexander, Mrs. Lucy G.	5 00	Cassedy, George A.	1 00
Allee, D. A.	2 00	Champion, F. R.	2 00
Allen, Miss Charlotte	1 00	Chrisler, Leonora V.	1 00
Allen, Miss Eleanor J.	2 00	Christopher, G. E.	1 00
Allen, John	10 00	Clark, Louisa H.	2 00
Allen, Miss Mary	1 00	Clarke, Mrs. W. H.	1 00
Alplaus Sunshine Circle	5 00	Clements, Joseph H.	5 00
Altes, Carolyn H. Korthals	2 00	Clements, Jr., Mr. and Mrs.	
Andrews, Col. James M.	5 00	Joseph H.	15 00
Andrews, W. S.	1 00	Coffin, C. A.	20 00
Armer, Wallace	2 00	Cohen, Mrs. Edward F.	1 00
Armstrong. A. H.	2 00	Cohen, Blanche B.	1 00
Atkinson, E. G.	1 00	Colburn, Hattie Leonard	1 00
Backus, Miss Mary W.	1 00	Collins, Anna E.	5 00
Baird, James	1 00	Conover, W. R.	1 00
Baldwin, E. A.	3 00	Conover, J. S.	5 00
Banker, L. G.	2 00	Coolidge, W. D.	1 00
Barhydt, Mrs. Jane	2 00	Cox, Miss Emma	2 00
Barhydt, Mrs. T. Low	2 00	Cozzens, Frank M.	2 00
Barringer, Mrs. L. E.	1 00	Curtis, Miss Mary	1 00
Basley, F. E.	2 00	Curtis, Wooster B.	1 00
Baum, Max	1 00	Dallam, Mrs. A. C.	1 00
Baumgartner, Mrs. Marie C.	2 00	Dalton, Mrs. Ida H.	10 00
Beller, Mrs. Charles A. G.	1 00	Darling, Henry W.	5 00
Bellinger, Myron	2 00	Deininger, Mrs. J. C.	2 00
Benham, Mrs. Anna F.	2 00	DeMarco, Peter	5 00
Bernardi, Peter	2 00	Deming, W. M.	5 00
Birge, N. R.	5 00	Devenpeck, Mrs. L. W.	1 00
Bishop, S. M.	2 00	Dewey, Mrs. H. F.	2 00
Boardman, H. B.	5 00	DeWitt, Mrs. John E.	5 00
Boston Store	2 00	Dickhoff, Samuel	5 00
Bowman, J. W.	1 00	Dutton, Edgar F.	5 00
Bradshaw, Walter B	5 00	Eggleston, Mrs. Mary E.	3 00
Brandhorst, Mrs. Fred	1 00	Ellis, Mrs. Edward	10 00
Brown, Charles	10 00	Emmet, W. L. R.	5 00
Brown & Son Co., A.	5 00	Emmons, George E.	15 00
Brownell, Mrs. Ira	1 00	Erben, H. F. T.	2 00
Brower, Jr., Charles de Hart		Eveleth. Mrs. Elizabeth L.	3 00
Buck, Mrs. A. A.	1 00	Fagan, Hugh J.	1 00
Buell, Miss Mary L.	1 00	Fairlee, Hon. Alvah	5 00
Bullen, D. R.	5 00	Faust, Dr. William P.	2 00
Callahan, E. F.	2 00	Faust, Dr. Louis	5 00
Callanan, James H	5 00	Ferguson, Mrs. Harriet R.	2 00
Carey, Mrs. B. R.	1 00	Ferguson, John	5 00
Carey, W. Gibson	1 00	Field, Mrs. J. A.	1 00

Wanted: An endowment to safeguard the future of the work

Finch & Hahn	5 00	Jeffers, Prof. G. B.	1 00
Fitzgerald, M. C.	5 00	Jenkins, Mrs. J. H.	1 00
Flinn & Company	5 00	Jesmain, Mrs. A.	5 00
Fodder, Mrs. W. L.	1 00	Johnson, Miss Marian E.	3 00
Footman, Harold	1 00	Johnson, Edward A.	1 00
Fortenbaugh, S. B.	2 00	Johnston, A. M.	1 00
Foster, William J.	1 00	Johnston, A. W.	1 00
Frame, Mrs. W. S.	1 00	Jones, Mrs. A. W.	1 00
Franchot, Katherine F.	1 00	Junggren, O.	2 00
Freeman, H. C.	2 00	Juno, Mrs. J. S.	5 00
Friend	2 00	Kathan, Anna Banker	2 00
Friend	1 00	Kellogg, Mrs. James W.	5 00
Frumkin, M.	1 00	Kelly, Mrs. John	1 00
Fuller, Bertha M.	1 00	Kilgallen, James	1 00
Furman, Catharine A.	1 00	Killian, Joseph H.	1 00
Gallup, Mrs. W. J.	1 00	Kimball, Mary Anderson	2 50
Gardner, I. L.	2 00	Kinney, Mrs. E. M.	2 00
Garlock & Vedder	2 00	Knight, C. D.	2 00
Garrison, W. A.	1 00	Knight, Prosper	1 00
Geisenhoner, E. L.	1 00	Kniskern, H. B.	1 00
Giblin, James	1 00	Koch, Theodore A.	1 00
Gifford, George	1 00	Kruesi, A. H.	1 00
Gilbert, George and Judson	2 00	Laden, Hon. John	1 00
Gilbert, E. E.	5 00	Lambert, F. M.	1 00
Gilmore, Mrs. Mary L.	1 00	Langley, P. G.	1 00
Gilmour, William Ellis	5 00	Levi, Miss Ruth	2 00
Ginster, F. E.	1 00	Lewin, P. L.	3 00
Goddard, Mrs. W. W.	10 00	Lewis, J. W.	1 00
Gregg, Mrs. John	1 00	Lewis, Mrs. Katherine R.	1 00
Grimm, William C. F.	2 00	Liddle, Mrs. Harriet	5 00
Gross, Dr. O.	1 00	Lieety, Sally B.	5 00
Grupe, Mrs. E. H.	1 00	Link, N. V.	1 00
Grupe, Mrs. Henry	1 00	Lovejoy, J. R.	25 00
Hall, Mrs. Mabel	5 00	Luffman, Mrs. E. G.	2 00
Hagadorn, John B.	1 00	Lunt, Mrs. A. D.	3 00
Hanrahan, Joseph J.	1 00	Lyon, J. T.	2 00
Hanson, Jr., W. T.	5 00	Lyon, Harvey	2 00
Hanson, Mrs. Willis T.	5 00	Lyon, Mrs. J. A.	5 00
Hardstock, William F.	5 00	Mackintosh, Frederick	2 00
Hardstock, Louisa	1 00	MacMinn, Dr. C. A.	1 00
Hartley, Mrs. E. C.	1 00	MacNee, Miss Ella	1 00
Haselo, F. W.	1 00	Magarvey, John R.	10 00
Hathaway, Mrs. W. H.	1 00	Magill, Rev. C. B.	2 00
Hawkins, Lawrence A.	2 50	Marcellus, John N.	1 00
Hayden, Mrs. J. Leroy	3 00	McAleer, C. J.	1 00
Heatley, Dr. John A.	2 50	McCabe, Mrs. Kathleen	1 00
Heilbronner, Cora D.	1 00	McClellan, F. W.	3 00
Heilbronner, Mrs. Henry	1 00	McDermott, P. H.	1 00
Herman, Mrs. William	1 00	McDonald Brothers	1 00
Hild, Johanna	1 00	McKinley, J. G.	1 00
Hoffman, Ph.D., Prof. Frank S.	2 00	McMullen, Mrs. Henry	1 00
Hollister, J. M.	1 00	Middlemiss, Peter R.	10 00
Holtzmann, Sr., Charles	1 00	Milbank, Louise	1 00
Holtzman, George	2 00	Milmine, E. L.	1 00
Hoppman, Frank	1 00	Moir, Mrs. R. T.	1 00
Horne, Jessie Van Dyck	1 00	Moon, Mrs. George Church	1 00
Houck, H. C.	2 00	Moore, Mrs. Rachel	1 00
Howe, W. F.	1 00	Moore, Mrs. E. W.	50
Hyndman, Mrs. Rachel K.	2 00	Murphy, Mrs. S. E.	1 00
Jackson, A. H.	5 00	Murray, Dr. Janet	1 00

Wanted: An endowment to safeguard the future of the work

Myers, Mrs. John	1 00	Slaght, G. William	2 00
Mynderse, H. V.	5 00	Smith, Mrs. Paul	1 00
Nagahama, I.	1 00	Smith, Miss Ellen	3 00
Naylon, Jr., Hon. Daniel	5 00	Smith, Hon. Everett	1 00
Neubauer, R. P.	4 00	Smith, Gerardus	5 00
Nisbet, A. W.	1 00	Smith, Eleanor F.	3 00
O'Brien, Dr. John J.	1 00	Smitley, Mr. and Mrs. Joseph.	10 00
Oudin, Mrs. M. A.	2 00	Steinmetz, Charles P.	25 00
Overton, Dr. P. W.	1 00	Stern, Mrs. F. L.	1 00
Palmer, Mrs. Robert	1 00	Stevenson, Rev. A. Russell	1 00
Parker, John R.	5 00	Stoddard, Julia E.	1 00
Parker, James C.	2 00	Stoller, Ph. D., Prof. James H.	2 00
Parsons, Jessie B.	2 00	Stone, Harriet A. W.	5 00
Patterson, Roger W.	5 00	Stone, Mrs. E. M. O.	1 00
Patton & Hall.	5 00	Stoodley, Alfred	2 00
Peckham, Mrs. W. H.	1 00	Strong, Alonzo P.	5 00
Phillips, Mrs. William	1 00	Strong, Miss Florence	1 00
Potter, W. B.	5 00	Swanker, Minnie	2 00
Pratt, Henry C.	1 00	Switz, Harmon	1 00
Pratt, Mrs. F. C.	3 00	Swits, Mrs. Harmon D.	1 00
Priest, E. D.	5 00	Talbot, Mrs. Walter Eugene	1 00
Prince, C. L.	10 00	Tayler, D. D., Rev. B. W. R.	1 00
Putman, Mrs. G. H.	5 00	Taylor, Mrs. F. K.	1 00
Quackenbush, A. J.	5 00	Taylor, Mrs. J. B.	3 00
Quinn, William H.	5 00	Taylor, Mrs. W. C.	1 00
Rasher, C. F.	1 00	Telkes, Dr. Magda	1 00
Rector, Miss Emma	1 00	Tenney, A. E.	1 00
Reicherter, Charles	8 00	Tetro, W. F.	1 00
Reilly, George C.	2 00	Thomas, W. S.	1 00
Reilly, Margaret R.	1 00	Thompson, Louise A.	5 00
Reilly, Rt. Rev. Msgr. J. L.	5 00	Thornton, A. R.	1 00
Reist, H. G.	2 00	Timeson & Fronk	5 00
Rice, Jr., Mrs. E. W.	5 00	Tinnerholm, August F.	1 00
Rindfleisch, Jacob	1 00	Towne, Dr. H. L.	5 00
Ripton, LL. D., Dean B. H.	5 00	Unitarian Sunday School Children	5 00
Roach, Michael A.	5 00		
Roberts, John	1 00	Upp, John W.	2 00
Rogers, Mrs. L. R.	1 00	Van Brunt, Charles	5 00
Rohrer, Albert L.	5 00	Van Deusen, Mrs. W. E.	3 00
Rohrer, Mrs. Albert L.	2 00	Van Eps, Mr. and Mrs. Jewett E.	1 00
Rohrer, Miss Marian	1 00		
Rosa, Mrs. Nelson W.	1 00	Van Voast, Miss Isabelle	5 00
Rosenthal, Mrs. Sophia L.	1 00	Van Vranken, Mrs. A. B.	1 00
Rubenstein, L.	1 00	Vaughen, Mrs. F. G.	1 00
Rynex, Mrs. J. W.	1 00	Vedder, John N.	5 00
Rynex, Miss Edna	1 00	Veeder, James W.	2 00
Ryon, E. J.	1 00	Vrooman, Mrs. William C.	1 00
Salmon, Edna Stern	1 00	Waldron, C. N.	1 00
Sanborn, Juta	1 00	Walton, Roger P.	5 00
Schermerhorn, W. G.	10 00	Ward, Mrs. G. E. T.	2 00
Schermerhorn, Miss Mary V.	2 00	Warnick, Mr. and Mrs. H. T.	10 00
Schermerhorn, Clarence	1 00	Washburn, C. S.	10 00
Schermerhorn, Mrs. M. H.	1 00	Washington, Miss	1 00
Schieffelin, Mrs. Ethel P.	1 00	Wasylevsky, Alex	1 00
Schoolcraft, Dr. John L.	1 00	Weber, John	5 00
Seede, Mrs. Keziah Lewis	1 00	Weber, A.	15 00
Semple, William	1 00	Wellman, Miss Elizabeth F.	10 00
Shaible, W. G.	1 00	Wellman, Walter	10 00
Shop 49 — G. E. Co.	8 55	Wemple, Mrs. W. W.	1 00
Simmons, Cornelia C.	1 00	Weston, Frederick H.	1 00

Wanted: An endowment to safeguard the future of the work

Westover, M. F.............. 5 00
White, Mrs. J. H............ 2 00
Whitehead, Mrs. William..... 1 00
Whitestone, Laura J......... 3 00
Whitmyer, C. 1 00
Whitmyer, Mrs. E. C......... 2 00
Whitmyer, Mrs. Henry....... 1 00
Whitney, Prof. E. R......... 10 00
Williams, C. W.............. 1 00
Wiltshire, C. J.............. 10 00
Winne, Miss 1 00

Wissenbach, Alex. 1 00
Witbeck, Clark 10 00
Woman's   Branch   Alliance,
  Unitarian Church 10 00
Woodard, W. E.............. 1 00
Wright, Margaret 1 00
Yates, Miss Elizabeth M..... 1 00
Yates, Mrs. O. I............. 1 00
Yelverton, E. E............. 1 00
Yelverton, James W......... 25 00
Zeiser, Edward E............ 1 00

List of deceased members of the Central and other departments will be found found on page 39.

MISCELLANEOUS CONTRIBUTIONS TO THE SCHENEC-TADY COUNTY DEPARTMENT

Buell & McDonald, one new dresser.
Endicott-Johnson, 10 pairs new shoes.
Fish, Miss, canned fruit and jelly.
Gardner, I. L., fruit and vegetables.
Hyser, Mrs. Elliott, dresser, chairs, pictures, etc.
MacGill, Mrs. Frank, all pillows used in the Shelter.
Public Market, fruit.
Robinson's Bakery, 100 hot cross buns.
Rennie, Mrs., bed and springs.
Rohrer, Mrs. A. L., bed and springs.
Rosa, Nelson, 20 books and one-half ton of coal.
Sewing Circle, Presbyterian Church, 9 aprons and other articles of clothing.
Sommers, Mrs. R. F., bread, rolls, etc.
Stone, Mrs. C. W., large rocking horse.
Switchboard Department, General Electric Co., at Christmas time, gave clothing and toys to the amount of $70, which was distributed among children in needy families.
Woman's Needlework Guild, quantity of new clothing.
Fourteen purple stamp books and one yellow stamp book, filled from boxes placed in the Boston Store, Boston Store Annex, Crescent Market, and The Carl Company's store, by Mrs. Frank MacGill. Twenty-three pairs of shoes, 5 pairs of rubbers, 7 pairs of mittens, 15 pairs of stockings, 7 union suits, waists, trousers, etc., were purchased with these books for children in emergency cases.
Many others have given clothing and toys.
The Society wishes to thank Mr. Theodore Avlon for taking photographs for the Society without cost.

Wanted: An endowment to safeguard the future of the work

THE COLUMBIA COUNTY DEPARTMENT

OF THE

MOHAWK AND HUDSON RIVER HUMANE SOCIETY

———————

REPORT FOR 1916

[57]

THE COLUMBIA COUNTY DEPARTMENT

OF THE

MOHAWK AND HUDSON RIVER HUMANE SOCIETY

ORGANIZATION AND REPORT FOR 1916

Office at Police Headquarters. Telephones: Bell 376; Home 376.

President
* Mr. JAMES McNEILL.

Secretary
Miss BLANCHE B. MEMBERT.

Treasurer
Mrs. LUELLA DOWD SMITH.

Acting Superintendent
Mr. WILLIAM C. MESICK.

Counsel
Mr. EDWARD G. MacARTHUR, Mr. HERBERT L. RICKARD,
Miss CATHERINE MURPHY.

Veterinary Surgeons
J. H. LUFF, D. V. S.; S. L. HONEYFORD, D. V. S.;
F. B. D. SMITH, D. V. S.

Board of Managers
Rev. George C. Yeisley, *Mr. James McNeill, Miss Blanche B. Membert, Mrs.
C. P. B. Williams, Mrs. Luella D. Smith, Mrs. Willard Peck.

Executive Committee
*Mr. James McNeill, Miss Blanche B. Membert, Mrs. Luella D. Smith, Mrs. James
W. DeFrate.

Kennel Department Staff
Mr. William LaRose, Agent; Mr. William S. Heermance, Kennelmaster.

Special Committees
Homeless Dogs.— Mrs. James W. De Frate.
Suffering Cats.— Miss Blanche B. Membert.
Injured Birds.— Mrs. Luella D. Smith.
Misued Horses.— Miss Kathryn Krick.

* Deceased.

Wanted: An endowment to safeguard the future of the work

REPORT OF COLUMBIA COUNTY DEPARTMENT

Prefatory Remarks by Treasurer Mrs. Luella D. Smith

When the Columbia County Branch was formed in 1905, Mr. James McNeill was elected president. He has given strength, time, money and pains to this humane work during these years. We have had no other president. A few years ago Mr. McNeill began to pass his winters in Florida. The burden of the work, which had fallen almost entirely upon him before this time, was now shared to a greater extent by the few officers in charge.

Last year we worked, practically, as a committee under the parent society. In the spring Mr. McNeill returned to Hudson for the summer. His health was not good, and in October he was called from earth. He was faithful, unassuming and self-sacrificing, a lover of truth and justice and mercy.

Our work must go on. The need is great — greater than ever before. Many of our helpers have been taken, and now the active workers are few. We face our two problems: the financial, for this work can only be continued by the continuance of cash; and the anti-cruelty work, itself, to which we are ever urged by the calls of the suffering, neglected and abused, who have " no language but a cry ". We thank all who have helped and we ask you to continue your aid in support of this worthy cause. " Blessed are the merciful."

Wanted: An endowment to safeguard the future of the work

COLUMBIA COUNTY DEPARTMENT

CHILDREN'S STATISTICS

JANUARY 1, 1916, TO JANUARY 1, 1917

Complaints received 232
Children involved:
Boys.. 232
Girls.. 97
                                                         ───── 329

CHARGES

Neglect by father............	21	Violation Labor Law............	1
Neglect by mother............	1	Assault, third degree.........	15
Desertion by father.........	4	Held as witness.............	1
Improper guardianship	38	Petit larceny	37
Endangering morals	4	Vagrancy	6
Violation parole	1	Disorderly children	51
Admitting to theatre without		Burglary...................	30
parent	4	Riding on freight trains......	1
Rape and attempted rape.....	3	Destitute	1
Application to take from asy-		Carrying firearms	11
lum	1	Miscellaneous	1

DISPOSITION OF CASES

Complaints sustained	224	Advised and warned..........	94
Complaints unsustained	6	Summoned to court..........	27
Action undesirable	2	Warned by court.............	25
Prosecution (against adults).	15	Compelled to pay by court....	1
Convictions (against adults)..	15	Placed in institutions........	13
Prosecutions (against minors).	73	Pending settlement	10
Convictions (against minors).	69	Relieved in other ways.......	5
Imprisonment imposed: 1 year,		Returned to homes...........	8
8 months and 29 days.		Referred to public officer......	3
Sentence suspended	65		

PLACED IN INSTITUTIONS

State Industrial School.......	3	Reformatory for Women, Bed-	
St. Margaret's House.........	1	ford	1
Randall's Island	2	Other institutions	6

Wanted: An endowment to safeguard the future of the work

COLUMBIA COUNTY DEPARTMENT

PROBATION REPORT

January 1, 1916, to January 1, 1917

Continued on probation from 1915..................................	13
Boys placed on probation from January 1, 1916, to January 1, 1917...	30
Girls placed on probation from January 1, 1916, to January 1, 1917...	16

Nature of Charges

Burglary...................	32	Petit larceny	18
Disorderly children	8	Assault	1

Terms of Probation

Three months	6	One year	19
Six months	34		

Disposition of Cases

Discharged with improvement.	43	Re-arrested and committed....	2
Discharged without improve-		Transferred to other officers...	4
ment	3	Moved to other cities.........	3
Still on probation...........	4		

Ages

Nine years	4	Thirteen years	6
Ten years	10	Fourteen years	10
Eleven years	11	Fifteen years	3
Twelve years	15		

Nativity of Child

American	36	Polish	14
Italian	7	Hebrew	2

Color

White......................	58	Black	1

Religion

Catholic....................	48	Protestant	11

Number of Times on Probation

First time..................	45	Second time	14

Regarding Parents

Father dead	8	Mother dead	3
Both parents living..........	48		

Wanted: An endowment to safeguard the future of the work

COLUMBIA COUNTY DEPARTMENT

ANIMAL STATISTICS

JANUARY 1, 1916, TO JANUARY 1, 1917

Complaints received 88
Animals involved 148

CHARGES

Horses worked when sick.....	2	Starved and neglected........	3
Horses worked when lame.....	4	Maliciously torturing ......,.	5
Horses worked with sores.....	6	General neglect and cruelty...	5
Unblanketed in winter........	4	Poisoning animals	2
Cock fighting	7	Cats rescued from trees......	2
Sick or suffering............	15	Beating and abusing.........	5
Lost and strayed............	1	Vicious animals	3
Disabled animals	10	Carried in cruel way.........	2
Suffering from exposure......	1	Crates of fowl overcrowded...	1
Homeless	1	Overloading	2

Miscellaneous 7

DISPOSITION OF CASES

Complaints sustained	74	Homes found	1
Complaints unsustained	10	Sent to blacksmith...........	2
Action not needed...........	4	Relieved by padding.........	2
Advised and warned.........	41	Cock fights stopped.........	1
Prosecutions	2	Veterinarians called	3
Convictions	2	Relieved in other ways.......	3
Fines imposed	$10	Disabled horses killed........	1
Sentence suspended	1	Suspended from labor........	3
Referred to public officers.....	1	Compelled to repair stable....	1

Other animals killed........ 32

KENNEL REPORT

Dogs received on orders....................................... 41
Dogs seized 35
Dogs redeemed and released.................................. 3
Dogs humanely destroyed 42
Homes found for dogs.. 31
Cats received 54
Homes found for cats.. 16
Cats humanely destroyed..................................... 38

INSPECTION OF DUMPING GROUNDS

During the year visits to dumping grounds, freight yards, etc., were made as follows:

To dumping grounds 14
To freight yards 22
To poultry yards 8
To building excavations 11
Number of horses inspected on streets........................ 32

87

Wanted: An endowment to safeguard the future of the work

COLUMBIA COUNTY DEPARTMENT

REPORT OF TREASURER

JANUARY 1, 1916, TO JANUARY 1, 1917

RECEIPTS

Annual membership	$36 00	
Annual sustaining membership	90 00	
Annual memorial membership	6 00	
Gifts	139 98	
Fines	11 00	
Dog tax, 90 per cent	385 20	
		$668 18

EXPENDITURES

Deficit from 1915	$20 07	
Salaries and expenses of superintendents	163 33	
Traveling expenses . . . . : . .	119 00	
Veterinary surgeons	84 50	
Kennels and gas	106 46	
Expenses of court trials	39 50	
Telephones and telegrams	2 35	
Board, aid, food, shelter and chloroform	21 20	
Burials	13 25	
Advertising	2 54	
Postage	4 79	
		$576 99
Balance		91 19
		$668 18

MRS. LUELLA D. SMITH,
Treasurer.

Wanted: An endowment to safeguard the future of the work

MEMBERS OF COLUMBIA COUNTY DEPARTMENT

LIFE MEMBERS

(A life member is one who has given $100 in one payment)

Miss M. I. Bevan   Miss Amanda Limbrick   Mr. Herbert DuBois

MEMBERS AND CONTRIBUTORS FOR 1916

Aken, Mrs. Delia A.	$25 00	McNeill, Miss Margaretta (in	
Ambler, Mrs. J. M. B.	1 00	memory of Mrs. William	
Butler, Mrs. Angelica J	1 00	Tough).	1 00
Cochrane, Hon. A. V. S.	10 00	Murphy, Miss Catherine S.	1 00
Cole, Rev. Thomas L.	2 00	Newkirk, Miss Agnes.	5 00
Collier, Miss Anna C.	5 00	Nichols, Miss Susan D. (paid	
Collier, Miss Anna C. (in mem-		in 1915).	1 00
ory of Miss Mary T. Collier)	5 00	Nixon, Mrs. Mattie E.	1 00
Davis, Mrs. Cassius M.	19 00	Peck, Mrs. Willard.	1 00
Day, W. P. (for 1916 and 1917)	10 00	Potts, Miss Ida C.	50 00
DeFrate, Mrs. James W.	50	Powell, George T.	2 00
Dowd, Miss Alice M.	1 00	Powell, Mrs. Marcia C.	1 00
DuBois, Miss Rachel.	1 00	Punderson, Mrs. J. M.	1 00
Elmer, Miss Ellen F.	1 00	Punderson, Miss Louise M.	1 00
Evans, Mrs. C. H., Sr.	5 00	Seymour, Miss J. Adelaide.	1 00
Finnerty, Mrs. Anna.	1 00	Seymour, William	5 00
Gillette, Mrs. John W.	5 00	Seymour, Miss Julia D.	1 00
Hall, Mrs. C. V. R.	1 00	Seymour, Miss Mary Howard.	1 00
Hallenbeck, Mrs. Fred S.	1 00	Smith, Dr. H. Hadley.	2 00
Huntington, C. W.	1 00	Smith, Mrs. Luella Dowd.	5 00
Jones, Miss Bessie L.	7 00	Smock, Professor J. C.	2 00
*Jones, Mrs. Mary E.	5 00	Smock, Mrs. J. C.	1 00
*Kisselburgh, Mrs. Austin		Thompson, Mrs. Sarah H.	25 00
(paid in 1915).	1 00	Wardle, Miss Emma.	3 00
Lampman, Mrs. John T.	5 00	Wardle, Miss Ethelwyn.	1 00
Limbrick, Miss Amanda (to		W. C. T. U of North German-	
balance deficit of 1915 and		town	1 00
for 1916)	30 00	Williams, Mrs. C. P. B.	2 00
Macbeth, Mrs. S. J.	1 00	Wilsey, Mrs. Mary L. (paid in	
Mack, Mrs. Mary E.	1 00	1915)	1 00
McNamee, Judge D. V.	2 00	Yeisley, Mrs. George C.	5 00
McNeill, Miss Margaretta.	1 00	Yeisley, Rev. George C.	5 00

* Deceased.

List of deceased members of the Central and other departments will be found on page 39.

Wanted: An endowment to safeguard the future of the work

3

THE SARATOGA COUNTY DEPARTMENT

OF THE

MOHAWK AND HUDSON RIVER HUMANE SOCIETY

REPORT FOR 1916

[67]

THE SARATOGA COUNTY DEPARTMENT

OF THE

MOHAWK AND HUDSON RIVER HUMANE SOCIETY

ORGANIZATION AND REPORT FOR 1916

Office, G. A. R. Hall, Pavilion Place, Saratoga Springs, N. Y. Telephone No. 1302-W.
Kennels, No. 55 Warren Street, Saratoga Springs, N. Y.

President
MR. IRVING I. GOLDSMITH.

First Vice-President
* MR. CHARLES F. WELLS.

Second Vice-President
MRS. R. J. C. WILLIAMS.

Secretary
MRS. FRANK JENKINS.

Treasurer
MISS MARGARET WALBRIDGE.

Superintendent
MR. ROBERT S. RIMINGTON.

Counsel
MR. IRVING I. GOLDSMITH.

Veterinary Surgeon
EUGENE J. SULLIVAN, D. V. S.

Kennel Department Staff
MR. MOSES B. CAPEN, Poundmaster.

Board of Managers
Mr. Irving I. Goldsmith, Mrs. E. T. Brackett, Miss Sara Putnam, Mrs. R. J. C. Williams, Mrs. Frank M. Jenkins, Miss Margaret Walbridge, Mrs. A. S. Downs, Mrs. R. C. McEwen, Mrs. Thomas Sheehan.

Executive Committee
Mrs. R. C. McEwen, Mrs. J. B. Ledlie, Mrs. A. S. Downs, Mrs. John Foley, Mrs. E. T. Brackett, Miss Elizabeth Shackelford, Miss Ingham, Mrs. Thomas Sheehan.

* Deceased,

Wanted: An endowment to safeguard the future of the work

REPORT OF SARATOGA COUNTY DEPARTMENT

PREFATORY REMARKS BY PRESIDENT IRVING I. GOLDSMITH

The Saratoga County Department is pleased to report that its work has progressed satisfactorily during the past year. The substitution of motor vehicles for horses for commercial purposes has noticeably reduced the number of cases of cruelty to horses in the cities and larger villages of Saratoga county, although in the country districts and smaller communities the number of these cases requiring the attention of this Society remain about the same.

Unfortunately the number of children's cases requiring attention has been increasing, but this Society has been successful in handling most of these cases and has been able to remedy conditions so that the households have been improved and the children benefited. It is always with reluctance that this Department takes a child away from its parents and places it in an institution, and every effort is made to improve home conditions and make the home a suitable place for the child.

The work of this Society is greatly facilitated by the courtesy and interest shown by the courts and public officials throughout the county.

Wanted: An endowment to safeguard the future of the work

SARATOGA COUNTY DEPARTMENT

CHILDREN'S STATISTICS
JANUARY 1, 1916, TO JANUARY 1, 1917

Number of complaints received..................................... 77
Number of children involved:

Boys.	89	
Girls.	69	
		158

CHARGES

Neglect by father............	6	Disorderly children	6
Neglect by mother...........	5	Vagrancy	1
Desertion by father..........	1	Truancy	2
Improper guardianship	27	Petit larceny	3
Endangering morals	1	Using tobacco	1
Abandonment of child.......	1	Destitute	6
Rape and attempted rape.....	1	Without home	3
Abduction	1	Violation Education Law.....	1
Bastardy	1	Feeble-minded child	1
Application to place in asylum	1	Held as witness.............	1
Miscellaneous	7		

DISPOSITION OF CASES

Complaints sustained	70	Sentence suspended	15
Complaints unsustained	4	Warned by court.............	6
Action undesirable	1	Held for grand jury.........	1
Advised and warned.........	40	Referred to public officers.....	1
Prosecutions (against adults).	12	Placed in institutions........	11
Convictions (against adults)..	12	Placed in families...........	1
Prosecutions (against minors).	5	Receiving hospital treatment..	1
Convictions (against minors).	5	Relieved in other ways.......	7
Compelled to pay by court....	3	Summoned to court..........	4

PLACED IN INSTITUTIONS

St. Margaret's House.........	1	Hawley Home	3
State Industrial School.......	3	Troy Orphan Asylum.........	2
Training School	1	Other institution	1

Wanted: An endowment to safeguard the future of the work

SARATOGA COUNTY DEPARTMENT

ANIMAL STATISTICS
JANUARY 1, 1916, TO JANUARY 1, 1917

Number of complaints received.................................... 69
Number of animals involved...................................... 106

CHARGES

Horses worked when sick.....	1	Sick or suffering.............	5
Horses worked with sores.....	1	Disabled animals	13
Horses worked when lame.....	8	Lost or strayed..............	3
Suffering from exposure......	1	Cock fighting	1
Starved and neglected........	7	Vicious animals	9
General neglect and cruelty...	5	Homeless	2
Overdriven	3	Carried in cruel way.........	2
Beating and abusing.........	4	Overloading	1

Miscellaneous 3

DISPOSITION OF CASES

Complaints sustained	66	Referred to public officer......	1
Action not needed...........	1	Disabled horses killed........	9
Not found	1	Other animals killed.........	23
Referred to other society.....	1	Veterinarians called	2
Advised and warned..........	34	Returned to owners..........	1
Prosecutions	1	Suspended from labor........	6
Convictions	1	Compelled to furnish food....	5
Imprisonment imposed, 10 days.		Relieved in other ways.......	7

KENNEL REPORT

Dogs voluntarily surrendered..................................... 140
Dogs seized during period....................................... 10
Dogs humanely put to death...................................... 150

Cat Department

Cats voluntarily surrendered..................................... 100
Cats humanely put to death...................................... 100

Fowls

Fowls inspected (crates)... 25
Overcrowded and warned... 15

Wanted: An endowment to safeguard the future of the work

SARATOGA COUNTY DEPARTMENT

REPORT OF TREASURER
From September 1, 1915, to September 1, 1916

RECEIPTS

Annual dues and gifts............................	$98	00
Interest on bonds................................	72	00
County money	100	00
City check for dog licenses.......................	476	81
Last year's ball (August, 1915)..................	25	00
Charity ball, 1916...............................	206	00
	$977	81
Bank balance, September 7, 1915..............	313	69
		$1,291 50

DISBURSEMENTS

Humane officer and his expenses...................	$793	76
Printing	16	05
Dog pound	169	50
Insurance on pound...............................	5	00
Postage...	1	50
Ball expenses	63	50
	$1,049	31
Checks out last reckoning........................	7	90
		1,057 21
Bank balance, September 7, 1916........................		$234 29

Miss Margaret Walbridge,
Treasurer.

Wanted: An endowment to safeguard the future of the work

WARREN COUNTY DEPARTMENT

OF THE

MOHAWK AND HUDSON RIVER HUMANE SOCIETY

REPORT FOR 1916

[75]

WARREN COUNTY DEPARTMENT

OF THE

MOHAWK AND HUDSON RIVER HUMANE SOCIETY

ORGANIZATION AND REPORT FOR 1916

Office, 56 Warren Street, Glens Falls, N. Y. Telephone, 572-J.

President
MR. DANIEL L. ROBERTSON.

First Vice-President
MR. FREDERICK B. RICHARDS.

Second Vice-President
DR. T. H. FOULDS.

Secretary and Officer in Charge of Children's Work
MISS LAURA L. SWEET.

Treasurer
DR. ANNETTA E. BARBER.

Superintendent of Children's Department
MRS. EDWARD REED.

General Director of Animal Work
MAJOR D. J. HOGAN.

Counsel
MR. FRANK D. MOREHOUSE.

Physicians and Surgeons
DR. H. S. PAINE, DR. J. J. DEVER.

Veterinarian
DR. HENRY MURRAY, D. V. S.

Dentist
DR. THOMAS H. FOULDS.

In Charge of Kennel Department
MR. CHARLES MILLER.

Board of Managers
Dr. Thomas H. Foulds, Dr. Annetta Barber, Mr. and Mrs. James H. Seaman, Mr. Frederick B. Richards, Mr. F. D. Morehouse, Dr. Henry Murray, Dr. James J. Dever, Mr. Daniel F. Keefe, Dr. Howard S. Paine, Mr. George F. Bayle, Miss Nell K. Pruyn, Mrs. Allison B. Abbott, Mr. Daniel L. Robertson, Miss Anna Lossee, Major D. J. Hogan, Dr. H. D. Sweet, Mrs. George Brown, Mrs. Edward Reed.

Executive Committee
Mr. Frederick B. Richards, Chairman ; Dr. Thomas H. Foulds, Dr. Annetta Barber, Mrs. Edward Reed.

Wanted: An endowment to safeguard the future of the work

WARREN COUNTY DEPARTMENT

PREFATORY REMARKS BY SECRETARY LAURA L. SWEET

The year's work has been a profitable and useful one to the community. The complaints come from all sources. All cases take a great deal of time and thought, but it has done a great deal of good.

The Humane Society for the Prevention of Cruelty to Children and Animals is a power when brought before men. They stop and think and try to do better, so let us keep up the good work which is making better citizens every day.

Wanted: An endowment to safeguard the future of the work

WARREN COUNTY DEPARTMENT

CHILDREN'S STATISTICS

JANUARY 1, 1916, TO JANUARY 1, 1917

Number of complaints received.................................... 23
Number of children involved:
 Boys 25
 Girls 26
                          51

CHARGES

Neglect by father...........	1	Disorderly children 2
Neglect by mother...........	1	Destitute 2
Improper guardianship	11	Feeble-minded child 1
Truancy	2	Application to place in asylum 1
Miscellaneous	2	

DISPOSITION OF CASES

Complaints sustained	22	Referred to public officers.... 2
Complaints unsustained	1	Placed in institutions........ 7
Advised and warned........	12	Relieved in other ways....... 5
Prosecutions (against minors)	3	Receiving hospital treatment.. 1
Convictions (against minors).	3	Pending settlement 1

PLACED IN INSTITUTIONS

Albany Orphan Asylum......	1	State Industrial School....... 1
Charlton Industrial School....	2	Rome Custodial Asylum...... 1
Hawley Home	1	Hudson Training School...... 1

Wanted: An endowment to safeguard the future of the work

WARREN COUNTY DEPARTMENT

ANIMAL STATISTICS

Number of complaints received.................................... 3
Number of animals involved....................................... 3

CHARGES

Beating and abusing.........   2   Starved and neglected........   1

DISPOSITION OF CASES

Complaints sustained   3   Prosecutions   1
Advised and warned.........   2   Discharged   1

REPORT OF TREASURER

JANUARY 1, 1916, TO JANUARY 1, 1917

RECEIPTS

Balance on hand................................ $60 11
Received during year............................   10 00
                                                              $70 11

DISBURSEMENTS

Miscellaneous expenses 61 70

Balance on hand, December 31, 1916..................... $8 41

DR. ANNETTA E. BARBER,
Treasurer.

Wanted: An endowment to safeguard the future of the work

HOOSICK FALLS BRANCH

OF THE

MOHAWK AND HUDSON RIVER HUMANE SOCIETY

REPORT FOR 1916

[81]

HOOSICK FALLS BRANCH

OF THE

MOHAWK AND HUDSON RIVER HUMANE SOCIETY

ORGANIZATION AND REPORT FOR 1916

Office, " The Pines," and 90 High Street, Hoosick Falls, N. Y.

President
Mr. FRED N. STEVENS.

Vice-President
Mr. ERNEST C. JONES.

Secretary
Mr. CLYDE L. HARVEY.

Treasurer
Mr. HENRY W. HUDSON.

Board of Managers
Mr. Fred N. Stevens, Mr. Ernest C. Jones, Mr. Henry W. Hudson, Dr. William B. Putnam, Mr. Clyde L. Harvey, Mr. Michael J. Dillon, Mr. James M. Carpenter, Mr. J. H. McEachron, Mr. John Marshall.

Executive Committee
Mr. Fred N. Stevens, Mr. Ernest C. Jones, Mr. Clyde L. Harvey, Mr. M. J. Dillon, Mr. H. W. Hudson.

Auditing Committee
Mr. Fred N. Stevens, Mr. M. J. Dillon, Mr. J. H. McEachron.

Finance Committee
Mr. Fred N. Stevens, Mr. J. H. McEachron, Mr. Clyde L. Harvey, Mr. H. W. Hudson.

Special Agents of the Branch
Mr. John Marshall, Hoosick Falls, N. Y.; Mr. Richmond L. Perry, Hoosick Falls, N. Y.

Wanted: An endowment to safeguard the future of the work

REPORT OF THE HOOSICK FALLS BRANCH

PREFATORY REMARKS BY PRESIDENT FRED N. STEVENS

Our present report must necessarily be more or less a repetition of our former reports. The work here is about the same as usual except that there seem to be a fewer number of cases to investigate, which is good evidence that our past efforts are bearing fruit. We are not, however, relaxing our interest on this account and the work of the Society is being followed up with attention whenever the occasion demands.

We anticipate some difficulty this year in raising funds as easily as in the past because of the many war contributions the people are called upon to contribute to. All societies, however, I presume, will have the same difficulty.

The winter months will probably bring a greater number of cases to our attention but we do not look forward to as much work as in the past owing to a seeming better condition in the community.

Wanted: An endowment to safeguard the future of the work

HOOSICK FALLS BRANCH

CHILDREN'S STATISTICS
JANUARY 1, 1916, TO JANUARY 1, 1917

Number of complaints received.................................... 4
Number of children involved:
    Boys.. 3
    Girls... 4
                                                       7

CHARGES

Improper guardianship	1	Application to take from asy-	
Truancy	1	lum	
		Rape and attempted rape..... 1	

DISPOSITION OF CASES

Complaints sustained	3	Advised and warned	2
Complaints unsustained	1	Returned to homes...........	4
Prosecutions (against minor)..	1	Placed in institution (Troy Or-	
Convictions (against minor)..	1	phan Asylum).............	

Wanted: An endowment to safeguard the future of the work

HOOSICK FALLS BRANCH

ANIMAL STATISTICS

Number of complaints received..................................... 1
Number of animals involved.. 2

CHARGE

Beating and abusing... 1

DISPOSITION OF CASE

Complaints unsustained 1

REPORT OF TREASURER

JANUARY 1, 1916, TO JANUARY 1, 1917

Cash on hand, January 1, 1916............................. $174 70

DISBURSEMENTS

Salary of special agents...........................	$37 00	
Stationery and extras.............................	2 00	
Livery hire	4 50	
		43 50
Cash on hand, February 7, 1917.........................		$131 20

MR. HENRY W. HUDSON,
Treasurer.

Wanted: An endowment to safeguard the future of the work

THE FULTON COUNTY DEPARTMENT

OF THE

MOHAWK AND HUDSON RIVER HUMANE SOCIETY

REPORT FOR 1916

THE FULTON COUNTY DEPARTMENT

OF THE

MOHAWK AND HUDSON RIVER HUMANE SOCIETY

ORGANIZATION AND REPORT FOR 1916

Offices: 41 West Fulton Street, Gloversville, N. Y.; Telephone No. 2289.   Recorder's Office, Johnstown, N. Y.; Telephone No. 28.

President
MR. WILLIAM M. GRANT.

First Vice-President
REV. E. M. BRADY.

Second Vice-President
PROF. E. L. MERRITT.

Third Vice-President
MR. WILLIAM C. HUTCHENS.

Secretary
MR. H. W. SCHUMANN, JR.

Treasurer
MR. F. S. SEXTON.

Counsel
Hon. A. L. Graff, Mr. John T. Morrison, Mr. Harwood Dudley, Mr. Alfred D. Dennison.

Physicians and Surgeons
Dr. M. Kennedy, Dr. Vernon R. Ehle, Dr. R. J. Palmer.

Board of Managers
Mr. Charles T. Bowen, Mr. Charles English, Mr. Charles Stahl, Mr. E. K. Cassidy, Mr. Martin Kennedy, Mr. William M. Grant, Mr. E. L. Merritt, Rev. E. M. Brady, Mrs. Anna M. Bellows, Mr. William C. Hutchens, Mr. Albert Lyke, Mrs. Albert Hertz, Rev. A. P. Manwell, Mr. F. S. Sexton, Mr. John H. Mackin.

Executive Committee
Mr. William M. Grant, Mr. William C. Hutchens, Mr. E. K. Cassidy, Rev. E. M. Brady, H. W. Schumann, Jr., Mr. E. L. Merritt, Mr. F. S. Sexton.

Executive Staff
Superintendent, H. W. Schumann, Jr.; Stenographer, Miss Katherine Mullins.

Special Agents
Mr. A. S. Gustin, Mr. Charles Furness, Mr. A. B. Rhodes, Mr. F. S. Sexton, Mr. Martin Kennedy.

Wanted: An endowment to safeguard the future of the work

REPORT OF FULTON COUNTY DEPARTMENT

PREFATORY REMARKS BY PRESIDENT WILLIAM M. GRANT

A humane society represents the crystallized sentiment of humanity which exists in any given community. For many generations mankind has been growing, in the personal aspect, more kind and considerate toward the weak, the helpless and the suffering, than during ages before. Philosophers are fond of calling the motive or spirit which actuates unselfish devotion to others altruism. The altruism of the past 100 years has shown itself in the abolishment of human slavery, in legislative enactments to stop, or protect, child labor, in the abolition of padronism and other form of chattel service on the part of human beings.

The work has grown from less than 50 children and animals a year, coming under the care of the Society to nearly 1,400, both of children and animals. During the year 1916 the Society's work in this department affected 689 children. A very large variety of charges were involved in these cases, the largest class being that of neglect by father, and the next largest being that of improper guardianship. The details of the charges concerned in these cases will be found in the statistics presented in this report. The total number of prosecutions, or court cases, involving children, conducted by the Department during 1916 amounted to 73, with convictions aggregating 64. No reader of this report can for one moment realize the unutterable sadness and heartrending character of many of these cases which the Society was called upon to adjust in the interest of child protection.

The total number of animals cared for during the year amounted to 676. The largest number of complaints in any one classification was in regard to sick and suffering, which involved 156. There were many charges of general neglect and cruelty; also of using disabled animals. The details of this department may be found in our statistical report. Most cases were adjusted by advice and warning. The number of prosecutions amounted to three and the convictions three, while 13 horses were so badly disabled as to require killing in order to relieve their suffering.

Wanted: An endowment to safeguard the future of the work

Most of this important work, which has grown to develop year by year, is carried on largely from the support of friends and patrons of this work. The grateful thanks of the Society are due the large number of persons who have made many contributions to this work and assisted it to defray its necessary expenses; also to many persons who have contributed gratuitous services, during the past year, including our legal counsel, special agents and physicians. Magistrates, district attorneys, and the police, as well as many poor officers, have shown great kindness and consideration to the Society, and have evinced their confidence in its practical and successful work. The Board of Managers and elective officers of the Society, as well as the ladies' committee, have done a valuable· work in aiding its operations. It would be unfair not to mention the wise, conscientious and able work which has been done by its paid employees, who have largely made the work of the Society a matter of personal interest and devotion, and have raised it far above the plane of mere perfunctory paid service.

Wanted: An endowment to safeguard the future of the work

FULTON COUNTY DEPARTMENT

CHILDREN'S STATISTICS
JANUARY 1, 1916, TO JANUARY 1, 1917

Number of complaints received.................................... 415
Number of children involved:
    Boys... 388
    Girls.. 301
                                                                    ———
                                                                    689

CHARGES

Neglect by father.............	81	Burglary	1
Neglect by mother............	18	Grand larceny	2
Desertion by father..........	2	Petit larceny	5
Desertion by mother.........	3	Disorderly children	51
Improper guardianship	50	Vagrancy	1
Assault, first and second degree....................	1	Carrying firearms	1
		Lost or strayed child.........	1
Assault, third degree.........	3	Using tobacco	2
Abandonment of child........	1	Runaway	1
Endangering morals	27	Employed in street trades....	1
Endangering life or limb.....	36	Feeble-minded child	1
Rape and attempted rape.....	5	Violation parole	15
Sodomy	3	Violation Education Law.....	3
Abduction...................	2	Violation Labor Law.........	3
Sending for liquor...........	2	Destitute	11
Selling liquor	3	Admitting to pool room or bowling alleys	3
Selling tobacco	16	Application to place in asylum	6
Receiving stolen property.....	2	Not permitted to appear in theatricals	4
Application to take from asylum........................	1	Miscellaneous	44
Permitted to appear in theatricals	3		

DISPOSITION OF CASES

Complaints sustained	358	Sentence suspended	34
Complaints unsustained	44	Summoned to court..........	28
Action undesirable	6	Warned by court............	22
Advised and warned.........	261	Compelled to pay by court....	18
Prosecutions (against adults).	33	Not in jurisdiction...........	17
Convictions (against adults)..	30	Referred to public officers.....	15
Prosecutions (against minors)	12	Placed in institutions........	11
Convictions (against minors)..	12	Receiving hospital treatment.	2
Imprisonment imposed, 2 months, 4 days.		Pending settlement	5
		Bailed to grand jury..........	2
Fines imposed	$50	Placed in families...........	2
Transferred to other societies.	5	Relieved in other ways.......	13

PLACED IN INSTITUTIONS

Troy Orphan Asylum........	3	Training School, Hudson......	3
Other institutions	5		

Wanted: An endowment to safeguard the future of the work

FULTON COUNTY DEPARTMENT

PROBATION REPORT

JANUARY 1, 1916, TO JANUARY 1, 1917

Number continued under probationary oversight from 1915:
Boys, 2; women, 2; men, 28; total............................ 32
Number placed on probation January 1, 1916 to January 1, 1917:
Boys, 4; women, 1; men, 24; total........................... 29

Total on probation for year.................................. 61

NATURE OF CHARGES

Burglary, third degree.......	4	Grand larceny, second degree..	4
Petit larceny	7	Assault, third degree........	1
Public intoxication	7	Carrying concealed weapon...	1
Rape, second degree.........	2	Common gambler	1
Burglary, second degree.....	1	Assault, second degree.......	2
Violation city ordinance......	1	Violation Conservation Law...	1
Juvenile delinquency	1	Grand larceny, first degree....	3
Disorderly person	25		

TERMS OF PROBATION

Six months	17	Two years	1
One year	38	Three years	1
Indefinite.................	1		

DISPOSITION OF CASES

Rearrested and committed violation of probation (men)............. 4
Discharged with improvement (boys, 2; women, 3; men, 21).......... 32
Remaining on probation, January 1, 1917 (boys, 2; men, 23)......... 25

NUMBER OF TIMES ON PROBATION

First time	49	Third time	2
Second time	10		

AGES

9 years	1	32 years	1
10 years	2	35 years	2
13 years	1	36 years	2
15 years	2	37 years	2
16 years	2	38 years	3
17 years	2	39 years	2
18 years	2	41 years	2
19 years	6	42 years	1
20 years	3	43 years	1
21 years	1	44 years	1
23 years	2	45 years	1
24 years	1	48 years	3
26 years	1	49 years	1
28 years	2	50 years	2
30 years	6	56 years	1
31 years	2		

Wanted: An endowment to safeguard the future of the work

RELIGION

Protestant 51   Jewish   3
Catholic   7

COLOR

White..................... 59   Black...................   2
Money collected from disorderly persons during 1916........... $2,107 05
Money collected in restitution during 1916...................   179 00

Total collected and paid out........................... $2,286 05

Wanted: An endowment to safeguard the future of the work

FULTON COUNTY DEPARTMENT

ANIMAL STATISTICS

January 1, 1916, to January 1, 1917

Number complaints received...................................... 474
Number animals involved... 676

Charges

Horses worked when sick.....	3	Disabled animals............	41
Horses worked when lame....	15	Lost or strayed............,......	6
Horses worked with sores.....	6	Abandoned animals	4
Horses worked without shoes..	1	General neglect and cruelty...	50
Starved and neglected........	5	Vicious animals	17
Unblanketed in winter........	12	Beating and abusing.........	9
Sick and suffering...........	156	Homeless	87
Maliciously torturing	17	Cats rescued from trees......	9
Overdriven	5	Overloading	3
Poisoning animals...........	7	Suffering from exposure......	14
Miscellaneous	7		

Disposition of Cases

Complaints sustained	394	Disabled horses killed........	13
Complaints unsustained	19	Other animals killed..........	339
Action not needed...........	27	Returned to owners..........	2
Referred to other societies....	2	Homes found	8
Not found	32	Suspended from labor........	12
Advised and warned..........	110	Veterinarians called	8
Relieved in other ways.......	5	Warned by court............	2
Prosecutions	3	Compelled to furnish food....	4
Convictions	3	Relieved by padding.........	3
Sent to blacksmith...........	2	Referred to public officers.....	3
Fines imposed	$15	Sentence suspended	1

Wanted: An endowment to safeguard the future of the work

FULTON COUNTY DEPARTMENT

REPORT OF TREASURER

JANUARY 1, 1916, TO JANUARY 1, 1917

Overdraft January 1, 1916................................. $32 40

RECEIPTS

Board of Supervisors (appropriation)........................	$1,500 00
Membership and contributions...............................	282 00
Fines...	165 00
Total receipts	$1,947 00
Total disbursements	2,041 74
Overdraft January 1, 1917..............................	$94 74

DISBURSEMENTS

H. W. Schumann, Jr., salary and expenses as superintendent....	$1,173 53
Katherine Mullins, salary as stenographer....................	306 00
J. F. Morgan, salary and expenses acting superintendent during vacation	35 75
Ruth Sitterly, salary as sub-stenographer during vacation......	12 00
Fulton County Gas & Electric Co., lighting office..............	9 59
E. S. Parkhurst & Co., rent of office........................	99 00
Harry Scribner, repairing and overhauling auto, gasoline, etc....	97 71
Krit Motor Car Co., parts for auto and express on same........	37 33
Glen Telephone Co...................................	8 18
Frank Wadsworth, horse hire, country cases..................	7 50
Morning Herald Co., printing.............................	11 00
J. W. Thyne, chloroform for small animals...................	8 35
F. S. Houck, chloroform for small animals...................	4 48
Leader Republican, printing of supplies.....................	7 00
Monarch Carbon Paper Co., supplies.......................	3 96
J. R. Conover, tires for auto..............................	35 50
Cowles & Casler, supplies.................................	11 83
Keystone Garage, repairs on auto, gasoline, etc..............	14 50
City of Johnstown R. R., fares taking girl to New York City....	20 04
A. L. Graff, legal services...............................	25 00
Fisk Rubber Co., tires and tubes for auto....................	38 10
A. S. Gustin, expenses as special agent.....................	5 00
C. J. Heacock, supplies for office..........................	3 35
Gloversville Garage Repair Shop, repairs on auto.............	5 00
Leonard Arnold, stands for watering troughs, small animals....	3 00
Gloversville Rubber & Vulcanizing Works, repairs on tubes, auto.	4 60
Dr. Henry Cady, services as veterinary......................	6 00
Charles H. Miller, expenses as special agent.................	4 50
F. N. Ward, insurance on office fixtures.....................	3 09
Fulton Co. Veterinary Hospital, services veterinary............	1 50
W. H. Ecker, printing...................................	1 75
Charles E. Lair, horse hire, country cases...................	4 45
Royal Typewriter Co., supplies............................	75
Overdraft January 1, 1916...............................	32 40
Total disbursements	$2,041 74

Respectfully submitted,

FRANK S. SEXTON,
Treasurer.

Wanted: An endowment to safeguard the future of the work

CONTRIBUTIONS TO THE FULTON COUNTY DEPART-MENT OF THE MOHAWK AND HUDSON RIVER HUMANE SOCIETY FOR 1916 ·

Argersinger, Mrs. P. P.	$10 00	Keck, Miss Flora	1 00
Argersinger, John	1 00	Keck, Mr. Jeremiah	1 00
Argersinger, Scott	1 00	Kennedy, Martin, Jr	5 00
Argersinger, Mrs. Sidney	1 00	Kennedy, Mrs. Martin, Jr	1 00
Adler, Jacob, & Co	5 00	Kennedy, Eleanor	1 00
Board of Supervisors of Fulton		Knox, Mrs. C. B	25 00
County, appropriation	1,500 00	Kennedy, Everett M	10 00
Bowen, Charles T	2 00	Keiner, Mrs. E. A	5 00
Bellows, Mrs. Anna M	1 00	Lachmeyer, Mrs. Julia	1 00
Beyerline, A. C	2 00	Moore, Alice	1 00
Bowman, Miss Catherine	1 00	Manwell, Rev. A. P	1 00
Banker, Mrs. Albert	1 00	McGuire, James	1 00
Burdick, Margaret	1 00	McCulloch, Stephen	2 00
Baker, Hon. A. D. L	10 00	McIntyre, P. C	1 00
Brown, George N	5 00	Mierson, E. H	10 00
Conover, J. R	1 00	Meyers, Louis, & Son	10 00
Carroll, Fred Linus	1 00	Merrick, Mrs. L. A	1 00
Day, Mrs. R. W	2 00	Mosher, Mrs. L. D	2 00
Darling, Mr. Hiram	5 00	Mayfield Glove Co	1 00
Dawes, William, & Co	2 00	Mills, Marion D	1 00
De Beer, Jacob	5 00	Naylor, E. C	5 00
Decker, Mrs J. H	1 00	Northrup, Mrs. H. B	1 00
Dempster, Mrs. D. S	5 00	Petter, George C	5 00
Evans, Mrs. Mary B	1 00	Parsons, R. B	5 00
Evans, Mrs. Richard	1 00	Rohr, Louise	2 00
Eldridge, Louise	1 00	Raymond, Grace	1 00
Estee, Mr. James A	5 00	Richheimer, Miss Sadie	1 00
Fraser, Mrs. McIntyre	1 00	Streeter, Mrs. J. B	1 00
Fraser, Mrs. Sarah	1 00	Streeter, Amy	1 00
Filmer, Darius	5 00	Streeter, Maria G	1 00
Folmsbee, V. R	1 00	Streeter, Kate	1 00
Green, Mary	3 00	Streeter, L. P	2 00
Garnsey, Dr. W. S	5 00	Smith, Borden D	1 00
Gardiner, Mr. and Mrs.		Streeter, J. B	1 00
Charles E	5 00	Streeter, L. L	2 00
Graff, Elsie L	1 00	Shotwell, E. C	10 00
Green, G. G. W	1 00	Sutliff, H. M	1 00
Hann, Percy	1 00	Ten Eyck, H. B	5 00
Hees, J. L	10 00	Thorne, Henry W	1 00
Harrison, Hon. A	1 00	Topp & Vosburgh	1 00
Hutchens, William C	5 00	Uhlinger, J. W	5 00
Hosmer, Mrs. Caroline	1 00	Vedder, Dr. J. D	1 00
Humphrey, Mrs. George M	1 00	Wells, S. Margaret	10 00
Judson, Charles W	10 00	West, Mrs. W. D	3 00
Johnson, Catherine M	5 00	Younglove, Miss Anna	1 00
King, Charles	5 00		

List of deceased members of the Central and other departments will be found on page 39.

Wanted: An endowment to safeguard the future of the work

4

MISCELLANEOUS DONATIONS TO FULTON COUNTY DEPARTMENT

———

Mr. Newman, manager 5 and 10 cent store, Gloversville, toys and clothing.

Miss Jean Fraser, school nurse, Gloversville, clothing.

Glen Telephone Co., free telephone.

F., J. & G. R. R. Co., free transportation.

Mr. F. S. Sexton, sweater.

Mrs. R. D. Noble, clothing.

This Society desires to thank the police officials, judges, superintendents of schools, truant officers and the school nurses of Gloversville and Johnstown, N. Y., for the valuable assistance they rendered us during the past year.

We also desire to thank the Leader-Republican and the Morning Herald Company for the publishing of the work done by this Society in their daily papers during the past year.

Wanted: An endowment to safeguard the future of the work

THE CLINTON COUNTY DEPARTMENT

OF THE

MOHAWK AND HUDSON RIVER HUMANE SOCIETY

REPORT FOR 1916

[99]

THE CLINTON COUNTY DEPARTMENT

OF THE

MOHAWK AND HUDSON RIVER HUMANE SOCIETY

ORGANIZATION AND REPORT FOR 1916

Office, No. 109 Cornelia Street, Plattsburg, N. Y.   Mountain Home Telephone No. 581-W.

President
ELMER F. BOTSFORD, Esq.

First Vice-President
MR. R. F. DANIS.

Second Vice-President
DR. J. H. LaROCQUE.

Third Vice-President
MRS. WILLIAM M. LEVY.

Secretary
MR. JAMES H. BURNS, Esq.

Treasurer
MR. O. T. LARKIN.
MRS. O. T. LARKIN, *Assistant.*

Superintendent
MR. WILLIAM A. HENNESSEY.

Kennell Department Staff
MR. WILLIAM BOURASSA, Assistant Poundmaster.

Stenographer
MISS BESSIE M. WEATHERWAX.

Veterinary Surgeon
DR. John A. McCRANK, D. V. S.

Board of Managers

Mr. Elmer F. Botsford, Mr. F. Robert Danis, Mr. Orrin T. Larkin, Mr. William C. Pike, Mr. Benjamin S. Ramsay, Mrs. William M. Levy, Mrs. Charles P. Watson, Miss Mary McCaffery, Miss Mary Barber, Dr. John A. McCrank, Dr. Joseph H. LaRocque, Dr. Ethan A. Barnes, Miss Helen I. Smith, Mrs. Cassius D. Silver, Mrs. Samuel S. Whittelsey, Mrs. John H. Booth, Dr. Charles E. Bentley, Mrs. Corydon S. Johnson, Mrs. Ida M. Hayes, Mrs. William E. Parkhurst, Mrs. Henry B. Billings, Mr. Solomon S. Kempner, Mrs. Mary H. H. Chase, Mr. George F. Hutchinson, Mr. Abraham M. Markstone.

Committee to Inspect Reports on Children's Cases

Mrs. John H. Booth, Mrs. William M. Levy, Mrs. Corydon S. Johnson, Mrs. Cassius D. Silver, Mrs. Ida M. Hayes.

Committee to Inspect Reports on Animal Cases

Mrs. Henry B. Billings, Mrs. Helen I. Smith, Mrs. Elmer F. Botsford, Mrs. F. Robert Danis, Mrs. Samuel S. Whittelsey.

Wanted: An endowment to safeguard the future of the work

CLINTON COUNTY DEPARTMENT

PREFATORY REMARKS BY PRESIDENT E. F. BOTSFORD

The good work accomplished by the Plattsburgh Branch of the Mohawk and Hudson River Humane Society is most gratifying. The knowledge that the work of our Society is being actively looked after and that our representative will always listen to a complaint and act immediately has deterred many a would-be law breaker from daring to perpetrate a crime.

Superintendent Hennessey not alone looks after the humane work in Clinton and Essex counties but is Truant Officer for the schools of the city of Plattsburgh, enforces the dog tax and distributes the tags and is Probation Officer for the several courts of the county and our judges have ordered many youthful delinquents to make weekly or monthly reports for a stated period to our Superintendent.

In our Children's Department 703 complaints, involving 1,203 children, were investigated, with 93 prosecutions and 88 convictions; sentences being suspended upon 40 and fines of $95.00 being imposed; 33 were committed to institutions; advice and warnings were given to 549.

In our Animal Department 567 complaints, involving 923 animals, with five prosecutions and four convictions; fines collected, $50.00; 28 disabled horses, 650 dogs and cats were humanely put to death. Homes were found for many valuable dogs and cats.

A new committee was named by the president to look after the conservation and protection of our song and insectivorous birds. The president had a large exhibit of bird houses, feeding stations, baths, bird supplies and literature on exhibition at the annual fair of the Clinton County Agricultural Society and has also equipped a room 15 x 18 feet, with Audubon charts and bird houses, as well as all kinds of feeding stations and plans for making bird houses so that anyone can see how to construct and erect homes for our feathered friends. Many bird houses are being erected, feeding stations established and maintained and special work is being done among the farmers to interest them in the protection of the birds. The vagrant cat has been proven to be one of the greatest menaces to bird life, and over 517 cats have been humanely put to

Wanted: An endowment to safeguard the future of the work

death. It is estimated by Dr. A. K. Fisher of the Biological Survey that the cats in New York destroy 3,500,000 birds annually. While this great destruction is going on all over the United States, pestivorous insects, cut-worms and beetles are taking an enormous toll of nearly a billion dollars annually from our farmers, orchardists, fruit growers and gardeners, and the return of bird life is the only relief from this enormous loss.

I would recommend that each Humane Society make as a special feature of their animal work the destruction of vagrant cats and insisting on the licensing of all valuable cats and the protection of our song and insectivorous birds.

The Society has lost by death its secretary, James H. Burns; Hon. John B. Riley, Fred W. Chase, C. H. Hopkins, Fred E. Pierce, Frank P. Lobdell, A. Alpert and Marcus Miller. These with members moving away from our city made a total loss of 22, but this was offset by a gain of new members of 32, making our total membership 243, the largest in the history of the Society. The sources of financial income are from membership fees, percentage of licensing and collecting dog taxes, court fines and the generous annual contribution of $100.00 from Mrs. Fred W. Chase of Loon Lake.

The report of Superintendent Hennessey was one that showed admirable work in his department during the year 1916. While the 20 cases of which he spoke is only a small part of what has been done in aid of what is really necessary in this regard.

In the matter of enforcing the law looking to the prevention of children under 16 years from entering motion picture theatres the Society will seek co-operation from the city in enforcing the provisions of this statute.

In the matter of the nuisance in Jockey Lane during Fair days steps will be taken at that time to keep this avenue of travel cleared of objectionable characters.

Owing to the increased work of the Superintendent in visiting the surrounding towns in Clinton county in humane work, the Society, on motion, decided to furnish gasoline and pay for repairs for an automobile to be used by the Humane Officer. On motion it was also decided to raise the salary of the Superintendent especially in view of the splendid work he has been doing in the cause of humanity.

Wanted: An endowment to safeguard the future of the work

CLINTON COUNTY DEPARTMENT

CHILDREN'S STATISTICS

JANUARY 1, 1916, TO JANUARY 1, 1917

Number of complaints received...................................   703
Number of children involved:

Boys	703	
Girls	485	
		1,203

CHARGES

Neglect by father	104	Carrying firearms............	6
Neglect by mother...........	6	Violation Labor Law.........	4
Desertion by father..........	12	Application to place in asylum	7
Desertion by mother.........	6	Application to take from asy-	
Improper guardianship.......	69	lum	7
Abandonment of child........	16	Using tobacco	6
Assault, first and second de-		Burglary, first degree.........	1
grees	2	Begging or peddling..........	6
Assault, third degree.........	24	Intoxication	2
Violation Education Law.....	56	Vagrancy	18
Endangering morals	35	Truancy	34
Endangering life or limb......	16	Disorderly children	121
Rape and attempted rape.....	5	Destitute	50
Bastardy	3	Grand larceny	1
Admitting to saloons.........	1	Petit larceny	8
Action to compel parent to pay		Runaway	3
asylum	1	Riding on freight trains......	1
Without homes	4	Children gambling	1
Child in disorderly house.....	1	Lost or strayed children......	4
Violation city ordinance......	1	Employed in street trades....	1
	Miscellaneous	60	

DISPOSITION OF CASES

Complaints sustained	694	Imprisonment imposed, 3 years,	
Complaints unsustained......	5	1 month, 16 days.	
Action undesirable...........	3	Advised and warned.........	540
Prosecutions (against adults).	60	Returned to homes...........	11
Convictions (against adults)..	49	Pending settlement	5
Prosecutions (against minors)	39	Sentence suspended	47
Convictions (against minors).	39	Referred to public officers....	11
Transferred to other society..	1	Placed in institutions........	27
Summoned to court..........	15	Placed in families............	6
Warned by court.............	20	Receiving hospital treatment..	7
Bailed to grand jury.........	5	Relieved in other ways.......	38
Fines imposed $45 00		Compelled to pay by court....	4
	Compelled to furnish food....	2	

PLACED IN INSTITUTIONS

Troy Catholic Male Orphan		State Industrial School.......	3
Asylum	1	Training School, Hudson......	3
Troy Orphan Asylum........	5	Other institutions	15

Wanted: An endowment to safeguard the future of the work

CLINTON COUNTY DEPARTMENT

JUVENILE PROBATION REPORT
JANUARY 1, 1916, TO JANUARY 1, 1917

Continued under probationary oversight from 1915................... 24
Boys placed on probation during 1916............................. 5
Girls placed on probation during 1916............................. 7

NATURE OF CHARGES

Improper guardianship....... 5   Ungovernable child 3
Burglary, third degree....... 1   Truancy 3

DISPOSITION OF CASES

Discharged with improvement. 25   Rearrested and committed.... 2
Still on probation........... 9

TERMS OF PROBATION

Six months.................. 1   One year 11

AGES

Two years 1   Eleven years 1
Four years 1   Twelve years 2
Seven years 1   Thirteen years 1
Nine years 1   Fourteen years 2
Fifteen years 2

RELIGION

Catholic.................... 9   Protestant 3

COLOR

White 12

NUMBER OF TIMES ON PROBATION

First time 12

Wanted: An endowment to safeguard the future of the work

CLINTON COUNTY DEPARTMENT

ADULT PROBATION REPORT

JANUARY 1, 1916, TO JANUARY 1, 1917

Continued under probationary oversight from 1915:
Men, 28; women, 1.. 29
Placed on probation during 1916:
Men, 31; women, 6.. 37
Discharged with improvement:
Men, 37; women, 2.. 39
Still on probation:
Men, 22; women, 5.. 27

NATURE OF CHARGES

Non-support	11	Assault, third degree	5
Endangering morals	1	Burglary, third degree	4
Discharging firearms	1	Abandonment	1
Public intoxication	5	Disorderly conduct	2
Petit larceny	1	Vagrancy	2
Grand larceny, second degree	2	Common prostitution	2

TERMS OF PROBATION

Two months	1	Eight months	2
Three months	4	One year	11
Five months	1	Two years	1
Six months	14	Five years	1
	Indefinite	2	

COLOR

White 37

RELIGION

Catholic..................... 25   Protestant 12

Money collected during year of 1916 from disorderly persons for
the support of their families at home and at institutions, and
paid over to families and authorities...................... $1,525 41
In court fines.. 25 00
Reparation 5 00
                                                          _____
                                                           $1,555 41

Number of parole men from State institutions remaining under my probationary oversight, January 1, 1916............................ 2
Number of parole men placed under probationary oversight from January 1, 1916, to January 1, 1917................................. 1
Number of parole men discharged with improvement................ 2
Number of parole men from State institutions remaining under my probationary oversight, January 1, 1917............................ 1

Wanted: An endowment to safeguard the future of the work

CLINTON COUNTY DEPARTMENT

ANIMAL STATISTICS
January 1, 1916, to January 1, 1917

Number of complaints received.................................... 567
Number of animals involved...................................... 923

Charges

Horses worked when lame.....	15	Lost and strayed.............	18
Horses worked when sick.....	2	Cock fighting................	1
Horses worked without shoes..	1	Abandoned animals	1
Unblanketed in winter........	27	Maliciously torturing.........	4
Overdriven	5	Vicious animals..............	29
Disabled animals	29	Beating and abusing.........	8
Starved and neglected........	14	Homeless animals............	17
Sick and suffering............	378	Overloading	2
Checked too high.............	1	Carried in cruel way.........	1
Suffering from exposure......	3	Crates of fowl overcrowded...	1

Miscellaneous 10

Disposition of Cases

Complaints sustained........	564	Fines imposed $50	00
Complaints unsustained......	1	Disabled horses killed........	19
Not found	1	Veterinarians called	2
Action not needed...........	1	Other animals killed.........	542
Prosecutions	5	Sent to blacksmith...........	1
Convictions	4	Homes found	19
Sentence suspended	1	Advised and warned..........	132
Compelled to repair stable....	3	Returned to owners..........	13
Compelled to furnish food....	7	Cock fights stopped..........	1
Sent to kennels..............	534	Suspended from labor........	5

Relieved in other ways....... 7

Wanted: An endowment to safeguard the future of the work

CLINTON COUNTY DEPARTMENT

ANIMAL STATISTICS
January 1, 1916, to January 1, 1917

Dog Department

Dogs in kennel January 1, 1916.....................................	0
Dogs voluntarily surrendered	65
Dogs seized during period..	75
	140
Homes found for dogs..	4
Dogs redeemed and released..	13
Dogs humanely put to death..	123
	140

Cat Department

Cats in kennels January 1, 1916....................................	0
Cats voluntarily surrendered	528
	528
Homes found for cats...	11
Cats humanely put to death...	517
	523

INSPECTION OF DUMPING GROUNDS, ETC.

During the year visits to dumping grounds, etc., were made as follows:

To freight yards.............	39	To poultry districts..........	20
To dumping grounds........	35	To building operations and ex-	
To wharves and docks........	22	cavations	12

Horses inspected on streets.... 27

Wanted: An endowment to safeguard the future of the work

CLINTON COUNTY DEPARTMENT

REPORT OF TREASURER

JANUARY 11, 1916, TO JANUARY 8, 1917

RECEIPTS

Balance in treasury January 11, 1916	$256 69
From contributing membership	483 50
From city of Plattsburgh, N. Y., share enforcing dog tax law	406 25
From Essex county, N. Y., for services and expenses on humane work	186 88
From court fines in cruelty to animals cases	50 00
From Mrs. Mary H. H. Chase, Loon Lake, N. Y., contribution	50 00
From Mr. John Zetmichrovich, Lyon Mountain, N. Y., contribution in finding his wife and her return to her children	10 00
From release on dogs from Humane Society Kennel	4 00
Total receipts	$1,447 32

DISBURSEMENTS

Salary and expenses and office rent of Superintendent William A. Hennessey	$922 98
Salary of William Bourassa, assistant poundmaster at Humane kennel	171 00
Salary of Miss Emily McMasters, stenographer at Humane office	24 00
A. Mason & Sons, Humane Society kennel box and ten fitting report boxes	16 37
Salary of Miss Bessie M. Weatherwax, stenographer at Humane office	21 00
Brandow Printing Co., Albany, N. Y., letter heads and envelopes	8 50
Spear Bros., lining Humane Society kennel animal box	4 10
Isaac Merkel & Son, gas for Humane kennel to kill animals	4 50
John W. Guibord, trustee for bankrupt of J. Ochsner, for gas	2 00
Jacob Ochsner, gas for Humane Society kennel to kill animals	2 50
Dr. John A. McCrank, D. V. S., examining sick horses	2 00
H. A. Cook, sundries	10 29
Total disbursements	$1,189 24
Balance in treasury January 8, 1917	$258 08

O. T. LARKIN,
Treasurer.

Wanted: An endowment to safeguard the future of the work

MEMBERS AND CONTRIBUTORS TO THE CLINTON
COUNTY DEPARTMENT FOR 1916

Abraham, Joseph............ $1 00	Cahoon, Hon. George, Ausable
Akey, Peter 1 00	Forks, N. Y............... 5 00
Andress, George W.......... 1 00	Carroll, George H........... 2 00
Avery & Light, Morrisonville,	Clark, Robert J............. 2 00
N. Y. 1 00	Conway, Miss Flora.......... 1 00
Annuis, G. W., Peru, N. Y.... 1 00	Cavanaugh, Mrs. James....... 1 00
Alpert, A., Dannemora, N. Y.. 1 00	Cook, Mrs. Ora W., Danne-
Alpert, Simon, Dannemora,	mora, N. Y................ 1 00
N. Y. 1 00	Caffery, Arthur J............ 1 00
Armstrong, Miss Ethel....... 1 00	Childs, William A........... 1 00
Bentley, Mrs. J. E., in Memory	Couture, J. Harvey, Rouse's
of John E. Bentley......... 5 00	Point, N. Y................ 1 00
Bentley, Dr. and Mrs. C. S... 10 00	Caplan, Caleb 1 00
Billings, Mr. and Mrs. H. B.,	Couture, Arthur, Rouse's Point,
Valcour, N. Y............. 10 00	N. Y. 1 00
Booth, Hon. and Mrs. John H.,	Curtis, S. D................. 1 00
and family 5 00	Cady Drug Company......... 1 00
Barnes, Dr. and Mrs. Ethan A. 5 00	Cahalan, William R., Peru,
Barber, Miss Mary........... 5 00	N. Y. 1 00
Brown, Eugene 3 00	Carmody, John 1 00
Boire, Hon. V. F.............. 2 00	Cavanagh & Co., James....... 1 00
Barber, Hubert L............ 2 00	Conway, Miss Mary J........ 1 00
Bowron, John W., Rouse's	Clark, Datus, Peru, N. Y..... 1 00
Point, N. Y................ 2 00	Callanan, M. J., Keeseville,
Boylan, Mr. and Mrs. John P.. 2 00	N. Y. 1 00
Barton, Dr. and Mrs. L. G.... 3 00	Driscoll, Rev. Dr. J. H., D. D.,
Botsford, Elmer F., Esq...... 1 00	D. C. L. 2 00
Botsford, Mrs. Elmer F...... 1 00	Danis, F. Robert............. 2 50
Botsford, Benedict 1 00	Daily, Felix 1 00
Belmore, Joseph 1 00	Dare, Dr. Gilbert D., Mor-
Boomhower, Harry, in Memory	risonville, N. Y............ 1 00
of A. D. Boomhower........ 1 00	Dominy, Eben N............. 1 00
Byrnes, William J........... 1 00	Dunton, F. E................ 1 00
Brando, Mrs. A. F.......... 1 00	Desjardin, Charles 1 00
Blanch, Jerry, Lyon Mountain,	DeLoffre, Mrs. Captain S. M.
N. Y. 1 00	U. S. A. 1 00
Bedore, W. N................ 1 00	Delaney, James L............ 1 00
Byrnes, F. E................ 1 00	Everett, Dr. W. H., Peru, N. Y. 2 00
Baker, H. E., Peru, N. Y...... 1 00	Edwards, Mr. and Mrs. C. E. M. 2 00
Buttler, George A............ 1 00	Elmore, Elmore F., Esq., Peru,
Baker, Ned 1 00	N. Y. 2 00
Burdick, Mrs. W. L., Danne-	Finn, Frank A............... 2 00
mora, N. Y................ 1 00	Foot, William M............. 2 00
Brando, Mrs. F. E........... 1 00	Fitzpatrick, Mrs. F. P....... 1 00
Baber, J. A., Keeseville, N. Y. 1 00	Farrell, Miss Catherine...... 1 00
Bramer, Mrs. Arnold......... 1 00	Fitzpatrick, Mrs. S. E........ 1 00
Brunet, Mrs. J. H., Redford,	Freeman, J. A............... 1 00
N. Y. 1 00	Finney, W. W., Peru, N. Y.... 1 00
Chase, Mrs. Mary H. H., Loon	Goyette, J. O., Rouse's Point,
Lake, N. Y................ 50 00	N. Y. 1 00
Cole, George M., and family... 5 00	Goff, Hon. William H........ 1 00
Cartwright, Mr. and Mrs. John	Guibord, Robert H........... 2 00
H., Lyon Mountain, N. Y... 5 00	Garriety, Miss Margaret...... 1 00
Carter, Mrs. John L., in Mem-	Gale. Rev. Albert............ 1 00
ory of John L. Carter...... 5 00	Hayes, Mrs. Ida M.......... 2 00

Wanted: An endowment to safeguard the future of the work

Holland, James, & Bros	2 00
Hodges & Robinson	2 00
Holcomb & Bruso, Rouse's Point, N. Y.	2 00
Hadley, Howard D	2 00
Hopkins, C. N., Keeseville, N. Y.	2 00
Henshaw, Dr. and Mrs. A. N..	2 00
Houghran, John H	5 00
Hutchinson, George F	5 00
Heyworth, H. E., Peru, N. Y..	2 00
Howcroft, William	1 00
Hart, William J., Lyon Mountain, N. Y.	1 00
Haley, William F	1 00
Hennessy, Mrs. William A	1 00
Hawkins, Mrs. George K	1 00
Hall, Miss E. J	1 00
Hanlon, Miss Mary G	1 00
Holden, B. E., Peru, N. Y	1 00
Hull, Miss Kate E	1 00
Heyworth, George R., Peru, N. Y.	1 00
Hitchcock, H. C	1 00
Haley, S. D., Lyon Mountain, N. Y.	1 00
Hagez, George, Lyon Mountain, N. Y.	2 00
Hogue, J. A	1 00
Howell, William H	1 00
Hyde, Dr. R. E	1 00
Johnson, C. S., and family	5 00
Justin, Mr. and Mrs. F. H	5 00
Johnson, H. S., Esq	2 00
Justin, Frank S	1 00
Juvet, Alfred	1 00
Kellogg, Mr. and Mrs. Geo. C.	5 00
Kelly, Rev. John Bailey	1 00
Kelly, Mrs. Rev. John Bailey..	1 00
Kurtz, J. H., Dannemora, N.Y.	1 00
Kempner, Louis	1 00
Keysor, G. D., Standish, N.Y.	1 00
Kempner, S. S	1 00
LaRocque, Dr. John H	2 00
Levy, Mrs. William M	3 00
Laundrie, J. and W. H., Rouse's Point, N. Y	2 00
Lubin, Rev. Jacob	1 00
Larkin, O. T	1 00
Lapham, Miss Eliza A., Peru, N. Y.	1 00
Larkin, Mrs. O. T	1 00
Lobdell, Mrs. F. P	1 00
Leonard, Frank H	1 00
Larkin, Mrs. E. E	1 00
Long, Frank A., Ausable Forks, N. Y.	1 00
Larvia, Napoleon A	1 00
Ladue, Dr. William H., Morrisonville, N. Y.	1 00
Lagoy, Adolph, Ausable Forks, N. Y.	1 00
Lombardoni, L	1 00
McCaffrey, Mrs. William J	3 00
McCrank, Dr. John A	2 00
McKeefe & Co., James	1 00
McCadden, Frank	1 00
McDougall, Crosby	1 00
McLean, Miss Katherine	2 00
McClellan, L. H., Standish, N. Y.	1 00
McGaulley, John H	1 00
McHattie, A	1 00
McKinzie, M. K., Keeseville, N. Y.	1 00
Moore, Mr. and Mrs. E. G	5 00
Mason, A. & Sons, Peru, N. Y.	5 00
Myers, Mrs. John H	5 00
Myers, Mr. and Mrs. J. R., Rouses's Point, N. Y	5 00
Moffitt, Hon. John H	2 00
Morehouse, Mrs. A. E., Peru, N. Y.	3 00
Myers and Belden	2 00
Merkle, Isaac	2 00
Myers, Mrs. M. P	1 00
Markstone, A. M	1 00
Merkle, Mrs. David	1 00
Merrihew, D. A., Town of Plattsburgh, N. Y	1 00
Myers, John P	1 00
Morrison, Miss A. M., in Memory of Miss Sophia	1 00
Merritt, Mrs. Nancy H	1 00
Macdonald, Dr. R. S	1 00
Manix, Mrs. T. F	1 00
Miller, Marcus, & Sons	1 00
Morgan, S. P	1 00
Marshall, A. H	1 00
North, Dr. and Mrs. C. H., Dannemora, N. Y	2 00
Newton, Mrs. S. A	1 00
Newton, Dr. S. H., Rouse's Point, N. Y	1 00
O'Brien, Hon. John F., West Chazy, N. Y	5 00
O'Bryan, M. J	2 00
Ochsner, Jacob	1 00
Parkhurst & Taylor	3 00
Payette & Mendelsohn	2 00
Pike, William C	2 00
Palmer, Miss Helen	1 00
Parshall, F. C	1 00
Palmer, Miss Kate	1 00
Purdy, F. M., Morrisonville, N. Y.	1 00
Percey, John H	1 00
Plattsburgh Plumbing & Electric Co.	1 00
Plattsburgh Feed Co	1 00
Ricketson, H. C	1 00
Riley & Rugar, Morrisonville, N. Y.	1 00
Rogers, Dr. T. A	1 00

Wanted: An endowment to safeguard the future of the work

Riley, Hon. John B..........	5 00
Rogers, Mrs. Chastine H......	10 00
Ross, Dr. and Mrs. John R., Dannemora, N. Y.........	2 00
Ramsay, B. S...............	2 00
Ransom, Dr. and Mrs. J. B., Dannemora, N. Y..........	2 00
Ross, Mr. and Mrs. L. P......	3 00
Reed, Charles V., Peru, N. Y..	1 00
Robert, Dr. H. R., Dannemora, N. Y.	1 00
Reid, J. E., Lyon Mountain, N. Y.	1 00
Smith, Misses Helen I. and Grace	5 00
Silver, Dr. and Mrs. C. D.....	3 00
Sharron, Albert	2 00
Sirois, Rev. Fr. J. A.........	2 00
Sartwell, Dr. Edwin W., Peru, N. Y.	1 00
Shedden, Mrs. L. L..........	1 00
Sartwell, Mrs. Edwin W., Peru, N. Y.	1 00
Smith, Mrs. J. Ovette........	1 00
Siddon, Frank F., Morrisonville, N. Y...............	1 00
Shedden, Mr. and Mrs. J. S. Esq.	5 00
Stratton, James A............	1 00
Schier, Henry	1 00
Stower, Mrs. J. N............	1 00
Schuyler, William H.........	1 00
Sherman, Miss Alice.........	1 00
Stilles, Miss Minnie, West Chazy, N. Y..............	1 00
Stevenson, Dr. George, Mooers, N. Y.	1 00

Studholm, J. M..............	1 00
Schiff, Mrs. Dr. Leo..........	1 00
Seymour, Eli Z..............	1 00
Schiff, Morris	1 00
Smith Bros.	1 00
Stiles, Lestley	1 00
Schiff, Mrs. Eliza............	1 00
Statham, Rev. George K......	1 00
Schiff, Mrs. Abraham........	1 00
Stackpool & Co., C. H........	1 00
Speir Bros.	2 00
Sisco, Mrs. Edward..........	1 00
Tuttle, Mr. and Mrs. George F., and family	5 00
Thomas, Harry A............	1 00
Trombly, John B., Dannemora, N. Y.	1 00
Traynor, Mrs. Martin L......	1 00
Vert, Hon. and Mrs. Chas. J..	10 00
Watson, Mr. and Mrs. Charles P.	5 00
Weir, Mr. and Mrs. O. B......	5 00
Wilcox, W. G., & Sons........	3 00
Whittlesey, S. S.............	1 00
Whittlesey, Mrs. S. S.........	1 00
Williams, A. F..............	1 00
Warren, A. M...............	1 00
Wood, H. A.................	1 00
Watson, Prof. Frank K.......	1 00
Zetmichrovich, John, Lyon Point, N. Y................	1 00
Weir, G. A.	1 00
Wood, Rev. R. D.............	1 00
Zetmichrovich, John, Lyon Mountain, N. Y............	1 00

List of deceased members of the Central and other departments will be found on page 39.

Wanted: An endowment to safeguard the future of the work

MISCELLANEOUS CONTRIBUTIONS TO CLINTON
COUNTY DEPARTMENT

Twenty-five dollars from Mrs. James J. Rogers of Ausable Forks, N. Y., for transportation, meals and livery, investigating cases in and about Ausable Forks. Of this sum $12.93 was spent investigating cases, leaving a balance of $12.07.

James McKeefe & Co. and Mr. W. N. Bedore, meat for animals; Plattsburgh Morning Press and Plattsburgh Daily Republican, daily papers; The Adirondack Record, of Ausable Forks, N. Y., weekly paper; Dr. John A. McCrank, furnishing a horse to Superintendent Hennessey; Miss Margaret Tallon, clothing; Mrs. Edward Bates, clothing and shoes; Mrs. William Soper, clothing; Mrs. E. Kempner, clothing and shoes; Mr. and Mrs. Frank McCadden, clothing, shoes and stove; Mrs. B. S. Ramsay, clothing; Mrs. Frank Smith, clothing and shoes; Mrs. A. M. Warren, clothing and shoes; Mrs. Crosby McDougall, clothing; Miss Ryan, coat; Mrs. Ned Baker, clothing and shoes; Mrs. G. Gilmour, clothing; Mrs. E. E. Larkin, clothing and shoes; Mrs. G. E. Wilson, clothing; Miss Grace O'Connor, clothing; Miss Bertha Laravie, coat; Mrs. William Sweeney, clothing; Mrs. Charles Anderson, clothing; Miss Flora Conway, clothing and hat; Mrs. George Bixby, clothing; Mrs. F. R. Danis, clothing; Women's Missionary Society of Dannemora, N. Y., barrel of clothing; Mrs. Minnie Palmer, coat; Mrs. Charles Rexford, clothing and books; Mrs. J. A. McCrank, clothing; Mrs. James O'Hara, clothing; Mrs. Ida Murphy, clothing; from Rummage Sale, through Mrs. W. H. Chappel, clothing, shoes and hats; Mrs. J. Cronin, one-half bushel potatoes; Mrs. S. H. Legett, of Peru, N. Y., clothing; Mrs. Frank S. Smith, clothing and hat.

Wanted: An endowment to safeguard the future of the work

THE SCHOHARIE COUNTY DEPARTMENT

OF THE

MOHAWK AND HUDSON RIVER HUMANE SOCIETY

REPORT FOR 1916

[115]

THE SCHOHARIE COUNTY DEPARTMENT

OF THE

MOHAWK AND HUDSON RIVER HUMANE SOCIETY

ORGANIZATION AND REPORT FOR 1916

Office, Farmers and Merchants' Bank, Cobleskill.

President
MR. VERNON M. BELLINGER.

Vice-President
DR. HOWARD H. FOX.

Secretary
MR. JOHN V. S. ELDREDGE.   -

Treasurer
REV. GRANT L. BICE.

Board of Managers

Mr. Vernon M. Bellinger, Rev. Grant L. Bice, Dr. Howard H. Fox, Dr. L. R. Becker, Mr. John V. S. Eldredge, Mr. H. R. Berger, Mr. Leroy Moore, Mr. John Mack, Jr., Mr. Wallace H. Sidney, Dr. S. A. Scranton, Mr. F. A. Guernsey, Mr. D. P. Bulson, Mr. Frank X. Straub.

Executive Committee

Mr. Vernon M. Bellinger, Dr. Howard H. Fox, Rev. Grant L. Bice, Mr. J. V. S. Eldredge.

Counsel

Hon. George M. Palmer, Mr. William H. Golding, Esq., Mr. Wallace H. Sidney.

Physician and Surgeon
DR. LeROY BECKER.

Dentist
DR. HOWARD H. FOX.

Special Agents

Mr. Vernon M. Bellinger, Dr. H. H. Fox, Cobleskill; Mr. Fred Rickard, Schoharie; Mr. Frank X. Straub, Mr. Henry D. Lawyer, Mr. Dorr P. Bulson, Middleburg; Mr. Ten Eyck Kilmer, Esperance.

Wanted: An endowment to safeguard the future of the work

SCHOHARIE COUNTY DEPARTMENT

Prefatory Remarks by President Vernon M. Bellinger

The work in Schoharie county during the past year has been carried on with as much vigor as could be expected with only volunteer agents to do the work. We are more and more impressed with the need of a paid officer, who is properly trained, to look after both animal and children work. Many of the cases coming to our attention are serious and require a thorough investigation if the proper results are to be secured.

We sincerely hope that in the near future some means will be found by which the rural counties will be provided with a paid officer for a day or two a week at least. In the meantime we will continue to carry on the work as best we can with volunteer officers.

During the past year quite a number of serious cases, involving both children and animals, have been handled by the volunteer agents and good results have been secured. We have the hearty endorsement of the right thinking people of our county, and while we have not been able to cover the field as fully as we would like because of our limited means and the fact that we must depend upon volunteer agents, we still feel that much good has been accomplished in our county. I take this opportunity of expressing our appreciation for the splendid work which has been done by our volunteer agents.

Wanted: An endowment to safeguard the future of the work

SCHOHARIE COUNTY DEPARTMENT

CHILDREN'S STATISTICS
JANUARY 1, 1916, TO JANUARY 1, 1917

Number of complaints received..................................... 13
Number of children involved....................................... 29

CHARGES

Neglect by father............	3	Improper guardianship.......	4
Desertion by father..........	1	Held as witness.............	1
Without home	1	Vagrancy	1
Endangering morals..........	1	Miscellaneous	1

DISPOSITION OF CASES

Complaints sustained	13	Imprisonment imposed......100 days	
Prosecutions (against adults).	2	Relieved in other ways.......	4
Convictions (against adults)..	2	Advised and warned..........	8
Pending settlement	1	Placed in institution.........	1

INSTITUTION

Sent to St. Vincent's Male Orphan Asylum, Albany.................   ▲

SCHOHARIE COUNTY DEPARTMENT

ANIMAL STATISTICS
JANUARY 1, 1916, TO JANUARY 1, 1917

Number of complaints received.................................... 11
Number of animals involved...................................... 21

CHARGES

Horses worked with sores.....	1	Overdriven	1
Disabled animals............	1	Carried in cruel way........	1
Poisoning animals...........	1	Beating and abusing.........	2
Sick and suffering...........	1	General neglect and cruelty...	2
	Miscellaneous	1	

DISPOSITION OF CASES

Complaints sustained........	11	Sentence suspended..........	1
Prosecutions	1	Advised and warned..........	10
Convictions	1	Disabled horse killed........	1

Wanted: An endowment to safeguard the future of the work

SCHOHARIE COUNTY DEPARTMENT

REPORT OF TREASURER

JANUARY 1, 1916, TO JANUARY 1, 1917

RECEIPTS

Balance on hand January 1, 1916.............................	$24	32
Received from Board of Supervisors..........................	34	81
	$59	13

DISBURSEMENTS

One thousand letter heads and envelopes............	$10	00		
Livery and auto hire..............................	9	00		
J. T. Clark in Baker case.........................	5	14		
Telephone expenses	4	70		
D. P. Bulson in Wilson case.......................	3	00		
Hotaling — Veterinary surgeon	2	54		
Postage and envelopes	2	43		
			36	81
Balance on hand January 1, 1917.......................			$22	32

GRANT L. BICE,
Treasurer.

Wanted: An endowment to safeguard the future of the work

THE GREENE COUNTY DEPARTMENT

OF THE

MOHAWK AND HUDSON RIVER HUMANE SOCIETY

———

REPORT FOR 1916

[121]

THE GREENE COUNTY DEPARTMENT

OF THE

MOHAWK AND HUDSON RIVER HUMANE SOCIETY

ORGANIZATION AND REPORT FOR 1916

Office, 370 Main Street, Catskill.

President
Mr. GEORGE W. IRWIN.

Vice-President
Dr. GEORGE E. ENGLERT.

Secretary and Treasurer
Miss G. A. JACKSON.

Board of Managers

Mr. Charles H. Van Orden, Mr. Clarence E. Bloodgood, Dr. George E. Englert, Dr. Robert Seldon, Miss Mary L. Van Orden, Miss Mary Bedell, Miss Emily F. Becker, Miss Anna Van Orden, Mr. Frank H. Osborn, Mr. E. M. Jackson.

Counsel
Mr. G. HOWARD JONES.

Superintendent
Mr. L. J. HUBBARD.

Special Agents

Rev. Samuel T. Clifton, Coxsackie; Mr. George T. Mackay, Dr. E. H. Merriam, West Coxsackie; Mr. William H. Baldwin, New Baltimore; Rev. Conrad E. Metzger, Oak Hill; Mr. Frank E. Ryan, Catskill; Mr. A. Melvin Stewart, Hensonville.

Wanted: An endowment to safeguard the future of the work

REPORT OF GREENE COUNTY DEPARTMENT

PREFATORY REMARKS BY PRESIDENT GEORGE W. IRWIN

The year 1916 has been one of unusual activity on the part of our Society. We feel that much suffering has been relieved through our efforts, and acknowledge with thanks the assistance and advice received from the Albany Society headquarters. Our work during the year has taken us to all parts of the county, and includes the examination of horses in lumber camps in the mountains and horses in different summer resorts, as well as animals on farms and in villages. The condition of animals generally throughout the county is good. Through the efforts of our active superintendent an old offender has again been rounded up and sentenced for a long term in the county jail and a heavy fine. The first sentence received some years ago was for a term in the penitentiary. We trust that his labors along the inhumane line are now terminated.

Among the objects accomplished this year one at least deserves special mention. Through the efforts of some of the members of our Society a petition was circulated throughout the village asking the trustees to take action against the setting of steel traps within the corporate limits as numbers of animals had been caught and either left to die or were terribly maimed. The trustees took the matter up in a broad-spirited and kindly manner and eventually passed an ordinance forbidding the use of the traps as prayed for in the petition.

The work among children, other than litigated cases, has been largely performed by a committee of two, a short report of which is given below. The report, however, gives no adequate idea of the amount of work performed nor of the constant following up of the cases undertaken by these devoted women.

Wanted: An endowment to safeguard the future of the work

REPORT OF SPECIAL COMMITTEE

The undersigned, a committee appointed by the Humane Society, reports that during the past year they have sent out twenty-two baskets at Christmas containing everything for the day in quantities sufficient for the family, fruit and flowers for the sick. In co-operation with a benevolent order they received for distribution among the poor, shoes for 150 children. During the winter they have rendered assistance to over fourteen families, comprising over fifty children. To some of these only temporary assistance was given, such as food and clothing; to others nursing, medical attention, hospital care, and to others continuous care for months, such as supervision of household provisions, and the entire buying of the same. We have acted with the clergy of all the churches in the village, and also with the truant officer and the poor-masters, and in that way no overlapping has occurred.

Very respectfully,

MISS EMILY F. BECKER,
MISS MARY LAYMAN.

GREENE COUNTY DEPARTMENT

CHILDREN'S STATISTICS

JANUARY 1, 1916, TO JANUARY 1, 1917

Number of complaints received.....................................	5
Number of children involved:	
Boys..	4
Girls..	3
	7

CHARGES

Application to place in asylum.	1	Application to take from asy-	
Disorderly children	2	lum	
	Improper guardianship	1	

DISPOSITION OF CASES

Complaints sustained	5	Relieved in other ways........	2
Advised and warned..........	4	Pending settlement	1
	Placed in families...........	1	

Wanted: An endowment to safeguard the future of the work

GREENE COUNTY DEPARTMENT

ANIMAL STATISTICS

JANUARY 1, 1916, TO JANUARY 1, 1917

Number of complaints received.....................................   7
Number of animals involved.......................................   21

CHARGES

Horses worked with sores.....   2   General neglect and cruelty...   1
Suffering from exposure......   1   Overloading   1
Starved and neglected........   2

DISPOSITION OF CASES

Complaints sustained   7   Disabled horses killed........   5
Advised and warned..........   6   Suspended from labor........   4
Prosecutions   1   Compelled to furnish food....   1
Convictions   1   Compelled to repair stable....   1
Fines imposed $25

GREENE COUNTY DEPARTMENT

REPORT OF TREASURER

JANUARY 12, 1916, TO MARCH 16, 1917

RECEIPTS

Balance reported January 12, 1916................. $78 05
Fines received 15 00
Dues of members..................................   49 00
                                                                $142 05

DISBURSEMENTS

Paid for services and expenses of agent............ $62 75
Telephone charges 3 19
Veterinary..   2 00
Printing..   3 50
Livery..   17 22
Incidental..   10 90
                                                                  99 56

Balance, March 16, 1917.............................. $42 49

MISS GEORGINA A. JACKSON,
Treasurer.

Wanted: An endowment to safeguard the future of the work

STATE OF NEW YORK

No. 65

IN SENATE

MAY 4, 1917

Proceedings of the Senate relative to lands at Rockaway Point

THE PRESIDENT: The Senator from the Tenth (Senator Gilchrist) asks unanimous consent to make a statement.

Senator GILCHRIST: The other day the Senator from the Second called the attention of the Senate to the fact that in 1812 there was established on the peninsula known as the Rockaway peninsula, at or about the westerly extension thereof, a fort of the United States government and that the property was then owned by the United States. Since that time the land has increased to the west until it passed what was known then, and is still known as Barren Island. Beyond the westerly extension of that peninsula was an island, the property of the State of New York. The continued accretions finally closed the inlet between the westerly extension of the peninsula and this island so that the island, the property of the State of New York, became the extreme westerly point of the peninsula, and accretions from that time continued on the property of the State of New York.

In 1887 it appears there was an act passed by this Legislature which permitted the sale of the land which was included in the original government reservation to one Henry Y. Attrell. By chapter 150 (?) of the Laws of 1887, the interest of the State was to be turned over to Mr. Attrell for the sum of $20,000, and such expenses as the State had incurred in settling its title to the land. From the best information I can receive, the latest report from the Comptroller, it appears that that money was never paid, and so the land is still either the property of the United States government by accretions from the fort to the original inlet, or the property of the State of New York, that is so far as the land which is about to be used, or is now being used, or has been taken by this State for the purpose of a government fortification.

There are accessible, living in and about Jamaica bay and Canarsie, a number of pilots and captains who recall the original inlet which existed between the former extreme westerly portion of the peninsula and the island I have mentioned, and who recall the time when that inlet was closed up by natural accretions.

Under the circumstances, I deem it proper at this time to ask that these facts, together with those that Senator Daly was able to present the other day, be incorporated in a Senate document and sent to the attorney-general for his investigation, and I accordingly submit the maps showing the situation, together with the names of the steamship men and other facts which we have in our possession and I offer the following resolution:

By Mr. GILCHRIST:

WHEREAS, Certain alleged facts relative to the ownership or alleged ownership of lands at Rockaway Point have been laid before the Senate, indicating that the land recently acquired by the State and transferred to the Federal government for fortification purposes as well as all that portion of the Rockaway peninsula lying to the west thereof is and, for a century has been, the property of the United States and the State of New York,

Resolved, That the Clerk of the Senate be directed to have these facts printed as a Senate Document, and be it further

Resolved, That such information be transmitted by the Clerk of the Senate to the Attorney-General for his guidance, with a request that he take such action upon it as he may deem necessary for the protection of the interests of the State and report his findings to the Senate in January, 1918.

In Senate, *May* 1, 1917.

Senator Daly.—Mr. President, I would ask unanimous consent to make a statement.

The President.— The Senator from the Second asks unanimous consent to make a statement.

Senator Daly.—At some time past we had quite an agitation in this body with regard to the fortifications at Rockaway. This particular section, Rockaway peninsula, as everybody knows, is in the Second Senatorial District. Naturally people in Queens county became very much interested in the proposition of the fort and in the proposition of the land values so far as the Rockaway peninsula was concerned. As a result, feeling that I should interest myself to a great extent in the matter, I had a search made at the Queens County Clerk's office in Jamaica, Long Island, with regrad to the title of the property where this Fort was to be located. After due search and due diligence, I find these to be the facts:

About 1807, the first record deed that is there was made to one William Cornwell. This deed was recorded in April, 1899. Now, from every indication at that particular time, the Rockaway peninsula, so far as geography was concerned, was far different than it is today. What I mean to say by that is this: Today Barren island is about three miles off the Rockaway peninsula, whereas at that particular time Barren island was about a mile northwest of the Rockaway peninsula. To make my point clear, I wish to state that there seems to have been a great deal of land added to the point by accretion. In this deed recorded in the County Clerk's office on August 23, 1879, in giving the boundaries of the land of this William Cornwell, there is exception made to land held at that time by the United States government. Upon looking into the facts, we find in 1812, during the war of 1812, the United States government erected and had at this particular point a blockhouse. Following the deeds down from Cornwell's

deed, we find that in each and every deed in giving the boundaries
that exception is held to. In other words, the description of the
property sold passed on from Cornwell to Nathaniel Rider, and
there is excepted in the deed all that parcel of land held by the
United States government.

Now, not to take up too much time, not to go into it in too much
detail, but to summarize briefly, I wish to state that as each deed
is examined you find the same exception. There are a number of
litigations recorded, such as foreclosures of mortgage and parti
tion sales, and all that sort of thing, from 1807 down. However
we go on to about 1881 — Henry Montfort, referee, to Frederick
A. Phipps, recites a judgment of foreclosure and sale at a Special
Term of the Supreme Court, April 11, 1881. The sale was held
on June 4, 1881, to Albert Billings for one hundred and eighty-five
thousand dollars, and assignment by Billings of his purchase to
Frederick A. Phipps conveys same premises with same exception
as in Liber 546, p. 33.

Now, we go on and find that exception of land is carried right
down until the final deed before the Rockaway Pacific Company.
This deed conveys to one Huntington the above-named lots, sub
ject to the right of the United States government. Then we find
the following deed, Arabella D. Huntington, Edward Huntington
and Mary Huntington, deed dated February 11, 1901, acknow
edged February 12, 1901, and recorded September 27, 1902, the
consideration being forty-four thousand dollars, and it recites th
the grantors are the residuary devisees under the last will an
testament of Collis P. Huntington, deceased, who held the lan
and premises described on behalf of the beneficiary; the grant
above-named conveys the same premises as Liber 1172, p. 59,
Andrew K. Van Deventer, and he then conveys to the Rockaw:
Pacific Company this particular tract without any reservation
to this land formerly held by the United States government.

Now, I lay these facts before the Senate, realizing as I do th
for the purchase of this land there has been placed upon the Sta
presumably a debt of two million five hundred thousand dolla:
going into it as I have, knowing as I do there is a resolution on
question of an investigation, I felt I would state these facts befo
the members of this body and in any way possible, either throu

the Attorney-General's office or any other office in which I might help, so far as this title of this land is concerned, I wish to take and place before the body the facts I have found so far as the record in the County Clerk's office in Queens county is concerned.

Senator SAGE.— Can I ask what part of the land is excepted to the United States?

Senator DALY.— The United States government formerly claimed the western point of the peninsula, and, as I stated in the beginning, there has been added by accretion.

Senator BROWN.—Is there any description of the property held by the United States government anywhere?

Senator DALY.— The only thing is the exception of the property held by the United States.

Senator BROWN.— Doesn't describe it?

Senator DALY.— No.

Senator BROWN.— That is the trouble.

Memoranda of Title of United States of America, to all that portion of Rockaway Beach or Rockaway Point owned and occupied by the United States, consisting of about 83 acres and the accretions:

The early title to the above land and land adjoining on the east is assumed to have been good in William Cornwell, prior to the year 1809, and the said William Cornwell conveyed the land in question by the following deed.

William Cornwell and	**Deed**
Nelly, his wife,	Date July 1, 1809
To	Ack. Nov. 8, 1810
Nathaniel Rider.	Rec. Aug. 23, 1879
	Liber 546 cp. 331
	Con. $200.00

Conveys: All that certain lot of beach situate, lying and being on the south side of Long Island in Queens county, bounded southerly by the sea or ocean, westerly by the inlet, northerly by the bay, and easterly by beach belonging to Ruloff Duryea, containing 200 acres of beach, more or less.

Nathaniel Rider died at Hempstead, L. I., on or about the 12th day of April, 1832, and some of his heirs conveyed their interest in the premises above described to George Durland, by the following deed:

Uriah Ryder and Mary Ann, his wife; Richard Ryder, Benjamin Ryder and Mary Ann, his wife; Ruleff Van Clief and Mary Ann, his wife; Edward T. Oakley and Emma A., his wife; Gilbert S. Thatford and Eliza, his wife; George W. Rogers and Helen M., his wife; Henry D. Allen, Charles E. Allen, Thomas H. Rogers and Fannie H., his wife; Jacob S. York and Amelia, his wife; Nathaniel Carman and Phoebe, his wife; Smith Ryder and Mary, his wife, and Andrew Jackson Ryder	Deed Dated Aug. 25, 1872 Ack. Aug. & Sept., 1872 Rec. Oct. 5, 1872 Liber 391 cp. 1 Cons. $1.00

To

George Durland, of Jamaica,

Conveys: Same premises by same description as above.

George Durland after acquiring title by the above deed, brought a suit in partition against the remaining heirs of Nathaniel Rider, deceased, shown as follows:

SUPREME COURT— QUEENS COUNTY.

GEORGE DURLAND, *Plaintiff,*
              against
GABRET V. W. ELDERT and others,
                    Defendants.

Final amended summons and complaint and lis pendens were filed in the office of the County Clerk December 27, 1873.

The complaint sets forth the rights of all the parties, plaintiff and defendants and their respective interests in the premises, and in due course of proceedings a judgment of partition and sale was entered June 17, 1874, wherein Edward M. Shepard was appointed referee to sell, and pursuant to such judgment the referee sold the said premises on the 27th day of August, 1874, to Alonzo B. Wright, as shown by the following deed:

	Deed
Edward M. Shepard, Referee,	Date Oct. 26, 1874
To	Ack. Oct. 26, 1874
Alonzo B. Wright.	Rec. Oct. 26, 1874
	Liber 450, cp. 374
	Cons. $900.00

Recites judgment Durland v. Eldert and others, June 17, 1874, and sale to Alonzo B. Wright August 27, 1874, conveys premises as described in Liber 546, cp. 334, but makes no exception as to the land belonging to the United States government.

	Deed
Aaron A. Degraw	Dated Jan. 2, 1879
To	Ack. Jan. 2, 1879
Alonzo B. Wright.	Rec. Aug. 23, 1879
	Liber 546 of Deeds, p.333
	Cons. $1.00

Conveys same premises as in Liber 546, cp. 334, containing 600 acres, more or less, and recites " Being the land on which the United States government in the War of 1812 erected a block-house by permission of Nathaniel Rider, the then owner."

	Deed
Alonzo B. Wright and Martha A.,	Dated Aug. 15, 1879
his wife,	Ack. Aug. 23, 1879
To	Rec. Aug. 23, 1879
Benjamin E. Smith.	Liber 546, cp. 334
	Cons. $200,000

Conveys property at Rockaway Beach or Point with buildings and improvements thereon erected and being all that part of Rock-away Beach or Point lying west of a line running due north and south from the Atlantic ocean to Jamaica bay and intersecting a line running south 75 degrees west from the land formerly of Rothery Rider but now or late of Garret V. W. Eldert, at a point on said line distant 144 chains from said land of Rothery Rider, the land hereby conveyed being bounded on the east by said line running due north, on the north by Jamaica bay, on the west by the inlet, and on the south by the Atlantic ocean, containing by estimation 610 acres, more or less. Excepting and reserving out of said above described lands so much of said premises as are now occupied, used and required by the United States government for life-saving purposes, also excepting two other parcels.

Benjamin E. Smith	Mortgage $170,000 at 6%
To	Dated Aug. 15, 1879
Alonzo B. Wright.	Due July 21, 1900
	Rec. Aug. 23, 1879

Conveys same premises as in Deed L. 546, cp. 334.

The above mortgage was foreclosed by Alonzo B. Wright, against Benjamin E. Smith and Henry Y. Atrill and Helen M. Atrill, his wife, as will hereafter appear.

	Deed
Benjamin E. Smith and Catherine,	Dated Aug. 25, 1879
his wife,	Ack. Aug. 25, 1879
To	Rec. Aug. 26, 1879
Henry Y. Atrill.	Liber 546, cp. 380
	Cons. $200,000

Conveys same premises by same description and exception as in Deed L. 546, cp. 334.

Note.— In 1874, at the time of the purchase by Wright at foreclosure sale, a map of this property was made and filed in the office of the County Clerk dividing the beach into lots, numbered from 1 to 30, both inclusive; the property in question being located on the lots numbered 1 and 2.

In a deed made by DeWitt C. Littlejohn and others to Henry Y. Atrill, dated July 11, 1879, conveying about 140 acres adjoining the easterly line of land " commonly called land of the United

States," a map attached to this deed shows the United States is in possession of the property in question.

Deed

| Henry Y. Atrill and Helen F., his wife,   To   John P. Kennedy. | Dated Nov. 20, 1880   Ack. Nov. 20, 1880   Rec. Jan. 26, 1881   Liber 571, cp. 152 |

Conveys same premises by same description and exceptions as in Liber 546, cp. 380.

NOTE.—This deed having been made subsequent to the filing of the summons and complaint in the action brought by Wright v. Smith and Attrill, was of no effect and is inserted only for reference.

Kennedy by deed dated March 30, 1881, recorded Liber 574, cp. 405, conveyed any possible interest he might have acquired by the above deed to one Albert M. Billings.

SUPREME COURT— QUEENS COUNTY.

ALONZO B. WRIGHT, *Plaintiff,*

against

BENJAMIN E. SMITH, HENRY Y. ATTRILL and HELEN F. ATTRILL, his wife, *Defendants.*

Summons, complaint and lis pendens filed in the office of the County Clerk September 20, 1880. In due course this action terminated in a judgment of foreclosure and sale April 11, 1881, wherein Henry A. Montfort was appointed referee to sell, as more fully appears by the following deed:

Deed

| Henry A. Montfort, Referee,   To   Frederick A. Phipps. | Dated July 11, 1881   Ack. July 11, 1881   Rec. July 12, 1881   Liber 579, cp. 207   Cons. $185,000 |

Recites judgment of foreclosure and sale at Special Term of Supreme Court April 11, 1881; sale June 4, 1881, to Albert M.

Billings for $185,000, and assignment by Billings of his purchase to Frederick A. Phipps; conveys same premises with same exceptions as in Liber 546, cp. 334.

	Deed
Frederick A. Phipps	Dated July 11, 1881
To	Ack. July 11, 1881
Albert M. Billings.	Rec. July 12, 1881
	Liber 579, cp. 232

Conveys same premises with same exceptions as in L. 546, cp. 334.

	Deed
Albert M. Billings and Augusta S.	Dated Oct. 3, 1881
his wife,	Ack. Oct. 3, 1881
To	Rec. May 12, 1882
Edward D. Moore.	Liber 593, cp. 341
	Cons. $100,000

Conveys same premises with same exceptions as in Liber 546, cp. 334.

	Deed
Edward D. Moore,	Dated Sept. 11, 1882
To	Ack. Sept. 11, 1882
George L. Geraw.	Rec. Feb. 26, 1883
	Liber 607, cp. 244
	Cons. $110,000

Conveys same premises with same exceptions as in Liber 546, cp. 334.

	Deed
George L. Geraw and Nettie H., his	Dated Sept. 11, 1882
wife,	Ack. Sept. 12, 1882
To	Rec. July 10, 1884
Henry Y. Attrill.	Liber 635, cp. 56

Conveys same premises with same exceptions as in Liber 546, cp. 334.

By virtue of a judgment in an action brought by A. S. Hatch

against Henry Y. Attrill, et al., docketed December 21, 1885, for the sum of $164,835.52, all right, title and interest of Henry Y. Attrill in property at Rockaway Beach was sold by the sheriff under execution.

Matthew J. Goldner, sheriff, etc.,	Deed July 27
	Dated 1891
To	Ack. July 30, 1891
William Parkin.	Rec. Aug. 4, 1891
	Liber 880, cp. 37

Recites judgment December 21, 1885, in action of Hatch against Attrill, et al. $164,835.52, sold to William Parkin for $208,000; conveys same premises with same exceptions as in Liber 546, cp. 334.

William Parkin,	Deed
	Dated Dec. 11, 1891
To	Ack. Dec. 11, 1891
Isaac E. Gates.	Rec. Dec. 14, 1891
	Liber 899, cp. 259

Isaac E. Gates,	Deed
	Dated Dec. 1, 1897
To	Ack. Dec. 1, 1897
Collis P. Huntington.	Rec. Dec. 2, 1897
	Liber 1172, cp. 59
	Cons. $1.00

Recites deed to Parkin as above and judgment in partition and action to determine title brought by Chittenden as assignee of Alfred S. Hatch v. Isaac E. Gates and others, November 22, 1897. In this action a map of the beach was made and filed in the county clerk's office, entitled " Map of Rockaway Point, surveyed June, 1897, by Walter M. Meserole " (Map No. 74) in which Collis P. Huntington was allotted lots 39 to 52 inclusive. (Lot 52 is at the extreme end of Rockaway Point and is a part of the land in question.)

This deed conveys to Huntington the above named lots subject to right of United States Government.

Arabella D. Huntington, Edward Huntington and Mary A. Huntington, his wife,
To
Andrew K. Van Deventer.

Deed
Dated Feb. 11, 1901
Ack. Feb. 12, 1901
Rec. Sept. 27, 1902
Liber 1287, cp. 14
Cons. $44,048.00

Recites that grantors are the residuary devisees under the last will and testament of Collis P. Huntington, deceased, who held the land and premises hereinafter described on behalf of a beneficiary, the grantee above named; conveys same premises as in Liber 1172, p. 59.

Andrew K. Van Deventer, Ella H, his wife,
To
Rockaway Pacific Corporation.

Deed
Dated Dec. 26, 1913
Ack. Dec. 26, 1913
Rec. Jan. 6, 1914
Liber 1924, cp. 164
Cons. $1.00

Conveys lots numbers 39 to 52 inclusive as shown on Map No. 74 noted above.

LIST OF WITNESSES.

Following is a list of names and addresses of men who for past fifty years have been engaged in and about Rockaway Point and the waters of Jamaica Bay, and who I am informed will testify to facts substantiating the statement I have made: A. J. Gilchrist, James Bailey, Barren Island; Smith Foster, Barren Island; Cornelius Vreeland, East 92d Street, Canarsie; Hon. John Wilson, East 96th Street, Canarsie; William Schmeelk, East 94th Street, Canarsie; Captain Arthur McAvoy, Canarsie; Captain Louis Klee, East 92d Street, Canarsie; Walter Ryder (oil boat), Canarsie Dock; Jacob Wise, 6th Street, near Shoor Avenue; George Schlenk, Union Course, near Pitkin Avenue, Brooklyn; Herman Eckhard, 7th Street, near Show Avenue, Union Course, L. I.; Steven McNamara, Schenck Lane, near 91st Street, Canarsie;

Captain Bevency, 1045 East 96th Street, Canarsie; John Green-
wood, Plum Beach, Sheepshead Bay; Captain Schwarzbach, Captain Yacht "Amphion," Sheepshead Bay; Frank Hammer, Captain Yacht " Whitney," Sheepshead Bay.

CHAPTER 560.

An Act for the release of any interest of the State in lands in the
town of Hempstead, Queens County, to Henry V. Attrill.

Passed June 13, 1889, by a two-thirds vote.

*The People of the State of New York represented in Senate
and Assembly, do enact as follows:*

Section 1.   All right, title and interest, claim and and demand,.
of the State of New York, in and to all that point and peninsula.
of land known as Rockaway Beach, in the town of . Hempstead,.
County of Queens, and State of New York, which lies west of a.
line running due north from the Atlantic Ocean to Jamaica Bay,.
and intersecting a line running south, seventy-five degrees west,
from the land formerly of Rothery Ruder, but now or late of
Garrett Eldert, at a point on said line, distant one hundred and
forty-four chains from said land formerly of Rothery Ruder, said
premises being bounded easterly by the said line running north.
from the Atlantic Ocean to Jamaica Bay; south by the Atlantic
Ocean; west by the inlet; and north by Jamaica Bay; is hereby
released to *Henry Y. Attrill* upon the payment by him within
sixty days after the passage of this act, to the Comptroller of the
State, of the sum of twenty thousand dollars, and of all sums of
money which the Attorney-General and Comptroller shall certify
to have been expended or incurred by the State in and about the
investigation of the claim of the State to the said lands, and in
establishing its title thereto.

§ 2. This act shall take effect immediately.

NOTE.— Recent inquiry at the office of the State Comptroller
failed to disclose any evidence that the $20,000 purchase price
had been paid or any deed executed.

65th Congress, 1st Session.   S. 1852.

IN THE SENATE OF THE UNITED STATES.

April 17, 1917.

Mr. Calder introduced the following bill; which was read twice
and referred to the Committee on Military Affairs.

A BILL

Authorizing the Secretary of War to transfer to the city of New
York the title of the United States to certain lands in Kings
County, State of New York.

*Be it enacted by the Senate and House of Representatives of
the United States of America in Congress assembled,* That the
Secretary of War be, and he is hereby, authorized to transfer to
the city of New York, in partial consideration for the transfer to
the United States of the city's right and title to certain lands on
Rockaway Point, the title of the United States to the reservation
on Plumb Island, in the town of Gravesend, in Kings County,
State of New York, and containing an area of approximately fifty
acres.

STATEMENT CONCERNING THE MAPS.

Map No. 1 is a tracing of part of an original map found in
volume 14, page 15, of the Colonial History of the State of New
York which is accessible in the Brooklyn Library at Montague
Street, Brooklyn. This map indicates that Canarsie Bay had no
outlet to the west subsequent to the time of this map which was
known as a plot of the situation of the town and place of the
waters and of Long Island to Hempstead by Mr. Hubbard and
dated July 3rd, 1666.

It will be found that what is indicated as " Broken Lands " on
this map afterward became Barren Island and that the " Sand
Hills " were changed in location so that a channel ran through
and between what is there indicated as " Sand Hills " and

ed evi-
e near

penin-
hannel
n con-
United
ie pen-
s west,
known
h map
ns, in
ployed
Aaron
accre-
beyond

pears,

icated
on of
d the
il the
a rren
1 890.
t here
Duck
ween
et of
bay-
boats
point
the
the
ance
upon

65th Cc

I:

Mr. Ca

s

Authori
York
Coun

Be it
the Uni
Secretal
the city
the Uni
Rockaw
on Plux
State of
acres.

Map
volume
York w
Street,]
outlet to
known (
waters (
dated J
It wil
this ma
Hills "
and bet

. evi-
near

enin-
annel
con-
nited
pen-
west,
town
map
s, in
oyed
a ron
cre-
yond

ears,

nated
n of
, the
l the
rren
890.
here
Duck
veen
t of
bay-
oats
oint
the
the
ance
upon

65th

Mr.

Auth
Y
Co
Be
the
Secr
the o
the t
Rock
on P
State
acres

Me
volun
York
Stree
outlet
know
water
dated
It
this
Hills
and 1

æd evi-
re near

ι penin-
channel
on con-
United
he pen-
es west,
ι known
ch map
tens, in
nployed
ι Aaron
e accre-
beyond

ιppears,

ιdicated
rtion of
and the
.ntil the
Barren
ιt 1890.
n, there
r, Duck
between
inlet of
nd bay-
ιn boats
he point
ιlly, the
l to the
ιntrance
ιst upon

65th

Mr.

Autl
Y
C

B
the
Secr
the c
the l
Rock
on F
State
acres

.

M
volun
York
Stree
outle
know
watei
dated
It
this
Hills
and

"Broken Lands." The peninsula was accordingly formed evidently by the closing of an inlet which existed somewhere near what is now known as Edgemeer.

It will seen then that the action of the tides caused the peninsula to make land a little southwesterly because it left a channel between Barren Island and the peninsula. This condition continued until in 1812 when there was a fortification of the United States Government at the extreme westerly extension of the peninsula beginning at a point on the Atlantic Ocean 375 degrees west, 144 chains from the land of Rothery Rider and afterwards known as Garret Eldert's land as indicated on Map No. 2, which map is recorded in the County Clerk's office, County of Queens, in Liber 386 of Conveyances at page 210. This map was employed and filed in connection with a lease by the Government to Aaron A. De Graw, on March 19, 1872, although at that time the accretions to the point had extended westerly some distance beyond what the map indicated.

(Note error on this map where the name Robert Rider appears, it should be Rothery Rider.)

It will be observed that the point of the peninsula as indicated on this map lay about opposite the extreme easterly portion of what was then Barren Island. The accretion continued and the land made westerly on and from the Government station until the point lay almost directly south of the westerly end of Barren Island. This was the end of the peninsula in and about 1890. Shortly beyond, a short distance from the west therefrom, there was an island or sand bar. This was known as Dry Bar, Duck Bar or West Bar, and formed no part of the peninsula for between that island and the point last described was the inlet; an inlet of 30 feet in depth of water and through which the pilots and baymen, yacht captains and those who piloted the iron steam boats to Rockaway Beach entered Canarsie Bay. This bar and the point of the peninsula continued to increase in size until finally, the inlet just spoken of was closed and a new inlet formed to the west of this bar or island. That inlet now constitutes the entrance to Jamaica Bay and accretions are continuing to the west upon the island or bar that was last mentioned.

A chart of the Government Survey made in 1845, showing the Rockaway Peninsula and its then location is on file in the Government Station at Tompkinsville, S. I.

There is, we believe, a deed affecting the title of this property from Nathaniel Rider who owned the land between that of Rothery Rider and the extreme westerly point of the peninsula to the State of New York, and this deed will doubtless be found in the archives of the Secretary of State at Albany.

The Government Life Saving Station which was at Barren Island until 1870 was forced to move from Barren Island over to the Rockaway Peninsula for two reasons: Barren Island was being cut down by the waters, a large portion of it having been and since has been washed away and the Rockaway Peninsula increasing to the westward, had passed to the south of Barren Island, so that the Life Saving Station was forced to take this new position in order to be on the ocean. This occurred, we are informed, in or about 1870 or 1871.

Assuming for the purpose of this situation that pursuant to the terms of the act of 1887, such title as the State had to these lands was actually passed, the title to the land which was formerly Duck Bar, as mentioned above, did not pass under that act and as this and its accretions now constitute the point of the beach, it is submitted that no consequential damages can be claimed in connection therewith.

In the decision of the case of Van De Venter against Lott, tried before Judge Chatfield in the United States District Court for the Eastern District of New York, some time in or about the year 1900, the judge intimated that the Government of the United States had the best title to the point of the beach as it then existed. This was about the time Duck Bar was becoming connected with the main land.

The facts above stated were brought to my attention by Mr. Louis Jaeger, whom I have known for 20 years or more. He is an architect and builder with a residence at 170 Shore Avenue, Union Course, Borough of Queens, New York City. He, himself, is an old yachtsman to whom I would respectfully refer for any further detailed information.

ALFRED J. GILCHRIST.

ANNUAL REPORT

OF

THE ADJUTANT GENERAL

OF THE

STATE OF NEW YORK

FOR THE YEAR 1916

TRANSMITTED TO THE LEGISLATURE MAY 9, 1917

ALBANY
J. B. LYON COMPANY, PRINTERS
1917

STATE OF NEW YORK

No. 66

IN SENATE

MAY 9, 1917.

REPORT OF THE ADJUTANT-GENERAL

STATE OF NEW YORK:

EXECUTIVE CHAMBER,

ALBANY, *May* 9, 1917.

To the Legislature:

I have the honor to transmit herewith the annual report of the Adjutant-General, the same being for the year 1916.

CHARLES S. WHITMAN.

ANNUAL REPORT OF THE ADJUTANT-GENERAL OF THE STATE

THE ADJUTANT-GENERAL'S OFFICE,

ALBANY, *December* 31, 1916

To the Governor:

SIR.—The following report covering the operations of the military establishment during the past year is submitted in compliance with the provisions of Section 16 of the Military Law.

GENERAL REMARKS

Since the last report, the National Guard of the State has been subjected to every test of warfare except the actual clash upon the battlefield.

For the first time in eighteen years the President summoned it to the national colors to meet a grave emergency. The Guard was assembled almost overnight, recruited, equipped, concentrated in mobilization camps, mustered in part into the Federal service and transported thousands of miles to the extreme southern frontier of the country, where at the end of the year there still remained three regiments of infantry, two regiments of field artillery, one field hospital and part of another, the rest of the State troops having been returned, mustered out of the Federal service and received again into the State control.

Coincident with the transfer of troops to the Federal service was the enlargement of the Guard by recruiting and by the formation of new elements, by the establishment of depot units, and by numerous changes made in conformity with legislation of a radical sort, including the National Defense act which became law June 3, 1916, and required the increase of the National Guard of this State to double its previous maximum.

It is a matter of legitimate pride to this administration that New York State has in all its legislation cooperated with the National government in every step toward preparedness, and in

many instances has anticipated all other states and the National
government itself in the advancement of this cause.

While the mobilization by its speed and magnitude undoubtedly
saved the nation from a bloody conflict with Mexico, it exposed the
Guard to strains, difficulties, and criticisms which would have
been less severe in many respects or at least less conspicuous if
there had been the compensating glory of combat. It is in some
ways a far simpler thing to die for the country than to live for it.

Much of the criticism would be changed to praise if the conditions were fully set forth and the blame shifted to the responsible
shoulders. Many of the faults of the mobilization were due to
conditions from which the Guard had vainly endeavored to be
relieved. This is not the place, however, for apology or recrimina-
tion, but rather for a plain record of accomplishments in so far
as they affect the value of the service, and a discussion of failures
in so far as they offer lessons for the future. The National
Guard faces with the new year even greater responsibilities and
consequent opportunities.

It is permissible to emphasize the fact that the efforts of this
department in anticipation of just such a crisis were justified by
the event. Such measures as it was enabled to put into effect
saved the Guard from making a much worse showing than it did,
while if the entire programme had been carried out, the showing
would have been far better than it was.

As the President's call came at almost exactly the middle of the
year, it will be necessary to defer a discussion of it until a statement has been made of the previous activities, most of them undertaken in the expectation of a summons.

FEDERALIZATION OF THE GUARD

The opening of the year witnessed an increased national agitation in the matter of preparedness, owing to the peril of embroil-
ment in the European War, and the complexities of the Mexican
situation.

During the long and stormy discussions of measures in Congress
the National Guard was the object of much obloquy. Various
legislative factions planned to ignore it, annul it, deprive it of
every national significance, and reduce it to the functions of a

state police.   But no substitute could be agreed upon, and at length the National Guard was federalized, at least theoretically, and recognized as the mainstay of the Regular Army.

In the meanwhile, without waiting for the conclusion of the Congressional debates, an effort was made to stimulate in New York the recruiting and the efficiency of the various units of the Guard and to give them the advantages of field training on a more elaborate scale than ever before.   These preparations were well under way when the President called out the troops.   If his call had been delayed three weeks it would have found the entire National Guard of this state assembled in its entirety at the very camp in which it was prematurely and hastily mobilized.

In addition to these activities steps were taken to place the whole theory of military service on a more sound and practical basis, working toward the establishment of vital principles of obligation in the laws and the hearts of our people.

Though there was much outcry from certain quarters that these were new, dangerous and even pernicious principles, they were in fact the original ideas of the founders of the republic; they are dangerous only to the enemies of the republic, and it was their long neglect that was pernicious.

It is only human nature for citizens to be far more ready to assert the rights of citizens than to acknowledge the obligations that are reciprocal.   But those who would enjoy equality of privilege cannot escape equality of responsibility.   It is of the very essence of democracy that those who would reap the harvests and know the unbroken slumbers of security must take their turns in the watch towers and not leave the gates to mercenaries.

Universal military service is not a step toward militarism but an insurance against it.   People can hardly fear the tyranny of a power which the people themselves constitute and control.   Furthermore, in the new and enormously complex system of warfare, the word " military " has acquired so broad a significance that it no longer means merely the carrying of a sword or the brandishing of a firearm.   The farmer, the railroad man, the bookkeeper, the telephone operator, the coal miner, the manufacturer, the weaver, the merchant, the physician, the members of almost all the trades and professions, are as much a part of the military establishment as the rifleman or the cannoneer. The European war has shown that the efficient mobilization of all womanhood is as necessary to military success as of manhood, and an increasing attention must be paid to the organizing of the entire citizenry, beginning with the schoolboy and the schoolgirl.

During the year 1916 this office worked successfully with the Legislative Committee to embody in our laws important measures to supplement the voluntary efforts of the National Guard, by making sure that it should not lack necessary reenforcement from the manhood of the State, and that its manhood should be in turn reenforced from the youth of the State, properly trained physically as well as mentally before its entry into citizenship.

MILITARY TRAINING COMMISSION

Upon attaining the age of 18 every able-bodied male citizen becomes *ipso facto* a member of the militia. It is an important duty of the state to see that in so far as possible every male citizen shall reach the age of 18 able bodied. It is important also that he should be imbued with the ideals of duty to the state.

With this end in view an amendment of the Education Law was prepared, recommended and enacted into the law, providing for courses of instruction in physical training for the pupils of elementary and secondary schools, and prescribing specifically that the purpose of the training during such period was to develop correct physical posture and bearing, mental and physical alertness, self-control, discipline and initiative, sense of duty and the spirit of cooperation under leadership.

A Military Training Commission was appointed, composed of the President of the University of the State of New York, the Major General commanding the New York National Guard, a member appointed by the Board of Regents of the University of the State, and a fourth member appointed by the Governor.

It is provided in this measure that all boys above the age of 16 years, and not over the age of 19 years, with certain exceptions, be given military training to be prescribed by the commission, for periods aggregating not more than three hours in each week during the school year, or for like periods between September 1st of each year and the 15th day of June next ensuing, for boys who are not pupils in public schools or colleges.

The law also provides for the establishment and maintenance of state military camps of instruction for the field training of boys between the ages of 16 and 19.

The Military Training Commission has adopted a comprehensive program of military instruction which is now in successful operation and which has the hearty approval and co-operation of the school authorities and the teachers throughout the State.

Military Training camps are to be established during the coming summer, at which it is expected 5,000 boys between the ages of 16 and 19 will receive field training.

Compulsory Service

On May 15, 1916 a law was passed to confirm in the Governor a power which had lapsed from neglect and indifference so long that the law was regarded as a revolutionary act granting a new power, though a brief consideration will prove it to be a return to original principles.

All of the colonies had compulsory service before the Declaration of Independence. The first Constitution of the State of New York, adopted in 1777, in its provisions relative to a defensive department of the State, began with the declaration that it is the duty of every man who enjoys the protection of society to be prepared and willing to defend it. But the effort to write this policy into effective legislation was never satisfactorily carried out.

George Washington asserted that the obligation of service was the main pillar of a free government. In other words, the theory upon which We, the People, ordained and established the Constitution of the United States was that We, the People should defend it.

In the first Militia Law enacted by the Congress in 1792 power was given to the states to create such exemptions as the Legislatures of the several states should provide. Up to 1848 the system of universal military training required all of the militia not exempted by law to devote three days in each year to military training. But the exemptions were increased, and laxity of administration gradually led to the abandonment of the whole system of universal obligatory military training and service. This indifference of the citizens toward the government eventually seemed to establish a universal exemption in place of the universal obligation. Certain volunteer organizations assumed the entire responsibility, and training disappeared in a system dividing the organized militia from the general body of the militia. The active militia was recognized as including the National Guard and Naval Militia, and the reserve militia as consisting of all others liable to service in the militia.

The active militia was thereafter required to undergo prescribed training during the term of enlistment; the reserve militia had no prescribed duty, but remained liable, in a case of insurrection, invasion, tumult, riot or breach of the peace, or imminent danger thereof, to be ordered into the active service of the State.

The power of the Governor to call out all of the militia is unquestioned. Our Military Law has prescribed the manner in which the call shall be made, either by draft or by accepting as many volunteers as may be necessary for the purpose.

The new National Defense Act, which was pending before the Congress at the time of our last legislative session, provided for a substantial increase in the number of the National Guard, that is, the active militia, to be maintained in each State. The number of enlisted men of the National Guard to be organized under the act, within one year from its passage, was regulated in the proportion of 200 men for each Senator and Representative in Congress, this number to be increased each year thereafter, in the proportion of not less than 50 per centum, until a total peace strength of not less than 800 enlisted men for each Senator and Representative in Congress shall have been reached.

The total number of the National Guard required in the State of New York, under the National Defence Act, amounts therefore approximately to 35,000.

In anticipation of this Federal legislation, the Military Law of this State was amended by what is generally referred to as the Stivers Bill (Chapter 568, Laws of 1916), under which the Governor is authorized, at any time, to call for such number of volunteers, in any city or town, as may be required to make up or complete the complement of organizations of the National Guard or Naval Militia, in conformity with any requirement as to strength which may be prescribed by the laws of the United States.

The act further provides that if a sufficient number of volunteers is not secured to enable the State to keep up to its requirements under the laws of the United States, the Governor may direct his order to the Mayor of any city, or the Supervisor of any town, specifying the number required, and upon the receipt of such order, the Mayor or the Supervisor, as the case may be, shall either accept as volunteers as many as are required to make up such quota, or proceed to make an enrollment of the reserve militia residing within the city or town, and to draft therefrom the number required.

This feature of the Stivers Bill, providing for a draft from the reserve militia, has been the subject of considerable criticism by those who have failed to understand its purport, and the necessity of maintaining the quota required by the Federal statute, if New York State is to be in a position to do its part in the plan of national defense.

The Stivers Bill makes no one subject to military service who has not always been liable to military service under our Constitution when necessity should require it. The draft provision has been incorporated in our Military Law since the adoption of the first Military Code in 1870, and appears as section 9 of the present Military Law.

While it is improbable that it should ever become necessary to resort to the draft in order to keep up the required number in our National Guard and Naval Militia organizations, it is essential, in view of the Federal statute requiring the force to be maintained at certain strength, that such a provision be incorporated in our Military Law, and that the State should possess the means to enforce the fulfillment of its obligation, should the usual volunteer method fail in the accomplishment of that result. The State has never been compelled to resort to the draft in case of insurrection, invasion, tumult, riot or breach of the peace, but that the power to do so, is, nevertheless, a most necessary provision of our Military Law, has never been doubted.

The amendment referred to (the Stivers Bill) applies the volunteer principle to the limit, providing that the Governor may call for volunteers in any city or town where additional forces are required. It is only upon failure of this method, that the wise precaution is incorporated in our statute, providing for the application of the sovereign right of compelling its able-bodied citizens to render service in the defense of the State. The mere statement of the provisions of the act demonstrates its necessity. If the militia of the State fails to respond voluntarily to its obligation of service, the State must possess the power of compulsion, and it is well that the method of applying it should be carefully prescribed and well understood.

The act is purely precautionary, co-ordinating our own military policy with the new National Defense Act. It must be remembered, that, under the Constitution of the United States, Congress has full power to provide for the organization of the militia. The states must conform. It is the part of wisdom and of patriotism that the State should do its part in the scheme of national defense and should evidence its willingness to cooperate by incorporating in its military statute authority which will enable it to do its full share in the face of any contingency which might arise.

In order to enlarge the scope of the volunteer principle as well as to increase the sources of supply, a further amendment was successfully advocated.

TRAINING DETACHMENTS

Hitherto the Military Law (by section 241 as amended in 1911) had prohibited the formation of military organizations other than those provided for. It declared that "no body of men shall associate themselves together as a military company or organization or parade in public with firearms in any city or town of this State." It forbade cities and towns from raising money toward "arming, equipping, uniforming or in any other way supporting, sustaining or providing drill rooms or armories for any such body of men."

This made it illegal to impart military training even to the reserve militia in times of peace. To meet the demand for preparedness, section 41 of the Military Law was so amended May 9, 1916, as to authorize the Governor to organize from time to time at places other than the station of a command, training detachments of officers and men who shall form a part of such command. It was provided that "whenever in the opinion of the Major-General a training detachment has an enlisted strength which entitles it to armory accommodations, he may issue a certificate," and that, " if and when the certificate is approved by the Adjutant-General the training detachment shall be deemed a company and shall be entitled to all the benefits, including the allowances of money."

The effect of this amendment is that patriotic citizens of smaller localities where there are no armories may enjoy the advantages of military training. At the same time additional numerical strength is provided for units already located in armories, but unable to secure in their immediate neighborhoods the great increase of strength required by the National Defense Act.

Following this legislation in the State of New York the War Department has authorized the formation of like detachments in all of the States.

POWER TO SUMMON THE GUARD

A further step in the direction of economy and efficiency was taken in the amendment of May 1, 1916. Section 115 of the Military Law hitherto gave authority to various State, County and City officials to order out the State military forces in case of breach of the peace, tumult, riot, or resistance to process of the State, or imminent danger thereof. It was found that this right was not always judiciously exercised, more troops being called for in a number of instances than were needed for the purposes desired, thereby entailing unnecessary expense on the counties concerned. This power was therefore vested in the Governor alone, to be exercised upon the request of the local authority when it shall be made to appear to the Governor that such action is necessary.

Various other amendments were enacted in order to make the organization of the state troops conform to the models prescribed by the National Government.

THE CHARGE OF DISCRIMINATION AGAINST JEWS

. During the heat of the recruiting campaign, when the regiments were using every device for stimulating public enthusiasm, an incident occurred which threatened to discredit the essential democracy of the Guard.

While it is desirable that every encouragement be given to the good fellowship and congeniality of organization, in order to stimulate *esprit de corps,* the Guard must be protected against any charge of being a merely social organization or of being used for the encouragement of snobbery or racial prejudice.

It is above all important that any man eager to serve his country and qualified to do so, should meet encouragement and not rebuff. Fortunately, occasions of complaint have been rare.

In the first instance arising under this administration the opportunity was seized not only to emphasize the principle of equality but to confirm it with an amendment to the Regulations.

On May 10, 1916, Max J. Klein of 948 Union Avenue, Bronx, 26 years old, born abroad, but naturalized, applied to join Battery D of the Second Field Artillery, Captain H. E. Sullivan. He complained that he and other Jews were told that there were no vacancies though men of other races were being accepted for enlistment.

The Committee for the Protection of the Good Name of Immigrant Peoples on May 19, 1916, made a formal complaint to the Governor who transmitted the charges to this department with instructions to investigate and report. On May 24, 1916, this department issued a statement that such conditions would not be tolerated in the National Guard and ordered all persons concerned to appear at a hearing in New York City at the State Arsenal May 25th.

After four hearings were held and the testimony of forty-nine witnesses taken, the Governor directed that the scope of the investigation be broadened to include the complaint of any others who had met with similar discrimination.

The President's call and the mobilization compelled the deferment of the proceedings until October 11, 1916, when this office reported that the evidence showed a discrimination in individual instances by officers of sub-units, though there was no generally prevailing sentiment of prejudice, and that several of those who complained of unjust treatment in one organization were subsequently welcomed by another.

This office further advised that, while the law of the State vested in an enlisting officer and in the commanding officer of an organization a discretion in the matter of accepting or rejecting applicants, it should be rendered illegal for any officer to use such discretion as an arbitrary and unlimited weapon of personal prejudice. General Orders No. 36 was accordingly published October 25, 1916, and the Regulations amended as follows:

> "All officers who are connected with the enlistment of recruits and those who are authorized to approve or disapprove of such enlistments, shall, in determining whether an applicant should be accepted or rejected, be guided by an honest judgment, deliberately exercised, as to his fitness for the service, and no applicant shall be rejected on account of his race or religion.
>
> " It shall also be the duty of officers charged with making enlistments to see that their subordinates are free from such bias or prejudice and conform to the requirements of this paragraph."

NEW ORGANIZATIONS

The organization of the New York Division has not hitherto satisfied the requirements of the Tables of Organization prescribed for the organized Militia by the War Department in that headquarters, supply and machine gun companies and troops for all regiments of infantry and cavalry did not exist. Two headquarters companies, only one machine gun company and one machine gun troop and no supply companies, were previously established, while the Tables of Organization prescribe one of each for each regiment — a total of 14 of each for the National Guard of the State. Action was at once taken looking to the correction of these deficiencies and at present all regiments of infantry and cavalry have these units completely organized.

The Division also lacked two Field Hospitals and one Ambulance Company, as well as a complete Field Bakery Company and Supply Train. These were organized, equipped, and mustered in.

Two Aero Companies were formed during the past year. Although these units are not required for a division by the Tables of Organization it was deemed advisable to organize them, their importance in obtaining information in active service being beyond question. The Federal authorities being unable to

extend any assistance in the way of equipment, four aeroplanes
were presented to the National Guard by patriotic citizens through
the Aero Club of America and funds obtained through the same
source for the training of the personnel. Other aeroplanes were
rented for training purposes and both of the Aero Companies had
several months of instruction at the U. S. Aviation Station at
Mineola, Long Island.

An Armored Motor Battery has been organized in New York
City. Four Armored Motor cars, eight auxiliary cars, seventy
motor cycles, and eight motor cycle trailers were purchased for
the use of this organization by Captain H. G. Montgomery,
Commanding Officer of the battery, from funds obtained by
private subscription. Although the usefulness of an organization
of this character has been amply demonstrated during the present
war in Europe, the Federal authorities have been unable to
recognize this unit for the reason that the organization of the
Regular Army does not provide for such an organization.

The Coast Artillery Corps is charged with the duty of manning
the coast defense of the nation in time of war. It was found that
the Coast Artillery Corps of this State was short four companies.
Two of these companies have been mustered into the State
service and the requisite number of men have been enrolled for the
remaining companies, which will shortly be mustered.

The Military Law of 1913 provided that within three months
the Adjutant-General should organize and equip a Colored Regiment of Infantry in the State of New York. But no action was
taken looking to a compliance with its provisions until the present
administration came into office. Twelve companies of a colored
regiment, which has been designated the 15th Infantry, N. G.,
N. Y., have been organized and mustered into the State service,
by S. O. 138, June 29, 1916.

Equipment for the regiment will be obtained from the War
Department as soon as the federal authorities extend the necessary
recognition, which is assured at an early date.

THE MOBILIZATION CAMP

The choice of a mobilization centre had been a matter of discussion since the summer of 1915. The Camp at Peekskill had
accommodations for only one-eighth of the state troops. Various

sites were examined and finally the State Industrial Farm at Beekman, Dutchess County, was chosen as the most excellent situation. It was a tract of 825 acres at a point within one-and-a-half hour's railroad journey for two-thirds of the National Guard organizations. The site was inspected by the Federal authorities and pronounced ideal in every way.

The Board of Managers granted the temporary use and occupation of the land to the Armory Commission and early in May 1916 contracts were entered into for the installation of an adequate water system, the construction of buildings, latrines, baths, etc. On May 18, 1916 an order was issued directing the Commanding General Division to assume possession and control. The reservation was designated Camp Whitman, Green Haven, N. Y.

That the choice of this site was wise was shown by the fact that no serious cases of sickness occurred and communicable diseases were entirely absent, though some of the organizations remained in camp as long as five weeks. This State record equalled that of the Federal service in Texas and furnished a striking contrast with the disease records of both State and National mobilization camps in 1898.

Due credit for the result should be given to the invaluable services of the Division Surgeon, Lieutenant-Colonel Harlow Brooks, whose report contains so much matter of importance to military hygiene that it is published herewith as Appendix C.

PLANS FOR STATE MOBILIZATION

For the expenses and mobilization of its own forces the State made the unprecedented appropriation of $500,000 on May 20th, 1916.

Having secured the funds, the site, and the authority for the mobilization of the State troops there was no further delay. On May 27th, 1916, General Orders, No. 14 was issued by this office directing the entire National Guard, less the Coast Defense Commands, one battalion of Engineers, and one Machine Gun troop, to mobilize at Camp Whitman for a period of two weeks July 9–22, 1916.

The Coast Defense Commands were directed June 10, 1916 by General Orders, No. 17, to participate in joint Coast Defense exercises at Fort H. S. Wright, N. Y., during the month of July. The battalion of Engineers was to be sent to Belvoir Tract, Va., for field service and the Machine Gun troop to Fort Ethan Allen, Vt.

In preparation for this tour of duty Schools of Application were held for officers at Peekskill for three weeks May–June. Every officer of the Guard was compelled to spend one week there under the tuition of officers assigned from the Regular Army. This school completed its invaluable course of training just one day before the President's call.

Foreseeing the inevitable confusion that must arise upon receipt of a call to national service this department had endeavored for some time to forestall one great obstacle to efficiency,— lack of clothing and equipment.

All clothing and equipment for the National guard are drawn from the Federal Government under annual appropriations by Congress, which are allotted to the various states in proportion to the number of enlisted men in the service in each State as shown by the last annual inspection. Section 13 of the Federal Militia Law fixes $8.33 as the annual clothing allowance for each enlisted man in the National Guard as shown by the last Federal inspection. This allowance is ample for the purpose for which it is intended but it makes no provision for the large increase in strength which would result by recruitment to full war strength required for mobilization under the President's call, the peace (minimum) strength being less than one-half of the war (maximum) strength of organization. Nor was provision made elsewhere by the Federal Government whereby the State authorities could obtain the clothing and equipment required for recruitment to war strength. It is true that the State of New York had clothing and equipment in excess of requirements for the minimum strength of its National Guard but it had been unable from its allotments from the Federal Government to obtain a sufficient supply for war strength.

To meet these conditions the War Department had formulated a plan whereby property sufficient to clothe and equip the difference between the minimum and maximum strength of organization was stored at the Federal Supply Depot, Philadelphia, ready for shipment to the mobilization camp immediately upon the National Guard's being ordered into the service of the United States, where it would be issued to the troops after their arrival at that point and muster into the United States service. This plan did not take into consideration the fact that the troops were to remain at their home stations for from one to two weeks to recruit to war strength, nor the fact that there would be unavoidable delays of from three days to two or more weeks in mustering the troops after their arrival at mobilization camps. Futhermore, no provisions were made for clothing and equipping the troops during these periods.

The faults of this system of issue are apparent, and were pointed out to the War Department by this State on June 2, 1913, again on July 20, 1914, and for the third time on June 4, 1916. In the letter of June 2, 1913, a plan was submitted whereby all war strength property was to be stored in the armories of the organizations for which intended in rooms provided by the State for that purpose, which were to be under the control of Federal officers or State officers as the War Department might prefer. In the former case the rooms were to be considered as Federal Supply Depots and the State authorities were to have no control over them. In the latter case the property was to be issued without charge to the State's allotment and the War Department was to make such regulations concerning its care and safe-keeping as it considered necessary.

In all of these letters the delay and confusion which would result from the shipment of property to mobilization points were clearly pointed out. The following is quoted from the communication of July 20, 1914: " This (State plan) would place the property where it would be readily available in time of war, and not in a general supply depot, where it may be ready for prompt shipment but where it would not be available for prompt use by the individuals who would need it. * * * On the other hand to ship it in bulk from the Philadelphia depot to the mobilization camp would involve endless confusion, delay and property losses. * * * Such a plan (War Department) necessitates the transportation of the War strength personnel from the home station to the mobilization camp where they would have to subsist and be provided for in some manner while dressed as civilians, and would have a bad effect on the discipline of new men at the very time when they should be under rigid discipline."

The State plan, while approved by many Regular Army Officers, was never adopted by the War Department, the result being that many recruits were without proper uniforms and equipment for a considerable length of time after arrival at the mobilization camp.

The matter was further complicated by the War Department's stopping all issues under the allotments to the State on June 20 and returning unfilled all requisitions previously submitted.

Section 17 of the Federal Militia Law provides that any State may with the approval of the Secretary of War, purchase for cash from the War Department for the use of its militia, stores, supplies, material of war or military publications in addition to those issued. This right was also withdrawn by the War Department, the State being thus deprived of all sources of supply.

Considerable criticism has appeared because the troops or a part of them were sent to the border in olive drab woolen uniforms instead of olive drab cotton or khaki. This criticism is generally directed to the Federal Government but some inquiries have been made as to why the State did not have a supply of this light weight clothing on hand. In reply to this it may be stated that the issue of khaki or olive drab cotton uniforms to the National Guard was discontinued by the United States Government on May 29, 1914, and all requisitions subsequently made by the State were returned disapproved. Statement was made at that time by the War Department that the service uniform for troops within the continental limits of the United States would thereafter be the olive drab woolen cloth. No cotton clothing, therefore, had been issued to the National Guard of New York State for over two years. Some of the organizations had on hand a limited supply of cotton clothing which was recived by them before the issue was discontinued by the Federal Government.

THE PRESIDENT'S CALL

The first call was the telegram from the Secretary of War to the States of Texas, Arizona and New Mexico, May 9th, 1916, ordering out the organized militia for Federal service.

The second call was issued on the night of June 18th, 1916, and contained in a telegram to all the States, except those above mentioned, and Nevada.

The telegram to New York was as follows:

"June 18

HON. CHARLES S. WHITMAN, *Albany, N. Y.:*

Having in view the possibilities of further aggression upon the territory of the United States and the necessity for proper protection of the same, the President has thought proper to exercise the authority vested in him by the Constitution and laws and to call out the organized Militia and the National Guard necessary for that purpose. I am consequently instructed by the President to call into the service of the United States forthwith through you the following units of the organized Militia and the National Guard of the State of New York, which the President directs shall be assembled at the State Mobilization Camp at New Dorp (or at a place to be designated to you by the Commanding General, Eastern Department) and for muster into the service of the United States, as follows:

One division of three brigades of three regiments each of infantry.
One regiment, one squadron, and one machine group troop of cavalry.
Two regiments of field artillery.
Two battalions of engineers.
One battalion of signal corps.
Three field hospitals.
Four ambulance companies.

Organizations to be accepted into the Field Service shall have the minimum peace strength now prescribed for organized militia. The maximum strength at which organizations will be accepted and to which they should be raised as soon as possible is prescribed in section 2, Tables of Organization, U. S. Army. In case any regiment, battalion or squadron now recognized as such contains an insufficient number of organizations to enable it to conform on muster to regular army organization tables, the organization necessary to complete such unit may be moved to Mobilization Camp and there inspected under orders of the Department Commander to determine fitness for recognition as organized militia by the War Department. Circular 19 D. M. A. 1914, prescribes the organization desired from each State as part of the local tactical division and only those organizations will be accepted into the service.

It is requested that all officers of the Adjutant General's Department, Quartermaster Corps and Medical Corps duly recognized as pertaining to state headquarters under Table 1, Tables of Organization, Organized Militia and any elsewhere required for duty in State administration, be ordered to camp for duty as camp staff officers. Such number of these staff officers as the Department Commander shall determine may be mustered into the service of the United States for the purpose of proper camp administration and will be mustered out when their services are no longer required. Where recognized brigades or divisions are called into service from a state and the staff officers pertaining to these units under Tables of Organization U. S. Army will be mustered into service, and also the authorized inspectors of small arms practice pertaining thereto. Except for these two purposes and mobilization camp service and the prescribed staff service with tactical units, officers of state headquarters under Table 1 above mentioned will not be mustered into service at this time. If tactical divisions are later organized the requisite additional number of staff officers with rank as prescribed for division staff will as far as practicable be called into service from those states which have furnished troops to such divisions. Acknowledge.

(Signed)   BAKER, Secretary of War."

FIVE AMENDMENTS TO THE PRESIDENT'S CALL

On June 29, 1916, a telegram from the Chief Militia Bureau, called for a supply train, an ammunition train, a pack train company, a field bakery company, and an aero company.

On June 28, 1916, a telegram called for the 3d Regiment of Field Artillery.

On July 11, 1916, the second aero company of Buffalo was called for.

On July 19, 1916, the call for two battalions of engineers was changed to a call for one regiment.

On July 21, 1916, the organization of a fourth field hospital was asked. This was accomplished in time for its mustering in August.

THE MOBILIZATION

The first call arrived on the night of June 18, 1916.

On June 19, 1916, this Department issued G. O. 18 ordering the Commanding General Division to " cause the organizations of his command less Coast Artillery troops, to assemble forthwith at their respective home stations in the equipment prescribed for field duty, preparatory to their muster into the service of the United States."

On June 21, 1916, G. O. 19 was issued for the information and guidance of all concerned in the mobilization which was proceeding with feverish enthusiasm.

In this Order the recruiting of all organizations was directed, and the examination by the Medical Department of all officers and enlisted men with a view to guarding against the presence of any infectious or contagious disease. It was directed that no recruit should be accepted who failed to conform to the physical standard prescribed for the Regular Army. The new oath for officers and the new oath and enlistment contract for enlisted men set forth in the National Defense Act of June 3, 1916, were prescribed and the forms issued as soon as they could be printed. Inventory and inspection were ordered of all property of the United States and the State to be taken into the Federal Service. It was directed that all property not to be taken into the Federal service was to be promptly invoiced, turned over and receipted for by the commanding officers of the depot units, the immediate organization of which according to the Military Law, section 120, was also directed.

Requisitions for all clothing, equipment and supplies necessary for the enlisted strength were called for and authority was given for the organization of machine gun companies and troops in regiments in which they had not already been authorized.

As soon as organizations had completed their inventories and made suitable arrangements the Commanding General Division, was instructed to move them to the mobilization camp at Green Haven, N. Y.

Owing to the anxiety of the War Department to place troops on the border at the earliest possible moment, orders were received later for the muster-in at their home stations and immediate departure of a number of organizations.

The Headquarters Division was mustered in at New York June 28th and departed for McAllen, Texas, July 2nd, arriving July 6th.

The Seventh and Seventy-first regiments of infantry were mustered in at their armories June 26th and entrained for the border June 27th, on which date the Fourteenth Infantry also departed though it was not mustered in until July 31st, August 1st and 2d at Mission, Texas.

The Twelfth Infantry was mustered at its armory on June 28th and departed for the border the same day, as did Batteries D and E of the First Field Artillery, Battery F following the next day.

These Batteries and Battery B were mustered in at Van Cortlandt Park June 28th. Battery B departed July 3rd. Batteries A and C were mustered in at Camp Whitman July 4th and departed July 9th.

At Van Cortlandt Park the Headquarters First Brigade was mustered June 28th, departing July 7th. Here also Squadron A Cavalry was mustered in June 30th, departing July 6th, as well as the Machine Gun Troop, mustered in June 30th and departing July 6th.

At Van Cortlandt Park the First Cavalry was assembled as its various organizations arrived. Troops A, F, K and L were mustered in June 28th and departed June 29th; Troops C, E, G, H and M were mustered in June 30th, departing July 1st.

Troops B and D were mustered in June 30th and departed July 6th, on which date Troop I also departed after being mustered in July 1st.

In order to respond to the second amendment to the President's call, which required a third regiment of artillery, permission was asked and granted for the reorganization of the Sixty-fifth Infantry. (See Appendix A, Exhibit D.)

This was accomplished. By General Orders No. 22, July 11, 1916, the regiment was so constituted, and designated the Third Field Artillery. The regiment was mustered into Federal service at Camp Whitman, August 5, 1916, receiving on that date complete equipment for a regiment of 2 battalions of 3 batteries each. The wheeled material consisted of 24 4.7 howitzers, 72 caissons, 6 battery wagons, 6 store wagons, and 3 reel carts. On August 18th 300 horses were received.

Captain Daniel W. Hand of the Fifth Field Artillery, U. S. A., was commissioned Colonel and assigned to the command. The regiment was held in training at Camp Whitman until October 3rd, when it departed for the border with an enlisted strength of 750 men. It was still in Texas at the close of the year.

To meet the requirements of the National Defense Act and to comply with the fourth amendment to the President's call, the Twenty-second Corps of Engineers was reorganized by G. O. 25, July 11, 1916, to constitute the Twenty-second Regiment of Engineers with two battalions of three companies each and two additional companies for duty as army troops. The First Battalion departed for the border on July 12th; the Second Battalion departed July 14th.

The First Field Hospital was among the first units to leave for the border, being mustered in at Camp Whitman June 28th and departing the same day, as did the Third Ambulance Company of the Fourth Field Hospital.

The Twenty-third Infantry was mustered in at its armory in Brooklyn July 1st and departed July 4th. The Seventy-fourth Infantry was mustered in at Buffalo July 1st and 2nd, and departed July 5th.

Of the Signal Corps, First Battalion, Company A, was mustered in at New York, and Company B at Brooklyn July 3rd, both departing for Texas July 5th.

The remaining organizations were moved to Camp Whitman as fast as the Camp could be made ready to receive them, the earliest organizations to arrive, the Twenty-second Engineers arriving June 21st, the Sixty-ninth Infantry June 21st, the Second and Third Infantry June 27th, devoting their energies to the completion of the installation of the water system, the building of roads, etc.

There were delays in equipping the regiments taken to Camp Whitman on two accounts, neither of them due to the Department. The first cause was the decision of the Federal authorities to deliver equipment to no organization till after it was mustered in; the second being a confusion in the War Department as to the destination of the equipment.

Though the mobilization camp had been changed from New Dorp to Camp Whitman, Green Haven, N. Y., and the Camp inspected and approved in May, through some oversight the alteration was not recorded and the President's call ordered mobilization at New Dorp or at a place to be designated by the Commanding General, Eastern Department. Verbal approval of the change to Camp Whitman was asked by the Commanding General, received and confirmed in writing, June 23, 1916, but much of the equipment was labelled and made ready for shipment to New Dorp, and delay ensued.

More troops were mobilized than were required by the call of the President. The reasons were ample. Plans had been in order for months to gather the entire National Guard of the State into one camp. Preliminary contracts had been entered into for transportation, subsistence, horse hire, installation of water system and other incidentals and it was thought advisable not to change the plans to a greater extent than necessary.

Thus the troops not called for would have the benefit of the contemplated field exercises, and would be immediately available should their services be required by the Federal Government.

The wisdom of this step was seen in the fact that the Government actually did amend its call until all the organizations were mustered in except three regiments of infantry and substantial numbers of their personnel were mustered in as members of organizations of special arms of the service.

The order in which the remaining units were accepted into the
Federal service at Camp Whitman is as follows:

Second Infantry, July 1st (departed July 7th).
Third Infantry, July 5th (departed July 13th).
Sixty-ninth Infantry, July 6th (departed July 11th).
First and Second Ambulance Companies, July 3rd (departed July 10th)
Twenty second Engineers, 1st Battalion, July 4th (departed July 12th).
Second Battalion, July 7th (departed July 14th).
Second Field Hospital July 10th (departed July 15th).
Third Field Hospital, July 26th (departed October 12th).
Third Field Artillery, August 5th (departed October 3rd).

The First Aero Company was mustered in at Mineola, L. I.,
June 13th, but was not called to the border, remaining at the
aviation camp.

The Quartermaster Corps was mustered in at New York City
July 21st (departed July 25th); the Field Bakery was mustered
in at Peeskill July 4th and departed for the border July 9th.

The Division Supply Train was mustered in at Peekskill September 24th and departed October 17th.

October 5th, at New York City, the Fourth Field Hospital was
mustered in and departed.

The importance of providing for the maintenance of an armed
force to replace automatically the Guard when it is called into
Federal service, was emphasized by the threat of serious labor
distubances during the absence of the Guard at the border.

In order to reassure the public that the State had not been
denuded of its power to preserve order, and at the same time to
avoid making any demonstration likely to arouse hostility as a
repressive measure, the three infantry regiments not taken into
the Federal service were ordered to make practice marches, and
due publicity was given to their movements.

The Tenth Infantry was ordered to proceed from Camp Whitman to the Camp of Instruction at Peekskill for rifle practice
from August 4th to August 7th, returning to its home stations by
battalions from August 5th to August 8th. The companies of
the First Infantry were ordered to their home stations by rail.

The Forty-seventh Infantry after having marched from Peekskill to Van Cortlandt Park, was ordered to return to its home
station in Brooklyn.

REGULAR ARMY OFFICERS

A significant feature of the mobilization was the wise policy of attaching regular army officers to National Guard organizations. After thorough consideration, the War Department finally decided not to allow any officers of the regular establishment to accept a commission below the grade of lieutenant-colonel.

Vacancies through physical disability, resignation or through the consent of certain officers to accept a lower rank, enabled the Guard to take advantage of the services of experienced regulars, and the following served with the Guard at the border:

Major Harry H. Bandholtz as Colonel, Chief of Staff, New York Division.
Captain Daniel W. Hand as Colonel of the Third Field Artillery.
Captain William E. Welsh as Lieutenant Colonel of the Twenty-third Infantry.
Captain William N. Haskell as Colonel of the Sixty-ninth Infantry.
Colonel Gordon Johnston as Colonel of the Twelfth Infantry.

THE SECOND DIVISION

Once the organizations were mustered into the Federal service, the State lost its authority over them but not its responsibility to them. Their welfare remained a matter of grave concern, since they were but a loan to the Government and it was important that on their return they should be ready to resume their service for the State and should find their places ready, their interests conserved, and their property cared for.

Furthermore the State, having transferred almost its entire armed power to the United States, required some substitute for the preservation of the civil peace.

To serve these and other ends the depot units were organized according to the Military Law. Officers who were prevented from entering the Federal service but were well able and willing to serve the State, were designated to organize a unit at each depot, and to these units were assigned, by General Orders No. 20, June 22, 1916, such enlisted men as, for various reasons, failed to take the new oath and subscribe to the new contract of enlistment.

This office issued General Orders No. 21, July 7, 1916:

" 1. The organizations of the National Guard of this State less organizations mustered into the service of the United States under the call of the President, dated June 18, 1916, together with the depot units now or hereafter organized in pursuance to M. L. 120, and such other organizations as are now or may hereafter be organized as part of the military forces of the State, are hereby constituted the Second Division, National Guard.

" 2. Brevet Major-General Daniel Appleton, heretofore placed on active duty under his brevet commission as Major-General to supervise the organization of depot units, is hereby assigned to the command of the Second Division, National Guard, created by this order."

THE DEPOT UNITS AND RECRUITING

The battalion was the model of organization and the duties included not only the making of inventories and the protection of property left behind by the troops at the border, but also the collection, training and forwarding of recruits to their parent organizations.

There would have been greater success if there had been more excitement and allurement in the border service. It was difficult to enlist men in a service that seemed to promise little danger and great discomfort. The depot units, however, labored with energy and were accomplishing results when their authority to enlist men was unfortunately terminated by the act of the War Department, which found it inconsistent with its policy to make use of these recruiting facilities. A Federal recruiting system was substituted but was found to be ill adapted to the National Guard situation.

The reasons for the failure of the Federal system are manifest. Its lessons are so important to the future that a somewhat frank statement of the case is imperative.

The purpose of the depot unit is not only to provide an organization immediately available to take charge of the Armory and property of the organization not carried into the Federal service, but also to co-ordinate and encourage and make use of the loyalty, enthusiasm and efficiency of those veterans of the organizations who for various reasons have given up their active service but are still ready in every way to support and back up the parent organization during its absence in the Federal service, and to make all necessary sacrifices to that end.

.The veterans of an organization understand its sentiments and its local pride and can stimulate it. Moreover, the armory is the natural place where applicants for enlistment in that neighborhood would report.

The spirit of territorial enlistment is eminently worth fostering and neighborhood sentiment and enthusiasm cannot wisely be ignored, either in the recruitment of men or their after employment. In the regular establishment where men take up military life as a career, it is a matter of indifference, but the power of *esprit de corps* has been firmly established in history.

The method put in operation in this State took full advantage of this principle of territorial recruitment, which all experts recognize. It permitted the man who wanted to serve with his friends and comrades to find a place near them, and it permitted the men already enlisted to act as recruiting agents, appealing to their old friends to come out of the civil life and join the cause.

After the President's call had taken the parent organization into the Federal service, the depot units assumed the task of their reinforcement heartily and effectively. The problems of providing equipment and uniforms were out of their control, but they were accomplishing the work of recruiting in a satisfactory manner.

As a result of conferences held two years before the President's call, the War Department had authorized in advance under a general mobilization plan, the appointment of what was called a "recruiting officer for war." It was provided that he should in each case be a member of the active organization mustered into the Federal service, who had taken the Federal oath but would remain at the home station with authority to enlist men for that organization.

The first inconsistent order from the War Department was that this recruiting officer for war, being an officer of the parent organization, had no right to remain at home, but must straightway report and proceed to his unit. Otherwise he was to be mustered out of service.

We proceeded to recruit through the depot commander. Orders were then received establishing as the recruit rendezvous for infantry, Fort Hamilton, and for other arms, Fort Totten. This meant that any recruits from any part of the state must report at Fort Hamilton.

New complications ensued at once. An instance in point is the fate of the recruits gathered by a certain depot commander. Exercising what he thought to be his authority under state laws to recruit classes A and B, he recruited a number of class A men, signed their papers, provided them as far as possible with uniforms and equipment, and under orders from the War Department through the Eastern Department, shipped them to Fort Hamilton.

These men had all been physically examined by a surgeon but by the time they reached Fort Hamilton, new and unusual conditions had been established for recruits. It was announced that married men, men with dependents, etc., would not be accepted. Out of one group of fifty men sent to Fort Hamilton twenty were rejected. This opened yet another problem: who was to assume the obligation imposed by the delivery of recruits to Fort Hamilton, their pay from the time they were enlisted, their transportation, subsistence, and return to their homes?

The War Deparment decided to refuse this obligation, stating that it would regard these men as merely "applicants" for enlistment, since the officer who enlisted them was not in the Federal service. This department was asked what it intended to do with the men. Reply was made that since the War Department had ordered them down it should order them back. Our interpretation was denied and this department was compelled to assume the entire responsibility and expense of these luckless patriots.

While this first transaction was taking place, another group of twenty arrived at Fort Hamilton. Ten of these were rejected. It was necessary for this department to issue an immediate order to the depot commanders that they had no authority for recruitment and to discontinue their efforts.

FAILURE OF THE FEDERAL SYSTEM OF RECRUITMENT

In the meantime the psychological moment for recruiting had passed and this experience further discouraged enthusiasm. It was at this stage, that the regular army scheme of recruiting was introduced which it was said, had worked well in other states. It was suggested that the State should muster into the service regular recruiting officers, forming a special organization, with authority to recruit, and it was stated that the proper organization of this state would require a quota of 50 officers and 150 non-commissioned officers who would be allowed pay, subsistence, commutation of subsistence, and transportation.

This office telegraphed the parent organizations at the border, asking their commanding officer in each case to designate a recruiting officer. The commanding officers in the field felt unable to make such nominations, since the men who were competent to serve, were expected to serve at the border.

Officers who had been doing good work with the depot units were not willing to undertake recruiting as a business. The Reserve list and other sources finally provided the necessary quota, and these officers were ordered to report at the 22d Regiment Armory in New York city for instruction in the art of recruiting according to army methods.

The accomplishment of this group under the conditions imposed upon them was practically nil, though they were distributed about the State and made every effort.

Their organization and distribution went counter to the whole idea of territorial recruitment. Men enlisted in the New York East Side, for example, were assigned to a Buffalo organization. The result was that the system had to be disbanded, because it cost too much, averaging about forty-five dollars per man. Few recruits were secured and these not always of an adaptable quality. And the expense of the officers added to the costliness of the experiment.

As the various organizations returned from the border certain of the recruiting officers were mustered out, the entire service being abolished by order November 20, 1916. The total number of enlistments was 840 as a result of three months' work. The total number required to bring organizations in the Federal service to war strength was 6261.

The reasons for the failure have been indicated. A typical example is that of a recruiting officer who enlisted 200 recruits at the armory during the three weeks while the organization was at Camp Whitman prior to its departure for the border. The same officer in the Federal service obtained only eleven recruits in seven weeks for all branches of the service, though he had an extra recruiting station and made liberal use of advertisements.

Discouraging as the results were, they taught anew the lesson that the principle of territorial recruitment and neighborhood organization can not wisely be defied, and that in the National Guard *esprit de corps* is the best reliance for recruitment.

DISBANDING OF THE SECOND DIVISION

On October 6th, 1916, in view of the return to the State of many organizations, the Second Division was disbanded by General Orders No. 33. The command of the National Guard then in service within the State devolved upon Brigadier General Dyer, who had been mustered out of the Federal service. The brigade organizations constituted of depot units were disbanded, and the brigade commanders relieved from duty. The commanding officers of the depot units were instructed to report to the commanding officers of the parent organizations or of the brigade to which they belonged.

· The depot units have been continued in existence. Their personnel was by G. O. 19, June 21, 1916, divided into two classes, Class A consisting of men available to fill vacancies in organizations in Federal service, Class B consisting of all other enlisted men. General Orders No. 27, August 3rd, 1916, directed that on the return to the home stations of the parent organization all Class A enlisted men should be transferred to that organization, Class B enlisted men to be continued in depot unit service administered under Regulations 954–959.

The depot unit is so valuable that every effort will be made in this State to keep it in existence even when the parent organization is at the home station. The two should coexist and work together so that in the crisis of another sudden call, the depot unit will be ready and trained for the immediate assumption of its duties. Its functions are analogous to those of the vice-president toward the president of a corporation. It would be no worse policy to postpone the selection of a vice-president till the president was called away than it is to defer the organization of the depot units till the parent organization has marched out.

Furthermore, according to the plan contemplated in the military law requiring that the State shall never be left without a minimum of 10,000 troops, the upkeep of the depot units is obligatory.

These depot organizations will be strictly a State force and not called on for duty outside of the State, but the members thereof, at their own request may be transferred to fill vacancies in the unit represented by the new organizations. After the departure of the parent organization for service, enlistments in the depot organization will be of two classes: Class A— men who desire to be transferred to fill vacancies in the unit represented by the depot organization, and Class B — men who enlist for strictly State service.

By this system will be maintained at all times in the State the required force of not less than 10,000 enlisted men fully uniformed, armed, equipped, disciplined, and available for any service within the State.

All former National Guardsmen who do not find it possible or expedient to rejoin the colors for active service, can and should immediately re-enlist in their depot organizations and assist in the important work of recruiting and training. Ample opportunity is thus offered for all whether in or out of the service to show their loyalty and patriotism.

DEPENDENTS

A development that materially affected the efficiency of this mobilization and is of high importance in the matter of future military policy, concerned the man eager to volunteer and perhaps highly qualified by experience and ability but unable to give up his civil occupation except by leaving one or more persons without support.   The dependents included wives, children, elderly parents, young brothers or sisters, or other relatives.

The pay of the enlisted man while much larger than in foreign nations, is very small according to American standards.   The allotted 50 cents a day is hardly sufficient to provide for the soldier's immediate comforts.   It was not contemplated that it should serve for the support of a family.   The recent increase in the cost of living has rendered it still less elastic.   In the case of officers, while the pay is better, the demands are greater and the standards of life of the families have usually been established on such a plane that positive hardship and social distress result when this pay is the only income.

In a state efficiently organized the calling out of troops should not disorganize the civil life of the community, especially as in any prolonged campaign it is essential to success that numberless non-military activities be continued. It does not help the fighting spirit, indeed it dampens the patriotic ardor of any volunteer, to feel that an ungrateful republic ignores the wants of the family he has left at home.

The President's call in 1916, found, as such a summons will always find, great numbers of good soldiers in an economical situation where they were quite unprepared to leave their families endowed for an indefinite period. Their departure for a long campaign must mean lasting disaster. Also their businesses, which in many cases had been built up by a lifelong devotion, could not but suffer. On the other hand a country cannot afford to depend for military support entirely upon those who are so young or so unsocial that they have acquired no families and no positions.

When the National Guard was called out, it was announced that Congress would provide a fund of a million dollars for the dependents of absent soldiers. This fund was opposed and postponed for months.

In the first flush of patriotic enthusiasm many employers promised either to continue their employees on their pay-rolls or to make up the difference between their established wages and the Federal pay. The announcement that men with dependents would be released together with the project of a Congressional relief fund led many of these to withdraw their promises to the great embarrassment of the men. Other employers continued to pay for a time then quietly withdrew or postponed the payment.

On these accounts numbers of Guardsmen found themselves at the Border engaged in a monotonous patrol duty, while their families struggled with penury and wrote appeals for help.

The situation was rendered the more irritating by the stories of the prosperity of less patriotic citizens who stayed at home and filled the posts of the absentees; and by the fact that the border service lacked excitement and glory. There was further resentment at the failure of the regular establishment to recruit the forces to a point where it could relieve the Guard from what had come to be hardly more than police duty.

So many men applied for release on the ground of dependents that the force at the border was threatened with disintegration. The War Department finally issued an order forbidding their release entirely or checking it with impediments and delays that acted as a practical annulment of the privilege.

In the case of the few men who were finally granted their discharge, there was a new hardship. The journey home was expensive and sleeping car accommodations were not generally provided.

Much assistance was given to families of soldiers by charitable societies, and by societies especially organized, but much suffering and much injustice were caused by the lack of an established plan for relief in all such cases.

Provision should be fully made now for this situation, which is bound to occur in the future. In time of peace preparation should be made, not only to train and equip the soldier, but to insure his dependents against privation.

CONDITIONS OF BORDER SERVICE

During the absence of the troops under Federal authority, there was so much more than the amount of grumbling normal to soldiers in a remote country, and there was so much newspaper agitation over the hardships unnecessarily inflicted on the men, that it seemed wise to send a representative to inspect and report on the exact state of affairs for the purpose of determining in what way it might be possible for the State to contribute to the health, comfort and convenience of its troops in the United States service.

By Special Orders No. 139, July 6, 1916, Lieutenant-Colonel J. Mayhew Wainwright of the Inspector General's Department, was authorized to proceed to Texas and report as to troops of the State in service of the United States.

Colonel Wainwright after a conference with the Governor, left New York July 15th. Arriving at San Antonio, Texas, on July 20th, he had a conference with General Funston, then proceeded to McAllen, where he conferred with the Major-General of the New York Division.

Colonel Wainwright found among the important needs were cots and board floors, screens for the company kitchens, mess shacks so that the men could eat in comfort under shelter from sun and storm, a more abundant water supply, and cash to supply necessary augmentation of the ration until the ration saving was available.

Few of the organizations had company funds and having just entered the Federal service, they were provided with neither the money nor the experience for properly provisioning themselves.

The general health was excellent, the majority of the hospital cases being dysentery and heat prostration.

But there was a considerable shortage of suitable clothing, some of the organizations not having received their cotton cloth uniforms and still wearing the heavy olive-drab of winter.

Some of the hardships were due to the fact that the organizations were considered to be technically in the field though they were actually in permanent camp. The character of the hospital was maintained as that of a field hospital rather than a base or camp hospital, thus restricting its facilities and equipment and staff of nurses, to the distress of those who feel ill.

Colonel Wainwright informally visited every organization and talked with numerous officers and men on all phases of their l' at the border. His experiences and conclusion give so vivid a picture and so valuable a statement of the conditions and difficulties of transportation and tropic encampment, the amount of training received, the hardships encountered, the sanitary and other problems faced and overcome, including the epidemic of paratyphoid fever, that his communication is published herewith in its entirety as Appendix D.

In an effort to assist the purchase of necessaries, this Department on July 14, 1916, placed on deposit in a McAllen bank $5,000 to be expended for the comfort of the men.

PAYMENT OF THE TROOPS

The Military Law provides that each officer and enlisted man ordered for duty by the Governor, or, under his authority, by the Major-General or the Commanding Officer of the Naval Militia, shall receive the pay specified by the State law for every day actually on duty, except for service for a single day when ordered for inspection, muster, small arms practice, parade, etc.

The rate of pay provided by the State law is, for enlisted men an average of from 30 to 150 per cent more than the rates provided for similar grades in the regular service. Thus, the rate for a private in the regular army is 50 cents a day, in the State troops, $1.25; for a corporal, 70 cents as against $1.40; for a sergeant, $1.00 as against $1.60; for a first sergeant, $1.50 as against $2.00. For officers, the base rate of pay is the same, but in the State service commissioned officers, up to and including majors, are given an additional allowance of 25 per cent for each five years of service up to an aggregate of 40 per cent. The increase for lieutenant-colonels and colonels stops at 30 per cent. For brigadier and major-generals there is no service increment.

These provisions of our Military Law were inserted before there was any thought of federalization. The order calling out the troops was always a matter for the action by the Governor, or, under his direction, by the Major-General. The occasion for the call and the duration of the service were determined by the Governor and were necessarily measured by the amount of appropriations available.

While the National Defense Act did not, in language, extend the power of the President to call the National Guard into the Federal service, the provision in the law for a draft made the National Guard available for service without the United States, and definitely removed that obstacle to its usefulness which had been urged for many years, viz., the contention that the National Guard could not be used beyond the territorial limits of the United States. The act involving this change of policy had barely been signed when there was a call for the Mexican Border service.

While the call was actually made by the President, it was made through the Governor of the State, as the act provided. It was issued under circumstances which the State could not resist, and the actual order of service came from the Governor, so that the men ordered for service came within the provisions of section 210 of the Military Law.

It raised an interesting question, therefore, as to whether, during the whole or any part of the service for which the Guard was called out, they were within the provisions of section 210 and entitled to the rate of pay provided by that section. Heretofore, when organizations had been ordered out by the Governor for camp duty or in aid of civil authorities, there was no question that during the entire period of service they were entitled to the rate of pay provided by our State law. In 1898, however, the precedent was established that the responsibility or obligation of the State ceased when organizations were mustered into the Federal service. Therefore, in connection with this call for Mexican Border service, the State assumed no legal obligation for making up the difference between the Federal and State pay after the organizations had been actually mustered. In the case of the 14th Regiment of Brooklyn, there had to be a slight modification of this policy, because the Federal authorities ordered the organization to the border before it was mustered into Federal service. In that case we had, therefore, to resort to the interpretation that the State was relieved from any obligation or responsibility when the organization was moved beyond its bounds by superior authority, and this organization was paid up only to date of departure from the State. Other organizations remaining in Camp Whitman, before being taken into the Federal service, were entitled to, and received, State pay for longer periods.

In view of the new policy of the War Department, and the fact that under the Defense Act all organizations are required to have at least fifteen days' camp service in each year in order to participate in the appropriations and secure recognition under the act, it may become a question of grave State policy whether there should not be a modification of this State pay provision, so that when organizations are called out by the Federal authorities, whether by the Governor or by direct action of the President, they shall be limited to the pay provisions of the Federal act.

It does seem, however, that when called out for purely State purposes, as in aid of the civil authorities in case of disorder, the rate of pay provided by the State law is by no means excessive. It has been held, furthermore, and we believe it is the proper conclusion, that under the Defense Act there should be no future occasion for formal muster into the United States service, since organizations are actually in the Federal service from the time they are called under presidential authority.

The theory of State pay was less difficult of solution than the practice. The President's call brought immediately a great rush of applicants for enlistment. Some men not found had to be dropped at least temporarily; great numbers of old members asked to be " taken up from dropped;" many others asked for transfer to organizations more convenient. New descriptive lists and efficiency records had to be made up.

The matter of the new oath and contract of enlistment and the weeding out of men whom disabilities or dependents made it necessary to release, also complicated the bookkeeping essential to all military organizations.

Furthermore, the War Department had just adopted a new form of payroll, with which the State officers had had no opportunity to become familiar. Ordinarily, when organizations are summoned for mobilization they are notified in advance to appear at a certain date. The President's call, however, came without warning, summoning the individuals to report immediately at their armories.

Numbers of men were caught at great distances from their home stations and came in from day to day, many of them not appearing till their organizations had moved out from the armories.

The officers, overtasked by the necessity for recruiting from peace to war strength and busied with requisitions for enlarged equipment, were swamped by an avalanche of details. Some of the items most important in a payroll, particularly the essential matter of the date of reporting, were neglected or lost.

The confusion of equipping the men, making requisitions and inventories and transfer of property from State to Federal service and compiling muster rolls was aggravated by the inability to secure from the War Department blank forms in sufficient quantity. This Department printed quantities of them on its own initiative, but in the meanwhile forms had been improvised crudely and hastily with resulting inaccuracy.

There were, indeed, so many things to be done by the organizations that the matter of the personal interest of the individual was not approached until nearly all of the officers and enlisted men were reduced to extremity and living on credit. Then only they found time to approach the matter of the payroll.

While the Federal representatives were most insistent on the matter of muster-in rolls and other paper-work, they evinced no impatience in the question of the payrolls. Most of the organizations had left the State before they could take up the matter.

Here there were new difficulties and it was discovered that many of the records had been left behind. The regiments were

at such a distance from their home stations and from the administrative office that correspondence required ten days in transit.

By the Governor's direction, the Adjutant-General was sent to
the Texas border to adjust the matter and to make payment with
the greatest dispatch possible. He left Camp Whitman August
9th, taking with him Major Hoppin, Lieutenant Kerwin and six
civilian clerks.

The rolls were promptly gotten into legal shape to meet the
requirements, both of State and Federal law, and within ten days
payments were made in cash in the aggregate amount of $135,000,
which cleared up the difference in pay for all those organizations
then on the border. In this connection a word of appreciation
should be made of record in regard to the splendid co-operation
extended by the local banking interest at McAllen, Mission and
Pharr. Mr. R. E. Horn, cashier of the First National Bank of
McAllen, was especially helpful, enabling the officers to make cash
payments averaging $15,000 a day, for four days before actual
confirmation of credit was received.

The Adjutant-General left McAllen on August 24th, stopping
at the Headquarters, Southern Department, San Antonio, to pay
respects to General Funston, and arriving at Camp Whitman on
August 28th.

MUSTER OUT

When it was discovered that there was no likelihood of active
hostilities with Mexico, there arose a great impatience for the
return of the National Guard of the United States to its homes.
The expense of the service was a heavy drain on the country's
resources. It was a heavy drain also on the families of the soldiers
and on the employers who were still paying the wages of absent
men and conducting their business with difficulty.

The men themselves betrayed a natural resentment at being
detained on the border, especially as conditions prevented any
great variety of training.

The typical Guard officer and men are too ambitious and too
important in their communities to be indifferent to the disposition made of their time, energies and liberties.

There seemed, however, still to be enough unrest and menace
across the border to make a general withdrawal inadvisable.

Some regiments, however, were relieved by sending South organizations that had not yet seen border service. The Third Field Artillery departed for McAllen October 3d; the Third Field Hospital departed October 12th.

The organizations not accepted into the federal service were returned to their home stations and relieved of duty: the Forty-seventh Infantry, July 26th; the First Infantry, August 3d; the Tenth Infantry, August 5-8; the First Armored Motor Battery, August 10th; the Second Aero Corps, September 18th.

Of the organizations mustered into the Federal service the First Aero Company was mustered out at Mineola, L. I., September 30th and November 2, 1916. The other organizations were returned from Texas to the State and mustered out on the dates designated. The first to arrive were sent to Camp Whitman, but for men fresh from the tropics, the climate was found too severe, and the remaining organizations were mustered out at their armories. Camp Whitman was closed for Federal use October 25, 1916, and the property, trucks, etc., taken to the camp at Peekskill for storage.

Muster Out

ORGANIZATION	Departure from border	Arrival at Camp Whitman	Arrival at home station	Date of muster out
71st Infantry..........	Sept. 6	Sept. 11	Sept. 21	Oct. 6.
14th Infantry.........	Sept. 8	Sept. 13	....	Oct. 11.
3rd Infantry, Cos. A, B, C, D, E, F, H, K, L, M.	Sept. 8	Sept. 15–21	....	Mustered out at Camp Whitman, Oct. 5.
Co. I.................	Sept. 9			
Co. G................	Sept. 13			
2nd Infantry, Cos. A, B, C, D, I, K, L, M.	Sept. 21	....	Sept. 27	Co. I, Oct. 7
Cos. E, F, G, H.......	Sept. 23	....	Sept. 29	Co. K, Oct. 8 M, Oct. 13. L, Oct. 16. B, Oct. 17. G and H, Oct. 19 E and F, Oct. 20 and Supply Co., headquarters, Cos. A, C, D, October 23. Machine Gun, Oct. 30
1st Battalion, 22nd Engineers.	Oct. 13	....	Oct. 21	Oct. 30.

MUSTER OUT —(*Continued*)

ORGANIZATION	Departure from border	Arrival at Camp Whitman	Arrival at home station	Date of muster out
1st Field Hospital......	Oct. 13	....	Oct. 20	Oct. 25.
1st Ambulance Company, 4th Field Hospital.	Oct. 14	....	Oct. 19	Oct. 24.
1st Field Artillery, Batteries A, B, C.	Oct. 19	....	Oct. 26	Battery B, Nov. 1. A, Nov. 4. C, Nov. 8.
Headquarters, Batteries D, E, F..............	Oct. 27	....	Nov. 3	Nov. 15.
7th Infantry..........	Nov. 22	....	Nov. 28	Dec. 2.
1st Battalion, Signal Corps.	Dec. 13	....	Dec. 20	Dec. 23.
Headquarters Division..	Dec. 14	....	Dec. 21	Dec. 23.
2nd Field Hospital.....	Dec. 14	....	Dec. 22	Dec. 27.
2nd Ambulance Company, 4th Field Hospital.	Dec. 14	....	Dec. 21	Dec. 27.
Quartermaster Corps...	Dec. 14	....	Dec. 21	Dec. 23.
Squadron A, Cavalry...	Dec. 15	....	Dec. 23	Dec. 28.
Machine Gun Troop....	Dec. 15	....	Dec. 23	Dec. 28.
Headquarters and 2d Battalion, 22nd Engineers.	Dec. 16	....	Dec. 24	Jan. 4, 1917.

The Third Ambulance Company and the Second Field Artillery were under orders to entrain at an early date.

The organizations left on the border on December 31st were the following: Twelfth Infantry, Twenty-third Infantry, Sixty-ninth Infantry, Third Field Artillery, the Third Field Hospital, the Headquarters and the Fourth Ambulance Company of the Fourth Field Hospital, the Supply Train, and the Field Bakery.

ARMORY INSTRUCTION

For those organizations which had not been received into the Federal service and for the others as they were mustered out, the resumption of regular armory instruction was directed by General Orders No. 34, October 11, 1916.

The number of required drills was set at forty-eight in accordance with the National Defense Act, and the conditions of attendance and payment for officers and men under that act set forth.

In General Orders No. 35, October 13, 1916, the conditions were set forth governing the discharge of enlisted men, their furlough to the National Guard Reserves and the credit to be given them for previous service.

In General Orders No. 38, October 27, 1916, instructions were issued for the reduction of all organizations to the maximum peace strength, and the retention of excess strength until by transfer to other organizations, furloughs to the reserve, authorized discharges, etc., the reduction was affected.

Aggregate Number

It is difficult to give an accurate statement of the total response of New York manhood to the President's call, since the shifting of numbers and of organizations, handling of recruits and rejections threw a great and for a time unmanageable burden on everybody concerned, on all the individuals and all the departments.

An approximation can, however, be made and an idea gained of the magnitude of the enrollment and equipment under difficulties.

In the first place the total strength of the organizations taken into the Federal service was at their respective dates of muster in, 690 officers, 16,657 enlisted men, 91 medical officers, 788 hospital corps men.

Recruits gathered by the depot units and sent to their parent organizations numbered 5,056 enlisted men. After the recruiting service was taken under Federal control 840 enlisted men were forwarded.

The organizations not accepted into the federal service were of the following strength: Staff officers, 30; Armored Motor Battery — 4 officers, 151 men; the Second Aero Company — 2 officers, 28 men; the First Infantry — 46 officers, 1,875 men, 7 medical officers, 24 hospital corps men; the Tenth Infantry — 46 officers, 1,721 men, 4 medical officers, 24 hospital corps men; the Forty-seventh Infantry — 46 officers, 1,412 men, 3 medical officers and 24 men.

The Fifteenth Infantry (colored) mustered into State service but not yet recognized by the War Department, showed a strength September 30, 1916, of 8 officers, 737 men, 1 medical officer, 2 hospital corps men.

On September 9, 1916, the Second Division composed of 27 depot units, showed a total strength of 200 officers and 2,598 enlisted men.

The Coast Defense troops were naturally not included in the call for border mobilization, but during the summer the 8th and 9th Coast Defense Commands carried out the tours of duty planned in G. O. No. 17. The 13th did not participate, G. O. 28 for its tour of duty being cancelled by G. O. 29 at the direction of the War Department on account of prevalence of poliomyelitis at the home station. The total strength of these three commands was 127 officers, 3,219 men, 5 medical officers, 47 hospital corps men.

As a part of the State's organized force, the Naval Militia which had an active summer, belongs in the list with 86 officers, 1,664 men, 12 medical officers and 20 hospital corps men.

The aggregate mobilization, therefore, combining the medical officers and men with the others, totalled 1,408 officers and 36,887 men.

It is interesting to add to this total the number of men who applied for enlistment and were rejected for disability; a total of 1,436 men in the accepted organizations and of 763 men in those not accepted for Federal service. Applicants rejected because of dependents were 108 men.

The numbers of those on the rolls who were relieved on account of physical disability, dependents or failure to take the new oath of enlistment, amount to 40 officers and 1,249 men.

A certain number of members of the National Guard were inevitably unable to respond to the President's call owing mainly to removal from the State, or in some cases from the United States. In the aggregate enrollment they made a total of 2 medical officers and 310 enlisted men, or less than one per cent.

Summing up all these figures we find that the State called forth through its organized militia, a grand total of 1,448 commissioned officers and 40,416 men. This number would have been far larger of course, as stated before, if there had been a greater peril or a more inspiring mission.

NAVAL MILITIA

Though not called to the federal service, the Naval Militia has been active, has performed its tours of duty afloat, has enjoyed an increase of numbers, and received very high commendations from the Navy Department.

The Military Law was amended May 15, 1916, in section 50, concerning the composition, strength and command of the Naval . Militia.

In conformity with General Orders No. 153 of the Navy Department standardizing the organization of the Naval Militia of the various states, General Orders No. 8, March 6, 1916, were issued to carry them into effect.

To complete the brigade formation of the Naval Militia forces of the State two line divisions, one signal division, one marine company, and two aeronautic sections have been organized and equipped since January 1, 1915. The Naval Militia Brigade was thereby conformed to the requirements of the Navy Department as to number of units but it was believed desirable to increase this force and three further divisions, one more marine company and a third aeronautic section were organized and equipped.

A bill was submitted to the Legislature December 18, 1916, authorizing the increase of the Naval Militia from 2,000 to not exceeding 4,500 officers and men.

Two flying boats were presented to the force; the first battalion receiving one as a gift from the Curtiss Aeroplane Company; the second battalion receiving one from a committee of patriotic citizens headed by Vincent Astor, Esq. This hydroaeroplane was tested the following day and flew 58 miles in 42 minutes. The third battalion is still in need of one.

On September 15th the U. S. S. *Luzon* was transferred from Illinois to Rochester, permitting the transfer of the U. S. S. *Sandoval* to Watertown, where there had been no vessel.

Early in the morning of Sunday, July 30, 1916, the first battalion received an urgent call from Ellis Island for a detail of officers and men to patrol and rescue property after the disastrous explosion of the munition plants on Black Tom's Island. This work was performed to the satisfaction of the Navy Department.

The full report of the Naval Militia is appended hereto.

THE FALLACY OF "PEACE STRENGTH"

There is probably no other principle of organization from which spring so many confusions as from the system of making a distinction between "peace strength" and "war strength." It is based on a theory that regiments are indefinitely elastic; that they may be managed like sponges, condensed to their minimum in dry times and expanded to double their size without difficulty by merely dipping them in water.

But regiments are not sponges. They are incapable of sudden expansion and contraction. They are more analogous to athletic organizations in which teamwork is vital to success. Base ball clubs are not organized in skeleton. They do not practice with diminished numbers. A football team does not organize and train six men for months, then on the morning of the contest call on five strangers ignorant of the rules and untrained in exertion to complete the eleven.

Yet that is exactly what the National Guard regiments are expected and required to do. A custom that would be considered ludicrous in sport is adopted for the desperate necessities of war.

The familiarity of officers with their men and their individual qualities, is of the utmost importance. Discipline is a habit acquired only by association. Team-work is impossible to strangers.

At the time of a sudden call to the field when the officers should be exercising their men and themselves in battle problems, they are confined to an endless grind of paper-work, of equipment and inventory, and the teaching of the rudimentary manuals to new recruits. New men thrown into the companies disrupt the squad formations which are the basis of efficiency. Old soldiers who know their tasks are hindered and exasperated by the association with ignorant newcomers. The previous training of the organization goes largely for naught, since the entire company is held back for the awkward squads.

Most of the criticism directed against the manner in which the National Guard performed its service, was due to this phase of Federal policy with its resultant introduction of the untrained, untried, undisciplined and unequipped war strength.

In the New York division it has been found that 80 per cent of all the delinquency in disciplinary cases arising during the service came from the war strength element attached upon the eve of departure. Sixty per cent of the hospital cases came from the war strength element.

It should be adopted as a basic principle of our military system, that organizations shall be maintained in time of peace at the strength they are to utilize in time of war.   No recruits should be sent forward or attached until they have been thoroughly trained and disciplined.   The policy was forced upon England by her experience in the present war, that at least six months' arduous training was required before recruits could be advanced to the firing line.   This country should not make the mistake of burdening regiments which have had none too much training at best, with a large percentage of absolutely green men.

Every effort was made in this State to prepare for the strain of war but it was impossible to complete a revolution in policy and practice in every detail before the President's call.   In view of the nature of the problem before the Government it was believed, and the result proved the wisdom of the belief, that it was of the utmost importance to transfer the entire organized militia of the nation to the southern border.

The object was rather to forestall war than to wage it.   The immediate necessity was for a patrol and garrison of important points along a frontier thousands of miles long.   The Guard was expected to release the Regular Army from this onerous duty so that it might be free for use as a weapon of offence.

The National Guard accomplished its mission and it should not be criticized for being unready for other tasks.   Those tasks loom upon its future, however, and every lesson of the mobilization should be applied in all wisdom.

APPROPRIATIONS

Of primary importance was the demonstration that a call to actual service ought not to cause an interruption of the work of the office or a dislocation of the mechanism.   It is for the emergency that the mechanism exists.   It should, therefore, be at all times in readiness for instant adjustment to a sudden increase of demands.

Like an electric plant it must be constantly able to take care of an enormous overload.

The organization of this department as planned will place it in a state of high efficiency and preparedness, if sufficient appropriation is made for its completion and its maintenance.

BOARDS OF EXAMINATION

According to the new system the State boards of examination are done away with entirely; their place being taken by boards appointed by the War Department and consisting of one regular army officer and two National Guard officers.

DECORATIONS AND PRIZES

The usual decorations and prizes for long and faithful service for individual efficiency in small arms firing, for competition firing with the rifle, and for secondary battery practice have been awarded this year.

SMALL ARMS PRACTICE

Several of the organizations completed their regular annual small arms practice at Peekskill before the President's call. Others were interrupted in that tour of duty by their removal to the border, where under many handicaps a certain amount of practice was received near Sharyland, McAllen, and later a more thorough training under well-emulated battle conditions at a range especially constructed at La Gloria ranch.

RECORDS OF BORDER SERVICE

It has been deemed advisable to prepare a volume containing the records of the New York State men called into the Federal service for border duty while those records are still complete and accessible. The compilations of similar records of previous Federal service have been greatly appreciated, but owing to long delay have been achieved with much difficulty and an inevitably large percentage of error. The volume of border service records now in preparation will therefore be unusually accurate and complete. It will be issued during the coming year.

PROPERTY DIVISION, STATE ARSENAL.

During the past year, the State Arsenal has been called upon to handle a very large quantity of property owing to the mobilization of troops for service upon the Mexican border. The force was augmented sufficiently to carry out this work promptly and efficiently.

On July 14, 1916, a very serious fire took place in the Arsenal destroying a considerable amount of property, necessitating the rental of a warehouse at 152 West 36th street, as the floors of the Arsenal were so weakened by the fire as to make it impossible to store any large quantity ·: property therein. Until extensive repairs are made, it will be impossible to use the Arsenal for storage of large quantities of material, but it is expected that during the coming years repairs will be undertaken so as to make this possible.

During the first six months of the year, cash sales of property to the amount of $16,568.39 were made, but on July 1, 1916, following instructions from the Federal Government cash sales were discontinued.

The amount of property handled during the year 1916, from Government and State sources, amounted to a total of about $1,000,000. The return of the troops from the Mexican border, followed by the condemnation of a large amount of property by the muster-out officers will make it necessary for us to provide for the equipment of a large number of men, and unless the Federal Government can supply such equipment, it will be necessary for the State to purchase same in order that the Guard may be fully equipped.

ORGANIZATION

National Guard. The organization of the several arms, corps and departments now conforms to the Tables of Organization prescribed by the War Department.

The organization of the Division is complete, the following new units having been formed during the year:

(a) Headquarters, supply and machine gun companies or troops for each regiment of infantry or cavalry and headquarters and supply companies for each regiment of field artillery.

(b) Two field hospitals.

(c) Three companies of coast artillery.

(d) One regiment of infantry.

(e) One regiment of field artillery (Formed by reorganizing 65th N. Y. Infantry).

(f) One regiment of engineers (22d Corps of Engineers reorganized to form a· regiment).

(g) One aero company.

(h) One field bakery.

(i) One supply train.

Naval Militia. The organization of the Naval Militia by enactment of Chapter 565, Laws of 1916, now conforms to that prescribed by the Navy Department, namely, a brigade of three battalions.

The 1st battalion consists of nine divisions, and one aeronautic section; the 2nd battalion of seven divisions, one marine company, and one aeronautic section; the 3rd battalion of eight divisions.

The equipment includes the U. S. S. *Granite State*, serving as an armory for the 1st Battalion, which has also the U. S. S. *Wasp*, the U. S. S. *Gloucester*, assigned to the 2nd battalion and stationed at Brooklyn; the U. S. S. *Hawk,* stationed at Buffalo; the U. S. S. *Sandoval* at Watertown, and the U. S. S. *Isla de Luzon* at Rochester; these three assigned to the 3rd battalion. The 1st battalion has two hydroaeroplanes, the 2nd battalion has three.

New Organizations. The following new organizations have been authorized during the year.

Aeronautic Section, 2nd Battalion, with station at Brooklyn, N. Y., March 9, 1916.

Marine Company, 2nd Battalion, with station at Brooklyn, N. Y., May 1, 1915.

Eighth Division, 3rd Battalion, with station at Niagara Falls, N. Y., May 4, 1916.

Ninth Division, 3rd Battalion, with station at Oswego, N. Y.. December 20, 1916.

APPENDICES

The report of the Commanding General, is transmitted herewith as Appendix A; the report of the Commodore, commanding Naval Militia as Appendix B; the report of the Division Surgeon as Appendix C; the report of Lieutenant-Colonel Wainwright on conditions of service at the border as Appendix D; the summary of the financial operations of the office as Appendix E; personnel tables as Appendix F.

Very respectfully,

LOUIS W. STOTESBURY,

The Adjutant-General.

APPENDIX "A"

Report of Major-General John F. O'Ryan, Commanding Division National Guard.

HEADQUARTERS DIVISION, NATIONAL GUARD

STATE OF NEW YORK

MUNICIPAL BUILDING

NEW YORK CITY, *December* 31, 1916

During the past year the most important incidents affecting the National Guard were the passage of the National Defense Act, which makes radical changes in the government, supply, administration and utilization of the National Guard, and its service on the Mexican Border, pursuant to the President's call of June 18, 1916. For purposes of convenience this report will be divided into three parts, Part I covering the mobilization pursuant to the President's call aforesaid, Part II covering the effect of the National Defense Act and of the Mexican Border Service upon the Guard, and Part III other matters affecting the Guard.

PART I

MOBILIZATION

On Sunday evening, June 18, 1916, the Division Commander, then on duty at the Infantry School of Application at Peekskill, N. Y., received a telephone message from His Excellency the Governor, to the effect that the President had called into the active service of the United States for the purpose mentioned in the call, the National Guard of the United States and the Organized Militia of the several States, and that the quota from the

State of New York was a tactical Division, the composition of which was specified in the call, although the particular regiments to constitute the composition of the division were not named in the call. The call by its terms covered the National Guard and the Organized Militia as separate and distinct forces, for reasons that appear in Part II of this report and in order to insure the inclusion of all officers and men, no matter in which force they might technically be serving at the time of the call.

The order of the Governor was later confirmed by printed order, copy of which is attached hereto and marked Exhibit "A." Telegraphic and telephonic orders were immediately transmitted to such staff officers of the Division as were not on duty at Peekskill at that time, to report for duty at once. A Special Order was issued relieving from further duty student officers at the School of Application, and directing them to return at once to their commands. Telegrams were prepared and sent to all Commanding Officers the following morning, directing them to assemble their commands at 8.00 p. m., June 19th, in field service uniform and equipment, to cancel all leaves, to recruit to war strength, and to organize depot units. Copy of this telegram is attached hereto and marked Exhibit " B." Attached hereto is copy of Division Order confirming telegraphic orders, directing the mobilization of the troops of the Guard, less the Coast Artillery Corps. This order is marked Exhibit " C."

The Legislature of the State of New York during the preceding winter had appropriated $500,000 for field exercises and training of the entire National Guard during the summer of 1916, and plans had been perfected to provide such field training and instruction at Green Haven, Dutchess county New York, beginning July 9th. At the time of the President's call there was on duty at Green Haven a detachment of engineers engaged in the work of installing a water supply, mapping the terrain and doing other work incidental to the preparation of the ground for the use contemplated. It was in view of the proposed field exercises that the State order to mobilize included not only the number of units necessary to compose a tactical Division, but all the remaining units of the Guard.

Pursuant to the order to mobilize there were assembled at the home stations of organizations at 8.00 p. m., on June 19th, within less than twenty-four hours of the first telephone call, ready for service, clothed, armed and equipped, with all that it was the duty of the State authorities to provide, 15,289 officers and men. The strength, in detail, of this force is shown in the following table.

Organization.	Officers.	Men.
Headquarters, Division	20	0
Headquarters, First Brigade	9	2
Headquarters, Second Brigade	6	2
Headquarters, Third Brigade	9	2
Headquarters, Fourth Brigade	10	2
Quartermaster Corps	13	7
First Battalion, Signal Corps	9	149
Twenty-second Engineers	30	562
First Cavalry	55	904
Squadron A	13	206
Machine Gun Troop, Cavalry	2	63
First Field Artillery	35	755
Second Field Artillery	38	627
First Armored Motor Battery	4	73
First Infantry	53	951
Second Infantry	55	1197
Third Infantry	51	986
Seventh Infantry	52	869
Tenth Infantry	54	891
Twelfth Infantry	37	673
Fourteenth Infantry	43	646
Twenty-third Infantry	39	661
Forty-seventh Infantry	47	560
Sixty-fifth Infantry (later reorganized as Third Field Art.).	39	646
Sixty-ninth Infantry	45	872
Seventy-first Infantry	47	884
Seventy-fourth Infantry	45	649
First Field Hospital	5	62
Second Field Hospital	3	56
Third Field Hospital	1	67
First Ambulance Company	4	79
Second Ambulance Company	4	63
Third Ambulance Company	4	76
Fourth Ambulance Company	2	72
Field Bakery	1	6
Total	884	14,405
Grand total		15,289

In addition to this the strength of the Coast Artillery Corps, not included in the call, aggregated 3,398 officers and men.

At the time of the President's call, the National Guard of this State was administered as a Territorial Division, included within which there were all the units necessary for the composition of a Tactical Division. About this time the War Department had concluded, in view of the teachings of experience abroad, to increase the Field Artillery of the Tactical Division from two regiments to three regiments, the additional regiment to be composed of batteries armed with guns heavier in type than the three-inch, up to that time exclusively used by the divisional artillery. On June 19th, therefore, on recommendation of the Division Commander, the Adjutant-General wired the War Department, requesting that the Sixty-fifth Infantry, stationed in Buffalo, a regiment not a part of the Divisional infantry, be reorganized as the Third Field Artillery Regiment of the Division, so that the Divisional artillery might consist of a brigade of three complete regiments. A copy of this telegram is attached hereto and marked Exhibit "D." This recommendation was approved June 28, 1916.

On June 20th orders were issued for a Detachment of the Signal Battalion, two Battalions of Engineers and the Sixty-ninth Infantry, to move by rail to the mobilization camp at Green Haven, to aid in the work of preparing the camp for immediate occupation. This site, consisting of 825 acres, had been secured from another department of the State government in the spring, and the President's call necessitated additional work to advance the time from the date of its contemplated occupation for field training, namely on July 9th, to the earliest practicable date after the call. The work to be done involved the clearing of land, the sinking of wells for water, the installation of a water system for a large command, the construction of spurs, switches and railroad sidings, connecting with the main railroad line, the erection of storehouses, the construction of incinerators, shower baths, mess shacks and latrines.

The following day, June 21st, the organizations named arrived at the mobilization camp, the Telephone Detachment consisting of one officer and 13 men, the Engineers consisting of 29 officers and 689 enlisted men, and the Sixty-ninth Infantry consisting of 38 officers and 860 enlisted men. This detachment of troops made camp promptly during a spell of wet weather, and began the routine of camp and the performance of the labor incidental to their mission. These troops and all others assembled within this short space of a few hours after the President's call, were ready for duty anywhere. During the previous three years they had been immunized against typhoid fever by the administration of typhoid prophylaxis. The organizations on the date of assembly did not possess more than the normal percentage of recruits. The strength of the commands exceeded the average strength of similar Regular Army units.

A proper comprehension of the mobilization of the National Guard cannot be had without an undertanding of the features affecting this phase of the mobilization and the incidents immediately following it. Much matter has been circulated in the public press concerning the shortcomings of the mobilization and what is referred to as the " National Guard System," whatever that may be. In general these criticisms have emphasized the fact that the National Guard was not at war strength or promptly brought to war strength, and that many delays occurred between the date of the call and the arrival of National Guard units on the border.

In reference to the first point, the so-called war strength of organizations had been a paper ideal never attained in our military history, either by Regulars, Volunteers, Organized Militia or National Guard, until the recent mobilization, when it was attained by most of the units of the New York Division in the face of much matter circulated in the press tending to injure recruiting. There was further no authority from the Federal Government to recruit organizations to war strength prior to the call. In another part of this report there appears a table, Exhibit " E," showing the strength by units of the organizations of the New York Division during the period of the Mexican Border Service. The records will show that the United States never had in its military service throughout the history of the country, a tactical unit of the strength of the New York Division during the period of the Mexican service. During that service the New York Division was officially known as the Sixth Division, U. S. Army.

As to the other criticisms affecting the alleged delays in forwarding the troops after the assembly mentioned above, these delays, where they occurred, are to be attributed to the system prescribed by the War Department and by the manner in which the system was administered, and not to any regulations or methods of the National Guard. An appreciation of this may be had from the following:

As stated above, the tactical division, ordered out on June 19th, was clothed, armed, equipped, immunized against typhoid, and ready to move anywhere, pursuant to the President's call, the following day. See Table No. 17, p. 261, Report of the Acting Chief of Militia Bureau, 1916. The first circumstance to consider in relation to what followed, is that the emergency which called forth the troops was not considered by the Federal Government sufficient to warrant the subordination of commercial railroad transportation to the use by the War Department of the railroads for the immediate transportation of troops as fast as they could be entrained for the Mexican border. Apparently it was determined to transport the troops by rail with such dispatch as was possible, without interference with the normal railroad traffic. This decision was undoubtedly justified, and it explains in lar measure the period of time involved in transporting troops from various parts of the country to the Mexican Border.

The next consideration relates to the system imposed by the War Department Regulations upon the National Guard when it is to be utilized in the active Federal service. As stated above, the President's call included the organized militia as well as the National Guard, because at the time of the call, while the National Defense Act creating the National Guard of the United States had become a law, no regulations to make the Act effective had been adopted and published, and as a matter of fact there were not at the time of the President's call, any troops constituting the National Guard of the United States. The only military force other than the Regular Army was the Organized Militia of the several States, known variously as National Guard of New York, the Massachusetts Volunteer Infantry, and by such other names as were in force in the several States. The War Department system referred to did not in effect consider the Organized Militia as a Federal force to be used promptly upon being called into the service by Presidential proclamation, but the regulations governing its use were such as might appropriately apply to a volunteer force to be created by the muster into the Federal service of those citizens who volunteered. True, the regulations contemplate the physical examination of each and every officer and man, either before or immediately following what was termed a " muster-in " to the Federal service. Here it is to be noted that no "muster-in" of officers or enlisted men of the National Guard of the States was required by law for the reasons that are herein set forth in detail.

The magnitude of the task connected with physical examinations was one that should have presented itself to those responsible for the system. It is apparent that a vast amount of time would necessarily be consumed by medical examining officers in making proper physical examinations, or on the other hand that under the stress of emergency the examinations would be hasty and therefore fail in their purpose. It is obvious that to make an effective physical inspection of a man, involving test of the eyesight, of the hearing, an examination of the teeth and throat, of the heart and lungs, of the fingers, toes and feet, and to inspect for hernia and other disqualifying disabilities, would involve at least ten minutes of time, including the interval between the termination of the examination of one man and the commencement of the examination of the next, and this assuming also that the Medical Officer is assisted by several efficient non-commissioned officers who will do all the clerical work, make the measurements of height, record weights, and keep the flow of men appearing stripped before the Medical Examiner without delays. Examinations so conducted are made at the rate of six an hour. The work is exacting, but under stress of emergency the Medical Examiner might be required to work efficiently ten hours in each twenty-four. In addition to this he would be required to devote other time to making his daily reports.

He would therefore examine at the rate of sixty men per day of ten examining hours. On this basis he would complete the examination of a regiment of 1,200 men in twenty working days.

The War Department had on duty with this Division at the time of the mobilization order one Regular Medical Officer, Major Sanford H. Wadhams. At the rate mentioned Major Wadhams would have examined the strength of this Division in nearly a year's time.

Obviously, to avoid this result, the number of medical examining officers should be increased, or the time devoted to each individual examination cut down. Assuming that the time of examination were limited to but five minutes per man, and enough medical officers supplied so that there might be one to each regiment the time involved in making the examinations, assuming that everything moved without a hitch, would still be ten days.

Any intelligent consideration given this subject will clearly indicate that physical examinations should have been supervised and made uniform throughout the country by the Federal Government in time of peace, so that nothing might remain to be done on the occasion of a call for active duty except the physical inspection of the personnel by each company commander at the time of the call for the purpose of determining with the aid of a regimental medical officer what men, if any, should be left behind temporarily or permanently by reason of special circumstances such as injury or illness suffered at the time. Such inspections are made in all armies before troops move for active service.

The system criticized, or something approximating it, was in a measure unavoidable under the Federal law as it existed prior to the passage of the National Defense Act, for there was no authority for the War Department under the old law to supervise the physical examination of officers and men in the Organized Militia.

In this State the physical requirements for service were those prescribed for enlistment in the Regular Army, and here it should be noted that these standards of the Regular Army are not permanent. They vary from time to time, and are dependent upon what might be termed " the recruit market ". In periods when economic conditions throughout the country are unsatisfactory there are many applicants for enlistments in the Regular Army and the physical standards are high. When there is industrial prosperity the standards are lower, in order to increase the number enlisted.

Under the new National Defense Act the physical requirements for enlistment in the National Guard of the United States are fixed by the War Department, and doubtless when regulations are published to make the provisions of the Act effective physical examinations will be supervised in such manner that the readiness of the National Guard for active field service will be identical with that of the Regular Army so far as the existence or non-existence of physical defects in the personnel is concerned. There should be no such interruption of other work for the conduct of physical examinations, as was witnessed immediately following the mobilization of the troops on this occasion.

To Major Wadhams of the Medical Corps of the Army, who was charged with making the physical examinations of the personnel of this Division, were finally assigned as assistants, Major Albert E. Truby and Captain W. Cole Davis, M. C., U. S. A., and Major Edward R. Maloney, Captain Robert B. Kennedy and Captain John S. Maeder, M. C., N. G., N. Y. These officers worked with untiring zeal and fidelity, frequently until they were forced to suspend their work through complete physical exhaustion. They were victims of an impossible system.

All the incongruities and inefficiency of system that transpired were fully understood and predicted by National Guard officers charged with the efficiency of the Guard and by the Regular Officers regularly on duty with the Division preceding the call. The system imposed and the results flowing from it were not chargeable to the National Guard. On more than one occasion the Division Commander endeavored to have such physical examinations as the War Department desired made by its Medical Officers during the winter and spring preceding the call. Had this plan been carried out the entire matter of physical examinations could have been disposed of in advance of the call in a systematic, thorough and careful manner.

The next feature which would have delayed the utilization of troops had the transportation facilities been available to move them at dates earlier than those fixed was the requirement that all military property to be taken into the active service of the United States should be inventoried, inspected and receipted for, in pursuance of a transaction apparently based upon the theory that the property was property of the State to be loaned to the United States for the use of the troops while in the service of the latter, and later to be accounted for to the State by the United States.

So far as can be learned the regulations governing the matter (and they were all Federal regulations) were survivals of the old

Militia days when the Militia was largely equipped by the States, and hence held much property over which the United States had no control and exercised no ownership unless the same could be brought about by a formal transfer of the property from the States to the United States. To accomplish this an inventory in quadruplicate, carefully setting forth every item of military property, was made the basis for transfer. This requirement imposed an apparently needless amount of paper work upon regimental supply officers and company officers, which was complicated by endless inquiry, discussion and rulings as to the methods involved and the manner of describing various articles. The clerical work alone, assuming the perfection of all other details, would condemn the system.

As a matter of fact the clothing, arms, equipment, equipage and material of the Guard at the time of the President's call, and for some years prior thereto, were all the property of the United States, and no transfer of the same was needed to establish ownership and control.

The system imposed was one that had no relation to the situation as it existed. It served only to exasperate all concerned. A national emergency requiring the use of troops for military purposes should be devoid of such incidents as resulted from the imposition of this system. Property supply and accountability in the National Guard should be conducted by the Federal Government in peace as well as in war by the same methods and pursuant to the same system that exists in the Regular Army. This is so obvious as to need no supporting argument.

The next cause for criticism relates to the system which governed the so-called "muster-in" of organizations.

To understand this process it is necessary to note that in former wars, when volunteers were largely depended upon, it was necessary to fix by documentary evidence the date on which the personnel of a volunteer company or other unit entered the service of the United States. This documentary evidence took the form of what was called a muster-in roll, which contained the names, grades and other desirable data affecting the personnel of the unit, and at the time of the muster-in there was present an officer of the Army of the United States who called the roll to ascertain whether all the men whose names appeared thereon were actually present, after which they raised their right hands and repeated after the mustering officer the oath of enlistment, whereupon, having already signed the muster roll, they were sworn in. At the end of the muster roll there was a form of certificate signed by the muster officer that these requisites had been followed.

The National Defense Act became a law June 8, 1916, and this Act created a new force which the Organized Militia could join, the officers by taking the oath of office, and the enlisted men by taking the oath of enlistment prescribed in the Act.

The forms of these oaths are attached hereto and marked Exhibit " F." They establish the status of Federal soldier. Those who take that oath enter the service of the United States from the date of such contract.

The War Department apparently failed to provide the necessary forms prescribed by this Act between the date when the Act took effect, June 8th, and the date of the President's call, June 18th, and for some time thereafter.

The State, however, caused to be printed a sufficient number of such forms for the use of the troops of this Division, and these forms were promptly distributed to our organizations. With practical unanimity the officers and enlisted men of the Division subscribed to the new oath and became soldiers of the National Guard of the United States.

Attached hereto is a table showing the number of men by organizations who joined the new force and those who exercised the option of declining to do so. This table is marked Exhibit " G."

It would seem that the personnel of the New York Division having become soldiers of the United States by enlisting in the National Guard of the United States did not require to be " mustered in ", as if they were civilian volunteers. This was finally decided by the War Department, the Adjutant-General of the Army telegraphing that as to organizations which qualified as National Guard under the provisions of the National Defense Act no muster in was necessary. This information was received by telegram on July 24th, six days after the President's call. In the meantime muster-in rolls had been prepared by all organizations pursuant to directions of United States Mustering Officers.

It would be difficult to adequately portray the unnecessary effort, annoyance, amount of clerical work and supervisory labor connected with the preparation of these " muster-in " rolls.

There were approximately seven officers of the Regular Army detailed· for duty as mustering officers with the New York Division. Most of them were unfamiliar with the duties assigned them. These duties were prescribed by Army Regulations, Organized Militia Regulations, Mustering Regulations, and were varied from time to time during the mobilization period as decisions were made or conclusions arrived at by officers of the War Department. All the regulations referred to constituted a considerable amount of reading matter, to understand which would require careful study by any officer expected to execute their provisions.

A great amount of administrative machinery had been built up and apparently existed as necessary in relation to the National Guard and the Organized Militia, although the system appears to have been built wholly upon the peculiar conditions affecting the induction of volunteers into the service of the United States as soldiers.

This complicated system was not prescribed by the National Guard authorities but was imposed upon the National Guard by the War Department. The object sought to be attained by the so-called muster is to fix in documentary way the status of each individual officer and man of the unit in the military service, and to determine authoritatively the date when under such status he begins to receive the full pay of his grade. Some record is also necessary to fix definitely the date when Federal liability for possible pension occurs.

With these considerations in mind it must be apparent that the only paper necessary is the last muster roll of the unit, as all subsequent changes in the composition of the company, with all necessary data, will appear on the following bi-monthly muster roll. This can readily be prescribed because the National Guard as a military force is in existence as fully and to the same extent between periods of active operations as it is during such active operations. In this respect it differs from a volunteer force which comes into being after the call for troops and necessarily must have an initial or muster-in roll.

The military conservatism connected with the ancient practice of mustering may be indicated by the fact that until recent years the making of muster rolls on the typewriter was prohibited and the use of ditto marks under the word "Private" was also prohibited. In order that the muster rolls might adequately embarrass the clerical force engaged in their preparation it was the custom to require their several copies to be made in long hand and to write out the word "Private" after the name of each private soldier of the command in all the copies of the roll.

Doubtless under regulations to make the National Defense Act effective the National Guard will no longer be regarded as a volunteer force requiring the preparation of "muster-in" rolls at a time of national emergency, but will be administered in this regard as are organizations of the Regular Army.

The next cause for delay, inconvenience and confusion relates to the matter of the supply of military property to clothe, arm and equip the men necessary to raise regiments from peace strength to war strength. Under the system prescribed by the War Department the National Guard troops were notified that in the event of a call no requisitions for such property should be made by organization commanders, but that the same would be shipped direct from the Federal Supply Depot to the State mobilization camp.

After a study of the proposed system I mentioned as far back as 1914 in an official report that "it would be difficult for the most cunning mind to devise a scheme better calculated to create confusion, indecision and disorganization at a time of National stress." Attached hereto and marked Exhibit "H" are copies of recommendations and extracts from correspondence on this subject.

The plan recommended by the National Guard of this State was approved by Major-General Leonard Wood, Commanding the Eastern Department, and was later approved by Major-General A. L. Mills, Chief, Division of Militia Affairs, but the same was never adopted by the War Department, with the result that the military property for this Division would have been shipped to the mobilization camp at Green Haven after the President's call, although in view of the emergency it had been determined to send some organizations directly from their armories to the Mexican border. Accordingly, by direction of Major-General Wood, Commanding the Eastern Department, the military property necessary for the organizations to move direct was diverted and sent to the armories of such organizations.

It has been claimed that this action which constituted a departure from the plan of the War Department caused confusion and embarrassment to the mustering officers who were also charged with certain duties in relation to this property. On the other hand if this initiative had not been taken we should have had the spectacle of regiments ready in all respects to entrain for the border except for the possession of war strength property, required first to move to the mobilization camp for the purpose of receiving, fitting, issuing and marking such property under conditions incomparably inferior to the accommodations afforded by the modern armory, and then leaving such camp for the border.

One of the redeeming features of the mobilization as conducted under the system which then obtained was the readiness of the Commanding General of the Eastern Department to disregard the system when its application would have led to results entirely out of keeping with the mission in hand. And here it should be noted that the Department Commander or some other representative of the War Department was the only authority who could modify the system, for it was a Federal system.

The reports of some civilian bodies which have assumed to criticize the mobilization have referred to inconsistencies of dual control and referred vaguely to the relation of Federal and State authority. There was no dual control in relation to the mobilization. Under the law not only the National Guard of the United States under the new act but the Organized Militia under the old law were automatically in the Federal service from the date of the President's call, and were solely under the orders of the War Department. The regulations governing the issue of property, like all other regulations governing the subject of mobilization, were Federal regulations administered by Federal officers throughout.

The next embarrassment affecting the mobilization was lack of Federal forms to comply with Army Regulations governing the examination and enlistment of recruits, obtaining their finger prints, giving typhoid prophylaxis and vaccination, and furnishing the many reports and papers required to be made in the course of military administration.

Although these and other forms were essential for orderly administration many of them were not only not supplied at the time of mobilization, but some were not furnished until after the Division had been in service on the border for several months.

This shortcoming was not one that could have been avoided by the National Guard. Our officers were instructed pursuant to directions from the Commanding General, Eastern Department, to use the most appropriate State form available, indorsing thereon the fact that the prescribed forms had not been furnished. The practice carried on pursuant to these directions was necessarily continued for months after the President's call.

Under the new National Defense Act it is probable that the regulations to be framed will prescribe the use of Regular Army forms in the administration of the Guard. If so there will be no likelihood in the future of difficulty in this connection for the reason that such forms will be constantly on hand in all organizations and furthermore the officers will be familiar with their use.

The regulations in force at the time of the President's call, governing the mobilization of the National Guard, provided that mounted organizations would receive their animals from the War Department. Prior to the date of the President's call the quartermaster of the New York Division had made a contract for the hire of 2,500 animals for the use of mounted organizations of the Division during the period of field training planned for the month of July, and in anticipation of a possible call for service on the border we secured a provision in the contract whereby the option was given the State to purchase any or all of the animals at an agreed price.

After the President's call the option contained in this contract was offered to and accepted by the War Department. A board of army officers was appointed by the Commanding General, Eastern Department, to inspect animals offered by the contractor and to make purchase under the option referred to.

3

All the mounted organizations of the New York Division owned a nucleus of animals, and many of these were promptly purchased by the Federal Government for the use of such organizations during the period of active Federal service. It thus transpired that our mounted organizations moved to the border with a substantial number of animals.

Some of the animals purchased were unsuited for the service. Some of these died in transit, others were condemned after arrival on the border, and some succumbed from the extreme heat prevalent in that section during the month of July. It is doubted, however, whether ground for criticism exists in respect to the manner in which the animals were supplied the New York troops during the period of the mobilization.

No Government maintains in its military service in time of peace the full complement of animals needed in time of war. . In every army the call to the colors is the signal for a large increase in the number of animals maintained. Unlike motor transportation, horses and mules are as costly to maintain in idleness as they are in activity, and under any system of mobilization there will always be large numbers of animals to be hurriedly obtained, and these animals will have to be gathered, inspected, hoof marked, branded, transported and issued to the units needing them under conditions of stress, which will make it difficult if not impossible to limit the issue of animals to those fitted in all respects for the service they are expected to perform. The New York Division, as stated, went to the border with a substantial number of animals, approximately 3,377 in number, so the command was self-maintaining for camp purposes upon reaching the border.

Reference to the subject of mobilization would not be complete without some mention of the so-called dual control of the National Guard. It has been made to appear in defense of the responsibilities for the shortcomings of the mobilization that in some way unexplained they were the result for the most part of dual control by the Federal Government and the State concerning the mobilization, which resulted in friction and ineffectiveness.

There was, to repeat, no dual control, nor could there be under the law. On the date of the President's call the National Guard of the United States and the Organized Militia as well were automatically in the active Federal service, and subject only to the orders of the Federal Government.

This statement is based upon the decisions of the Federal courts and upon the orders and regulations of the War Department, and was at the time thoroughly understood by all responsible officers in the military service. The supreme and complete authority of the Federal Government was not questioned, and was well understood by the State authorities. The mobilization of this Division was not embarrassed in any manner by State officers.

The entrainment of troops for the border was in charge of the Quartermaster of the Eastern Department. There was assigned to assist him in the work of arranging details affecting the movement of organizations of this division the Assistant Quartermaster of the Division, Captain James T. Loree, Q. M. C. The work performed by Captain Loree is worthy of special mention. By reason of his railroad experience, this officer, being the General Manager of the Delaware & Hudson Railroad Company, had intimate knowledge of all details affecting the subject, and this combined with his military training and exceptional capacity made him an asset of inestimable value in all that pertained to the troop movement. Attached hereto is a table, Exhibit " I," indicating the dates of entrainment of units of the Division for the Mexican border and arrival thereat. These movements were made pursuant to orders of the Commanding General, Eastern Department.

Relying upon our experience in this mobilization I am of the opinion that in the future mobilization should be governed by regulations quite different from those in force in June, 1916. These regulations in my opinion should be based upon the following principles:

1. That no physical examinations of the personnel as it exists on the date of call need be made, except such as are necessary to determine the fitness of individuals reported by company commanders to be unfit at the time for active field service, either by

reason of accident or illness. That to make this rule sound the physical examination of all recruits during times of peace be checked up and supervised by the War Department.

2. That no "muster-in" is necessary. That in place of "muster-in," a simple regulation provide that for the purpose of fixing definitely the status of each man in each unit on the date of the call to active service, each company commander be required to prepare a muster roll similar in form to the bi-monthly muster roll, such roll to show the condition of his company on the date of the call. All subsequent changes in personnel of the company will necessarily be indicated on the next bi-monthly muster roll. The muster roll required to be prepared might be officially designated "Initial muster roll, Mexican Border Service," substituting in the place of Mexican Border Service the designation of the particular occasion which calls for the use of troops. Such rolls could readily be made up by the first Sergeants of Companies, supervised by Company Commanders, and the necessary number of copies forwarded as might be prescribed by regulations.

3. Recruits necessary to bring organizations to war strength should be clothed, armed and equipped in the armories of the organizations which they are to join, and then sent to the mobilization camp for training, whether the organization is sent there or not.

4. Property necessary to fully clothe, arm and equip recruits should be kept in a Federal Supply Depot maintained on the basis of one for each tactical Division. From the stores in such depot there should be withdrawn therefrom and stored in each armory the arms and equipment necessary to arm and equip the difference between peace and war strength of the organization. In addition to this property there should also be maintained in the armory Federal storeroom such clothing as is necessary for the recruits to have in order to be moved from the armory to the mobilization camp in satisfactory manner. This would make unnecessary the maintenance in the armory storeroom of underclothing or any uniforms except what is essential for the recruit to have in the first instance. To keep clothing and equipment from becoming obsolete or shopworn, current requisitions should

be filled from property on hand, the latter to be replaced from the Division Supply Depot which in turn should draw upon the proper Supply Department.

5. The National Guard during time of peace should be administered in the same manner as is the Regular Army. For this purpose the necessary forms should be supplied by the Federal Government. A sufficient quantity of these forms should be on hand in the armory of each organization to ensure opportunity for proper administration after the call.

PART II

THE EFFECT OF THE NATIONAL DEFENSE ACT, AND OF THE MEXICAN BORDER SERVICE UPON THE NATIONAL GUARD

Undoubtedly the provisions of the National Defense Act affecting the National Guard constitute an important and even radical step toward greater Federal control, national uniformity and high standards of military efficiency.

The first consideration affecting the efficiency of a military force is the manner of its organization. Military efficiency requires that a military force shall be organized in accordance with certain principles. The first of these is that there must be uniformity of obligation of those in each class constituting the force. Thus the obligation of the officers should be based upon a uniform oath of office, and the obligations of the enlisted men should be based upon a uniform oath of enlistment. In similar manner infantry units should be uniformly organized and the same comment applies to units of the other arms of the service.

Prior to the passage of the National Defense Act the Organized Militia of the several States did not constitute a national force which met even this fundamental requirement of military organization. The States fixed the nature of the officer's oath and his tenure of office. In some States officers were commissioned for short periods, subject to re-election, while in others they were commissioned for life subject to retirement for age and to removal pursuant to sentence of court-martial in accordance with the rule in the Regular Army. Contracts of enlistment varied in the different States. In some States officers were required to swear allegiance to the United States, while in others they were not.

In some States the obligation of the enlisted men differed from similar obligations in other States. Even the period of enlistment varied materially.

The National Defense Act has changed all this. Under Section 73 of the Act, officers upon being commissioned are required to take and subscribe the oath set forth in Exhibit " F," while enlisted men are required by the provision of Section 70 to take and subscibe the form of oath set forth in the same Exhibit.

It will therefore be seen that by virtue of these two sections of the Act alone the fundamental shortcomings in relation to the obligations of officers and men which existed prior to the passage of the Act had been eliminated by prescribing a uniform obligation. Not only this, but these two sections by their terms constitute of the officers and men so commissioned and enlisted a force having a Federal status and designated the National Guard of the United States.

Another principle governing the organization of a military force is that the officers and enlisted men composing it should meet prescribed standards of qualification. Prior to the passage of the National Defense Act there were as many standards for qualifying officers for appointment and promotion as there were States, and similar comment applies to the methods affecting the physical qualifications of enlisted men.

Under the new Act all officers, although technically appointed by the Governors of the several states, are required to be appointed, under the provisions of Section 74 of the Act, from among those constituting one of the five following classes of citizens:

(a) Officers and enlisted men of the National Guard.

(b) Officers on the reserve or unassigned list of the National Guard.

(c) Officers, active or retired, and former officers of the United States Army, Navy and Marine Corps.

(d) Graduates of the United States Military and Naval Academies, and graduates of schools, colleges and universities where military science is taught under the supervision of an officer of the Regular Army.

(e) For technical branches and staff, corps and departments such other civilians as may be especially qualified for duty therein.

The effect of this provision is to limit the appointment of officers to those classes qualified at least as to fundamental education and training.

A further limitation is provided in the following section of the Act which prescribes that appointments of officers shall not be made unless the candidates have successfully passed such tests as to physical, moral and professional fitness as the President may prescribe, and that such qualifications shall be determined by a board of three commissioned officers appointed by the Secretary of War. Prior to the enactment of these sections the qualifications for officers depended upon the methods and procedure which obtained in each State and these varied in effectiveness from high standards to very low standards.

Prior to the passage of the National Defense Act there was no uniform method throughout the Organized Militia of the several States to secure the elimination of officers whose record had demonstrated their unfitness. The new act provides for a uniform system of eliminating the unfit.

Prior to the passage of the National Defense Act it was within the power of the Governors or of the Legislatures of the several States to disband the whole or any portion of the Organized Militia of that State without reference to the rights and vested interests of the Federal Government, because Congress had never placed any limitation upon such acts under its constitutional power to organize the Militia. The National Defense Act by Section 68 prohibits the disbandment or reduction by the States, without the consent of the President, of any National Guard organization within the State.

One of the vital factors entering into the efficient organization of a military force is the character and procedure of its system to punish offenders against the discipline of the force. Prior to the passage of the National Defense Act this important detail of military organization was completely left to the States to provide for. Systems of military jurisprudence were organized pursuant to the laws of the States, and these varied greatly in principle and in detail. Under the National Defense Act the number and character of the courts for the maintenance of discipline, and the procedure to make such courts effective, are prescribed in detail.

All of these vital matters affecting the organization of the National Guard have been prescribed by Congress in the uniform manner referred to, and under the powers granted to the Congress by the Federal Constitution to organize the Militia. Congress in other words has the same power to provide for the organization of the Militia as it has to provide for the organization of the Regular Army. Accordingly it would appear that the power so completely exercised by Congress in the matter of organization under the provisions of this Act is a power that cannot be questioned. The Act further provides for compensating officers and men for attendance at prescribed drills and provides appropriations for furnishing the National Guard with clothing, arms and equipment.

From the foregoing it will be observed that the National Defense Act is far-reaching in its application to the National Guard, and that during the next few years as a result of the recognition and application of the fundamental principles of military organization referred to there should be a great increase in the efficiency of the force from a national point of view.

It is true that the National Defense Act falls short of accomplishing all in relation to the National Guard that military training and experience indicate as necessary to make of the force an efficient national army. But the criticism, based upon what the National Defense Act has not accomplished have obscured the great importance and value of the things it has made practicable of accomplishment.

Nevertheless it is believed generally among students of military organization that dual control of a military force, even in time of peace, is not satisfactory, and that military forces subject to such dual jurisdiction must necessarily suffer in efficiency. Responsibility for supply, discipline and training must be fixed, definite and certain. I share these views.

Accordingly it is believed to be for the best interests of the United States, of the States and of the National Guard that responsibility for everything relating to the efficiency of the force should be vested in the Federal Government in peace as well as in war, and that provision should be made in the Federal law bringing this about for the use by the States of the troops stationed within their confines for the suppression of insurrection, in return for which right the States shall lease to the Federal Government for nominal consideration for the use of Guard organizations the rifle ranges, camp grounds, armories, supply depots, barracks and stables now maintained by the States.

What the States need is the *use* of the Guard, not the right to control it. Hand in hand, however, with the grants to the Federal Government should necessarily go proper provision for representation of the Guard in the War Department at Washington, in order that its rights, interests, traditions and efficiency may be conserved by those who know the conditions affecting it, and who are primarily interested in its development.

PART III

Other Matters Affecting the Guard

The most important service rendered by the Division during the past year was the Mexican border service.

Exhibit " I " shows the organizations which constituted the Division, the date of departure for the Mexican border, the date of arrival at the border, and the date of returning to home station therefrom.

Upon arrival at the border the commands were stationed as follows:

Organization	Station	Commander
Headquarters, Division	McAllen	Major-General John F. O'Ryan.
Signal Battalion	McAllen	Major William L. Hallahan.
Engineers	McAllen	Lt.-Col. William S. Conrow.
st Cavalry	McAllen	Colonel Charles I. DeBevoise.
Squadron A Cavalry	McAllen	Major William R. Wright.
Machine Gun Troop, Cavalry	McAllen	Captain Henry Sheldon.
Field Artillery Brigade	McAllen	Brig.-General William S. McNair.
1st Field Artillery.		
2nd Field Artillery.		
3rd Field Artillery.		
1st Field Hospital	McAllen	Major John F. Dunseith.
2nd Field Hospital	McAllen	Major Louis H. Ga us.
3rd Field Hospital	McAllen	Major Arthur W. Slee.
4th Field Hospital	McAllen	Major Frank Harnden.
1st Ambulance Company	Mission	Captain Frank W. Sears.
2nd Ambulance Company	Pharr	Captain Charles O. Boswell.
3rd Ambulance Company	McAllen	Captain Leander H. Shearer.
4th Ambulance Company	McAllen	Captain Jefferson B. Latta.
1st Infantry Brigade	Mission	Brig.-Genl. James W. Lester.
2nd Infantry.		
14th Infantry.		
69th Infantry.		

Organization	Station	Commander
2nd Infantry Brigade...........	McAllen......	Brig.-Genl. George R. Dyer.
7th Infantry.		
12th Infantry.		
71st Infantry.		
3rd Infantry Brigade...........	Pharr........	Brig.-Genl. William Wilson.
3rd Infantry.		
23rd Infantry.		
74th Infantry.		
3rd Tennessee Infantry.		
Supply Train..................	McAllen......	Major T. Harry Shanton.
Bakery Company..............	McAllen......	Captain Jesse A. Millard.

Under date of July 11, 1916, a Military Police was established as provided for in G. O. No. 2, attached hereto and marked Exhibit " J."

The usual sanitary orders were prescribed and enforced.

A General Order, known as G. O. 7, was issued, prohibiting officers and enlisted men of the Division using alcoholic drink in any form during their service on the border and entering houses of prostitution or places where liquor was sold. This order was lived up to in really remarkable manner by the 19,000 officers and men constituting the New York Division.

To ensure its enforcement a permanent guard was maintained by the Military Police at the front and rear doors of each saloon and house of prostitution. These guards prohibited soldiers of the New York Division from entering such places. Within three weeks time every house of prostitution had been driven from the sector occupied by the New York Division. So far as liquor places were concerned they were not numerous, not more than a dozen being in the sector, but many enterprising citizens from other sections of the country, as well as from that locality, were planning to open saloons about the time of the arrival of the Division on the border.

When this order went into effect numerous inquiries, requests, applications and threats were made with a view to establishing such places within our sector under conditions which would secure traffic. A rigid enforcement of the order and the provision for guards had the effect of deterring the establishment of these contemplated places.

The result of this order and the high standards of conduct of the personnel of the Division resulted in perhaps the most remarkable health record ever made by any organization of similar size in the history of the Army. Venereal diseases practically did not exist in the Division throughout the period of its service. The same comment applies to the commission of crime. Attached hereto and marked Exhibit " K " is a table showing the sick rate and venereal record of the Division from July 19, to November 30, 1916.

The Infantry and Cavalry organizations of the Division made a 110-mile practice march. Details of this march were prescribed in S. O. 109, 122, 155, and 156, N. Y. D. 1916, copies of which are attached hereto and marked Exhibit " L."

All the batteries of artillery had target practice at La Gloria and later near Point Isabel.

The Division Headquarters organization consisted of the General Staff group, which was divided into

  (a) The Combat Section,
  (b) The Administrative Section,
  (c) The Intelligence Section, and the Technical and
       Administrative Staff group, divided into
         (a) Inspector's Section,
         (b) Judge Advocate's Section,
         (c) Supply Section,
         (d) Ordnance Section,
         (e) Medical Section,
         (f) Headquarters Detachment Section.

The functions of these sections were prescribed in G. O. 20, N. Y. D. 1916, copy of which is attached hereto and marked Exhibit " M."

The units of the Division armed with the rifle, having completed elementary practice at improvised ranges, were in October sent to La Gloria, Texas, for instruction in combat firing. This instruction was provided for in G. O. 33, 36 and 45, N. Y. D. 1916, copies of which are attached hereto and marked Exhibit " N."

In October a line of detached posts was established along the Rio Grande river, covering the New York sector. The details of this duty were provided for in G. O. 37, N. Y. D. 1916, copy of which is attached hereto and marked Exhibit " O." This order was later supplemented by G. O. 46, N. Y. D. 1916, under date of November 1st, copy of which is attached hereto and marked Exhibit " P."

Practically all of the organizations of the New York Division arrived on the Mexican Border disciplined and fairly well-trained commands. They profited much by their service.

Attached hereto are photographs, the titles of which explain features indicated in each Exhibit. These photographs present special features affecting the work of the troops.

Attached hereto is table, marked Exhibit " Q," showing the names, grades, organizations and causes of death of officers and men who died in the service of the United States, between July 19 and November 25, 1916.

In addition to the Mexican Border Service, Companies G, H, I, and L of the 10th Infantry were ordered on duty April 19, 1916, by the Sheriff of Westchester County, to suppress rioting in connection with a strike of the employees of the National Conduit & Cable Company at Hastings-on-Hudson. These companies were relieved from duty on April 27, 1916.

Attached hereto and marked Exhibit " R " is report of Small Arms Firing of organizations of this Division during 1916; also results of Matches.

JOHN F. O'RYAN,
Major-General.

EXHIBIT "A"

(G. O. 18.)

STATE OF NEW YORK,
THE ADJUTANT-GENERAL'S OFFICE,
STATE ARSENAL, NEW YORK CITY.

June 19, 1916.

GENERAL ORDERS, }
    No. 18.   }

In accordance with a proclamation of the President of the United States dated June 18, 1916, calling out under the Constitution and laws of the United States, a part of the Organized Militia to be employed in the service of the United States, the Commanding General, Division, will cause the organization of his command less coast artillery troops to assemble forthwith at their respective home stations in the equipment prescribed for field duty, preparatory to their muster into the service of the United States.

BY COMMAND OF THE GOVERNOR:
LOUIS W. STOTESBURY,
The Adjutant General.

STATE OF NEW YORK
THE ADJUTANT GENERAL'S OFFICE

ALBANY, *June* 21, 1916.

GENERAL ORDERS,
No. 19.

I. The organizations of the National Guard of this State, less Coast Artillery Troops, having been directed to be assembled forthwith at their respective home stations by General Orders No. 18, this office, dated June 19, 1916, pursuant to a call from the President of the United States, the following instructions relative to the mobilization of troops under said order are hereby published for the information and guidance of all concerned.

II. The Commanding General, Division, is authorized to detail for duty as Camp Staff Officers, such officers of The Adjutant General's Department, Quartermaster Corps and Medical Corps, as may be required for administrative purposes.

III. Regimental and other separate organization commanders are charged with subsisting the enlisted men of the National Guard, reporting at their respective home stations, and for this purpose they will be limited to an allowance of seventy-five cents per day for each enlisted man actually present for duty as shown by the morning report. They are also charged with providing necessary fuel, bedding, and forage, and for shoeing of authorized horses, pertaining to their respective organizations. The allowances authorized for such purposes are specified by Army Regulations (Paragraphs 1044–1077). Purchases will be made covering periods of not more than five days at time. Receipted vouchers will be obtained on Forms 330 and 335, War Department, and forwarded for settlement direct to The Adjutant General of the State, accompanied by consolidated ration returns.

IV. The Commanding General, Division, is authorized, while troops remain at their home stations and where armory facilities do not exist for sleeping, to allow organization commanders to permit such enlisted men of their respective commands as they may designate to sleep at home.

V. All officers and enlisted men will be examined by an officer of the Medical Department prior to their leaving their company rendezvous, with a view to determining the presence of any infectious or contagious disease.

VI. Drill and instructions of all organizations will be commenced at once and carried out in accordance with the Drill Regulations of the arm of which the organization is a part. The Commanding General, Division, will issue necessary instructions in regard to the character and time to be devoted daily to drills while organizations are at their home stations.

VII. Commanding officers of organizations will cause them to be recruited to the maximum enlisted strength given below:

Company of infantry	150
Regiment of infantry	1836
Troop of cavalry	100
Regiment of cavalry	1236
Battery light artillery	171
Regiment of field artillery	1128
Company of engineers	164
Battalion of engineers	494
Company of signal troops	77
Field battalion of signal troops	163
Ambulance company	79
Field hospital	67

The maximum enlisted strength of sanitary troops attached to organizations is given in General Orders No. 3, A. G. O. 1916.

VIII. No recruit will be accepted in any organization until he has been given a thorough physical examination, by a medical officer and has been found to conform to the physical standard prescribed for the Regular Army. Such physical standard is given in Circular 5, D. M. A., 1916.

IX. The National Defense Act approved by the President of the United States, June 3, 1916, contemplates the transition of the present Organized Militia into National Guard upon fulfillment of the requirements prescribed in Sections 70 and 73 of the Act cited relative to enlistment contracts and oaths. The form of new oath to be taken by officers and the form of new oath and enlisted contract to be subscribed and sworn to by enlisted men must conform to the requirements of the Act. Forms of oath and contract will be sent to each organization for use as soon as possible. The oath for officers and contract and oath for enlisted men will be subscribed and sworn to before a recognized officer of the National Guard. To be qualified for this duty the officer must have subscribed to the oath for commissioned officers of the National Guard before a Notary Public or an officer of the Regular Army; that is to say, no officer of the National Guard is authorized to administer the oath, until he has himself qualified under the provisions of the Act. Three copies of each form should be made in the case of each commissioned officer and organization (company, troop, battery, etc.), one to be retained by the organization for record and two to be forwarded direct to The Adjutant-General of the State.

X. The accountable officers in each organization are designated as the representatives of the Governor to act with the designated mustering officers of the United States to inventory and inspect all property of the United States and the State taken by the National Guard into the Federal service. Preparatory to the transfer, every officer accountable for public property will immediately take or cause to be taken, an inventory of the same. The inventory, which will be made by actual count, should include all the property issued by the State to, or purchased with the military funds or allowances of the organization, whether on hand in the storeroom or lockers, so as to show all property now in the possession of the organization. All property not to be taken into the service of the United States will be promptly invoiced, turned over and receipted for by the commanding officer of the depot unit. All property to be taken into the service of the United States will as soon as a regiment or other separate organization has been mustered into the service of the United States, be invoiced by the proper officer of the regiment or separate organization as follows:

(a) Clothing, camp and garrison equipage, subsistence and quartermaster supplies, to the Quartermaster.

(b) Property pertaining to medical department to the Senior Medical Officer.

(c) Property pertaining to the corps of engineers, ordnance department and signal corps, to an accountable officer detailed by the Regimental or other Commander of a separate organization from his staff.

Property pertaining to each department will be invoiced separately.

Transfers of property will be accomplished on Form No. 25, which will be supplied for the purpose by this office without requisition.

Receipts will be obtained in triplicate, one copy to be retained by the accountable officer, and two copies to be forwarded direct to the Adjutant-General of the State. When the property is transferred in accordance with the foregoing authority, the accountable officers upon invoicing the same and obtaining the prescribed receipts therefor, are relieved of further accountability for the property so transferred.

XI. Regimental and other commanders of separate organizations will forward direct to the Adjutant-General of the State, State Arsenal, 463 Seventh Avenue, New York City, requisitions for clothing, equipment and supplies necessary to care for their organizations at the enlisted strength stated in paragraph VII of this order.

XII. Commanding Officers of regiments not heretofore authorized to organize machine gun companies and troops and the detailed portion of headquarter's companies and troops and of supply companies are hereby authorized to form such units.

XIII. When the organizations have completed their inventories and have made suitable arrangements for caring for the property to be left at their home stations, the Commanding General, Division, will issue the necessary orders to move the organizations of his command, assembled pursuant to

G. O. 18, A. G. O. 1916, to the mobilization camp, now established and owned by the State at Green Haven, Town of Beekman, Dutchess County, N. Y.

XIV. In order to carry out the provisions of M. L. 120, depot units will be at once organized for each regiment or other unit assembled for service. A depot company will be formed for each separate company, troop or battery and a depot battalion for all other organizations. A depot battalion may consist of any number of companies not exceeding twelve. The enlisted personnel of depot units will be divided into two classes designated respectively Class A and Class B. Class A will consist of men available to fill vacancies in the organizations of the National Guard in the service of the United States. Class B will consist of all other enlisted men of such organizations.

XV. Muster in rolls will be prepared upon the blank forms supplied for that purpose, and in accordance with models and detailed instructions accompanying the same. Commanding officers should be directed to personally see that these rolls contain all information that might in any way affect pay, or which it might be necessary to consider in the setttlement of claims for pensions. The muster into the service of the United States will be carried out in accordance with the detailed regulations therefor prescribed by the Secretary of War.

XVI. The pay of the National Guard called into the service of the United States begins from the day on which it appears at the place of company rendezvous. It is essential that the date on which each member reports at the rendezvous, or joins his organization, be accurately noted on muster in and pay rolls, in order that men may receive proper pay, and that all prescribed records be accurately and fully kept, in order that the State may be reimbursed for the actual expense incurred in mobilization.

XVII. The Commanding General, Division, will direct the Chief Quartermaster to furnish the transportation necessary for the execution of this order.

XVIII. General Orders No. 14, A. G. O., 1916, will be deemed superseded by G. O. 18 and G. O. 19, A. G. O., 1916

BY COMMAND OF THE GOVERNOR:

LOUIS W. STOTESBURY,

The Adjutant General.

EXHIBIT " B "

(TELEGRAM)

PEEKSKILL, N. Y., *June* 19, 1916.

· COMMANDING OFFICERS, ORGANIZATIONS OF NEW YORK DIVISION:

Assemble your command eight p. m. today, field service uniform and equipment, all leaves recalled, recruit to war strength, organize depot unit.

OLMSTED,

Adjutant General.

EXHIBIT " C "

[G. O. 14.]

HEADQUARTERS DIVISION, NATIONAL GUARD, NEW YORK.

ALBANY, *June* 19, 1916.

GENERAL ORDERS, \
 No. 14. }

In compliance with General Orders No. 18, The Adjutant General's Office, June 19, 1916, the organizations of the National Guard, less Coast Artillery Corps, will assemble in their respective armories at 8:00 p. m. this date for service under Federal authority, and will await further orders. Instructions of the War Department governing the mobilization of the Organized Militia under the call of the President, will be carefully observed.

BY COMMAND OF MAJOR GENERAL O'RYAN:

CHAUNCEY P. WILLIAMS,

Colonel, Adjutant General.

Exhibit "D"

(TELEGRAM)

PEEKSKILL, N. Y., *June* 19, 1916.

Chief, Division of Militia Affairs,
Washington, D. C.

Governor of this State requests authority of Secretary of War to reorganize 65th Infantry which is not part of Divisional Infantry, as a heavy field artillery regiment, and to prepare it for muster into Federal service as Third Field Artillery Regiment of Division, and to requisition for material, clothing and equipment therefor. Request for detail of a Regular Field Artillery officer to command same will follow.

Louis W. Stotesbury,
The Adjutant General.

Exhibit "E"

STRENGTH OF THE N. Y. DIVISION ON THE BORDER.

	Officers.	Enlisted men
Headquarters, Division	16	0
Signal Battalion	9	166
Engineers	34	712
1st Cavalry	56	1,288
Squadron A Cavalry	15	382
Machine Gun Troop, Cavalry	4	86
Field Artillery Brigade Headquarters	4	0
1st Field Artillery	42	1,030
2nd Field Artillery	47	1,068
3rd Field Artillery	34	695
1st Field Hospital	6	74
2nd Field Hospital	5	65
3rd Field Hospital	4	66
4th Field Hospital	6	61
1st Ambulance Company	5	78
2nd Ambulance Company	5	78
3rd Ambulance Company	5	79
4th Ambulance Company	5	81
1st Brigade Headquarters	4	3
2nd Infantry	56	1,660
14th Infantry	51	1,028
69th Infantry	54	1,011
2nd Brigade Headquarters	5	13
7th Infantry	56	1,218
12th Infantry	53	1,133
71st Infantry	57	1,543
3rd Brigade Headquarters	2	5
3rd Infantry	53	1,535
23rd Infantry	47	1,037
74th Infantry	53	1,306
Quartermaster Corps Detachment, Division	....	14
Medical Department Detachment, Division	....	4
Supply Train	5	185
Bakery Company	1	29
Total	799	17,733
Grand Total	....	18,532

EXHIBIT "F"

NO. 1.

OATH AND CONTRACT OF ENLISTMENT OF...............................

Company, Troop, Battery,

IN THE NATIONAL GUARD OF THE UNITED STATES AND OF THE STATE OF........

I do hereby acknowledge to have voluntarily enlisted this .... day of ...., 1916, as a soldier in the National Guard of the United States and of the State of .... for the period of three years' service and three years in the reserve, under the conditions prescribed by law, unless sooner discharged by proper authority. And I do solemnly swear that I will bear true faith and allegiance to the United States of America and to the State of ...., and that I will serve them honestly and faithfully against all their enemies whomsoever, and that I will obey the orders of the President of the United States and of the Governor of the State of ...., and of the officers appointed over me according to law and the rules and articles of war. This oath is subscribed to with the understanding that credit will be given in the execution of this contract for the period which I have already served under my current enlistment in the Organized Militia of the State of ....

SIGNATURE	Date of current enlistment in Organized Militia

[SEAL]

Subscribed and duly sworn to before me this .... day of .... A. D., 1916.

....

....
(Rank in National Guard)
or
Notary Public.

NO 2.

OATH FOR COMMISSIONED OFFICERS OF THE NATIONAL GUARD.

I, ..., do solemnly swear that I will support and defend the Constitution of the United States and the constitution of the State of ...., against all enemies, foreign and domestic; that I will bear true faith and allegiance to the same; that I will obey the orders of the President of the United States and of the Governor of the State of ....; that I make this obligation freely, without any mental reservation or purpose of evasion, and that I will well and faithfully discharge the duties of the office of .... in the National Guard of the United States and of the State of .... upon which I am about enter, so help me God.

.... [SEAL]
(Signature)

Subscribed and duly sworn before me this .... day of ...., A. D., 1916.

....
(Rank in National Guard)
or
Notary Public

EXHIBIT "G"

NUMBER OF MEN BY ORGANIZATIONS WHO JOINED THE NEW FORCE AND THOSE WHO EXERCISED THE OPTION OF DECLINING TO DO SO.

ORGANIZATION	Number that joined new force. Strength on date of muster into U. S. Service.			Number that declined to take dual oath under National Defense Act.		
	Officers.	Men.	Total.	Officers.	Men.	Total.
‡Headquarters Division..........	17	......	17	1	....	1
*Quartermaster Corps...........	16	......	16	....	....	....
Quartermaster Corps Detachment Division	....	14	14	....	....	....
Medical Department Detachment Division	....	4	4	....	....	....
‡Headquarters, 1st Brigade......	7	2	9	....	....	....
*Headquarters, 2d Brigade......	5	2	7	....	....	....
‡Headquarters, 3d Brigade.......	7	2	9	....	....	....
‡Headquarters, 4th Brigade......	8	2	10	....	....	....
1st Battalion, Signal Corps....	9	166	175	....	1	1
1st Aero Company	4	38	42	....	....	....
†2d Aero Company	1	28	29	....	....	....
22d Regiment Engineers........	35	733	768	....	5	5
1st Cavalry	57	1,092	1,149	....	8	8
Squadron A, Cavalry..........	15	383	398	....	2	2
Machine Gun Troop, Cavalry...	3	86	89	....	....	....
1st Field Artillery............	41	1,083	1,124	....	1	1
2d Field Artillery.............	47	1,019	1,066	1	27	28
3d Field Artillery.............	40	893	933	....	34	34
*1st Motor Battery.............	4	153	157	....	8	8
*1st Infantry	54	1,812	1,866	1	31	32
2d Infantry	55	1,824	1,879	....	4	4
3d Infantry	53	1,644	1,697	....	4	4
7th Infantry	55	1,211	1,266	....	....	....
*10th Infantry	55	1,687	1,742	....	....	....
12th Infantry	52	1,191	1,243	....	6	6
14th Infantry	52	1,026	1,078	2	10	12
23d Infantry	45	1,031	1,076	....	1	1
*47th Infantry	47	1,058	1,105	....	7	7
69th Infantry	47	1,003	1,050	1	1	2
71st Infantry	55	1,385	1,440	....	....	....
74th Infantry	54	1,145	1,199	....	8	8
1st Field Hospital	6	64	70	....	....	....
2d Field Hospital.............	6	67	73	....	....	....
3d Field Hospital.............	5	40	45	....	3	3
4th Field Hospital	6	61	67	....	....	....
1st Ambulance Company.......	3	79	82	....	1	1
2d Ambulance Company.......	4	78	82	....	....	....
3d Ambulance Company.......	5	79	84	....	....	....
4th Ambulance Company.......	5	79	84	....	....	....
Field Bakery	1	19	20	....	....	....
Division Supply Train.........	2	186	188	....	8	8
Totals	983	22,469	23,452	6	170	176

* Strength of Headquarters, 2d Brigade, Quartermaster Corps, 1st, 10th and 47th Infantry, and 1st Motor Battery, on June 30, 1916.

† Strength of 2d Aero Company, on July 1, 1916.

(These organizations did not go into active Federal service.)

‡ Strength of Headquarters Division, and Headquarters, 1st, 3d and 4th Brigades includes officers mustered into active service, and State Administrative Officers.

EXHIBIT " H "

PEEKSKILL, N. Y., *June* 4, 1916.

HEADQUARTERS DIVISION,

NATIONAL GUARD, NEW YORK.

From: Commanding General,

To: The Adjutant-General of the State.

Subject: Mobilization of the Division and supply of property necessary to bring organizations to war strength.

1. Attention is invited to communication, dated June 2, 1913, addressed to The Adjutant-General of the State, on the subject of the mobilization of the Division and supply of property necessary to bring organizations thereof to war strength, and to the subsequent correspondence in relation thereto with the War Department, more particularly to communication dated May 21, 1914, from the Acting Chief of Ordnance to the Chief, Division of Militia Affairs, and to the indorsement of the Chief, Division of Militia Affairs under date of of June 18, 1914, to The Adjutant-General of the State, and to my indorsement of July 20, 1914, to The Adjutant-General of the State.

2. This correspondence and the indorsements, indicate the desire of the Chief, Division of Militia Affairs, to be kept advised of conclusions arrived at and the action the State may be able to take in the premises.

3. In view of the possibility of service by this Division, it is believed to be desirable to again point out the delays which are inherent in the existing system of attempting to rapidly transfer military property from the Supply Depot at Philadelphia to the possession of the troops after the order to mobilize is given. As I understand the existing plan it is that upon mobilization the Commanding Officer of the Depot at Philadelphia will promptly ship to the State mobilization camp all military property required by all the organizations of the Division to clothe and equip the excess number of men necessary to bring organizations to war strength. I understand that this property is all boxed and ready to be placed on cars, but I do not understand that this shipment constitutes the problem which is by a proper system of accountability and physical transfer to put the property in the possession of the individuals who are to use it. It is submitted that any system devised to accomplish this in the most efficient manner, must be harmonized with other problems which will be in process of solution at the same time. For example a retrospect of the volunteer camps at the outbreak of the Spanish War will indicate that much of what was objectionable was due to the presence at such camps at the time they were organized, of large numbers of recruits and prospective recruits, with little or no military clothing or equipment — men whose lack of discipline was stimulated by their relatively large numbers, by their lack of uniformity as to clothing, and by the psychological effect upon them of an apparent lack of system and order. It is submitted that if there is any one place where undisciplined recruits should not be in the first week after a mobilization call, it is at the mobilization camp. If upon the call for mobilization, organizations were authorized to move promptly to the mobilization camp and there establish themselves without the unnecessary distraction caused by the presence of large numbers of men with little or no training, the work at the mobilization camp could proceed with greater system and efficiency. If at the same time all prospective recruits were received, examined, enlisted, clothed and equipped at the several home stations of the organizations, it must be apparent that this work could proceed under the most favorable circumstances. The armories in the State are adequately constructed for just such purposes, and moreover they would be wholly relieved at that time from the presence of the regular organizations which would be at the mobilization camp. The reserve unit of each organization should be in possession of the armory, and such organization with its trained personnel could aid in receiving, caring for and placing in the minds of the new recruits correct notions of soldierly conduct. Physical examinations could be made much more rigidly in the regular medical officers' quarters than amid the activity of the mobilization camp. Only after the mobilization camp is prepared and the regular routine begun, and after the new recruits at the home

stations have been organized into detachments, clothed, armed and equipped, should they be sent to join their organizations at the mobilization camp. Everything connected with the latter plan, so far as the psychological effect on new men is concerned, will make for impressions of system, order and respect for the service. Conversely everything connected with the former plan will tend to create impressions of confusion, haste and license. If the latter plan is preferable and is to be followed, it means that the property necessary to clothe, arm and equip the personnel between existing strength and war strength should be shipped to and held in Federal storerooms at the home stations of organizations, as recommended in the correspondence referred to. As heretofore pointed out, this will not mean any transfer of the legal possession, accountability or responsibility of the property in time of peace from Federal to State officers. The so-called Federal storerooms provided for in the modern armories may be made as satisfactory for Federal storage purposes as is the storeroom in the Philadelphia Depot, by requiring the State to meet whatever regulations may be prescribed to insure complete control of the property by the Federal accountable officer. The plan will conform to the best methods abroad in that it establishes the property where the men are located, who are to use it. The present plan contemplates a maneuver at a particular time, whereby the property leaves one point and the recruits another in the expectancy that they will effect a meeting under satisfactory conditions at a third point, which may not occur. The problem of "turning over" property so stored, in order that it may be kept up to date was discussed, and a solution offered in the corespondence referred to. Furthermore the plan, if adopted, will free the Philadelphia Depot of a large amount of property, thus making available the space so occupied for other purposes.

4. It is understood that this plan when originally submitted was approved by the Chief, Division of Militia Affairs, and in anticipation of its adoption arrangements were made in 1914 for Federal storerooms in the armories of the 7th and 23d Infantry, and such storerooms have been included in the plans of all new armories constructed since that time.

5. It is recommended that this communication be referred to the Chief, Division of Militia Affairs for further consideration by the War Department and with a view to the adoption of the plan recommended, and its application to the organizations of this Division, as fast as the Federal storerooms may be provided by us and inspected and approved by the War Department.

(Signed)   JOHN F. O'RYAN,
Major-General.

HEADQUARTERS DIVISION, NATIONAL GUARD, NEW YORK.

SCHOOL OF APPLICATION, N. Y. INFANTRY.

PEEKSKILL, N. Y., June 2, 1913.

From: Commanding General, Division, N. G., N. Y.,

To: The Adjutant-General of the State.

Subject: Mobilization of the Division and supply of property necessary to bring organizations to war strength.

1. In the event of any mobilization of the 6th (New York) Division, much avoidable delay would result in connection with the supply of equipment and other property necessary to outfit the various organizations at war strength. Much of this property would come from the Philadelphia Depot, involving boxing, shipping, freighting, transportation from terminal points to the New York Arsenal, inspection, checking up of invoices, correspondence, marking and stenciling, and all this at a time when the Philadelphia Depot will be taxed perhaps beyond its limit with the demands of other Divisions equally as important. The situation would doubtless be complicated as it has always been in the past by the introduction and enforcement of demands, not now in the contemplation of the supply departments of the army, of states and organizations thereof, backed by political influence which could not be ignored.

2. In order to carry out in a practical manner the policy of the present Governor to render to the Federal Government in full measure the obligation of the State in the matter of military preparedness, we have given much thought to this subject of supply, and recommend that the matter be taken

up with the War Department with a view to supplying the organizations of this State, constituting the tactical Division, with the property necessary to bring them up to war strength, this to be done according to the following plan:

a. The State to provide as soon as practicable the storehouses and supply depots necessary for that purpose.

b. The clothing, property and stores to be furnished by the War Department without charge against the allotment of Federal funds. If there is legal objection to the supply by the War Department of the property involved, without charging the same against the State's allotment of Federal funds, it is suggested that the War Department might legally ship (not issue) such property to the indicated supply depot or storehouse, consigned to a Federal or State Supply Officer, for the purpose of storage only. For example in an effort to carry out in practical manner the plan herein suggested, I have conferred with Colonel Daniel Appleton, Commanding Officer, 7th Infantry, concerning the storage of all property necessary to fit out his command at war strength. The armory of the 7th Infantry occupies an entire city block. Additions have lately been added to the building, with large increase in storage facilities. The property accountability in that command leaves little or nothing to be desired. Colonel Appleton has agreed to provide the storage facilities and to care for the arms, clothing and other property necessary to bring his regiment to war strength. This places the war strength property where it belongs according to the principles of efficiency methods — namely, with the organization that will be required to account for, issue and use the property on short notice. I am also prepared to make the same arrangement in the case of the property necessary to bring the Battalion of four companies of pioneers to war strength. The new armory of the Engineers, commanded by Colonel Walter B. Hotchkin, is the most recently constructed of the armories in the City of New York, and the most up-to-date in its equipments and appointments. The discipline of the command and its property accountability and methods, leave little or nothing to be desired.

3. If the above plan meets the approval of the War Department we will proceed with reasonable dispatch to provide similar facilities in other selected commands, and make application from time to time when such facilities are ready for the receipt of the necessary property.

4. The mobilization camp of the 6th (New York) Division is at Peekskill, New York. The buildings already erected and other plans will permit the storage of a large amount of property for organization of the Division, which have not at present storage facilities, necessary to care for their excess property.

5. It is requested that this communication be referred to the War Department for consideration and decision.

(Signed)   JOHN F. O'RYAN,
Major-General.
May 21, 1914.

From: The Ordnance Office.

To: The Chief, Div. Mil. Affairs.

Subject: Equipments — New York.

1. In connection with the matter of the ordnance stores being set aside at the Army Field Supply Depot No. 1 for equipping the increase in the Organized Militia troops of the State of New York, there is inclosed herewith a statement prepared from the records of this office showing the total number of certain principal articles of personal equipment required to equip, at the strength prescribed by Tables of Organization, U. S. Army, based on Field Service Regulations, 1914, the Organized Militia of the above mentioned State. Against this number, required to equip the troops at this strength, there is shown the number on hand at Federal inspection, in April, 1913. There are also shown the articles set aside for Coast Artillery companies at coast defense forts, and the number set aside at Army Field Supply Depot No. 1. It will be noted that a deficit exists in most of the articles shown on this tabulation.

2. Information is requested as to whether it is the intention that this office shall set aside the additional articles sufficient to eliminate the deficits referred to, or whether it is the intention of the Militia Division to have the State

procure as a charge against its allotment the articles in which the deficits are shown.

3. It is recommended that this matter be taken up with the Adjutant-General of the State of New York with a view to determining whether there were any articles of equipment on hand procured through purchase or otherwise which were not accounted for at the Federal inspection, 1913, or whether a greater or less supply of the articles enumerated is now on hand.

4. In connection with the matter of determining the surplus or deficit of the equipment required for the Organized Militia of the State of New York, attention is invited to the following extract taken from letter to this office from the Adjutant-General, February 23, 1911, relative to the method to be followed in determining the articles which should be kept on hand at Army Field Supply Depot No. 1 for the equipment of Organized Militia troops:

" From the articles and quantities of such supplies necessary to place the regular and militia organizations above mentioned in the field at full war strength, deduct the quantities in the hands of those organizations."

(Signed)   JNO. T. THOMPSON,
Col. Ord. Dept.,
Acting C. of O.

1st Ind.   300 N. Y.

WAR DEPT., DIV. MILITIA AFFAIRS, O. C. S.

To the Adjutant-General:
June 18, 1914.

1. It may be stated in reference to the inquiry in the second paragraph of the foregoing letter that the States are now expected to maintain a supply of all necessary equipment sufficient in quantity to equip the minimum authorized strength of the Militia.

The War Department insists on this requirement.

It is believed that the States will, with proper care of property and economical use of funds, in a few years be able to accumulate a stock of supplies sufficient to equip the Militia at war strength. Steps to this end have already been taken in some of the States.

It is requested that the subject of accumulating war strength supplies be taken under consideration and the Division of Militia Affairs advised of the conclusions arrived at and the action the State may be able to take in the premises.

2. It is further requested that the information asked for by the Chief of Ordnance in the third paragraph of his letter be given in an indorsement hereon.

(Signed)   A. L. MILLS,
Brig. Gen. G. S., Chief of Div'n,
For the Chief of Staff.

2nd Ind.

THE ADJUTANT-GENERAL'S OFFICE.

ALBANY, *June* 27, 1914.

To, Commanding General Division, for remark in connection with 1st indorsement. The records of this office, as per attached sheet, show the following as on hand June 20, 1914:

*   *   *   *   *   *   *   *

2. The War Department has included officers in their statement of equipment required, but officers' equipment is not included in our figures. Each officer supplies his own equipment, and therefore the only deficit would be about 421 cups and 897 gun slings. Requisitions are now in the hands of the War Department for 218 gun slings.

BY COMMAND OF THE GOVERNOR:

(Signed)   JOHN P. TREANOR,
Lt. Col. Asst. Adj.-General,
For the Adjutant-General.
J. F. O'R.— W. H. N.

3rd Ind.

HEADQUARTERS DIVISION, NATIONAL GUARD OF NEW YORK.

To the Adjutant-General of the State:

NEW YORK CITY, N. Y., *July* 20, 1914.

1. It would seem apparent that in New York State there is sufficient property on hand and in possession of troops, to more than equip and clothe the minimum authorized strength of each organization, which is the requirement stated in the first paragraph of the 1st Indorsement.

2. It is the purpose, as soon as the Federal store rooms in each armory are inspected and approved by the War Department, to recommend that the State undertake to maintain by charge against its share of the Federal allotment all the property required for companies of infantry, on the basis of 100 enlisted men to the company, whether or not the companies have that number of men, so that the War Department may have a fixed and unvarying number of articles in each class to be stored in the regimental Federal store rooms. On this basis there would be approximately 800 of each class of single articles to be supplied by the Federal Government at Federal expense, and maintained in each regimental Federal store room. It will require a number of years, even in this State, before all the regiments could be provided with the Federal store rooms, on account of the expense involved in constructing them.

3. The "turning over" of this reserve property so as to get it up to date would seem to be entirely practicable. A requisition, from the 7th Infantry for 50 haversacks, for example, when finally approved, could, instead of being filled from the Philadelphia Depot, be filled from the regimental store room by authority given to the Inspector Instructor accountable for the property in the Federal store room, to transfer by regular invoice to the regimental Quartermaster the required number of haversacks. To keep his reserve property up to the amount required, the Federal accountable officer will then make requisition to the War Department to replace the property issued to the regiment. This arrangement would not appear to involve expense to the War Department, for it is not contemplated that the plan involves the purchase of any greater amount of reserve property than existing plans provide for, but that such property as is classed as reserve property shall be placed in a Federal store room with the organization which is to use the property, as fast as such store rooms may be provided at the expense of the State. This would place the property where it would be readily available in time of war, and not in a general supply depot, where it may be ready for prompt shipment, but where it would not be available for prompt use by the individuals who will need it. Our mobilization tests of six organizations, just completed, show that approximately 90 per cent of the men volunteered for service in the Volunteer Army, passed the physical examination, conducted by the regular Medical Officer assigned for that purpose, and were men whose family and business arrangements made it practical for them to enter the Volunteer Army as enlisted men. The test, furthermore, showed that all the companies subjected to the test had lists of men ready and fit to enlist on call to bring the commands to immediate war strength. In perfecting our plans here for mobilization, the one missing factor is that of military property. If the reserve property was stored with the command, the war strength recruits could be enlisted and equipped within forty-eight hours of the call, and ready for muster in, thus enabling commands to move to the mobilization camp at war strength all properly clothed and equipped. This plan means decentralization of reserve property in such manner that it can be handled and accounted for with facility and promptness, and simultaneously throughout the Division. On the other hand to ship it in bulk from the Philadelphia Depot to a mobilization camp, would involve endless confusion, delay and property losses. The reserve property, considerable in bulk for one regiment at its post, when shipped with the property of all other regiments to the mobilization camp furnishes a total mass of property at the mobilization camp which would add materially to the difficulties of handling it. At the mobilization camp there would be no ready facilities for protecting the property from

the elements and from theft, for checking it, transferring and issuing it. Such a plan necessitates the transportation of the war strength personnel from the home station to the mobilization camp, where they would have to subsist and be provided for in some manner while dressed as civilians, and would have a bad effect on the discipline of new men at the very time when they should be under rigid discipline.

4. It is recommended that the War Department be advised that if reserve property will be shipped to the Federal store rooms in regimental armories, as soon as such store rooms can be provided and inspected and approved by Federal officers, that the State of New York will, as a charge against its share of the Federal allotment, maintain on hand in the State all the property required for service in the field on the basis of 100 men per company of infantry, 133 for a battery of artillery, 90 for a troop of cavalry, and 100 men for a company of engineers. With the large force maintained by the State of New York, and with the great and necessary demands made upon the State's allotment from Federal funds, it is doubted whether the State would be able to accumulate within a reasonable time property in amount sufficient to equip the Division at war strength. If the State maintains equipment on the basis of the above figures it would seem to be meeting its obligations. The subject of reserve property and the storage thereof in Federal regimental store rooms, was the basis of a previous communication, and it is understood that the plan was finally approved by the Chief of Staff.

5. As to the information requested in the third paragraph of the foregoing communication, this can be furnished by the records of the Adjutant-General's Office, and by the tables attached hereto.

(Signed)   . JOHN F. O'RYAN,

Major-General.

Status of Equipment Required by State of New York to Equip Organizations at Strength Prescribed by Tables of Organization, 1914

ORGANIZATIONS, APRIL 1, 1914	Haversacks	Cartridge belts, cal. 30	Canteens	Cups	Meat cans	Knives	Forks	Spoons	Gun slings
Infantry (4 Brigades and 1 Regiment)	24,100	23,881	24,883	24,883	24,883	24,883	24,883	24,883	23,897
Cavalry (1 Regiment, 1 Squadron and 1 Machine Gun Patrol)		1,706	1,774	1,774	1,774	1,774	1,774	1,774	1,706
Field Artillery (2 Regiments)	816		2,340	2,343	2,340	2,340	2,340	2,340	
Engineers (4 Battalions)	1,676	1,976	2,036	2,036	2,036	2,036	2,036	2,036	1,976
Signal Corps (2 Battalions)	196		342	342	342	342	342	342	
Coast Artillery (31 Companies)	3,317	3,224	3,317	3,317	3,317	3,317	3,317	3,317	3,317
Sanitary (3 Ambulance Companies)	198		252	252	252	252	252	252	
Sanitary (2 Field Hospitals)	118		146	146	146	146	146	146	
Sanitary (19 Detachments)	304		532	532	532	532	532	532	
Total	30,725	30,787	35,622	35,622	35,622	35,622	35,622	35,622	30,896
On hand at Federal Inspection, April 1913	17,966	17,508	22,601	20,679	21,203	21,041	20,646	20,816	16,707
Set aside for Coast Artillery	1,398	1,398	1,398	1,398	1,398	1,398	1,398	1,398	1,398
Set aside, Field supply Depot No. 1	11,568	11,728	12,454	12,454	12,454	12,454	12,454	12,454	11,774
Total	30,932	30,634	36,453	34,531	35,055	34,893	34,498	34,668	29,879
Surplus	207		831						
Deficit		153		1,091	567	729	1,124	954	1,017
On hand June 30, 1914	18,765	17,632	21,961	20,349	21,347	21,628	21,472	21,862	16,827
On hand April, 1913	17,966	17,508	22,601	20,679	21,203	21,041	20,646	20,816	16,707
Gained	799	124	640	330	144	587	826	1,046	120
Lost									
Surplus now	1,006		191					92	
Deficit now		29		1,421	423	142	298		897

EXHIBIT "I"

Dates of Entrainment of Units of the New York Division for the Mexican Border, and Arrival Thereat and Return Therefrom.

ORGANIZATION	Date of leaving for border (1916)	Date of arrival at border (1916)	Date of return from border (1916–17)
Headquarters, N. Y. Division....	July 2............	July 6.........	Dec. 14, 1916
Headquarters, 1st Brigade.......	July 7............	July 15........	Still at border
Headquarters, 2d Brigade........	June 29..........	July 2.........	Sept. 6, 1916
Headquarters, 3d Brigade........	July 5............	July 10........	Dec. 15, 1916
1st Battalion, Signal Corps.......	July 5............	July 10........	Dec. 13, 1916
22d Engineers:			
1st Battalion.................	July 12...........	July 18........	Oct. 14, 1916
2d Battalion.................	July 14...........	July 22........	Dec. 16, 1916
1st Cavalry:			
1st Squadron................	June 29..........	July 5.........	Stil1 at border
3d Squadron.................	July 1............	July 7.........	Still at border
Headquarters and 2d Squadron.	July 6............	July 12........	Still at border
Squadron A, Cavalry............	July 6............	July 12........	Dec. 15, 1916
Machine Gun Troop, Cavalry....	July 6............	July 12........	Dec. 15, 1916
1st Field Artillery:			
2d Battalion................	June 29.....	July 5 (Hdqrs.).	Oct. 27, 1916
Hdqrs. and 1st Bln. (less Btys. A and C)	July 3............	July 11 (less)...	Oct. 19, 1916
Batteries A and C............	July 9............	July 16 (Hdqrs.).	Oct. 19, 1916
2d Field Artillery:			
2d Battalion................	July 8............	July 15........	Dec. 30, 1916
Hdqrs. and 1st Battalion......	July 9............	July 16........	Dec. 30, 1916
3d Field Artillery..............	Oct. 3d, 1st section	Oct. 9....	Still at border
	Remainder.	Oct. 10........	Still at border
2d Infantry...................	July 7............	July 15........	Still at border
3d Infantry...................	July 13...........	July 21....	Sept. 8, 1916
7th Infantry..................	June 27..........	July 2.........	Nov. 22, 1916
12th Infantry.................	June 29..........	July 5.........	Still at border
14th Infantry.................	June 27..........	July 3.........	Sept. 8, 1916
23d Infantry..................	July 4............	July 11........	Still at border
69th Infantry.................	July 11...........	July 18	Still at border
71st Infantry.................	June 27..........	July 2.........	Sept. 6, 1916
74th Infantry.................	July 5............	July 10........	Still at border
1st Field Hospital.............	June 28..........	July 5.........	Oct. 13, 1914
2d Field Hospital..............	July 15...........	July 21........	Dec. 14, 1916
3d Field Hospital..............	Oct. 13..........	Oct. 17........	Still at border
4th Field Hospital.............	Nov. 10..........	Nov. 15........	Still at border
1st Ambulance Company.......	July 10...........	July 17........	Oct. 13, 1916
2d Ambulance Company.......	July 10...........	July 17........	Dec. 15, 1916
3d Ambulance Company.......	June 28..........	July 5.........	Dec. 28, 1916
4th Ambulance Company.......	July 15...........	July 21........	Still at border
Supply Train.................	Oct. 17..........	Oct. 24........	Still at border
Field Bakery, Detachment.......	July 9............	July 16........	Still at border
2 Bakery Units................	July 12	July 18........	Still at border

EXHIBIT "J"

HEADQUARTERS, NEW YORK ·DIVISION.

McALLEN, TEX., *July* 11, 1916.

GENERAL ORDERS, }
No. 2. }

I. A detachment of Military Police is organized to police the towns of Pharr, McAllen and Mission, and the roads connecting the same. The detachment will be organized and commanded by Lieutenant-Colonel Robert McLean, 7th Infantry, and will consist of three lieutenants of the line, one medical officer, four non-commissioned officers and 15 privates of cavalry, eight non-commissioned officers and 50 privates of infantry, three of whom shall be provided with motor cycles.

II. Details of officers for service with the Military Police will be made on recommendation of the Commanding Officer of the detachment. Detail of enlisted men will be made on an equitable basis among organizations at the three stations of the Division, by organization commanders after conference with the Detachment Commander. Enlisted men will be selected for their physical bearing, judgment and previous experience. The personnel of the detachment will mess with their organizations, and will be changed in part from time to time.

III. In addition to the functions prescribed for Military Police, Article VII, F. S. R., the detachment is charged with reporting violations of all camp orders, and where the offenses warrant such action to arrest soldier offenders. The detachment will co-operate with the civilian police authorities.

IV. Officers and enlisted men of the Military Police when actually performing their duties will wear a blue brassard on the left arm, half-way between the elbow and shoulder, bearing the letters M. P. in white.

V. In cases of emergency the Military Police may call on any troops to assist them. All persons belonging to the military service are required to give every assistance to the Military Police in the execution of their duties.

BY COMMAND OF MAJOR GENERAL O'RYAN:

EDWARD OLMSTED,
Major, Assistant Chief of Staff.

OFFICIAL:

FRANKLIN W. WARD,
Major, Assistant Chief of Staff.

EXHIBIT " K "

SICK RATE AND VENEREAL RECORD OF THE NEW YORK DIVISION
FROM JULY 19th TO NOVEMBER 30th, 1916.

Month.	Percentage sick.	Venereal rate.
July	.0145	.00294
August	.0139	.00165
September	.0248	.000336
October	.0266	.00062
November	.0283	.00167

The rate of admissions to sick report for alcoholism during these months has been practically nil.

Deaths.

From injury	8
From disease	16
Total	24

Any sick rate below 3 per cent is excellent.

Two cases of typhoid fever, neither had been innoculated.

Venereal rate negligible. Few cases on hand are largely in Tennessee regiment, and Division Supply Train, which reported here about November 1, having been at Camp Whitman all summer.

EXHIBIT " L"

HEADQUARTERS, NEW YORK DIVISION.

MCALLEN, TEX., *August* 2, 1916.

SPECIAL ORDERS, }
  No. 109.   }

1. Squadron A, and Machine Gun Troop, N. Y. Cavalry, with one Radio Platoon Pack, N. Y. Signal Corps, and one motor ambulance, 1st N. Y. Field Artillery, will proceed on the morning of 3rd August, 1916, on a practice march as follows:

McAllen to Sterling's Ranch to Gloria Ranch
  to Sterling's Ranch to McAllen.

2. Equipment A, the necessary rations and forage, and the necessary wagon transportation will be taken, less combat wagons (G. O. 66, W. D. 1911).

3. During the march every opportunity will be taken advantage of for tactical instruction appropriate to the terrain.

4. Arrival at each camp will be reported, and such other communications as may be desirable for instruction will be sent to these Headquarters by Radio.

5. Route sketches will be prepared, and any information of military value will be reported to these Headquarters on return of the detachment.

6. The march will be so regulated that the detachment will arrive at its present camp by noon either the 7th instant or the 8th instant.

BY COMMAND OF MAJOR-GENERAL O'RYAN:

H. H. BANDHOLTZ,
Colonel, Chief of Staff.

OFFICIAL:
(Signed)   ALLAN L. REAGAN,
Adjutant.

NEW YORK DIVISION.

MCALLEN, TEX., *August* 5, 1916.

SPECIAL ORDERS,
No. 122.

1. First N. Y. Cavalry, less two squadrons, will proceed on the morning of 6th August, 1916, on a practice march as follows:

McAllen to Sterling's Ranch to Gloria Ranch to Sterling's Ranch
to Young's Ranch to Sterling's Ranch to McAllen.

2. Equipment A, the necessary rations and forage, and the necessary wagon transportation will be taken, less combat wagons (G. O. 66, W. D. 1911).

3. During the march every opportunity will be taken advantage of for tactical instruction appropriate to the terrain.

4. Route sketches will be prepared, and any information of military value will be reported to these Headquarters on return of the detachment.

5. The march will be so regulated that the detachment will arrive at its present camp by noon either the 10th or the 11th instant.

·6. Another Squadron to be designated by the Commanding Officer, 1st N. Y. Cavalry, will proceed on the morning 7th August, 1916, on a practice march identical with above, returning to present camp by noon either the 11th instant or the 12th instant.

7. The remaining Squadron 1st N. Y. Cavalry will proceed on a practice march on the morning of 8th August, 1916, identical with above, returning to present camp by noon either the 12th instant or 13th instant.

8. Commanding Officer, 3rd Ambulance Company will furnish one ambulance from his command to accompany each of the above three detachments.

BY COMMAND OF MAJOR-GENERAL O'RYAN:

H. H. BANDHOLTZ,
Chief of Staff.

OFFICIAL:
(Signed)   ALLAN L. REAGAN,
Adjutant.

HEADQUARTERS, NEW YORK DIVISION.

MCALLEN, TEX., *August* 14, 1916.

SPECIAL ORDERS,
No. 155.

1. Squadron A, Cavalry (less one troop) and Machine Gun Troop with one motor ambulance will proceed on the morning of August 15, 1916, for a practice march.

2. Route followed will be:
Sam Fordyce.
Ojo De Agua,
Hidalgo,
Donna Pump,
Mercedes,
McAllen.

3. Equipment A, forage, rations and necessary transportation will be taken, less combat wagons (G. O. 66, W. D. 1911).

4. During the march every opportunity will be utilized for tactical exercises appropriate to the terrain.

5. Route sketches and all information of military value will be reported to these Headquarters on return of the detachment.

6. The march will be so conducted that the detachment will return to its present camp by noon of August 20th, 1916.

BY COMMAND OF MAJOR-GENERAL O'RYAN:

H. H. BANDHOLTZ,
Colonel, Chief of Staff.

OFFICIAL:

(Signed)   ALLAN L. REAGAN,

Major, Adjutant.

HEADQUARTERS, NEW YORK DIVISION.

MCALLEN, TEX., August 14, 1916.

SPECIAL ORDERS, }
  No. 156.   }

1. The infantry commands of the division will proceed on practice marches, on the mornings of the dates indicated, as follows:

    Aug. 16.— 1st Brigade (less 2nd and 69th Inf.).
    Aug. 16.— 2nd Brigade (less 7th and 12th Inf.).
    Aug. 17.— 3rd Brigade (less 23rd and 74th Inf.).
    Aug. 22.— 2nd Infantry.
    Aug. 22.— 7th Infantry.
    Aug. 22.— 23rd Infantry.
    Aug. 26.— 69th Infantry.
    Aug. 28.— 12th Infantry.
    Aug. 28.— 74th Infantry.

2. The regiments of the 2nd Brigade will proceed from McAllen to Mission. The regiments of the 3rd Brigade will proceed from Pharr via McAllen to Mission.

All regiments will proceed from Mission via:

Alton,
Sterling's Ranch,
La Gloria,
Sterling's Ranch,
Laguna Seca,
Young's Ranch,
Laguna Seca,
Sterling's Ranch,
Edinburg.

The regiments of the 1st Brigade will proceed from Edinburg via McAllen to Mission.

The regiments of the 2nd Brigade will proceed from Edinburg to McAllen.

The regiments of the 3rd Brigade will proceed from Edinburg to Pharr.

All regiments will halt and camp for one night at each place in the above sequence and as indicated in the attached march tables.

3. From the initial points field rations and forage will be carried as follows:

Regiments of the 1st Brigade — 2 days.
Regiments of the 2nd Brigade — 3 days.
Regiments of the 3rd Brigade — 4 days.

After their first arrival at Sterling's Ranch all regiments will draw, from the refilling point at Monte Cristo, sufficient rations, and forage to supply themselves until their next return to Sterling's Ranch. On their final departure from Sterling's Ranch they will supply themselves for a return to their original camps.

One day's reserve rations will be carried in the haversack from the first day until utilized for practical instruction in individual cooking as required in paragraph 1205, Army Regulations, which instruction will be given during the march on such day as the regimental commander may select.

4. During the entire practice march advantage will be taken by each organization of every opportunity to give instruction required by paragraph 109, F. S. R. Security measures, appropriate to the terrain and exercise, will always be taken and outposts will be established every night.

War diaries will be kept as required by paragraph 35, F. S. R. and will be forwarded through intermediate channels to division headquarters.

Daily field orders will be issued covering the march and any maneuvers connected therewith.

Route sketches will be made, and with all information of military value, will be forwarded to division headquarters within 24 hours after the conclusion of the last day's march.

Full field equipment will be worn during all marches and exercises.

No ammunition will be carried on the person.

After leaving in their camps such transportation as may be required for policing and other necessary purposes, all available transportation will be taken by each regiment on the march.

Combat wagons, with their appropriate loads only, will be taken by each regiment.

5. Field Hospital Co., No. 2, will proceed by the most practicable route so as to arrive and establish at Sterling's Ranch not later than the afternoon of August 17th, and will remain there until further orders.

6. The Division Surgeon will arrange to send one ambulance to report to the surgeon of each infantry regiment not later than 3:00 p. m. of the day before the regiment starts on its march, and for two ambulances to report to and proceed with Field Hospital Co., No. 2, to Sterling's Ranch, and will remain there until further orders.

7. The commanding officer, Signal Battalion, will establish one radio section at Sterling's Ranch, not later than August 17th, and one radio section at Young's Ranch, not later than August 20th, which will remain at the places mentioned until further orders.

8. The Division Quartermaster will establish a refilling point at Monte Cristo not later than August 12, which will be prepared to supply all the troops mentioned herein, and will be maintained until further orders. He will arrange for the possible necessity of adding to the water supply at Alton by the use of motor truck transportation.

9. Troop C, 1st Cavalry, will take station at Monte Cristo not later than August 12th as guard and on duty at the refilling point under the exclusive orders of the Division Quartermaster.

10. Equipment A is prescribed for all organizations.

BY COMMAND OF MAJOR-GENERAL O'RYAN:

H. H. BANDHOLTZ,
Colonel, Chief of Staff.

OFFICIAL:
(Signed)   ALLAN L. REAGAN,
Major-Adjutant.

1st BRIGADE

14	2	69	REGIMENT		
	Dates		From	To	Miles
16	22	26	Mission	Alton	7
17	23	27	Alton	Sterling's	6
18	24	28	Sterling's	La Gloria	3
19	25	29	La Gloria	Sterling's	3
20	26	30	Sterling's	Laguna Seca	10
21	27	31	Laguna Seca	Young's	6
22	28	1	Young's	Laguna Seca	6
23	29	2	Laguna Seca	Sterling's	10
24	30	3	Sterling's	Edinburg	14
25	31	4	Edinburg	McAllen	11
26	1	5	McAllen	Mission	6

2d BRIGADE

71	7	12	REGIMENT		
Dates			From	To	Miles
16	22	28	McAllen	Mission	6
17	23	29	Mission	Alton	7
18	24	30	Alton	Sterling's	6
19	25	31	Sterling's	La Gloria	3
20	26	1	La Gloria	Sterling's	3
21	27	2	Sterling's	Laguna Seca	10
22	28	3	Laguna Seca	Young's	6
23	29	4	Young's	Laguna Seca	6
24	30	5	Laguna Seca	Sterling's	10
25	31	6	Sterling's	Edinburg	14
26	1	7	Edinburg	McAllen	11

3d BRIGADE

3	23	74	REGIMENT		
Dates			From	To	Miles
17	22	28	Pharr	McAllen	3
18	23	29	McAllen	Mission	6
19	24	30	Mission	Alton	7
20	25	31	Alton	Sterling's	6
21	26	1	Sterling's	La Gloria	3
22	27	2	La Gloria	Sterling's	3
23	28	3	Sterling's	Laguna Seca	10
24	29	4	Laguna Seca	Young's	6
25	30	5	Young's	Laguna Seca	6
26	31	6	Laguna Seca	Sterling's	10
27	1	7	Sterling's	Edinburg	14
28	2	8	Edinburg	Pharr	8

HEADQUARTERS, NEW YORK DIVISION.

McALLEN, TEX., *August* 14, 1916.

(IN CONNECTION WITH S. O. 156.)

Memorandum to all Regimental and Battalion Commanders of Infantry.

The Division Commander desires that particular attention be paid to the following, and that all of the recommendations and requirements be carefully observed.

1. The people at Sterling's Ranch and Young's Ranch are most hospitably inclined, but owing to the large number of troops that will be located at or near those places during the coming practice march, Regimental Commanders will station guards at both Sterling's Ranch and Young's Ranch, with instructions to notify all officers and enlisted men that they are not to enter the house or premises during the march.

2. Instructions will be given and every precaution taken to prevent damage of any kind to personal or public property.

3. Officers and enlisted men will be instructed not to trespass on private property.

4. Officers and enlisted men are to be warned that the appropriation of any articles, small or large, as souvenirs, may work a hardship on the owners, and such conduct is prohibited.

5. The most careful sanitary precautions will be adopted on the march, during halts and in camps. Regimental Commanders will charge their Regimental surgeons with seeing that every care is exercised in maintaining the health of the command.

6. Whenever a camp is vacated, the ground will be thoroughly policed, and policing means leaving it in such a condition that practically no evidence will be visible to the casual observer that the site had been occupied by troops.

7. Recruits are usually inclined to drink up all the water in their canteens during the first stages of the march or at the first halt, and then refill them

at the first opportunity regardless of the kind of water. The contemplated marches are all so short, that during very few of them will it be necessary to drink any water whatever; in any event, all company commanders will be instructed to see that the canteens of all of the men in their command are filled with good potable water before starting, and that there is no waste of same during the march.

8. As it may be difficult at some of the camp sites to supply large quantities of water, all Commanding Officers are charged with seeing that the men are economical in the use of water for any purpose.

9. All Officers before starting on the march should carefully read over those paragraphs of Field Service Regulations and Infantry Drill Regulations which pertain to marches, and should instruct their men to do the same.

10. It is seldom practicable to establish a typical camp as indicated in the Field Service Regulations. The location and arrangement of regimental, battalion and company camps will be such as to preserve the health of the command, and to interfere as little as possible with the comfort of the men.

11. Commanding Officers are cautioned to see that the men in pitching their shelter tents have the closed ends towards the prevailing wind.

12. Just before starting on all marches, maneuvers or military exercises, all troops will be inspected for ball ammunition.

13. Company Commanders are charged with seeing that the men's equipments are properly adjusted.

14. Regimental Commanders will require that all their animals be taken from the picket line at the same time and watered together. This to avoid the possibility of any animal being overlooked.

15. Regimental, Battalion and Company Commanders will, from time to time, march at the rear of their organizations to see that the march is being properly conducted.

16. Company Commanders will see that sufficient oil and cleaning material for the arms is carried on the march, and that all arms are oiled and cleaned as many times each day as may be necessary to keep them in proper condition.

17. The old established armory custom of "grounding arms" is prohibited. The men under no circumstances will lay their guns upon the ground, either collectively or individually. Ordinarily slings may be loosened so as to sling the piece over the shoulder and in any ordinary emergency requiring freedom of movement and, if a large detachment or company is required for any purpose, it will be moved to a suitable place and arms stacked.

18. It has been noted that mounted orderlies and others are inclined to slouch in the saddle. All officers are charged with observing mounted enlisted men, and requiring them to sit squarely and properly in the saddle.

19. The different regiments will be observed and inspected at various places along the line of march by officers especially detailed for that purpose, and the efficiency of the commands will be judged by the number of stragglers, extent to which the commands are closed up, the general appearance of the men, etc.

20. Each regimental commander will have full charge of the selection of his own camp site, and the making of all arrangements connected with the camp.

21. Company Commanders are particularly enjoined to keep the feet of the men in good condition.

22. Only field and staff officers will be mounted.

23. A guard of one squad with belts filled with ball ammunition will accompany and guard each combat wagon. This detail will be changed daily, and will also be charged with guarding any prisoners. This guard will not participate in maneuvers and exercises. Battalion Commanders will make suitable arrangements for promptly supplying their commands with ball ammunition in case of emergency.

BY COMMAND OF MAJOR GENERAL O'RYAN:

H. H. BANDHOLTZ,
Colonel, Chief of Staff.

OFFICIAL:

ALLAN L. REAGAN,
Major, Adjutant.

EXHIBIT " M "

NEW YORK DIVISION.

McALLEN, TEX., *Sept.* 1, 1916.

GENERAL ORDERS, }
   No. 20.   }

I. The Headquarters personnel is hereby subdivided, under the Chief of Staff as prescribed in Paragraph 261, F. S. R., as follows:

THE GENERAL STAFF DIVISION.

(a) The Combat Section.
(b) The Administrative Section.
(c) The Intelligence Section.

THE TECHNICAL AND ADMINISTRATIVE STAFF DIVISION.

(a) Inspector's Section.
(b) Judge Advocate's Section.
(c) Supply Section.
(d) Ordnance Section.
(e) Medical Section.
(f) Headquarters Detachment Section.

Colonel H. H. Bandholtz is announced as Chief of Staff.

II. The duties of the divisions and sections above enumerated will be:

THE GENERAL STAFF DIVISION.

(a) *The Combat Section* will concern itself with orders governing movements and dispositions of the forces, war diaries, maneuvers, problems, programs and schedules of instruction, critiques, bridge and road repairs, etc.

Major Edward Olmsted is announced as First Assistant Chief of Staff, and is assigned to the Combat Section, and in general as Assistant to the Chief of Staff.

(b) *The Administrative Section* will concern itself with organization, gains and losses, police and discipline, reports and returns, signal and general communication service, promulgation of orders, circulars, etc., compilation and care of records, and with correspondence in general.

Major A. L. Reagan is announced as Division Adjutant, and is assigned to the Administrative Section, which is further sub-divided as follows:

Report Sub-section. Consolidated morning reports, camp returns, programs and schedules of instruction, survey reports and ordnance requisitions.

Record Sub-section. Receiving and posting all Headquarters mail, entering and recording all papers, seeing that all outgoing papers are signed and lead pencil marks removed, preparing returns, checking up all returns due from subordinate organizations, etc.

Orders Sub-section. Preparing and checking up court-martial cases, keeping records of same, preparing all orders pertaining to court-martials, keeping all records concerning prisoners, and all data concerning the Military Police, preparing muster and pay-rolls of the Headquarters Detachment, descriptive lists and discharges of casuals, distributing and keeping War Department, Southern Department, and other orders, bulletins, etc., and correcting regulations and manual to conform to changes.

Distributing Sub-section. Having charge of orderlies, messengers, telephone operators, etc., the preparation and distribution of division orders, memoranda, circulars, etc., the care and cleaning of the offices, and the systematic and hourly collection of papers from the desk baskets, and their prompt distribution.

Printing Sub-section. Printing and mimeographing of orders, memoranda, etc., performing any special work that may be assigned.

Miscellaneous Sub-section. Preparing all papers and having charge of all miscellaneous work not assigned to another section.

The civilian and enlisted office force will be assigned to sub-sections by the Division Adjutant.

The work in the sub-sections of the Administrative Section will be governed by the following rules:

4

(1) The Chief Clerk, under the Adjutant, will have charge of the clerical force and the general distribution of work. Routine work as above assigned to the several sub-sections will be performed by each, but additional work may be assigned to any sub-section, and one sub-section may be required to assist another.

(2) All clerks will acquaint themselves with the work of the entire office and use of typewriters. They will familiarize themselves with all orders, circulars, memoranda and general instructions, and will be held responsible for the correct application of same.

(3) Action once taken in a particular case will establish a precedent and all similar cases will be handled in a like manner. Samples of the various forms of orders in frequent use will be prepared and followed until changed.

(4) Letters, indorsements, memoranda, etc., pertaining to the work of any section will be prepared and initialed in lead pencil by the clerk in charge as an indication of its correctness.

(5) All papers prepared by the Commanding General, the Chief of Staff and his Assistants, the Adjutant, or any other staff officer, will be checked before being submitted for signature.

(c) *The Intelligence Section* will concern itself with the movements and dispositions of the emeny, reconnaissance, gathering and distribution of information, newspapers, correspondence, deserters, prisoners of war, relations with inhabitants, etc.

Major F. W. Ward is announced as Second Assistant Chief of Staff, and is assigned to the Intelligence Section.

III. THE TECHNICAL AND ADMINISTRATIVE STAFF DIVISION.

(a) *The Inspector's Section* will concern itself with Inspections of the various organizations, their camps, means of transportation, morale, etc., and will make such investigations as may from time to time be required.

Major C. Vanderbilt is announced as Division Inspector.

(b) *The Judge Advocate's Section* will concern itself with the investigation and preparation of court-martial charges, the submitting of legal opinions on doubtful questions, the examination of all court-martial proceedings that are forwarded to these Headquarters, and in rendering any general assistance that may be required.

Major J. L. Kincaid is announced as Division Judge Advocate.

(e) *The Supply Section* will concern itself with the questions of quarters, subsistence, pay, transportation, clothing, fuel, light, water-supply and forage.

Lieut. Col. H. S. Sternberger is announced as Division Quartermaster and Captain J. T. Loree as Assistant Division Quartermaster.

The Supply Section is further sub-divided as follows:

Transportation Sub-section. Having charge of all transportation under the direct orders of the Division Quartermaster, having charge of the assignment and keeping in accurate record of all auto-transportation on duty in the division so that any vehicle can be immediately located, and keeping a record, to be verified monthly, of all the transportation with the various organizations.

Supply Sub-section. Having charge of all matters affecting the supply and equipment of the units of the division.

Record Sub-section. Having charge of all records not cared for by the Transportation Sub-section, and in charge of miscellaneous affairs.

The officers and enlisted men of the Supply Section will be assigned to duty by the Quartermaster.

(d) *The Ordnance Section* will concern itself with the supply of ammunition for the entire division, and with the target practice of all units.

Major F. M. Waterbury is announced as Division Ordnance Officer.

(e) *The Medical Section* will concern itself in general with the questions of the health and sanitation of the command and will be sub-divided by the Division Surgeon in such manner as he may deem best.

Lieut. Col. W. S. Terriberry is announced as Division Surgeon and Major E. R. Maloney as Assistant Surgeon.

Major W. H. Steers is announced as Division Sanitary Inspector.

(f) *The Headquarters Detachment* will consist of the entire enlisted personnel on duty at Division Headquarters.

First Lieut. R. R. Molyneux, Aide-de-Camp, is announced as Detachment Commander.

First Lieut. F. J. McCann, Aide-de-Camp, is charged with the general supervision of the destruction of refuse.

IV. All office work of whatever nature at Division Headquarters will be considered as strictly confidential.

V. No changes of any kind will be made in the Headquarters personnel without the approval of the Chief of Staff. Staff Officers, except when accompanying or summoned by the Commanding General, will not absent themselves from Headquarters over twelve hours at a time without the approval of the Chief of Staff, and all absences and returns will be indicated on the board prepared for the purpose.

VI. Official telegrams and mail will be opened by the Chief of Staff or by an officer designated by him. Official communications from Divisional units or individuals, unless otherwise marked on the envelope, will be opened by the Adjutant, who will handle routine matters but will submit any questions of importance or concerning general policy to the Chief of Staff.

VII. The Headquarters reference slips will habitually be used for intercommunication at Headquarters. They may frequently be used for the informal transmission or reference of papers to subordinate organizations, and in general their purpose will be to minimize clerical work.

VIII. Officers will endeavor to accomplish results with a minimum of office work. Whenever practicable, penciled notes, memoranda, personal conferences, etc., will be resorted to instead of formal letters. Communications will be made as brief as consistent with clarity. Officers desiring an official communication to be sent, will draft same in its proposed final form and place it in the " Incoming " basket of the Adjutant. Stenographers will be asked for only for rush work or lengthy papers.

IX. Whenever a division staff officer requires the services of a stenographer or clerk, he will apply verbally to the Division Adjutant for same.

X. All Division Staff Officers will consult the Headquarters bulletin board at least once every twenty-four hours.

XI. The North (central) office entrance will habitually be used by officers and enlisted men from organizations of the division who come to headquarters on business.

XII. Office furniture will not be removed from Headquarters except by permission of the Division Adjutant.

XIII. Division Staff Officers requiring automobile transportation will apply to the Division Quartermaster, and any officers desiring to have a mounted orderly assigned to him, will confer with the Commanding Officer of the Headquarters Detachment.

XIV. Regular office hours at Division Headquarters will be:

Daily (Sundays excepted) 8 A. M. to 12.30 P. M.; 1.30 P. M. to 5 P. M. Sundays, 8.30 A. M. to 12.30 P. M.

In addition to the foregoing, one stenographer will be on duty Sunday afternoons from 2.00 to 5.30 o'clock and daily, including Sundays, from 7.00 to 8.30 P. M. The Division Adjutant will arrange to have at least one man constantly present at Headquarters from 7.00 A. M. to 9.00 P. M. daily, to answer telephone calls, etc. The entire force is subject to call outside of the indicated hours to meet emergencies.

XV. On completion of the day's work, the desks will be cleared and neatly arranged; uncompleted papers cared for and typewriters covered. Every effort will be made to keep the office at all times in a neat and orderly condition.

XVI. The Division Surgeon's office will conform to the foregoing insofar as applicable.

BY COMMAND OF MAJOR-GENERAL O'RYAN:

H. H. BANDHOLTZ,

Chief of Staff.

OFFICIAL:

ALLAN L. REAGAN,

Adjutant.

EXHIBIT "N"

HEADQUARTERS, NEW YORK DIVISION.

McALLEN, TEX., *October* 3, 1916.

GENERAL ORDERS, }
No. 33.. }

1. Instructions Combat, Practice, suitable to the terrain and the experience of the participants, will begin at La Gloria on October 6th, for the detachment of the New York Division stationed at McAllen.

2. Major George F. Chandler, Adjutant, 1st Brigade, is detailed as Officer in Charge of Firing and as Range Officer during the entire practice. (Pars. 104 and 105, S. A. F. M.)

3. The Commanding Officer, 22d Engineers, will detail one officer and thirty men to remain at the range, under the orders of the officer in Charge of Firing, until the completion of the practice.

4. The Commanding Officer, Ambulance Company No. 2, will send one officer and sixteen men, four ambulances, and the dressing station equipment and will establish and maintain a station for the care of the sick and injured at La Gloria during the combat practice. Such patients as may require transfer will be transported to the Camp Hospital, at McAllen.

5. One battalion at a time will engage in two days' Instruction Combat Practice at La Gloria, and the battalions of each regiment will be sent singly at two day intervals.

All of the battalions will march from McAllen to La Gloria via Mission, Alton and Sterling's, in two marches. On the outward march they will camp over night at Alton.

On the return march, they will leave La Gloria on the afternoon of the second day's practice, camp that night at Sterling's and return, over the original route, in two marches to McAllen, camping over night at Alton.

6. The Commanding Officer of each Battalion, upon arrival at La Gloria, will report to the Officer in Charge of Firing.

7. Each regimental commander will detail one officer to report as assistant to the Officer in Charge of Firing during the entire practice of the regiment.

8. Each company commander through his battalion commander will submit to the Officer in Charge of Firing, a list of men too inexperienced to justify their participation in combat practice, and such men will be given a special elementary course each afternoon.

9. The regiments of the 1st Brigade will hold combat practice in the following order: 7th Infantry, 12th Infantry, 69th Infantry.

10. The 1st Battalion of the 7th Infantry will leave McAllen on the morning of October 4th, the 1st Battalion of the 12th Infantry on the morning of October 10th, and the 1st Battalion of the 69th Infantry on the morning of October 16th.

11. The Officer in charge of firing will make adequate provision for the safety of the operating personnel and of the organizations firing. He will deliver a short explanatory talk to each battalion before the commencement and at the conclusion of its practices, and a critique (Pars. 227, S. A. F. M.) will be given after each exercise. A figure of merit will be given each company.

12. Especial care will be taken that no unit is allowed to fire while one or more men of the adjoining unit are in advance of its front.

13. Equipment A will be carried, and each regiment is charged with arranging for the subsistence of its units.

14. The Quartermaster Corps will furnish any necessary additional transportation, and will make suitable arrangements for camp sites, wood and water at Alton and at Sterling's.

BY COMMAND OF MAJOR-GENERAL O'RYAN:

H. H. BANDHOLTZ,

Colonel, Chief of Staff.

OFFICIAL:

EDWARD OLMSTED,

Major, Acting Adjutant.

HEADQUARTERS, NEW YORK DIVISION.

McAllen, Tex., *October* 11, 1916.

General Orders, }
No. 36.   }

1. Instruction combat practice for the New York Infantry Regiments stationed at Pharr and for the Division Cavalry will begin at La Gloria on October 24th. The organizations will have their combat exercises in the following order: 23rd Infantry, 74th Infantry, 1st Cavalry, Squadron A.

2. One battalion or squadron at a time will engage in two days' practice at La Gloria, and such organizations will be sent singly at two day intervals.

3. The infantry will march from Pharr to La Gloria via Edinburg and Sterling's, halting the first night at Edinburg and the second night at Sterling's The following morning each battalion will start early enough from Sterling's to arrive at La Gloria in time to put in a full day's practice. The third night will be spent at La Gloria, leaving there after combat practice on the following day, and spending the fourth night at Sterling's, returning from there to Pharr in two marches via Edinburg.

4. The commanding officers of organizations, while encamped at Edinburg, will allow no officers or men to leave camp except in case of emergency, and then only for a brief time and on a written pass.

5. The cavalry will march from McAllen to Sterling's where each squadron will camp during its practice, proceeding early each morning to La Gloria and returning the same afternoon to Sterling's. After the third night each squadron will return direct to McAllen.

6. The 1st battalion, 23d Infantry, will leave Pharr on the morning of October 22d, and the first battalion, 74th Infantry, on the morning of October 26th. The 1st squadron, 1st Cavalry, will leave McAllen on the morning of November 4th.

7. Upon completion of all the foregoing, the 3d Tennessee Infantry will engage in combat practice, conforming to the above instructions for the New York Infantry regiments and sending its 1st Battalion from Pharr on the morning of November 11th.

8. G. O. No. 33, current series, these headquarters, except Paragraphs 1, 3, 9 and 10, will apply.

By command of Major-General O'Ryan:

H. H. BANDHOLTZ,
Colonel, Chief of Staff.

Official:

Edward Olmsted,
Major, Acting Adjutant.

HEADQUARTERS, SIXTH DIVISION.

McAllen, Tex., *November* 1, 1916.

General Orders, }
No. 45.   }

1. So much of Paragraphs 6 and 7, G. O. 36, New York Division, as affects the dates of departure of the 1st New York Cavalry and the 3d Tennessee Infantry for combat practice are amended as follows:

The 1st Battalion, 3d Tennessee Infantry, will leave Pharr on the morning of November 3, 1916.

The 1st Squadron, 1st N. Y. Cavalry, will leave McAllen on the morning of November 10, 1916.

By command of Major-General O'Ryan:

H. H. BANDHOLTZ,
Colonel, Chief of Staff.

Official:

Frank E. Bamford,
Major, 26th U. S. Inf., Acting Adjutant.

Exhibit "O"

HEADQUARTERS, NEW YORK DIVISION.

McAllen, Texas, *October* 14, 1916.

General Orders, }
No. 37.   }

1. A line of detached posts will be established along the Military Road from Madero to San Juan Hacienda.

Upon receipt of proper orders, each commanding officer of the regiments designated will establish and maintain one two-company detached post as follows:

        7th N. Y. Infantry at Madero,
        12th N. Y. Infantry at Granjeno Ranch,
        69th N. Y. Infantry at Hidalgo,
        23rd N. Y. Infantry at Capote Ranch,
        74th N. Y. Infantry at San Juan Hacienda.

2. The *Madero Sector* extends from Cavazos (inclusive) about one mile Southwest of Madero, to the Reported Crossing (exclusive), about three miles down the Rio Grande River from Madero, and about two miles southwest of Granjeno Ranch.

The *Granjeno Ranch Sector* extends from the "Reported Crossing" (inclusive) down the Rio Grande River to the Rio Bravo Pump plant (exclusive).

The *Hidalgo Sector* extends from the Rio Bravo Pump Plant (inclusive) down the Rio Grande River to a point one mile from the Hidalgo Pump Plant.

The *Capote Ranch Sector* extends from the down-stream limits of the Hidalgo Sector to Smuggler's crossing (inclusive) directly South of the Crossing of the Pharr road with the Military Road.

The *San Juan Hacienda Sector* extends from Smuggler's Crossing (exclusive) to a point three miles down the Rio Grande River.

Each commanding officer upon arriving at his post will arrange with adjoining commands to mark sector divisions by a stake or otherwise.

3. The two companies at each detached post will be relieved every four days.

4. All questions involving equipment to be used, camp sites, fuel, water, transportation and supply will be handled by the regimental commanders.

5. One medical officer and a suitable hospital corps detachment from the regiment concerned will be stationed at each detached post, and need not be changed unless so desired by the regimental commander.

6. Each detached post commander will provide himself with a good map of his own sector and the neighboring country, and immediately upon taking station will have a sketch (scale 6" to 1 mile) made of that portion of his sector one-half mile north or east of the Military Road to the Rio Grande River and clearly indicating thereon all outguards, regular patrols and other dispositions.

7. Each detached post commander will keep a diary showing in detail the dispositions made, the number of patrols used, information received, and in general containing a record of all matters of military value.

8. Each detached post commander, upon being relieved, will explain his sketch and diary to his successor, and will transmit to him all orders and information pertaining to the station; upon joining his regiment he will forward his sketch and a detailed written report, compiled from his diary, to these Headquarters, through channels.

9. Brigade, regimental and battalion commanders will make at least one careful inspection of each two companies during their tour of detached post duty.

10. All crossings of the Rio Grande River are now illegal, except at Hidalgo. Each detached post commander will prevent illegal crossings or traffic within his sector. Any person arrested will be sent at once to Hidalgo and turned over to the immigration authorities for examination. Such persons arrested in the Madero and San Juan Hacienda Sectors will be turned over to the commanding officers of the Granjeno Ranch and Capote Ranch Sectors

respectively, and by them sent to Hidalgo as above prescribed. Any boats found on the American side of the Rio Grande river will be seized and the matter immediately reported to the immigration authorities at Hidalgo.

11. Each morning the river bank will be carefully examined for evidence of crossings.

12. Fords and crossings will be under constant observation, and roads and trails leading to the river will be covered.

13. Each detached post commander will establish an outpost formation that will effectively and appropriately cover his entire sector by suitable outguards and patrols by day and night. Taking advantage of every opportunity to give his command as much instruction and training as possible, he will impress upon them the fact that their work while on these duties is essentially practical, and that the situation is real and not assumed.

14. Regimental commanders will see that suitable defenses are prepared at their respective detached posts, that the works are of appropriate character and as progressive in construction as practicable, so that each relief will have its proportionate share of work, and in this connection, the troops will be instructed in the making of gabions, fascines, hurdles, and other revetting material, as described in the Engineer Field Manual, pages 371 to 376. The outguards will also be given practical field instruction by intrenching their positions. See Infantry Drill regulations, paragraphs 584 to 595.

15. Each detached post commander will inform himself and notify his command as to the location of neighboring troops, and especial care will be taken to avoid accidents in the way of firing upon cavalry patrols or other troops whose duties may require them to pass along the front covered by the New York Division.

16. The entire command is reminded that many of the inhabitants of the Texas Border do not understand English, and nobody should be fired at unless clearly a dangerous enemy. Commanding officers are strictly enjoined to take every possible precaution to prevent accidents from excess of zeal, from overwrought imaginations, or otherwise; and they are cautioned that ordinary objects are frequently distorted in appearance at night so that floating logs look like boats, stumps like men, etc.

17. The commanding officer of the Divisional Cavalry will maintain in his discretion a one troop or two troop detached post at Mission and will conform to as much of the foregoing instructions as may be applicable to the case.

18. The commanding officer of the Signal Battalion will arrange for the communication of the detached posts with each other and with regimental, brigade and division headquarters. ·

19. The commanding officer, 22d New York Engineers is charged with keeping all connecting roads in condition for quick movements, and he will also frequently inspect the defenses and make recommendations to the detached post commanders in case he considers any changes in construction or plans advisable.

20. The Division Surgeon will see that all proper sanitary precautions are taken at the various detached posts.

21. The troops of this division will at all times co-operate with the forces in the Brownsville District.

BY COMMAND OF MAJOR-GENERAL O'RYAN:

H. H. BANDHOLTZ,
Colonel, Chief of Staff.

Official:

EDWARD OLMSTED,
Major, Acting Adjutant.

EXHIBIT "P"

HEADQUARTERS, SIXTH DIVISION.

MCALLEN, TEXAS, *November* 1, 1916.

Confidential.

GENERAL ORDERS, }
    No. 46. }

I. On November 3d, the line of detached posts established along the Military Road from Madero to San Juan Hacienda by G. O. 37, these Headquarters, October 14, 1916, will be extended on the west to 1 mile east of Penitas, and on the east to La Donna Canal. Total length of road covered as line of resistance about 28 miles, and of river front as line of observation about 52 miles.

II. The Rio Grande River front is divided into sectors as follows:

(1) The Ojo De Agua (Abram) Sector extends from "Crossing" (inclusive), west of San Pedro Ranch, downstream to Sgt. Smith's Crossing (exclusive).

(2) The Madero (La Lomita) Sector extends from Sgt. Smith's Crossing (inclusive) downstream to a point about ½ mile southwest of the Catholic Novitiate School (inclusive).

(3) The Granjeno Sector extends from the downstream limits of the Madero Sector to a point on the north bend of the river about 1 mile east of Granjeno and about ⅛ mile south of the Military Road.

(4) The Hidalgo Sector extends from the downstream limits of the Granjeno Sector downstream to the Hidalgo Pump (inclusive).

(5) The Louisiana Rio Grande Canal Sector extends from the Hidalgo Pump (exclusive) downstream to "Reported Crossing" (inclusive) about 1¼ miles southwest of Capote Ranch.

(6) The Capote Ranch Sector extends from "Reported Crossing" (exclusive), downstream to Jackson (inclusive) opposite Jalisco on the Mexican side.

(7) The San Juan Hacienda Sector extends from Jackson (exclusive) downstream to south of Esperanza Ranch '(T. J. Handy) (inclusive).

(8) The Jackson Sector extends from a point south of Esperanza Ranch (exclusive) to La Donna Canal (exclusive).

III. The Divisional Cavalry will cover to Ojo De Agua and Jackson Sectors with one squadron as follows:

Two or three troops — Ojo De Agua Sector.

One or two troops — Jackson Sector.

The detached post at Mission will be discontinued.

IV. The 1st Brigade will cover the Madero, Granjeno and Hidalgo Sectors as follows:

7th N. Y. Infantry one battalion — Madero Sector.

12th N. Y. Infantry one battalion — Granjeno Sector.

69th N. Y. Infantry one battalion — Hidalgo Sector.

V. The 3rd Brigade will cover the Louisiana Rio Grande Canal, Capote Ranch, and San Juan Hacienda Sectors as follows:

3d Tenn. Infantry one battalion — Louisiana Rio Grande Canal Sector.

23d N. Y. Infantry one battalion — Capote Ranch Sector.

74th N. Y. Infantry one battalion — San Juan Hacienda Sector.

VI. Each Brigade commander will arrange so that the Machine Gun Company of one of his regiments is constantly on or near the line of resistance. In case one regiment is temporarily detached for combat exercises or other duty, he will cover his three sectors with the two remaining battalions.

VII. Each command will march to and from its post as though in the presence of an enemy. March, camp and outpost orders will be issued.

VIII. Each Commanding Officer, upon arriving at his station will get in touch with the commanders of adjoining stations, and will arrange to mark sector divisions by stakes or otherwise. Brigade Commanders will decide all questions of jurisdiction in their own commands and will refer other such questions to these Headquarters.

IX. The Commanding Officer in each sector will suitably locate his command in one or more detached posts along the line of resistance.

X. Each sector commander will establish an outpost formation that will effectively and appropriately cover his entire sector by suitable outguards, and patrols by day and night. Advantage will be taken of every opportunity to give his command as much instruction and training as possible. He will impress upon them the fact that their work, while on these duties, is essentially practical and that the situation is real and not assumed.

XI. Each sector commander will require the officers and enlisted men of his command to learn a few words of Spanish. A small English-Spanish vocabulary will be found in the "Manual for Non-commissioned Officers and Privates of Infantry of the Organized Militia and Volunteers of the United States," pages 252–261. There are numerous other small books available for acquiring an elementary knowledge of Spanish. The following are given as necessary for sentinels:

English	Spanish	Pronunciation
Halt!	Alto!	Ahl-to.
Who comes there?	Quien vive?	Kee-Ain-Vee-veh.

XII. All crossings of the Rio Grande River along our line of observation are now illegal, except at the 'Hidalgo Immigration Crossing. Each detached post commander will prevent illegal crossings or traffic within his sector. Any person arrested will be sent at once to the immigration authorities at Hidalgo by suitable transportation or by being turned over to successive commanding officers en route. Prisoners will be treated courteously and kindly.

XIII. Each morning the river bank will be carefully examined for evidence of crossing.

XIV. Fords and crossings will be under constant observation. All roads and trails leading to the river will be covered.

XV. Each sector commander will provide himself with a good map of his own sector and contiguous country. Immediately upon taking station he will have a sketch (scale 6″ to 1 mile) made of that portion of his sector one-half mile north or east of the Military Road to the Rio Grande River and clearly indicating thereon all outguards, regular patrols and other dispositions.

XVI. Detached post and sector commanders will keep a diary showing in detail the dispositions made, the number and kind of patrols, information received and in general containing a record of all matters of military value.

XVII. In case of attack by a small hostile force, each regiment will support its own line and adjoining posts will support each other. In case of any large movement these headquarters will have sufficient advance notice to give the necessary orders.

XVIII. Each detached post commander and each sector commander, upon being relieved, will explain his sketch and diary to his successor, and will transmit to him all orders and information pertaining to the station. Upon joining his regiment, he will forward his sketch and a detailed written report, compiled from his diary, to these Headquarters, through channels.

XIX. The troops in each sector will be relieved weekly in such rotation as will insure an equal distribution of this class of duties among the organizations of each regiment, or arm.

XX. All questions involving equipment to be used, rental of camp sites, fuel, water, transportation, supply and medical attendance will be handled by the regimental commanders.

XXI. Regimental commanders will see that suitable defenses are prepared along their respective lines, that the works are of appropriate character and as progressive in construction as practicable, so that each relief will have its proportionate share of work, and in this connection, the troops will be instructed in the making of gabions, fascines, hurdles, and other revetting material, as described in the Engineer Field Manual, pages 371 to 376. The outguards will also be given practical field instruction by intrenching their positions. See Infantry Drill Regulations, paragraphs 584 to 595.

XXII. Each regimental and organization commander will send to these Headquarters, at least 24 hours in advance of a change, the designation of his new outpost detail, with the name of its commander.

XXIII. To make compliance with the foregoing more practicable, par. 3, G. O. 37 is amended to read as follows: The two companies at each detached post on November 2nd may remain until relieved by operation of this order.

XXIV. Brigade and regimental commanders will make at least one careful inspection of each battalion or detachment during its tour of outpost duty.

XXV. The entire command is reminded that many inhabitants of the border are unacquainted with the English language and no one should be fired upon unless clearly identified as an enemy. Commanding officers are strictly enjoined to take every precaution to prevent accidents which may result from excess of zeal, over-wrought imagination, or partial identification. In this connection troops are cautioned that at night ordinary objects are frequently distorted in appearance, floating logs and stumps of trees resembling boats, men, etc. An animate object failing to halt or answer when challenged, may prove to be an animal.

XXVI. The Commanding Officer of the Signal Battalion will arrange for the communication of the detached posts with each other and with regimental, brigade and division headquarters.

XXVII. The Commanding Officer, 22nd New York Engineers is charged with keeping all connecting roads in condition for quick movements; he will frequently inspect the defenses and make recommendations to the detached post commanders in case he considers any changes in construction of plans advisable. He will add to the progressive military map the data submitted by the various detachments.

XXVIII. The Division Surgeon will see that all proper sanitary precautions are taken at the various detached posts, and will have one ambulance for emergency service stationed at each of the headquarters of the Ojo De Agua, Hidalgo and San Juan Hacienda Sectors. The ambulance personnel will be subsisted with the organizations at the stations to which attached.

XXIX. The Commanding General, Artillery Brigade, will prepare data for promptly covering the various crossings along the line of observation and for supporting the defense of any sector that may be threatened with attack.

XXX. Commanding Officers of organizations may modify the requirements as to periods of instruction in Training Memorandum of October 27th so that the course prescribed therein will be interfered with as little as possible.

XXXI. The troops of this division will at all times cooperate with the forces in the Brownsville District. There is a company of 28th U. S. Infantry at Penitas and the 2d Provisional Cavalry Regiment, Brownsville District, at Donna.

BY COMMAND OF MAJOR-GENERAL O'RYAN:

H. H. BANDHOLTZ,
Colonel, Chief of Staff.

Official:

Frank E. Bamford,
Major, 28th U. S. Inf., Act. Adjutant.

EXHIBIT "Q"

List of Deaths with Causes in New York Division, July 19th to November 25th, 1916

NAME	Rank	Co.	Organization	Cause of death
Martin, Clarke..........	Private...	Hq.	69th N. Y. Inf......	Pneumonia.
Loc'er, Joseph..........	Corp....	M	12th N. Y. Inf......	Typhoid.*
Healy, Clinton..........	Private...	.....	23d N. Y. Inf......	Tuberculosis.*
Whelan, Hans S.........	2d Lt....	.....	69th N. Y. Inf......	Tubercular meningitis.*
Chichester, George B.....	1st Sgt...	H	7th N. Y. Inf......	Dysentery.
Winslow, Claude........	Private...	B	N. Y. Sig. Corps....	Gastroenterocolitis.
Lockwood..............	Sgt......	.....	12th N. Y. Inf......	Accidental drowning.
Boldtman, Harold O.....	Private...	L	7th N. Y. Inf......	Paratyphoid " A."
Cohn. Joseph	Private...	B	12th N. Y. Inf......	Intestinal obstruction.
Johnson. William...... ..	Private...	E	2d N. Y. F. A......	Accidental kick by horse.
Bishop, Fred E.........	Private...	.....	N. Y. Amb Co. No. 1.	Gunshot wound.
Riley, Peter.......... ..	'Private...	B	1st N. Y. Cav......	Dysentery.
Baker, Willett........	MSE....	.....	N. Y. Sig. Corps....	Interstitial nephritis.
Smith, Robert J.........	Private...	D	12th N. Y. Inf......	Paratyphoid " A."
Webster, William J......	Private...	B	N. Y. Sig. Corps....	Paratyphoid " A."
McEvoy, James F.......	Private...	F	12th N. Y. Inf......	Tuberculosis.
Vassar, Rufus P........	Private...	E	7th N. Y. Inf......	Nephritis.
Smith, William N.......	Private...	E	12th N. Y. Inf......	Paratyphoid " A."
Flynn, Richard J........	Private...	B	3d N. Y. F. A......	Gunshot wound.
Murtaj, Peter..........	Private...	K	69th N. Y. Inf......	Endocarditis.
....	.....	.....	3d Tenn. Inf.......	Accidental drowning.

* Died at base hospital, Fort Sam Houston, Tex.

The above list does not include two members of the 14th N. Y. Inf. accidentally drowned, nor one man from the 1st N. Y. Field Artillery accidentally killed while en route from Camp Whitman to McAllen, Texas, nor those who died at home stations.

EXHIBIT "R"

HEADQUARTERS DIVISION, NATIONAL GUARD, NEW YORK.

MUNICIPAL BUILDING

NEW YORK CITY, *January* 26th. 1917.

FMW–WHM

No: .

From: Ordnance Officer, Division,
To: Commanding General, Division,
Subject: Annual Report of Small Arms Firing, 1916.

1. The annual report of Small Arms Firing for the year 1916, is submitted as follows:

The course for small arms firing, prescribed in Article V, Small Arms Firing Manual, 1913, for the practice of the Organized Militia, was followed during the season of 1916, by a majority of the organizations, Mexican Border Service preventing the annual practice of many organizations.

2. The record practice of the troops of Greater New York began at Peekskill on Monday, April 17th, 1916, and completed on May 19th, 1916. On Saturday, May 20th, Companies G, H, I and L of the 10th Infantry, completed their record firing. On Tuesday and Wednesday, May 23rd and 24th, the 1st and 2nd Battalions, Naval Militia, practiced at Peekskill. The record practice of the troops was supervised by Lieutenant-Colonel N. B. Thurston, Chief Ordnance Officer, assisted by me.

3. Under authority of the Governor, a detail of four officers and one hundred enlisted men from the various organizations of Greater New York, formed a Provisional Detachment under command of Captain Joseph J. Daly, 22nd Corps of Engineers, assisted by Captain Frederick C. Ringer, 22nd Corps of Engineers, Captain Charles A. Bodin, 13th Coast Defense Command and 1st Lieutenant Leo F. Knust, 7th Infantry, for duty as scorers and mark-

ers on the Peekskill Ranges. This detachment was placed on duty on Saturday, April 15th, and was relieved on Wednesday, May 24th. The work performed by this detachment was efficient and satisfactory.

4. The record practice of other organizations of the 3rd Brigade was supervised by me on the State Range at Rensselaerwyck and the various company ranges throughout the State, up to and including June 17th, the practice being then taken up and supervised by Captain Howard E. Crall, Acting Ordnance Officer, 2nd Division, assisted by Lieutenant Eugene McK. Froment.

5. No record practice was held this year in the Fourth Brigade, the 3rd Infantry and 74th Infantry being away on Mexican Border Service and the 65th Infantry having been converted into a regiment of Field Artillery and also mustered into Federal Service on the border.

6. With the exception of Troop B, 1st Cavalry, Albany, the up-State Cavalry Troops and Batteries of Artillery attached to Headquarters did not have annual small arms record firing for the same reasons as stated in paragraph 5.

7. The following table shows the results of the season's small arms practice:

For the Government Decoration Prescribed by the War Department for Organized Militia

Organization	Expert riflemen	Sharp-shooters	Marks-men	Total
Headquarters Division, Departments, etc....	11	2	0	13
22nd Regt. of Engineers....................	27	33	48	108
1st Regt. of Cavalry......................	*85	38	73	196
Squadron A and Machine Gun Troop.......	45	59	120	224
1st Armored Motor Battery..............	2	6	11	19
Total	170	138	252	560

Coast Artillery Corps

Organization	Marksmen	Total
8th Coast Defense Command....................	6	6
9th Coast Defense Command....................	8	8
13th Coast Defense Command.................	17	17
Total	31	31

First Brigade

Organization	Expert riflemen	Sharp-shooters	Marks-men	Total
Headquarters, 1st Brigade.................	1	....	....	1
7th Infantry	89	117	271	477
12th Infantry	16	8	33	57
69th Infantry	10	8	23	41
71st Infantry	34	31	61	126
Total	150	164	388	702

Second Brigade

Organization	Expert riflemen	Sharp-shooters	Marks-men	Total
Headquarters, 2nd Brigade................	1	....	....	1
14th Infantry	14	7	22	43
23rd Infantry	15	27	63	105
47th Infantry	8	9	25	42
Total	38	43	110	191

* Five troops not practicing on account of Mexican Border Service.

For the Government Decoration Prescribed by the War Department for
Organized Militia — *Continued*

Third Brigade

Organization	Expert riflemen	Sharp-shooters	Marks-men	Total
Headquarters, 3rd Brigade.................	3	....	1	4
1st Infantry	†136	85	168	389
2nd Infantry	‡102	36	58	196
10th Infantry	§56	50	98	204
Total	297	171	325	793

Fourth Brigade

Organization	Expert riflemen	Sharp-shooters	Marks-men	Total
Headquarters, 4th Brigade.....(Holdovers)	5	....	....	5
3rd Infantry ....(Holdovers)	¶139	....	....	139
74th Infantry ....(Holdovers)	¶72	....	....	72
Total	216	....	....	216

65th Infantry converted into 3rd Field Artillery.
No practice. Mexican Border Service.

Recapitulation

Organization	Expert riflemen	Sharp-shooters	Marks-men	Total
Headquarters, Division, etc...............	170	138	252	560
Coast Artillery Corps.....................	....	....	31	31
1st Brigade	150	164	388	702
2nd Brigade	38	43	110	191
3rd Brigade	297	171	325	793
4th Brigade ....(Holdovers)	216	....	....	216
Total	871	516	1106	2493

The following table shows the result of

Pistol Practice
Under S. A. F. M. 1913

Organization	Expert	1st Class	Total
Headquarters, Division	1	2	3
1st Battalion, Signal Corps...........	3	1	4
1st Field Artillery....................	‖8	6	14
2nd Field Artillery...................	2	5	7
13th Coast Defense Command..........	1	......	1
1st Infantry	3	......	3
2nd Infantry	1	......	1
3rd Infantry	2	......	2
10th Infantry	......	2	2
12th Infantry	1	......	1
Total	22	16	38

† Two companies excused from practicing.
‡ Seven companies not practicing on account of Mexican Border Service.
§ One company not practicing, rifle range condemned.
¶ Not practicing on account of Mexican Border Service.
‖ Two batteries not practicing on account of Mexican Border Service.

The Figure of Merit Prizes authorized by M. L. 112, consist of the three prizes in Headquarters, Division, National Guard, and in each Brigade, of the value of $100.00, $75.00 and $50.00, respectively, to be awarded to the three companies in organizations or corps attached to the Headquarters, Division, National Guard, and of each Brigade attaining the highest general figure of merit.   The firing for these prizes resulted as follows:

FIGURE OF MERIT, 1916

Headquarters, Division......	Troop B, Squadron A, Cavalry......	88.48
	Troop B, 1st Cavalry..............	85.00
	Troop C, Squadron A, Cavalry....	81.56
1st Brigade................	Company D, 7th Infantry.........	78.29
	Company F, 7th Infantry..........	76.73
	Company I, 7th Infantry..........	73.18
2nd Brigade...............	Company K, 23rd Infantry........	38.97
	Company I, 23rd Infantry........	36.47
	Company A, 23rd Infantry........	31.32
3rd Brigade...............	Company G, 1st Infantry..........	101.62
	Company L, 2nd Infantry.........	80.00
	Company K, 10th Infantry........	71.78
4th Brigade...............	No practice.— Mexican Border Service.	

THE NATIONAL DEFENSE TROPHIES

Were won as folows:

Organization	Expert riflemen	Sharp-shooters	Marks-men	Total
Co. "G," 1st Infantry	23	39	36	98
Co. "F," 7th Infantry	6	13	41	60
Troop "B," Squadron A..................	11	18	27	56

THE NATIONAL TROPHY

(Circular No. 5, W. D., D. M. A., March 14, 1914)
Was won as follows:

ORGANIZATION	Expert riflemen	Sharp-shooters	Marks-men	First Class	Second Class	Figure of merit
Co. "G", 1st Infantry......	23	39	36	3	0	99.80

COMPANY	Expert riflemen	Sharp-shooters	Marks-men	First Class	Second Class	Divisor	Figure of merit
Co. G, 1st Inf.................	13	25	20	10	0	68	101.62
Troop B, Squad. A.............	10	19	27	16	1	79	88.48
Troop B, 1st Cav..............	6	20	21	10	4	68	85.00
Troop C, Squad. A.............	4	22	23	14	6	77	81.56
Co. L, 2nd Inf.................	6	14	20	25	6	75	80.00
Co. D, 7th Inf.................	6	12	22	20	1	70	78.29
Co. F, 7th Inf.................	6	13	41	28	7	107	76.73
Troop A, Squad. A.............	2	14	26	16	0	70	76.29
Co. I, 7th Inf..................	7	12	29	12	11	85	73.18
Co. K, 10th Inf................	4	12	22	16	7	73	71.78
Co. K, 7th Inf.................	7	21	18	19	17	99	68.38
Machine Gun Troop, Cav.......	2	8	23	18	5	69	68.12
Co. C, 7th Inf.................	2	11	31	15	11	88	66.93
Troop D, Squad. A.............	0	12	25	10	6	70	66.57
Co. L, 7th Inf.................	3	11	22	11	8	73	65.07
Co. G, 7th Inf.................	6	9	18	11	8	74	60.68
Co. M, 1st Inf.................	5	7	25	28	6	99	58.48
Co. I, 1st Inf..................	4	13	17	27	0	91	57.47
Co. H, 1st Inf.................	3	10	18	40	9	106	56.79
Co. B, 1st Inf.................	2	2	19	30	2	78	51.36
Co. E, 10th Inf................	0	11	15	17	1	73	51.64
Co. D, 2nd Inf.................	0	8	11	22	5	68	51.47
Co. B, 7th Inf.................	1	11	21	8	13	94	47.13
Co. E, 7th Inf.................	1	6	15	9	9	68	46.76
Co. B, 2nd Inf.................	2	5	12	18	5	71	46.06
Co. F, 1st Inf.................	2	6	17	13	6	79	45.82

The National Trophy — *Continued*

COMPANY	Expert riflemen	Sharp-shooters	Marks-men	First Class	Second Class	Divisor	Figure of merit
Co A, 7th Inf	1	9	11	5	10	68	42.79
Co. M, 7th Inf	1	8	16	4	8	75	42.13
Co. A, 1st Inf	4	3	16	21	7	95	41.58
Co. F, 10th Inf	6	8	11	17	7	98	40.82
Co. K, 1st Inf	0	5	21	13	5	90	40.33
Co. K, 23rd Inf	1	5	13	6	8	68	38.97
Co. H, 7th Inf	3	5	12	3	7	68	37.79
Troop C, 1st Cav	3	3	12	5	9	68	37.50
Troop A, 1st Cav	3	5	8	6	11	68	36.91
Co. D, 1st Inf	1	3	12	23	2	85	36.59
Co. I, 23rd Inf	2	2	10	11	9	68	36.47
Co. D, 1st Batt. Eng	5	6	6	3	9	69	34.78
Troop K, 1st Cav	4	3	9	5	11	72	34.03
Co. C, 2nd Inf	1	6	6	15	7	76	33.68
Co. C, 10th Inf	3	5	6	9	5	67	33.58
Co. A, 1st Batt. Eng	4	4	9	7	3	73	32.33
Co. A, 23rd Inf	1	7	8	4	5	68	31.32
Co. G, 2nd Batt. Eng	1	2	10	6	9	68	30.29
Co. E, 2nd Batt. Eng	4	2	4	9	10	68	30.00
Co. A, 10th Inf	1	4	7	7	11	72	29.44
Co. I, 10th Inf	1	4	12	4	13	89	28.31
Co. B, 10th Inf	2	4	8	3	6	68	27.94
Troop L, 1st Cav	1	6	9	1	10	77	27.79
Troop F, 1st Cav	0	4	8	5	8	67	27.76
Co. A, 2nd Inf	1	6	7	8	11	88	27.27
Co. D, 10th Inf	2	4	5	7	5	68	26.47
Co. L, 71st Inf	3	1	9	3	5	67	26.12
Co. H, 2nd Batt. Eng	1	3	6	8	5	68	25.44
1st Armored Motor Bty	2	6	11	13	23	151	24.51
Co. H, 71st Inf	4	3	5	6	7	81	24.07
Co. G, 71st Inf	0	4	6	4	8	68	23.53
Co. B, 12th Inf	2	4	5	6	4	76	22.37
Co. G, 23rd Inf	1	3	8	0	6	68	21.91
Co. L, 10th Inf	1	3	5	5	4	68	20.74
Troop E, 1st Cav	1	1	5	6	9	70	20.70
Co. E, 71st Inf	5	4	7	8	7	121	20.66
Co. C, 71st Inf	0	4	7	3	5	76	20.00
Co. H, 10th Inf	1	1	8	4	7	78	19.87
Co. C, 1st Batt. Eng	1	6	5	5	8	97	19.79
Co. K, 71st Inf	4	5	5	7	12	126	19.29
Co. F, 23rd Inf	0	2	2	6	12	68	18.53
Co. F, 2nd Batt. Eng	1	7	4	3	9	101	18.12
Co. B, 71st Inf	1	5	4	0	7	79	17.09
Co. F, 69th Inf	1	2	3	5	5	68	16.76
Co. M, 69th Inf	1	2	5	1	5	67	16.42
Co. A, 71st Inf	2	1	5	1	3	66	15.61
Co. H, 23rd Inf	0	3	2	4	7	68	15.44
Co. C, 1st Inf	2	4	6	6	17	150	15.41
Co. E, 14th Inf	0	4	4	4	6	87	15.17
Co. B, 1st Batt. Eng	0	4	3	2	4	68	15.00
Co. D, 71st Inf	2	1	3	1	12	80	14.88
Co. K, 47th Inf	1	2	3	3	4	68	14.41
Co. G, 14th Inf	5	0	2	2	1	68	14.12
Co. F, 12th Inf	2	1	4	0	5	68	13.97
Co. B, 23rd Inf	0	0	3	7	5	68	13.53
Co. L, 12th Inf	0	2	3	3	6	71	13.24
Co. I, 71st Inf	0	0	3	4	8	68	12.65
Co. E, 23rd Inf	1	2	3	1	4	68	12.65
Co. G, 12th Inf	0	1	3	1	8	67	11.79
Co. C, 23rd Inf	0	0	2	3	11	70	11.71
Co. E, 12th Inf	1	0	3	4	3	68	11.47
Co. M, 71st Inf	0	1	3	3	5	71	11.13
Co. L, 69th Inf	1	0	4	1	4	68	10.88
Co. G, 10th Inf	0	3	1	4	6	84	10.83
Co. M, 23rd Inf	0	1	5	2	4	87	10.23
Co. D, 23rd Inf	0	1	3	2	4	68	10.15
Co. A, 71st Inf	0	1	2	2	7	70	10.14
Co. I, 12th Inf	0	1	2	1	7	68	9.56
Co. D, 12th Inf	0	0	1	3	8	69	8.70
Co. G, 47th Inf	0	0	2	2	4	68	8.68
Co. E, 47th Inf	0	0	2	1	8	68	8.18
Co. L, 23rd Inf	1	0	3	1	5	68	8.53
Co. A, 47th Inf	0	1	3	0	4	68	8.38
Co. D, 47th Inf	0	0	3	1	4	68	7.65
Co. C, 14th Inf	0	0	2	3	5	75	6.93
Co. B, 47th Inf	0	1	3	0	1	68	6.62
Co. I, 69th Inf	0	0	2	1	5	76	6.05
Co. H, 47th Inf	0	1	2	0	2	68	5.74
Co. H, 14th Inf	0	0	2	1	3	67	5.67

THE NATIONAL TROPHY — *Concluded*

COMPANY	Expert riflemen	Sharpshooters	Marksmen	First Class	Second Class	Divisor	Figure of merit
Co. F, 14th Inf	0	0	3	0	2	68	5.59
Co. H, 69th Inf	0	0	2	2	3	79	5.57
Co. A, 12th Inf	0	0	3	0	2	68	5.51
Co. E, 69th Inf	1	1	0	0	3	68	5.15
Co. C, 69th Inf	0	2	0	0	3	68	5.00
Co. B, 69th Inf	1	1	0	1	1	68	4.85
Co. A, 14th Inf	0	1	1	0	3	68	4.85
Co. M, 14th Inf	0	0	2	0	3	68	4.71
Co. I, 47th Inf	1	0	1	1	1	68	4.71
Co. H, 12th Inf	0	1	1	0	1	67	3.73
Co. L, 14th Inf	0	1	0	1	2	68	3.68
Co. F, 47th Inf	0	0	0	3	1	67	3.28
Co. M, 12th Inf	0	0	1	2	0	68	3.24
Co. D, 14th Inf	0	0	1	0	3	68	3.24
Co. C, 47th Inf	0	1	1	0	0	68	3.09
Co. C, 12th Inf	0	0	1	1	1	68	2.94
Co. L, 47th Inf	0	0	0	2	2	68	2.94
Co. G, 69th Inf	0	0	1	0	2	67	3.69
Co. M, 47th Inf	0	0	1	0	2	68	2.65
Co. K, 14th Inf	0	0	1	1	0	68	2.35
Co. K, 12th Inf	0	0	0	2	1	68	2.31
Co. K, 69th Inf	0	0	1	0	1	67	2.09
Co. A, 69th Inf	0	0	1	0	1	68	2.06
Co. I, 14th Inf	0	0	1	0	0	68	1.47
Co. B, 14th Inf	0	0	1	0	0	68	1.47
Co. D, 69th Inf	0	0	0	0	1	68	0.59

FIGURE OF MERIT OF COAST ARTILLERY BY COMPANIES

COMPANY	Marksmen	First class	Second class	Divisor	Figure of merit
D. C.	3	8	5	91	10.77
. D. C.	2	4	6	68	10.00
. D. C.	2	6	0	68	8.24
D. C.	2	3	6	83	7.47
C. D. C.	0	6	3	68	7.06
C. D. C.	0	7	1	68	6.76
C. D. C.	2	3	2	68	6.76
C. D. C.	0	9	1	88	6.59
C. D. C.	1	5	2	74	6.49
C. D. C.	3	2	0	68	6.18
C. D. C.	1	2	5	70	6.00
C. D. C.	0	5	2	68	5.59
C. D. C.	0	4	3	68	5.29
C. D. C.	1	3	2	68	5.29
. D. C.	0	3	4	68	5.00
D. C.	1	1	4	68	4.71
8th C. D. C.	0	4	2	68	4.71
9th C. D. C.	1	3	1	68	4.71
8th C. D. C.	1	2	2	71	4.23
. 9th C. D. C.	0	3	2	68	3.83
13th C. D. C.	1	4	1	105	3.63
3 lrd Company, 8th C. D. C.	0	2	3	68	3.53
29th Company, 8th C. D. C.	0	4	0	68	3.53
29th Company, 8th C. D. C.	0	4	0	68	3.53
34th Company, 8th C. D. C.	1	2	0	68	3.24
19th Company, 9th C. D. C.	0	3	1	92	2.39
17th Company, 9th C. D. C.	0	2	1	67	2.39
13th Company, 9th C. D. C.	0	2	1	68	2.35
20th Company, 9th C. D. C.	0	2	1	68	2.35
22nd Company, 9th C. D. C.	0	1	2	67	2.09
28th Company, 8th C. D. C.	0	1	2	68	2.06
25th Company, 8th C. D. C.	0	1	2	68	2.03
15th Company, 9th C. D. C.	0	2	0	67	1.79

As a majority of the Division was called to Mexican Border Service in June, the competitive firing for the State and Brigade prizes, authorized by M. L. 112, was not held this year, and as there were no matches held by either the New York State Rifle Association or the New Jersey State Rifle Association the annual McAlpin and Dryden Trophy Matches also lapsed for the year.

A report on the team which represented the State of New York in the National Trophy Match held at Jacksonville, Fla., in October, is submitted with this report.

The group firing problem prescribed by paragraph XIV, G. O. 6, D. 1916, was shot at Peekskill Range at 500 yards this year for all organizations, except the Coast Defense Commands, the latter firing the problem at last year, at 300 yards. It proved more interesting and a keener contest at this longer range.

The splendid work of Captain Howard E. Crall and Lieutenant Eugene McK. Froment in supervising the practice of the remaining companies in the 1st and 10th Infantry after June 17th, under assignment as Ordnance Officers, 2nd Division, cannot be too highly recommended.

FRED M. WATERBURY,
Major.

HEADQUARTERS DIVISION, NATIONAL GUARD OF NEW YORK
MUNICIPAL BUILDING

G. V. M.

NEW YORK CITY, December 31, 1917.

No:

From: Ordnance Officer, Division,

To: Commanding General, Division,

Subject: Report of New York State Team's Work at National Matches.

1. Having been nominated by you, and appointed by the Governor of New York State, to captain the team in the National Matches held at the State Camp Grounds, Jacksonville, Fla., October 20–25, I herewith submit my report.

2. Following the suggestions of the Adjutant General of the State of New York, the team was selected both from those in Federal Service and those in the Guard in the State, some of whom had just been mustered out of the service, the personnel of the team being as follows:

> Captain, Major Fred M. Waterbury, O. O. N. Y. Div.
> Coach, Lieutenant Ernest C. Dreher, 71st Inf.
> Spotter, Captain Ernest F. Robinson, Corps of Eng.
> Principals, Sergt. Fred M. Dardingkiller, Q. M. Corps; Sergt. Francis J. Wellenberger, 74th Inf.; Capt. D. J. Cadotte, Sergt. Joseph F. Sulger, 7th Inf.; Supply Sergt. Fred C. Smith, 1st Inf.; Lieut. Walter K. Whitley, 3rd Inf.; Lieut. George E. Bryant, 23rd Inf.; Corp. John F. Enders, 1st Cavalry; Lieut. Elwood Groesbeck, 2nd Inf.; Capt. Elisha H. Janes, 12th Inf.; Lieut. John H. Kneubel, 74th Inf.; and Sergt. Alexander Jokl, 74th Inf.
> Alternates, Sergt. Major Alex Eakin, Squadron A; Sergt. Theo. Crane, Squadron A; Sergt. Austin J. Fischer, 74th Inf., and Corp. Ralph Pollock, 2nd Inf..
> Range Officer, Captain Charles E. Fiske, 1st Cavalry.
> Surgeon, Lieut. C. C. Zacharie, 10th Infantry.
> Cook, Howard I. Marshall, 74th Infantry.

3. The team members from McAllen and Pharr left for Jacksonville, Fla., on the 6th of October, arriving at the camp on the 10th, where they were joined by the members from the State of New York. The team was assigned to Street No. 15, maintained its own mess for the seventeen days' encampment, had no sickness or casualties, broke camp October 26, the National Guardsmen returning north and those in the federal service returning to their regular posts, arriving and reporting back to duty with their several organizations, October 30.

4. The team practiced every day from October 11 to 23, either by entering the matches of the Southern Association, the National Rifle Association, or in straight team pair work, and were in excellent condition for the National match which is shown by the results accomplished.

5. The team steadily worked its way to the top of the list, from fifth at the close of the 200 yard rapid fire, to third place at the finish of the 600 yard stage, being led by Iowa for second place with a 25 point margin and the U. S. Marine Corps for first place by a margin of 47 points. Despite the very bad conditions at the 1,000 yard range, New York moved steadily up until it had passed, with a safe margin, all the National Guard teams, the

match only being decided by the last two pairs when the Service team won with the scant margin of 10 points. This gave the National Trophy to the Service team and the Hilton trophy, for the winning team of the National Guard organizations, to New York.State. The trophy, "A Soldier of Marathon," was captured by the California Civilian Rifle Club and the University trophy by the Washington, D. C. High School.

SCORES OF THE NEW YORK STATE TEAM IN THE NATIONAL TROPHY MATCH, JACKSONVILLE, FLA., OCTOBER 24 AND 25, 1916

Name	R. F. 200 yds.	S. F. 600 yds.	S. F. 1000 yds.	Aggre- gate
Q. M. Sergt. Frederick M. Dardingkiller....	78	88	79	245
Sergt. Francis J. Wallenberger.............	70	83	85	238
Captain Damase J. Cadotte...............	85	90	89	264
Sergt. Joseph F. Sulger..................	84	90	90	264
Supply Sergt. Frederick C. Smith..........	77	93	81	251
1st Lieut. Walter K. Whitley..............	88	89	82	259
1st Lieut. George E. Bryant..............	81	89	71	241
Corporal John F. Enders.................	84	86	80	250
1st Lieut. Elwood Groesbeck..............	85	89	78	252
Captain Elisha H. Janes.................	87	91	85	263
Sergt. Alexander Jokl....................	84	92	78	254
1st Lieut. John H. Kneubel, Jr...........	84	90	82	256
	987	1,070	980	3,037

How the fifty-five competing teams finished:

CLASS "A "

No.	RF200	Yards. 600	1000	Agg.
1. U. S. M. C..........................	1,017	1,083	947	3,047
2. N. Y. Nat. Gd......................	987	1,070	980	3,037
3. Penn N. G..........................	964	1,080	961	3,005
4. Minnesota N. G.....................	990	1,045	960	2,995
5. Iowa N. G..........................	1,011	1,067	912	2,990
6. N. J. N. G.........................	940	1,058	983	2,981
7. Indiana N. G.......................	1,005	1,045	926	2,978
8. Georgia N. G.......................	967	1,064	941	2,972
9. California civilian	965	1,047	952	2,964
10. N. C. N. G.........................	970	1,048	934	2,952
11. Wyoming N. G......................	953	1,068	927	2,948
12. Ohio N. G..........................	928	1,046	973	2,947
13. Delaware N. G......................	943	1,011	992	2,946
14. D. of C. civilian....................	937	1,058	949	2,946
15. New Mexico N. G...................	955	1,043	936	2,934
16. Kansas N. G.	956	1,067	910	2,933

CLASS " B "

No.	RF200	600	1000	Agg.
17. Miss. N. G..........................	949	1,030	951	2,930
18. Colorado N. G......................	961	1,036	931	2,928
19. California N. G.....................	958	1,033	932	2,923
20. Maryland N. G......................	981	1,026	916	2,923
21. Oklahoma N. G.....................	940	1,028	940	2,908
22. Florida N. G.......................	954	1,026	926	2,906
23. Tenn. N. G.........................	949	1,058	885	2,892
24. Indiana civilian	927	1,043	915	2,885
25. North Dakota N. G..................	909	1,013	959	2,881
26. Ohio civilian	928	1,029	923	2,880
27. Wash., D. C., H. S..................	951	1,032	893	2,876
28. Florida civilian	941	1,002	924	2,867

CLASS "B" — continued

29. Missouri civilian	961	1,050	845	2,856
30. D. of C. N. G.........................	949	977	926	2,852
31. South Car. M. A......................	922	1,045	872	2,839
32. West Va. N. G........................	972	1,010	850	2,832
33. Idaho civilian	964	1,002	862	2,828

CLASS "C"

34. Idaho civilian	943	995	881	2,819
35. Texas N. G............................	950	1,002	853	2,805
36. Arkansas N. G.........................	970	992	835	2,797
37. Michigan civilian	897	1,027	866	2,790
38. Virginia N. G.........................	962	1,018	792	2,772
39. Nebraska N. G.........................·	897	979	894	2,770
40. Kansas civilian	896	997	867	2,760
41. Oklahoma civilian	891	954	870	2,715
42. Wyoming civilian	917	975	821	2,713
43. Texas civilian	883	989	840	2,712
44. Minnesota civilian	880	958	824	2,662
45. Alaska civilian	904	906	815	2,625
46. Nevada civilian	929	910	785	2,624
47. Penn. civilian	856	907	852	2,615
48. South Dakota civilian.................	915	945	717	2,577
49. Maryland civilian	851	966	757	2,574
50. Utah civilian	920	924	633	2,477
51. West Va. civilian.....................	824	872	686	2,382
52. Georgia civilian	815	777	643	2,235
53. Arkansas civilian	838	778	579	2,195
54. Alabama civilian	695	723	549	1,967
55. Fla. Mil. Ac..........................	733	742	460	1,935

6. During its stay at the Jacksonville Rifle Range, the New York State team entered one of the matches of the Southern Association, and nearly all of the events of the National Rifle Association, besides taking part in the National Matches. It was necessary to participate in these matches in order to obtain practice, as the attendance was so large that the various events kept all the 150 targets, available on this range, fully occupied. In both team and individual competitions, New York State team, captured about $175.00 in prize money, 56 medals, the Hilton trophy, two team competitions, finishing third in another team competition and sixth in the fourth team competition, in which they were defeated only by five U. S. Marine Service teams.

In the individual National Match, New York won sixth place, Sergeant Jokl of the 74th Infantry winning one of the ten gold medals and five other members of the team, Capt. Cadotte, Sergt. Crane, Sergt. Sulger, Sergt. Fischer and Lieut. Kneubel, coming within the hundred prize winners in a field of 953 competitors.

In the Leech Cup Match, 1,000 yards, New York had five men, Capt. Cadotte, Lieut. Whitley, Sergt. Dardingkiller, Lieut. Groesbeck and Capt. Robinson in the first fifty, 332 competing.

In the President's Match, at 200, 600 and 1,000 yards, New York scored five places in the first forty with Capt. Cadotte, Sergt. Sulger, Lieut. Groesbeck, Sergt. Dardingkiller and Lieut. Kneubel, 683 competing.

In the Marine Corps Match, at 600 and 1,000 yards, New York had two men, Capt. Cadotte and Sergt. Jokl in the first twenty-five, 519 competing.

In the Members Match, 600 yards, 684 competing, 1st Lieut. Groesbeck won second prize and Q. M. Sergt. Dardingkiller and Corp. Enders also finished in the first fifty.

In the Wimbleton Cup Match, 1,000 yards, Capt. Cadotte, New York team, was ninth and Q. M. Sergt. Dardingkiller and 1st Lieut. Dreher finished within the first twenty-five, 629 competing.

In the Individual Pistol Match, National Pistol Match Course, New York had two men, Sergt. Major Eakin and Sergt. Crane in the first fifty, 359 competing.

Two days after the arrival of the New York State team, two teams of eight men each were entered in the State Team Match of the Southern Rifle Association; one of these teams won the match, defeating the other twelve contestants and also the three teams put in by the U. S. Marine Corps, for practice only. New York was not eligible for the trophy, but won the first cash prize.

In the Regimental Team Match of six men, the 74th Infantry, New York, won third place with a total of 793, being defeated for second place by the First Minnesota with 797 points, and for first place by the First Iowa Infantry with 808 points.

At the close of all the matches, there is annually held under the auspices of the N. R. A., what is termed a Service Match, which is competed for by a team composed of sixteen highest percentage men in all the National Guard teams, sixteen highest percentage men in all the Service teams, and this year, sixteen of the highest men in all the Civilian teams. The New York team secured 25 per cent of the membership of this team, namely, Capt. Cadotte, Sergt. Sulger, Sergt. Jokl and Lieut. Kneubel. Colonel Brookhart of Iowa was selected to captain the team, Major Waterbury of New York as Adjutant and Major Anderson, the Adjutant-General of Wyoming, as coach. The course is the same as in the National Match, and owing to the very threatening weather conditions, it was moved forward to Thursday afternoon following the National Match in place of Friday morning, as at first scheduled, thus giving the National Guard and Civilian teams no chance to practice their team pairs, who in fact were not acquainted with each other, while the Marine Corps, being the only Service team, were enabled to match trained pairs, thus accounting, in a measure for the defeat of the National Guard team by about 100 points. Another factor in the higher score of the Marine Corps team was due to the fact that the kind of ammunition is not specified in this match and this team used the 180 grain bullet, which was very efficient at the long ranges in the heavy wind that prevailed, while the National Guard and Civilian teams were obliged to use the regulation service ammunition carrying 150 grain bullet, it being impossible to purchase any of the heavier ammunition in time for the match. It is understood that next year the conditions of the match will prevent the use of any ammunition except the regular service ammunition for all teams.

FRED M. WATERBURY,
Major, Ordnance Officer.

Report of Commodore Robert P. Forshen, Commanding Naval Militia

HEADQUARTERS NAVAL MILITIA, N. Y., U. S. S. GRANITE STATE, FOOT NINETY-SEVENTH STREET, NORTH RIVER

NEW YORK CITY, *December* 30, 1916.

The following report is submitted concerning the operations and condition of the Naval Militia, New York, for the year ending September 30, 1916:

1. In compliance with instructions received from the Adjutant-General, S. N. Y., Tours of Duty afloat were performed as follows:

First Battalion, N. M. N. Y.; U. S. S. *Kentucky,* July 15th to July 29th, 1916, both dates inclusive.

Second Battalion, N. M. N. Y.; U. S. S. *Maine* and U. S. S. *Gloucester,* July 15th to July 29th, 1916, both dates inclusive.

Third Battalion, N M. N. Y.: U. S. S. *New Jersey,* July 14th to July 30th, 1916, both dates inclusive.

In addition to the above, the following Tours of Duty ashore were performed:

Aeronautic Sections, First and Second Battalions, N. M. N. Y.: Bay Shore, N. Y., July 15th to July 29th, 1916, both dates inclusive.

Marine Company, Second Battalion, N. M. N. Y.: Wakefield, Mass., July 15th to July 29th, both dates inclusive.

It is proper to mention that the U. S. Naval Officers commanding the vessels on which this duty was performed, and the Commanding Officer of the U. S. Marine Corps Camp at Wakefield, Mass., reported most favorably on the discipline and efficiency of the Naval Militia, N. Y., taking part in this duty.   There was no U. S. Naval Observer at the Aeronautic Camp but an inspection made by myself convinces me that this duty was well and intelligently performed.

2. The usual Small Arms Practice Returns are attached, marked Exhibit A. The Figure of Merit Prizes for the Naval Militia were won by the Second Division, Second Battalion; Third Division, First Battalion; and, Eighth Division, First Battalion, N. M. N. Y.

The Inter-Battalion Secondary Battery Match was won by the First Battalion with a Final Merit of 37.81.

The Inter-Divisional Secondary Battery Match of the First Battalion was won by the Eighth Division with a Final Merit of 84.7.

The Inter-Divisional Secondary Battery Match of the Second Battalion was won by the Fifth Division with a Final Merit of 64.10.

3. The aggregate strength of this command on June 30, 1915, was 1,437, and on June 30, 1916, it was 1,801, and increase of 364.

4. The regular annual inspections of the organizations of the Naval Militia, N. Y., by the State and United States were held as follows:

First Battalion: April 10, 11, 12, 14 and 18, 1916.
Second Battalion: March 27, 1916.
Third Battalion: March 6, 7, 8 and 9, 1916.

5. The following units were mustered into the Naval Militia, N. Y., during the past year:

An Aeronautic Section in the First Battalion on January 17, 1916;

An Aeronautic Section in the Second Battalion on May 15, 1916;

A Marine Company in the Second Battalion on May 1, 1916;

A line division designated the Eighth Separate Division, Third Battalion, at Niagara Falls, N· Y., on May 5, 1916.

6. The Annual Reports of the Commanding Officers of the First, Second and Third Battalions are attached hereto.

7. On November 1, 1915, a Flying Boat was presented to the First Battalion, N. M. N. Y., by the Curtiss Aeroplane Company. On July 1, 1916, a Flying Boat was presented to the Second Battalion by a Committee of Citizens headed by Mr. Vincent Astor. These Flying Boats were in constant use until the end of the season. It is hoped that either through the Navy Department or some other source a flying boat may be secured for the Third Battalion.

8. On September 15, 1916, five officers and forty-two enlisted men were ordered to Chicago where on the following day the U. S. S. *Isla De Luzon* was transferred from Illinois to New York for the use of that portion of the Naval Militia located at Rochester.

The *Luzon* arrived at Charlotte on September 24th. The acquisition of the *Luzon* by the Rochester contingent of the Naval Militia permitted the transfer of the U. S. S. *Sandoval* to the 4th Division, Third Battalion at Watertown, N. Y.

9. During the year, there were performed special Tours of Duty under section 13, General Orders No. 77, Navy Department, as follows:

Fifteen enlisted men, Marine Corps Rifle Range, Winthrop, Maryland;

Two officers and six enlisted men on Battleship Cruise;

One officer, U. S. N. Aeronautic Station at Pensacola, Florida.

10. The Navy Department has placed the U. S. S. *Kentucky* at the disposal of the First Battalion for instruction purposes, and her Commanding Officer, Captain D. E. Dismukes, U. S. N., has been assigned by the Navy Department as Inspector-Instructor for the First and Second Battalions. The assignment of this ship will be most beneficial to the First Battalion but in order to retain her a suitable wharf must be obtained. Efforts to this end are now being made with the Commissioner of Docks and Ferries of the City of New York. Eventually it is hoped to secure the assignment of a second battleship for the Second Battalion, N. M. N. Y. It is believed, however, that this latter matter will hinge very largely on the obtaining of a desirable

berth for the U. S. S. *Kentucky*. The placing of this latter ship at this Port will eventually result in having a trained crew, for this ship, of Naval Militiamen ready for prompt and efficient duty at a minimum expense to the State and to the Navy Department.

11. During the year, there were issued General Orders No. 8, c. s., A. G. O. making changes in the organization of the Naval Militia to conform with General Orders No. 153, Navy Department which standardizes the organization of the Naval Militia of the various States.

12. The physical and professional examinations called for by General Orders No. 150 and 153, Navy Department, are well under way.

13. By virtue of an Act of Congress approved August 29, 1916, an organization known as the National Naval Volunteers was formed in which only Naval Militiamen are eligible. This new organization is intended as a vehicle of transfer of the Naval Militia to active service, and is intended merely as a paper organization designed to give the President the immediate use of the Naval Militia in case of emergency.

By an Act of Congress approved June 3, 1916, popularly known as the National Defense Act, States maintaining a Naval Militia may be credited to the extent of the number thereof to the quota of National Guard that would otherwise be required from that State. This is an important factor, and calculated to be helpful to the military as well as the naval forces of the State.

The Division of Naval Militia Affairs in a letter, marked Exhibit B, has commented handsomely on the organization, energy, zeal and efficiency of the Naval Militia of this State, and has at the same time stated that the requirements of the Naval Defense Act set the quota of Naval Militiamen from this State at 4,500 officers and men. An expansion of the numbers of the Naval Militia is most desirable but to obtain the additional number and to properly train them, as well as to keep the organization up to its present high standard, the Commanding Officer of the Naval Militia should be enabled to give his entire time and efficiency to this most important work.

14. The Commanding Officer of the Naval Militia has previously reported the death of Commander Charles O. Brinckerhoff on January 5, 1916, who at the time was commanding the Second Battalion, Naval Militia. This officer enlisted as a seaman in the Naval Militia and had risen through the successive grades to commander, was a veteran of the Spanish-American War, was an officer of high standing and efficiency, and his loss is deeply regretted.

ROBERT P. FORSHEW,
Commodore.

REPORT OF FIRST BATTALION

NEW YORK, *December* 28, 1916.

FROM: Commanding Officer.

To: Commodore, Commanding Naval Militia.

SUBJECT: Annual Report.

1. During the year ending September 30, 1916, the battalion in addition to the regular winter drill season performed extra duty both ordered and voluntary. The schools for officers and petty officers which were conducted during the drill season gave excellent results. The special school on Navigation, conducted by Lieutenant-Commander R. R. Riggs, U. S. N., Retired, the Navigation Officer, for petty officers and enlisted men, was of much value. Lectures in navigation were also held for the commissioned officers. The drills this season were conducted under the jurisdiction of the individual divisional officers instead of by classes. In comparison with the methods of the previous season it is found that this is not as good except a systematic routine is carried out through the entire season. A Board for the purpose of systematizing drills is now in session and is preparing a drill schedule for the coming season.

2. On November 1, 1915, the Curtiss Flying Boat presented the battalion was christened by the daughter of the Governor of the State, Honorable Charles S. Whitman, who was present. The battalion was ordered out on this occasion. On November 23, 1915, the battalion was reviewed by Captain H. O. Dunn, U. S. Navy. On February 28, 1916, the battalion was reviewed by

Real Admiral W. II. Brownson, U. S. Navy, Retired. On March 16, 1916 there was a battalion review. On March 23, 1916, the battalion conducted its annual small-arms practice on the State range at Peekskill, N. Y. On May 30, 1916, the battalion was ordered out in connection with Memorial Day parade.

3. The annual Federal Inspections were held as follows:

April 10, 1916: Music C. P. O. staff, 5th and 9th division, Lieutenant A. S. Farquhar, U. S. Navy.

April 11, 1916, 2nd and 3rd divisions, Lieutenant Farquhar.

April 12, 1916, 1st, 4th and 6th divisions, Lieut.-Comdr. P. B. Dungan, U. S. Navy, and Lieut. Farquhar, U. S. Navy.

April 14, 1916, 8th division: Lieut.-Comdr. Dungan U. S. Navy.

April 18, 1916, 7th division, Lieut.-Comdr. Dungan, U. S. Navy.

4. The annual secondary battery practice of the battalion was conducted in Gardiner's Bay, L. I., on board the U. S. S. *Wasp,* September 2nd to 5th, inclusive. There was noted a decided improvement in this practice and the results were encouraging.

The annual tour of ordered federal duty was performed on board the U. S. S. *Kentucky,* from July 15th to 29th, inclusive, 1916 (see special report herewith appended as Exhibit " C ").

5. During the summer the launches and cutters were in constant use by the volunteer crews from the various divisions, who made numerous cruises in which the men gained practical knowledge in the handling of small boats under steam, sail and oars. The aggregate distance steamed by the launches was 11,257½ miles.

6. The U. S. S. *Wasp* was in frequent use for short cruises and instruction, as follows:

October 2nd to 4th, 1915, cruise to Gardiner's Bay, L. I.

May 10, 1916, North River to Navy Yard.

June 16, 1916, Navy Yard to North River.

June 17th to 19th, 1916, cruise in North River.

July 1st to 4th, 1916, Long Island Sound to Gardiner's Bay.

August 20th to 21st, Long Island Sound to Block Island.

September 2nd to 5th, Gardiner's Bay.

7. The Aviation Section of the First Battalion was mustered in by the Commanding Officer under Special Orders of the Adjutant-General of the State of New York, on January 17, 1916. This section during the past summer has been in camp at Bay Shore, L. I., where much valuable practice was obtained. The section during this period made many flights for the qualifying of officers and men. During the period from July 15th to 29th, inclusive, the Aviation Section was under federal orders for its annual tour of duty.

The report of the Officer in Command of the Aviation Section has been sent forward separately.

8. Early in the morning of Sunday, July 30, 1916, the Battalion received an urgent call from Ellis Island, the Government Emigration Station, for a detail of officers and men to patrol there and assist in rescuing the property and for general service, consequent upon the disastrous explosion on Black Tom Island on that date. Lieut-Commander Earl Farwell took charge of a detachment of men from the battalion, proceeded to Ellis Island, where he remained for some hours assisting in the work there. This service was the subject of a commendatory letter, from the federal official in charge. (See Exhibit " D.")

CHARLES L. POOR.

REPORT OF SECOND BATTALION

BROOKLYN, N. Y., *December* 15, 1916.

FROM: Commanding Officer

To   Commodore, Commanding Naval Militia, New York.

SUBJECT: Annual Report.

1.   There is submitted herewith report of the operations of the Second Battalion, N. M., N. Y. for the year ending September 30th, 1916.

2.   The indoor season began early in November and continued until May 1st, when small boat work began.

3.   The Engineer Divisions followed their usual course of instruction, consisting of instruction in the engine and fireroom of the *Gloucester* and machine shop work in the Armory. Much

favorable comment was expressed by the Engineer Officers of the U. S. S. *Maine* during the recent Federal Cruise on the ability and interest displayed by the members of these divisions. Their good showing was due entirely to the course of instruction given during the winter months by the officers and chief petty officers of the Engineer Divisions.

4.   A Marine Company, Lieutenant J. F. Rorke, Commanding, was mustered into the service of the State on May 1, 1916. This Company performed its annual tour of duty at the Marine Encampment, Wakefield, Mass., from July 15th to 29th, inclusive with one hundred per cent of attendance.   This I consider remarkable when it is considered that this tour of duty was performed within three months from the date of mustering in. From reports received from the Commandant of Marine Corps, this tour of duty was satisfactory in every respect, the men showing great interest in their work.   The success of this Company is due in a great measure to the untiring zeal, personal interest and self-sacrifice on the part of the Commanding Officer, Lieutenant J. F. Rorke.

5.   The Annual Federal and State Inspection was held on March 27, 1916.   The inspection was very satisfactory in all respects, not only to the Commanding Officer, but to the Inspecting Officers as well; the percentage present (.954) being one of the highest ever attained by this Battalion.

6.   The Small Arms Practice of the Battalion was held at Peekskill on May 24, 1916, and with more satisfactory results than in 1915, due mainly to the greater amount of preliminary practice on the indoor ranges, which was made possible by the allowance of indoor ammunition allowed by the Department, and it is hoped that the Division of Naval Militia Affairs can see its way clear to make the same provision for the coming year.

7.   After extensive repairs at the Navy Yard, New York, the U. S. S. *Gloucester* was put in commission on June 25, 1916, which is a month later than usual.   During the season just closed, 15 cruises, including the Federal Cruise, was made, 3620 knots steamed, approximately 1100 officers and men taking part.

8.   On May 15, 1916, an Aeronautic Section, Ensign Vincent Astor, Commanding, was mustered into the Service of the State,

and on July 1, 1916, the Hydroaeroplane presented to the Battalion by a Committee of Patriotic Citizens was officially accepted with appropriate ceremonies. The next day, July 2, the Hydroaeroplane was flown to Bayshore, L. I. (56 miles in 42 minutes), which is a record considering the short time the machine was under the jurisdiction of the Second Battalion.

9. The enrolled strength of the Battalion on September 30th, was 569 officers and men, a net increase of 137 over that of September 30th, 1915, which shows that recruiting has been very extensive during the past year, and it is the opinion of the writer that when the new Naval Militia Law becomes fully in operation, the coming year will show substantial increase in numbers and efficiency.

E. T. FITZGERALD.

REPORT OF THIRD BATTALION

EAST ROCHESTER, N. Y., *December* 16, 1916.

FROM: Commanding Officer.

To: Commodore Commanding, Naval Militia, N. Y.

SUBJECT: Annual Report.

1. The Fall and Winter Indoor Drill season held from December 1st to May 30th, 1916, consisting of infantry, artillery, signal work and seamanship, together with lectures and instructions in Engineering Work by Engineer Divisions, schools for Petty Officers, were held weekly by the various divisions.

2. The drill season afloat covered period from June 1st to September 20th, and consisted of small boat work, under oars, sails, and week end cruises, for 1st, 3rd, 5th, 8th, Divisions aboard the U. S. S. *Hawk,* and 2nd, 6th and 7th Divisions aboard the U. S. S. *Sandoval* and launches on Rochester station.

3. Indoor Rifle Practice was greatly stimulated by competition for the trophy presented the Third Battalion by Paymaster L. W. Josephthal, was won by the 7th (Engineer) Division.

4. Small Arms Practice was held at Kenilworth Range on September 2nd, 3rd and 4th, for the 1st, 2nd, 3rd, 5th, 6th, 7th and 8th Divisions, and at Stoney Point, U. S. Army Range on

July 2nd for the 4th Division.   There were twenty-four officers and 328 men who participated in Small Arms Practice.

5.   The Annual Inspection was held on dates below:

Watertown, March 6th

Rochester, March 7th

Dunkirk, March 8th

Buffalo, March 9th

The Federal inspection was made by Lieutenant Commander C. H. Fisher, U. S. N. Inspector N. M. Great Lakes, and State Inspection by Commander A. B. Fry accompanied by Commander E. N. Walbridge.

6.   Annual cruise aboard the U. S. S. *New Jersey* from July 14th to 30th, which was participated in by seventeen officers and 400 men.

7.   During the year there were performed tours of duty under section 13, G. O. 77, Navy Department as follows: Six men from 2nd and 6th Division with Atlantic Fleet, three months; one Petty Officer, Marine Corps Rifle Range, Winthrop, Md., fifteen days.

8.   These tours of duty have proven very instructive and all encouragement is being given men of this Battalion to take advantage of the opportunity thus offered by the Navy Department.

9.   During the year an additional division was organized, the 8th (Deck) Division at Niagara Falls, which was mustered in on May 1st, with forty-three men.   On September 15th, five officers and forty-two men were ordered to Chicago where on the following day the U. S. S. *Isla de Luzon* was transferred from Illinois to New York Naval Militia, and proceeded on September 17th to Rochester arriving at Rochester on September 24th. This transfer of the Luzon to Rochester on September 24th, permitted the transfer of the U. S. S. *Sandoval* to the 4th Division at Watertown.   It is now stationed at Sackett's Harbor, New York, for the use of that organization, who heretofore have been greatly handicapped by lack of such floating equipment as this affords, and it is much appreciated.   The acquisition of the U. S. S. *Isla de Luzon* to Rochester station will greatly stimulate the three

Divisions located at Rochester. As the vessel did not arrive until very late during the season of navigation no report can be offered showing her operations.

10. The strength of the Battalion on October 1st, 1915, was as follows: Commissioned Officers twenty-five; enlisted men 416; and on September 30th, 1916, Commissioned Officers twenty-eight, and enlisted men 464, all of which is submitted, gain for period of fifty-one.

E. N. WALBRIDGE,

Captain, Comdg. 3rd Batt. N. M., N. Y.

EXHIBIT "A"

November 10, 1916.

General Orders

No. 10.

1. The particulars of the competition for Figure of Merit prizes for the organizations of the Naval Militia, N. Y., for the season of 1916, are given hereunder.

	Qualified as marksmen	Strength	Figure of merit
2nd Div., 2nd Batt.........................	28	74	37.84
3rd Div., 1st Batt..........................	26	72	34.72
8th Div., 1st Batt..........................	19	56	33.93
4th Div., 1st Batt..........................	23	70	32.66
2nd Div., 1st Batt..........................	19	59	32.20
3rd Div., 3rd Batt.........................	21	89	30.43
1st Div., 2nd Batt.........................	15	52	28.85
1st Div., 1st Batt..........................	21	77	27.27
7th Div., 2nd Batt.........................	12	49	24.49
7th Div., 1st Batt..........................	16	74	21.63
4th Div., 3rd Batt.........................	20	95	21.05
5th Div., 3rd Batt.........................	15	74	20.37
6th Div., 1st Batt..........................	11	59	18.64
9th Div., 1st Batt..........................	9	63	14.29
4th Div., 2nd Batt.........................	10	72	13.69
6th Div., 2nd Batt.........................	7	51	13.73
6th Div., 3rd Batt.........................	9	68	13.24
7th Div., 3rd Batt.........................	6	50	12.00
5th Div., 2nd Batt.........................	6	51	11.76
5th Div., 1st Batt..........................	7	64	10.94
2nd Div., 3rd Batt.........................	7	67	10.45
3rd Div., 2nd Batt.........................	6	72	8.33
1st Div., 3rd Batt..........................	5	61	8.20
8th Div., 3rd Batt..........................	4	64	6.25

2.   The prizes are won by the first three divisions named in their sequence; and Commanding Officers thereof will designate suitable prizes for purchase by the Adjutant General, State Arsenal, 7th Avenue and 35th Street, New York City.

By command of Commodore FORSHEW,

HERBERT WALDO YORK,

Lt. Comdt. and Ordnance Officer, N. M. N. Y.

EXHIBIT "B"

NAVY DEPARTMENT, DIVISION OF NAVAL MILITIA AFFAIRS, WASHINGTON, D. C.

December 18, 1916.

To Chief of Staff, New York Naval Militia,

SUBJECT: Increase of members of New York Naval Militia.

1.   In accordance with the requirements of the Naval Defense Act, this Division has estimated that there will be required for reserves for the Navy in time of war by 1921, 25,000 Naval Militiamen.   Upon the basis of population of the States bordering the seaboard and great lakes, this Division estimates that a proper quota for the State of New York will be 4500 officers and men.

2.   If agreeable to the Naval Militia of New York, this Division would be pleased to have the necessary steps taken to increase the organizations to a total of 4500.   In view of the experience and training of the Naval Militia officers of New York, it is extremely desirable that that State increase its quota of Naval Militia, since it has the organization that has developed battalions upon which the Navy now depends for an expansion of the Fleet.

3.   In this connection it may not be amiss for the Division to express its satisfaction at the energy, zeal and efficiency of the Naval Militia organizations of the State of New York as reported to this Division by the Commanding Officers of the ships upon which these organizations made their annual cruise.

T. P. MAGRUDER.

EXHIBIT "C"

U. S. S. KENTUCKY, NAVAL MILITIA CRUISE, JULY 15–29, 1916.

DATE	Arrived	Distance	Average speed
July 15–16....	New York, N. Y..................	....	....
July 16–16....	Fort Pond Bay, Long Island Sound......	155 miles...	10 knots
July 21–16....	Newport, R. I.........................	60 miles...	10 knots
July 24–16....	Block Island Sound..................	22 miles...	10 knots
July 26–16....	Maneuvers........................	....	10 knots
July 27–16....	Tactical maneuvers.................	....	10 knots
July 28–16....	New York, N. Y.....................	150 miles...	10 knots

Complement-Naval. 1. Itinerary Militia Officers.

NAME	Rank	Duty
Poor, Charles L.............	Captain (L)........	Auxiliary command.
Wait, William B., Jr........	Commander (L)....	Executive officer.
Riggs, Roland R............	Lt. Comdr. (L)......	Nav. Sig. Off. and Div. Off.
DeKay, Eckford C..........	Lt. Comdr. (L)......	Asst. Nav. Sig. Off. J. O.
Farwell, Earle.............	Lt. Commdr. (L)....	Fire Control J. O. Div.
Macfarlane, James..........	Lt. Comdr. (L).....	Assistant to executive.
Boone, Charles.............	Lt. Comdr. (E) (L)..	Engine and fireroom deck.
Mallon, William L..........	Lieut. (L)...........	J. O. Div.— Div. Off.
Moore, Clarence A..........	Lieut (L)............	J. O. Division.
Raff, Lemuel E.............	Lieut (L)............	Not qualified.
Bensel, Walter.............	Lieut (L)............	J. O. Div. in fire control.
Condon, Richard...........	Lieut. (L)..........	J. O. Division.
Brown, Harry R............	Lieut. (jg) (L)......	Not qualified.
Ketcham, Berkeley S.......	Lieut. (jg) (L)......	J. O. Division.
MacCollom, Augustus, Jr....	Lieut. (jg) (L)......	Not qualified.
Mason, Charles A..........	Lieut. (jg) (L)......	J. O. Division.
Williams, Henry T.........	Lieut. (jg) (L)......	J. O. Division.
Browne, Harold W..........	Ensign (L)..........	J. O. Division.
Kenyon, Albert J..........	Ensign (L).........	Fire control, plotting room.
Moore, John R., Jr........	Ensign (L).........	J. O. Division.
Murray, Leo J.............	Ensign (L).........	Fire control party.
Oatley, Henry B...........	Ensign (E)........	Engine and fireroom.
Kimball, Cleaveland C.....	Surgeon...........	Operative surgery and genito urinary work.
Boyd, William H..........	Paymaster.........	Not qualified.
Willis, Walter J...........	Lieut. (L) (R)......	Engine and fireroom.

Total officers, 25.

5

2. Naval Militia Enlisted Men.

Seaman branch	266
Artificer branch (deck force)	12
Artificer branch (engineer force)	61
Special branch	21
Total enlisted men	380

3. Drills held.

KIND OF DRILLS	MANNER OF PERFORMING
(a) General quarters (day and night)	Good
(b) Battery drill	Good
(c) Handling and treatment of wounded. Instruction given.	
(d) Fire (day and night)	Very Good
(e) Collision	Very Good
(f) Abandon ship	Good
(g) Man overboard	Good
(h) Boats under sail and oars	Little opportunity
(i) Signalling	Good

INSTRUCTION

(j) Naval customs.
(k) Routine in port and at sea.
(l) Aim and object of all general drills.
(m) Marking clothes.
(n) Personal cleanliness.
(o) Boats.
(p) Marlinspike seamanship.
(q) Duties of a lockout.
(r) Deck seamanship.
(s) Ground tackle.
(t) Steering.
(u) Gunnery.
(v) Signals.

All drills were performed very well with very little noise or confusion.

Before any drills were held the Divisions were thoroughly instructed in regard to the duties to be performed.

D. E. DISMUKES.

EXHIBIT "D"

U. S. S. KENTUCKY, NEW YORK, N. Y., *July 29, 1916.*

FROM: Commanding Officer.

To: The Secretary of the Navy. (Navigation Naval Militia Affairs).

Via: Commander, Reserve Force.

SUBJECT: Cruise of Naval Militia, 1st Battalion, N. Y., report on.

1. In accordance with orders of the Commander of the Reserve Force, the *Kentucky* embarked the battalion at New York, July 15, and sailed the same day for the rendezvous at Fort Pond Bay. The battalion was disembarked at New York at 10:30 a. m., July 29.

2. Upon arrival on board the divisions fell in at their stations and the work of the cruise began immediately. Drills and exercises were planned from day to day, this being the most practical way of utilizing the short time of the cruise to the best advantage. The plan in general was as follows: First, the various divisions were organized and the men made acquainted with their respective parts of the ship, both as regards to the batteries and cleanings. Second, all officers and men taken by squads over the ship, including engine and firerooms and handling-rooms and shellrooms. The daily schedules of drills are appended.

3. The Militia officers were detailed for deck and engine-room watch, and junior officers of the watch in accordance with their commissions, while under way a regular ship's officer was always on hand to render advice and assistance when necessary. While steaming in formation and in North River, the deck was not turned over to the Militia. At all other times the Commanding Officer of the battalion and the Militia officers-of-the-deck had entire charge of the ship. Likewise the navigating and engineering duties were performed respectively by the Militia officers assigned to the duties. There were not enough engineer officers to take complete charge of the engine room. One officer was assigned a regular watch in the engine room.

4. The officers of the battalion took great interest in their work and performed their duties with credit to themselves and to the organization. The enlisted men were remarkably well disciplined and were uniformly clean and well behaved. Their bags, as shown on inspections, were in excellent shape.

5. I consider that this battalion is a very valuable asset to the Navy, and in case of need could be utilized at once in the regular service. With two months' drill the organizations would be an efficient portion of the crew on any ship.

D. E. DISMUKES.

AUGUST 2, 1916.

FROM: Commander, Reserve Force, Atlantic Fleet.

To: Secretary of the Navy (Division of Naval Militia Affairs).

1. Forwarded approved.

J. M. HELM.

Report of Lieutenant-Colonel Harlow Brooks, Division Surgeon,
National Guard

CAMP WHITMAN, GREEN HAVEN, N. Y.,

AUGUST 14, 1916.

It has seemed wisest to consider in this report, conclusions,
criticisms and deductions to which the service at this camp have
led me rather than to recapitulate the various occurrences which
have led to these conclusions.

GENERAL CONDITIONS IN THE CAMP

Camp Location. The somewhat isolated location of this camp
has been a very great advantage however it may have affected the
work of other corps. The difficulty of access has made the number
of visitors small. With a consequent decrease in social attractions
there has been an exactly parallel rise in efficiency. Litter has
been perceptibly less than in most previous camps. There has also
been apparently less discontent and homesickness among the soldiers and an undeniably smaller list of digestive disorders due to
undesirable articles of food brought into camp by relatives and
friends.

Contagious diseases, notably such disorders as measles, diphtheria and the like have also been few, probably for the same
reason, but the most notable and fortunate result in this respect
has been the very small rate of venereal infections developed in
men who came to camp uninfected. This is in itself a cogent
reason for an isolated military camp with poor and expensive
transportation facilities.

Climatic Characteristics. Taken altogether, it is very doubtful
if more desirable climatic conditions could have been obtained
elsewhere in the State of New York. While the exceedingly wet

and delayed season caused considerable discomfort, this could be in no way laid to the natural or usual climatic conditions of the camp. The rolling and naturally excellently drained character of terrain on the contrary greatly improved camp conditions, while the sandy soil and frequent and rapid streams made it possible for the excess of water to be easily disposed of.

Size. There was sufficient space for each organization, and each was able to select, even during the most crowded periods of the camp, suitable and clean camping grounds. It was unnecessary for the same ground to be occupied by succeeding organizations without permitting sufficient time for the cleansing powers of nature, with sun, air and rain to act upon it.

Water Supply

That there was great danger when the camp was first established from its water supply does not even admit of debate. The quantity of water furnished was inadequate, derived chiefly from a greatly overtaxed and obviously infected source. The excreta infected drainage known to enter this single supply chanced to be free from typhoid or dysentery infection. Conditions were quickly remedied by the driving of numerous wells which within a reasonably short time were found to yield abundant and pure water, sufficient for cooking, bathing and the cleansing of clothing. The experimental chlorination of a portion of the early water supply failed in this camp, probably because the men were able to secure good tasting water from the creeks and ponds more palatable than the chlorinated water with its slightly disagreeable flavor. As the camp now stands, abundant pure water may be supplied for many more men than were encamped here during this mobilization, and this immediate supply may be insured in perpetuity for any future mobilizations, no matter how extensive or sudden, by the expenditure now of a moderate sum to install permanent instead of the present temporary mains.

Attention should be drawn to the fact that the deliberate installation of a simple sewerage system would insure this important feature indefinitely for all the future and would eventually save much money by cheapening the now expensive liquid garbage disposal.

Food

The food supply, even in the early days of the camp, seems to have been sufficient. In most cases it has been more than sufficient. A good many criticisms may be made in regard to the food supply, in addition to the fact that it was wastefully extravagant. The meat ration has been proportionately too high for the best health of the men, and the waste in this particular has been most shocking. This has been chiefly due to two factors: first, the quantity of meat furnished was altogether too abundant for health; secondly, the handling of this food was not well carried out. As a rule the meat was well iced and was kept in a cleanly manner in the quartermaster storehouses (usually the original iced cars in which the meat was shipped), it was delivered in a cleanly way, and after a little instruction from the sanitary inspectors it was generally well and cleanly handled by cooks and organization quartermasters. Few cooks, however, had the judgment or the facilities for properly utilizing the fat. The great value of fat in warfare has been shown recently in Europe, but in Camp Whitman the fat was usually thrown into the garbage, where it became one of the most difficult and danger-breeding elements in garbage disposal. Bone, which should enter largely into the manufacture of soup and which is highly prized in most military establishments, was almost wholly wasted in this camp. It would seem that the addition of the " Goulash Canonen " to the equipment of our kitchens would contribute greatly to attractiveness, effectiveness and economy of our extravagant meat ration. Under present conditions, tasteful and satisfying soup has been rarely served.

Errors on the side of caution have been made in several cases in condemning slightly and only slightly questionable meat, such as would be served as in prime condition in the most expensive restaurants and hotels.

It is always difficult even in the heart of such a farming community as that in which Camp Whitman is located to supply a sufficient quantity of certain fresh vegetables. For these food elements may however be readily substituted such easily obtained foods as cabbages, onions, beets, oatmeal, rice, beans, corn and peas, which in the dried form enter largely into the foreign military ration and which are little utilized in America. Macaroni, cheese and noodles might also be very advantageously and more widely used with a positive benefit insofar as the health of the men is concerned. Egg powder and dried milk, both comparatively cheap and nutritious, might also be used to good advantage in our ration. Butter, while generally of excellent quality in this camp, often becomes slightly tainted in taste or odor, without becoming necessarily dangerous. A much cheaper, better and more constantly flavored and infinitely more easily kept substitute is oleomargerine.

Although enlisted cooks have in the end given far better service than so-called professional cooks, still a little instruction by competent out-door or regular army cooks would greatly improve the health, comfort and pleasure of the men. Considerable effort was expended by the sanitary inspectors in instruction in the care of cooking utensils, and on the whole this was fairly satisfactory, but only after the inspectors had persistently brought up this subject and demonstrated its direct bearing on health.

SANITARY PROVISIONS

Latrines. In general, most officers and men fully appreciate the importance of proper care of the latrines and sanitary details, and are usually quite willing and competent to police them, especially when the imperative nature of this duty is frequently emphasized and illustrated by the inspecting sanitarians. One very important step in this direction however has been very generally neglected. When organizations are first marched out on their camp ground, the very first step after dismissal should always be the selection of proper sites and the immediate establishment of latrines and urinals. Very frequently these were left until the general camp had been established, etc., and as an inevitable and universal result, the brush and environs of the camp ground had become polluted. Where proper latrines are not immediately available, trenches should be dug and the straddle rail or pole latrine established.

I have been satisfied from a study of conditions in this camp that the present latrine, if properly constructed and properly policed, offers very little danger to the camp, and if it does become dangerous it is entirely due to improper care. The latrine problem appears to be solved in just so far as human responsibility and cleanliness can be depended upon. We have found without exception that poor latrines are an exact index of the character and discipline of the superior officers of any organization.

Garbage Disposal. Quite a different problem lies in the disposal of the garbage, and especially of the liquid garbage, which in my opinion now offers the most serious problem in camp sanitation. The kitchen incinerators now in use are efficient only to the degree of willingness and intelligence of those who use them. When properly constructed (and this is often a very difficult matter, largely dependent upon the drainage and the character of the soil) and when sufficient fuel is supplied, they are efficient, provided that they are properly managed. One man of intelligence must be put in charge of each incinerator and he must have complete and consecutive charge of it. The chief difficulty lies in the disposal of the liquid portions of the garbage. If this is not properly carried out, the incinerator becomes a fly clearing house and a constant menace to the health, both during and after suspension of any camp.

Considerable ingenuity in the construction of the incinerator is important. By far the most satisfactory of those in use at Camp Whitman were constructed of brick after the general model of one first built by the very efficient Machine Gun Company of the Tenth Infantry. This was later extensively copied throughout the camp.

The incinerator method of garbage disposal is expensive in time, material and in personnel, and it is dangerous to health unless very punctiliously supervised. In my opinion, as it now exists, it forms one of the most dangerous features of camp life from the sanitarian's standpoint. It would seem that a more extensive trial of the methods of chemical disposal of garbage should be undertaken, and some brief experiments conducted at this camp indicate that the borax method may be more satisfactory. Where time and material permit, such an incinerator as that in use at the Peekskill Camp of Instruction is far more efficient and much cheaper to operate.

Picket Lines. In general the policing of the picket lines in this camp has been very satisfactory, simply because this matter has been carefully supervised. In our experience, it is not well to depend upon the outside disposal of horse manure unless immediately controlled by military authorities. Either the manure should be carted away by military authorities and perhaps disposed of by sale at prices sufficient to pay cartage, or it should be spread, winnowed and burned, if necessary by sanitary details. In this camp, the picket lines with one noticeable exception have never at any time become the usual menace because of fly breeding, but only because persistent care has prevented this problem. The picket lines of the quartermaster corps have been notably excellent. Proper garbage and manure disposal, with correct policing of the cook and supply tents, in our opinion largely disposes of the fly problem, at least in this climate. Fly traps constructed on the grounds and for use chiefly in the kitchens have been extensively used. In our opinion the proper screening of the food is more important.

HEALTH AND MEDICAL CONDITIONS

Mosquitoes. These have not been a serious problem in Camp Whitman, notwithstanding the fact that many breeding places for mosquitoes existed. These were however immediately recognized and appropriately treated. When because of military necessities, the sanitary details were cut down, this problem did again assert itself, but this camp has amply illustrated that even in unfavorable locations the mosquito pest may be kept well in abeyance by intelligent sanitation. Among the mosquitoes found in this camp, the anopheles seemed to be most abundant. Although several recognized malarial cases were in camp, no spread of this infection took place.

Body Parasites. As is inevitably the case, lice of various varieties, especially the pediculis pubis, have been a factor of considerable importance. The chief medium of transmission has been the latrines, no matter how well policed. In our experience an effective measure is frequent body inspections, conducted openly and under sufficient censure so that personal cleanliness becomes a matter of mental as well as of bodily comfort.

Venereal Inspections. These have been notably of minor importance in this camp, doubtless because of the isolation of the camp and the prompt expulsion from the neighborhood of undesir-

able females. The use of the venereal phophylactics has therefore been mostly unnecessary though available. Several cases of
both syphilis and gonorrhea were discovered, but never became a
matter of serious concern since the physical examinations and
body inspections made its early recognition possible.

Sanitary Details. These have been difficult to obtain and insufficient in numbers. Oftentimes also, men detailed for this
work were of the lesser intelligence. It would appear that medical
officers should have more direct control in these respects if the best
result is to be expected. It was found in this camp that the actual
supervision of these parties, though not so provided for in regulations, should be under the absolute command of medical officers.
If the authority of this corps should be extended in this direction
and the sanitary details should be made up of privileged rather
than of punished personnel this absolutely necessary and vital
work would be greatly facilitated.

Sanitary Inspections. Where possible, sanitary inspections
have been made accompanied by line or engineer officers who have
been found almost without exception very willing and anxious to
improve the sanitary conditions of their commands, and since they
were also competent to command instead of to recommend alone,
the results have been correspondingly good.

Epidemics. Camp Whitman has been notably free from epidemic camp diseases. No cases of infection, except for the para-
sitic ones previously considered, have spread in this camp. Dysentery occurred in three instances, each promptly recognized, diag-
nosed clinically and verified by bacterial examinations. These
three instances have been apparently traced to extramural infection, to be considered later in this report, and we feel that we are
justified in the statement that they were in no way dependent upon
negligence or inapprehension on the part of the Medical Corps,
who had long previous to this outbreak given warning to this
probable source of infection and strongly recommended its eradi-
cation.

Typhoid. No cases of typhoid fever developed in this camp
nor have we been able to learn of any which developed in soldiers
from this camp subsequent to their leaving Whitman. Nonethe-
less, four instances of typhoid carriers were detected and promptly

reported to proper authorities since, when confirmed, these men
had left this station. Routine faeces examinations were made of
the cooks, and doubtless this precaution, the technic of which was
carried out through the courtesy of the Health Board, S. N. Y.,
saved disease dissemination.

Typhoid Vaccination. This was insisted upon in every unprotected soldier in the camp. There can be no doubt that this
precaution, especially in view of the unsatisfactory water supply
in the early days of the camp, prevented untold misery and sickness. Vaccination against small pox was also a matter of routine
and while perhaps a matter of unimportance in this neighborhood,
its value to those troops destined for border service cannot be
overestimated. A few but no serious cases of vaccine sickness
naturally resulted, but none was serious.

Hospital Cases. Naturally a few serious illnesses, both medical
and surgical, as appendicitis and a small number of fractures,
have occurred. These cases were promptly sent to base hospitals,
where proper medical care was provided. These removals were
greatly facilitated by the prompt purchase of a motor ambulance
under the immediate direction of the Adjutant-General. The
system of base hospitals has not worked out satisfactorily because,
in some instances, of the special character of some of the hospitals
and chiefly because of the total lack of military supervision of
soldiers sick in these institutions. It is recommended that for the
future, arrangements be made for base hospitals in which at least
some staff members are either active or reserve members of the
Medical Corps. Members of the Medical Reserve Corps, U. S. A.,
have been entirely unsatisfactory for this purpose because of their
total lack of knowledge in military procedure.

GENERAL HYGIENE

Post Exchanges. One of the most serious features from
the hygienic standpoint has been the attempt to control the sale
of various articles to soldiers by outside authorities. Early in
the history of the camp the surroundings became infested with
all sorts of irregular establishments for the sale of various
articles, chiefly foods. Some attempt was made to instruct these
persons in hygienic matters and to indicate to them how their
places could be kept in a reasonably clean condition. Some of

the dealers responded and did actually run clean and orderly establishments, while others through lack of intelligence or desire did not. An attempt was made to control these places through the State Board of Health, but without any result, save for a series of interesting letters. An appeal to military authorities was equally futile until the Adjutant-General was directly reached when finally sentries were posted and ordered to forbid soldiers to trade at these places. Still several remained open, selling to soldiers at will. No authority was invested in the Medical Corps to arrest, nor could any military authority be induced to do so, yet the three cases of dysentery were directly traced to this traffic and throughout it remained the most frequent cause of the numerous gastro-intestinal diseases to which the camp as usual was prone.

But very little difference existed in this respect between these extramural sources of disease production and the official Post Exchanges conducted under a concession by a commercial firm and supposedly under military control. Instructions given to managers of these places met in some instances with polite attention and respectful promises, but absolutely nothing was done to correct conditions fully as serious as those presented by outside institutions. Articles forbidden to be sold were sold as frequently as desired. In pleasing contrast to these experiences was the Post Exchange conducted by the Chaplain of the 10th Infantry, in which the articles on sale, the persons handling the materials and the premises were in as commendable condition as any model company kitchen. It is unfortunate that those most concerned and best qualified to judge as to these serious matters are not permitted to enforce as well as recommend. I strongly recommend that in the future, M. L. 240 be strictly enforced, and that no concessions be granted to outside parties, but that each organization be expected to maintain its own exchange or exchanges and that these be absolutely under military control.

Instruction. It is to be regretted that instruction in matters of general hygiene has not been given as a matter of routine in the National Guard. It would be far better to devote less time to the instruction of line officers and men in the care of the feet, etc., and more to matters of general and camp hygiene. In order to produce results our inspectors have found it most advisable to explain in detail the reasons for each recommendation. When this

has reached a responsible line officer in most instances immediate
correction of the fault has been effected, and if these officers could
be thoroughly grounded in the elements of sanitary science before
they came to camp much time and much sickness might be prevented.   An inspector has graphically stated that he could place
the colonel of any regiment by the condition of his garbage incinerators.

Bacteriological Tests.   Experience, notably in this camp, has
shown the imperative necessity in every large camp of an expert
bacteriologist to conduct examinations of water, cultures from
suspicious disease conditions and especially to make such
tests as may be necessary to determine specific infections
as dysentery, typhoid, diphtheria, malaria, and the like.   This
work during this encampment has been efficiently performed
by Dr. Van Winkle, generously detailed for that purpose by
Dr. Augustus Wadsworth, of the State Research Laboratories.
For thorough co-operation in these matters, it is however necessary that familiarity with military methods and procedures
as well as objects should exist and this is very difficult when such
work is performed by civilian physicians.   There are several men
now serving as medical officers in the National Guard of New
York who are perfectly competent to do such work.   A suitable
equipment is obtainable from the U. S. Army supply lists and
there is no reason whatever why this work should not be added
to that of our corps, thereby greatly increasing its efficiency and
at the same time adding to the attractiveness of the service for a
very desirable class of physicians.   In the armies abroad this work
is entirely in charge of the medical corps and there is no reason
why this should not also pertain to our service.

CONCLUSION

It would be unfair to conclude this report without some reference to those who have contributed most generously to the
results achieved in the hygienic work at Camp Whitman.
Major Wadhams, of the Medical Corps, U. S. A., is above all to be
commended in this respect.   He has given most generously of his
wide experience and learning, which has been in all ways asso-
ciated with a remarkable understanding of National Guard con-

ditions and personnel.   He has at all times cheerfully instructed, advised and admonished.   The value of his services to the National Guard of New York cannot be estimated and is deserving of recognition which is beyond us to give.   Major Daniel Lucas, who has been alternately Camp Surgeon, Chief Inspector and general utility man in every sanitary way, also deserves special credit for his industry and efficiency.   The Medical Corps is deeply indebted to Lieutenant-Colonel Townsend, of the Quartermaster Corps for his always cheerful and loyal assistance, and wise advice often on matters quite outside his multifarious duties.   Every possible facility has been extended to us by the Quartermaster Corps at all times without respect to whether the matter was distinctly in its province or not.   This has been much appreciated.

Finally, the Division Surgeon wishes to chronicle the most unusual fact that the Major-General, Commanding the Second Division, and The Adjutant-General of the State of New York, have promptly and most generously granted precisely 100 per cent. of the requests made upon them by this department. This has been the real reason why Camp Whitman has been remarkable for the small percentage of sickness which has characterized it and why its soldiers have gone away better physically than when they came to this camp.

HARLOW BROOKS
Lieutenant-Colonel, Division Surgeon.

Report of Lieutenant-Colonel J. Mayhew Wainwright, Inspector-General's Department, National Guard, State of New York

NEW YORK, *December* 14, 1916.

To the Adjutant-General, State of New York, Albany, N. Y.:

SIR.— I have the honor to submit the following report of my service in compliance with Special Orders No. 139 A. G. O., Albany, July, 1916 (copy attached).

I was directed to proceed to McAllen, Texas, to report as to New York troops in service of the United States and to confer with Major-General John F. O'Ryan. In addition to this order I was directed by the Governor in person at a conference held with him at the Executive Mansion on July 12, 1916, to report to him direct any action which might be recommended and which could be properly taken by the State authorities to add. to the comfort, health and convenience of our troops in Federal service. Deeming it wise before visiting McAllen to call on Major-General Funston, U. S. A., Commander of the Southern Department, to state to him the nature of my mission and secure his sanction thereto, I secured the sanction both of yourself and the Governor to such course.

Leaving New York on July 15th on the 6:57 p. m. train, I arrived at San Antonio, Texas, on July 20th, having through misinformation as to the whereabouts of General Funston first gone to El Paso. I called on General Funston at Department Headquarters at Fort Sam Houston in the forenoon, and explained to him the object of my visit to McAllen, stating. that I con- ceived I was in no sense to inspect in a military sense, but was to observe conditions in a general way, principally for the purpose of determining in what way it might be possible for the State to contribute to the health, comfort and convenience of its troops in the United States service, consistent with army regulations, and the fact that they were in Federal service. He did not think that there was much that could be done but stated he was very glad to have me proceed upon my mission and requested that after I had familiarized myself with conditions, I should again come and see him (see my telegram to the Governor of July 20th).

I then proceeded to McAllen, arriving there at about two o'clock on the afternoon of July 21st. I at once called on General O'Ryan, presenting to him a personal letter from the Governor stating the nature of my service, and requesting that all facilities be extended to me to carry out my mission. General O'Ryan received me most courteously, assigned me a tent at headquarters and invited me to join the headquarters mess. In fact, I was made to understand that during my stay I was expected to be a member of his official family, and throughout my whole stay I was treated accordingly.

McAllen is a city of about twenty-five hundred inhabitants situated upon a branch of the St. Louis, Brownsville & Mexican Railroad about thirty-seven miles from Harlingen, the junction point, Harlingen being about twenty-five miles north of Brownsville. Both the main line and branch are single track lines of more or less inferior construction, running west for a distance of about fifty miles parallel with the Rio Grande river to a station known as Sam Fordyce, about a mile back from an important ford of the river. The railroad is at no place more than eight miles from the river and generally much nearer. Brownsville is a city of about fifteen thousand inhabitants situated on the Rio Grande opposite the Mexican city of Matamoras at a point about twenty-five miles up the river from the Gulf of Mexico.

The whole region is flat or slightly undulating, generally at about the river level, the natural growth being a chapparal of cactus and mesquite except where cleared for cultivation. Much of the region between the railroad and the river is intersected by irrigation canals to which the Rio Grande water is pumped from pumping stations along the river. The soil is naturally fertile growing an abundance and variety of crops where irrigated. Farther back from the river it is grazing country. The whole region is known as the San Benito valley. The great majority of the population is Mexican, mostly of a low order. The character of the soil is such that when subjected to heavy rains it becomes a clinging and persistent mud, the roads when subjected to rain becoming quagmires.

THE CAMPS

The Camp of Division Headquarters is situated about half a mile east of the railroad station at McAllen on the south side of the track, the General occupying a newly constructed hut or bungalow. The camp at McAllen extends south from Division Headquarters, being in a right angle formed by the Pharr, McAllen and Mission highway and the highway running directly south to Hidalgo and the river, the organizations being camped in the orders named north and south, each practically adjoining the other, as follows:

Second Brigade, Brigadier-General Dyer, Seventh, Twelfth and Seventy-first Regiments Infantry, First and Second Field Artillery, Twenty-second Engineers, First Cavalry and Squadron A, Brigade Headquarters, the Field Hospital, First Ambulance Company and Signal Corps being camped in line north to south on the east flank of the camps first named. There were in McAllen camp over ten thousand men and thirty-five hundred animals. The camp ground had been uncleared chapparal, undulating, with some low spots in which the water remained after the heavy rains. To the south and parallel with the line of camps at a distance of about one-third of a mile is an irrigation ditch leading from the Rio Grande river. It had been necessary for each organization to clear its camp ground, a most laborious and hard task in view of the temperature and the nature of the growth to be removed. The distance of the line of camps from Division Headquarters on the north to Squadron A on the south is about two miles. There being plenty of space, the camps are laid out on generous lines with broad streets. For the infantry latrines and corrals are on the west flank along the Hidalgo road, kitchens and officers are on the east, this being reversed in the cavalry and artillery camps in which picket lines are on the east flank on account of proximity to the water in the irrigation canal.

The tentage appeared good and new, although the Twelfth Regiment had much old white tentage. The source of water supply for drinking and cooking was the municipal water system of McAllen from driven wells which, although said to be of good quality, was insufficient in quantity owing to a one-inch supply pipe running north and south through the whole camp having erroneously been considered sufficient to supply all needs. The depot quartermaster was in a building facing the railroad at McAllen.

The bread for this camp was baked at a field bakery at McAllen.

The First Brigade, Brigadier-General Wilson, Seventy-fourth, Twenty-third and Third Regiments Infantry, and Second Ambulance Company was camped three miles east of McAllen at Pharr in line parallel to and about half a mile south of the railroad. Pharr is a small city about the same size and nature as McAllen. The camps ran from east to west and practically adjoining as follows: Third, Twenty-third, Brigade Headquarters, Seventy-fourth, the Ambulance Company in the center on the north flank. Water for drinking and cooking was from the local water supply procured from wells; for the animals, from the irrigation ditch. Most of the tentage of the Seventy-fourth was old style white. Several of the companies of the Third were very short of tentage, causing overcrowding of tents. There were about thirty-five hundred men in the Pharr camp.

The Third Brigade, Brigadier-General Lester, was camped on the north side of the railroad about a half mile west of Mission, a small city possibly larger than McAllen from which it is distant about five miles west. The camps were parallel to the railroad in order as follows: Fourteenth Regiment, Brigade Headquarters, Sixty-ninth and Second running from north to south. There were about four thousand men at Mission. The water supply was Rio Grande water pumped from the irrigation ditches. At Pharr and Mission the local people had installed the piping system, building and presenting each of the organizations with ample shower baths. The Mission camp was supplied with bread from the field bakery located on the south side of the track in the Mexican quarter. There were no regular troops at McAllen.

At Mission there were a company of the Twenty-eighth Regular Infantry and a troop of the Third Cavalry; at Pharr a company of the Twenty-eighth' Infantry. On the river at Hidalgo there was one company of the Twenty-eighth Infantry and at Madero south of Mission, one company of the Second Texas Infantry guarding the pumping station.

General Funston informed me that the location of the camps for our division was selected, not with reference to its availability for concentration camps, but for strategic reasons, having regard to the protection of the border from raids and proximity to the ford or crossing over the Rio Grande river at Sam Fordyce. Sam Fordyce, fifteen miles west of Mission, is the terminus of the railroad and the pontoon train and a detachment of the engineers were here located. Hidalgo is a place of some importance, owing to the ferry across to Reynosa, a considerable Mexican town on the other side of the railroad which parallels the river from Matamoras to Camargo and thence to Monterey. Here and at Madero, a point on the river about three miles to the south of Mission, are two important irrigation pumping stations. The old military road which runs close to and parallel with the river along the river front was constantly patrolled.

Pursuant to my orders I took the earliest opportunity of conferring with General O'Ryan, brigade commanders and commanding officers of the various organizations. I append a memorandum (Exhibit A) of interviews with all such.

From such memorandum it will appear that the important needs were cots and board floors to keep the men off the ground; proper screening of the company kitchens to keep out the flies; some sort of structure in which the men could sit and have their meals with some reasonable degree of comfort; a more abundant water supply, cash to supply necessary augmentation of the ration and other articles till the ration saving was available.

The first ten days of my stay were devoted to interviews with responsible officers and to visiting companies, troops and batteries for the purpose of interviewing non-commissioned officers and enlisted men. I append also (Exhibit B) a partial memorandum of such interviews with enlisted men.

At the time of my arrival most of the organizations had been at their stations for about two weeks. The Third Regiment, however, had just arrived and was making camp. Camps were by no means well settled. Much manual labor still remained to complete the equipment of the camps.

General Conditions

The health of the men generally at the time of my arrival was excellent. Notwithstanding the uncomfortable features of the service there had been practically no cases of sun stroke. But at first owing to the excessive heat and necessary exertions in preparing camps, there had been many cases of heat prostration from which, however, recovery was rapid, with rest and proper treatment.

The general appearance, demeanor and spirit of men and officers were excellent. Notwithstanding the many discomforts owing to lack of supplies there was little complaint or grumbling. There was an apparently general disposition to make the best of everything and allowances for all shortcomings on the score of the suddenness of the call and the remoteness and inaccessibility of the region.

Tentage was conical or pyramidal with the quota of eight men to a tent. No cots had been issued, so men were sleeping on the ground with ponchos under their blankets. Some had been able to procure cots at their own expense, and there were some sleeping bags, but the great majority slept on the bare ground. There were no board floors except in officers' tents where they had been procured at private expense.

Company kitchens were unscreened leaving free access to the swarms of flies. Fly traps had not been issued, although some had been procured. In most of the organizations most of the men messed unprotected from the sun or weather in the company streets as, of course, they were not permitted to mess in their tents. In some few cases tent flies were used as mess shelters and in the cavalry some wooden mess shelters were under construction at organization expense.

Mosquito bars or mosquito netting had not been issued. Latrines were for the most part uncovered. In some organizations, notably the Second and Sixty-ninth, they were entirely unscreened.

At McAllen there were very limited facilities for washing owing to lack of water. Showers were contemplated as soon as the supply could be increased.

There was no cover for the animals of the infantry organizations. Picket lines of the artillery and cavalry were entirely without cover or shelter for the animals except in the case of some troops of cavalry where they had been procured at private expense.

Health and Hospital Conditions

The percentage of sick was surprisingly low, under two per cent. The field hospital was located on the east flank at McAllen in several regulation hospital tents, which had no board floors, and were unscreened. Owing to lack of cots the sick men were obliged to lie on the ground or upon litters. The sick from all camps were concentrated at the field hospital. The medical officers in charge and in attendance at the hospital appeared zealous, faithful and assiduous in the performance of their duties, yet the lack of supplies undoubtedly occasioned much unnecessary hardship and suffering.

The seriously sick were sent in daily parties in charge of a non-commissioned officer of the Ambulance Company to the base hospital at Fort Sam Houston at San Antonio, necessitating a railway journey in a local passenger train from McAllen to Harlingen with change of cars into Pullman sleepers at Harlingen, the time consumed being about twenty hours.

The hospital cases for the most part were dysentery and heat prostration. Besides those in hospital there was always a considerable number incapacitated for ordinary duty and returned for light duty or to quarters. There was no typhoid or malaria, but there had been some serious cases, mostly appendicitis, sent to San Antonio for operation.

On the second day after my arrival there were two cases requiring immediate operation, one for appendicitis and the other for strangulated hernia. The operations were performed in an improvised operating room in the hospital tent and both men recovered.

The low sick rate was remarkable among men so recently come from a temperate climate to the torrid atmosphere of this the most southerly portion of the United States, where the daily temperature in the shade at midday was usually well above one hundred degrees, and at night rarely below eighty, and where there were much dampness and humidity owing to the torrential rains.

SANITATION

Sanitary arrangements appeared excellent and well enforced. Incinerators had been constructed at the kitchens where all garbage and kitchen refuse were completely consumed. Sinks and latrines were daily sprayed or burned out though they were neither covered nor adequately screened. Litter from the corrals and other refuse which could not be burned in the incinerators was conveyed to a great plain or open space about two and one-half miles down the Hidalgo road south of the camp known as the "dump" by the company wagons, where it was spread and burned. Carcasses of all dead animals were transported thither and cremated. The "dump" was in charge of a detail under a staff officer who was also supplied with a corps of laborers. At first and before they were acclimated the mortality among the horses and mules was considerable.

Although the region abounds in insects and creeping things of all varieties, there were comparatively few mosquitoes. Flies there were in abundance, particularly at the company kitchens where it appeared impossible to keep them from the food on which they literally swarmed. Prevalence of intestinal troubles was undoubtedly due to this cause, as well as to the heat and the alkali water. All measures of sanitation were prescribed and enforced under the direction of the Division Surgeon. (See Exhibit C.)

Drinking water at all three of the camps though unpleasant was officially reported not unwholesome or necessary to be boiled. No provision was made for filtering, It would appear that every company and regimental infirmary should have been provided with some kind of filter to at least clear the water. It was commonly believed that the paratyphoid epidemic which broke out principally in the organizations at the Mission camp was due in large measure to the irrigation ditch water there in use.

Drainage was necessarily poor owing to the flat contour. During the first few weeks, owing to the constant downpours, the camps and company streets were deep in mud. Tents had to be diked in some cases to a height of eighteen inches to prevent the incursion of water. Constant traffic over the streets and cleared spaces rendered them quagmires. The low portions in some camps, particularly at McAllen became and remained inundated at times to a depth of eighteen inches to two feet until a deep trench running through the centre of the camp to the irrigation canal was constructed owing to the insistence and indefatigable efforts of Colonel Gordon Johnson whose regiment, the Twelfth Infantry, was the worst sufferer.

After every rain for several hours portions of the west flank of the camp of this regiment was simply a lake, many of the tents having to be abandoned. Although possibly the volume of water was excluded, obviously tent floors were rendered damp and uncomfortable and unsanitary as places of habitation. Horses on the picket line stood for days in mud well over fetlocks. Grooming and horse care was usually done by men standing in mud above their ankles.

FOOD

Food was the regular army field ration. There were few complaints as to its quality or quantity, although in the beginning there was a great lack of variety and too much meat to be suitable for the climate.

Owing to lack of funds in most companies for the first month or six weeks, it was necessary for the men to subsist entirely on the ration. Undoubtedly some hardship was occasioned, although after the " saving from the ration " became available, they were able to buy green vegetables, extras and delicacies. There appeared to be a great difference in the bills of fare and character of cooking in the different companies, due to the difference in skill and experience of the company cooks; yet the following are some typical menus taken at random:

Company A, 74th Regiment: .Breakfast, hash, coffee, bread. Dinner, roast beef, potatoes, turnips, iced tea, ice cream (bought with company funds.) Supper, canned tomatoes, bread and tea.

Company H, 69th Regiment: Breakfast, hash, coffee and bread. Dinner, cabbage, bacon, beans, bread, tea. Supper, soup, bread and coffee.

Company —, 2nd Regiment: Breakfast, boiled rice, coffee, bread, milk, beans. Dinner, puree of bean soup, tea and bread. Supper, cold roast beef, boiled potatoes, stewed corn, bread and tea.

Much weakness and unevenness in cooking were evident. Some companies were exceedingly well fed; others complained bitterly of the food suggesting a more satisfactory system of procuring experienced company cooks.

The bread seemed generally wholesome and well-baked, yet there was complaint of some unbaked and moldly bread.

Ice was procured from the local ice plants. The daily allowance was two pounds per man but there were complaints of considerable shortage. Refrigerators were required to be constructed but materials for the purpose were not issued. Still many companies managed to construct good and ingenious ice boxes, one company of the Third Infantry having a spacious refrigerating cellar six or eight feet underground.

Inequalities in the issue of food or rations were doubtless due in some measure to inexperience or lack of enterprise on the part of supply officers and commissary sergeants, but defect or unevenness of supply was probably the main cause.

CLOTHING

There was considerable shortage of suitable clothing. Some organizations were still in the heavy olive cloth, not having received their cotton cloth uniforms.

There appeared to be a great unevenness in the supplies and equipment of the various organizations. Some had received a complete supply of all articles; on the other hand, in one company of the Sixty-ninth I found four men still in their black civilian shoes and was informed that no second pair of shoes had been issued and that many men still had but the one set of underclothing in which they left the North.

It would seem obvious that no organization should have been permitted to leave its home station without being fully and suitably equipped for campaign in this climate and region. The suddenness of the call and lack of available stores on hand with the War Department will account for much of the shortage.

Most of the organizations, although considerably under war strength at the time of the call had been by no means equipped for the actual strength. No reserve stores were on hand at the armories or in sufficient quantity at depots to supply the increased strength.

It is safe to say that no organization left its home station fully equipped or thoroughly prepared to take the field. The difficulty of supplying deficiencies after reaching the border was, of course, much greater than it would have been at the home stations.

For a long time after arrival the troops were considered technically in the field and little provision was made to transform the camps from field camps to permanent camps. Without any definite order changing their status, they became by force of circumstances-permanent camps.

The War Department apparently was in no way prepared to provide the necessary equipment and supplies for permanent camps for any such number of men. Materials and supplies were procured largely from local sources. Upon the Chief Quartermaster at Fort Sam Houston, who was to a great extent limited to the possibilities of local markets and industries, devolved the task of providing and furnishing the necessary supplies and making up deficiencies in equipment.

The fact that for a number of weeks the character of the principal hospital was maintained as that of a field rather than a base or camp hospital restricting its facilities and equipment to those of a field hospital resulted in hardship and distress to the men who had the misfortune to fall seriously sick. Nothing could have exceeded the industry, zeal and fidelity of the Chief Medical officer of our Division, his assistants and the regimental medical officers. The trouble was in the system which maintained a field hospital in a situation in which a camp hospital was required, and which failed to supply necessary supplies and experienced nurses.

There was much and not unnatural complaint of the medical service upon the part of the men. The system prohibited the retention in regimental infirmaries of any sick beyond those returned to light duty or sick in quarters; so that those requiring hospital treatment were obliged to go to a field hospital inadequately equipped, or to undergo the long and fatiguing journey to the base hospital at Fort Sam Houston, above described.

Undoubtedly, a considerable sum of money could well have been spent by the State or from private sources to improve the facilities of the field hospital during the first two months. I recommend that a fund of at least two thousand dollars be made immediately available for this purpose, as will appear from my communication to the Adjutant General on the subject. Brigadier General Dyer was able to raise the sum of one thousand dollars providing board floors, screens, cots, sheets, pillow and other much needed equipment for the field hospital.

Soldiers discharged for physical disability underwent considerable hardship. To be sure they were given transporation to their homes, but no provision was made for their care or comfort on the journey home. It would seem obviously proper that no soldier discharged for disability should be permitted to undertake the journey home unless proper provision be made for his comfort, and that it is inappropriate to permit a man recently recovered from a serious illness or who is in a weakened or debilitated condition to undergo a long journey alone and with merely his transportation furnished.

Several cases of great hardship occurred which came to my attention where sick men discharged for disability were obliged to remain a considerable length of time at Harlingen or Brownsville owing to clerical defects in their papers which might have been overlooked, cured on the spot or rectified by telephone or telegraph. The inflexibility of our military system often appears to business or civilian minds as unnecessarily severe.

ANTI-DRINK ORDER

The fine condition, low sick rate and general good condition of health and morale may in considerable measure be attributed to the order issued by the Division Commander prohibiting not only the purchase, but the consumption of liquor. It appeared to be realized by both officers and enlisted men that total abstinence in that climate was most desirable. Voluntary observance of this order was general; though, on the other hand, it was rigidly enforced. Too much importance cannot be attributed to this measure so wise owing to the climate and nature of the service.

PAY

No pay was received by the men until the middle of August. Although, of course, men have little personal need of cash under conditions of such service, nevertheless much inconvenience and possibly some hardship, particularly to the dependents of those in the service was occasioned. All of the organizations had been called into service on June 19 and mustered into the United States service on or about June 30th and became entitled to State pay during the period from call to muster, Federal pay beginning from muster. It seemed unfortunate that provision could not be made for their receiving State pay at least by the middle of July and their Federal pay for the month of July early in August.

Delay in Federal pay was occasioned by the difficulties encountered in complying with regulations in regard to payrolls and in many cases to the different views as to particular questions of different pay officers.

It would seem as though in so important a subject as pay with its effect on the spirts and contentment of the men, there should be ample practical instructions while in State service as to the Government's requirements as to payrolls and indeed as to all prescribed Army forms, in view of the complexity and the rigid insistence of the regular Army upon compliance with every detail.

Indeed, if any simplification of the complicated system of forms and reports is possible, it would be highly desirable, if for no other reason than to relieve officers and non-commissioned officers of the nervous strain and vast amount of time required to meet the Government's requirements in this respect.

During the second week of August, General Stotesbury, our Adjutant General, arrived receiving a warm welcome. During his stay of ten days, the troops received State pay.

I interviewed all commanding officers, many company, troop and battery commanders, company officers and some enlisted men in practically every infantry company, and in most of the batteries and troops.

My course of procedure was as follows: After procuring the permission of the commanding officer, I went unaccompanied by any commissioned officer to the first sergeant's tent and stated to him the nature of my errand. After interviewing him, I proceeded down the company street, entered unannounced the most crowded tent I could find, or approached any group at hand; told them I was there as the Governor's representative to find out how they were faring, whether there was anything that the State could do for them and requested a free expression, which I believe I secured.

Little dissatisfaction, discontent or complaint was expressed. The men seemed universally to realize the nature of their service; that they had become Federal soldiers, that there were great difficulties owing to remoteness and lack of transportation in supplying all their needs. They expressed confidence that in time they would have everything they required.

I venture to say that no government could show the service of more loyal and willing men than those of our National Guard. There was shown a general cheerfulness, strong soldierly spirit and willingness to take things as they came; in fact, in my judgment, the highest form of patriotism was displayed on all sides. They drew my attention to the lack of cots and other discomforts and articles needed generally, not in the spirit of criticism but more as a matter of inquiry. They wanted to know how long they were to be kept sleeping on the ground; it was pretty uncomfortable. Did I think they would have board floors? Was it not possible to vary the rations or to improve the cooking? Did I not think that the doctors might be a little more sympathetic and not treat them in such an off-hand manner when they reported at sick call?

The general morale and discipline were of a high order. There were comparatively few cases to engage the general or summary court martial and hardly any due to violence or intoxication.

As stated, there was great need of cots, properly screened kitchens, proper shacks, improved water supply and cash to purchase necessary or desirable articles to enable them to secure many things which, although the subject of issue, had not been received by the Quartermaster. I found no occasion to make specific recommendation except that a certain amount of cash might be sent to the regimental or company commanders to supply accessories and that representations be made to the War Department to expedite much needed materials and supplies.

Many organizations spent of their private or civil funds to supply articles which should have been supplied by the Government.

Provision should be made by which, if they are not able to secure reimbursement from the Government, they may be reimbursed out of the public funds of this State. It would seem unjust that funds accumulated often over a long period of time through dues or voluntary subscription by members should be exhausted or devoted to the purchase of necessary articles and supplies to which the organization or its members are entitled but which they were prevented from having by the slow processes of the Government.

A violent rain and wind storm on the 29th of July having blown down and flooded tents, the need of cots or board floors became pressing. Accordingly on the 1st of August, I went to San Antonio to see General Funston on the subject. I was informed that it was found not possible to procure a supply of more than one thousand cots a week; that the General was much concerned and that he had issued instructions to supply officers to procure all the lumber necessary for board floors, as well as for the kitchens, mess shacks and other shelter.

Notwithstanding the difficulty for the Government to procure cots, it appeared to be possible at all times to purchase all desired from local merchants, from which source both the 7th Regiment and Squadron A were practically completely supplied.

When I left on September 12th comparatively few cots had been issued. Though the lumber for board floors was being issued, but few board floors yet existed. The kitchen and mess shack structures were in process of construction but few were completed. The one-inch water pipe that supplied the McAllen camp had been replaced with a *two-inch* pipe, which again was to be replaced with one of larger calibre, as there was still a considerable shortage in the cavalry and artillery camps. It was a matter of not unnatural surprise that there was so much delay in these matters.

The camp hospital authorized in the latter part of July was completed and received patients early in September. It consisted of several well-constructed, one-story wooden pavilions with offices, laboratories, doctors' and nurses' quarters and capacity for two hundred patients. It was a most desirable change from the previous field hospital. A corps of female nurses arrived during the second week of September.

DEPENDENTS

One of the subjects of most concern was the dependents of those required to go to the front. His Excellency referred to me a telegram of Mr. R. Fulton Cutting to the effect that great distress was being occasioned by the absence of the men; that probably forty per cent. of the men had dependents who were prejudiced by their absence, and that such men should be discharged in order that their places might be taken by recruits differently situated.

It was manifestly impracticable, if not undesirable, to conduct an inquiry calculated to elicit the exact facts; therefore, I made inquiries on the subject in every organization visited. The result of such inquiries led to the conclusion that although there was in every company a certain number so situated, that there were by no means so many as supposed.

Early in July the order was issued providing for the discharge of men having dependents who were suffering by their absence. I was informed that down to the middle of August less than three hundred applications for discharge under this order had been made. This, of course, did not represent the actual conditions since many men who were entitled to discharge and who should have applied on account of home conditions refrained from doing so on account of a natural disinclination to have their courage or patriotism questioned.

Also there was much delay in action on the applications owing to the evidence required to sustain the application, namely the affidavits of two disinterested citizens at home as to the facts of dependence. Owing to the provision made by Congress for money payments for the relief of dependents, the order was revoked to take effect August 31st.

The provision made by Congress was entirely inadequate in the very large number of cases of men on salary or whose ordinary income from their occupation or profession had provided for a scale of living much higher than that contemplated by Congress. As to these latter it will be practically impossible ever to furnish relief from public funds commensurate with their needs.

I gathered the impression that after the first few weeks either through the efforts of home relief agencies or on account of the men's being paid, the condition as to the dependency of relatives was very much relieved; at all events little further was heard on this subject, in relation to the lower paid men. The condition was however but little relieved and has grown probably more acute as to those receiving salaries or higher pay.

Many employers who had agreed to continue salary or pay and to keep open jobs have discharged men or stopped their pay, which was, of course, inevitable, as it is out of the question to expect employers to carry men indefinitely under these circum-. stances.

No system either of governmental or private relief will ever prove adequate or will result in more than the relief of cases of pressing necessity, and it is inevitable that the inconvenience or distress of dependents and injury or loss in business or occupation must be inseparable from any prolonged service of National Guard or volunteers.

Transportation

The regulations require that troops shall be transported in tourist sleepers. Some organizations were despatched in ordinary and in many cases dilapidated day coaches, and there was much unnecessary crowding even in these. In some cases they were changed into tourist sleepers en route; in others, the entire journey was made in day coaches.

The necessities of the situation were undoubtedly largely responsible for despatching some organizations in ordinary cars before tourist sleepers could be provided, since they were not on hand in sufficient numbers at points of departure. The food appeared in most cases to have been ample, it having been possible to supplement the travel ration with meals cooked on the train or procured en route, though in some cases the men received little in addition to the issued travel ration of coffee, canned corned beef and beans and crackers.

There had been ample opportunity offered for exercise by short marches at stops, at which some organizations had also been afforded the opportunity to bathe in nearby streams or rivers.

The press stories as to hardships and talk of food were, I believe, either utterly unfounded or greatly exaggerated.

The story, for instance, of the detachment of recruits from the 71st Regiment having raided a bakery at Erie, Pennsylvania,

6

owing to having had no food since leaving home had no basis in fact, the fact having been that their particular detachment had three good meals a day during the entire journey.

Early in September the 14th, 71st and 3rd and 2nd Regiments were returned to New York. I inspected the train and witnessed the entrainment and loading of the 71st Regiment which left McAllen in one train with Pullmans for officers and tourist sleepers with berths for the men, two men to a section as required by regulations, the cars being apparently clean and in good order.

Drill and Instruction

There was limited opportunity for drill or military exercise or instruction during the first few weeks. The necessities of making camp occupied most of the time and besides the lack of cleared ground and the nature of the country precluded any extended field of instruction. The drill periods, however, for those not on detail were two hours in the forenoon before ten-thirty and one hour in the afternoon. There was company and battalion drill in close and extended order and instruction of recruits in the school of the soldier.

Companies and in some cases battalions were sent on practice marches of two or three days duration to and along the river, bivouacking in shelter tents at night, confining the march to the early morning and late afternoon, covering from eight to ten miles a day. These marches were most useful in accustoming men and officers to campaign conditions and imparting familiarity with the country and a spirit of self-reliance.

By the middle of July opportunities for rifle practice were afforded at an improvised range constructed under the direction of Major Waterbury, Division Ordance Officer. The ranges were but fifty and one hundred yards with sufficient targets to afford practice for one battalion a day. Although the ranges were short and the facilities crude, the practice afforded undoubtedly proved of benefit as a large proportion of the men were new recruits who had never before handled a rifle, to say nothing of rifle practice. Unfortunately the limited number of targets did not insure more than one day's practice a month to each organization.

Owing to the condition of the roads and of the horses there was little opporuntity for drill for the cavalry, although even in

July single troops too were given experience in patrol duty and bivouac on marches of several days from camp.

Little opportunity was afforded for drill or practice by the artillery owing to shortage of equipment, and poor condition of horses. No fire practice was had until September when field firing by battery was held at the Gloria ranch about twenty miles from McAllen. By early September, however, the artillery was in condition for battery drill and fully horsed, though many of the horses appeared light for artillery. I attended a quite impressive and imposing view of all the artillery by Brigadier General McLeer, Chief of Artillery, early in September.

CAVALRY PRACTICE MARCH

Early in August all the cavalry were despatched by successive squadrons on a practice ride of five days over a ninety mile route, Squadron A going first and the squadrons of the 1st Regiment Cavalry following successively.

The first night camp was at Sterling's Ranch, about fourteen miles North of Mission or twenty from McAllen. The second day was taken in a ride out to the Gloria Ranch and back to Sterling's, about twelve miles, with camp for the second night at Sterling's; the third of eighteen miles to the northwest to Young's, a large cattle ranch, with a halt for dinner at Laguna Seca, a Mexican ranch about half-way; the fourth day returning to Sterling's and camping for the night, and thence on the fifth back to McAllen.

I accompanied and camped with the 3rd Squadron of the 1st Cavalry as the guest of Captain Shiverick commanding M Troop. The tour was of great value to both horses and men, notwithstanding the heat and bad roads and both returned much improved in every way. At the same time as the infantry hike next detailed Squadron A was despatched on another five days march out.

THE "HIKE"

The infantry regiments in succession were given a march covering the same route except that on the return they marched from Sterling's, fourteen miles to Edinburg, the county seat, and thence to their various camps, eight miles for those at Pharr, eleven for those at McAllen and sixteen for those at Mission, making a total march of about eight-six miles, the tour covering eleven days.

The Fourteenth and Seventy-first Regiments started from Mission and McAllen respectively on the 16th of August, the Seventy-first camping the first night at Mission, the Fourteenth at Alton, six miles north of Mission. The marches and camps were as follows: From Mission to Alton six miles, to Sterling's ranch fourteen, to Gloria five and a half, return to Sterling's five and a half; to Laguna Seca eleven miles, to Young's ranch seven miles, return to Laguna Seca seven miles, to Sterling's eleven, to Edinburg fourteen, to Pharr eight, McAllen eleven, to Mission seventeen, as the case might be.

After the Fourteenth and Seventy-first the regiments followed each day in the following order: Third, Second, Seventh, Seventy-fourth, Sixty-ninth, Twelfth and Twenty-third, the last completing the "hike" on September 8th.

I accompanied the Seventy-first for three days, the Fourteenth for four, the Third for three, the Second for four and was one night each with the Twelfth and Seventy-fourth and visited the Sixty-ninth at Gloria. The duty appeared on the whole most profitable for all concerned.

The experience gained by the officers in the care of the men and by the men in the care of themselves was most valuable, and all returned much improved both physically and in morale. The march was ordered to be conducted in heavy marching order with company baggage wagons and battalion combat wagons.

An advance supply base or refitting station was established at the rail head of a branch line from Mission at Monte Cristo, in charge of Captain Loree, the efficient divisional assistant quartermaster, at which the regimental supply wagons were loaded with the field rations. There was also a detachment of auto trucks assigned to this station and some of the organizations had one or two such of their own. Motor transportation proved very unsatisfactory over such roads, the main reliance being the mules which, as usual, proved their worth under such campaign conditions.

Troops C, D and B of Squadron A were each in turn detailed to furnish a guard for and to help unload the quartermaster stores at Monte Cristo, the rail head. While on such duty they were in a shelter tent camp about a third of a mile from Monte Cristo, Troop C being on such duty for two weeks. The zeal, cheerfulness, efficiency and readiness for any duty of all in Squadron A was most marked. At Monte Cristo also was established an advance field hospital in charge of Major Gaus, Medical Corps and one of the Ambulance Companies.

The general health of all on the "hike" was excellent, all things considered. About three hundred men in all were treated at the advance hospital, those incapacitated from continuing being returned to the hospital at McAllen in the ambulances, the journey of twenty miles being a great ordeal for the really sick. Most of the cases were of prostration and heat exhaustion.

There was surprisingly little foot trouble: whether on account of the shoe or the soft "footing" is hard to say. The requirements as to foot inspection were fairly well observed. Invaluable experience in the care of the feet was gained by both officers and men. Considerable trouble due to fallen arches developed.

The army shoe proved comfortable but hardly sufficiently serviceable. I doubt if one-half the shoes were serviceable at the end of the "hike", although they had been constantly subjected to water and mud. The roads were soft so that there was little hard wear. They appeared to be too light for continuous marching. The march was conducted as though in enemy country with advance and rear guards.

The hours of marching were within the discretion of the regimental commander and varied in different organizations. Reveille was usually at five-thirty, the advance guard clearing camp at seven, and getting into the next camp before eleven. Some organizations, notably the Second, started much earlier. Colonel Andrews' hours of reveille varied from 2 A. M for the march to Laguna Seca to midnight for that from Edinburg to Mission.

The advantage of the early start obviously avoided much exertion under the hot sun and resulted generally in a command arriving in camp in fresher, better condition than those which started later. There was considerable discussion as to whether the advantage of marching in the cooler hours made up for the consequent loss of sleep.

There was also considerable variance as to method of conducting the march. In the Second it was a fifteen minute halt after the first twenty-five minutes marching and then five minutes halt after every twenty-five minutes. In others, after the first fifteen minutes ten in every hour, with still different periods in others, and much discussion as to results. It appeared to me that the shorter period of both march and halt proved better under the conditions. There was little straggling and comparatively few were picked up by the ambulances.

Valuable experience in the habit of abstention from the use of water on the march was gained. On the first day great difficulty was found in prevailing on the men not to drain their canteens in the first two hours of the march; but experience, often of a bitter nature, soon demonstrated the advantage of drinking little or any water on the march and that it was far better to do without it. After the first two or three days most men came into camp at the end of the march with much water still in their canteens.

The issue of food on the "hike" was well sustained and there was little apparent dissatisfaction, though occasionally the train of some organizations became mired or delayed by the bad roads necessitating a late meal or encroaching on the supply of an adjoining company.

While the "hike" was in progress, a severe hurricane visited the region, proving a greater ordeal for the Seventy-first, which arrived in camp at Sterling's in the pouring rain just as the storm was beginning, and the Fourteenth which was at the remotest point of the "hike" at Gloria than for the other organizations which were in the permanent camps.

The hurricane lasted about fourteen hours and at its height the wind was said to have blown over one hundred miles an hour. The Fourteenth had absolutely no shelter but literally stood and took it all day and most of the night grouped about their camp fires, since all tentage went down.

I was with the Seventy-first, all of whom finally got under cover of some kind, two battalions either in the Sterling pump house or ranch outbuildings, the Third, Major Delamater's, being marched a mile and a half just before dark when the wind was at its height to Monte Cristo where sufficient empty buildings, including the station, were found to shelter them. The hurricane disrupted the march programme for two days. It blew down all the wind mills at Laguna Seca from which alone water could be procured.

Owing to the energy and efficiency of a detachment from the Twenty-second Engineers under Captain Woodward, the pumps of several of the more important mills were sufficiently repaired to be workable at least by hand power.

Notwithstanding considerable criticism as to its utility I believe that the " hike " proved of the utmost benefit to all concerned. Every one in any way related to the duty was much benefited from · the experience. It was, to say the least, a valuable, excellent preparation for the necessary conditions and incidents of real field service and campaigning. The Second and Twelfth Regiments both took out their bands which contributed much to the cheer and enlivenment of their camps during the tour.

The efficiency of the Signal Corps under Major Halahan was well demonstrated during the " hike." Radio stations were established at Sterling's and the Young ranch which maintained constant communication with Division Headquarters. The neatness of the camp, the discipline and high order of every feature of the work of this organization at the border reflect great credit on its commander and personnel.

PARATYPHOID EPIDEMIC

Near the end of August a mild epidemic of paratyphoid developed principally in the regiments at Mission. In the Fourteenth, forty cases developed in one day on the return from the " hike ", also a number in the Second and Sixty-ninth and later a few cases in every regiment. The exact cause was not determined. The field battery at Mission appeared to be a focus, as a number of those who had worked there developed the disease. The general impression was that it was principally due to the water supply at Mission (Rio Grande water taken from the irrigation ditch). Fortunately the new and thoroughly equipped camp hospital which had just been completed was able to receive the patients and suspects.

The situation was taken in hand most energetically and efficiently by Colonel Terriberry, the Division Surgeon, and Lieut.

Colonel Reynolds, U. S. A., the district medical officer. Temperatures of all men in the Mission regiments were taken and all men showing any rise were at once segregated and despatched to the Base Hospital at San Antonio for observation.

After the middle of September no further new cases developed and the epidemic was over (see memorandum of conditions September 10th attached). There were in all, including suspects as well as positive cases not over two hundred cases. The epidemic naturally occasioned great concern.

The effectiveness of the typhoid prophylactic was never more clearly demonstrated, as no case of true typhoid developed, notwithstanding that the conditions or causes that produced the paratyphoid would probably, except for the preventive, have produced a severe typhoid epidemic. (Report as to Origin, Recommendations, etc., of Division Surgeon, Exhibit D).

The paratyphoid epidemic drew attention forcibly to the crude and inadequate provision for the transportation of sick from camp to the Base Hospital. This had been to send them by ordinary passenger car in the case of those able to sit up, and by litter on the floor of the baggage car in the case of those obliged to lie prone to the Harlingen junction where after a wait sometimes of several hours they were transferred to the San Antonio express into drawing room cars, often upper berths.

It was a very severe and trying ordeal for the really sick. Possibly soldiers would be obliged to undergo much worse conditions of transportation in time of actual warfare, but under the circumstances of the present border service some different or special provision might be expected.

After the despatch of one lot of sixty-one men, some of them very ill, in this manner, following the despatch of a large number on previous days, an unofficial telegram to the Department Commander asking for some different provision resulted in the arrival at McAllen on the following day of a thoroughly equipped hospital train of converted Pullmans in which a comfortable and unbroken journey for the sick was afforded.

Recreation

Opportunities for recreation were afforded. The Y. M. C. A. with their usual energy and foresight erected at each of the camps a commodious, substantial, high and well ventilated structure with attendants in charge where the men could write and gather in the evenings and where religious services, meetings of various kinds and entertainments are held. The advantages and influence of the Y. M. C. A. were invaluable and appreciated by all.

Also, a stage or platform was erected near the Division Commander's Headquarters where boxing contests, band concerts and other forms of entertainment were afforded. On every Saturday night a show or entertainment of some sort was given under the auspices of one of the organizations at some of which there were audiences of several thousand soldiers. Also there was the inevitable moving picture show established in a large arena at the McAllen camp where very good and well attended shows were given. In addition there was the usual baseball and much voluntary pedestrianism. Latterly special rates were made to the soldiers to Corpus Christi and liberal leave was granted to those who desired to take advantage of this opportunity for change.

THE RIO GRANDE RATTLER

A weekly newspaper has been established, the "Rio Grande Rattler." It has proved a great source of attraction and interest. It will prove an invaluable record of this tour of service. Its excellence has attracted widespread attention and favorable comment from the press of the country and reflects great credit on Major Franklin W. Ward of the Division Staff and his able assistants.

GENERAL CONCLUSIONS

On September 12th, pursuant to a telegram from you I returned to New York and reported in person to the Governor on September 16th and to you on September 17th.

I would express the view that our troops on the border at the date of my departure were in an excellent condition of health and discipline, and that most of the camp equipment necessary to their comfort and physical welfare which were lacking in the beginning had finally been supplied. I doubt, however, if they were yet full equipped for field service, or sufficiently trained t actually take the field for active service either in Mexico or elsewhere.

The responsibility for and deficiencies or shortages of equipment which existed at the time of the call would appear not to be with the military authorities of our own State. The delay in furnishing necessary equipment and supplies after the State troops were mustered in may doubtless fairly be charged to lack of an adequate system or of any· preparation or plan commensurate with the emergency and numbers of State troops involved in the call.

The situation that exists at the border has undoubtedly furnished a valuable experience for all concerned and an object lesson as to what is required both as to preparation and training for any subsequent mobilization entailing the incorporation into the Federal service of all or a considerable portion of the State's militia for immediate service. The nature of the response of our National Guard to this call and the zeal and spirit displayed by all not only in the response but in the service rendered must always be a subject of pride to the citizens of our State. They responded cheerfully and willingly, assuming without cavil or complaint their new duties and obligations.

Notwithstanding the inconvenience and injury to their material concerns involved in very many cases, they have proved themselves ready to meet the perils and hardships of active service even beyond our own borders.

Their service and record on the Mexican border in this emergency must always be a bright page in the military record of the State of New York.

Respectfully,

J. MAYHEW WAINWRIGHT,

Lieutenant-Colonel.

Inspector General's Department.

STATE OF NEW YORK,

THE ADJUTANT GENERAL'S OFFICE.

ALBANY, *July* 6, 1916.

SPECIAL ORDERS ⎱
No. 139. ⎰

EXTRACT

*   *   *   *   *   *   *   *   *

XVII. J. Mayhew Wainwright, having qualified as Lieutenant Colonel, Inspector General's Department, and reported in accordance with instructions from this office, July 6, 1916, is hereby placed on duty. He is authorized to proceed to McAllen, Texas, and report to these headquarters as to troops of this State now in service of the United States, and in connection therewith will confer with Major-General John F. O'Ryan. The necessary travel is authorized.

BY COMMAND OF THE GOVERNOR:

LOUIS W. STOTESBURY,

The Adjutant-General.

Official:

(Signed)   W. A. NIVER.

(Seal)   Major, Adjutant-General's Department,

Assistant to the Adjutant-General.

EXHIBIT A

Memorandum of conferences with Major-General Frederick Funston at San Antonio, Major-General commanding New York Division, Brigade Commanders and Commanders of organizations of New York troops at camps at McAllen, Pharr and Mission, Texas.

Major-General Frederick Funston:

Arrived San Antonio, July 20th. Called on General Funston, stated my mission. He said he would be very glad to have me go to camps of New York Division upon my errand. Express concern of necessity of locating the Division at such a remote point but said it had been necessary owing to strategic reasons. That he had its interest very much on his mind and proposed to do everything he could for their comfort and convenience and general welfare and believed that it would be possible later to provide some diversion for the men, mentioning the ·contemplated plan of sending the organizations later successively to the sea shore to the Gulf of Mexico for sea bathing and change. He requested that I see him again after I had visited the camps.

Major-General John O'Ryan:

Arrived at McAllen, July 21st. Called on General O'Ryan at Division Headquarters. Was most cordially received. Was assigned to tent and invited to become during my stay one of the Division Staff family. Presented my letters and stated my errand. The General said he considered all conditions good and the troops in excellent condition and that the facilities, supplies and equipment furnished by the government were coming in and that many needs were still lacking but of course this was to be expected in view of the distance from supply points and facilities of transportation. He had nothing to suggest that the Government or State might do to supplement the provision or the amount which the troops may buy.

Brigade-General George R. Dyer:

Conferred with General Dyer, commanding 2nd Brigade Infantry, McAllen, on the same day. Expressed his opinion that conditions were good but that cots for the men and screening for kitchens and better facilities at Field Hospital were desirable. Had no specific suggestions to make as to what could be done by State in behalf of the troops.

Colonel Bates, (Commanding 71st Infantry):

Stated conditions in his regiment were excellent. Men generally in good health and spirits. Inquired why the State did not pay the men that pay which was due them between rendezvous and muster. Stated that cots and board floors for tents extremely desirable. He knew of no complaint as to clothing.

Brigadier-General John Wilson (Commanding First Brigade, Headquarters at Pharr, Texas:

Cots and covers and screened mess shacks badly needed. Had some doubts as to quality of water supply. Water was abundant. Called attention to lack of tourist cars for transportation down. Had been told by a New York Central transportation official that that railroad had been instructed not to furnish tourist sleepers as were required by regulations (Section No. 1143) unless specifically instructed so to do. Same official had informed him that on 24 hours' notice he could have secured all needed for Buffalo troops who had not secured them until they arrived at Kansas City. Bread sometimes unsatisfactory. Called attention to the mouldy bread issued to two companies of the 23rd. Had no specific suggestions as to anything the State could do.

Colonel Thurston (74th Infantry):

Men were still in woolen cloth uniforms but confident that necessary clothing would soon arrive. Have board screened sinks and a central system of shower baths. Food plenty and good and improving as to variety. Considered a well balanced ration and confident of savings, will have ample for sufficient green vegetables in a week. Meat was good. Stressed importance of cots, 1200 of which had been requisitioned. Also badly needed screens for kitchens. Understood contract for which and for screened mess shacks had been provided. Had plenty of food and water down and turned in four days' ration on arrival. Thought supplement of 5 cents per man from State until the saving from exchange and ration available would be very useful. Hoped the State would be able to send down the 1910 equipment which he understood was on hand. In addition as to health and spirits of men, excellent.

Colonel Norton (23rd Infantry):

Men short of bed sacks so that they had to sleep on ponchos. Screened kitchen and mess shacks needed. Understood materials coming. Cots essential. Satisfied that they are on the way. Also needed fly paper and fly traps. Abundance of water. Have large central shower baths similar to 74th Regiment. Ration good as to quantity and quality. Had bought much lumber out of their own fund. One company in particular had expended a large part of a $1200.00 company fund for lumber, vegetables and other things. Abundance of ice. Only four companies had been able to secure brick for incinerators. Had paid out of their own funds for lumber for covering for horses on picket line. Badly in need of transportation facilities. Would like a motor truck or a Ford car. Motor cycle out of business owing to bad roads.

Colonel Jennings (3rd Infantry):

Anxious to use military fund. In doubt if permissible. Would like ruling. Wanted to use it until exchange and ration saving available. Doubted if there would be any saving from ration. Our men want to eat better things than the army and our cooks are different. They are fed on basis of a ration of 40 cents per day. Screens for kitchens and sinks much needed. The water supply was limited, essential it should be increased and that proper bathing facilities which were lacking, should be furnished. His judgment more ice be issued; allowance of two pounds per man not enough. One per cent. of his command sick in hospital. Expressed as his judgment that there should be more than one in each seat of a day coach while travelling and a barrel of water be provided on each car preferably on the front platform.

Called attention to the absence of shower baths. Lumber for board floors should be authorized. But 1200 shoes had been issued. He had not enough for the necessary two pairs for each man. Called attention to the fact that his sinks were covered but not screened. Mosquito bars were also necessary and they had been requisitioned but not supplied. Sufficient equipment so as to be able to supply regiment at war strength should at all times be kept on hand at the Armory. Still far short of equipment. Fifty per cent. of intrenching tools lacking and only 20 mules received. His regiment was entitled to 104. Believe refrigerating plant in each organization could be procurable at comparatively small expense, as it was highly desirable to make ice cream and frozen dishes as men in this climate craved cold things. The ration lacked variety but was improving in this respect. Said that if State would provide 10 or 5 cents per man per day in addition to ration it would be very much in the interest of the men as they could then procure oranges and lemons, acids being desirable in this climate, green dishes and other rations. Not to piece out the rations but simply to furnish the men with extra delicacies not in the rations.

Colonel Fiske (Commanding 7th Regiment).

The health of his command was good and the sick list small. Some diarrhoea but no dysentery. The important things needed cots and bathing facilities. The pipe system in the street was a tap at each company. Pipe not large enough to supply sufficient water. Showers for men very necessary. Animal life in this country makes it uncomfortable without cots. Objected to using the beds sacks as an invitation to creeping things. The regiment has spent about $2,000.00 out of its own funds for lumber for latrines, mess tables and benches but there was no covering for the tables. In many cases the men were obliged to eat their meals in the sun as they could not take them into their tents. Thought the kitchen should not be screened as it was doubtful if the flies could be prevented as the strong breezes would be a better preventive than the screens. Believe board floors should be provided and the latrines covered. They found great difficulty in getting lumber. They requisitioned for cots and requested showers on arrival. Understood he could not requisition for lumber. The fresh meat was often not in good condition and it comes late in the afternoon. Men buy out of their own fund fruit, fresh vegetables, peas, beans, oranges and lemons. Their clothing requisition has been filled and have received sufficient for extra needs. Believe the price would be so high that it would be difficult to make any saving from ration. Thought that if the State gave the 10 cents per man as suggested by Colonel Bates, it would be a great help. The variety of the ration now better and improving. Objected to receiving no cereal except rice. Getting among other things bacon, coffee, sugar, beans, hard tack but much of that received has to be condemned. The bread often not good, so fresh it falls apart. Every Armory ought to have on hand property sufficient to equip regiment to full strength. Called attention to harsh Treasury rule that pay of Government employees in National Guard in Federal Service with salaries of $2,000.00 and over stops, so that they receive only soldiers' pay while pay of those with salaries under $2,000.00 continues while in Federal Military service.

Colonel Gordon Johnson (Commanding 12th Infantry):

Essentials lacking in order of importance, as follows: 1. Screened kitchens. 2 Cots. 3. Mess shack should be screened. 4. Tables and benches. 5. More water supply. 6. Showers essential. Out of private fund has provided showers for regiment at irrigation canal about half mile distance. Food at present adequate. There has been a serious shortage of food. Fifteen days without dried fruit. Bread supply insufficient, irregular. Believe washing or laundry machines extremely desirable, one such to wash the clothes of entire company in a half day. Two would be sufficient for each battalion. Did not think cash allowance to supplement ration necessary or desirable. Was confident that the profit from the exchange and the saving from ration would net each company $75.00 per month. Did not believe cold things desirable for men in this climate. Proper ice boxes were needed. As to general conditions nothing to worry about as long as sick report does not exceed 3 per cent. As to health and conditions everything is all right. Had sufficient clothing.

Division Hospital:

Same day called at the Field Hospital of the Division. No board floors, cots, mosquito bars or screens. Sick lying on bed sacks or blankets on ground. Deem it extremely necessary that this should be rectified. Division Surgeon Terriberry informs me that these will be ultimately provided, that stay of men very short at Division Hospital as hospital cases were transferred to Base Hospital at Brownsville and San Antonio, that regulations did not provide for board floors or cots for Field Hospitals.

Lieut.-Colonel J. C. McLeer ([Colonel C. I. De Bevois absent on detached service] First Regiment, New York Cavalry):

Two troops have board floors purchased with private funds. Others not. They have mess tables and benches for each troop constructed from lumber purchased from Quartermaster. Some troops have wooden mess shelters provided from their own funds. Most important needs cots and water. Water supply very limited. Pipe line entirely too small for needs of regiment. Can only get along by storing in barrels. No bathing facilities except in shallow and muddy and practically impossible irrigation canal. Showers certainly should be provided. Need a wooden frame regimental infirmary or hospital with screened sides, board floors and cots and some comforts so that the men could be decently taken care of and avoid being taken to field or base hospitals. Food all right, no complaint. If State could provide 10 cents or some amount per day to supplement the ration, it certainly would be very acceptable. His men generally in good health and spirits.

Major Wright (Squadron "A" Cavalry):

At the end of the pipe line have not even enough water to drink. None for washing. Essential kitchen should be screened. Health of command good, sick list less than 2 per cent. They have built their own refrigerators. Fund for purchase of supplementary medical supplies such as ginger tonics and other items not provided at the hospital very desirable. Suggested that a few civilian hospital orderlies be hired to give practical training in hospital work to hospital stewards. Suggested that the Government or State should reimburse the men for a good many things that they had paid for which they were entitled to draw but not able to procure, i, e., lumber of shelters, horse covers and board floors.

Colonel Wingate (Second Field Artillery):

Cots, screened kitchens and mess sheds badly needed. Lacks underclothes for men. Too small water supply, not enough for washing. Bathing facilities greatly needed. No suggestions.

Colonel Rogers (First Field Artillery):

No provision had been made for water when they arrived. No lumber received from Government until yesterday. All lumber in sight purchased with funds of organization. Horses badly affected by heat due to lack of shelter. Believe health of men affected by the failure to screen kitchen and latrines. Some diarrhœa from this cause. 46 cases today, 36 yesterday. No serious cases. Health of command fair. Believed sickness of his horses due to tremendous journey from Oklahoma to New York and then here. It would have been better to ship the horses direct to here. Washing facilities lacking but understand they will be remedied. Complained they had taken away his regular army adjutant under the ruling that no regular officer could be commissioned in the National Guard below rank of Lieut.-Col. No specific suggestions.

Major Whitley (Engineers):

Regiment had recently arrived. Not yet settled. Changing camp site. Men hardly yet accustomed to surroundings. Some diarrhœa, but no illness to cause apprehension. No complaints or suggestions. Hard to adjust to regular army ration of 28 cents. Understands also that men in regular army are assessed from one to two dollars for company fund. These things possible in the army where organizations are long established. not practical in the militia. Strongly urged allowance of 10 cents per day per man by the State. Thought it just they should be reimbursed for private funds spent for articles imperatively needed or which could not wait until received on requisition. Material for shelters for horses badly needed. Doubted if provision for discharge of married men would prove of much use owing to reluctance of men incurring risk of being called quitters. Many who ought to apply will not. Spirit of men good, not discontented or unhappy, quite the reverse. Funds needed to supply extra diet in regimental infirmary. If such diet available woud prevent sending men to Field Hospital. Also a filter at regimental infirmary very desirable so as to be able to give men slightly indisposed clear, pure looking water which will go far in many cases to cure slight indispositions.

Brigadier-General Lester (Commanding 3rd Brigade, Headquarters at Mission, Texas:

Everything in good shape. Health and spirits of men good. Believe everything possible being done. Strongly urge that State pay be expedited.

Colonel Foote (14th Infantry):

Had received 800 cots which he believes had been shipped direct from Fort Sam Houston on requisition through Depot Quartermaster. Said "Haven't got any kick coming." Have abundance of everything.

Colonel Andrews (2nd Infantry):

If anything more done than had been done or was contemplated believe it would be to their detriment than advantage. Condition of command all that could be desired in every way.

Major Lynch (69th Infantry):

Had no complaints or suggestions. Believes everything possible is being done for them. Believed his command contented and in good spirits. Strongly urged that State pay be sent down, for both officers and men in great need of cash.

Memorandum of Conversation with Captain Steger, Regular Army Quartermaster at McAllen, Texas.

He reported McAllen on Friday, the 21st. Lack of water at McAllen camp at once came to his attention. Decided new pipe line necessary. Had been able to secure $8,000.00 worth of pipe at Houston which was now on the cars and sent an enlisted man familiar with the transportation to stay with it in transit to expedite its delivery. He was certain this would give an abundance of water as far as cavalry camps. Had necessary authority to procure necessary shower baths as soon as additional water available. Division Surgeon advises undesirable to install such until drainage or sewerage provided. Proposed to put them in anyway. Had secured an engineer skilled in sewerage (Major Hutchinson) to make survey and specifications for drainage system.

Had received ample authority to procure material to put in screened kitchens and sheds. Understands that 12,000 cots had been requisitioned but this had been done by predecessor not aware when they would be shipped. As to mess sheds, etc., had sent officer of his department to New York accompanied by sergeant to act as master carpenter to develop plans for approval of depot quartermaster. Confident that these will be up in less than two weeks. Telegram had been received on July 17th from Quartermaster stating that materials for these purposes would be on hand two weeks from that date. Had no authority to floor, screen or provide cots for Field Hospital nor to furnish wood to screen regimental infirmary. Suggested, however, that if requisition for these was sent him for Field Hospital there would be no trouble in filling it. Believe that if camp was to be permanent board floors for all tents would be provided.

Illustrative of steps being taken to supply these camps I penned memoranda of communications passing between Assistant Depot Quartermaster here and Depot Quartermaster at Brownsville to which attention is particularly called.

HEADQUARTERS, NEW YORK DIVISION

MCALLEN, TEXAS, *July* 26, 1916.

MEMORANDA

July 17th, 1916, the Depot Quartermaster at Brownsville communicated with the assistant depot quartermaster here and authorized the construction of screen kitchens, dining rooms, and incinerators for the New York Division. At this time he stated that an allotment had been made for material only and that the troops would furnish labor. Authority, however, was given him for the employment of civilian foreman carpenters to properly supervise construction. The material required for the construction work was purchased by the depot Quartermaster at Brownsvilte. He concludes the letter by saying that it cannot possibly arrive at McAllen for at least two weeks.

On July 22nd, the Depot Quartermaster, Captain Steger, wired request to Department Quartermaster for authority to purchase sufficient wrought iron pipe for water supply and estimated the cost therefor at $4200.00. This wire concludes "need urgent wire action." On the same date he received a wire from the Department Quartermaster requesting information as to the condition of water supply at McAllen and asking him if bath facilities for the entire command had been completed, also whether he had plenty of hay or straw for use in bed sacks, and whether supplies reached him promptly.

To the above he answered that water supply was ample but pipe was insufficient and referred to first telegram this date. He further stated that ample hay and straw for bed sacks was on hand and that supplies reach this station five or six days after shipment from San Antonio. On the same date the Department Quartermaster wired as follows: "You have authority to purchase everything necessary for water supply for troops in camp. Purchase whatever is necessary. Your office has previously been authorized and directed to provide necessary water supply; construct latrines, latrine seats, bath shelters and necessary fixtures for all troops at your station."

The Depot Quartermaster at Brownsville is now purchasing wherever he can get material quickest, lumber and other material, to construct incinerators and kitchens and mess shelters for troops in Brownsville District. Wire me at once if you cannot obtain necessary pipe and fittings and they will be shipped to you at once."

Captain Steger procured a quantity of 4 and 6 inch pipe in Houston on the 24th inst., and sent an enlisted man familiar with transportation from the Division to Houston with orders to remain with the car until it was delivered; delivery expected three days from shipment. Upon arrival of this pipe a 6 inch main' will be installed from power plant at McAllen to a point midway in the camp where 4 inch connections will be made and continued to the cavalry camp.

EXHIBIT B

NOTES OF SOME INTERVIEWS WITH ENLISTED MEN

74th *Regiment.* July 27th, 1916.

Co. C.— Clothing badly needed.

Co. E.— 16 men applied for discharge on account of dependency.

C. F.—No ice box. No proper incinerator. "Don't think men get what's coming to them at the hospital tent."

Co. G.— Asked about tobacco; also candy.

Co. H.—Complained of no board floors, also of lack of variety of food.

Bill of Fare, (day visited)

Breakfast: Hash, coffee, bread.

Dinner: Roast Beef, potatoes, turnips, ice cream, (but with own funds).

Often no sugar in coffee, no milk.   Asked about fruit, oranges and lemons.

Co. K.—Food coming down "rotten," not enough of it.   Three men to a seat in ordinary cars, tourist sleepers much better.   Only one man worrying about dependent.   No one worrying as to job.

Co. L.—Complaint of hospital treatment.   Object to constant rice for breakfast.

Co. M.—Ask for oatmeal and hominy.   Much cramps and diarrhœa.   Men should have ditty bags for their clothing and belongings.   No bread today, but good dinner otherwise, but not enough of it. Want ice tea.   Insufficient facilities for washing mess kits.   Should have two tins of dishwater.

3rd Regiment.   July 28th, 1916.

Co. B.— *Geneva.*   Thirteen men sick in quarters.   One man Churchill six days in Field Hospital.   Not given opportunity to wash or shave.   Two men have applied for discharge on account of dependency.

Co. C.— *Syracuse.*   Eleven men with diarrhœa.   Some married men worrying. Employers not paying them.

Co. G.— *Rochester.*   Want board floors.   First sergeant says everything O. K., except a good deal of diarrhœa.   19 on sick report.

69th Regiment.   July 30th, 1916.

Captain Dillon calls attention to the fact that City is not paying its employees in the service.   Prison keeper who went to paymaster to have his check sent to his mother, but only up to January 31st, understands that those sent in prior to June 1st will not be paid.

Co. A.—Complain of water not good, milky and bubbles up.   Food good and coming better all the time.   Ask for cots.   No green things yet, as no company fund and no cash anywhere.   Making some saving from ration.   Seldom have lemons.   Four or five married men with dependents and some worrying about jobs.   Have bed sacks but no straw.   (Q. M. tells me they can have plenty of straw if they will only draw it).   No extra shoes, have two suits underclothing.

Captain Lilly says short big tools, shovels and rakes.   No lumber for ice boxes.

Co. B.—Not getting what we apply for in food.   No condensed milk for five days.   One day without potatoes.   Fresh meat only three times since arrival.   Four days not even pork.   Get canned spinach and beans.   No lemons, oranges or eggs.   Clamor for pay as no cash in company.   No straw for bed sacks.   Nobody worrying about jobs.   One man says, "Field Hospital fine."   Another, "Man just back from field hospital given light duty — ought to be sick in quarters — men don't like the treatment of the hospital."

Bill of Fare (this morning) ·

Breakfast: Rice and coffee without sugar.

Dinner: Salmon, potatoes and bread and tea.   No lemons or oranges.   Haven't seen a cent in four weeks.   No washing facilities, no buckets, tub or wash board.   Told they would get goggles and ties.   (sic) Water often don't run in shower baths.   Four men with *no underclothes.*   Many only one suit.   Four *without stockings.*

Co. C.—Short of clothing.   Some have military shoes, some still in the old civilian black shoes.   One man has lost 30 lbs.   Diseased meat was issued, but was condemned.   Many defective shoes issued, several without regulation shoes.   Short of underclothing.   Ninety per cent. of men have received no Government underclothing. Some only 1 pair socks. Food insufficient quantity and variety. Quality excellent. No fresh vegetables. Complain of tea. All meat now carefully examined. Don't fill food requisitions. Sixty men got only 45 lbs of meat and no bacon. Ask for soups and delicacies for sick men. Throughout regiments sinks neither covered nor screened.

Captain Ford, Assistant Surgeon, says water is unpalatable and does not believe it is healthy and that in some companies food is badly cooked.

Co. D.—Six men excused from duty. Two in Field Hospital. None sick in quarters. No straw in bed sack. Requisitions for workmen all promptly filled. Don't get enough to eat.

Breakfast: (this morning).

Coffee, oatmeal and bread, no sugar.

Dinner: String beans, potatoes, bread and jelly, no meat.

Supper: Boiled beef, boiled potatoes and coffee. Coffee served without milk (no seconds). Food not enough. Apparently not a happy company. No soap, no ditty bags. Cooking bad. Asked me to get after the medical corps. Told they had no castor oil, bismuth or salts. Complain of water.

Co. E.— First Sergeant says Company generally in good spirits, healthy and happy. No kick on grub. Have mess fund and have had lemonade and oranges. Know of only one man who is worrying about dependents. Men say not enough food. Don't get what they ask for. No milk, no sugar on oatmeal, no fruit. Only 25 lbs. potatoes. Generally, no ice. Never draw more than 75 lbs a day. Some days none. Coffee poor. Complain as to medical corps. Won't examine you. Tell you you are a faker. No soup. Ask. about cots. No hay for bed sack. Ask if a man can get his discharge here at expiration of his National Guard term of service.

Co. F.— First Sergeant. Company generally satisfied with food and clothes. Some complaint of food.

Dinner: Thick soup, two potatoes, no milk in coffee, 3 prunes and some rice.

Co. G.— Health good. Only one man in hospital. Only half a cake of ice weighing not over 75 lbs., for entire company. Drew only 100 lbs. ice in three days. Complain of milky appearance of water, strong in lime — milky and bubbles up, then clears off. Six or seven married men with dependents worrying.

Co. H.— Insufficient food and ice. Men satisfied with cooking. Four or five with dependents. Only one applied for discharge. Andrew Murray sick in quarters for last four days. Diarrhoea and cramps. Don't get enough to eat.

Bill of Fare

Supper: (Last night.) Soup, bread, coffee, too little sugar.

Breakfast: Hash, coffee, bread, no prunes or dried fruit.

Dinner: Cabbage, bacon, beans, bread, tea. No preserves or jam.
Complain of the medical service. Man gets something in his eye, they give him a pill. The men on guard got coffee that made them all sick.

Co. I.— First Sergeant says the food as to quality is rank. Hams had to thrown into the incinerators. Complain of sleeping conditions, absence of cots, no hay for bed sacks. No lemons. Weadenhorn and Shea have only old torn pants. Cannot get them others. Three sick in quarters. Four have applied for discharge.

Co. K.— Cots, food, quantity and quality all right but not enough milk, short on sugar. Only two men worrying as to dependents. No ice box because no lumber. Have requisitioned but cannot get it. Ice very irregular. No stand for evaporating pan. Food good but shortage of milk.

Co. L.— All happy and feeling good. City men worrying about their city positions. Machine Gun Company, trouble of drawing stuff from Commissary. Very uneven issue. Chaplain Father O'Keefe says only six or seven cases of dependents brought to his attention. Bad cooking giving trouble. Much more contented than a week ago. Believes regiment is good for a term of service.

First Artillery.— July 24th, 1916.
Troop D.—Lieutenant Gibbons. Give them plenty of grub and plenty of work and they will be all right.

Second Regiment.— July 24th, 1916.
Co. F.— Plenty of Ice. 260 lbs. a day on the average. All the meat they want. Get it once a day, short of sugar. Mess Sergeant, 1898 Veteran, Tampa, says this is paradise compared. Pork three times a week. Up to 15th had a saving of $100. Get seconds. Don't get many prunes or fresh fruits. Have a company fund and expect to draw butter.
Breakfast: (Friday) Boiled rice, coffee, bread, milk and prunes.
Dinner: Puree of bean soup, tea and bread.
Supper: Cold roast beef, boiled potatoes, stewed corn, bread and tea.
Supply officers say up to last Friday the canned goods were short and hard to get. Chief complaint is meat, but this morning very good. Plenty of sugar. Potatoes and onions in abundance. Expect cots today. No butter. Plenty of evaporated milk, prunes, canned fruits, jam. No apple butter. Water good and plenty of it. Difficulty as to washing clothes. Privilege to wash in bath houses had to be stopped, should have more than one tub to each company and at least two wash boards. Colonel Andrews thinks they will soon get board floors.

Co. A.— *Troy.*— First Sergeant says mess on arrival poor, both as to quan-
Citizens' tity and quality. One day all he could get for breakfast was two
Corps. spoonfuls cream of wheat, coffee and bread. Mid-day meal potato salad, bread and water. At night, corn and potatoes and tea, no bread. Asked for cots. Got sacks for only sixty-six men, need 133. No straw. Food lacks variety. Well cooked and palatable. Making out with funds from home. Health good. Six sick in quarters, none seriously ill. Like definite information as to how long going to be here. Cannot get new clothes, breeches, leggins and hats. Some woolen breeches available, some men still with civilian shoes. Twelve or fifteen men worrying about dependent families. Citizens' Organizations not giving much relief. Not getting full allowance of ice, only half cake. Two days no ice. Much diarrhœa. Six sick men in quarters. One man sick in quarters three days. Complain of hospital. Get no medicines coming down. Fellow with high fever and nose bleed coming down. Understood the Doctor short of equipment but believe he was doing all he could. Raymond C. Ide says he had no travel ration coming back from base hospital. Got one sandwich. Went back Saturday and is still sick in quarters. Also Corporal Fenton. Some still have their woolen clothing. Sergeant Cluth had to buy shoes in town, as they did not have his size. Complain of uneven drilling.

Co. B.— *Cohoes.*—Cots, rations, quality and quantity good. Ice irregular, not enough for 140 men. Short of canned stuff. Spirits and health good but don't like camp life. Unable to get proper sizes of shoes. Six married men worrying. One application. Sick get good care. Attribute good condition of company to sticking to Government ration, in which great improvement. Much diarrhœa, at first, now over. Held too close to camp.

Co. C.—*Troy.*—Spirits and health good. Food good, quantity and quality and variety. Three or four days without ice. Now get 240 lbs. Three men sick. Two in quarters. Short breeches, shirts, shoes and underclothing. Not worrying about dependents. Happy company. Short of tentage. Seventeen in one tent. Capacity for eight. Understand tents have arrived. No poles.

Co. D.—*Troy.*—First Sergeant says men dissatisfied. Better food than '98. Buying our own food, couldn't get on if we didn't. No milk. Only draw beef and bacon.

Dinner: Beefsteak, boiled potatoes, stewed corn, tea and bread.

Breakfast: Potatoes, prunes, coffee, bread. No oatmeal or cream of wheat issued. The only cereal rice.

Mid-day meal: Creamed salmon, macaroni soup, bread and rice pudding.

Two days last week no ice. Drawn little underwear. Men never able to draw any underclothes. Complain of water as unpalatable. Company appears dissatisfied. Bought wash tub and board, cannot draw brooms. Post-office employee doubtful if he will get his pay. Short tents. Fourteen men to a tent. Have been short blankets. 123 men. No fly to eat under. Use Burkfield filter. Complain of hospital. " Pills for twisted finger." No medicine for skin diseases. Food is better. Eleven tents for fourteen squads. Extra tentage has been heretofore supplied but no poles and pins. Short of lumber.

Co. E.—*Schenectady.*—Five men applied for discharge. None dissatisfied. Feeling well. Clothing short in some particulars. No telling how many men should apply for discharge. Praying for cots. First Sergeant says complaints few. Some say unless American Locomotive Company paid us we could not have gone.

Co. F.—*Schenectady.*—Happy Company. Praying for cots. Complain of too much soup. Meat every other day. Average four or five men with diarrhœa a day. Only know of one man worrking about dependents, mother. No married men worrying. Private Bonds three days sick in quarters.

Co. G.—*Gloversville.*—112 men. Representing young men of the place. Generally speaking happy, spirits good. Are satisfied with meals. Now things O. K. as to quantity, quality and cooking. Little dysentery. Three sick in quarters but are in dispensary. Nine applied for discharge. No men suffering as to jobs. Mostly piece workers, will not lose their jobs. Very good attention at the hospital. Every man three suits of underclothing. Four pairs of socks. Every man extra shoes. Got them at Camp Whitman. Ask for board floors. Should issue lime juice. Three men, Arnold J. Feldman, R. F. Rose, Geo. Wenkirk, entitled to get discharge but cannot get applications.

Co. H.—*Amsterdam.*—More or less have diarrhœea. Seven sick in quarters. Six light cases. Corporal Robert Brunnigan sick one week in quarters. Three days at hospital. Food all right. Kick on cooking. No complaint as to quantity. Well equipped as to clothing. Every man two pairs. Claim don't get enough attention at the hospital, but can go any time day or night. Thirty-four married men have applied for discharge because employers are not paying men. Only one good meal.

Supper: Gravy soup, lemonade, bread, one-half pear.

Breakfast: Maple flakes, bread, coffee, bacon and eggs.

Dinner: Meat (poor) two or three potatoes, gravy, bread and coffee. No preserves.

Co. I.—*Whitehall.*— Complain regimental dispensary. Six with diarrhœa. Seem to do nothing for them, although no sick in quarters. One at Field Hospital. Food fine. " Couldn't be better." Clothing all right. Nobody yet applied. Some men with no bed sacks. "All hardy laboring men mostly satisfied with their lot."

Co. K.— *Glens Falls.*— First Sergeant says conditions much better than '98.
Apparently contented company. Food good. ·Plenty of ice. Few
sick. Two in quarters. Some worrying about dependents.

Co. L.—*Saratoga.*—Food good. Clothing O. K.. General health good. Good
care at hospital. Some little diarrhœa. Two have applied for
discharges.

Co. M.—*Hoosick Falls.*—Now contented with food. Generally good condition.
Are not very happy company. All right as to clothing and underclothing, but some trouble with sizes. One-tenth company has
diarrhœa.

Co. K.—J. T. Shanley detailed from Company C. to Supply Company, asked
me to look into bill for over $200 against the State for team hire
at Whitman. Said " Need it badly."

14th Regiment, July 31st, 1916.

Co. A.—Food good, but not enough. First Sergeant says cannot draw enough.
Employers who agreed to pay don't.

Co. C.—First Sergeant said men in good spirits and food all right. Two men
sick. No men worrying about jobs or families. Men interviewed
say everything O. K.

Co. B.—Happy Company. Old mildewed and leaky tentage. More than eight
men to a tent. Five applications. No sick. First Sergeant says
happy Company. Live on Government ration, but don't get enough.

Co. E.—First Lieutenant says food O. K. First Sergeant, not enough.
Breakfast: Beef stew, coffee and bread.
Dinner: Canned corn, beef and potatoes, coffee and bread, sugar, no
milk, stewed dried apricots.
Supper: Cornmeal, ice tea, no bread.
No sick. None on charges. Ice irregular some days. Short tentage.

Co. F.—Health good. No kick on food or clothing. Know of only one man
worrying about his family. Tentage not over crowded but two
tents with nine men each.

Co. G.—Three men applied for discharge. Health fine. Can't get enough
food. Bad bread. Mess Sergeant cannot get what he asks. Short
shoes and underwear. Have a man without shoes, so bad he has
to stay in his tent.

Co. H.—Call for board floors. Crowded in tents. Sergeant says not satisfied with food, cooking and quantity. Health good. Spirits good.

Co. I.—Getting on all right. Don't get enough food. Don't get enough
meat or ice. Mess Sergeant says can only get what they give him.
Loose Mexican beans unpalatable. Canned beans not good. Don't
get enough bread. Apparently contented company. Cannot get
potatoes.
Supper: Evaporated apple sauce, tea and bread, canned peaches,
jam and crackers.
Breakfast: Fried bacon, coffee, no bread.
Dinner: Beef stew, coffee and crackers, no bread.
Health fine. Eight men have applied for discharge owing to
employers failing to pay.

Co. K.—Say have credit of being best company, having the cleanest street.
Good spirit. Two sick. Stick to Government ration. Have been
short of clothing, now getting all required. Two applied for discharge.

Co. L.—First Sergeant says everything O. K. Fine, good men, healthy.
Only one sick. Two applied for discharge. Some few more
will. No bed sacks for recruits. Private J. Emlock complains he
can't get proper treatment for scabs at the dispensary.
Musician Smith, Co. K. 3rd Infantry, Brownsville Hospital. Positive
sputum examination at McAllen discloses T. B. Can't he be discharged without bringing him back for examination by Regimental
Board. Can his discharge not be expedited. Supply officer of the
3d asked me if not possible to get horse medicines. Have had and
apparently can procure none.

Co. M.—Happy Company. Sometimes not enough food. Only one sick in quarters.. No men have applied for discharge. Ice irregular. Variety of food not sufficient. Private Lyman Seeley sick in quarters. Weak, can't walk to latrines. One of best soldiers First Sergeant says. Short only two canteens.

Note: Is it not possible for some one to explain to Company Commanders in a practical way about clothing issues.

N. B.— Besides above visited in various company streets and interviewed enlisted men in the same manner as above, to wit: July 22nd, 7th and 12th, First Cavalry and Squadron A; July 24th, First and Second Artillery; July 27th, 12th and 71st; July 28, 23d, Engineers and Signal Corps, but neglected to make notes.

EXHIBIT C

NEW YORK DIVISION

MCALLEN, TEXAS, *July* 17, 1916.

GENERAL ORDERS, }
    No. 6.   }

The following regulations for camp sanitation are published for the information and guidance of all concerned:

I. *Division Surgeon:* The Division Surgeon is charged with the general conduct and supervision of the Medical Department in the performance of its duties and will recommend to the Commanding General such assignments of personnel as may be required.

II. *Sanitary Inspectors:* The Sanitary Inspector is charged specially with the supervision of the sanitation of the camp. It is the duty of commanders to remedy defects called to their attention by the Inspector. He will keep a careful record of all inspections and recommendations and the action taken to remedy reported defects. He is authorized to issue orders in the name of the Commanding General for the immediate correction of such sanitary defects as he may observe. All failures to remedy sanitary defects will be reported in writing to the Commanding General, Division.

III. *Regimental Surgeons:* The senior medical officer on duty with a regiment or lesser unit will be held strictly responsible for the sanitary inspection of the organization to which he is attached and for the recommendations which he makes to his commanding officer. He will inspect the camp once daily, and oftener if necessary. All sanitary defects, with proper recommendations to remedy the same, will reported to the regimental commander and he will immediately take the steps necessary to make the correction.

IV. *General Police:* At inspections special attention will given to the condition of the grounds, tents, kitchens, food, bathing facilities, latrines and picket lines. The interior of the tents will be kept clean, and clothing, blankets and bedding will be exposed to the sunlight daily, weather permitting. Tents will be raised during the daytime in good weather and will be adequately ventilated at night. All tents will be furled or struck occasionally.

V. *Kitchens:* All food and water in camp will be protected from dust, flies and sun. An ice box will be built at each kitchen, care being taken that there is a provision made for adequate drainage, and that the earth from the roof and the ground about the box will not fall upon or become mixed with the ice or food contained therein.

An eating place will be designated in each company, and men will not be allowed to take food into their tents. Garbage, until destroyed in kitchen incinerators, will not be allowed to accumulate about the kitchens. In all cases kitchen refuse will be placed in the kitchen incinerator at once. No other disposition of food refuse will be made.

The throwing of water from kitchens or water in which eating or cooking utensils have been washed is prohibited.

The use of garbage cans will not be permitted. Empty tin cans or containers will be placed in the fire, thoroughly burned out and when raked from the incinerator flattened with an axe.

Water barrels or cans for drinking water will be kept securely covered and set on a framework so as to have the faucets 3 inches from the ground. Water will not be taken from the barrels or cans in any other way than by drawing it from the faucets. The use of powder hypochloride of lime tubes, one tube to each thirty (30) gallons of drinking water is prescribed. Tubes of hypochloride of lime will be procured from the Quartermaster Corps.

VI. *Food and Drinks:* No food, drinks or like commodities will be sold in camp except in the authorized exchanges, for which permits will be obtained from the camp commander at the several camps of the division.

VII. *Disposal of Waste:* Organization commanders will be held responsible for the police of their respective camps. Each company, or similar organization, will construct incinerators of brick and evaporating pans in such a manner that waste water from the kitchen and from the washing of cooking and mess utensils will be evaporated quickly and completely. Solid garbage will be placed immediately in the fires. No other disposition of liquid or solid garbage will be permitted.

Manure from picket lines or corrals will be hauled to the designated dumping grounds and there disposed of in a manner to be prescribed by the Division Quartermaster. The ground at the picket lines will be burned over with crude oil or kerosene at least once each five (5) days.

Tin cans, paper and general refuse will be hauled to the designated dumping ground.

VIII. *Latrines:* Latrines will be constructed at the rate of one for each company and one for officers, and one for headquarters detachments in each regiment, and in the same proportion for lesser units. The pits will be dug 2 feet wide, 7 feet 6 inches long and 5 feet deep, and the excavated dirt will be removed at least 4 feet from the pit, and if necessary the pit will be ditched to prevent flooding.

The pits will be covered by boxes which will be so constructed that all the joints are fly and light proof. These boxes will have covers for holes so constructed that by means of stop blocks or spring hinges the covers will remain closed when not in use. Each day the latrine boxes will be removed from the pits and the pits thoroughly burned out by the use of not less than one gallon crude oil and sufficient straw, or they will be treated by the use of a spray of lamp black and kerosene oil. The tops of the seats will be scrubbed with soap and water each day, and if necessary be disinfected by the use of a strong solution of bichloride of mercury. Suitable urinals will be provided at each latrine connected with the pit by a pipe, and the interior of such urinal will be kept smeared at all times with crude oil.

Toilet paper will be furnished and care must be taken that it is kept from blowing or lying on the ground. It will be protected by a suitable box or cover.

A lantern will be kept burning in each latrine during the hours of darkness.

A urinal can will be placed in each company street at night and its contents emptied at reveille in the latrine. Care will be taken that these urinal cans occupy the same area of ground each night and that when removed for emptying, the ground upon which they have stood will be burned off each morning with crude oil or kerosene. Urinal cans will be stored during the daytime in the latrines after being burned out with crude oil or straw. Defilement of the ground in or about the camps is prohibited.

IX. *Personal Cleanliness:* All persons whose duty requires them to handle food supplies will observe the greatest care in their personal cleanliness, particularly the hands, which must be washed whenever they are about to handle any food supply. This applies especially to all men detailed as cooks and kitchen police. All soldiers must wash their hands thoroughly before each meal, and after having gone to the latrine. A rack or table will be provided in each company at which men will wash their persons and clothing, and adequate provision will be made by means of clothes lines for the drying of clothing and equipment which has been washed. Bath houses must be kept clean and thoroughly policed of cast off clothing, ends of soap and other refuse.

X. *Picket Lines:* Picket lines, corrals and places where horses are tied will be kept thoroughly clean. Care will be taken to see that horse droppings are immediately collected and piled, and in addition to the careful raking of manure the ground will be swept at least three times a day. Manure will be removed at least once each day.

XI. *Sanitary Squads:* The senior medical officer of each regiment or lesser unit will organize a specially instructed squad of noncommissioned officers and privates of the Hospital Corps which will, under his supervision, make inspections of all parts of the camp at least every two (2) hours and report to the senior medical officer the result of their inspections. The enlisted men comprising this squad are not authorized to make any comment or criticism to any whatsoever except the organization surgeon. Defects reported by the Sanitary Squad will be immediately investigated by a medical officer and the necessary recommendations to correct the defects made to the commanding officer of the organization.

XII. *Venereal Inspections:* Venereal inspections will be made once each week, at which time all enlisted men of the command will be inspected. At these inspections a careful record will be made of all cases of venereal diseases discovered and a report made to the man's commanding officer. The duty of performing these inspections is charged to the senior medical officer of each regiment or lesser unit, and will be made by him personally, or by a junior officer under the supervision of the organization surgeon.

BY COMMAND OF MAJOR GENERAL O'RYAN:

EDWARD OLMSTED,
Major, Assistant Chief of Staff.

OFFICIAL:

....

Major, Assistant Chief of Staff,
In the absence of the Division Adjutant.

EXHIBIT D

NEW YORK DIVISION

MCALLEN, TEX., *August* 30, 1916.

FROM: Division Surgeon,
TO: Commanding General, Division.
SUBJECT: Report on Paratyphoid.

I submit a report in re paratyphoid cases in this Division.

The first information that we had that paratyphoid had been found in cases of undetermined fever sent from here to the Base Hospital, at San Antonio, was obtained through conversation with Capt. James E. Baylis, M. C., U. S. A., and Capt. George F. Lull, M. C., U S. A., on August 22nd, 1916, the day upon which they reported for duty with this Division. They informed us that they learned while at San Antonio that there were three cases of paratyphoid among the men sent from Mission. The next morning, about 5 o'clock, Capt. Edgar W. Miller, M. C., U. S. A., Camp Sanitary Inspector at Mission, informed Major Maloney over the 'phone that he had been notified by the Base Hospital, San Antonio, that the following men had paratyphoid, as shown by blood examinations.

Sergt. Harold J. Forshay, Hdqrs. Co., 14th Inf.

Private Alfred V. Parker, Co. L, 14th Inf.
Private William Helgers, M. D., 69th Inf.
Capt. Miller requested the clinical histories of these men while in Field Hospital No. 1, at McAllen, which were sent him from this office. On August 26th, a telegram to the Division Surgeon was received from Lt. Col. Reynolds, M. C., U. S. A., General Sanitary Inspector, sent from Brownsville, with the information that the following men were reported from the Department Laboratory as having paratyphoid:

Sullivan, Co. A, 14th Inf.,
Keegan, Co. K, 14th Inf.

On August 28th, a telegram was received from Lt. Col. Reynolds from Ft. Brown stating that "San Antonio reports two new cases of paratyphoid, Privates Garrney and Martin Hain, Fourteenth New York Inf., also one case typhoid, Corporal John Leins, Seventy-Fourth N. Y. Infantry, Pharr."

The files of this office show that Private Martin Hain, Co. C, 14th Inf., was sent to San Antonio on August 14th with a diagnosis of alcoholic gastritis. We have no record of any man named Garrney, but have a record of Private Timothy Gaffney, Co. C, 14th Inf., sent to San Antonio on August 24th with a diagnosis of undetermined fever. In all probability Gaffney is meant instead of Garrney, as in the telegram.

Major Maloney went to Pharr and investigated the case of Corp. John Leins, 74th Inf., and found that they had no such man in the regiment, but had a corporal Charles F. Lewis, Co. F, sent to San Antonio, August 24th, whose vaccination card showed no record of his ever having been inoculated against typhoid.

On August 29th, a letter addressed to the Commanding Officer, 1st N. Y. Field Hospital, McAllen, Texas (through Division Surgeon), was received at this office from Capt. E. W. Miller, M. C., U. S. A., Mission, Texas, stating that "the Department Laboratory reports positive findings of paratyphoid 'A' in the cases of the following additional members of this command who had been transported to your hospital:

Reuchenberg, Charles, Cook, H. Co., 14th Inf. Aug. 21, 1916.
Harkey, Eugene F., Pvt. Hdqrs. Co., 14th Inf., Aug. 22, 1916.
Sullivan, J. J., Pvt. A. Co., 14th Inf, Aug. 24, 1916."

and asking for complete reports of these cases for Department Surgeon and Surgeon General's office. This letter was forwarded to the First Field Hospital for compliance.

At no time has any information been furnished this office direct from the Base Hospital at San Antonio, and no notification as to the Laboratory findings in these cases has been received from Captain Miller, except as to asking for histories of cases reported to him as having paratyphoid. All information received by this office as to the diagnosis of these cases has been obtained either accidentally through conversation with officers who happened to know of them, or as in two instances by telegrams from Lt. Col. Reynolds, or through requests to the Field Hospital for their records by Capt. Miller.

On August 25th, I requested Capt. Miller to make an investigation of the food, milk and water supply at Mission. I detailed to assist him two medical officers of the 1st Ambulance Co., only one of whom, Lt. U. S. Kahn, reported as Lt. S. B. Whitbeck had left on leave of absence. Up to date no report has been received from Capt. Miller.

On August 23rd, I directed Major W. H. Steers, Division Sanitary Inspector, to proceed to Mission and investigate into the possible causes of infection. Major Steers submitted a report to me which is enclosed.

On August 29th, I accompanied Major Steers to Mission and directed him to have a conference with the Regimental Surgeon, Major John J. Lyons and the regimental commander and make a complete and thorough and complete investigation of conditions in the regiment, particularly as to Headquarters and Supply Companies and the attendants at the regimental exchange. At the time of this visit I found a patient in the regimental infirmary suffering from undetermined fever and learned upon investigation he was a member of the Headquarters Company. This patient presented every evidence of infection with paratyphoid. I directed his transfer to the Camp Hospital at McAllen with a view to his transfer to the Base hospital at San Antonio for Laboratory investigation. On the afternoon of August 29th, Major Steers transferred a large number of cases of undetermined fever which he had found existing in the Headquarters Company and Supply Company of the 14th Inf. and from the Sanitary Troops attached to this regiment.

The list of paratyphoid cases given below was handed to me today by Lt. Col. Reynolds.

August 11 to 22, four in 14th N. Y. Inf. One in 69th N. Y. Inf.
August 19th, one in N. Y. Signal Corps.
August 22, one in N. Y. Ambulance Co. No. 3.
Pvt. James J. Sullivan, " a " 14th N. Y. Inf., Mission.
August 25, 1st Sergt. William Keegan, " k," 14th N. Y., Mission.
August 25, Pvt. John Marstelar, " n," 12th N. Y., McAllen.
August 27, Timothy Gaffney, " c," 14th N. Y., Mission.
August 27, Pvt. Martin Haris, " c," 14th N. Y., Mission.
August 28, Pvt. Thomas Ramsey, " a," 2nd N. Y., Mission.
August 28, Maj. Walter Robinson, 2nd N. Y., Mission.
August 28, Pvt. Gerard Byrne, " L," 2nd N. Y., Mission.
August 28, Pvt. James Donachy, " L," 14th N. Y., Mission.
August 28, Pvt. George Cummings, " i," 14th N. Y., Mission.
August 28, Pvt. James Brady, " b," 60th N. Y., Mission.
August 28, Pvt. Will I. Neary, H. C., 14th N. Y., Mission.

This is the first definite and complete information we have ever received at this office regarding paratyphoid cases from this Division.

Lt. Col., Medical Corps, N. G., U. S.

NEW YORK DIVISION   •

MCALLEN, TEX., *September 2, 1916.*

FROM: Division Surgeon,
To: Commanding General, Division.
SUBJECT: Paratyphoid, Mission, Texas.

1. In view of the reports received from Lt. Col. F. P. Reynolds, M. C., U. S. A., General Sanitary Inspector, relative to certain unsanitary conditions existing at Mission, Texas, and its surroundings, and in view of the fact that it is desirable to segregate the regiments in which there have appeared cases of paratyphoid infection, I recommend, after consultation with Lt. Col. Reynolds, that the 69th Inf. be retained in camp at Sterling's and that the 2nd Inf. be directed to proceed to Sterling's and encamp there.

2. I recommend that the above mentioned regiments be retained in camp at Sterling's until such a time as further danger of the spread of infection has passed.

3. Sterling's is recommended for the reason that there is an ample water supply of good quality at this point and that it is readily accessible by rail for supply and in case of a troop movement.

4. Enclosed herewith is a copy of a telegram from Lt. Col. Reynolds to the Department Surgeon embodying a recommendation that the 2nd Inf. and the 69th Inf. be removed from Mission.

5. I further recommend that the section of the Field Bakery now at Mission also be removed elsewhere.

WM. S. TERRIBERRY,
Lt. Colonel, Medical Corps, N. G., U. S.

NEW YORK DIVISION

MCALLEN, TEX., *Sept. 5, 1916.*
BULLETIN No. 11

1. The Division Surgeon reports that paratyphoid fever is spreading among the units of the Division and that only extreme and conscientious care on

the part of organization commanders and their surgeons, will prevent the situation from becoming grave.

2. In case matters become worse in any organization, it will be necessary to quarantine such an organization in its present camp or move it into the interior and leave it behind in case the remainder of the Division is transferred elsewhere.

3. The following is a copy of a letter received from the Division Surgeon:

NEW YORK DIVISION

MCALLEN, TEX., *Sept.* 5, 1916.

FROM: Division Surgeon,

TO: Commanding General, Division.

SUBJECT: Paratyphoid Infection.

1. After consultation with Lt. Col. F. P. Reynolds, M. C., U. S. A., Major E. R. Maloney, M. C., N. G., U. S., Major Wm. H. Steers, Division Sanitary Inspector the following report of the situation as it exists relative to the outbreak of paratyphoid fever in this Division is submitted:

2. Reports received from the regiments, from the Divisional Camp Hospital and from the Laboratory indicate that the paratyphoid fever is spreading throughout the various regiments of the Division. The spread appears to be one due to contact with cases originating from the primary focus at Mission. From these secondary cases, other cases are developing and are likely to develop by reason of personal contact directly or indirectly through the infection of food supplies or by transmission by flies.

3. It is the opinion of all officers at this conference that prevention of the secondary infection rests largely upon the strict enforcement of disciplinary measures which will insure the carrying out of sanitary orders and regulations already promulgated. It is further the opinion that no new sanitary orders or regulations are necessary.

4. *Recommendations*   It is recommended that the provisions of General Order No. 6, this Division, and General Order No. 13, Headquarters Southern Department, be carried out in every detail, and that regimental commanders make full use of the sanitary troops attached to their command in the supervision of the carrying out of these orders.

(Signed.)   WM. S. TERRIBERRY,

Lt. Colonel, Medical Corps, N. G., U. S.

4. Upon receipt of this circular, organization commanders will assemble their officers and read it to them. All officers are hereby directed to study the General Orders referred to and obey them in letter and in spirit.

5. The Division Surgeon or his representatives will make frequent sanitary inspections of all camps and will report upon any officer or man who, in their opinion, is not complying with the requirements of existing sanitary orders.

6. By a faithful observance of the instructions already given, all danger of an epidemic will be avoided, but this will require perfect team work for some time to come.

BY COMMAND OF MAJOR-GENERAL O'RYAN:

H. H. BANDHOLTZ,

Chief of Staff.

Official:

ALLAN L. REAGAN,

Adjutant.

MEMORANDUM AS TO PARATYPHOID EPIDEMIC CONDITIONS AS GIVEN ME BY COLONEL REYNOLDS FROM OFFICIAL RECORDS, SEPTEMBER 10, 1916

2nd Regiment Infantry: Total confirmed cases 16; no new cases since September 6th; one on that date; one officer.

3rd Regiment Infantry: Total confirmed 2; 15 with temperature all negative under test.

12th Regiment Infantry: Total confirmed 4; 3 recent.

14th Regiment Infantry: Total confirmed 40; increase of 8 in four days generally distributed through companies; 2 still under suspicion.

69th Regiment Infantry: Total confirmed 9; no new cases since September 5th on which date 1.

1st Regiment Cavalry: Total confirmed 3 in three different troops.

Squadron A: Total confirmed 3 all in Troop C.

71st Regiment Infantry: Total confirmed 1, September 4th.

22nd Regiment Engineers: Total confirmed 1 on September 2nd.

74th Regiment Infantry: Total confirmed 1 on September 9th

23rd Regiment Infantry: Total confirmed 1 on September 9th

7th Regiment Infantry: Total confirmed 1.

Field Artillery: None.

Ambulance Company No. 3:   Total confirmed 1.

Forty-five suspects in this hospital (Camp Hospital); 5 new cases in three days.

Colonel Reynolds informs me, in his judgment, the trouble is practically over.

APPENDIX " E "

Financial Statement

DETAILED STATEMENT SHOWING EXPENDITURES FOR THE FISCAL YEAR ENDING JUNE 30, 1916

Salary of the Adjutant General:

Balance, September 30, 1915		....	
Appropriation, chap. 725, Laws 1915		$5,500 00	$5,500 00

Expended:

Service to June 30, 1916			4,125 00
			$1,375 00

Salaries: Officers and Employees, the Adjutant General's Office, Albany:

Balance, Sept. 30, 1915	$1,603 22		
Lapsed, balance, chap. 834, Laws 1913, $458 33			
Lapsed, balance, chap. 529, 1914....1,144 89			
	1,603 22		
Appropriation, chap. 725, 1915		$39,500 00	
			$39,500 00

Expended:

Services to June 30, 1916			28,768 03
Balance, June 30, 1916			$10,731 97

Salaries: Employees, the Adjutant General's Office, New York:

Balance, Sept. 30, 1915	$287 50		
Lapsed, balance, chap. 529, 1914	287 50		
Appropriation, chap. 725, Laws 1915		$27,500 00	$27,500 00

Expended:
Services to June 30, 1916 ·

Clerical force		$9,900 00	
Laborers		10,725 00	
			20,625 00
Balance, June 30, 1916			$6,875 00

NATIONAL GUARD

Salary of the Major General:

Balance, Sept. 30, 1916		....	....
Appropriation, chap. 725, Laws 1915		$8,000 00	$8,000 00

Expended:

Services to June 30, 1916			6,000 00
Balance, June 30, 1916			$2,000 00

Salaries: Staff of the Major General and Graded Employees:

Balance, Sept. 30, 1915	$598 41		
Lapsed, balance, chap. 529, Laws 1914	598 41		

Appropriation, chap. 725, Laws 1915.........			$29,360 00
Expended:			
Services to June 30, 1916:			
Officers.................................		$15,075 00	
Graded employees.......................		6,932 56	
			22,007 56
Balance, June 30, 1916.................			$7,352 44
Allowances to Headquarters:			
Balance, Sept. 30, 1915.....................	$12,104 36		
Lapsed, balance, chap. 529, 1914.............	79 36		
		$12,025 00	
Appropriation, chap. 725, Laws 1915.........		35,000 00	
			$47,025 00
Expended:			
Brigades....................................		$6,600 00	
Headquarters, Division (Coast Defense Officer).		1,150 00	
Field artillery..............................		2,625 00	
Cavalry....................................		2,775 00	
Infantry...................................		21,000 00	
Coast Defense Command....................		4,062 50	
Engineers..................................		1,125 00	
Signal Corps...............................		500 00	
			39,837 50
Balance, June 30, 1916.................			$7,187 50
Allowances to Officers and Organizations:			
Balance, Sept. 30, 1915.....................		$530 31	
Appropriation, chap. 725, Laws 1915.........		213,750 00	
Appropriation, chap. 646, Laws 1916..........		35,000 00	
Appropriation, chap. 646, Laws 1916..........		4,500 00	
			$253,780 31
Expended:			
Officers...................................		$39,684 94	
Organizations:			
Allowances, per capita.:...................	$119,893 20		
Separate companies.......................	12,750 00		
Horse allowance.........................	78,250 00		
		210,893 20	
			250,578 14
Balance, June 30, 1916			$3,202 17
General Expense of the National Guard and Office			
of the Adjutant General:			
Balance Sept. 30, 1915.....................	$160,748 09		
Lapsed, balance, chap. 529, Laws 1914........	2,382 78		
		$164,365 31	
Appropriation, chap. 725, Laws 1915.........		205,000 00	
			$369,365 31
Expended:			
Office of the Adjutant General:			
Travel expense....	$3,138 27		
Office furniture and fixtures.................	312 92		
Office supplies and expenses.................	799 54		
Telephone and telegraph....................	953 46		
Printing and binding.......................	6,304 70		
Engrossing................................	311 70		
Publications...............................	256 32		
Labor.....................................	555 45		
		$12,632 36	

Headquarters, division:

Travel expense	$1,406 61	
Office supplies and expenses	1,600 20	
Printing and binding	2,504 21	
Telephone and telegraph	1,298 37	
Publications	119 35	
Supervision, small arms firing	1,991 44	
Inspection, troops and property	1,565 01	
Indexing general orders	36 00	
Extra stenographic service	289 90	
Motor trucks, repairs and supplies	898 72	
State horses	270 19	
Diplomas and maps	221 58	
Bond indemnity	10 00	
Hauling escort wagons	3 75	
		12,215 33

New York Arsenal:

Repairs, equipment and supplies	$230 32	
Freight, cartage and express	1,257 18	
Fuel, gas and electricity	1,086 33	
Office supplies and expenses	1,260 06	
Telephone and telegraph	273 43	
Motor trucks, repairs and supplies	456 65	
Extra labor	1,239 40	
Extra stenographic service	360 50	
Advertising	18 00	
Veterinary service	7 00	
Publications	6 00	
New typewriters	142 10	
Travel expense	118 10	
		6,455 07

Governor's Staff:

Transportation	$2,000 54	
Subsistence	1,458 00	
Pay orderly	12 00	
		3,470 54

Officers on Special Duty:

Examining boards for officers	$8,897 44	
Enlisted specialists	3,677 60	
Armory boards	611 21	
Pay-rations and expense enlisted men	1,863 70	
Adjustment of property	100 00	
Inventory of property	155 33	
Surveying office	59 20	
Other special duty	1,251 69	
		16,616 17

Decorations and Prizes:

Long service decorations	$4,126 00	
Prizes, small arms firing	3,014 25	
Campaign badges	5 29	
Cleaning and engraving trophies	28 50	
Repairing McAlpen trophey	155 00	
Medals of valor	46 00	
		7,375 04

Small Arms Firing:

Maintenance, state range	$423 89	
Maintenance, separate company ranges	809 86	
Transportation	15,625 90	
Provisional detachment, Peekskill	7,129 04	
Civilian markers and scorers	4,641 33	
Service rangekeepers	999 92	
Expenses, state team	2,185 88	

State brigades matches......................	47 22	
Carrying mail.............................	50 00	
		31,923 04
Camp of Instruction:		
Service, custodian.........................	$333 33	
Employees.................................	2,652 00	
Cost of filling ice house....................	398 75	
Medical attendance........................	9 00	
		3,393 08
Field Service:		
Pay of troops.............................	$8,376 49	
Transportation............................	3,145 73	
Subsistence...............................	15,305 57	
Civilian employees.........................	214 25	
Team, cartage and freight..................	6,735 76	
Horse hire and stable accommodation........	3,842 22	
Forage and straw..........................	2,721 78	
Motor trucks and automobiles...............	1,618 46	
Animals, injured and destroyed.............	4,815 75	
Fuel and illuminants.......................	776 46	
Hardware and lumber......................	1,387 73	
Latrines and bath houses...................	173 37	
Rental and damage........................	412 33	
Medical stores and supplies.................	18 81	
Telephone and telegraph....................	408 47	
Disinfectants.............................	120 14	
Water supplies............................	4,424 31	
Installing side track.......................	253 74	
Lighting equipment........................	219 09	
Supplies and expense......................	710 85	
		55,681 31
Supplies and Equipment:		
Color flags and guidons....................	$443 21	
Dress coats...............................	6,162 09	
Dress trousers............................	2,603 74	
Buttons, caps and collar ornaments..........	3,352 16	
Shoes.....................................	5,925 55	
Bed sacks.................................	432 00	
Purchase of mules.........................	5,000 00	
Forage, state horses.......................	1,907 34	
Repairs, escort wagons.....................	1,313 49	
Motion picture machine....................	259 00	
Pay, employees............................	126 00	
Cartage and freight........................	300 97	
Repairs to tents...........................	305 82	
Packing boxes and lumber..................	80 59	
Binders...................................	2,252 50	
Repairs to auto truck......................	580 00	
Motor trucks..............................	5,425 00	
Miscellaneous supplies.....................	22 56	
Trail mobiles.............................	558 00	
		37,050 02
Militia Council:		
Pay......................................	$61 24	
		61 24
Field Firing Auxiliary Arms:		
Target practice, machine gun company.		
Transportation..........................	$105 23	
Ammunition.............................	3,817 00	
Pay employees..........................	4 00	
		3,926 23

Exercises and instruction:

Bakers and cooks school, pay................	$282 70	
Military exhibition, high school boys, music....	201 00	
Special course, army service school, pay........	195 84	
Operating motion picture machine............	5 40	
Office furniture............................	25 60	
Tactical exercises, subsistence................	304 40	
Army service school, Fort Leavenworth........	455 56	
Field officers course, Gettysburg subsistence....	54 00	
Liberty Bell escort..........................	431 15	

School of the Line:

Pay of troops....................	$905 91	
Subsistence......................	502 35	
Transportation...................	266 60	
Stationery.......................	184 04	
Publications.....................	614 28	
Maps, diplomas and drawing material.......................	65 50	
Furniture........................	19 20	
Horse hire.......................	58 50	
Supplies and expense..............	80 34	
Advertising......................	57 75	
		2,754 47	4,710 12

Inspection and Instruction, U. S. A.:

Expenses, Sergeant Instructors:

Quarters.........................$4,905 33		
Transportation...................	850 22	
Pay.............................	274 00	
	$6,029 55	

Expenses, Inspector, Instructors:

Transportation...................	$360 01	
Subsistence......................	808 20	
Witness machine gun company.....	20 29	
	1,188 50	
Medical attendance.........................	4 00	
		7,222 05

General Expense:

Expense procuring band.....................	$10 00	
Funeral expense, transportation..............	130 45	
Duty, New York Arsenal, Adj. property accounts..............................	1,002 65	
Publications...............................	2 50	
	1,145 60	

Contingent Reserve:

Pay rolls detachment farm boys camps........	$398 86	
Freight charges, headquarters division.........	41 51	
Freight, New York arsenal....................	48 73	
Gloversville anniversary, 4th July celebration..	109 36	
	598,46	
		204,475 66

Balance, June 30, 1916..................		$164,889 65

NAVAL MILITIA

Salaries: Graded Employees, Naval Militia Division, the Adjutant General's Office:

Balance September 30, 1915.................		
Appropriation, chap. 725, Laws 1915.........	$2,700 00	$2,700 00
Expended:		
Service to June 30, 1916....................		2,025 00
Balance, June 30, 1916..................		$675 00

7

Allowances to Headquarters:
Balance, September 30, 1915................   1,352 01
Appropriation, chap. 725, Laws 1915........   4,600 00
                                                           $5,952 01
    Expended:
Headquarters............................ $2,389 92
Battalions...............................   2,317 74
                                                           4,707 66

    Balance, June 30, 1916................. $1,244 35

Allowances to Officers and Organizations:
Balance, September 30, 1915................ $585 70
Appropriation, chap. 725, Laws 1915........   13,500 00
                                                           $14,085 70
    Expended:
Officers................................. $1,657 50
Organizations:
Allowances per capita..................... $9,861 80
Allowances, separate divisions.............   2,250 00
                                               12,111 80
                                                           13,769 30

    Balance, June 30, 1916................. $316 40

General Expense of the Naval Militia:
Balance, September 30, 1915................ $22,173 86
Appropriation, chap. 725, Laws 1915........   35,000 00
                                                           $57,173 86
    Expended:
Officers on Special Duty:
Examining board for officers................. $582 77
Armory board............................   300 06
Aeronautic course.........................   171 06
Conference winter work.....................   30 71
Desk office expense.......................   58 01
Other special duty.........................   832 13
Testing aeroplane.........................   170 25
Inspection, muster........................   290 96
                                               2,425 97
U. S. Vessels and Launches:
Employees................................ $10,938 42
Scraping deck, U. S. S. Gloucester............   52 50
Berthing U. S. S. Sandoval..................   56 15
Storage and repairs.......................   937 15
Removal ashes, Gloucester..................   320 00
                                               12,304 22
Decorations and Prizes:
Prizes, small arms firing.................... $422 00
Decorations, long service...................   150 00
                                               572 00
Supplies and Equipment:
Coal, oil and wood......................... $430 69
Ammunition..............................   658 50
                                               1,089 19
Exercises and Instruction:
Aviation course........................... $637 43
                                               637 43
Target Practice:
Supervision.............................. $44 08
Target Practice:
Transportation................... $167 31
Markers and scorers..............   587 59
Towing.........................   200 00
                                               954 90

Subsistence............................	472 96		
Maintenance of ranges...................	23 97		
Secondary battery practice, pay...........	1,825 40		
		3,321 31	

General Expense, Naval Militia:
Contingent Reserve:

Dues, naval militia association..............	$143 70		
National naval militia convention...........	82 02		
Engrossing................................	10 50		
National naval reserve convention...........	129 50		
Travel expense............................	20 80		
		386 52	
			20,736 64

Balance, June 30, 1916.................			$36,437 22

Summer Cruise:

Balance, September 30, 1915.................		$14,916 90	
Appropriation, chap. 725, Laws 1915........		13,000 00	
			$27,916 90

Expended:

Pay.......................................		$5,351 85	
Subsistence...............................		609 35	
			5,961 20

Balance, June 30, 1916.................			$21,955 70

MISCELLANEOUS

Postage and Transportation, The Adjutant General's Office:

Balance, September 30, 1915.................		$371 45	
Appropriation, chap. 725, Laws 1915........		2,000 00	
			$2,371 45

Expended:

Postage...................................		$1,697 00	
Express...................................		520 91	
			2,217 91
			$153 54

Postage and Transportation, Division National Guard:

Balance, September 30, 1915.................	$54 12		
Lapsed, balance chap. 529, 1914..............	5 80		
		$48 32	
By appropriation, chap. 725, 1915...........		1,000 00	
			$1,048 32

Expended:

Postage...................................		$800 00	
Express...................................		159 64	
			959 64

Balance, June 30, 1916.................			$88 68

Pensions and Care of Disabled:

Balance, September 30, 1915.................	$717 01		
Appropriation, chap. 725, Laws, 1915........	12,000 00		
			$12,717 01

```
    Expended:
    Pensioners................................    $7,968 21
    Temporary disability.......................    2,734 56
    Pension examiner...........................      207 70
    Medical examiner...........................      337 31
    Stenographic service.......................      101 00
                                                 ------------
                                                              11,368 78
                                                             ------------
        Balance, June 30, 1916.................               $1,348 23
                                                             ============

War Records:
    Balance, September 30, 1915................     $98 20
    Appropriation, chap. 725, Laws, 1915.......  12,000 00
    Appropriation, chap. 646, Laws, 1916.......     201 80
                                                 ------------
                                                             $12,300 00
    Expended:
    Services to June 30, 1916..................               12,300 00
                                                             ============

Spanish War Claims:
    Balance, September 30, 1915................    $669 35
    Appropriation, chap. 646, Laws, 1916.......      80 65
                                                 ------------
                                                              $750 00
    Expended:
    Services to June 30, 1916..................                750 00
                                                             ============

Campaign Badges:
    Balance, September 30, 1915................               $1,000 00
    Expended:
    Medals.....................................    $800 00
    Postage....................................     200 00
                                                 ------------
                                                               1,000 00
                                                             ============

Military Record Fund:
    Balance, September 30, 1915................    $107 66
    Appropriation, chap. 725, Laws, 1915.......   2,000 00
                                                 ------------
                                                              $2,107 66
    Expended:
    Services to June 30, 1916..................               1,500 00
        Balance, June 30, 1916.................                 607 66
                                                             ============

Delegates National Guard Convention, San Fran-
    cisco, Cal.:
    By appropriation, chap. 726, Laws, 1915.....              $1,000 00
    Expended:
    Travel expenses............................               1,000 00
                                                             ============

Maintenance and Operation:
    The Adjutant General's Office, Moving Furniture
        and Equipment:
    By appropriation, chap. 646, Laws, 1916.....               $250 00
    Expended:
    Moving furniture and equipment.............                250 00
                                                             ============

Taking Down and Assembling Metal Filing Cases:
    By appropriation, chap. 646, Laws, 1916.....               $406 95
    Expended:
    Services...................................                406 95
```

STATEMENT, SPANISH WAR REFUND

ALBANY TRUST COMPANY, ALBANY, N. Y

Date	Item	Principal	Interest	Total
Sept. 30, 1915	Balance...........................	$26,859 21	$411 04	$27,270 25
June 30, 1916	Increment.........................	....	412 52	412 52
		$26,859 21	$823 56	$27,682 77
	Disbursement.....................	418 14	262 50	680 64
June 30, 1916	Balance...........................	$26,441 07	$561 06	$27,002 13

UNION TRUST COMPANY, ALBANY, N. Y.

Date	Item	Principal	Interest	Total
Sept. 30, 1915	Balance...........................	$22,937 12	$342 88	$23,280 00
June 30, 1916	Increment.........................	....	701 86	701 86
		$22,937 12	$1,044 74	$23,981 86
	Disbursement.....................	238 00	....	238 00
June 30, 1916	Balance...........................	$22,699 12	$1,044 74	$23,743 86

STATE CASH PURCHASES

(Military Stores and Supplies)

Statement Showing Receipts by The Adjutant General Against Sales From Stock, New York Arsenal, and Disbursements for Stores Procured to June 30, 1916.

1915
Sept. 30 Balance on hand... $1,147 78

Receipts

Oct.	6	12th Infantry....................................	$6 96
		71st Infantry....................................	1 00
	8	23d Infantry.....................................	50
		8th Coast Defense Command......................	2 82
		23d Infantry.....................................	2 47
		Reserve List.....................................	2 47
		Reserve List.....................................	2 47
	27	23d Infantry.....................................	4 94
		Co. I, 1st Infantry (24th Separate Co.).............	9 98
Nov.	12	W. T. Romaine, Major, R. L......................	2 47
		7th Infantry.....................................	7 41
	30	1st Field Artillery...............................	1 00
		12th Infantry....................................	1 50
		10th Infantry....................................	7 76
		7th Infantry.....................................	2 47
		12th Infantry....................................	4 94
		9th Coast Defense Command......................	2 47
		2d Infantry......................................	9 88
Dec.	6	23d Infantry.....................................	9 88
	17	Troop B, 1st Cavalry.............................	5 14
		Machine Gun Troop..............................	7 66
		Quartermaster Corps.............................	2 47

1915			
Dec.	17	10th Infantry..	$5 19
		1st Field Artillery................................	2 47
·		2d Infantry..	22 40
		Battery B, 1st Field Artillery.....................	1 00
	21	8th Coast Defense Command......................	2 67
		Retired List.......................................	2 67
		12th Infantry......................................	2 67
		12th Infantry......................................	5 24
		8th Coast Defense Command.....................	2 47
1916			
		Headquarters Division...........................	37 23
Jan.	6	12th Infantry......................................	2 67
		12th Infantry..:...................................	2 47
		23d Infantry.......................................	4 94
		Battery C, 1st Field Artillery......................	1 19
	8	Co. G, 1st Infantry................................	2 47
	13	Co. G, 1st Infantry................................	56
		Co. M, 2d Infantry................................	1 75
		Battery D, 1st Field Artillery......................	3 40
		Co. B, 10th Infantry..............................	1 33
		Co. D, 3d Infantry................................	98
		Co. F, 2d Infantry................................	2 24
		Co. C, 3d Infantry................................	14
	25	7th Infantry.......................................	1 00
		2d Field Artillery.................................	1 12
		2d Field Artillery.................................	60
		12th Infantry......................................	2 47
	28	47th Infantry......................................	12 00
		Battery B, 1st Field Artillery.....................	1 89
			$225 89
Jan.	31	23d Infantry.......................................	1 50
		Co. A, 3d Infantry................................	2 03
Feb.	17	10th Infantry......................................	70
		7th Infantry.......................................	10 94
		Headquarters Division...........................	2 47
		71st Infantry......................................	4 55
	21	10th Infantry......................................	7 39
		Co. M, 3d Infantry................................	35
	26	1st Cavalry..	14 10
		1st Cavalry..	15 00
		Troop G, 1st Cavalry.............................	19
		7th Infantry.......................................	1 92
March	6	12th Infantry......................................	2 47
		1st Field Hospital.................................	5 00
		Co. E, 1st Infantry................................	1 56
		12th Infantry......................................	5 19
	15	Reserve List.......................................	14 20
		Allan L. Reagan, Major, I. G.....................	2 67
		23d Infantry.......................................	4 94
	29	1st Cavalry..	3 75
	27	Co. G, 3d Infantry................................	1 64
April	8	7th Infantry.......................................	7 19
May	9	Co. C, 1st Infantry................................	7 86
		Reserve List.......................................	19 59
		12th Infantry......................................	50
	18	Settlement Property Shortage's, account Troop M, 1st Cavalry...................................	7 80
	19	23d Infantry.......................................	27 97
		Battery F, 1st Field Artillery.....................	2 47
June	7	Medical Corps.....................................	2 67
		7th Infantry.......................................	10 19
			$1,562 47

Disbursements

1915

Oct.   28 Adjustment to correct entry of October 6, 1915 . . . . $6 96

1916

Jan.   31 Transferring funds, Purchase made from U. S. C. P . . .   7 41
May   8 Revising entry of January 6, 1916 . . . .   2 47
                                                                    ─────────
                                                                      $16 84

                                                                  ═════════
                                                                  $1,545 63
                                                                  ═════════

UNITED STATES CASH PURCHASES

Statement of Receipts by The Adjutant General From Officers and Organizations, for the purchase from the War Department, Stores, Supplies, Etc., in Accordance With Section 17, Organized Militia Regulations, and Disbursements Against Same to June 30, 1916.

1915

Sept.   30 Balance on hand $1,711 64

Receipts

Oct.	6	12th Infantry	$5 88
		23d Infantry	3 10
		1st Infantry	28 25
		71st Infantry	3 15
		71st Infantry	12 75
		7th Infantry	2 57
		14th Infantry	14 73
		12th Infantry	1 74
		Squadron A, Cavalry	11 75
		7th Division, 1st Battalion, N. M	14 73
		General Division	2 47
		1st Field Hospital, Medical Corps	4 47
		Hospital Corps, 1st Battalion Signal Corps	2 67
		Battery D, 1st Field Artillery	17 31
		12th Infantry	6 10
		12th Infantry	4 94
		7th Infantry	4 43
		23d Infantry	3 10
		9th Coast Defense Command	1 69
		12th Infantry	76
		3d Battalion, N. M	8 35
	8	Battery F, 1st Field Artillery	7 25
		Battery F, 1st Field Artillery	12 95
		N. B. Thurston, Colonel	37 62
		7th Division, 1st Battalion, N. M	32
		23d Infantry	12 75
		Battery B, 2d Field Artillery	75
		23d Infantry	2 24
		23d Infantry	9 73
		8th Coast Defense Command	4 86
		23d Infantry	3 10
		23d Infantry	2 01
		69th Infantry	1 15
		23d Infantry	1 09
		23d Infantry	6 07
		Co. F, 2d Infantry	1 00
		8th Coast Defense Command	50
		Reserve List	3 15
		Headquarters Division	1 34
		Headquarters Division	4 25

1915				
Oct.	8	1st Field Hospital...............................	$6	10
		69th Infantry...................................	10	72
		1st Field Artillery.............................	14	04
		Reserve List....................................	1	35
	27	23d Infantry....................................	6	43
		Battery C, 2d Field Artillery...................	15	62
		1st Cavalry.....................................	85	82
		10th Infantry...................................	2	52
		7th Infantry....................................	15	92
		Co. I, 1st Infantry, (24th Separate Co.)........	9	96
		Co. H, 3d Infantry..............................	34	65
		Co. A, 3d Infantry..............................	25	41
		Co. D, 10th Infantry, (45th Separate Co.).......	2	40
		P. O. Mills, R. L...............................	5	25
		4th Division, 3d Battalion, N. M................	5	32
Nov.	12	47th Infantry...................................	6	15
		W. T. Romaine, Major, R. L......................	9	88
		47th Infantry...................................	12	05
		47th Infantry...................................	14	99
		10th Infantry...................................	21	98
		7th Infantry....................................	23	13
		Co. L, 1st Infantry.............................	6	05
		Battery B, 1st Field Artillery..................	1	19
	23	Headquarters, 2d Division.......................	7	37
		Quartermaster Corps.............................		10
		1st Infantry....................................	2	67
		69th Infantry...................................	2	67
		71st Infantry...................................	3	10
		12th Infantry...................................	17	58
		2d Field Hospital...............................	3	85
		1st Cavalry.....................................	24	20
		1st Field Hospital..............................	13	28
		1st Field Hospital..............................	24	07
		1st Cavalry.....................................	13	94
	30	Headquarters, 2d Division.......................	5	61
		1st Cavalry.....................................	7	40
		12th Infantry...................................	9	20
		3d Infantry.....................................	14	83
		1st Field Artillery.............................	3	70
		12th Infantry...................................	1	24
		1st Infantry....................................	14	04
		1st Infantry....................................	15	95
		Signal Corps....................................	10	77
		47th Infantry...................................	6	15
		7th Infantry....................................	31	10
		12th Infantry...................................	1	92
		2d Infantry.....................................	1	38
		69th Infantry...................................	37	75
		3d Infantry.....................................	13	72
		7th Infantry....................................	27	76
		1st Cavalry.....................................		83
		1st Cavalry.....................................	27	38
		1st Infantry....................................	8	80
		9th Coast Defense Command.......................	5	09
		2d Infantry.....................................	19	79
Dec.	6	2d Field Artillery..............................	25	47
		Headquarters Division...........................	14	20
		1st Field Artillery.............................	1	47
		22d Corps of Engineers..........................	15	61
		Squadron A, Cavalry.............................	17	90
		1st Field Artillery.............................	21	85
		2d Field Artillery..............................	31	28

```
1915
Dec.    6  71st Infantry...................................  $14 24
           71st Infantry...................................      49
           23d Infantry...................................    9 14
           10th Infantry..................................   14 18
           Reserve List...................................   26 33
       17  10th Infantry..................................    3 10
           10th Infantry..................................   18 30
           Battery B, 1st Field Artillery.................   91 35
           14th Infantry..................................   15 07
           2d Infantry....................................   15 93
           12th Infantry..................................    6 81
           2d Infantry....................................   15 82
           1st Battalion, Signal Corps....................      98
           Troop B, 1st Cavalry...........................   13 22
           Troop I, 1st Cavalry...........................  127 23
           10th Infantry..................................    5 89
           Quartermaster Corps............................    5 42
           8th Coast Defense Command......................    6 40
           14th Infantry..................................   17 59
           Troop B, 1st Cavalry...........................    2 52
       17  Troop B, 1st Cavalry...........................   14 39
           Battery D, 2d Field Artillery..................   92 07
           7th Infantry...................................    2 24
           7th Infantry...................................      65
           Headquarters Division..........................    8 00
           1st Field Artillery............................    1 89
           12th Infantry..................................    1 55
           Battery B, 1st Field Artillery.................    2 77
           12th Infantry..................................   10 47
           2d Infantry....................................    3 32
           Battery E, 1st Field Artillery.................   46 13
           3d Infantry....................................   14 37
           Headquarters Division..........................    2 36
           10th Infantry..................................    6 76
       21  7th Infantry...................................  109 00
           8th Coast Defense Command......................    7 62
           8th Coast Defense Command......................    1 56
           12th Infantry..................................   12 91
           Adjutant General's Office......................    1 80
           12th Infantry..................................    1 61
           8th Coast Defense Command......................    3 20
           1st Infantry...................................   12 15
           Battery E, 2d Field Artillery..................   31 25
           Retired List...................................    5 38
           1st Brigade....................................   10 62
           Reserve List...................................   15 04
           12th Infantry..................................    8 52
           7th Infantry...................................   29 01
           10th Infantry..................................   19 74
           3d Infantry....................................    3 55
           12th Infantry..................................   11 88
           12th infantry..................................   40 13
1916
Jan.    6  12th Infantry..................................   14 51
           9th Coast Defense Command......................   13 79
           9th Coast Defense Command......................   18 98
           23d Infantry...................................   13 56
           23d Infantry...................................    3 10
           H. A. Bostwick, Lieut. Col.....................    1 75
           12th Infantry..................................      96
           Co. K, 74th Infantry...........................    5 73
           Co. K, 74th Infantry...........................    3 60
```

1916			
Jan.	6	Co. K, 74th Infantry	$0 88
		Co. F, 10th Infantry	1 75
		14th Infantry	23 65
		Battery B, 1st Field Artillery	2 41
		Battery C, 1st Field Artillery	9 91
		Battery C, 1st Field Artillery	5 60
		Co. F, 2d Infantry	7 42
		Co. B, 10th Infantry	27
		Co. B, 10th Infantry	50
		2d Ambulance Company	4 86
		2d Ambulance Company	2 55
	8	65th Infantry	1 60
		Battery C, 1st Field Artillery	2 99
		Battery C, 1st Field Artillery	21 99
		1st Field Artillery	10 75
		Co. F, 1st Infantry	5 02
		Co. G, 1st Infantry	4 52
		47th Infantry	8 42
		2d Infantry, M. C.	24 13
		Co. B, 10th Infantry	2 37
		2d Infantry	67 09
		2d Field Artillery	989 70
	13	Headquarters, 1st Brigade	17 65
		Co. F, 1st Infantry	4 16
		Co. M, 2d Infantry	35
		Co. G, 1st Infantry	99
		Co. G, 1st Infantry	1 75
		12th Infantry	14 29
		Battery D, 2d Field Artillery	10 48
		Co. M, 2d Infantry	17 96
		Co. M, 2d Infantry	65
		3d Infantry, M. C.	9 26
		3d Infantry	6 47
		First Field Hospital	34 96
		47th Infantry	12 52
		Troop I, 1st Cavalry	3 94
		Troop I, 1st Cavalry	9 48
		2d Ambulance Company	39 47
		Battery D, 1st Field Artillery	24
		Co. A, 3d Infantry	4 70
		Battery B, 1st Field Artillery	17 47
		Co. F, 1st Infantry	9 97
		Division, National Guard	7 25
		3d Brigade	1 05
		Battery B, 2d Field Artillery	13 87
		Co. F, 1st Infantry	17 51
		Co. F, 1st Infantry	5 02
		71st Infantry	61 56
		Co. B, 10th Infantry	51 97
		Co. D, 3d Infantry	19 38
		Co. F, 3d Infantry	3 79
		Co. F, 2d Infantry	59 39
		Adjutant General's Office	5 80
		47th Infantry	26 27
		Co. C, 3d Infantry	18 20
	14	Armory Commission	1,275 44
	25	Co. D, 3d Infantry	8 06
		1st Ambulance Company	49 49
		7th Infantry	55 68
		Co. F, 2d Infantry	12 90
		10th Infantry	7 84
		2d Field Artillery	15 68

1916

Jan.	25	2d Field Artillery....................................	$0 50
		2d Field Artillery....................................	10 36
		2d Field Artillery....................................	7 94
		12th Infantry......................................	2 13
		9th Coast Defense Command.......................	06
		71st Infantry......................................	2 67
		8th Coast Defense Command.......................	1 53
		Troop F, 1st Cavalry..............................	14 92
		E. B. Bruch, Lt. Col., R. L........................	15 11
	28	2d Field Artillery....................................	2 30
		2d Field Artillery....................................	9 66
		22d Corps of Engineers............................	14 73
		Co. A, 1st Infantry................................	1 11
		Troop I, 1st Cavalry...............................	2 66
		13th Coast Defense Command.......................	1 10
		Co. K, 1st Infantry................................	2 83
		Co. K, 1st Infantry................................	2 57
		Battery B, 1st Field Artillery......................	1 84
		Co. E, 71st Infantry...............................	57 81
Jan.	31	10th Infantry......................................	4 46
		1st Brigade..	17 65
		1st Brigade..	17 65
		Co. D, 1st Infantry................................	11 17
		Co. D, 1st Infantry................................	9 76
		2d Ambulance Company............................	2 83
		Co. E, 3d Infantry.................................	10 77
		Co. I, 1st Infantry................................	1 73
		Transferring funds................................	7 41
		Co. L, 1st Infantry................................	4 83
		1st Infantry.......................................	11 99
		1st Infantry.......................................	10 43
		1st Infantry.......................................	6 69
		23d Infantry.......................................	54 25
		7th Infantry.......................................	2 71
		7th Infantry.......................................	4 92
		Co. F, 1st Infantry................................	8 36
		Co. F, 1st Infantry................................	14 74
		Co. F, 3d Infantry.................................	9 25
		Co. A, 3d Infantry.................................	36 47
		22d Corps of Engineers............................	17 07
		Co, F, 1st Infantry................................	10 82
		Co. F, 1st Infantry................................	25
		Co. F, 3d Infantry.................................	10 77
Feb.	17	2d Field Artillery..................................	28 45
		Battery F, 2d Field Artillery.......................	162 00
		Co. M, 3d Infantry................................	30 66
		10th Infantry......................................	10 36
		7th Infantry.......................................	218 00
		7th Infantry.......................................	155 52
		Co. B, 3d Infantry.................................	1 04
		Co. B, 3d Infantry.................................	59 58
		7th Infantry.......................................	12 27
		12th Infantry......................................	10 77
		Headquarters Division.............................	4 69
		12th Infantry......................................	7 65
		23d Infantry.......................................	3 10
		7th Infantry.......................................	5 15
		Battery E, 2d Field Artillery.......................	72
		71st Infantry......................................	5 86
		Co. H, 10th Infantry...............................	2 47
		Reserve List.......................................	18 99
		Reserve List.......................................	1 91

1916			
Feb.	17	10th Infantry.....................................	$0 53
		2d Infantry......................................	2 00
	21	N. B. Thurston, Col..............................	17 68
		3d Infantry......................................	13 79
		Co. C, 3d Infantry...............................	15 90
		Troop D, 1st Cavalry.............................	59 00
		J. S. Ballman, R. L..............................	9 30
		9th Coast, Defense Command......................	14 34
		Battery D, 2d Field Artillery....................	35 61
		12th Infantry....................................	2 73
		47th Infantry....................................	5 50
		1st Battalion, Signal Corps......................	11 55
		Co. M, 3d Infantry...............................	2 76
		Co. M, 3d Infantry...............................	2 74
	26	Headquarters, 2d Field Artillery, 1..............	3 81
		2d Field Artillery...............................	36 20
		1st Cavalry......................................	153 54
		Co. H, 1st Battalion, S. C.......................	29 50
		Troop G, 1st Cavalry.............................	20 50
		Troop G, 1st Cavalry.............................	24
		Co. I, 3d Infantry...............................	88
		Co. I, 1st Infantry.............................	19
		Co. D, 1st Infantry..............................	12 50
		3d Brigade.......................................	2 06
		12th Infantry....................................	1 36
		12th Infantry....................................	1 89
		Battery F, 1st Field Artillery.,.................	3 53
		Battery F, 1st Field Artillery...................	15 34
		9th Coast Defense Command........................	1 60
		Battery F, 2d Field Artillery....................	42 35
		10th Infantry	2 40
		Battery F, 2d Field Artillery....................	40 74
		71st Infantry....................................	28 70
		Co. B, 1st Infantry..............................	1 40
		7th Infantry.....................................	16 38
Mar.	6	1st Cavalry......................................	4 60
		2d Field Artillery...............................	3 25
		Co. D, 7th Infantry..............................	16 62
		Troop B, 1st Cavalry.............................	3 10
		Co. I, 10th Infantry.............................	1 13
		The Veteran Corps of Artillery...................	63 71
		10th Infantry....................................	6 41
		12th Infantry....................................	33 13
		1st Battalion, 2d Field Artillery................	3 21
		Battery D, 2d Field Artillery....................	31 09
		69th Infantry....................................	7 92
		1st Cavalry......................................	136 07
		2d Infantry......................................	135 82
		1st Field Hospital...............................	5 25
		1st Field Hospital...............................	5 16
		1st Field Hospital...............................	124 19
		Co. E, 1st Infantry..............................	1 44
		Co. E, 1st Infantry..............................	1 04
		Battery D, 1st Field Artillery...................	17 45
		Troop I, 1st Cavalry.............................	33 35
		2d Field Artillery...............................	46 61
		Quartermaster Corps..............................	7 75
		12th Infantry....................................	40
		8th Coast Defense Command........................	1 80
		47th Infantry....................................	17 13
		9th Coast Defense Command........................	2 73
		Troop I, 1st Cavalry.............................	2 24

1916			
Mar.	6	Co. D, 1st Infantry	$12 66
		Troop B, 1st Cavalry	21 81
		Co. E, 65th Infantry	26 44
		12th Infantry	15 43
		12th Infantry	1 42
	15	1st Cavalry	295 75
		69th Infantry	20 20
		Co. K, 10th Infantry	7 06
		1st Field Artillery	27 44
		1st Field Artillery	34 54
		1st Field Artillery	10 65
		1st Field Artillery	58 09
		1st Field Artillery	6 15
		1st Field Artillery	5 82
		2d Ambulance Company	19 74
		H. A. Bostwick, Lt. Col.	22 48
		Reserve List	12 80
		2d Infantry	6 10
		Co. B, 1st Battalion, S. C.	10 86
		Co. A, 10th Infantry	48
		22d Corps of Engineers	62 44
		Co. H, 10th Infantry	16 08
		H. G. Ridabock, Lt. Col., Retired List	3 10
		9th Coast Defense Command	2 42
		23d Infantry	48 75
		1st Field Hospital	5 43
		12th Infantry	69
		9th Coast Defense Command	13 79
		12th Infantry	17 64
		12th Infantry	15 96
		12th Infantry	3 77
		9th Coast Defense Command	13 00
		1st Battalion, Signal Corps	12 75
		Co. A, 1st Battalion, S. C.	27 48
		Co. H, 10th Infantry	7 06
		1st Field Artillery	13 06
	17	8th Coast Defense Command	17 26
		1st Brigade	3 82
		12th Infantry	2 04
		12th Infantry	2 34
		12th Infantry	4 25
		8th Coast Defense Command	18 82
		8th Coast Defense Command	2 75
		69th Infantry	14 24
		Squadron A, Cavalry	183 65
		Battery B, 1st Field Artillery	1 58
		Reserve List	10 36
	20	12th Infantry	4 10
		Co. H, 1st Infantry	1 30
		71st Infantry	12 44
		Co. L, 3d Infantry	3 07
		M. C., 3d Infantry	22 67
		8th Coast Defense Command	1 64
		Battery D, 2d Field Artillery	6 11
		Lt.-Col. Bruch, Reserve List	16 23
	27	Co. G, 3d Infantry	3 63
		Co. G, 3d Infantry	31 32
		Co. M, 3d Infantry	10 47
		Battery F, 1st Field Artillery	18 16
		Co. K, 74th Infantry	1 70
		Co. B, 10th Infantry	38
		9th Coast Defense Command	9 74

1916			
Mar.	27	12th Infantry..................................	87 53
		Co. L, 10th Infantry..........................	11 67
		12th Infantry.................................	2 06
		12th Infantry.................................	5 22
		8th Coast Defense Command....................	1 60
		2d Field Artillery.............................	37 77
		65th Infantry.................................	46 00
		9th Coast Defense Command....................	31 70
		12th Infantry.................................	4 90
		Battery C, 2d Field Artillery..................	90
		Troop H, 1st Cavalry..........................	25 53
		8th Coast Defense Command....................	6 16
		8th Coast Defense Command....................	13 17
		9th Coast Defense Command....................	18 50
		3d Infantry...................................	15 44
		3d Infantry...................................	20 31
		Co. H, 1st Infantry...........................	10 84
		Headquarters, 3d Infantry.....................	41 35
		1st Field Artillery............................	12 75
		Headquarters, 3d Infantry.....................	18 68
		Headquarters, 1st Brigade.....................	14 69
		Co. L, 10th Infantry..........................	3 79
		12th Infantry.................................	75
		12th Infantry.................................	5 22
April	8	Headquarters, 3d Brigade......................	10 80
		Headquarters Division.........................	2 43
		7th Infantry..................................	45 60
		7th Infantry..................................	228 00
		Machine Gun Tr., Cavalry......................	2 25
		Co. E, 65th Infantry..........................	12 00
		Co. B, 3d Infantry............................	49 65
		Co. L, 2d Infantry............................	17 77
		Reserve List..................................	10 61
		9th Coast Defense Command....................	15 38
		Battery B, 2d Field Artillery..................	30
		Headquarters, 1st Brigade.....................	1 64
		1st Armored Motor Battery.....................	1 86
		1st Armored Motor Battery.....................	24 05
		1st Armored Motor Battery.....................	27 69
		1st Field Hospital............................	2 54
		2d Infantry...................................	14 29
		7th Infantry..................................	30 81
		Co. C, 3d Infantry............................	18 21
		Headquarters, 3d Infantry.....................	10 77
		Co. C, 1st Infantry...........................	23 95
	11	2d Field Artillery.............................	17 50
		1st Cavalry...................................	209 77
		12th Infantry.................................	5 63
		Troop B, 1st Cavalry..........................	5 15
		Co. M, 10th Infantry..........................	33 43
		Co. L, 3d Infantry............................	24
		Co. E, 3d Infantry............................	31 65
		14th Infantry.................................	5 07
		8th Coast Defense Command....................	27 68
		Corps of Engineers............................	4 47
		9th Coast Defense Command....................	27 53
		2d Infantry...................................	4 65
		Co. B, 1st Battalion, S. C.....................	31 44
		2d Ambulance Company.........................	2 24
		Co. G, 2d Infantry............................	8 00
		Co. L, 1st Infantry...........................	65 58
		Reserve List..................................	12 75

1916			
April	11	Co. D, 10th Infantry..............................	$1 17
		71st Infantry.....................................	2 62
		12th Infantry....................................	2 59
		Quartermaster Corps..............................	1 56
		9th Coast Defense Command........................	9 87
		9th Coast Defense Command........................	3 44
		23d Infantry.....................................	4 43
		Headquarters, Detach., S. C......................	6 10
		2d Field Hospital................................	2 67
		Troop B, 1st Cavalry.............................	33 00
		Co. C, 3d Infantry...............................	9 25
		Co. C, 1st Infantry..............................	6 20
		Co. A, 1st Battalion, S. C.......................	12 75
		Squadron A, Cavalry	416 50
	25	Co. H, 1st Infantry..............................	8 35
		Troop M, 1st Cavalry.............................	12 44
		Co. M, 1st Infantry..............................	10
		Co. M, 1st Infantry..............................	15 80
		Co. L, 2d Infantry...............................	5 57
		65th Infantry....................................	38 25
		Co. F, 74th Infantry.............................	14 4
		12th Infantry....................................	8 29
		12th Infantry....................................	2 76
		1st Armored Motor Battery........................	20 20
		1st Armored Motor Battery........................	14 34
May	8	Revising entry Jan. 3, 1916......................	2 47
		Adjust entry, April 29, 1916.....................	2,299 48
	9	Headquarters Division............................	1 61
		Headquarters, 1st Brigade........................	14 34
		Headquarters Division............................	1 90
		Co. B, 12th Infantry.............................	33 91
		Co. C, 1st Infantry..............................	2 37
		Battery B, 2d Field Artillery....................	1 60
		13th Coast Defense Command.......................	66 07
		Battery F, 1st Field Artillery...................	1 64
		12th Infantry....................................	90
		Quartermaster Corps..............................	40
		1st Cavalry......................................	71 70
		1st Cavalry......................................	154 88
		1st Battalion, Signal Corps......................	6 75
		10th Infantry....................................	9 46
		69th Infantry....................................	4 47
		13th Coast Defense Command.......................	119 40
		Headquarters, 3d Infantry........................	38 13
		8th Coast Defense Command........................	14 34
		Battery D, 2d Field Artillery....................	11 50
		Co. F, 10th Infantry.............................	10 23
		Headquarters, 1st Brigade........................	14 34
		Headquarters, 1st Brigade........................	14 34
		H. Q. Detach. Bn. S. C...........................	2 66
		William H. Robinson, 1st Lt., R. L...............	17 17
		47th Infantry....................................	4 12
		22d Corps of Engineers...........................	1 61
		12th Infantry....................................	60
		Co. B, 65th Infantry.............................	2 41
		2d Field Artillery...............................	40 47
		7th Infantry.....................................	10 00
		Troop F, 1st Cavalry	2 50
		22d Corps of Engineers...........................	2 50
		2d Infantry.....................................	10 00
		Battery D, 2d Field Artillery....................	2 00
		Reserve List.....................................	2 50

1916			
May	9	Battery B, 1st Field Artillery.......................	$5 23
		2d Field Artillery................................	2 13
		Headquarters, 1st Brigade........................	2 65
		Headquarters, 1st Brigade........................	2 65
	12	10th Infantry....................................	26 11
		Co. G, 10th Infantry.............................	6 10
		12th Infantry....................................	70 95
		Co. G, 10th Infantry.............................	2 67
		Headquarters, 2d Field Artillery..................	122 46
		1st Field Artillery...............................	12 75
		8th Coast Defense Command.......................	14 44
		9th Coast Defense Command.......................	4 39
		Headquarters Division............................	8 29
		2d Field Artillery................................	9 64
		8th Coast Defense Command.......................	18 49
	19	2d Field Artillery................................	1 16
		47th Infantry....................................	16 78
		Co. B, 1st Infantry...............................	104 07
		Battery F. 2d Field Artillery......................	82 70
		Battery F, 2d Field Artillery......................	14 42
		9th Coast Defense Command.......................	1 73
		23d Infantry.....................................	103 61
		Battery F, 1st Field Artillery.....................	1 87
		Battery F, 1st Field Artillery.....................	4 53
		Reserve List.....................................	4 04
	20	10th Infantry....................................	18 85
		2d Battalion, 2d Field Artillery...................	14 39
		3d Ambulance Company...........................	199 00
		10th Infantry....................................	3 99
		Reserve List.....................................	39 38
		Reserve List.....................................	11 53
		Reserve List.....................................	91 02
		12th Infantry....................................	2 60
		8th Coast Defense Command.......................	2 54
		8th Coast Defense Command.......................	24 03
		12th Infantry....................................	90
	24	Headquarters, 1st Brigade........................	14 34
		Battery C, 2d Field Artillery......................	1 60
		Co. L, 10th Infantry..............................	24 45
		Co. M, 14th Infantry.............................	15 07
		Headquarters Division............................	17 31
		13th Coast Defense Command......................	1 68
		12th Infantry....................................	10 27
		12th Infantry....................................	26 18
May	24	13th Coast Defense Command......................	3 10
		69th Infantry....................................	3 15
		12th Infantry....................................	3 10
June	7	Headquarters, 3d Brigade.........................	9 11
		12th Infantry....................................	12 75
		12th Infantry....................................	5 62
		Co. I, 3d Infantry................................	20 52
		Co. G, 10th Infantry.............................	4 87
		74th Infantry....................................	11 95
		9th Coast Defense Command.......................	15 43
		9th Coast Defense Command.......................	15 43
		9th Coast Defense Command.......................	17 27
		9th Coast Defense Command.......................	14 39
		14th Infantry....................................	15 59
		12th Infantry....................................	3 10
		12th Infantry....................................	267 50
		12th Infantry....................................	1 36
		2d Ambulance Company...........................	14 74
		71st Infantry....................................	158 87

1916
June 7

Battery C, 1st Field Artillery	$31	07
Battery C, 1st Field Artillery	81	66
7th Infantry	6	98
4th Ambulance Company	254	15
2d Field Artillery	5	85
10th Infantry	7	00
Co. M, 10th Infantry	6	20
3d Infantry	6	13
Battery C, 1st Field Artillery	28	49
8th Coast Defense Command	285	05
74th Infantry		22
74th Infantry	2	24
8th Coast Defense Command	4	47
10th Infantry	4	47
69th Infantry	3	54
1st Field Hospital	8	94
1st Field Hospital		30
Headquarters, 8th Coast Defense Command	7	57
Co. F, 2d Infantry	90	79
74th Infantry	5	17
Co. F, 3d Infantry	4	80
Quartermaster Corps	1	69
12th Infantry	6	15
Reserve List	4	47
8th Coast Defense Command	12	75
1st Cavalry	17	57
74th Infantry	3	38
Co. G, 3d Infantry	4	27
Co. I, 2d Infantry	25	58
12th Infantry	3	00
1st Field Artillery	62	67
9th Coast Defense Command	20	55
9th Coast Defense Command	1	65
8th Coast Defense Command	31	99
8th Coast Defense Command	9	45
Deposit, 1st National Bank	2,349	92

$20,960 30

Disbursements

1915
Oct. 22

Depot Q. M., Philadelphia, purchases	$626	62
C. O. Springfield Armory, purchase	48	35
Paymaster, Navy Yard, Washington, D. C.	8	10
31 C. O. Rock Island Arsenal	461	03
Depot Q. M., New York	3	58
Officer in charge, Medical Supply Depot	5	78
Frankford Arsenal	56	30
C. O., Springfield Armory	143	41
C. O., Springfield Armory		24
First National Bank, account Depot Q. M., Phila	126	00
Nov. 23 C. O., New York Arsenal, purchases	11	55
D. O., Signal Corps, U. S. A., purchases	1	15
Depot Q. M., Jeffersonville, purchases	10	94
C. O., Springfield Armory, purchases	53	12
C. O., Rock Island Arsenal, purchases	29	18
Depot Q. M., Philadelphia, purchases	51	18
Depot Q. M., Philadelphia, purchases	5	34
Dec. 31 C. O., Frankford Arsenal	61	01
C. O., Springfield Armory		23
C. O., Springfield Armory	68	30
C. O., Rock Island Arsenal	36	97
D. O., Signal Corps	1,275	44
C. O., Frankford Arsenal	107	75
First National Bank, Depot Q. M., Philadelphia	228	02

1916

Jan.	31	C. O., Springfield Armory.........................	$375	71
		C. O., Frankford Arsenal..........................	65	12
		Andrew Moses, Major Secretary....................	2	17
		John R. Hegeman, Jr., refund......................	16	51
		Officer in charge, Federal Medical Supply Depot.....	5	10
		C. O., Springfield Armory.....:...................	12	75
		C. O., Springfield Armory, purchases...............	7	50
		C. O., Rock Island Arsenal.......................	195	87
		First National Bank, account Depot Q. M., Phila.....	547	11
		Revising entry, January 31, 1916..................	4	27
Feb.	21	First National Bank, account Depot Q. M., Phila.....	10	53
		Major, A. Moses, Secretary W. C. Division..........	11	57
		C. O., Springfield Armory.........................	531	07
	29	C. O., Frankfort Arsenal..........................	386	50
		First National Bank, account Depot Q. M., Phila.....	166	17
		Officer in charge, Federal Medical Supply Depot.....	23	18
		First National Bank, account Depot Q. M., Phila....	708	52
Mar.	31	Officer in charge, Engineer Department, property....	1	55
		First National Bank, account Depot Q. M., Phila....	2	58
		C. O., Rock Island Arsenal, property...............	9	75
		First National Bank, account Depot Q. M., Phila....	21	79
		Secretary, War College Division...................	18	90
April	29	C. O., Frankford Arsenal, purchases...............	45	10
		C. O., Frankford Arsenal, purchases...............	1	20
		First National Bank, account Depot Q. M., Phila.....	2,299	48
		C. O., Frankford Arsenal, purchases...............	312	50
		C. O., Rock Island Arsenal, purchases...............		16
		Officer in charge, Federal Medical Supply Depot, purchases...	36	01
		C. O., Rock Island Arsenal, purchases...............	1,204	38
		Depot Q. M., U. S. A., New York, purchases........	171	10
		First National Bank, account Depot Q. M., Phila., purchases.......................................	195	87
May	8	To adjust entry, April 29, 1916....................	5	88
	31	Officer in charge, Engineer Department, Washington Barracks, purchases.............................	4	65
		C. O., Frankford Arsenal, purchases................	2	88
		Depot Q. M., Philadelphia, purchases...............	2	53
		Depot Q. M., Philadelphia, purchases...............	920	71
		C. O., Frankford Arsenal, purchases................	297	50
		Depot Q. M., Philadelphia, purchases..............	227	00
May	31	C. O., Augusta Arsenal, purchases.................	59	40
		Depot Q. M., Philadelphia, purchases..............	20	38
		C. O., Frankford Arsenal, purchases...............	16	00
June	16	C. O., Frankford Arsenal, purchases...............	8	00
		First National Bank, account Depot Q. M., Philadelphia, purchases.............................	6	42
		C. O., Rock Island Arsenal, purchases...............	86	91
		C. O., Frankford Arsenal, purchases................	115	25
		Depot Q. M., U. S. A., New York, purchases........	49	30
		First National Bank, account Depot Q. M., Philadelphia, purchases.............................	1	06
	20	C. O., Springfield Armory.........................	615	67
		C. O., Augusta Arsenal............................	44	55
		Depot Quartermaster, Philadelphia.................	648	88

$13,942 63

$7,018 17

APPENDIX " F "

STATEMENTS SHOWING STRENGTH, COMPOSITION, AND GAINS IN THE
NATIONAL GUARD AND NAVAL MILITIA

	NATIONAL GUARD			NAVAL MILITIA			Aggre-gate
	Officers	Enlisted men	Total	Officers	Enlisted men	Total	
Strength Sept. 30, 1915....	1,023	15,996	17,019	90	1,345	1,435	18,454
Strength Sept. 30, 1916....	1,105	25,841	26,946	98	1,684	1,782	28,728
Net gain............	82	9,845	9,927	8	339	347	10,274

COMPOSITION OF THE NATIONAL GUARD ON SEPTEMBER 30, 1916

	2ND DIVISION		6TH DIVISION		Total
	Officers	Enlisted men	Officers	Enlisted men	
Major Generals.........................	1	....	1	....	2
Brigadier Generals......................	2	....	4	....	6
Adjutant General's Department..........	3	....	5	....	8
Inspector General's Department..........	4	....	1	....	5
Judge Advocate General's Department.....	3	....	1	....	4
Quartermaster Corps....................	6	13	17	328	364
Ordnance Department...................	4	4	1	....	9
Medical Department....................	21	167	92	788	1,068
Aides to General Officers...............	3	....	6	....	9
Signal Corps..........................	8	105	9	164	286
Corps of Engineers.....................	1	....	34	676	711
Cavalry..............................	......	....	73	1,695	1,768
Field Artillery........................	......	....	116	2,763	2,879
Coast Artillery Corps..................	122	3,275	......	....	3,397
Motor Battery........................	3	136	......	....	139
Infantry.............................	148	4,616	416	11,111	16,291
Total...........................	329	8,316	776	17,525	26,946

OFFICIAL REGISTER

OF THE

Organized Land and Naval Forces

OF THE

STATE OF NEW YORK

December 31, 1916

[213]

ABBREVIATIONS

a g........	Adjutant General
adj........	Adjutant
a.d.c......	Aide-de-Camp
amb.......	Ambulance
artif.......	Artificer
arty.......	Artillery
ass't.......	Assistant
bat........	Battalion
batty......	Battery
bvt.......	Brevet
brig.......	Brigade
brig.gen...	Brigadier General
capt.......	Captain
cav.......	Cavalry
c.a.c.......	Coast Artillery Corps
c.d.c.......	Coast Defense Command.
cert.......	Certificate
col.......	Colonel
c. g.......	Commanding General
c.o........	Commanding Officer
com'dr....	Commander
com'dg....	Commanding
com......	Command
comy......	Commissary
c.of e......	Corps of Engineers
corp.......	Corporal
dept.......	Department
dep......	Deputy
det.......	Detailed
eng.......	Engineers
ex........	Executive
f.a.......	Field Artillery
f.h........	Field Hospital
f.m.......	Field Music
1 lt.......	First Lieutenant
gov.......	Governor
hdqrs.....	Headquarters
hdqrs.co....	Headquarters Company
hon.dis....	Honorable discharge
h.c........	Hospital Corps
hosp.stwd..	Hospital Steward
inf........	Infantry
insp.......	Inspector
i.s.a.p.....	Inspector Small Arms Practice
j.a.g......	Judge Advocate General
j.g........	Junior Grade
lt.col.....	Lieutenant Colonel
m.g co....	Machine Gun Company
maj.......	Major
maj.gen....	Major General
m.c.......	Medical Corps
mus......	Musician
M. V.....	Medal of valor
N.G......	National Guard
n.m......	Naval Militia
off.......	Officer
ord.......	Ordnance
o.d.......	Ordnance Department
o.o.......	Ordnance Officer
o.r.......	Original Rank
pvt.......	Private
qm.......	Quartermaster
regt......	Regiment
r. l......	Reserve List
2 lt......	Second Lieutenant
sep.co.....	Separate Company
sgt.......	Sergeant
sig.corps...	Signal Corps
sq.........	Squadron
stwd.....	Steward
sub.......	Subsistence
supn......	Supernumerary
sup.co.....	Supply Company
surg......	Surgeon
trs.......	Transferred
tr........	Troop
U.S.M.A...	United States Military Academy
U.S.N.A...	United States Naval Academy
W.D......	War Department

OFFICIAL REGISTER

THE ORGANIZED LAND AND NAVAL FORCES OF THE STATE OF NEW YORK

NATIONAL GUARD

HEADQUARTERS, 158 STATE STREET, ALBANY, N. Y.

The National Guard constitutes a Division consisting of four brigades of infantry (12 regiments); 1 regiment, 1 separate squadron and 1 machine gun troop, cavalry; 1 brigade of field artillery (3 regiments organized); 1 corps of engineers (2 battalions); 1 battalion of signal corps (2 companies organized); 2 aero companies; 4 field hospitals; 4 ambulance companies; 1 mounted motor battery, 1 ammunition train,* 1 supply train, 1 pack train,* 1 field bakery. The coast artillery corps (35 companies) is attached for purposes of administration.

Stations and awards of organization

FIRST BRIGADE
Headquarters, 104 East 34th Street, New York City
The Brigade consists of the 7th, 12th, 15th, 69th and 71st Regiments of Infantry

SECOND BRIGADE
Headquarters, 1322 Bedford Avenue, Brooklyn
The Brigade consists of the 14th, 23d and 47th Regiments of Infantry

THIRD BRIGADE
Headquarters, 176 State Street, Albany
The Brigade consists of the 1st, 2d and 10th Regiments of Infantry

FOURTH BRIGADE
Headquarters, 431 Main Street, Buffalo
The Brigade consists of the 3d and 74th Regiments of Infantry

COMMANDER-IN-CHIEF

Name, grade, date of rank and highest brevet rank	In the armies of the U. S. or foreign states	In the National Guard	Born
GOVERNOR			
Charles S. Whitman, 1 jan. '15	....	....	Conn. 28 aug. 68
LIEUTENANT GOVERNOR			
THE ADJUTANT GENERAL			
Brigadier General Louis William Stotesbury, 1 jan. 15	....	See Office of The Adjutant General.	N. Y. 21 oct. 70
MILITARY SECRETARY			
Lieutenant Colonel Lorillard Spencer, 28 sept. 16	....	See 15th inf....................	N. Y. 4 jul. 83

* Not organized.

STAFF OF THE GOVERNOR.

Name, grade, date of rank and highest brevet rank.	Service		Born
	In the armies of the U. S. or foreign states.	In the National Guard	
STAFF OF THE GOVERNOR—*Continued*			
Aides-de-camp — Detailed.			
Lieutenant Colonel Reginald L. Foster, 12 inf detailed, 1 jan. 15.	....	See 12 inf...................	China. 25 nov. 69
Major Henry J. Cookinham, Jr., 1 inf. detailed, 1 jan. 15.	....	See 1 inf...................	N. Y. 26 aug. 74
Major Francis L. V. Hoppin, Adj. Gen.'s Dept. detailed, 1 jan. 15.	....	See Adj. Gen.'s Dept...........	R. I. 7 oct. 68
Major James L. Kincaid, 1 cav..... detailed, 4 oct. 15.	....	See 1 cav...................	N. Y. 28 nov. 85
Major Walter F. Gibson, 74 inf..... detailed, 1 jan. 15.	....	See qm. c...................	N. Y. 29 sep. 76
Lieutenant Commander Louis M. Josepthal, paymaster, n. m. detailed, 1 jan. 15.	....	See n. m...................	N. Y. 17 oct. 69
Captain Lyman P. Hubbell, 74 inf.. detailed, 4 oct. 15.	....	See 74 inf...................	N. Y. 19 nov. 74
Captain Joseph J. Kingsbury, R. L. detailed 26 jan. 15.	....	See r. l...................	N. Y. 11 sep. 72
Captain Henry E. Greene, 2 inf.... detailed, 1 jan. 15.	....	See 2 inf...................	N. Y. 2 may 80
Captain Howard E. Crall, 7 inf.... detailed, 26 jul. 15.	....	See 7 inf...................	D. C. 19 sep. 87
Captain Alvan W. Perry, 1 f. a..... detailed, 1 jan. 15.	....	See 1 f. a...................	Mass. 17 sep. 73
First Lieutenant John W. Goff, Jr., 71 inf. detailed, 1 jan. 15.	....	See 71 inf...................	N. Y. 26 sep. 80
First Lieutenant Maunsell S. Crosby 10 inf. detailed, 1 jan. 15.	....	See 10 inf...................	N. Y. 14 feb. 87

OFFICE OF THE ADJUTANT GENERAL OF THE STATE

Name, grade, date of rank and highest brevet rank	Service		Born
	In the armies of the U. S. or foreign states	In the National Guard	
THE ADJUTANT GENERAL			
Brigadier General			
Stotesbury, Louis William 1 jan. 15	....	pvt., corp., sgt. co. F, 7 inf.............. 6 apr. 92 to 15 mar. 01 2 lt. 7 inf............15 mar. 01 1 lt............... 8 aug. 05 cap............... 6 feb. 06 a. d. c. to gov....... 1 jan. 09 to 31 dec. 10 resigned............. 2 feb. 11 insp. gen. lt. col.....19 sep. 12 accepted..........23 sep. 12 The a. g., S. N. Y., brig. gen......... 1 jan. 15	N. Y. 21 oct. 70
ASSISTANT ADJUTANTS GENERAL			
Lieutenant Colonels			
Howard, Edward Vicars, 8 jun. 11 bvt. maj............29 oct. 09	....	pvt., corp., sgt., 1 sgt., co. I, 23 inf....... 2 oct. 84 to 16 mar. 00 pvt. corp. sgt. co. B, 10 bat...............16 mar. 00 to 28 jul. 03 hon. dis............30 jul. 03 2 lt. (B), 10 bat......28 jul. 03 1 lt...............18 feb. 04 bat. adj. with o. r.....26 apr. 04 supn., assigned com. 35 sep. co .... 1 may 05 cap. 35 sep. co.......12 may 05 asst. a. g. S. N. Y. lt. col 8 jun. 11 accepted.........13 jun. 11	Va. 4 jul. 64
Bostwick, Henry Anthon, 11 feb. 15 bvt. maj............30 jul. 12	....	pvt. cos. B and I, 7 inf., bat. qm. sgt., bat. sgt. maj.........19 jun. 85 to 21 feb. 01 1 lt. asst. i. s. a. p.....21 feb. 01 supn., reassigned.....21 jan. 08 1 lt. o. d............ 7 feb. 08 cap. o. d.............29 feb. 12 cap. 7 inf............. 1 may 14 accepted............. 6 may 14 lt. col. qm. corps.....11 feb. 15 accepted............11 feb. 15	N. Y. 21 aug. 64
ASSISTANT TO THE ADJUTANT GENERAL			
Major			
Westcott, Edward John, 19 jun. 16	pvt. 203 N. Y. inf...14 jul. 98 to 13 jan. 99	pvt., corp., co. A, 10 bat., post qm. sgt., 3 brig.............28 feb. 01 to 23 may 12 2 lt. 10 inf.........23 may 12 accepted............24 may 12 asst. to the A. G.....16 aug. 15 accepted............31 jul. 16	N. Y. 14 oct. 73

NATIONAL GUARD — GENERAL OFFICERS

Name, grade, date of rank & highest brevet rank	Service		Born	Attached to
	In the armies of U. S. or foreign states	In the National Guard		

Major General				
O' Ryan, John Francis, 1 may 12 graduate U. S. Army War College, 1914.	mustered into u. s. ser.....30 june 16 out dec. 22, 16	pvt. co. G, 7 inf....12 mar. 97 to 22 nov. 00 trs. 2 batty.........22 nov. 00 2 lt............... 6 dec. 00 1 lt............... 9 apr. 04 cap. 1 batty........10 may 07 a. d. c. to gov....... 1 jan. 11 to 16 apr. 12 maj. 2 bat. f. a......19 sep. 11 maj. gen. div. N. G. 16 apr. 12 accepted........... 1 may 12	N. Y... 21 aug. 74	com'dg div.
Brigadier Generals				
Lester, James Westcott, 6 jun. 11 bvt. maj. gen. 7 jan. 13	maj. 2 N. Y. inf., 2 may 98 to 25 oct. 98 mustered into u. s. ser.....28 June 16	pvt., sgt. 22 sep. co...............25 nov. 84 to 15 jan. 92 cap...............15 jan. 92 maj. 14 bat........29 mar. 98 maj. 2 inf. with o. r. 18 nov. 98 lt. col...........31 mar. 99 col...............11 dec. 03 brig. gen. 3 brig..... 6 jun 11 accepted........... 7 jun. 11	N. Y... 8 sep... 59	com'dg 3 brig.
Dyer, George Rathbone, 28 feb. 12 bvt. maj. gen. 8 apr. 15	cap. 12 N. Y. inf., 2 may 98 maj.....13 may 98 to 20 apr. 99 mustered into u. s. ser.....jun. 28, 16 out sep. 27, 16	pvt. co. K, 7 inf....10 jun. 89 to 16 may 92 2 lt. 12 inf. (G)......16 may 92 1 lt............... 7 mar. 93 cap............... 2 may 93 maj. 12 inf.........28 jun. 99 col............... 7 sep. 99 brig. gen. 1 brig.....28 feb. 12 accepted...........29 feb. 12	R. I... 24 jun. 69	com'dg 1 brig.
Wilson, William, 9 jun. 15 bvt. brig. gen. 29 oct. 07	maj. 3 N. Y. inf., 1 may 98 to 10 dec. 98 mustered into u. s. ser.....july 6, 16 out dec. 31, 16	pvt. 34 sep. co.....21 jan. 80 to 23 feb. 82 1 lt...............23 feb. 82 cap............... 6 oct. 84 maj. 2 bat.........22 dec. 98 a. d. c. to gov.......17 jan. 00 to 1 jan. 01 assigned 3 inf 30 mar. 07 col. 3 inf........... 9 may 07 brig. gen. 4 brig..... 9 jun. 15 accepted...........10 jun. 15	N. Y... 16 jun... 55	com'dg 4 brig.
AIDES TO GENERAL OFFICERS				
First Lieutenants				
Davis, Chester Wyman, 9 mar. 07	mustered into u. s. ser.....28 june 16	pvt., qm. sgt. 44 sep. co., bat. qm. sgt., 1 inf............22 apr. 04 to 9 mar. 07 1 lt. asst. i. s. a. p. 1 inf............... 9 mar. 07 supn., reassigned....21 jan. 08 1 lt. o. d....... 6 feb. 08 det. aide 3 brig....28 aug. 11	N. Y... 6 nov. 80	hdqrs. 3 brig.
Green, Griswold, 17 aug. 08 bvt. cap. 16 oct. 09	pvt. co. A, 2 N. Y. inf.....2 may 98 2 lt. 201 N. Y. inf. 6 july 98 to 8 sep. 98 mustered into u. s. ser.....28 june 16	pvt. 6 sep. co........26 jan. 97 1 lt. asst. i. s. a. p. 2 inf............15 sep. 99 a. d. cap. 3 brig....24 may 01 supn., reassigned....21 jan. 08 1 lt. 1 inf...........23 july 08 supn. own request, det. aide staff c. g. 3 brig. 17 aug. 08 a. d. c. to gov....... 1 jan. 11 to 31 dec. 12	N. Y... 28 dec. 76	hdqrs. 3 brig.

NATIONAL GUARD — GENERAL OFFICERS — (Concluded)

Name, grade, date of rank & highest brevet rank	Service		Born	At-tached to
	In the armies of U. S. or foreign states	In the National Guard		
AIDES TO GENERAL OFFICERS — (Continued)				
First Lieutenants — (Continued)				
Underwood, Harry Gregory, 10 dec. 10	....	1 lt. 2 inf. ....10 dec. 10 accepted...........12 dec. 10 a. d. c. to gov.......1 jan. 11 to 31 dec. 12 relieved from duty 2 inf. det. additional aide 3 brig.. 5 sep. 11	N. Y... 25 oct. 82	hdqrs. 3 brig.
Montant, Louis Townsend, 19 dec. 12	.... mustered into u. s. ser..... 6 july 16 out 27 sep. 16	pvt. tr. 2 sq. A......26 apr. 07 to 6 aug. 12 2 lt. 12 inf. .... 6 aug. 12 accepted............. 7 aug. 12 aide 1 brig..........11 sep. 12 1 lt. 12 inf. ....19 dec. 12 accepted...........20 dec. 12	N. Y... 27 dec. 85	hdqrs. 1 brig.

ADJUTANT GENERAL'S DEPARTMENT

Name, grade, date of rank & highest brevet rank	Service		Born	At- tached to
	In the armies of U. S. or foreign states	In the National Guard		
ADJUTANTS GENERAL *Colonel*				
Williams, Chauncey Pratt, 4 may 99 bvt. brig. gen. 12 nov. 09	....	pvt., sgt., 1 sgt. co. A, 10 bat............10 nov. 84 to 23 dec. 89 2 lt................23 dec. 89 insp. 3 brig........11 nov. 91 sig. off. sig. and tel corps, 3 brig............10 feb. 93 a. d. c. maj. div. N. G., 24 feb. 96 of the N. G. with o. r., 5 apr. 98 asst. a. g. S. N. Y., lt. col., 30 jan. 99 col............... 4 may 99 a. g. lt. col......... 8 sep. 09 accepted........... 8 sep. 09 col............... 4 may 99 accepted........... 4 may 99	N. Y...6 dec. 69	hdqrs. div.
Bandholts, Harry H., 22 july 16	cadet M. A. 1 july 86 2 lt. 6 inf., 12 june 90 1 lt. 24 inf., 12 feb. 97 trs. to 7 inf., 29 mar. 97 cap. 2 inf., 15 nov. 99 major....12 mar. 11 trs. to 22 inf., 1 dec. 11 unassigned, 23 mar. 13 assigned to 29 inf., 9 oct. 13 trs to 30 inf., 19 jan. 15 mustered out u. s. ser.....22 dec. 16	col. chief. staff, div.22 july 16 accepted ....22 jul. 16	Mich. 18 dec. 64	hdqrs. div.
Majors				
Hoppin, Francis Lauren Vinton, 18 mar. 12	1 lt. 12 N. Y. inf., 13 may 98 to 14 sep. 98 mustered into u. s. ser.....28 june 16 out 27 sep. 16	2 lt. 12 inf..........23 apr. 96 a. d. c. cap. 1 brig....14 june 99 supn................ 1 july 04 assigned duty 12 inf.. 1 june 02 to 7 june 02 assigned duty 12 inf..10 sep. 02 relieved............. 1 aug. 06 assigned duty 12 inf..11 mar. 08 relieved and reassigned, 30 dec. 08 relieved............19 feb. 09 assigned duty hdqrs. 1 brig., 11 mar. 12 a. g. maj.........18 mar. 12 accepted...........18 mar. 12	R. I... 7 oct. 66	hdqrs. 1 brig.
Ward, Franklin Wilmer, 28 june 16 W. D. Cert. in course No. 1 (Basic)	mustered into u. s. ser.....28 june 16 out 22 dec. 16	pvt., corp., co. I, 1 inf. N. G. Pa......17 may 88 hon. dis............ 1 may 91 pvt., corp., sgt., 1 sgt. co. I, 1 inf., N. G. Pa.........18 june 91 hon. dis............ 5 june 94 pvt., 1 sgt.........18 june 94 hon. dis............ 5 july 97 2 lt. 109 N. Y. inf. (D)31 aug. 98 supn................22 dec. 98 assigned to duty with 9 regt.........12 jan. 99 1 lt. 9 regt. (D).....24 nov. 99 cap................ 3 may 02 maj. 9 regt.........28 may 07	Pa..... 4 dec. 70	hdqrs. div.

ADJUTANT GENERAL'S DEPARTMENT — (*Concluded*)

Name, grade, date of rank & highest brevet rank	Service		Born	At-tached to
	In the armies of U. S. or foreign states	In the National Guard		
ADJUTANT GENERAL — (*Continued*) *Majors* — (Continued) Ward, Franklin Wilmer — (*Continued*)	....	maj. c. s. c ....23 jan. 08 a. g. lt. col .... 1 june 12 accepted .... 1 june 1 major, staff major 2 gen. com'dg div. . . 28 june 1s accepted ....28 june 16		
Reagan, Allan Lawrence, 28 june 16	mustered into u. s. ser.....30 june 16 out dec. 22 16	pvt., corp., sgt. co. A, 10 bat............. 8 nov. 00 to 1 may 05 1 lt. bat. adj. 10 inf.. 1 m ay 05 cap...............11 oct. 06 asst. a. g., S. N. Y., lt. col .... 1 oct. 10 accepted .... 1 oct. 10 asst. a. g., S. N. Y., col...............21 mar. 12 accepted...........21 mar. 12 supn............15 feb. 13 insp. gen. maj........ 6 apr. 15 accepted........... 7 apr. 15 major, staff major gen. com'dg div...28 june 16 accepted...........28 june 16	Pa..... 11 dec. 64	hdqrs. div.
Olmsted, Edward 28 june 16 graduate, g a r r i s o n schools, cavalry, 1914 especial course for field officers, army service schools, 1916	mustered into u. s. ser.....30 june 16 out 22 dec. 16	pvt., artif., corp., sgt., tr. 1 sq. A........17 may 98 to 14 may 07 1 lt. (4) sq. A.......14 may 07 cap. sq. A.........12 sep. 08 assigned aide staff maj. gen. com'dg div. N. G........25 sep. 12 a. g. lt. col.........23 apr. 15 accepted...........23 apr. 15 major, asst. chief staff, C. G. div...28 june 16 accepted...........28 june 16	Cal.... 5 jan. 72	hdqrs. div.
Smith, Leonard Bacon, 25 july 16 L. S. D., Class IV	mustered into u. s ser.....27 oct. 16	pvt., corp. sq. A, cav., trs. tr. 3, trs. tr. 4, corp., sgt........27 nov. 03 to 25 feb. 13 1 lt. o. d............25 feb. 13 1 lt. 1 f. a.........20 apr. 14 cap................20 oct. 14 accepted...........22 oct. 14 major.............25 july 16 accepted...........25 july 16	N. Y. 18 may 73	hdqrs. f. a. brig.
Tuck, Andrew Edward, 16 aug. 16	mustered into u. s. ser.....17 sep. 16 out 23 sep. 16	2 lt. 3 inf........24 july 11 accepted...........25 july 11 cap................ 8 oct. 12 accepted........... 9 oct. 12 major, J. A. Gen'l's dept.............21 dec. 16 accepted...........23 dec. 16 major, A. G. dept., 3 brig., u. s.........16 aug. 16 accepted...........16 aug. 16 assigned to duty as A. G. 4 brig. S. O. 241, A. G. O ....15 nov. 16	N. Y... 11 may 74	hdqrs. 4 brig.
Captain Butler, Henry Langdon, 1 dec. 15	....	pvt., corp., sgt., 1 sgt. co. H, 7 inf...16 apr. 00 to 1 dec. 15 a. g., cap........... 1 dec. 15 accepted........... 1 dec. 15	S. I.... 6 jul. 76	A. G. O.

INSPECTOR GENERAL'S DEPARTMENT

Name, grade, date of rank & highest brevet rank	Service		Born	Attached to
	In the armies of U. S. or foreign states	In the National Guard		

INSPECTORS GENERAL

Colonels

Chapin, William Henry, 4 nov. 15 brevet brigadier general, 8 july 16	lt. col. 65 N. Y. inf., 1 may 98 to 19 nov. 98	1 lt. 65 inf............22 mar. 80 adj. 74 inf........ 5 nov. 81 maj............13 aug. 83 resigned........... 8 may 84 adj. 1 lt. 65 inf.....22 mar. 86 lt. col............28 jan. 92 a. d. c. to gov....... 1 jan. 99 relieved...........17 jan. 00 insp. staff maj. gen. com. N. G. lt. col. with o. r........ 9 jan. 00 col.................27 feb. 02 supn., reassigned....21 jan. 08 insp. gen. lt. col.....30 jan. 08 insp. gen. col........ 4 nov. 15 accepted........... 8 nov. 15	N. Y... 16 may 56	hdqrs. div.

Majors

Farquharson, James Hammill, 2 may 11	2 lt. 9 N. Y. inf., 23 july 98 to 15 nov. 98	pvt., corp. co. F, 74 inf...............12 mar. 94 to 16 june 97 bat. adj. 1 lt. 74 inf..16 june 97 cap. (F)............ 7 june 00 a. d. c. 4 brig. cap. with o. r........10 mar. 05 supn., reassigned....21 jan. 08 1 lt. 65 inf..........17 july 08 supn. own request det. aide staff c. g. 4 brig...........31 july 08 insp. gen. maj....... 2 may 11 accepted........... 2 may 11	N. Y... 25 apr. 74	hdqrs. 4 brig.

JUDGE ADVOCATES

Lieutenant Colonel

From the retired list Ladd, William Whitehead, 25 feb. 98 bvt. col 21 may 01	....	asst. j. a. g., S. N. Y. lt. col.........25 feb. 87 resigned............29 may 88 asst. j. a. g., S. N. Y. col.................26 jan. 91 j. a. div., N. G. lt. col. 25 feb. 98 of the N. G. with o. r. 5 apr. 98 supn., reassigned....21 jan. 08 j. a. lt. col.........30 jan. 08	N. Y... 24 sep. 52	hdqrs. div.

Majors

Lawyer, George, 28 feb. 01	....	pvt. tr. A.......... 2 apr. 89 to 31 may 90 j. a. maj. 3 brig......28 feb. 01 supn., reassigned....21 jan. 08 j. a. maj...........30 jan. 08	N. Y... 24 sep. 64	hdqrs. 3 brig.
Sanford, Henry Gansevoort, 2 july 13	....	pvt. tr. 3, sq. A.....22 mar. 97 to 1 june 99 j. a. maj............ 2 july 13 to r. l............. 1 may 14 reassigned.......... 1 may 14	N. Y... 29 aug. 71	hdqrs. 1 brig.
Kincaid, James Leslie, 30 june 15	mustered into u. s. ser.....30 june 16 out 22 dec. 16	pvt., tr. D..........26 apr. 04 to 19 sep. 04 pvt., corp., sgt., 1 sgt., tr. D........ 8 oct. 04 hon. dis.......... 6 may 09 pvt., 1 sgt.......... 6 may 09 hon. dis.......... 5 may 10 pvt. tr. D.......... 6 may 10 to 5 july 11 2 lt. tr. D.......... 5 july 11	N. Y.... 28 nov 85	hdqrs. div.

INSPECTOR GENERAL'S DEPARTMENT — (Continued)

Name, grade, date of rank & highest brevet rank	Service		Born	At- tached to
	In the armies of U. S. or foreign states	In the National Guard		

Name, grade, date of rank & highest brevet rank	In the armies of U. S. or foreign states	In the National Guard	Born	At- tached to
JUDGE ADVOCATES — (Continued)				
Majors — (Continued)				
Kincaid, James Leslie — (Continued)	....	trs. 1 cav.......... 28 dec. 11 det. aide staff di- vision commander. 8 may 12 to 20 nov. 14 1 lt. 1 cav......... 2 aug. 12 trs. 2 cav......... 5 nov. 13 assigned 1 cav...... 10 dec. 13 maj..........30 june 15 accepted......... 2 july 15		
QUARTERMASTER CORPS				
Colonel				
Townsend, Arthur Far- ragut, 18 aug. 16	....	pvt., corp., co. F, 7 inf............... 5 mar. 87 hon. dis.......... 3 oct. 92 pvt., corp.; tr. 1, sq. A, sgt. maj. sq. A ..25 mar. 01 to 22 mar. 06 2 lt. (1)...........23 mar. 06 cap..............14 may 07 dep. qm. gen. lt. col.. 8 may 12 qm. corps.......... 1 nov. 14 col............... 7 dec. 14 accepted......... 8 dec. 14 placed on r. l....... 8 mar. 16 lt. col. qm. c ......19 june 16 col...............19 aug. 16 accepted..........21 aug. 16	Mass... 17 may 65	hdqrs div.
Lieutenant Colonels				
Sternberger, Henry Sher- man, 28 june 16	2 lt. 22 N. Y. inf., 9 may 98 1 lt......25 sep. 98 1 lt. and reg. qm., 14 oct. 98 to 23 nov. 98 mustered into u. s. ser.....30 june 16	pvt. co. E, 22 inf..... 7 june 89 hon. dis.........11 june 98 bat. qm. 1 lt. 22 inf..22 july 95 cap. comy. of sub.... 6 feb. 99 cap. c. of e........23 jan. 08 dep. comy. gen. lt. col.............. 5 june 12 accepted.......... 6 june 12 qm. corps.......... 1 nov. 14 lt. col............28 june 16 accepted..........28 june 16	N. Y... 65	hdqrs. div.
Bostwick, Henry Anthon, 11 feb. 15 bvt. maj.....30 july 12	....	pvt. cos. B I, 7 inf., bat. qm. sgt., bat. sgt. maj........19 june 85 to 21 feb. 01 1 lt. asst. i. s. a. p....21 feb. 01 supn., reassigned....21 jan. 08 1 lt. o. d........... 7 feb. 08 cap. o. d...........29 feb. 12 cap. 7 inf.......... 1 may 14 accepted.......... 6 may 14 lt. col............11 feb. 15 accepted..........11 feb. 15	N. Y. 21 aug. 64	A. G. O.
Majors				
Hislop, Thomas Wallace, 30 june 04 bvt. lt. col.... 6 may 08	corp. co. A, 2 N. Y. inf....2 may 98 1 lt. bat. adj., 23 may 98 to 2 nov. 98 mustered into u. s. ser.....30 june 16	pvt., corp., sgt., 6 sep. co.............. 7 may 83 to 11 july 93 2 lt.............11 july 93 1 lt............. 8 feb. 94 1 lt. i. s. a. p. 13 bat. with o. r..........12 apr. 98 cap. i. s. a. p. 2 inf...25 nov. 98 comy. of sub. with o. r...........16 feb. 04 maj...............30 june 04 qm. maj...........11 jul. 11 accepted........ .12 july 11 qm. corps .... 1 nov. 14	N. Y... 3 nov. 61	hdqrs. 3 brig.

INSPECTOR GENERAL'S DEPARTMENT —(Continued)

Names, grade, date of rank & highest brevet rank	Service		Born.	Attached to
	In the armies of U. S. or foreign states	In the National Guard		
QUARTERMASTER CORPS — (Continued)				
Majors — (Continued)				
Steers, Alfred Ernest; 22 dec. 04 bvt. lt. col....18 feb. 14	....	2 lt. (K) 14 inf......27 sep. 86 1 lt...............15 nov. 86 resigned............ 6 june 88 1 lt. (B) 14 inf......16 apr. 89 cap. (G) 32 inf....15 may 90 maj. 32 inf.......... 7 jan. 91 resigned...........17 mar. 92 pvt. co. H, 13 inf....19 may 92 to 14 mar. 93 insp. rifle practice cap. 13 inf............14 mar. 93 resigned...........14 aug. 94 asst. insp. rifle practice, 1 lt. 14 inf....14 oct. 95 cap. comy. of sub....15 feb. 00 qm. 2 brig. maj......22 dec. 04 supn., resigned....21 jan. 05 qm. maj............ 6 feb. 09 qm. corps.......... 1 nov. 14	N. Y... 20 mar. 00	hdqrs. 2 brig
Foley, Frank Joseph, 18 mar. 12	....	2 lt. 12 inf..........16 mar. 08 1 lt................. 3 dec. 08 cap................ 8 may 09 qm. maj...........18 mar. 12 accepted...........18 mar. 12 qm. corps.......... 1 nov. 14	N. Y... 23 june. 84	hdqrs. 1 brig.
Ahern, Charles Joseph, 1 oct. 15	mustered into u. s. ser.....30 june 16 out 10 aug. 16	mus. f. m. 22 inf., corp. co. I........30 apr. 00 hon dis.........12 nov. 06 pvt. 3 batty........28 sep. 07 to 3 june 08 2 lt. 12 inf.......... 3 june 08 1 lt...............26 mar. 09 accepted...........29 mar. 09 assigned aide 1 brig.. 6 mar. 12 maj. qm. corps...... 1 oct. 15 accepted............ 1 oct. 15	N. Y... 14 sep. 81	hdqrs. 1 brig.
Gibson, Walter Fraser, 24 jan. 16 Graduate, Garrison Schools, 1915.	mustered into n. s. ser....30 june 16	1 lt. co. C, 74th inf... 7 mar. 06 cap. 74 inf....... 7 apr. 09 accepted.........12 apr. 09 a. d. c. to gov....... 1 jan. 11 to 31 dec. 12 major...........24 jan. 16 accepted...........25 jan. 16	N. Y. 20 sep. 76	Div.
Breed, Carl H., 23 june 16	mustered into u. s. ser.....30 june 16 out 9 oct. 16	pvt. 29 sep. 00......10 may 99 to 5 apr. 01 2 lt................ 5 apr. 01 1 lt................ 7 aug. 07 relieved from duty 3 inf., det. aide 4 brig............. 2 dec. 11 major qm. c.......28 june 16 accepted...........28 june 16	N. Y... 21 july 77	hdqrs. 4 brig.
Ringer, Frederick Charles, 23 june 16 bvt. maj ....31 mar. 05	1 lt. bat. adj. 22 N. Y. inf. 9 may 98 to 23 nov. 98 mustered into u. s. ser.....30 june 16 out 9 oct. 16	pvt., corp., sgt. co. B, 22 inf............ 7 oct. 78 hon. dis........... 1 feb. 90 pvt., sgt., 1 sgt. co. B, 22 inf........10 july 91 to 19 feb. 94 2 lt..............19 feb. 94 bat. qm. 1 lt. 22 inf..29 oct. 96 cap., reg. qm........ 5 july 00 cap. c. of e.........23 jan. 08	N. Y. 23 nov. 63	22d engs.

8

INSPECTOR GENERAL'S DEPARTMENT — (Continued)

Name, grade, date of rank & highest brevet rank	Service		Born	Attached to
	In the armies of U. S. or foreign states	In the National Guard		

QUARTERMASTER CORPS — (Continued)

Majors — (Continued)

Name, grade, date of rank & highest brevet rank	In the armies of U. S. or foreign states	In the National Guard	Born	Attached to
Ringer, Frederick Charles — (Continued)	....	r. l. and re-assigned..24 dec. 14 cap. qm. corps....... 1 june 15 accepted........... 2 june 15 major.............28 june 16 accepted...........28 june 16		
Shanton, Thomas Harry, 25 july 16	mustered into u. s. ser.....24 sep. 16	pvt. co. E, 69 inf....30 nov. 01 to 5 aug. 02 1 lt. (C), 69 inf...... 5 aug. 02 cap. qm. corps.....21 dec. 14 accepted...........26 dec. 14 major.............25 july 16 accepted...........25 july 16	Wyo. 25 sep. 68	field train
Captains				
Millard, Jesse Alvro, 7 dec. 14	mustered into u. s. ser..... 4 july 16	pvt., corp., 3 sep. co.12 dec. 05 to 4 may 07 2 lt................ 4 may 07 1 lt. 1 inf........... 1 june 10 cap. qm. corps..... 7 dec. 14 accepted........... 8 dec. 14	N. Y. 5 feb. 80	div. field bakery
Farrell, Joseph William, 20 june 16	mustered into u. s. ser.....13 july 16 out 20 july 16	pvt. co. E, 71 inf.... 7 may 01 dropped for removal.10 jan. 02 taken up from dropped co G 22 engs.. 3 jan. 06 regtl. c. sgt.........23 mar. 06 post c. sgt.......... 5 feb. 08 post q. m. sgt....... 1 sep. 09 qm. sgt. qm. c...... 1 nov. 14 f. and h. dis........ 7 may 15 re-enlisted same date sgt. 1 cl...........19 may 15 cap. qm. c.........20 june 16 accepted...........20 june 16	West Point N. Y... 17 feb. 76	Div.
Monis, Raymond Thomas, 20 june 16	mustered in co. D, 201 N. Y. Vols inf.....17 july 98 corporal..17 july 98 qm. sgt...18 jan 99 mustered out 3 apr 99 mustered into u. s. ser.....30 june 16	pvt. co. E, 23 inf.... 6 june 98 qm. sgt.............23 sep. 07 post c. sgt.........14 jan. 13 qm. sgt. f. & h. dis... 5 june 15 re-enlisted........... 6 june 15 cap. qm. c.........20 june 16 accepted...........20 june 16	N. Y. 25 sep. 80	Div.
Loree, James T. 21 june 16	mustered into u. s. ser.....30 june 16 out 22 dec. 16	cap. qm. c.........21 june 16 accepted...........21 june 16	Ind.... 6 apr. 71	Div.
Nellis, Merwyn Humphrey, 23 aug. 16	mustered into u. s. ser.....24 sep. s. 16	pvt. tr. B........... 6 jul. 08 hon. dis........... 2 feb. 10 pvt., corp., sgt., co. A, 10 inf........ 1 dec. 10 to 1 feb. 12 2 lt. 10 inf.......... 1 feb. 12 1 lt...............31 jan. 13 accepted........... 3 feb. 13 captain...........23 aug. 16 accepted...........23 aug. 16	N. Y... 10 aug. 85	field train
First Lieutenants				
Kerwin, John F. 25 july 16	....	pvt. co. B, 10 inf....25 sep. 12 corp.............. 4 feb. 14 1 lt. qm. c........25 july 16 accepted...........25 jul. 16	Blk'yn. N. Y. 21 feb. 87	

INSPECTOR GENERAL'S DEPARTMENT — (*Concluded*)

Name, grade, date of rank & highest brevet rank	Service		Born	At-tached to
	In the armies of U. S. or foreign states	In the National Guard		
QUARTERMASTER CORPS — (*Continued*)				
Majors				
Waterbury, Frederick Martin, 22 nov. 09	mustered into u. s. ser. 30 june 16 out 22 dec. 16	pvt., corp., sgt., 22 sep. co.......... 5 feb. 91 to 8 may 96 2 lt............... 8 may 96 cap. 122 sep. co.....17 may 98 supn............... 9 dec. 98 assigned to duty, acting asst. i. s. a. p. 2 inf...........15 nov. 00 relieved...........17 apr. 01 assigned to duty acting asst. i. s. a. p. 2 inf..........19 june 01 cap. i. s. a. p. 2 inf...26 apr. 04 supn., reassigned.....21 jan. 08 cap. o. d...........24 feb. 08 maj................27 nov. 09 accepted.........30 nov. 09 assigned staff div. commander, o. o., maj.............. 1 jan. 13	N. Y... 11 may 68	hdqrs. div.
Bird, Harrison Kerr, 24 dec. 12	....	2 lt. (D), 171 inf.... 3 june 98 supn.............. 3 jan. 99 assigned to duty (I), 71 inf............26 jan. 00 military secretary to gov., maj........ 1 jan. 01 reappointed with o. r. 1 jan. 03 a. d. c. to gov., col... 2 jan. 05 resigned...........21 dec. 06 maj. o. d..........24 dec. 12 accepted...........26 dec. 12	N. Y. 20 dec. 74	hdqrs. 1 brig.
Barker, John Hammond, 11 feb. 13	....	pvt. corp. 18 sep. co.23 jan. 05 to 9 aug. 06 1 lt. asst. i. s. a. p. 2 inf.............. 9 aug. 06 supn., reassigned....21 jan. 08 1 lt. o. d...........24 feb. 08 1 lt. 2 inf...........21 june 09 cap. o. d...........13 jan. 10 maj. o. d..........11 feb. 13 accepted...........12 feb. 13	N. Y... 28 oct. 77	hdqrs. 3 brig.
Tumbridge, John William, 4 june 14	....	maj. eng. 2 brig.....20 june 98 supn. reassigned.....21 jan. 08 maj. c. of e......... 6 feb. 08 retired...........24 sep. 10 maj. o. d.......... 4 june 14 accepted.......... 8 june 14	N. Y... 9 oct. 70	hdqrs. 2 brig.

DIVISION SUPPLY TRAIN
(Attached to Division Headquarters)

Mustered in September 20, 1916.

Mustered into United States Service, September 24, 1916; recognition extended by War Department under Act of June 3, 1916, on June 29, 1916.

FIRST ARMORED MOTOR BATTERY
(Attached to Division Headquarters)
216 Fort Washington Avenue, New York City
Authorized December 1, 1915
Mustered in March 18, 1916

Name, grade, date of rank and highest brevet rank	Line No.	Service		Born
		In the armies of U. S. or foreign states	In the National Guard	
Captain Montgomery, Henry Granville, 3 feb. 16	2	....	2 lt. 12 inf..............21 feb. 14 accepted..............25 feb. 14 cap.................... 3 feb. 16 accepted.............. 4 feb. 16	D. C. 8 june 80
Second Lieutenant Hubbell, George W. Jr., 22 mar. 16	...	....	pvt. tr. A, sq. A......... 2 oct. 03 trs. tr. C, 1 cav.......... 2 feb. 12 f. and h. dischg..........29 mar. 15 2 lt. 1 a. m. bty..........22 mar. 16 accepted..............24 mar. 16	N. J. 25 aug. 78

MEDICAL DEPARTMENT
FIRST FIELD HOSPITAL
(Attached to Division Headquarters.)
56 West Sixty-sixth Street, New York City
Mustered in as Field Hospital March 14, 1906
Designation changed to First Field Hospital, Jan. 19, 1911

SECOND FIELD HOSPITAL
(Attached to Division Headquarters.)
195 Washington Avenue, Albany
Authorized December 10, 1910, as the First Ambulance Company
Reorganized, Nov. 29, 1911, as the Second Field Hospital

THIRD FIELD HOSPITAL
(Attached to Division Headquarters.)
355 Marcy Avenue, Brooklyn
Authorized May 5, 1916
Recognition extended by War Department under Act of June 3, 1916, on
July 25, 1916

FOURTH FIELD HOSPITAL
(Attached to Division Headquarters.)
216 Fort Washington Avenue, New York City
Mustered in September 22, 1916
Recognition extended by War Department under Act of June 3, 1916, on
September 22, 1916

FIRST AMBULANCE COMPANY
(Attached to Division Headquarters.)
State Armory, 227–241 Washington Street, Binghamton
Authorized Nov. 29, 1911

SECOND AMBULANCE COMPANY
(Attached to Division Headquarters.)
State Armory, 920 Main Street, East, Rochester
Authorized Dec. 20, 1911

THIRD AMBULANCE COMPANY
(Attached to Division Headquarters.)
56 West Sixty-sixth Street, New York City
Mustered in January 29, 1912

FOURTH AMBULANCE COMPANY
(Attached to Division Headquarters.)
State Armory, West Jefferson Street, Syracuse
Mustered in November 10, 1915

Name, grade, date of rank & highest brevet rank	Service		Born	Attached to
	In the armies of U. S. or foreign states	In the National Guard		
MEDICAL CORPS				
Lieutenant Colonel				
Terriberry, William Stotenborough. 9 aug. 13 Army Field Service School, Medical Officers, 1912. Fort Leavenworth, Kan.	asst. surg. 1 lt. 2 N. J. inf...15 may 98 to 30 sep. 98 acting asst. surg. U. S. A... 1 oct. 98 to 11 apr. 99 mustered into u. s. a. ser.....30 june 16 out 22 dec. 16	asst. surg. 12 inf. cap............. 1 nov. 02 surg. f. h. maj....... 9 jan. 06 supn., reassigned....21 jan. 08 surg. maj...........30 jan. 08 maj. m. c...........17 may 09 lt. col. m. c......... 9 aug. 13 accepted...........12 aug. 13	N. J... 3 july 71	hdqrs. div.

MEDICAL DEPARTMENT — (Continued)

Name, grade, date of rank & highest brevet rank	Service		Born	Attached to
	In the armies of U. S. or foreign states	In the National Guard		
MEDICAL CORPS — Continued Majors				
Dye, Daniel Chauncey, 8 june 07	acting asst. surg. U. S. A...14 nov. 98 to 24 feb. 99	pvt. corp. 44 sep. co.. 8 may 88 to 18 oct. 90 asst. surg. 1 lt......18 oct. 90 asst. surg. cap. 4 bat. 26 may 99 supn................1 may 05 asst. surg. 1 inf. cap. with o. r..........5 may 05 surg. 1 inf. maj......8 june 07 supn., reassigned....21 jan. 08 surg. maj..........6 feb. 08 maj. m. c..........17 may 09 accepted..........24 june 09	N. Y... 23 june 60	1 inf.
Hotchkiss, Henry Thomas, 29 feb. 08	....	asst. surg. cap. 47 inf..............23 july 99 supn., reassigned....21 jan. 08 surg. maj..........11 mar. 08 maj. m. c..........17 may 09 accepted..........23 aug. 09	N. Y... 22 june 63	47 inf.
Kevin, John Richard, 30 dec. 09	mustered into u. s. ser..... 2 july 16	pvt. Lacrosse light inf. N. G. Wis..... 7 feb. 80 to 5 oct. 81 asst. surg. 14 inf. N. G. N. Y. cap...25 apr. 06 supn., reassigned....21 jan. 08 asst. surg. cap.......11 feb. 08 cap. m. c..........17 may 09 maj................13 jan. 10 accepted..........17 jan. 10	Wis.... 8 sep. 63	23 inf.
Connell, Carl, 31 may 11	mustered into u. s. ser.....26 june 16 out 6 oct. 16	asst. surg. cap....... 9 nov. 08 cap. m. c..........17 may 09 maj................31 may 11 accepted.......... 6 june 11	Neb... 4 july 78	71 inf.
Montgomery, Walter Clark 7 oct. 11	mustered into u. s. ser..... 2 july 16	asst. surg. cap.......30 dec. 08 cap. m. c..........17 may 09 accepted..........23 aug. 09 maj.............. 7 oct. 11 accepted..........10 oct. 11	N. Y... 19 may 78	12 inf.
Maloney, Edward Robert, 27 jan. 10	mustered into u. s. ser.....30 june 16 out 22 dec. 16	asst. surg. 9 inf. cap..............28 sep. 07 supn., reassigned....21 jan. 08 asst. surg. cap......11 feb. 08 cap. m. c..........17 may 09 maj................27 jan. 12 accepted..........29 jan. 12	Conn. 6 feb. 74	Div.
Corbett, Stratford Francis, 11 feb. 13	mustered into u. s. ser.....30 june 16	pvt. hosp. corps, sgt., sgt. 1 class, 1 bat. f. a..............21 june 10 to 14 mar. 12 1 lt. m. c..........14 mar. 12 maj................11 feb. 13 accepted..........13 feb. 13	N. Y... 6 mar. 73	2 f. a.
Gaus, Louis Herbert, 27 mar. 13	mustered into u. s. ser.....10 july 16	pvt. 22 sep. co.......30 july 06 to 24 nov. 06 1 lt. m. c..........25 apr. 11 maj................27 mar. 13 accepted..........31 mar. 13	N. Y... 7 aug. 84	2 f. h.

MEDICAL DEPARTMENT — (Continued)

Name, grade, date of rank & highest brevet rank	Service		Born	Attached to
	In the armies of U. S. or foreign states	In the National Guard		
MEDICAL CORPS — Continued				
Majors — Continued				
Percy, William Wellesley, 20 may 13	pvt. co. C, 3. N. Y. inf..... 1 may 98 trs. hosp. corps, U. S. A.; assigned to 2 div. 2 army corps...18 june 98 trs. co. C, 3 N. Y. inf.....11 sep. 98 mustered out, 30 nov. 98 mustered into u. s. ser..... 5 july 16 out 5 oct. 16	pvt. 41 sep. co.......18 apr. 98 hon. dis...........30 dec. 98 asst. surg. 8 sep. co., 1 lt.............. 9 mar. 06 supn., reassigned....21 jan. 08 asst. surg. 1 lt.......11 mar. 08 cap. m. c..........17 may 09 maj.................20 may 13 accepted..........21 may 13	N. Y. 31 jan. 74	3 inf.
Dunseith, John Franklin, 1 oct. 13	mustered into u. s. ser.....28 june 16 out 25 oct. 16	pvt. lance corp. f. h. .25 nov. 07 to 15 mar. 09 asst. surg. 1 lt.......15 mar. 09 1 lt. m. c..........17 may 09 cap................18 mar. 12 maj............. 1 oct. 13 accepted.......... 9 oct. 13	N. Y. 27 oct. 75	1 f. h.
Bebee, Edwin Lorendus, 18 mar. 14	mustered into u. s. ser.....	asst. surg. 74 inf., cap., 23 may 04 supn., reassigned....21 jan. 08 asst. surg., cap......24 feb. 08 cap. m. c..........17 may 09 maj.................18 mar. 14 accepted..........19 mar. 14	N. Y. 29 oct. 70	74 inf.
Harnden, Frank, 18 may 14	mustered into u. s. ser..... 5 oct. 16	pvt. h. c., 13 arty. dist............ 5 oct. 13 to 19 june 12 1 lt. m. c..........19 june 12 maj.................18 may 14 accepted..........19 may 14	N. Y. 3 feb. 86	4 f. h.
Wadhams, Robert Pelton, 19 may 14	mustered into u. s. ser.....28 june 16 out 15 nov. 16	1 lt. m. c.......... 6 mar. 12 maj.................19 may 14 accepted..........20 may 14	Conn... 10 jan. 79	1 f. a.
Maguire, Thomas Francis, 13 june 14	mustered into u. s. ser..... 6 july 16	asst. surg. 69 inf., cap., 28 may 02 supn., reassigned....21 jan. 08 asst. surg., cap......21 feb. 08 cap. m. c..........17 may 09 maj.................13 june 14 accepted..........19 june 14	N. Y. 27 oct. 69	69 inf.
Purdy, Sylvanus, 11 nov. 14	....	asst. surg. 11 sep. co., 1 lt..............26 sep. 06 supn., reassigned....21 jan. 08 asst. surg., 1 lt......31 jan. 08 cap. m. c..........30 nov. 09 maj.................11 nov. 14 accepted..........12 nov. 14	N. Y. 20 dec. 76	10 inf.
Fowler, Edmund Prince, 16 mar. 15	mustered into u. s. ser.....26 june 16 out 12 dec. 16	pvt., corp., co. B, 7 inf., sgt., co. B, 7 inf., asst. hosp. stwd., sgt. h. c. sgt. 1 class....... 5 may 92 to 10 jan. 11 1 lt. m c.............10 jan. 11 cap................11 jan. 14 accepted..........19 jan. 14 maj.................16 mar. 15 accepted..........18 mar. 15	N. Y. 19 dec. 72	7 inf.

MEDICAL DEPARTMENT — (Continued)

Name, grade, date of rank & highest brevet rank	Service		Born	At-tached to
	In the armies of U. S. or foreign states	In the National Guard		

MEDICAL CORPS — Continued

Majors — Continued

Lipes, Harry Judson,
25 may 15

mustered into u. s. ser...... 1 july 15
out 23 oct 16

pvt. 1 sep. co.......12 apr. 39
hon. dis............. 3 jan. 98
pvt., corp., co. A,
116 bat.......... 9 may 98
hon. dis...........15 mar. 99
pvt. co. A, 10 bat....21 may 02
to 6 june 03
asst. surg. 1 lt. 10
inf...............3 dec. 08
1 lt. m. c..........17 may 09
cap............28 nov. 11
accepted........... 6 dec. 11
maj..............25 may 15
accepted...........25 may 15

Ill..... 29 dec. 71

2 inf.

Lyons, John James,
3 june 15

mustered into u. s. ser..... 2 aug. 16
out 11 oct. 16

seaman, 3 div. 2 bat.
N. M., tre. h. c., 1
class petty off.....14 june 97
hon. dis...........18 nov. 07
1 lt. m. c. N. G. N.
Y...........11 oct. 09
cap...........19 oct. 12
accepted........21 oct. 12
maj..............3 june 15
accepted........... 4 june 15

N. Y... 25 apr. 76

14 inf.

Pilcher, James Taft,
3 july 15

mustered into u. s. ser.....28 june 15

pvt. tr. 5, sq. C.....14 jan. 05
to 26 mar. 06
2 mar. 08
to 20 apr. 08
7 nov. 10
to 29 oct. 13
16 feb. 14
to 15 may 14
1 lt. m. c..........15 may 14
accepted..........16 may 14
maj.............. 3 jul. 15
accepted........... 5 jul. 15

N. Y... 31 mar. 80

1 cav.

Steers, William Henry,
6 apr. 16

mustered into u. s. ser.....30 june 16
out accepted.
22 dec. 16

1 lt. m. c..........14 mar. 11
cap..............17 mar. 14
accepted..........19 mar. 14
major.......... 6 apr. 16
accepted........... 8 apr. 16

N. Y... 23 jun. 69

Div.

Slee, Arthur Waller,
21 july 16

mustered into u. s. ser..... 4 july 16
out 19 Oct. 16

pvt., corp., sgt. 3
1 batty..........26 feb. 94
hon. dis.........20 mar. 99
lt. m. c.......... 8 dec. 13
accepted..........15 dec. 13
major....21 july 16
accepted..........21 july 16

Pa.... 28 feb. 84

3 f. h.

Hinds, Robert Watson,
21 july 16

mustered into u. s. ser..... 5 aug. 16

1 lt. m. c..........21 jun. 12
cap........... 3 nov. 15
rank from.........21 jun. 15
accepted..... 4 nov. 15
major.............21 july 16
accepted...........7 aug. 16

Iowa.. 7 mar. 81

3 f. h.

Captains

Muren, George Morgan,
7 mar. 00

acting asst. surg. u. s. a.. .27 mar. 99
to 11 dec. 99
mustered into u. s. ser..... 4 apr. 16

asst. surg., cap. 47
inf.............. 7 mar. 00
asst. surg. f. h. cap.
with o. r.........19 mar. 06
supn., reassigned...21 jan. 08
asst. surg. cap....19 feb. 08
cap. m. c.........17 may 09
accepted..........21 jun. 09

N. Y... 4 oct. 69

47 inf.

MEDICAL DEPARTMENT — (Continued)

Name, grade, date of rank & highest brevet rank	Service		Born	Attached to
	In the armies of U. S. or foreign states	In the National Guard		

MEDICAL CORPS — Continued

Captains — Continued

Sears, Frank Walker, 30 mar. 07	mustered into u. s. ser..... 3 july 16 out 24 oct. 16	pvt., sgt., 1 sgt. 30 sep. co.......... 1 mar. 78 to 8 mar. 81 1 lt................ 8 mar. 81 resigned............24 apr. 83 asst. surg. 1 lt. 6 batty...........23 apr. 96 1 lt. 6 batty, with o. r............26 feb. 02 resigned..........19 dec. 05 asst. surg. 1 inf. cap.............30 mar. 07 supn., reassigned....21 jan. 08 asst. surg. cap....... 6 feb. 08 cap. m. c..........17 may 09 accepted...........14 jun. 09	N. Y... 16 aug. 57	1 amb. co.
Addy, Arthur Rockwell, 25 may 07	mustered into u. s. ser.....26 june 16 out 6 oct. 16	asst. surg. 71 inf. cap., 25 may 07 supn., reassigned....21 jan. 08 asst. surg. cap....... 7 feb. 08 cap. m. c..........17 may 09 accepted...........10 aug. 09	Ohio... 18 aug. 70	71 inf.
Stivers, Moses Ashby, 13 july 07	mustered into u. s. ser.....26 july 16	pvt. 24 sep. co...... 9 dec. 90 to 20 feb. 92 27 may 92 to 2 jan. 93 11 june 94 to 6 oct. 94 pvt. 124 sep. co., trs. 24 sep. co. corp....19 may 98 to 10 aug. 00 asst. surg. 1 lt.......10 aug. 00 asst. surg. 1 inf. cap..13 july 07 supn., reassigned.....21 jan. 08 asst. surg. cap....... 6 feb. 08 cap. m. c..........17 may 09 accepted...........16 june 09	N. Y... 14 nov. 72	1 inf.
Bishop, Eliot, 29 feb. 08	....	pvt. hosp. corps, asst. hosp. stwd., sgt. hosp. corps, 13 inf. 2 apr. 07 to 4 mar. 08 asst. surg. cap....... 4 mar. 08 cap. m. c..........17 may 09 accepted...........10 aug. 09	N. Y... 18 jan. 80	2 f. a.
Dunseith, James Gracey, 31 dec. 12	mustered into u. s. ser.....28 june 16 out 25 oct. 16	Pvt. 1 class pvt. f. h. 3 dec. 07 to 28 dec. 09 1 lt. m. c..........28 dec. 09 cap................ 2 jan. 13 accepted........... 6 jan. 13	N. Y... 17 apr. 80	12 inf.
Rodden, Hugh Aloysius, 3 jan. 13	mustered into u. s. ser..... 2 aug. 16 out 11 oct. 16	pvt., tr. 8, sq. C.....13 jan. 08 to 8 feb. 08 pvt. tr. 8, sq. C.....22 mar. 08 to 28 dec. 09 1 lt. m. c..........28 dec. 09 cap................29 jan. 13 accepted...........13 feb. 13	N. Y... 9 jul. 78	14 inf.
Hooks, Don Melville, 9 june 13	mustered into u. s. ser.....10 july 16	pvt. h. c., sgt. h. c., 20 sep. co......... 3 dec. 03 to 7 june 10 1 lt. m. c.......... 7 june 10 cap................ 9 june 13 accepted...........12 june 13	N. Y... 29 mar. 88	1 amb. co.

MEDICAL DEPARTMENT — *(Continued)*

Name, grade, date of rank & highest brevet rank	Service — In the armies of U. S. or foreign states	In the National Guard	Born	Attached to
MEDICAL CORPS — *Continued*				
Captains — Continued				
Lawrence, George James Joseph, 17 july 14	mustered into u. s. ser.....28 june 16 out 10 mar. 16	pvt. 17 sep. co......28 dec. 08 to 17 july 11 1 lt. m. c...........17 july 11 cap...............17 july 14 accepted...........22 july 14	N. Y... 25 july 81	12 inf.
Hall, Edward William, 27 mar. 09	....	asst. surg. cap...... 2 apr. 09 accepted........... 9 apr. 09 cap. m. c...........17 may 09 accepted...........19 july 09	N. Y... 17 june 64	8 c. d. c.
Simonds, Grant H., 17 may 09	....	asst. surg. 1 lt. 29 sep. co..........27 june 95 supn., reassigned....21 jan. 08 asst. surg. 1 lt...... 3 mar. 08 cap. m. c...........17 may 09 accepted...........18 june 09	N. Y... 3 may 65	3 inf.
Boswell, Charles Oliver, 17 may 09 Army Field Service School, Medical Officers, 1915, Fort Leavenworth, Kan.	mustered into u. s. ser..... 3 july 16 out 27 dec. 16	pvt. 1 sep. co......23 dec. 99 to 9 mar. 00 asst. surg. 1 lt...... 9 mar. 00 supn., reassigned....21 jan. 08 asst. surg. 1 lt...... 9 mar. 08 cap. m. c...........17 may 09 accepted...........15 june 09	N. Y... 16 aug. 71	2 amb. co.
Cranston, William Johnston, 17 may 09	mustered into u. s. ser.....oct. 5, 16	asst. surg. 33 sep. co. 1 lt..............17 mar. 04 supn., reassigned....21 jan. 08 asst. surg. 1 lt...... 6 feb. 08 cap. m. c...........17 may 09 accepted...........29 june 09	N. Y... 21 jan. 66	10 inf.
Babcock, Archer Dorval, 17 may 09	....	pvt. tr. D..........26 apr. 04 to 5 may 04 asst. surg. 1 lt...... 5 may 04 supn., reassigned....21 jan. 08 asst. surg. 1 lt...... 5 feb. 08 cap. m. c...........17 may 09 accepted........... 6 aug. 09	N. Y... 16 feb. 70	1 cav.
Turnbull, Raymond Alexander, 23 may 09	mustered into u. s. ser..... 5 july 16 out 5 oct. 16	pvt. 30 sep. co.....18 oct. 04 to 23 may 06 asst. surg. 1 lt......23 may 06 supn., reassigned....21 jan. 08 asst. surg. 1 lt......11 mar. 08 cap. m. c...........11 oct. 09 accepted...........15 oct. 09	N. Y... 29 aug. 80	3 inf.
Parker, Jason Samuel, 3 aug. 10	mustered into u. s. ser..... 5 oct. 16	asst. surg. 49 sep. co. 1t.............3 aug. 08 supn., reassigned....21 jan. 08 asst. surg. 1 lt......31 jan. 08 1 lt. m. c...........17 may 09 cap...............13 oct. 10 accepted...........19 oct. 10	N. Y... 18 apr. 79	10 inf.
Augustin, George William, 13 nov. 12	....	1 lt. m. c...........12 nov. 09 cap............... 4 dec. 12 accepted........... 7 dec. 12	N. J... 14 nov. 76	1 inf.
Albertson, Harvey Sprague, 5 apr. 13	mustered into u. s. ser..... 5 july 16 out 5 oct. 16	1 lt. m. c........... 1 apr. 10 cap............... 5 apr. 13 accepted........... 7 apr. 13	N. Y... 14 dec. 75	3 inf.

MEDICAL DEPARTMENT — (*Continued*)

Name, grade, date of rank & highest brevet rank	Service		Born	At-tached to
	In the armies of U. S. or foreign states	In the National Guard		

MEDICAL CORPS — *Continued*

Captains — Continued

Name, grade, date of rank & highest brevet rank	In the armies of U. S. or foreign states	In the National Guard	Born	At-tached to
Salisbury, Lucius Albert, 7 mar. 14	mustered into u. s. ser.....26 june 16 out 6 oct. 16	pvt. co. B, 1 inf. N. G. R. I.........29 oct. 02 hon. dis.. . .....20 may 04 pvt. co. M, 23 inf., N. G. N. Y....... 9 may 10 to 28 feb. 11 1 lt. m. c.........28 feb. 11 cap.............. 7 mar. 14 accepted..........13 mar. 14	N.Y... 1 jan. 82	71 inf.
Schaefer, Arthur Charles, 27 apr. 14	mustered into u. s. ser..... 2 july 16	1 lt. m. c.... ...... 25 apr. 11 cap.............27 apr. 14 accepted.........29 june 14	N.Y... 25 jan. 83	74 inf.
Maeder, John Samuel, 5 jan. 15	....	1 lt. m. c.........30 dec. 11 cap.............. 5 jan. 15 accepted..........11 jan. 15	N.Y... 2 june 81	9 c. d. o.
Gillen, Henry Blacklidge, 4 jan. 15	mustered into u. s. ser..... 1 july 16 out 22 oct. 16	1 lt. m. c.......... 3 jan. 12 cap.............. 4 jan. 15 accepted.......... 6 jan. 15	N.Y... 7 apr. 84	2 inf.
Allerton, Samuel Miller, 8 feb. 15	mustered into u. s. ser..... 5 july 16 out 15 nov. 16	pvt., sgt., 1 amb. co. and h. c., 1 inf..19 nov. 08 to 30 jan. 12 1 lt. m. c.........30 jan. 12 cap.............. 8 feb. 15 accepted..........17 feb. 15	N.Y... 16 aug. 81	1 f. a.
Lynn, Charles Willard, 6 mar. 15	mustered into u. s. ser.....28 june 16 out 10 nov. 16	1 lt. m .c......... 5 mar. 12 cap.............. 6 mar. 15 accepted.......... 8 mar. 15	N.Y... 3 nov. 78	12 inf.
Latta, Jefferson Brown, 15 may 15	pvt. co. L, 202 N. Y. inf. 29 july 98 mus..... 1 aug. 98 returned to ranks, 25 aug. 98 mustered out, 15 apr. 99 mustered in u. s. ser..... 9 july 16	pvt. tr. D, trs. h. c. corp............. 2 apr. 07 hon. dis.........25 apr. 12 1 lt. m. c.........14 may 12 assigned com. med. reserve.........18 dec. 14 cap.............15 may 15 accepted..........18 may 15	N.Y... 30 july 80	4 amb. co.
Seymour, Frederick Ward, 16 may 15	....	pvt. tr. H, 1 cav .... 16 apr. 12 to 15 may 12 1 lt. m. c.........15 may 12 cap.............16 may 15 accepted..........24 may 15	Mass... 10 jun. 80	1 cav.
Richman, Raynauld Dobson, 29 may 15	mustered into u. s. ser..... 3 july 16 out 27 dec. 16	pvt. 2 amb. co....... 2 may 12 to 28 may 12 1 lt. m. c.........28 may 12 cap.............29 may 15 accepted.......... 8 june 15	N.Y... 11 oct. 85	2 amb. co.
Papen, George Washington, Jr., 1 june 15	mustered into u. s. ser.....10 july 16	1 lt. m. c.........28 may 12 cap.............. 1 june 15 accepted.......... 4 june 15	N.Y... 29 jan. 83	2 f. h.
Petersen, Leo Smith, 15 oct. 15	mustered into u. s. ser.....28 june 16 out 25 oct. 16	pvt., corp. 1 batty. f. a.24 nov.05 hon. dis...........12 dec. 10 1 lt. m. c.........15 oct. 12 cap.............. 3 nov. 15 rank from.........15 oct. 15 accepted......... 8 nov. 15	N.Y... 14 mar. 87	1 f. h.

MEDICAL DEPARTMENT — (Continued)

Name, grade, date of rank & highest brevet rank	Service		Born	At-tached to
	In the armies of U. S. or foreign states	In the National Guard		

MEDICAL CORPS — Continued

Captains—Continued

Quell, John Adam, 16 Nov. 15	....	pvt. tr. 5 and hosp. corps. sq. C......24 apr. 05 to 5 may 10 1 lt. m. c........... 5 may 10 cap.................17 may 13 hon. dis........... 8 dec. 14 1 lt. m. c........22 july 15 cap..............16 nov. 15 accepted ....22 nov. 15	N. Y... 5 sep. 81	1 cav.
Kennedy, Robert Buchanan, 11 mar. 13	mustered into u. s. ser..... 3 july 16 out 23 dec. 16	1 lt. m. c.........11 mar. 13 accepted........14 mar. 13 cap.................14 mar. 16 accepted..........17 mar. 16	N. Y... 23 aug. 85	1 a. c.
Connally, Eugene Francis, 1 july 16	mustered into u. s. ser......1 july 16 out 23 oct. 16	1 lt. m. c........... 1 july 13 accepted.......... 2 july 13 cap............... 1 july 16 accepted.......... 1 july 16	N. Y... 1 june 85	2 inf.
Ford, William M., R. L., 22 june 16	mustered into u. s. ser..... 6 july 16	asst. surg. 69 inf., cap., 5 may 03 supn., reassigned....21 jan. 08 asst. surg., cap.....21 feb. 08 cap. m. c........17 may 09 accepted.......... 7 july 09 reserve list..........25 feb 16 det. active duty as cap., 22 june 16 accepted..........22 june 16	N. Y... 30 nov. 78	69 inf.
Brown, Charles Augustus, 26 june 16	mustered into u. s. ser.....28 june 16	pvt., corp. co. K, 23 inf...............19 mar. 94 to 24 feb. 96 hon. dis............27 mar. 99 pvt. tr. C...........27 mar. 99 to 17 dec. 01 asst. surg. tr. C, 1 lt..17 dec. 01 assigned duty, acting asst. surg. sq. C...28 dec. 04 asst. surg. sq. C, cap.18 apr. 05 supn., reassigned....21 jan. 08 asst. surg., cap......10 feb. 08 cap. m. c...........17 may 09 maj.................23 jan. 12 accepted............27 jan. 12 f. h. dis............22 june 15 maj. r. l...........19 apr. 16 accepted............20 apr. 16 cap................26 june 16 accepted..........26 june 16	N. Y... 17 sep. 73	1 cav.

First Lieutenants

Oaksford, Homer Hollett, 2 oct. 13	mustered into u. s. ser..... 1 july 16 out 23 oct. 16	1 lt. m. c .... 2 oct. 13 accepted........... 8 oct. 13	N. Y... 12 aug. 88	2 inf.
Hacker, Philip Conrad, 11 nov. 13	mustered into u. s. ser.....10 july 16 out 27 dec. 16	1 lt. m. c.........11 nov. 13 accepted.........13 nov. 13	N. Y... 6 oct. 88	2 f. h.
Goldstein, Emanuel, 12 jan. 14	mustered into u. s. ser..... 5 july 16 out 30 oct. 16	pvt., corp., sgt., h. c. 22 eng........... 6 nov. 02 to 12 jan. 14 1 lt. m. c.........12 jan. 14 accepted..........19 jan. 14	N. Y... 20 mar. 86	c. of e.

MEDICAL DEPARTMENT. — (Continued)

Name, grade, date of rank & highest brevet rank	Service		Born	At-tached to
	In the armies of U. S. or foreign states	In the National Guard		

MEDICAL CORPS — *Continued*

First Lieutenants — Continued

Name, grade, date of rank & highest brevet rank	In the armies of U. S. or foreign states	In the National Guard	Born	At-tached to
Hutton, Lafferts, 22 jan. 14	mustered into u. s. ser.....26 june 16 out 2 dec. .16	pvt. co. C, 7 inf., trm co. K, corp., bat. agt. med.........30 dec. 08 to 22 jan. 14 1 lt. m. c........22 jan. 14 accepted.........23 jan. 14	N. Y... 25 may 88	7 inf.
Ackerman, Stephen Hulbert, Jr., 12 mar. 14	....	1 lt. m. c........12 mar. 14 accepted.........17 mar. 14	N. Y... 8 jul. 85	13 c.d.c.
Riley, Henry Alsop, 23 apr. 14	mustered into u. s. ser.....28 june 16	pvt. h. c. sq. A......17 dec. 09 to 23 apr. 14 1 lt. m. c........23 apr. 14 accepted.........26 apr. 14	N. Y... 23 july 87	sq. A.
Newton, Charles Irving, 28 apr. 14	mustered into u. s. ser.....28 june 16	pvt. tr. M, 1 cav.....21 mar. 14 to 28 apr. 14 1 lt. m. c........23 apr. 14 accepted.........30 apr. 14	N. Y... 5 sep. 85	1 cav.
Cooley, Elias Earl, 21 may 14	....	1 lt. m. c........21 may 14 accepted.........26 may 14	S. C... 4 jan. 90	1 inf.
Hall, George McKensie, 11 nov. 14	mustered into u. s. ser..... 2 july 16	1 lt. m. c........11 nov. 14 accepted.........12 nov. 14	Can... 27 sep. 78	74 inf.
Robertson, Ransom Smith, 2 dec. 14	mustered into u. s. ser..... 2 july 16	1 lt. m. c......... 2 dec. 14 accepted......... 8 dec. 14	N. Y... 7 nov. 87	13 c. d. c.
Clark, James Jay, 19 dec. 14	mustered into u. s. ser..... 5 july 16 out 5 oct. 16	1 lt. m. c........19 dec. 14 accepted.........22 dec. 14	N. Y... 29 jan. 89	3 inf.
Miller, George Leslie, 19 dec. 14	mustered into u. s. ser.....10 july 16 out 27 dec. 16	1 lt. m. c........19 dec. 14 accepted.........22 dec. 14	Can.... 3 july 88	3 inf.
Marsh, Edward Harvey, 31 dec. 14	mustered into u. s. ser..... 2 aug. 16 out. 11 oct. 16	corp. co. D, 2 corps cadets, M. V. M...30 oct. 03 to 10 mar. 05 1 lt. m. c., N. G., N. Y. 31 dec. 14 accepted......... 4 jan. 15	N. Y... 7 sep. 86	14 inf.
Cassebeer, Alfred Frederick, 31 dec. 14	mustered into u. s. ser..... 3 july 16 out 27 dec. 16	pvt. hosp. corps, 2 am. co..............4 dec. 14 to 31 dec. 14 1 lt. m. c........31 dec. 14 accepted..........4 jan. 15	N. Y... 31 aug. 88	2 amb. co.
Shelley, Hilton Jewell, 31 dec. 14	....	pvt., corp., sgt. co. L, inf., 21 oct. 08 hon. dis.........14 june 09 pvt., corp., sgt. hosp. det., 26 feb. 12 to 31 dec. 14 1 lt. m. c........31 dec. 14 accepted......... 2 jan. 15	Conn... 26 mar. 64	1 inf.
Malcolm, Robert, 1 apr. 15	....	1 lt. m. c......... 1 apr. 15 accepted......... 8 apr. 15	N. J... 14 sep. 86	10 inf.
O'Connor, John Henry, 20 apr. 15	....	1 lt. m. c........20 apr. 15 accepted.........26 apr. 15	N. Y... 13 june 69	9 c. d. c.

MEDICAL DEPARTMENT — (Continued)

Name, grade, date of rank & highest brevet rank	Service		Born	Attached to
	In the armies of U. S. or foreign states	In the National Guard		
MEDICAL CORPS — Continued				
First Lieutenants — Continued				
Kahn, Ulysses Silver, 22 apr. 15	mustered into u. s. ser.....3 july 16 out 24 oct. 16	1 lt. m. c..........22 apr. 15 accepted..........24 apr. 15	Switserland, 2 feb. 73	1 amb. co.
Mead, Theodore Fletcher, 24 apr. 15	mustered into u. s. ser.....28 june 16 out 15 nov. 16	1 lt. m. c..........24 apr. 15 accepted..........3 may 15	N. Y... 29 june 85	1 f. a.
von Roeder, Ludwig Robert, 3 june 15	mustered into u. s. ser.....26 june 16 out 2 dec. 16	pvt. co. B, 7 inf.....10 nov. 04 to 3 june 15 1 lt. m. c..........3 jun. 15 accepted..........4 june 15	Texas.. 30 jan. 76	7 inf.
Bles, Charles David, 12 july 15	....	1 lt. m. c..........12 july 15 accepted..........13 july 15	N. Y... 19 apr. 78	22 c.ofe.
Zacharie, Charles Cowing, 28 oct. 15	....	1 lt. m. c..........28 oct. 15 accepted..........29 oct. 15	N. Y... 11 oct. 73	10 inf.
Ballantyne, Lowyd Whitcombe, 29 oct. 15	mustered into u. s. ser.....28 june 16 out 25 oct. 16	1 lt. m. c..........29 oct. 15 accepted..........1 nov. 15	Can.... 7 apr. 87	3 inf.
Grabau, John Christopher, 4 nov. 15	....	1 lt. m. c..........4 nov. 15 accepted..........8 nov. 15	N. Y... 19 sep. 89	3 f. a.
Dunning, Ralph Henry, 12 nov. 15	....	1 lt. m. c..........12 nov. 15 accepted..........14 nov. 15	N. Y... 1 aug. 85	4 amb. co.
Truax, William Elmer, 12 nov. 15	mustered into u. s. ser.....9 july 16	1 lt. m. c..........12 nov. 15 accepted..........13 nov. 15	N. Y... 10 jan. 84	4 amb. co.
Gulick, John Duncan, 20 dec. 15	mustered into u. s. ser.....7 july 16	1 lt. m. c..........20 dec. 15 accepted..........28 dec. 15	N. J... 21 apr. 81	22 engs.
Benson, Edward George, 29 dec. 15	mustered into u. s. ser.....22 july 16	1 lt. m. c..........29 dec. 15 accepted..........30 dec. 15	N. Y... 12 oct. 82	1 aero co.
McClintock, Thomas H., 4 jan. 16	mustered into u. s. ser.....2 aug. 16 out 11 oct. 16	1 lt. m. c..........4 jan. 16 accepted..........10 jan. 16	N. Y... 7 feb. 76	14 inf.
Pawling, Jesse R., 1 feb. 16	mustered out of u. s. ser.....24 oct. 16	1 lt. m. c..........1 feb. 16 accepted..........12 feb. 16	N. Y... 23 apr. 84	1 amb. co.
Worthing, Harry J., 8 feb. 16	mustered into u. s. ser.....2 july 16	1 lt. m. c..........8 feb. 16 accepted..........9 feb. 16	N. Y... 14 apr. 88	23 inf.
Nichol, Charles F., 9 feb. 16	mustered into u. s. ser.....2 july 16	1 lt. m. c..........9 feb. 16 accepted..........15 feb. 16	N. Y... 25 dc. 89	23 inf.
Schwarts, Seymour C., 7 mar. 16	mustered into u. s. ser.....9 july 16	1 lt. m. c..........7 mar. 16 accepted..........10 mar. 16	Japan. 30 sep. 86	4 amb. co.
Moore, Francis W., 9 mar. 16	....	1 lt. m. c..........9 mar. 16 accepted..........18 mar. 16	N. Y... 19 july 87	47 inf.

MEDICAL DEPARTMENT — (Continued)

Name, grade, date of rank & highest brevet rank	Service — In the armies of U. S. or foreign states	Service — In the National Guard	Born	Attached to
MEDICAL CORPS — Continued				
First Lieutenants — Continued				
Kayser, Charles D., 22 mar. 16	mustered into u. s. ser.....26 june 16 out 6 oct. 16	1 lt. m. c..........22 mar. 16 accepted..........30 mar. 16	N. Y... 19 july 76	71 inf.
Ormsby, Elmer H., 29 apr. 16	mustered into u. s. ser..... 9 july 16	1 lt. m. c..........29 apr. 16 accepted..........29 apr. 16	N. Y... 5 jan. 90	2 inf.
Houghton, James T., 15 may 16	....	1 lt. m. c..........15 may 16 accepted..........22 may 16	N. Y... 23 july 85	69 inf.
Costigan, Leo H., 26 may 16	mustered into u. s. ser..... 5 oct. 16	1 lt. m. c..........26 may 16 accepted..........29 may 16	N. Y... 17 nov. 80	13 c. d. c.
Smith, Henry B., 6 july 16	mustered into u. s. ser.....26 july 16	1 lt. m. c.......... 6 july 16 accepted.......... 8 july 16	N. Y... 28 aug. 89	3 f. h.
Reynolds, Robert J., 7 july 16	mustered into u. s. ser.....16 july 16	1 lt. m. c.......... 7 july 16 accepted.......... 7 july 16	N. Y... 30 apr. 91	3 f. h.
McSweeney, Geo. W., 6 july 16	....	1 lt. m. c.......... 6 july 16 accepted.......... 7 july 16	N. Y... 30 apr. 89	15 inf.
Harding, Read B., 6 july 16	mustered into u. s. ser.....26 july 16	1 lt. m. c.......... 6 july 16 accepted..........11 july 16	N. Y... 1 apr. 91	3 f. h.
Cromwell, Chas. D., 24 july 16	mustered into u. s. ser..... 5 oct. 16	1 lt. m. c..........24 july 16 accepted..........24 july 16	N. Y... 10 aug. 77	4 f. h.
Stehl, Henry J., 13 sep. 16	....	1 lt. d. c..........13 sep. 16 accepted..........15 sep. 16	N. Y... 2 may 86	71 inf.
Oeder, Lambert R., 13 sep. 16	....	1 lt. d. c..........13 sep. 16 accepted..........15 sep. 16	N. J... 10 jan. 91	2 f. a.
Bamford, Austin C., 15 sep. 16	mustered into u. s. ser.....12 oct. 16	1 lt. d. c..........15 sep. 16 accepted..........19 sep. 16	N. Y... 22 oct. 76	69 inf.
Loughlin, Jos. T., 21 sep. 16	....	1 lt. m. c..........21 sep. 16 accepted..........26 sep. 16	N. Y... 21 may 92	47 inf.
Coughlin, James F., 7 oct. 16	mustered into u. s. ser.....15 nov. 16	1 lt. m. c.......... 7 oct. 16 accepted.......... 7 oct. 16	....	2 f. a.
Smith, Martin D. F., 23 sep. 16	....	1 lt. m. c..........23 sep. 16 accepted..........28 sep. 16	N. Y... 3 dec. 88	3 f. a.
Gray, Chas. P., 9 oct. 16	mustered into u. s. ser..... 2 dec. 16 out 2 dec. 16	1 lt. m. c.......... 9 oct. 16 accepted.......... 2 dec. 16	Me... 31 jan. 75	7 inf.
Warren, David D., 13 oct. 16	mustered into u. s. ser.....30 oct. 16 out 2 dec. 16	1 lt. d. c..........13 oct. 16 accepted..........14 oct. 16	N. J... 7 aug. 94	7 inf.

MEDICAL DEPARTMENT — (Concluded)

Name, grade, date of rank & highest brevet rank	Service — In the armies of U. S. or foreign states	Service — In the National Guard	Born	Attached to
MEDICAL CORPS — Continued				
First Lieutenants — Continued				
Timmeson, Earl, 23 nov. 16	....	1 lt. d. c............23 nov. 16 / accepted...........28 nov. 16	N. Y... 26 jun. 83	2 inf.
Powers, George A., 28 nov. 16	mustered into u. s. ser.....27 dec. 16	1 lt. d. c............28 nov. 16 / accepted.......... 4 dec. 16	....	3 f. h.
Girvin, Walter V., 4 dec. 16	mustered into u. s. ser..... 8 dec. 16	1 lt. d. c............. 4 dec. 16 / accepted........... 5 dec. 16	Mich... 22 jan. 82	3 f. a.
Donovan, James C., 7 dec. 16	....	1 lt. d. c........... 7 dec. 16 / accepted...........11 dec. 16	....	1 inf.
Ballantyne, Reginald M., 16 dec. 16	.	pvt. tr. B, 1 cav..... 2 may 16 / 1 lt. m. c........16 dec. 16 / accepted...........23 dec. 16	Can... 7 apr. 85	4 amb. co.
VETERINARY CORPS				
Second Lieutenants				
Goubeaud, George J., 6 may 12	....	veterinarian........ 6 may 12 / accepted...........11 may 12	N. Y... 15 june 70	2 cav.
Nimphius, Harry F., 25 mar. 14	mustered into u. s. ser.....30 june 16	veterinarian........25 mar. 14 / accepted...........31 mar. 14	N. Y... 8 may 86	2 f. a.
McAuslin, Robert A., 9 nov. 14	mustered into u. s. ser. 30 june 16	veterinarian........ 9 nov. 14 / accepted...........16 nov. 14	Scot. 1 nov. 77	2 f. a.
MacDonald, Jay, 9 july 15	....	veterinarian........ 9 july 15 / accepted...........10 july 15	Can. 24 july 87	qm. c.
Johnson, August F., 30 june 16	mustered into u. s. ser.... 30 june 16	veterinarian........30 june 16 / accepted...........30 june 16	N. Y... 1 sep. 75	1 cav.
Wermuth, John J., 3 july 16	mustered into u. s. ser..... 6 july 16	asst. veterinarian.... 3 july 16 / accepted........... 3 july 16	N. Y... 23 jan. 88	qm. c.
Anderson, Charles E., 1 aug. 16	....	asst. veterinarian.... 1 aug. 16 / accepted........... 1 aug. 16	....	hdqrs.
Causney, Frank J., 1 aug. 16	....	asst. veterinarian.... 1 aug. 16 / accepted........... 5 aug. 16	....	hdqrs.

FIRST BATTALION, SIGNAL CORPS

The Battalion has received authority to place silver rings on the lances of its colors, engraved
as follows:
On the National Color.— Spanish-American War, 1898.
On the State Color.— Buffalo, August, 1892; Brooklyn, January, 1895.

COMPANY A
(Attached to Division Headquarters)
Armory, 104 East 24th Street, New York City

COMPANY B
(Attached to Division Headquarters)
Armory, 801 Dean Street, Brooklyn

Name, grade, date of rank and highest brevet rank	Company	Service		Born
		In the armies of U. S. or foreign states	In the National Guard	
SIGNAL CORPS				
Major				
Hallahan, William Leo, 11 mar. 10	......	mustered into u. s. ser...... 3 july 16 out 23 dec. 16	pvt., corp., sgt., sgt. 1 class, 1 sig. corps. 2 dec. 01 to 30 dec. 06 1 lt. sig. corps......30 dec. 08 cap...............18 mar. 10 maj...............19 feb. 15 accepted..........23 feb. 15 chief signal officer div............. 1 mar. 15	N. Y. 24 sep. 80
Captains				
Schenk, George Edmund, 9 may 11 Honor graduate N. Y. School of the Line, 1915	B	mustered into u. s. ser...... 3 july 16 out 23 dec. 16	pvt., pvt. 1 class, corp., sgt., sgt. 1 class, 2 co. sig. corps.........17 aug. 03 to 11 jul. 10 1 lt. sig. corps......11 july 10 cap............... 9 may 11 accepted..........15 may 11	Pa. 7 nov. 80
Howe, Arthur Lenox, 30 apr. 14	bat. adj. and qm.	mustered into u. s. ser...... 3 july 16 out 23 dec. 16	pvt., pvt. 1 class, sgt. 1 sig. corps......17 jun. 01 to 8 oct. 10 1 lt. sig. corps...... 8 oct. 10 cap...............30 apr. 14 accepted.......... 4 may 14	N. Y. 19 may 80
First Lieutenants				
Maloney, Robert Walter, 25 apr. 14	A	mustered into u. s. ser...... 6 dec. 16 out 23 dec. 16	pvt., pvt. 1 class, corp., sgt, sgt. 1 class. 1 co., sig. corps........... 5 oct. 05 to 25 apr. 14 1 lt. sig. corps......25 apr. 14 accepted.........27 apr. 14	N. Y. 16 sep. 81
Watson, Herbert Leslie, 10 july 15	A	mustered into u. s. ser...... 3 july 16 out 23 dec. 16	pvt., sgt., 1 class sgt. 1 co. sig. corps.... 5 dec. 07 to 10 feb. 15 1 lt...............10 jul. 15 accepted..........12 july 15	N. H. 11 feb. 76
Steeves, Frederick Manly, 12 july 15	B	mustered into u. s. ser...... 3 july 16 out 23 dec. 16	pvt., corp., sgt., 1 class sgt. 1 co. sig. corps...........18 june 03 to 12 july 15 1 lt...............12 july 15 accepted..........12 july 15	N. Y. 15 dec. 79

FIRST BATTALION, SIGNAL CORPS — (Concluded)

Name, grade, date of rank and highest brevet rank	Company	Service		Born
		In the armies of U. S. or foreign states	In the National Guard	
SIGNAL CORPS — Continued				
First Lieutenants — Continued				
Sullivan, Jerome Benedict. 26 june 16	A	mustered into u. s. ser...... 3 july 16 out 23 dec. 16	pvt. co. A, bn. s. c...10 jan. 07 corp.............. 8 sep. 11 sergt..............28 feb. 13 1 cl. segt...........28 june 15 1 lt.................26 june 16 accepted...........26 june 16	N. Y. 28 may 89
De Baun, Lewis Henry, 1 july 16	B	mustered into u. s. ser...... 3 july 16 out 23 dec. 16	pvt. co. B, 1 bn, s. c. 7 nov. 10 1 cl. pvt............27 may 12 corp...............27 june 12 sergt............... 8 july 15 1 cl. sergt..........20 june 16 1 lt................. 1 july 16 accepted........... 1 july 16	N. J. 14 nov. 85
Ireland, Gordon, 1 july 16	B	mustered into u. s. ser...... 3 july 16 out 23 dec. 16	1 corps cadets M. V. M., 1903–1904............. pvt. co. I, 7 inf......13 oct. 05 f. & h. discharge.....24 mar. 12 pvt. co. A, 1 bn. Signal corps......24 mar. 12 pvt. 1 cl. pvt. sergt.. 1 july 16 1 lt................ 1 july 16 accepted........... 1 july 16	Mass. 23 dec. 80

FIRST AERO COMPANY

(Attached to Division Headquarters)

Armory, 104 East 34th Street, New York City

Mustered in June 22, 1916

Recognition extended by War Department under Act June 3, 1916, on June 30, 1916

Name, grade, date of rank and highest brevet rank	Service		Born
	In the armies of U. S. or foreign states	In the National Guard	
Captain			
Bolling, Raynauld C., 1 july 16	mustered into u. s. ser......july 13 16 out 23 sep. 16	pvt. squad A....... 8 feb. 07 corp...............23 dec. 10 sergt...............17 nov. 13 f. & h. dis.........20 may 14 1 lt. sig. cps........12 nov. 15 accepted............16 nov. 15 cap. 1 aero co....... 1 july 16 accepted.......... 1 july 16	Ark. 1 sep. 77
First Lieutenants			
Carolin, Norbert, 26 june 16	mustered into u. s. ser......13 july 16 out 23 sep. 16	pvt. 1 co. sig. corps..14 may 08 1 cl. pvt............22 june 10 corp...............22 apr. 13 discharged..........22 sep. 13 re-enlisted.......... 9 an. 14 1 lt. sig. corps......26 june 16 accepted..........26 june 16	N. J. 25 nov. 88
Miller, James E., 1 july 16	mustered into u. s. ser......13 july 16 out 23 sep. 16	pvt. squad. A, cav...30 apr. 06 discharged.......... 8 dec. 11 1 lt. 1st bn. s. c..... 1 july 16 accepted.......... 1 july 16	N. Y. 24 mar. 83
Thaw, Alexander B., jr., 13 july 16	mustered into u. s. ser......13 july 16 out 23 sep. 16	priv. 1 aero co......22 jun. 16 1 lt.................13 july 16 accepted...........13 july 16	Pa. 3 dec. 97

SECOND AERO COMPANY
(Attached to Division Headquarters)
Armory, 29 Masten Street, Buffalo
Mustered in June 20, 1916

Name, grade, date of rank and highest brevet rank	Service		Born
	In the armies of U. S. or foreign states	In the National Guard	
Captain			
Satterfield, John M., 1 july 16	....	cap. 2 aero co. 1 bn. signal corps........ 1 july 16 accepted........... 1 july 16	Pa. 5 aug. 76
First Lieutenants			
More, Morgan B., 1 aug. 16	....	pvt. 2 aero co. 1 lt... 1 aug. 16 accepted........... 2 aug. 16	N. Y. 3 jan. 89
Bryant, Russell W. 12 sep. 16	....	pvt. 2 aero co...... 28 jun. 16 1 cl. sergt, 1 lt......12 sep. 16 accepted...........12 sep. 16	sep. 9 84

CORPS OF ENGINEERS

Name, grade, date of rank and highest brevet rank	Company	Service		Born
		In the armies of U. S. or foreign states	In the National Guard	
CORPS OF ENGINEERS				
Majors				
Metzger, George Jacob, 15 july 98 bvt. lt. col.... 3 feb. 10	....	....	pvt. co. A, 65 inf.....10 oct. 82 to 7 dec. 82 qm. 1 lt. 65 inf...... 7 dec. 82 insp. rifle practice cap. 1 nov. 87 hon. dis..............13 dec. 92 qm. maj. 4 brig.....21 apr. 94 hon dis............. 6 june 98 eng. maj. 4 brig.....15 july 98 supn., reassigned....21 jan. 08 maj. c. of e........16 mar. 08	N. Y. 17 nov. 55
Fairchild, John Fletcher, 7 feb. 12	......	mustered out of u. s. ser......28 nov. 16	pvt. corp., sgt., 1 sgt. 11 sep. co.....11 june 00 to 20 mar. 05 2 lt................20 mar. 05 cap...............20 jan. 06 1 lt. o. d...........26 nov. 10 maj. c. of e...... 7 feb. 12 placed on r. l. and reassigned....24 dec. 14 maj. c. of e........22 jan. 15 accepted..........25 jan. 15	D. C. 22 dec. 67
Captains				
Walsh, Patrick Joseph, 17 jan. 10	....	....	pvt., corp., sgt., co. A, 22 inf......... 7 feb. 02 to 16 feb. 06 2 lt. (A), 22 eng.....16 feb. 06 2 lt. c. of e........23 jan. 08 1 lt...............29 oct. 09 cap...............24 jan. 10 a. d. c. to gov....... 1 jan. 13 to 1 jan. 15 r. l...............23 dec. 14 cap...............22 jan. 15 accepted..........23 jan. 15	Ire. 1 jan. 78
First Lieutenants				
McEwen, Alexander Milloy, 15 may 13	......	gunner, corp., 2d regt. Canadian arty 17 nov. 86 to 25 apr. 89 2 lt 31 dec. 90 lt........30 jan. 91 cap.......24 may 92 maj....... 9 aug. 94 resigned...17 aug. 95	pvt., corp., sgt., 1 sgt. co. E, 22 eng..29 sep. 02 to 11 oct. 09 2 lt. c. of e.. ......11 oct. 09 r. l...............23 dec. 14 1 lt.............22 jan. 15 accepted..........25 jan. 15	Can. 19 may 68

TWENTY-SECOND REGIMENT OF ENGINEERS

(Six Companies)

(Two Battalions)

(Attached to Division Headquarters)

Armory, 216 Fort Washington Avenue, New York City

This regiment was organized in April, 1861; it entered the United States service May 28, 1862, for three months, and was mustered out September 5, 1862, having been stationed at Washington, D. C., and later forming part of the garrison at Harper's Ferry, Va.; June 18, 1863, it was again mustered in the service of the United States for thirty days, and was mustered out July 24, 1863. In 1867 the regiment took up rifle practice as part of its drill, and in 1871 it established for itself a rifle range and system of practice which was in 1873 adopted by the National Rifle Association. Co. G was disbanded March 22, 1878, and new Co. G organized April 30, 1879. Co. F was disbanded October 10, 1890, and new Co. F organized January 8, 1891. Co. I was disbanded October 10, 1890, and new Co. I organized October 6, 1892. May 7, 1898, it was authorized to be temporarily consolidated into eight companies, and four companies of the 18th Regiment were attached to it, preparatory to entry into the United States service, into which it was mustered on May 24, 1898, as the 22d Regiment, Infantry, N. Y. Vols., and it was mustered out November 23, 1898. February 20, 1902, the regiment was constituted a regiment of engineers and designated 22d Regiment, Engineers.

By the law of May 7, 1908, the 22d Regiment became a part of the Corps of Engineers, and on Nov. 10, 1908, Companies L and M were authorized, completing the three battalion organization. The regimental organization of the Corps of Engineers, known as 22d Regiment, Corps of Engineers, and all battalions and companies, except band, were disbanded by General Orders No. 27, A. G. O., December 28, 1914.

The Engineer troops were organized into two battalions, known and designated as the 1st Battalion, Corps of Engineers, consisting of four pioneer companies (Companies A, B, C and D), and the 2d Battalion, Corps of Engineers, to consist of four ponton companies (Companies E, F, G and H). General Orders No. 2, A. G. O., January 15, 1915, changed the designation to 22d Corps of Engineers.

Reorganized and designated as 22d Regiment of Engineers by S. O. 187, September 2, 1916; and S. O. 190, September 9, 1916. Companies changed as follows: Companies B and F disbanded; Company D changed to B; Company H to Company F; Company G to Company D, by G. O. 22, 6th N. Y. Div., Sept. 4, 1916.

Recognition extended by War Department, under Act June 3, 1916, on June 26, 1916.

The regiment has received authority to place silver rings on the lances of its colors, engraved as follows:

On the National Color. — Harper's Ferry, 1862; Gettysburg Campaign, 1863; Sporting Hill, Pa., June 30, 1863; Carlisle, Pa., July 1, 1863; Spanish-American War, 1898.

On the State Color. — Draft riots, 1863; Orange riots, 1871; Buffalo, 1892; Brooklyn, 1895.

TWENTY-SECOND REGIMENT OF ENGINEERS

Name, grade, date of rank and highest brevet rank	Company	Service		Born
		In the armies of U. S. or foreign states	In the National Guard	
CORPS OF ENGINEERS				
Colonel				
Vanderbilt, Cornelius, 4 dec. 16	......	mustered into u. s. ser......30 june 16	2 lt. 12 inf. (G)......20 sep. 01 1 lt. (D)............ 2 dec. 02 a. d. c. to gov......29 sep. 03 to 31 dec. 04 cap. (F), 12 inf......11 jun. 07 supd. own request det. aide staff maj. gen. com. div. N. G......... 1 oct. 08 insp. gen. lt. col..... 1 june 12 accepted........... 1 june 12 col................ 4 dec. 16 accepted..........13 dec. 16	N. Y. 5 sep. 73

TWENTY-SECOND REGIMENT OF ENGINEERS — (Continued)

Name, grade, date of rank and highest brevet rank	Company	Service		Born
		In the armies of U. S. or foreign states	In the National Guard	
CORPS OF ENGINEERS — Continued				
Lieutenant Colonel				
Conrow, William Stevens, 5 sep. 16	......	1 lt. 22 N. Y. inf., 9 may 98 to 23 nov. 98 1 lt. 43 U. S. vol., 19 aug. 99 to 30 june 01 mustered into u. s. ser...... 7 july 16	pvt., corp., sgt., co. C, 22 inf..........14 nov. 87 hon. dis...........17 jan.93 pvt., corp., sgt., co. C, 22 inf..........17 jan. 93 2 lt. (C), 22 inf......18 mar. 98 1 lt.................24 jan. 99 resigned............ 3 oct. 99 1 lt. bat. adj. 22 eng. 2 nov. 05 1 lt. (H), 22 eng. with o. r..........16 mar. 06 cap...............30 may 07 cap. c. of e.........23 jan. 08 r. l................23 dec. 14 cap...............22 jan. 15 maj...............15 may 15 accepted..........17 may 15 lt. col............ 5 sep. 16 accepted.......... 5 sep. 16	N. J. 1 jun. 62
Captains				
Bates, Guy, 28 may 15	adj.	mustered into u. s. ser...... 4 july 16	pvt., corp., sgt., co. D, 22 eng.......... 4 jan. 04 to 8 apr. 11 2 lt. c. of e.......... 8 apr. 11 1 lt................26 mar. 12 r. l................23 dec. 14 1 lt................22 jan. 15 cap...............28 may 15 accepted ....30 may 15	N. J. 11 oct. 80
Robinson, Ernest Franklin, 2 aug. 11	D	mustered into u. s. ser...... 4 july 16	pvt., pvt. 1 class, co F, 22 regt. c. of e....11 apr. 10 to 22 july 10 2 lt. c. of e..........22 july 10 with rank from......15 july 10 1 lt................23 dec. 10 cap............... 2 aug. 11 r. l................23 dec. 14 cap...............22 jan. 15 accepted..........25 jan. 15	Iowa. 23 jun. 82
Dunn, John Joseph, 9 sep. 16 bvt. cap......11 aug. 08	supply officer	reg. qm. sgt. 22 N. Y. inf... 9 may 98 to 19 oct. 98 mustered into u. s. ser..... 7 july 16	pvt., qm. sgt., co. C, 22 inf., bat. qm. sgt., 22 inf.... ...18 july 83 to 3 may 99 1 lt. bat. qm........ 3 may 99 supn., reassigned....21 jan. 08 2 lt. c. of e......... 5 feb. 08 r. l................23 dec. 14 2 lt...............22 jan. 15 1 lt...............25 may 15 accepted..........27 may 15 captain............ 9 sep. 16 accepted..........12 sep. 16	N. Y. 7 dec. 64
Burns, Peter Francis, 26 june 16	qm.	sgt., 1 sgt., co. G, N. Y. inf., 9 may 98 to 23 nov. 98	pvt., corp., sgt., 1 sgt., co. G, 22 inf..29 jan. 92 hon. dis............ 6 oct. 99 pvt., sgt., co. G, 22 inf.............. 5 feb. 00 hon. dis...........17 mar. 05	N. J. 20 nov. 69

TWENTY-SECOND REGIMENT OF ENGINEERS — *(Concluded)*

Name, grade, date of rank and highest brevet rank	Com-pany	Service		Born
		In the armies of U. S. or foreign states	In the National Guard	
CORPS OF ENGINEERS — *Continued*				
Captains — Continued				
Burns, Peter Francis — *Continued*		....	2 lt. c. of e.. ......11 mar. 08 r. l................23 dec. 14 2 lt...... .....22 jan. 15 1 lt...............25 may 15 accepted..........31 may 15 captain............26 june 16 accepted. . ...26 june 16	
Chaplain				
First Lieutenants				
Fell, Horace Requa, 15 dec. 13	......	mustered into u. s. ser......12 sep. 16	chaplain.... .. ...15 dec. 13 r. l................23 dec. 14 chaplain.... . ...22 jan. 15 accepted..........28 jan. 15	N. Y. 73
Lane, Wm. Edw., Jr., 9 sep. 16	adjt.	mustered into u. s. ser...... 7 july 16	captain.... . . ... 9 sep. 16 accepted.......... 9 sep. 16	

FIRST BATTALION—TWENTY-SECOND REGIMENT OF ENGINEERS

Name, grade, date of rank and highest brevet rank	Company	Service		Born
		In the armies of U. S. or foreign states	In the National Guard	
FIRST BATTALION				
Major				
Garrison, Harvey, 5 sep. 16	......	pvt. U. S. M. A. detachment of cav., 22 apr. 81 to 21 apr. 86 sgt. co. C, 22 N. Y. inf..... 9 may 98 2 lt......24 may 98 to 23 nov. 98 2 lt. 47 N. Y. inf., 17 aug. 99 1 lt...... 4 nov. 99 to 2 july 01 mustered into u. s. ser...... 4 july 16 out 30 oct. 16	pvt., corp., sgt., co. C, 22 inf.........23 may 87 hon. dis.........26 oct. 96 pvt., sgt. co. C, 22 inf...............21 feb. 98 to 27 mar. 99 2 lt. (C), 22 inf......27 mar. 99 resigned............ 3 oct. 99 pvt. (C), 22 eng.... 3 aug. 03 to 1 apr. 04 2 lt. (C), 22 eng..... 1 apr. 04 1 lt................23 may 04 cap. c. of e.........19 nov. 08 r. l................23 dec. 14 cap................22 jan. 15 accepted..........25 jan. 15 maj................ 5 sep. 16 accepted.......... 5 sep. 16	N. Y. 26 mar. 60
Captains				
Dieges, Charles Joseph, 3 mar. 08	B	mustered into u. s. ser...... 7 july 16	pvt., corp., sgt., co. F, 22 eng.........27 oct. 02 to 30 mar. 06 2 lt................30 mar. 06 1 lt................18 may 06 cap. c. of e.........11 mar. 08 r. l................23 dec. 14 cap................22 jan. 15 accepted..........25 jan. 15	N. Y. 25 oct. 65
Ross, William Alexander, 5 may 13	A	pvt. co. H, 22 N. Y. inf., 24 may 98 to 23 nov. 98. mustered into u. s. ser...... 4 july 16	pvt., corp., sgt., 1 sgt., co. F, 22 inf... 7 feb. 99 to 11 jun+ 05 2 lt. 22 eng........11 jun. 06 1 lt...............20 apr. 08 hon. dis........... 1 nov. 10 2 l t c. of e........28 mar. 11 1 lt...............20 sep. 11 cap............... 5 may 13 r. l................23 dec. 14 cap. c. of e.........22 jan. 15 accepted..........26 jan. 15	N. J. 20 july 77
First Lieutenants				
Koop, Louis Dietrich, 14 june 15	A	mustered into u. s. ser...... 4 july 16 out 30 oct. 16	pvt., corp., co. F, 22 c of e.......... 5 sep. 13 to 13 apr. 14 r. l. reassigned.... 23 dec. 14 2 lt. c. of e........22 jan. 15 1 lt...............14 june 15 accepted..........15 june 15	N. Y. 30 dec. 86
Gray, Maxwell Henderson, 27 june 16	B	mustered into u. s. ser...... 4 july 16 out 30 oct. 16	pvt., 1 class pvt., corp., co. D, 22 engs........... 5 may 14 to 30 june 15 2 lt................30 june 15 accepted..........30 june 15 1 lt................27 june 16 accepted..........27 june 16	Ga. 8 dec. 87
Bregenser, Charles Emil, 27 june 16	C	mustered into u. s. ser...... 4 july 16 out 30 oct. 16	pvt. co. H, 22 c. of e.21 dec. 14 to 5 oct. 15 2 lt................ 5 oct. 15 accepted.......... 7 oct. 15 1 lt...............27 june 16 accepted..........27 june 16	Ger. 28 aug. 77

FIRST BATTALION — TWENTY-SECOND REGIMENT OF ENGINEERS — *(Continued)*

Name, grade, date of rank and highest brevet rank	Com-pany	Service		Born
		In the armies of U. S. or foreign states	In the National Guard	
FIRST BATTALION—Con-tinued				
First Lieutenants — Con-tinued				
Crimmins, Thomas, 2 july 16	A	mustered into u. s. ser...... 4 july 16 out 30 oct. 16	1 lt. c. of e......... 2 july 16 accepted ..... . 2 july 16	N. Y. 6 jan. 80
Mellen, Henry Luther, 28 june 16	B	mustered into u. s. ser...... 4 july 16 out 30 oct. 16	pvt., 1 class pvt., corp., co. D, c. of e. 9 may 14 to 30 june 15 2 lt.....30 june 15 accepted.....30 june 15 1 lt.....28 june 16 accepted.....28 june 16	Vt. 4 jan. 89
Palmer, Augustus Wright, 26 may 16	C	mustered into u. s. ser...... 4 july 16 out 30 oct. 16	pvt., 1 class pvt., corp., co. K, 22 c. of e........14 apr. 13 to 25 june 15 2 lt.....25 june 15 accepted.....28 june 15 1 lt.....26 may 16 accepted.....27 may 16	N. Y. 4 feb. 86
Second Lieutenants				
Wagner, Charles Bragdon, 27 june 16	C	mustered into u. s. ser...... 4 july 16 out 30 oct. 16	pvt., co. c., 22 c. of e., 2 lt. c. of e.....27 june 16 accepted.....27 june 16	Pa. 17 oct. 83
SECOND BATTALION				
Major				
Humphreys, Frederic Erastus, 5 sep. 16	......	cadet, U. S. M. A., 12 june 02 to 12 june 06 2 lt. U. S. C. E., 12 june 06 1 lt.......— apr. 10 to 1 aug. 10 mustered into u. s. ser...... 7 july 16	1 lt. c. of e.....10 june 15 cap.....6 dec. 15 accepted.....9 dec. 15 maj.....5 sep. 16 accepted.....5 sep. 16	N. J. 16 sep. 83
Captains				
Johnson, George Howard, 25 nov. 07	F	pvt. co. H, 22 N. Y. inf.....24 may 98 to 23 nov. 98 mustered into u. s. ser...... 7 july 16	pvt., corp., sgt., co. H, 22 inf.....22 sep. 97 to 1 feb. 06 2 lt. (H), 22 eng..... 1 feb. 06 1 lt.....26 june 07 cap i. s. a. p. 22 engr.25 nov. 07 supn., reassigned....21 jan. 08 cap. c. of e.....5 feb. 08 r. l.....23 dec. 14 cap.....22 jan. 15 accepted.....27 jan. 15	Swed. 10 dec. 77
Snyder, George D, 12 sep. 16	D	2 lt. 12 Pa. vol. inf.....26 apr. 98 mustered in, 12 may 98 asst. to chief eng., 2 army corps, 29 may 98 relieved...12 oct. 98 mustered out, 29 oct. 98 mustered into u. s. ser...... 7 july 16	pvt., corp., sgt., co. D, 12 Pa. inf.....5 jan. 94 to 7 may 98 2 lt.....7 may 98 cap.....11 dec. 99 resigned.....27 dec. 01 2 lt. r. l. N. G. N. Y.15 oct. 15 1 lt. c. of e.....21 dec. 15 accepted.....23 dec. 15 cap.....12 sep. 16 accepted.....19 sep. 16	Pa. 25 sep. 66

FIRST BATTALION — TWENTY-SECOND REGIMENT OF ENGINEERS — (Continued)

Name, grade, date of rank and highest brevet rank	Company	Service		Born
		In the armies of U. S. or foreign states	In the National Guard	
SECOND BATTALION — Continued				
Captains — Continued				
Daly, Joseph James, 13 june 13	E	mustered into u. s. ser...... 7 july 16	pvt. co. I, 22 eng. trs. co. M, pvt. 1 class, corp., sgt....21 aug. 05 to 8 apr. 11 2 lt. c. of e........ 8 apr. 11 1 lt....................28 may 12 cap..................13 june 13 r. l..................23 dec. 14 cap. c. of e.........22 jan. 15 accepted...........25 jan. 15	N. Y. 9 sep. 84
Barrett, Alexander Mo-Cook, 28 aug. 18	Bat. ajt.	Trumpeter, Astor Batty... 1 june 98 to 2 feb. 99 pvt. tr. B. U. S. cav.....11 apr. 99 to 10 apr. 02 pvt., tr. H, 15 U. S. cav.... 9 july 02 to 8 july 05 mustered into u. s. ser...... 7 july 16 out 30 oct. 16	pvt. 2 class, pvt. 1 class, sgt., 1 sgt. co. H, c. of e........20 feb. 12 to 10 june 14 2 lt................10 june 14 r. l.................23 dec. 14 2 lt................22 jan. 15 1 lt................21 dec. 15 accepted...........23 dec. 15 cap................28 aug. 16 accepted............ 1 sep. 16	Texas. 12 sep. 70
First Lieutenants				
Bobb, Clarence Henry, 5 apr. 09	F	pvt. co. C, 22 N. Y. inf......20 sep. 98 to 23 nov. 98 mustered into u. s. ser...... 7 july 16	pvt., corp., qm. sgt., co. C, 22 inf.....14 mar. 99 to 12 apr. 09 1 lt. c. of e.........12 apr. 09 r. l..................23 dec. 14 1 lt..................22 jan. 15 accepted...........25 jan. 15	Pa. 9 sep. 74
Donovan, Lawrence Collins, 14 june 15	F	mustered into u. s. ser...... 7 july 16	pvt., co. G, eng., trs. co. K, corp......11 jan. 99 to 29 may 13 2 lt. c. of e.........29 may 13 r. l..................23 dec. 14 2 lt..................22 jan. 15 1 lt..................14 june 15 accepted...........21 june 15	N. Y. 25 jul. 90
Stockwell, Norris Parmly, 22 june 15 graduate, N. Y. School of the Line, 1915.	F	mustered into u. s. ser...... 7 july 16 di	pvt., corp., co. M, 5 Ohio N. G.......13 dec. 94 s. removal....... 2 aug. 97 pvt., corp., sgt., 1 sgt., co. K, 22 c. of e............. 1 mar.04 to 10 june 14 2 lt. c. of e.........10 june 14 r. l..................23 dec. 14 2 lt..................22 jan. 15 1 lt..................22 june 15 accepted...........29 june 15	Eng. 2 jul. 73
Baker, Joseph Edwards, 27 june 16	D	seaman, U. S. N., 27 nov. 06 to 26 nov. 10 mustered into u. s. ser...... 7 july 16	2 lt. c. of e.........21 dec. 15 accepted...........29 dec. 15	D. C. 15 jan. 87

FIRST BATTALION — TWENTY-SECOND REGIMENT OF ENGINEERS — (Concluded)

Name, grade, date of rank and highest brevet rank	Company	Service		Born
		In the armies of U. S. or foreign states	In the National Guard	
SECOND BATTALION — Continued				
First Lieutenants — Continued				
Davis, Frederick A. W., 17 june 16	A	mustered into u. s. ser...... 4 july 16 out 30 oct. 16	2 cl. pvt. co. D, 22 c. of engs........... 8 nov. 15 2 lt................17 june 16 accepted........ ...19 june 16	N. Y. 14 aug. 93
Lamb, Andrew Francis, 27 june 16	B	mustered into u. s. ser.....30 july 16 out 30 oct. 16	pvt. co. B, 22 engs...24 may 15 1 cl. pvt............— apr. 16 2 lt......27 june 16 accepted...... ...27 june 16	N. Y. 24 may 92
Whittlesey, Edward B. 27 june 16	D	mustered into u. s. ser.....30 july 16 out 30 oct. 16	1 year in co. E, 8 inf Mass. Vols. pvt. co. B................27 apr. 14 corp . ... 29 may 16 2 lt . ...27 june 16 accepted...... .. . 27 june 16	Mass. 1 may 84

CAVALRY

FIRST REGIMENT

(Twelve Troops)

(Attached to Division Headquarters)

Headquarters, 1579 Bedford Avenue, Brooklyn

On March 11, 1912, the 2d Regiment of Cavalry was organized by General Orders No. 11, A. G. O., by detaching Troops C, H, I, K and M from the 1st Cavalry, which were thereupon designated Troops A, B, C, D and E, respectively. Troop F, located at West Brighton, was added April 23, 1912, and Troop G, located at Utica, on June 21, 1912.

On November 5, 1913, General Orders No. 27, A. G. O., transferred Troops B, D, H and I of 1st Cavalry to the 2d Cavalry as Troops B, D, H and I. Troops B and D, 2d Cavalry, were changed to Troops K and L by G. O. 28, A. G. O., December 10, 1913. Troop M was authorized to be organized by G. O. 27, A. G. O., November 5, 1913, and the designation of 2d Cavalry was changed to 1st Cavalry by the same order. Troop M was mustered in March 21, 1914. Troop D of this regiment performed duty at riots, Syracuse, May, 1913, and Troop I performed riot duty at Depew, N. Y., in April, 1914.

The appointive system was adopted by the 1st Cavalry, March 1, 1915, by S. O. 33, A. G. O., 1915.

Recognition extended by the War Department under Act of June 3, 1916, to Troop A, June 27; Troops B and F, I, L and Sanitary Detachment, June 26; Troops C and E, June 30; Troops D, H and M, June 24; Troops I and L, June 26; Troop C, July 9, 1916; Headquarters Troop, June 30, 1916; Machine Gun Troop, July 21, 1916; Supply Troop, Aug. 2, 1916.

The regiment has received authority to place silver rings on the lances of its colors, engraved as follows:

On the National Color.— Spanish-American War, 1898; Porto Rico, 1898; Coamo, August 9, 1898; Asomanta, August 9 to 12, 1898.

On the State Color.— Croton Dam, April, 1900; Coeymans, May, 1906.

CAVALRY — FIRST REGIMENT

Name, grade, date of rank and highest brevet rank	Company	Service		Born
		In the armies of U. S. or foreign states	In the National Guard	
CAVALRY				
Colonel				
DeBevoise, Charles I., 14 mar. 12	......	sgt. tr. C, N. Y. cav., 2 may 98; to 25 nov. 98 mustered into us. ser. 30 june 16	pvt., 1 guidon sgt., tr C. ......16 dec 95 to 27 apr. 98 2 lt ....27 apr. 98 1 lt ....18 mar. 99 cap .... 7 sep. 99 a. d. c. to gov .. 1 jan. 01 to 31 dec. 04 assigned com. sq. C..28 dec. 04 maj. sq. C......... 4 jan. 05 trs. 1 cav..........28 dec. 11 trs. 2 cav..........11 mar. 12 col. 2 cav..........14 mar. 12 accepted..........15 mar. 12 assigned 1 cav .. .10 dec. 13	N. Y. 17 oct. 72
Lieutenant Colonel				
McLeer, James Crooke, 22 mar. 15 Distinguished graduate, Garrison Schools, 1914.	......	sgt. tr. C, N. Y. cav., 2 may 98 to 25 nov. 98 mustered into u. s. ser.... .30 june 16	pvt., corp , sgt., tr. C, 16 dec. 95 to 9 feb. 99 2 lt .... 9 feb. 99 1 lt ....18 mar. 99 assigned duty sq. C. 28 dec. 04 cap. (5) sq. C...... 9 feb. 05 trs. 1 cav..........28 dec. 11 trs. 2 cav..........11 mar. 12 maj. 2 cav..........13 apr. 12 assigned 1 cav......10 dec. 13 lt. col..........22 mar. 15 accepted..........25 mar. 15	N. Y. 15 sep. 72

CAVALRY — FIRST REGIMENT — (Continued)

Name, grade, date of rank and highest brevet rank	Company	Service		Born
		In the armies of U. S. or foreign states	In the National Guard	
CAVALRY — *Continued*				
Majors				
McLeer, Edward, Jr., 3 june 15 Graduate, Garrison Schools, 1915:	......	qm. sgt., sgt., tr. C, N. Y. cav., 2 may 98 to 25 nov. 98 mustered into u. s. ser......30 june 16	pvt., qm. sgt., tr. C..16 dec. 95 to 22 apr. 99 2 lt...............22 apr. 99 1 lt............... 2 nov. 99 assigned duty sq. C..28 dec. 04 1 lt. sq.qm. sq. C, with o. r...............11 feb. 05 supn., reassigned...21 jan. 08 cap. sq. C.........18 mar. 08 trs. 1 cav.........28 dec. 11 trs. 2 cav.........11 mar. 12 assigned 1 cav......10 dec. 13 maj............... 3 june 15 accepted.......... 4 june 15	N. Y. 31 may 72
Bryant Mortimer Drake, 3 june 15 Graduate, Garrison Schools, 1914.	......	pvt. tr. C, N. Y. cav. 2 may 98 to 25 nov. 98 mustered into u. s. ser......30 june 16	pvt., corp., sgt., tr. C............... 1 nov. 97 to 9 feb. 05 1 lt. (6) sq. C...... 9 feb. 05 cap............31 july 09 trs. 1 cav.........28 dec. 11 trs. 2 cav.........11 mar. 12 assigned 1 cav......10 dec. 13 maj............... 3 june 15 accepted.......... 5 june 15	N. Y. 14 mar. 78
Tobin, Charles M., 15 nov. 16	......	mustered into u. s. ser. .... 5 dec. 16	pvt. 5 inf. Texas N. G., — —84 to — —88 cap. co. D ....to— —90 cap. 1 cav. N. G., N. Y., 26 sep. 14 accepted..........28 sep. 14 maj...............15 nov. 16 accepted..........21 nov. 16	Tex. 30 mar. 71
Captains				
Miller, Ernest Livingston, 8 nov. 11 Graduate, Garrison Schools, 1914.	B	mustered into u. s. ser.... .30 june 16	pvt., corp., sgt., 1 sgt., 3 sig. corps, pvt. tr. B......... 1 feb. 93 hon. dis........... 1 feb. 00 pvt., 1 sgt.......... 6 feb. 00 hon. dis...........15 jan. 02 2 lt...............27 jan. 02 1 lt............... 6 oct. 03 cap. 3 sq.......... 8 nov. 11 trs. 1 cav.........28 dec. 11 trs. 2 cav......... 5 nov. 13 assigned 1 cav......10 dec. 13	N. Y. 19 apr. 73
Fiala, Antony...19 jan. 12	M. G. trp.	pvt. tr. C, N. Y. cav., 2 may 98 to 25 nov. 98 mustered into u. s. ser... .30 june 16	pvt. tr. C..........12 may 98 to 18 june 00 1 lt. bat. qm. 14 inf..18 june 00 resigned........... 9 july 01 2 lt. sq. C......... 3 june 08 cap. 1 cav.........19 jan. 12 cap. 2 cav.........13 apr. 12 accepted...........15 apr. 12 assigned 1 cav......10 dec. 13	N. J. 19 sep. 69
Curie, Charles, 13 apr. 12 Graduate, Garrison Schools, 1914.	adj.	sgt. tr. C, N. Y. cav., 2 may 98 to 25 nov. 98 mustered into u. s. ser......30 june 16	pvt., corp., sgt., gui- don sgt., tr. C.....16 dec. 95 to 9 feb. 05 1 lt. sq. adj. sq. C.... 9 feb. 05 a. d. c. to gov....... 1 jan. 11 to 31 dec. 12 trs. 1 cav.........28 dec. 11 trs. 2 cav.........11 mar. 12 cap. 2 cav.........13 apr. 12 accepted...........15 apr. 12 assigned 1 cav......10 dec. 13	N. J. 4 mar. 72

CAVALRY — FIRST REGIMENT — (Continued)

Name, grade, date of rank and highest brevet rank	Company	Service		Born
		In the armies of U. S. or foreign states	In the National Guard	
CAVALRY — Continued				
Captains — Continued				
Fiske, Charles Edward, 1 may 12 Graduate, Garrison Schools, 1915.	H	pvt. tr. C, N. Y. cav., 2 may 98 to 25 nov. 98 mustered into u. s. ser...30 june 16	pvt. tr. C... .... 16 dec. 95 to 31 may 97 1 nov. 97 to 17 mar. 05 1 lt. i. a. s. p. sq. C ..17 mar. 05 supn., reassigned....21 jan. 08 1 lt. o. d..........10 feb. 08 cap.............. 1 may 12 a. d. c. to gov .. .. 1 jan. 13 to 31 dec. 14 cap., i. s. a. p .. . 1 may 14 accepted .... 6 may 14	Va. 17 oct. 69
Donovan, William Joseph, 11 oct. 12 Distinguished Graduate, Garrison Schools, 1914.	I	mustered into u. s. ser .....30 june 16	pvt. tr. I, 1 cav .... 7 may 12 to 11 oct. 12 cap. 1 cav .. ..11 oct. 12 accepted..........12 oct. 12 trs. 2 cav.......... 5 nov. 13 assigned 1 cav.. .. 10 dec. 13	N. Y. 1 jan. 83
Platt, Abner Hunter, 11 dec. 13 Distinguished Graduate, Garrison Schools, 1914.	F	mustered into u. s ser......30 june 16	pvt. tr. 6, sq. C, trs. tr. 8, corp., sgt 15 apr. 07 to 7 may 12 2 lt. 2 cav .... 7 may 12 assigned 1 cav.. .. 10 dec. 13 cap...............11 dec. 13 accepted..........13 dec. 13	Cal. 10 may 81
Donaldson, Harold Homer, 23 nov. 14 Graduate, Garrison Schools, 1915.	A	mustered into u. s. ser.... 30 jun. 16	pvt. tr C, assigned tr. 5, sq C, corp., sgt.............29 feb. 04 to 4 mar. 10 2 lt. sq. C..........4 mar. 10 trs. 1 cav..........28 dec. 11 trs. 2 cav..........11 mar. 12 1 lt. 2 cav..........25 jun. 12 assigned 1 cav.. ..10 dec. 13 cap...............23 nov. 14 accepted..........24 nov. 14	N. Y. 1 may 84
Pickard, Arthur Walker, 6 jan. 15	G	1 lt. co. E, N. Y. inf.... 1 may 98 cap...... 7 jul. 98 to 21 feb. 99 mustered into u. s. ser.....30 june 16	pvt. 24 sep. co.....16 feb. 86 hon. dis..........11 mar. 87 pvt., sgt , 44 sep. co..13 mar. 88 hon. dis............25 oct. 92 re-enlisted ... ..25 oct. 92 to 5 jun. 96 2 lt............. 5 jun. 96 1 lt.... .. ..12 nov. 97 cap............24 may 05 resigned.. . . 1 oct. 07 1 lt. 2 cav... ... ..11 oct. 12 assigned 1 cav......10 dec 13 accepted .... 7 jan. 15	Eng. 14 mar. 66
Spencer, Harry Hovey, 22 jun. 15 Graduate, Garrison Schools, 1915.	K	seaman, 2 bat. N M , N. Y. Vol., 8 jun. 98 coxswain.. 1 jul. 98 to 27 sep. 98 mustered into u. s. ser.....30 jun. 16	seaman, 3 div. 2 bat. N. M., trs. 1 div...14 jun 97 hon. dis........11 apr. 00 pvt., corp., sgt., 1 sgt,. tr. 6, sq C ...11 jul. 05 to 19 apr. 12 2 lt. 2 cav. ......19 apr. 12 1 lt............... 3 jun. 12 assigned 1 cav.....10 dec. 13 cap ....22 jun. 15 accepted..........25 jun. 15	N. Y. 11 may 80

CAVALRY — FIRST REGIMENT — (Continued)

Name, grade, date of rank and highest brevet rank	Company	Service		Born
		In the armies of U. S. or foreign states	In the National Guard	
CAVALRY — *Continued*				
Captains — Continued				
Alpers, George Frederic, 24 nov. 15	L	mustered into u. s. ser.....30 jun. 16	pvt. tr. C, assigned tr. 6, sq. C, corp., sgt., trs. pvt. tr. 8, sgt...........24 dec. 00 to 13 may 10 2 lt. sq. C.......13 may 10 trs. 1 cav...........29 dec. 11 trs. 2 cav...........11 mar. 12 1 lt. 2 cav..........10 apr. 12 assigned 1 cav......19 dec. 13 cap...............24 nov. 15 accepted..........29 nov. 15	N. Y. 27 jul. 80
King, Chester Harding, 15 july 14 Graduate, Garrison Schools, 1914.	D	mustered into u. s. ser.....30 june 16	pvt., corp., com'y sgt., tr. D, post com'y sgt., color sgt., 1 cav.............26 apr. 04 hon. dis...........5 may 10 pvt., color sgt.......6 may 10 to 12 nov. 12 2 lt. 1 cav.........12 nov. 12 trs. 2 cav........'..5 nov. 13 assigned, 1 cav...10 dec. 13 1 lt................15 july 14 accepted..........21 july 14	N. Y. 31 aug. 80
Backhouse, George Garrison, 9 feb. 16 Graduate, Garrison Schools, 1915.	C	mustered into u. s. ser......5 dec. 16	pvt., corp., sgt., sq. C................24 apr. 04 to 1 july 14 2 lt. 1 cav.........1 july 14 accepted...........8 july 14 1 lt...............24 apr. 15 accepted...........26 apr. 15 captain...........9 feb. 16 accepted..........12 feb. 16	N. Y. 21 july 80
Maclin, James Chives, Jr., 4 july 16	(Sup. ofr.)	mustered into u. s. ser......6 dec. 16	enlisted trp. C.......16 dec. 95 to 30 june 16 1 lt. 1 cav........1 july 16 accepted..........1 july 16 cap..............4 july 16 accepted..........4 july 16	Va. 21 july 69
Newton, Dallas Casper, 6 nov. 16	M	mustered into u. s. ser......5 dec. 16	pvt. co. K, 2 bat....23 apr. 01 to 10 june 03 taken up, trans. to tr. M, 1 cav........23 apr. 14 to 19 apr. 15 2 lt...............19 apr. 15 accepted..........20 apr. 15 captain.............6 nov. 16 accepted..........11 nov. 16	N. Y. 18 jan. 83
First Lieutenants				
Briggs, Benjamin Robert, 16 jan. 15	H	mustered into u. s. ser.....30 june 16	pvt., qm. sgt. 1 cav. 16 apr. 12 to 6 jan. 15 1 lt................16 jan. 15 accepted...........18 jan. 15	N. Y. 1 may q 73
Eadie, Bertram George, 10 feb. 15	F	mustered into u. s. ser.....30 june 16	pvt. co. B. 7 inf....31 mar. 04 hon. dis ....4 nov. 09 pvt. tr. F, 1 cav....23 apr. 12 to .0 feb. .5 1 lt................10 feb. 15 accepted........,....13 feb. 15	N. Y. 11 jan. 84

CAVALRY — FIRST REGIMENT — (Continued)

Name, grade, date of rank and highest brevet rank	Company	Service		Born
		In the armies of U. S. or foreign states	In the National Guard	
CAVALRY — Continued				
First Lieutenants — Continued				
Ogilvie, Donald Manson, 12 apr. 15 Graduate, Garrison School, N. Y. Service	A	mustered into u. s. ser......28 june 16	pvt. tr. 5, sq. C.....13 nov. 05 to 30 apr. 06 pvt., corp., sgt., 1 sgt.............18 mar. 07 to 1 feb. 15 2 lt................. 1 feb. 15 1 lt.............12 apr. 15 accepted..........15 apr. 15	N. Y. 19 oct. 86
Keegan, John Sloane, 6 jul. 15	K	mustered into u. s. ser......30 june 16 out 23 dec. 16	pvt. tr. C, assigned tr. 6, sq. C, corp., sgt..19 oct. 03 to 12 jul. 12 2 lt. 2 cav.........12 jul. 12 assigned 1 cav.......10 dec. 13 1 lt................. 6 july 15 accepted..........12 july .5	Eng. 25 nov. 78
Molyneux, Robert Rice, 17 july 15	sq. adj.	mustered into u. s. ser......30 june 16 out 23 dec. 16	pvt. tr. D, 1 cav., corp., sgt.........22 sep. 11 to 17 jul. 15 1 lt...............17 jul. 15 accepted..........20 jul. 15	N. Y. 9 dec. 89
Devereux, Nicholas Edward, Jr., 16 feb. 16	G	mustered into u. s. ser......30 june 16	pvt., corp., sgt., tr. G, 1 cav.........28 aug. 12 to 25 june 15 2 lt............25 june 15 accepted..........26 june 15 1 lt...............16 feb. 16 accepted..........17 feb. 16	N. Y. 16 dec. 86
Adsit, Henry, 6 nov. 16	M	mustered into u. s. ser......28 june 16	pvt. co. M, 5 inf. Md. N. G.........11 feb. 04 hon. dis.........15 dec. 04 pvt. tr. 1 cav. N. G. N. Y......... 3 may 12 to 10 dec. 12 1 lt. m. c.........10 dec. 12 cap...............22 dec. 15 rank from..........12 dec. 15 accepted..........27 dec. 15 1 lt...............10 dec. 16 accepted..........11 nov. 16	Mo. 30 jan. 80
Barnes, Harry Hamilton, 14 mar 16	D	mustered into u. s. ser......30 june 16	pvt., corp. tr. D, 1 cav...............18 sep. 07 hon. dis............12 dec. 12 pvt., sgt., 1 sgt...... 7 jan. 13 hon. dis............ 8 feb. 15 pvt............... 8 feb. 15 to 12 may 15 2 lt...............12 may 15 accepted..........14 may 15 1 lt...............14 mar. 16 accepted..........24 mar. 16	N. Y. 11 sep. 84
Olmstead, Harold Neergaard, 30 mar. 16	C	mustered into u. s. ser.. ...30 june 16	pvt., corp., sgt., sq. C..............12 mar. 06 to 24 feb. 13 pvt., sgt., 1 sgt...... 6 oct. 13 to 19 may 15 hon. dis............ 1 mar. 15 2 lt...............19 may 15 accepted..........20 may 15 1 lt...............30 mar. 16 accepted.......... 4 apr. 16	N. Y. 12 nov. 81

9

CAVALRY — FIRST REGIMENT — (Continued)

Name, grade, date of rank and highest brevet rank	Company	Service — In the armies of U. S. or foreign states	Service — In the National Guard	Born
CAVALRY — Continued				
First Lieutenant's — Continued				
Morgan, Charles Nordquist, 22 mar. 16 Graduate, Garrison Schools, 1911.	B	mustered into u. s. ser......30 june 16	pvt., corp:, sgt., tr. B, 1 cav. . . . . .26 may 10 to 20 dec. 13 hon. dis . . . . . . .20 dec. 13 2 lt.... ....16 feb. 14 accepted......19 feb. 14 1 lt . . . . .22 mar. 16 accepted. . . . .23 mar. 16	N. Y. 25 jan. 84
Hinckley, George Wright, 27 june 16	sq. adjt	mustered into u. s ser......28 june 16	pvt. tr. 8. . . . . . .24 may 09 corp. . . . . .12 dec. 10 sgt. . . . . .22 dec. 13 f. and h. dis......11 mar. 15 re-enlisted tr. i, 1 cav.11 mar. 15 warrant as sgt., contd. f. and h. dis......13 mar. 16 re-enlisted.........13 mar. 16 1 lt. squad. A, cav...27 june 16 accepted...........28 june 16	Mass. 6 nov. 80
Pearson, Charles, Jr., 30 june 16	I	mustered into u. s. ser......30 june 16	pvt., sgt., tr. I, 1 cav...............20 may 12 to 18 june 14 2 lt....... ....18 june 14 accepted...........19 june 14 1 lt.. . . . . .30 june 16 accepted...........30 june 16	N. J. 31 jul. 85
Blauvelt, Clarence H. K., 30 june 16	sq. adjt.	mustered into u. s. ser......15 dec. 16	pvt. squad. C......20 nov. 05 corp...............5 apr. 09 sergt.. . . . . .18 mar. 12 f. & h. dischg . . .5 mar.15 re-enlisted . . . . . .5 mar.15 1 sergt . . . . .19 july 15 f. & h. dis.........4 mar. 16 re-enlisted . . . . . .6 mar.16 1 lt..............30 june 16 accepted...........30 june 16	N. Y. 13 feb. 79
Harbinson, James R., 21 july 16	M. G. trp.	mustered into u. s. ser....... 5 dec. 16	Pvt. trp. F, 3 u. s. c 17 dec. 84 corp...........16 mar. 87 sergt...........12 may 88 f. & h. dis . . . .16 dec. 89 re-enlisted, 1 sergt... 1 aug. 91 f. & h. dis . . . . . . .26 jan. 99 pvt. trp. C.......31 may 01 f. & h. dis.........8 mar. 15 re-enlisted . . . . . .23 mar. 15 farrier, f. & h. dis . . .24 mar. 16 re-enlisted....25 mar. 16 1 lt. 1 cav...........21 july 16 accepted...........21 july 16	Ind. 22 feb. 62
Keevers, Edwin F., 20 nov. 16	chap.	mustered into u. s. ser...... 8 dec. 16	chaplain, 1 lt.......20 nov. 16 accepted ....22 nov. 16	
Second Lieutenants				
Gillespie, William Lane, 7 feb. 12	sq. qm. and comy.	mustered into u. s. ser......30 june 16	pvt. tr. B, sgt. maj. 3 sq. . . . . .30 apr. 08 to 7 feb. 12 2 lt. 1 cav...... .. 7 feb. 12 accepted . . . . 8 feb. 12 trs. 2 cav ... . 5 nov. 13 assigned 1 cav.......10 dec. 13	N. Y. 1 jan. 81

CAVALRY — FIRST REGIMENT — (Continued)

Name, grade, date of rank and highest brevet rank	Company	Service		Born
		In the armies of U. S. or foreign states	In the National Guard	
CAVALRY — (Continued)				
Second Lieutenants — Continued				
Loebs, Carl Herman, 26 jan. 15	H	mustered into u. s. ser.....30 june 16	pvt., corp., sgt., tr. H, 1 cav.........16 apr. 12 to 26 jan. 15 2 lt................26 jan. 15 accepted...........27 jan. 15	N. Y. 27 nov. 92
McDougall, Charles, 8 mar. 15	sup. co.	mustered into u. s. ser.....28 june 16	pvt. co. B, 7 inf.....19 june 85 to 20 oct. 97 hon. dis...........20 oct. 97 pvt...............10 may 98 to 30 sep. 98 pvt............... 8 feb. 00 to 23 jan. 02 pvt., trans. to tr. C, assigned tr. 6, sq. C, qm. sgt., trans. to tr. 8, sq. 6, regt. qm. sgt.......... 9 may 02 to 8 mar. 15 2 lt............... 8 mar. 15 accepted.......... 9 mar. 15	N. Y. 26 sep. 65
Schelling, George Louis, 30 apr. 15	A	mustered into u. s. ser......28 june 16	pvt. tr. A, 1 cav.....18 oct. 10 to 11 mar. 14 pvt., corp..........23 aug. 14 to 30 apr. 15 2 lt................30 apr. 15 accepted.......... 7 may 15	N. Y. 16 apr. 86
Black, Harley, 25 may 16	M. D.	mustered into u. s. ser... ..30 june 16	pvt. tr. D, 1 cav... 15 feb. 10 corp.............. 5 aug. 12 sergt. 1 cav.......23 may 14 f. & h. dis.........20 feb. 15 re-enlisted.........20 feb. 15 1 sergt............10 apr. 16 2 lt................25 may 16 accepted....29 may 16	N. Y. 21 nov. 85
Munro, Daniel Colin, 14 june 16	G	mustered into u. s. ser.....30 june 16	pvt. corp. G, 1...... cav............... 6 sep. 12 to 6 may 15 1 lt. m. c......... . 6 may 15 accepted..........13 may 15 2 lt................14 june 16 accepted..........16 june 16	Nova Scotia 4 jan. 82
Franchot, Charles P., 4 july 16	I	mustered into u. s. ser...... 5 dec. 16	pvt. tr. I, 1 cav..... 9 nov. 14 2 lt................ 4 july 16 accepted.......... 4 july 16	N. Y. 8 oct. 86
Raldiris, Edward J. L., 24 july 15	K	mustered into u. s. ser.....30 june 16	pvt., corp., sgt., 1 sgt. tr. 6, sq. C....16 apr. 06 to 21 july 15 2 lt................21 july 15 accepted..........24 july 15	N. Y. 20 sep. 80

CAVALRY — FIRST REGIMENT — *(Concluded)*

Name, grade, date of rank and highest brevet rank	Company	Service		Born
		In the armies of U. S. or foreign states	In the National Guard	
CAVALRY — *(Continued)*				
Second Lieutenants — Continued				
Lester, William B., 21 july 16	M G. co.	....	pvt. tr. C..... ....16 dec. 95 pvt. tr. C, N. Y. vols. 2 may 98 to 25 nov. 98 qm. sgt...........15 july 99 dis. re-enlisted.....24 may 04 assgd to tr. 5, sq. C..29 dec. 04 qm. sgt............ 8 mar. 05 1 sgt.............. 3 may 09 sgt. maj............27 may 12 regtl. sgt. maj.......12 july 15 f. & h. dis........16 mar. 15 re-enlisted.........17 mar. 15 f. & h. dis........16 mar. 16 re-enlisted.........16 mar. 16 2 lt...............21 july 16 accepted...........21 july 16	N. Y. 20 aug. 70
		mustered into u. s. ser...... 5 dec. 16		
Shants, Alson, 13 sep. 15	qm. and comy	mustered into u. s. ser. 30 june 16	pvt., corp., tr. H, 1 cav.............16 apr. 12 hon. dis.........16 apr. 15 pvt., 1 sgt........ 16 apr. 15 to 13 sep. 15 2 lt..............13 sep. 15 accepted..........15 sep. 15	Canada 19 may 81
Menzie, James Trueman, 5 dec. 16	M	mustered into u. s. ser..... 24 dec. 16	pvt. tr. M.........21 mar. 14 sgt..............18 jan. 15 2 lt............... 5 dec. 16 accepted........... 9 dec. 16	N. Y. 17 sep. 88

SQUADRON A, CAVALRY
(Four Troops)
(Attached to Division Headquarters)
Headquarters, 1889–1849 Madison Avenue, New York City

Squadron A was organized as Troop A on April 3, 1889, and performed duty at Buffalo during the switchmen's riot in August, 1892, and at Brooklyn during the motormen's riot in January, 1895. It was divided into two troops, to be known as Troops 1 and 2, and these organised into one squadron, designated Squadron A, February 9, 1895. November 27, 1896, Squadron A was divided into three troops, to be known as Troops 1, 2 and 3. Troop 4 was added May 2, 1907. The squadron was on duty at the riot at Croton Dam, April, 1900. One troop (Troop A), made up of members of the three troops of the squadron, was in United States service from May 20, 1898, to November 28, 1898.

This squadron was assigned to 1st Cavalry December 28, 1911 (G. O. 60) and the numerical designation of troops was changed January 18, 1912 (G. O. 2) to letter designation, viz.: Troops A, E, F and G.

Troops A, E, F and G, 1st Cavalry, were detached and organized as a separate squadron by General Orders No. 27, A. G. O., November 5, 1913. On December 10, 1913, the designation of Troops E, F and G, 1st Squadron, Cavalry, was changed to Troops B, C and D, respectively, by General Orders No. 28, A. G. O.

The designation of 1st Squadron, Cavalry, was changed to Squadron A, Cavalry, by General Orders 3, A. G. O., March 5, 1914. The band attached to Squadron A was mustered out December 7, 1914.

Recognition extended by War Department under Act of June 3, 1916, to Troops B, C and D. June 26, 1916; to Headquarters Troop and Troop A, June 30, 1916; to Supply Troop June 27, 1916.

The squadron has received authority to place silver rings on the lances of its colors, engraved as follows:

On the National Color.— Spanish-American War, 1898; Porto Rico, 1898; Coamo, 1898; Asomanta, 1898.

On the State Color.— Buffalo, August, 1892; Brooklyn, January, 1895; Croton Dam, April, 1900; Coeymans, May, 1906.

Name, grade, date of rank and highest brevet rank	Company	Service		Born
		In the armies of U. S. or foreign states	In the National Guard	
Major				
Wright, William Runk, 26 jan. 12	......	pvt., corp., tr. A, N. Y. cav... 2 may 98 to 28 nov. 98 mustered into u. s. ser.....30 june 16 out 28 dec. 16	pvt., corp, guidon sgt., sgt., 1 sgt., tr. 3, sq. A . . . . 2 dec. 96 to 10 nov. 02 2 lt................10 nov. 02 1 lt................11 june 07 cap. sq. A.......12 sep. 08 trs. 1 cav.........28 dec. 11 maj. 1 cav.......26 jan. 12 accepted.........26 jan. 12 assigned, 1 sq......5 nov. 13 assigned, sq. A......5 mar. 14	N. Y. 29 aug. 73
Captains				
Cowperthwait, Howard Morgan, 4 june 12 Graduate, Garrison Schools, 1914.	A	mustered into u. s. ser.... 30 june 16. out 28 dec. 16.	pvt. co. A, 23 inf, trs sq A, corp., sgt. 1 sgt ....4 oct 02 to 12 june 08 2 lt. sq. A . ....12 june 08 trs 1 cav.. ....28 dec. 11 cap. 1 cav ... 4 june 12 accepted 5 june 12 assigned, 1 sq . 5 nov. 13 assigned sq. A 5 mar. 14	N. Y. 28 july 73
Putnam, Albert William, 8 oct. 14 Distinguished Graduate, Garrison Schools, 1914.	B	mustered into u. s. ser.....30 june 16 out 28 dec. 16	pvt. tr. 1, sq. A, trs. tr 2, corp, 1 sgt.... 8 dec. 98 to 11 june 07 2 lt. (2) sq. A.. ....11 june 07 1 lt.... ....7 jun. 10 trs. 1 cav ....28 dec. 11 assigned, 1 sq......5 nov. 13 assigned, sq. A......5 mar. 14 cap. . ...8 oct. 14 accepted.. ....13 oct. 14	N. Y. 22 sep. 77

SQUADRON A — CAVALRY — (Continued)

Name, grade, date of rank and highest brevet rank	Company	Service — In the armies of U. S. or foreign states	Service — In the National Guard	Born
Captains — Continued				
Youngs, Graham, 19 june 16 Graduate, Garrison Schools, 1914.	D	mustered into u. s. ser......30 june 16 out 28 dec. 16	pvt., corp., sgt., tr. 3, sq. A, pvt. tr. L, 1 cav........26 feb. 00 hon. dis......2 feb. 12 2 lt. 1 cav ...19 feb. 12 1 lt.... 1 july 12 accepted...........2 july 12 assigned machine gun tr., 5 nov. 13 cap.................19 june 6 accepted............——16	N. Y. 26 aug. 77
Nicholas, Ridgley, 1 dec. 16	C	mustered into u. s. ser..... 13 dec. 16 out 28 dec. 16	corp. sq. A.......28 aug. 07 sergt..............10 july 11 1 sgt.............25 apr. 12 2 lt ... .14 july 16 accepted. ....14 july 16 1 lt...............3 nov. 16 accepted. . ...6 nov. 16 cap ....1 dec. 16 accepted.... .. .. 5 dec. 16	L. I. 82
First Lieutenants				
Gillespie, Samuel Hazard, 29 july 13 Graduate, Garrison Schools, 1914.	A	mustered into u. s. ser .....30 june 16 out 28 dec. 16	pvt., artif., corp., sgt., 1 sgt.. tr. 1, sq. A............25 nov. 01 to 1 july 12 2 lt. 1 cav .... . 1 july 12 1 lt...............29 july 13 accepted...........30 july 13 assigned, 1 sq....... 5 nov. 13 assigned, sq. A..... 5 mar. 14	N. Y. 16 dec. 77
Wurster, Frederick William, Jr., 16 june 14	C	mustered into u. s. ser......30 june 16 out 28 dec. 16	pvt., h. c., sq. A, cav., trs. tr. 1, corp. guidon sgt., sgt.... 5 nov. 03 hon. dis...........5 aug. 12 pvt., tr. A, 1 cav., trs. o. d.........29 june 13 to 16 june 14 1 lt., asst. i. s. a. p., sq. A..........16 june 14 accepted ....17 june 14	N. Y. 22 jan. 81
Egleston, Nathaniel Hillyer, 7 july 15	D	mustered into u. s. ser......30 june 16 out 28 dec. 16	pvt. tr. 1, sq. A, trans. tr. 4, corp., sgt., 1 sgt........18 feb. 07 to 11 mar. 15 2 lt. ....11 mar. 15 1 lt...............7 july 15 accepted...........8 july 15	N. J. 13 feb. 84
Bartholomew, Robert Bradford, 18 jan. 15	B	mustered into u. s. ser..... 30 june 16 out 28 dec. 16	pvt. hosp. corps, tr. 2, sq. A, corp., sgt., 1 sgt........10 nov. 05 to 18 jan. 15 2 lt.. ....18 jan. 15 accepted..........20 jan. 15 1 lt...............21 june 16 accepted..........23 june 16	Conn. 21 dec. 80
Second Lieutenants				
Wingham, Reginald Effingham, 8 oct. 13 Graduate, Garrison Schools, 1914.	A	mustered into u. s. ser .....30 jun 16 out 28 dec. 16	pvt. artif., corps, sgt., 1 sgt., tr. 1, sq. A .... 9 dec. 98 to 8 oct. 13 2 lt...............8 oct. 13 accepted...........9 oct. 13 assigned, sq. A...... 5 mar. 14	N. Y. 18 jan. 78

CAVALRY — SQUADRON A — *(Concluded)*

Name, grade, date of rank and highest brevet rank	Com-pany	Service — In the armies of U. S. or foreign states	Service — In the National Guard	Born
Second Lieutenants — Continued				
Cole, Milton Douglas, 3 nov. 15	D	mustered into u s. ser.... .30 june 16 out 28 dec. 16	pvt. tr. 4 sq. A, corp., sgt........28 jan. 10 hon. dis.... .. .29 june 15 pvt. tr. D, sq. A. . 30 june 15 to 3 nov. 15 2 lt.............. 3 nov. 15 accepted....... . 5 nov. 15	W. Va. 6 june 82
Cooper, Dudley M., 27 dec. 15	sq. qm and comy	mustered into u. s. ser......30 june 16 out 28 dec. 16	pvt., trumpeter, tr. 4, sq. A .... 4 dec. 08 hon. dis .... 8 dec. 11 pvt., farrier, qm., sgt., tr. G, 1 cav. .30 july 12 to 27 dec. 15 1 lt. ... . .27 dec. 15 accepted........ 28 dec. 15	N. Y. 18 july 84
Leake, Robert H., 1 dec. 16	C	mustered into u. s. ser.... .13 dec. 16 out 28 dec 16	pvt. tr. 3, sq. A..... 2 dec. 07 f. and b. dischg......17 june 15 re-enlisted.........18 june 15 discharged..........17 june 16 dropped........... 4 nov. 14 taken up......... . 4 jan. 15 corp..............25 apr. 12 corp.............22 !an. 15 sergt... ....29 apr. 15 1 sgt...........4 feb. 16 2 lt.............. 1 dec. 16 accepted.......... 5 dec. 16	N. Y. 20 oct. 83

MACHINE GUN TROOP, CAVALRY

(Attached to Division Headquarters)

Headquarters, 1389–1349 Madison Avenue, New York City

General Orders No. 27, A. G. O., November 5, 1913, authorized the organization of a machine gun troop by detaching Troop C of the 1st Cavalry.

Name, grade, date of rank and highest brevet rank	Company	Service		Born
		In the armies of U. S. or foreign states	In the National Guard	
Captain				
Sheldon, Henry, 11 june 12 Graduate, Garrison Schools, 1914.		mustered into u. s. ser.... 30 june 16 out 28 dec. 16	pvt. tr. 2, sq A, trs tr 1, trs. tr. 3, artif., corp., guidon sgt. sgt., pvt. tr. L, 1 cav... ....26 nov. 00 hon. dis . . .. 2 feb. 12 1 lt. 1 cav...... 19 feb. 12 cap ....11 june 12 accepted...........12 june 12 assigned machine gun tr.............. 5 nov. 13	N. Y. 9 oct. 74
First Lieutenant				
Whitney, Stanton, 22 june 16 Graduate, Garrison Schools, 1914.	......	mustered into u. s. ser.... .30 june 16 out 28 dec. 16	pvt., corp., sgt., tr. 3, sq. A..........27 may 01 hon. dis .... 20 may 11 pvt , 1 sgt., tr. L, 1 cav.......... 2 feb. 12 to 18 july 12 2 lt. 1 cav.. .. ...18 july 12 accepted..........22 july 12 assigned machine gun tr.......... 5 nov. 13 1 lt................22 june 16 accepted...........	Mass. 17 feb. 79
Second Lieutenant				
Hoyt, Colgate, Jr , 28 june 16	m. g. co.	mustered into u. s ser 30 june 16 out 28 dec. 16	2 lt , . accepted ... 28 june 16 28 june 16	....

FIELD ARTILLERY

FIRST REGIMENT

(Formerly Second Battalion)

(Six Batteries)

(Two Battalions)

(Attached to Division Headquarters)

Headquarters, 1988 Broadway, New York City

On August 30, 1911, the 2d Battalion, Field Artillery, composed of Batteries D, E and F, was organized by General Orders No. 31, A. G. O., from the 1st Battery, previously detached from the 1st Battalion, Field Artillery.

The late 1st Battery was organized April 3, 1867, as Battery K, 1st Regiment of Artillery. The regiment was disbanded December 10, 1869, but the battery retained as Separate Battery K, which designation was changed December 17, 1881, to 1st Battery. The battery was on duty during the railroad riots in July, 1877, and at Brooklyn during the motormen's strike in January, 1895

The First Regiment, Field Artillery, was organized from the 2d Battalion, composed of Batteries D. E and F and Separate Battery A, May 28, 1912, by G. O. 33, A. G. O. October 26, 1912, Battery A was detached and carried as a separate battery by G. O. 64, A. G. O. On the same date the headquarters 1st Battalion and Batteries A, B and C of the late 2d Field Artillery were transferred to the 1st Field Artillery to be known as the 1st Battalion and Batteries A, B and C of that regiment. Battery C was detached and designated a separate battery, November 26, 1912, by G. O. 70. A. G. O. The new Battery A was detached and designated Separate Battery B by G. O 74, December 16, 1912. General Orders No. 74, authorized the organization of two additional batteries from Battery B, 1st Field Artillery, to replace Batteries A and C, detached.

On May 19, 1913, Battery E, 2d Field Artillery, was detached and transferred to 1st Field Artillery as Battery A, 1st Field Artillery, by G. O. 16. A. G. O.

A new battery, known and designated as Battery B. was organized May 19. 1913.

Recognition extended by the War Department under Act of June 3, 1916, to Batteries E and F, June 25, 1916; to Batteries B, D, Sanitary Detachment. June 26, 1916; to the Headquarters Company. June 27, 1916.

BATTERY A. FIRST FIELD ARTILLERY

(Formerly Battery E, 2d Field Artillery)

Armory, East Jefferson Street, Syracuse

Organized August 31, 1911, by General Orders No. 33, A. G. O. On May 28, 1912, it was assigned as Battery A, 1st Field Artillery, by G. O. 33, A. G O., October 26, 1912. It was detached from the 1st Field Artillery and designated Separate Battery A, Field Artillery, by G. O. 64, A. G. O. On December 16, 1912, the battery was assigned to the 2d Battalion, Field Artillery, as Battery A, 2d Battalion, Field Artillery, by G. O. 74, A. G. O.

On May 19, 1913. the battery was changed to Battery A and transferred to 1st Field Artillery, by G. O. 16, A. G. O. The battery performed duty at riots, Syracuse, May. 1913.

Recognition extended by War Department under Act of June 3, 1916, on June 23, 1916.

BATTERY C, FIRST FIELD ARTILLERY

(Formerly Sixth Battery)

Armory, 227–235 Washington Street, Binghamton

Organized as Battery of Artillery, 28th Brigade, 6th Division. September 15, 1870. Designation changed to Battery L, December 8, 1877; designation changed to 6th Battery, December 17, 1881. Designation changed to Battery C, 1st Battalion, Field Artillery, August 30, 1911. Was designated Battery C, 2d Regiment. Field Artillery, May 28, 1912, by G. O. 33, A. G. O. Designation was changed to Battery C, 1st Regiment. Field Artillery, October 26, 1912, by G. O. 64. Was detached from 1st Regiment, Field Artillery, by G. O. 70, November 26. 1912, and designated a separate battery, to be known as Battery C, Field Artillery. On December 16, 1912, was designated Battery C, 2d Battalion. Field Artillery, by G. O. 74. The battery in August. 1892, was on duty during riot at Waverly.

Designated as Battery C, 1st Field Artillery, January 10, 1913, by G. O. 5, A. G. O.

Recognition extended by War Department under Act June 3, 1916, to Battery C, June 27, 1916.

FIELD ARTILLERY — FIRST REGIMENT — (Continued)

Name, grade, date of rank and highest brevet rank	Company	Service — In the armies of U. S. or foreign states	Service — In the National Guard	Born
FIELD ARTILLERY *Lieutenant Colonel* Smith, Merritt Haviland, 23 may 12	......	cap. 1 U. S. Vol. eng..... 7 june 98 maj...... 24 jan. 99 to 25 jan. 99 mustered into u. s. ser......28 june 16 out 15 nov. 16	pvt., corp., co. F, 7 inf.......... ...19 oct. 80 hon. dis...........19 sep. 89 pvt., corp., sgt., tr. 1 sq. A.............. 2 jan. 96 hon. dis........... 6 jan. 02 1 lt. sq. A.......... 6 jan. 02 cap................ 3 feb. 06 resigned..........24 apr. 07 cap. 1 cav......... 7 feb. 12 lt. col............23 may 12 trs. 2 cav.........10 dec. 13 assigned 1 cav......10 dec. 13 lt. col. 1 f. a.......20 oct. 14 accepted.........22 oct. 14	N. Y. 21 may 62
Majors Seymour, Charles Robert, 2 oct. 15	......	mustered into u. s. ser......28 june 16 out 15 nov. 16	pvt., corp., 20 sep. co., trs. 1 20 sep. co.29 nov. 88 to 9 june 98 1 lt............... 9 june 98 supn.........24 feb. 99 assigned duty asst. surg. 20 sep. co.. .31 mar. 99 1 lt. asst. i. s. a. p. 1 inf............. 5 feb. 03 supn............. 1 may 05 cap. i. s. a. p. 1 inf... 1 may 05 supn., reassigned....21 jan. 08 cap. o. d........... 8 feb. 08 cap. 1 bat. f. a....25 apr. 12 trs. 2 bat. f. a......16 dec. 12 a. d. c. to gov...... 1 jan. 13 to 31 dec. 14 maj.... .... 2 oct. 15 accepted.......... 6 oct. 15	N. Y. 11 mar. 70
Austin, James Edward, 2 oct. 15	......	mustered into u. s. ser..... 28 june 16 out 15 nov. 16	pvt. co. G, 9 inf... 1 apr. 02 hon. dis ....31 mar. 07 pvt., corp., sgt. 1 batty.......... 30 may 07 to 1 may 12 2 lt. 2 bat. f. a..... 1 may 12 1 lt...............17 may 12 cap. 1 f. a......... 4 nov. 12 maj.............. 2 oct. 15 accepted....... . 5 oct. 15	N. Y. 25 dec. 84
Captains Verbeck, Guido Fridolin, 19 sep. 11	A	mustered into u. s. ser...... 4 july 16 out 15 nov. 16a	2 lt. 3 inf..........17 july 11 cap. batty. A, f. a....19 sep. 11 ccepted...........22 sep. 11 trs. 2 bat. f. a.......16 dec. 12 assigned 1 f. a..... .19 may 13	N. Y. 2 may 87
Delaney, John Thomas, 4 mar. 14	E	mustered into u. s. ser...... 4 july 16 out 15 nov. 16	pvt., 1 batty., corp., sgt, batty. F, 2 bat. f. a .... 21 dec. 09 to 25 nov 12 2 lt. 1 f. a....... ...25 nov. 12 1 lt...............13 feb. 13 cap.. .... 4 mar. 14 accepted... ....10 mar. 14	N. Y. 20 june 87

FIELD ARTILLERY — FIRST REGIMENT — (Continued)

Name, grade, date of rank and highest brevet rank	Company	Service		Born
		In the armies of U. S. or foreign states	In the National Guard	
FIELD ARTILLERY — Continued				
Captains — Continued				
Reid, Raymond Macfarlane, 1 july 15	F	mustered into u. s. ser...... 4 july 16 out 15 nov. 16	pvt. 1 batty. 1 bat. f. a., trs. batty. F, 2 bat., corp. sgt....25 jan. 10 to 19 feb. 13 2 lt...............19 feb. 13 1 lt...............17 nov. 13 cap...............1 july 15 accepted..........8 july 15	N. Y. 6 sep. 90
Bowne, Francis Draper, 15 mar. 15	sup. co.	qm. sgt. tr. A, N. Y. cav. 14 apr. 98 to 28 nov. 98. mustered into u. s. ser......4 july 16 out 15 nov. 16	pvt., artif., tr. A, cav., trs. tr. 2, trs. tr. 3, qm. sgt., trs. tr. 2, artif., qm. sgt., ord. sgt., qm. sgt. ....10 apr. 04 hon. dis...........18 apr. 04 pvt., farrier, qm. sgt. tr. 4 sq. A ......8 oct. 09 to 8 dec. 11 pvt., wagoner, tr. 4, sq. A...........10 oct. 12 to 16 apr. 14 1 lt. 1 f. a..........16 apr. 14 cap....16 mar. 15 accepted..... .16 mar. 15	N. Y. 21 july 68
Perry, Alvan Williston, 6 may 15	adjt.	mustered into u. s. ser......28 june 16 out 15 nov. 16	pvt., corp. co. F, 7 inf.23 mar. 98 hon. dis...........14 apr. 03 pvt. tr. 1, sq. A, qm., tr. 4, regt. qm., sgt., regt. sgt. maj. 1 cav...........23 nov. 06 hon. dis... ... ...24 dec. 13 pvt. machine gun tr., cav., post qm. sgt. sq. A... ....16 feb. 14 to 25 apr. 14 1 lt. 1 f. a..........25 apr. 14 cap...............6 may 15 accepted..........7 may 15	Mass. 17 sep. 73
VanRaden, Benjamin, 29 nov. 15	bat. adjt.	mustered into u. s. ser......28 june 16 out 15 nov. 16	pvt. 1 batty. trs. batty. D, 2 bat. f. a. sgt...........15 may 06 to 9 dec. 12 2 lt. 1 f. a...........9 dec. 12 1 lt...............12 nov. 13 cap...............29 nov. 15 accepted..........30 nov. 15	Neb. 9 mar. 86
Blakeslee, Charles Gray, 1 dec. 15	C	mustered into u. s. ser......4 july 16 out 8 nov. 16	pvt. corp, 6 batty. 18 mar. 07 to 1 june 10 2 lt. 6 batty........1 june 10 accepted..........2 june 10 trs. 2 bat. f. a......16 dec. 12 assigned, 1 f. a......1 jan. 13 cap....... 1 dec. 15 accepted..........2 dec. 15	N. Y. 7 dec. 84
Simpson, Sylvester, 11 feb. 16	D	mustered into u. s. ser......28 june 16 out 15 nov 16	pvt., corp., 1 batty. trs. batty. F, 2 bat., sgt., trs. batty. D, 1 f. a...25 mar. 08 to 27 feb. 13 2 lt...............27 feb. 13 1 lt....... ....20 oct. 14 accepted..........27 oct 14 cap...............11 feb. 16 accepted..........12 feb. 16	N. Y. 9 sep. 89

FIELD ARTILLERY — FIRST REGIMENT —(*Continued*)

Name, grade, date of rank and highest brevet rank	Company	Service		Born
		In the armies of U. S. or foreign states	In the National Guard	

FIELD ARTILLERY — *Continued*

Captains — Concluded

Ryan, Frederick Hamilton, 8 dec. 14 17 aug. 16	bat. adjt.	mustered into u. s. ser..... 28 june 16 out 15 nov. 16	seaman, sig. div. 1 bat. N. M ... ... 1 sep. 05 hon. dis............29 mar. 11 pvt. co. M, 7 inf., trs. batty. E, 1 f. a.14 apr. 11 to 4 feb. 14 2 lt. 1 f. a........... 4 feb. 14 1 lt..... ..... 8 dec. 14 accepted..........23 dec. 14 cap...............17 aug. 16 accepted..........21 aug. 16	N. Y. 6 oct. 84
McClure, Walter Cecil, 4 apr. 16	B	mustered into u. s. ser......28 june 16 out 15 nov. 16	pvt., corp., sq. A....10 may 07 trs. tr. 3............23 jan. 08 returned to ranks, trs. tr. L, 1 cav., sgt., qm. sgt., returned to ranks....12 feb. 12 trs. batty. E, 1 f a...14 nov. 14 2 lt. 1 f. a......... 3 feb. 15 1 lt ....12 july 15 accepted..........15 july 15 cap .... 4 apr. 16 accepted.. ...... 5 apr. 16	N. Y. 21 nov. 88

First Lieutenants

Toy, Channing Rust, 16 aug. 15	B	mustered into u. s. ser .....28 june 16 out 1 nov. 16	pvt tr. 2, sq. A... ...29 apr. 08 to 2 oct. 08 pvt. tr. F, 1 cav. Ill. N. G............ 7 nov. 10 to 29 feb. 12 pvt. tr. A, sq. A, cav. N. G. N. Y....... 4 mar. 12 to 16 june 14 2 lt. 1 f. a...........16 june 14 1 lt................16 aug. 15 accepted ....25 aug. 15	Va. 20 nov. 83
Weir, Matthew S., 29 nov. 15	E	pvt., corp., batty. C, 6 f. a. U. S. A., 4 apr. 08 to 4 apr. 11 pvt., corp., trs. batty. F, 6 U. S. f. a., sgt., 3 f. a. U. S. A., 18 apr. 12 to 17 apr. 15 mustered into u. s. ser......28 june 16 out 15 nov. 16	pvt., sgt., batty. D, 1 f. a............11 may 15 to 29 nov. 15 1 lt................29 nov. 15 accepted..........30 nov. 15	N. Y. 14 sep. 89
Thomas, William Henry, 19 aug. 16	A	mustered into u. s. ser...... 4 july 16 out 1 nov. 16	pvt. co. H, 3 inf.....28 apr. 03 to 28 mar. 05 pvt. batty. A, 1 f. a..11 oct. 11 to 1 july 13 2 lt................ 1 july 13 accepted........ ... 2 july 13 1 lt. f. a..........19 aug. 16 accepted..........23 aug. 16	N. Y. 16 aug. 83
Koch, Frederick Jacob, 11 feb. 16	D	mustered into u. s. ser......28 june 16 out 15 nov. 16	pvt. 1 batty. trs. batty. D, corp.. sgt.............. 7 apr. 07 to 16 june 14 2 lt................16 june 14 accepted..........16 june 14 1 lt................11 feb. 16 accepted..........23 feb. 16	N. Y. 6 feb. 81

FIELD ARTILLERY — FIRST REGIMENT — (Continued)

Name, grade, date of rank and highest brevet rank	Company	Service — In the armies of U. S. or foreign states	In the National Guard	Born
FIELD ARTILLERY — Continued *First Lieutenants — Continued*				
Kaeppel, Arthur Edward, 24 jan. 16	C	mustered into u. s. ser...... 4 july 16 out 8 nov. 16	pvt., corp. 6 batty. f. a. .... 7 apr. 05 to 18 nov. 09 pvt., sgt. 6 batty.... 7 feb. 10 hon. dis........ .15 nov. 10 pvt. 1 f. a...... .16 nov. 10 to 21 dec. 14 2 lt 1 f. a........ .21 dec. 14 accepted.......... .26 dec. 14 1 lt. f. a. ....24 jan. 16 accepted......... 25 jan. 16	N. Y. 3 aug. 86
Gibbons, George Billings, 15 feb. 16	D	mustered into u. s. ser.... .28 june 16 out 15 nov. 16	pvt. sq. A, cav.. . .11 aug. 09 hon dis ..... .26 oct. 14 pvt. batty. E, 1 f. a. corp............22 oct. 14 to 1 feb. 15 2 lt........ ... . . 1 feb. 15 accepted........ . 4 feb. 15 1 lt.... ....15 feb. 16 accepted ....19 feb. 16	Mich 5 june 84
Russell, Robert Law, 17 aug. 16	E	mustered into u. s. ser.... .28 june 16 out 15 nov. 16	pvt. 32 co. c. a. c., trs. batty. E, 1 f. a. corp............11 dec. 08 to 4 mar. 15 2 lt. 1 f. a...... ... 4 mar. 15 accepted........... 9 mar. 15 1 lt. f. a. ....17 aug. 15 accepted.........26 aug. 16	Scotl'd, 28 mar. 81
Giles, James Harrison, 3 mar. 16	B	mustered into u. s. ser......28 june 16 out 15 nov. 16	pvt., batty. B, 1 f. a., corp., sgt .... 3 feb. 14 to 2 oct. 15 2 lt. 1 f. a.......... 2 oct. 15 accepted........... 8 oct. 15 1 lt. f. a. .... 3 mar. 16 accepted..........11 mar. 16	N. Y. 22 july 91
Michalis, Clarence Gayler, 17 aug. 16	sup. co.	mustered into u. s. ser......28 june 16 out 15 nov. 16	pvt., tr. D, sq. A ....18 feb. 14 to 21 dec. 15 2 lt.............21 dec. 15 accepted..........31 dec. 15 1 lt.............17 aug. 16 accepted..........21 aug. 16	Ohio, 85
O'Mahoney, Jeremiah William, 5 june 15 *W. D. Cert. in course No. 1 (Basic).*	B	mustered into u. s. ser......28 june 16 out 15 nov. 16	pvt., co. L, Mass. V. M............. 4 aug. 03 to 1 sep. 04 2 lt. 17 co. c. a. c..... 8 apr. 13 1 lt..... .... 5 june 15 accepted... ......10 june 15	Mass. 5 feb. 84
Sinnock, Albert James, 15 aug. 16	C	mustered into u. s. ser.......4 july 16 out 8 nov. 16	pvt. 6 batty f. a...... 3 dec. 09 corp..............19 mar. 12 retired to ranks at own request......12 may 12 assgd. musician......11 june 12 hon. dis............29 aug. 13 re-enlisted..........13 aug. 14 corp............... 3 mar. 15 2 lt................ 7 mar. 16 accepted........... 8 mar. 16 1 lt................15 aug 16 accepted..........21 aug. 16	N. Y. 30 oct 91

FIELD ARTILLERY — FIRST REGIMENT — (Concluded)

Name, grade, date of rank and highest brevet rank	Company	Service		Born
		In the armies of U. S. or foreign states	In the National Guard	

FIELD ARTILLERY — Continued

Second Lieutenants

Name, grade, date of rank and highest brevet rank	Company	In the armies of U. S. or foreign states	In the National Guard	Born
Granger, Edward Ross, 11 mar. 14	A	mustered into u. s. ser.......4 july 16 out 1 nov. 16	pvt. batty. A, 1 f a..28 sep. 11 hon. dis ...... 5 mar. 12 2 lt. 1 f. a.......... 11 mar. 14 accepted..........12 mar. 14	Mich. 6 oct. 89
Lucas, Clinton Mansfield, 12 aug. 15	D	mustered into u. s. ser...... 16 out 16	pvt. batty. D, 1 f. a. corp. ....22 apr. 14 to 12 aug. 15 2 lt. 1 f. a..........12 aug. 15 accepted..........14 aug. 15	Mass. 22 july 92
Welsh, William Peter, 2 dec. 15	B	mustered into u. s ser......28 june 16 out 1 nov. 16	pvt., corp., sgt., batty. B, 1 f. a.... 6 nov. 14 to 2 dec. 15 2 lt................. 2 dec. 15 accepted.......... 6 dec. 15	Ky. 20 sep. 89
Bettleheim, Edwin N., 21 june 16	F	mustered into u. s. ser......21 june 16 out 15 nov. 16	pvt. batty. F, 2 btn. f. a............... 2 apr. 12 lance corp..........23 jan. 13 corp...............30 jan. 13 sgt............... 2 june 14 2 lt. 1 f. a..........21 june 16 accepted..........22 june 16	N. Y. 11 apr. 87
Wotkyns, Steele, 3 july 16	C	mustered into u. s. ser...... 4 july 16 out 8 nov. 16	pvt., corp., Conn. N. G............. 4 feb. 10 to 20 nov. 12 2 lt. Conn. N. G....20 nov. 12 1 lt................24 nov. 12 hon. dis..........27 nov. 14 2 lt. 12 inf., N. G., N. Y............24 mar. 15 1 lt................25 may 15 cap................12 july 15 accepted..........13 july 15 2 lt. 1 f. a.......... 3 july 16 accepted.......... 3 july 16	Conn. 26 dec. 90
Weld, Philip B., 10 aug. 16	C	mustered out u. s. ser...... 8 nov. 16	pvt. batty. C.......12 jan. 16 corp................ 9 may 16 2 lt................10 aug. 16 accepted..........15 aug. 16	
Petersen, Fred A., 10 aug. 16	D	mustered out u. s. ser......15 nov. 16 16	pvt. batty. D, 1 f. a.23 jan. 12 f. & h. discharge....28 jan. 15 re-enlisted.......... 2 feb. 15 2 lt................10 aug. 16 accepted..........15 aug. 16	N. Y. 15 jan. 81
Whitney, Harold LeR., 17 aug. 16	E	mustered out u. s. ser......15 nov. 16	pvt. batty E........ 4 feb. 16 sgt................26 july 16 2 lt................17 aug. 16 accepted ....17 aug. 16	

FIELD ARTILLERY — (*Continued*)

SECOND REGIMENT

(Formerly First Battalion)

(Six Batteries)

(Two Battalions)

(Attached to Division Headquarters)

Armory, 165–179 Clermont Avenue, Brooklyn

Organized February 28, 1908, by General Orders No. 7, A. G. O., and composed of the 1st, 2d and 3d Batteries.

On August 30, 1011, the battalion was reorganized by General Orders No. 81, A. G. O., the 1st Battery being detached, and the 6th Battery assigned. The 2d. 3d and 6th Batteries composing the battalion, were thereupon designated as Batteries A, B and C, respectively.

Organized as a regiment from the 1st Battalion, Field Artillery, composed of Batteries A, B and C, and designated Batteries A, B and C, 2d Field Artillery, May 28, 1912, by G. O. 33, A. G. O. On October 26, 1912, regimental headquarters was disbanded and the 1st Battalion and Batteries A. B and C were transferred to the 1st Field Artillery by G. O. 64, A. G. O.

General Orders No. 5, A. G. O., January 10, 1913, organized the 2d Regiment as follows: 1st Battalion of Batteries A, B and C of Brooklyn; 2d Battalion consists of Battery D of Bronx; Battery E of Syracuse, and Battery F, unorganized. General Orders No. 16, A. G. O., May 19, 1913, transferred to 1st Field Artillery Battery E, and authorized the organization of Batteries E and F.

In accordance with the requirements of the National Defense Act, June 3, 1916, the Headquarters Company and Supply Company, were organized July 24, 1916.

Recognition extended by the War Department under Act of June 3, 1916, to Battery B, June 28, 1916; to Battery E, June 29, 1916; to Batteries A' and F, June 30, 1916; to Battery C, July 1, 1916; to Sanitary Detachments, June 26, 1916.

BATTERY D, SECOND FIELD ARTILLERY

(Formerly Second Battery)

Armory, Franklin Avenue and 166th Street, Bronx, New York City

Organized February 4, 1833, as Washington Gray Troop, Horse Artillery, part of 3d Regiment, New York State Artillery. July 27, 1847, the designation of the regiment was changed to 8th Regiment, and of the troop to Co. I; January 22, 1867, the troop was formed into a battalion of cavalry, which in 1870 was consolidated into one troop. In 1879 the troop was reorganized as Battery E, which designation was changed to 2d Battery, December 17, 1881. Designation changed to Battery A, 1st Battalion, Field Artillery, August 30, 1911. Designated Battery A, 2d Regiment, Field Artillery, May 28, 1912, by G. O. 33, A. G. O.; transferred as Battery A to the 1st Regiment, Field Artillery, by G. O. 64, A. G. O., October 26, 1912; detached from that regiment and designated Separate Battery B. Field Artillery, by G. O. 74, A. G. O., December 16, 1912. Attached to the 2d Battalion as Battery B, December 16, 1912.

The organization rendered service to the State and City of New York at the abolition riot, July 14, 1834; stevedore riot, February 24, 1836; Croton water riots, April 22 and 23, 1840; great fire, July 19, 1845; Astor Place riot, May 10, 1849; quarantine riots, September, 1858; draft riots, July, 1863; Orange riots, July 12. 1871; railroad riots, July, 1877; motormen's riot, Brooklyn, January, 1895. It was in the United States service for three months, from April 18 to July 20, 1861, and for thirty days, from June 20 to July 23, 1863; and was in action near Annapolis, Md., and Fairfax Court House in 1861; at Carlisle, Shippensburg, Scotland, Chambersburg, Oyster Point and Kingston in 1863.

Recognition extended by the War Department under Act of June 3, 1916, on June 28, 1916.

FIELD ARTILLERY — SECOND REGIMENT — *(Continued)*

Name, grade, date of rank and highest brevet rank	Company	Service		Born
		In the armies of U. S. or foreign states	In the National Guard	
FIELD ARTILLERY *Colonel*				
Wingate, George Albert, 25 june 12		mustered into u. s. ser......30 june 16 out	pvt., corp., sgt., 1 sgt. co. D, sgt. maj. 23 inf.......18 mar. 89 to 11 nov. 95 regt. adj. 1 lt.......11 nov. 95 cap.................22 may 96 a. d. c. to gov........ 1 jan. 99 to 1 jan. 01 asst. a. g. staff maj. gen. com. N. G. lt. col...............28 mar.03 supn., reassigned....21 jan. 08 a. g. lt. col.........30 jan. 08 retired............. 1 may 12 col. 2 f. a.........25 june 12 supn., assigned 1 f. a.26 oct. 12 col. 1 f. a.........31 oct. 12 assigned 2 f. a.......11 jan. 13 col. 2 f. a.........21 jan. 13 accepted...........22 jan. 13	N. Y. 24 feb. 71
Lieutenant Colonel				
Hines, Frank Harrington, 31 jan. 12 School of Fire, Fort Sill, Okla, 1913.		mustered into u. s. ser......30 june 16 out	pvt., lance corp., corp., qm. sgt. co. D, 7 inf.......13 feb. 93 to 13 apr. 08 1 lt. 1 bat. f. a......13 apr. 08 maj...............31 jan. 12 assigned to com. 2 bat. f. a.........16 dec. 12 lt. col. 2 f. a......14 jan. 13 accepted...........15 jan. 13	N. Y. 21 aug. 68
Majors				
Berry, Joseph Ignatius, 1 july 13 School of Fire, Fort Sill, Okla., 1913.		mustered into u. s. ser.... .30 june 16 out	pvt co. G, 71 inf....19 may 03 to 9 jan. 06 2 lt. 2 batty......... 9 jan. 06 1 lt...............22 may 07 cap. 1 bat. f. a...... 2 apr. 08 assigned 2 bat. f. a...16 dec. 12 assigned 2 f. a.......10 jan. 13 maj. 2 f. a......... 1 july 13 accepted........... 2 july 13	N. Y. 31 july 78
Weld, DeWitt Clinton, Jr., 7 sep. 16		mustered into u. s. ser......30 june 16	pvt., copr., sgt., 1 sgt. co. A, 23 inf... 8 mar. 87 to 16 nov. 92 2 lt. 23 inf..........16 nov. 92 1 lt............... 3 feb. 96 resigned............18 sep. 02 cap. 2 f. a........ 8 oct. 12 supn., assigned to 1 f. a..............26 oct. 12 cap. 1 f. a.........16 nov. 12 assigned 2 f. a.......11 jan. 13 cap. 2 f. a.........20 jan. 13 accepted............23 jan. 13 maj. 2 f. a......... 7 sep. 16 accepted...........11 sep. 16	N. Y. 18 july 68
Richardson, James Barbour, 20 jan. 16		mustered into u. s. ser......30 june 16	pvt., corp., guidon sgt., 2 batty....... 4 oct. 00 to 31 may 07 2 lt...............31 may 07 trs. 2 bat. f. a......16 dec. 12 assigned 2 f. a.......10 jan. 13 cap. 2 f. a.........13 aug. 13 accepted...........15 aug. 13 major..:...........20 jan. 16 accepted...........21 jan. 16	Conn. 25 aug. 75

FIELD ARTILLERY — SECOND REGIMENT — (*Continued*)

Name, grade, date of rank and highest brevet rank	Company	Service		Born
		In the armies of U. S. or foreign states	In the National Guard	
FIELD ARTILLERY — (Continued)				
Captains				
Wright, Wilbur Teed, 18 sep. 12	E	mustered into u. s. sor......30 june 16	pvt., corp., co B, 71 inf...............14 apr. 91 hon. dis............26 apr. 98 cap. 171 inf.........21 june 98 supn...............3 jan. 99 resigned............23 jan. 00 pvt. hosp. corps, 1 bat. f. a., sgt. 1 class, trs. pvt. 1 bat. f. a., sgt. maj.. 7 june 10 hon. dis............7 mar. 12 cap. 2 f. a..........18 sep. 12 supn., assigned 1 f. a..26 oct. 12 cap. 1 f. a..........16 nov. 12 assigned 2 f. a......11 jan. 13 cap 2 f. a..........20 jan. 13 accepted...........21 jan. 13	N. Y. 7 apr. 72
Hamilton, Albert Scales, 23 jan. 13	C	mustered into u. s. ser......30 june 16	pvt., corp., sgt., 3 batty...........4 feb. 01 to 14 nov. 10 2 lt. 1 bat. f. a.....14 nov. 10 1 lt................30 apr. 12 trs. 1 f. a..........26 oct. 12 cap. 2 f. a..........23 jan. 13 accepted...........27 jan. 13	N. Y. 8 july 81
Kunts, Louis Francis, 25 mar. 13	sup. co.	mustered into u. s. ser......30 june 16	pvt., sgt., qm. sgt., h. c. 1 bat. f. a....21 june 10 to 9 mar. 12 2 lt. 1 bat. f. a......9 mar. 12 1 lt................6 may 12 cap. 2 f. a..........5 sep. 12 supn...............26 oct. 12 1 lt. 1 f. a.........26 oct. 12 trs. 2 bat. f. a......10 dec. 12 assigned 2 f. a......10 jan. 13 cap 2 f. a..........25 mar. 13 accepted...........27 mar. 13	N. Y. 21 nov. 78
Richardson, William Ormiston, 18 aug. 13	F	corp. 4 batty. N. Y. arty....21 july 98 to 21 oct. 98 mustered into u. s. ser......30 june 16	pvt., 2 batty.........5 may 98 to 15 aug. 98 pvt., corp., sgt., 1 sgt., 2 batty.....16 jan. 99 to 24 jan. 08 2 lt................24 jan. 08 1 lt. 1 bat. f. a......14 may 08 assigned 2 f. a......10 jan. 13 cap. 2 f. a..........18 aug. 13 accepted...........20 aug. 13	N. Y. 6 aug. 79
Fox, Walter Parke, 24 jan. 13	A	mustered into u. s. ser......30 june 16	pvt., corp., sgt., 1 sgt., 3 batty.......15 jan. 06 to 24 jan. 13 2 lt. 2 f. a..........24 jan. 13 1 lt................8 aug. 13 cap...............5 nov. 13 accepted...........10 nov. 13	N. Y. 26 jul. 86
Fox, Lester Cecil, 7 nov. 13	B	mustered into u. s ser......30 june 16	pvt., corp., 3 batty., pvt. batty. A, 2 f. a..............9 mar. 08 to 18 mar. 13 2 lt. (B)............18 mar. 13 1 lt................30 july 13 cap...............7 nov. 13 accepted...........12 nov. 13	N. Y. 20 june 88

FIELD ARTILLERY — SECOND REGIMENT — (Continued)

Name, grade, date of rank and highest brevet rank	Company	Service — In the armies of U. S. or foreign states	Service — In the National Guard	Born
FIELD ARTILLERY — (Continued)				
Captains — Continued				
Washington, Albert Daniel, 10 apr. 16	comy.	mustered into u. s. ser......30 june 16	pvt., corp., 3 batty., acting sgt. batty. C, sgt. maj.......16 oct. 11 to 2 july 13 1 lt...............2 july 13 accepted...........3 july 13 captain............10 apr. 16 accepted..........11 apr. 16	N. Y. 12 mar. 86
Sullivan, Howard E., 21 feb. 16	D	mustered into u. s. ser......30 june 16	pvt., corp., 2 batty., trs. pvt. hdqrs., 1 bat., bat. sgt. maj..............26 jan. 08 to 26 aug. 13 2 lt. 2 f. a..........26 aug. 13 1 lt............11 feb. 14 accepted........16 feb. 14 cap............21 feb. 16 accepted........23 feb. 16	N. Y. 4 may
Marshall, Robert Waddell, 25 sep. 16	bat. adjt.	mustered into u. s. ser......30 june 16	pvt., corp., 2 batty.. 6 sep. 04 to 12 sep. 13 hon. dis..........20 oct. 11 pvt. 2 batty........20 oct. 11 to 12 sep. 13 2 lt. 2 f. a..........12 sep. 13 1 lt............27 apr. 14 accepted..........1 may 14 cap. 2 f. a.......25 apr. 16 accepted........26 apr. 16	N. Y. 30 nov. 83
Butt, John Diedrich, 26 sep. 16	bat. adjt.	mustered into u. s. ser......30 june 16	pvt. batty. B, 2 f. a., trs. batty. A, trs. batty. B, corp....18 nov. 12 to 3 jan. 14 2 lt.............3 jan. 14 1 lt...........11 may 14 accepted.........12 may 14 cap...........26 sep. 16 accepted........26 sep. 16	N. Y. 4 apr 88
e Figaniere, Frederick, 20 sep. 16	adjt.	mustered into u. s. ser......30 june 16	2 lt..............26 june 16 accepted..........26 june 16 1 lt.............19 aug. 16 accepted........24 aug. 16 cap...........20 sep. 16 accepted........21 sep. 16	Pa. 11 apr. 69
First Lieutenants				
King, Charles Henry, 4 may 14	F	mustered into u. s. ser......30 june 16	pvt., corp., 2 batty., trs. batty. B, trs. batty. F, corp., sgt.23 mar. 09 to 3 jan. 14 2 lt. 2 f. a..........3 jan. 14 1 lt.............4 may 14 accepted..........7 may 14	N. Y. 1 may 89
Albrecht, Horst Adolf Christian, 11 may 14	B	mustered into u. s. ser......30 june 16	pvt. 3 batty........9 oct. 05 hon. dis..........21 may 11 pvt., sgt. batty. B, 2 f. a..............30 dec. 12 to 22 dec. 13 2 lt..........22 dec. 13 1 lt...........11 may 14 accepted.........13 may 14.	N. Y. 9 feb. 84

FIELD ARTILLERY — SECOND REGIMENT — (Continued)

Name, grade, date of rank and highest brevet rank	Company	In the armies of U. S. or foreign states	In the National Guard	Born
FIELD ARTILLERY — (Continued)				
First Lieutenants — Continued				
Holmes, Eugene Albert, 13 may 14	C	mustered into u. s. ser......30 june 16	pvt., corp., sgt., 2 co. 13 a. d.......27 feb. 06 hon. dis...........26 sep. 11 pvt., corp., sgt., batty. C, 2 f. a.... 9 june 13 to 6 mar. 14 2 lt................. 6 mar. 14 1 lt................13 may 14 accepted...........20 may 14	N. Y. 18 june 87
Miller, Harry Charles, 4 mar. 15	B	mustered into u. s. ser......30 june 16	pvt., corp., sgt. batty. B, 2 f. a..........19 may 13 to 16 june 14 2 lt................16 june 14 1 lt................ 4 mar. 15 accepted...........11 mar. 15	N. Y. 6 july 87
Clark, Rogers Pratt, 12 aug. 15	A	mustered into u. s. ser......30 june 16	pvt. batty. C, 2 f. a., trs. batty. A, corp., sgt................29 sep. 13 to 9 july 14 2 lt................ 9 july 14 1 lt................12 aug. 15 accepted...........18 aug. 15	N. J. 5 july 91
McGrosan, Charles Joseph, 14 mar. 16	D	mustered into u. s. ser......30 june 16	pvt. batty. B, 2 f. a..11 nov. 13 to 16 june 14 2 lt................16 june 14 accepted...........19 june 14 1 lt................14 mar. 16 accepted...........15 mar. 16	N. Y. 18 may 81
Brennan, Edward Leo, 18 oct. 16	hdq'rs co.	mustered into u. s. ser .....26 oct 16	pvt., sgt. batty. B, 2 f. a..............15 sep. 13 to 20 aug. 15 2 lt................20 aug. 15 accepted...........23 aug. 15 1 lt................18 oct. 16 accepted...........18 oct. 16	N. Y. 3 mar. 92
Nelson, Dean, 11 apr. 16	E	1 lt. 8 N. Y. vols., 19 may 98 to 3 nov. 98 mustered into u. s. ser......30 june 16	pvt. co. F, 7 inf......19 oct. 92 hon. dis...........19 oct. 97 2 lt. 8 regt.........30 apr. 98 1 lt................17 may 98 pvt., tr. 6 sq. C.....14 jan. 05 to 19 oct. 08 2 lt. 2 f. a.......... 2 oct. 15 accepted........... 8 oct. 15 1 lt................11 apr. 16 accepted...........20 apr. 16	N. Y. 7 feb. 69
Cox, Henry W. G., 15 may 16	D	mustered into u. s. ser......30 june 16	pvt. 1 f. h..........14 feb. 07 pvt. 1 cl........... 5 may 08 sgt................ 2 dec. 12 f. and h. discharge...29 nov. 13 pvt. 3 amb. co....... 1 dec. 13 sgt................ 7 jan. 14 2 lt................23 feb. 16 accepted...........28 feb. 16 1 lt................15 may 16 accepted...........16 may 16	Pa. 30 june 87
Gilmore, Edward Owen, 26 may 16	C	mustered into u. s. ser......30 june 16	pvt. batty. B, 2 f. a., acting corp., sgt....25 jan. 15 to 11 dec. 15 2 lt. f. a...........11 dec. 15 accepted...........13 dec. 15 1 lt. f. a...........26 may 16 accepted...........29 may 16	N. Y. 11 jan. 95

FIELD ARTILLERY — SECOND REGIMENT — *(Concluded)*

Name, grade, date of rank and highest brevet rank	Company	Service		Born
		In the armies of U. S. or foreign states	In the National Guard	
FIELD ARTILLERY — *(Continued)*				
First Lieutenants — Continued				
Shedden, George Alden, 28 june 16	bat. qm. and com'sy	mustered into u. s. ser.....30 june 16	pvt. tr. C, sq. A.....12 feb. 16 trs. to tr. D, sq. A...— june 16 2 lt. 2 f. a...........28 june 16 accepted...........28 june 16	......
Spencer, Frank A., Jr.	E.	mustered into u. s. 30 june 16	pvt. tr. C, M. G. tr...18 sep. 13 2 lt. 2 f. a..........11 may 16 accepted..........13 may 16 1 lt..............9 oct. 16 accepted..........9 oct. 16	N. Y. 18 may 84
Second Lieutenants				
Hoffman, Raymond Lithgow, 2 june 14	F	mustered into u. s. ser.....30 june 16	pvt., 2 batty. f. a., trs. batty. F, 2 f. a., corp..............1 mar. 10 to 2 june 14 2 lt. 2 f. a...........2 june 14 accepted...........6 june 14	N. Y. 9 apr. 87
Veterinarians				
Nimphius, Harry Frank.	......	mustered into u. s. ser.....30 june 16	appointed veterinarian, 2 f. a...........25 mar. 14 accepted...........31 mar. 14	N. Y. 8 may 86
McAuslin, Robert Anderson.	......	mustered into u. s. ser........30 june 16	appointed veterinarian, 2. f. a.............9 nov. 14 accepted..........16 nov. 14	Scot. 1 nov. 77
McSweeney, James Hubert, 27 apr. 16	C	mustered into u. s. ser .....30 june 16	pvt. batty. C........24 mar. 13 corp............26 jan. 14 sgt...............7 july 14 f. and h. discharge...24 mar. 16 re-enlisted..........3 apr. 16 2 lt...............27 apr. 16 accepted..........1 may 16	N. Y. 24 oct. 88
Floor, Arthur Munro, 19 may 16	C	mustered into u. s. ser........30 june 16	pvt. batty. C, corp...21 sep. 14 2 lt...............19 may 16 accepted..........22 may 16	N. Y. 3 oct. 86
Andrews, Thomas H. S., 2 june 16	A	mustered into u. s. ser.... .30 june 16	pvt. batty. A.......17 jan. 16 2 lt............21 june 16 accepted..........22 june 16	N. J. 27 sep. 88
Hereth, Walter Henry, 28 june 16	B	mustered into u. s. ser.... .30 june 16	pvt. batty. B.......11 may 14 corp.............24 may 16 sgt..............20 mar. 16 1 sgt.............10 apr. 16 2 lt.............28 june 16 accepted...........28 june 16	N. Y. 9 jan. 93
Herbert, Weyman D., 17 oct. 16	E	mustered into u. s. ser......30 june 16	pvt. tr. M. G. Trp...23 jan. 14 wagoner...........10 dec. 15 corp..............1 mar. 16 sgt..............18 july 16 2 lt.............17 oct. 16 accepted..........22 oct. 16	N. Y. 19 oct. 88
Hayes, Francis V., 10 may 16	F	mustered into u. s. ser......30 june 16	pvt. batty F........16 june 15 2 lt...............10 may 16 accepted..........13 may 16	N. Y. 15 aug. 89

FIELD ARTILLERY — *(Continued)*

THIRD REGIMENT

(Formerly SIXTY-FIFTH REGIMENT)

(Six Batteries)

(Two Battalions)

(Attached to Division Headquarters)

Armory, 29 Masten Street, Buffalo

The regiment was organized in 1848. Cos. K and I were disbanded, the latter in 1875. A new Co. I was organized in 1879, and Co. E was consolidated with Co. H the same year. In 1880 Co. B was consolidated with Co. A, and Troop D, Cavalry, Eighth Division, was reorganized as a company of infantry and attached to the regiment as Co. E. In 1881 Cos. D and E were disbanded. A new Co. B and a new Co. D were organized in 1885. It entered the service of the United States June 19, 1863, and was mustered out July 30, 1863. In October, 1864, practically the whole of this regiment, as part of the 187th Regiment, N. Y. Volunteers, was again mustered into the United States service for one year and mustered out July 1, 1865. April 28, 1898, the regiment received authority to organize as a twelve-company regiment, preparatory to entry into the United States service, the 13th Separate Company becoming for the time one of the additional companies. It was mustered into the United States service May 17, 1898, as the 65th Regiment, N. Y. Infantry, and mustered out of such service November 19, 1898. Cos. K, L and M were ordered disbanded May 31, 1899. June 10, 1907, the 13th Separate Company was attached to the 65th Regiment as Co. E. July 9, 1909, the regiment received authority to organize a new company to be known as Company K. Companies L and M were authorized to be organized December 2, 1910. This regiment performed duty at the riots in Buffalo, April, 1913.

Co. E of this regiment, the 13th Separate Company, is quartered in the State Armory, South Main street, Jamestown. It was organized August 22, 1875, as the 1st Separate Company, 31st Brigade. Designation changed to 4th Separate Company, December 5, 1877, and to the 13th Separate Company, September 4, 1882. Became Co. G, 3d Regiment, March 30, 1907, and Co. E, 65th Regiment, June 10, 1907. It was in the State service in Buffalo during the switchmen's strike in August, 1892, and the street car strike, Buffalo, April, 1913. In United States service, as Co E, 65th Regiment, N. Y. Infantry, from May 17, 1898, to November 17, 1898.

Appointive system adopted by the 65th Infantry, January 27, 1916, S. O. 22, A. G. O., 1916.

The regiment was constituted a regiment of field artillery of two battalions, and designated 3d Field Artillery, by G. O. 22, A. G. O., July 11, 1916.

Company L and M consolidated and designated Battery A.
Company A and F consolidated and designated Battery B.
Company H and K consolidated and designated Battery C.
Company C and D consolidated and designated Battery D.
Company B and G consolidated and designated Battery F.
Company I designated Battery C.

Recognition extended by the War Department under Act of June 3, 1916; to Battery E and Sanitary Detachment, June 27, 1916; to Battery D, July 1, 1916; to Battery B, July 20, 1916; to Headquarters Company, September 6, 1916.

The regiment has received authority to place silver rings on the lances of its colors, engraved as follows:

On the National Color.— Gettysburg campaign, 1863; before Petersburg, Va., October 20, 1864, to April 2, 1865; Hatcher's Run, Va., October 27-28, 1864; Hicksford raid, Va., December 6-11, 1864; Hatcher's Run, Va., February 5-7, 1865; Appomattox campaign, Va., March 28 to April 9, 1865; Gravelly Run, March 29, 1865; White Oak Ridge, March 29-31, 1865; Five Forks, April 1, 1865; Fall of Petersburg, April 2, 1865; Appomattox Court House, April 9, 1865; Spanish-American War, 1898.

On the State Color.— Canal riot, Buffalo, 1849; draft riots, New York, 1863; railroad strike, Buffalo, 1877; riots, Buffalo, 1892; riots, Tonawanda, 1898.

FIELD ARTILLERY — THIRD REGIMENT — *(Continued)*

Name, grade, date of rank and highest brevet rank	Company	Service		Born
		In the armies of U. S. or foreign states	In the National Guard	
FIELD ARTILLERY				
Colonel				
Hand, Daniel W., 10 july 16	......	cap., 45 u. s. inf., 17 aug. 99 hon. muster out, 3 june 01 1 lt., art. corps., 22 aug. 01 cap......25 jan. 07 assigned to 1 f. a., 6 june 07 q. m. by detail, 6 aug. 08 unassigned.29 may 10 assigned to 1 f. a., 27 june 10 trs. to 2 f. a., 3 dec. 12 trs. to 5 f. a., 16 june 13 mustered into u. s. ser......10 july 16	col. . a.............10 july 16 accepted...........10 july 16	Pa.
Lieutenant Colonel				
Howland, John David, 1 oct. 14	......	maj. 65 N. Y. inf., 1 may 98 1 lt. regt. adj. 202 N. Y. inf., 6 nov. 98 to 15 apr. 99 mustered into u. s. ser......5 aug. 16	2 lt. (D), 65 inf.....20 mar. 89 1 lt............. 27 nov. 89 cap................28 dec. 92 maj...............10 nov. 02 lt. col............. 1 oct. 14 accepted........... 2 oct. 14	Mass. 12 june 65
Majors				
Eller, Louis Henry, 16 dec. 11	......	cap. 65 N. Y. inf, 1 may 98 to 19 nov. 98 mustered into u. s ser......5 aug. 16	pvt., corp , sgt., 1 sgt., co. F, 65 inf...16 feb. 85 to 29 june 97 2 lt................29 june 97 cap (M). .... 1 may 98 supn., assigned to co. C, 65 inf.........25 oct. 99 cap. 65 inf........11 dec. 01 maj................16 dec. 11 accepted...........18 dec. 11	N. Y 11 feb. 69
Fowler, James Porter, 5 may 13	......	1 lt. 65 N. Y. inf., 1 may 98 to 19 nov. 98 mustered into u. s ser......5 aug. 16	pvt., corp., sgt., co. G, 65 inf.......... 8 may 93 to 28 may 9 2 lt................28 may 93 1 lt.......25 feb. 98 cap................14 sep 93 maj................ 5 may 13 accepted........... 6 may 13	Can. 13 jan. 74
Captains				
Keeler, Patrick James, 26 june 07	B	mustered into u. s ser.....5 aug. 16	pvt. co. A, 65 inf....10 aug. 03 to 29 june 04 2 lt. (A), 65 inf.....29 june 04 1 lt.............29 may 07 cap................26 june 07	N. Y. 10 may 76
Barrett, Nelson True, 27 Feb. 09	E	2 lt. 65 N. Y. inf., 1 may 98 to 19 nov. 98 mustered into u. s. ser ....5 aug. 16	pvt , corp., sgt., co. I, 65 inf......... 3 apr. 93 to 12 dec. 95 2 lt................12 dec. 95 1 lt ....11 june 01 cap. 65 inf.........15 mar. 09 accepted...........22 mar. 09	N. Y. 14 dec. 68

FIELD ARTILLERY — THIRD REGIMENT — (*Continued*)

Name, grade, date of rank and highest brevet rank	Company	Service		Born
		In the armies of U. S. or foreign states	In the National Guard	
FIELD ARTILLERY — (*Continued*)				
Captains — Continued				
William, Charles Hoyt, 2 aug. 13	sup. co.	pvt. batty A, 1 Mass. Heavy Artillery... 4 may 98 to 14 nov. 98 mustered into u. s. ser...... 5 aug. 16	pvt. co. C, 65 inf .. 9 apr. 00 to 12 july 00 2 lt.................12 jul. 00 1 lt. ....14 dec. 01 1 lt. bat. qm. 65 inf. with o. r........ 9 aug. 07 supn., reassigned....21 jan. 08 2 lt 65 inf......... 7 feb 08 cap .... 2 aug. 13 accepted........... 4 aug. 13	N. Y. 27 nov. 76
Schohl, William Frederick, 1 apr. 15	F	mustered into u. s ser...... 5 aug. 16	pvt., sgt., co. M, 65 inf............. 3 may 11 to 10 june 12 2 lt. 65 inf..........10 june 12 cap.... ....1 apr. 15 accepted.......... 5 apr. 15	N. Y. 14 sep. 84
Marks, Thomas, 14 july 16	bat. adjt.	15 f. bty. art corps, 20 apr. 03 to 19 apr. 05 baty. E, 3 f. a., 22 apr. 06 to 21 apr. 09 baty. D, 5 f. a., 8 aug. 09 to 7 aug. 15 schl. musketry, 8 aug. 15 to 14 july 16 mustered into u. s ser...... 5 aug. 16	cap .. ..14 july 16 accepted... ....14 july 16	Mich. 22 oct. 83
Webber, John D., 16 dec. 16	......	U. S. V ... 1 may 99 to 30 apr. 01 2 cav..... 1 feb. 02 to 1 jan. 05 3 f. a..... 4 feb. 05 to 4 aug. 16 mustered into u. s ser......26 dec. 16	2 lt ....28 july 16 accepted........... 5 aug. 16 1 lt ... . 4 sep. 16 accepted...... .... 6 sep. 16 cap . ...16 dec. 16 accepted...........26 dec. 16	
Brost, Jacob, 11 nov. 16	C	pvt. co. I, 65 N Y inf.... 14 june 98 to 19 nov. 98 mustered into u. s ser... ..26 dec. 16	pvt., corp., sgt , co. I, 65 inf.......... 4 sep. 99 to 13 jan. 12 2 lt 65 inf..........13 jan. 12 accepted...........15 jan. 12 cap ....11 nov. 16 accepted.........11 nov. 16	N. Y. 30 dec. 79
Kennedy, Wm. Henry, 29 sep. 16	adjt.	tr. M, 2 u. s. cav., 29 sep. 02 to 23 oct. 05 u. s. navy, 21 july 05 to 20 july 10 tr. M, n. c. s. 2 cav., 10 oct. 10 to 9 oct. 13 n. c. s. 2 cav., 10 oct. 13 to 12 july 16 mustered into u. s. ser......29 sep. 16	cap.... . ...29 sep. 16 accepted.... .. ...29 sep. 16	Wis 10 apr 82

FIELD ARTILLERY — THIRD REGIMENT — (*Continued*)

Name, grade, date of rank and highest brevet rank	Company	Service		Born
		In the armies of U. S. or foreign states	In the National Guard	
FIELD ARTILLERY — (*Continued*)				
Captains — Continued				
Hamlin, Chauncey J., 11 nov. 16	D	mustered into u. s. ser...... 5 aug. 16	2 lt 65 inf........ ... 2 feb. 16 accepted............ 3 feb. 16 2 lt. 3 f . a..........11 july 16 accepted............ 2 feb. 16 1 lt. .... 3 aug. 16 accepted............ 3 aug. 16 cap............11 nov. 16 accepted............15 nov. 16	N. Y. 11 jan. 81
Goodyear, Bradley, 6 sep. 16	C	mustered into u. s. ser...... 5 aug. 16	1 lt. 65 inf.......... 8 feb. 16 accepted............ 9 feb. 16 1 lt. 3 f. a..........11 july 16 rank from.......... 8 feb. 16 accepted..........29 july 16	N. Y. 18 oct. 85
First Lieutenants				

Gilchriese, Harry Lyons, 1 june 15	D	mustered into u. s. ser...... 5 aug. 16	pvt., corp. co. D, 65
			  inf...............18 apr. 10
			  to 30 apr. 15
			1 lt..............1 june 15
			accepted........... 3 jun. 15
				Can.
				4 june
				92

Merwin, Miles Herbert, 21 dec. 15	F	mustered into u. s. ser...... 5 aug. 16	pvt. 27 sep. co......24 mar. 02
			  to 28 sep. 03
			  4 jan. 04
			  to 30 apr. 04
			  31 may 04
			  to 21 nov. 04
			  16 feb. 07
			  to 20 apr. 07
			pvt., corp., sgt. co.
			  B, 22 eng........ 1 may 07
			  to 8 mar. 11
			2 lt. c. of e......... 8 mar. 11
			1 lt............26 mar. 12
			r. l............23 dec. 14
			1 lt. 65 inf..........21 dec. 15
			accepted..........27 dec. 15
				N. Y.
				3 aug.
				81

Curtin, John Joseph, 4 sep. 16	D	mustered into u. s. ser...... 5 aug. 16	pvt., corp., co. C, 65
			  inf...............25 jan. 09
			  to 30 july 12
			2 lt. 65 inf..........30 july 12
			accepted........... 1 aug. 12
			1 lt.............. 4 sep. 16
			accepted........... 6 sep. 16
				N. Y.
				25 oct.
				90

Parker, Howard K., 4 sep. 16	B	Tr. C, 2 U. S. cav., 26 dec. 12 to 17 july 16 mustered into u. s. ser...... 5 aug. 16	2 lt................14 july 16 accepted............14 july 16 1 lt.............. 4 sep. 16 accepted........... 6 july 16	......
Burkhardt, Howard K., 29 sep. 16	F	mustered into u. s. ser...... 5 aug. 16	2 lt.............. 4 sep. 16 accepted........... 6 sep. 16 1 lt.............29 sep. 16 accepted..........29 sep. 16	
Williams, Edw. Levi, 11 nov. 16	D	mustered into u. s. ser......24 nov. 16	2 lt. 65 inf..........20 apr. 16 accepted..........21 apr. 16 2 lt. 3 f. a..........11 july 16 rank from..........20 apr. 16 1 lt.............11 nov. 16 accepted..........15 nov. 16	W. Va.
Gutelius, Edwin Chas., 16 dec. 16	E	mustered into u. s. ser...... 5 aug. 16	2 lt................15 july 16 accepted..........15 july 16 1 lt................16 dec. 16 accepted..........26 dec. 16	

FIELD ARTILLERY—THIRD REGIMENT—(*Continued*)

Name, grade, date of rank and highest brevet rank	Company	Service		Born
		In the armies of U. S. or foreign states	In the National Guard	
FIELD ARTILLERY—Con-tinued)				
First Lieutenants—Con-tinued				
Allen, Leonard S., 16 dec. 16	C	mustered into u. s. ser......26 dec. 16	pvt. co. M, 65 inf. ..20 june 16 sergt............11 aug. 16 t.............. 4 sep. 16 accepted.......... 9 sep. 16 1 lt.............16 dec. 16 accepted.........26 dec. 16	N. Y. 14 june 92
Briggs, Carleton B., 16 dec. 16	C	mustered into u. s. ser......26 dec. 16	pvt. co. H, 65 inf., 7 june 15 corp............ 2 jan. 16 sgt. batty. C...... 5 aug. 16 2 lt............. 4 sep. 16 accepted.......... 9 sep. 16 1 lt.............16 dec. 16 accepted.........26 dec. 16	N. Y. 28 sep. 85
Marcus, Marvin M. Jr., 16 dec. 16	A	mustered into u. s. ser...... 5 aug. 16	2 lt. f. a ....30 july 16 accepted..... ....30 july 16 1 lt. . ...16 dec. 16 accepted..... ....26 dec. 16	......
Sprague, Eben C., 16 dec. 16	A	mustered into u. s ser.... .dec. 26 16	pvt. tr. I, 1 cav......17 june 13 dropped...........22 apr. 14 taken up.........20 july 14 trs. to co. M, 65 inf..14 mar. 16 2 lt............. 4 sep. 16 accepted.......... 9 sep. 16 1 lt.............16 dec. 16 accepted.........26 dec. 16	N. Y. 12 july 89
Second Lieutenants				
Wojtkowski, Louis, 4 sep. 16	E	mustered into u. s. ser.....	pvt. co. I, 65 inf.....19 june 11 corp., sgt., 1 sgt., trs. batty. E, 3 f. a.12 july 16 2 lt............. 4 sep. 16 accepted..........10 sep. 16	N. Y. 13 aug. 80
Scheu, Henry, 29 sep. 16	A	pvt. co A, 65 u. s. vols. 19 nov. 98 from 17 may 98 mustered into u. s ser...... 1 oct. 16	2 lt.............12 nov. 16 accepted..........15 nov. 16	......
Howard, John B., 12 nov. 16	B	mustered into u. s. ser...... 6 dec. 16	furloughed to reserve..17 sep. 16 re-enlisted batty. F, 3 f. a........... 2 oct. 16 2 lt.............29 sep. 16 accepted..........30 sep. 16 pvt. co. B, 65 inf..... 4 mar. 00 corp............18 feb. 02 sgt.............12 mar. 06	N. Y. 12 jan. 83
Gaskin, Wm. J., 12 nov. 16	B	pvt. 22 batty. f. a. u. s. 23 oct. 04 discharged 22 oct. 07 re-enlisted. 5 sep. 08 batty. B, 6 f. a. u. s dis......10 feb. 10 mustered into u. s. ser.......6 dec. 16	2 lt ,........12 nov. 16 accepted..........15 nov. 16	N. Y. 24 mar. 83

FIELD ARTILLERY—THIRD REGIMENT—(Concluded)

Name, grade, date of rank and highest brevet rank	Company	Service		Born
		In the armies of U. S. or foreign states	In the National Guard	
FIELD ARTILLERY — (Concluded)				
Second Lieutenants — Concluded				
Philips, Edw. C., 3 dec. 16	D	pvt. tr. A, 6 u. s. cav. 9 aug. 00 to 8 aug. 03 pvt. co. H, 16 u. s. inf...... 7 dec. 03 to 15 feb. 05 re-enlisted.16 feb. 05 discharged 15 feb. 08 mustered into u. s. ser......15 dec. 16	2 lt................ 3 dec. 16 accepted ....15 dec. 16	Conn. 1 july 81
P our, Walter D., 16 dec. 16	A	mustered into u. s ser ... 26 dec 16	pvt. co. H, 65 inf 14 sep. 08 2 lt. 65 inf..........20 june 11 accepted .....21 june 11 1 lt................22 apr. 12 accepted........23 apr. 12 cap................ 2 sep. 15 accepted ...... 4 sep. 15 f. and h. discharge ..31 dec. 15 pvt. 3 f. a........ 1 oct. 16 color sgt.......... 2 oct. 16 2 lt...............16 dec. 16 accepted .....26 dec. 16	Cal. 3 may 90
Chaplain				
Fornes, Walter Francis, 4 apr. 11	......	mustered into u. s. ser.... 5 aug. 16	chaplain 65 inf...... 4 apr. 11 accepted........... 8 apr. 11	N. Y. 6 mar. 83

COAST ARTILLERY CORPS

Name, grade, date of rank and highest brevet rank	Company	Service		Born
		In the armies of U. S. or foreign states	In the National Guard	
COAST DEFENSE OFFICER *Lieutenant Colonel* Taylor, Washington Irving, 26 may 09, *W. D. Cert. in course Nos. 1 (Basic), 2 (Emplacement Officer), 3 (Range and Communication Officer), 4 (Battery Commander), 5 (Searchlight Officer) and 6 (Fire and Battle Commander).*			2 lt. (D), 13 inf......17 dec. 89 1 lt. (I)............11 june 90 trs. co. E..........13 dec. 93 cap...............23 mar. 94 insp. rifle practice with o. r......27 july 97 supn............ 7 may 98 resigned.........27 may 98 cap. i. s. a. p. 13 inf.. 1 june 00 maj. art. eng. and o. o............22 may 07 supn., resigned.....21 jan. 08 maj. c. a. c......... 6 feb. 08 det. asst. to chief c. a........... 6 nov. 08 lt. col. c. a. c....... 4 june 09 accepted.......... 7 june 09	N. Y. 13 dec. 64

EIGHTH COAST DEFENSE COMMAND

(Ten Companies)

Armory, 75 East Ninety-fourth Street, New York City

On the 4th of April, 1786,* the 1st Brigade, 1st Division, was formed in New York city into a brigade of artillery, and was to consist of the 1st and 2d Regiments and *a battalion*. In April, 1807, the 3d Regiment of New York Artillery was organized by including *this* battalion and other troops. July 27, 1847, the designation of the regiment was changed to the 8th Regiment. In December, 1893, it was reduced to a battalion of four companies. It was reorganized, as a regiment, February 14, 1896. New companies were organized for the battalion as follows: On July 8, 1895, Co. A; on October 30, 1895, Co. E; on January 27, 1896, Co. H, and on February 14, 1896, Co. G, when it was reorganized as a regiment. April 28, 1898, it was authorized to be organized as a twelve-company regiment to enter the service of the United States. It was in the service of the United States from September 15 to December 15, 1812; from April 23 to August 2, 1861; from May 29 to September 9, 1862; and from June 17 to July 23, 1863. It was mustered into the United States service as the 8th Regiment Infantry, New York Volunteers, May 14, 17 and 19, 1898, and mustered out of such service November 3, 1898. Companies L and M were disbanded December 22, 1898. December 10, 1906, Companies A, C and E were disbanded and the regiment reduced to a battalion of seven companies and designated the 8th Battalion. January 18, 1908, Co. A was reorganized and on January 21, 1908, the battalion was again constituted a regiment under its original designation. January 23, 1908, a coast artillery corps was organized, the 8th Regiment being constituted coast artillery and the companies respectively designated as the 25th, 26th, 27th, 28th, 29th, 30th, 31st and 32d Companies, Coast Artillery Corps, constituting the 8th Artillery District. November 10, 1908, an additional company was directed to be organized and attached to the 8th Artillery District, as the 33d Company, Coast Artillery Corps. November 11, 1911, authority was given to organize an enlisted band, to be designated the 8th Band, Coast Artillery Corps. The 34th Company was mustered in May 29, 1914, and attached to the 8th Coast Defense Command. The 34th Company is to be designated as a mortar company and assigned to the coast defenses of Eastern New York.

The 35th Company was mustered in March 6, 1916; accepted by S. O. 58, A. G. O., March 22, 1916. The 36th Company was mustered in June 27, 1916, and accepted by S. O. 228, A. G. O., October 28, 1916.

Recognition extended by the War Department under Act of June 3, 1916, to 25th, 28th, 31st, 34th Companies, June 26, 1916; to Band and 27th, 29th, 32d, 35th, 36th Companies, June 27, 1916; to 26th, 30th, 33d Companies, June 28, 1916; to F. S., N. C. S., and Sanitary Detachment, June 30, 1916.

* Date in dispute.

Authority has been granted to place silver rings on the lances of its colors, engraved as follows:

On the National Color.— Fort Gansevoort, 1812; Fort Greene, 1812; Washington, April, 1861; Bull Run, July 21, 1861; Yorktown, 1862; Gettysburg campaign, 1863; Spanish-American War, 1898.

On the State Color.— Flour riots, 1826; stonecutters' riot, 1835; great fire, New York city, 1845; Astor Place riot, 1849; police riot, 1857; Dead Rabbit riot, 1857; Sepoy riot, 1858; Camp Corcoran Legion, 1862; draft riots, 1863; Orange riots, 1871; Syracuse, 1877; Brooklyn, 1895.

COAST ARTILLERY CORPS — EIGHTH COAST DEFENSE COMMAND

Name, grade, date of rank and highest brevet rank	Company	Service		Born
		In the armies of U. S. or foreign states	In the National Guard	
Colonel				
‡Austin, Elmore Farrington 24 feb. 08 W. D. Cert. in course Nos. 1 (Basic), 2, (Emplacement Officer), 3 (Range and Communication), 4 (Battery Commander), 5 (Searchlight Officer), and 6 (Fire and Batt. Commander).	......	cap. 71 N. Y. inf.. 2 may 98 to 15 nov. 98	pvt., corp., sgt., ord. sgt., co. B, 71 inf..29 nov. 87 to 14 may 94 insp. rifle practice, cap...............14 may 94 cap. (L) with o. r.....30 apr. 98 eng. maj. 5 brig...... 1 dec. 98 supn............ 1 july 01 assigned to duty 1 brig............ 1 july 01 eng. 1 brig. maj. with o. r.............19 nov. 01 supn., reassigned....21 jan. 08 col. c. a. c.........26 mar. 08 chief, c. a. brig. gen..18 jan. 12 assigned to com. 8 arty. dist. in addition to other duties.............18 jan. 12 col. c. a. c......... 5 may 14 accepted......... 6 may 14	N. Y. 9 may 64
Majors				
Wilson, Henry Clinton.... 25 feb. 08 W. D. Cert. in course Nos. 1 (Basic), 2 (Emplacement Officer), 3 (Range and Communication Officer), and 4 (Battery Commander).	......	1 lt. 1 regt. u. 's. vol. eng......... 7 june 98 cap......19 jan. 99 to 25 jan. 99	pvt. 1 regt. N. G. D. C............ 3 sep. 94 hon. dis......... 4 mar. 95 pvt. 1 regt. N. G. D. C...........23 apr. 00 to 7 may 00 1 lt. bat. adj........ 7 may 00 hon. dis.........25 mar. 01 2 lt. (G), 71 inf. N. G. N. Y......... 3 jan. 02 1 lt...........26 sep. 05 maj. c. a. c.........26 mar. 08	D. C. 5 june 76
Ames, Asel, 26 may 09 Nos. 1 (Basic), 2 (Emplacement Officer), 3 (Range and Communication Officer), 4 (Battery Commander), 5 (Searchlight Officer) and 6 (Fire and Battle Commander).	arty. eng.	cap. 1 U. S. V. eng. to 25 jan. 9 to 25 jan. 99	2 lt., c. a. c.........26 oct. 08 accepted.......... 4 june 0 accepted........... 7 june 09	Mass. 93 jan. 73
Loeser, Paul, 22 sep. 09 W. D. Cert. in course Nos. 1 (Basic), 2 (Emplacement Officer), 3 (Range and Communication Officer), 4 (Battery Commander), 5 (Searchlight Officer) and 6 (Fire and Battle Commander).	......		pvt. co. C, 7 inf.....14 apr. 00 to 23 may 05 1 lt. (K), 8 regt.....23 may 05 cap...............19 dec. 07 cap. c. a. c.........23 jan. 08 maj...........11 oct. 09 accepted...........15 oct. 09	N. Y. 21 nov. 80

COAST ARTILLERY CORPS—EIGHTH COAST DEFENSE COMMAND—*(Continued*

Name, grade, date of rank and highest brevet rank	Company	Service		Born
		In the armies of U. S. or foreign states	In the National Guard	
Captains				
Cowdrey, John Jay, 8 nov. 00 *W. D. Cert. in course Nos.* 1 *(Basic),* 2 *(Emplacement Officer)* 3 *(Range and Communication Officer) and* 4 *(Battery Commander)*	31	....	pvt. co. K, 1 regt. Conn. N. G........— aug. 86 to — jan. 89 pvt. 109 regt. N. G. N. Y.............12 may 98 to 22 dec. 98 1 lt. (C), 8 regt......30 apr. 00 cap..............8 nov. 00 supn.............10 dec. 06 assigned to com. 31 co. c, a c........24 apr. 08 cap. c. a. c.........23 july 00	Ohio. 24 june 64
Bremer, Alexander Magnus, 20 jan. 08 *W. D. Cert. in course Nos.* 1 *(Basic),* 2 *(Emplacement Officer),* 3 *(Range and Communication Officer),* 4 *(Battery Commander)* 5 *(Searchlight Officer) and* 6 *(Fire and Battle Commander).*	25	....	pvt., corp., sgt., co. K, 8 regt........13 apr. 00 hon. dis..........17 nov. 05 2 lt. (A), 8 regt.....17 apr. 06 supn.............10 dec. 06 assigned to duty with 8 bat. (F)......10 dec. 06 2 lt. 8 bat. (F), with o. r............11 june 07 cap. (A), 8 arty....22 jan. 08 cap. c. a. c........23 jan. 08	N. Y. 12 may 76
Spear, William Duroy, 29 may 08 *W. D. Cert. in course Nos* 1 *(Basic),* 2 *(Emplacement Officer),* 3 *(Range and Communication Officer),* 4 *(Battery Commander)* 5 *(Searchlight Officer) and* 6 *(Fire and Battle Commander).*	28	....	pvt. co. A, 5 Mass. inf...............21 dec. 83 to 21 aug. 85 19 jul. 86 to 19 july 87 1 lt. (C), 8 regt. N. G. N. Y.......25 jan. 01 supn.............10 dec. 06 1 lt. (A), 8 arty....22 jan. 08 cap. c. a. c......... 3 june 08	D. C. 31 oct. 67
McKenzie, Abraham Lincoln, 8 dec. 09	27	2 lt. 8 N. Y. inf., 2 may 98 to 3 nov. 98	pvt., corp., sgt., 1 sgt., co. D, 8 regt.. 8 july 90 to 14 dec. 99 2 lt............14 dec. 99 1 lt.............30 apr. 00 1 lt. c. a. c........23 jan. 08 cap.............21 dec. 09 accepted..........27 dec. 09	N. Y. 11 feb. 70
Gray, William, 14 jan. 10 *W. D. Cert. in course Nos.* 1 *(Basic),* 2 *(Emplacement Officer),* 3 *(Range and Communication Officer) and* 5 *(Searchlight Officer).*	o. o.	....	pvt., qm. sgt., 2 batty 27 dec. 99 to 26 sep. 05 2 lt. (I), 71 inf....26 sep. 05 2 lt. c. a. c......... 5 may 08 cap.............24 jan. 10 accepted..........25 jan. 10	N. Y. 11 jan. 64
Schussler, Ferdinand Conrad, 22 dec. 13 *W. D. Cert. in course Nos.* 1 *(Basic),* 2 *(Emplacement Officer)* 3 *(Range and Communication Officer),* 4 *(Battery Commander) and* 5 *(Searchlight Officer).*	32	....	pvt., co. K, 171 inf., trs. co. K, 71 inf., corp., sgt......15 may 98 to 26 feb. 10 2 lt. c. a. c.........26 feb. 10 1 lt.............28 june 11 cap.............22 dec. 13 accepted..........29 dec. 13	N. J. 27 june 74

COAST ARTILLERY CORPS—EIGHTH COAST DEFENSE COMMAND—*(Continued)*

Name, grade, date of rank and highest brevet rank	Company	Service — In the armies of U. S. or foreign states	Service — In the National Guard	Born
Captains — Continued				
Stewart, Samuel Townsend, 14 june 15 *W. D. Cert. in course Nos. 1 (Basic), 2 (Emplacement Officer), 3 (Range and Communication Officer), 4 (Battery Commander) 5 Searchlight Officer) and 6 (Fire and Battle Commander).*	26	pvt., sgt., 10 Ohio vol. inf..25 june 98 to 23 mar. 99	pvt., 1 class pvt., 1 co sig. corps.....11 aug. 03 to 16 jan. 03 pvt., corp., sgt., sgt. 1 class, 1 co. sig. corps...........14 may 06 to 1 july 12 2 lt. c. a. c.......... 1 july 12 1 lt................25 sep. 13 cap....... ......14 june 15 accepted..........16 june 15	Ohio. 25 dec. 79
Trull, William Evans, 1 july 15 *W. D. Cert. in course No. 1 (Basic).*	30	2 lt. 71 N. Y. inf. 10 may 98 to 13 nov. 98	pvt., corp., co. B, 71 inf., bat. qm. sgt., regt. qm. sgt...... 7 apr. 92 to 26 apr. 98 2 lt. c. a. c.........16 july 13 cap................ 1 july 15 accepted........... 1 july 15	W. Va. 26 sep. 73
Newcomb, Robert Scott, 25 apr. 12 *W. D. Cert. in course Nos. 1 (Basic), 2 (Emplacement Officer) 3 (Range and Communication Officer) 4 (Battery Commander) 5 (Searchlight Officer) and 6 (Fire and Battle Commander).*	33	....	1 lt. c. a. c.........25 apr. 12 accepted.. ....29 apr. 12	Fla. 5 jun. 85
Munson, Frederic Granville, 1 apr. 12 *W. D. Cert. in course Nos. 1 (Basic), 2 (Emplacement Officer), 3 (Range and Communication Officer), 4 (Battery Commander), 5 (Searchlight Officer) and 6 (Fire and Battle Commander).*	36	....	pvt. co. E, 7 inf...... 7 jan. 10 to 26 feb. 10 1 lt. c. a. c..... 26 feb. 10 cap..... .... 1 apr. 12 accepted .... 3 apr. 12	Pa. 21 nov. 82
Haseltine, Robert Henry, 22 mar 16 *W. D. Cert. in course Nos. 1 (Basic), 2 (Emplacement Officer), 3 (Range and Communication Officer) and 4 (Battery Commander).*	35	....	2 lt. c. a. c. ..... 17 june 13 1 lt..... .... 1 july 14 accepted.. . ..... 2 july 14 captain...........22 mar. 16 accepted ....24 mar. 16	N. Y. 24 mar. 76
Day, Arthur Mortimer, 28 june 16	adjt.	....	pvt. tr. 1, sq. A.... 23 mar. 97 dropped.......... 24 oct. 97 2 lt. c. a. c.........26 oct. 08 with rank from.....21 oct. 08 1 lt................30 dec. 08 with rank from.. ...23 dec. 08 cap. . ...13 may 10 with rank from...... 2 may 10 accepted...........16 may 10 f. & h. dis...........18 june 13 captain r. 1.........18 may 15 captain........ ..28 june 16 accepted........28 june 16	N. Y. 9 mar. 74

COAST ARTILLERY CORPS—EIGHTH COAST DEFENSE COMMAND—*(Continued)*

Name, grade, date of rank and highest brevet rank	Company	Service		Born
		In the armies of U. S. or foreign states	In the National Guard	

Captains — Concluded

Name, grade, date of rank and highest brevet rank	Company	In the armies of U. S. or foreign states	In the National Guard	Born
Tannenbaum, Julius, 8 aug. 16 *W. D. Cert. in course Nos. 1 (Basic), 2 (Emplacement Officer), 3 (Range and Communication Officer)*	qm.	. . . .	pvt., asst. hosp. stwd. hosp. stwd. h. c., 8 regt . . . . 9 july 99 to 6 feb. 06 2 lt. (G), 8 regt . . . . . 6 feb. 06 1 lt. (G), 8 bat . . . . 8 may 07 cap. c. a. c . . . . 3 june 08 1 lt . . . . 10 mar. 10 cap . . . . 7 june 12 1 lt . . . . 9 mar. 14 accepted . . . . 15 mar. 15 captain . . . . 8 aug. 16 accepted . . . . 9 aug. 16	Russia 1 may 71
Miller, Arthur Harrison, 29 june 16 *W. D. Cert. in course Nos. 1 (Basic) and 2 (Emplacement).*	34	. . . .	pvt. co. F, 7 inf . . . . . 1 nov. 12 to 23 june 14 2 lt. c. a. c . . . . 23 june 14 1 lt . . . . 14 june 15 accepted . . . . 16 june 15 captain . . . . 29 june 16 accepted . . . . 29 june 16	N. Y. 9 nov. 86
Perry, Alexander, 26 sep. 16	29	. . . .	pvt. co. K, 7 inf . . . . 10 oct. 00 to 30 dec. 03 26 may 04 to 8 feb. 05 29 apr. 05 to 4 oct. 05 12 oct. 06 hon. dis . . . . 7 may 09 pvt. co. K, 7 inf . . . . 7 may 09 to 1 may 10 27 june 12 to 22 oct. 13 2 lt. c. a. c . . . . 1 july 14 accepted . . . . 3 jul 14 captain . . . . 26 sep. 16 accepted . . . . 29 sep. 16	N. J. 31 aug. 82

First Lieutenants

Name, grade, date of rank and highest brevet rank	Company	In the armies of U. S. or foreign states	In the National Guard	Born
Miller, John, 17 aug. 08 *W. D. Cert. in course Nos. 1 (Basic), 2 (Emplacement Officer), 3 (Range and Communication Officer), 4 (Battery Commander) and 5 (Searchlight Officer).*	unattached	. . . .	pvt., corp., sgt., co. K, 71 inf., sgt. maj. 11 sep. 85 hon. dis . . . . 9 nov. 07 1 lt. 171 inf . . . . 3 jun. 98 resigned as supn. off. and returned to duty with 71 inf. sgt. maj . . . . 20 june 99 hon. dis . . . . 4 dec. 00 2 lt. (G), 8 bat . . . . . . 28 dec. 07 1 lt. c. a. c . . . . 25 aug. 08	N. Y. 20 june 66
Daly, John Thomas, 18 may 16 *W. D. Cert. in course Nos. 1 (Basic) and 2 (Emplacement Officer).*	33	. . . .	pvt., corp., 9 co. c. a. c. Conn. N. G . . . . 28 jan. 07 to 7 dec. 09 2 lt . . . . 7 dec. 09 resigned . . . . 21 apr. 10 2 lt. c. a. c. N. G. N. Y . . . . 1 june 10 1 lt . . . . 3 feb. 12 accepted . . . . 5 feb. 12 resigned . . . . 24 feb. 16 1 lt . . . . 18 may 16 accepted . . . . 22 may 16	Conn. 27 jan. 87

COAST ARTILLERY CORPS — EIGHTH COAST DEFENSE COMMAND — (*Continued*)

Name, grade, date of rank and highest brevet rank	Company	Service — In the armies of U. S. or foreign states	Service — In the National Guard	Born
First Lieutenants — Continued				
Smith, St. Clair, Jr., 17 june 13 *W. D. Cert. in course Nos. 1 (Basic), 2 (Emplacement Officer) 3 (Range and Communication Officer) 4 (Battery Commander) and 5 (Searchlight Officer).*	34	....	pvt., lance corp., corp. co. I, 7 inf...24 apr. 02 hon. dis............12 nov. 08 2 lt c. a. c........30 dec. 08 1 lt.... ....17 june 13 accepted..........19 june 13	N. Y. 12 apr. 82
Alden, Herbert Clarendon, 29 sep. 13 *W. D. Cert. in course Nos. 1 (Basic), 2 (Emplacement Officer), 3 (Range and communication Officer), 4 (Battery Commander), 5 (Searchlight Officer) and 6 (Fire and Battle Commander).*	36	....	pvt., corp., sgt., 4 sep. co..........27 dec. 00 to 7 june 07 1 lt. bat. qm. 10 inf.. 7 june 07 supn., reassigned....21 jan. 08 2 lt. 10 inf.........20 feb. 08 cap. c. a. c......... 2 dec. 10 1 lt.............29 sep. 13 accepted.......... 4 oct. 13	N. J. 28 oct. 59
Hatfield, Marshall Granville, 14 apr. 15	27	1 sgt. co. M, 8 N. Y. inf... 2 may 98 to 3 nov. 98	pvt., corp., sgt., 1 sgt. 11 sep. co., ret. to ranks, trs. to co. M, 8 regt., 1 sgt.............1 apr. 89 hon. dis..........22 dec. 98 pvt., sgt., 1 sgt. co. I, 8 regt......... 3 mar. 99 hon. dis..........11 nov. 99 2 lt. 8 regt........12 oct. 99 1 lt.............25 apr. 02 resigned..........13 aug. 04 pvt., 1 sgt., 28 co....16 apr. 08	Conn. 22 oct. 70
Brown, Harold Haskell, 14 june 15 *W. D. Cert. in course Nos. 4 (Battery Commander) and 6 (Fire and Battle Commander).*	28	1 div. sig. corps, U. S. N..22 apr. 98 to 31 july 98	seaman, Mass. naval brig. 30 mar. 97 to 11 aug. 98 1 co. c. a. c. trs. sig. corps, 13 feb. 05 to 29 may 13 2 lt. c. a. c........29 may 13 2 lt. c. a. c. N. G., N. Y., 28 dec. 14 1 lt.............14 june 15 accepted..........16 june 15	Mass. 4 nov. 72
Monell, Harry Stanbrough, 2 june 14 *W. D. Cert. in cert. No. 1 (Basic).*	31	....	pvt. 3 batty........ 1 oct. 06 hon. dis........... 6 feb. 07 2 lt. c. a. c........10 feb. 13 r. l.............31 aug. 14 1 lt.............14 june 15 rank from.......... 2 june 14 accepted..........16 june 15	N. Y. 22 sep. 87
Stahl, Edward Canning Muhlenbruch, 22 june 15 *W. D. Cert. in course Nos. 1 (Basic), 2 (Emplacement), and 3 (Range and Communication Officer).*	26	....	2 lt. c. a. c........19 june 14 1 lt.............22 june 15 accepted..........25 june 15	Minn. 10 mar. 91

COAST ARTILLERY CORPS — NINTH COAST DEFENSE COMMAND — (Continued)

Name, grade, date of rank and highest brevet rank	Company	Service		Born
		In the armies of U. S. or foreign states	In the National Guard	
First Lieutenants—Continued				
Dupuy, Richard Ernest, 3 may 16	32	....	pvt., corp., sgt. co. A, sig. corps......18 nov. 09 hon. dis............24 feb. 15 2 lt. c. a. c.........13 apr. 15 accepted..........16 apr. 15 1 lt. c. a. c.......... 3 may 16 accepted.......... 5 may 16	N. Y. 24 mar. 87
Meinecke, Otto J., 16 aug. 16	adjt.	pvt. 112 N. Y. vols., 6 june 98 disbanded . 10 jan, 99	pvt. co. C, 22 engs... 9 apr. 0 corp...............24 oct. 04 sgt................22 may 05 1 sgt...............10 apr. 07 f. and h. dis........28 dec. 08 pvt. 8 c. d. c.. ....12 apr. 09 sgt. maj., jr. gd......12 apr. 09 sgt. maj. sr. gd...... 8 may 11 2 lt. c. a. c.......... 4 apr. 16 accepted.......... 5 apr. 16 1 lt................16 aug. 16 accepted..........23 aug. 16	N. Q Y. 20 jan. 77
Gavit, Walter P., 19 aug. 16	35	....	pvt. 8 c. a. c....... 1 oct. 15 master eltrn....... 8 nov. 15 2 lt. c. a. c........ 6 apr. 16 accepted.......... 8 apr. 16 1 lt................19 aug. 16 accepted..... ..26 aug. 16	N. Y. 25 june 86
Callender, William Edwin, Jr., 16 sep. 16	25	....	pvt. co. G, 7 inf ....10 oct. 10 to 13 oct. 11 pvt., sgt..........27 sep. 12 to 21 dec. 15 2 lt................21 dec. 15 accepted..........22 dec. 15 1 lt................16 sep. 16 accepted..........20 sep. 16	N. Y. 11 jan. 90
Phinney, Harry B., 8 nov. 16	29	....	pvt. 26 co. c. a. c.....28 may 15 2 lt. c. a. c.......... 3 may 16 accepted..........10 may 16 1 lt................ 8 nov. 16 accepted..........10 nov. 16	N. Y.
Fieux, Ernest Daniel, 21 nov. 16	arty. eng.	....	pvt. 30 co. c. a. c.... 4 oct. 15 elect. sgt. 1 cl...... 3 mar. 15 2 lt. c. a. c........ 6 june 16 accepted.......... 7 june 16 1 lt................21 nov. 16 accepted..........22 nov. 16	N. Y. 28 feb. 85
Second lieutenants				
Dayton, Harry Leeds, 7 jan. 16	26	....	pvt. 7 inf..........26 oct. 11 corp...............27 nov. 14 2 lt. 8 c. d. c....... 7 jan. 16 accepted..........10 jan. 16 accepted..........10 jan. 16	N. Y. 24 feb. 87
Suydam, John Richard, 27 apr. 16	32	....	pvt. co. K, 7 inf..... 4 nov. 08 dropped for removal. 19 nov. 13 taken up...........28 apr. 14 2 lt. c. a. c.........13 june 14 accepted..........16 june 14 placed on r. l.......24 dec. 14 2 lt. c. a. c.........27 apr. 16 accepted..........28 apr. 16	N. Y. 9 may 86

10

COAST ARTILLERY CORPS — NINTH COAST DEFENSE COMMAND — *(Continued)*

Name, grade, date of rank and highest brevet rank	Company	Service		Born
		In the armies of U. S. or foreign states	In the National Guard	
Second Lieutenants — Continued				
Doll, Clarence E., 26 may 16	30	....	pvt. co. E, 7 inf..... 1 may 14 2 lt. c. a. c.........26 may 16 accepted..........29 may 16	N. Y. 30 mar. 85
Farrell, William James, 6 june 16	28	....	pvt. unassigned, 8 d. c., 23 feb. 14 trs. to 34 co........29 may 14 sgt............ 2 july 14 2 lt. c. a. o......... 6 june 16 accepted........... 7 june 16	N. Y. 21 oct. 91
Gunther, Albert E. P., 28 june 16	36		2 lt. c. a. c.........28 june 16 accepted..........28 june 16	N. Y. 25 feb. 87.
Davis, Francis Perry, 28 june 16	33		pvt. 26 co. 8 c. d. c... 6 oct. 15 1 cl. el. sgt......... 3 mar. 16 1 cl. gunner........20 apr. 16 2 lt. 8 c. d. c....... 28 june 16 accepted......... 28 june 16	R. I. 20 aug. 90
Orr, William C., Jr., 28 june 16	27	....	pvt. 7 inf.......... 7 feb. 12 f. and h. discharge...19 oct. 15 2 lt. c. a. c.........28 june 16 accepted..........28 june 16	N. Y. 29 apr. 89
Hansen, Howard A., 30 sep. 16	qm.	....	pvt. 32 co. 8 c. d. c... 6 june 12 corp............. 2 may 13 sgt............. 2 july 15 1 cl. gunner........19 dec. 13 plotter.............26 may 16 2 lt...............30 sep. 16 accepted.......... 3 oct. 16	N. Y. 27 dec. 93
Purcell, Thomas Edw., Jr., 26 oct. 16	35	....	pvt. 8 c. d. c........26 jan. 16 2 cl. gunner.......18 mar. 16 1 cl. gunner........20 april 16 2 cl. observer.......19 may 16 corp.............17 mar. 16 2 lt...............26 oct. 16 accepted..........26 oct. 16	N. Y. 25 oct 89
Shelby, Joseph B., 31 oct. 16	34	....	pvt. 35 co..........18 apr. 16 corp.............14 june 16 el. sgt. 1 cl sgt......18 sep. 16 2 lt...............31 oct. 16 accepted........... 2 nov. 16	Ky. 11 oct. 90
Weibesahl, Robert L., 16 dec. 16	29	....	pvt. co. B, 60 inf.... 4 jan. 06 to 23 mar. 06 pvt. 5 co. 13 c. d. c ..20 apr. 09 to 15 mar. 10 pvt. 26 co. 8 c. d. c...25 aug. 15 to 5 dec. 16 2 lt................ 6 dec. 16 accepted........... 8 dec. 16	N. Y. 19 mar. 84
Scofield, Thomas, 6 dec. 16	31	....	pvt. 36 co..........28 june 16 2 lt................ 6 dec. 16 accepted........... 8 dec. 16	N. Y. 22 aug. 85
Siggelkow, John, 22 dec. 16	unassigned	....	pvt. 30 co..........11 june 15 master gunner......27 sep. 16 2 lt...............22 dec. 16	N. C.
Chaplain Pelton, DeWitt Lincoln, 25 nov. 12		......	chaplain, c. a. c ....25 nov. 12 accepted...........29 nov. 12	Iowa. 10 dec. 66

COAST ARTILLERY CORPS — (*Continued*)
NINTH COAST DEFENSE COMMAND
(Eleven Companies.)

Armory, 125 West Fourteenth Street, New York City

By virtue of an order from Governor John Jay to Brigadier-General James Miles Hughes, New York, N. Y., dated Albany, June 24, 1799, the preliminary organization of the 6th Regiment, New York State Infantry, *of which this regiment is the successor*, took place, by transfer of four companies from the 1st Regiment, three companies from 2d Regiment, five companies from 3d Regiment, two companies from 4th Regiment, all organized March 4, 1786; three companies from the 5th Regiment, organized May 11, 1789, and the Independent Rifle Co., organized August 28, 1798.

The 6th Regiment, New York State Infantry, was permanently organized with 16 companies, under the command of Lieutenant-Colonel Commandant Jacob Morton, on March 8, 1800. This regiment was changed by General Orders, Adjutant General's Office, Albany, to the 2d New York State Artillery, March 27, 1805, and to the 9th Regiment, New York State Artillery, June 13, 1812; it was reduced to a battalion, December 13, 1813, and became a regiment again, by orders of Council of Appointment, June 6, 1816. By orders from Adjutant General's Office, the state was divided in division, brigade, regiment and company districts, May 13, 1847. Three of the regiment's companies were transferred to the 8th Regiment, New York State Militia, May 27, 1850; some of the officers and men elsewhere, but Colonel B. Clinton Ferris retained command of the 9th Regiment as reorganized May 29, 1850. It was again partly disbanded May 31, 1858, but the district of the 9th Regiment, New York State Militia, was kept intact, under Colonel Lucius Pitkin, and once more the regiment made — anew, June 25, 1859.*

Under this title it entered the service of the United States, May 27, 1861, and was mustered in at Washington, D. C., June 8. 1861. A further change was made in numerical designation; it became known as the 83d New York Volunteers, December 7, 1861, by which title it was mustered out of the United States service, June 23, 1864.

Under orders from the authorities of the State, the 9th District was retained for the regiment during its three years of war service, and formally retook position in the National Guard of the State as the 9th Regiment, National Guard, State of New York, June 13, 1864, which was continued until 1898, when the title was changed to the 9th Regiment Infantry, New York Volunteers, May 2, 1898. It was redesignated the 9th Regiment, National Guard, New York, January 12, 1899.

April 28, 1898, it was authorized to be organized into a twelve-company regiment, preparatory to entry into the United States service, into which it was mustered as the Ninth Regiment Infantry, New York Volunteers, May 17, 19 and 20, 1898, and mustered out November 15, 1898. Companies L and M were disbanded December 22, 1898.

To conform to the Military Law (1903), General Orders No. 7, Adjutant General's Office, dated Albany, January 23, 1908, reorganized the 9th Regiment Infantry, as Coast Artillery and made it a part of the Coast Artillery Corps, National Guard, New York, as the 9th Artillery District, and the designation of companies from letters A to K, to be the 13th to 22d Companies, Coast Artillery Corps, respectively.

Authorized to nominate officers for appointment February 1, 1909.

The designation of the 9th Artillery District was changed to the 9th Coast Defense Command by G. O. 14. A. G. O., August 10, 1914, to consist of the 13th, 14th, 15th, 16th, 17th, 18th, 19th, 20th, 21st and 22d Companies.

The 13th, 19th and 21st Companies transferred to mortar batteries, 1915.

The 23d Company was mustered into the service of the State, December 5, 1916. Accepted by S. O. 267. A. G. O., December 18. 1916.

Recognition extended by the War Department under Act of June 3, 1916, to F. S., N. C. S., Band, Sanitary Detachment, and 13th, 14th, 15th, 16th, 17th, 18th, 20th, 21st, 22d Companies, June 29, 1916; to 19th Company, June 30, 1916; to 23d Company, December 6, 1916.

The regiment was authorized to place silver rings on the lances of its colors, engraved as follows:

On the National Color.— War against Great Britain. 1812-15; New York Harbor. June 22 to December 15, 1812 (North Battery); New York Harbor, September 2 to December 3, 1814 (West Battery); War of the Rebellion, 1861–65; Harper's Ferry, Va., July 4, 1861; Warrenton Junction, Va., April 6, 1862; Warrenton Junction, Va., April 16, 1862; North Fork River, Va., April 18, 1862; Rappahannock River, Va., May 5, 1862; Cedar Mountain, Va., August 9, 1862; Rappahannock River, Va., August 22, 1862; Rappahannock Station, Va., August 23, 1862; Thoroughfare Gap, Va., August 28, 1862; Bull Run, Va., August 30, 1862; Chantilly, Va., September 1, 1862; South Mountain, Md., September 14, 1862; Antietam, Md., September 17, 1862; Fredericksburg, Va., December 11–15, 1862; Pollock's Mill Creek, Va., April 29, 1863; Chancellorsville, Va., May 2–3, 1863;

———
* Date in dispute.

Gettysburg, Pa., July 1–4, 1863; Hagerstown, Md., July 12–13, 1863; Liberty, Va., November 21, 1863; Mine Run, Va., November 26 to December 2, 1863; Wilderness, Va., May 5–7, 1864; Spottsylvania Court House, Va., May 1, 1864; Piney Branch Church, Va., May 8, 1864; Laurel Hill, Va., May 10, 1864; Spottsylvania, Va., May 12, 1864; North Anna, Va., May 22, 1864; Totopotomoy, Va., May 27–31, 1864; Cold Harbor, Va., June 1–7, 1864; Spanish-American War, May 2 to November 15, 1898.

On the State Color. Execution of George Hart, January 3, 1812; New York Harbor, June 5 to July 28, 1812; West Battery, New York Harbor, May 23 to June 1, 1813; Sag Harbor, L. I., May 1 to August 1, 1814; Brooklyn Heights, August 15, 1814; Brooklyn Heights, October 4, 1814; abolition riot, January 11–12, 1835; great fire, December 17, 1835; police riot, June 16–18, 1857; Dead Rabbit riot, July 5–6, 1857; Orange riot, July 12–13, 1871; West Albany, July 24–28, 1877; Buffalo, August 18–27, 1892; Brooklyn, January 20–24, 1895; Albany, May 17–19, 1901.

COAST ARTILLERY CORPS — NINTH COAST DEFENSE COMMAND

Name, grade, date of rank and highest brevet rank	Company	Service		Born
		In the armies of U. S. or foreign states	In the National Guard	
Lieutenant Colonel				
Byrne, John James, 15 june 12 W. D. Cert. in course No. 1 (Basic).	......	1 lt. 9 N. Y. inf., 2 may 98 cap......17 aug. 98 to 15 nov. 98	pvt. co. H, 7 inf.....13 jan. 90 to 16 july 94 1 lt. co. K, 9 regt..16 july 94 cap..................20 may 99 a. d. c. to gov.......1 jan. 01 to 31 dec. 04 maj. 9 regt........14 feb. 02 maj. c. a. c.........23 jan. 08 lt. col..............15 june 12 accepted..........17 june 12	N. Y. 13 sep. 71
Majors				
Thiery, Lewis Marie, 27 sep. 12 W. D. Cert. in course Nos. 1 (Basic), 2 (Emplacement Officer), 3 (Range and Communication Officer), 4 (Battery Commander), 5 (Searchlight Officer) and 6 (Fire and Battle Commander).	......		pvt. tr. A, trs. tr. 1 sq. A, artif......19 jan. 95 to 11 dec. 99 1 lt. bat. qm. 9 regt..11 dec. 99 bat. adj. with o. r...1 may 00 cap. regt. qm.......7 nov. 02 regt. adj. with o. r..14 aug. 03 cap. c. a. c.........23 jan. 08 maj................27 sep. 12 accepted..........28 sep. 12	N. Y. 5 sep. 71
Miller, Mills, 4 oct. 12 W. D. Cert. in course Nos. 1 (Basic), 2 (Emplacement Officer), 3 (Range and Communication Officer), 4 (Battery Commander), 5 (Searchlight Officer) and 6 (Fire and Battle Commander).	......		pvt. co. I, 109 inf., trs. co. I, 9 regt., corp., sgt.........4 may 98 to 15 nov. 04 2 lt. co. I, 9 regt.....15 nov. 04 1 lt................11 apr. 05 cap. co. C........16 july 07 cap. c. a. c.........23 jan. 08 maj..................4 oct. 12 accepted...........7 oct. 12	Md. 11 july 74
Allyn, Robert Starr, 21 jan. 16 W. D. Cert. in course Nos. 1 (Basic), 2 (Emplacement Officer), 3 (Range and Communication Officer), 4 (Battery Commander), 5 (Searchlight Officer) and 6 (Fire and Battle Commander).	......		pvt., lance corp., corp., co. F, 7 inf..15 dec. 03 hon. dis.............2 sep. 09 pvt., 1 sgt., 3 co. c. a. c..............28 sep. 09 to 1 june 10 1 lt. c. a. c.........1 june 10 cap...............25 oct. 10 accepted..........25 oct. 10 maj..............21 jan. 16 accepted...........24 jan. 16	Conn. 27 nov. 75

COAST ARTILLERY CORPS — NINTH COAST DEFENSE COMMAND —(*Continued*)

Name, grade, date of rank and highest brevet rank	Company	Service		Born
		In the armies of U. S. or foreign states	In the National Guard	
Captains				
Wetzelberg, Bruno Frederick, 19 apr. 09 W. D. Cert. in course Nos. 1 (Basic), 2 (Emplacement Officer) and 3 (Range and Communication Officer).	18	....	pvt., corp., co. D, 9 regt.............27 dec. 02 to 27 nov. 06 2 lt. co. C.........27 nov. 06 1 lt.................15 oct. 07 1 lt. c. a. c.........23 jan. 08 cap.................22 apr. 09 accepted...........26 apr. 09	Ger. 12 nov. 83
Walsh, James Joseph, 21 jan. 10	unattached	sgt., 1 sgt., co. A, 9 N. Y. inf., 2 may 98 to 27 aug. 98 1 lt......28 oct. 98 to 15 nov. 98	pvt., corp., sgt., 1 sgt., co. A, 9 regt..19 feb. 94 to 17 oct. 99 2 lt.................17 oct. 99 1 lt............... 2 aug. 00 bat. adj. 9 regt...... 2 jan. 03 1 lt. c. a. c.........23 jan. 08 cap.................28 jan. 10 accepted........... 7 feb. 10	N. Y. 3 sep. 75
Baldwin, Thomas William, 9 jan. 12 W. D. Cert. in course Nos. 1 (Basic), 2 (Emplacement Officer) 3 (Range and Communication Officer) and 4 (Battery Commander).	21	....	pvt., corp., sig. and tel. corps. 1 brig. (1 sig. corps.)..... 1 mar. 94 to 6 june 98 2 lt. (C), 108 regt... 6 june 98 supn..............22 dec. 98 resigned...........16 jan. 00 pvt., corp., sgt., 1 sig. corps........17 jan. 00 to 24 nov. 03 2 lt. 1 co. sig. corps...24 nov. 03 1 lt.................21 oct. 04 1 lt. sig. corps.......23 jan. 08 1 lt c. a. c.........24 mar. 10 cap................. 9 jan. 12 accepted...........15 jan. 12	Mass. 24 jan. 71
Cole, Wilmot Lawrence, 3 mar. 13 W. D. Cert. in course Nos. 1 (Basic), 2 (Emplacement Officer), 3 (Range and Communication Officer) and 4 (Battery Commander)	13	....	1 lt. c. a. c.........15 mar. 11 cap................. 3 mar. 13 accepted........... 5 mar. 13	N. Y. 4 nov. 86
Mackin, Robert Neville, Jr., 8 may 15 W. D. Cert. in course Nos. 1 (Basic), 2 (Emplacement Officer), 3 Range and Communication Officer), 4 Battery Commander) and 5 (Searchlight Officer).	20	....	pvt. 11 co. c. a. c....10 july 11 to 6 july 12 2 lt. c. a. c......... 6 july 12 1 lt.................16 july 13 cap................. 8 may 15 accepted...........14 may 15	N. Y. 22 feb. 88
Gates, George Upfold, 16 dec. 15	22	....	pvt., corp. co. E, 171 regt............. 9 may 98 to 14 jan. 99 hon. dis............14 jan. 99 pvt., corp., sgt. co. H, 13 regt........20 sep. 00 2 lt. c. a. c.........23 jan. 08 1 lt.................24 jan. 11 hon. dis............ 5 feb. 15 1 lt.................15 mar. 15 cap................16 dec. 15 accepted...........20 dec. 15	N. Y. 4 sep. 74

COAST ARTILLERY CORPS — NINTH COAST DEFENSE COMMAND — *(Continued)*

Name, grade, date of rank and highest brevet rank	Company	Service		Born
		In the armies of U. S. or foreign states	In the National Guard	
Captains — Concluded				
Higgins, Lucius Cornelius, 3 apr. 16 *W. D. Cert. in course No.* 1 *(Basic).*	14	....	2 lt. 71 inf..........16 may 12 1 lt. c. a. c.........12 nov. 14 accepted.... ....16 nov. 14 cap................ 3 apr. 16 accepted........... 6 apr. 16	D. C. 28 mar. 60
Meyer, James Julius, 27 mar. 16 *W. D. Cert. in course No.* 1 *(Basic).*	21	....	pvt., corp., sgt., gun com'dr. 16 co. c. a. c.............25 apr. 02 to 20 apr. 14 2 lt............20 apr. 14 1 lt............22 june 15 accepted..........25 june 15 cap................27 mar. 16 accepted..........30 mar. 16	N. Y. 13 june 83
Ford, Martin Francis, 3 june 16 *W. D. Cert. in course Nos.* 1 *(Basic),* 3 *(Range and Communication Officer) and* 5 *(Searchlight Officer).*	unattached	....	pvt. co. F, 9 regt., trs. co. I, comy. sgt. 9 regt....... 9 sep. 01 to 8 aug. 05 1 lt. co. C, 9 regt.... 8 aug. 05 1 lt. asst. i. s. a. p. with o. r ......23 nov. 06 supn., reassigned....21 jan. 08 1 lt. c. a. c.........11 feb. 08 accepted.... ....24 feb. 08 cap .... 6 june 16 accepted........... 8 june 16	N. Y. 9 nov. 66
First Lieutenants				
Gilmore, John Winfield, 1 july 15 *W. D. Cert. in course No.* 1 *(Basic).*	23	asst. eng. U. S. N., grade of ensign, 14 may 98 to 17 sep. 98	2 lt. c. a. c ... ... 11 jan. 15 1 lt .... 1 july 15 accepted. .... 3 july 15	N. J. 25 may 73
Knudson, Foulke Olaf Eric, 24 jan. 16 *W. D. Cert. in course Nos.* 1 *(Basic) and* 2 *(Emplacement Officer).*	19	....	pvt., corp , 19 co. c. a. c.... ..... 12 jan. 12 to 4 may 14 2 lt. c. a. c........ 4 may 14 accepted.......... 6 may 14 1 lt................24 jan. 16 accepted..........26 jan. 16	N. Y. 26 nov. 91
Bernheimer, Charles Daly, 15 may 16	15	....	2 lt. c. a. c ......18 may 14 accepted..........21 may 14 1 lt................15 may 16 accepted... ....22 may 16	N. Y. 26 june 68
Paine, Albert Ignatius, 19 may 16	14	....	2 lt. c. a. c.......... 6 july 15 accepted..........12 july 15 1 lt................19 may 16 accepted..........22 may 16	Mass. 4 oct. 91
Brown, Frank Harold, 1 mar. 16	22	....	2 lt. c. a. c.........20 july 15 accepted..........29 july 15 1 lt. c. a. c........ 1 mar. 16 accepted.......... 6 mar. 16	N. Y. 13 apr. 82
Higgins, Gilbert Henry, 6 june 16	17	....	2 lt. c. a. c ....21 dec. 15 accepted..........27 dec. 15 1 lt............ 6 june 16 accepted.......... 9 june 16	N. J. 19 may 15

COAST ARTILLERY CORPS — NINTH COAST DEFENSE COMMAND — (Continued)

Name, grade, date of rank and highest brevet rank	Company	Service		Born
		In the armies of U. S. or foreign states	In the National Guard	
First Lieutenants — Concluded				
Bosca, Ernest Eugene, 29 may 16	arty., engr.	....	pvt. co. H, 9 regt....27 sep. 89 corp...............20 mar. 90 sergt...............13 jan. 93 retd. to ranks......15 jan. 94 dropped............16 feb. 94 taken up...........11 feb. 07 1 sgt............. 6 may 07 1 lt. 9 regt.........28 dec. 07 captain c. a. c......22 apr. 09 accepted...........26 apr. 09 resigned...........21 dec. 09 1 lt...............29 may 16 accepted.......... 5 june 16	N. Y.
Austen, Charles A., 15 july 16	13	....	pvt. 1 co. s. c.......30 nov. 04 1 cl. pvt...........23 dec. 07 corp...............28 june 09 2 lt. c. a. c.........13 june 10 with rank from..... 8 june 10 accepted...........14 june 10 f. and h. dis........14 nov. 10 1 lt. c. a. c.........28 feb. 12 accepted........... 2 mar. 12 f. and h. dis........15 july 12 1 lt. c. a. c.........15 july 16 accepted...........15 july 16	N. Y. 1 nov. 83
Force, Malcolm W., 15 july 16	16	....	2 lt. 9 c. d. c.......12 jan. 16 accepted..........12 jan. 16 1 lt...............15 july 16 accepted...........15 july 16	N. J. 25 nov.
Fairbairn, Russell A., 10 oct. 16	21	....	2 lt. c. a. c........ 6 mar. 16 accepted.......... 9 mar. 16 1 lt...............10 oct. 16 accepted...........13 oct. 16	N. Y. 3 jan. 91
Norton, Kenneth B., 5 dec. 16	16	....	2 lt. c. a. c...... .11 mar. 16 accepted..........13 mar. 16 1 lt............... 5 dec. 16 accepted.......... 6 dec. 16	N. Y. 7 dec. 90
Second Lieutenants				
Travis, Pierce Mason, 13 mar. 16	19	....	N. G., Wyoming.....14 july 04 to 30 may 05 2 lt. c. a. c........13 mar. 16 accepted...........16 mar. 16 1 lt...............12 apr. 17 accepted...........16 apr. 17	N. Y. 3 sep. 87
Shipway, George Edward, 29 may 16	unassigned	....	2 lt............... 8 may 16 accepted...........15 may 16	N. Y. 1 mar. 87
Warren, William Henry, 9 may 16	22	....	pvt. 16 co. c. a. c.... 6 mar. 11 dropped............20 oct. 13 taken up, 22 co......28 dec. 14 hon. dis............10 may 15 re-enlisted 14 co.....27 sep. 15 2 lt. c. a. c......... 9 may 16 accepted...........13 may 16	N. Y. 29 july 84
Nichols, Joseph A., 17 may 16	13	....	pvt. 14 co. c. a. c....27 sep. 15 2 lt...............17 may 16 accepted...........22 may 16	N. Y. 6 feb. 84

COAST ARTILLERY CORPS — NINTH COAST DEFENSE COMMAND — (*Concluded*)

Name, grade, date of rank and highest brevet rank	Company	Service		Born
		In the armies of U. S. or foreign states	In the National Guard	
Second Lieutenants — Concluded				
Crosby, Hiram Bedford, 29 may 16	unassigned	enltd. 4 batty. N. Y. vols.....20 july 98 dis........21 oct. 98	pvt. 2 batty........ 5 sep. 95 hon. dis............28 oct. 01 2 lt. c. a. c..........29 may 16 accepted........... 5 june 16	N. Y. 24 july 72
Guidera, Albert M., 9 july 16	15	....	pvt. 21 co.......... 9 mar. 16 2 lt................ 9 june 16 accepted...........16 june 16	N. Y. 17 aug. 92
Macurda, William H., 21 june 16	unassigned	....	2 lt. c. a. c..........21 june 16 accepted..........23 june 16	Mass.
Seligman, Walter, 17 oct. 16	21	....	pvt. 21 co..........12 june 16 2 lt................17 oct. 16 accepted ....19 oct. 16	N. Y. 28 feb. 94
Ford, Martin Ambrose, 21 nov. 16	14	....	pvt................13 mar. 16 corp...............16 june 16 2 lt................21 nov. 16 accepted..........22 nov. 16	N. Y. 9 may 78
Peck, Alexander W., 24 nov. 16	20	....	pvt. 20 co..........23 june 16 2 lt................24 nov. 16 accepted..........27 nov. 16	N. Y. 20 oct. 88

COAST ARTILLERY CORPS — (Continued)
THIRTEENTH COAST DEFENSE COMMAND
(Twelve Companies.)
Armory, 357 Sumner Avenue, Brooklyn

This regiment was organized July 5, 1847; there were changes in the organization a few years later, again in April, 1859, and in 1860. It was disbanded May 7, 1898, except one battalion of four companies which had volunteered to enter the United States service, and authority was given to reorganize it May 15, 1898, November 28, 1898, such portion of the regiment as had been organized was disbanded, and authority was given to re-establish the regiment, the battalion which was in the United States service forming the nucleus of the new organization. Companies L and M were organized March 11, 1899; February 8, 1900, it was constituted a regiment of heavy artillery and designated 13th Regiment of Heavy Artillery of the National Guard, New York. This designation was changed to Coast Artillery, September 1, 1906. The regiment was in the service of the United States for three months from April 23, 1861, and was mustered out August 6, 1861; again from May 28 to September 12, 1862, and for the third time from June 20 to July 20, 1863, for thirty days; it was in the State service during the draft riots in July and August, 1863; the Orange riots, July 12, 1871; the railroad riots, July, 1877; the switchmen's strike at Buffalo, August, 1892; the quarantine disturbances at Fire Island, September, 1892, and the motormen's strike at Brooklyn, January, 1895. The battalion which volunteered to enter the United States service as part of the 22d Regiment, New York Volunteer Infantry, in the war with Spain, was mustered into such service May 24, 1898, and was mustered out November 23, 1898. January 23, 1908, the Coast Artillery Corps was organized; the companies of the 13th Regiment, Coast Artillery, becoming Companies 1 to 12 inclusive, Coast Artillery Corps, and constituting the 13th Artillery District.

The 13th Artillery District is changed to the 13th Coast Defense Command by G. O. 14, A. G. O., Aug. 10, 1914. It will consist of the 1st, 2d, 3d, 4th, 5th, 6th, 7th, 8th, 9th, 10th, 11th and 12th Companies.

The appointive system was adopted by the 13th Coast Defense Command, Oct. 29, 1914.

Recognition extended by the War Department under Act of June 3, 1916, on June 27, 1916.

The regiment has received authority to place silver rings on the lances of its colors, engraved as follows:

On the National Color:
    U. S. April 23–August 6, 1861.
    U. S. May 28–September 12, 1862.
    U. S. June 20–July 20, 1863.
    Spanish-American War, 1898.

On the State Color:
    Draft riots, 1863.
    Orange Riots, 1871.
    Railroad Riots, 1877.
    Buffalo, 1892.
    Fire Island, 1892.
    Brooklyn, 1895.

COAST ARTILLERY CORPS — THIRTEENTH COAST DEFENSE COMMAND

Name, grade, date of rank and highest brevet rank	Company	Service — In the armies of U. S. or foreign states	Service — In the National Guard	Born
Colonel				
Grant, Sydney, 29 apr. 15 bvt. lt. col....21 june 16 W. D. Cert. in course Nos. 1 (Basic), 2 (Emplacement Officer), 3 (Range and Communication Officer) and 4 (Battery Commander).		....	pvt., corp., qm. sgt., co. D, 13 regt.... 2 aug. 81 hon. dis. ....22 nov. 88 re-enlisted..........22 nov. 88 cap............23 sep. 95 supn...............16 may 98 assigned duty with 13 regt...........21 may 98 relieved............28 nov. 98 assigned duty with 13 regt...........24 dec. 98 cap. (D)............ 6 feb. 99 recommissioned.....12 may 03 cap. c. a. c.........23 jan. 08 maj................15 mar. 09 lt. col..............29 apr. 15 accepted........... 4 may 15 colonel............21 june 16 accepted..........24 june 16	Ill. 12 oct. 62

COAST ARTILLERY CORPS — THIRTEENTH COAST DEFENSE COMMAND —
(Continued)

Name, grade, date of rank and highest brevet rank	Company	Service		Born
		In the armies of U. S. or foreign states	In the National Guard	
Lieutenant Colonel				
Pendry, Bryer Hamilton, 20 july 16 *W. D. Cert. in course Nos. 1 (Basic), 2 (Emplacement Officer), 3 (Range and Communication Officer), 4 (Battery Commander), 5 (Searchlight Officer) and 6 (Fire and Battle Commander).*	......		pvt., corp., co. F, 13 regt............19 mar. 95 to 16 may 98 hon. dis............16 may 98 pvt. co. F, 13 regt., trs. co. H, sgt.....13 dec. 98 to 31 jan. 00 2 lt................31 jan. 00 cap................23 apr. 02 cap. c. a. c........23 jan. 08 maj................8 sep. 09 accepted...........15 sep. 09 lt. col............20 july 16 accepted...........21 july 16	Can. 7 dec. 75
Major				
Orr, Robert Peebles, 20 aug. 15 *W. D. Cert. in course Nos. 1 (Basic), 2 (Emplacement Officer), 3 (Range and Communication Officer), 4 (Battery Commander), 5 (Searchlight Officer) and 6 (Fire and Battle Commander).*	......		pvt., corp., sgt., 1 sgt. co. D, 13 regt....29 nov. 92 hon. dis............16 may 98 pvt................24 may 98 hon. dis............24 nov. 98 pvt., 1 sgt., co. D, 13 regt...............13 dec. 98 to 9 may 02 2 lt................9 may 02 1 lt................19 dec. 02 cap. c. a. c........26 may 08 maj................20 aug. 15 accepted...........26 aug. 15	Ire. 29 may 71
Captains				
Reilly, Edward James, 11 nov. 02	qm.	....	pvt. co. E, 13 regt., trs. co. D, corp., sgt................26 dec. 90 to 17 jan. 93 1 lt................17 jan. 93 supn...............7 may 98 assigned duty with 13 regt............21 may 98 relieved...........15 dec. 98 assigned duty with co. D, 13 regt.....23 jan. 99 1 lt................25 feb. 99 cap. (F)............11 nov. 02 cap. i. s. a. p. 13 regt. with o. r.........27 july 07 supn., reassigned....21 jan. 08 cap. c. a. c........6 feb. 02	Eng. 28 may 65
Johnston, George William, 14 may 08 *W. D. Cert. in course Nos. 1 (Basic), 2 (Emplacement Officer), 3 (Range and Communication Officer), 4 (Battery Commander), 5 (Searchlight Officer) and 6 (Fire and Battle Commander).*	3	....	pvt. co. A, 13 regt.... 2 apr. 92 to 18 sep. 94 5 may 96 hon. dis............16 may 98 2 lt. (C), 147 regt.... 9 aug. 98 supn...............24 jan. 99 2 lt. (C), 13 regt....22 aug. 99 1 lt................12 apr. 01 trs. co. M..........14 sep. 03 cap................17 may 04 resigned...........22 jan. 07 cap. c. a. c........26 may 08	Ky. 11 may 71
Finke, William Drexler, 7 june 09 *W. D. Cert. in course Nos. 1 (Basic), 2 (Range and Communication Officer) and 5 (Searchlight Officer).*	adjt.	....	pvt., corp., co. A, 13 regt..............5 june 01 to 6 apr. 03 1 lt. bat. adj. 13 regt. 6 apr. 03 1 lt. c. a. c........23 jan. 08 cap................14 june 09 accepted...........14 june 09 a. d. c. to gov.......1 jan. 13 to 31 dec. 14	N. Y. 17 dec. 66

COAST ARTILLERY CORPS — THIRTEENTH COAST DEFENSE COMMAND — (*Continued*)

Name, grade, date of rank and highest brevet rank	Company	Service		Born
		In the armies of U. S. or foreign states	In the National Guard	
Captains — Continued				
Van Auken, Harry Vermilyea, 23 nov. 10 *W. D. Cert. in course Nos.* 1 (*Basic*), 2 (*Emplacement Officer*), 3 (*Range and Communication Officer*), 4 (*Battery Commander*), 5 (*Searchlight Officer*) and 6 (*Fire and Battle Commander*).	8	sgt. co. L, 22 N. Y. inf......24 may 98 to 23 nov. 98	pvt., corp., sgt., co. E, 13 regt . : ....24 aug. 95 to 1 mar. 99 1 lt..............1 mar. 99 resigned...........14 feb. 00 pvt. tr. 6, sq. C, trs. tr. 7............13 jan. 08 to 3 june 09 1 lt. c. a. c.......... 3 june 09 cap........ 2 dec. 10 accepted .. .. 6 dec. 10	N. Y. 2 july 78
Meekes, Harry, 16 nov. 11 *W. D. Cert. in course Nos.* 1 (*Basic*), 2 (*Emplacement Officer*), 4 (*Battery Commander*) and 5 (*Searchlight Officer*).	9	....	pvt., corp., sgt., co. D, 13 regt.......21 may 86 hon. dis..........23 july 91 pvt. co. D, 13 regt.... 7 jan. 92 hon. dis..........11 may 93 pvt...........24 feb..96 hon. dis..........16 may 98 pvt...........24 may 98 hon. dis..........28 nov. 98 pvt., corp., sgt., qm. sgt., co. D, 13 regt.13 dec. 98 hon. dis..........12 sep. 05 2 lt. c. a. c.......... 3 dec. 08 cap..............16 nov. 11 accepted...........17 nov. 11	N. Y. 30 jan. 62
Jennings, John Dollo, 12 july 12 *W. D. Cert. in course Nos.* 1 (*Basic*), 2 (*Emplacement Officer*), 3 (*Range and Communication Officer*) and 4 (*Battery Commander*).	2	sgt. co. F, 22 N. Y. inf......12 may 98 to 23 nov. 98	pvt. co. B, 13 regt... 9 feb. 93 to 29 aug. 03 pvt., corp., sgt., co. B, 13 regt.......19 nov. 95 to 15 nov. 07 1 lt. (B), 13 regt.....15 nov. 07 1 lt. c. a. c.........23 jan. 08 cap..............12 july 12 accepted...........13 july 12	N. Y. 21 nov. 74
Aikman, Robert, 22 aug. 13	4	....	pvt., corp., sgt., 1 sgt., 4 co. c. a. c...26 feb. 01 to 19 jan. 12 2 lt. c. a. c.........19 jan. 12 cap.............22 aug. 13 accepted...........26 aug. 13	N. Y. 24 may 81
Clifton, Clarence Anthony, 22 aug. 13 *W. D. Cert. in course Nos.* 1 (*Basic*), 2 (*Emplacement Officer*), 3 (*Range and Communication Officer*), 4 (*Battery Commander*), 5 (*Searchlight Officer*) and 6 (*Fire and Battle Commander*).	7	....	pvt., corp., co. E, 7 inf..............28 dec. 06 to 12 july 12 1 lt. c. a. c.........12 july 12 cap.............22 aug. 13 accepted...........26 aug. 13	Col. 19 oct. 75
Comstock, George Spaulding, 23 june 14 *W. D. Cert. in course Nos.* 1 (*Basic*), 2 (*Emplacement Officer*), 3 (*Range and Communication Officer*) and 5 (*Searchlight Officer*).	5	pvt. h. c., 22 N. Y. inf...... 9 may 98 to 23 nov. 98	pvt. h. c., asst. hosp. stwd., 13 regt.....26 apr. 98 to 28 sep. 06 1 lt. asst. i. s. a. p. 13 regt...........28 sep. 06 supn., reassigned....21 jan. 08 1 lt. c. a. c.......... 6 feb. 08 cap..............23 june 14 accepted...........24 june 14	Iowa. 6 feb. 77

COAST ARTILLERY CORPS — THIRTEENTH COAST DEFENSE COMMAND —
(*Continued*)

Name, grade, date of rank and highest brevet rank	Company	Service		Born
		In the armies of U. S. or foreign states	In the National Guard	
Captains — Continued				
Cunningham, William Augustine, 21 apr. 15 *W. D. Cert. in course Nos 1 (Basic), 2 (Emplacement Officer), 3 (Range and Communication Officer), 4 (Battery Commander) and 5 (Searchlight Officer).*	6	....	pvt., corp., rgt., 1 class gunner, 12 co. c. a. c......... 9 nov. 09 to 25 june 12 1 lt. c. a. c.........25 june 12 cap.............. 21 apr. 15 accepted...........23 apr. 15	N. Y. 30 oct. 82
Wright, Harry McIndoe, 20 aug. 15 *W. D. Cert. in course Nos. 1 (Basic), 2 (Emplacement Officer), 3 (Range and Communication Officer), 4 (Battery Commander), 5 (Searchlight Officer) and 6 (Fire and Battle Commander).*	10	....	pvt. co. A, 9 regt., trs. co. D, 13 regt., corp .... 7 may 94 hon. dis .... 16 may 98 pvt. co. D, 13 regt...24 may 98 hon. dis..........28 nov. 98 pvt., sgt., 1 sgt., co. D, 13 regt........16 dec. 98 to 2 mar. 03 2 lt................ 2 mar. 03 1 lt. c. a. c.........12 june 08 cap.............. 20 aug. 08 accepted...........26 aug. 15	Ire. 4 jan. 74
Harris, Edward Tisdale, 22 sep. 15 *W. D. Cert. in course Nos. 1 (Basic), 2 (Emplacement Officer), 3 (Range and Communication Officer), 4 (Battery Commander), 5 (Searchlight Officer) and 6 (Fire and Battle Commander).*	12	....	pvt. co. H, 13 regt., trs. co. M, corp., 1 oct. 01 to 20 oct. 03 pvt., sgt., 1 sgt., co. H, 13 regt........23 feb. 04 hon. dis........... 5 feb. 07 pvt.............. 5 feb. 07 to 2 apr. 08 2 lt. c. a. c......... 2 apr. 08 1 lt................10 feb. 10 cap..............22 sep. 15 accepted...........25 sep. 15	N. Y. 16 july 83
Nelson, Frank Rogers Morse, 22 sep. 15 *W. D. Cert. in course No. 1 (Basic).*	11	....	pvt., corp., co. I, 13 inf.............. 5 feb. 00 hon. dis........ . 7 jan. 04 pvt., corp., sgt., 1 sgt., 9 co. c. a. c. 9 nov. 09 to 19 june 14 1 lt. c. a. c....... . 19 june 14 cap..............22 sep. 15 accepted...........25 sep. 15	N. Y. 10 aug. 81
Bodin, Charles Arthur, 10 apr. 16 *W. D. Cert. in course No. 1 (Basic).*	arty. engs.	....	pvt., corp., sgt., co. K, 13 regt........13 jan. 92 hos. dis..........16 may 98 pvt., sgt., 1 sgt., co. K, 13 regt., bat. qm. sgt., regt. qm. sgt., 13 regt.... ..20 dec. 98 to 22 may 07 1 lt. bat. adj. 13 regt..22 may 07 1 lt. c. a. c.........23 jan. 08 cap ... .10 apr. 16 accepted..... ......11 apr. 16	Eng. 3 july 73
Clifford, Charles S., 26 july 16	1	....	pvt. co. D, 7 regt., 15 dec. 02 dropped.. .... 5 oct. 04 2 lt. (A), 65 regt.....26 june 07 1 lt. 65 inf... .....17 july 08 withrank from...10 july 08 1 lt., c. a. c.......... 1 june 10 with rank from..10 july 08	S. C. 31 mar. 77

COAST ARTILLERY CORPS — THIRTEENTH COAST DEFENSE COMMAND — (Continued)

Name, grade, date of rank and highest brevet rank	Company	Service		Born
		In the armies of U. S. or foreign states	In the National Guard	
Captains — Continued				
Clifford, Charles S.— *Continued*	....	....	accepted............ 3 june 10 cap.................28 aug. 11 accepted............11 sep. 11 f. and h. dis.........19 jan. 12 cap. r. l............ 2 may 16 cap. c. a. c.........26 july 16 accepted...........26 july 16	
First Lieutenants				
Gibson, Walter Livingstone, 27 june 06 W. D. Cert. in course Nos. 1 (Basic), 2 (Emplacement Officer) and 3 (Range and Communication Officer).	adjt.	....	pvt., corp., sgt., co. A, 13 regt........ 4 oct. 00 to 27 june 06 1 lt. (A), 13 regt....27 june 06 1 lt. c. a. c.........23 jan. 08	N. Y. 20 feb. 77
Murray, Joseph Francis, 3 jan, 14 W. D. Cert. in course No. 1 (Basic).	7	....	pvt., corp., sgt., 1 class gunner, 7 co. c. a. c............19 mar. 00 to 3 jan. 14 1 lt. c. a c......... 3 jan. 14 accepted........... 6 jan. 14	N. Y. 16 sep. 81
Welch, George Morgan, 30 dec. 14 W. D. Cert. in course No. 1 (Basic).	5	....	pvt. co. E, 7 inf.....14 nov. 05 hon. dis...........22 nov. 10 1 lt. c. a c.........30 dec. 14 accepted........... 2 jan. 15	N. J. 7 jan. 82
Franklin, Edward Louis, 16 jan. 15 W. D. Cert. in course Nos. 1 (Basic), 2 (Emplacement Officer), 3 (Range and Communication Officer) and 4 (Battery Commander).	8	....	pvt., corp., sgt., 1 sgt., 8 co. c. a. c...17 jan. 05 to 23 nov. 11 2 lt. c. a. c.........23 nov. 11 1 lt................16 jan. 15 accepted...........19 jan. 15	N. Y. 1 oct. 84
Wahle, William Carl Gross, 21 oct. 15 W. D. Cert. in course No. 1 (Basic).	12	....	pvt., corp., qm. sgt 12 co. c. a. c.......28 feb. 11 to 20 apr. 14 2 lt. c. a. c.........20 apr. 14 1 lt................21 oct. 15 accepted...........25 oct. 15	N. Y. 15 jan. 92
Dwinall, George W. I., 25 oct. 15 W. D. Cert. in course Nos. 1 (Basic) and 2 (Emplacement Officer).	4	....	pvt., corp., sgt., 1 class gunner, plotter, 4 co. c. a. c... 4 may 09 t0 18 may 14 2 lt. c. a. c.........18 may 14 1 lt................25 oct. 15 accepted...........26 oct. 15	N. Y. 10 nov. 76
Patterson, Edward Walter, 15 june 16	11	....	pvt. co. B, 47 inf.....28 apr. 02 hon. dis........... 7 feb. 10 pvt., qm. sgt., co. D.14 aug. 11 to 11 may 14 2 lt. c. a. c.........11 may 14 accepted...........12 may 14 1 lt. c. a. c.........15 june 16 accepted...........16 june 16	N. Y. 30 apr. 83
Foster, Valentine Pearsal, 24 may 15	asst. adjt.	....	pvt., corp.; qm. sgt. 1 co. c. a. c........ 9 apr 07 to 30 june 15 2 lt................30 june 30 accepted........... 2 july 15	N. Y. 22 jan. 87

COAST ARTILLERY CORPS — THIRTEENTH COAST DEFENSE COMMAND — *(Continued)*

Name, grade, date of rank and highest brevet rank	Company	Service		Born
		In the armies of U. S. or foreign states	In the National Guard	
First Lieutenants — Continued				
Austin, Thomas Bennett, 19 may 16	1	....	pvt., corp , sgt., master. gunner, 5 co. 7 feb. 10 c. a. c......... 1 dec. 08, to 2 july 15 2 lt. c. a. c.......... 2 july 15 accepted.......... 6 july 15 1 lt. c. a. c.........19 may 16 accepted.........21 may 16	N. Y. 30 apr. 26 nov. 85
Gleim. Charles Sailor. 25 apr. 16	6	....	pvt., sgt. co. L, 71 inf.... ....27 nov. 08 hon. dis.. . ... . 1 mar. 12 2 lt. c. a. c.... ... 7 july 15 accepted... .... 9 july 15 1 lt. c. a. c.........25 apr. 16 accepted.. ....27 apr. 16	Pa. 16 nov. 87
Edwards, Archibald Crawford, 26 july 16 W. D. Cert. in course Nos. 1 (Basic), 2 (Emplacement Officer), 3 (Range and Communication Officer) and 4 (Battery Commander).	2	....	pvt., co. K, 13 regt., trs. co. B, corp., sgt............... 9 apr. 88 hon. dis........... 1 june 97 pvt., corp., sgt., 2 co. c. a. c......... 7 apr. 08 to 3 apr. 13 2 lt. c. a. c .... 3 apr. 13 accepted..........7 apr. 13 1 lt ... .26 july 16 accepted..........27 july 18	Eng. 8 jan. 70
Van Nost, Eugene A., 7 jan. 16	10	....	pvt. co. A, 13 inf ... 2 jan. 99 trs. co. C.......... 5 apr. 00 corp..............17 may 00 dropped...........22 jan. 01 taken up, co. M.. . 26 feb. 01 1 lt..............22 may 01 resigned...... ...10 feb. 03 1 lt .. . .20 mar. 03 f. and h. dis....... 6 mar. 06 1 lt. 13 c. d. c....... 7 jan. 16 accepted..........11 jan. 16	N. Y. 25 mar. 74
De Forest, Arthur E 24 jan. 16	9	....	mus. 13 regt. h. a.... 9 nov. 00 f. and h. dis... ....16 oct. 06 mus, 5 co. c. a. c.... 4 may 09 trs. to 13 band and apptd. sgt..... 7 dec. 09 retd to ranks..... ..14 oct. 13 trs. to 9 co..........14 oct. 13 sgt................14 oct. 13 2 cl. gunner.........20 may 14 1 sgt.........28 june 14 1 cl. gunner..... 5 may 15 f. and h. dis .... 20 july 15 re-enlisted..........21 july 15 warrant 1 sgt. continued 1 lt, c. a. c.24 jan. 16 accepted..........25 jan. 16	N. Y. 13 oct. 78
Second Lieutenants				
Baird, Andrew, 19 june 12	9	....	pvt., corp., qm. sgt., 1 class gunner, co. I, 13 regt...... ..29 aug. 05 to 19 june 12 2 lt. c. a. c . ...19 june 12 accepted.. ....22 june 12	N. Y. 19 dec. 86

COAST ARTILLERY CORPS — THIRTEENTH COAST DEFENSE COMMAND — (Continued)

Name, grade, date of rank and highest brevet rank	Company	Service		Born
		In the armies of U. S. or foreign states	In the National Guard	
Second Lieutenants — Continued				
Carroll, William Hughes, 12 apr. 15	8	....	pvt., corp. co H, 13 arty. dist........25 sep. 00 to 14 oct. 02 pvt., corp., sgt......28 mar. 05 hon. dis...........20 dec. 10 pvt., 1 sgt. 8 co. c. a. c................23 sep. 13 to 12 apr. 15 2 lt................12 apr. 15 accepted..........13 apr. 15	N. Y. 22 apr. 75
Davenport, Harry Augustus, 10 july 15	10	....	pvt., 2 class gunner, corp., 1 class gunner, sgt., gun commander, 12 co. c. a. c................19 sep. 11 hon. dis...........26 jan. 15 pvt., sgt..........27 jan. 15 to 10 jul. 15 2 lt................10 july 15 accepted.. ....13 july 15	N. Y. 22 jan. 92
Tice, John Henry, Jr., 28 oct. 15	11	....	pvt , sgt., 1 sgt., reduced to sgt. at own req., 1 class gunner, gun commander, 11 co. c. a. c............. 8 feb. 10 hon. dis...........26 june 14 2 lt. c. a. c........28 oct. 15 accepted...........29 oct. 15	N. Y. 2 feb. 91
Cording, Frederick William, 11 dec. 15	4	....	pvt , corp., sgt., 4 co. c. a. c....... . 3 oct. 05 hon. dis...........19 mar. 12 pvt., corp., sgt., 2 class gunner, 1 class gunner, gun commander......27 oct. 14 to 11 dec. 15 2 lt................11 dec. 15 accepted..........14 dec. 15	N. Y. 12 apr. 88
Van Wagenen, Elmer Harnden, 22 dec. 15	3	....	2 lt. c. a. c...... .22 dec. 15 accepted.......... ...28 dec. 15	N. Y. 16 oct. 93
Saunders, Irving M., 13 jan. 16	12	....	pvt. 12 co. c. a. c....12 mar. 12 corp..............16 june 14 sgt.......... .... 6 july 15 2 lt. c. a. c.... ...13 jan. 16 accepted..........18 jan. 16	N. Y. 7 feb. 94
Clark, Chas. Irvine, 18 jan. 16	5	....	pvt. 8 co. c. a. c.....13 feb. 12 corp..............17 nov. 14 sgt...............29 june 15 observer..........26 june 14 gun pointer........26 dec. 14 gun commander.....31 dec. 14 f. and h. dischg......26 feb. 15 re-enlisted......... 2 mar. 15 2 lt. c. a. c........18 jan. 16 accepted..........25 jan. 16	N. Y. 21 feb. 93

COAST ARTILLERY CORPS — THIRTEENTH COAST DEFENSE COMMAND —
(*Concluded*)

Name, grade, date of rank and highest brevet rank	Company	Service		Born
		In the armies of U. S. or foreign states	In the National Guard	
Second Lieutenants — Continued				
Kerby, Frank Edgar, 2 feb. 16	un.	....	pvt. co. K, 13 regt . . .27 dec. 94	......
			corp...............23 aug. 99	
			sgt...............19 may 03	
			1 sgt...............27 dec. 04	
			sgt. maj ....8 may 11	
			f. and h. dischg.....26 dec. 14	
			pvt..............22 jan. 15	
			f. and h. dischg.....21 jan. 16	
			2 lt. c. a. c.......2 feb. 16	
			accepted..........4 feb. 16	
Thomas, Francis Paul, 22 may 16	2	....	pvt. 13 c. d. c 11 dec.12	N. Y.
			corp...............26 may 14	25 jan.
			sgt...............29 june 15	93
			f. and h. dischg.....21 dec. 15	
			re-enlisted..........22 dec. 15	
			warrant continued	
			2 lt. c. a. c........22 may 16	
			accepted..........23 may 16	
Smith, James Axtell, 13 june 16	6	....	pvt. 4 co. c. a. c.....11 june 15	N. Y.
			corp...............26 oct. 15	24 mar.
			2 lt. c. a. c ....13 june 16	90
			accepted ....18 june 16	
Alman, Samuel, 19 june 16	q. & c.	....	pvt. 3 batty. f. a.....13 mar. 05	N. Y.
			corp...............11 jan. 07	21 mar.
			sgt...............22 nov. 07	
			hon. dis...........7 june 10	
			pvt. tr. D, 1 cav.....10 mar. 13	
			corp...............7 june 15	
			f. and h. dis........17 apr. 16	
			pvt. 3 co. c. a. c .....25 apr. 16	
			corp...............29 may 16	
			2 lt...............19 june 16	
			accepted..........20 june 16	
White, William C., 26 july 16	7	....	pvt. 7 co. c. a. c .....2 mar. 07	N. Y.
			corp.....;.....24 jan. 11	31 oct.
			f. and h. dis........2 apr. 12	88
			re-enlisted..........10 mar. 14	
			sgt...............15 june 15	
			1 sgt....`.......2 nov. 15	
			f. and h. dis.. ....11 mar. 16	
			re-enlisted..........11 mar. 16	
			2 cl. gunner... ....3 mar. 15	
			1 cl. gunner.....15 may 15	
			2 lt. c. a. c........26 july 16	
			accepted..........28 july 16	
Ross, James Munro, 27 july 16	1	....	pvt. 1 co. c. a. c ....22 jan. 07	N. Y.
			f. and h. dis.......9 mar. 15	6 june
			re-enlisted..........10 mar. 15	91
			corp.. ....25 may 15	
			2 cl. gunner........	
			2 lt. c. a. c ... .26 july 16	
			accepted..........27 july 16	
Chaplain				
Boynton, Nehemiah, 7 june 12		....	chaplain, c. a. c.....7 june 12	Mass.
			accepted....... ...12 june 12	21 nov.
				56

INFANTRY
FIRST REGIMENT
(Twelve Companies.)
(Third Brigade.)
Headquarters, State Armory, 227-241 Washington Street, Binghamton

By General Orders No. 10, Adjutant General's Office, the 1st Regiment and 4th Battalion were disbanded on May 1, 1905, and the 5th, 10th, 24th, 33d, 3d, 20th, 28th, 44th, 27th, 31st, 39th and 40th Separate Companies organized as the 1st Regiment, and designated respectively as companies L, E, I, F, G, H, A, B, K, M, C and D of that organization. November 29, 1911, the regiment received authority to organize a detachment of the Hospital Corps, to be stationed at Middletown.

The regiment has received authority to place silver rings on the lances of its colors engraved as follows:
On the National Color.— Spanish-American War, 1898 ; Hawaii, 1898.
On the State Color.— Buffalo, 1892 ; New York Mills, April, 1912.

COMPANY A, FIRST INFANTRY
(Twenty-eighth Separate Company.)
(Third Brigade.)
State Armory, Steuben and Rutger Streets, Utica

Organized June 8, 1873, as Co. C, 26th Battalion, and designated 28th Separate Co., December 17, 1881. Attached to Fourth Battalion as Co. A, April 19, 1899, and to 1st Regiment as Co. A, May 1, 1905. It was on duty at Buffalo during the riots in August, 1892, and at New York Mills, April, 1912.

Recognition extended by the War Department under Act of June 3, 1916, on June 26, 1916.

COMPANY B, FIRST INFANTRY
(Forty-fourth Separate Company.)
(Third Brigade.)
State Armory, Steuben Park, Utica

Organized September 13, 1887. Attached to 4th Battalion, as Co. B, April 19, 1899, and to 1st Regiment, as Co. B, May 1, 1905. On duty at Buffalo during the riots in August, 1892. In United States service as Co. E, 1st Regiment, N. Y. Infantry, from May 20, 1898, to February 21, 1899. New York Mills, April, 1912.

Recognition extended by the War Department under Act of June 3, 1916, on June 25, 1916.

COMPANY C, FIRST INFANTRY
(Thirty-ninth Separate Company.)
(Third Brigade.)
State Armory, 44 Arsenal Street, Watertown

Originally Co. C, 35th Battalion. Designation changed December 17, 1881. Attached to 4th Battalion as Co. C, April 19, 1899; to 1st Regiment, as Co. C, May 1, 1905. On duty at Buffalo during the riots in August, 1892, and at Massena July 31 to August 8, 1915, and also at Deferiet, September 3-13, 1915.

Recognition extended by the War Department under Act of June 3, 1916, on June 24, 1916.

COMPANY D, FIRST INFANTRY
(Fortieth Separate Company.)
(Third Brigade.)
State Armory, 33 Elisabeth Street, Ogdensburg

Organized February 27, 1894. Attached to 4th Battalion, as Co. D, April 19, 1899; to 1st Regiment as Co. D, May 1, 1905. On duty during riots at Massena, July 31 to August 6, 1915.

Recognition extended by the War Department under Act of June 3, 1916, on June 27, 1916.

COMPANY E, FIRST INFANTRY
(Tenth Separate Company.)
(Third Brigade.)
State Armory, 145 Broadway, Newburgh

Organized and designated Co. E, 17th Battalion, September 13, 1878. December 17, 1881, on the disbandment of the 17th Battalion, it was retained in service as the 10th Separate Company. Attached to 1st Regiment as Co. E, March 15, 1899. Designation retained on reorganization of regiment, May 1, 1905. December 26, 1881, it was on duty quelling a riot among railroad laborers at Cornwall, and in August, 1892, at Buffalo.

During the Spanish-American War this company furnished 66 officers and enlisted men to New York volunteer regiments.

Recognition extended by the War Department under Act of June 3, 1916, on June 25, 1916.

INFANTRY — (Continued)

COMPANY F, FIRST INFANTRY

(Thirty-third Separate Company.)

(Third Brigade.)

State Armory, 139–141 Stockton Avenue, Walton

Organized May 20, 1879. Attached to 1st Regiment as Co. F, March 15, 1899. Designation retained on reorganization of regiment, May 1, 1905. In United States service, as Co. F, 1st Regiment, N. Y. Infantry, from May 20, 1898, to February 25, 1899.

Recognition extended by the War Department under Act of June 3, 1916, on June 29, 1916.

COMPANY G, FIRST INFANTRY

(Third Separate Company.)

(Third Brigade.)

State Armory, 4 Academy Street, Oneonta

Organized August 10, 1875, as the 1st Separate Company, 28th Brigade. December 8, 1877, its designation was changed to 3d Separate Company. Attached to 1st Regiment as Co. G, March 15, 1899. Designation retained on reorganization of regiment May 1, 1905. On duty during the railroad riots in July, 1877, and at Buffalo during riots in August, 1892, and New York Mills, April 17–29, 1912. In United States service as Co. G, 1st Regiment, N. Y. Infantry, from May 20, 1898, to February 25, 1890.

Recognition extended by the War Department under Act of June 3, 1916, on June 26, 1916.

COMPANY H, FIRST INFANTRY

(Twentieth Separate Company.)

(Third Brigade.)

State Armory, 227–241 Washington Street, Binghamton

Organized February 28, 1878. Attached to 1st Regiment as Co. H, March 15, 1899. Designation retained on reorganization of regiment, May 1, 1905. On duty at Waverly during the riots in August, 1892, and New York Mills, April 17–29, 1912. In United States service as Co. H, 1st Regiment, N. Y. Infantry, from May 20, 1898, to February 26, 1899.

Recognition extended by the War Department under Act of June 3, 1916, on June 25, 1916.

COMPANY I, FIRST INFANTRY

(Twenty-fourth Separate Company.)

(Third Brigade.)

State Armory, John Street and Wickham Avenue, Middletown

Organized March 17, 1857. Attached to 1st Regiment, as Co. I, March 15, 1899. Designation retained on reorganization of regiment May 1, 1905. In the United States service, as Co. I, 1st Regiment, N. Y. Infantry, from May 20, 1898, to February 20, 1899.

Recognition extended by the War Department under Act of June 3, 1916, on June 26, 1916.

COMPANY K, FIRST INFANTRY

(Twenty-seventh Separate Company.)

(Third Brigade.)

State Armory, 116 West Main Street, Malone

Organized July 10, 1878. Attached to 4th Battalion as Co. E, April 19, 1899. To 1st Regiment, as Co. K, May 1, 1905. On duty during riots at Massena from July 31 to August 7, 1915.

Recognition extended by the War Department under Act of June 3, 1916, on June 24, 1916.

COMPANY L, FIRST INFANTRY

(Fifth Separate Company.)

(Third Brigade.)

State Armory, 145 Broadway, Newburgh

Organized February 27, 1878, as Co. A of the 17th Battalion, and on the disbandment of that battalion the company was detached from it and its designation changed December 17, 1881, to 5th Separate Company. Attached to 1st Regiment. as Co. L, March 15, 1899. Designation retained on reorganization of regiment, May 1, 1905. The company, with the 10th Separate Company, was on duty suppressing a riot and arresting the leaders thereof, December 26, 1881, at Cornwall, and also at Buffalo during the riots in August, 1892. In United States service, as Co. L, 1st Regiment, N. Y. Infantry, from May 20, 1898, to February 26, 1899.

Recognition extended by the War Department under Act of June 3, 1916, on June 24, 1916.

INFANTRY — (*Continued*)
COMPANY M, FIRST INFANTRY
(Thirty-first Separate Company.)
(Third Brigade.)

State Armory, East Main Street, Mohawk.

Organized November 25, 1878. Assigned as Co. G, to 2d Regiment, November 19, 1898; transferred as Co. G to 4th Battalion, November 9, 1900. Attached to 1st Regiment as Co. M, May 1, 1905. In the United States service as Co. G, 2d Regiment. N. Y. Infantry, from May 16, 1898, to November 1, 1898. New York Mills, April, 1912.

Recognition extended by the War Department under Act of June 3, 1916, on June 26, 1916.

INFANTRY — FIRST REGIMENT

Name, grade, date of rank and highest brevet rank	Company	Service		Born
		In the armies of U. S. or foreign states	In the National Guard	
Colonel				
Hitchcock, Charles Henry, 26 apr. 05 bvt. brig. gen. 19 july 10 Graduate, Garrison Schools, 1914.	......	cap. 1 N. Y. inf., 1 may 98 to 26 feb. 99	pvt., 1 sgt., 20 sep. co 30 may 82 to 19 apr. 89 2 lt................19 apr. 89 1 lt................31 jan. 93 cap................1 oct 97 maj. 1 inf..........17 mar. 99 supn...............1 may 05 col. 1 inf............1 may 05	N. Y. 12 nov. 57
Lieutenant Colonel				
Boyer, James Starbuck, 26 apr. 05 bvt. col.....25 feb. 07	......	enrolled 6 july 98 and mustered in cap. 203 N. Y. inf., 19 july 98 maj ... 2 feb. 99 to 25 mar. 99	pvt., corp., sgt., co. C, 35 bat. 39 sep. co................29 mar. 81 to 13 apr. 88 1 lt................13 apr. 88 cap.. .... 21 mar. 93 maj 4 bat .. .. 9 nov. 99 supn...............1 may 05 lt. col. 1 inf ....1 may 05	N. Y. 25 june 62
Majors				
Cookinham, Henry Jared, Jr., 26 apr. 05 Graduate, Garrison Schools, 1914.	......	sgt. co. E, 1 N. Y inf...... 2 may 98 to 21 feb. 99	pvt. corp., sgt, 44 sep. co .... 4 june 96 to 16 june 99 cap................16 june 99 maj. 1 inf........26 apr. 05 a. d c. to gov......2 jan. 05 to 31 dec. 06	N. Y. 26 aug. 74
Sheehan, James Francis, 15 apr. 16		cap. 1 N. Y. inf., 2 may 98 to 26 feb. 99	pvt., corp., 5 sep. co..30 july 87 to 6 july 92 2 lt.............. 6 july 92 1 lt................ 5 oct. 93 cap................28 apr. 98 major..............15 apr. 16 accepted..........19 apr 16	Ire. 7 nov. 63
Seymour, Lewis, 27 mar. 16	......	regt. qm. sgt 1 N. Y. inf...... 1 may 98 to 26 feb. 90	pvt. 20 sep. co....... 8 apr. 98 to 2 may 99 1 lt. bat. adj. 1 inf ... 2 may 99 supn., reassigned .... 1 may 05 cap. regt. adj. 1 inf...22 may 05 major..............27 mar. 16 accepted...........28 mar. 16	N. Y. 14 mar 63
Captains				
Parish, Edward Jenkins, 26 mar. 10 Distinguished Graduate, Garrison Schools, 1915	G	....	asst. surg. 3 sep. co 1 lt................31 may 05 supn., reassigned....21 jan. 08 asst. surg. 1 lt...... 6 feb. 08 1 lt. 1 inf ..... 5 june 08 cap................1 apr. 10 accepted .... 4 apr. 10	N. Y. 15 june 74

INFANTRY — FIRST REGIMENT —(Continued)

Name, grade, date of rank and highest brevet rank	Company	Service — In the armies of U. S. or foreign states	Service — In the National Guard	Born
Captains — Continued				
Merselis, Lewis B., 2 mar. 16	M. G. co.	sgt. co. H, 1 N. Y. inf......23 june 98 to 26 feb. 99	pvt., corp., sgt., 1 sgt. 20 sep. co.........20 june 95 to 2 mar. 05 2 lt................ 2 mar. 05 1 lt. 1 inf...........17 nov. 08 cap.................21 dec. 09 resigned...........13 jan. 11 cap. 1 inf..........23 may 11 accepted...........24 may 11 cap............. 2 mar. 16 accepted.......... 6 mar. 16	Pa. 24 july 74
Sherman, Thomas Moore, 22 july 11 Graduate, Garrison Schools, 1915.	B	....	pvt. 44 sep. co......14 dec. 06 to 12 june 08 2 lt. 1 inf...........12 june 08 cap.................22 july 11 accepted.........25 july 11 det. aide staff of comdg. gen. div... 5 dec. 14	N. Y. 24 dec. 85
Yeomans, Charles Willis, 14 jan. 13	sup. co.	....	pvt. 20 sep. co., bat. sgt. maj. 1 inf.....31 mar. 98 to 1 may 05 cap., comy. of sub... 1 may 05 resigned...........13 may 10 cap. 1 inf..........14 jan. 13 accepted...........15 jan. 13	N. Y. 17 mar. 70
Witherbee, Rex Gould, 20 nov. 13	M	....	pvt., corp., 44 sep co., bat. qm. sgt., post qm. sgt., bat. sgt. maj. 1 inf........12 oct. 00 to 28 sep. 02 pvt. 44 sep. co.......11 june 03 to 2 oct. 03 25 june 04 to 4 oct. 04 pvt., corp., 44 sep. co., bat. qm. sgt., bat. sgt. maj. 1 inf.15 aug. 05 to 23 dec. 10 2 lt. 1 inf...........23 dec. 10 1 lt................19 jan. 12 cap.................20 nov. 13 accepted...........21 nov. 13	N. Y. 15 jan. 84
Briggs, Clark Arthur, 10 dec. 13	D	....	pvt., corp., sgt., 1 sgt. 40 sep. co.....25 oct. 97 hon. dis...........28 may 06 1 lt. 40 sep. co......17 oct. 07 cap.................10 dec. 13 accepted...........12 dec. 13	N. Y. 28 aug. 77
Ryan, Richard John, 30 mar. 14	C	pvt., E batty. Royal Canadian artillery..... 9 jan. 00 to 9 jan. 01	pvt., corp., qm. sgt., co. C, 1 inf.......23 feb. 04 hon. dis........... 1 mar. 09 pvt. co. C, 1 inf..... 1 mar. 09 to 16 aug. 09 1 lt................24 feb. 13 cap.................30 mar. 14 accepted.......... 2 apr. 14	Can. 10 sep. 76
Miller, Edward Kook, 1 june 14	A	....	pvt., corp., sgt., 28 sep. co..........12 feb. 94 to 30 july 07 hon. dis...........13 feb. 00 pvt., sgt..........16 feb. 00 hon. dis...........14 june 06 2 lt. 28 sep. co......30 july 07 1 lt................10 may 12 cap............. 1 june 14 accepted..........10 june 14	N. Y. 4 nov. 73

INFANTRY — FIRST REGIMENT —(Continued)

Name, grade, date of rank and highest brevet rank	Company	Service		Born
		In the armies of U. S. or foreign states	In the National Guard	
Captains — Continued				
Steedman, Harry Livingston, 24 mar. 15	I	pvt., corp. co I, 1 N. Y. inf., 2 may 98 to 21 feb. 99	pvt., corp., sgt., 24 sep co.........26 apr. 94 to 3 june 09 pvt.............25 may 06 hon. dis.........25 may 06 2 lt. 1 inf..........3 june 09 1 lt.............5 july 1: accepted..........7 july 11 captain...........24 mar. 15 accepted.........26 mar. 15	N. J. 27 june 72
Egan, Raphael Augustin, 6 may 15	E	....	pvt., co. D, 7 inf ....13 dec. 09 to 3 dec. 10 pvt., corp., 10 sep. co.............30 jan. 11 to 26 jan. 12 2 lt. inf...........26 jan. 12 1 lt..............13 oct. 14 cap..............6 may 15 accepted..........6 may 15	N. Y. 12 may 87
Marshall, Alvin Inman, 14 july 15	K	....	pvt. 27 sep. co......20 feb. 03 to 15 nov. 04 pvt., corp., sgt. 27 sep. co.........29 july 07 hon. dis..........30 jan. 11 1 lt. 1 inf.........28 dec. 11 cap..............14 july 15 accepted..........20 july 15	N. Y. 10 feb. 85
Keepers, George S........ 26 may 16	adjt.	....	pvt. mtd. det........2 july 13 corp.............22 jan. 14 sgt. major.........26 may 15 1 lt..............2 mar. 16 accepted...........4 mar. 16 cap.............26 may 16 accepted..........29 may 16	Ill. 3 mar. 81
Blythe, Harry Thomas.... 9 june 16	L	corp. co. L, 1 N. Y. inf......2 may 98 to 26 feb. 99	pvt., corp., 5 sep. co.21 apr. 93 hon. dis............9 mar. 99 pvt. corp., 5 sep. co.26 dec. 99 hon. dis...........26 dec. 00 2 lt. 5 sep. co.......2 june 05 1 lt. 1 inf..........1 feb. 11 accepted...........2 feb. 11 captain............9 june 16 accepted...........10 june 16	N. Y. 10 jan. 74
Moody, Edwin H........ 5 feb. 15	H	....	pvt., corp., mtd. detach. comy sgt., 1 inf..............28 june 13 to 30 sep. 14 2 lt..............30 sep. 14 1 lt..............5 feb. 15 accepted..........6 feb. 15	N. Y. 3 may 79
First Lieutenants				
Wilbur, Julian Roy, 15 feb. 10	H	corp. co. H, 1 N. Y. inf......1 may 98 to 26 feb. 99	pvt., corp., sgt., 1 sgt., 20 sep. co....23 jan. 96 hon. dis...........23 may 06 pvt..............23 may 06 to 30 dec. 08 2 lt. 1 inf.........30 dec. 08 1 lt..............26 feb. 10 accepted...........5 mar. 10	N. Y. 11 apr. 74

INFANTRY — FIRST REGIMENT —(Continued)

Name, grade, date of rank and highest brevet rank	Company	Service		Born
		In the armies of U. S. or foreign states	In the National Guard	
First Lieutenants — Continued				

Roberts, Edward Angelle, 2 aug. 12	B	....	pvt., corp., 144 sep. co..............24 may 98
			hon. dis...........15 mar. 99
			pvt., corp. 44 sep. co.,16 nov. 00
			      to 2 oct. 02
			pvt., sgt., 44 sep. co.,26 may 06
			hon. dis...........30 mar. 09
			pvt., sgt...........30 mar. 09
			      to 16 aug. 10
			pvt................16 aug. 10
			      to 6 feb. 12
			2 lt. 1 inf...........6 feb. 12
			1 lt................2 aug. 12
			accepted............3 aug. 12
				Wales 27 june 78

Beebee, Fred Emerson, 12 may 13	C	....	pvt., corp., sgt., 1 sgt., 39 sep. co....23 oct. 93 hon. dis............6 apr. 06 pvt................6 apr. 06 to 9 feb. 11 2 lt. 1 inf...........9 feb. 11 1 lt...............12 may 13 accepted...........13 may 13	N. Y. 9 feb. 67
Goodnow, Henri Delbert, 13 mar. 14	D	....	pvt., corp., 40 sep. co................28 oct. 01 hon. dis............6 apr. 07 re enlisted..........6 apr. 07 to 16 may 08 2 lt. 1 inf..........16 may 08 1 lt...............13 mar. 14 accepted...........14 mar. 14	N. Y. 22 june 71

Mahoney, Francis Sylvester, 19 oct. 14	M. G. co.	....	pvt., corp., sgt., 28
			sep. co............7 oct. 07
			hon. dis...........11 jun. 06
			re-enlisted.........11 june 06
			      to 16 oct. 12
			re-enlisted..........24 oct.
			      to 23 dec. 12
			2 lt. 1 inf..........23 dec. 12
			1 lt...............19 oct. 14
			accepted...........23 oct. 14
				N. Y. 1 apr. 76

Wilbur, Harry Andrew, 23 nov. 14	F	....	pvt., corp., sgt., 1 sgt., 33 sep. co....23 nov. 00 hon. dis...........23 may 06 re-enlisted.........23 may 06 hon. dis...........23 jan. 11 re-enlisted.........23 june 11 to 18 sep. 12 2 lt. 1 inf..........18 sep. 12 1 lt...............23 nov. 14 accepted...........25 nov. 14	N. Y. 6 may 83
Vernon, Russell Montgomery, 13 may 15	I	....	pvt., corp., sgt., 1 sgt., 24 sep. co....22 dec. 03 to 1 aug. 11 2 lt................1 aug. 11 1 lt...............13 may 15 accepted...........14 may 15	N. Y 23 apr. 73
Penoyar, William Brewster, 4 june 15	E	....	pvt., corp., sgt., qm. agt. co. E, 1 inf...23 nov. 08 to 11 dec. 14 2 lt...............11 dec. 14 1 lt................4 june 15 accepted...........9 june 15	N. Y. 20 jan. 82

INFANTRY — FIRST REGIMENT —(*Continued*)

Name, grade, date of rank and highest brevet rank	Company	Service		Born
		In the armies of U. S. or foreign states	In the National Guard	
First Lieutenants — Continued				
Belfield, William H., 11 dec. 15	G	....	pvt., lance corp., sgt., co. G, 1 inf...27 july 1(to 11 dec. 15 1 lt................11 dec. 15 accepted..........15 dec. 15	Pa. 1 aug. 86
McLean, Charles M., 2 mar. 16	Bn. adjt.	....	pvt. mtd. det......28 june 13 q. m. sgt...........12 feb. 15 1 lt............... 2 mar. 16 accepted.......... 6 mar. 16	N. Y. 10 june 87
Hinds, John Barry, 21 mar. 16	K	....	pvt., corp., sgt., 27 sep. co.......... 6 dec. 04 hon. dis..........30 jan. 11 2 lt. 1 inf..........28 dec. 11 accepted., ... 4 jan. 12 1 lt..............21 mar. 16 accepted..........24 mar. 16	N. Y. 26 mar. 82
Adams, Frederick B.,	Bn. adjt.	....	pvt. co. B.......22 nov. 04 corp............22 jan. 06 rtd. to ranks........14 apr. 08 dropped for removal.28 dec. 08 taken up trp. G, 1 cav............. 9 sep. 12 f. and h. dis......... 8 mar. 15 re-enlisted.......... 7 mar. 15 corp............24 july 15 sgt................ 6 dec. 15 1 lt................23 may 16 accepted..........24 may 16	N. Y. 19 oct. 75
Wallace, James Monroe Henderson, 28 june 16	L	....	pvt.,1 sep. co...... 3 dec. 00 to 22 mar. 04 pvt., corp., 1 sgt., 6 sep. co..........30 jan. 09 to 5 apr. 11 2 lt. 1 inf.......... 5 apr. 11 accepted............ 6 apr. 11 1 lt................28 june 16 accepted..........28 june 16	N. Y. 22 june 80
Wightman, David Chase, 14 aug. 16	M	....	pvt., co. M, 1 inf....18 apr. 10 to 12 oct. 10 8 june 11 to 27 sep. 11 pvt., corp., co. M, 1 inf..............22 jan. 14 to 11 may 14 2 lt................11 may 14 accepted............18 may 14 1 lt................14 aug. 16 accepted..........21 aug. 16	N. Y. 1 jan. 92
Spencer, James A., 8 jan. 14	m. g. co.	....	pvt., corp., sgt., co. C, 1 inf., bat. sgt. maj................ 7 jan. 07 hon. dis..........23 jan. 12 re-enlisted..........23 jan. 12 2 lt................ 8 jan. 14 accepted..........10 jan. 14	N. Y. 19 jun. 85
Hones, William, Jr., 5 feb. 15	F	....	pvt., corp., sgt., co. F, 1 inf..........26 feb. 12 to 5 feb. 15 2 lt. 1 inf......... 5 feb. 15 accepted......... 6 feb. 15	N. Y. 21 oct. 92

INFANTRY — FIRST REGIMENT — (Concluded)

Name, grade, date of rank and highest brevet rank	Company	Service — In the armies of U. S. or foreign states	Service — In the National Guard	Born
First Lieutenants — Continued				
McLean, Floyd Dana, 18 mar. 15	H	....	pvt. mt. det. 1 inf.... 7 jul. 13 to 18 mar. 15 2 lt................18 mar. 15 accepted..........20 mar. 15	N. Y. 21 may 85
Cockinham, Walter Sherman, 15 may 14	sup. co.	....	pvt. co. B, 1 inf.....20 nov. 03 to 7 aug. 04 5 dec. 05 to 2 oct. 06 pvt., corp., sgt., co. B, 1 inf..........16 dec. 11 to 15 may 14 2 lt................15 may 14 accepted..........18 may 14	N. Y. 3 mar. 86
Second Lieutenants				
Jenks, Addison Elmore, 30 jun. 10	G	....	pvt., 3 sep. co......16 feb. 04 to 31 dec. 06 pvt., corp., 3 sep. co., 4 may 07 hon. dis............26 jun. 09 2 lt. 1 inf.......... 1 jul. 10 accepted.......... 1 jul. 10	N. Y. 3 sep. 85
Dedell, Thomas Clark, 31 dec. 14	A	....	pvt. co. A, 1 inf....24 feb. 02 to 14 nov. 06 pvt..............13 feb. 09 to 7 dec. 09 pvt..............26 july 13 hon. dis.........15 july 14 2 lt. 1 inf..........31 dec. 14 hon. dis.........15 jul. 15 re-enlisted........16 july 14 to 31 dec. 14 accepted.......... 2 jan. 15	N. Y. 12 apr. 83
Bowman, Robert W., 21 feb. 16	C	....	pvt. co. C..........26 aug. 15 2 lt................21 feb. 16 accepted..........28 feb. 16	Pa. 2 july 69
Brundage, Arthur Edward, 28 sep. 15	E	....	pvt., corp., sgt., co. E, 1 inf..........18 jul. 07 to 28 sep. 15 2 lt................28 sep. 15 accepted.......... 1 oct. 15	N. Y. 4 apr. 86
Korschen, John Anthony, 5 oct. 15	I	....	pvt., post qmr. sgt. h. c., 1 inf........26 feb. 12 to 5 oct. 15 2 lt................ 5 oct. 15 accepted.......... 7 oct. 15	Denmark. 24 jan. 84
Shaver, Herbert F., 9 jun. 16	D	....	pvt. co. D.......... 1 jan. 06 corp..............31 mar. 09 qm. sgt..............12 jul. 13 2 lt................ 9 jun. 16 accepted..........10 jun. 16	N. Y.
Judson, Frank S., 22 july	m. g. 16 co.	....	pvt., co. H, 22 engrs.10 feb. 91 corp..............23 apr. 94 retired to ranks..... 3 jun. 99 sgt..............28 aug. 99 1 sgt.............. 8 jan. 00 f. and h. dis........11 jan. 04 pvt., co. B, 1 inf.... 3 apr. 08 f. and h. dis........ 9 may 09 re-enlisted........11 oct. 10 post qm. sgt........13 oct. 11 2 lt................22 jul. 16 accepted..........22 july 16	N. Y. 6 may 70

INFANTRY — (*Continued*)

SECOND REGIMENT

(Twelve Companies.)

(Third Brigade.)

Headquarters, State Armory, 7 Ferry Street, Troy

April 27, 1898, the Governor directed the commanding officer of the Third Brigade to organize two regiments of such portions of his command as desired to volunteer for service in the United States Volunteer Army. The Second Regiment was composed of the 6th, 7th, 9th, 12th, 18th, 21st, 22d, 31st, 32d, 36th, 37th and 46th Separate Companies, the companies being designated as A, B, I, C, K, D, L, G, M, E, F and H, respectively. It entered the service of the United States, May 16 and 17, 1898, and was mustered out of such service: Companies A, B, C and D on October 25, Co. M on October 26, Co. L on October 27, Co. I on October 28, Co. K on October 29, Cos. E and F on October 31, Cos. G and H on November 1, and the field and staff on October 31, 1898. On its re-entry into the State service it was, on November 19, 1898, continued as a twelve-company regiment, composed as in the volunteer service as stated above. The 31st Separate Company was detached from this regiment on November 9, 1900, and assigned to the 4th Battalion. The 19th Separate Company was organized November 9, 1900, at Gloversville, N. Y., and assigned to this regiment as Co. G. The regiment was authorized to organize a detachment of mounted scouts by Special Orders, No. 73, March 25, 1912.

Machine Gun Company mustered into the service of the State, G. O. 19, A. G. O., June 21, 1916, accepted by S. O. 262, A. G. O., December 12, 1916. Recognition extended by the War Department under Act of June 3, 1916, on June 28, 1916.

Supply Company mustered into the service of the State in accordance with G. O. 19, June 21, 1916, accepted by S. O. 274, December 27, 1916. Recognition extended by War Department under Act of June 3, 1916, on June 23, 1916.

Headquarters Company mustered into the service of the State, G. O. 19, June 21, 1916.

Recognition extended by the War Department under Act of June 3, 1916, on June 23, 1916.

Recognition extended by the War Department under Act of June 3, 1916, on June 23, 1916, to Sanitary Detachment.

The regiment has received authority to place silver rings on the lances of its colors, engraved as follows:

On the National Color.— Spanish-American War. 1898.

On the State Color.—Buffalo, 1892; Albany, 1901; Hudson Valley, 1902; Corinth — South Glens Falls — Fort Edward, 1910.

COMPANY A, SECOND INFANTRY

(Sixth Separate Company)

(Third Brigade.)

State Armory, 7 Ferry Street, Troy

The Troy Citizens' Corps was organized September 23, 1835, and chartered by act of Legislature May 20, 1836; at the beginning of the War of the Rebellion the members of the company practically all joined the United States forces, and the company was compelled to suspend all action as an organization. February 3, 1877, the company was reorganized, and February 20, 1877, was mustered into the State service as the 6th Separate Company, 10th Brigade. Its designation was changed to 20th Separate Company, December 8, 1877, and to 6th Separate Company, February 4, 1878. Under the orders of the Governor of the State the company aided the civil authorities in December, 1839, in quelling resistance by the anti-renters; again in 1844, under the order of the mayor of Troy; in 1850 it assisted in suppressing a riot in the northern part of the city of Troy, and in July, 1877, during the railroad riots, it performed duty in West Albany. It was on duty at Buffalo during riots in August, 1892; at Albany during the street railway riots, May 16–18, 1901; during Hudson Valley riots, 1902, at Corinth in April, 1910, and at Troy, March, 1913, Hudson River flood. In the United States service as Co. A, 2d Regiment, N. Y. Infantry, from May 17, 1898, to October 25, 1898.

Recognition extended by the War Department under Act of June 3, 1916, on June 30, 1916.

COMPANY B, SECOND INFANTRY

(Seventh Separate Company.)

(Third Brigade.)

State Armory, 4 Hart Street, Cohoes

Organized February 26, 1876, as the 3d Separate Co. of the 10th Brigade, 3d Division. Its designation was changed to 7th Separate Co. on December 8, 1877. It performed duty during the railroad riots in 1877; at Buffalo during riots in August, 1892; at Albany during street railway riots, May 16–18, 1901, and during Hudson Valley riots, 1902. In the United States service as Co. B, 2d Regiment, N. Y. Infantry, from May 16, 1898, to October 25, 1898.

Recognition extended by the War Department under Act of June 3, 1916, on June 23, 1916.

INFANTRY — (Continued)

COMPANY C, SECOND INFANTRY

(Twelfth Separate Company.)

(Third Brigade.)

State Armory, 7 Ferry Street, Troy

Organized March 20, 1876, as the 4th Separate Company, 10th Brigade. Designation changed to 12th Separate Company, December 8, 1877. Was in the State service at West Albany during the railroad riots in July, 1877; at Albany during street railway riots, May 16–18, 1901; during Hudson Valley riots, 1902, at Fort Edward in May, 1910, and at Troy, March, 1913, Hudson River flood. In the United States service as Co. C, 2d Regiment, N. Y. Infantry, from May 17, 1898, to October 25, 1898.

Recognition extended by the War Department under Act of June 3, 1916, on June 23, 1916.

COMPANY D, SECOND INFANTRY

(Twenty-first Separate Company.)

(Third Brigade.)

State Armory, 7 Ferry Street, Troy

Organized February 16, 1877, as the 7th Separate Company of the 10th Brigade. Designation was changed to 21st Separate Company, December 8, 1877. On duty at Buffalo during riots in August, 1892; at Albany, May 16–18, 1901, during street railway riots; during Hudson Valley riots, 1902, and at Troy, March, 1913, Hudson River flood. In United States service, as Co. D, 2d Regiment, N. Y. Infantry, from May 16, 1898, to October 25, 1898.

Recognition extended by the War Department under Act of June 3, 1916, on June 23, 1916.

COMPANY E, SECOND INFANTRY

(Thirty-sixth Separate Company.)

(Third Brigade.)

State Armory, 700 State Street, Schenectady

Organized June 9, 1880. On duty at Buffalo during riots in August, 1892; at Albany during street railway riots, May 16–18, 1901; during Hudson Valley riots, 1902; and at Corinth, March, 1910. In United States service, as Co. E, 2d Regiment, N. Y. Infantry, from May 16, 1898, to October 31, 1898.

Recognition extended by the War Department under Act of June 3, 1916, on June 22, 1916.

COMPANY F, SECOND INFANTRY

(Thirty-seventh Separate Company.)

(Third Brigade.)

State Armory, 700 State Street, Schenectady.

Organized June 10, 1880. On duty at Buffalo during riots in August, 1892; at Albany during street railway riots, May 16–18, 1901; during Hudson Valley riots, 1902; and at Corinth, March, 1910. In United States service, as Co. F, 2d Regiment, N. Y. Infantry, from May 16, 1898, to October 31, 1898.

Recognition extended by the War Department under Act of June 3, 1916, on June 22, 1916.

COMPANY G, SECOND INFANTRY

(Nineteenth Separate Company.)

(Third Brigade.)

Armory, 87 Washington Street, Gloversville

Organized November 9, 1900. Was on duty at Albany during street railway riots, May 16–18, 1901; and during Hudson Valley riots, 1902.

Recognition extended by the War Department under Act of June 3, 1916, on June 23, 1916.

COMPANY H, SECOND INFANTRY

(Forty-sixth Separate Company.)

(Third Brigade.)

State Armory, Florida Avenue and De Witt Street, Amsterdam

Organized September 6, 1888. On duty at Buffalo during riots in August, 1892; at Albany during street railway riots, May 16–18, 1901; during Hudson Valley riots, 1902; and at Corinth, March, 1910. In United States service, as Co. H, 2d Regiment, N. Y. Infantry, from May 16, 1898, to November 1, 1898.

Recognition extended by the War Department under Act of June 3, 1916, on June 23, 1916.

INFANTRY — *(Continued)*

COMPANY I, SECOND INFANTRY

(Ninth Separate Company.)

(Third Brigade.)

Armory, Poultney and William Streets, Whitehall

Organized as 2d Separate Company, 10th Brigade, April 26, 1876. Designation changed to 9th Separate Company, December 8, 1877. On duty during labor riots in July, 1877; at Albany, May 16–18, 1901; during Hudson Valley riots, 1902; and at Fort Edward, March, 1910. In United States service as Co. I, 2d Regiment, N. Y. Infantry, from May 16, 1898, to October 28, 1898.

Recognition extended by the War Department under Act of June 3, 1916, on June 23, 1916.

COMPANY K, SECOND INFANTRY

(Eighteenth Separate Company.)

(Third Brigade.)

State Armory, 85–89 Warren Street, Glens Falls

Organized as the 5th Separate Company, 10th Brigade, in November, 1876. Its designation was changed to the 18th Separate Company, December 8, 1877. Was in the State service at Troy during the railroad riots in July, 1877; at Albany during street railway riots, May 16–18, 1901; during Hudson Valley riots, 1902; and at South Glens Falls and Fort Edward, March, 1910. In United States service, as Co. K, 2d Regiment, N. Y. Infantry, from May 16, 1898, to October 29, 1898.

Recognition extended by the War Department under Act of June 3, 1916, on . June 23, 1916.

COMPANY L, SECOND INFANTRY

(Twenty-second Separate Company.)

(Third Brigade.)

State Armory, 61–65 Lake Avenue, Saratoga Springs

Organized March 14, 1878. On duty at Albany, May 16–18, 1901, during street railway riots; during Hudson Valley riots, 1902; and at Corinth and South Glens Falls, March, April and May, 1910. In United States service, as Co. L, 2d Regiment, N. Y. Infantry, from May 16, 1898, to October 27, 1898.

Recognition extended by the War Department under Act of June 3, 1916, on June 23, 1916.

COMPANY M, SECOND INFANTRY

(Thirty-second Separate Company.)

(Third Brigade.)

State Armory, 80 Church Street, Hoosick Falls

Organized March 20, 1885. On duty at Buffalo during riots in August, 1892; at Albany during street railway riots, May 16–18, 1901; during Hudson Valley riots, 1902; and at Fort Edward, April and May, 1910. In United States service, as Co. M, 2d Regiment, N. Y. Infantry, from May 16, 1898, to October 26, 1898.

Recognition extended by the War Department under Act of June 3, 1916, on June 23, 1916.

INFANTRY — SECOND REGIMENT

Name, grade, date of rank and highest brevet rank	Company	Service		Born
		In the armies of U. S. or foreign states	In the National Guard	
Colonel				
Andrews, James Madison..... 28 dec. 12	....	cadet, U. S. M. A. 15 june 86 2 lt. 5 U. S. cav . 90 resigned... 9 nov. 02 cap. 2 N. Y inf , 2 may 98 to 31 oct. 98 mustered into u. s ser...... 1 july 16 out 23 oct. 16	1 lt. 36 sep. co..... 1 nov. 95 cap ....28 apr. 98 a. d. c. to gov....... 1 jan. 99 to 1 jan. 01 maj. 2 inf.......... 8 feb. 01 lt. col...............31 jul. 11 col.... ....28 dec. 12 accepted ....30 dec. 12	N. Y. 2 apr. 68

INFANTRY — SECOND REGIMENT — (*Continued*)

Name, grade, date of rank and highest brevet rank	Company	Service — In the armies of U. S. or foreign states	Service — In the National Guard	Born
Lieutenant Colonel				
Taylor, William Aloysius, 5 july 16 Field Officers' Course, Army Service Schools, 1915.	......	mustered into u. s. ser...... 1 july 16 out 23 oct. 16	pvt., corp. 121 sep. co.............. 6 may 98 hon. dis............ 6 dec. 98 pvt., co. D, regt. qm. dgt. 2 inf. ...16 aug. 00 to 21 june 09 2 lt. 2 inf..........21 june 09 cap.................20 sep. 11 insp. gen. maj., 3 brig............17 oct. 12 maj. 2 inf..........27 apr. 14 accepted..........27 apr. 14 lt. col..........5 july 16 accepted..........5 july 16	N. Y. 22 aug. 76
Majors				
Robinson, Walter George, 30 mar. 15	......	mustered into u. s. ser...... 1 july 16 out 23 oct. 16	1 lt. 36 sep. co......13 dec. 07 cap....... ....11 dec. 11 maj.................30 mar. 15 accepted..........2 apr. 15	N. Y. 11 apr. 77
Pateman, Everett Eugene, 11 june 15	......	pvt., corp. co. D, 2 N. Y. inf., 2 may 98 to 25 oct. 98 mustered into u. s. ser...... 1 july 16 out 23 oct. 16	pvt., corp., qm. sgt., 21 sep. co.... ..28 may 06 to 25 may 05 2 lt................25 may 05 1 lt................26 july 06 cap. 2 inf..........3 apr. 12 maj................11 june 15 accepted..........14 june 15	N. Y. 19 june 76
Button, Jesse Scott, 5 july 16	......	corp. co. F, 2 N. Y. inf...... 2 may 93 to 31 oct. 98 mustered into u. s. ser...... 1 july 16 out 23 oct. 16	pvt. 37 sep. co......3 dec. 96 hon. dis.......... 4 may 99 29 aug. 99 to 8 jan. 00 pvt., corp., sgt. 37 sep. co., bat. sgt. maj.............17 mar. 00 to 20 dec. 04 2 lt. 37 sep. co......20 dec. 04 1 lt........ ...... 31 jul. 07 cap. 2 inf.... 12 apr. 12 accepted........ 14 apr. 12 major.. 5 july 16 accepted.. .... 5 july 16	N. Y. 24 oct. 74
Captains				
Thiessen, Frederick Allen, 3 apr. 16	sep. co.	mustered into u. s. ser...... 1 july 16 out 30 oct. 16	pvt., corp., sgt., 6 sep. co. ... 18 feb 03 to 1 aug. 11 2 lt. 2 inf..... ....1 aug. 11 1 lt.... ....31 jan. 13 accepted.. . 5 feb. 13 captain..... 3 apr. 16 accepted..........3 apr. 16	N. Y 24 apr 85
Tiffany, Stewart David, 3 may 16	m. g. co.	mustered into u s ser...... 1 july 16 out 20 oct. 16	pvt, co. H, 2 inf 27 mar. 06 hon. dis.......... 3 apr 11 pvt., corp., sgt. co. H..............21 dec. 11 to 15 may 14 2 lt................15 may 14 1 lt................28 jan. 15 accepted.... ..30 jan. 15 captain ... . 3 may 16 accepted........ . 8 may 16	N. Y. 10 nov. 90

INFANTRY — SECOND REGIMENT — (Continued)

Name, grade, date of rank and highest brevet rank	Company	Service		Born
		In the armies of U. S. or foreign states	In the National Guard	
Captains — Continued				
Sullivan, Hermon E., 1 may 16	I	mustered into u. s. ser...... 1 july 16 out 7 oct. 16	captain............. 1 may 16 accepted............. 1 may 16	N. Y. 23 may 74
Crounse, Herbert Duane, 5 july 16	F	mustered into u. s. ser...... 1 july 16 out 4 oct. 16	pvt., corp., sgt., 37 sep. co................28 apr. 03 hon. dis............24 jan. 11 re-enlisted.........24 jan. 11 to 6 sep. 12 2 lt. 2 inf............. 6 sep. 12 1 lt................10 june 15 accepted............11 june 15 captain............. 5 july 16 accepted............ 5 july 16	N. Y. 30 oct. 78
Hay, Frank McElroy, 20 sep. 11	B	sgt. co. B, 2 N. Y inf...... 2 may 98 to 25 oct. 98 mustered into u. s. ser...... 1 jul. 16 out 17 oct. 16	pvt., corp., sgt., 7 sep. co................ 9 jun. 90 hon. dis.........29 may 01 pvt., corp., sgt., 7 sep. co................25 nov. 01 to 20 feb. 03 2 lt.................20 feb. 03 1 lt.................21 sep. 03 cap. 2 inf...........20 sep. 11 accepted...........22 sep. 11	N. Y. 20 jul. 71
Compton, C. H. Ranulf,	L	mustered into u. s. ser.............. out 16 oct. 16	cap. 2 inf...........26 nov. 12 1 jul. 16 accepted...........27 nov 12	Ind. 16 sep. 78
Bradshaw, George Frederick, 3 apr. 13 Graduate, Garrison Schools, 1915.	C	1 lt. co. C, 2 N. Y. inf...... 2 may 98 to 25 oct. 98 mustered into u. s. ser...... 1 jul. 16 out 23 oct. 16	pvt., corp., 12 sep. co., regt. sgt. maj., 2 inf................24 jun. 95 to 6 dec. 09 1 lt. 2 inf........... 6 dec. 09 cap............. 3 apr. 13 accepted............ 4 apr. 13	N. Y. 10 nov. 74
MacArthur, Charles Abner, 12 may 13	A	mustered into u. s. ser...... 1 jul. 16 out 23 oct. 16	pvt., corp., 6 sep. co..26 jul. 04 to 22 mar. 11 1 lt. 2 inf..........22 mar. 11 cap............12 may 13 accepted...........14 may 13	N. Y. 3 mar. 84
Hall, Robert Stewart, 16 jun. 13	K	pvt. co. K, 2 N. Y. inf...... 2 may 98 to 29 oct. 98 mustered into u. s. ser...... 1 jul. 16 out 8 oct. 16	pvt., lance corp., corp., sgt., 18 sep. co................ 6 apr. 98 to 21 sep. 03 2 lt.................21 sep. 03 1 lt. 2 inf........... 3 dec. 08 cap............16 jun. 13 accepted...........17 jun. 13	N. Y. 10 aug. 76
Trumble, Roscoe Bradley, 15 jul. 13	G	mustered into u. s. ser...... 1 jul. 16 out 19 oct. 16	pvt., sgt., 1 sgt., co. G, 2 inf.........26 oct. 00 to 15 jul. 13 cap.............1 jul. 13 accepted...........16 jul. 13	N. Y. 23 mar. 76
Greene, Henry Eckford, 17 feb. 14	adj.	mustered into u. s. ser...... 1 jul. 16 out 19 oct. 16	pvt. 146 sep. co., trs. 46 sep. co., corp., sgt., 1 sgt........ 12 jul. 98 hon. dis.........19 nov. 03 1 lt. 2 inf........... 9 dec. 12 cap................17 feb. 14 accepted.. ....19 feb. 14	N. Y. 2 may 80

INFANTRY — SECOND REGIMENT — (Continued)

Name, grade, date of rank and highest brevet rank	Company	Service — In the armies of U. S. or foreign states	Service — In the National Guard	Born
Captains — Continued				
Curtis, William Hanford, 1 mar. 14	M	mustered into u. s. ser...... 1 jul. 16 out 13 oct. 16	pvt. co. M, 2 inf.....13 mar. 08 to 30 dec. 08 2 lt.................30 dec. 08 resigned............16 sep. 10 cap................. 1 mar. 14 accepted.......... 3 mar. 14	N. Y. 15 jan. 84
Clinton, Jacob Sanders, 29 apr. 15	E	pvt. co. F, 2 N. Y. inf...... 2 may 98 to 31 oct. 98 mustered into u. s. ser..... 1 july 16 out 20 oct. 16	pvt., corp., sgt., 37 sep. co............ 3 mar. 98 hon. dis............ 3 mar. 10 2 lt. 2 inf............23 dec. 10 1 lt......... 29 may 12 cap...........29 apr. 15 accepted.........30 apr. 15	N. Y. 4 nov. 79
Livingston, John, 8 nov. 15	D	mustered into u. s ser...... 1 july 16 out 23 oct. 16	pvt., corp., sgt., 21 sep. co............28 feb. 99 to 29 dec. 06 2 lt. 2 inf............29 dec. 06 1 lt. 2 inf............14 jun. 12 resigned............ 4 apr. 14 cap.............. 8 nov. 15 accepted.......... 9 nov. 15	Scot. 27 aug. 80
First Lieutenants				
McEwan, Henry Gansevoort, 11 dec. 11	bat. adj.	mustered into u. s. ser...... 1 july 16 out 23 oct. 16	pvt., corp., sgt., tr. B.................18 jun. 00 to 11 dec. 11 1 lt.................11 dec. 11 trs. 1 cav.............28 dec. 11 1 lt. 2 inf..........29 july 13 accepted.........31 july 13	N. Y. 5 jan. 80
Plumley, Charles Burton, 13 dec. 11	B	mustered into u. s. ser...... 1 july 16 out 17 oct. 16	pvt., corp., 7 sep. co..25 may 03 hon. dis........... 3 aug. 08 re-enlisted......... 3 aug. 08 to 13 dec. 11 1 lt. 2 inf..........13 dec. 11 accepted...........14 dec. 11	Vt. 24 sep. 83
Young, Harry Jay, 5 june 12	L	mustered into u. s. ser...... 1 july 16 out 16 oct. 16	pvt., corp., sgt., 22 sep. co............19 feb. 01 to 5 june 12 1 lt. 2 inf.... 5 jan. 12 accepted.......... 7 june 12	N. Y. 25 aug. 69
Groesbeck, Elwood, 28 june 14	I	mustered into u. s. ser...... 1 july 16 out 30 sep. 16	pvt., corp., sgt., co. F, 2 inf....... 7 may 07 hon. dis........... 7 june 12 re-enlisted.......... 7 june 12 to 29 sep. 13 1 lt. o. d.........29 sep. 13 1 lt. 2 inf....... 4 may 14 accepted.......... 6 may 14 1 lt......... 8 june 16 accepted.........28 june 16	N. Y. 22 jan. 78
Buckley, Benjamin, 11 may 14	C	mustered into u. s ser...... 1 july 16 out 23 oct. 16	pvt., corp., sgt., co. C, 2 inf.......... 1 aug. 04 to 11 may 14 1 lt.............11 may 14 accepted ....12 may 14	Eng. 10 feb. 79
Benedict, Chester Levi, 28 sep. 15	G	mustered into u. s. ser...... 1 july 16 out 19 oct. 16	pvt., corp., sgt., co. G, 2 inf............31 mar. 05 hon. dis...........21 aug. 11 pvt., sgt., co. G......25 july 13 to 20 oct. 14 2 lt.................20 oct. 14 1 lt.................28 sep. 15 accepted..........29 sep. 15	N. Y. 18 june 81

INFANTRY — SECOND REGIMENT — (Continued)

Name, grade, date of rank and highest brevet rank	Company	Service		Born
		In the armies of U. S. or foreign states	In the National Guard	
First Lieutenants — Continued				
Whipple, Charles R., 1 may 16	M	mustered into u. s. ser...... 1 july 16 out 13 oct. 16	1 lt... .... 1 may 16 accepted........... 2 may 16	N. Y. 22 sep. 89
Ramsey, George Ellis, 27 may 16	E	pvt. co. L, 2 N. Y. inf......16 may 98 to 27 oct. 98 mustered into u. s. ser...... 1 july 16 out 20 oct. 16	pvt., 22 sep. co..... 23 nov. 94 to 14 nov. 00 pvt., corp., sgt., 1 sgt. 36 sep. co.........21 feb. 01 to 20 may 12 2 lt. 2 inf............20 may 12 accepted..........27 may 12 1 lt...............27 mar. 16 accepted..........29 mar. 16	N. Y. 20 jan. 72
Pike, Seneca M., 21 june 16	bat. adj.	mustered into u. s. ser...... 1 july 16 out 23 oct. 16	pvt. co. K..........30 jan. 05 dropped........ 4 nov. 05 taken up, co. A......10 mar. 06 dropped...........15 nov. 08 taken up..........10 may 09 dropped........... 9 nov. 09 taken up..........28 feb. 10 dropped...........18 may 10 taken up.......... 1 jan. 16 1 lt............21 june 16 accepted.........22 june 16	N. Y. 28 sep. 82
Kriegsman, Arnold E., 5 july 16	F	mustered into u. s. ser...... 1 july 16 out 4 oct. 16	pvt., lance corp., corp., sgt. co. F, 2 inf....12 apr. 11 to 17 june 15 2 lt. 2 inf..........17 june 15 accepted...........18 june 15 1 lt............. 5 july 16 accepted........... 5 july 16	N. Y. 30 mar. 87
Bird, Howard,	M. C. co.	mustered out u. s. ser......20 oct. 16	pvt. co. F..........15 feb. 11 dropped...........23 nov. 11 taken up..........26 jan. 12 det. lance corp.... 10 apr. 13 corp...............10 apr. 13 f. and h. dis........ 4 aug. 14 re-enlisted.........12 aug. 14 discharged. . . ...12 nov. 15 re-enlisted.....19 may 16 sergt...............20 may 16 1 sgt. m. g. co 1 lt.............27 july 16 accepted.........27 july 16	Conn.
Rugge, George Folsom, 6 oct. 16	bat. adj.	mustered into u. s ser..... 1 july 16 out 4 oct. 16	pvt., corp., sgt., 18 sep. co ....6 july 04 hon. dis ....26 may 11 pvt. co. A, 10 inf... .15 june 11 to 20 may 12 2 lt. 2 inf ....20 may 12 accepted...........20 may 12 1 lt........... 6 oct. 16 accepted. .... 6 oct. 16	N. Y. 9 apr. 85
Second Lieutenants				
Davidson, Harry James, 6 sep. 12	D	corp., co. D, 2 N. Y. inf...... 2 may 98 to 25 oct. 98 mustered into u. s ser...... 1 july 16 out.23 oct. 16	pvt., corp , sgt., 1 sgt., 21 sep. co.....20 sep. 92 to 6 sep. 12 2 lt. 2 inf ....6 sep. 12 accepted............ 9 sep. 12	N. Y. 19 apr. 74
Van Schoonhoven, Jacob L. 22 jan. 16	A	mustered into u. s ser......23 oct. 16 out 23 oct. 16	pvt. co. A. ....11 apr. 11 corp. . ...25 june 13 2 lt ....22 jan. 16 accepted .. ..24 jan. 16	N. Y. 15 oct. 92

INFANTRY — SECOND REGIMENT — (*Concluded*)

Name, grade, date of rank and highest brevet rank	Company	Service		Born
		In the armies of U. S. or foreign states	In the National Guard	
Second Lieutenants — Continued				
Farrell, Michael J.,	C	mustered into u. s. ser...... 1 july 16 out 23 oct. 16	pvt. co. C..... 20 jan. 13 corp.............. 1 july 13 2 lt............... 25 jan. 16 accepted......... 28 jan. 16	N. Y. 18 apr. 87
Hall, John C. R., 22 mar. 16	I	mustered into u. s. ser...... 1 july 16 out 7 oct. 16	2 lt................ 22 mar. 16 accepted.. ...... 23 mar. 16	N. Y. 21 june 92
Howard, Leonard J., 7 apr. 16	K	mustered into u. s. ser..... 1 july 16 out 8 oct. 16	2 lt............... 7 apr. 16 accepted.......... 10 apr. 16	N. Y. 7 june 87
Stevens, Carl W., 28 apr. 16	M	mustered into u. s. ser...... 1 july 16 out 13 oct. 16	pvt. co. M......... 22 oct. 15 dropped, removal. . 3 dec. 15 taken up.......... 17 apr. 16 2 lt.......... 28 apr. 16 accepted......... 2 may 16	N. Y. 24 june 94
Root, William F. S., 10 may 16	Q & C	mustered into u. s. ser...... 1 jul. 16 out 30 oct. 16	pvt. co. F, 74 inf. 23 s p. 98 trs. to hosp. c. 65 inf. 9 feb. 00 2 lt. 65 inf........ 22 dec. 00 resigned.......... 8 nov. 01 pvt. co. D, 69 inf. .22 sep. 02 trs. co. B.......... 26 feb. 06 1 lt............... 6 mar. 06 f. and h. dis....... 20 feb. 08 pvt. hdqs. 2 inf.... 4 oct. 14 2 lt.......... 10 may 16 accepted..... 13 may 16	Conn. 14 jul. 75
Shuttleworth, Wright, 21 june 16	H	mustered into u. s. ser..... 1 jul. 16 out 19 Oct. 16	pvt. co. H .....11 jan. 13 corp .....22 dec. 13 dropped........... 26 sep. 14 taken up.......... 8 feb. 15 2 lt............... 21 jun. 16 accepted......... 21 june 16	N. Y.
Fuller, William H., 5 july 16	F	mustered into u. s. ser..... 5 july 16 out 4 oct. 16	pvt. co. F, 2 inf.... 21 feb. 01 dropped........... 11 oct. 02 taken up.......... 23 june 04 f. and h. dis........ 14 mar. 10 re-enld. co. F..... 3 mar. 11 corp.............. 3 may 11 sergt............... 17 oct. 11 f. and h. dis... ... 2 mar. 15 re-enld............ 3 mar. 15 2 lt.............. 5 july 16 accepted........... 5 july 16	.....
Degenaar, Christopher B., 5 july 16	E	mustered into u. s. ser...... 5 july 16 out 20 oct. 16	pvt. co. E........ 30 june 13 corp......... ...30 may 15 sergt.. .... 7 apr. 16 f. and h. dis... ... 30 june 16 re-enld............ 1 july 16 2 lt.............. 5 july 16 accepted......... 5 july 16	.... .
Fifield, Stephen H., 7 sep. 11	M. G. Co.	mustered into u. s ser..... 11 sep. 16 out 20 oct. 16	pvt. co. F.......... 11 mar. 13 corp............. 20 dec. 13 sergt............ 12 july 13 bn. sergt. major ....21 jan. 16 f. and h. dis....... 10 mar. 16 re-enld........... 11 mar. 16 2 lt.... .... 7 sep. 16 accepted........ 11 sep. 16	Iowa. 3 oct. 85

INFANTRY — (*Continued*)
THIRD REGIMENT
(Twelve Companies.)
(Fourth Brigade.)

Headquarters, 920 Main Street, East, Rochester

Organized under General Orders No. 14, Adjutant General's Office, March 30, 1907, by a consolidation of the 1st, 2d and 3d Battalions of Infantry. It is composed of the 8th, 34th, 41st, 48th, 42d, 29th, 50th, 1st, 43d, 47th, 30th, and 2d Separate Companies. designated as Companies A, B, C, D, E, F, G, H, I, K, L and M, respectively. Of these. Companies A, B, C, D, E, F, H, I, K, L, and M were in the Volunteer Army of the United States from May 17, 1898, to November 30, 1898, as the corresponding companies of the 3d Regiment, N. Y. Infantry. The regiment was authorized to organize a detachment of mounted scouts, by Special Orders No. 88, April 10, 1912. The regiment performed duty at the Buffalo street car strike, April, 1913.

Recognition extended by the War Department under Act of June 3, 1916, on July 5, 1916, to Headquarters Company, Machine Gun Company and Supply Company.

The regiment has received authority to place silver rings on the lances of its colors, engraved as follows:

On the National Color.— War with Spain, 1898.
On the State Color.— Buffalo. 1892.

COMPANY A, THIRD INFANTRY
(Eighth Separate Company.)
(Fourth Brigade.)

920 Main Street, East, Rochester

Organized as Co. E, 54th Regiment. September 8, 1863. Designation changed to 8th Separate Company. December 10, 1880. In service of United States at Elmira from July 26, 1864, to November 10, 1864. On duty in May, 1871, quelling a riot at Ox Bow Bend, Erie canal, Monroe county; on duty at Rochester, January 3–7, 1872, on call of the sheriff; on duty July, 1877, during the railroad riots, at Buffalo during riots in August, 1892, and Buffalo street car riot, April, 1913. In the United States service, as Co. A, 3d Regiment, N. Y. Infantry, from May 17, 1898, to December 5, 1898.

Recognition extended by the War Department under Act of June 3, 1916, on June 25, 1916.

COMPANY B, THIRD INFANTRY
(Thirty-fourth Separate Company.)
(Fourth Brigade.)

State Armory, 300 Main Street, Geneva

Organized January 6, 1880. On duty at Buffalo during riots in August, 1892, and Buffalo street car riot, April, 1913. In United States service, as Co. B, 3d Regiment, N. Y. Infantry, from May 17, 1898, to December 3, 1898.

Recognition extended by the War Department under Act of June 3, 1916, on June 25, 1916.

COMPANY C, THIRD INFANTRY
(Forty-first Separate Company.)
(Fourth Brigade.)

State Armory, West Jefferson Street, Syracuse

Originally Co. D, 51st Regiment. Designation changed December 17, 1881. On duty at Buffalo during riots in August, 1892; at Buffalo street car riot and mill riot, Auburn, April, 1913, and at riots. Syracuse, May, 1913. In United States service, as Co. C, 3d Regiment, N. Y. Infantry. from May 17, 1898, to November 30, 1898.

Recognition extended by the War Department under Act of June 3, 1916, on June 23, 1916.

COMPANY D, THIRD INFANTRY
(Forty-eighth Separate Company.)
(Fourth Brigade.)

State Armory, 257–271 West First Street, Oswego

Formed by consolidation of 29th and 38th Separate Companies, May 4, 1892. On duty in aid of the civil authorities at Syracuse in August, 1890, as the 29th and 38th Separate Companies; at Buffalo during the riots in August, 1892, at Oswego in July, 1884, during a riot at that place and at Buffalo street car riot, April, 1913. In United States service, as Co. D, 3d Regiment, N. Y. Infantry, from May 17, 1898, to December 1, 1898.

Recognition extended by the War Department under Act of June 3, 1916, on June 24, 1916.

11

INFANTRY — (Continued)

COMPANY E, THIRD INFANTRY
(Forty-second Separate Company.)

(Fourth Brigade.)

State Armory, 901 Main Street, Niagara Falls

Organized November 9, 1885. On duty at Tonawanda to suppress a riot June 14 and 15, 1892; at Buffalo during the riots in August, 1892; again at Tonawanda, June 16 to 18, 1893, during a riot at that place, and at Buffalo street car riot, April, 1913. In United States service, as Co. E, 3d Regiment, N. Y. Infantry, from May 17, 1898, to December 6, 1898.

Recognition extended by the War Department under Act of June 3, 1916, on June 26, 1916.

COMPANY F, THIRD INFANTRY
(Twenty-ninth Separate Company.)

(Fourth Brigade.)

Armory, 302 Pearl Street, Medina

Organized December 28, 1891. In United States service, as Co. F, 3d Regiment, N. Y. Infantry, from May 17, 1898, to December 5, 1898. Performed duty at street car riots, Buffalo, April, 1913.

Recognition extended by the War Department under Act of June 3, 1916, on June 26, 1916.

COMPANY G, THIRD INFANTRY
(Fiftieth Separate Company.)

(Fourth Brigade.)

State Armory, 920 Main Street, East, Rochester

Mustered in June 6, 1907. Performed duty at street car strike, Buffalo, April, 1913.

Recognition extended by the War Department under Act of June 3, 1916, on June 24, 1916.

COMPANY H, THIRD INFANTRY
(First Separate Company.)

(Fourth Brigade.)

State Armory, 920 Main Street, East, Rochester

Organized June 11, 1890. Served at Buffalo during the riots in August, 1892, and at Buffalo street car riots, April, 1913. In United States service, as Co. H, 3d Regiment, N. Y. Infantry, from May 17, 1898, to December 5, 1898.

Recognition extended by the War Department under Act of June 3, 1916, on June 26, 1916.

COMPANY I, THIRD INFANTRY
(Forty-third Separate Company.)

(Fourth Brigade.)

State Armory, 119 North Street, Olean

Organized March 17, 1887. On duty at Buffalo during the riots in August, 1892, and at Buffalo street car riots, April, 1913. In United States service, as Co. I, 3d Regiment, N. Y. Infantry, from May 17, 1898, to December 8, 1898.

Recognition extended by the War Department under Act of June 3, 1916, on June 26, 1916.

COMPANY K, THIRD INFANTRY
(Forty-seventh Separate Company.)

(Fourth Brigade.)

State Armory, 100 Seneca Street, Hornell

Organized October 21, 1891. On duty at Buffalo during the riots in August, 1892, and at Buffalo street car riots, April, 1913. In United States service, as Co. K, 3d Regiment, N. Y. Infantry, from May 17, 1898, to December 9, 1898.

Recognition extended by the War Department under Act of June 3, 1916, on June 26, 1916.

COMPANY L, THIRD INFANTRY
(Thirteenth Separate Company.)

(Fourth Brigade.)

State Armory, 307–310 East Church Street, Elmira

Organized as Co. D, 110th Battalion, October 1, 1874. Designation on disbandment of battalion changed to 30th Separate Company, November 22, 1878. On duty during the railroad riots in July, 1877; at Buffalo riots in August, 1892, and at Buffalo street car riots, April, 1913. On duty at Elmira from March 23, 1915, to March 28, 1915. In United States service, as Co. L, 3d Regiment, N. Y. Infantry, from May 17, 1898, to December 10, 1898.

Recognition extended by the War Department under Act of June 3, 1916, on June 28, 1916.

INFANTRY — *(Continued)*

COMPANY M, THIRD INFANTRY

(Second Separate Company.)

(Fourth Brigade.)

State Armory, 97 State Street, Auburn

Organized in May, 1881. Served at Buffalo during the riots in August, 1892, at mill riot at Auburn, April, 1913, and street car riots, Buffalo, April, 1913. In United States service, as Co. M, 3d Regiment, N. Y. Infantry, from May 17, 1898, to December 2, 1898.

Recognition extended by the War Department under Act of June 3, 1916, on June 24, 1916.

INFANTRY — THIRD REGIMENT

Name, grade, date of rank and highest brevet rank	Company	Service		Born
		In the armies of U. S. or foreign states	In the National Guard	
Colonel				
Jennings, Edgar Stilson, 29 dec. 15 Graduate, Garrison Schools, 1915.	......	1 sgt. co. M, 3 N. Y. inf...... 1 may 98 2 lt......21 june 98 1 lt....11 nov. 98 to 2 dec. 98 mustered into u. s. ser...... 5 july 16 out 5 oct. 16	pvt., corp., sgt., 1 sgt., 2 sep. co.....3 mar. 91 to 4 may 99 2 lt................4 may 99 1 lt................22 june 99 cap.............15 june 04 maj. 3 inf........17 mar. 11 col.............29 dec. 15 accepted..........30 dec. 15	N. Y. 25 aug. 71
Lieutenant Colonel				
Rees, Sanderson Alexander, 29 may 07	......	cap. 3 N. Y. inf., 1 may 98 to 5 dec. 98 mustered into u. s. ser...... 5 july 16 out 5 oct. 16	cap. 29 sep. co.......28 dec. 91 lt. col. 3 inf........29 may 07	N. Y. 21 aug. 63
Majors				
Shepard, George Gibson, 31 jan. 13 Graduate Garrison Schools, 1915. bvt. lt. col....25 nov. 16	......	mustered into u. s. ser...... 5 july 16 out 5 oct. 16	pvt., corp., sgt., 42 sep. co...........18 sep. 88 to 26 jan. 97 2 lt..............26 jan. 97 cap. 142 sep. co......19 july 98 supn., assigned duty adj. 1 bat......17 dec. 98 cap. 42 sep. co.......23 mar. 99 maj. 3 inf.........31 jan. 13 accepted.......... 1 feb. 13	N. Y. 16 oct. 65
Tuck, John Bennett, 10 feb. 13 Graduate, Garrison Schools, 1915.	......	cap. co. A, 203 N. Y. inf...... 6 july 98 to 25 mar. 99 mustered into u. s. ser...... 5 july 16 out 5 oct. 16	pvt. 35 sep. co.....17 may 87 to 5 jan. 91 1 lt. 141 sep. co...... 3 june 98 supn.............17 dec. 98 1 lt. 41 sep. co...... 7 nov. 06 cap.............24 july 07 maj. 3 inf........10 feb. 13 accepted..........11 feb. 13	N. Y. 5 apr. 68
Couchman, Frederick Stuart, 3 mar. 16	......	corp. co. A, 3 N. Y. inf..... 1 may 98 to 30 nov. 98 mustered into u. s. ser...... 5 july 16 out 5 oct. 16	pvt., lance corp., corp., sgt., 8 sep. co.............. 4 june 95 to nov. 01 2 lt.............26 nov. 01 1 lt.............26 mar. 02 cap............. 7 mar. 06 major............ 3 mar. 16 accepted.......... 4 mar. 16	Can. 13 jan. 74
Captains				
Charles, William Stuart, 5 dec. 00	K	1 lt. 3 N. Y. inf., 1 may 98 to 9 dec. 98 mustered into u. s. ser...... 5 july 16 out 5 oct. 16	pvt. 47 sep. co.......29 sep. 91 to 23 dec. 91 2 lt.............23 dec. 91 1 lt.............22 may 97 cap............. 5 dec. 00	N. Y. 7 sep. 60

INFANTRY — THIRD REGIMENT — (*Continued*)

Name, grade, date of rank and highest brevet rank	Company	Service — In the armies of U. S. or foreign states	Service — In the National Guard	Born
Captains — Continued				
Turnbull, William Arthur 29 june 09 Graduate Garrison Schools, 1915.	L	mustered into u. s. ser...... 5 july 16 out 5 oct. 16	pvt., 30 sep. co......19 oct. 01 to 28 june 02 pvt., corp., 30 sep. co..............30 aug. 02 to 9 june 04 2 lt................. 9 june 04 cap. 3 inf.......... 8 july 09 accepted..........10 july 09	N. Y. 21 may 78
Ball, Torrey Allen, 25 nov. 10 Graduate, Garrison Schools, 1915.	D	pvt. co. E, 3 N. Y. inf...... 1 may 98 to 30 nov. 98 mustered into u. s. ser...... 5 july 16 out 5 oct. 16	pvt. 48 sep. co...... 9 nov. 97 hon. dis.............14 nov. 02 pvt.................25 apr. 10 to 2 dec. 10 cap. 3 inf .... 2 dec. 10 accepted........... 5 dec. 10	N. Y. 23 aug. 78
Chormann, Otto Irving, 14 apr. 11 Graduate, Garrison Schools, 1915.	adj.	mustered into u. s. ser...... 5 july 16 out 5 oct. 16	pvt. co. H, 3 inf.....24 may 09 to 21 dec. 09 1 lt. 3 inf...........21 dec. 09 cap.................14 apr. 11 accepted...........18 apr. 11	N. Y. 18 nov. 82
Brown, Thurber Arnold, 11 mar. 12	i. s. a. p.	1 lt. 3 N. Y. inf., 1 may 98 to 10 dec. 98 mustered into u. s. ser...... 5 july 16 out 5 oct. 16	pvt., corp., sgt., 30 sep. co ....28 apr. 85 to 25 nov. 90 2 lt.................25 nov. 90 1 lt...............27 may 97 i. s. a. p. 3 bat. with o. r...............14 june 04 assigned to 3 inf.....30 mar. 07 1 lt. asst. i. s. a. p. 3 inf. with o. r.....24 june 07 supn., reassigned...21 jan. 08 1 lt. o. d...........21 feb. 08 cap. o. d...........11 mar. 12 cap. 3 inf.......... 1 may 12 accepted........... 9 may 12	N. Y. 6 apr. 61
Murray, Edwin Jesse, 3 apr. 13 Graduate, Garrison Schools, 1915.	E	pvt. co. E, 3 N. Y. inf...... 1 may 98 trs. co. C, 1 U. S. V. eng....28 june 98 to 25 jan. 99 mustered into u. s. ser...... 5 july 16 out 5 oct. 16	pvt. 42 sep. co......28 nov. 96 hon. dis............ 6 oct. 98 pvt., corp., 1 sgt., 42 sep. co..........25 sep. 99 to 18 nov. 08 pvt. 42 sep. co. 8 july 10 to 6 feb. 12 1 lt. 3 inf...... 6 feb. 12 cap............... 3 apr. 13 accepted.......... 4 apr. 13	N. Y. 6 apr. 77
Barnes, Charles Heber, 7 may 13 Graduate, Garrison Schools, 1915.	C	mustered into u. s. ser...... 5 july 16 out 5 oct. 16	pvt., corp., 41 sep. co..... 9 apr. 03 to 2 apr. 08. 2 lt. 3 inf... 2 apr. 08 1 lt. o. d...........25 june 12 cap. 3 inf.......... 7 may 13 accepted.......... 7 may 13	Conn. 4 mar. 71
Thompson, John Sylvester, 25 may 14	F	mustered into u. s. ser...... 5 july 16 out 5 oct. 16	pvt., corp., sgt., 29 sep. co...........29 jan. 00 to 25 oct. 07 2 lt...............25 oct. 07 1 lt. 3 inf.......... 2 mar. 12 cap...............25 may 14 accepted..........28 may 14	Can. 3 june 73

INFANTRY — THIRD REGIMENT — (Continued)

Name, grade, date of rank and highest brevet rank	Company	Service — In the armies of U. S. or foreign states	Service — In the National Guard	Born
Captains — Continued				
Smith, Copeland Edward, 26 may 14 Graduate, Garrison Schools, 1915.	I	pvt. co. I, 3 N. Y. inf., 1 may 98 to 30 nov. 98 mustered into u. s. ser...... 5 july 16 out 5 oct. 16	pvt., corp., sgt., 43 sep. co........... 7 may 96 hon. dis........... 3 oct. 06 pvt., corp., 43 sep. co.............26 june 07 to 29 feb. 08 2 lt. 3 inf.............29 feb. 08 1 lt................ 7 sep. 10 cap.............26 may 14 accepted.......... 1 june 14	N. Y. 23 mar. 76.
Merrill, Samuel Herbert, 19 oct. 14	B	mustered into u. s. ser...... 5 july 16 out 5 oct. 16	pvt. 134 sep. co., trs. 34 sep. co., corp., sgt., qm. sgt., 1 sgt.............20 may 98 to 14 dec. 06 1 lt.............14 dec. 06 cap.............19 oct. 14 accepted.........22 oct. 14	N. Y. 3 dec. 78
Mead, Benjamin Charles, 9 june 15 Graduate, Garrison Schools, 1915.	M	mustered into u. s. ser.. ... 5 july 16 out 5 oct. 16	pvt., corp., sgt., 2 sep. co...........24 nov. 03 to 3 oct. 10 2 lt. 3 inf. .... 3 oct. 10 1 lt.......... 5 june 11 cap ... 9 june 15 accepted ....10 june 15	N. Y. 17 feb. 73
Smith, Lawrence Newton, 18 nov. 15	G	mustered into u. s. ser...... 5 july 16 out 5 oct. 16	pvt., corp., sgt., 1 sgt., co. G, 3 inf ... 6 june 07 to 25 nov. 12 1 lt. 3 inf ....25 nov. 12 cap.............18 nov. 15 accepted...........19 nov. 15	N. Y. 9 nov. 84
Barager, Albert Manley, 27 mar. 16	H	pvt. co. H, 3 N. Y. inf...... 1 may 98 to 30 nov. 98 mustered into u. s. ser...... 5 july 16 out 5 oct. 16	pvt., corp., sgt., 1 sgt., 1 sep. co. ... 7 apr. 98 to 5 may 10 2 lt. 3 inf. .... 5 may 10 1 lt.............31 may 11 accepted........... 5 june 11 cap . ...27 mar. 16 accepted.........31 mar. 16	Mich. 27 apr. 78.
Smith, Arthur Thomas, 1 apr. 16	A	mustered into u. s. ser...... 5 july 16 out 5 oct. 16	pvt., lance corp., co. A, 3 inf...... 6 mar. 12 to 1 apr. 13 2 lt............ 1 apr. 13 1 lt.............11 dec. 14 accepted.........15 dec. 14 cap. . 1 apr. 16 accepted .... 3 apr. 16	N. Y. 6 nov. 86
Mohler, David D., 3 apr. 16	m. g. co.	mustered into u. s. ser...... 5 july 16 out 5 oct. 16	pvt., corp., sgt., tr. D............. 7 aug. 05 to 27 nov. 12 hon. dis. .... 8 oct. 10 1 lt. o. d...........27 nov. 12 r. l........ .... 1 may 14 2 lt. 3 inf.....18 nov. 14 accepted.........23 nov. 14 cap.............. 3 apr. 16 accepted....... .. 5 apr. 16	Mo. 1 mar. 80

INFANTRY — THIRD REGIMENT — (Continued)

Name, grade, date of rank and highest brevet rank	Company	Service — In the armies of U. S or foreign states	Service — In the National Guard	Born
Captains — Continued				
Johnston, Frederick S., 21 jan. 16	sup. co.	mustered into u. s. ser...... 5 july 16 out 5 oct. 16	pvt. 2 sep. co.......26 sep. 99 dropped...........3 may 02 taken up..........27 sep. 02 corp..............13 aug. 04 qm. sgt...........12 jan. 07 1 lt. 3 inf........26 nov. 10 with rank from.....17 nov. 10 accepted...........28 nov. 10 cap...............3 may 11 accepted...........4 may 11 f. and h. dis.......10 may 15 placed on r. l......19 july 15 on duty for 90 days..21 jan. 16 cap. 3 inf.........27 mar. 16 with rank from.....21 jan. 16 accepted...........29 mar. 16	N. Y. 16 nov. 75
First Lieutenants				
Elliott, George Albert, 30 sep. 07 Graduate, Garrison Schools, 1915.	bat. adj.	....	pvt. 41 sep. co. ..20 july 03 to 1 nov. 06 2 lt..........1 nov. 06 1 lt..........30 sep. 07	N. Y. 24 july 80
Martin, Clarence Stewart, 26 mar. 12 Graduate, Garrison Schools, 1915.	D	pvt. co. D, 3 N. Y. inf......15 may 98 to 30 nov. 98 mustered into u. s. ser...... 5 july 16 out 5 oct. 16	pvt. 48 sep. co......12 may 98 hon. dis..........10 jan. 99 pvt. 48 sep. co......25 mar. 11 to 26 mar. 12 1 lt. 3 inf..........26 mar. 12 accepted..........27 mar. 12	N. Y. 16 oct. 72
Farmer, Harry Haile, 2 july 13	C	mustered into u. s. ser..... 5 july 16 out 5 oct. 16	pvt. 141 sep. co......21 may 98 hon. dis..........27 dec. 98 2 lt. 3 inf..........23 dec. 12 1 lt...............2 july 13 accepted...........3 july 13	N. Y. 26 june 71
Welch, John Joseph, Jr., 13 aug. 13	E	mustered into u. s. ser...... 5 july 16 out 5 oct. 16	pvt., corp., sgt., co. E, 3 inf...........13 feb. 00 to 13 aug. 13 1 lt................13 aug. 13 accepted...........14 aug. 13	N. Y. 20 july 79
Considine, Francis Joseph, 13 oct. 14	I	mustered into u. s. ser. ... 5 july 16 out 5 oct. 16	pvt., corp., sgt., 1 sgt., co. I, 3 inf... 24 oct. 04 to 13 oct. 14 1 lt...............13 oct. 14 accepted...........16 oct. 14	N. Y. 2 dec. 82
Coursey, Thomas Joseph, 31 dec. 14	B	mustered into u. s. ser...... 5 july 16 out 5 oct. 16	pvt. 34 sep. co......10 dec. 00 to 18 june 02 20 oct. 02 to 20 apr. 03 13 oct. 03 to 7 apr. 04 pvt., corp., sgt., 1 sgt., 34 sep. co.....13 dec. 04 to 28 may 12 2 lt. 3 inf..........28 may 12 1 lt...............31 dec. 14 accepted...........1 jan. 15	N. Y. 13 sep. 76
Hodder, William Lord, 17 july 15	M	mustered into u. s. ser...... 5 july 16 out 5 oct. 16	pvt., corp., sgt., 2 sep. co...........26 apr. 04 to 28 dec. 11 2 lt. 3 inf..........28 dec. 11 1 lt...............17 july 15 accepted...........22 july 15	N. Y. 18 may 11 79

INFANTRY — THIRD REGIMENT — (*Continued*)

Name, grade, date of rank and highest brevet rank	Company	Service — In the armies of U. S. or foreign states	In the National Guard	Born
First Lieutenants — Continued				
Bentley, De Lancey, 2 mar. 16	bat. adj.	mustered into u. s. ser...... 5 july 16 out 5 oct. 16	pvt. mtd. det ....20 june 12 corp............... 9 may 13 sgt............... 1 oct. 15 1 lt............... 2 mar. 16 accepted........... 3 mar. 16	N. Y. 29 nov. 87
Staudenmaier, William George, 3 may 16	m. g. co.	mustered into u. s ser...... 5 july 16 out 5 oct. 16	pvt. co. A, 3 inf......26 july 11 hon. dis............ 9 oct. 14 pvt. co. A,.... 9 oct. 14 to 24 nov. 15 2 lt.............24 nov. 15 accepted...........26 nov. 15 1 lt............... 3 may 16 accepted........... 5 may 15	N. Y. 12 july 87
Taylor, George E., 16 mar. 16	K	mustered into u. s. ser...... 5 july 16 out 5 oct. 16	1 lt ....16 mar. 16 accepted...........18 mar. 16	N. Y. 12 mar. 90
Simes, Frank L., 9 june 16	H	mustered into u. s. ser...... 5 july 16 out 5 oct. 16	pvt., 1 sep. co. .... 3 aug. 99 corp....... ....22 dec. 04 sgt................10 mar. 06 1 sgt...............24 may 10 2 lt. 3 inf..........26 july 11 accepted...........27 july 11 f. and h. dis........16 mar. 15 1 lt............. 9 june 16 accepted........12 june 16	Can. 19 dec. 80
Second Lieutenants				
Chapin, Henry Burlingame, 21 apr. 05	m. g. co.	corp. co. H, 3 N. Y. inf...... 1 may 98 to 5 dec. 98 mustered into u. s. ser...... 5 july 16 out 5 oct. 16	pvt., corp., sgt., 1 sep. co...........26 nov. 94 to 26 sep. 01 2 lt...............26 sep. 01 1 lt...............21 apr. 05 1 lt. bat. qm., 3 inf., with o. r.........11 jun. 07 supn., reassigned....21 jan. 08 2 lt. 3 inf..........21 feb. 08	N. Y. 14 jan. 71
Riffe, James, 21 july 09	L	mustered into u. s. ser...... 5 july 16 out 5 oct. 16	pvt., corp., sgt., co. L, 3 inf.........23 dec. 02 to 2 aug. 09 2 lt. 3 inf........: ... 2 aug. 09 accepted........... 4 aug. 09	N. Y. 22 feb. 75
Vogt, Jacob Whitney, 8 oct. 14	E	mustered into u. s. ser...... 5 july 16 out 5 oct. 16	pvt., corp., sgt., 1 sgt. co. E, 3 inf...10 apr. 01 to 8 oct. 14 2 lt............... 8 oct. 14 accepted...........14 oct. 14	N. Y. 1 jan. 78
Oakleaf, James Francis, 16 nov. 14	I	mustered into u. s. ser...... 5 july 16 out 5 oct. 16	2 lt. 3 inf..........16 nov. 14 accepted...........25 nov. 14	N. Y. 25 dec. 82
Winnek, Edward Francis, 10 aug. 15	B	mustered into u. s. ser...... 5 july 16 out 5 oct. 16	pvt., corp., sgt., 1 sgt. co. B, 3 inf...23 dec. 07 hon. dis...........29 dec. 14 2 lt...............10 aug. 15 accepted...........11 aug. 15	Mass. 7 oct. 88
Roberts, Edwin Morris, 10 sep. 15	M	mustered into u. s. ser...... 5 july 16 out 5 oct. 16	pvt., corp., sgt., 1 sgt. 20 sep. co......11 apr. 87 hon. dis............ 2 feb. 94 pvt............... 2 feb. 94 to 10 sep. 15 2 lt...............10 sep. 15 accepted...........13 sep. 15	N. Y. 28 apr. 68

INFANTRY — THIRD REGIMENT — (Concluded)

Name, grade, date of rank and highest brevet rank	Company	Service — In the armies of U. S. or foreign states	Service — In the National Guard	Born
Second Lieutenants — Continued				
Barnes, Ezra Andrew, 2 dec. 15	D	mustered into u. s. ser..... 5 july 16 out 5 oct. 16	2 lt................. 2 dec. 15 accepted.......... 4 dec. 15	N. Y. 11 may 79
Blades, Archie L., 16 mar. 16	K	mustered into u. s. ser...... 5 july 16 out 5 oct. 16	pvt. Co. K......... 2 dec. 01 dropped............31 dec. 01 taken up...........24 oct. 02 dropped............ 4 aug. 05 corp. 31 jul. 09 reduced to ranks.....15 july 11 sergt...............26 july 11 f. and h. dis ....22 apr. 12 2 lt................16 mar. 16 accepted...........17 mar. 16	N. Y. 24 sep. 84
Hartley, Henry J. 20 apr. 16	C	U.S.M.A., 15 june 13 to 29 june 14 mustered into u. s. ser..... 5 july 16 out 5 oct. 16	2 lt................20 apr. 16 accepted.... ...21 apr. 16	Pa. 24 may 94
Underwood, Kennard, 13 june 16	sup. co.	mustered into u. s. ser......24 june 16 out 5 oct. 16	pvt. co. L, 1 cav..... 2 feb. 12 dropped for removal. 16 oct. 14 taken up Co. M.....31 mar. 16 2 lt................13 june 16 accepted...........14 june 16	N. Y. 16 aug. 86
Mosher, Charles F, 6 july 16	H	mustered into u. s. ser......10 july 16 out 5 oct. 16	pvt. co. H.......... 1 apr. 07 corp...............14 may 09 sgt................10 june 11 f. and h. dis........ 1 feb. 12 re-enlisted........28 feb. 16 corp...............17 mar. 16 2 lt................ 6 july 16 accepted........... 6 july 16	N. Y. 26 june 89
Chaplain				
Jaynes, Almon Andrus, 7 may 13	......	mustered into u. s. ser...... 5 july 16 out 5 oct. 16	chaplain, 3 inf...... 7 may 13 accepted.......... 8 may 13	N. Y. 15 jan. 77

INFANTRY — *(Continued)*

SEVENTH REGIMENT

(Twelve Companies.)

(First Brigade.)

Armory, 643 Park Avenue, New York City

Companies A, B, C and D were organized during the excitement created by the firing of British at American vessels off Sandy Hook in April, 1806, as the first, second, third and fourth companies, and June 25th they were officially recognized by the State as part of the uniformed militia of the State, and attached to the battalion of artillery commanded by Major Andrew Sitcher. April 5, 1807, the battalion, in the organization of the 3d Regt. of New York Artillery, became its 2d Battalion. When war with England became imminent in 1807, these four companies, with other volunteers, were temporarily organized as a regiment, commanded by Colonel Peter Curtenius, and remained thus detached until April 20, 1809. In 1812 the 3d became the 11th Regiment of Artillery, the four companies remaining the 2d Battalion. August 25, 1824, the battalion was named "Battalion of National Guards" (its distinctive name until, in 1862, the Legislature appropriated it for the uniformed militia), and in December, 1824, the fifth company was organized and Captain Stevens' company of the 11th New York Artillery transferred to it as the sixth company. In January, 1825, the battalion was transferred to the 2d New York Artillery. October 1, 1825, the battalion was detached and organized as a separate and independent battalion, and during the month the seventh company was organized. May 4, 1826, the organization of the eighth company was completed, and May 6th the battalion was organized into a regiment, the 27th Artillery. April 17, 1838, a troop of cavalry was admitted to the regiment, which, in 1861, became the ninth company. In 1843 the State furnished the regiment with arms, it having heretofore provided them itself; July 27th the designation of the regiment was changed to 7th Regiment. In April, 1849, an engineer corps was organized which, in 1861, became the tenth company. May 11, 1909, the regiment received authority to organize a new company to be known as Company L. December 2, 1910, a new company, to be designated Company M, was authorized to be mustered in. The regiment was frequently ordered to hold itself ready for service, and did active service for the United States, the State and New York city, as follows: In United States service from September 15 to December 15, 1812; from September 2 to December 2, 1814; from April 19 to June 3, 1861; from May 26 to December 5, 1862; from June 17 to July 21, 1863. In support of State or municipal authority: Execution of James Reynolds, November 19, 1825; at the election riots, April 10, 1834; abolition riot, July 11 to 12, 1834; great conflagration in New York city, December 17, 1835; stevedore riot, February 24, 1836; flour riots, February 6 and March 6, 1837; anti-rent war, December 9 to 10, 1839; Croton water riots, April 22 to 23, 1840; fire in New York city, July 19 to 21, 1845; Astor Place riot, May 10, 12 and 14, 1849; police riot, June 16, 1857; Dead Rabbit riot, July 5, 1857; quarantine war, January 3, 1859; preserving order at camp of Spinola Brigade, September 12 to 19, 1862; draft riots, July, 1863; Orange riots, July, 1871; labor riots, July, 1877; motormen's riots, Brooklyn, January, 1895; and at riot, Croton Dam, April, 1900. The regiment was authorized to organize a detachment of mounted scouts by Special Orders No. 66, A. G. O., March 15, 1912, and a machine gun platoon by Special Orders No. 168, A. G. O., July 3, 1912. A machine gun company was organized April 24, 1914.

Recognition extended by the War Department under Act of June 3, 1916, to Companies A, B, C, D, E, F, G, H, I, K, L, and Sanitary Detachment, on June 25, 1916; to Company M on June 24, 1916; to Headquarters Company, on June 25, 1916; to Supply Company, on June 26, 1916.

INFANTRY — SEVENTH REGIMENT

Name, grade, date of rank and highest brevet rank	Company	Service		Born
		In the armies of U. S. or foreign states	In the National Guard	
Colonel				
Fisk, Willard Clinton, 15 apr. 16	......	mustered into u. s. ser......26 june 16 out 2 dec. 16	pvt. co. G, 7 inf., trs. co. A, sgt.........24 mar. 74 to 13 apr. 81 2 lt ....13 apr. 81 1 lt ....29 may 82 adj. 7 inf. with o. r...24 sep. 89 cap. (D)............29 dec. 90 maj. 7 inf.........30 oct. 01 lt. col. 7 inf......30 july 08 with rank from 14 july 08 appointed member militia council....28 july 11 term expired.......27 july 13 bvt. col............23 apr. 15 retired.............30 apr. 15 col 7 inf...........15 apr. 16 accepted...........18 apr. 16	N. Y. 26 mar. 56
Lieutenant Colonel				
McLean, Robert, 9 june 15 Graduate, Garrison Schools, 1915.	......	mustered into u. s. ser......26 june 16 out 2 dec. 16	pvt., corp., sgt. 1 sgt., co. K, 7 inf..13 dec. 80 to 12 dec. 88 2 lt ....12 dec. 88 1 lt ....25 may 91 cap...............16 apr. 95 maj. 7 inf.........14 may 07 lt. col............ 9 june 15 accepted...........10 june 15	Eng. 23 july 60
Majors				
Schuyler, James Everett, 8 dec. 09 Graduate, Garrison Schools, 1915.	......	mustered into u. s. ser......26 june 16 out 2 dec. 16	pvt., corp., sgt., 1 sgt., co. B, 7 inf.. 7 oct. 78 to 15 oct. 91 2 lt ....15 oct. 91 cap...............17 may 97 maj...............21 dec. 09 accepted...........29 dec. 09	N. Y. 23 nov. 60
Mazet, Robert, 1 july 15 bvt. maj..... 7 feb. 08 Graduate, Garrison Schools, 1915.	......	mustered into u. s. ser......26 june 16 out 2 dec. 16	pvt. 18 inf. N. G. Pa.—july 76 to — jan. 78 pvt., corp., sgt., co. H, 7 inf.........31 july 82 to 5 jan. 91 2 lt. (D)............ 5 jan. 91 1 lt ....26 july 93 cap...............20 dec. 01 maj............... 6 july 15 rank from .... 1 july 15 accepted........... 1 july 15	Pa. 15 may 57
Falls, DeWitt Clinton, 21 june 16	......	mustered into u. s. ser......26 june 16 out 2 dec. 16	pvt., corp., co. K, sgt., maj. 7 inf..27 jan. 86 to 5 july 95 bat. adj. 1 lt...... 5 july 95 cap. regt. adj...... 2 june 99 a. d. c. to gov...... 1 jan. 11 to 31 dec. 12 maj...............21 june 16 accepted...........21 june 16	N. Y. 29 sep. 64
Captains				
Myers, James Weston, 2 apr. 98 bvt. maj..... 3 dec. 08	sup. co.	mustered into u. s. ser..... .26 june 16 out 2 dec. 16	pvt. co. B, 7 inf.....22 june 83 to 21 june 88 pvt., corp., co. B, comy sgt., 7 inf.... 9 nov. 88 to 18 feb. 95 comy of sub. 1 lt....18 feb. 95 cap............... 2 apr. 98	N. Y. 64

INFANTRY — SEVENTH REGIMENT — (Continued)

Name, grade, date of rank and highest brevet rank	Company	Service — In the armies of U. S. or foreign states	Service — In the National Guard	Born
Captains — Continued				
Barnard, J. Augustus, 6 oct. 08 Graduate, Garrison Schools, 1914.	K	mustered into u. s. ser......26 june 16 out 2 dec. 16	pvt., corp., sgt., 1 sgt., co. K, 7 inf... 5 oct. 92 to 21 apr. 00 2 lt.............21 apr. 00 1 lt.............. 2 july 07 cap. 7 inf.........26 oct. 08	N. Y. 15 sep. 71
Engel, Nicholas, 30 jan. 09	C	mustered into u. s. ser.....26 june 16 out 2 dec. 16	pvt., corp., sgt., 1 sgt., co. C, 7 inf... 7 mar. 90 to 16 nov. 99 2 lt.............16 nov. 99 1 lt.............10 mar. 03 cap. 7 inf.......... 8 feb. 09 accepted...........16 feb. 09	N. Y. 18 aug. 69
Covell, William Simpson, 18 mar. 11 Graduate, Garrison Schools, 1915.	F	mustered into u. s. ser.....26 june 16 out 2 dec. 16	pvt. corp., sgt., co. F, 7 inf............24 dec. 90 to 26 sep. 05 2 lt. 7 inf. (F).......26 sep. 05 1 lt.............20 mar. 06 cap.............18 mar. 11 accepted...........28 mar. 11	N. Y. 1 jan. 72
Halsted, William Moore, 21 nov. 12 bvt. maj. 23 feb. 16	B	mustered into u. s. ser....26 june 16 out 2 dec. 16	pvt., corp., sgt., 1 sgt., co. B, 7 inf... 5 dec. 84 to 9 jan. 06 2 lt. 7 inf. (B).......9 jan. 06 1 lt.............26 feb. 10 cap.............21 nov. 12 accepted...........22 nov. 12	N. Y. 15 apr. 58
Nicoll, Fancher, 24 july 13 Graduate, Garrison Schools, 1915.	L	mustered into u. s. ser.....26 june 16 out 2 dec. 16	pvt., corp., sgt., co. K, 7 inf., trs. co. L.............21 mar. 00 to jun. 09 2 lt. 7 inf ....30 jun. 09 cap ....24 jul. 13 accepted.. ....26 jul. 13	N. Y. 29 oct. 78
Heylman, Henry Budelman, 14 apr. 14	A	mustered into u. s. ser......26 june 16 out 2 dec. 16	pvt., lance corp., corp., sgt., co. B, 7 inf............10 oct. 01 to 13 feb. 13 2 lt.............13 feb. 13 cap.............14 apr. 14 accepted...........14 apr. 14	N. Y. 13 sep. 72
Nesbitt, Maxwell Betts, 3 july 14 Graduate, Garrison Schools, 1915.	G	mustered into u. s. ser......26 june 16 out 2 dec. 16	pvt., corp., sgt., co. G, 7 inf..........14 mar. 90 to 25 may 99 2 lt.............25 may 99 1 lt.............30 july 08 cap............. 3 july 14 accepted........... 6 july 14	N. Y. 5 mar. 68
Hayes, Wade Hampton, 28 sep. 14	I	mustered into u. s. ser......26 june 16 out 2 dec. 16	pvt., lance corp., corp., sgt., 1 sgt., co. I, 7 inf........19 jan. 05 to 10 june 12 1 lt. 7 inf..........10 june 12 cap.............28 sep. 14 accepted...........30 sep. 14	Va. 12 may 79
Crall, Howard Elmer, 28 mar. 15 bvt. major 20 dec. 16	i. s. a. p.	....	pvt., corp., sgt., co. G, 7 inf.......... 9 jan. 91 to 23 feb. 99 1 lt.............23 feb. 99 resigned...........16 may 08 cap. 7 inf.........28 mar. 15 accepted...........31 mar. 15 a. d. c. to gov.......26 july 15	D. C. 18 aug. 67

INFANTRY — SEVENTH REGIMENT — (*Continued*)

Name, grade, date of rank and highest brevet rank	Com-pany	Service — In the armies of U. S. or foreign states	Service — In the National Guard	Born
Captains—Continued				
Fisk, Clinton Earle, 17 sep. 15	D	mustered into u. s. ser......26 june 16 out 2 dec. 16	pvt., corp., sgt., co. D, 7 inf...........24 mar. 00 to 19 oct. 14 2 lt.................19 oct. 14 cap................17 sep. 15 accepted...........20 sep. 15	N. J. 13 apr. 82
Gardner, Kenneth, 13 jan. 16	m. g. co.	mustered into u. s. ser......26 june 16 out 2 dec. 16	pvt., corp., sgt., 22 sep. co. (co. E, 3 inf.) Ind. N. G....28 mar. 00 to — mar. 03 pvt., bat. sgt. maj...13 may 03 2 lt., qm...........12 may 05 1 lt., adj.......... 7 july 06 pvt., co. H, 8 inf., N. G. N. Y. trs. co. B, 7 inf., corp. bat. sgt. maj........ 3 sep. 07 to 30 july 14 2 lt.................30 july 14 accepted........... 5 aug. 14 captain...........13 jan. 16 accepted...........13 jan. 16	Ind. 25 dec. 82
Despard, Douglas Cornell, 13 jan. 16	adj.	mustered into u. s. ser......26 june 16 out 2 dec. 16	pvt., corp., co. K, 7 inf., bat. sgt. maj., regt. segt. maj.....22 nov. 04 to 22 dec. 13 1 lt.. ....22 dec. 13 accepted...........23 dec. 13 captain...........13 july 16 accepted...........13 july 16	N. Y. 7 jan. 85
Colman, Richard Whiting, 19 sep. 16	M	sgt. co. K, 2 N. J. vols..... 2 may 98 to 17 nov. 98 mustered into u. s. ser......26 june 16 out 2 dec. 16	pvt., corp., 1 sgt., co. K, 2 inf., N. G. N. J.............13 june 95 hon. dis........... 2 may 00 pvt. batty. A, f. a....30 mar.01 hon. dis...........12 june 01 pvt., sgt., 1 sgt., co. K, 5 inf..........15 july 02 to 15 mar. 05 pvt., co. E, 7 inf., N. G. N. Y., trs. co. M, sgt., 1 sgt...15 may 08 to 13 feb. 13 2 lt.................13 feb. 13 accepted...........15 feb. 13 1 lt.................24 june 16 accepted...........24 june16 captain...........19 sep. 16 accepted...........19 sep. 16	N. Y. 17 oct. 76
Knust, Leo Frederick, 3 nov. 16 Graduate, Garrison Schools, 1915.	E	mustered into u. s. ser.... .26 june 16 out 2 dec. 16	pvt., lance corp., corp., sgt., 1 sgt., co. E, 7 inf.....11 may 98 to 23 feb. 12 1 lt. 7 inf ....23 feb. 12 accepted ....26 feb. 12 cap................ 3 nov. 16 accepted.... ....17 nov. 16	Ger. 28 feb. 78
First Lieutenants				
Daniell, John Francis, 19 dec. 07 Graduate, Garrison Schools, 1915.	bat. adj.	mustered into u. s. ser. ..26 june 16 out 2 dec. 16	pvt., lance corp., corp., co. G, bat. sgt. maj., regt. sgt. maj., 7 inf .....12 feb. 92 to 19 dec. 07 1 lt. bat. adj 7 inf...19 dec. 07 a. d. c. to gov. ..... 1 jan. 13	N. Y. 5 nov. 74

INFANTRY — SEVENTH REGIMENT — (Continued)

Name, grade, date of rank and highest brevet rank	Company	Service		Born
		In the armies of U. S. or foreign states	In the National Guard	
First Lieutenants — Continued				
Crane, Charles Bunker, 4 jan. 11 Graduate, Garrison Schools, 1915.	K	mustered into u. s. ser......26 june 16 out 2 dec. 16	pvt., lance corp., corp., sgt., 1 sgt., co. K, 7 inf......18 oct. 99 to 4 jan. 11 1 lt. 7 inf..........4 jan. 11 accepted..........5 jan. 11	N. Y. 24 apr. 74
Loeser Charles Peter, 27 nov. 12	bat. adj.	mustered into u. s. ser......26 june 16 out 2 dec. 16	pvt. co. D, 7 inf.....29 dec. 93 to 15 may 94 pvt., lance corp., corp., sgt., co. D, bat. sgt. maj., regt. sgt. maj. 7 inf.....11 june 94 to 27 nov. 12 1 lt. 7 inf..........27 nov. 12 accepted..........6 dec. 12	N. Y. 24 july 69
Clark, Francis Dayton, 24 dec. 12	B	pvt. co. A, 2 N. Y. inf......2 may 98 to 25 nov. 98 mustered into u. s. ser......26 june 16 out 2 dec. 16	pvt. 6 sep. co........19 apr. 98 to 17 may 98 pvt., corp., 6 sep. co., trs. co. B, lance corp., corp., sgt., 1 sgt............25 dec. 98 to 10 june 12 2 lt. 7 inf..........10 june 12 1 lt...............24 dec. 12 accepted..........31 dec. 12	N. J. 25 jan. 75
Conklin, Frederick Doane, 23 jan. 14 Distinguished graduate°, N. Y. School of the Line, 1915.	A	mustered into u. s. ser......26 june 16 out 2 dec. 16	pvt., corp., sgt., 1 sgt., co. A, 7 inf... 7 oct. 04 to 23 jan. 14 1 lt...............23 jan. 14 accepted..........28 jan. 14	N. Y. 26 june 83
Stratton, Gerald, 6 june 16 Graduate, Garrison Schools, 1915.	G	mustered into u. s. ser......26 june 16 out 2 dec. 16	pvt., lance corp., corp., sgt., 1 sgt., co. G, 7 inf......8 feb. 95 to 9 nov. 08 2 lt. 7 inf..........9 nov. 08 1 lt...............14 sep. 14 accepted..........17 sep. 14 1 lt. r. lt............6 june 16 accepted..........6 june 16	Can. 1 dec. 76
Nichols, George Pardee, 29 oct. 14	I	mustered into u. s. ser......26 june 16 out 2 dec. 16	pvt., corp., sgt., 1 sgt., co. I, 7 inf... 2 jan. 02 to 29 oct. 14 1 lt...............29 oct. 14 accepted..........30 oct. 14	N. Y. 1 jan. 81
Drake, Arthur, 18 jan. 15 Graduate, Garrison Schools, 1915.	H	mustered into u. s. ser......26 june 16 out 2 dec. 16	pvt., lance corp., corp., sgt., 1 sgt., co. H, 7 inf......13 june 87 to 23 may 05 2 lt. 7 inf. (H)......23 may 05 1 lt...............18 jan. 15 accepted..........20 jan. 15	N. Y. 19 feb. 68
Byrns, Robert Ainsworth, 10 feb. 15	L	mustered into u. s. ser......26 june 16 out 2 dec. 16	pvt., lance corp., corp., sgt., co. K, 7 inf., trs. co. L, 1 sgt...............7 apr. 99 to 18 sep. 13 2 lt...............18 sep. 13 1 lt...............10 feb. 15 accepted..........10 feb. 15	Ind. 31 dec. 73

INFANTRY — SEVENTH REGIMENT — (Continued)

Name, grade, date of rank and highest brevet rank	Company	Service — In the armies of U. S. or foreign states	Service — In the National Guard	Born
First Lieutenants — Continued				
Raecke, Louis Charles, 1 june 10	C	mustered into u. s. ser......26 june 16 out 2 dec. 16	pvt., lance corp., corp., 1 sgt., co. C, 7 inf............10 may 95 to 13 june 10 2 lt. 7 inf.........13 june 10 accepted.........16 june 10	Ohio 17 aug. 77
Kent, Edward H., 22 july 16	bat. adj.	mustered into u. s. ser......26 june 16 out 2 dec. 16	pvt. co. B.........4 jan. 06 corp..............20 dec. 07 sgt..............10 may 12 bat. sgt. maj........3 feb. 13 sgt. maj...........9 jan. 14 f. and h. dis........3 jan. 15 re-enlisted.........4 jan. 15 warrant contd. 2 lt...24 june 16 accepted.........24 june 16 1 lt.............22 july 16 accepted.........22 july 16	......
Smith, Arthur Mathews, 7 oct. 16	F	mustered into u. s. ser......26 june 16 out 2 dec. 16	pvt., lance corp., corp., sgt., qm. sgt., 1 sgt. co. F, 7 inf............17 feb. 06 hon. dis..........16 feb. 15 pvt., 1 sgt. co. F, 7 inf............23 feb. 15 to 16 apr. 15 2 lt..............16 apr. 15 accepted.........19 apr. 15 1 lt.............7 oct. 16 accepted.........11 oct. 16	N. Y. 30 nov. 81
Cramer, Murray E., 23 oct. 16	M	mustered into u. s. ser......26 june 16 out 2 dec. 16	pvt. co. M.........5 oct. 11 lance corp.........20 mar.13 sgt..............10 apr. 14 2 lt..............24 june 16 accepted.........24 june 16 1 lt.............23 oct. 16 accepted.........28 oct. 16	N. Y. 4 sep. 86
Tompkins, Rowland, 30 oct. 16	D	mustered into u. s. ser...... 7 nov. 16 out 2 dec. 16	pvt., corp., sgt., co. D, 7 inf.........28 sep 06 hon. dis..........16 nov 14 pvt. co. D, 7 inf...17 nov 14 to 28 oct. 15 2 lt..............28 oct. 15 accepted.........1 nov. 15 1 lt.............30 oct. 16 accepted.........4 nov. 16	N. J. 15 dec. 81
Second Lieutenants				
Alleyn, Charles Gordon, 9 june 14	B	mustered into u. s. ser......26 june 16 out 2 dec. 16	pvt. co. E, 7 inf., trs. co. B, corp., sgt., 1 sgt.............5 feb. 89 to 9 june 14 2 lt..............9 june 14 accepted.........15 june 14	N. Y. 23 july 62
Grant, Gordon Hope, 31 oct. 14	I	mustered into u. s. ser......26 june 16 out 2 dec. 16	pvt., corp., sgt. co. I. 7 inf............8 may 07 to 31 oct. 14 2 lt..............31 oct. 14 accepted.........5 nov. 14	Cal. 7 june 75
Drake, Marston Elliott, 29 oct. 14	G	mustered into u. s. ser......26 june 16 . out 2 dec. 16	pvt., corp., sgt. co. G, 7 inf............5 feb. 09 to 29 oct. 14 2 lt..............29 oct. 14 accepted.........30 oct. 14	Cal. 27 apr. 91

INFANTRY — SEVENTH REGIMENT — (*Concluded*)

Name, grade, date of rank and highest brevet rank	Company	Service		Born
		In the armies of U. S. or foreign states	In the National Guard	
Second Lieutenants — Continued				
McKenna, Arthur James, 24 mar. 15	L	mustered into u. s. ser...... 2 dec. 16 out 2 dec. 16	pvt., lance corp., co. I, 7 inf., trs. co. L, 7 inf., corp., sgt., 1 sgt.............. 2 oct. 06 hon. dis........... 2 dec. 14 pvt. co. L, 7 inf...... 2 dec. 14 to 24 mar. 15 2 lt................24 mar. 15 accepted..........29 mar. 15	N. Y. 13 dec. 84
Wilson, Kenneth C., 4 nov. 16	M. G. co.	mustered into u. s. ser...... 2 dec. 16 out 2 dec. 16	pvt. co. I..........21 may 14 corp. m. g. co......21 june 15 trs. to co D........18 feb. 16 sgt................18 feb. 16 f. and h. dis.........21 may 16 re-enlisted..........22 may 16 1 sgt. m. g. co...... 8 oct. 16 2 lt................ 4 nov. 16 accepted..........10 nov. 16	N. Y. 14 july 86
Willis, Edward, 4 nov. 16	M. G. co.	mustered into u. s. ser...... 2 dec. 16 out 2 dec. 16	pvt. co. K..........24 oct. 12 corp. m. g. co......27 nov. 14 sgt................18 feb. 16 2 lt................ 4 nov. 16 accepted..........10 nov. 16	N. Y. 13 june 90
Brady, Thomas J........ 6 nov. 16	D	mustered into u. s. ser...... 2 dec. 16 out 2 dec. 16	pvt. co. D..........25 sep. 08 f. and h. dis......... 1 mar. 15 re-enlisted.......... 2 mar. 15 corp................. 1 july 14 1 sgt...............20 dec. 15 f. and h. dis......... 1 mar. 16 re-enlisted.......... 2 mar. 16 2 lt................ 6 nov. 16 accepted..........18 nov. 16	N. Y. 25 feb. 85
Hayward, Harry W., 14 nov. 16	K	mustered into u. s. ser...... 2 dec. 16 out 2 dec. 16	pvt. co. K..........30 may 03 f. and h. dis......... 3 dec. 14 re-enlisted.......... 4 dec. 14 f. and h. dis......... 1 june 16 re-enlisted.......... 2 june 16 2 lt................14 nov. 16 accepted..........20 nov. 16	Me. 17 sep. 75
Chaplain				
McCord, William Edgar, 30 aug. 01	......	mustered into u. s. ser..... 26 jun. 16 out 2 dec. 16	pvt. co. F, 7 inf......29 sep. 90 to 30 aug. 01 chaplain, 7 inf.......30 aug. 01	Ill. 19 sep. . 59

INFANTRY — (Continued)

TENTH REGIMENT

(Twelve Companies.)

(Third Brigade.)

Headquarters, State Armory, 195 Washington Avenue, Albany

The 10th Regiment was organized on December 29, 1860, by General Orders No. 60, A. G. O., of that year, Captain Ira W. Ainsworth's company of the 25th Regiment being detached from that regiment and assigned to the 10th as the nucleus of the new regiment; Captain Ainsworth subsequently becoming the first colonel of the 10th Regiment with rank from May 27, 1862.

On May 17, 1881, the 10th Regiment, with the exception of Companies A, B, D and K, was disbanded and these companies retained in the service as the 10th Separate Battalion. On October 1, 1884, the designation of Company K was changed to C.

April 28, 1898, the 1st Regiment was organized preparatory to entry in United States service and Companies A, B, C and D of the 10th Battalion became Companies A, B, C and D of the 1st Regiment. On the disbandment of this regiment on March 15, 1899, these companies resumed their former designations in the 10th Battalion.

The battalion organization of the 10th Battalion was disbanded on May 1, 1905, and Companies A, B, C and D constituted separate companies, designated respectively, as the 26th, 35th, 38th and 45th Separate Companies. On the same date the 10th Regiment, composed of separate companies, was reorganized and its headquarters established at Albany, and the 26th, 35th, 38th and 45th Separate Companies attached to it as Companies A, B, C and D, respectively. In addition the 16th, 23d, 4th, 11th, 17th, 15th and 14th Separate Companies were assigned to the regiment and designated respectively as E, F, G, H, I, K and M. May 28, 1907, the 49th Separate Company was mustered in at White Plains, and assigned to the 10th Regiment as Company L. On December 1, 1910, Company A was mustered out, and a new company mustered in, on the same date, and designated as Company A, 10th Infantry (26th Separate Company).

The 10th Regiment was mustered into the service of the United States as the 177th New York Volunteers, November 21, 1862, and was mustered out September 10, 1863. Companies A, B, C, D, K and M were mustered into the United States service as Companies A, B, C, D, K and M, 1st New York Infantry, May 20, 1898, and were mustered out February 20, 1899. The 10th Regiment was on duty in aid of the civil authorities in the Helderbergs in 1865, during the anti-rent war; during the railroad riots at West Albany in 1877; the 10th Battalion at Buffalo during the riots in 1892; at Albany during street railway riot in 1901; and a portion of the 10th Regiment at Coeymans during a riot in May, 1906. The regiment was authorized to organize a detachment of mounted scouts by Special Orders No. 66, A. G. O., March 15, 1912.

Recognition extended by the War Department under Act of June 3, 1916, to Sanitary Detachment on June 26, 1916; to the Machine Gun Company on July 9, 1916, and to the Supply Company on July 5, 1916.

The regiment has received authority to place silver rings on the lances of its colors, engraved as follows:

On the National Color.— McGill's Ferry, La., January 6, 1863; Poncharoula, La., March 24, 1863; McGill's Ferry, La., March 24, 1863; Civigne's Ferry, La., March 25, 1863; Amite River, La., May 10 and 11, 1863; Port Hudson, La., May 23 to July 8, 1863; Spanish-American War, 1898; Hawaii, 1898.

On the State Color.— Helderbergs, 1865; West Albany, 1877; Buffalo, 1892; Albany, 1901; Coeymans, 1906.

COMPANY A, TENTH INFANTRY

(Twenty-sixth Separate Company.)

(Third Brigade.)

State Armory, 195 Washington Avenue, Albany

Organized July 23, 1860, as an independent company, the "Albany Zouave Cadets;" joined the National Guard, and was attached to the 10th Regiment as Co. A, December 29, 1860; became Co. A, 10th Battalion, February 17, 1881; established as a separate company, designated the 26th Separate Company, and attached to the 10th Regiment as Co A, May 1, 1905. On December 1, 1910, this company was mustered out, and a new company mustered in the same date, designated the 26th Separate Company, and attached to the 10th Infantry as Company A.

The company was mustered into the United States service as Co A, 177th N. Y. Volunteers, November 21, 1862, for nine months, and was mustered out September 10, 1863; during the War of the Rebellion the company furnished for the armies of the United States nearly 75 commissioned officers. Was again mustered into the United States service as Co. A. 1st N. Y. Infantry, May 20, 1898, and mustered out February 20, 1899.

Recognition extended by the War Department under Act of June 3, 1916, on June 23, 1916.

INFANTRY — *(Continued)*

COMPANY B, TENTH INFANTRY
(Thirty-fifth Separate Company.)
(Third Brigade.)
State Armory, 195 Washington Avenue, Albany

Organized July 4, 1854, as an independent company, the "Washington Continentals;" joined the militia as a company of light artillery, August 28, 1856, and was attached to the 76th Regiment; was assigned to the 29th Regiment, December 20, 1860; to the 10th Regiment as Company B, December 29, 1860; became Company B, 10th Battalion, February 17, 1881; was constituted a separate company, designated the 35th Separate Company, and assigned to the 10th Regiment as Company B, May 1, 1905.

The company was mustered into the service of the United States as Co. B, 177th N. Y. Vols., November 21, 1862, and mustered out September 10, 1863; was again mustered into the United States service May 20, 1898, as Co. B, 1st N. Y. Infantry, and was mustered out February 20, 1899. During the War of the Rebellion the company furnished sixty officers to the volunteer armies of the United States.

Recognition extended by the War Department under Act of June 3, 1916, on June 24, 1916.

COMPANY C, TENTH INFANTRY
(Thirty-eighth Separate Company.)
(Third Brigade.)
State Armory, 195 Washington Avenue, Albany

Organized April 5, 1877, as Co. K, 10th Regiment. Assigned to 10th Battalion, February 17, 1881; designation changed to C, October 1, 1884; constituted a separate company, designated the 38th Separate Company, and assigned to the 10th Regiment as Co. C, May 1, 1905.

The company was mustered into the United States service as Co. C, 1st N. Y. Infantry, May 20, 1898, and was mustered out February 20, 1899.

Recognition extended by the War Department under Act of June 3, 1916, on June 23, 1916.

COMPANY D, TENTH INFANTRY
(Forty-fifth Separate Company.)
(Third Brigade.)
State Armory, 195 Washington Avenue, Albany

Organized July 2, 1861, as Company D, 10th Regiment. Became Company D, 10th Battalion, February 17, 1881; constituted a separate company, designated the 45th Separate Company, and attached to the 10th Regiment as Company D, May 1, 1905.

The company was mustered into the United States service as Company D, 177th N. Y. Vols., November 21, 1862; and was mustered out September 10, 1863; was again mustered into the United States service as Company D, 1st N. Y. Infantry, May 20, 1898, and was mustered out February 20, 1899.

Recognition extended by the War Department under Act of June 3, 1916, on June 23, 1916.

COMPANY E, TENTH INFANTRY
(Sixteenth Separate Company.)
(Third Brigade.)
State Armory, 78 Water Street, Catskill

Organized October 8, 1879. Attached to 10th Regiment as Co. C, March 15, 1899; to 10th Regiment, as Co. E, May 1, 1905. June 23, 1882, it was placed on duty to assist the civil authorities in suppressing a riot among Italian laborers on the line of the New York, West Shore and Buffalo Railroad at Coxsackie, and at Buffalo in August, 1892, during riots at that place.

Recognition extended by the War Department under Act of June 3, 1916, on June 23, 1916.

COMPANY F, TENTH INFANTRY
(Twenty-third Separate Company.)
(Third Brigade.)
Armory, Fifth and State Streets, Hudson

Organized May 24, 1878. Attached to 1st Regiment as Co. D, March 15, 1899; to 10th Regiment as Co. F, May 1, 1905. On duty at Buffalo riots in August, 1892, and near Stockport to enforce quarantine against smallpox in June, 1901.

Recognition extended by the War Department under Act of June 3, 1916, on June 23, 1916.

INFANTRY — (*Continued*)
COMPANY G, TENTH INFANTRY
(Fourth Separate Company.)
(Third Brigade.)
Armory, Waverly Street, Yonkers

Organized July 18, 1870, as Co. H, 3d Regiment, which regiment was disbanded and the companies formed into another organization designated the 27th Regiment, November 22, 1873, Co. H retaining its letter designation. It was transferred to the 16th Battalion, May 12, 1874, as Co. D, and on the disbandment of the battalion, December 17, 1881, was retained in service as the 4th Separate Company; attached to 1st Regiment, as Co. A, March 15, 1899; to 10th Regiment, as Co. G, May 1, 1905. It served during the riots at Buffalo in August, 1892, and riots at Croton Dam, April, 1900.

Recognition extended by the War Department under Act of June 3, 1916, on June 25, 1916.

COMPANY H, TENTH INFANTRY
(Eleventh Separate Company.)
(Third Brigade.)
State Armory, North Fifth Avenue and North Street, Mt. Vernon

Organized April 12, 1876, as 1st Separate Troop of Cavalry, 7th Brigade, 5th Division. Designation changed December 8, 1877, to Separate Troop E, and October 5, 1881, reorganized as the 11th Separate Co. Attached to 1st Regiment as Co. B, March 15, 1899; to 10th Regiment, as Co. H, May 1, 1905. On duty during the riots at Croton Dam, April, 1900.

Recognition extended by the War Department under Act of June 3, 1916, on June 26, 1916.

COMPANY I, TENTH INFANTRY
(Seventeenth Separate Company.)
(Third Brigade.)
State Armory, 147 Broadway, Flushing

Organized as the 1st Separate Company, 2d Division, in July, 1876; its designation changed to 17th Separate Company, December 8, 1877. Transferred to the 3d Brigade and assigned to the 10th Regiment as Company I, May 1, 1905.

Recognition extended by the War Department under Act of June 3, 1916, on June 24, 1916.

COMPANY K, TENTH INFANTRY
(Fifteenth Separate Company.)
(Third Brigade.)
State Armory, Market and Church Streets, Poughkeepsie

Organized immediately after the bombardment of Fort Sumter, S. C., as the Poughkeepsie Drill Guards; May 14, 1861, the name was changed to "Ellsworth Grays," and on October 27, 1862, the company joined the militia and became Co. A of the 21st Regiment and on disbandment of that regiment its designation was changed, December 17, 1881, to 15th Separate Company. Attached to 1st Regiment, as Co. K, March 15, 1899; to 10th Regiment, as Co. K, May 1, 1905. In the service of the United States from June 27 to August 6, 1863, and as Co. K, 1st Regiment, N. Y. Infantry, from May 20, 1898, to February 26, 1899. In the service of the State at Buffalo during the riots in August, 1892.

Recognition extended by the War Department under Act of June 3, 1916, on June 26, 1916.

COMPANY L, TENTH INFANTRY
(Forty-ninth Separate Company.)
(Third Brigade.)
Armory, South Broadway and Mitchell Place, White Plains

Mustered in May 28, 1907.

Recognition extended by the War Department under Act of June 3, 1916, on June 26, 1916.

COMPANY M, TENTH INFANTRY
(Fourteenth Separate Company.)
(Third Brigade.)
State Armory, Broadway and Hoffman Street, Kingston

Organized September 21, 1874, as Co. H, 20th Battalion. Designation changed to Co. B, November 13, 1874, and to 14th Separate Company, December 17, 1881. Attached to 1st Regiment as Co. M, March 15, 1899; and to the 10th Regiment, as Co. M, May 1, 1905. May 21 and 22, 1875, the company was on duty suppressing a riot at Rosendale; April 20 and 21, 1876, on similar duty at Rondout; in July and August, 1877, again at Rondout, and March 4, 1879, at Kingston. In United States service as Co. M, 1st Regiment, N. Y. Infantry, from May 20, 1898, to February 26, 1899.

Recognition extended by the War Department under Act of June 3, 1916, on June 25, 1916. ·

INFANTRY — TENTH REGIMENT

Name, grade, date of rank and highest brevet rank	Company	Service		Born
		In the armies of U. S. or foreign states	In the National Guard	
Colonel				
Klein, John Frederick, 1 feb. 11 bvt. brig. gen. 1 may 12	......	cap. 203 N. Y. inf., 21 july 98 to 7 sep. 98	pvt., corp., sgt., 17 sep. co............14 dec. 84 to 26 may 91 2 lt................26 may 91 1 lt................20 sep. 92 cap...............13 apr. 96 maj. 10 inf.........25 aug. 08 col................ 1 feb. 11 accepted........... 1 feb. 11	N. Y. 19 oct. 63
Lieutenant Colonel				
Saulpaugh, Albert, 3 nov. 11	......	sgt., qm. sgt. co. K, 203 N. Y. inf., 20 july 98 to 25 mar. 99	pvt., qm. sgt., 16 sep. co...........26 oct. 96 to 20 june 00 2 lt...............20 june 00 cap...............11 jan. 01 maj. 10 inf......... 4 june 09 lt. col.............. 3 nov. 11 accepted........... 4 nov. 11	N. Y. 16 june 79
Majors				
Chandler, George Fletcher, 9 jan. 12 Field Officers' course, Army Service Schools, 1915.	....		asst. surg. 14 sep. co. 1 lt...............21 nov. 06 supn., reassigned....21 jan. 08 asst. surg. 1 lt......31 jan. 08 cap. 10 inf.........18 dec. 08 maj............... 9 jan. 12 accepted...........11 jan. 12	N. Y. 13 dec. 73
lover, Ralph Murray, 20 mar. 14 Graduate, Garrison Schools, 1915.	......	1 lt. 202 N. Y. inf., 1 aug. 98 to 15 apr. 99	pvt. 11 sep. co.......20 sep. 82 hon. dis............25 oct. 87 pvt., corp., sgt., 1 sgt., 11 sep. co......13 june 89 to 14 jan. 98 2 lt...............14 jan. 98 1 lt...............15 oct. 00 resigned...........18 apr. 02 cap. 49 sep. co......21 june 07 maj...............20 mar. 14 accepted...........23 mar. 14	N. Y. 7 feb. 63
Captains				
Harris, Frank Salisbury, 1 may 05	m. g. co.	....	pvt., corp., sgt., co. A, 10 bat......... 9 oct. 86 to 22 may 96 comy of sub. 1 lt. 10 bat..............22 may 96 cap. (A), 110 bat....20 may 98 resigned to return to 10 bat. as comy of sub............. 9 mar. 99 cap. comy of sub. 10 inf............... 1 may 05 a. d. c. to gov......21 feb. 14 to 31 dec. 14	N. Y. 30 apr. 68
Dooley, Thomas Jefferson, 23 jan. 09 Graduate, Garrison Schools, 1915.	I	2 lt. 203 N. Y. inf., 21 july 98 to 1 oct. 98	pvt., corp., sgt., 17 sep. co...........20 jan. 91 to 21 feb. 98 2 lt...............21 feb. 98 supn., reassigned....21 jan. 08 relieved, reassigned..30 dec. 08 cap. 10 inf......... 8 feb. 09 accepted...........11 feb. 09	N. Y. 18 mar. 71

INFANTRY — TENTH REGIMENT — (*Continued*)

Name, grade, date of rank and highest brevet rank	Company	Service: In the armies of U. S. or foreign states	Service: In the National Guard	Born
Captains — Continued				
Burnett, William Lewis, 28 may 09	K	pvt., corp., co. K, 1 N. Y. inf., 2 may 98 to 26 feb. 99	pvt., corp., sgt., 1 sgt., 15 sep. co... .15 jan. 97 to 21 nov. 02 2 lt..............21 nov. 02 1 lt................ 5 nov. 03 cap............... 4 june 09 accepted.......... 9 june 09	N. Y. 28 june 79
Canfield, Charles Henry, 1 mar. 11	H	pvt., corp. co. M, 8 N. Y. inf., 2 may 98 to 3 nov. 98	pvt., 11 sep. co., trs. co. M, 8 inf......26 jan. 98 hon. dis...........22 dec. 98 pvt., corp., sgt., 1 sgt., 11 sep. co.....12 may 99 to 1 aug. 02 1 lt........ 1 aug. 02 cap. 10 inf......... 1 mar. 11 accepted.......... 4 mar. 11	N. Y. 1 mar. 77
Schenck, Gilbert Van Evera, 17 may 11	adj.	....	pvt., corp., co. A, 10 bat., sgt., 26 sep. co...............18 mar. 01 to 27 feb. 07 1 lt. bat. adj. 10 inf..27 feb. 07 cap. 10 inf.......17 may 11 accepted..........18 may 11	N. Y. 28 dec. 82
Bogert, Albert Cole, 25 may 11	G	corp., qm. sgt., co. B, 203 N. Y. inf., 10 july 98 to 2 feb. 99	pvt. 4 sep. co....... 8 july 98 to 29 sep. 98 pvt., qm. sgt., 4 sep. co.............. 8 june 99 to 13 june 02 2 lt..............13 june 02 1 lt..............18 may 06 cap............25 may 11 accepted..........26 may 11	N. Y. 21 dec. 69
Wheelock, William Fowler, 5 july 11	sup. co.	1 lt. 1 N. Y. inf., 2 may 98 to 20 feb. 99	pvt., corp., 1 sgt., co. D, 10 bat......13 feb. 94 to 20 dec. 95 2 lt..............20 dec 95 1 lt..............14 mar. 00 cap............25 jan. 01 1 lt. bat. adj. 10 inf.. 1 may 05 cap. 10 inf......... 5 july 11 accepted.......... 8 july 11	N. Y. 22 jan. 72
Callan, Albert Stevens, 6 feb. 12	D	....	pvt. 34 sep. co...... 1 feb. 06 to 14 dec. 06 2 lt..............14 dec. 06 2 lt. 10 inf........12 jan. 09 1 lt.............. 2 aug. 11 cap............... 6 feb. 12 accepted.......... 9 feb. 12	N. Y. 27 july 84
Ferguson, William Henry, 16 apr. 12	i. s. a. p.	....	pvt. co. I, 23 inf. . . 6 oct. 92 hon. dis .... 7 dec. 03 pvt., qm. sgt. tr. B...16 sep. 07 to 16 apr. 12 cap. o. d.........16 apr. 12 cap. 10 inf......... 1 may 14 accepted.......... 5 may 14	N. Y. 8 may 69
Meagher, Frank Leo, 23 apr. 12 Graduate, Garrison Schools, 1915.	M	....	pvt. 114 sep. co., trs. 14 sep. co., corp., sgt., 1 sgt........10 nov. 98 to 6 jan. 09 1 lt. 10 inf.......... 6 jan 09 cap............23 apr. 12 accepted..........24 apr. 12	N. Y. 7 apr. 76

INFANTRY — TENTH REGIMENT — (Continued)

Name, grade, date of rank and highest brevet rank	Company	Service		Born
		In the armies of U. S. or foreign states	In the National Guard	
Captains — Continued				
Townsend, Reynolds King, 26 nov. 12	A	....	pvt., corp., 26 sep. co..............30 dec. 07 hon. dis........... 1 dec. 10 1 lt. 10 inf.......... 2 dec. 10 cap..................26 nov. 12 accepted...........27 nov. 12 a. d. c. to gov...... 1 jan. 13 acting military secre- tary to gov......23 oct. 13 to 31 dec. 14	N. Y. 15 july 84
Best, Archland Miller, 17 mar. 14	F	....	pvt., corp., co. F, 10 inf............... 4 jan. 11 to 18 dec. 12 2 lt. 10 inf.........18 dec. 12 cap.................17 mar. 14 accepted...........18 mar. 14	N. Y. 23 oct. 87
Anderson, Harry Boardman, 30 apr. 14	C	....	pvt., corp., sgt., co. A, 10 bat., color sgt. 10 inf........16 oct. 01 hon. dis........... 7 nov. 10 pvt., sgt., co. C, 10 inf............. 1 dec. 10 to 3 july 11 31 july 13 to 19 feb. 14 1 lt.................19 feb. 14 cap.................30 apr. 14 accepted...........30 apr. 14	N. Y. 15 nov. 75
Cobb, Frederick William, 18 may 14 Graduate, Garrison Schools, 1915.	L	....	pvt. co. B, 7 inf..... 6 june 96 hon. dis........... 2 jan. 02 pvt., 1 sgt., 49 sep. co..............28 may 07 to 7 jan. 08 2 lt. 49 sep. co...... 7 jan. 08 1 lt. 10 inf.........16 oct. 12 cap.................18 may 14 accepted...........21 may 14	Conn. 6 june 75
Cassidy, Daniel John, 11 dec. 14	E	....	pvt., corp., sgt., 16 sep. co........... 3 oct. 03 hon. dis...........12 oct. 08 pvt., sgt., 16 sep. co.19 oct. 08 to 14 dec. 08 2 lt. 10 inf.........14 dec. 08 1lt..................30 nov. 09 cap.................11 dec. 14 accepted...........12 dec. 14	N. Y. 22 feb. 80
Thorne, Edward R........ 28 june 16	B	....	pvt. co. B, 10 bat., trs. co. B, 110 bat., trs. co. B, 10 bat., corp., sgt........11 feb. 97 to 30 may 05 2 lt. 35 sep. co......30 may 05 1 lt. 10 inf......... 4 june 09 accepted........... 7 june 09 cap.................25 july 11 accepted...........26 july 11 f. and h. dis........ 4 feb. 14 placed on r. l.......15 july 14 cap. 10 inf..........28 june 16 accepted...........28 june 16	N. Y. 24 june 76

INFANTRY — TENTH REGIMENT — (*Continued*).

Name, grade, date of rank and highest brevet rank	Company	Service		Born
		In the armies of U. S. or foreign states	In the National Guard	
First Lieutenants				
Hammond, Wilber Bird, 10 dec. 04	G	....	pvt. co. I, 22 inf., trs. 4 sep. co., corp., sgt., 1 sgt........30 mar. 94 to 6 dec. 04 1 lt. bat. adj. 1 inf.... 6 dec. 04 supn............... 1 may 05 1 lt. bat. adj. 10 inf. with o. r.......... 5 may 05	N. Y. 1 oct. 68
Clark, Edward James..... 19 may 11 Graduate, Garrison School, 1915.	I	....	pvt., corp., sgt., 1 sgt., 17 sep. co.... 8 mar. 98 to 17 feb. 10 2 lt. 10 inf..........17 feb. 10 1 lt................19 may 11 accepted...........23 may 11	N. Y. 31 aug. 70
Evans, Harold Brown, 25 feb. 13	bat. adj.	....	pvt. co. F, 10 inf.....30 mar. 07 to 27 apr. 07 2 apr. 12 to 25 feb. 13 1 lt................25 feb. 13 accepted...........26 feb. 13	N. Y. 6 feb. 89
Crosby, Maunsell Schieffelin, 6 feb. 14	D	....	2 lt. 10 inf..........19 nov. 12 1 lt................ 6 feb. 14 accepted.......... 9 feb. 14	N. Y. 14 feb. 87
Coffey, John Augustine, 6 july 14	C	....	pvt., corp., co. C, 10 inf...............27 may 12 to 27 mar. 14 2 lt................27 mar. 14 1 lt................ 6 july 14 accepted.......... 6 july 14	N. Y. 17 nov. 91
Dunning, Edward Clark, 21 july 14	L	pvt., acting sgt., h. c. U. S. Vols., 15 june 98 to 15 nov. 98	pvt., corp., h. c. 71 inf., trs. co. D, trs. co. C, corp....17 jan. 97 hon. dis............17 june 02 pvt , qm. sgt., 1 sgt., co. L, 10 inf......28 may 07 to 25 mar. 13 2 lt................25 mar. 13 1 lt................21 july 14 accepted...........22 july 14	N. Y. 29 july 71
Snyder, Louis Virtue, 1 oct. 14	H	....	pvt., corp., sgt., 1 sgt., 11 sep. co....26 nov. 06 to 28 july 11 2 lt. 10 inf..........28 july 11 1 lt................ 1 oct 14 accepted.......... 5 oct. 14	N. J. 16 sep. 82
Doty, Lucius Huntington, 5 feb. 15	E	....	pvt., h. c., 16 sep. co.,16 apr. 97 hon. dis............ 1 june 03 pvt., qm. sgt., 16 sep. co............... 1 jan. 04 hon. dis............28 apr. 06 2 lt. 10 inf..........23 dec. 10 1 lt................ 5 feb. 15 accepted.......... 6 feb. 15	N. Y. 25 may 76
Dittus, Rudolph C., 28 dec. 15	M	....	pvt., corp., co. M, 10 inf............11 dec. 03 hon. dis............17 feb. 10 pvt., sgt., 10 inf..... 2 mar. 10 hon. dis............ 2 mar. 15 pvt. 10 inf......... 2 mar. 15 to 28 dec. 15 1 lt................28 dec. 15 accepted...........30 dec. 15	N. Y. 12 dec. 85

INFANTRY — TENTH REGIMENT — (*Continued*)

Name, grade, date of rank and highest brevet rank	Company	Service		Born
		In the armies of U. S. or foreign states	In the National Guard	
First Lieutenants — Continued				
Coffin, Tristram, 28 dec. 14	F	....	2 lt. 10 inf.........28 dec. 14 accepted..........29 dec. 14	N. Y. 12 aug. 89
Niles, Edgar C., 13 jun. 16	C	pvt. 11 U. S. cav. 16 oct. 01 hon. dis. 15 oct. 04	pvt. co. C, 10 inf.....21 nov. 10 1 sgt...............11 jan. 11 2 lt. 10 inf.........16 jan. 12 accepted..........20 jan. 12 f. and h. dis........ 1 may 13 2 lt...............23 sep. 15 1 lt...............13 june 16 accepted..........13 june 16	N. Y. 26 may 84
Bayles, Frank Anthony, 7 july 16	bat. adjt.	....	pvt. co. L, 10 inf....11 feb. 89 to 21 apr. 94 pvt...............27 june 94 to 5 dec. 95 pvt. sgt. 1 sgt. post qm. sgt. co. L, 10 inf..............28 may 07 to 2 dec. 14 2 lt................ 2 dec. 14 accepted.......... 3 dec. 14 1 lt................ 7 july 16 accepted.......... 7 july 16	N. Y. 16 sep. 69
Parsons, Theophilus, 7 july 16	m. g. co.	....	1 lt................ 7 july 16 accepted.......... 8 july 16	N. Y. 20 june 77
Second Lieutenants				
Laraway, Frank John, 16 feb. 12	B	....	pvt., corp., sgt., 1 sgt., co. B, 10 bat.. 2 june 03 to 16 feb. 12 2 lt. 10 inf.........16 feb. 12 accepted..........17 feb. 12	N. Y. 26 aug. 77
Bragdon, George Douglas, 6 june 14	G	....	pvt. co. A, 10 inf..... 6 may 99 to 28 oct. 02 31 mar. 05 to 12 sep. 05 pvt., mus. sgt. co. A, 4 feb. 11 to 6 june 14 2 lt................ 6 june 14 accepted..........10 june 14	Minn. 13 jan. 78
Crump, Samuel, Jr., 9 july 14	D	....	pvt. co. D, 10 inf.... 1 dec. 13 to 9 july 14 2 lt............... 9 july 14 accepted..........11 july 14	N. J. 15 july 88
Callan, Francis Marvin, 11 sep. 14	A	....	pvt., corp., sgt., co. A, 10 inf..........27 july 11 to 11 sep. 14 2 lt...............11 sep. 14 accepted..........14 sep. 14	N. Y. 12 july 89
Heath, William, 28 may 15	E	....	pvt. co. E, 10 inf....22 mar. 06 to 11 june 11 pvt., corp., sgt., co. E, 10 inf..........27 june 11 to 28 may 15 2 lt...............28 may 15 accepted..........29 may 15	N. Y. 13 dec. 84

INFANTRY — TENTH REGIMENT — (Concluded)

Name, grade, date of rank and highest brevet rank	Company	Service		Born
		In the armies of U. S. or foreign states	In the National Guard	
Second Lieutenants — Continued				
Burtis, Edward Morrison,	H	....	pvt., corp., sgt., co. H, 10 inf.........29 nov. 09 to 15 june 15 2 lt.................15 june 15 accepted...........18 june 15	N. Y. 5 dec. 90
Cashin, Edward LeR., 11 jan. 16	M..	....	pvt. co. M.........19 dec. 08 dropped...........21 july 11 taken up...........29 aug. 11 corp...............14 nov. 12 f. and h. dis.........18 mar. 14 re-enlisted.........28 apr. 14 corp...............19 dec. 14 2 lt................11 jan. 16 accepted...........12 jan. 16	N. Y. 30 aug. 90
Decker, Percy W., 10 apr. 16	m. g. co.	....	2 lt. 16 sep. co....... 1 dec. 02 1 lt. 10 inf........... 3 june 08 with rank from......19 may 08 cap. 10 inf.........24 june 09 with rank from.....18 june 09 accepted...........24 june 09 reserve list.........13 oct. 14 2 lt................16 apr. 16 accepted...........11 apr. 16	N. Y. 14 july 73
Gritman, Edgar B., 7 july 16	m. g. co.	....	2 lt................ 7 july 16 accepted........... 9 july 16	L. I. 12 aug. 79
Morrison, Richard R., 14 aug. 16	bat. q. m. and com.	....	pvt. co. L.........28 may 07 to hosp. corps....... 5 aug. 07 to med. dept........ 7 mar. 08 sgt................ 5 july 09 1 cl. sgt........... 1 sep. 09 f. and h. dis........26 apr. 15 re-enlisted co. L.....27 apr. 15 bat. sgt. maj........ 5 may 15 2 lt................14 aug. 16 accepted...........16 aug. 16	N. J. 21 aug. 62
Odell, Albert C., 31 dec. 15	K	....	pvt. co. E.........13 dec. 97 trs. to 14 sep. co....27 apr. 98 2 lt................31 dec. 15 accepted........... 7 jan. 16	N. Y. 27 mar. 78
Chaplain, Captain				
Kelly, Francis A.,	......	....	chaplain...........10 july 16 accepted...........10 july 16	N. Y. 19 apr. 87

INFANTRY — (Continued)

TWELFTH REGIMENT

(Twelve Companies.)

(First Brigade.)

Armory, 120 West Sixty-second Street, New York City.

This regiment was organized as the 11th Regiment by a general order dated June 21, 1847, and was of eight companies, viz.: Light Guard of 100th Regiment; Bensen Guard, of 125th Regiment; Independence Guard, of 264th Regiment; Italian Guard, of 252d Regiment; Monroe Blues, of 235th Regiment; Tompkins Blues, of 51st Regiment; Independent Tompkins Blues, of 222d Regiment, and LaFayette Fusiliers, of 85th Regiment. By a general order dated July 27, 1847, the designation of the regiment was changed to the 12th. A new company, under command of Captain Henry Johnson, was organized and attached to the regiment, April 25, 1849. Co. H of the 3d Regiment was transferred to the 12th Regiment, April 25, 1849. Co. D was consolidated with Co. C, June 5, 1849. A new company under Captain Adolphus I. Johnson. was organized April 15, 1850. Co. L was transferred to the 11th Regiment, May 3, 1858. On March 16, 1859, Cos. A and C, B and H, and G and E were consolidated, and the consolidated companies, with Co. D, transferred to the 10th Regiment. On June 29, 1859, these transferred companies were disbanded. On November 16, 1859, five companies (A, B, C, D and G) were organized in the Twenty-second Regimental District. On November 22, 1859, Co. E was organized and an election ordered for field officers of the 22d Regiment. These companies were composed principally of former members of the old 12th Regiment. The designation of the 22d Regiment was changed December 19, 1859, to 12th Regiment. Co. H was organized January 28, 1860, and Co. F, February 2, 1860. Co. C was consolidated with Co. E, March 21, 1861, and Co. K was organized May 8, 1861. Co. I, 23d Regiment, was transferred to 12th Regiment as Co. I, April 2, 1861. New Co. C was organized December 31, 1861. Co. K was disbanded February 12, 1862, and new Co. K organized September 22, 1862. Co. C was consolidated with Co. I, January 12. 1876. Co. I was consolidated with Co. G, January 12, 1876. New Co. I was organized February 21, 1876. Co. D was consolidated with Co. E, March 11, 1876. New Co. D was organized July 16, 1884, and new Co. C was organized June 3, 1885. The regiment performed duty during the Astor Place riots in 1840. April 21, 1861, the regiment entered the United States service for three months; July 12, took part in a skirmish near Martinsburg, and July 15, near Bunkerhill, W. Va.; August 5, 1861, it was mustered out of service at New York city. May 27, 1862, the regiment again entered the United States service for three months, during which they were engaged in the defense of Harper's Ferry, and were present at the surrender, although their services expired August 27, 1862, having volunteered to remain in service until October 15, 1862; September 16, the regiment was paroled; October 8, it was mustered out, and January 11, 1863, declared exchanged. June 20, 1863, the regiment re-entered the service of the United States for thirty days, serving in Pennsylvania and Maryland, and in suppressing the draft riots at New York city; it was mustered out by companies between July 20 and 25, but remained in the service of the State until September, 1863. The regiment was on duty during the Orange riots in July, 1871; during the railroad riots in July, 1877; during the switchmen's strike at Buffalo, in August, 1892; and at Brooklyn during the motormen's strike in January, 1895. April 28, 1898, the regiment was authorized to be organized as a twelve-company regiment to enter the United States service, into which it was mustered as the 12th Regiment. N. Y. Infantry, May 18, 1898, and mustered out April 20, 1899; Companies L and M were disbanded April 24, 1899. December 2, 1910, the regiment received authority to muster in a new company to be known as Company M. The regiment was authorized to organize a detachment of mounted orderlies by Special Orders No. 167, July 2, 1912.

Recognition extended by the War Department to Supply Company, Companies A. D, E and G, on June 25. Company B, on June 24. Companies C, F, H, L and Sanitary Detachment, on June 27; Companies I and M, June 26; and Company K on June 28, 1916; Headquarters Company, on June 24, 1916, and to Machine Gun Company on November 3, 1916.

The regiment has received authority to place silver rings on the lances of its colors, engraved as follows:

On the National Color.— May 24, 1861, Arlington Heights, Va.; July 12, 1861, Martinsburg, Va.; July 15, 1861, Bunkerhill, W. Va.; September 12-13, 1862, Maryland Heights, Md.; September 12-15, 1862, Harper's Ferry, W. Va.; July 18, 1861, Blackburn's Ford, Va.; July 21, 1861, Bull Run, Va.; March 27, 1862, Reconnaissance at Big Bethel, Va.; April 5 to May 12, 1862, Yorktown, Va.; May 27, 1862; Hanover Court House, Va.; June 27, 1862, Gaines Mills, Va.; June 30, 1862, Turkey Bridge. Va.; July 1, 1862, Malvern Hill, Va.; August 30, 1862, Bull Run or Manassas, Va.; September 17, 1862, Antietam, Md.; December 13, 1862, Fredericksburg, Va.; May 3, 1863, Chancellorsville, Va.; July 1-4, 1863, Gettysburg, Pa.; May 5-7, 1864, Wilderness, Va.; May 8-21, 1864, Spottsylvania Court House, Va.; May 31 to June 2, 1864, Cold Harbor, Va.; Spanish-American War, 1898; Cuba, 1899.

On the State Color.— Astor Place riots, 1840; Dead Rabbit riot, July 3, 4, 5, 1857; quarantine riot, 1858; Draft riot, 1863; Orange riot, 1871; railroad riots, 1877; Buffalo, 1892; Brooklyn, 1895.

INFANTRY — TWELFTH REGIMENT

Name, grade, date of rank and highest brevet rank	Com- pany	Service		Born
		In the armies of U. S. or foreign states	In the National Guard	
Colonel				
Johnston, Gordon, 7 july 16	......	sgt. co. M, 2 Miss. inf. and pvt. tr. M, 1 u. s. cav. 8 june 98 to 15 sep. 98 2 lt. 43 u. s. inf., 17 aug. 99 accepted...25 aug. 99 hon. must. out, 5 july 01 2 lt. 10 cav. 2 feb. 01 accepted...25 sep. 01 1 lt. 15 cav..4 oct. 02 1 lt. sig. corps (by de- tail, act 2 mar. 03), 17 sep. 03 unassd.... 6 dec. 06 assd to 3 cav., 19 jan. 07 trs. to 7 cav, 25 feb. 10 unassd....11 mar. 11 assd. to 7 cav., 25 feb. 12 trs. to 15 cav., 27 june 12 cap. 11 cav., 27 mar. 13 mustered into u. s. ser......28 june 16	col................. 7 july 16 accepted........... 7 july 16	N. C. 25 may 74
Lieutenant Colonel				
Foster, Reginald Love, 6 sep. 16	......	mustered into u. s. ser.... .28 june 16	pvt., corp., sgt., co. G, 7 inf .... 6 may 93 to 4 apr. 00 1 lt. (G), 12 inf...... 4 apr. 00 cap. (E)........... 7 apr. 03 maj. 12 inf.........13 oct. 08 a. d. c. to gov...... 1 jan. 09 lt. col........... 6 sep. 16 accepted..........10 sep. 16	China 25 nov. 69
Majors				
Downs, William Edward, 11 oct. 12	......	1 lt. 12 N. Y. inf., 2 may 98 cap......20 oct. 98 to 17 nov. 98 mustered into u. s. ser.. ...26 june 16	pvt., corp., sgt., co. E, sgt. maj. 12 inf..29 apr. 89 to 26 feb. 96 2 lt. (E)...........26 feb. 96 1 lt...............18 dec. 96 1 lt. asst. i. s. a. p. 12 inf., with o. r...... 1 nov. 99 cap. i. s. a. p ......10 oct. 00 cap. (I), 12 inf., with o. r............17 may 02 resigned..........23 mar. 04 cap. 12 inf......... 3 jun. 08 maj............11 oct. 12 accepted...... ...14 oct. 1	N. J. 20 sep. 67
Quackenbos, Henry For- rest, 24 apr. 16	......	mustered into u. s. ser......28 june 16	2 lt. (E), 12 inf......14 june 06 1 lt. 12 inf ....27 apr. 09 cap...............15 mar. 09 accepted..........18 mar. 09 maj..............24 apr. 16 accepted..........26 apr. 16	N. Y. 18 feb. 72 *
Roosevelt, George Emlen, 6 sep. 16	......	mustered into u. s. ser......26 june 16	2 lt. 12 inf.......... 4 jan. 11 1 lt...............21 dec. 11 cap...............10 dec. 13 accepted..........15 dec. 13 major........ 6 sep. 16 accepted..........10 sep. 16	N. Y. 13 oct. 87

INFANTRY — TWELFTH REGIMENT — (Continued)

Name, grade, date of rank and highest brevet rank	Company	Service		Born
		In the armies of U. S. or foreign states	In the National Guard	
Captains				
Zorn, Jay, 13 feb. 09	F	mustered into u. s ser..... 28 jun 17	pvt., corp., sgt., 30 sep. co., trs. co. B, 7 inf ....1 oct. 96 hon. dis ....14 may 03 2 lt. (F), 9 inf......21 mar. 05 1 lt.................14 nov. 05 lt. 12 inf.........27 apr. 08 cap.................24 feb. 09 accepted.......... 1 mar. 09	Ja- maica, W. I. 9 mar. 71
Janes, Elisha Harris, 19 june 12	I	mustered into u. s. ser......28 june 16	2 lt. 12 inf.........13 jan. 10 1 lt................. 3 mar. 11 cap...............19 june 12 accepted...........24 june 12	N. Y. 25 nov. 74
Dean, John Joseph, 10 dec. 13	L	pvt. co. H, 22 N. Y. inf...... 9 may 98 to 23 nov. 98 mustered into u. s.ser... 28 jun.	pvt., corp., sgt., 1 sgt., co. H. 22 inf. 10 jan. 05 hon. dis............14 feb. 05 16trs. co. L., 1 sgt.. 1 mar. 05 to 3 dec. 08 2 lt. 12 inf......... 3 dec. 08 1 lt...............27 nov. 09 cap..............10 dec. 13 accepted..........11 dec. 13	N. Y. 6 sep. 75
de Peyster, Frederic Ashton, 16 dec. 13	A	mustered into u. s. ser......28 june 16	2 lt. 12 inf..........15 mar. 09 1 lt................. 6 apr. 11 cap. o. d...........16 dec. 13 cap. 12 inf......... 1 may 14 accepted..........12 may 14	N. Y. 29 oct. 74
Hildreth, Henry Snively, 27 dec. 13	K	pvt. 22 U. S. inf., 18 feb. 02 hon. dis....17 feb. 05 mustered into u. s. ser.....28 june 16	pvt. co. F. 23 inf....30 nov. 96 hon. dis ....21 feb. 02 pvt. co. F.........14 jan. 07 hon. dis...........12 june 08 pvt. co. F. 23 inf....22 jan. 12 to 6 dec. 12 2 lt. 12 inf......... 6 dec. 12 cap...............27 dec. 13 accepted..........29 dec. 13	N. Y. 7 aug. 78
deKay, Sidney Gilder, 22 jan. 14	D	mustered into u. s. 28 june 16	seaman, 2 div. 1 bat. N. M............20 feb. 11 to 6 dec. 12 2 lt. 12 inf. N. G. N. Y.............. 6 dec. 12 1 lt................15 may 13 cap..............23 jan. 14	N. Y. 18 nov. 80
McCoy, Frank James..... 19 feb. 15	B	mustered into u. s. ser......28 june 16	pvt., corp., co. B, 12 inf...............7 nov. 10 to 6 aug. 12 2 lt................. 6 aug. 12 1 lt................ 4 june 14 cap...............19 feb. 15 accepted..........20 feb. 15	Mass. 26 feb. 81
Cammack, Huette, 13 mar. 15	G	mustered into u. s. ser......28 june 16	2 lt. 12 inf.........23 may 13 1 lt................. 3 jun. 14 cap...............13 mar. 15 accepted..........16 mar. 15	N. Y. 9 may

INFANTRY — TWELFTH REGIMENT — (Continued)

Name, grade, date of rank and highest brevet rank	Company	Service		Born
		In the armies of U. S. or foreign states	In the National Guard	
Captains — Continued				
Holt, Henry Emil, 6 july 15	E	pvt. tr. A, I U. S. V. cav. —— ——98 mustered into u. s. ser......28 june 16	pvt., corp., tr. 2, sq. A................ 9 feb. 98 hon. dis. .... 1 apr. 03 pvt., guidon sgt., corn. tr. 2....... 9 mar. 06 hon. dis...........20 mar. 13 pvt. tr. 2 .... 4 apr. 13 1 lt. 12 inf.......... 4 apr. 13 cap................. 6 july 15 accepted..........12 july 15	N. Y. 1 jan. 78
Gauche, Edward Eugene, 6 july 15	adjt.	mustered into u. s. ser......28 june 16	pvt., corp., sgt., 1 sgt. Ohio N. G.... 6 apr. 03 to 25 may 04 2 lt...............25 may 04 1 lt............... 3 aug. 04 cap... .... 7 dec. 04 resigned........... 1 jun. 06 2 lt. 12 inf., N. G., N. Y..........30 jan. 15 1 lt...............25 may 15 cap................. 6 july 15 accepted..........12 july 15	Ohio 1 feb. 77
Mitchell, William S., 9 may 16	sup. co.	mustered into u. s. ser......28 june 16	pvt , trumpeter, chief trumpeter, sq. A................17 apr. 03 to 28 feb. 12 chief trumpeter, 1 cav...............23 feb. 12 hon. dis .... 8 dec. 13 2 lt. 12 inf .... 25 feb. 14 accepted...........26 feb. 14 captain.......... 9 may 16 accepted.......... 9 may 16	N. Y. 27 feb. 82
Scott, Julian Fairfax, 24 june 16	m g. co.	mustered into u. s. ser......28 june 16	pvt. co. I, 7 inf......26 may 03 to 17 oct. 05 2 lt. (K), 12 inf ....17 oct. 05 1 lt.. ....28 dec. 07 cap. 12 inf..........15 june 08 cap. r. l............14 dec. 15 cap 12 inf..........24 june 16 accepted..........24 june 16	Md. 23 june 77
Daly, George Augustine, 24 june 16	H	mustered into u. s ser......28 june 16	2 lt. 12 inf.......... 2 jan. 09 1 lt .... 3 jan. 13 accepted.......... 6 jan. 13 captain.............24 june 16 accepted...........24 june 16	N. Y. 23 aug. 78
Waltz, Millard Fillmore, Jr., 3 oct. 16	M	mustered into u. s. ser......28 june 16	2 lt. 12 inf..........19 june 15 accepted...........21 june 15 captain........... 3 oct. 16 accepted.......... 6 oct. 16	Md. 12 sep. 81
Brown, Charles Steele, Jr., 25 nov. 16	C	mustered into u. s ser......28 june 16	2 lt. 12 inf.......... 4 dec. 13 1 lt................26 may 14 accepted........... 1 june 14 captain.............25 nov. 16 accepted...........29 nov. 16	N. Y. 4 aug. 85
First Lieutenants				
Bramwell, George Moffat, 10 june 14	B	mustered into u. s ser......28 june 16	2 lt. 12 inf.......... 3 jan. 13 1 lt.................10 june 14 accepted...........12 june 14	N. Y. 10 oct. 87

INFANTRY — TWELFTH REGIMENT —(*Continued*)

Name, grade, date of rank and highest brevet rank	Company	Service		Born
		In the armies of U. S. or foreign states	In the National Guard	
First Lieutenants — Continued				
Taylor, Geoffrey Marshall, 14 july 15	I	mustered into u. s. ser......28 june 16	2 lt. 12 inf..........19 june 14 1 lt................14 july 15 accepted...........16 july 15	N. Y. 21 mar. 93
Ross, Carl G. R., 14 june 16	G	mustered into u. s. ser......28 june 16	2 lt. 12 inf..........16 sep. 15 accepted...........20 sep. 15 1 lt................14 june 16 accepted...........19 june 16	N. Y. 12 july 92
Cavanagh, Edward, 23 june 16	A	mustered into u. s. ser......28 june 16	pvt. trp. 7, sq. C....20 apr. 08 f. and h. dis........ 7 dec. 14 2 lt................24 june 16 accepted...........24 june 16 1 lt................23 sep. 16 accepted...........27 sep. 16	Mo. 29 mar. 86
Juskin, Joseph D., Jr., 24 june 16	F	mustered into u. s. ser......28 june 16	pvt., bty. A, N. G., Pa................— jan. 98 2 lt. 12 inf.......... 1 june 16 accepted............ 5 june 16	Pa. 9 nov. 79
Barber, Thomas Hunt, 24 june 16	C	mustered into u. s. ser......28 june 16	pvt. batty. A, Mass. V. M., 12 may 08 1 class gunner......20 dec. 09 dis................20 aug. 10 2 lt. 12 inf., N. G., N. Y., 4 jan. 11 accepted............ 5 jan. 11 1 lt................ 5 apr. 12 accepted............ 8 apr. 12 hon. dis............ 1 may 13 1 lt................24 june 16 accepted...........24 june 16	N. Y. 20 jan. 89
Koen, Joseph John, 6 july 15	bat. adj.	mustered into u. s. ser......28 june 16	pvt. co. E., 7 inf.....11 nov. 11 to 16 dec. 13 2 lt. 12 inf..........16 dec. 13 accepted...........22 dec. 13 1 lt................ 6 july 16 accepted...........14 july 16	N. Y. 22 dec. 87
Dowling, James F., 6 sep. 16	F	mustered into u. s. ser......28 june 16	pvt. co. D..........30 sep. 90 corp.............—22 sgt..............—96 1 sgt.............—98 bn. sgt. maj.......—00 f. and h. dis........ 1 apr. 03 re-enlisted co. F..... 1 apr. 93 1 sgt.............. 1 apr. 03 bn. sgt. maj.......19 june 16 2 lt................24 june 16 accepted...........24 june 16 1 lt................ 6 sep. 16 accepted...........11 sep. 16	N. Y. 27 nov. 73
Van Cortlandt, Augustus, Jr., 25 nov. 16	C	mustered into u. s. ser......28 june 16	2 lt. 12 inf..........12 july 15 accepted...........12 july 15 1 lt................25 nov. 16 accepted...........29 nov. 16	N. Y. 15 may
Taylor, Murray, 20 dec. 16	hqs. co.	mustered into u. s. ser......28 june 16	2 lt................24 june 16 accepted...........24 june 16 1 lt................20 dec. 16 accepted...........23 dec. 16	N. Y. 2 dec. 95

INFANTRY — TWELFTH REGIMENT — (Concluded)

Name, grade, date of rank and highest brevet rank	Company	Service		Born
		In the armies of U. S. or foreign states	In the National Guard	
Second Lieutenants				
Chadbourne, William Merriam, 19 mar. 14	sup. co.	mustered into u. s. ser......28 june 16	pvt. sq. A..........16 nov. 09 to 19 mar. 14 2 lt................19 mar. 14 accepted..........23 mar. 14	Cal. 11 feb. 79
Callahan, John F., 25 june 16	B	mustered into u. s. ser......28 june 16	pvt. co. B.......... 3 apr. 16 2 lt................25 june 16 accepted..........25 june 16	Cortland N. Y. 7 sep. 84
Clark, Frith D., 26 june 16	H	mustered into u. s. ser......28 june 16	pvt. co. B.......... 8 nov. 15 2 lt................26 june 16 accepted..........26 june 16	N. Y. 25 oct. 94
Captain				
Connolly, James Nicholas, 13 sep. 01	Chaplain	served by authority of the Secretary of War, as volunteer chaplain without rank or pay, on the U S. A hospital ship Relief, from 30 june 98 to sep. 98.	chaplain,'12 inf......13 sep. 01	N.'Y. 15 jan. 64

FOURTEENTH REGIMENT

(Twelve Companies.)

(Second Brigade.)

Armory, 1402 Eighth Avenue, Brooklyn

This regiment was organized in 1847. It entered the service of the United States for three years in May, June and July, 1861; June 1, 1864, those entitled to discharge were mustered out, and the re-enlisted men and recruits transferred to the 5th New York Volunteers. During this service the regiment was also known as the 84th New York Volunteers. April 28, 1898, it was authorized to be organised as a twelve-company regiment, preparatory to entering the service of the United States, into which service it was mustered May 13, 1898; it was mustered out of such service October 27, 1898. December 6th, the regiment was continued as a regiment of the National Guard composed of twelve companies. The regiment was authorized to organize a detachment of mounted orderlies by Special Orders No. 167, July 2, 1912.

The regiment was authorized to organize a machine gun platoon of 22 men, by S. O. 168, A. G. O., July 3, 1916.

Recognition extended by the War Department to Companies A, B, C, D, E, F, G, H, I, K, L, M and Sanitary Detachment on June 26, 1916.

The regiment has authority to place silver rings on the lances of its colors, engraved as follows:

On the National Color.— Advance into Virginia, May 24, 1861; Bull Run, Va., July 21, 1861; Ball's Cross Roads, Va., August 27, 1861; Upton's Hill, Va., October 5, 1861; Binn's Hill, Va., November 18, 1861; Falmouth, Va., April 17-18, 1862; Carmel Church, Va., July 23, 1862; Massaponax, Va., August 6, 1862; General Pope's campaign, Va., August 16–September 3, 1862; Rappahannock River, Va., August 21, 1862; Rappahannock Station, Va., August 23, 1862; Sulphur Springs, Va., August 26, 1862; Gainesville, Va., August 28, 1862; Groveton, Va., August 29, 1862; Second Bull Run, Va., August 30, 1862; South Mountain, Md., September 14, 1862; Keedysville, Md., September 15-16, 1862; Antietam, Md., September 17, 1862; Fredericksburg, Va., December 13-15, 1862; Port Royal, Va., April 22-23, 1863; Fitzhugh's Crossing, Va., April 29–May 2, 1863; Chancellorsville, Va., May 3, 1863; Gettysburg, Pa., July 1-3, 1863; Mine Run, Va., November 28-30, 1863; Wilderness, Va., May 5-7, 1864; Spottsylvania, Va., May 8-21, 1864; Piney Branch Church, Va., May 8, 1864; Laurel Hill, Va., May 10, 1864; Spanish-American War, 1898.

On the State Color.— Fire Island, September, 1892; Brooklyn, January, 1895.

INFANTRY — FOURTEENTH REGIMENT

Name, grade, date of rank and highest brevet rank	Company	Service		Born
		In the armies of U. S. or foreign states	In the National Guard	
Colonel				
Foote, John Henry, 14 may 06 bvt. brig. gen. 11 feb. 10	......	cap. 14 N. Y. inf., 2 may 98 to 27 oct. 98 mustered into u. s. ser...... 1 aug. 16 out 11 oct. 16	pvt., qm. sgt., 1 sgt., co. B, 14 inf., sgt. maj. 14 inf.......11 feb. 85 to 18 sep. 93 1 lt. adj.............18 sep. 93 cap. (B)............. 3 jun. 95 maj. 14 inf.......... 5 dec. 01 lt. col.............23 sep. 04 a. d. c. to gov...... 2 jan. 05 to 1 feb. 06 col. 14 inf..........14 may 06	N. Y., 10 july 66
Lieutenant Colonel				
Garcia, William Lewis, 7 june 06	......	cap. 14 N. Y. inf., 2 may 98 to 27 oct. 98 mustered into u. s. ser...... 1 aug. 16 out 11 oct. 16	pvt., corp., sgt., 1 sgt., co. E, 14 inf., comy. sgt. 14 inf...14 may 86 to 20 jan. 93 1 lt. (D), 14 inf.....20 jan. 93 cap................. 2 apr. 94 maj.... .... 5 dec. 01 lt. col........ . 7 june 06	N. Y. 28 oct. 68

INFANTRY — FOURTEENTH REGIMENT — (Continued)

Name, grade, date of rank and highest brevet rank	Company	Service — In the armies of U. S. or foreign states	Service — In the National Guard	Born
Majors				
Donovan, Timothy Fran⁻ cis, 11 feb. 11 Graduate, Garrison Schools, 1915.	......	1 lt. 14 N. Y. inf., 2 may 98 to 27 oct. 98 mustered into u. s. ser...... 1 aug. 16 out 11 oct. 16	pvt., corp., sgt., qm. sgt., co. B, 14 inf., bat. qm. sgt., 14 inf................19 apr. 92 to 12 july 97 2 lt. (B)............13 july 97 1 lt. (L)............ 6 may 98 trs. co. B.........26 sep. 99 cap................23 jan. 02 regt. adj. with o. r...12 june 06 maj. 14 inf.........11 feb. 11 accepted.........13 feb. 11	N. Y. 7 oct. 72
Captains				
Summers, Herbert Anderson, 11 july 07	Sup. co.	mustered into u. s. ser...... 1 aug. 16 out 11 oct. 16	pvt. co. D, 23 inf.... 6 may 96 to 28 nov. 99 2 lt. (B) 14 inf........ 6 dec. 06 cap. i. s. a. p. 14 inf..11 july 07 supn., reassigned....21 jan. 08 cap. o. d.........11 feb. 08 cap. 14 inf........ 1 may 14 accepted.........11 may 14	N. Y. 5 may 67
Campion, Howard Lester, 12 mar. 08 Graduate, Garrison Schools, 1914. Distinguished Graduate, N. Y. School of the Line, 1915.	I	mustered into u. s. ser...... 1 aug. 16 out 11 oct. 16	2 lt. (A) 14 inf......21 june 06 1 lt............... 4 oct. 06 cap. 14 inf.........26 mar. 06 accepted.......... 6 apr. 08	N. Y. 27 mar. 73
Jackson, William Randolph, 27 may 00 M. V.	adj.	mustered into u. s. ser...... 1 aug. 16 out 11 oct. 16	pvt., corp., sgt., 3 batty............16 jan. 99 hon. dis......... 1 july 07 2 lt. 14 inf.........16 mar. 08 1 lt...............19 nov. 08 cap.............. 4 june 09 accepted.......... 7 june 09	N. Y. 27 jan. 77
Hollander, Gabriel George, 16 feb. 10 Graduate, Garrison Schools, 1915.	M	pvt., corp. co. E, 22 N. Y. inf., 9 may 98 to 16 oct. 98 mustered into u. s. ser...... 1 aug. 16 out 11 oct. 16	pvt., corp., co. E, 22 regt................22 nov. 98 hon. dis.........14 apr. 99 pvt., sgt., co. K, 22 eng., bat. sgt. maj., regt. sgt. maj., 22 eng..............17 feb. 02 hon. dis......... 7 feb. 08 2 lt. 14 inf......... 1 oct. 08 1 lt...............23 mar. 09 cap.............26 feb. 10 accepted.......... 5 mar. 10	N. Y. 19 june 73
Wonderly, Elbert Eugene, 23 dec. 10	C	mustered into u. s. ser...... 1 aug. 16 out 11 oct. 16	pvt., corp., sgt., qm. sgt., 1 sgt., co. A, 1 inf., N. G. N. J...21 feb. 02 to 28 june 06 2 lt...............28 june 06 resigned.........28 dec. 06 2 lt. 14 inf. N. G. N. Y.............24 apr. 08 1 lt...............24 mar. 10 cap.............23 dec. 10 accepted.........27 dec. 10	N. J. 23 apr. 73
Carlson, Oscar, 19 apr. 12	G	pvt. co. G, 14 N. Y. inf...... 2 may 98 to 27 oct. 98 mustered into u. s. ser...... 1 aug. 16 out 11 oct. 16	pvt., corp., qm. sgt., 1 sgt., co. G, 14 inf................11 may 98 to 5 may 10 2 lt. 14 inf.......... 5 may 10 1 lt...............17 may 11 cap..............19 apr. 12 accepted..........22 apr. 12	Sweden 5 june 76

INFANTRY — FOURTEENTH REGIMENT — (Continued)

Name, grade, date of rank and highest brevet rank	Company	Service		Born
		In the armies of U. S. or foreign states	In the National Guard	
Captains — Continued				
Clements, Albert, 5 may 14	K	pvt. co. A, 14 N. Y. inf...... 2 may 98 to 27 oct. 98 mustered into u. s. ser...... 1 aug. 16 out 11 oct. 16	pvt., corp., sgt., co. A, 14 inf..........15 june 96 hon. dis............26 aug. 07 pvt., sgt., co. C, 14 inf.............26 aug. 07 to 18 dec. 08 2 lt 14 inf..........18 dec. 08 1 lt................29 oct. 09 cap................5 may 14 accepted..........11 may 14	N. J. 1 oct. 75
Sayles, Philip Allen, 5 may 14	B	mustered into u. s. ser...... 1 aug. 16 out 11 oct. 16	pvt. co. I, 22 regt., trs. 122 regt., trs. 22 inf., corp., sgt...27 apr. 96 to 27 may 04 1 lt. (I) 22 inf.......27 may 04 resigned............14 dec. 08 1 lt. o. d...........14 june 09 assigned 14 inf......26 june 12 cap................5 may 14 accepted..........6 may 14	N. J 28 aug. 77
Punger, John Carl, 17 may 16	K	mustered into u. s. ser...... 1 aug. 16 out 11 oct. 16	pvt., corp., sgt., 1 sgt., co. A, 14 inf... 4 may 03 2 lt. 14 inf..........26 june 12 1 lt................12 dec. 13 cap................6 may 14 accepted..........22 may 17	N. Y. 7 nov. 84
Byron, John Joseph, 28 jan. 15	H	mustered into u. s. ser...... 1 aug. 16 out 11 oct. 16	pvt., corp., sgt., co. H, 14 inf..........19 may 04 to 2 dec. 10 2 lt. 14 inf.......... 2 dec. 10 1 lt................ 6 feb. 13 cap................28 jan. 15 accepted.......... 1 feb. 15	N. Y. 12 may 82
Hetzel, Foster Greer, 12 mar. 15	F	mustered into u. s. ser...... 1 aug. 16 out 11 oct. 16	pvt., corp., sgt., 7 co. c. a. c............ 9 apr. 07 to 11 feb. 11 2 lt. 14 inf..........11 feb. 11 1 lt................23 jan. 13 cap................12 mar. 15 accepted..........15 mar. 15	N. J. 4 aug. 89
Thompson, Nelson Walter, 15 may 14	Sup. co.	mustered into u. s. ser...... 1 aug. 16 out 11 oct. 16	pvt., corp., sgt. 24 sep. co..........12 oct. 06 to 30 jan. 12 1 lt. o. d............30 jan. 12 cap. 1 inf..........15 may 14 accepted..........16 may 14	Mich. 21 aug. 76
Starrett, Harry Clarence, 27 june 14 Graduate, N. Y. School of the Line, 1915.	D	pvt. co. C, 14 N. Y. inf......16 may 98 to 27 oct. 98 mustered into u. s. ser...... 1 aug. 16 out 11 oct. 16	pvt. co. D, 14 inf., trs. co. C, corp., sgt..............16 may 98 to 15 may 01 pvt., corp., 1 sgt., post qm. sgt., trs. co. K, 1 sgt., sgt. maj., trs. co. D, 1 sgt.............15 aug. 04 to 25 may 14 1 lt................25 may 14 accepted..........30 may 14 captain............27 june 16 accepted..........27 june 16	Eng. 17 mar. 79

12

INFANTRY — FOURTEENTH REGIMENT — (*Continued*)

Name, grade, date of rank and highest brevet rank	Company	Service — In the armies of U. S. or foreign states	Service — In the National Guard	Born
Captains — Continued				
deGarmo, Leon Brookes, 4 june 14	A	mustered into u. s. ser...... 1 aug. 16 out 11 oct. 16	pvt., corp., co. K, 23 inf...............11 dec. 05 to 6 may 12 2 lt. 14 inf.......... 6 may 12 1 lt................ 4 june 14 accepted.......... 8 june 14	New Mex. 14 feb. 88
Blaisdell, William Edward, 27 june 16	L	mustered into u. s. ser...... 1 aug. 16 out 11 oct. 16	pvt. 3 batty., trs. co. C, 14 inf., corp....12 nov. 06 to 15 jan. 09 2 lt. 14 inf..........15 jan. 09 1 lt................27 nov. 09 resigned...........16 sep. 10 1 lt................ 9 july 15 accepted..........12 july 15 captain............27 june 16 accepted..........27 june 16	Mass. 16 july 87
First Lieutenants				
Lovell, Isaac James, 25 may 14	bat. adj.	mustered into u. s. ser...... 1 aug. 16 out 11 oct. 16	pvt., corp., sgt., co. D, 14 inf........ 8 nov. 09 to 25 may 14 1 lt................25 mar. 14 accepted..........30 may 14	Pa. 9 mar. 81
Gillmann, Joseph Lawrence, 4 june 14	G	mustered into u. s. ser...... 1 aug. 16 out 11 oct. 16	pvt. 5 co. c. a. c....23 sep. 02 hon. dis...........14 july 08 pvt., corp., co. G, 14 inf................23 oct. 11 to 9 may 12 2 lt. 14 inf...... 9 may 12 1 lt................ 4 june 14 accepted.......... 8 june 14	N. Y. 82
Frank, Charles H. E., 11 feb. 15	bat. adj.	mustered into u. s. ser...... 1 aug. 16 out 11 oct. 16	pvt., corp., sgt. 4 sig. corps...........27 feb. 00 to 15 jan. 02 pvt. 3 batty.......13 feb. 06 2 lt. 14 inf........ 12 dec. 07 1 lt................ 5 may 08 cap................31 july 09 hon. dis...........26 jan. 11 1 lt. 14 inf.........11 feb. 15 accepted..........15 feb. 15	Eng. 18 nov. 69
Jensen, Mads Frederik, 17 mar. 15	bat. adj.	pvt., under corp., coast arty., Denmark.... 4 june 98 to 4 june 99 2 lt....... 1 aug. 99 to 3 oct. 00 mustered into u. s. ser......1 aug. 16 out 11 oct. 16	pvt., sgt., 1 sgt. co. H, 14 inf........ 23 mar. 08 to 14 june 09 2 lt................14 june 09 hon. dis..........24 oct. 10 1 lt................17 mar. 15 accepted..........19 mar. 15	Denmark 15 apr. 75
Walsh, Stephen Phelan, 12 mar. 15	E	mustered into u. s. ser...... 1 aug. 16 out 11 oct. 16	pvt., corp, sgt , co. E, 14 inf..........13 june 04 to 27 dec. 13 2 lt................27 dec. 13 1 lt................12 mar. 15 accepted..........16 mar. 15	N. Y. 22 aug. 85
Nelson, John Arthur, 20 may 25	F	mustered into u. s. ser...... 1 aug. 16 out 11 oct. 16	pvt., corp., sgt. co. F, 14 inf.......... 6 mar. 11 to 4 june 14 2 lt................ 4 june 14 1 lt................20 may 15 accepted..........24 may 15	N. Y. 23 july 93

INFANTRY — FOURTEENTH REGIMENT — (*Continued*)

Name, grade, date of rank and highest brevet rank	Company	Service — In the armies of U. S. or foreign states	Service — In the National Guard	Born
First Lieutenants — Continued				
Howard, Dudley Blanchard, 9 july 15	C	mustered into u. s. ser...... 1 aug. 16 out 11 oct. 16	pvt., sgt., co. F, N. G., D. C..........14 july 10 to 27 july 12 2 lt................16 july 12 1 lt................24 july 12 resigned............ 5 mar. 15 2 lt. 14 nf., N. G., N. Y............ 1 apr. 15 1 lt............... 9 july 15 accepted..........10 july 15	D. C. 13 nov. 89
Haring, Harry B., 30 june 16	M. G. co.	mustered into u. s. ser...... 7 july 16 out 11 oct. 16	pvt. co. B, 23 inf.... 4 feb. 01 to 14 may 03 2 may 10 to 20 may 13 1 lt. o. d...........29 may 13 1 lt. 14 inf.......... 6 may 14 accepted...........11 may 14 f. and h. dis........27 jan. 14 1 lt................30 june 16 accepted..........30 june 16	N. J. 26 july 79
Wilson, Matthew J. A., 30 june 16	A	pvt. co. I, 14 N. Y. inf...... 2 may 98 to 27 oct. 98 mustered into u. s. ser...... 7 july 16 out 11 oct. 16	pvt. co. I, 14 inf ....14 mar. 98 corp...............22 jan. 00 sgt................24 mar. 02 qm. sgt..........20 june 04 1 sgt.............18 dec. 05 2 lt. (I) 14 inf ....29 feb. 08 with rank from......20 feb. 08 1 lt............. 9 nov. 08 with rank from.. ..22 oct. 08 cap...............18 apr. 12 accepted ....22 apr. 12 f. and h dis.. .... 8 dec. 14 1 lt................30 june 16 accepted..........30 june 16	N. Y. 12 feb. 80
Ostberg, Charles Gustaf, 22 july 16	D	mustered into u. s. ser...... 1 aug. 16 out 11 oct. 16	pvt., corp., sgt. co. D, 14 inf.........23 mar. 06 to 25 june 14 2 lt...............25 june 14 accepted ....29 june 14 1 lt..............22 july 16 accepted........22 july 16	Sweden 4 july 81
Sullivan, Harry F., 13 sep. 16	L	mustered into u. s. ser...... 2 aug. 16 out 11 oct. 16	pvt. co. A, 14 inf., trs. co. I, corp., sgt...............26 aug. 07 to 28 jan. 15 2 lt..............28 jan. 15 accepted.......... 1 feb. 15 1 lt..............13 sep. 16 accepted..... ...16 sep. 16	N. Y. 17 feb. 89
Aber, Daniel George, 13 sep. 16	B	pvt. 19 inf. U. S. A. 17 may 00 dis........17 may 03 mustered into u. s. ser...... 1 aug. 16 out 11 oct. 16	pvt., 1 sgt., co. G, 14 inf..............19 july 15 to 4 nov. 15 2 lt............... 4 nov. 15 accepted......... 8 nov. 15 1 lt..............13 sep. 16 accepted........16 sep. 16	N. Y. 4 sep. 82

INFANTRY — FOURTEENTH REGIMENT — (*Continued*)

Name, grade, date of rank and highest brevet rank	Company	Service — In the armies of U. S. or foreign states	Service — In the National Guard	Born
Second Lieutenants				
Clisset, John Thomas, Jr., 25 may 14	A	mustered into u. s. ser...... 1 aug. 16 out 11 oct. 16	pvt., corp., co. C, 14 inf............... 3 apr. 11 to 25 may 14 2 lt.................25 may 14 accepted.......... 1 june 14	N. Y. 26 oct. 89
Goudey, Clarence Irving, 25 june 15	H	mustered into u. s. ser......31 july 16 out 11 oct. 16	pvt., corp., sgt., qmr. sgt., 14 inf.......22 may 11 to 25 june 15 2 lt.................25 june 15 accepted..........28 june 15	N. Y. 8 sep. 78
McDonough, Thomas A., 9 july 15	E	mustered into u. s. ser......31 july 16 out 11 oct. 16	pvt., corp., sgt. co. C, 14 inf.........21 nov. 10 to 9 july 15 2 lt................. 9 july 15 accepted..........12 july 15	N. Y. 21 apr. 91
Atkinson, John Jason, Jr., 16 july 15	M	mustered into u. s. ser......31 july 16 out 11 oct. 16	pvt., corp., co. C, 14 inf............... 1 apr. 12 to 16 july 16 2 lt................16 july 15 accepted..........22 july 15	N. Y. 19 feb. 93
Hedes, Ira Irving,, 22 sep. 15	C	mustered into u. s. ser..... 31 july 16 out 11 oct. 16	pvt. 54 co. c. a. c., 19 mar. 08 hon. dis...18 mar. 11 2 lt. 14 inf.........22 sep. 15 accepted..........27 sep. 15	N. Y. 12 dec. 91
Moran, John Wm., 29 may 16	B	mustered into u. s. ser......31 july 16 out 11 oct. 16	sgt. co. G, 7 reg. Ill. N. G. vol.,......26 apr. 98 to 20 oct. 98 2 lt.................29 may 16 accepted.......... 1 june 16	Ohio 28 may 76
Bostick, John W., 22 june 16	D	mustered into u. s. ser......18 aug. 16 out 11 oct. 16	enld. 22 engrs....... 1 nov. 09 1 cl. pvt............22 may 11 corp............... 5 june 11 sgt.................22 apr. 12 2 lt.................22 june 16 accepted..........23 june 16	Pa. 11 dec. 83
Depp, Peter Michael, 10 july 16	F	mustered into u. s. ser......18 july 16 out 11 oct. 16	pvt. co. K...........22 apr. 12 corp...............16 mar. 14 sgt................ 9 nov. 14 f. and h. dis.........28 june 15 re-enlisted..........28 june 15 2 lt.................10 july 16 accepted...........10 july 16	N. Y. 16 jan. 94
Marshall, Herbert E., Jr., 13 sep. 16	L	mustered out u. s. ser.....11 oct. 16	pvt. co. L........... 6 oct. 08 dis. discharged (neglect of duty)......13 sep. 09 enlisted co. L.......13 jan. 11 corp...............30 nov. 14 1 sgt...............20 dec. 15 f. and h. dis.........24 jan. 16 re-enlisted..........24 jan. 16 2 lt.................13 sep. 16 accepted...........18 sep. 16	N. Y. 12 july 90
Kerrigan, Joseph A., 6 sep. 16	K	mustered out u. s. ser......11 oct. 16	pvt. co. D...........20 jan. 08 corp............... 7 dec. 14 qm. sgt.............21 june 15 1 sgt............... 8 nov. 16 2 lt................. 6 sep. 16 accepted...........16 sep. 16	N. Y. 31 oct. 89

INFANTRY — FOURTEENTH REGIMENT — (Concluded)

Name, grade, date of rank and highest brevet rank	Company	Service		Born
		In the armies of U. S. or foreign states	In the National Guard	
Second Lieutenants — Continued				
Ward, Thomas F., 6 sep. 16	m. g. co.	mustered out u. s. ser......11 oct. 16	pvt. co. E..........28 feb. 10 corp...............15 july 12 f. and h. dis......... 1 mar. 15 re-enlisted.......... 1 mar. 15 1 sgt............... 1 june 15 f. and h. dis........ 6 mar. 16 re-enlisted.......... 6 mar. 16 2 lt................ 6 sep. 16 accepted...........16 sep. 16	N. Y. 17 apr. 90
Miller, Elmer H., 13 sep. 16	sup. co.	mustered out u. s. ser......11 oct. 16	pvt. co. M..........13 mar. 16 1 sgt................... 2 lt................13 sep. 16 accepted...........18 sep. 16	Okla. 1 feb. 92

INFANTRY — *(Continued)*

FIFTEENTH REGIMENT

(Twelve Companies.)

(First Brigade.)

Armory, 2217 7th Ave., New York City

The 15th Regiment (Colored) was organized and mustered into the service of the State under S. O. 133, A. G. O., June 29, 1916.

Companies A, B and C were mustered into the State service July 12, 1916; Company D, July 20; Company E, July 25; Company I, Aug. 25; Companies F and G, Oct. 8, 1916; Companies K and L, Sept. 28 and Company M, Oct. 18, 1916.

INFANTRY — FIFTEENTH REGIMENT

Name, grade, date of rank and highest brevet rank	Company	Service		Born
		In the armies of U. S. or foreign states	In the National Guard	
Colonel				
Heyward, William, 18 nov. 16	......	entered into u. s. ser. in 98 and served as cap. 2 Neb. N. G., hon. dis. — nov. 98	mus. co. C, 2 rgt. Neb. N. G.......92 sgt..................... cap. co. C..........99 maj................99 col.................00 hon. dis...............03 col. r. l. N. . N. Y..23 june 16 col. 15 inf...........18 nov. 16 accepted........20 nov. 16	Neb.
Lieutenant Colonel				
Spencer, Lorillard, 28 sep. 16 *W. D. Cert. in course Nos. 1 (Basic), 2 (Emplacement Officer), 3 (Range and Communication Officer) and 4 (Battery Commander). L. S. D., Class IV.*	......	....	pvt. tr. 2, sq. A......1 june 04 to 29 sep. 09 pvt., wagoner, farrier, tr. 2.......4 nov. 09 to 1 july 12 2 lt. c. a. c........1 july 12 1 lt................2 jan. 13 a. d. c. to gov......1 jan. 15 cap................15 apr. 15 accepted...........16 apr. 15 mil. secy. to gov....20 oct. 15 lt. col.............28 sep. 16 accepted...........28 sep. 16	N. Y. 4 july 83
Majors				
Morris, Monson, R. L., 8 aug. 16	......	2 lt. 12 N. Y. inf., 2 may 98 1 lt.......7 sep. 98 to 20 apr. 99	2 lt. (E), 12 inf ....21 apr. 98 cap................7 sep. 99 1 lt. asst. i. s. a. p. 12 inf................6 jan. 03 bat. qm. with o. r....19 oct. 03 cap. comy of sub.....19 jan. 04 resigned...........17 mar. 05 cap. 12 inf.........29 feb. 08 a. d. c. to gov.......1 jan. 11 to 31 dec. 12 maj. 12 inf..........19 sep. 12 accepted...........20 sep. 12	S. C. 1 aug. 75
Captains				
Fillmore, Charles W., 18 july 16	D	1 lt. 9 u. s. vol. inf. Ohio N. G., 15 june 98 bat. adj., comdnt. co. F, dis...15 nov. 98	enlisted in Duquesne Blues, Ohio N. G..20 jan. 79 hon. dis...........20 jan. 84 re-enlisted pvt. co. A, 9 bn. inf............4 apr. 84 hon. dis............17 jan. 87 pvt. co. A, 9 bn. inf.........15 oct. 96 1 lt.............21 nov. 96 major.............25 feb. 97 hon. dis...........14 apr. 99 cap. 15 inf. N. Y. N. G.............18 july 16 accepted..........24 july 16	Ohio 17 apr. 69

INFANTRY — FIFTEENTH REGIMENT — (*Concluded*)

Name, grade, date of rank and highest brevet rank	Company	Service		Born
		In the armies of U. S. or foreign states	In the National Guard	
Captains — Continued				
Hinton, George F., 31 oct. 16	F	lt. col. Idaho N.G.,a. d. c. to gov., 11 apr. 91 resigned... 9 nov. 91	lt. col. r. l.......... 6 july 16 detailed to duty with 15 inf.......... 8 july 16 retd. to r. l..........29 sep. 16 cap. 15 inf..........31 oct. 16 accepted.......... 1 nov. 16	N. Y. 5 dec. 63
First Lieutenants				
Tandy, Vertner W., 29 june 16	K	....	pvt. co. K..........18 sep. 16 1 sgt..............26 sep. 16 1 lt................11 dec. 16 accepted..........13 dec. 16	Ala. 22 feb. 81
Parks, Vergil, 2 sep. 16	C	pvt. trp. A, 10 u. s. cav....13 july 98 f. and h. dis. 25 nov. 99 re-enlisted in co. G, 25 u. s. inf.. 3 mar. 00	pvt. co. C..........17 aug. 16 1 lt................ 2 sep. 16 accepted.......... 5 sep. 16	Ky. 24 mar. 82
Marshall, Napoleon B. 20 sep. 16	I	.	1 lt................20 sep. 16 accepted..........25 sep. 16	D. C.
Europe, James R. 11 dec. 16	K	....	pvt. co. K..........18 sep. 16 1 sgt..............26 sep. 16 1 lt................11 dec. 16 accepted..........13 dec. 16	Ala. 22 feb. 81
Whedon, Burt D. R. L., 10 oct. 16	E	....	pvt. co. H, 1 Neb. vols. 12 may 98 sgt.-maj..........20 m y 98 2 lt. co. C........15 june 98 1 lt. regt'l adjt......18 apr. 99 mustered out........23 aug. 99 placed on r. l. N. G., N. Y..........12 july 16 assigned to duty 15 inf.10 oct. 16	
Ripley, Henry Baldwin Hyde, R. L., 13 dec. 16	B	....	2 lt. 12 inf..........12 june 14 1 lt................ 6 july 15 accepted.......... 8 july 15	N. Y. 19 nov. 89
Second Lieutenants				
Wyatt, James Hovey, 2 sep. 16	D	pvt. 24 u. s. inf., 6 july 09 co. M, hon. dis. 17 june 12	pvt. co. D..........18 aug. 16 2 lt................ 2 sep. 16 accepted..........13 sep. 16	Ind. 22 july 90
Prunty, Peter P., 30 sep. 16	sup. co.	....	pvt. co. H, 12 inf....12 oct. 03 f. and h. dis........10 sep. 12 re-enlisted........10 sep. 12 f. and h. dis........ 1 oct. 15 corp. (re-enlisted)....27 feb. 07 sgt................15 jan. 08 1 sgt..............15 nov. 09 bn. sgt. maj........ 4 dec. 12 qm. sgt. qm. c......21 mar. 16 2 lt................30 sep. 16 accepted.......... 4 oct. 16	Eng. 28 june 85
Toney, Charles E., 20 dec. 16	M	....	pvt. co. M................ 2 lt................20 dec. 16 accepted..........22 dec. 16	Ala. 23 dec. 78

INFANTRY — (*Continued*)

TWENTY-THIRD REGIMENT

(Twelve Companies.)

(Second Brigade.)

Armory, 1322 *Bedford Avenue, Brooklyn*

The first company (A) was mustered into the State service January 20, 1862; the regimental organization was perfected July 14, 1862. It was in the service of the United States from June 18 to July 22, 1863. Co. L was mustered in June 4, 1906. November 10, 1908, an additional company was directed to be organized and attached to the 23d Infantry as Co. M. The regiment was authorized to organize a detachment of mounted orderlies by Special Orders No. 167, July 2, 1912.

The regiment was authorized to organize a machine gun platoon of 22 men, by S. O. 168, July 3, 1912.

Recognition extended by War Department under Act of June 3, 1916, to Companies A, B, C, D, E, F, G, H. I, K, L and M, and Sanitary Detachment, on June 26, 1916; to Headquarters and Machine Gun Companies, June 30, 1916; to Supply Company, July 1, 1916.

The regiment has received authority to place silver rings on the lances of its colors, engraved as follows:

On the National Color.— Gettysburg campaign, 1863.

On the State Color.— Draft riot, July and August, 1863; East New York, September 22, 1863; Brooklyn, November 6, 1864; Brooklyn, February 16, 1870; Orange riots, 1871; Hornellsville, July 22, 1877; Buffalo, August, 1892; Brooklyn, January, 1895; Albany, 1901.

INFANTRY — TWENTY-THIRD REGIMENT

Name, grade, date of rank and highest brevet rank	Company	Service		Born
		In the armies of U. S. or foreign states	In the National Guard	
Colonel				
Norton, Frank Hastings, 26 july 09 bvt. brig. gen. 3 nov. 11	.....	mustered into u. s ser ..... 2 july 16	pvt., corp., sgt., 1 sgt., co. F, 23 inf...28 sep. 85 hon. dis............ 6 june 98 1 lt. (F), 23 inf......20 may 99 cap................ 9 june 02 maj................22 dec. 04 lt. col.............. 1 may 07 col................31 july 09 accepted.......... 4 aug. 09	N. Y. 6 apr.
Lieutenant Colonel				
Welsh, William E., 7 aug. 16	......	cadet, Mil. Academy, 17 june 90 2 lt. 8 inf...12 june 94 1 lt. 10 inf. 26 apr. 98 cap. 30 inf. 2 feb. 01 grad., army school of the line.. 1910 grad ate, Army staff college.. 1911	lt. col.............. 7 aug. 16 accepted.......... 7 aug. 16	Pa. 23 nov. 72
Majors				
Blanton, David Burton, 16 feb. 10	......	mustered into u. s ser...... 2 july 16	pvt. co. C, 4 Va. inf.. 1 sep. 84 hon. dis............25 apr. 87 pvt., corp., co. G, 23 inf., N. G., N. Y., 14 nov. 90 to 11 may 96 pvt., corp., sgt., 1 sgt., co. G....... 17 july 96 to 26 apr. 01 2 lt................26 apr. 01 1 lt................ 2 apr. 03 cap................13 oct. 04 maj. 23 inf..........26 feb. 10 accepted..........26 feb. 10	Va. 11 mar 68

INFANTRY — TWENTY-THIRD REGIMENT — (Continued)

Name, grade, date of rank and highest brevet rank	Company	Service — In the armies of U. S. or foreign states	Service — In the National Guard	Born
Majors — Continued				
Addison, Matthew George, 16 mar. 16 Distinguished Graduate, N. Y. School of the Line, 1915.	......	sgt., 1 sgt., co. I, 47 N. Y. inf., 24 may 98 to 21 nov. 98 1 lt. (M) 21 nov. 98 to 31 mar. 99 mustered into u. s. ser..... 2 july 16	pvt., corp., sgt., co. B, 23 inf., trs. co. L, 47 inf., trs. co. B, 23 inf., 1 sgt .... 1 aug. 94 to 20 mar. 02 2 lt.................20 mar. 02 1 lt.................22 oct. 03 cap. 23 inf..........1 oct. 08 accepted............12 oct. 08 maj.................16 mar. 16 accepted............18 mar. 16	N. Y. 1 jan. 70
Sawyer, John Richard, 6 sep. 16	......	mustered into u. s. ser......1 july 16	pvt., co. G, 23 inf....15 oct. 94 to 5 apr. 97 pvt., corp., sgt., 1 sgt., co. G........10 may 97 to 22 dec. 04 2 lt. (G), 23 inf.....22 dec. 04 1 lt. 23 inf..........21 sep. 08 cap..................10 mar. 10 accepted...........10 mar. 10 maj...................6 sep. 16 accepted...........10 sep. 16	N. Y. 16 june 75
Captains				
Bangs, Bleecker, 12 july 97	sup. co.	mustered into u. s. ser......2 july 16	pvt., corp., qm. sgt., co. C, 23 inf., regt. qm. sgt., 23 inf.... 5 feb. 83 to 30 sep. 95 1 lt., bat. qm......30 sep. 95 cap., regt. qm......12 july 97	N. Y. 1 mar. 62
Walker, Clarence Joshua, 20 feb. 08	m. g. co.	mustered into u. s. ser..... 2 july 16	pvt., corp., sgt., qm. sgt., co. K, 23 inf., bat. qm. sgt., 23 inf..............9 mar. 96 to 25 oct. 06 1 lt. bat. qm. 23 inf...25 oct. 06 supn., reassigned....21 jan. 08 2 lt. 23 inf..........7 feb. 08 cap.................29 feb. 08	N. Y. 11 may 76
Stoll, George Matthew, 20 mar. 11	K	mustered into u. s. ser......2 july 16	pvt., corp., 1 sgt., co. K, 23 inf..........22 apr. 01 to 22 apr. 09 2 lt. 23 inf..........22 apr. 09 1 lt.................5 feb. 10 cap.................20 mar. 11 accepted............27 mar. 11	N. Y. 28 jan. 80
DeMott, James Boardman 24 july 12	F	mustered into u. s. ser......2 july 16	pvt. co. F, 23 inf....26 feb. 83 hon. dis............11 nov. 89 pvt.................5 may 91 hon. dis............18 may 92 pvt., corp., sgt. co. F, color bearer, bat. sgt. maj., 23 inf...24 jan. 98 to 18 sep. 09 2 lt. 23 inf..........18 sep. 09 1 lt.................26 jan. 11 cap.................24 july 12 accepted............29 july 12	N. J. 25 oct. 62
Ward, Charles Miron, 24 oct. 13	E	1 sgt. co. D, 201 N. Y. inf., 17 july 98; 2 lt. (K), 201 N. Y. inf., 6 dec. 98 to 3 apr. 99 mustered into u. s ser......1 july 16	pvt., corp., sgt., 1 sgt., co. E, 23 inf..25 oct. 95 to 30 nov. 04 2 lt. (E), 23 inf......30 nov. 04 1 lt.................17 feb. 06 cap.................24 oct. 13 accepted............27 oct. 13	N. Y. 13 aug. 70

INFANTRY—TWENTY-THIRD REGIMENT—(*Continued*)

Name, grade, date of rank and highest brevet rank	Company	Service — In the armies of U. S. or foreign states	Service — In the National Guard	Born
Captains — Continued				
Mundy, Joseph Aloys Sutten, 20 nov. 13	D	mustered into u. s. ser...... 2 july 16	pvt., corp., sgt., 1 sgt., co. D, 23 inf..22 apr. 01 to 25 may 11 2 lt. 23 inf..........25 may 11 1 lt...............17 july 12 cap................20 nov. 13 accepted...........24 nov. 13	N. Y. 25 mar. 80
Liebmann, Morris Nathaniel, 29 nov. 13	adjt.	mustered into u. s. ser..... 2 july 16	pvt., corp., sgt., co. I, 23 inf......21 oct. 01 to 15 feb. 08 2 lt. 23 inf..........15 feb. 08 1 lt.............. 3 june 03 cap................29 nov. 13 accepted........... 1 dec. 13	N. Y. 13 july 78
Congdon, Herbert Wheaton, 13 oct. 14 Graduate, Garrison Schools, 1915.	A	mustered into u. s. ser......2 july 16	pvt., corp., co. A, 23 inf...............25 oct. 97 hon. dis............ 2 june 04 pvt., corp., sgt., co. A,10 may 09 to 23 nov. 11 2 lt. 23 inf..........23 nov. 11 1 lt...............31 july 12 cap................13 oct. 14 accepted...........14 oct. 14	N. Y. 9 may 76
Shiebler, Joseph Prentice Durfey, 9 july 15 Distinguished Graduate, N. Y. School of the Line, 1915.	L	mustered into u. s. ser...... 1 july 16	pvt., corp., sgt., 1 sgt., co. H, 23 inf.. 5 jan. 93 to 27 mar. 02 2 lt..............27 mar. 02 1 lt..............12 mar. 03 bat. adj. 23 inf. with o. r.............. 1 mar. 06 cap............... 9 july 15 accepted...........25 july 15	N. Y. 29 may 74
Fairservis, Thomas, 17 nov. 15 Graduate, Garrison Schools, 1915.	C	mustered into u. s. ser..... 2 july 16	pvt., corp., sgt., co. C, 23 inf..........28 dec. 03 to 20 apr. 10 2 lt. 23 inf........ .20 apr. 10 1 lt............. 7 may 13 cap ....17 nov. 15 accepted...........19 nov. 15	N. Y. 22 dec. 84
Fenton, Willard Conklin, 7 may 12	G	mustered into u. s. ser......2 july 16	pvt., qm. sgt., 1 sgt., co. G, 23 inf.. ... 6 feb. 89 to 5 may 10 2 lt. 23 inf.......... 5 may 10 1 lt................ 7 may 12 accepted............13 may 12	N. Y. 13 aug. 78
Evans, William J., 6 oct. 16	M	mustered into u. s. ser......2 july 16	pvt. co. M..........14 apr. 13 corp................16 mar. 14 sgt.................15 feb. 15 1 sgt.... ....28 june 15 f. and h. dis........14 apr. 16 re-enlisted..........14 apr. 16 2 lt .... 3 july 16 accepted............ 3 july 16 cap........ .. ... 6 oct. 16 accepted...........10 oct. 16	N. Y. 18 june 93
Langer, Jerome Francis, 3 july 16	I	mustered into u. s. ser...... 2 july 16	pvt., corp., sgt , 1 sgt., co. I, 23 inf...21 oct. 01 to 21 sep. 08 2 lt. 23 inf..........21 sep. 08 1 lt....20 dec. 13 accepted...........22 dec. 13 cap.. .... 3 july 16 accepted........ 3 july 16	Neb. 4 jan. 81

INFANTRY — TWENTY-THIRD REGIMENT — *(Continued)*

Name, grade, date of rank and highest brevet rank	Company	Service — In the armies of U. S. or foreign states	Service — In the National Guard	Born
Captains—Continued				
Simonson, George Lefevre, 3 may 16	B	mustered into u. s. ser..... : 2 july 16	pvt., corp., sgt., co. B, 23 inf.......... 1 oct. 02 to 16 oct. 12 2 lt. 23 inf..........16 oct. 12 accepted..........21 oct. 12 cap.............. 3 may 16 accepted.......... 8 may 16	N. Y. 2 feb. 84
Cooke, James Pennoyer, 3 july 16	H	mustered into u. s ser ... . 2 july 16	pvt., corp, sgt., 1 sgt., co. H, 23 inf.. 6 mar 02 to 12 mar. 13 2 lt.... ....12 mar. 13 accepted ....15 mar. 13 cap.............. 3 july 16 accepted.......... 3 july 16	N. Y. 8 may 79
First Lieutenants				
Powers, Edwin Ambrose, 4 apr. 13	L	mustered into u. s. ser...... 1 july 16	pvt. co. K, 23 inf....11 apr. 98 hon. dis...........18 may 03 pvt. co. F, 23 inf..... 9 nov. 03 hon. dis...........29 oct. 06 pvt., sgt , 1 sgt., co. L, 23 inf.......... 3 dec. 06 to 4 apr. 13 1 lt............... 4 apr. 13 accepted.......... 7 apr. 13	N. Y. 13 feb. 77
Enderle, Charles Christopher .... 3 dec. 12	......	mustered into u. s ser.. ... 2 july 16	pvt., corp, sgt., co. sgt., co. F, 23 inf...17 jan. 98 to 3 dec. 12 2 lt. 23 inf.......... 3 dec. 12 accepted.......... 5 dec. 12	N. Y. 28 aug. 74
Johnson, John A., 18 jan. 16	C	mustered into u. s. ser...... 1 july 16	pvt. co. C.......... 10 dec. 06 corp...............15 mar. 09 sgt .... 6 june 10 actg. qm. sgt........ 1 apr. 12 1 sgt...............17 nov. 13 1 lt...............18 jan. 16 accepted...........22 jan. 16	N. Y. 31 may
Cook, Millard Fillmore, 8 nov. 06 bvt. cap...... 3 jan. 12	bat. adj.	mustered into u. s. ser...... 2 july 16	pvt , corp , sgt., co. K, 23 inf. ...... 4 dec. 76 to 8 nov. 06 1 lt. bat. adj. 23 inf.. 8 nov. 06	Mich. 20 july 55
Simonson, William Frederick, 3 july 16	B	mustered into u. s. ser...... 2 july 16	pvt., corp , sgt., sgt., co. B, 23 inf...26 apr. 98 to 9 nov. 08 1 lt. 23 inf. .... .. 9 nov. 08 resigned. ....24 feb. 16 1 lt. 23 inf.......... 3 july 16 accepted.......... 3 july 16	N. Y. 6 oct 77
McCann, Francis Joseph, 30 aug. 16 bvt. cap...... 3 dec. 08	M	mustered into u. s. ser...... 1 july 16	pvt., co. A, 23 inf and tr. C.......... 5 feb. 94 to 30 dec. 01 2 lt. (I), 47 inf.......30 dec. 01 1 lt. (G)........... 3 sep. 03 trs. co. I........... 2 aug. 05 bat. qm. with o. r.... 5 jan. 06 resigned...........27 july 07 a. d. c. 2 brig. cap....27 dec. 07 supn., reassigned.... 21 jan. 08 1 lt. o. d...........11 feb. 08 supn. own request det. aide staff c. g. 2 brig..........27 feb. 08 comy. maj..........13 oct. 11 accepted...........16 oct. 11 qm. corps.......... 1 nov. 14 1 lt................30 aug. 16 accepted.......... 1 sep. 16	N. Y. 19 oct. 74

INFANTRY—TWENTY-THIRD REGIMENT—(*Continued*)

Name, grade, date of rank and highest brevet rank	Company	Service		Born
		In the armies of U. S. or foreign states	In the National Guard	
First Lieutenants — Continued				
Ronalds, William A., 3 july 16	B	mustered into u. s ser...... 1 july 16	pvt. co. B.......... 9 feb. 14 corp............... 9 nov. 14 sgt...............12 july 15 2 lt............... 8 june 16 accepted..... ...12 june 16 1 lt............... 3 june 16 accepted.......... 3 july 16	N. Y. 18 oct. 86
Ireland, Rutherford, 3 july 16	L	....	pvt. 1 batty........23 mar. 94 dropped..........28 july 98 taken up..........27 oct. 98 trs. to co. I.......15 may 99 hon. dis..........23 june 99 re-enlisted.........23 june 99 corp............... 4 feb. 01 sgt............... 1 june 03 2 lt..............27 july 05 1 lt............... 7 nov. 07 f. and h. dis........20 apr. 08 1 lt............... 3 july 16 accepted.......... 3 july 16	......
Long, Frederic K., 3 july 16	bat. adjt.	....	pvt. co. G.........11 apr. 10 corp..............19 dec. 10 sgt...............16 mar. 14 f. and h. dis........11 apr. 15 re-enlisted.........11 apr. 15 f. and h. dis........11 apr. 16 re-enlisted..........11 apr. 16 warrant as sgt. contd. 1 lt............... 3 july 16 accepted.......... 3 july 16	N. J. 16 jan. 91
Bryant, George Edw., 6 sep. 16	m. g. co.	....	pvt. co. F.......... 1 dec. 91 corp............... 9 mar. 95 sgt...............17 apr. 99 color sgt...........27 may 01 retd. to ranks at own request and assigned to co. F.... 7 apr. 02 1 sgt............... 2 june 02 ord. sgt...........31 may 09 f. and h. dis........20 sep. 15 re-enlisted.........20 sep. 15 sgt. maj........... 2 july 16 1 lt............... 6 sep. 16 accepted..........10 sep. 16	N. Y. 7 nov. 73
Stoffregen, Lester F., 24 nov. 16	......	mustered into u. s ser .....29 nov. 16	pvt. co. K.......... 8 oct. 06 corp..............15 feb. 09 sgt............... 6 feb. 11 1 sgt............... 9 nov. 14 f and h. dis......... 8 mar. 15 warrant contd. f. and h. dis........ 6 apr. 16 re-enlisted..........10 apr. 16 warrant contd. 2 lt............... 3 july 16 accepted.......... 3 july 16 1 lt...............24 nov. 16 accepted..........29 nov. 16	N. Y. 29 mar. 87
Second Lieutenants				
Ulrichs, Charles Bartholomew, 3 jan. 13	sup. co.	mustered into u. s ser...... 2 july 16	pvt., co. A, 23 inf., regt. comy. sgt.... 9 oct. 99 to 3 jan. 13 2 lt............... 3 jan. 13 accepted.......... 6 jan. 13	N. Y. 27 sep. 77

INFANTRY — TWENTY-THIRD REGIMENT — (*Continued*)

Name, grade, date of rank and highest brevet rank	Company	Service		Born
		In the armies of U. S. or foreign states	In the National Guard	
Second Lieutenants — Continued				
Jones, Chester Prince, 27 mar. 14	L	mustered into u. s. ser...... 1 july 16	pvt., corp., sgt., co. L, 23 inf..........25 oct. 09 to 27 mar. 14 2 lt...............27 mar. 14 accepted..........30 mar. 14	N. Y. 24 oct. 91
E!munds, Euston, Fletcher, 17 mar. 15	A	mustered into u. s. ser...... 1 july 16	pvt., corp., sgt., co. A, 23 inf........ 3 apr. 11 to 17 mar. 15 2 lt...............17 mar. 15 accepted..........18 mar. 15	N. Y. 13 oct. 92
De Loiselle, Harold Cornell, 13 may 15	E	mustered into u. s. ser...... 1 july 16	pvt., corp., sgt., co. E, 23 inf..........26 oct. 08 hon. dis.........16 nov. 14 pvt., sgt...........16 nov. 14 to 13 may 15 2 lt...............13 may 15 accepted..........17 may 15	N. Y. 13 sep. 82
Keese, George M., 3 july 16	B	mustered into u. s. ser...... 1 july 16	pvt. co. A.......... 7 nov. 95 corp...............14 jan. 95 hon. dis...........28 feb. 00 re-enlisted.........31 dec. 04 qm. sgt............20 feb. 05 1 sgt............ 4 may 08 qm. sgt............11 apr. 10 f. and h. dis........ 2 nov. 14 re-enlisted co. K..... 5 apr. 15 sgt..............28 apr. 15 comsy. sgt..........19 june 16 color sgt............ 2 july 16 2 lt................ 3 july 16 accepted.......... 3 july 16	N. Y. 29 june 72
Brill, William F., 3 july 16	m. g. co.	....	pvt................ 3 mar. 02 corp.............. 2 nov. 03 sgt.............. 5 feb. 06 retd. to ranks.......12 nov. 06 dropped...........19 nov. 06 taken up...........27 jan. 08 dropped........... 2 nov. 08 taken up........... 1 dec. 11 sgt...............26 may 13 f. and h. dis........28 june 15 re-enlisted.........19 july 15 2 lt................ 3 july 16 accepted.......... 3 july 16	N. Y. 29 mar. 83
Mayor, Fred E., 3 july 16	D	....	2 lt................ 3 july 16 accepted.......... 3 july 16	N. Y.
Jewett, Everett B., 7 oct. 16	C	mustered into u. s. ser......30 oct. 16	pvt. co. D..........28 mar. 04 corp..............14 feb. 06 dropped...........24 feb. 08 taken up, co. K......16 june 13 trs. to co. C........ 7 jan. 14 sgt.............. 3 may 15 1 sgt............ 6 mar. 16 2 lt................ 7 oct. 16 accepted.......... 8 oct. 16	N. Y. 13 feb. 81
Davies, Samuel D., 3 nov. 16	I	mustered into u. s. ser......29 nov. 16	pvt. co. I..........25 may 14 corp.............. 3 apr. 16 1 sgt..............22 july 16 2 lt................ 3 nov. 16 accepted..........18 nov. 16	N. Y. 4 dec. 91

INFANTRY — TWENTY-THIRD REGIMENT — (*Concluded*)

Name, grade, date of rank and highest brevet rank	Company	Service		Born
		In the armies of U. S. or foreign states	In the National Guard	
Second Lieutenants — Continued				
Stevens, Harry C., Jr., 18 nov. 16	M	mustered into u. s. ser ......27 dec. 16	pvt. co. M.......... 8 july 12 corp...............14 dec. 14 sgt.................21 june 16 f. and h. dis........19 july 15 re-enlisted..........19 july 15 2 lt................18 nov. 16 accepted........... 9 dec. 16	Mont. 20 feb. 87
McMullen, William H., Jr., 18 dec. 16	K	....	pvt. co. K.........29 june 03 corp..............22 apr. 13 qm. sgt............19 oct. 14 f. and h. dis........ 8 mar. 15 re-enlisted. f. and h. dis........ 3 apr. 16 re-enlisted. sup. sgt............29 june 16 hon. dis...........22 dec. 16 2 lt................18 dec. 16 accepted..........23 dec. 16	N. Y. 14 apr. 82
Chaplain, 2d Lieutenant				
Cadman, Samuel Parkes, 14 jan. 10	......	....	chaplain, 23 inf......28 jan. 10 accepted..........12 feb. 10	Eng. 18 dec.

INFANTRY — *(Continued)*
FORTY-SEVENTH REGIMENT
(Twelve Companies.)
(Second Brigade.)

State Armory, 355 Marcy Avenue, Brooklyn

Companies A, B, C, D, E, F, G, H and I were organized in 1862, Co. K in 1872. Co. C was disbanded in 1878, and Cos· G and H in 1863. A new Co. G was organized in 1864 and a new Co. II in 1878; the latter was disbanded in 1885. The , 1862, and e, June 17, of service.

regiment preparatory to its entry into the United States service, into which service it was mustered as the 47th Regiment, N. Y. Infantry, May 24, 1898, and mustered out March 31, 1899. Cos. C, H, L and M were disbanded April 24, 1890. New Co. C organized, May 7, 1908. New Co. H organized June 24, 1912. New Cos. L and M were organized November 10, 1913.

Recognition extended by the War Department under Act of June 3, 1916, to Machine Gun Company on Nov. 24, 1916; Company C, Nov. 25, 1916; to Company A, June 26, 1916; to Companies B, C, D, E, F, G, H, I, K, L, M and Sanitary Detachment, June 25, 1916.

The regiment has received authority to place silver rings on the lances of its colors, engraved as follows:

On the National Color.— Fort McHenry, Md., 1862; Washington, D. C., 1863; Spanish-American War, 1898; Porto Rico, 1898–9.

On the State Color.— Draft riots, 1863; railroad riots, 1877; Fire Island, 1892; . Brooklyn, 1893.

INFANTRY — FORTY-SEVENTH REGIMENT

Name, grade, date of rank and highest brevet rank	Company	Service		Born
		In the armies of U. S. or foreign states	In the National Guard	
Colonel				
Jannicky, Ernest Ellsworth, 16 feb. 14	......	cap. 47 N. Y. inf., 2 may 98 to 14 dec. 98	pvt., corp., sgt., co. A, 47 inf......... 3 june 80 to 19 mar. 94 2 lt................19 mar. 94 1 lt................17 jan. 98 cap (B)...........13 july 99 lt. col. 47 inf.......27 dec. 07 col.................16 feb. 14 accepted..........19 feb. 14	N. Y. 7 aug. 71
Lieutenant Colonel				
Baldwin, Harry Beam, 11 mar. 14	......	....	pvt., corp., sgt., co. B, 13 inf.......... 5 may 84 hon. dis...........13 feb. 90 pvt., co. B.........21 july 92 hon. dis...........31 oct. 93 2 lt. (E), 47 inf......15 july 95 1 lt. (B), 13 inf......25 apr. 98 supn...............28 nov. 98 assigned to duty 4 bat. 47 inf........ 2 mar. 99 relieved...........24 apr. 99 cap. (E), 47 inf......20 june 99 maj................28 apr. 04 lt. col.............11 mar. 14 accepted..........16 mar. 14	N. Y. 21 july
Majors				
Ecke, Albert Daniel, 1 mar. 14	......	pvt. co. L, corp. co. H, 47 N. Y. inf., 2 may 98 to 31 mar. 99	pvt. co. L, 47 inf..... 2 may 98 hon. dis...........20 may 99 pvt., corp., co. A....20 sep. 99 to 3 dec. 00 2 lt................ 3 dec. 00 1 lt................28 jan. 04 cap. 47 inf..........14 may 08 maj................ 1 mar.14 accepted.......... 4 mar. 14	N. Y. 16 jan. 77

INFANTRY — FORTY-SEVENTH REGIMENT — (Continued)

Name, grade, date of rank and highest brevet rank	Company	Service		Born
		In the armies of U. S. or foreign states	In the National Guard	

Captains — Continued

Corwin, Walter Edmund, 3 apr. 14			pvt., corp., sgt., 1 sgt., co. D, 47 inf.....30 apr. 00 to 9 may 07 1 lt. (D), 47 inf..... 9 may 07 cap. 47 inf.........23 mar .09 maj............. 3 apr. 14 accepted........... 6 apr. 14	N. Y. 7 dec. 81
McAdam, William Arthur, 11 nov. 15 Honor Graduate, N. Y. School of the Line, 1915.			pvt., corp., co. E, 13 inf.............30 jan. 06 to 3 june 08 1 lt. 47 inf......... 3 june 08 cap............. 3 june 09 accepted........... 7 june 09 maj.............11 nov. 15 accepted.........13 nov. 15	N. Y. 10 may 83

Captains

May, Charles Henry, 27 feb. 08	m. g. co.		pvt., artif., tr. C, trs. tr. CC. qm. sgt., trs. tr. C.....16 dec. 95 to 4 dec. 99 pvt. tr. G.........17 sep. 01 to 17 oct. 01 1 lt. (D), 47 inf.....17 oct. 01 cap.............15 may 02 1 lt. asst. i. s. a. p...25 oct. 06 supn., reassigned....21 jan. 08 cap., 47 inf......... 4 mar.08	N. Y. 12 july 72
Fahnestock, Samuel Ferguson, 23 apr. 09 bvt. maj..... 9 dec. 13	i. s. a. p.	1 lt. 22 N. Y. inf., 2 may 98 cap. co. D., 24 may 98 to 23 nov. 98	pvt., corp., sgt., 1 sgt. co. I, 13 inf...26 june 85 to 29 dec. 93 1 lt............29 dec. 93 asst. i. s. a. p. with o. r.............13 apr. 00 resigned............17 aug. 00 1 lt. bat. qm. 14 inf.. 1 nov. 01 cap.............15 may 02 resigned.........15 mar.07 cap. o. d.............30 apr. 09 cap. 47 inf......... 1 may 14 accepted......... 7 may 14	Ind. 9 may 65
Wilson, George Aloysius, 17 may 11	K		pvt., corp., co. K, 47 inf.............15 jan. 00 to 28 apr. 04 2 lt. (K), 47 inf.....28 apr. 04 1 lt.............13 apr. 05 cap.............17 may 11 accepted.........22 may 11	N. Y. 26 oct. 79
Post, Frederick Ralph, 13 oct. 11	sup. co.		pvt., corp., co. E, 13 inf., trs. co. D, 13 inf., sgt., 1 sgt.....14 mar. 89, hon. dis.........28 sep. 97 1 lt. 114 inf.........12 july 98 supn.............10 dec. 98 assigned to duty with 14 inf.......17 oct. 00 1 lt. (I), 14 inf.....28 mar. 01 re-commissioned.....12 may 03 bat. adj. with o. r... 4 may 04 1 lt. (L), with o. r...18 apr. 05 cap. (C)...........30 dec. 05 resigned............16 sep. 10 2 lt. 47 inf.........25 feb. 11 cap.............13 oct. 11 accepted.........16 oct. 11	N. J. 10 may 64

INFANTRY — FORTY-SEVENTH REGIMENT — (Continued)

Name, grade, date of rank and highest brevet rank	Company	In the armies of U. S. or foreign states	In the National Guard	Born
Captains — Continued				
Hendricks, Marcus Tolman, 1 feb. 12	C	....	pvt., corp., sgt., qm. sgt., co. K, 23 inf. . 2 july 03 to 19 nov. 08 1 lt. 47 inf..........19 nov. 08 cap................. 1 feb. 12 accepted............ 2 feb. 12	Pa. 1 dec. 77
Young, James Lowen, 23 feb. 12	I	....	pvt., corp., sgt., co. A, 47 inf....... 5 may 02 to 9 may 07 2 lt................. 9 may 07 1 lt. 47 inf.......... 5 june 08 cap................23 feb. 12 accepted............26 feb. 12	N. Y. 20 oct. 83
Tiffany, Stephen Ralph, 3 july 12	B	....	pvt., corp., sgt., co. B, 47 inf.........26 nov. 06 to 16 mar. 11 1 lt. 47 inf..........16 mar. 11 cap................. 3 july 12 accepted............ 5 july 12	Pa. 2 feb. 83
Stockbridge, Morton Gorton, 17 july 12	G	....	pvt., tr. E, 1 cav. N. G., Ill.........19 nov. 01 dis. hon. dis., N. G., Ill...............15 mar. 02 disability removed...25 nov. 10 2 lt. 47 inf., N. G., N. Y...........26 jan. 11 1 lt................16 may 11 cap......17 july 12 accepted............18 july 12	N. Y. 22 nov.
Chase, George Salsbury, 28 mar. 13	D	pvt. co. B, 47 N. Y. inf., tra. h. c. U. S. A., acting hosp. stwd., 2 may 98 to 21 apr. 99	pvt. co. G, 47 inf: ... 1 oct. 90 hon. dis...........22 jan. 96 pvt., corp., sgt., h. c. 47 inf., bat. sgt. maj. 47 inf.......14 oct. 96 to 26 oct. 08 1 lt. 47 inf..........26 oct. 08 cap................28 mar. 13 accepted............29 mar. 13	N. Y. 4 july 72
Eldred, Hubert Willard, 14 jan. 14	L	....	pvt. co. I, 13 regt....19 mar. 00 to 1 oct. 01 12 may 03 to 14 feb. 05 2 lt. 47 inf.......... 3 dec. 12 1 lt................. 7 mar. 13 cap................14 jan. 14 accepted............16 jan. 14	Mass. 26 oct. 83
Snowball, Arthur Henry, 15 may 14	F	....	pvt., corp., sgt., co. C. 13 inf.........29 nov. 08 to 2 jan. 09 2 lt. 47 inf.......... 2 jan. 09 1 lt................13 jan. 10 cap................15 may 14 accepted............18 may 14	Eng. 19 mas. 76
Brown, Charles William, 25 july 15	A	pvt. tr. F, 2 U. S. cav.....—july 83 to — 88	2 lt. 47 inf.......... 3 apr. 14 1 lt................16 june 14 cap................25 july 15 accepted............25 july 15	N. B. 23 june 64
Coffin, Charles R., 21 mar. 16	adjt.	....	pvt., corp., sgt., 1 sgt., co. C, 23 inf.. 7 oct. 01 to 2 apr. 09 2 lt. 23 inf.......... 2 apr. 09 1 lt................26 feb. 10	N. Y. 25 nov. 81

INFANTRY — FORTY-SEVENTH REGIMENT — (*Continued*)

Name, grade, date of rank and highest brevet rank	Company	Service — In the armies of U. S. or foreign states	Service — In the National Guard	Born
Captains — Continued				
Coffin, Charles R. — *Continued*	.....	......	cap................. 3 apr. 13 accepted........... 5 apr. 13 f. and h. dis........ 1 nov. 15 cap. R. L.......... 8 dec. 15 cap. 47 inf........21 mar. 16 accepted...........22 mar. 16	
Tucker, Cornelius Joseph, 5 july 16	M	....	pvt., cor ., sgt., 1 sgt., co. I, 47 inf...17 nov. 02 to 19 jan. 12 2 lt. 47 inf.........19 jan. 12 1 lt............... 23 feb. 12 accepted...........26 feb. 12 cap................ 5 july 16 accepted.......... 5 july 16	N. Y. 25 may 81
Rogers, Charles H., Jr., 5 july 16 Distinguished graduate, N. Y. School of the Line, 1915.	H	....	pvt., corp., sgt., co. B, 47 inf........ 1 july 12 to 8 nov. 13 2 lt................ 8 nov. 13 1 lt.............. 5 may 14 accepted........... 6 may 14 cap............... 5 july 16 accepted........... 5 july 16	N. Y. 8 feb. 90
Jackson, William Joseph, 5 july 16	E	....	pvt , corp., sgt., 1 sgt., co., B, bat. sgt. maj., 47 inf... 3 feb. 03 to 2 jan. 09 2 lt................ 2 jan. 09 resigned...........19 jan. 11 1 lt. 14 inf.........25 june 14 accepted...........29 june 14 cap .... 5 july 16 accepted........... 5 july 16	N. Y. 23 aug. 83
First Lieutenants				
Thompson, Edwin Francis, 17 nov. 10	C	....	pvt., corp., sgt., co. E, 14 inf........30 apr. 00 to 26 apr. 10 2 lt. 14 inf.........26 apr. 10 1 lt............... 2 dec. 10 1 lt. 47 inf.......... 9 may 12 accepted..........14 may 12	N. Y. 24 sep. 82
Bohn, Charles Henry, 12 dec. 12	B	....	pvt., corp., sgt. 1 sgt., co. B, 47 inf...23 nov. 03 to 12 dec.12 1 lt. 47 inf.........12 dec. 12 accepted...........16 dec. 12	W. Va. 25 mar. 74
Googin, Ernest Benton, 9 july 14	D	pvt. co. A, Mass. inf......17 june 98 to 21 jan. 99	2 lt. 47 inf.......... 4 june 14 1 lt.............. 9 july 14 accepted...........10 july 14	Mass. 31 aug. 78
Frost, John William, 9 july 14	M	....	pvt. tr. E, 1 cav.....18 may 14 to 9 july 14 1 lt. 47 inf.......... 9 july 14 accepted...........13 july 14	Me. 4 jan. 85
Peterson, Edwin Cornelius, 2 jan. 15	F	....	pvt., corp., sgt. co. F. 47 inf........ 7 oct. 07 to 9 july 14 2 lt................ 9 july 14 accepted...........13 july 14 1 lt................ 2 jan. 15 accepted...........11 jan. 15 to 29 may 04	N. Y. 27 apr. 89 81

INFANTRY — FORTY-SEVENTH REGIMENT — (Continued)

Name, grade, date of rank and highest brevet rank	Company	Service		Born
		In the armies of U. S. or foreign states	In the National Guard	
First Lieutenants — Continued				
Simons, Leon Marvin, 22 jan. 15	bat. adjt.	....	pvt. co. D, 1 light inf.............23 apr. 03 pvt. co. C, 1 inf., R I. M............11 july 04 2 lt. 47 inf., N. G., N. Y............2 apr. 09 2 lt. 14 inf..........16 mar. 11 resigned............12 jan. 12 2 lt. 47 inf..........27 june 14 1 lt............22 jan. 15 accepted........30 jan. 15	N. H. 22 jul.
Brown, James Milton, 26 aug. 15	E	pvt., lance corp., corp., sgt., 1 sgt., tr. H. 6 U. S. cav., 15 apr. 96 to 3 dec. 98	2 lt. 47 inf.......... 6 mar. 15 1 lt.............26 aug. 15 accepted..........30 aug. 15	N. Y. 3 dec. 75
Hyames, Frederick Clare, 29 july 15	A	....	pvt., corp., sgt., ret. to 1 class pvt. co. G, 22 engs. trs; corp., sgt., co. K, 222 engs........28 june 05 to 1 july 14 2 lt..............1 july 14 r. l..............23 dec. 14 2 lt..............22 jan. 15 1 lt..............29 july 15 accepted.......... 8 aug. 15	N. Y. 9 june 83
Holloway, Edwin Leroy, 1 june 16	bat. adjt.	....	2 lt. 47 inf..........13 may 15 accepted..........14 may 15 1 lt..............1 june 16 accepted.......... 2 jan. 16	Pa. 23 mar. 90
Baldwin, Harry Beam, Jr., 17 june 16	G	....	pvt., corp., co. E, 47 inf............2 apr. 06 to 14 may 08 2 lt. (G), 47 inf....14 may 08 resigned............10 feb. 10 1 lt. 14 inf..........31 july 12 accepted..........2 aug. 12 placed on r. l........17 jan. 16 1 lt. 47 inf..........17 june 16 accepted..........25 june 16	N. Y. 23 feb. 88
Carlin, Thomas G., 28 june 16	K	....	pvt..............6 jan. 13 dropped..........19 oct. 14 taken up..........19 july 15 returned to duty....24 jan. 16 corp..............3 apr. 16 1 lt..............28 june 16 accepted..........28 june 16 assigned as permanent aid, C. G. 2 brig ...14 july 16	N. Y. 15 june 92
Smith, Albert Cummings, 5 july 16	I	....	pvt., co. I, 10 inf.... 7 feb. 12 to 9 nov. 14 2 lt. 47 inf..........9 nov. 14 accepted..........11 nov. 14 1 lt..............5 july 16 accepted..........5 july 16	N. Y. 19 apr. 93
Focardi, Pier Luigi, 5 july 16	F	....	2 lt. 47 inf..........10 june 15 accepted..........14 june 15 1 lt..............5 july 16 accepted..........5 july 16	Eng. 18 jan. 87
Frost, John W., 9 july 14	M	....	pvt. trp. E, 1 cav...18 may 14 1 lt., 47 inf.........9 july 14 accepted..........13 july 14	Me. 4 jan. 85

INFANTRY — FORTY-SEVENTH REGIMENT — (*Concluded*)

Name, grade, date of rank and highest brevet rank	Company	Service		Born
		In the armies of U. S. or foreign states	In the National Guard	

Second Lieutenants

Brotheridge, Herbert Joseph, R. L., 2 jan. 15	m. g. co.	....	pvt., vet. sgt., stable sgt., 3 batty...... 7 nov. 02 to 2 jan. 15 2 lt............... 2 jan. 15 accepted.......... 4 jan. 15	N. Y. 6 mar. 75
Strachan, Donald Cheyne, 11 june 15	M	....	2 lt. 47 inf.........11 june 15 accepted.........14 june 15	N. Y. 26 july 85
Jantzer, Harry Jackson, 6 july 15	sup. co.	....	pvt. co. C, 7 inf.....28 jan. 14 to 6 july 15 2 lt............... 6 july 15 accepted.......... 8 july 15	N. Y. 27 oct. 79
Grass, Allie Pleasant, 7 oct. 15	E	pvt., corp., co. L, 5 U. S. inf., 9 july 09 to 31 may 10 pvt., sgt., qm. sgt., 1 june 10 to 11 mar. 12	2 lt. 47 inf.......... 7 oct. 15 accepted...........11 oct. 15	Ohio. 27 oct. 87
Graham-Rogers, Chas. T., 11 dec. 15	D	....	2 lt. 47 inf.........11 dec. 15 accepted...........13 dec. 15	N. Y. aug. 1 74
MacElroy, Andrew J., 9 feb. 16	L	....	pvt. co. L..........14 june 15 2 lt............... 9 feb. 16 accepted...........14 feb. 16	Ohio 14 sep. 75
Curtis, Summerfield Samuel, 24 mar. 16	m. g. co.	sgt. co. K, 47 N. Y. inf...... 2 may 98 to 31 mar. 99	pvt., corp., sgt., 1 sgt., co. K, 47 inf.. 8 may 95 hon. dis...........19 may 02 pvt., corp., sgt., co. K............. 7 may 06 to 31 july 12 2 lt. 47 inf.........31 july 12 accepted.......... 8 aug. 12 placed on R. L.....25 jan. 16 2 lt...............24 mar. 16 accepted...........25 june 16	N. J. 1 jan. 74
McCahill, Peter B., 27 apr. 16	F	....	pvt. co. I, 71 inf....19 apr. 98 sgt............... 4 apr. 01 dishon. dis........22 july 02 dis. revoked by S. O. 98, 71 R....... 7 nov. 02 reduced to ranks at own request......15 dec. 02 f. and h. dis......... 5 may 03 pvt. co. E, 71 inf.... 3 mar. 04 dis................. 3 may 07 pvt................21 july 15 sgt................22 july 15 2 lt................27 apr. 16 accepted.......... 4 may 16	N. Y. 1 sep. 77
Madigan, Thomas M., 24 may 16	E	....	pvt. co. E......... 5 feb. 06 corp.............. 1 mar. 09 sgt................29 nov. 09 f. and h. dis........ 3 may 15 re-enlisted.......... 3 may 15 1 sgt..............27 sep. 15 2 lt...............24 may 16 accepted...........26 may 16	N. Y. 7 jan. 86

Chaplain

Edrop, Percy Tom, 1 june 16		....	chaplain........... 1 june 16 accepted.......... 5 june 16	Eng. 18 oct. 83

INFANTRY — (*Continued*)

SIXTY-NINTH REGIMENT

(Twelve Companies.)

(First Brigade.)

Armory, 68 *Lexington Avenue, New York City*

On October 12, 1851, a number of independent, uniformed military companies in the City of New York were organized into a regiment under the command of Colonel Charles S. Roe, and designated in General Orders No. 489, A. G. O., dated November 1, 1851, as the 69th Regiment, New York State Militia. In 1858 the regiment was reorganized as a regiment of artillery doing duty as infantry.

The regiment was mustered into the United States service on May 9, 1861, at Washington, D. C., for three months, during which service it participated in the battles of Blackburn's Ford and Bull Run, and was mustered out on August 3, 1861.

Immediately after its muster out and return practically the whole regiment, including the officers and enlisted men who had served in the three months' campaign, volunteered for three years, or the war, and the offer was accepted by the War Department in a letter to the commanding officer of the regiment under date of August 30, 1861, the regiment being mustered into the United States service on November 8, 1861, as the 69th Regiment, New York Volunteers. Its appellation of " militia " was changed to " volunteers " for the reason that the term for which the regiment volunteered exceeded the period of time established by the State of New York for which its militia regiments, to be recognized as such, could serve without the State. But its numerical designation, however, was, by authority of the State, retained in order to preserve and maintain the regiment's identity with the militia organisation. During this service the regiment was attached to the Army of the Potomac, forming part of the Irish Brigade (2d Brigade — 1st Division — 2d Corps). It was recruited in 1863 and again in 1864 and finally mustered out of the United States service at New York on June 30, 1865.

The militia organisation, having in the fall of 1861 been again reorganized and recruited, re-entered the United States service for three months on May 26, 1862, and on its return from this service the major part thereof entered the service of the United States for three years, being mustered in on November 17, 1862, as the 69th Regiment, New York National Guard Artillery, which designation was, to avoid confusion, changed on March 19, 1864, to the 182d New York Volunteers and mustered out of the United States service under that designation on July 15, 1865. During its term of service this organisation was one of the units in the brigade of New York regiments known as the " Irish Legion," officially designated as the 4th Brigade (afterwards 2d Brigade), 2d Division, 2d Corps, Army of the Potomac.

The militia regiment having been again reorganised, was mustered into the service of the United States on June 25, 1863, for thirty days, and was mustered out on July 25, 1863. Again for the fourth time, the militia organisation was, on July 6, 1864, mustered into the United States service for three months and was mustered out on October 6, 1864.

The regiment has rendered service to the State during the quarantine riots in 1858; the draft riots, 1863, and the quarantine disturbances in 1892. It was reduced December 6, 1893, to a battalion of five companies, A, C, D, I and K. The battalion was on duty at Brooklyn during the riots in January, 1895. New companies were organized for the battalion as follows: Co. B, June 5, 1894; Co. G, June 10, 1895; Co. E, June 11, 1895, and Co. F, September 7, 1900. The battalion was reconstituted a regiment September 4, 1896. April 28, 1898, the regiment received authority to organize as a twelve-company regiment, preparatory to its entry into the United States service, into which service it was mustered May 19, 1898, as the 69th Regiment, N. Y. Infantry, and mustered out January 31, 1899. The regiment formally re-entered the service of the State on March 15, 1899. Companies L and M were disbanded April 12, 1899; Co. F, February 8, 1900, and Co. B, March 5, 1900. Co. F was reorganized and mustered in May 31, 1900. New Co. B was organized January 4, 1900. New Co. L was mustered in July 14, 1911. Co. M was mustered in December 29, 1913.

Recognition extended by War Department under Act of June 3, 1916, to Companies A, B, E, G, H, I, June 26, 1916; to Companies C, D, F, K, L, M and Sanitary Detachment, June 28, 1916; to Headquarter and Supply Companies, June 26, 1916.

The regiment has received authority to place silver rings on the lances of its colors, engraved as follows:

On the National Color.— Civil War, 1861–1865: Blackburn's Ford, Va., July 18, 1861; Bull Run, Va., July 21, 1861; Rappahannock Station, Va., March 28–29, 1862; Yorktown, Va., April 16–May 4, 1862; Fair Oaks, Va., June 1, 1862; Gaines's Mill, Va., June 27–28, 1862; Savage Station, Va., June 29, 1862; Peach Orchard, Va., June 29, 1862; White Oak Swamp, Va., June 30, 1862; Glendale, Va., June 30, 1862; Malvern Hill, Va., July 1, 1862; Antietam, Md., September 17, 1862; Charlestown, W. Va., October 16–17, 1862; Snickers Gap, Va., November 2, 1862; Hartwood Church, Va., November 17, 1862; Fredericksburg, Va., December 11–15, 1862; Deserted House, or Kelley's Store, near Suffolk, Va., January 30, 1863; Suffolk, Va., April 11–May 4, 1863; Chancellorsville, Va., May 1–3, 1863; Carrasville, Va., May 16, 1863; Gettysburg, Pa., July 1–3, 1863; Auburn Mills, Va., October 14, 1863; Bristoe Station, Va., October 14, 1863; Mine Run, Va., November 26–December 2, 1863; Wilderness, Va., May 5–7, 1864; Po River, Va., May 9–10, 1864; Spottsylvania (angle), May 8–21, 1864; Landron House, Va., May 18,

1864; North Anna River, Va., May 22–26, 1864; Totopotomoy Creek, Va., May 27–31, 1864; Cold Harbor, Va., June 1–12, 1864; Petersburg (assault), Va., June 16, 1864; Weldon Railroad, Va., June 21, 23, 26–29, 1864; Deep Bottom, Va., July 27–29, 1864; Strawberry Plains, Va., August 14–18, 1864; Reams Station, Va., August 25, 1864; Boydton Plank Road, Va., October 27–28, 1864; Hatcher's Run, Va., December 8–9, 1864; Hatcher's Run or Dabney's Mills, Va., February 5–7, 1865; Skinner's Farm, Va., March 25, 1865; Crow's House, near Petersburg, Va., March 31, 1865; Hatcher's Run, Va., March 31, 1865; siege of Petersburg, Va., June 17, 1864–April 2, 1865; Sutherland Sta., Boydton Plank Road, Va., April 2, 1865; Sailor's Creek, Va., April 6, 1865; Farmville, Va., April 7, 1865; Appomattox Court House, Va., April 9, 1865; Spanish-American War, 1898.

On the State Color.— Quarantine riots, 1858; draft riots, 1863; Fire Island, 1892; Brooklyn, 1895.

INFANTRY — SIXTY-NINTH REGIMENT

Name, grade, date of rank and highest brevet rank	Company	Service		Born
		In the armies of U. S. or foreign states	In the National Guard	
Colonel				
Haskell, William N., 31 july 16	......	cadet, M. A., 19 june 97	col. 69 N. Y. inf.....31 july 16	N. Y.
		2 lt. 9 cav..18 feb. 01	accepted............ 4 aug. 16	13 aug.
		to rank.... 2 feb. 01		78
		1 lt. 4 cav., 26 apr. 06		
		1 lt. sig. corps by detail, Act Mar. 2, 1903.... 8 nov. 07		
		assgd. to 14 cav., 8 nov. 11		
		trs. to 8 cav., 22 apr. 12		
		trs. to 7 cav., 20 june 13		
		graduate, inf. and cav. schools, 1904..		
		graduate, staff college 1905		
		mustered into u. s. ser......16 aug. 16		
Lieutenant Colonel				
Reed, Latham Ralston, 3 nov. 16	......	mustered into u. s. ser...... 6 nov. 16	pvt. tr. 3, sq. A......12 oct. 04 to 12 may 05	N. Y. 8 july 86
			pvt., corp...........22 aug. 05	
			hon. dis............28 oct. 10	
			pvt., sgt., 1 sgt......18 mar. 12	
			hon. dis............17 mar. 15	
			1 lt................ 1 july 15	
			accepted............ 5 july 15	
			maj., 69 inf........ 8 oct. 16	
			accepted............ 5 oct. 16	
			lt. col. 69 inf........ 3 nov. 16	
			accepted............ 6 nov. 16	
Majors				
Stacom, William Benedict, 23 dec. 10	......	mustered into u. s. ser...... 6 july 16	pvt., corp., co. A, 69 inf............... 5 jan. 06 to 26 mar. 07	N. Y. 30 aug. 83
			2 lt. (A), 69 inf......26 mar. 07	
			1 lt................29 feb. 08	
			cap................23 dec. 10	
			accepted...........30 dec. 10	
Moynahan, Timothy Joseph, 7 mar. 16 Distinguished Graduate, N. Y. School of the Line, 1915.	......	mustered into u. s. ser...... 6 july 16	pvt., 1 sgt., co. A, 169 inf............ 4 may 98	Ire. 11 may
			hon. dis...........15 mar. 99	
			1 lt. 8 inf........... 4 june 00	
			cap................19 aug. 02	
			resigned...........24 apr. 07	
			1 lt. o. d...........25 may 11	
			cap. 69 inf..........26 sep. 11	
			accepted...........27 sep. 11	
			major.............. 7 mar. 16	
			accepted...........10 mar. 16	

INFANTRY — SIXTY-NINTH REGIMENT — (*Continued*)

Name, grade, date of rank and highest brevet rank	Company	Service		Born
		In the armies of U. S. or foreign states	In the National Guard	
Captains				
MeSherry, Felix Joseph, 18 oct. 00	C	2 lt. 69 N. Y. inf., 2 may 98 to 31 jan. 99	pvt., corp., co. C, 69 inf., sgt. co. C, 69 bat., 1 sgt. co. C, 69 inf..........10 feb. 90 to 19 july 00 1 lt.............19 july 00 cap.............18 oct. 00	Eng. 27 nov. 70
Dillon, Edward Maurice, 6 mar. 06	sup. co.	pvt. co. I, 71 N. Y. inf.... 2 may 98 to 15 nov. 98 mustered into u. s. ser..... 6 july 16	pvt., corp., qm. sgt., co. I, 71 inf......27 apr. 98 hon. dis...........26 aug. 02 pvt., qm., sgt., co. F, 69 inf..........10 feb. 03 to 24 aug. 04 1 lt. (F), 69 inf......24 aug. 04 cap. (B)...........6 mar. 06	Vt. 3 nov.
Doyle, William Thomas, 6 mar. 14	M	mustered into u. s. ser..... 6 july 16	pvt. co. E, 7 inf......3 feb. 05 to 29 jan. 07 2 apr. 07 to 8 oct. 09 pvt., lance corp., corp. co. E.......14 feb. 11 to 7 mar. 13 1 lt. 69 inf.........7 mar. 13 cap.............6 mar. 14 accepted..........9 mar. 14	N. Y. 31 jan. 82
Kelly, Michael Andrew, 5 july 16	F	....	pvt., corp., co. F, 69 inf.............21 apr. 03 to 22 may 06 1 lt. (F), 69 inf......22 may 06 cap............5 july 16 accepted........5 july 16	Ire. 29 oct. 79
Anderson, Alexander Edward, 15 apr. 16 Honor Graduate, N. Y. School of the Line, 1915.	E	....	pvt., corp., qm. sgt., co. G, 69 inf........7 jan. 10 to 5 aug. 12 1 lt. 69 inf.........5 aug. 12 accepted.........7 aug. 12 cap.............15 apr. 16 accepted........21 apr. 16	N. Y. 23 nov. 89
Lilly, John Joseph, 8 june 16	A	....	pvt. co. H, bat. sgt. maj. 69 inf.....20 oct. 11 to 13 apr. 14 1 lt.............13 apr. 14 accepted.........15 apr. 14 cap............8 june 16 accepted........12 june 16	N. Y. 14 nov. 83
Hurley, John Patrick, 26 june 16	M	....	pvt. co. H, 69 inf.....3 jan. 10 to 7 june 10 2 lt. 69 inf.........7 june 10 1 lt.............21 june 12 hon. dis.........3 mar. 13 1 lt. 69 inf.....15 may 15 accepted........17 may 15 cap............26 june 16 accepted........26 june 16	N. Y. 15 sep. 78
McKenna, Jas. A., Jr., 20 oct. 16	I	mustered into u. s. ser..... 6 july 16	pvt. 7 inf..........1 oct. 08 f. and h. dis......1 nov. 14 re-enlisted.........3 mar. 15 corp..........19 apr. 15 1 lt. 69 inf.......11 may 16 accepted.........19 may 16 cap.............20 oct. 16 accepted........24 oct. 16	N. Y. 23 sep. 85

INFANTRY — SIXTY-NINTH REGIMENT — (*Continued*)

Name, grade, date of rank and highest brevet rank	Company	Service		Born
		In the armies of U. S. or foreign states	In the National Guard	
Captains — Continued				
Powers, Walter E., 20 oct. 16	G	pvt. 7 u. s. cav., 26 jan. 01 agt., 1 agt., color agt., sq. agt. maj. 27 july 07 apptd. reg. agt. maj.; disch....12 sep. 16	2 lt...............15 sep. 16 accepted...........15 sep. 16 cap...............20 oct. 16 accepted...........23 oct. 16	Mass. 17 sep. 83
First Lieutenants				
Carroll, Michael Francis, 4 mar. 14	....		pvt., corp., co. H, 69 inf...............11 apr. 92 to 11 jan. 94 pvt., corp. agt., 1 agt., co. D, 71 inf..27 mar. 94 to 26 may 03 pvt. mtd. detach....10 apr. 13 to 4 mar. 14 2 lt. 69 inf.......... 4 mar. 14 accepted.......... 6 mar. 14	Ire. 14 oct. 71
Patton, William Henry, 13 may 14	K	mustered into u. s. ser...... 6 july 16	pvt. co. K, 69 inf......10 nov. 13 to 13 may 14 1 lt...............13 may 14 accepted...........16 may 14	N. Y. 20 apr. 78
Finn, James Gregory, 15 feb. 15	H	pvt., corp., 1 Maine inf.....10 may 98 to 20 oct. 98 mustered into u. s. ser...... 6 july 16	pvt. co. I, 1 inf. N. G., Maine.......— feb. 98 to 10 may 98 pvt., corp., agt., co. I.— jan. 99 to — jan. 02 2 lt. 69 inf. N. G. N. Y................13 june 14 1 lt...............15 feb. 15 accepted...........23 feb. 15	Me. 3 jan. 79
Smith, Samuel A 23 feb. 16	bat. adj.	mustered into u. s. ser...... 6 july 16	1 lt...............23 feb. 16 accepted...........28 feb. 16	Ky. 26 jan. 93
Reilly, Thomas T., 24 june 16	B	mustered into u. s. ser...... 6 july 16	pvt. co. F, 7 inf......21 apr. 11 lance corp.........23 jan. 13 corp...............28 nov. 13 dropped........... 4 oct. 15 1 lt...............24 june 16 accopted...........24 june 16	N. Y. 20 mar. 83
Kennelly, William, 24 june 16	K	mustered into u. s. ser...... 6 july 16	pvt. 7 inf...........12 may 06 lance corp.........13 nov. 08 corp............... 3 dec. 09 agt...............22 sep. 10 1 lt. 69 inf.........24 june 16 accepted...........24 june 16	N. J. 12 may 85
Archer, James Joseph, 5 july 16	F	mustered into u. s. ser...... 6 july 16	pvt., corp., agt., 1 agt., co. F, 69 inf...15 jan. 06 to 25 mar. 14 2 lt...............25 mar. 14 accepted...........27 mar. 14 1 lt............... 5 july 16 accepted........... 5 july 16	N. Y. 6 mar. 85
Hall, Patrick James, 7 july 16	bat. adj.	mustered into u. s. ser...... 6 july 16	pvt. co. K, 69 inf....30 nov. 14 to 6 apr. 15 2 lt............... 6 apr. 15 accepted........... 9 apr. 15 1 lt............... 7 july 16 accepted........... 7 july 16	Eng. 5 june 76

INFANTRY—SIXTY-NINTH REGIMENT—(*Continued*)

Name, grade, date of rank and highest brevet rank	Company	Service		Born
		In the armies of U. S. or foreign states	In the National Guard	
First Lieutenants — Continued				
Mangan, John J., 23 sep. 16	sup. co.	mustered into u. s. ser...... 6 july 16	pvt. co. F, 71 inf..... 1 may 16 2 lt. 69 inf......... 6 june 16 accepted.......... 8 june 16 cap.................23 sep. 16 accepted..........27 sep. 16	N. J.
Poore John Gooden, 16 nov. 16	D	mustered into u. s. ser...... 6 july 16	pvt., corp., co. A, 69 inf...............11 may 14 to 14 july 15 2 lt.................14 july 15 accepted..........15 july 15 1 lt.................16 nov. 16 accepted..........19 nov. 16	Del. 24 june 86
Murray, Francis W., Jr., 3 nov. 16	m. g. co.	....	pvt. tr. B, sq. A....30 mar.10 dropped.........17 nov. 11 taken up..........20 mar. 13 corp..............8 dec. 14 sgt...............3 mar. 16 1 lt. 69 inf......... 3 nov. 16 accepted.......... 4 nov. 16	
McKenna, Wm. F., 16 nov. 16	bat. adj.	....	pvt. co. F, 7 inf.....16 feb. 12 f. and h. dis.......25 feb. 15 re-enlisted......... 2 mar. 15 2 lt. 69 inf......... 4 sep. 16 accepted.......... 8 sep. 16 1 lt.................16 nov. 16 accepted..........19 nov. 16	L.I.City 7 june 90
McAdie, George, 16 nov. 16	K	....	pvt. co. E, 12 inf.....13 oct. 02 corp trs. to co. C, 7 inf...............30 mar. 06 corp.............21 may 09 sgt...............13 nov. 14 f. and h. dis......... 2 dec. 14 re-enlisted......... 3 dec. 14 1 lt. 69 inf.........16 nov. 16 accepted..........27 nov. 16	Ire. 3 sep. 84
Greene, John A., Jr., 1 dec. 16	m. g. co.	pvt. 8 Mass. inf., — july 05 dropped for removal, — jan. 06	pvt. 1 cav.........13 mar. 13 discharged........12 mar. 16 re-enlisted m. g. tr...13 mar. 16 corp............... 3 mar. 16 2 lt................. 1 dec. 16 accepted.......... 6 dec. 16	Mass. 13 may 83
Second Lieutenants				
Burns, William John, 4 apr. 14	m. g. co.	mustered into u. s. ser...... 6 july 16	pvt., corp., sgt., co. B, 69 inf.........11 apr. 11 to 4 apr. 14 2 lt................. 4 apr. 14 accepted.......... 6 apr. 14	N. Y. 1 feb. 90
Prout, John T., 5 july 16	m. g. co.	mustered into u. s. ser...... 6 july 16	pvt. co. F...........13 mar. 08 corp.............. 6 may 10 sgt............... 5 july 12 1 sgt.............22 may 14 2 lt............... 5 july 16 accepted.......... 5 july 16	Ire. 26 oct. 80
Martin, Thomas C. P., 9 sep. 16	K	....	pvt. co. K, 7 inf.....28 nov. 13 2 lt. 69 inf......... 9 sep. 16 accepted..........17 sep. 16	Penn. 23 mar. 88

INFANTRY — SIXTY-NINTH REGIMENT — (*Concluded*)

Name, grade, date of rank and highest brevet rank	Company	Service		Born
		In the armies of U. S. or foreign states	In the National Guard	
Second Lieutenants — Continued				
Cruger, Frederick H., 28 oct. 16	A	....	pvt. tr. B, sq. A.....26 june 16 2 lt. 69 inf..........28 oct. 16 accepted...........6 nov. 16	N. Y. 10 apr. 85
Crimmins, Clarence P., 28 oct. 16	D	mustered into u. s. ser......12 dec. 16	pvt. trp. B, sq. A,...26 june 16 2 lt. 69 inf..........28 oct. 16 accepted...........6 nov. 16	N. Y. 27 feb. 88
Philbin, Ewing R........ 2 nov. 16	sup. co.	mustered into u. s. ser......11 dec. 16	pvt. trp. B, sq. A....17 oct. 14 2 lt ....2 nov. 16 accepted...........18 nov. 16	Ill. 3 aug. 89
Lynch, Hampton S... 2 nov. 16	sup. co.	mustered into u. s. ser......6 dec. 16	pvt. trp. D, sq. A....16 oct. 15 1 cl. pvt............11 sep. 16 2 lt. 69 inf..........2 nov. 16 accepted...........18 nov. 16	
Merle-Smith, Van S...... 16 nov. 16	D	mustered into u. s. ser......13 dec. 16	pvt. trp. C. sq. A....17 nov. 14 corp.................3 mar. 16 2 lt.................16 nov. 16 accepted...........19 nov. 16	N. J. 22 june 89
Chaplain				
Duffy, Francis Patrick, 9 nov. 14	....	mustered into u. s. ser......6 july 16	chaplain............9 nov. 14 accepted...........16 nov. 14	Can. 2 may 71

INFANTRY — (*Continued*)
SEVENTY-FIRST REGIMENT
(Twelve Companies.)
(First Brigade.)
Armory, 104 Park Avenue, New York City

The regiment was organized in August, 1852. The American Rifles, a battalion of four companies, formed the nucleus of the regiment. September 21, 1870, the 37th Regiment was consolidated with the 71st Regiment, Cos. E, D, H, A, G, K and B of the 37th Regiment being consolidated with Cos. A, C, D, E, F, G and K of the 71st Regiment, respectively. In 1861 it entered the United States service for three months, from April 19 to July 30; in 1862 it re-entered the same service, May 29, for three months, at the expiration of which it volunteered to remain, and remained until September 1; in 1863 it was mustered into the United States service for thirty days, and served from June 17 to July 22. April 28, 1898, it received authority to organize as a twelve-company regiment, preparatory to its entry into the United States service, into which it was mustered May 10, 1898, as the 71st Regiment, N. Y. Infantry, and mustered out November 15, 1898. December 8, 1898, it was reorganized as a National Guard regiment, composed of ten companies, Cos. L and M being disbanded. Co. M was mustered in January 8, 1907. On November 10, 1908, an additional company was directed to be organized and attached to the 71st Infantry, as Co. L. The regiment was authorized to organize a detachment of mounted scouts by Special Orders No. 66, March 15, 1912.

Recognition extended by the War Department under Act of June 3, 1916, to Companies A, B, C, D, E, G, H, K, L, M and Sanitary Detachment, on June 25, 1916; to Companies F and I, on June 26, 1916; to Headquarters Company, Supply Company and Machine Gun Company, on Nov. 18, 1916.

The regiment has received authority to place silver rings on the lances of its colors, engraved as follows:

On the National Color.—Alexandria, Va., May 24, 1861; Aquia Creek, Va., May 31, 1861; Matthis Point, Va., June 27, 1861; Bull Run, Va., July 21, 1861; Tenallytown, D. C., 1862; Washington, D. C., 1862; Gettysburg campaign, 1863; Kingston, Pa., June 26, 1863; near Harrisburg, Pa., June 29, 1863; Spanish-American War, 1898; Cuba, June, July and August, 1898; San Juan Hill, July 1, 1898; Siege of Santiago de Cuba, July 2 to 17, 1898.

On the State Color.— Dead Rabbit riot, 1857; quarantine riots, 1858; draft riots, 1863; Orange riots, 1871; railroad riots, 1877; Buffalo, 1892; Brooklyn, 1895.

INFANTRY — SEVENTY-FIRST REGIMENT

Name, grade, date of rank and highest brevet rank	Company	Service		Born
		In the armies of U. S. or foreign states	In the National Guard	
Colonel				
Bates, William Graves, 23 nov. 99 bvt. brig. gen...14 aug. 03	......	1 lt. regt. adj., 71 N. Y. inf... 2 may 98 cap. asst. a. g. U. S. vols..... 3 june 98 to 15 oct. 98 mustered into u. s. ser......27 june 16	pvt., corp., sgt., co. K, 7 inf., sgt. maj. 7 inf.............5 dec. 77 to 16 may 92 1 lt. regt. adjt. 71 inf.16 may 92 cap................22 may 96 maj...............17 may 99 col................23 nov. 99	N. Y. 14 july 60
Lieutenant Colonel				
Beekman, William Schuyler, 14 may 07 bvt. lt. col....13 mar.12 Graduate, Garrison Schools, 1914.	......	1 lt. 71 N. Y. inf., 2 may 98 to 15 nov. 98 mustered into u. s. ser......27 june 16	pvt. corp., sgt., 1 sgt., co. B, 71 inf.....24 feb. 87 to 16 apr. 95 2 lt................16 apr. 95 1 lt................ 8 jan. 97 cap...............17 may 00 maj. 71 inf.........14 may 07 a. d. c. to gov....... 1 jan. 11 to 31 dec. 12	N. Y. 11 sep. 68
Majors				
Hutchinson, James Merrill, 16 june 10 Field Officers' Course, Army Service Schools, 1914.	......	pvt., sgt., co. M, 71 N. Y. inf......... 3 may 98 to 5 june 98 2 lt....... 5 june 98 to 15 nov. 98 mustered into u. s. ser......27 june 16	pvt., co. K, 7 inf.... 2 dec. 91 to 15 oct. 92 pvt. co. K, trs. co. M, 71 inf., trs. co. F, 71 inf., sgt.....15 apr. 99 to 18 oct. 01 2 lt................18 oct. 01 cap...............25 apr. 02 trs. co. M.........22 jan. 07 maj. 71 inf......... 1 july 10 accepted........... 4 july 10	Wis. 31 july 64

INFANTRY — SEVENTY-FIRST REGIMENT — (Continued)

Name, grade, date of rank and highest brevet rank	Company	Service		Born
		In the armies of U. S. or foreign states	In the National Guard	
Majors — *Continued*				
Wells, Arthur Edwin, 30 apr. 13 Graduate, Garrison Schools, 1914.	......	mustered into u. s. ser......27 june 16	pvt., corp., sgt., co. E, 7 inf.........20 jan. 93 to 7 april 03 1 lt. (H), 71 inf..... 7 apr. 03 cap................21 mar. 05 maj................30 apr. 13 accepted.......... 1 may 13	Pa. 17 dec. 70
Delamater, Walter Allen, 26 june 16 Graduate, Garrison Schools, 1914.	......	mustered into u. s. ser......27 june 16	pvt., qm. sgt., co. K, 71 inf.. .... 2 mar. 00 to 10 nov. 03 2 lt. (K), 71 inf.....10 nov. 03 1 lt.. ....15 nov. 04 cap................11 apr. 05 major.............26 june 16 accepted..........26 june 16	N. Y. 18 apr. 80
Captains				
True, Clarence Fagan, 3 june 98	F	mustered into u. s. ser......27 june 16	pvt. 17 sep. co.. ....31 mar. 82 hon. dis............30 may 87 cap. comy of sub. 171 inf............ 3 june 98 supn., assigned comy of sub. 71 inf.....14 jan. 99 cap. comy of sub. 71 inf..........23 feb. 00 re-commissioned.....11 may 03	Mass. 17 aug. 60
Fearn, William Royde, 19 apr. 04	sup. co.	mustered into u. s. ser......27 june 16	pvt. co. K, 71 inf.....15 june 89 hon. dis............15 aug. 94 1 lt. bat. qm. 71 inf.. 6 june 01 cap. regt. qm.......19 apr. 04 a. d. c. to gov....... 1 jan. 07 to 31 dec. 10	N. Y. 1 jan. 71
Maslin, Henry, 23 may 05	G	pvt., corp. sgt., 4 bat. Connaught Rangers, British Militia — mar. 83 to 27 nov. 84 pvt., 16 Queen's Lancers regular cav.....27 nov. 84 to — july 87 1 lt. 71 N. Y. inf., 2 may 98 to 15 nov. 98	pvt., corp., sgt., 1 sgt., co. G, 71 inf...17 sep. 89 to 22 jan. 97 1 lt...............22 jan. 97 cap..............23 may 05	Ire. 15 apr. 67
Lyon, John Wesley, 16 july 07	sup. co.	mustered into u. s. ser......27 june 16	pvt. co. B, 71 inf., trs. co. B, 171 inf...11 feb. 95 to 3 june 98 2 lt. (F), 171 inf..... 3 june 98 supn............... 3 jan. 99 pvt., qm. sgt., co. B, 71 inf............ 7 apr. 99 to 29 mar. 04 2 lt. (B), 71 inf......29 mar. 04 1 lt.................12 mar. 07 cap...............16 july 07	N. Y. 20 jan. 98
Eben, James, 7 apr. 09 Graduate, Garrison Schools, 1915.	E	mustered into u. s. ser......27 june 16	pvt., corp., co. B, 71 inf., trs. 171......12 jan. 92 to 3 june 98 2 lt................ 3 june 98 resigned to return to co. B, 71 inf. as rp..........12 jan 99 2 lt................17 may 00 1 lt...............30 aug. 00 bat. adj. 71 inf. with o. r.............28 dec. 06 cap. 71 inf.........15 apr. 09 accepted..........20 apr. 09	N. Y. 19 apr. 71

INFANTRY — SEVENTY-FIRST REGIMENT — (Continued)

Name, grade, date of rank and highest brevet rank	Company	Service		Born
		In the armies of U. S. or foreign states	In the National Guard	
Captains — Continued				
Perrine, George, 30 june 11 99	adj.	2 lt. 1 U. S. Vol. eng.... 7 june 98 1 lt......28 june 98 bat. qm.... 5 july 98 bat. adj...28 oct. 98 to 25 jan. 99 mustered into u. s. ser......27 june 16	pvt. co. I, 7 inf......30 apr. 95 hon. dis............ 7 june 98 pvt., lance corp., corp., sgt., co. I, 7 inf............ 3 mar.99 to 15 jan. 02 pvt., lance corp., co. I............31 mar.02 to 23 dec. 02 1 lt. bat. adj. 71 inf..23 dec. 02 cap............30 jun. 11 accepted........... 2 july 11	Wis. 11 jan. 71
Ely, William Allen Hall, 29 may 13	C	pvt. co. C, 71 N. Y. inf...... 2 may 98 to 28 july 98 2 lt. 201 N. Y. inf., 6 july 98 to 31 dec. 98 mustered into u. s. ser......27 june 16	pvt., corp., co. C, 71 inf...........27 apr. 98 to 14 feb. 05 2 lt. (C), 71 inf......14 feb. 05 1 lt. 10 dec. 07 cap...........29 may 13 accepted........... 3 june 13	N. Y. 5 july 77
Vogel, Frederick William, 1 july 13	H	pvt. co. H, 71 N. Y. inf......29 apr. 98 to 15 nov. 98 mustered into u. s. ser......27 june 16	pvt., corp., sgt., 1 sgt., co. H, 71 inf...25 apr. 98 to 1 oct. 07 1 lt. (H), 71 inf 1 oct. 07 cap............... 1 july 13 accepted........... 8 july 13	N. Y. 8 may 77
Kehlbeck, Harverd Albert, 22 july 13 Graduate, Garrison Schools, 1915.	L	mustered into u. s. ser......27 june 16	pvt., qm. sgt., co. K, 71 inf........... 2 apr. 01 to 11 apr. 05 2 lt. (K), 71 inf......11 apr. 05 1 lt................ 6 may 11 cap...........22 july 13 accepted..........23 july 13	N. Y. 18 june 79
Delanoy, Stephen James, 9 june 14 Graduate, Garrison Schools, 1915.	I	mustered into u. s. ser......27 june 16	2 lt. 71 inf.........21 june 09 1 lt............19 june 12 cap............... 9 june 14 accepted..........10 june 14	N. Y. 30 june 82
Potter, Frank Rawson, 3 may 15	D	wagoner, co. D, 71 N. Y. inf., 2 may 98 to 15 nov. 98 mustered into u. s. ser......27 june 16	pvt., corp., sgt., 1 sgt., co. D, 71 inf..15 oct. 95 to 28 jan. 10 2 lt. 71 inf.........28 jan. 10 1 lt................24 oct. 10 cap............... 3 may 15 accepted........... 7 may 15	N. Y. 12 june 76
McDermott, Joseph Holmes, 2 june 15	M	artif. co. D, 71 N. Y. inf...... 2 may 98 to 15 nov. 98 mustered into u. s. ser......27 june 16	pvt., corp., qm. sgt., 1 sgt., co. D, 71 inf...........22 may 96 hon. dis............11 june 01 pvt..............11 june 01 hon. dis............23 aug. 04 pvt., 1 sgt., co. M, 71 inf............... 8 jan. 07 to 24 sep. 10 2 lt. 71 inf.........24 sep. 10 1 lt................18 mar.12 cap.............. 2 june 15 accepted........... 8 june 15	N. Y. 10 feb. 74
Hodgdon, Raymond Fallon, 20 aug. 15 Distinguished Graduate, N. Y. School of the Line, 1915.	A	mustered into u. s. ser......27 june 16	pvt., corp., sgt., co. K, 71 inf......... 8 dec. 05 to 19 feb. 12 2 lt. 71 inf.........19 feb. 12 1 lt................28 mar. 13 cap...........20 aug. 15 accepted..........24 aug. 15	Mass. 24 mar. 84

INFANTRY — SEVENTY-FIRST REGIMENT — (*Continued*)

Name, grade, date of rank and highest brevet rank	Company	Service		Born
		In the armies of U. S. or foreign states	In the National Guard	
Captains — Continued				
Ranges, John Frederick, 31 july 13 Graduate, Garrison Schools, 1915.	K	mustered into u. s. ser......27 june 16	pvt., corp., qm. sgt., co. K, 71 inf......16 sep. 02 to 23 may 11 2 lt. 71 inf..........23 may 11 1 lt.................31 july 13 accepted.......... 5 aug. 13	N. Y. 10 june 80
Bulkley, Stanley, 26 may 16	B	mustered into u. s. ser......27 june 16	pvt., corp., co. C, 71 inf................ 5 feb. 07 to 16 may 12 2 lt. 71 inf..........16 may 12 1 lt................. 1 july 13 accepted.......... 8 july 13 captain..........26 may 16 accepted..........26 may 16	Minn. 27 jan. 85
Schroeder, Earnest, Charles, 23 june 16	m. g. co.	pvt. co. G, 10 Pa. inf., corp., qm., Philippine scouts, 29 apr. 98 to 30 apr. 00 pvt. 5 U. S. A., 16 july 00 to 24 apr. 03 2 lt....... 2 apr. 04 to 1 mar. 06 1 lt....... 1 mar. 06 to 1 june 08 1 june 08 to 30 nov. 12 mustered into u. s. ser......27 june 16	2 lt. 71 inf., N. G., N. Y............. 4 feb. 15 to 6 may 15 1 lt................. 6 may 15 accepted.......... 7 may 15 cap..........23 june 16 accepted..........23 june 16	Va. 3 june 80
First Lieutenants				
Mers, Harry, 12 nov. 07	B	mustered into u. s. ser......27 june 16	pvt. co. B, 171 inf., trs. co. B, 71 inf., corp., sgt........10 may 98 to 18 june 07 2 lt. (B), 71 inf......18 june 07 1 lt...............12 nov. 07	N. Y. 27 dec. 62
Callahan, John Jerome, 16 may 11	H	mustered into u. s. ser......27 june 16	pvt. co. A, 22 eng., trs. co. I, 71 inf., corp.............23 feb. 04 to 21 dec. 09 2 lt. 71 inf..........21 dec. 09 1 lt................16 may 11 accepted..........23 may 11	N. Y. 26 feb. 85
Goff, John William Jr., 25 sep. 11	bat. adj.	mustered into u. s. ser......27 june 16	pvt.,co. A, 7 inf., trs. co. I, lance corp., corp., sgt........16 apr. 00 hon. dis........... 7 may 10 pvt................30 may 11 to 13 aug. 11 1 lt. 71 inf..........25 sep. 11 accepted..........29 sep. 11 aide staff division commander....... 3 may 13 to 30 nov. 14	N. Y. 26 sep. 80
Warner, Selden Gloyd, 24 july 13	I	mustered into u. s. ser......27 june	pvt., corp., co. I, 71 inf............17 apr. 068 dec. to 28 june 11 2 lt. 71 inf..........28 june 11 1 lt................24 july 13 accepted..........29 july 13	N. Y. 84

INFANTRY — SEVENTY-FIRST REGIMENT — (Continued)

Name, grade, date of rank and highest brevet rank	Company	Service		Born
		In the armies of U. S. or foreign states	In the National Guard	
First Lieutenants — Continued				
Thomas, Edward Clark Oertel, 18 mar. 14 Distinguished Graduate, N. Y. School of the Line, 1915.	D	mustered into u. s. ser....27 june 16	pvt., corp., sgt., co. L, 22 eng........ 9 apr. 00 to 3 apr. 12 2 lt. c. of e........ 3 apr. 12 1 lt................18 mar. 14 r. l................23 dec. 14 1 lt. c. of e........22 jan. 15 1 lt. 71 inf........14 june 15 accepted..........15 june 15	N. Y. 29 dec. 90
Terry, George Francis, 15 dec. 14	L	mustered into u. s. ser......27 june 16	pvt. co. L, 71 inf.....31 mar. 11 to 6 aug. 12 2 lt. 71 inf......... 6 aug. 12 1 lt...............15 dec. 14 accepted..........18 dec. 14	N. Y. 18 may 87
Dreher, Ernest Carl, 28 dec. 14 Distinguished Graduate, N. Y. School of the Line, 1915.	A	mustered into u. s. ser......27 june 16	pvt., corp., sgt. h. c. 8 inf............ 4 dec. 03 hon. dis...........17 dec. 09 seaman, gunner's mate, 2 class, paymaster's yeoman, 1 div. 1 bat. N. M...20 dec. 09 hon. dis........... 6 jan. 12 2 lt. 71 inf........21 feb. 14 1 lt...............28 dec. 14 accepted.......... 7 jan. 15	N. Y. 25 oct. 88
Lovell, Frederic Kurcsyn, 20 sep. 15 Honor graduate, N. Y. School of the Line, 1915.	E	mustered into u. s. ser......27 june 16	pvt., corp., sgt., co. K, 71 inf..........28 aug. 06 to 9 aug. 13 2 lt............... 9 aug. 13 accepted..........12 aug. 13 1 lt...............20 sep. 15 accepted..........21 sep. 15	N. Y. 14 july 83
Robertson, Ellis Adelbert, 4 apr. 16	M	sgt. co. E, 203 N. Y. inf......11 july 98 mustered into u. s. ser.....27 june 16 to 25 mar. 99	pvt. 39 sep. co.......12 jan. 97 to 15 apr. 99 pvt., sgt. 39 sep. co...23 sep. 98 to 24 oct. 99 pvt., corp., sgt. co. G, 71 inf...........15 jan. 02 to 2 aug. 09 2 lt. 71 inf......... 2 aug. 09 accepted..........12 aug. 09 1 lt............... 4 apr. 16 accepted.......... 7 apr. 16	N. Y. 4 feb. 79
Reinhold, Edgar Van Court, 24 june 16	C	mustered into u. s. ser......27 june 16	pvt., corp., co. C, 71 inf............... 9 apr. 07 to 11 may 14 2 lt...............11 may 14 accepted..........16 may 14 2 lt...............24 june 16 accepted..........24 june 16	N. Y. 1 nov. 86
Beglin, Francis H., 24 june 16	bat. adjt.	mustered into u. s. ser......27 june 16	pvt. co. F..........23 oct. 00 f. and h. dis........23 oct. 06 re-enlisted co. M.... 8 jan. 07 corp.............. 9 june 03 sgt...............25 apr. 05 qm. sgt...........26 feb. 07 bat. sgt. maj.......19 mar. 09 regt. sgt. maj....... 9 nov. 15 1 lt...............24 june 16 accepted..........24 june 16	N. Y. 25 july 73

INFANTRY — SEVENTY-FIRST REGIMENT — *Continued*

Name, grade, date of rank and highest brevet rank	Company	Service — In the armies of U. S. or foreign states	Service — In the National Guard	Born
First Lieutenants — Continued				
Scott, Charles H., 26 june 16	F	mustered into u. s. ser......27 june 16	pvt. co. K..........25 jan. 99 corp...............30 nov. 00 sgt...............4 mar. 04 f. and h. dis........10 jan. 05 re-enlisted.........10 jan. 05 2 lt..............24 mar. 16 accepted..........27 mar. 16 r. l.............22 june 16 1 lt..............26 june 16 accepted..........26 june 16	N. Y. 10 july 74
Strong, Ernest Wales, 7 sep. 16	C	....	pvt. co. A, 5 inf. M. V. M. trs. co. K, 2 inf. M. V. M......7 apr. 02 to 20 feb. 05 pvt., corp., sgt., co. G, 71 inf. N. G., N. Y............16 oct. 04 to 9 nov. 14 2 lt...............9 nov. 14 accepted..........13 nov. 14 1 lt...............7 sep. 16 accepted..........12 sep. 16	Mass. 27 july 83
Second Lieutenants				
Keuhnle, Frederick Charles, 11 feb. 07	m. g. co.	pvt., corp., co. D, 71 N. Y. inf. 2 may 98 to 15 nov. 98 mustered into u. s. ser.....,...26 june 16	pvt., corp., co. D, 71 inf...............1 june 97 to 27 sep. 01 2 lt...............27 sep. 01 1 lt. bat. qm. 71 inf..11 feb. 07 supn., reassigned....21 jan. 08 2 lt. 71 inf.........7 feb. 08	Ger. 21 june 73
Groff, Frank Fisher, 3 june 08	bat. qm. and comy	mustered into u. s. ser.....26 june 16	pvt. co. M, 71 inf....30 dec. 07 to 9 june 08 2 lt. 71 inf.........9 june 08	N. J. 12 nov. 83
Palmer, Russell Booth, 21 june 11	B	pvt. co. B, 71 N. Y. inf......27 june 98 to 15 nov. 98 mustered into u. s. ser.....26 june 16	pvt., co. B, 171 inf...13 may 98 to 13 july 98 pvt., co. B, 71 inf.....16 nov. 98 to 21 june 11 2 lt. 71 inf.........21 june 11 accepted...........27 june 11	N. Y. 1 jan. 74
Hazen, Conrad Phillip, 10 dec. 13	m. g. co.	mustered into u. s. ser......26 june 16	2 lt. 71 inf..........10 dec. 13 accepted...........12 dec. 13	Vt. 7 apr. 84
Granat, Alexander, 26 june 16	K	mustered into u. s. ser......26 june 16 out 6 oct. 16	pvt. co. K..........16 mar. 09 corp...............2 july. 12 sgt...............23 apr. 15 f. and h. dis........25 apr. 15 reenlisted.........20 apr. 16 reenlisted co. K.....9 june 16 1 sgt..............9 june 16 2 lt..............26 june 16 accepted..........26 june 16	Rus. 17 jan. 86
Conway, Harry L., 26 may 16	E	mustered into u. s. ser.....26 june 16	pvt. co. E..........24 sep. 07 corp...............12 oct. 09 sgt...............31 may 10 1 sgt..............17 nov. 11 f. and hon. dis......13 nov. 14 re-enlisted........13 nov. 14 full and hon. dis.....29 feb. 16 re-enlisted.........29 feb. 16 2 lt..............26 may 16 accepted..........29 may 16	N. Y. 14 dec 8 88

INFANTRY — SEVENTY-FIRST REGIMENT — (*Concluded*)

Name, grade, date of rank and highest brevet rank	Company	Service		Born
		In the armies of U. S. or foreign states	In the National Guard	
Second Lieutenants — Continued				
Brown, Amos Thoradike, 19 feb. 15	M	mustered into u. s. ser......26 june 16	2 lt. 12 inf.........19 feb. 15 accepted.........24 feb. 15	Mass. 3 nov. 90
Paton, Thomas Bugard, Jr., 24 feb. 15	I	mustered into u. s. ser......26 june 16	pvt. co. I, 71 inf..... 8 feb. 13 2 lt................24 feb. 15 accepted...........27 feb. 15	N. Y. 6 feb. 90
Lane, John Joseph, 6 mar. 15	A	mustered into u. s. ser......26 june 16	pvt., corp., sgt., 1 sgt. co. A, 71 inf...11 apr. 05 hon. dis.............13 oct. 14 pvt. 71 inf..........13 oct. 14 2 lt. 71 inf.......... 6 mar. 15 accepted........... 9 mar. 15	N. Y. 15 nov. 81
Firth, William De Lamater, 15 may 15	F	mustered into u. s. ser.....26 june 16	pvt. co. G, 71 inf....30 sep. 99 hon. dis............28 jan. 08 pvt., corp., sgt., co. D, 71 inf........25 june 12 to 15 may 15 2 lt................15 may 15 accepted..........18 may 15	N. Y. 10 aug. 78
George, James H., 24 june 16	G	mustered into u. s. ser......26 june 16	pvt. co. F..........15 apr. 02 corp................ 1 dec. 03 sgt................17 jan. 05 1 sgt............... 5 june 08 f. and h. dis........16 mar.09 pvt. co. G.......... 6 july 09 corp................ 2 dec. 10 1 sgt............... 3 feb. 15 f. and h. dis........19 feb. 15 re-enlisted..........19 feb. 15 hon. dis............24 june 16 2 lt................24 june 16 accepted..........24 june 16	Pa. 2 aug. 83
Comstock, Albert E. 24 june 16	C	mustered into u. s. ser......26 june 16	pvt. co. C..........23 apr. 98 corp................26 feb. 07 sgt................25 nov. 10 f. and h. dis........ 5 mar. 15 re-enlisted.......... 2 apr. 15 1 sgt............... 9 nov. 15 2 lt................24 june 16 accepted..........24 june 16	N. Y. 3 nov. 75
Chaplain First Lieutenant				
Crocker, William Tufts, 22 nvo. 12	......	mustered into u. s. ser......26 june 16	corp. 5 co. Mass. provisional militia....29 aug. 98 hon. dis............15 apr. 99 chaplain, 71 inf. N. G., N. Y........22 nov. 12 accepted..........26 nov. 12	Mass. 9 sep. 62

13

INFANTRY — (*Continued*)
SEVENTY-FOURTH REGIMENT
(Twelve Companies)
(Fourth Brigade)
Armory, 184 Connecticut Street, Buffalo

In June 1854, the organization of the regiment commenced. Co. D of the 65th Regiment forming the nucleus. Co. B was organized in August, and Companies C and E in September, 1854; Co. A was formed in May, 1855; and these five companies constituted the regiment until February, 1858, when two companies, one of cavalry (R) and one of rifles (L) were organized and attached to it. In 1860 Companies F, G, H and I were organized, and the designation of Co. L was in 1865 changed to Co. K. Co. R was disbanded in 1865. Co. H in 1868; Co. I was consolidated with Co. B in 1870, and in 1882 Companies E and K were disbanded. Co. E was reorganized in 1886, and Co. H in 1891. New Co. I was organized January 4, 1906. In May, 1861, nearly the whole of Companies B, C, D and F joined and formed four companies of the 21st N. Y. Volunteers. June 19, 1863, the regiment was mustered into the service of the United States for thirty days, and mustered out August 8, 1863; it was remustered into the United States service November 16, 1863, for thirty days, and mustered out December 16, 1863. During the War of the Rebellion the regiment furnished to the country nearly 300 officers and over 1,000 men, who received their military instruction while members of it. Companies L and M were authorized by G. O. 64, A. G. O., November 10, 1908, to be mustered in. The regiment was authorized to organize a detachment of mounted scouts by Special Orders No. 89, April 11, 1912. The regiment performed duty at the street car riots, Buffalo, April, 1913, and riots at Depew, March, 1914.
Co. K of this regiment, is quartered in the State Armory at Tonawanda. It was organized May 29, 1891. Was assigned to 1st Battalion as Co. G, December 22, 1898; and to the 74th Regiment, as Co. K, March 30, 1907. On duty at Tonawanda to suppress a riot in June, 1892; at Buffalo during the riots in August, 1892, at Tonawanda again in June, 1893, during a riot at that place and at the street car riots, Buffalo, April, 1913. In United States service, as Co. G, 3d Regiment, N. Y. Infantry, from May 17, 1898, to December 7, 1898.
Recognition extended by War Department under Act of June 3, 1916, to Companies F, G, L, M, Machine Gun Company, on June 24, 1916; to Companies I and K, on June 26, 1916; to Company E, on June 28, 1916; to Company H, on June 30, 1916; to Companies A, B, D and Sanitary Detachment, on July 1, 1916; to Headquarters Company and Supply Company, on July 1, 1916.
The regiment has received authority to place silver rings on the lances of its colors, engraved as follows:
On the National Color.— Gettysburg campaign, 1863; Buffalo, November and December, 1863.
On the State Color.— Draft riots, 1863; negro riot, 1864; Fenian invasion of Canada, 1866; Hornellsville, 1877; Buffalo, 1892.

INFANTRY — SEVENTY-FOURTH REGIMENT

Name, grade, date of rank and highest brevet rank	Company	Service		Born
		In the armies of U. S. or foreign states	In the National Guard	
Colonel				
Thurston, Nathaniel Blunt, 27 june 16 bvt. col......18 sep. 02	hdqrs. div.	lt. col. 22 N. Y. inf., 1 may 98 to 23 nov. 98 mustered into u. s. ser...... 2 july 16	pvt., corp., 1 sgt., co. E, 22 inf...... 6 aug. 77 to 11 feb. 80 2 lt................11 feb. 80 1 lt................ 6 apr. 80 cap................20 dec. 86 maj. 22 inf........28 july 96 lt. col.............14 may 98 i. s. a. p. and o. o. staff, c. g., N. G. lt. col............31 dec. 98 reappointed with o. r.11 jan. 00 supn., reassigned....21 jan. 08 lt. col. o. d.........30 jan. 08 recommissioned with o. r............. 7 may 08 special duty, under brevet, rank of col. and assigned com. 13 C. D. C.......15 june 14 relieved from com. 13 C. D. C.........11 dec. 15 col................27 june 16 accepted..........27 june 16	N. Y. 12 apr. 57

INFANTRY — SEVENTY-FOURTH REGIMENT — (Continued)

Name, grade, date of rank and highest brevet rank	Company	Service		Born
		In the armies of U. S. or foreign states	In the National Guard	
Lieutenant Colonel				
White, George H., 7 july 16	......	1 lt. 35 Mich. inf. 9 july 98 hon. must. out, 31 mar. 99 1 lt. 42 u. s. inf., 17 aug. 99 accepted...26 aug. 99 h. m. out..27 june 01 1 lt. 16 inf. 2 feb. 01 accepted...14 sep. 01 trs. to 9 inf.31 may 10 cap. 16 inf.23 june 10 unassigned.19 may 13 mustered into u. s. ser...... 2 july 16	lt. col.............. 7 july 16 accepted........... 7 july 16	Mich. 17 sep. 70
Majors				
Kemp, Arthur, 20 apr. 11 Graduate, Garrison schools, 1915.	......	mustered into u. s. ser...... 2 july 16	pvt., corp., sgt., co., H, 74 inf........27 may 91 to 18 may 98 2 lt................18 may 98 1 lt................ 9 feb. 99 cap...............18 nov. 03 maj. 74 inf........20 apr. 11 accepted..........21 apr. 11	N. Y. 7 may 73
Pooley, William Richard, 16 nov. 11 Graduate, Garrison Schools, 1915.	......	mustered into u. s. ser...... 2 july 16	pvt., corp., sgt., co. F, 74 inf........31 mar. 92 to 3 apr. 03 1 lt................ 3 apr. 03 cap............... 5 apr. 05 maj...............16 nov. 11 accepted..........20 nov. 11	N. Y. 5 oct. 73
Wood, Lyman Adelbert, 1 july 16	D	mustered into u. s. ser...... 2 july 16	pvt., corp., sgt., 1 sgt., co. D, 74 inf..20 feb. 93 hon. dis..........25 apr. 98 pvt., 1 sgt., co. B, 74 inf..............13 sep. 99 to 25 mar. 03 2 lt................25 mar. 03 1 lt................21 july 04 major.............. 1 july 16 accepted.......... 1 july 16	N. Y. 17 mar. 66
Captains				
Hubbell, Lyman Parsons, 10 apr. 08	qm.	mustered into u. s. ser...... 2 july 16	pvt., co. F, color bearer, 74 inf.....23 mar. 96 to 25 aug. 05 1 lt. bat. qm........25 aug. 05 supn., reassigned....21 jan. 08 2 lt. 74 inf.........24 feb. 08 cap...............20 apr. 08	N. Y. 19 nov. 74
Minniss, George Stewart, 30 dec. 08	L	mustered into u. s. ser...... 2 july 16	pvt., co. F, 74 inf....1 mar. 97 to 27 oct. 00 pvt., lance corp., corp., sgt., 1 sgt. co. E...........17 nov. 00 to 17 july 05 1 lt (F), 74 inf......17 july 05 cap. 74 inf.......... 6 jan. 09 accepted............11 jan. 09	Pa. 26 oct. 71
Kendall, Charles Adams, 24 may 12	comy	mustered into u. s. ser...... 2 july 16	pvt., corp., co. H, 74 inf., regt. sgt. maj. 74 inf............11 sep. 99 to 15 mar. 04 1 lt. bat. adj. 74 inf..15 mar. 04 cap...............24 may 12 accepted..........25 may 12	Can. 30 dec. 71

INFANTRY — SEVENTY-FOURTH REGIMENT — (Continued)

Name, grade, date of rank and highest brevet rank	Company	Service		Born
		In the armies of U. S. or foreign states	In the National Guard	
Captains — Continued				
Gillig, Alexander Lorens, 25 may 12	H	mustered into u. s. ser..... 2 july 16	pvt., corp., sgt., co. A, 74 inf......... 5 nov. 98 to 18 nov. 03 2 lt...............18 nov. 03 1 lt................ 3 aug. 04 bat. adj. 74 inf. with o. r.............17 july 07 cap.............25 may 12 accepted.........27 may 12	N. Y. 22 jan. 81
Robertson, Ralph Kenyon, 1 apr. 13	I	mustered into u. s. ser..... 2 july 16	2 lt. (A), 74 inf......19 dec. 06 1 lt...............17 dec. 07 cap................ 1 apr. 13 accepted.......... 3 apr. 13	N. Y. 24 apr. 83
Branch, Clifford Ernest, 9 nov. 14	m. g. co.	mustered into u. s. ser...... 2 july 16	pvt., corp., sgt., co. E, 74 inf.........23 may 04 to 30 june 09 2 lt. 74 inf.........30 june 09 1 lt..............17 may 12 cap............. 9 nov. 14 accepted.........10 nov. 14	Pa. 15 oct. 79
Bagnall, Henry Dickson, 23 nov. 14 Graduate, Garrison Schools, 1915.	F	mustered into u. s. ser..... 2 july 16	2 lt. 74 inf.......... 1 apr. 10 1 lt........ .....11 jan. 13 cap.............23 nov. 14 accepted.........24 nov. 14	N. Y. 8 feb. 85
Sandburg, Charles Amel, 1 mar. 15	E	pvt. co. K, 202 N. Y. inf...... 1 aug. 98 to 15 apr. 99 mustered into u. s. ser..... 2 july 16	pvt. 113 sep. co.... .23 may 98 to 31 nov. 98 pvt., corp., sgt., 13 sep. co..........25 may 99 to 15 july 13 2 lt...............15 july 13 cap.............. 1 mar. 15 accepted.......... 2 mar. 15	Pa. 21 feb. 74
Maldiner, Frank John, 18 june 15	K	mustered nto u. s. ser...... 2 july 16	pvt. co. G, 74 inf....10 jan. 06 to 12 oct. 06 pvt. co. K, 74 inf....24 june 07 to 7 dec. 08 9 aug. 09 to 6 dec. 09 25 mar. 12 to 21 feb. 14 2 lt................21 feb. 14 1 lt................ 5 aug. 14 cap...........18 june 15 accepted.........21 june 15	N. Y. 13 dec. 89
Kean, Thomas Vincent, 2 dec. 15	G	mustered into u. s. ser...... 2 july 16	pvt., corp., sgt., 1 sgt., co. G, 74 inf..29 apr. 03 to 6 may 11 2 lt. 74 inf.......... 6 may 11 1 lt...............27 jan. 13 cap................ 2 dec. 15 accepted.......... 6 dec. 15	N. Y. 25 mar. 85
Millar, Oliver Frank, 10 aug. 16	bat. adj.	mustered into u. s. ser...... 2 july 16	pvt., corp., sgt. co. D., 74 inf.........29 jan. 02 2 lt. 74 inf.........29 sep. 11 1 lt..............12 nov. 14 accepted.........16 nov. 14 cap..............10 aug. 16 accepted...........16 aug. 16	N. Y. 16 july 83

INFANTRY — SEVENTY-FOURTH REGIMENT — (*Continued*)

Name, grade, date of rank and highest brevet rank	Company	Service		Born
		In the armies of U. S. or foreign states	In the National Guard	
Captains — Continued				
Cadotte, Damase Joseph, 6 oct. 16	B	mustered into u. s. ser...... 2 july 16	pvt., corp., sgt., co. F, 74 inf..........28 mar. 98 to 26 sep. 05 2 lt. (F) 74 inf.......26 sep. 05 1 lt. 74 inf.........15 mar. 09 cap. o. d.............20 nov. 12 cap. 74 inf.........15 may 14 accepted..........18 may 14 cap.............. 6 oct. 16 accepted.......... 6 oct. 16	Can. 9 aug. 74
Taggart, Charles Joseph, 3 nov. 16	M	mustered into u. s. ser...... 2 july 16	pvt., corp., sgt., co. H, 74 inf........ 3 aug. 99 to 14 oct. 12 1 lt. 74 inf.........14 oct. 12 accepted..........20 nov. 16 cap.............. 3 nov. 16 accepted..........20 nov. 16	Can. 12 sep. 79
Knuebel, John Herman, Jr., 25 nov. 14	I	mustered into u. s. ser...... 1 dec. 16	pvt., corp., sgt., co. H, 74 inf........ 6 may 07 to 9 aug .13 2 lt............. 9 aug. 13 hon. dis.........29 dec. 13 1 lt............. 3 aug. 14 accepted.......... 4 aug. 14 cap.............25 nov. 16 accepted..........28 nov. 16	N. Y. 10 feb. 89
First Lieutenants				
Ziegler, Edwin George, 19 june 12	bat. adj.	mustered into u. s. ser...... 2 july 16	pvt., corp., co. H, 74 inf., trs. co. I..... 2 dec. 01 to 1 mar. 06 2 lt. (I), 74 inf....... 1 mar. 06 1 lt...............19 june 12 accepted..........20 june 12	N. Y. 17 oct. 83
Kaffenberger, Karl Gustav, 18 nov. 14	C	mustered into u. s. ser...... 2 july 16	2 lt. 74 inf..........15 july 13 1 lt...............18 nov. 14 accepted..........20 nov. 14	N. Y. 22 june 90
Pilcher, Edward Sargent, 3 nov. 14	A	mustered into u. s. ser...... 2 july 16	pvt. co. G, 23 inf., trs. tr. C, att. 2 brig.............26 dec. 96 to 10 may 04 pvt., sgt., tr. 7, 1 cav.. 7 may 12 hon. dis......... 8 aug. 13 2 lt. 74 inf.........15 aug. 13 1 lt...............30 nov. 14 accepted.......... 2 dec. 14	Mich. 3 oct. 76
McMichael, Clarence R., 24 nov. 14	L	mustered into u. s. ser...... 2 july 16	pvt. co. A, 74 inf.....12 may 91 to 9 apr. 94 pvt. co. A, trs. f. m. agt., trs. band..... 8 nov. 97 hon. dis.........13 apr. 08 pvt., 1 sgt., co. L, 74 inf..............29 dec. 08 to 2 aug. 09 2 lt. 74 inf......... 2 aug. 09 1 lt...............24 nov. 14 accepted..........26 nov. 14	N. Y. 14 mar. 73
Baxter, Melvin Leonard, 5 feb. 15	F	mustered into u. s. ser...... 2 july 16	1 lt. 74 inf.......... 5 feb. 15 accepted........... 8 feb. 15	Wyo. 7 jan. 89

INFANTRY — SEVENTY-FOURTH REGIMEN — (Continued)

Name, grade, date of rank and highest brevet rank	Company	Service		Born
		In the armies of U. S. or foreign states	In the National Guard	
First Lieutenants — Continued				
Fast, Harold Rea, 16 feb. 16	E	mustered into u. s. ser..... 2 july 16	pvt., corp., sgt., co. E, 74 inf..........18 may 08 2 lt.............. 4 mar. 15 accepted.......... 8 mar. 15 1 lt..............16 feb. 16 accepted..........21 feb. 16	Ind. 30 july 88
Rignel, Charles Homer, 26 apr. 16	bat. adj.	mustered into u. s. ser..... 2 july 16	pvt., corp., sgt., co. H, 74 inf..........15 dec. 02 to 18 apr. 12 2 lt. 74 inf.......18 apr. 12 accepted..........22 apr. 12 1 lt..............26 apr. 16 accepted.......... 1 may 16	N. Y. 2 aug. 80
Roos, James J., 22 mar. 16	G	74 co. c. a. c. u. s. a., — june 08 corp......13 oct. 08 sgt.......25 mar. 09 observer 1 cl. and gunner 1 cl., 27 oct. 10 f. and h. dis., — june 11 mustered into u. s. ser...... 1 july 16	pvt. co. F..........19 jan. 04 corp..........22 july 07 hon. dis............ 1 june 08 1 lt..............22 mar. 16 accepted..........22 mar. 16	N. Y. 24 july 83
Harp, Alonzo Mordecai, 10 may 16	D	pvt. co. A, 202 N. Y. inf......14 july 98 to 16 jan. 99	pvt., corp., sgt., 1 sgt. co, D, 74 inf...19 apr. 99 to dec. 14 2 lt........... 2 dec. 14 accepted.......... 5 dec. 14 1 lt..............10 may 16 accepted..........12 may 16	N. Y. 5 oct. 78
Peterson, Auguste B., 21 june 16	E	mustered into u. s. ser...... 1 july 16	pvt. co. E..........14 apr. 10 dropped...........17 oct. 10 taken up..........29 feb. 12 dropped........... 1 sep. 13 taken up..........14 oct. 13 dropped...........13 apr. 14 taken up..........24 jan. 16 corp............19 apr. 16 1 lt. 65 inf.........21 june 16 accepted..........23 june 16 trs. to co. E, 74 inf...27 june 16	N. Y. 8 feb. 88
Shaw, Lyman Aldrich, 21 june 16	M	mustered into u. s. ser...... 1 july 16	pvt. co. F, 74 inf.....23 mar. 09 hon. dis...........10 mar. 13 2 lt..............18 mar. 15 accepted..........20 mar. 15 1 lt..............21 june 16 accepted..........28 june 16	Miss. 23 jan. 90
Smith, Joseph W., 23 june 16	A	mustered into u. s. ser...... 4 july 16	pvt. co. D, M. V. M.. 2 aug. 04 discharged.......... 5 june 08 2 lt..............23 mar. 14 discharged.........30 nov. 15 2 lt. 74 inf.......16 june 16 accepted..........17 june 16 1 lt..............23 june 16 accepted..........23 june 16	Eng. 11 july 84

INFANTRY — SEVENTY-FOURTH REGIMENT — *(Continued)*

Name, grade, date of rank and highest brevet rank	Company	Service		Born
		In the armies of U. S. or foreign states	In the National Guard	
First Lieutenants — Continued				
Crosby, Harry Edmund, 23 sep. 16	K	pvt. co. H, 3 N. Y. inf......17 may 98 to 30 nov. 98 mustered into u. s. ser......1 july 16	pvt., corp., 1 sep. co..............1 feb. 98 to 3 apr. 00 pvt., corp., sgt., 1 sgt. co. F, 74 inf......12 nov. 01 hon. dis..........16 sep. 07 pvt. co. F, bat. sgt. maj............8 june 11 to 12 dec. 13 2 lt. 74 inf..........12 dec. 13 accepted..........13 dec. 13 1 lt...............23 sep. 16 accepted..........23 sep. 16	N. Y. 11 may 79
Moyer, Charles Samuel, 14 nov. 16	H	mustered into u. s ser......1 july 16	pvt., co. G, 74 inf.... 3 oct. 10 to 14 mar. 13 2 lt..........14 mar. 13 accepted..........17 mar. 13 1 lt...........14 nov. 16 accepted..........18 nov. 16	N. Y. 5 june 84
Tuttle, Albert Leon, 25 nov. 16	I	mustered into u. s. ser......1 july 16	pvt., corp., sgt., co. I, 74 inf..........16 jan. 11 to 16 july 13 2 lt...........16 july 13 accepted..........23 july 13 1 lt...........25 nov. 16 accepted..........28 nov. 16	N. Y. 24 july 84
Wallace, George Francis, 25 nov. 16	hdqr. co.	mustered into u. s. ser......1 july 16	pvt., corp., sgt., co. L, 74 inf..........9 nov. 09 to 13 oct. 13 pvt. co. L, 74 inf.....17 feb. 15 to 1 june 15 2 lt...............1 june 15 accepted..........5 june 15 1 lt...........25 nov. 16 accepted..........28 nov. 16	N. Y. 8 nov. 90
Donnocker, Chas. J., 25 nov. 16	H	mustered into u. s. ser......1 dec. 16	pvt. co. E..........15 may 11 corp..........8 dec. 13 sgt..........30 dec. 14 f. and h. dis........7 june 15 2 lt...............22 mar. 16 accepted..........22 mar. 16 1 lt...........25 nov. 16 accepted..........29 nov. 16	N. Y. 5 june 93
Second Lieutenants				
Phillips, Charles R, 22 mar. 16	F	mustered into u. s. ser......1 july 16	2 lt...............22 mar. 16 accepted..........22 mar. 16	Iowa 17 feb. 87
Robinson, Joseph H., 1 july 16	D	mustered into u. s. ser......1 july 16	pvt. co. D, ...25 sep. 99 corp..............16 oct. 05 sgt..........26 july 09 1 sgt..........22 mar. 15 f. and h. dis........1 june 15 re-enlisted..........1 june 15 2 lt...............14 aug. 16 accepted..........24 aug. 16	N. Y. 26 nov. 3
Coulter, Wm. D., 1 july 16	M	mustered into u. s. ser......1 july 16	pvt. co. D..........9 nov. 89 f. and h. dis........14 dec. 96 re-enlisted..........22 feb. 09 f. and h. dis........1 mar. 15 re-enlisted..........1 mar. 15 2 lt...............1 july 16 accepted..........1 july 16	Can. 11 sep. 69

INFANTRY — SEVENTY-FOURTH REGIMENT — (*Concluded*)

Name, grade, date of rank and highest brevet rank	Company	Service		Born
		In the armies of U. S. or foreign states	In the National Guard	
Second Lieutenants — Continued				
Taggart, William E., 1 july 16	K	mustered into u. s. ser...... 1 july 16	pvt. co. H......... 3 apr. 00 corp.............25 apr. 02 1 sgt.............30 apr. 06 f. and h. dis........ 7 june 15 re-enlisted......... 7 june 15 f. and h. dis........23 june 16 re-enlisted.........23 june 16 2 lt.............. 1 july 16 accepted.......... 1 july 16	Can. 21 jan. 78
Spawton, Fred G., 1 july 16	M	mustered into u. s. ser...... 1 july 16	pvt. co. M.........11 feb. 11 corp.............28 july 11 sgt.............19 july 15 f. and h. dis........21 feb. 16 re-enlisted.........21 feb. 16 2 lt.............. 1 july 16 accepted......... 1 july 16	N. Y. 2 jan. 82
Milsom, George A., 1 july 16	sup. co.	pvt. co. B, 19 u. s. inf. 1894; disch. as 1 sgt; re-enlisted as 1 sgt; disch. aug. 98; clerk on transport Meade, aug. 98 to sep. 99; chief clerk, qm. dept., Tacoma, Wash.; Zamboanga P. I., Manila, P. I. and N. Y. City.	pvt. co. A.......... 4 aug. 88 corp.............11 aug. 90 pvt. co. F.......... 4 aug. 93 2 lt.............. 1 july 16 accepted............. july 16	N. Y. 6 mar. 73
Kline, Charles L., 7 oct. 16	K	mustered into u. s. ser...... 2 july 16	pvt. co. C.........21 may 13 1 sgt.............30 may 13 f. and h. dis........12 june 16 re-enlisted, 2 lt...... 7 oct. 16 accepted.......... 8 oct. 16	Ger. 19 feb. 86
O'Rourke, Edw. H., 14 nov. 16	A	mustered into u. s. ser......12 dec. 16	pvt. co. D.........29 dec. 13 corp.............25 jan. 15 sgt.............. 1 july 16 2 lt.............14 nov. 16 accepted.........19 nov. 16	......
Wright, Richard D., 25 nov. 16	I	mustered into u. s. ser......12 dec. 16	pvt. co. C.........21 oct. 12 corp............. 7 apr. 13 dropped.........20 july 14 taken up......... 8 nov. 15 sgt.............10 feb. 16 2 lt.............25 nov. 16 accepted.........28 nov. 16	N. Y. 24 mar. 95
King, Delaney, 25 nov. 16	m.g. co.	mustered into u. s. ser......14 dec. 16	pvt. co. F.........21 feb. 16 corp.............25 june 16 2 lt.............25 nov. 16 accepted..........28 nov. 16	N. Y. 22 dec. 93 nn
Mackay, Harold G., 27 dec. 16	m. g.	....	pvt. co. E.........15 may 11 dropped......... 8 jan. 12 taken up.........23 sep. 12 corp.............23 feb. 14 sgt.............22 feb. 15 f. and h. dis........24 may 15 re-enlisted.......... 2 lt.............27 dec. 16 accepted.........27 dec. 16	Mass. 22 dec.
Chaplain				
Ward, John C., 20 jan. 16	......	....	chaplain...........20 jan. 16 accepted..........22 jan. 16	N. Y. 27 aug. 73

RETIRED OFFICERS

NAME, GRADE AND DATE OF RANK	RETIRED		Residence
	Organisation	Date	
MAJOR GENERAL			
Roe, Charles Francis, 9 feb. 98........	National Guard......	1 may 12	New York.
BRIGADIER GENERALS			
Austen, David Elwell (bvt. maj. gen.), 12 sep. 08.	chief of c. a..,......	31 dec. 11	Brooklyn.
Eddy, John G., 11 nov. 07...........	2 brig............	17 aug. 16	Brooklyn.
Fox, George C., 15 jul. 11...........	National Guard.....	15 jul. 11	Buffalo.
Henry, Nelson Herrick (bvt. maj. gen.), 1 jan. 02.	The a. g. S. N. Y....	31 may 10	New York.
McLeer, James (bvt. maj. gen.), 13 oct. 85.	2 brig..............	11 nov. 07	Brooklyn.
Morris, William F., 7 may, 1914......	chief, c. a...........	15 jun. 14	New York.
Oliver, Robert Shaw, 30 dec. 90......	3 brig.............	1 sep. 03	Washington, D. C.
Pettebone, Lauren Woodruff (bvt. maj. gen.), 4 feb. 02.	4 brig.............	10 apr. 11	Niagara Falls.
Smith, George Moore (bvt. maj. gen.), 4 mar. 98.	1 brig............	31 dec. 11	New York.
Welch, Samuel M. (bvt. maj. gen.), 16 jun. 11.	4 brig.............	1 may 15	Buffalo.
COLONELS			
Appleton, Daniel (bvt. maj. gen.), 6 aug. 89.	7 inf...............	23 feb. 16	New York.
Barthman, Henry Charles, 7 dec. 07...	47 inf..............	5 feb. 14	Brooklyn.
Camp, John T., 18 jan. 86...........	22 regt............	15 jun. 96	New York.
Cavanagh, James (bvt. brig. gen.), 29 nov. 67.	69 inf..............	1 dec. 93	New York.
Cole, Ashley William, 11 jan. 95......	supn...............	24 may 15	England.
Davis, Charles Otis (bvt. brig. gen.), 23 nov. 08.	13 c. d. c.........	15 jun. 14	Brooklyn.
Depew, Chauncey M., 7 jul. 12.......	j. a. 5 div.........	26 feb. 12	New York.
Duffy, Edward (bvt. brig. gen.), 13 apr. 98.	69 inf..............	12 mar. 09	New York.
Francis, Augustus T. (bvt. brig. gen.), 3 jun. 98.	171 inf.............	23 jun. 99	New York.
Gildersleeve, Henry A., 5 oct. 74.....	supn...............	19 mar. 12	New York.
Huston, Thomas William, 18 mar. 12..	12 inf..............	23 apr. 13	New York.
Jussen, Carl, 7 oct. 74..............	1 div..............	18 mar. 12	New York.
Kline, Ardolph Loges (bvt. brig. gen.), 6 may 01.	14 regt............	1 jan. 06	Brooklyn.
Ladd, William W., 11 jan. 16........	J. A. G. dept......	26 sep. 16	New York.
Olin, Stephen Henry, 24 feb. 98......	asst. a. g. N. G...	5 mar. 03	New York.
Pruyn, John Isaac (bvt. brig. gen.), 25 jun. 08.	10 inf.............	24 jun. 10	Yonkers.
Reichert, Louis P., 6 may 78.........	supn..............	21 may 15	Buffalo.
Sanger, William Cary, 31 dec. 99......	insp. National Guard.	27 feb. 02	Sangerfield.
Sauvan, Frank Olin, 23 apr. 14.......	8 c. d. c.........	27 apr. 14	New York.
Stokes, William A. (bvt. brig. gen.), 23 sep. 04.	23 inf.............	24 jun. 09	Brooklyn.
Story, Joseph Grafton (bvt. maj. gen.), 20 jan. 80.	asst. a. g. S. N. Y....	31 dec. 11	New York.
Wolf, Charles J., 31 aug.. 11........	74 inf.............	26 jun. 16	Buffalo.
LIEUTENANT COLONELS			
Bakewell, Allan C., 11 oct. 98........	supn..............	22 may 15	New York.
Bendell, Herman, (bvt. col.), 11 dec. 11	National Guard......	11 dec. 11	Albany.
Bogart, John, 21 apr. 98............	eng. National Guard..	15 jan. 06	New York.
Cleveland, James Wray (bvt. col.), 27 feb. 02.	insp.-gen...........	15 aug. 08	New York.
Cottle, Edmund Petrie (bvt. col.), 20 jun. 94.	74 inf..............	18 feb. 11	Buffalo.
Crego, Floyd Stranahan, 2 apr. 98.....	surg. 4 brig.......	6 jan. 04	Buffalo.
Cushman, Harry Curtis, 8 jan. 91.....	asst. a. g. 3 brig...	8 feb. 04	Albany.
Fisk, Willard Clinton (bvt. col.), 30 apr. 15.	7 inf..............	30 apr. 15	New York.
Healy, Charles, 5 sep. 11............	69 inf..............	24 mar. 14	New York.
Hurry, Gilford, 26 mar. 98...........	chief comy. div.......	1 may 12	New York.

RETIRED OFFICERS — (Continued)

NAME, GRADE AND DATE OF RANK	RETIRED		Residence
	Organization	Date	

LIEUTENANT COLONELS — Continued

Japha, Solomon E., 3 jan. 02.........	c. a. c...............	10 apr. 12	New York.
Kipp, William H. (bvt. brig. gen.), 14 sep. 95.	7 inf................	3 feb. 08	New York.
Kirkland, William James, 5 aug. 98....	supn................	24 may 15	New York.
Knapp, Louis H., 3 jun. 82........	4 div...............	18 nov. 12	Buffalo.
La Rose, Anthime Watson, 30 jun. 11..	National Guard.....	30 jun. 11	Albany.
Lawrence, Abram B., 2 jan. 83........	4 div...............	11 mar. 12	Warsaw.
Lilliendahl, John G. R. (bvt. col.), 9 may 06.	22 eng..............	6 may 14	New York.
Manning, James Hilton, 30 jun. 11....	National Guard.....	30 jun. 11	Albany
Palmer, Charles N., 27 Oct. 79.......	4 div...............	12 mar. 12	Lockport.
Rasmus, Carl Gerhard, (bvt. col.), 30 dec. 10.	23 inf...............	25 aug. 13	Cedarhurst, L. I.
Ridabock, Henry G., 2 mar. 99........	8 inf................	19 jan. 06	New York.
Russell, George D. (bvt. col.), 11 may 99.	c. a. c...............	26 feb. 08	Norwalk, Conn.
Schilling, Francis A., 14 dec. 70.......	8 arty...............	20 apr. 12	New York.
Storey, James H., 15 mar. 80........	2 div...............	20 feb. 12	Brooklyn.
Todd, Charles Griswold (bvt. col.), 25 nov. 04.	23 inf...............	15 mar. 07	Brooklyn.
Treadwell, Harry Hayden (bvt. col.), 24 jan. 99.	22 eng..............	6 oct. 05	New York.

MAJORS

Abeel, Alfred Havens, 23 aug. 00......	a. g. dept............	11 mar. 12	New York.
Babcock, Louis Locke, 20 jan. 03......	4 brig..............	13 aug. 15	Buffalo.
Barnie, Alexander, 17 jun. 92........	o. d.................	5 mar. 12	Brooklyn.
Barrett, Frank Brower, 23 oct. 12.....	1 f. a...............	5 may 14	New York.
Bascom, George J., 3 jun. 98........	171 inf..............	26 mar. 12	Mt. Vernon.
Bissell, William Grosvenor, 7 oct. 97..	74 inf...............	24 feb. 14	Buffalo.
Briggs, Albert Henry (bvt. lt. col.), 23 apr. 83.	m. c................	31 dec. 11	Buffalo.
Burr, Daniel Swift (bvt. lt. col.), 2 may 99.	surg. 1 inf..........	25 mar. 07	Binghamton.
Butler, Mighells B. (bvt. lt. col.), 22 dec. 98.	3 inf................	4 jan. 13	Niagara Falls.
Chase, James T., 29 mar. 98..........	12 bat..............	9 mar. 99	New York.
Christoffel, John B. (bvt. lt. col.), 8 oct. 08.	o. d.................	1 aug. 10	Brooklyn.
Cipollari, Joseph, 8 mar. 09..........	8 c. d...............	5 feb. 14	Lynnbrook, L. I.
Cleminshaw, Charles G., 8 sep. 99.....	comy. of sub. 3 brig...	6 jan. 04	Troy.
Cochran, Henry Lord (bvt. lt. col.), 21 mar. 98.	m. c................	18 sep. 09	Brooklyn.
Colles, Christopher John (bvt. lt. col.), 28 aug. 99.	m. c................	23 feb. 15	New York.
Content, Washington, 22 jan. 97......	12 inf...............	24 jan. 01	New York.
de Forest, Henry P., 17 jan. 00........	m. c................	18 may 12	New York.
de Russy, Rene A., 3 oct. 08.........	12 inf...............	1 jul. 10	New York.
Disbrow, Robert N., 16 apr. 13.......	m. c................	6 oct. 16	New York.
Doty, Alvah H., 8 mar. 88...........	surg. 9 regt.........	20 may 97	New York.
Earle, Eugene M., 6 may 75..........	supn................	21 may 15	Brooklyn.
Fisher, Harris B., 1 dec. 98..........	1 brig..............	11 mar. 12	Pelham Manor.
Gedney, Frederick G., 17 jan. 81......	supn................	24 may 15	New York.
Green, Lansdale B., 13 jan. 04........	q. m. c.............	5 jul. 16	Troy.
Hicks, Horace Madison, 17 feb. 10.....	m. c................	15 jul. 12	Amsterdam.
Holland, John B. (bvt. col.), 25 feb. 98	a. d. c. staff maj. gen. com. N. G.	15 jan. 08	New York.
Houston, David Walker, 25 nov. 98....	m. c................	24 jan. 10	Troy.
Hyatt, James Levinus (bvt. lt. col.), 11 may 00.	10 bat..............	15 jan. 03	Albany.
Jackson, Thomas Edmund (bvt. lt. col.), 2 apr. 03.	47 inf..............	21 dec. 11	Brooklyn.
Jarrett, Arthur Richard, 19 jun. 12....	m. c................	22 apr. 14	Brooklyn.
Jarvis, Nathan S., 14 dec. 99.........	m. c................	19 feb. 12	New York.
Jones, Samuel Case, 8 jun. 07........	3 inf................	2 may 13	Rochester.
Kirby, William Maurice (bvt. maj. gen.), 31 dec. 98.	o. d.................	31 dec. 11	Auburn.
Linson, William H. (bvt. lt. col.), 14 jun. 00.	71 inf..............	8 apr. 10	New York.

RETIRED OFFICERS — (*Continued*)

Name, Grade and Date of Rank	Retired		Residence
	Organization	Date	

MAJORS — *Continued*

Marsh, Edward T. T., 4 mar. 85......	surg. 71 inf..........	23 may 06	New York.
Martin, Frank Adrian, 24 may 07....	23 inf...............	26 mar. 09	Brooklyn.
Mitchell, Edmund Harmon, 13 dec. 97.	14 inf...............	12 jan. 05	Brooklyn.
Mott, Seldon Whitney (bvt. lt. col.), 20 aug. 08.	2 inf...............	1 may 13	Hudson Falls.
Mynotte, William Thomas, 5 jan. 10...	23 inf...............	28 oct. 13	Brooklyn.
Nugent, Arthur Wellesley (bvt. lt. col.), 6 apr. 11.	10 inf...............	29 jan. 14	Yonkers.
Pettit, James F., 5 jan. 77...........	44 bat..............	11 mar. 12	Binghamton.
Poillon, Richard H., 17 sep. 79........	4 brig..............	5 aug. 86	New York.
Reville, Philip E., 23 may 07.........	69 inf..............	16 may 13	Brooklyn.
Richmond, Harry Signa, 7 oct. 11.....	1 cav...............	10 jun. 14	Albany.
Russell, Nelson G., 13 mar. 10.......	m. c...............	25 jan. 13	Buffalo.
Sadler, John Timothy (bvt. lt. col.), 25 mar. 04.	3 inf...............	16 oct. 12	Elmira.
Scott, Walter, 1 apr. 98.............	17 bat.............	9 mar. 99	Oneonta.
Sheldon, Theodore Butler (bvt. lt. col.), 9 dec. 02.	a. g. dept..........	25 feb. 11	Buffalo.
Smith, Eugene Alfred, 10 feb. 04.....	m. c...............	28 jan. 10	Buffalo.
Smith, Harrie Eugene, 1 may 05......	m. c...............	10 feb. 10	Mt. Vernon.
Smith, Lee H., 30 mar. 00...........	ord. dept...........	5 jul. 16	Buffalo.
Stevenson, Frederick Harper, 13 sep. 06	14 inf...............	3 dec. 13	Brooklyn.
Thomas, Frederic Chichester, 8 mar. 00.	1 brig..............	11 mar. 12	New York.
Walton, John D. (bvt. lt. col.), 14 feb. 02.	9 arty.............	19 may 13	New York.
Wood, Frederick J. J. (bvt. lt. col.), 22 dec. 07.	m. c...............	8 apr. 10	Brooklyn.
Yates, Austin A., 1 apr. 98..........	2 inf...............	29 jan. 01	Schenectady.
Young, Horace Greeley, 22 jan. 91.....	3 brig..............	11 apr. 01	Albany.

CAPTAINS

Acker, Eben E., 17 apr. 08...........	c. a. c.............	10 aug. 16	New York.
Badgley, Howard Gardner, 18 feb. 95.	sq. A..............	18 sep. 05	Nutley, N. J.
Barker, Edward (bvt. maj.), 3 may 75..	supn...............	21 may 15	New York.
Barlow, Joseph Richard Kenrick, 18 nov. 95.	14 inf...............	21 mar. 00	Brooklyn.
Baum, Henry Clay, 2 mar. 00.........	asst. surg. 3 bat......	10 mar. 05	Syracuse.
Beasley, Crawford D., 17 may 09......	m. c...............	31 jul. 11	Brooklyn.
Bell, James Alexander (bvt. maj.), 24 jan. 99.	22 eng..............	2 jun. 05	Richmond Hill, L. I.
Brooks, Henry Harlow, 26 mar. 15.....	m. c...............	14 may 15	New York.
Bruckmann, Gustav T., 22 nov. 99....	14 inf...............	3 mar. 11	Brooklyn.
Buck, Willis Ripley (bvt. maj.), 19 apr. 98.	74 inf..............	9 apr. 12	Buffalo.
Bush, Robert P., 1 dec. 87...........	26 sep. co..........	5 mar. 12	Branchport.
Butler, John G., 12 apr. 88..........	41 sep. co..........	1 jan. 01	Syracuse.
Carroll, John Francis, 15 jul. 95.......	14 inf...............	20 dec. 05	Brooklyn.
Coleman, Hugh, 4 jan. 75...........	69 inf..............	8 mar. 12	New York.
Conlon, James, 27 dec. 81...........	69 inf..............	4 dec. 90	New York.
Crooks, George W., 6 apr. 88........	27 sep. co..........	11 nov. 98	Binghamton.
Delany, John A., 26 apr. 98..........	69 inf..............	27 nov. 09	New York.
Dixon, John J. (bvt. maj.), 10 jan. 84..	i. s. a. p. 14 inf......	6 dec. 99	Brooklyn.
Dixon, John James (bvt. maj.), 6 jul. 99	14 inf...............	6 apr. 08	Brooklyn.
Dwyer, Michael J., 25 jan. 01........	69 inf..............	6 mar. 16	New York.
Finlay, John J., 16 aug. 16..........	c. a. c.............	22 aug. 16	New York.
French, William A., 15 jun. 98.......	13 regt.............	12 mar. 12	Brooklyn.
Green, John Kneeland, 28 jan. 13.....	div n. g...........	12 apr. 13	New York.
Greer, Louis Morris, 27 feb. 08.......	div. n. g...........	1 may 12	New York.
Hall, Albert C., 10 oct. 77..........	supn...............	21 may 15	Brooklyn.
Hamlin, George Francis (bvt. lt. col.), 8 mar. 94.	23 inf...............	29 jul. 01	Philadelphia, Pa.
Hart, Charles L., 6 dec. 84..........	7 brig..............	11 mar. 12	Elmira.
Hart, Joseph (bvt. maj.), 9 mar. 92...	47 inf..............	20 feb. 08	Brooklyn.
Haubennestel, William (bvt. maj.), 12 nov. 66.	19 sep. co..........	11 mar. 12	Poughkeepsie.
Hayes, Almeron Deloss, 10 jul. 93.....	supn...............	16 mar. 12	Syracuse.
Hegeman, John R., Jr., 22 jul. 12......	o. d...............	17 oct. 13	New York.
Herron, Hugh H., 1 mar. 77..........	29 sep. co..........	1 oct. 90	Rochester.
Hornbeck, Benjamin Johnson, 28 sep. 98	supn...............	8 mar. 12	Kingston.

RETIRED OFFICERS — (*Continued*)

Name, Grade and Date of Rank	RETIRED Organization	Date	Residence
CAPTAINS—*Continued*			
Hughes, George, 6 jul. 06.............	2 inf...............	26 nov. 13	Amsterdam.
Hunter, William Goldsmith, 25 sep. 93.	10 sep. co.............	3 jul. 06	Newburgh.
Ingraham, John Henry, (bvt. maj.) 11 feb. 05.	22 inf...............	28 oct. 12	Brooklyn
Jewett, Sherman Skinner, 5 nov. 02....	74 inf...............	28 oct. 12	Buffalo.
Kerby, William H., Jr., 20 jun. 82.....	12 regt............	17 jan. 93	New York.
Lents, Charles B., 17 oct. 01.........	74 inf...............	17 mar. 13	Tonawanda.
Lovenberg, Eugene, 18 may 03........	c. a. c.............	23 jul. 13	Summit, N. J.
McCutcheon, Henry D., 27 dec. 07....	47 inf...............	17 jan. 16	Brooklyn.
Maidhof, William J., 10 dec. 88.......	22 regt............	7 jul. 97	Jersey City, N. J.
Marks, William Wolcott, 10 nov. 85...	9 inf...............	14 feb. 00	New York.
Martyne, Charles William, 12 dec. 12..	23 inf...............	13 aug. 15	Brooklyn.
Marvin, Matthew W., 20 may 79......	33 sep. co.........	31 may 92	Binghamton.
Maxfield, Charles Evans, 15 aug. 00...	47 inf...............	20 feb. 11	Newark, N. J.
Morgan, George, Jr., 13 dec. 70......	74 inf...............	11 mar. 12	Bath.
Mortimer, Thomas, 23 mar. 85........	supn...............	25 may 15	New York.
Musson, George Thomas (bvt. maj.), 5 may 98.	c. d...............	27 aug. 09	Brooklyn.
Myers, Berthold, 11 sep. 79..........	15 sep. co.........	2 jan. 92	Albany.
Napier, Charles Dwight (bvt. maj.), 15 may 93.	m. c...............	7 aug. 12	Brooklyn.
Nursey, Walter F. (bvt. maj.), 22 may 96.	65 inf...............	14 aug. 11	Buffalo.
O'Brien, John Emmett, 5 jul. 95......	69 inf...............	4 apr. 99	New York.
O'Connell, John, 14 feb. 94..........	69 inf...............	15 jun. 98	New York.
O'Donnell, James Matthew, 11 dec. 99.	c. a. c.............	1 nov. 12	New York.
Olmsted, Laurel L. (bvt. maj.), 13 nov. 74.	6 batty............	2 oct. 01	Binghamton.
Onderdonk, John D. A. (bvt. maj.), 5 dec. 01.	23 inf...............	2 sep. 08	Brooklyn.
Palmer, William H. (bvt. maj.), 1 may 83.	c. d...............	31 dec. 11	New York.
Phelan, James J., 11 nov. 98.........	2 inf...............	7 feb. 08	New York.
Praeger, Louis Jewett, 6 jan. 96......	23 inf...............	6 jan. 06	Brooklyn.
Rafferty, Peter Francis, 19 jul. 98.....	supn...............	25 may 15	New York.
Rasquin, Henry S. (bvt. maj.), 22 may 82.	3 batty............	17 jan. 07	Brooklyn.
Royce, Henry Herbert (bvt. maj.), 14 sep. 00.	c. a. c.............	1 jun. 10	Brooklyn.
Scanlon, John Joseph, 30 apr. 00......	69 inf...............	18 may 12	New York.
Schuyler, Walter G. (bvt. lieut. col.), 22 may 96.	7 inf...............	12 jul. 15	New York.
Sherry, Lansford Franklin (bvt. maj.), 27 mar. 08.	f. a...............	13 mar. 12	New York.
Stacey, James G. (bvt. maj.), 19 jan. 06	34 sep. co.........	29 dec. 13	Geneva.
Teets, Sylvanus Gibson, 21 mar. 05....	c. a. c.............	30 jun. 15	New York.
Tompkins, Arthur M., 29 may 93......	c. a. c.............	21 dec. 09	New York.
Vunk, Darwin E., 3 sep. 88..........	46 sep. co.........	11 jun. 06	Amsterdam.
Webb, William E., 10 oct. 77.........	2 brig............	19 mar. 12	New York.
Williams, Alfred H., 6 dec. 73........	23 inf...............	2 apr. 12	Philadelphia.
Winslow, George Justin, 7 mar. 12.....	1 inf...............	17 apr. 14	Utica.
Worthing, Harry Preston, 23 jun. 99...	1 inf...............	27 aug. 09	Binghamton.
Young, Thomas M., 15 mar. 86.......	8 regt............	17 apr. 96	New York.
FIRST LIEUTENANTS			
Barnum, Edward H. (bvt. cap.), 25 sep. 03.	c. d...............	12 jan. 10	Brooklyn.
Bridges, Charles W., 3 dec. 88........	14 inf...............	11 oct. 99	Brooklyn.
Calkins, Frederic R., 25 may 07.......	m. c...............	26 nov. 10	Watertown.
Clute, William T., 31 dec. 83........	asst. surg. 36 sep. co...	31 jan. 94	Schenectady.
Dorval, Alphonso C. (bvt. cap.), 12 dec. 98.	asst. surg. 9 sep. co...	10 may 04	Whitehall.
Gresham, Christopher (bvt. cap.), 29 apr. 98.	10 inf...............	16 jun. 10	Albany.
Haviland, George W., Jr. (bvt. cap.), 18 may 96.	10 inf...............	3 jun. 09	Flushing.
Johnson, Frank Abirt, (bvt. cap.), 5 jan. 04.	65 inf...............	24 feb. 14	Jamestown.
Knight, Archibald Stephen, 4 mar. 08..	m. c...............	28 mar. 11	Rochester.

RETIRED OFFICERS — (*Concluded*)

NAME, GRADE AND DATE OF RANK	RETIRED		Residence.
	Organization	Date	
FIRST LIEUTENANTS—*Continued*			
Laing, George Edgar (bvt. cap), 22 oct. 98.	3 batty.............	10 apr. 12	Brooklyn.
List, John, 30 apr. 00..............	71 inf..............	7 jun. 10	New Rochelle.
Loughran, Elbert DuBois, 23 jan. 09...	m. c..............	2 feb. 12	Kingston.
McNamara, John Patrick, 15 jul. 95...	14 inf	31 aug. 06	Brooklyn.
Mason, Samuel John (bvt. cap.), 14 sep. 99.	3 inf...............	6 nov. 11	Niagara Falls.
Meyers, John Henry, 3 dec. 03........	74 inf..............	21 mar. 14	Buffalo.
Philcox, Frederick James, 30 jun. 11...	65 inf..............	10 jun. 14	Buffalo.
Platt, William John, 13 apr. 06........	74 inf..............	28 sep. 14	Buffalo.
Smith, Joseph M., 7 jul. 87...........	22 regt............	13 oct. 97	New York.
Tracy, William J., 8 apr. 13..........	m. c..............	5 may 16	Hornell.
Travis, William Jewett (bvt. maj.), 8 nov. 00.	23 inf.............	1 feb. 06	Brooklyn.
Underwood, John N. (bvt. cap.), 22 aug. 81.	6 batty............	7 oct. 02	Binghamton.
Vanamee, Talcott Ostrom, 6 feb. 11....	1 inf..............	6 feb. 11	Newburgh.
Wilkins, George T., 5 oct. 85.........	supn...............	26 jan. 14	Penn Yan.
SECOND LIEUTENANTS			
Beutell, Martin L., 2 jan. 78.........	19 sep. co...........	13 mar. 96	Troy.
Conklin, Albert L., Jr., 19 dec. 02.....	c. a. c...........	10 mar. 13	So. Orange, N. J.
Dick, Adolph E., 20 apr. 81.........	22 regt...........	3 aug. 93	New York.
Gombers, Alexander Stevens, 5 mar. 08	23 inf.............	27 aug. 09	Brooklyn.
Gross, John H. (bvt. 1 lt.), 10 jun. 81..	6 batty............	14 jun. 06	Binghamton.
Masten, Daniel Westley, 28 sep. 93...	46 sep. co...........	26 oct. 03	Troy.
Merritt, Graham B., 29 jul. 79.......	16 bat.............	14 mar. 12	Ossining.
McGreevey, John, 25 may 87........	7 inf..............	19 apr. 99	New York.
Nickerson, Lorenzo Miller, 6 nov. 93...	3 batty............	16 jun. 05	Brooklyn.
Post, Henry, 9 dec. 12..............	74 inf.............	7 jul. 14	Buffalo.
Raymond, Edward Denton, 25 nov. 95.	14 inf.............	3 oct. 06	Brooklyn.
CHAPLAINS			
Converse, Rob Roy McNulty, 5 jun. 07.	3 inf..............	31 dec. 11	Rochester.
Dunnell, William N., (bvt. maj.), 15 apr. 74.	22 eng.............	15 apr. 05	New York.
Morgan, David P., 30 jul. 85.........	sq. A..............	11 dec. 06	New York.
Parker, Lindsay, 19 mar. 94.........	23 inf..............	4 nov. 09	Brooklyn.
Rhoades, William C. P., 31 jan. 00.....	c. a. c...........	31 dec. 11	Brooklyn.
Richards, George B., 26 dec. 99......	65 inf.............	14 nov. 10	Buffalo.
Tenney, Albert Francis, 9 may 99.....	10 inf.............	31 dec. 11	Pelham Manor.
Tilton, Edgar, Jr., 8 nov. 00.........	71 inf.............	11 mar. 12	New York.

BREVET COMMISSIONS AS SECOND LIEUTENANTS ISSUED TO ENLISTED MEN RETIRED AFTER TWENTY-FIVE YEARS' SERVICE

Name	Grade and organization when brevetted	Date of rank	Residence
Brewster, Joseph	qm. sgt. co. B 23 inf	3 may 98	Brooklyn.
Woodcock, Thomas	sgt. color bearer 13 regt	18 may 98	Brooklyn.
MacVeety, Robert J	pvt. co. K 23 inf	28 nov. 98	Brooklyn.
Holt, Charles J	qm. sgt. co. G 23 inf	30 jan. 99	Brooklyn.
Lent, Whitman S	pvt. co. I 7 inf	9 may 00	New York.
Kemp, William Cullen Bryant	pvt. co. B 7 inf	30 oct. 00	New York.
Page, John McC	pvt. 36 sep. co. 2 inf	14 jun. 01	Schenectady.
Mingay, Richard	pvt. 22 sep. co. 2 inf	18 jul. 02	Saratoga Springs
Miller, Charles A	sgt. co. E, 47 inf	9 may 03	Brooklyn.
Kelly, John	sgt. co. G 47 inf	23 oct. 03	Brooklyn.
Brown, George W	drum. maj. 23 inf	10 dec. 03	Brooklyn.
Guardineer, Theodore	qm. sgt. co. C 10 bat	15 mar. 04	Albany.
Wright, Joseph H	mus. 47 inf	21 mar. 04	Brooklyn.
Arthur, Frank	pvt. 31 sep. co. 4 bat	28 mar. 04	Mohawk.
Narwood, Edward H	color bearer 13 regt	25 apr. 05	Brooklyn.
Hagin, Edward	pvt. 37 sep. co. 2 inf	21 nov. 05	Schenectady.
Adgate, Joseph J	sgt. maj. 71 inf	11 dec. 05	New York.
Cornell, Reuben Lovel	drum maj. 14 inf	22 jan. 06	Brooklyn.
Wood, Samuel M	qm. sgt. co. H 23 inf	13 feb. 06	Brooklyn.
Haws, Philip H	mus. co. C 7 inf	16 jun. 06	New York.
Everdell, Henry	qm. sgt. co. D 7 inf	30 jun. 06	New York.
Way, Edward	color bearer 2 inf	24 jul. 06	Troy.
Breen, Robert B., Jr	pvt. co. B 8 inf	29 oct. 06	New York.
Perl, Frederick Christopher	mus. 28 sep. co. 1 inf	28 dec. 06	Utica.
Flett, William Alexander	1 sgt. co. B 74 inf	5 jan. 07	Buffalo.
Daniell, John, Jr	pvt. co. G 7 inf	19 feb. 07	New York.
Sontag, George J	pvt. co. G 7 inf	19 feb. 07	New York.
Bruford, Noah	color bearer 71 inf	25 feb. 07	New York.
Hildreth, Hirschel P	pvt. co. K 23 inf	10 apr. 07	Brooklyn.
Moog, John J	qm. sgt. 3 bat	23 may 07	Brooklyn.
Unger, Joseph	1 sgt. co. B 22 eng	29 may 07	New York.
Fox, Horace E	pvt. co. D 7 inf	22 oct. 07	New York.
Dederer, Joseph R	pvt. co. F 7 inf	22 oct. 07	New York.
Williams, Joseph	qm. sgt. co. H 7 inf	28 oct. 07	New York.
Cornee, Victor	sgt. 18 co. c. a. o	29 feb. 08	New York.
Logan, Edward D. B	1 sgt. co. H 14 inf	27 apr. 08	Brooklyn.
Menzies, Alexander G	regt. qm. sgt. 12 inf	16 may 08	New York.
Robinson, William A	1 sgt. co. D 23 inf	2 sep. 08	Brooklyn.
Warren, William W	post qm. sgt. qm. dept	26 oct. 08	New York.
Oliver, Thomas	pvt. co. G 10 inf	7 apr. 09	Yonkers.
Tillotson, George Harrison	pvt. co. G 10 inf	7 apr. 09	Yonkers.
Buckhorn, Frank	sgt. 26 co. c. a. c	16 aug. 09	New York.
	ord. sgt. 14 inf	15 sep. 09	Brooklyn.
Dutcher, Dewitt P	pvt. co. G 23 inf	10 feb. 10	Brooklyn.
Edwards, Joseph	pvt. co. L 3 inf	26 feb. 10	Elmira.
Massa, James	qm. sgt. co. A 12 inf	1 jun. 10	New York.
Van Heusen, Anthony B	sgt. co. B 12 inf	1 jun. 10	New York.
McDowell, Patrick	qm. sgt. co. A 69 inf	24 jun. 10	New York.
Schiebel, Henry	mus. co. G 71 inf	11 jul. 10	New York.
Arbuckle, John W	corp. co. G 10 inf	24 sep. 10	Yonkers.
Gendar, William S	sgt. maj. j. g. c. a. c	14 nov. 10	Brooklyn.
Schoonmaker, Edward C	pvt. co. D 7 inf	26 nov. 10	New York.
McNevin, James	ord. sgt. c. a. c	2 dec. 10	Brooklyn.
Elliss, Herman F. C	qm. sgt. 16 co. c. a. c	23 dec. 10	New York.
Place, Joseph F	sgt. co. C 47 inf	3 mar. 11	Brooklyn.
Delafield, Albert	qm. sgt. co. I 7 inf	27 apr. 11	New York.
Harvey, Thomas Mackness	sgt. maj. s. g. c. a. c	31 may 11	Brooklyn.
Ross, William	qm. sgt. co. B 2 inf	18 dec. 11	Cohoes.
Schneider, August	drum. maj. 74 inf	10 jun. 12	Buffalo.
Macy, Frank W	1 sgt. co. F 10 inf	17 jun. 12	Hudson.
Kinney, James T	pvt. co. F 23 inf	31 oct. 12	Brooklyn.
Hyson, William	regt. qm. sgt 47 inf	6 nov. 12	Brooklyn.
Reisig, Charles H	qm. sgt. co. E 7 inf	23 dec. 12	New York.
Brintnall, Charles S	pvt. co. A 2 inf	14 jan. 13	Troy.
Sullivan, John J	2 class pvt. co. B 22 eng	2 may 13	New York.
Meisner, John F	sgt. band 74 inf	2 may 13	Buffalo.
Mever, Daniel C	pvt. co. C 7 inf	12 may 13	New York.
Adair, John S	sgt. maj. 12 inf	16 may 13	New York.
Lane, James H	comy. sgt. 10 inf	4 sep. 13	Albany.
Lethbridge, Melvin W	pvt. co. H 2 inf	21 oct. 13	Amsterdam.
Graham, Chauncey B	post qm. sgt. 13 arty. dist	5 nov. 13	Brooklyn.
Pennoyer, Charles H	pvt. co. G 23 inf	3 dec. 13	Brooklyn.
Summers, William M	pvt. co. E 23 inf	3 dec. 13	Brooklyn.
Sweeney, John W	pvt. co. D 23 inf	3 dec. 13	Brooklyn.

BREVET COMMISSIONS AS SECOND LIEUTENANTS ISSUED TO ENLISTED
MEN RETIRED AFTER TWENTY-FIVE YEARS' SERVICE — (*Concluded*)

Name	Grade and organization when brevetted	Date of rank	Residence
McDermott, John	color sgt. 12 inf	19 dec. 13	New York.
Nimmo, William H. D.	pvt. co. I 10 inf	17 dec. 13	Flushing.
Gleason, Charles E.	pvt. co. E 7 inf	19 dec. 13	New York.
Morris, John J.	pvt. 15 co. a. a. c.	9 mar. 14	New York.
Meeker, James H.	pvt. co. H 1 inf	13 mar. 14	Binghamton.
Olin, Frank Lester	qm. sgt. co. G 1 inf	3 apr. 14	Oneonta.
Rowe, Chester A.	pvt. co. F 2 inf	3 apr. 14	Schenectady.
Scobie, Andrew J.	mus. co. D 1 inf	1 may 14	Ogdensburg.
Rauschkolb, Louis	chief trumpeter, c. a. c.	11 may 14	New York.
Prull, Charles W.	pvt. co. M 10 inf	18 may 14	Kingston.
Knight, Frank M.	post qm. sgt. 7 inf	17 jun. 14	New York.
Simons, Andrew J.	post qm. sgt. 2 inf	15 jul. 14	Troy.
Bush, Amos J.	1 sgt. batty. C 1 f. a.	24 jul. 14	Binghamton.
Morgan, William M.	pvt. co. H 7 inf	10 oct. 14	New York.
Tallon, Edward	pvt. co. D 69 inf	30 oct. 14	New York.
Hand, Anthony	pvt. co. D 69 inf	30 oct. 14	New York.
Dillon, Joseph M.	1 sgt. co. L 1 inf	5 nov. 14	Newburgh.
Johnston, John	mus. co. B 14 inf	9 nov. 14	Brooklyn.
Howard, Joseph F.	sgt. co. E 14 inf	16 nov. 14	Brooklyn.
Leonard, George W.	pvt. co. E 14 inf	16 nov. 14	Brooklyn.
Kretscham, Emil A.	sgt. band 7 inf	23 nov. 14	New York.
Scriven, Marshall W.	qm. sgt. co. A 7 inf	31 dec. 14	New York.
Jansen, John G.	regt. sgt. maj. 1 f. a.	15 dec. 14	New York.
Walker, Edward	pvt. co. D 23 inf	14 dec. 14	Brooklyn.
Easson, Alfred I.	qm. sgt. c. a. c. 13 c. d. c.	11 jan. 15	Brooklyn.
Shumway, Albert	pvt. co. H, 7 inf	20 jan. 15	New York.
Kerr, Thomas F.	sgt. co. K, 69 inf	27 jan. 15	New York.
Plate, Edward D.	pvt. 8 co. c. a. c.	10 feb. 15	Brooklyn.
Bailey, James	pvt. 8 co. c. a. c.	10 feb. 15	Brooklyn.
Scheurer, Charles T.	1 sgt. co. C, 10 inf	10 feb. 15	Albany.
Maxwell, John	bat. sgt. maj. 65 inf	15 mar. 15	Buffalo.
Rogers, James C.	1 sgt. co. C, 71 inf	29 mar. 15	New York.
Wilson, George A.	qm. sgt. 13 c. d. c.	31 mar. 15	Brooklyn.
Arnot, Raymond	pvt. 19 co. c. a. c.	8 apr. 15	New York.
Kellogg, Benjamin A.	pvt. co. G, 7 inf	15 apr. 15	New York.
Martin, Isaac S.	qm. sgt. 12 inf	26 apr. 15	New York.
Wenk, Augustus J.	qm. sgt. 12 inf	30 apr. 15	New York.
Mason, Walter C.	regt. sgt. maj. 65 inf	19 may 15	Buffalo.
McCarthy, Joseph A.	pvt. co. H, 23 inf	21 may 15	Brooklyn.
Brown, Charles H.	drum maj. 7 inf	20 may 15	New York.
Guerra, Theodore	sgt. co. C, 7 inf	19 jun. 15	New York.
Halliday, Charles G.	pvt. co. C, 7 inf	24 jun. 15	New York.
Schaffner, Samuel S.	sgt. qm. corps	9 jul. 15	Buffalo.
Murray, Charles	pvt. co. D, 7 inf	14 jul. 15	New York.
Dixon, William A.	sgt. co. G, 7 inf	14 jul. 15	New York.
McCoy, Frank	pvt. co. C, 7 inf	21 jul. 15	New York.
Davis, Richard N.	drum major, band, 71 inf	6 jul. 15	New York.
Wanty, Edward	pvt. co. B, 7 inf	15 oct. 15	New York.
Rose, Emerson F.	qm. sgt. co. I, 1 inf	28 oct. 15	Middletown.
Stevens, William B.	color sgt. co. K, 2 inf	9 nov. 15	Glens Falls.
Parker, Alexander	qm. sgt. 8 co. c. a. c.	21 dec. 15	New York.
Barrier, William W.	pvt. co. C 7 inf	28 jan. 16	New York.
Hedenberg, Frank B.	pvt. co. F 23 inf	13 mar. 16	Brooklyn.
May, Martin	pvt. 2 co. 13 c. d. c.	1 may 16	Brooklyn.
Howland, Edward A. J.	sgt. co. G 7 inf	25 may 16	New York.
Taylor, Frederick N.	1 sgt. co. K 71 inf	25 may 16	New York.
Graham, Thomas	qm. sgt. co. K 47 inf	1 jun. 16	Brooklyn.
Berg, Charles F.	pvt. co. C 7 inf	7 jun. 16	New York.
Drake, Archie T.	sgt. H. corps 74 inf	8 june 16	Buffalo.
Burton, William H. jr.	regt. sgt. maj. 10 inf	27 jun. 16	Albany.
Hessels, Francis H.	pvt. co. H 10 inf	27 jun. 16	Mt. Vernon.
Schick, Henry J.	1 sgt. co. H 65 inf	5 jul. 16	Buffalo.
Donovan, George	qm. sgt. 12 inf	8 jul. 16	New York.
Loughlin, Francis J.	comy. sgt. 12 inf	8 jul. 16	New York.
Youngs, George B.	1 sgt. co. I 71 inf	21 jul. 16	New York.
Busse, Courtney	pvt. 7 inf	21 dec. 16	New York.

RESERVE OFFICERS

Name, Grade and Date of Rank	To Reserve List		Residence
	Organization in which last served	Date	
BRIGADIER GENERALS			
Bridgman, Oliver Benedict, 1 aug. 16..	d. b. 1 brig..........	6 oct. 16	New York.
Butt, McCoskry, 3 mar. 98............	1 brig.............	1 jul. 01	New York.
Hamilton, Henry De Witt, 1 jan. 13...	The a. g., 8. N. Y....	31 dec. 14	New York.
COLONELS			
Austin, Eugene Kelly, 12 jul. 98......	106 inf..............	22 dec. 98	New York.
Babcock, Charles Edward Payne, 8 jun. 14.	65 inf..............	11 jul. 16	Buffalo.
Beals, Pascal P., 8 jan. 84............	asst. in dept. of rifle practice.	24 dec. 91	Buffalo.
Collins-Stanfurth, Frank S.,29 mar. 86.	supn...............	24 dec. 91	New York.
Davis, Loyal Lefisey, 5 jul. 1.........	2 inf...............	1 jul. 15	Glens Falls.
Griffith, William Morton, 14 jan. 97...	asst. chief of arty....	31 dec. 98	Jamaica, L. I.
Hilton, Albert B., 1 jan. 86...........	supn...............	31 dec. 94	New York.
Hotchkin, Walter B., (bvt. brig. gen.), 26 apr. 06,	22 eng...............	23 dec. 14	New York.
Jarvis, James Morgan, 26 jan. 99.....	8 inf...............	10 dec. 06	New York.
Kavanaugh, George Washington, 24 feb. 96.	asst. qm. gen........	31 dec. 98	New York.
Kellogg, Frederick Sheffield, 3 jan. 95..	asst. qm. gen.......	31 dec. 98	Utica.
Low, James Thomas, 9 aug. 95.......	asst. in o. d.........	31 dec. 98	Niagara Falls.
Luscomb, Charles Harris, 16 may 96	13 inf..............	28 nov. 98	Brooklyn.
Moss, Royal Emile, 30 jan. 95........	asst. comy. gen. of sub.	31 dec. 98	Red Bank, N. J.
O'Grady, James M. E., 25 feb. 98.....	asst. a. g...........	31 dec. 98	Rochester.
Rice, William G., 17 feb. 75..........	asst paymaster gen..	2 mar. 85	Albany.
Treadwell, George Curtis, 6 oct. 10....	mil. sec...........	9 oct. 16	Albany.
Trevor, Henry Graff, 3 mar. 98........	asst. comy. gen. of sub	31 dec. 98	Southampton, L. I.
Wadsworth, Clarence Seymour, 6 may 13.	12 inf	27 sep. 16	New York.
NATIONAL DEFENSE ACT, JUNE 30, 1916			
Dunspaugh, Merrill Mandville, 9 sep. 09.	3 brig..............	20 jun. 16	Hoosick Falls.
LIEUTENANT COLONELS			
Alden, George Marshall, 24 feb. 16....	2 inf...............	18 may 16	Troy.
Amory, William Nowland, 5 apr. 98....	supn...............	31 dec. 98	New York.
Brennan, Edward C., 2 jul. 98........	supn...............	10 jan. 99	Brooklyn.
Brooks, Henry Harlow, 7 jul. 16......	d. b. 7 inf..........	28 oct. 16	New York.
Broun, Heywood C., 14 mar. 94.......	asst. in dept. of rifle practice.	31 dec. 98	New York.
Bruch, Edward Blair, 11 may 10.......	insp. gen's. dept......	12 jul. 15	New York.
Burr, Nelson Beardsley, 7 jun. 12.....	12 inf..............	12 jun. 15	New York.
Burton, Wingfield G., 12 jan. 80......	supn...............	19 dec. 85	New York.
Clark, Henry S., 25 mar. 98..........	asst. a. g. 1 brig.....	1 jul. 01	New York.
Culver, John Y., 3 may 80............	eng. 2 div...........	5 aug. 86	Mt. Kisco.
Endress, William Fries, 13 apr. 98.....	supn...............	31 dec. 98	New York.
Flynn, John, Jr., 11 jul. 98..........	asst. chief of eng.....	31 dec. 98	Troy.
Goldman, Henry J., 28 jun. 16........	U. S. cav...........	28 june 16	Menands.
Hayte, Edward D., 27 aug. 78........	17 battn............	17 dec. 81	New York.
Heilner, George Corson, 12 jul. 98.....	108 inf.............	22 dec. 98	New York.
Hess, Frank Judson, 30 mar. 97......	asst. gen. insp. of rifle practice.	31 dec. 98	Rochester.
Kerby, John Edward, 7 apr. 06.......	8 inf...............	10 dec. 06	New York.
Lambert, Walter Eyre, 2 apr. 98......	surg. 1 brig..........	1 jul. 01	New York.
Mather, Adrian Whitford, 18 feb. 04...	3 brig..............	1 apr. 09	Albany.
Middleton, Clifford L., 19 apr. 86.....	asst. a. g. 4 brig......	5 aug. 86	Brooklyn.
Moran, James, 12 mar. 88............	69 inf..............	6 dec. 93	Brooklyn.
Olyphant, Robert (bvt. brig. gen.), 18 dec. 80.	asst. j. a. 1 brig......	5 aug. 86	New York.
Porter, Augustus Drum, 18 nov. 12...	12 inf..............	25 may 16	New York.
Schermerhorn, Arthur F., 1 nov. 98...	112 inf.............	24 jan. 99	New York.
Sickles, George Stanton, 28 may 97...	supn...............	31 dec. 98	New York.
Simmons, Charles Alonso, 6 jun. 11...	asst. a. g...........	6 jul. 15	Ithaca.
Weber, Abraham L., 10 dec. 79......	5 reg..............	17 dec. 81	New York.
Wells, Frederick Adams, 18 sep. 13...	23 inf..............	29 jul. 16	Brooklyn.
NATIONAL DEFENSE ACT, JUNE 30, 1916			
Wells, James H., 4 oct., 01............	71 inf..............	27 jun. 16	New York.
Barnes, Walter F., 29 nov. 07........	2 brig..............	29 dec. 16	Brooklyn.

RESERVE OFFICERS — (*Continued*)

NAME, GRADE AND DATE OF RANK	To RESERVE LIST		Residence
	Organization in which last served	Date	
MAJORS			
Bacon, James, 6 dec. 84	supn.	5 aug. 86	Elmira.
Banks, David, Jr., 1 nov. 98	112 inf.	10 jan. 99	New York.
Banks, Robert Lenox, 17 mar. 86	5 brig.	5 aug. 86	Albany.
Berry, Joseph Ignatius, 1 jul. 13	2 f. a.	13 jan. 16	New York.
Bigelow, Elliot, Jr., 2 mar. 08	sig. corps.	5 sep. 14	Brooklyn.
Bishop, Edwin F., 13 apr. 86	supn.	5 aug. 86	Buffalo.
Brown, Herbert P., 10 aug. 85	supn.	5 aug. 86	New York.
Bruce, Charles E., 23 apr. 83	surg. 8 bat.	16 nov. 94	New York.
Campbell, William Francis, 30 apr. 10	m. c.	13 aug. 15	Brooklyn.
Cochran, George G., 25 oct. 92	13 inf.	7 may 98	Brooklyn.
Cochran, John A., 24 may 88	surg. 13 inf.	28 nov. 98	Brooklyn.
Collins, George William, 12 jul. 98	supn.	24 feb. 99	New York.
Conklin, Charles C., 20 may 74	supn.	18 dec. 75	New York.
Dana, Paul, 7 may 83	o. o. 1 brig.	9 feb. 98	Glen Cove, L. I.
Duffy, John Edward, 7 jun. 04	69 inf.	2 may 16	New York.
Dyett, Albert Henry, 2 may 07	22 c. of e.	21 apr. 15	New York.
Edwards, Robert, Jr., 19 sep. 99	8 inf.	10 dec. 06	New Rochelle.
Eliot, Walter Graeme, 24 nov. 11	asst. to chief c. a.	1 sep. 14	New York.
Erlandsen, Oscar, 28 feb. 08	sig. corps.	5 sep. 14	Jamaica.
Fleming, Thomas Robertson, 26 may 09	asst. to chief c. a.	1 sep. 14	Brooklyn.
Gerard, James Watson, Jr., 31 may 00	1 brig.	1 jul. 01	New York.
Hart, Stephen F., 24 may 98	22 regt.	25 aug. 15	New York.
Hogan, Daniel John, 24 may 13	2 inf.	8 may 16	Glens Falls.
Honey, Saunders Thomas, 14 oct. 98	108 reg.	22 dec. 98	New York.
Keck, Frank, 16 dec. 15	maj. 71 inf.	16 dec. 15	New York.
Keech, Frank Brown, 28 mar. 98	1 brig.	1 july 01	New York.
Kemp, George Henry, 14 apr. 09	13 c. d. c.	2 jul. 15	Brooklyn.
Koch, Joseph, 27 oct. 79	2 brig.	6 sep. 80	Brooklyn.
Landon, Henry H., 3 jun. 98	171 inf.	3 jan. 99	New York.
Luckey, R. Livingston (bvt. lt. col.), 8 sep. 75.	insp. 7 brig.	17 dec. 81	New York.
MacGrotty, Edward F., 20 mar. 10	22 eng.	23 dec. 14	Glen Rook, N. J.
Macumber, John L., 18 jun. 97	14 inf.	19 apr. 15	Brooklyn.
Maxfield, Traverse Roche, 21 jun. 98	surg. 114 inf.	10 dec. 98	Brooklyn.
Meyer, Edward John, 9 sep. 98	surg. 165 regt.	22 dec. 98	Buffalo.
Murray, Francis Wisner, 11 feb. 85	surg. 1 brig.	5 aug. 86	New York.
Neff, Lewis Knode, 16 mar. 96	surg. 8 inf.	10 dec. 06	New York.
O'Rourke, John Francis, 9 aug. 09	asst. to chief c. a.	19 may 14	New York.
Parsons, Herbert, 8 apr. 98	j. a. 1 brig.	1 jul. 01	New York.
Perrine, Howland D., 8 may 86	chief sig. off. 2 div.	5 aug. 86	New York.
Porter, Walter B., 5 apr. 13	22 eng.	23 dec. 14	Bound Brook, N. J.
Read, Harmon Pumpelly, 1 mar. 86	insp. of rifle practice 2 brig.	5 aug. 86	Albany.
Roberts, Winfred Henry, 26 may 09	asst. to chief c. a.	1 sep. 14	Brooklyn.
Rodgers, George Washington, 17 apr. 08	13 c. d. c.	1 sep. 14	Brooklyn.
Romaine, Washington Tyson, 22 jan. 00	insp. 1 brig.	1 jul. 01	New York.
Sanford, Henry Gansevoort, 2 july 13	1 brig.	1 may 14	Poughkeepsie.
Schermerhorn, Edward Gibert, 24 jan. 99 (Restored to supernumerary list by act of Legislature as of Oct. 13, 1913).	military secretary to gov.	18 oct. 13	New York.
Schieffelin, Schuyler, 11 mar. 98	i. s. a. p. and o. o. 1 brig.	1 jul. 01	New York.
Schlereth, William John, 14 oct. 98	169 reg.	24 feb. 99	New York.
Smith, Clarence Wilbur, 10 jun. 09	insp. gen. dept.	1 sep. 14	Mountain Lakes, N. J.
Snyder, Edward Havemeyer, 5 nov. 08	47 inf.	19 jun. 15	Brooklyn.
Staats, Charles Bleeker, 13 sep. 06	10 inf.	23 june 16	Albany.
Stonehouse, John B., 24 july 16		24 july 16	Albany.
Strevell, Clarence, 6 mar. 30	10 inf.	19 jul. 15	Albany.
Templeton, Richard H., 1 apr. 12	74 inf.	20 oct. 15	Buffalo.
Thompson, Hobart Warren, 20 dec. 88.	qm. 3 brig.	16 jan. 91	Troy.
Van Benthuysen, Charles Frederick, 24 feb. 97.	asst. comy. gen. of sub	31 dec. 98	Albany.
Walbridge, Charles Eliphaet, Jr., 5 june 13.	4 brig.	29 may 16	Buffalo.
Warren, Charles Elliott, 25 may 15	5 brig.	25 may 15	New York.
Webb, Francis Egerton, 14 nov. 85	insp. 1 brig.	5 aug. 86	New York.
Weston, Albert Theodore, 9 jun. 13	med. corps.	8 jul. 14	New York.
Whitney, Alfred Rutgers, jr., 16 aug. 16	d. b. 1 brig.	6 oct. 16	New York.
Winterroth, Emil John, 16 feb. 11	qm. dept.	1 sep. 14	New York.
Wood, John Henry, 3 aug. 98	109 inf.	22 dec. 98	New York.
Wylie, Charles, 23 nov. 11	9 c. d. c.	25 aug. 15	New York.

RESERVE OFFICERS — *(Continued)*

Name, Grade and Date of Rank	To Reserve List		Residence
	Organisation in which last served	Date	

NATIONAL DEFENSE ACT, JUNE 30, 1916

MAJORS

Name, Grade and Date of Rank	Organisation	Date	Residence
Cluett, Sanford Lockwood, 26 dec. 08..	3 brig................	4 july 16	Hoosick Falls.
Denison, Alfred Edgar, 24 mar. 14....	10 inf................	23 sep. 16	Albany.
Landon, Francis Griswold, 8 dec. 08...	7 inf.................	6 june 16	New York City.
Roberts, Caroll Julian, 8 apr. 13......	65 inf. m. c.........	16 june 16	Buffalo.

CAPTAINS

Name, Grade and Date of Rank	Organisation	Date	Residence
Adriance, I. Reynolds, 11 feb. 75.....	a. d. c. 8 brig. 5 div...	17 dec. 81	Poughkeepsie.
Allen, Henry Raymond, 5 aug. 12.....	1 cav................	22 sep. 14	Rochester.
Anderson, John A., 9 mar. 96........	13 inf................	7 may 98	Brooklyn.
Anhalt, Abram, 21 jul. 81..........	5 regt................	17 dec. 81	New York.
Arbogast, Joseph Charles, 18 sep. 06..	65 inf................	18 july 16	Williamsville.
Archer, William James, 26 jul. 98....	165 inf................	22 dec. 98	Buffalo.
Baker, Floyd Eugene, 15 sep. 98......	169 inf................	24 feb. 99	New York.
Baker, Guy Ellis, 1 sep. 85.........	5 brig................	5 aug. 86	Ballston Lake.
Barron, Hugh James, 30 apr. 98......	69 inf................	5 may 99	New York.
Bartholomaei, Albert S., 19 july 98...	108 reg...............	22 dec. 98	New York.
Baxter, Malcolm, Jr., 8 may 06......	l. s. a. p. 8 inf.......	10 dec. 06	New York.
Bell, Walter Lincoln, 19 dec. 14......	9 marine corps........	6 dec. 15	New York.
Bernardi, Peter, 3 jun. 98..........	136 sep. co...........	10 dec. 98	Schenectady.
Bishop, George W., 30 dec. 12.......	a. g. o. S. N. Y.......	25 may 15	New York.
Boughain, Ben Austin, 4 feb. 15......	14 inf................	28 apr. 16	Brooklyn.
Bourne, George L., 1899...........		15 july 16	
Boyle, John, Jr., 28 dec. 09........	71 inf................	3 jul. 15	New York.
Breckenridge, Lucian S., 26 jul. 10...	71 inf................	25 mar. 15	New York.
Bronx, John Mortimer, 9 may 98.....	47 inf................	16 may 99	Brooklyn.
Brower, George Andrew, 28 nov. 98...	bat. adj. 114 inf......	10 dec. 98	Brooklyn.
Burnton, Maurice Evans, 18 oct. 98...	l. s. a. p. 122 inf.....	17 dec. 98	New York.
Callahan, John J., Jr., 18 nov. 79....	65 inf................	24 jan. 83	Buffalo.
Carmody, Michael F., 20 aug. 15.....	11 sep. co...........	20 aug. 15	New York.
Chapin, Charles Pierson, 26 july 98...	165 inf................	22 dec. 98	Buffalo.
Chard, James Alfred, 3 jun. 98......	171 inf................	3 jan. 99	New York.
Chilton, William Wiltshire, 6 june 98..	171 inf................	3 jan. 99	New York.
Clark, William N. G., 8 june 98......	169 inf................	24 feb. 99	New York.
Cluett, Walter H., 26 may 04........	asst. insp. 3 brig......	21 jan. 08	Saranac.
Coan, C. Arthur, 27 sep. 15.........	23 inf................	27 sep. 15	South Nyack.
Coates, William Benjamin, 1 may 05...	10 inf................	17 may 10	Albany.
Collins, Charles H., 6 feb. 88.......	11 reg................	14 jan. 89	New York.
Corwin, George Wood, 2 dec. 02.....	71 inf................	1 may 14	New York.
Coster, William Bay, 9 july 96.......	1 brig................	9 feb. 98	New York.
Cowen, George William, 21 may 98...	regt. qm. 13 inf.......	28 nov. 98	So. Orange, N. J.
Cruikshank, Barton, 10 may 04.......	8 C. D. C.............	19 jan. 16	Brooklyn.
Daly, Robert Joseph, 26 may 02......	22 corps of engs.......	23 dec. 14	New York.
Davidson, Harold A., 26 jul. 15......	23 inf................	26 jul. 15	New York.
Day, Arthur M., 18 may 15.........	8 c. d. c.............	18 may 15	New York.
Decker, Edward Madden, 20 jan. 09...	1 inf.................	18 dec. 15	Middletown.
Decker, Percy Wile, 18 jun. 09......	10 inf................	13 oct. 14	Catskill.
Deevy, Nicholas Alphonsus Thomas, 24 sep. 09.	22 engrs.............	17 jan. 11	New York.
Dessar, Harry L., 18 nov. 92........	9 inf.................	14 dec. 15	New York.
Dressel, John August Henry, 28 feb. 98.	13 inf................	7 may 98	Brooklyn.
Du Bois, Charles A., 10 feb. 88......	22 regt...............	10 oct. 90	New York.
Dudley, James Bliss, 9 june 98......	171 reg...............	27 july 98	New York.
Dusenbury, George, 14 jan. 10.......	47 inf................	13 july 16	Brooklyn.
Ellison, Francis, Joseph, 1 july 98....	165 reg...............	22 dec. 98	Buffalo.
Erikson, Alfred J., 1 may 98........	65 inf................	25 oct. 99	Philadelphia, Pa.
Fish, William Louis, 5 may 98.......	47 inf................	16 may 99	New York.
Ford, John, 12 sep. 00............	comy of sub...........	6 dec. 15	New York.
Fornachon, Joseph Louis, 6 jun. 98...	108 inf................	22 dec. 98	Newark, N. J.
Fraser, James Stanley, 28 feb. 13.....	c. a. c...............	2 feb. 15	New York.
Francis, Lloyd West, 3 jun. 97......	171 inf................	3 jan. 99	Brooklyn.
French, George Lew, 10 may 98......	106 sep. co...........	10 dec. 98	Troy.
Gibson, Kasson C., 6 sep. 86........	insp. of rifle practice 9 inf.	3 jan. 90	New York.
Gomes, Vincent, 9 may 98..........	112 reg...............	24 jan. 99	New York.
Graff, Edwin D., 7 jan. 16.........	9 inf.................	7 jan. 16	New York.
Grandy, Harvey Loomis, 15 mar. 16...	65 inf................	11 july 16	Buffalo.

RESERVE OFFICERS — *(Continued)*

NAME, GRADE AND DATE OF RANK	To RESERVE LIST		Residence
	Organization in which last served	Date	

CAPTAINS — *Continued*

NAME, GRADE AND DATE OF RANK	Organization in which last served	Date	Residence
Graves, Henry Bronson, 3 jun. 98.....	134 sep. co..........	17 dec. 98	Geneva.
Gridley, Abraham, 3 jul. 85..........	1 sep. co............	3 jan. 90	Penn Yan.
Grout, Paul, 9 feb. 05...............	sq. c.	12 apr. 16	New York City.
Guise, Philip, 25 feb. 11............	14 inf...............	25 july 16	Brooklyn.
Hacker, Adam, 1 apr. 80.............	25 regt.............	12 feb. 81	Albany.
Hackley, Alexander Strachan, 14 may 08.	23 inf...............	6 july 16	Brooklyn.
Hamblen, Arthur J., 23 aug. 15.......	9 c. d. c..........	23 aug. 15	New York.
Hamilton, Arthur McWhinney, 19 jul. 98.	asst. surg. 114 inf.....	10 dec. 98	Denver, Colo.
Haskell, William Cook, 3 jun. 98.....	171 inf.............	3 jan. 99	New York.
Hearn, George Henry, 4 may 09.....	22 corps of eng......	23 dec. 14	New York.
Herman, Harry, 8 july 07.........	13 C. D. C.......	15 aug. 16	Brooklyn.
Herriman, Frank R, 13 nov. 06......	23 inf.............	16 nov. 15	Brooklyn.
Heuel, Emil, 15 nov. 13............	m. c...............	13 apr. 15	New York.
Heun, Robert Ernest, 2 may 05......	71 inf.............	7 jan. 16	New York.
Hicks, Howard Ogden, 11 june 07....	65 inf.............	22 july 16	Buffalo.
Hobby, Frederick Howard, 22 oct. 03..	47 inf.............	21 jan. 08	Richmond Hill, L.I.
Holland, Henry, 8 feb. 87..........	35 sep. co..........	6 dec. 93	Ogdensburg.
Howell, George, 23 feb. 1900.......	7 inf.............	27 june 16	New York.
Hoyt, Charles Herbert, 18 aug. 98...	171 inf.............	3 jan. 99	New York.
Johnson, William Richmond, 1 apr. 14.	1 cav.............	2 jul. 15	New York.
Kelley, John Thornton, 26 may 98...	112 sep. co..........	10 dec. 98	Troy.
Kenyon, Harold Edward, 20 mar. 06...	9 C. D. C..........	27 june 16	New York.
Kingsbury, Walter Elliott, 16 dec. 12..	13 c. d. c..........	19 apr. 15	Brooklyn.
Kingston, Robert John, 12 apr. 98.....	asst. surg. 12 bat.....	15 mar. 99	Newburgh.
Kopetsky, Samuel Joseph, 14 mar. 02..	asst. surg. 8 inf.....	10 dec. 06	New York
Kurts, Henry William, Jr., 24 jan. 02.	8 inf.............	10 dec. 06	Pelham Manor.
Lediard, Charles, 30 nov. 04........	23 inf.............	5 aug. 15	Brooklyn.
Lent, Abraham F., 21 jul. 98..........	asst. surg. 147 inf.....	10 jan. 99	Brooklyn.
Leo, John P., 18 feb. 85............	22 inf.............	10 oct. 90	New York.
Levien, Christopher L., 23 nov. 15....	22 c. of e..........	23 nov. 15	New York.
Lewis, Calom Leslie, 24 jun. 98.....	114 inf.............	10 dec. 98	Brooklyn.
Livingston, Philip, 22 apr. 09.......	12 inf.............	7 july 16	New York City.
Lock Ambrose Maria, 13 may 98.....	8 reg.............	10 dec. 06	New York.
Long, Charles Edward, 23 sep. 98.....	asst. surg. 165 inf.....	22 dec. 98	Buffalo.
Louvot, Edward, 31 may 11..........	9 c. d. c..........	1 sep. 16	Brooklyn.
Luthy, William, 15 may 91..........	32 regt.............	26 may 92	Brooklyn.
Lynch, James, 30 aug. 15..........	9 inf.............	30 aug. 15	New York.
Lyon, Theodore Edward, 7 may 97....	comy. of sub. 8 inf.....	10 dec. 06	Montclair, N. J.
McMoran, William, 21 june 98......	169 inf.............	24 feb. 99	New York.
McNevin, Alfred C. B., 15 mar. 11....	13 c. d. c..........	5 mar. 15	Brooklyn.
Mackey, Martin Luther, 7 apr. 09....	71 inf.............	31 june 16	New York.
Mann, Alfred Christian, 27 nov. 08....	14 inf.............	4 july 16	Brooklyn.
Mansfield, John Collison, 13 oct. 14...	22 corps of eng......	23 dec. 14	New York.
Marshall, Richard Cranston, 20 may 98.	121 sep. co..........	10 dec. 98	Troy.
Mason, Jarvis W., 25 aug. 90........	8 reg.	13 mar. 16	New York.
Maxson, Wesley Searles, 28 mar. 90...	32 regt.............	17 may 92	New York.
Mets, Herman August, 20 dec. 06.....	14 inf.............	21 may 15	Brooklyn.
Miller, Douglas Winslow, 19 may 98...	103 sep. co..........	24 feb. 99	Cleveland, O.
Mills, Robert Doremus, 17 sep. 14....	1 f. a.............	7 feb. 16	Brooklyn.
Mora, Edward, 19 jul. 98............	108 inf.............	22 dec. 98	Bridgeport, Conn.
Morris, William Ephraim, 22 nov. 12..	69 inf.............	6 mar. 16	New York.
Morro, August T., 18 oct. 15........	23 inf.............	18 oct. 15	Brooklyn.
Napier, Charles Dwight, 15 may 93....	23 inf.............	14 july 16	Brooklyn.
Nelson, Guy L., 7 aug. 03..........	10 inf.............	18 dec. 15	New York.
Newton, Franklin Jonathan, 16 may 98.	137 sep. co..........	10 dec. 99	Schenectady.
Oliver, Edward, 23 oct. 06.........	10 inf.............	17 may 10	Albany.
Orr, Gilbert Franklin, 16 oct. 06.....	regt. qm. 8 inf.......	10 dec. 06	New York.
Osborn, Charles Wytlaw, 20 may 10,..	9 c. d. c..........	14 apr. 15	New York.
Outerbridge, Vivian L., 19 jun. 12....	23 inf.............	31 dec. 15	Brooklyn.
Owen, Walter G., 27 mar. 89........	12 inf.............	22 july 16	New York.
Paris, William F., 6 jun. 98........	108 inf.............	22 dec. 99	New York.
Peabody, Charles J., 8 sep. 86........	a. d. c. 3 brig......	9 jan. 91	New York.
Plunket, James.................	69 inf.............	10 july 16	New York.
Raborg, Thomas M. T., 7 mar. 00.....	12 inf.............	14 dec. 15	Utah.
Rae, Giles, 8 june 98................	169 inf.............	24 feb. 99	New York.
Rich, Fred Reed, 29 jul. 98..........	102 sep. co..........	17 dec. 98	Auburn.

RESERVE OFFICERS — (Continued)

Name, Grade and Date of Rank	To Reserve List		Residence
	Organization in which last served	Date	
CAPTAINS — Continued			
Robertson, Arthur Leslie, 15 mar. 99..	71 inf...............	11 apr. 16	New York.
Roe, William Clarke, 22 may 96......	regt. adj. 13 inf......	7 may 98	Great Neck, L. I.
Rulison, George W., 13 oct. 14......	c. of e...........	16 nov. 15	New York.
Ryan, John J., 2 may 87...........	69 inf...........	6 dec. 93	New York.
Salladin, Henry Lamppin, 7 mar. 07....	ord. dept........	1 may 14	Utica.
Sayre, Reginald Hall, 24 jan. 12....	unassigned.........	1 may 14	New York.
Schake, George Frederick, 4 jun. 98..	108 sep. co.......	17 dec. 96	Rochester.
Schoeneck, Charles C., 23 jan. 91....	32 regt..........	26 may 92	Brooklyn.
Scott, Julian F., 12 jun. 08........	12 inf...........	14 dec. 15	New York.
Scott, William Sherman, 21 jan. 08....	aide 1 brig.......	19 mar. 08	Mt. Kisco.
Short, William Byfeld, 20 jan. 13....	2 f. a...........	11 jan. 16	New York.
Singleton, Frederick William, 9 july 06.	23 inf...........	19 june 16	Brooklyn.
Skinner, Harry Hall, 18 aug. 98......	171 inf..........	3 jan. 99	New York.
Skinner, Le Roy Jance, 5 jul. 07.....	3 inf...........	21 jun. 15	Medina.
Smith, Arthur Crosaley, 12 apr. 13....	22 engrs.........	13 may 16	New York.
Smith, Edward Charles, 6 jun. 98.....	112 inf..........	24 jan. 99	New York.
Smith, L. Bertrand, 20 jun. 98......	tr. CC...........	3 jan. 99	Brooklyn.
Smith, Sydney J., 22 apr. 96........	a. d. c. 1 brig....	9 feb. 98	New York.
Sparrenberger, Frederick H , 7 feb. 01..	U. S. A. M. C......	5 may 16	New York.
St. John, Julius William, 25 may 98..	133 sep. co.......	24 feb. 99	Walton.
Stevens, John Jacob, Jr., 26 july 13..	2 f. a...........	25 feb. 16	New York.
Stevenson, Charles G., 9 oct. 15.....	8 c. d. c........	9 oct. 15	New York.
Stewart, Henry C. H., 9 oct. 15.....	9 inf...........	9 oct. 15	New York.
Stone, Charles B., 11 jun. 13.......	65 inf...........	24 may 15	Buffalo.
Strong, Prentice, 20 jan. 13........	1 f. a...........	2 dec. 15	New York.
Sullivan, Daniel Patrick, 10 june 14..	69 inf...........	22 may 16	New York.
Sweeny, Lawrence Alfred, 28 may 09..	22 engrs.........	6 july 16	New York.
Sylvester, Franklin Elmer, 24 june 98.	109 reg..........	22 dec. 98	New York.
Taylor, Irving K, 26 mar. 97........	7 inf...........	8 mar. 16	New York.
Taylor, Oscor Thomas, 8 july 98.....	165 inf..........	22 dec. 98	Buffalo.
Thompson, John M., 27 feb. 06......	9 c. d. c........	19 jul. 15	New York.
Thompson, Lynn Wentworth, 3 jun. 14.	71 inf...........	28 oct. 15	New York.
Thorne, Edward Rodger, 25 jul. 11....	10 inf...........	15 jul. 14	Albany.
Thum, William George, 11 mar. 91....	32 reg..........	26 may 92	New York.
Tilden, Philip S., 24 nov. 15.......	71 inf...........	24 nov. 15	New York.
Timpson, Lawrence, 14 nov. 02......	i. s. a. p. 1 inf......	1 may 05	Barrytown-on-Hudson.
Tompson, Frederick Bernard, 9 nov. 11	22 engrs.........	5 july 16	New York.
Townsend, John Henry, 12 jul. 98....	asst. insp. 1 brig......	21 jan. 08	New York.
Trimble, Walter, 25 oct. 83........	a. d. c. 1 brig.....	5 aug. 86	New York.
Tucker, Wentworth, 26 apr. 12......	12 inf...........	4 oct. 16	New York.
Tupper, Charles Ford, 9 jun. 98.....	120 sep. co.......	24 feb. 99	Binghamton.
Van Olinda, William Kinsley, 21 may 98	13 regt..........	28 nov. 98	New York.
Ward, John Bryan, 14 jul. 98.......	114 inf..........	10 dec. 98	Brooklyn.
Warring, Francis B., 21 may 98......	115 sep. co.......	15 mar. 99	Poughkeepsie.
Welch Thomas Cary, 5 jul. 98.......	165 inf..........	22 dec. 98	Manila, P L
Werner, Charles, 22 may 96........	13 c. d. c........	2 jul. 15	New York.
Westermann, Julius T., 22 jun. 11....	71 inf...........	4 may 15	New York.
White, Major Ambrose, 4 nov. 15.....	7 inf...........	5 jan. 16	New York.
White, S. Reynolds, 27 oct. 15......	47 inf...........	27 oct. 15	New York.
Whitehead, Otthoudt Z., 2 may 99....	1 regt...........	1 may 05	New York.
Whittle, John Henry, 23 sept. 92....	71 inf...........	27 june 16	New York.
Winne, Robert L., 16 dec. 15.......	9 inf...........	16 dec. 15	Long Island.
Winthrop, Bronson, 5 apr. 01........	regt. qm. 1 inf......	1 may 05	New York.
Wolff, Daniel, 6 feb. 05...........	22 corps of eng......	13 sep. 15	New York.
Wolff, Henry, 12 july 98...........	108 regt.........	22 dec. 98	New York.
Young, Warner S., 25 aug. 15.......	71 inf...........	25 aug. 15	New York.
Zabriskie, Andrew C., 5 feb. 96......	71 inf...........	18 dec. 15	Blithewood, N. Y.

NATIONAL DEFENSE ACT, JUNE 30, 1916

CAPTAINS			
Boyd, Thomas Edward, 11 aug. 03....	74 inf...........	15 june 16	Buffalo.
Doorty, Charles Tilden, 16 feb. 12....	3 f. a...........	24 july 16	Buffalo.
Hill, Henry Albert, 14 july 04......	74 inf...........	16 june 16	Buffalo.
Kingsbury, Joseph John, 15 mar. 12...	65 inf...........	3 mar. 15	Albany.
Maguire, Patrick Joseph, 8 dec. 03....	69 inf...........	13 july 16	New York.
Newman, Charles Howard, 18 nov. 12.	23 inf...........	24 july 16	Brooklyn.
Ritch, Amos Mead, 11 nov. 10......	47 inf...........	15 aug. 16	Brooklyn.
Stoddard, Francis R. Jr., 27 may 15...	1 heav. arty. M. V. M.	27 may 15	Albany.

RESERVE OFFICERS — *(Continued)*

NAME, GRADE AND DATE OF RANK	To Reserve List		Residence
	Organization in which last served	Date	
FIRST LIEUTENANTS			
Agnew, George B., 11 apr. 05.........	asst. i. s. a. p. 12 inf...	21 jan. 06	New York.
Arnold, Harrison B., 25 may 10......	o. d. c.............	3 mar. 15	New York.
Barton, Samuel Taylor, 28 sep. 98....	120 sep. co........	24 feb. 99	Binghamton.
Basil, Charles Joseph, 6 june 98......	108 regt...........	22 dec. 98	New York.
Beach, Oren Milton, 26 june 16......	D. B. 7 inf........	26 june 16	New York.
Bell, Charles Hamilton, 21 jan. 05....	bat. qm. 8 inf......	10 dec. 05	Mt. Vernon.
Bibby, Elias, 22 jan. 94..............	asst. surg. 18 sep. co..	19 nov. 98	Milwaukee, Wis.
Blair, Alexander McNeil, 30 jul. 01...	asst. surg. 4 sig. corps.	15 jan. 02	New York.
Booth, Arthur Woodward, 3 aug. 98...	130 sep. co.........	17 dec. 98	Elmira.
Booth, Charles Alfred, 19 july 98.....	108 regt...........	22 dec. 98	New York.
Bradley, Henry Hobart, 1 july 98.....	165 inf............	22 dec. 98	Buffalo.
Britton, Reuben A. (bvt. cap.), 29 mar. 79.	qm. 9 regt.........	7 dec. 85	New York.
Brodeur, William Henry, 4 apr. 11....	3 inf..............	2 feb. 15	Rochester.
Burdge, Harrie, 22 nov. 00..........	8 inf..............	10 dec. 06	New York.
Butler, Robert W. 13 sep. 1900......	12 inf.............	22 june 16	New York.
Campbell, Alfred B., 4 aug. 84.......	adj. 14 inf........	29 jul. 89	Brooklyn.
Carroll, Otis Swan, 23 apr. 12.......	co. B, 1 sig. corps....	28 jul. 15	New York.
Case, Wheeler Chapin, 30 jun. 11....	3 inf..............	20 aug. 15	Auburn.
Cattell, James Bernard, 28 june 98...	171 regt...........	3 jan. 99	New York.
Catuna, George Vande Bise, 15 nov. 07.	13 C. D. C........	5 july 16	Brooklyn.
Cipperly, Henry Darius.............	47 inf.............	2 sep. 16	Brooklyn.
Clark, John Paulus, 1 mar. 11.......	10 inf.............	9 jul. 15	Boston, Mass.
Clarke, Thomas B., Jr., 26 jan. 12...	1 cav..............	9 sep. 15	New York.
Clarke, Thomas Curtis, 16 sep. 15...	71 inf.............	16 sep. 15	New York.
Cohen, David B., 10 aug. 98........	109 regt...........	22 dec. 98	New York.
Colby, Francis Thompson, 29 jan. 13..	2 f. a.............	3 jul. 15	New York.
Conklin, Elwood Cline, 3 june 98.....	171 regt...........	3 jan. 99	New York.
Cooley, Benjamin Franklin, 12 jul. 98	132 sep. co........	10 dec. 98	Oyster Bay, L. I.
Curtis, Frederick Walter, 23 dec. 10..	13 c. d. c.........	3 may 15	New York.
Curtis, George, 4 may 00...........	13 regt...........	21 july 16	New York.
Daggett, Byron B., 23 feb. 00.......	4 sig. corps.......	15 jan. 02	Buffalo.
Daniel, Richard C., 9 may 02........	14 inf.............	14 jun. 15	Brooklyn.
Davis, Joseph William, 10 june 15....	13 c. d. c.........	8 mar. 16	Brooklyn.
Deeves, Richard Anderson, 26 feb. 10..	22 engrs..........	29 sep. 16	New York.
Denn, John Joseph, 12 may 05.......	14 inf.............	23 sep. 15	Brooklyn.
Dowden, Clarence Oswald, 1 oct. 00...	military pharmacist 47 inf.	22 apr. 01	Brooklyn.
Edwards, Frank Burch, 21 apr. 98....	adj. 17 bat........	15 mar. 99	Ft. Wingate, N. M
Edwards, James Howard, 11 may 98...	110 bat...........	15 mar. 99	Albany.
Fairfax, Charles Washington, 3 jun. 98	134 sep. co........	17 dec. 98	Geneva.
Fancher, Louis Delton, 14 sep. 14....	1 f. a.............	6 aug. 15	New York.
Farrington, Robert Webster, 20 dec. 09.	ord. dept.........	1 may 14	Buffalo.
Farrington, William Doty, 14 may 08..	8 c. d. c..........	24 jul. 15	New York.
Field, Robert Baxter, 15 may 14.....	47 inf.............	15 jan. 15	Brooklyn.
Field, William Putnam, 17 aug. 98....	109 inf............	22 dec. 98	New York.
Ford, Robert C., 1 may 87..........	69 regt...........	6 dec. 93	New York.
Francis, Eugene Mitchell, 22 aug. 98..	109 regt...........	22 dec. 98	New York.
Gleason, Andrew Chase, 26 jul. 98....	108 sep. co........	17 dec. 98	Rochester.
Gleed, James W., 12 may 98.........	131 sep. co........	10 dec. 98	Mohawk.
Glynn, George Alexander, 9 mar. 91...	48 sep. co.........	14 mar. 93	Albany.
Golding, John Noble, 18 june 88......	71 regt...........	20 june 16	New York.
Goodale, Walter S., 29 jul. 98.......	165 inf............	22 dec. 98	Buffalo.
Goodfellow, Eugene H..............	m. c..............	6 july 16	New York.
Graham, Wilmot Cornish, 22 jan. 97..	19 sep. co.........	21 jun. 97	Poughkeepsie.
Halpin, Francis, 15 oct. 15.........	squad. A..........	15 oct. 15	New York.
Hannan, Cornelius, 26 may 98.......	112 sep. co........	10 dec. 98	Watervliet.
Hardy, George J., 16 june 93........	9 regt............	22 dec. 98	New York.
Hathaway, Frank Bradner, 19 apr. 98.	comy. of sub. 12 bat..	15 mar. 99	Middletown.
Hayes, William A.................	9 c. d. c..........	8 oct. 15	New York.
Haseltine, Laban, 9 sep. 98.........	asst. surg. 113 sep. co.	20 dec. 98	Jamestown.
Hegeman, John Comstock, 17 may 11..	aide to chief e. a....	1 sep. 14	Jersey City, N. J.
Henry, John Joseph, 30 apr. 98......	69 regt...........	15 mar. 00	New York.
Herron, Joseph A., 2 dec. 15........	4 N. J. vols.......	2 dec. 15	New York.
Hill, Thomas Alfred, 3 june 98.......	171 regt...........	3 jan. 99	New York.
Hildenbrand, Christopher B., 12 aug. 98.	bat. adj. 108 inf....	22 dec. 98	New York.
Hitchcock, Wilbur J., 24 dec. 15.....	9 inf..............	24 dec. 15	New York.
Hoffman, Harry Natt. 18 sep. 06.....	bat. qm. 3 inf......	21 jan. 08	Elmira.
Hoyer, William Edmund, 29 may 08...	8 c. d. c..........	7 july 16	New York.
Humbert, Arthur C., 16 june 98......	171 regt...........	3 jan. 99	New York.

RESERVE OFFICERS — (Continued)

Name, Grade and Date of Rank	To Reserve List		Residence
	Organisation in which last served	Date	
FIRST LIEUTENANTS — *Continued*			
Ireland, Edward V., 2 dec. 15	12 inf	2 dec. 15	New York.
Janes, Edward Foster, 24 june 16	12 inf	27 sep. 16	New York.
Jeffrey, Stewart Lee, 10 july 12	10 inf. m. c	7 july 16	Yonkers.
Jessup, Charles M., 13 july 87	12 regt	29 oct. 90	New York.
Johnson, Edward, 14 june 98	171 regt	27 july 98	New York.
Jones, Elijah, 17 may 98	144 sop. co	24 feb. 99	Utica.
Joslin, Edward, 24 may 98	109 sep. co	10 dec. 98	Whitehall.
Kelley, Eugene, 21 dec. 15	23 inf	21 dec. 15	New York.
Kenney, Parker John, 28 feb. 16	3 inf	20 june 16	Ogdensburg.
Kernochan, Frederic, 23 aug. 04	bat. qm. 12 inf	21 jan. 08	New York.
Ladew, Edward W., 27 feb. 12	22 corps of engs	23 dec. 14	New York.
Lane, Henry, 6 june 98	108 regt	22 dec. 98	New York.
Lathrop, Henry Stebbins, 15 sep. 98	108 inf	22 dec. 98	Elizabeth, N. J.
Lloyd, William R., 6 june 98	108 regt	22 dec. 98	New York.
Lord, James Couper, 10 apr. 12	8 c. d. c	17 jun. 15	New York.
Lucey, Dennis Benedict, 1 jul. 08	qm. 16 bat	15 mar. 99	Ogdensburg.
McConkey, Thomas A., 9 jun. 98	109 inf	24 feb. 99	Scarsdale
McCoy, James John, 3 feb. 92	69 regt	6 dec. 93	New York.
McDowell, Frederick Lowman, 9 dec. 92	45 sep. co	6 dec. 93	Cortland.
McGrath, Denis Joseph, 12 jul. 98	169 inf	24 feb. 99	Brooklyn.
McKibbon, George N., 24 nov. 15	1 bat. sig. corps	24 nov. 15	New York.
McNeil, Thomas J.		8 july 16	New York.
Mackin, Robert N., 13 dec. 15	9 c. d. c	13 dec. 15	New York.
Magonigle, Harold Van Buren, 15 aug. 98	bat. adj. 109 inf	22 dec. 98	New York.
Maher, John D., 9 july 98	114 regt. n. y. v	16 may 16	New York.
Mahon, Charles, 1 aug. 90	69 regt	6 dec. 93	New York.
Marsh, Valentine, 22 aug. 98	109 regt	22 dec. 98	New York.
Martin, Edward Elsworth Irwin, 11 Aug. 16.	d. b. 71 regt	6 oct. 16	Brooklyn.
Maxwell, Frederick Stevens	d. b. 71 regt	10 july 16	New York
Mills, Clarence, 26 jan. 14	13 c. d. c	15 jun. 15	Brooklyn.
Minton, James V., 8 nov. 80	11 sep. co	17 jun. 81	Westfield.
Moon, John H., 6 jun. 98	108 inf	22 dec. 98	New York.
Morgan, John W., 12 aug. 98	108 regt	22 dec. 98	New York.
Moore, Frederick Charles, 98 apr. 07	71 regt	28 june 16	New York.
Mould, Erwin, 13 may 98	114 sep. co	24 feb. 99	Rochester.
Mulford, Joseph Parker, 30 apr. 98	8 inf	22 dec. 98	Brooklyn
Nelson, Lewis Henry, 21 may 98	107 sep. co	10 dec. 98	Winston-Salem, N. C.
O'Donohue, Louis V., 18 mar. 95	comy. of sub. sq. A	21 jan. 08	New York.
O'Keefe, Maurice Davis, 23 june 98	169 regt	24 feb. 99	New York.
O'Malley, Joseph, 15 oct. 15	23 inf	15 oct. 15	New York.
O'Reilley, Thomas Joseph, 4 feb. 08	69 regt	31 july 16	New York.
Paine, Henry Gallup, 6 jun. 98	112 inf	24 jan. 99	New York.
Parke, Floyd B., 20 may 87	asst. surg 26 sep. co	21 jun. 97	Elmira.
Paterson, Henry Augustus, 3 jun. 98	171 inf	3 jan. 99	New York.
Patton, Herbert W., 14 may 98	104 sop. co	24 feb. 99	Boston, Mass.
Pedersen, John Douglas, 19 feb. 14	1 inf	26 june 16	Mohawk.
Piers, Henry Philip, 30 dec. 11	10 inf	17 apr. 16	Albany
Radcliffe, Clarence Van Ness, 16 june 09.	7 inf	17 june 16	New York.
Reagan, James Henry, 17 may 98	122 sep. co	9 dec. 98	Saratoga Springs
Reynolds, Reginald, 30 dec. 08	12 regt	10 mar. 16	New York.
Ripley, Henry Baldwin Hyde, 6 july 15	12 inf	8 may 16	New York.
Roberts, William, 3 nov. 09	22 engrs	23 dec. 14	New York.
Roewer, John Edward, 6 jun. 98	112 inf	24 jan. 99	New York.
Rogers, Rochester H., 14 dec. 15	3 inf	14 dec. 15	New York.
Romer, Charles Baetsel, 11 jun. 98	130 sep. co	17 dec. 98	Elmira.
Rothenmeyer, Herbert Norris, 10 june	65 inf	11 july 98	Buffalo.
Rousseau, Theodore Duncan, 2 dec. 15	1 brig	25 may 16	New York.
Russell, Thomas Hendrick, 5 mar. 12	med. corps	24 nov. 14	New York.
Sagona, Charles Benedict, 2 dec. 14	14 inf	23 june 16	Brooklyn.
Scott, John Alexander, 21 sep. 98	110 bat	15 mar. 99	Albany.
Shields, William Hamilton, 10 may 98	106 sep. co	10 dec. 98	Troy.
Shirley, Rufus G., 15 oct. 15	9 c. d. c	15 oct. 15	New York.
Sisk, Maurice, 8 june 98	169 regt	24 feb. 99	New York.
Smith, Albert Rockwell, 3C jun. 03	comy. of sub. 1 bat	17 jul. 07	No Tonawanda.
Smith, Frederick William, 28 dec. 08	1 sig. cor	9 aug. 16	New York.

RESERVE OFFICERS — (Continued)

NAME, GRADE AND DATE OF RANK	To RESERVE LIST		Residence
	Organisation in which last served	Date	

FIRST LIEUTENANTS — Continued

Stebbins, Rowland, 27 feb. 12	8 c. d. c	19 may 14	New York.
Steers, Philip John, 30 mar. 14	47 inf	4 july 16	Brooklyn.
Stevenson, Mayne Reed, 9 jun. 98	113 sep. co	29 dec. 98	Jamestown.
Stivers, John Dunning, 26 apr. 98	qm. 12 bat	15 mar. 99	Middletown.
Stranahan, J. Orley, 23 sep. 98	asst. surg. 115 sep. co.	15 mar. 99	Rome.
Stuart, Malcolm. 21 jun. 98	bat. adj. 171 inf	3 jan. 00	New York.
Tansley, Frank D., 29 may 06	9 c. d. c	20 sep. 15	New York.
Thomas, Charles E. L., 6 apr. 15	69 inf	24 nov. 15	New York.
Thomas, James Winthrop, 25 may 10	8 c. d. c	19 may 14	New York.
Thompson, Leslie Eugene, 5 nov. 09	9 c. d. c	24 aug. 15	New York.
Thompson, William Bryan. 19 sep. 98	i. s. a. p, 11 bat	15 mar. 99	Mount Vernon.
Tomlinson, Burt Franklin, 22 june 15	9 c. d. c	8 may 16	New York.
Voroe, Walter Herbert, 4 june 98	101 sep. co	26 dec. 98	Rochester.
Waldron, Leonard Truman,3 june 98	171 regt	3 jan. 99	New York.
Walker, Henry Halsey, 6 may 98	47 regt	16 may 99	Brooklyn.
Walker, Willis Harvey, 17 jun. 14	22 c. of e	16 nov. 15	New York.
Ward, James Joseph, 5 sep. 82	69 regt	24 june 95	New York.
Waters, John T. C., 12 dec. 13	23 inf	20 aug. 15	Brooklyn.
Weir, James. 17 mar. 05	comy. of sub. sq. C.	21 jan. 08	Brooklyn.
Whaley, Arthur Mounder, 25 july 98	165 regt	22 dec. 98	Buffalo.
White, Robert A., 18 .eo. 13	1 f. a.	16 jul. 14	New York.
Wood, Franklin Thomas, 26 may 99	comy. of sub. 4 bat	1 may 05	Albany.
Wood, Lansing Pruyn, 16 dec. 08	110 bat	15 mar. 99	New York.
Woodruff, Henry Adsit, 14 june 98	171 regt	3 jan. 99	New York.
Woodward, Rigeal D., 6 jun. 98	112 inf	24 jan. 99	New York.
Wright, Clarence 8., 19 jul. 98	133 sep. co	24 feb. 99	Walton.
Young, William Joseph, 2 apr. 08	47 regt	2 july 14	Brooklyn.
Yurg. Fred, 30 sep. 85	qm. 11 regt	11 jan. 90	New York.
Zimpel, Rudolph L., 20 jan. 14	22 corps of engs	29 may 15	New York.

FIRST LIEUTENANTS, NATIONAL DEFENSE ACT, JUNE 3), 1916

Johnson, William Arthur, 13 mar. 16	3 f. a.	31 july 16	Buffalo.
McDougall, Philip Sidney, 26 june 16	3 f. a	10 aug. 16	Buffalo.
Malone, Paul, 13 sep. 10	65 inf	8 june 16	Buffalo.
Morris, Edward Joseph, 25 may 14	23 inf. m. c.	16 june 16	Brooklyn.
Walton, Lester Roberts, 4 apr. 11	9 c. d. c	5 june 16	New York.
Yund, Walter Charles, 19 june 16	2 inf.	20 dec. 16	Amsterdam.

SECOND LIEUTENANTS

Arnold, John Welles, 10 jun. 14	8 c. d. c	31 dec. 14	New York.
Atwater, Charles Anson, 31 july 11	3 inf	24 feb. 16	New York.
Barrett, Louis Stanley, 28 june 11	13 c. d. c	8 june 16	Brooklyn.
Berning, Henry Rudolph, 7 apr. 14	22 corps of engs	23 dec. 14	New York.
Bitroff, George Fred Jr., 17 apr. 14	47 inf	8 july 16	New York.
Boud, Montcalm Dunham. 23 sep. 98	148 sep. co	17 dec. 98	Oswego.
Burke, Frank Martin, 11 feb. 11	14 inf	4 july 16	Brooklyn.
Callaghan, John Henry, 23 jun. 98	169 inf	24 feb. 99	New York.
Carpenter, Frec. 13 may 08	144 sep. co	24 feb. 99	Kingston.
Chambers, Albert Walter, 16 june 98	171 regt	6 jan. 99	New York.
Chambers, James, 14 jul. 98	114 inf	10 dec. 98	New York.
Colburn, Arthur Daniel, 22 mar. 16	74 inf	1 july 16	Buffalo.
Conklin, Albert Lewis Jr., 19 dec. 02	c. a. c	11 nov. 16	New York City.
Croffut, Thomas D., 3 feb. 98	13 inf	7 may 98	Brooklyn.
Crowley, Patrick Joseph, 12 july 15	69 inf	29 june 16	New York.
Dawson, Woodson H., 22 dec. 13	22 eng	23 dec. 14	New York.
Denning, Charles Hovey, 17 may 98	144 sep. co	24 feb. 99	New York.
De Houville, Herman H., 14 may 98	110 bat	15 mar. 99	Albany.
Dillman, Frederick C., 28 oct. 08	14 inf	23 nov. 15	Brooklyn.
Doscher, William Stanley, 18 june 09	23 inf	27 june 16	Brooklyn.
Doulon, Richard Joseph, 21 may 98	107 sep. co	10 dec. 98	Cohoes.
Drew, Patrick Monahan, 2 aug. 93	69 inf	6 dec. 93	Brooklyn.
Feery, Denis J., 25 oct. 88	69 regt	6 dec. 93	New York.
Foley, Patrick John, 29 jul. 98	131 sep. co	10 dec. 98	Ilion.
Freid, Mortimer Edward, 5 may 14	14 inf	3 mar. 16	New York.
Furner, Ralph Herbert, 29 dec. 13	3 inf	30 oct. 14	Rochester.
Gardner, William Jr., 14 june 98	171 regt	27 july 98	New York.
Gaylord, Melvin Snow, 3 jun. 98	134 sep. co	17 dec. 98	Geneva.
Gerhardt, Christian, 7 apr. 08	71 regt	15 july 16	New York.

RESERVE OFFICERS — *(Continued)*

NAME, GRADE AND DATE OF RANK	To RESERVE LIST		Residence
	Organisation in which last served	Date	
SECOND LIEUTENANTS — *Continued*			
Gonzalez, Antonio C., Jr., 8 jul. 12....	9 c. d. c............	9 sep. 15	New York.
Gonzales, Eugene Raymond, 10 may 98	47 inf...............	16 may 99	Brooklyn.
Green, George E., 26 apr. 02.........	9 c. d. c............	13 sep. 15	New York.
Hamilton, Arthur Augustus, 26 may 98.	112 sep. co.........	10 dec. 98	Troy.
Hamilton, Wells, 6 jul 98............	114 inf.............	10 dec 98	Brooklyn.
Hasselbauer, Harry J., 23 apr. 13....	22 eng..............	23 dec. 14	New York.
Hemingway, Marshall Freeman, 15 jul. 98.	121 sep. co.........	10 dec. 98	Troy.
Higgins, William F. J., 7 jul. 15.....	9 c. d. c............	7 jul. 15	New York.
Himrod, Edwin Hanford, 29 jun. 98...	114 inf.............	10 dec. 98	Brooklyn.
Hollers, Carl H. B., 6 jun. 98.......	108 inf.............	22 dec. 98	Havana, Cuba.
Kenny, John Adams, 4 jun. 98........	110 bat.............	15 mar. 99	No Yakima, Wash.
Klein, Walter G., 12 nov. 4..........	47 inf..............	15 dec. 15	Brooklyn.
Klock, Karl Theodore, 30 jul. 13.....	3 inf...............	31 jul. 15	Syracuse.
Knapp, John Thomas, 14 may 98.....	103 sep. co.........	24 feb. 99	New York.
Kyle, James Orr, 7 june 04...........	71 inf..............	8 july 16	New York.
Lahens, Louis Emile, 13 feb. 12 (bvt. 1st lt.)	7 inf...............	21 june 16	New York.
Laughlin, Frank Dunlap, 31 aug. 98...	109 regt............	22 dec. 98	New York.
Livingston, Duncan McII., 30 apr. 98..	8 regt..............	22 dec 98	New York.
Ludlum, Nathaniel B., 11 dec. 03.....	65 regt.............	27 july 16	Buffalo.
Lund, Charles Joseph, 4 june 98......	101 sep. co.........	26 dec. 98	Rochester.
McKeever, Isaac C., 31 aug. 98.......	112 inf.............	22 jan 99	New York.
McLoud, Paul, 22 sep. 11............	1 f. a..............	27 june 16	Binghamton.
McMahon, Austin John, 3 june 98....	141 sep. co.........	17 dec. 98	Syracuse.
McManus, Terence Belleau, 30 june 09	71 regt.............	6 may 16	New York.
Magee, Walter Charles, 11 mar. 92...	69 regt.............	6 dec. 93	New York.
Manley, Arthur Lindley, 26 mar. 95..	26 sep co...........	21 jun. 97	Elmira.
Mann, Ellery W., 20 jan. 14.........	22 eng..............	23 dec. 14	New York.
Moore, Frederick F., 12 nov. 13......	1 f. a..............	31 jul. 15	New York.
Mullen, William Joseph, 20 jan. 09...	14 regt.............	5 july 16	Brooklyn.
Niles, Edgar C., 16 jan. 12..........	10 inf..............	23 sep. 15	Albany.
O'Shaughnessy, Charles Lawrence, 9 june 15.	65 inf..............	11 july 16	Buffalo.
O'Sullivan, Mortimer McCarthy, 30 apr. 98.	60 inf..............	15 mar. 00	New York.
Page, Raymond, 3 apr. 12............	13 c. d. c..........	12 jan. 15	Brooklyn.
Parenteau, Maxine John, 11 jan. 10...	12 inf..............	25 feb. 16	New York.
Paret, Frank Murray, 31 aug. 98.....	109 regt............	22 dec. 98	New York.
Pink, George Albert, 22 may 14......	47 inf..............	17 may 16	Brooklyn.
Pitts, Clarence Elwyn, 25 nov. 10....	3 inf...............	20 oct. 15	Oswego.
Potter, Joseph Boies, 24 may 98......	109 sep. co.........	10 dec. 98	Whitehall.
Renean, Michael Joseph, 26 jul. 04...	10 inf..............	19 may 14	New York.
Reidy, Michael Edward, 27 mar. 14...	69 inf..............	6 nov. 16	New York.
Reynolds, Robert Edward Lee, 14 may 98.	146 sep. co.........	10 dec. 98	Amsterdam.
Rich, Albert Edward, 25 sep. 90......	13 regt.............	17 dec. 92	New York.
Roberts, George Eleaser, 26 jul 98....	108 sep. co.........	17 dec. 98	Rochester.
Roberts, William, 7 mar. 13..........	22 eng..............	23 dec. 14	New York.
Robinson, Edward Augustus, 12 jul. 98	120 sep. co.........	24 feb. 99	Binghamton.
Robinson, Edward Heaword, 24 may 98.	137 sep. co.........	10 dec. 98	Detroit, Mich.
Rowell, Edwin Lewis, 21 may 98......	133 sep. co.........	24 feb. 99	Walton.
Sage, Edward E., 10 jan. 84.........	7 regt..............	28 apr. 16	New York.
Santee, Ellis Monroe, 10 apr. 93.....	45 sep. co..........	6 dec. 93	Cortland.
Schaefer, Robert G., 4 may 14.......	22 eng..............	23 dec. 14	New York.
Scheff, Bertram Rogers, 14 june 98...	171 regt............	3 jan. 99	New York.
Shaw, Albert Embree, 3 june 07......	13 c. d. c..........	10 june 12	Brooklyn.
Shaw, Edward R., 1 july 98..........	165 regt............	22 dec. 98	Buffalo.
Sly, Hiram Belden, 10 aug. 98.......	130 sep. co.........	17 dec. 98	Newtonville, Mass.
Smith, Charles Telfer, 3 june 98......	171 regt............	3 jan. 99	New York.
Smith, Frederick Crooker, 5 aug. 98..	143 sep. co.........	17 dec. 98	Port Arthur, Tex.
Smith, Sanford Edward, 18 may 10....	71 inf..............	9 aug. 16	New York.
Smith, Sidney L., 7 sep 98...........	112 inf.............	24 jan. 99	New York.
Smock, Daniel P., 21 jan. 91.........	13 regt.............	17 may 92	Brooklyn.
Steurer, William, 16 feb. 11.........	14 inf..............	19 july 16	Brooklyn.
Stewart, Thomas, 12 aug. 98.........	108 regt............	22 dec. 98	New York.
Stockham, Joseph Godfrey, 12 nov. 14.	23 inf..............	26 jan. 16	Brooklyn.
Suydam, John Richard, Jr., 13 jun. 14.	8 c. d. c...........	24 dec. 14	New York.
Throop, George Enos, 20 jan. 99......	112 regt............	24 jan. 99	New York.
Tierney, Dennis G., 24 oct. 98.......	105 sep. co.........	24 feb. 99	Ridgewood, L. I.

RESERVE OFFICERS — *(Concluded)*

NAME, GRADE AND DATE OF RANK	To Reserve List		Residence
	Organization in which last served	Date	
SECOND LIEUTENANTS — *Concluded*			
Timony, Arthur K., 19 july 98......	169 regt..............	24 feb. 99	New York.
Torberg, John George, 21 may 98.....	13 regt..............	28 nov. 98	Brooklyn.
Torborg, John George, 21 may 98.....	13 inf..............	28 nov. 98	Brooklyn.
Tracey, Charles Amasa, 8 feb. 16.....	1 cav..............	28 mar. 16	Brooklyn.
Tucker, Carl E., 15 feb 01...........	3 inf..............	21 jan. 08	Niagara Falls.
Ward, Theodore Hackett, 7 mar. 08...	12 regt.............	13 sep. 16	New York.
Warrick, Stanley Cummings, 17 jun.98.	102 sep. co.........	17 dec. 98	West Palm Beach, Fla.
Warner, Robert Louis Livingston, 27 feb. 08.	47 regt..............	29 june 16	Brooklyn.
Wolstenholme, Alfred J., 5 july 98....	165 regt.............	22 dec. 98	Buffalo.
Young, Oliver Curtiss, 8 sep. 15......	65 inf..............	23 mar. 16	Buffalo.
Zier, Calvin Valentine, 1 july 11	47 inf..............	8 july 16	Brooklyn.

SECOND LIEUTENANTS, NATIONAL DEFENSE ACT, JUNE 30, 1916

Albro, Preston Maurice, 22 may 16....	65 inf..............	18 july 16	Buffalo.
Barnum, Charles H., 7 dec. 11........	23 inf..............	7 july 16	Brooklyn.
Innes, William Henry, 20 apr. 16.....	2 inf..............	7 july 16	Scotia.
Steger, Charles Frederick, 16 june 14..	65 inf..............	6 july 16	Buffalo.
Stone, Steven Grant, 12 jan. 16.......	9 c. d. c.	10 oct. 16	New York.

CHAPLAINS

Bradshaw, Archibald Harmon, 1 sep. 98	171 inf.	3 jan. 99	New York

CHAPLAINS, NATIONAL DEFENSE ACT, JUNE 30, 1916

McCaffrey, Charles, 14 dec. 03..	1 inf...............	30 june 16	Oneonta.

RETIRED

Brigadier General

John G. Eddy, 2d Brigade, August 17, 1916.

Colonels

Daniel Appleton (bvt. Major General), 7th Infantry, February 23, 1916.
William Whitehead Ladd, Judge Advocate General's Department, September 26, 1916.
Charles Joseph Wolff, 74th Infantry, June 20, 1916.

Majors

Robert Newton Disbrow, Medical Corps (8th C. D. C.), October 6, 1916.
Lansdale Boardman Green, 3d Brigade, July 5, 1916.
Lee Herbert Smith, 4th Brigade, July 5, 1916.

Captains

Eben Elisha Acker, 8th Coast Defense Command, August 10, 1916.
Henry Daniel McCutcheon (bvt. Major), 47th Infantry, January 17, 1916.

First Lieutenants

William Joseph Tracy, Medical Corps (3d Infantry), May 15, 1916.

Brevet Second Lieutenants

William N. Bavier, late private, 7th Infantry, January 28, 1916.
William H. Burton, Jr., late regimental sergeant major, 10th Infantry, June 27, 1916.
Courtney S. Busee, late private, 7th Infantry, December 21, 1916.
George Donovan, late quartermaster sergeant, 12th Infantry, July 8, 1916.
Frank B. Hodenberg, late private, 23d Infantry, March 13, 1916.
Francis H. Hessels, late private, 10th Infantry (Company " H "), June 27, 1916.
Edward A. Howland, Jr., late sergeant, 7th Infantry, May 25, 1916.
Martin May, late private, 13th Coast Defense Command, May 1, 1916.
Henry J. Schick, late first sergeant, 65th Infantry, July 5, 1916.
George B. Youngs, late first sergeant, 71st Infantry, July 21, 1916.
Frederick W. Taylor, late first sergeant, 71st Infantry, May 25, 1916.
Thomas Graham, late quartermaster sergeant, 47th Infantry, June 1, 1916.
Charles F. Berg, late private, 7th Infantry, June 7, 1916.
Archie T. Drake, la
Francis J. Loughlin, late commissary sergeant, 12th Infantry, July 8, 1916.

DETAILED

Captain, Arthur M. Day, Reserve List, to duty with 8th Coast Defense Command, January 13, 1916.

Captain Frederick S. Johnston, Reserve List, to duty as Acting Commissary, 3d Infantry, January 21, 1916.

First Lieutenant, Theodore D. Rousseau, 69th Infantry, for duty as aide on 1st Brigade staff, to be a permanent assignment, January 3, 1916.

Captain, Frederick S. Couchman, 3d Infantry, detailed as aide on Governor's staff, January 19, 1916.

First Lieutenant, Jeremiah W. O'Mahoney, 9th Coast Defense Command, relieved from duty with that command and assigned to Quartermaster Corps, February 11, 1916.

First Lieutenant, William J. Young, Reserve List, to duty with 47th Infantry as I. S. A. P., February 17, 1916.

Captain, Joseph J. Kingsbury, Reserve List, detailed to duty with Company " M", 65th Infantry, March 9, 1916.

First Lieutenant, Clarence Radcliffe, to duty with Company F, 1st Infantry, for 90 days, March 21, 1916.

Second Lieutenant, Summerfield S. Curtiss, Reserve List, to duty with 47th Infantry for 90 days, March 24, 1916.

Colonel, Oliver B. Bridgman, Reserve List, to duty with Division Headquarters, for 90 days, March 22, 1916.

Second Lieutenant, Edgar C. Niles, detailed for 90 days with 10th Infantry, April 10, 1916.

Captain, Frederick E. Humphreys, 22d Corps of Engineers, detailed as aide on Division staff, May 18, 1916.

Captain, Walter L. Bell, Reserve List, to Division, N. G., June 10, 1916.

First Lieutenant, Harry B. Baldwin, Reserve List, to 47th Infantry, June 17, 1916.

Second Lieutenant, Antonio C. Gonsalas, Jr., Reserve List, to 2d Field Artillery, 90 days, June 20, 1916.

First Lieutenant, James N. Wadsworth, Jr., Reserve List, to Troop M, Depot Unit, 1st Cavalry, June 21, 1916.

Second Lieutenant, John H. Hendrick, Reserve List, to Company H, 7th Infantry, 90 days, June 21, 1916.

First Lieutenant Gerald Stratton, Reserve List, to Company G, 7th Infantry, 90 days, June 21, 1916.

First Lieutenant, Wheeler C. Case, Reserve List, to Company G, 3d Infantry, 90 days, June 22, 1916.

Captain, William M. Ford, Reserve List, to M. C. 69th Infantry, 90 days, June 22, 1916.

Captain, Henry H. Brooks, Retired, to M.C., Depot Unit, 7th Infantry, June 22, 1916.

Lieutenant Colonel, Edward B. Bruch, Reserve List, to Depot Unit, 71st Infantry, June 22, 1916.

Detailed — Continued

Captain Lynn W. Thompson, Reserve List, to Depot Unit, 71st Infantry, June 22, 1916.

Captain, Francis R. Stoddard, Jr., Reserve List, to Depot Unit, 71st Infantry, June 22, 1916.

Captain, Robert E. Heun, Reserve List, to Depot Unit, 71st Infantry, June 22, 1916.

Bvt. Brigadier General, Daniel Appleton, retired to 2d Division, N. G., June 22, 1916.

Chaplain, Herbert Shinman, Reserve List, to 1st Field Artillery, 90 days, June 24, 1916.

Colonel, Charles J. Wolf, Retired, to Depot Battalion, 74th Infantry, June 26, 1916.

Colonel, Eugene K. Austin, Reserve List, to State Arsenal, 90 days, June 26, 1916.

Colonel, Oliver B. Bridgman, Reserve List, to State Arsenal, 90 days, June 26, 1916.

First Lieutenant, George P. Hill, Reserve List, to State Arsenal, 90 days, June 26, 1916.

First Lieutenant, Oren M. Beach, Reserve List, to State Arsenal, 90 days, June 26, 1916.

Colonel, Nathaniel B. Thurston, Ordnance Department, to 74th Infantry, June 26, 1916.

Colonel, William Hayward, Reserve List, to 15th Infantry, June 27, 1916.

Second Lieutenant, William A. Niver, Reserve List, to State Arsenal, June 27, 1916.

Second Lieutenant, Patrick J. Crowley, Reserve List, to State Arsenal, June 29, 1916.

Captain, Lorillard Spencer, Reserve List, to Military Secretary, June 29, 1916.

Major, H. F. Hotchkiss, M. C., to 15th Infantry, June 29, 1916.

First Lieutenant, David N. Barrows, M. C., to 15th Infantry, June 29, 1916.

First Lieutenant, Joseph B. Hydorn, Reserve List, to Troop B, Depot Unit, 1st Cavalry, June 30, 1916.

Major, John L. Macumber, M. C., Reserve List, to State Arsenal, June 30, 1916.

Captain, James H. Chard, Reserve List, to Depot Battalion, 71st Infantry, June 30, 1916.

Captain, Frederick C. Moore, Reserve List, to Depot Battalion, 71st Infantry, June 30, 1916.

Captain, C. D. Van Wagenen, Reserve List, to Depot Battalion, 71st Infantry, June 30, 1916.

Captain, L. C. Breckenridge, Reserve List, to Depot Battalion, 71st Infantry, June 30, 1916.

First Lieutenant, Burton C. Wager, Reserve List, to Depot Battalion, 71st Infantry, June 30, 1916.

First Lieutenant, Harold Lawson, Reserve List, to 1st Field Artillery, 90 days, June 30, 1916.

First Lieutenant, John A. Coffey, Reserve List, to Armory Commission, June 30, 1916.

Brigadier General, Samuel M. Welch, retired, to President Examining Board, 4th Brigade Depot Units, June 30, 1916.

Lieutenant Colonel, Henry A. Bostwick, Q. M. C., to Property and Disbursing Office, U. S., June 30, 1916.

Captain, Walter L. Bell, Reserve List, to Chief Quartermaster, July 1, 1916.

Major, Charles F. Van Benthuysen, Reserve List, to Depot Battalion, 10th Infantry, July 1, 1916.

Second Lieutenant, Karl T. Klock, Reserve List, to Company A, 3d Infantry, July 1, 1916.

First Lieutenant, Robert S. Field, Reserve List, to Depot Battalion, 22d Corps of Engineers, July 1, 1916.

Major Edward H. Snyder, Reserve List, to Depot Battalion, 47th Infantry, July 3, 1916.

Captain, George H. Teats, Reserve List, to Depot Battalion, 47th Infantry, July 3, 1916.

First Lieutenant, George W. Hudtwalker, Reserve List, to Depot Battalion, 47th Infantry, July 3, 1916.

Major Henry H. Royce, Retired, to Depot Battalion, 2d Field Artillery, July 3, 1916.

Captain, George H. Davis, Reserve List, to Depot Battalion, 47th Infantry, July 3, 1916.

Captain, August T. Morro, Reserve List, to Depot Battalion, 1st Infantry, July 3, 1916.

Major, George G. Cochran, Reserve List, to Depot Battalion, 14th Infantry, July 3, 1916.

Lieutenant Colonel, J. Mayhew Wainwright, Reserve List, to State Arsenal, July 3, 1916.

Lieutenant Colonel, Percy E. Nagle, Retired, to Chief Quartermaster, July 3, 1916.

Captain, Arthur E. Connor, Reserve List, to Depot Battalion, 1st Infantry, July 5, 1916.

Second Lieutenant, Herbert C. Dienst, Reserve List, to Depot Battalion, 2d Field Artillery, July 5, 1916.

Second Lieutenant, Charles T. Whelan, Reserve List, to Depot Battalion, 3d Infantry, July 5, 1916.

Captain, Prentice Strong, Reserve List, to Depot Battalion, 1st Field Artillery, July 5, 1916.

First Lieutenant, Charles A. Hickey, Reserve List, to Depot Battalion, 69th Infantry, July 5, 1916.

Captain, Michael J. Dwyer, Retired, to Depot Battalion, 69th Infantry, July 5, 1916.

Captain, William J. Costigan, Reserve List, to Depot Battalion, 69th Infantry, July 5, 1916.

Captain, Daniel P. Sullivan, Reserve List, to Depot Battalion, 69th Infantry, July 5, 1916.

Captain, Walter C. Woods, Reserve List, to Depot Battalion, 69th Infantry, July 5, 1916.

Second Lieutenant, John G. Poore, Jr., Reserve List, to Depot Battalion, 69th Infantry, July 5, 1916.

Major, Philip E. Reville, Reserve List, to Depot Battalion, 69th Infantry, July 5, 1916.

Second Lieutenant, Melvin B. Gaylord, Reserve List, to Depot Battalion, 3d Infantry, July 5, 1916.

Captain, John A. Anderson, Reserve List, to Depot Battalion, 14th Infantry, July 5, 1916.

First Lieutenant, John H. Bogardus, Reserve List, to Depot Battalion, 23d Infantry, July 5, 1916.

First Lieutenant, Joseph E. Kunsmann, Reserve List, to Depot Battalion, 23d Infantry, July 5, 1916.

First Lieutenant, Eugene Kelley, Reserve List, to Depot Battalion, 23d Infantry, July 5, 1916.

Second Lieutenant, Robert G. Schaefer, Reserve List, to Depot Battalion, 22d Corps of Engineers, July 5, 1916.

Colonel, Loyal L. Davis, Reserve List, to Depot Battalion, 2d Infantry, July 5, 1916.

Major, Samuel C. Jones, Retired, Depot Unit 2d Ambulance Company, July 5, 1916.

First Lieutenant, John A. Scott, Reserve List, to Depot Battalion, 10th Infantry, July 5, 1916.

Captain, Charles D. Napier, Reserve List, to Depot Battalion, 14th Infantry, July 5, 1916.

First Lieutenant, John M. Morrison, Reserve List, to Depot Battalion, 1st Infantry, July 5, 1916.

Second Lieutenant, Charles F. Hinman, Reserve List, to Depot Battalion, 1st Infantry, July 5, 1916.

Detailed — Continued

Captain Henry B. Graves, Reserve List, to Depot Battalion, 3d Infantry, July 5, 1916.

Captain, Frank R. Harriman, Reserve List, to Depot Battalion, 23d Infantry, July 5, 1916.

First Lieutenant, Arthur R. Overfield, Reserve List, to Depot Battalion, 74th Infantry, July 5, 1916.

Captain, Nicholas A. Deevy, Reserve List, to Depot Battalion, 22d Corps of Engineers, July 6, 1916.

Captain, Laurence A. Sweeney, Reserve List, to Depot Battalion, 22d Corps of Engineers, July 6, 1916.

Captain James A. Bell, Reserve List, to Depot Battalion, 22d Corps of Engineers, July 6, 1916.

Captain, Daniel Wolff, Reserve List, to Depot Battalion, 22d Corps of Engineers, July 6, 1916.

First Lieutenant, Frederick Wendel, Reserve List, to Depot Battalion, 22d Corps of Engineers, July 6, 1916.

Captain, John Mansfield, Reserve List, to Depot Battalion, 22d Corps of Engineers, July 6, 1916.

First Lieutenant, William Roberts, Reserve List, to Depot Battalion, 22d Corps of Engineers, July 6, 1916.

Captain, Dana L. Jewell, Reserve List, to Depot Battalion, 3d Infantry, July 6, 1916.

First Lieutenant, Fred W. Plank, Reserve List, to Depot Battalion, 3d Infantry, July 6, 1916.

Brigadier General, Samuel M. Welch, Retired, to 4th Brigade, July 6, 1916.

Second Lieutenant, Alonson B. Wilson, 7th Infantry, to aide Commanding General, 2d Division, July 7, 1916.

First Lieutenant, David N. Barrows, M. C., to Div. Com., July 7, 1916.

Captain, John W. Elmes, Reserve List, to Depot Battalion, 69th Infantry, July 7, 1916.

Second Lieutenant, Antonio C. Gonzales, Reserve List, to State Arsenal, July 7, 1916.

Major, David Banks, Reserve List, to Depot Battalion, 12th Infantry, July 7, 1916.

Captain, Howland Pell, Reserve List, to Depot Battalion, 12th Infantry, July 7, 1916.

First Lieutenant, Elisha Sniffin, Reserve List, to Depot Battalion, 12th Infantry, July 7, 1916.

Major, Edwin N. Dayton, Reserve List, to Aide Div., July 7, 1916.

Lieutenant Colonel, Henry H. Brooks, M. C., to Camp Whitman, July 7, 1916.

Lieutenant Colonel, George F. Hinton, Reserve List, to 15th Infantry, July 8, 1916.

Captain, Cornelius S. DeBevoise, Reserve List, to Depot Battalion, 1st Cavalry, July 8, 1916.

Major, Howard K. Brown, Reserve List, to Depot Battalion, 1st Cavalry, July 8, 1916.

Captain, Philip Livingston, Reserve List, to Depot Battalion, 12th Infantry, July 8, 1916.

Major, William S. Cherry, Reserve List, to Depot Unit, 1st Field Hospital, July 8, 1916.

First Lieutenant, David L. Conway, Reserve List, to Depot Unit, 4th Ambulance Company, July 8, 1916.

First Lieutenant, F. G. Englehardt, Reserve List, to Depot Unit, 4th Ambulance Company, July 8, 1916.

First Lieutenant, John A. Scott, Reserve List, to Depot Battalion, 10th Infantry, July 8, 1916.

Captain, John A. C. Jansen, Reserve List to Depot Battalion, 1st Cavalry, July 8, 1916.

Second Lieutenant, George F. Bittrolff, Jr., Reserve List, to Depot Battalion, 47th Infantry, July 8, 1916.

Captain James S. Angus, Reserve List, to Depot Battalion, 47th Infantry, July 8, 1916.

Second Lieutenant, Calvin V. Zier, Reserve List, to Depot Battalion, 47th Infantry, July 8, 1916.

Captain, Alfred F. Hodgman, Reserve List, to Depot Battalion, 3d Infantry, July 10, 1916.

First Lieutenant, Clarence V. Radcliff, Reserve List, to State Camp, Peekskill, July 10, 1916.

Second Lieutenant, Joseph J. Keegan, Reserve List, to Depot Battalion, 69th Infantry, July 10, 1916.

First Lieutenant, John P. Devane, Reserve List, to Depot Battalion, 69th Infantry, July 10, 1916.

Second Lieutenant, John H. Callaghan, Reserve List, to Depot Battalion, 69th Infantry, July 10, 1916.

First Lieutenant, Henry L. Stockbridge, Reserve List, to Depot Battalion, 47th Infantry July 10, 1916.

Captain, Schuyler Blankley, Reserve List, to Depot Battalion, 1st Cavalry, July 10, 1916.

First Lieutenant, Oscar W. Guelich, Reserve List, to Depot Battalion, 3d Infantry, July 10, 1916.

Captain, Charles J. Lamb, Reserve List, to Depot Battalion, 1st Infantry, July 10, 1916.

Second Lieutenant, Carl E. Tucker, Reserve List, to Depot Battalion, 3d Infantry, July 11, 1916.

First Lieutenant, John T. C. Waters, Reserve List, to Depot Battalion, 23d Infantry, July 11, 1916.

Captain, Francis De F. Kemp, Reserve List, to Depot Battalion, 2d Infantry, July 11, 1916.

Captain, Alex M. Jackson, Reserve List, to Depot Battalion, 2d Infantry, July 11, 1916.

Second Lieutenant, Frank Fremmer, Reserve List, to Depot Battalion, 2d Infantry, July 11, 1916.

Captain, Henry D. McCutcheon, Retired, to Commanding General, 2d Brigade, July 12, 1916.

Major, Clarence Strevell, Reserve List, to Adjutant General's Office, July 14, 1916.

Captain, Henry L. Butler, Adjutant General's Department, to Adjutant General's Office, July 14, 1916.

Captain, George H. Norton, Reserve List, to Depot Battalion, 3d Field Artillery, July 15, 1916.

Captain, Peter Cantline, Reserve List, to Depot Battalion, 1st Infantry, July 15, 1916.

Captain, Henry S. Ball, Reserve List, to Depot Battalion, 1st Infantry, July 15, 1916.

Captain, Edward E. Powell, Reserve List, to Depot Battalion, 1st Infantry, July 15, 1916.

First Lieutenant, Fred M. H. Jackson, Reserve List, to Depot Battalion, 1st Infantry, July 15, 1916.

Colonel, Charles E. P. Babcock, Reserve List, to 4th Brigade, Examining Board, July 17, 1916.

Major, Carroll J. Roberts, Reserve List, to 4th Brigade, Examining Board, July 18, 1916.

Captain, Daniel Wolff, Reserve List, to Camp Whitman, July 19, 1916.

Second Lieutenant, Antonio C. Gonzalez, Reserve List, to Commanding General Division, July 20, 1916.

First Lieutenant, Frederick J. Maxwell, Reserve List, to Depot Battalion, 71st Infantry, July 21, 1916.

First Lieutenant, John T. Shinners, Reserve List, to Depot Battalion, 1st Field Artillery, July 21, 1916.

Detailed — Continued

Captain, George H. Hearn, Reserve List, to Depot Battalion, 22d Corps of Engineers, July 21, 1916.

Captain, Joseph M. Gwinner, Reserve List, to 3d Field Artillery, July 22, 1916.

Captain, Walter A. Scott, Reserve List, to Depot Battalion, 3d Infantry, July 24, 1916.

First Lieutenant, Charles W. Fairfax, Reserve List, to Depot Battalion, 3d Infantry, July 24, 1916.

Captain, John T. Kennedy, Reserve List, to Depot Battalion, 69th Infantry, July 24, 1916.

Captain, John J. Roche, Reserve List, to Depot Battalion, 69th Infantry, July 24, 1916.

Second Lieutenant, Edmund J. Connelly, Reserve List, to Depot Battalion, 69th Infantry, July 24, 1916.

Major, Frank A. Martin, Retired to Depot Battalion, 23d Infantry, July 25, 1916.

First Lieutenant, Henry R. Berning, Reserve List, to Depot Battalion, 22d Corps of Engineers, July 26, 1916.

Captain, Joseph W. Farrell, Q. M. C. to Commanding General Division, July 28, 1916.

Second Lieutenant, John J. Curtin, Reserve List, to 3d Field Artillery, July 28, 1916.

Major, Joseph A. Cox, Reserve List, to 4th Field Hospital, July 28, 1916.

Major, Charles E. Warner, Reserve List, to Adjutant General's Department, July 31, 1916.

Captain, Frederick W. Hyde, Reserve List, to Depot Battalion, 74th Infantry, July 31, 1916.

Lieutenant Colonel, Henry H. Brooks, M. C., to A. G., Camp Whitman, August 1, 1916.

Major, Henry W. Brendel, Reserve List, to Depot Battalion, 3d Field Artillery, August 3, 1916.

Captain, James H. Kenyon, Reserve List, to Depot Battalion, 1st Field Artillery, August 3, 1916.

Captain, Frank M. Chapin, Reserve List, to Depot Battalion, 3d Field Artillery, August 3, 1916.

Captain, Gustav A. Frisch, Reserve List, to Depot Battalion, 3d Field Artillery, August 3, 1916.

First Lieutenant, Walter M. Wilson, Reserve List, to Depot Battalion, 3d Field Artillery, August 3, 1916.

First Lieutenant, John D. Clute, Reserve List, to Depot Battalion, · 3d Field Artillery, August 3, 1916.

First Lieutenant, Walter C. Barker, Reserve List, to Depot Battalion, 3d Field Artillery, August 3, 1916.

Second Lieutenant, Frederick C. Fornes, Reserve List, to Depot Battalion, 3d Field Artillery, August 3, 1916.

Second Lieutenant, George W. Powell, Reserve List, to Depot Battalion, 3d Field Artillery, August 3, 1916.

Second Lieutenant, John K. White, Reserve List, to Depot Battalion, 3d Field Artillery, August 3, 1916.

Second Lieutenant, Daniel S. Ferry, Reserve List, to Depot Battalion, 3d Field Artillery, August 3, 1916.

First Lieutenant, William P. Hennessy, Reserve List, to Depot Battalion, 3d Infantry, August 3, 1916.

First Lieutenant, Henry Chorman, Reserve List, to Depot Battalion, 3d Infantry, August 3, 1916.

Second Lieutenant, Philip F. Stephens, Reserve List, to Depot Battalion, 3d Infantry, August 3, 1916.

Major, Daniel H. Cowe, Q. M. C., to 2d Brigade, August 4, 1916.

Second Lieutenant, Fred C. Fleming, Reserve List, to Depot Battalion, 23d Infantry, August 4, 1916.

First Lieutenant, William J. Kavanaugh, Reserve List, to Depot Battalion, 1st Cavalry, August 8, 1916.

Captain, Jason S. Parker, M. C., to 4th Field Hospital, August 9, 1916.

First Lieutenant, Robert Malcolm, M. C., to 4th Field Hospital, August 9, 1916.

First Lieutenant, Charles D. Cromwell, M. C., to 4th Field Hospital, August 9, 1916.

First Lieutenant, Thomas L. Reynolds, Reserve List, to Depot Battalion, 69th Infantry, August 9, 1916.

First Lieutenant, Edward M. Kirkpatrick, Reserve List, to Depot Battalion, 69th Infantry, August 15, 1916.

First Lieutenant, Karl F. Eschelman, M. C., Reserve List, to Depot Battalion, 74th Infantry, August 16, 1916.

Captain, William T. Getman, M. C., Reserve List, to Examining Board, 4th Brigade, August 16, 1916.

Major, Albert T. Weston, M. C., Reserve List, to Depot Battalion, 12th Infantry, August 16, 1916.

Brigadier General, John G. Eddy, Retired to 2d Brigade District, August 17, 1916.

Second Lieutenant, Morton F. Sanborn, Reserve List, to Depot Battalion, 22d Corps of Engineers, August 21, 1916.

Major, Joseph A. Cox, M. C., Reserve List, to Depot Unit, 2d Field Hospital, August 21, 1916.

First Lieutenant, Charles P. Roberts, M. C., Reserve List, to Depot Unit, 1st Ambulance Company, August 22, 1916.

Major, Frank Harnden, M. C., to 4th Field Hospital, August 22, 1916.

First Lieutenant, Leo H. Costigan, M. C., to 4th Field Hospital, August 22, 1916.

First Lieutenant, Charles P. Roberts, M. C., to 4th Field Hospital, August 22, 1916.

First Lieutenant, Richard A. Deeves, Reserve List, to Depot Battalion, 22d Corps of Engineers, August 23, 1916.

Major, Harrison K. Bird, Ordnance Department, to 1st Brigade, August 23, 1916.

Major, Charles J. Ahern, Q. M. C., to 1st Brigade, August 23, 1916.

First Lieutenant, Francis H. Richardson, M. C., to Depot Battalion, Signal Corps, September 2, 1916.

Colonel, William Hayward, Reserve List, to 15th Infantry, 90 days, September 22, 1916.

First Lieutenant, Eugene McK. Froment, Reserve List, to Aide Division, September 23, 1916.

Colonel Eugene K. Austin, Reserve List, to Division, September 25, 1916.

Captain, Alex M. Jackson, Reserve List, to Depot Unit, 2d Infantry, September 29, 1916.

Captain, Walter L. Bell, Reserve List, to Chief Q. M. Division, September 30, 1916.

Lieutenant Colonel, Lorillard Spencer, 15th Infantry, to Military Secretary to Governor, September 29, 1916.

Captain, William Getman, M. C., to Depot Unit, Troop I, 1st Cavalry, October 3, 1916.

First Lieutenant, Burt D. Whedon, Reserve List, to 15th Infantry, October 10, 1916.

Second Lieutenant, Harry G. Kettner, Q. M. C., to Division Supply Train, October 13, 1916.

Second Lieutenant, Herbert J. Brotheridge, Reserve List, to 47th Infantry, October 17, 1916.

Detailed — Concluded

Colonel, William W. Ladd, Retired, to National Guard Headquarters, October 24, 1916

First Lieutenant, Thomas B. Laurie, Reserve List, to 3d Infantry, November 6, 1916

Captain, Andrew B. Gilfillan, Reserve List, to Depot Battalion, 3d Field Artillery, November, 10, 1916.

Captain, William T. Doane, Reserve List, to Depot Battalion, 3d Field Artillery, November 10,

List, to Novem-

William N. Barbour, 12th

1910.

First Lieutenant, Orsen M. Beach, Reserve List, to N. Y. Arsenal, November 23, 1916.

Major, Monson Morris, Reserve List, to 15th Infantry, November 28, 1916.

Second Lieutenant, Michael E. Reidy, Reserve List, to Depot Battalion, 69th Infantry, December 6, 1916.

First Lieutenant, Stanislaus Scheon, Reserve List, to Depot Battalion, 3d Field Artillery, December 7, 1916.

Second Lieutenant, Henry B. H. Ripley, Reserve List, to 15th Infantry, December 13, 1916.

RELIEVED

Captain, Lorillard Spencer, Coast Artillery Corps, relieved from duty as aide-de-camp to Governor, January 20, 1916.

First Lieutenant, Joseph de Rivera, relieved from duty as aide on Division Staff, May 18, 1916.

Second Lieutenant, Antonio C. Gonzalez, from duty at State Arsenal, July 17, 1916.

Major, John H. Barker, from duty, 3d Brigade Staff, July 24, 1916.

Major, Sanford Cluett, from 3d Brigade Staff, July 24, 1916.

Major, George Lawyer, from 3d Brigade Staff, July 2, 1916.

Colonel, Ernest E. Jannicky, 47th Infantry, from command, August 2, 1916.

Major, Clarence Strevell, Reserve List, from active duty, August 2, 1916.

Captain, Henry L. Butler, Adjutant General's Department, from active duty, August 2, 1916.

Captain, Lawrence A. Sweeney, Reserve List, from Depot Battalion, 22d Corps of Engineers, August 3, 1916.

First Lieutenant, Clarence V. Radcliffe, Reserve List, from State Arsenal, August 8, 1916.

First Lieutenant, Harold J. Hinchman, Q. M. C., from State Arsenal, August 8, 1916.

Major, Joseph A. Cox, Reserve List, from 4th Field Hospital, August 9, 1916.

First Lieutenannt, Ransom S. Robertson, M.C. from State Arsenal, August 14, 1916.

First Lieutenant, Leo H. Costigan, M. C., from State Arsenal, August 14, 1916.

Major, William A. Niver, Adjutant General's Department, from State Arsenal, August 16, 1916.

Major, Carroll J. Roberts, M. C., from Examining Board, 4th Brigade, August 16, 1916.

Lieutenant Colonel, Henry H. Brooks, M. C., from Camp Whitman, August 21, 1916.

First Lieutenant, Charles P. Roberts, M. C., from Depot Battalion, 1st Ambulance Company, August 22, 1916.

Lieutenant Colonel Percival E. Nagle, Supply, from duty, Camp Whitman, September 2, 1916.

First Lieutenant, Eugene McK. Froment, Reserve List, from Arsenal, September 2, 1916.

First Lieutenant, John A. Coffey, Reserve List, from Armory Commission, September 2, 1916.

Second Lieutenant, Harry G Kettner, V. C, Q. M. C., from Division Field Train, September 6, 1916.

First Lieutenant, Jay McDonald, V. C., Q. M. C., from Division Field Train, September 11, 1916.

First Lieutenant, Charles P. Roberts, Reserve List, from 4th Field Hospital, September 22, 1916.

Colonel, Eugene K. Austin, Reserve List, from Arsenal, September 23, 1916.

First Lieutenant, William Roberts, Reserve List, from Depot Battalion, 22d Corps of Engineers, September 24, 1916.

First Lieutenant, Richard A. Deeves, Reserve List, from Depot Battalion, 22d Corps of Engineers, September 29, 1916.

Lieutenant Colonel, George F. Hinton, Reserve List, from 15th Infantry, September 29, 1916.

First Lieutenant, Oren M. Beach, Reserve List, from duty at Arsenal, October 10. 1916.

Captain, Joseph M. Gwinner, Reserve List, from duty with 3d Field Artillery, October 20, 1916.

Colonel, William H. Chapin, National Guard Headquarters, from duty at State Camp, October 21, 1916.

First Lieutenant, Louis Montant, aide, 1st Brigade, from duty with 69th Infantry, October 24, 1916.

Major, Charles J. Ahern, Q. M. C., from duty, 1st Brigade, November 1, 1916.

Second Lieutenant, Walter Seligman, Coast Artillery Corps, from 18th Company, November 1, 1916.

First Lieutenant, William G. Staudenmaier, from Company A, 3d Infantry, November 6, 1916.

Second Lieutenant, Henry B. Chapin, from Supply Company, 3d Infantry, November 6, 1916.

First Lieutenant, James F. Coughlan, M. C., from 1st Field Hospital, November 15. 1916.

Second Lieutenant, Kennard Underwood, from M. G. Company, 3d Infantry, November 6, 1916.

Major, Mills Miller, Coast Artillery Corps, from Engineer Officer, November 23, 1916.

Captain, Henry E. Greene, from Company H, 2d Infantry, November 24, 1916.

Major, Monson Morris, from Recruiting Officer, November 25, 1916.

Relieved — Concluded

First Lieutenant, Walter L. Gibson, from 1st Company, Coast Artillery Corps, December 2, 1916.
First Lieutenant, Lowyd N. Ballantyne, from 1st Field Hospital, December 8, 1916.
Lieutenant Colonel, Edward B. Bruch, from Depot Battalion, 71st Infantry, December 14, 1916.
First Lieutenant, Theophilus Parson, from Company B, 10th Infantry, December 19, 1916.

Second Lieutenant, Edgar B. Gritman, from Company L, 10th Infantry, December 19, 1916.
Captain, Thurber A. Brown, from Company K, 3d Infantry, December 22, 1916.
First Lieutenant, J. Winfield Gilmore, from 18th Company, Coast Artillery Corps, December 22, 1916.
Major, Charles J. Ahern, from Headquarters, National Guard, December 26, 1916.

TRANSFERRED TO RESERVE LIST

Brigadier Generals

Oliver Benedict Bridgman, D. B., 1st Brigade, October 6, 1916.

Colonels

Charles Edward Payne Babcock, 65th Infantry, July 11, 1916.
Clarence Seymour Wadsworth, 12th Infantry, September 27, 1916.
Merrill Manleville Dunapaugh, 3d Brigade, June 20, 1916.

Lieutenant Colonels

George Marshall Alden, 2d Infantry, May 18, 1916.
Henry Harlow Brooks, D. B., 7th Infantry, October 28, 1916.
Augustus Drum Porter, 12th Infantry, May 25, 1916.
James H. Wells, 71st Infantry, June 27, 1916.
Walter F. Barnes, 2d Brigade, December 29, 1916.

Majors

Joseph Ignatius Berry, 2d Field Artillery, January 13, 1916.
John Edward Duffy, 69th Infantry, May 2, 1916.
Charles Eliphalet Walbridge, 4th Brigade, May 29, 1916.
Alfred Rutgers Whitney, D. B., 1st Brigade, October 6, 1916.

Sanford Lockwood Cluett, 3d Brigade, July 4, 1916.
Alfred Edgar Denison, 10th Infantry, September 23, 1916.
Francis Griswold Landon, 7th Infantry, June 6, 1916.
Caroll Julian Roberts, 65th Infantry, M. C., June 16, 1916.

Captains

Joseph Charles Arbogast, 65th Infantry, July 18, 1916.
Harvey Loomis Grandy, 65th Infantry, July 11, 1916.
Howard Ogden Hicks, 65th Infantry, July 22, 1916.
Robert Doremus Mills, 1st Field Artillery, February 7, 1916.
William Ephraim Morris, 69th Infantry, March 6, 1916.
Arthur Crossley Smith, 22d Corps of Engineers, May 13, 1916.
John Jacob Stevens, Jr., 2d Field Artillery, February 25, 1916.
Thomas Edward Boyd, 74th Infantry, June 15, 1916.

Charles Tilden Doorty, 3d Field Artillery, July 24, 1916.
Henry Albert Hill, 74th Infantry, June 16, 1916.
Joseph John Kingsbury, 65th Infantry, March 3, 1915.
Patrick Joseph Maguire, 69th Infantry, July 13, 1916.
Charles Howard Newman, 23d Infantry, June 24, 1916.
Amos Mead Ritch, 47th Infantry, August 15, 1916.
Francis R. Stoddard, Jr., 1st Heavy Artillery, M. V. M., May 27, 1915.

First Lieutenants

Joseph William Davis, 13th Coast Defense Command, March 8, 1916.
John Douglas Pedersen, 1st Infantry, June 26, 1916.
Henry Philip Piers, 10th Infantry, April 17, 1916.
Henry Baldwin Hyde Ripley, 12th Infantry, May 8, 1916.
Herbert Norris Rothenmeyer, 65th Infantry, July 11, 1916.
Theodore Duncan Rousseau, 1st Brigade, May 25, 1916.

Burt Franklin Tomlinson, 9th Coast Defense Command, May 8, 1916.
William Arthur Johnson, 3d Field Artillery, July 31, 1916.
Philip Sidney McDougall, 3d Field Artillery, August 10, 1916.
Paul Malone, 65th Infantry, June 8, 1916.
Edward Joseph Morris, 23d Infantry, M. C., June 16, 1916.
Lester Roberts Walton, 9th Coast Defense Command, June 5, 1916.
Walter Charles Yund, 2d Infantry, December 20, 1916.

Transferred to Reserve List — Concluded

Second Lieutenants

Charles Andson Atwater, 3d Infantry, February 24, 1916.
Patrick Joseph Crowley, 60th Infantry, June 20, 1916.
Louie Emilo Lahens, 7th Infantry, June 21, 1916.
William Joseph Mullen, 14th Regiment, July 5, 1916.
Maxine John Parenteau, 12th Infantry, February 23, 1916.
Charles Amasa Tracey, 1st Cavalry, March 23, 1916.

Oliver Curtiss Young, 65th Infantry, March 23, 1916.
Preston Maurice Albro, 65th Infantry, July 18, 1916.
Charles H. Barnum, 23d Infantry, July 7, 1916.
William Henry Innes, 2d Infantry, July 7, 1916.
Charles Frederick Steger, 65th Infantry, July 6, 1916.
Steven Grant Stone, 9th Coast Defense Command, October 10, 1916.

Chaplains

Charles McCaffrey, 1st Infantry, June 30, 1916.

CHANGES IN ASSIGNMENT

Captain, George H. Johnson, from I. S. A. P., to command Company H, 2d Battalion, 22d Corps of Engineers, December 24, 1915.
First Lieutenant, Clarence H. Bobb, I. S. A. P., to I. S. A. P. Headquarters, 22d Corps of Engineers, December 24, 1915.
Captain, Frederick Granville Munson, 9th Coast Defense Command, from duty with 19th Company to duty with 1st Company, February 16, 1916.
Captain, James J. Walsh, 9th Coast Defense Command, from 14th Company to unassigned 9th Coast Defense Command, February 26, 1916.
Captain, Otto Irving Chormann, 3d Infantry, from Company H, to Adjutant, February 26, 1916.
First Lieutenant, Jeremiah W. O'Mahoney, 9th Coast Defense Command, from 17th Company, to unassigned, February 1, 1916.
First Lieutenant, Alfred Winthrop Cook, 12th Infantry, from Company A, to Battalion Adjutant, February 11, 1916.
First Lieutenant, Walter Finney Siegmund, 65th Infantry, from Company K, to Company B, February 23, 1916.
Second Lieutenant, Gilbert H. Higgins, 9th Coast Defense Command, from 21st Company, to 20th Company, February 23, 1916.
Captain, Benjamin Van Raden, 1st Field Artillery, from Battery D, to Adjutant, March 1, 1916.
Captain, Wilbur Teed Wright, 2d Field Artillery, from Commissary to Battery E, March 10, 1916.
Captain, Sylvester Simpson, 1st Field Artillery, from Battery B, to Battery D, March 18, 1916.
First Lieutenant, Henry A. Allen, Jr., 2d Infantry, from Company F, to Battalion Adjutant, February 1916.
First Lieutenant, Joseph John Koen, 12th Infantry, from Company I, to Battalion Adjutant, March 1, 1916.
First Lieutenant, Harry C. Starrett,. 14th Infantry, from Company A, to Company D, March 11, 1916.
First Lieutenant, Leon B. de Garmo, 14th Infantry, from Company M, to Company A, March 11, 1916.
First Lieutenant, St. Clair Smith 8th Coast Defense Command, from 31st Company, to 25th Company, March 22, 1916.

First Lieutenant, Harry L. Monell, 8th Coast Defense Command, from 32d Company to 31st Company, March 22, 1916.
Second Lieutenant, Clarence I. Goudey, 14th Infantry, from Company F, to Company H, March 11, 1916.

Second Lieutenant, Russell A. Fairbairn, 9th Coast Defense Command, from 13th to 21st Company, March 21, 1916.
Second Lieutenant, Geoffrey J. O'Flynn, 69th Infantry, from Company I, to Company C, March 29, 1916.
Second Lieutenant, Eugene M. Dwyer, 69th Infantry, from Company C, to Company A, March 29, 1916.
Second Lieutenant, Malcolm W. Force, 9th Coast Defense Command, from 18th Company, to unassigned, April 17, 1916.
First Lieutenant, Herbert C. Alden, 8th Coast April 22, 1916.
First Lieutenant, Alexander Perry, 8th Coast Defense Command, from 23d Company, to 29th Company, April 22, 1916.
Captain, Herbert A. Summers, 14th Infantry, from I. S. A. P., to Commissary, May 10, 1916.
Captain, Arthur C. Smith, 22d Corps of Engineers, from Company E, to unassigned, May 9, 1916.
Captain, Joseph J. Daly, 22d Corps of Engineers, from Adjutant, to Company E, May 9, 1916.
Captain, Patrick J. Walsh, Company B, to Post Adjutant, May 9, 1916.
Captain, Harold C. Woodward, 22d Corps of Engineers, from Adjutant, to Company B, May 9, 1916.
First Lieutenant, Lawrence C. Donovan, 22d Corps of Engineers, from Company C, to Adjutant, May 9, 1916.
First Lieutenant, William Blaisdell, 14th Infantry, from Company H, to Company L, May 17, 1916.
First Lieutenant, John C. Hardy, 14th Infantry, from Company L, to Company M, May 17, 1916.
First Lieutenant, Arthur W. Slee, M. C., frp., 47th Infantry, to 3d Field Hospital, May 27, 1916.

Changes in Assignment — Concluded

Captain, Frederick G. Munson, 13th Coast Defense Command, from 1st Company to 29th Company, 8th Coast Defense Command, May 29, 1916.

Major, Edward R. Maloney, M. C., from 9th Coast Defense Command, to Division National Guard, May 26, 1916.

Second Lieutenant, Malcolm W. Force, 9th Coast Defense Command, from unassigned to 18th Company, May 19, 1916.

Second Lieutenant, John R. Suydam, Jr., 8th Coast Defense Command, from 27th Company to 32d Company, May 22, 1916.

Second Lieutenant, George Shipway, 9th Coast Defense Command, from 18th to unassigned, May 22, 1916.

First Lieutenant, Fred C. Hyames, 22d Corps of Engineers, to 47th Infantry, July 5, 1916.

Major, Francis L. V. Hoppin, Adjutant General, 1st Brigade, to State Arsenal, July 6, 1916.

Second Lieutenant, George Magee, Supply Company, 69th Infantry, to Company F, July 6, 1916.

Second Lieutenant, Edward J. Westcott, 10th Infantry, to Adjutant General's Office, State Arsenal, July 7, 1916.

Captain, William H. Ferguson, 10th Infantry, to Adjutant General's Office, Albany, July 10, 1916.

First Lieutenant, James T. Houghton, M. C., 2d Infantry, to 69th Infantry, July 10, 1916.

First Lieutenant, St. Clair Smith, Coast Artillery Corps, 25th Company, to 34th Company, July 12, 1916.

Captain, Frederick G. Munson, Coast Artillery Corps, 36th Company, to 19th Company, July 16, 30, 1916. July 14, 1916.

Second Lieutenant, Harry B. Phinney, 8th to 9th Coast Defense Command, July 16-30, 1916. July 15, 1916.

First Lieutenant, Frank E. Sidman, Battalion Adjutant, 69th Infantry, to Company D, July 16, 1916.

Captain, Moses A. Stivers, M. C., 1st Infantry, to 3d Field Hospital, July 24, 1916.

Second Lieutenant, Francis P. Thomas, Coast Artillery Corps, to 2d Company, July 26, 1916.

Captain, Alex M. Jackson, 2d Infantry, Depot Battalion, to Pay Department, July 26, 1916.

First Lieutenant, Charles D. Cromwell, M. C., Camp Whitman, to 10th Infantry, July 31, 1916.

First Lieutenant, Jeremiah W. O'Mahoney, M. C., to 22d Corps of Engineers, July 28, 1916.

First Lieutenant, Wilbur B. Hammond, Battalion Adjutant, 10th Infantry, to Company G, June 3, 1916.

Second Lieutenant, Joseph A. Nichols, Coast Artillery Corps, 21st Company, to 13th Company, June 6, 1916.

Second Lieutenant, James H McSweeney, Battery A, 2d Field Artillery, to Battery C, June 5, 1916.

Second Lieutenant, Ralph Kluge, Company E, 12th Infantry, to Company D, June 5, 1916.

Captain, Nelson W. Thompson, I. S. A. P., 1st Infantry, to 14th Infantry, I. S. A. P., June 5, 1916.

Captain, Alfred Wondt, Squadron A, Cavalry, to Aide Division, June 11, 1916.

First Lieutenant, Ernest E. Bosca, 21st Company, to Coast Artillery Corps, unassigned, June 16, 1916.

Second Lieutenant, Edward S. Moale, Company A, 22d Corps of Engineers, to Company E, June 19, 1916.

First Lieutenant, Frederick M. Steeves, 1st Battalion, Signal Corps, to Tel. & Tel. Detachments, June 24, 1916.

First Lieutenant, Raynal C. Bolling, Tel. & Tel. Detachments, to Company B, Signal Corps, June 24, 1916.

First Lieutenant, Raynal C. Bolling, Company B, Signal Corps, to Aero Company, June 27, 1916.

First Lieutenant, Norbert Carolin, Company B, Signal Corps, to Aero Company, June 28, 1916.

Captain, Frederick C. Munson, 29th Company, Coast Artillery Corps, to 36th Company, June 18, 1916.

First Lieutenant, Herbert C. Alden, Company C, unassigned, to 36th Company, June 25, 1916.

Captain, William J. Cranston, 10th Infantry, to Division Supply Train, August 3, 1916.

First Lieutenant, Elmer H. Ormsby, 2d Infantry, to Division Supply Train, August 3, 1916.

First Lieutenant, Charles D. Cromwell, 10th Infantry, to Division Supply Train, August 3, 1916.

Major, Lee H. Smith, retired to 4th Brigade, August 4, 1916.

First Lieutenant, Thomas G. Carlin, 47th Infantry, to 2d Brigade, August 4, 1916.

First Lieutenant, Guilford W. Francis, Battery F, 3d Field Artillery, to Supply Company, 3d Field Artillery, August 8, 1916.

Assistant Veterinary, Henry G. Kettner, Quartermaster Corps, to Division Supply Train, August 14, 1916.

Captain, Thurber A. Brown, I. S. A. P., to Company K, 3d Infantry, August 15, 1916.

Second Lieutenant, John W. Bostick, 47th Infantry, to 14th Infantry, August 16, 1916.

Captain, Arthur M. Day, 29th Company Coast Artillery Corps, to Adjutant, August 19, 1916.

First Lieutenant, Edward E. I. Martin, Depot Battalion, 71st Infantry to 1st Brigade, August 23, 1916.

First Lieutenant, Edward A. Roberts, 1st Infantry, to 14th Infantry, August 29, 1916.

Captain, Thomas M. Sherman, 1st Infantry, to 14th Infantry, August 29, 1916.

Captain, Frederick A. de Peyster, Staff, 12th Infantry, to Company M, September 12, 1916.

Captain, Thomas M. Sherman, 14th Infantry, to Company B, 1st Infantry, September 29, 1916.

First Lieutenant, Edward A. Roberts, 14th Infantry, to Company B, 1st Infantry, September 29, 1916.

Captain, William J. Cranston, Medical Corps, Division Field, Train, to 4th Field Hospital, September 30, 1916.

Second Lieutenant, William H. Macurda, 14th Company, Coast Artillery Corps, to unassigned, October 17, 1916.

14

ASSIGNED

Major, Charles J. Ahern, Quartermaster Corps, to Division National Guard, November 1, 1916.

Second Lieutenant, Walter Seligman, Coast Artillery Corps, to 21st Company, November 1, 1916.

First Lieutenant, Elmer H. Ormsby, Medical Corps, to 2d Infantry, November 6, 1916.

First Lieutenant, William G. Staudenmaier, 3d Infantry to Machine Gun Company, 3d Infantry, November 6, 1916.

Second Lieutenant, Leonard Underwood, 3d Infantry, to Supply Company, 3d Infantry, November 6, 1916.

Second Lieutenant, Henry B. Chapin, 3d Infantry, to Machine Gun Company, 3d Infantry, November 6, 1916.

First Lieutenant, Ernest E. Bosca, Coast Artillery Corps, as Ordnance Officer, and Artillery Engineer, November 23, 1916.

Major, Andrew E. Tuck, Adjutant General's Department, to 4th Brigade. November 15, 1916.

First Lieutenant, James T. Coughlan, Medical Corps, to 2d Field Artillery, November 15, 1916.

Second Lieutenant, Edgar B. Gritman, 10th Infantry, to Machine Gun Company, December 19, 1916.

Captain, Thurber A. Brown, 3d Infantry, to I. S. A. P., December 22, 1916.

Captain, William W. Charles 3d Infantry, to Company K, December 22, 1916.

Major, Charles J. Ahern, Quartermaster Corps, to 1st Brigade, December 26, 1916.

First Lieutenant, J. Winfield Gilmore, Coast Artillery Corps, to 23d Company, December 22, 1916.

Captain, Henry E. Greene, 2d Infantry, to Adjutant, 2d Infantry, November 24, 1916.

First Lieutenant, Walter L. Gibson, Coast Artillery Corps, Assistant to Adjutant, 13th Coast Defense Command, December 2, 1916.

First Lieutenant, Lowyd W. Ballantyne, M. C., to 3d Infantry, December 8, 1916.

Second Lieutenant, William C. Orr, Coast Artillery Corps, to 27th Company, 8th Coast Defense Command, December 12, 1916.

Captain, Karl B. Kloer, 23d Infantry, to Depot Battalion, 23d Infantry, December 13, 1916.

Lieutenant Colonel, Edward B. Bruch, Reserve List, to Division Headquarters, December 14, 1916.

First Lieutenant, Theophilus Parsons, 10th Infantry, to Machine Gun Company, December 19, 1916.

CASUALTIES

FULL AND HONORABLE DISCHARGES

Colonels

Henry H Rogers, 1st Field Artillery, December 18, 1916.

Lieutenant Colonels

John McGaffin, 2d Infantry, January 13, 1916.
Frederick A. Wells, 23d Infantry, July 29, 1916.

Majors

John P. Everett, 69th Infantry, February 4, 1916.

Richard B. Dawson, 23d Infantry, July 12, 1916.

Walter F. Barnes, 2d Brigade, November 11, 1916.

Charles F. Hader, 14th Infantry, November 1916.

Frederick W. Baldwin, 14th Infantry, November 14, 1916.

Walter J. Carlin, Inspector General's Department, November 15, 1916.

Almet R. Latson, Judge Advocate General's Department, November 15, 1916.

Daniel R. Lucas, Medical Corps, November 24, 1916.

Captains

Charles R. Coffin, 23d Infantry, November 1, 1915.

Harry L. Loop, Medical Corps, November 8, 1915.

Walter D. Parlour, 65th Infantry, December 31, 1915.

George E. Gasper, 3d Infantry, January 6, 1916.

John A. C. Jensen, 1st Cavalry, January 17, 1916.

Edwin W. Kellogg, Medical Corps, February 24, 1916.

William C Walker, 2d Infantry, February 24, 1916.

Haskell C. Billings, 47th Infantry, February 25, 1916.

Joseph G. Ten Eyck, 13th Coast Defense Command, March 9, 1916.

John Van B. Mitchell, 9th Coast Defense Command, March 15, 1916.

John J. Kelly, 2d Infantry, April 13, 1916.

Archie B. Zahn, 14th Infantry, April 28, 1916.

George B. Hartley, 8th Coast Defense Command, May 8, 1916.

Edwin Emerson, Ordnance Department, May 11, 1916.

Philip T. Stallman, Squadron A, Cavalry, May 27, 1916.

Cornelius I. DeBevoise, 1st Cavalry, June 6, 1916.

Frank P. Goodwin, Medical Corps, June 8, 1916.

Charles E. Taller, Coast Artillery Corps, July 6, 1916.

Frank C. Westphal, 65th Infantry, July 6, 1916.

Alfred F. Hodgman, Medical Corps, July 10, 1916.

Louis D Collins, 4th Brigade, July 8, 1916.

Stanley Tumbridge, Reserve List, October 20, 1916.

Charles W. Berry, 14th Infantry, November 14, 1916.

Casualties — Concluded

First Lieutenants

Joseph G. Hardmeyer, 13th Coast Defense Command, November 1, 1915.
John T. Shinnars, 1st Field Artillery, November 1, 1915.
Andrew J. Tarpey, 69th Infantry, November 9, 1915.
Arthur S. Douglas, 1st Field Artillery, November 22, 1915.
Sterling F. Higley, 2d Infantry, December 15, 1915.
George D. Vincent, 1st Cavalry, December 18, 1915.
Richard H. Vose, 14th Infantry, January 7, 1916.
Edward C. Bailey, 12th Infantry, February 1, 1916.
Joseph B. Hydorn, 1st Cavalry, February 4, 1916.
William F. Simonson, 23d Infantry, February 21, 1916.
John T. Daly, 8th Coast Defense Command, February 21, 1916.
Philip J. Steers, 47th Infantry, March 13, 1916.
Richard R. Westphal, 65th Infantry, March 17, 1916.
Addison R. Prudden, 65th Infantry, March 28, 1916.
Robert Hall, 23d Infantry, March 30, 1916.
Parker J. Kenney, 3d Infantry, April 3, 1916.
John E. Chiquette, 69th Infantry, April 29, 1916.

Charles B. Sagona, 14th Infantry, June 6, 1916.
Walter H. Powers, Squadron A, Cavalry, June 6, 1916.
Frederick C. Brown, Aide, 2d Brigade, June 15, 1916.
Thorne W. Jackson, Coast Artillery Corps, June 21, 1916.
Wallace M. Brown, 1st Cavalry, June 22, 1916.
Charles L. Yost, Coast Artillery Corps, June 23, 1916.
George G. Bailey, 1st Field Artillery, August 8, 1916.
Charles A. Baker, 10th Infantry, September 18, 1916.
Lawrence H. Gardner, 4th Brigade, September 22, 1916.
John A. Victor, Medical Corps, October 5, 1916.
Rowland Stebbins, Reserve List, November 17, 1916.
Walter K. Whitley, 3d Infantry, November 24, 1916.
John C. Hardy, 14th Infantry, December 8, 1916.
Thomas E. Hitchcock, 1st Field Artillery, December 18, 1916.
Robert Williamson, 2d Infantry, December 13, 1916.
John B. Bland, 3d Infantry, December 13, 1916.

Second Lieutenants

Lewis E. Travis, 65th Infantry, November 24, 1915.
Lewis H. Brown, Squadron A, Cavalry, November 30, 1915.
Richard E. Brown, 13th Coast Defense Command, December 14, 1915.
Barton Cruikshank, 8th Coast Defense Command, January 8, 1916.
Paul D. Owen, 2d Infantry, February 24, 1916.
Alfred Broadbent, 1st Infantry, February 24, 1916.

George C. Hart, 71st Infantry, May 19, 1916.
James D. Herriman, 12th Infantry, July 5, 1916.
Samuel S. Rapp, 23d Infantry, July 12, 1916.
Ira U. Travis, Jr., 10th Infantry, October 5, 1916.
Ignatius A. Scannell, 47th Infantry, November 10, 1916.
Egbert Bagg, 1st Infantry, November 11, 1916.

Chaplains

John H. Sattig, 14th Infantry, November 24, 1916.

HONORABLE DISCHARGES

Lieutenant Colonels

Eugene Van C. Lucas, Corps of Engineers, October 6, 1916.

Majors

Donald H. Cowe, Quartermaster Corps, August 23, 1916.
William S. Cherry, Medical Corps, August 29, 1916.
Edwin A. Strong, Corps of Engineers, November 3, 1916.

Frank S. Sidway, Depot Battalion, 74th Infantry, December 13, 1916.
Newbold Morris, Reserve List, December 28, 1916.

Captains

Arthur E. Conner, 1st Infantry, March 13, 1916.
Louis C. Trumble, Reserve List, April 7, 1916.
Steele Wotkyns, 12th Infantry, June 6, 1916.
Albert T. Rich, 71st Infantry, June 6, 1916.
Eldred W. Kennedy, Medical Corps, July 6, 1916.
Dawson Olmstead, 1st Field Artillery, July 25, 1916.

Karl Isburgh, 2d Infantry, November 11, 1916.
William H. Robinson, Depot Battalion, 10th Infantry, November 22, 1916.
George L. Baker, Reserve List, December 4, 1916.
George H. Fox, Medical Corps, December 18, 1916.

Honorable Discharges — Concluded

First Lieutenants

Arthur W. Copp, 1st Field Artillery, November 5, 1915.
Henry E. Lewis, 65th Infantry, January 4, 1916.
John S. Braun, 71st Infantry, January 26, 1916.
Reginald K. Fessenden, 12th Infantry, February 4, 1916.
Dewey A. Forbush, 2d Infantry, February 24, 1916.
John A. Coffey, 10th Infantry, April 13, 1916.
Edmund H. Parizot, 13th Coast Defense Command, April 19, 1916.
Davis T. Dunbar, 1st Cavalry, June 6, 1916.
David N. Barrows, Medical Corps, July 6, 1916.
Rudolph L. Zimpel, Reserve List, July 7, 1916.
Malcolm R. Matheson, 47th Infantry, August 14, 1916.
Joseph E. R. Kunsmann, Depot Battalion, 23d Infantry, August 29, 1917.
Stuart B. Blakely, Medical Corps, September 11, 1916.

William C. Rausch, Medical Corps, September 18, 1916.
Robert R. Haslett, 47th Infantry, September 25, 1916.
Warner J. Roberts, Coast Artillery Corps, October 9, 1916.
Francis K. Stoddard, Jr., 71st Infantry, October 18, 1916.
Charles A. McCarthy, 69th Infantry, November 2, 1916.
Walter H. Wells, 47th Infantry, November 14, 1916.
Jay D. B. Lattin, Reserve List, December 11, 1916.
Paul S. Barrett, Medical Corps, December 14, 1916.
James S. Larkin, 1st Field Artillery, December 18, 1916.
Frederick L. Farrell, Coast Artillery Corps, December 18, 1916.
Vincent C. Welsh, 2d Infantry, December 26, 1916.

Second Lieutenants

Edward W. Falanders, 65th Infantry, November 24, 1915.
Albert B. Mason, 71st Infantry, December 14, 1915.
James R. Miller, 1st Infantry, January 4, 1916.
Lydig Hoyt, 12th Infantry, February 4, 1916.
Byron E. Hupman, 2d Infantry, February 24, 1916.
Walter H. Simonson, 2d Field Artillery, May 25, 1916.
Philip F. Stephen, 3d Infantry, June 22, 1916.
Edgar B. Burchell, 12th Infantry, June 30, 1916.
William J. Platka, 47th Infantry, July 6, 1916.
Joseph L. Gravel, 65th Infantry, July 15, 1916.

Milton C. Guggenheimer, 3d Field Artillery, July 18, 1916.
Dudley Olcott, 3d 1st Armored Motor Battery, September 22, 1916.
John G. Goets, 2d Infantry, October 28, 1916.
Alfred P. Posner, 71st Infantry, November 2, 1916.
George S. Norman, 14th Infantry, November 14, 1916.
Frank L. Couch, 3d Infantry, November 24, 1916.
Robert L. Bacon, 1st Field Artillery, November 25, 1916.
Aiden E. Kelly, 1st Field Artillery, December 18, 1916.

Veterinaries

Eugene Combs, 1st Field Artillery, March 10, 1916.

Chaplains

Howard E. Snyder, 10th Infantry, July 5, 1916.
Herbert Shipman, 1st Field Artillery, December 18, 1916.

DISCHARGED

First Lieutenants

Philip N. Lawes, 1st Field Artillery, December 30, 1915.

DISMISSED UNDER M. L. 84

Second Lieutenants

Jay H. Johnson, 9th Coast Defense Command, February 10, 1916.

OFFICERS WHO RESIGNED WHILE IN FEDERAL SERVICE

Colonels

Clarence S. Wadsworth, 12th Infantry, August 23, 1916.

Majors

Edmund D. McCarthy, Adjutant General's Department, August 10, 1916.

Frederick N. Whitley, 22d Regiment of Engineers, August 15, 1916.

Chauncey Matlock, 2d Field Artillery, August 24, 1916

Michael Lynch, 69th Infantry, September 18, 1916.

George Beavers, Jr., 69th Infantry, December 19, 1916.

Captains

Wentworth Tucker, 12th Infantry, August 9, 1916.

James V. McKay, 3d Field Artillery, August 17, 1916.

George S. Towle, 7th Infantry, August 21, 1916.

Elmer E. Adler, 3d Field Artillery, August 23, 1916.

Bernard J. Glynn, 69th Infantry, August 24, 1916.

Henry C. Elwood, 74th Infantry, August 24, 1916.

Eugene F. Lohr, 2d Field Artillery, August 26, 1916.

Alphonse W. Weiner, 2d Field Artillery, August 31, 1916.

Edward J. Robbins, 23d Infantry, September 1, 1916.

Andrew B. Gilfallan, 3d Field Artillery, September 15, 1916.

Charles O. Boyd, 3d Field Artillery, September 21, 1916.

Felix A. Donnelly, 69th Infantry, September 28, 1916.

Rupert Hughes, 69th Infantry, September 28, 1916.

Joseph G. Fogarty, 69th Infantry, September 29, 1916.

Christopher A. Dunnigan, 3d Field Artillery, October 1, 1916.

Samuel K. Thomas, 7th Infantry, October 11, 1916.

Alexander R. Robertson, 74th Infantry, October 13, 1916.

Nathan C. Shiverick, 1st Cavalry, September 20, 1916.

Frederick W. Rice, Medical Corps, 69th Infantry, October 21, 1916.

Charles W. Floyd, 74th Infantry, October 23, 1916.

Robert Saunders, 12th Infantry, October 27, 1916.

James P. Askin, 69th Infantry, October 31, 1916.

William M. Ford, Medical Corps, 69th Infantry, November 1, 1916.

Walter F. Siegmund, 3d Field Artillery, November 2, 1916.

Thomas D. Lucus, Medical Corps, 7th Infantry, November 2, 1916.

Dennis Hogan, 69th Infantry, November 8, 1916.

Robert W. Bush, Squadron A, Cavalry, November 8, 1916.

William S. Collins, 7th Infantry, November 15, 1916.

Bernard F. Cummings, Jr., 69th Infantry, November 28, 1916.

Samuel McCullagh, Medical Corps, Squadron A, Cavalry, December 2, 1916.

First Lieutenants

August von Kleist, 74th Infantry, August 8, 1916.

Edward F. Janes, 12th Infantry, August 10, 1916.

Constantine J. MacGuire, Jr., 3d Ambulance Company, August 15, 1916.

Henry F. Davidson, 71st Infantry, August 18, 1916.

Herbert H. Glosser, Medical Corps, 74th Infantry, August 22, 1916

Henry A. Allen, Jr., 2d Infantry, August 23, 1916.

Stanislaus Schoen, 3d Field Artillery, August 26, 1916.

Arthur B. Chase, 14th Infantry, August 26, 1916.

Floyd L. Stevens, 23d Infantry, September 1, 1916.

Samuel J. Mack, 7th Infantry, September 15, 1916.

Henry Hafner, 3d Field Artillery, September 23, 1916.

Alfred L. Golab, 7th Infantry, September 27, 1916.

Sherwood V. Whitbeck, Medical Corps, 10th Infantry, September 30, 1916.

Samuel E. McRickard, 2d Field Artillery, October 7, 1916.

Harry C. Guess, Medical Corps, 3d Field Artillery, October 9, 1916.

Chauncey A. Pierce, 23d Infantry, October 13, 1916.

Aaron V. Frost, 12th Infantry, October 20, 1916.

George T. Strodl, Medical Corps, 1st Field Hospital, October 23, 1916.

William D. Sherwood, Medical Corps, 2d Field Artillery, October 24, 1916.

Alfred W. Cook, 12th Infantry, October 28, 1916.

James S. Burns, 74th Infantry, November 7, 1916.

Alfred Wendt, 1st Cavalry, November 1, 1916.

Louis B. Rice, 69th Infantry, November 9, 1916.

Edward A. Fitch, 7th Infantry, November 10, 1916.

Geoffrey O'Flynn, 69th Infantry, November 14, 1916.

William T. Doane, 3d Field Artillery, November 15, 1916.

Guilford W. Francis, 3d Field Artillery, November 15, 1916.

Rieman D. Dumont, 23d Infantry, November 15, 1916.

Frederick S. Wetherell, Medical Corps, 4th Ambulance Company, November 17, 1916.

Spencer F. Weaver, 12th Infantry, November 22, 1916.

Otto C. Pickhardt, Medical Corps, 3d Ambulance Company, November 24, 1916.

Joseph L. Donhauser, Medical Corps, 1st Cavalry, November 28, 1916.

John M. Waldron, 69th Infantry, November 28, 1916.

Francis B. O'Connor, 22d Regiment of Engineers, November 29, 1916.

Frederick M. Schwerd, Medical Corps, 1st Cavalry, December 2, 1916.

Augustin S. Hart, 1st Cavalry, December 11, 1916.

Officers Who Resigned While in Federal Service—Concluded

Second Lieutenants

Robert H. Lelie, 2d Infantry, August 4, 1916.

Eugene J. Orsenigo, 71st Infantry, August 18, 1916.

Spencer L. Safford, 2d Infantry, August 21, 1916.

John F. Hyland, 12th Infantry, August 24, 1916.

James F. Curtis, Jr., 14th Infantry, August 26, 1916.

Hathorne C. Geer, 2d Field Artillery, August 31, 1916.

Augustus H. Harvey, 23d Infantry, September 1, 1916.

Eugene Warner, 3d Field Artillery, September 13, 1916.

Arthur B. Wolf, 74th Infantry, September 15, 1916.

George A. Hall, 7th Infantry, September 22, 1916.

Michael E. Reidy, 69th Infantry, September 29, 1916.

Samuel J. Fisher, Jr., 12th Infantry, October 4, 1916.

John B. Gordon, 74th Infantry, October 23, 1916.

Heyworth Campbell, 1st Field Artillery, October 28, 1916.

John H. Hendrick, 7th Infantry, November 1, 1916.

Alfred B. Wade, 7th Infantry, November 2, 1916.

Charles E. Kinskey, 3d Field Artillery, November 8, 1916.

Marcus R. R. Monsarrat, 69th Infantry, November 11, 1916.

Clarence R. Baines, 12th Infantry, November 24, 1916.

Hugh S. Stange, 69th Infantry, December 1, 1916.

Irving R. Boody, 1st Cavalry, December 4, 1916.

James R. Knapp, Squadron A, Cavalry, December 5, 1916.

D. Rumsey Wheeler, 3d Field Artillery, December 18, 1916.

Chaplains

John B. Ridley, 2d Field Artillery, October 7, 1916.

OFFICERS DISCHARGED FROM FEDERAL SERVICE FOR PHYSICAL DISABILITY

Colonels

Louis D. Conley, 69th Infantry, July 7, 1916.

Lieutenant Colonels

John J. Phelan, 69th Infantry, July 12, 1916.

Howard L. Beck, 74th Infantry, July 13, 1916.

Captains

Robert L. Bigelow, 12th Infantry, August 17, 1916.

Leander H. Shearer, 3d Ambulance Company, August 31, 1916.

Jacob Dorst, 3d Field Artillery, September 6, 1916.

John S. Doorty, 3d Field Artillery, September 28, 1916.

First Lieutenants

John J. Egan, 69th Infantry, July 8, 1916.

Joseph H. de Rivera, 1st Field Artillery, July 26, 1916.

Alson J. Hull, Medical Corps, 2d Infantry, August 14, 1916.

John B. Mergler, 3d Field Artillery, September 25, 1916.

Ernst A. Wiedeman, 23d Infantry, November 25, 1916.

Second Lieutenants

Rodman Gilder, Squadron A, Cavalry, July 7, 1916.

Donald S. Brown, 74th Infantry, July 13, 1916.

George W. Magee, 69th Infantry, September 7, 1916.

Chaplains

Ulysses G. Warren, 1st Cavalry, November 17, 1916.

DROPPED FROM ROLLS TO ACCEPT APPOINTMENT IN U. S. A.

First Lieutenants

Truman Smith, 12th Infantry, December 21, 1916.

DIED

Major Generals

Joseph G. Story, Adjutant General's Department, April 8, 1916.

Colonels

James Cavanaugh, 69th Infantry.

Majors

Amos E. McIntyre, 1st Infantry, September 3, 1916.

Captains

George E. Crowley, Depot Battalion, 9th Coast Defense Command, April 11, 1915.
George B. Baldwin, 7th Infantry, March 22, 1916.

Harry P. Worthing, 1st Infantry, August 8, 1916.
George M. Teats, 47th Infantry, November 10, 1916.

First Lieutenants

Gerald P. Bagnall, 32d Regiment.

Second Lieutenants

John McGreevey, 7th Infantry.
Robert N. Peters, 23d Infantry, March 26, 1916.

Hans S. Whalen, 69th Infantry, July 26, 1916.

RELATIVE RANK OF OFFICERS IN ACTIVE SERVICE IN THE NATIONAL GUARD

No.	NAME AND DATE OF RANK	Corps or organization
	Major General	
1	John Francis O'Ryan, May 1, 1912	Commanding, Division.
	Brigadier Generals	
1	James Westcott Lester, June 6, 1911	3d Brigade.
2	George Rathbone Dyer, Feb. 28, 1912	1st Brigade.
3	William Wilson, June 9, 1915	4th Brigade.
	Colonels	
1	Chauncey Pratt Williams, May 1, 1899	Adjutant General's Dept.
2	William Graves Bates, Nov. 23, 1899	71st Infantry.
3	Charles Henry Hitchcock, April 26, 1905	1st Infantry.
4	John Henry Foote, May 14, 1905	14th Infantry.
5	Elmore Farrington Austin, Feb. 24, 1908	Coast Artillery Corps.
6	Frank Hastings Norton, July 26, 1909	23d Infantry.
7	John Frederick Klein, Feb. 1, 1911	10th Infantry.
8	Charles I. De Bevoise, March 14, 1912	1st Cavalry.
9	George Albert Wingate, June 25, 1912	1st Field Artillery.
10	James Madison Andrews, Dec. 28, 1912	2d Infantry.
11	Ernest Ellsworth Jannicky, Feb. 16, 1914	47th Infantry.
12	William Henry Chapin, Nov. 4, 1915	Inspector General's Dept.
13	Edgar Stilson Jennings, Dec. 29, 1915	3d Infantry.
14	Willard Clinton Fisk, April 15, 1916	7th Infantry.
15	Gordon Johnston, July 7, 1916	12th Infantry.
16	Daniel W. Hand, July 10, 1916	3d Field Artillery.
17	Harry H. Bandholts, July 22, 1916	Headquarters Division.
18	Arthur Farragut Townsend, Aug. 18, 1916	Quartermaster Corps.
19	William Hayward, Nov. 18, 1916	15th Infantry.
20	Cornelius Vanderbilt, Dec. 4, 1916	Inspector General's Dept.
	Lieutenant Colonels	
1	Nathaniel Blunt Thurston, May 14, 1898	Ordnance Dept.
2	James Starbuck Boyer, April 26, 1905	1st Infantry.
3	William Lewis Garcia, June 7, 1906	14th Infantry.
4	Sanderson Alexander Ross, May 29, 1907	3d Infantry.
5	Washington Irving Taylor, May 26, 1909	Coast Defense Officers.
6	Albert Saulpaugh, Nov. 3, 1911	10th Infantry.
7	Merrit Haviland Smith, May 23, 1912	1st Field Artillery.
8	Henry S. Sternberger, June 5, 1912	Quartermaster Corps.
9	John James Byrne, June 15, 1912	Coast Artillery Corps.
10	Frank Harrington Hines, Jan. 14, 1913	2d Field Artillery.
11	William Stoutenborough Terriberry, Aug. 8, 1913	Medical Corps.
12	Harry Beam Baldwin, Mar. 11, 1914	47th Infantry.
13	John David Howland, Oct. 1, 1914	3d Field Artillery.
14	Henry Arthur Bostwick, Feb. 11, 1915	Quartermaster Corps.
15	James Crooke McLeer, March 22, 1915	1st Cavalry.
16	Sydney Grant, April 29, 1915	Coast Artillery Corps.
17	Robert McLean, June 9, 1915	7th Infantry.
18	William Schuyler Beekman, Jan. 26, 1916	71st Infantry.
19	William Aloysius Taylor, July 5, 1916	2d Infantry.
20	Bryer Hamilton Pendry, July 20, 1916	Coast Artillery Corps.
21	Reginald Love Foster, Sept. 6, 1916	12th Infantry.
22	Lorillard Spencer, Sept. 28, 1916	15th Infantry.
23	Latham Ralston Reed, Nov. 3, 1916	Squadron A, Cavalry.
	Majors	
1	George Jacob Metzger, July 15, 1838	Corps of Engineers.
2	George Lawyer, Feb. 28, 1901	Judge Advocate General's Dept.
3	Thomas Wallace Hislop, June 30, 1904	Quartermaster Corps.
4	Alfred Ernst Steers, Dec. 22, 1904	Quartermaster Corps.
5	Henry Jared Cookinham, Jr., April 26, 1905	1st Infantry.
6	Daniel Chauncey Dye, June 8, 1907	Medical Corps.
7	Henry Clinton Wilson, Feb. 25, 1908	Coast Artillery Corps.
8	Henry Thomas Hotchkiss, Feb. 29, 1908	Medical Corps.
9	Axel Ames, May 26, 1909	Coast Artillery Corps.
10	Paul Loeser, Sept. 22, 1909	Coast Artillery Corps.
11	Frederick Martin Waterbury, Nov. 22, 1909	Ordnance Dept.
12	James Everett Schuyler, Dec. 8, 1909	7th Infantry.

No.	NAME AND DATE OF RANK	Corps or organization
	Majors — Continued	
13	John Richard Kevin, Dec. 30, 1909	Medical Corps.
14	David Burton Blanton, Feb. 16, 1910	23d Infantry.
15	James Merrill Hutchinson, June 16, 1910	71st Infantry.
16	Timothy Francis Donovan, Feb. 11, 1911	14th Infantry.
17	Arthur Kemp, April 20, 1911	74th Infantry.
18	James Hammill Farquharson, May 2, 1911	Inspector General's Dept.
19	Karl Connell, May 31, 1911	Medical Corps.
20	Walter Clark Montgomery, Oct. 7, 1911	Medical Corps.
21	William Richard Pooley, Nov. 16, 1911	74th Infantry.
22	Louis Henry Eller, Dec. 16, 1911	2d Field Artillery.
23	George Fletcher Chandler, Jan. 9, 1912	10th Infantry.
24	William Runk Wright, Jan. 26, 1912	Squadron A, Cavalry.
25	Edward Robert Maloney, Jan. 27, 1912	Medical Corps.
26	John Fletcher Fairchild, Feb. 7, 1912	Corps of Engineers.
27	Francis Lauren Vinton Hoppin, March 18, 1912	Adjutant General's Dept.
28	Frank Joseph Foley, March 18, 1912	Quartermaster Corps.
29	Lewis Marie Thiery, Sept. 27, 1912	Coast Artillery Corps.
30	Mills Miller, Oct. 4, 1912	Coast Artillery Corps.
31	William Edward Downes, Oct. 11, 1912	12th Infantry.
32	Harrison Kerr Bird, Dec. 24, 1912	Ordnance Dept.
33	George Gibson Shepard, Jan. 31, 1913	3d Infantry.
34	John Bennett Tuck, Feb. 10, 1913	3d Infantry.
35	John Hammond Barker, Feb. 11, 1913	Ordnance Dept.
36	Stratford Francis Corbett, Feb. 11, 1913	Medical Corps.
37	Louis Herbert Gaus, March 27, 1913	Medical Corps.
38	Arthur Edwin Wells, April 30, 1913	71st Infantry.
39	James Porter Fowler, May 5, 1913	3d Field Artillery.
40	William Wellesley Percy, May 20, 1913	Medical Corps.
41	John Franklin Dunseith, Oct. 1, 1913	Medical Corps.
42	Albert Daniel Ecke, March 1, 1914	47th Infantry.
43	Edwin Lorendus Bebee, March 18, 1914	Medical Corps.
44	Ralph Murray Glover, March 20, 1914	10th Infantry.
45	Walter Edmund Corwin, April 3, 1914	47th Infantry.
46	Frank Harnden, May 18, 1914	Medical Corps.
47	Robert Pelton Wadhams, May 19, 1914	Medical Corps.
48	John William Tumbridge, June 4, 1914	Ordnance Dept.
49	Thomas Francis Maguire, June 13, 1914	Medical Corps.
50	Sylvanus Purdy, Nov. 11, 1914	10th Infantry.
51	William Leo Hallahan, Feb. 19, 1915	1st Battalion Signal Corps.
52	Edmund Price Fowler, March 16, 1915	Medical Corps.
53	Walter George Robinson, March 30, 1915	2d Infantry.
54	Allan Lawrence Reagan, April 6, 1915	Adjutant General's Dept.
55	William Stevens Conrow, May 15, 1915	Corps of Engineers.
56	Harry Judson Lipes, May 24, 1915	Medical Corps.
57	Edward McLeer, Jr., June 3, 1915	1st Cavalry.
58	Mortimer Drake Bryant, June 3, 1915	1st Cavalry.
59	John James Lyons, June 3, 1915	Medical Corps.
60	Everett Eugene Pateman, June 11, 1915	2d Infantry.
61	James Leslie Kincaid, June 30, 1915	Adjutant General's Dept.
62	James Taft Pilcher, July 3, 1915	Medical Corps.
63	Robert Mazet, July 6, 1915	7th Infantry.
64	Robert Peebles Orr, Aug. 20, 1915	Coast Artillery Corps.
65	Charles Joseph Ahern, Oct. 1, 1915	Quartermaster Corps.
66	Charles Robert Seymour, Oct. 2, 1915	1st Field Artillery.
67	James Edward Austin, Oct. 2, 1915	1st Field Artillery.
68	William A. McAdam, Nov. 11, 1915	47th Infantry.
69	Frederick Stuart Couchman, March 3, 1916	3d Infantry.
70	Matthew George Addison, March 16, 1916	23d Infantry.
71	Lewis Seymour, March 27, 1916	1st Infantry.
72	James Francis Sheehan, April 15, 1916	1st Infantry.
73	Henry Forrest Quackenbos, April 24, 1916	12th Infantry.
74	Edward John Westcott, June 19, 1916	Adjutant General's Dept.
75	De Witt Clinton Falls, June 21, 1916	7th Infantry.
76	Carl H. Breed, June 23, 1916	Quartermaster Corps.
77	Walter Allen DeLamater, June 26, 1916	71st Infantry.
78	Frederick Charles Ringer, June 28, 1916	Quartermaster Corps.
79	Arthur Waller Slee, July 21, 1916	Medical Corps.
80	Leonard Bacon Smith, July 25, 1916	Adjutant General's Dept.
81	Thomas Harry Shanton, July 25, 1916	Quartermaster Corps.
82	Andrew E. Tuck, Aug. 16, 1916	Adjutant General's Dept.
83	Henry Adsit, Nov. 6, 1916	1st Cavalry.
84	Charles M. Tobin, Nov. 15, 1916	1st Cavalry.

RELATIVE RANK OF OFFICERS IN ACTIVE SERVICE IN THE NATIONAL GUARD — (Continued)

No.	NAME AND DATE OF RANK	Corps or organization
	Captains	
1	Bleecker Bangs, July 12, 1897	23d Infantry.
2	James Weston Myers, April 2, 1898	7th Infantry.
3	Clarence Fagan True, June 3, 1898	71st Infantry
4	George Morgan Muren, March 7, 1900	Medical Corps.
5	Felix Joseph McSherry, Oct. 18, 1900	69th Infantry.
6	John Jay Cowdrey, Nov. 8, 1900	Coast Artillery Corps.
7	William Stuart Charles, Dec. 5, 1900	3d Infantry.
8	Robert Joseph Daly, May 26, 1902	Corps of Engineers.
9	Edward James Reilly, Nov. 11, 1902	Coast Artillery Corps.
10	William Royde Fearn, April 19, 1904	71st Infantry.
11	Frank Salisbury Harris, May 1, 1905	10th Infantry.
12	Henry Maslin, May 23, 1905	71st Infantry.
13	Edward Maurice Dillon, March 6, 1906	69th Infantry.
14	Frank Walker Sears, March 30, 1907	Medical Corps.
15	Arthur Rockwell Addy, May 25, 1907	Medical Corps.
16	George Ellsworth Gasper, June 7, 1907	3d Infantry.
17	Patrick James Keeler, June 26, 1907	3d Field Artillery.
18	Herbert Anderson Summers, July 11, 1907	14th Infantry.
19	Moses Ashby Stivers, July 13, 1907	Medical Corps.
20	John Wesley Lyon, July 16, 1907	71st Infantry.
21	Lyman Adelbert Wood, July 29, 1907	74th Infantry.
22	George Howard Johnson, Nov. 25, 1907	22d Regt. of Engineers.
23	Alexander Magnus Bremer, Jan. 20, 1908	Coast Artillery Corps.
24	Clarence Joshua Walker, Feb. 20, 1908	23d Infantry.
25	Eliot Bishop, Feb. 29, 1908	Medical Corps.
26	Charles Joseph Dieges, March 3, 1908	22d Regt. of Engineers.
27	Howard Lester Campion, March 12, 1908	14th Infantry.
28	Lyman Parsons Hubbell, April 10, 1908	74th Infantry.
29	George William Johnston, May 14, 1908	Coast Artillery Corps.
30	William Duroy Spear, May 29, 1908	Coast Artillery Corps.
31	J. Augustus Barnard, Oct. 6, 1908	7th Infantry.
32	Harvey Garrison, Nov. 13, 1908	Corps of Engineers.
33	George Stewart Minniss, Dec. 30, 1908	74th Infantry.
34	Thomas Jefferson Dooley, Jan. 23, 1909	10th Infantry.
35	Nicholas Engel, Jan. 30, 1909	7th Infantry.
36	Jay Zorn, Feb. 13, 1909	12th Infantry.
37	Nelson True Barrett, Feb. 27, 1909	3d Field Artillery.
38	Edward William Hall, March 27, 1909	Medical Corps.
39	James Eben, April 7, 1909	71st Infantry.
40	Bruno Frederick Wetzelberg, April 19, 1909	Coast Artillery Corps.
41	Samuel Ferguson Fahnestock, April 23, 1909	47th Infantry.
42	Grant H. Simonds, May 17, 1909	Medical Corps.
43	Charles Oliver Boswell, May 17, 1909	Medical Corps.
44	William Johnston Cranston, May 17, 1909	Medical Corps.
45	Archer Dorval Babcock, May 17, 1909	Medical Corps.
46	Raymond Alexander Turnbull, May 23, 1909	Medical Corps.
47	William Randolph Jackson, May 27, 1909	14th Infantry.
48	William Lewis Burnett, May 28, 1909	10th Infantry.
49	William Drexler Finke, June 7, 1909	Coast Artillery Corps.
50	Alexander Roy Robertson, June 14, 1909	74th Infantry.
51	William Arthur Turnbull, June 29, 1909	3d Infantry.
52	Abraham Lincoln McKenzie, Dec. 8, 1909	Coast Artillery Corps.
53	William Gray, Jan. 14, 1910	Coast Artillery Corps.
54	Patrick Joseph Walsh, Jan. 17, 1910	Corps of Engineers.
55	Gabriel George Hollander, Feb. 16, 1910	14th Infantry.
56	John Richard Sawyer, March 2, 1910	23d Infantry.
57	Edward Jenkins Parish, March 26, 1910	1st Infantry.
58	Jason Samuel Parker, Aug. 3, 1910	Medical Corps.
59	Robert Starr Allyn, Oct. 17, 1910	Coast Artillery Corps.
60	Harry Vermilye Van Auken, Nov. 23, 1910	Coast Artillery Corps.
61	Torrey Allen Ball, Nov. 25, 1910	3d Infantry.
62	William Benedict Stacom, Dec. 23, 1910	69th Infantry
63	Elbert Eugene Wonderly, Dec. 23, 1910	14th Infantry.
64	Charles Henry Canfield, March 1, 1911	10th Infantry.
65	William Simpson Covell, March 18, 1911	7th Infantry.
66	George Matthew Stoll, March 20, 1911	23d Infantry.
67	Otto Irving Chormann, April 14, 1911	3d Infantry.
68	George Edmund Schenk, May 9, 1911	Signal Corps.
69	George Aloysius Wilson, May 17, 1911	47th Infantry.
70	Gilbert Van Evera Schenck, May 17, 1911	10th Infantry.
71	Lewis B. Marselis, May 23, 1911	1st Infantry.

RELATIVE RANK OF OFFICERS IN ACTIVE SERVICE IN THE NATIONAL
GUARD — (Continued)

No.	NAME AND DATE OF RANK	Corps or organization
	Captains — Continued	
72	Albert Cole Bogert, May 25, 1911	10th Infantry.
73	George Perrine, June 30, 1911	71st Infantry.
74	William Fowler Wheelock, July 5, 1911	10th Infantry.
75	Thomas Moore Sherman, July 22, 1911	1st Infantry.
76	Ernest Franklin Robinson, Aug. 2, 1911	Corps of Engineers.
77	Guido Fridolin Verbeck, Sept. 19, 1911	1st Field Artillery.
78	Frank McElroy Hay, Sept. 20, 1911	2d Infantry.
79	Frederick Ralph Post, Oct. 13, 1911	47th Infantry.
80	Ernest Livingston Miller, Nov. 8, 1911	1st Cavalry.
81	Harry Meekes, Nov. 16, 1911	Coast Artillery Corps.
82	Thomas William Baldwin, Jan. 9, 1912	Coast Artillery Corps.
83	Anthony Fiala, Jan. 19, 1912	1st Cavalry.
84	Marcus Tolman Hendricks, Feb. 1, 1912	47th Infantry.
85	Albert Stevens Callan, Feb. 6, 1912	10th Infantry.
86	James Lowen Young, Feb. 23, 1912	47th Infantry
87	Frederic Granville Munson, April 1, 1912	Coast Artillery Corps
88	Jesse Scott Button, April 12, 1912	2d Infantry.
89	Charles Curie, April 13, 1912	1st Cavalry.
90	William Henry Ferguson, April 16, 1912	10th Infantry.
91	Charles White Berry, April 18, 1912	14th Infantry.
92	Oscar Carlson, April 19, 1912	14th Infantry.
93	Frank Leo Meagher, April 23, 1912	10th Infantry.
94	Charles Edward Fiske, May 1, 1912	1st Cavalry.
95	Charles Adam Kendall, May 24, 1912	74th Infantry.
96	Alexander Lorenz Gillig, May 25, 1912	74th Infantry
97	Howard Morgan Cowperthwait, June 4, 1912	Squadron A, Cavalry.
98	Henry Sheldon, June 11, 1912	Machine Gun Troop, Cavalry.
99	Stephen Ralph Tiffany, July 3, 1912	47th Infantry.
100	John Dollo Jennings, July 12, 1912	Coast Artillery Corps.
101	Morton Gorton Stockbridge, July 17, 1912	47th Infantry.
102	James Boardman De Mott, July 24, 1912	23d Infantry.
103	Wilbur Teed Wright, Sept. 18, 1912	2d Field Artillery.
104	De Witt Clinton Weld, Jr., Oct. 8, 1912	2d Field Artillery.
105	William Joseph Donovan, Oct. 11, 1912	1st Cavalry.
106	Henry Simeon Ball, Oct. 28, 1912	1st Infantry.
107	Charles Henry Smith, Nov. 11, 1912	Quartermaster Corps.
108	George William Augustin, Nov. 13, 1912	Medical Corps.
109	Damase Joseph Cadotte, Nov. 20, 1912	74th Infantry.
110	William Moore Halsted, Nov. 21, 1912	7th Infantry.
111	Karl Baldwin Kloer, Nov. 26, 1912	23d Infantry.
112	Reynolds King Townsend, Nov. 26, 1912	10th Infantry.
113	C. H. Ranulf Compton, Nov. 26, 1912	2d Infantry.
114	Harry Cornelius Elwood, Dec. 18, 1912	74th Infantry.
115	James Gracey Dunseith, Dec. 31, 1912	Medical Corps.
116	Hugh Aloysius Rodden, Jan. 3, 1913	Medical Corps.
117	Charles Willis Yeomans, Jan. 14, 1913	1st Infantry.
118	Albert Scales Hamilton, Jan. 23, 1913	2d Field Artillery
119	Wilmot Lawrence Cole, March 3, 1913	Coast Artillery Corps.
120	Louis Francis Kunts, March 25, 1913	2d Field Artillery.
121	George Salisbury Chase, March 28, 1913	47th Infantry.
122	Ralph Kenyon Robertson, April 1, 1913	74th Infantry.
123	Edwin Jesse Murray, April 3, 1913	3d Infantry.
124	George Frederick Bradshaw, April 3, 1913	2d Infantry.
125	Harvey Sprague Albertson, April 5, 1913	Medical Corps.
126	William Alexander Ross, May 5, 1913	2d Regt. of Engineers.
127	Charles Heber Barnes, May 7, 1913	3d Infantry.
128	Charles Abner MacArthur, May 12, 1913	2d Infantry.
129	William Allen Hall Ely, May 29, 1913	71st Infantry.
130	Don Melville Hooks, June 9, 1913	Medical Corps.
131	Joseph James Daly, June 13, 1913	Corps of Engineers.
132	Robert Stewart Hall, June 16, 1913	2d Infantry.
133	Frederick William Vogel, July 1, 1913	71st Infantry.
134	Roscoe Bradley Trumble, July 15, 1913	2d Infantry.
135	Harvard Albert Kehlbeck, July 22, 1913	71st Infantry.
136	Fancher Nicoll, July 24, 1913	7th Infantry.
137	Charles Hoyt Williams, Aug. 2, 1913	65th Infantry.
138	James Barbour Richardson, Aug. 13, 1913	2d Field Artillery.
139	Robert Aikman, Aug. 15, 1913	Coast Artillery Corps.
140	William Ormiston Richardson, Aug. 18, 1913	2d Field Artillery.
141	Clarence Anthony Clifton, Aug. 22, 1913	Coast Artillery Corps.
142	Charles Miron Ward, Oct. 24, 1913	23d Infantry

RELATIVE RANK OF OFFICERS IN ACTIVE SERVICE IN THE NATIONAL
GUARD— (Continued)

No.	NAME AND DATE OF RANK	Corps or organization
	Captains — Continued	
143	Harold Lawson, Nov. 3, 1913....................	1st Field Artillery.
144	Walter Parke Fox, Nov. 5, 1913....................	2d Field Artillery.
145	Lester Cecil Fox, Nov. 7, 1913....................	2d Field Artillery.
146	Rex Gould Witherbee, Nov. 20, 1913..............	1st Infantry.
147	Joseph A. S. Mundy, Nov. 20, 1913..............	23d Infantry.
148	Morris N. Liebmann, Nov. 29, 1913..............	23d Infantry.
149	John Joseph Dean, Dec. 10, 1913..............	12th Infantry.
150	George Emlen Roosevelt, Dec. 10, 1913..............	12th Infantry.
151	Clark Arthur Briggs, Dec. 10, 1913..............	1st Infantry.
152	Abner Hunter Platt, Dec. 11, 1913..............	1st Cavalry.
153	Frederic Ashton de Peyster, Dec. 16, 1913..........	12th Infantry.
154	Ferdinand Conrad Schussler, Dec. 22, 1913.........	Coast Artillery Corps.
155	Henry Snively Hildreth, Dec. 27, 1913..............	12th Infantry.
156	Hubert Willard Eldred, Jan. 17, 1914..............	47th Infantry.
157	Sidney Gilder de Kay, Jan. 23, 1914..............	12th Infantry.
158	Henry Eckford Greene, Feb. 17, 1914..............	2d Infantry.
159	William Hanford Curtis, March 1, 1914..............	2d Infantry.
160	John Thomas Delaney, March 4, 1914..............	1st Field Artillery.
161	William Thomas Doyle, March 6, 1914..............	69th Infantry.
162	Lucius Albert Salisbury, March 7, 1914..............	Medical Corps.
163	Archland Miller Best, March 17, 1914..............	10th Infantry.
164	William Henry Steers, March 17, 1914..............	Medical Corps.
165	Richard John Ryan, March 30, 1914..............	1st Infantry.
166	Henry Budelman Heylman, April 14, 1914..........	7th Infantry.
167	Arthur Lenox Howe, April 30, 1914..............	1st Battalion, Signal Corps.
168	Harry Boardman Anderson, April 30, 1914..........	10th Infantry.
169	Albert Clements, May 5, 1914.	14th Infantry.
170	Philip Allen Sayles, May 5, 1914..............	14th Infantry.
171	Arthur Henry Snowball, May 15, 1914..............	47th Infantry.
172	Nelson Walter Thompson, May 15, 1914..............	14th Infantry.
173	Frederick William Cobb, May 18, 1914..............	10th Infantry.
174	John Sylvester Thompson, May 25, 1914..........	3d Infantry.
175	Copeland Edward Smith, May 26, 1914..............	3d Infantry.
176	Edward Kook Miller, June 1, 1914..............	1st Infantry.
177	George Spaulding Comstock, June 23, 1914..........	Coast Artillery Corps.
178	Maxwell Betts Nesbitt, July 3, 1914..............	7th Infantry.
179	George J. J. Lawrence, July 17, 1914..............	Medical Corps.
180	Wade Hampton Hayes, Sept. 28, 1914..............	7th Infantry.
181	Albert William Putnam, Oct. 8, 1914..............	Squadron A, Cavalry.
182	Herbert Wheaton Congdon, Oct. 13, 1914..........	23d Infantry.
183	Samuel Herbert Merrill, Oct. 19, 1914..............	3d Infantry.
184	Clifford Ernest Branch, Nov. 9, 1914..............	74th Infantry.
185	Harold Homer Donaldson, Nov. 23, 1914..........	1st Cavalry.
186	Henry Dickson Bagnall, Nov. 23, 1914..............	74th Infantry.
187	Jesse Alvro Millard, Dec. 7, 1914....................	Quartermaster Corps.
188	Daniel John Cassidy, Dec. 11, 1914..............	10th Infantry.
189	Henry Blacklidge Gillen, Jan. 4, 1915..............	Medical Corps.
190	John Samuel Maeder, Jan. 5, 1915..............	Medical Corps.
191	Arthur Walter Pickard, Jan. 6, 1915	1st Cavalry.
192	Edward Louis Franklin, Jan. 16, 1915..............	Coast Artillery Corps.
193	John Joseph Byron, Jan. 28, 1915..............	14th Infantry.
194	Edwin H. Moody, Feb. 5, 1915..............	1st Infantry.
195	Samuel Miller Allerton, Feb. 8, 1915..............	Medical Corps.
196	James Gregory Finn, Feb. 15, 1915..............	69th Infantry.
197	Frank James McCoy, Feb. 20, 1915..............	12th Infantry.
198	Charles Amel Sandburg, March 1, 1915..............	74th Infantry.
199	Charles Willard Lynn, March 6, 1915..............	Medical Corps.
200	Eldred Weston Kennedy, March 9, 1915..............	Medical Corps.
201	Foster Greer Hetzel, March 12, 1915...	14th Infantry.
202	Huette Cammack, March 13, 1915..............	12th Infantry.
203	Francis Draper Bowne, March 15, 1915.	1st Field Artillery.
204	Henry Livingstone Steedman, March 24, 1915	1st Infantry.
205	Howard Elmer Crall, March 29, 1915	7th Infantry.
206	William Frederick Schohl, April 1, 1915..............	65th Infantry.
207	John A. C. Jansen, April 6, 1915..............	1st Cavalry. Depot Battalion.
208	William Augustine Cunningham, April 21, 1915......	Coast Artillery Corps.
209	Jacob Sanders Clinton, April 20, 1915..............	2d Infantry.
210	Frank Rawson Potter, May 3, 1915..............	71st Infantry.
211	Raphael Augustine Egan, May 6, 1915..............	1st Infantry.
212	Alvan Williston Perry, May 6, 1915	1st Field Artillery.
213	Robert Neville Mackin, Jr., May 8, 1915............	Coast Artillery Corps.

RELATIVE RANK OF OFFICERS IN ACTIVE SERVICE IN THE NATIONAL
GUARD — *(Continued)*

No.	NAME AND DATE OF RANK	Corps or organization
	Captains — Continued	
214	Jefferson Brown Latta, May 15, 1915	Medical Corps.
215	Frederick Ward Seymour, May 16, 1915	Medical Corps.
216	Guy Bates, May 28, 1915	23d Regiment.
217	Ray Dobson Richman, May 29, 1915	Medical Corps.
218	George Washington Papen, Jr., June 1, 1915	Medical Corps.
219	Joseph Holmes McDermott, June 2, 1915	71st Infantry.
220	Benjamin Charles Mead, June 9, 1915	3d Infantry.
221	Samuel Townsend Stewart, June 14, 1915	Coast Artillery Corps.
222	Frank John Maldiner, June 18, 1915	74th Infantry.
223	Robert Watson Hinds, June 21, 1915	Medical Corps.
224	Harry Hovey Spencer, June 22, 1915	1st Cavalry.
225	William Evans Trull, July 1, 1915	Coast Artillery Corps.
226	Raymond Macfarlane Reid, July 1, 1915	1st Field Artillery.
227	Henry Emil Holt, July 6, 1915	12th Infantry.
228	Edward Eugene Gauche, July 6, 1915	12th Infantry.
229	Joseph P. D. Schiebler, July 9, 1915	23d Infantry.
230	Alvan Inman Marshall, July 14, 1915	1st Infantry.
231	Charles William Brown, July 25, 1915	47th Infantry.
232	Harry McIndoe Wright, Aug. 20, 1915	Coast Artillery Corps.
233	Raymond Fallon Hodgdon, Aug. 20, 1915	71st Infantry.
234	Clinton Earle Fisk, Sept. 17, 1915	7th Infantry.
235	Edward Tisdale Harris, Sept. 22, 1915	Coast Artillery Corps.
236	Frank R. M. Nelson, Sept. 25, 1915	Coast Artillery Corps.
237	Leo Smith Peterson, Oct. 15, 1915	Medical Corps.
238	John Livingstone, Nov. 8, 1915	2d Infantry.
239	John Adam Quell, Nov. 16, 1915	Medical Corps.
240	Thomas Fairservis, Nov. 17, 1915	23d Infantry.
241	Lawrence Newton Smith, Nov. 18, 1915	3d Infantry.
242	Benjamin Van Raden, Nov. 29, 1915	1st Field Artillery.
243	Henry Langdon Butler, Dec. 1, 1915	Adjutant-General's Dept.
244	Charles Gray Blakeslee, Dec. 1, 1915	1st Field Artillery.
245	Thomas Vincent Kean, Dec. 2, 1915	74th Infantry.
246	Frederic E. Humphreys, Dec. 6, 1915	Corps of Engineers.
247	George Upfold Gates, Dec. 16, 1915	Coast Artillery Corps.
248	Chester Harding King, Jan. 13, 1915	1st Cavalry.
249	Kenneth Gardner, Jan. 13, 1915	7th Infantry.
250	Robert Scott Newcomb, Jan. 16, 1916	Coast Artillery Corps.
251	Fred S. Johnston, Jan. 21, 1916	3d Infantry.
252	Walter Fraser Gibson, Jan. 24, 1916	Quartermaster Corps.
253	Henry Granville Montgomery, Feb. 3, 1916	1st Motor Battery.
254	George Garrison Backhouse, Feb. 9, 1916	1st Cavalry.
255	Sylvester Simpson, Feb. 11, 1916	1st Field Artillery.
256	Howard Edmunds Sullivan, Feb. 21, 1916	2d Field Artillery.
257	Timothy Joseph Moynahan, March 7, 1916	69th Infantry.
258	Robert Buchanan Kennedy, March 14, 1916	Medical Corps.
259	Charles R. Coffin, March 21, 1916	47th Infantry.
260	Robert Henry Haseltine, March 22, 1916	Coast Artillery Corps.
261	Stanley Bulkley, Mar. 26, 1916	71st Infantry.
262	James Julius Meyer, March 27, 1916	Coast Artillery Corps.
263	Arthur Thomas Smith, April 1, 1916	3d Infantry.
264	David D. Mohler, April 3, 1916	3d Infantry.
265	Lucius Cornelius Higgins, April 3, 1916	Coast Artillery Corps.
266	Frederick Allen Thiessen, April 3, 1916	2d Infantry.
267	Walter Cecil McClure, April 4, 1916	1st Field Artillery.
268	Charles Arthur Bodin, April 10, 1916	Coast Artillery Corps.
269	Alexander Edward Anderson, April 15, 1916	69th Infantry.
270	Herman E. Sullivan, May 1, 1916	2d Infantry.
271	George Lefevre Simonson, May 3, 1916	23d Infantry.
272	William Springler Mitchell, May 9, 1916	12th Infantry
273	George S. Koepers, May 26, 1916	1st Infantry.
274	John Carl Punger, May 17, 1916	14th Infantry.
275	Martin Francis Ford, June 6, 1916	Coast Artillery Corps.
276	John Joseph Lilly, June 8, 1916	69th Infantry.
277	Harry Thomas Blythe, June 9, 1916	1st Infantry.
278	Graham Youngs, June 19, 1916	Cavalry.
279	Raymond T. Monis, June 20, 1916	Quartermaster Corps.
280	Joseph William Farrell, June 20, 1916	Quartermaster Corps.
281	James T. Loree, June 21, 1916	Quartermaster Corps.
282	William M. Ford, R. L., June 22, 1916	69th Infantry.
283	Earnest Charles Schroeder, June 23, 1916	71st Infantry.
284	George Augustin Daly, June 24, 1916	12th Infantry.

RELATIVE RANK OF OFFICERS IN ACTIVE SERVICE IN THE NATIONAL GUARD — (Continued)

No.	Name and Date of Rank	Corps or organization
	Captains — Continued	
285	Peter Francis Burns, June 26, 1916	22d Regiment.
286	Charles A. Brown, June 26, 1916	1st Cavalry.
287	John Frederick Ranges, June 26, 1916	71st Infantry.
288	Harry Clarence Starrett, June 27, 1916	14th Infantry.
289	Leon Brooks de Garmo, June 27, 1916	14th Infantry.
290	William Edward Blaisdell, June 27, 1916	14th Infantry.
291	Arthur Mortimer Day, June 28, 1916	8th Coast Defense Corps.
292	Edward R. Thorne, June 28, 1916	10 Infantry.
293	Arthur Harrison Miller, June 29, 1916	Coast Artillery Corps.
294	Raynauld C. Bolling, July 1, 1916	1st Aero Company.
295	John M. Satterfield, July 1, 1916	2d Aero Company.
296	Oliver Frank Miller, July 1, 1916	74th Infantry.
297	James Pennoyer Cooke, July 3, 1916	23d Infantry.
298	Jerome Francis Langer, July 3, 1916	23d Infantry.
299	William James Evans, July 3, 1916	23 Infantry
300	James Chives Maclin, July 4, 1916	1st Cavalry.
301	William Joseph Jackson, July 5, 1916	47th Infantry.
302	Charles H. Rogers, Jr., July 5, 1916	47th Infantry.
303	Herbert Duane Crounse, July 5, 1916	2d Infantry.
304	Cornelius Joseph Tucker, July 5, 1916	47th Infantry.
305	Michael Andrew Kelly, July 5, 1916	69th Infantry.
306	Douglas Cornell Despard, July 13, 1916	7th Infantry
307	Thomas Marks, July 14, 1916	3d Field Artillery
308	Charles W. Fillmore, July 18, 1916	15th Infantry.
309	Charles S. Clifford, July 26, 1916	13th Coast Defense Corps.
310	John Patrick Hurley, July 26, 1916	69th Infantry.
311	George William Hudtwalker, Aug. 2, 1916	47th Infantry.
312	Julius Tannenbaum, Aug. 8, 1916	Coast Artillery Corps.
313	Frederick Hamilton Ryan, Aug. 17, 1916	1st Field Artillery.
314	Merwyn Humphrey Nellis, Aug. 23, 1916	Quartermaster Corps.
315	Alexander McCook Barrett, Aug. 25, 1916	Engineers, 22d Regiment.
316	Bradley Goodyear, Sept. 6, 1916	3d Field Artillery.
317	John Joseph Dunn, Sept. 9, 1916	Engineers, 22d Regiment.
318	William Edward Lane, Jr., Sept. 9, 1916	Engineers, 22d Regiment.
319	George Duncan Snyder, Sept. 12, 1916	Engineers, 22d Regiment.
320	Richard Whitney Colman, Sept. 19, 1916	7th Infantry.
321	Fred de Figaniere, Sept. 20, 1916	2d Field Artillery.
322	Robert Waddell Marshall, Sept. 25, 1916	3d Field Artillery.
323	Alexander Perry, Sept. 26, 1916	Coast Artillery Corps.
324	John Diedrich Butt, Sept. 26, 1916	2d Field Artillery.
325	William H. Kennedy, Sept. 29, 1916	3d Field Artillery.
326	Millard Fillmore Waltz, Jr., Oct. 3, 1916	12th Infantry.
327	Willard Conklin Penton, Oct. 6, 1916	23d Infantry.
328	James A. McKenna, Jr., Oct. 20, 1916	69th Infantry.
329	Frank Elliott Sidman, Oct. 20, 1916	69th Infantry.
330	Walter E. Powers, Oct. 22, 1916	69th Infantry.
331	George F. Hinton, Oct. 31, 1916	15th Infantry.
332	Dallas Casper Newton, Nov. 5, 1916	1st Cavalry.
333	Chauncey J. Hamlin, Nov. 11, 1916	3d Field Artillery.
334	Leo Colprice, Nov. 11, 1916	3d Field Artillery.
335	Jacob Brost, Nov. 11, 1916	65th Infantry.
336	John Herman Knuebel, Nov. 25, 1916	74th Infantry.
337	Nicholas Ridgley, Dec. 1, 1916	Squadron A, Cavalry.
338	Henry B. H. Ripley, Dec. 13, 1916	15th Infantry.
339	John D. Webber, Dec. 16, 1916	3d Field Artillery.
	First Lieutenants	
1	Wilber Bird Hammond, Dec. 16, 1904	10th Infantry.
2	Walter Livingstone Gibson, June 27, 1906	Coast Artillery Corps.
3	Millard Fillmore Cook, Nov. 8, 1906	23d Infantry.
4	Chester Wyman Davis, March 9, 1907	Aide, 3d Brigade.
5	George Albert Elliott, Sept. 30, 1907	3d Infantry.
6	Harry Merz, Nov. 12, 1907	71st Infantry.
7	John Francis Daniell, Dec. 19, 1907	7th Infantry.
8	Griswold Green, Aug. 17, 1908	Aide, 3d Brigade.
9	John Miller, Aug. 17, 1908	Coast Artillery Corps
10	Clarence Henry Bobb, April 5, 1909	Corps of Engineers.
11	Charles Allen Baker, Nov. 9, 1909	10th Infantry.
12	Julian Roy Wilbur, Feb. 15, 1910	1st Infantry.
13	Edwin Francis Thompson, Nov. 17, 1910	14th Infantry.

RELATIVE RANK OF OFFICERS IN ACTIVE SERVICE IN THE NATIONAL GUARD — (Continued)

No.	NAME AND DATE OF RANK	Corps or organization
	First Lieutenants — Continued	
14	Harry Gregory Underwood, Dec. 10, 1910	Aide, 3d Brigade.
15	Charles Bunker Crane, Jan. 4, 1911	7th Infantry.
16	Arthur Charles Schaefer, April 25, 1911	Medical Corps.
17	John Jerome Callahan, May 16, 1911	71st Infantry.
18	Edward James Clark, May 19, 1911	10th Infantry.
19	Albert Manley Barager, May 31, 1911	3d Infantry.
20	Arthur Russell Overfield, July 17, 1911	74th Infantry.
21	John William Goff, Jr., Sept. 25, 1911	71st Infantry.
22	Henry Gansevoort McEwan, Dec. 11, 1911	2d Infantry.
23	Charles Burton Plumley, Dec. 13, 1911	2d Infantry.
24	John Thomas Daly, Feb. 3, 1912	Coast Artillery Corps.
25	Clarence Stewart Martin, March 26, 1912	3d Infantry.
26	George Frederic Alpers, April 19, 1912	1st Cavalry.
27	John Horton Morrison, May 23, 1912	1st Infantry.
28	Harry Jay Young, June 5, 1912	2d Infantry.
29	Edwin George Ziegler, June 19, 1912	74th Infantry.
30	Stephen James De Lanoy, June 19, 1912	71st Infantry.
31	John Joseph Curtin, July 30, 1912	3d Field Artillery.
32	Harry Beam Baldwin Jr., July 31, 1912	47th Infantry.
33	Edward Angelle Roberts, Aug. 2, 1912	1st Infantry.
34	Charles Peter Loeser, Nov. 27, 1912	7th Infantry.
35	Louis Townsend Montant, Dec. 19, 1912	Aide, 1st Brigade.
36	Francis Dayton Clark, Dec. 24, 1912	7th Infantry.
37	Harold Brown Evans, Feb. 25, 1913	10th Infantry.
38	Edwin Ambrose Power, April 4, 1913	23d Infantry.
39	Fred Emerson Beebee, May 12, 1913	1st Infantry.
40	Alexander Milloy McEwen, May 15, 1913	Corps of Engineers.
41	St. Clair Smith, Jr., June 17, 1913	Coast Artillery Corps.
42	Eugene Francis Connolly, July 1, 1913	Medical Corps.
43	Harry Haile Farmer, July 2, 1913	3d Infantry.
44	Albert Daniel Washington, July 2, 1913	2d Field Artillery.
45	Samuel Hazard Gillespie, July 22, 1913	Squadron A, Cavalry.
46	Selden Gloyd Warner, July 24, 1913	71st Infantry.
47	John Joseph Welch, Jr., Aug. 13, 1913	3d Infantry.
48	Elwood Groesbeck, Sept. 29, 1913	2d Infantry.
49	Herbert Clarendon Alden, Sept. 29, 1913	Coast Artillery Corps.
50	Homer Hollett Oaksford, Oct. 2, 1913	Medical Corps.
51	Philip Conrad Hacker, Nov. 11, 1913	Medical Corps.
52	Joseph Francis Murray, Jan. 3, 1914	Coast Artillery Corps.
53	Emanuel Goldstein, Jan. 12, 1914	Medical Corps.
54	Lofferts Hutton, Jan. 22, 1914	7th Infantry.
55	Frederick Doane Conklin, Jan. 23, 1914	7th Infantry.
56	Lucius Huntington Doty, Feb. 5, 1914	10th Infantry.
57	Maunsell Schieffelin Crosby, Feb. 6, 1914	10th Infantry.
58	Wallace Macdonald Brown, Feb. 9, 1914	1st Cavalry.
59	Stephen Hulbert Ackerman, Jr., March 3, 1914	Medical Corps.
60	Harry Charles Miller, March 4, 1914	2d Field Artillery.
61	Henri Delbert Goodnow, March 13, 1914	1st Infantry.
62	James Walcott Wadsworth, Jr., March 26, 1914	1st Cavalry.
63	Charles Irving Newton, April 28, 1914	Medical Corps.
64	Charles Henry King, May 4, 1914	2d Field Artillery.
65	Horst A. C. Albrecht, May 11, 1914	2d Field Artillery.
66	Benjamin Buckley, May 11, 1914	2d Infantry.
67	William Henry Patton, May 13, 1914	69th Infantry.
68	Eugene Albert Holmes, May 13, 1914	2d Field Artillery.
69	Elias Earl Cooley, May 21, 1914	Medical Corps.
70	Isaac James Lovell, May 25, 1914	14th Infantry.
71	Harry S. Monell, June 2, 1914	Coast Artillery Corps.
72	Joseph Lawrence Gillmann, June 4, 1914	14th Infantry.
73	George Moffatt Bramwell, June 10, 1914	12th Infantry.
74	Frederick William Wurster, Jr., June 16, 1914	Squadron A, Cavalry
75	Edward Clark Dunning, July 21, 1914	10th Infantry.
76	Gerald Stratton, Sept. 14, 1914	7th Infantry.
77	Louis Virtue Snyder, Oct. 1, 1914	10th Infantry.
78	Francis Joseph Considine, Oct. 13, 1914	3d Infantry.
79	Francis Sylvester Mahoney, Oct. 19, 1914	1st Infantry.
80	George Pardee Nichols, Oct. 29, 1914	7th Infantry.
81	Frank Miller Foote, Oct. 30, 1914	23d Infantry.
82	George McKenzie Hall, Nov. 11, 1914	Medical Corps.
83	Carl Gustav Kaffenberger, Nov. 18, 1914	74th Infantry.
84	Harry Andrew Wilbur, Nov. 23, 1914	1st Infantry.

RELATIVE RANK OF OFFICERS IN ACTIVE SERVICE IN THE NATIONAL GUARD — (Continued)

No.	NAME AND DATE OF RANK	Corps or organization
	First Lieutenants — Continued	
85	Clarence R. McMichael, Nov. 24, 1914	74th Infantry.
86	Edward Sargent Pilcher, Nov. 30, 1914	74th Infantry.
87	George Francis Terry, Dec. 15, 1914	71st Infantry.
88	James Jay Clark, Dec. 19, 1914	Medical Corps.
89	George Leslie Miller, Dec. 19, 1914	Medical Corps.
90	Ernest Carl Dreher, Dec. 28, 1914	71st Infantry.
91	Alfred Frederick Cassebeer, Dec. 31, 1914	Medical Corps.
92	Edward Harvey Marsh, Dec. 31, 1914	Medical Corps.
93	Thomas Joseph Coursey, Dec. 31, 1914	3d Infantry.
94	Hilton Jewell Shelley, Dec. 31, 1914	Medical Corps.
95	George Morgan Welch, Dec. 30, 1914	Coast Artillery Corps.
96	Edwin Cornelius Peterson, Jan. 2, 1915	47th Infantry.
97	Benjamin Robert Briggs, Jan. 16, 1915	1st Cavalry.
98	Arthur Drake, Jan. 18, 1915	7th Infantry.
99	Leon Marvin Simons, Jan. 22, 1915	47th Infantry.
100	Melvin Leonard Baxter, Feb. 5, 1915	74th Infantry.
101	Robert Ainsworth Byrns, Feb. 10, 1915	7th Infantry.
102	Bertram George Eadie, Feb. 10, 1915	1st Cavalry.
103	Charles H. E. Frank, Feb. 11, 1915	14th Infantry.
104	Stephen Phelan Walsh, March 12, 1915	14th Infantry.
105	Mads Frederick Jensen, March 17, 1915	14th Infantry.
106	Robert Malcolm, April 1, 1915	Medical Corps.
107	Alson Joye Hull, April 1, 1915	Medical Corps.
108	Ellis Adelbert Robertson, April 4, 1915	71st Infantry.
109	Donald Manson Ogilvie, April 12, 1915	1st Cavalry.
110	Marshall Granville Hatfield, April 14, 1915	Coast Artillery Corps.
111	John Henry O'Connor, April 20, 1915	Medical Corps.
112	Ulysses Silver Kahn, April 22, 1915	Medical Corps.
113	Theodore Fletcher Mead, April 24, 1915	Medical Corps.
114	Russell Montgomery Vernon, May 13, 1915	1st Infantry.
115	John Arthur Nelson, May 20, 1915	14th Infantry.
116	Harry Lyons Gilchriese, June 1, 1915	3d Field Artillery.
117	Ludwig Robert von Roeder, June 3, 1915	Medical Corps.
118	William Brewster Penoyar, June 4, 1915	1st Cavalry.
119	Jeremiah William O'Mahoney, June 5, 1915	Coast Artillery Corps.
120	Laurence Collins Donovan, June 14, 1915	Engineers.
121		Engineers.
122		Coast Artillery Corps.
123		Coast Artillery Corps.
124	Norris Parmly Stockwell, June 22, 1915	Engineers.
125	John Winfield Gilmore, July 1, 1915	Coast Artillery Corps.
126	John Sloane Keegan, July 6, 1915	1st Cavalry.
127	Joseph John Koen, July 6, 1915	12th Infantry.
128	Nathaniel Hillyer Egleston, July 7, 1915	Squadron A, Cavalry.
129	Dudley Blanchard Howard, July 9, 1915	14th Infantry.
130	Herbert Leslie Watson, July 10, 1915	1st Battalion, Signal Corps
131	Frederick Manley Steeves, July 12, 1915	1st Battalion, Signal Corps.
132	Charles David Bles, July 12, 1915	Medical Corps.
133	William Lord Hodder, July 17, 1915	3d Infantry.
134	Robert R. Molyneux, July 17, 1915	1st Cavalry.
135	Frederick Clare Hyames, July 29, 1915	17th Infantry.
136	Roger Pratt Clark, Aug. 12, 1915	2d Field Artillery.
137	Channing Rust Toy, Aug. 16, 1915	1st Field Artillery.
138	Frederic Kurczyn Lovell, Sept. 20, 1915	71st Infantry.
139	Chester Levi Benedict, Sept. 28, 1915	2d Infantry.
140	William C. G. Wahle, Oct. 21, 1915	Coast Artillery Corps.
141	George W. I. Dwinell, Oct. 25, 1915	Coast Artillery Corps.
142		Medical Corps.
143	Lowyd Whitcomb Ballantyne, Oct. 29, 1915	Medical Corps.
144	John Christopher Grabau, Nov. 4, 1915	Medical Corps.
145	Frank Howard Richardson, Nov. 8, 1915	Medical Corps
146	Ralph Henry Dunning, Nov. 12, 1915	Medical Corps.
147	William Elmer Truex, Nov. 12, 1915	Medical Corps.
148	Raynal Cawthorne Bolling, Nov. 12, 1915	Signal Corps.
148a	Matthew Stanley Weir, Nov. 29, 1915	1st Field Artillery.
149	Walter F. Siegmund, Nov. 29, 1915	65th Infantry.
150	William Henry Belfield, Dec. 11, 1915	1st Infantry.
151	John Duncan Gulick, Dec. 20, 1915	Medical Corps.
152	Miles Herbert Merwin, Dec. 21, 1915	3d Field Artillery.
153	Rudolph C. Dittus, Dec. 28, 1915	10th Infantry.
154	Edward George Benson, Dec. 29, 1915	Medical Corps.

RELATIVE RANK OF OFFICERS IN ACTIVE SERVICE IN THE NATIONAL GUARD — (*Continued*)

No.	NAME AND DATE OF RANK	Corps or organization
	First Lieutenants — Continued	
155	Henry Wenman Allen, Dec. 29, 1915	1st Cavalry
156	Thomas H. McKlintock, Jan. 4, 1916...............	14th Infantry.
157	Tristram Coffin, Jan. 6, 1916....................	10th Infantry.
158	Eugene A. Van Nest, Jan. 7, 1916.......	13th Coast Defense Company.
159	John C. Ward, Jan. 20, 1916..	74th Infantry.
160	Arthur Edward Kaeppel, Jan. 24, 1916.............	1st Field Artillery.
161	Arthur E. DeForest, Jan. 24, 1916...............	13th Coast Defense Company.
162	Foulke O. E. Knudson, Jan. 24, 1916.............	Coast Artillery Corps.
163	Jesse R. Pawling, Feb. 1, 1916.....	1st Ambulance Company.
164	George Billings Gibbons, Feb. 5, 1916.............	1st Field Artillery.
165	Harry J. Worthing, Feb. 8, 1916..................	23d Infantry.
166	Charles F. Nichol, Feb. 9, 1916..................	23d Infantry.
167	Harold Rea Fast, Feb. 16, 1916................. , ..	74th Infantry.
168	Nicholas Edward Devereux, Jr., Feb. 16, 1916......	1st Cavalry
169	Samuel A. Smith, Feb. 23, 1916..................	69th Infantry.
170	Frank Harold Brown, Mar. 1, 1916................	Coast Artillery Corps.
171	Delancey Bentley, March 2, 1916.................	3d Infantry.
172	Charles McLean, March 2, 1916..................	1st Infantry.
173	James Harrison Giles, March 3, 1916....	1st Field Artillery.
174	Seymour C. Schwartz, March 7, 1916..............	4th Field Hospital.
175	Francis W. Moore, March 9, 1916.................	47th Infantry.
176	Charles Joseph McGronan, March 14, 1916..........	2d Field Artillery.
177	Harry Hamilton Barnes, March 14, 1916...........	1st Cavalry
178	George F. Taylor, March 16, 1916................	3d Infantry.
179	John Barry Hinds, March 21, 1916................	1st Infantry.
180	Charles D. Kayser, March 22, 1916...............	71st Infantry.
181	James J. Roos, March 22, 1916..................	74th Infantry.
182	Charles Nordquist Morgan, March 22, 1916.	1st Cavalry.
183	George Ellis Ramsey, March 27, 1916............	2d Infantry.
184	Harold Neergaard Olmstead, March 30, 1916	1st Cavalry.
185	Ellis Adelbert Robertson, April 4, 1916...........	71st Infantry.
186	Dean Nelson, April 11, 1916...................	2d Field Artillery.
187	Henry Hafner, April 12, 1916...................	3d Field Artillery.
188	Charles Sailor Gleim, April 20, 1916	Coast Artillery Corps.
189	Charles Homer Rignel, April 26, 1916.............	74th Infantry.
190	Elmer H. Ormsby, April 29, 1916................	2d Infantry.
191	Charles R. Whipple, May 1, 1916	2d Infantry.
192	Richard Earnest Dupuy, May 3, 1916..............	Coast Artillery Corps.
193	Valentine Pearsal Foster, May 4, 1916.............	Coast Artillery Corps.
194	Charles Christian Enderle, May 10, 1916...........	23d Infantry.
195	Alonzo Mordecai Harp, May 10, 1916..............	74th Infantry.
196	Henry W. G. Cox, May 15, 1916.................	2d Field Artillery.
197	James T. Houghton, May 15, 1916.	69th Infantry.
198	Thomas Bennett Austin, May 19, 1916.............	Coast Artillery Corps.
199	Albert Ignatius Paine, May 19, 1916...............	Coast Artillery Corps.
200	Fred B. Adams, May 23, 1916...................	1st Cavalry.
201	Edward Owen Gilmore, May 23, 1916.............	2d Field Artillery.
202	Augustus Wright Palmer, May 23, 1916........	Engineers.
203	Leo H. Costigan, May 24, 1916	13th Coast Defense Company.
204	Ernest Eugene Bosca, May 29, 1916..............	9th Coast Defense Company.
205	Edwin LeRoy Holloway, June 1, 1916.............	47th Infantry.
206	Gilbert Henry Higgins, June 6, 1916.............	Coast Artillery Corps.
207	Edgar C. Niles, June 13, 1916..................	10th Infantry.
208	Carl G. R. Ross, June 14, 1916.................	12th Infantry.
209	Edward Walter Patterson, June 15, 1916..........	Coast Artillery Corps.
210	Frederick A. W. Davis, June 17, 1916............	22d Regiment of Engineers.
211	Frank L. Simes, June 19, 1916.................	3d Infantry.
212	Seneca M. Pike, June 21, 1916.................	2d Infantry.
213	Lyman Aldrich Shaw, June 21, 1916	74th Infantry.
214	Robert Bradford Bartholomew, June 21, 1916..	Squadron A, Cavalry.
215	Auguste Petersen, June 21, 1916................	74th Infantry.
216	Stanton Whitney, June 22, 1916................	Machine Gun Troop, Cavalry.
217	Joseph W. Smith, June 23, 1916....	74th Infantry.
218	Thomas H. Barber, June 24, 1916...............	12th Infantry.
219	Joseph D. Junkin, Jr., June 24, 1916..........;..	12th Infantry.
220	Thomas Reilley, June 24, 1916 .... ;...	69th Infantry.
221	William Kennelly, June 24, 1916................	69th Infantry.
222	Francis H. Berlin, June 24, 1916...............	71st Infantry.
223	Jerome Benedict Sullivan, June 26, 1916.........	Signal Corps.
224	Norbert Carolin, June 26, 1916..................	1st Aero Company.
225	Charles H. Scott, June 26, 1916.................	71st Infantry.

RELATIVE RANK OF OFFICERS IN ACTIVE SERVICE IN THE NATIONAL
GUARD — (*Continued*)

No.	NAME AND DATE OF RANK	Corps or organisation
	First Lieutenants — Continued	
226	Charles Emil Bregenzer, June 27, 1916	22d Regiment of Engineers.
227	Edward B. Whittlesey, June 27, 1916	22d Regiment of Engineers.
228	Maxwell Henderson Gray, June 27, 1916	22d Regiment of Engineers.
229	Joseph Edwards Baker, June 27, 1916	22d Regiment of Engineers.
230	Andrew Francis Lamb, June 27, 1916	22d Regiment of Engineers.
231	George Wright Hinckley, June 27, 1916	1st Cavalry.
232	James Monroe Henderson Wallace, June 28, 1916	1st Infantry.
233	Harold Lawson, June 28, 1916	1st Field Artillery.
234	Henry Luther Mellen, June 28, 1916	22d Regiment of Engineers.
235	George A. Shedden, June 28, 1916	2d Field Artillery.
236	Thomas C. Carlin, June 28, 1916	47th Infantry.
237	Vertner W. Tandy, June 29, 1916	15th Infantry.
238	Clarence H. K. Blauvelt, June 30, 1916	1st Cavalry.
239	Charles Pearson, Jr., June 30, 1916	1st Cavalry.
240	Harry B. Haring, June 30, 1916	14th Infantry.
241	Matthew J. A. Wilson, June 30, 1916	14th Infantry.
242	James E. Miller, July 1, 1916	1st Aero Company.
243	Gordon Ireland, July 1, 1916	Signal Corps.
244	Lewis Henry De Baun, July 1, 1916	Signal Corps.
245	Morgan B. More, July 1, 1916	2d Aero Company.
246	Thomas Crimmins, July 2, 1916	22d Regiment of Engineers.
247	Rutheford Ireland, July 3, 1916	23d Infantry.
248	William Frederick Simonson, July 3, 1916	23d Infantry.
249	Frederick K. Long, July 3, 1916	23d Infantry.
250	William A. Ronalds, July 3, 1916	23d Infantry.
251	Lugi Focardi, July 5, 1916	47th Infantry.
252	James Joseph Archer, July 5, 1916	69th Infantry.
253	George W. McSweeney, July 6, 1916	15th Infantry.
254	Read B. Harding, July 6, 1916	3d Field Hospital.
255	Henry B. Smith, July 6, 1916	4th Field Hospital.
256	Robert J. Reynolds, July 7, 1916	3d Field Hospital.
257	Frank Anthony Bayles, July 8, 1916	10th Infantry.
258	Patrick James Hall, July 7, 1916	69th Infantry.
259	Theophilus Parsons, July 8, 1916	10th Infantry.
260	John W. Frost, July 9, 1916	47th Infantry.
261	Ernest Bentin Gogin, July 9, 1916	47th Infantry.
262	John W. Frost, July 9, 1916	47th Infantry.
263	Alexander B. Thaw, Jr., July 13, 1916	1st Aero Company.
264	Malcolm Wise Force, July 15, 1916	9th Coast Defense Company.
265	Charles Augustus Austen, July 15, 1916	9th Coast Defense Company.
266	James R. Harbinson, July 21, 1916	1st Cavalry.
267	Edward H. Kent, July 22, 1916	7th Infantry.
268	Charles Gustaf Ostberg, July 22, 1916	14th Infantry.
269	Charles D. Cromwell, July 24, 1916	4th Field Hospital.
270	John F. Kerwin, July 25, 1916	Quartermaster Corps.
271	Archibald Crawford Edwards, July 26, 1916	Coast Artillery Corps.
272	Howard Bird, July 27, 1916	2d Infantry.
273	David Chase Wightman, Aug. 14, 1916	1st Infantry.
274	Albert James Sinnock, Aug. 15, 1916	1st Field Artillery.
275	Otto J. Meinecke, Aug. 16, 1916	8th Coast Defense Company.
276	Clarence Gayler Michalis, Aug. 17, 1916	1st Field Artillery.
277	Robert Law Russell, Aug. 19, 1916	1st Field Artillery.
278	William Henry Thomas, Aug. 19, 1916	1st Field Artillery.
279	Walter Palmer Gavit, Aug. 19, 1916	8th Coast Defense Company.
280	James Milton Brown, August 25, 1916	47th Infantry.
281	Vergil H. Parks, Sept. 2, 1916	15th Infantry.
282	Howard K. Parker, Sept. 4, 1916	3d Field Artillery.
283	James F. Dowling, Sept. 6, 1916	12th Infantry.
284	George Edward Bryant, Sept. 6, 1916	23rd Infantry.
285	Ernest Wales Strong, Sept. 7, 1916	71st Infantry.
286	Russell W. Bryant, Sept. 12, 1916	2d Aero Company.
287	Harry Francis Sullivan, Sept. 13, 1916	14th Infantry.
288	Lambert R. Oeder, Sept. 13, 1916	2d Field Artillery.
289	Henry J. Stehl, Sept. 13, 1916	71st Infantry.
290	Daniel George Aber, Sept. 13, 1916	14th Infantry.
291	Austin C. Bamford, Sept. 15, 1916	69th Infantry.
292	William Edward Callender, Jr., Sept. 16, 1916	Coast Artillery Corps.
293	Napoleon B. Marshall, Sept. 20, 1916	15th Infantry.
294	Joseph F. Loughlin, Sept. 21, 1916	47th Infantry.
295	Martin D. F. Smith, Sept. 23, 1916	3 Field Hospital.
296	Harry Edmund Crosby, Sept. 23, 1916	74th Infantry.

RELATIVE RANK OF OFFICERS IN ACTIVE SERVICE IN THE NATIONAL
GUARD — (Continued)

No.	NAME AND DATE OF RANK	Corps or organization
	First Lieutenants — Continued	
297	John J. Mangan, Sept. 23, 1916	69th Infantry.
298	Edward Cavanaugh, Sept. 23, 1916	12 Infantry
299	Howard K. Burkhardt, Sept. 29, 1916	3d Field Artillery.
300	Peter P. Prunty, Sept. 30, 1916	15th Infantry.
301	George Folsom Rugge, Oct. 6, 1916	2d Infantry
302	Arthur Mathews Smith, Oct. 7, 1916	7th Infantry.
303	James F. Coughlin, Oct. 7, 1916	2d Field Artillery.
304	Charles P. Gray, Oct. 9, 1916	7th Infantry
305	Frank A. Spencer, Jr., Oct. 9, 1916	2d Field Artillery.
306	Russell A. Fairbairn, Oct. 10, 1916	9th Coast Defense Corps
307	David D. Warren, Oct. 13, 1916	7th Infantry.
308	Burt D. Whedon, R. L., Oct. 16, 1916	15th Infantry.
309	Edward Leo Brennan, Oct 16, 1916	2d Field Artillery
310	Murray F. Cramer, Oct. 23, 1916	7th Infantry.
311	Rowland Tompkins, Oct. 30, 1916	7th Infantry.
312	Francis W. Murray, Jr., Nov. 2, 1916	69th Infantry.
313	Michael Francis Carroll, Nov. 6, 1916	69th Infantry.
314	Frank H. Richardson, Nov. 8, 1916	1st Signal Corps.
315	Harry Brougham Phinney, Nov. 8, 1916	8th Coast Defense Corps.
316	Edward L. Williams, Nov. 11, 1916	3d Field Artillery.
317	William Ex Truex, Nov. 12, 1916	4th Field Hospital.
318	Harry Woodford Hayward, Nov. 14, 1916	7th Infantry.
319	Charles Samuel Moyer, Nov. 14, 1916	74th Infantry.
320	William F. McKenna, Nov. 16, 1916	69th Infantry.
321	John Gooden Poore, Nov. 16, 1916	69th Infantry.
322	George McAddie, Nov. 16, 1916	69th Infantry.
323	Ernest Daniel Fieux, Nov. 21, 1916	8th Coast Defense Corps.
324	Earl Timeson, Nov. 23, 1916	2d Infantry.
325	William George Staudenmaior, Nov. 24, 1915	3d Infantry.
326	Lester Edward Stoffregen, Nov. 24, 1916	23 Infantry.
327	Augustus Van Cortlandt, Jr., Nov. 25, 1916	12th Infantry.
328	Charles J. Donnocker, Nov. 25, 1916	74 Infantry.
329	George Francis Wallace, Nov. 25, 1916	74th Infantry.
330	Albert Leon Tuttle, Nov. 25, 1916	74th Infantry.
331	George A. Powers, Nov. 28, 1916	3d Field Hospital.
332	John A. Greene, Jr., Dec. 1, 1916	69th Infantry.
333	Walter V Girvin, Dec. 4, 1916	3d Field Hospital.
334	Kenneth Berkley Norton, Dec. 5, 1916	9th Coast Defense Corps
335	James C. Donovan, Dec. 7, 1916	1st Infantry.
336	James R. Europe, Dec. 11, 1916	15th Infantry.
337	Henry B. H. Ripley, Dec. 13, 1916	15th Infantry.
338	Carleton B. Briggs, Dec. 16, 1916	3d Field Artillery.
339	Marvin N. Marcus, Jr., Dec. 16, 1916	3d Field Artillery.
340	Leonard S. Allen, Dec. 16, 1916	3d Field Artillery.
341	Eben C. Sprague, Dec. 16, 1916	3d Field Artillery.
342	Harry L. Gutelius, Dec. 16, 1916	3d Field Artillery.
343	Reg. M. Ballantyne, Dec. 16, 1916	4th Field Hospital.
344	Murray Taylor, December 20, 1916	12 Infantry.
	Second Lieutenants	
1	Henry Burlingame Chapin, April 21, 1905	3d Infantry.
2	Frederick Charles Kuehnle, Feb. 11, 1907	71st Infantry.
3	Frank Fisher Groff, June 8, 1908	71st Infantry.
4	James Riffe, July 21, 1909	3d Infantry.
5	Louis Charles Raecke, June 1, 1910	7th Infantry.
6	Addison Elmore Jenks, June 30, 1910	1st Infantry.
7	Russell Booth Palmer, June 21, 1911	71st Infantry.
8	Ira Underhill Travis, Jr., July 22, 1911	10th Infantry.
9	William Lane Gillespie, Feb. 7, 1912	1st Cavalry.
10	Frank John Laraway, Feb. 16, 1912	10th Infantry.
11	Andrew Baird, June 19, 1912	Coast Artillery Corps.
12	Summerfield Samuel Curtis, July 31, 1912	47th Infantry.
13	Harry James Davidson, Sept. 6, 1912	2d Infantry.
14	Charles Bartholomew Ulrichs, Jan. 3, 1913	23d Infantry.
15	Conrad Philip Hasen, Dec. 10, 1913	71st Infantry.
16	James A Spencer, Jan. 8, 1914	1st Infantry
17	Edward Ross Granger, March 11, 1914	1st Field Artillery
18	William Merriman Chadbourne, March 19, 1914	12th Infantry.
19	Chester Finch Jones, March 27, 1914	23d Infantry
20	William John Burns, April 4, 1914	69th Infantry.

RELATIVE RANK OF OFFICERS IN ACTIVE SERVICE IN THE NATIONAL
GUARD — *(Continued)*

No.	NAME AND DATE OF RANK	Corps or organization
	Second Lieutenants — Continued	
21	Edgar Van Court Reinhold, May 11, 1914..........	71st Infantry.
22	Walter Sherman Cookinham, May 15, 1914..........	1st Infantry.
23	John Thomas Clisset, Jr., May 25, 1914..........	14th Infantry.
24	Raymond Lithgow Hoffman, June 2, 1914..........	2d Field Artillery.
25	George Douglas Bragdon, June 6, 1914..........	10th Infantry.
26	Charles Gordon Alleyn, June 9, 1914..........	7th Infantry.
27	John Richard Suydam, Jr., June 13, 1914..........	Coast Artillery Corps.
28	Walter Howard Simonson, June 16, 1914..........	2d Field Artillery.
29	Frederick Jacob Koch, June 16, 1914..........	1st Field Artillery.
30	Samuel Crump, Jr., July 9, 1914..........	10th Infantry.
31	Francis Marvin Callan, Sept. 11, 1914..........	10th Infantry.
32	Jacob Whitney Vogt, Oct. 8, 1914..........	3d Infantry.
33	Marston Elliott Drake, Oct. 29, 1914..........	7th Infantry.
34	Gordon Hope Grant, Oct. 31, 1914..........	7th Infantry.
35	James Francis Oakleaf, Nov. 16, 1914..........	3d Infantry.
36	Herbert Joseph Brotheridge, Jan. 2, 1915..........	47th Infantry.
37	Carl Herman Lorbs, Jan. 26, 1915..........	1st Cavalry.
38	William Hones, Jr., Feb. 5, 1915..........	1st Infantry.
39	Amos Thorndyke Brown, Feb. 19, 1915..........	71st Infantry.
40	Thomas Bugard Paton, Jr., Feb. 24, 1915..........	71st Infantry.
41	John Joseph Lane, March 6, 1915..........	71st Infantry.
42	Charles McDougall, March 8, 1915..........	1st Cavalry.
43	Euston Fletcher Edmunds, March 17, 1915..........	23d Infantry.
44	Floyd Dana McLean, March 18, 1915..........	1st Infantry.
45	Arthur James McKenna, March 24, 1915..........	7th Infantry.
46	William Hughes Carroll, April 12, 1915..........	Coast Artillery Corps.
47	George Louis Schelling, April 30, 1915..........	1st Cavalry.
48	Harold Cornell DeLoiselle, May 13, 1915..........	23d Infantry.
49	William De La Mater Firth, May 15, 1915..........	71st Infantry.
50	William Heath, May 28, 1915..........	10th Infantry.
51	Donald Cheyne Strachan, June 11, 1915..........	47th Infantry.
52	Edward Morrison Burtis, June 15, 1915..........	10th Infantry.
53	15..........	2d Infantry.
54	....	14th Infantry.
55	....	47th Infantry.
56	....	14th Infantry.
57	15..........	Coast Artillery Corps.
58	....	14th Infantry.
59	1915..........	1st Cavalry.
60	....	3d Infantry.
61	....	1st Field Artillery.
62	5..........	3d Infantry.
63	....	1st Cavalry.
64	....	14th Infantry.
65	1915..........	1st Infantry.
66	5..........	1st Infantry.
67	....	47th Infantry.
68	....	Coast Artillery Corps.
69	....	Squadron A, Cavalry.
70	....	3d Infantry.
71	....	1st Field Artillery.
72	Charles Theodore Graham-Rogers, Dec. 11, 1915.....	47th Infantry.
73	Frederick William Cording, Dec. 11, 1915..........	Coast Artillery Corps.
74	Elmer Harnden Van Wagenen, Dec. 22, 1915..........	Coast Artillery Corps.
75	Dudley Martindale Cooper, Dec. 27, 1915..........	Squadron A, Cavalry.
76	Albert Casterline Odell, Dec. 31, 1915..........	10th Infantry.
77	Thomas Clark Dedell, Dec. 31, 1915..........	1st Infantry.
78	Albert C. Odell, Dec. 31, 1915..........	10th Infantry.
79	Harry Leeds Dayton, Jan. 7, 1916..........	8th Coast Defense Corps.
80	Edward Le Roy Cashin, Jan. 11, 1916..........	10th Infantry.
81	Irving Mitchell Saunders, Jan. 13, 1916..........	13th Coast Defense Corps.
82	Charles I. Clark, Jan. 18, 1916..........	13th Coast Defense Corps.
83	Jacob L. Van Schoonhoven, Jan. 22, 1916..........	2d Infantry.
84	Michael J. Farrell, Jan. 25, 1916..........	2d Infantry.
85	Frank Edgar Kerby, Feb. 2, 1916..........	13th Coast Defense Corps.
86	Andrew Jackson MacElroy, Feb. 9, 1916..........	47th Infantry.
87	Robert W. Bowman, Feb. 21, 1916..........	1st Infantry.
88	Pierce Mason Travis, Mar. 13, 1916..........	9th Coast Defense Corps.
89	Archie L. Blades, March 16, 1916..........	3d Infantry.
90	John C. R. Hall, March 22, 1916..........	2d Infantry.
91	Charles R. Phillips, March 22, 1916..........	74 Infantry.

RELATIVE RANK OF OFFICERS IN ACTIVE SERVICE IN THE NATIONAL
GUARD — (Continued)

No.	NAME AND DATE OF RANK	Corps or organization
	Second Lieutenants — Continued	
92	George W. Hubbell, Jr., March 22, 1916	1st A. M. Battery.
93	Harry F. Nimphius, March 31, 1914	2d Field Artillery.
94	Leonard J. Howard, April 7, 1916	2d Infantry.
95	Carl W. Stevens, April 8, 1916	2d Infantry.
96	Percy W. Decker, April 10, 1916	10th Infantry.
97	Henry J. Hanley, April 20, 1916	3d Infantry.
98	James Hubert McSweeney, April 27, 1916	2d Field Artillery.
99	John Richard Suydam, Jr., April 27, 1916	8th Coast Defense Corps.
100	Peter B. McCahill, April 27, 1916	47th Infantry.
101	George Edward Shipway, May 8, 1916	9th Coast Defense Corps.
102	William Henry Warren, May 9, 1916	9th Coast Defense Corps.
103	Francis Vincent Hayes, May 10, 1916	2d Field Artillery.
104	William F. S. Root, May 10, 1916	2d Infantry.
105	George J. Goubeaud, May 11, 1912	1st Cavalry.
106	Joseph A. Nichols, May 17, 1916	9th Coast Defense Corps.
107	Arthur Munro Floor, May 19, 1916	2d Field Artillery.
108	Francis Paul Thomas, May 22, 1916	13th Coast Defense Corps.
109	Thomas M. Madigan, May 24, 1916	47th Infantry.
110	Harley Watson Black, May 25, 1916	1st Cavalry.
111	Harry L. Conway, May 26, 1916	71st Infantry.
112	Clarence Emil Doll, May 26, 1916	8th Coast Defense Corps.
113	Hiram Bedford Crosby, May 29, 1916	9th Coast Defense Corps.
114	John William Moran, May 29, 1916	14th Infantry.
115	Thomas H. S. Andrews, June 2, 1916	2d Field Artillery.
116	William James Farrell, June 6, 1916	8th Coast Defense Corps.
117	Herbert F. Shavor, June 9, 1916	1st Infantry.
118	Albert Michael Guidera, June 9, 1916	9th Coast Defense Corps.
119	James Axtell Smith, June 13, 1916	13th Coast Defense Corps.
120	Kennard Underwood, June 13, 1916	2d Infantry.
121	Daniel Colin Munro, June 14, 1915	1st Cavalry.
122	Samuel Alman, June 19, 1916	13th Coast Defense Corps.
123	William Hayward Miscurda, June 21, 1916	9th Coast Defense Corps.
124	Wright Shuttleworth, June 21, 1916	2d Infantry.
125	Edwin Sumner Bettlehrim, June 21, 1916	1st Field Artillery.
126	John F. Callahan, June 22, 1916	12th Infantry.
127	John Warner Bostick, June 22, 1916	14th Infantry.
128	Comstock, Albert E., June 24, 1916	71st Infantry.
129	James H. George, June 24, 1916	71st Infantry.
130	Alex Granato, June 26, 1916	71st Infantry.
131	Frith D. Clark, June 26, 1916	12th Infantry.
132	Harry G. Kettner, June 26, 1915	Quartermaster Corps.
133	Charles B. Wagner, June 27, 1916	2d Regiment of Engineers.
134	Colgate Hoyt, Jr., June 28, 1916	M. G. Troop, Cavalry.
135	Walter Henry Hereth, June 28, 1916	2d Field Artillery.
136	Albert Edward Gunther, Jr., June 28, 1916	8th Coast Defense Corps.
137		8th Coast Defense Corps.
138	Francis Perry Davis, June 26, 1916	8th Coast Defense Corps.
139	August F. Johnson, June 30, 1916	1st Cavalry.
140	Fred G. Spawton, July 1, 1916	74th Infantry.
141	William D. Coulter, July 1, 1916	74th Infantry.
142	George A. Milsom, July 1, 1916	74th Infantry.
143	Joseph H. Robinson, July 1, 1916	74th Infantry.
144	William P. Taggart, July 1, 1916	74th Infantry.
145	William Fred Brill, July 3, 1916	23d Infantry.
146	John J. Wermuth, July 3, 1916	Quartermaster Corps.
147	Fred E. Mayor, July 3, 1916	23d Infantry.
148	Leo M. Keese, July 3, 1916	23d Infantry.
149	Charles P. Franchot, July 4, 1916	1st Cavalry.
150	Chris B. Degenaar, July 5, 1916	2d Infantry.
151	John T. Prout, July 5, 1916	69th Infantry.
152	William H. Fuller, July 5, 1916	2d Infantry.
153	Charles F. Mosher, July 6, 1916	3d Infantry.
154	Edgar B. Gritman, July 7, 1916	10th Infantry.
155	Jay MacDonald, July 9, 1915	Quartermaster Corps.
156	Peter Michael Depp, July 10, 1916	14th Infantry.
157	William B. Lester, July 21, 1916	1st Cavalry.
158	Frank S. Judson, July 22, 1916	1st Infantry.
159	William Charles White, July 26, 1917	13th Coast Defense Corps.
160	James Munro Ross, July 27, 1916	13th Coast Defense Corps.
161	Frank J. Caveney, Aug. 1, 1916	3d Field Artillery.
162	Charles E. Anderson, Aug. 1, 1916	3d Field Artillery.

RELATIVE RANK OF OFFICERS IN ACTIVE SERVICE IN THE NATIONAL
GUARD — (*Concluded*)

No.	NAME AND DATE OF RANK	Corps or organization
	Second Lieutenants — Concluded	
163	Herbert E. Marshall, Jr., Aug. 4, 1916	14th Infantry.
164	Fred A. Petersen, Aug. 10, 1916	1st Field Artillery.
165	Richard R. Morrison, Aug. 14, 1916	10th Infantry.
166	Harold LeRoy Whitney, Aug. 17, 1916	1st Field Artillery.
167	James H. Wyatt, Sept. 2, 1916	15th Infantry.
168	Louis Wojtkowski, Sept. 4, 1916	3d Field Artillery.
169	Thomas Ward, Sept. 6, 1916	14th Infantry.
170	Joseph A. Kerrigan, Sept. 6, 1916	14th Infantry.
171	Stephen H. Fifield, Sept. 7, 1916	2d Infantry.
172	Elmer H. Miller, Sept. 13, 1916	14th Infantry.
173	Thomas P. Martin, Sept. 17, 1916	69th Infantry.
174	Henry Scheu, Sept. 29, 1916	3d Field Artillery.
175	Howard Agaton Hansen, Sept. 30, 1916	8th Coast Defense Corps.
176	Everett B. Jewett, Oct. 7, 1916	23d Infantry.
177	Charles L. Kline, Oct. 8, 1916	74th Infantry.
178	Walter Seligman, Oct. 17, 1916	9th Coast Defense Corps.
179	Weyman D. Herbert, Oct. 17, 1916	2d Field Artillery.
180	Thomas Edward Purcell, Jr., Oct. 26, 1916	8th Coast Defense Corps.
181	Frederic H. Cruger, Oct. 28, 1916	69th Infantry.
182	Clarence P. Crimmins, Oct. 28, 1916	69th Infantry.
183	Joseph Bryan Shelby, Oct. 31, 1916	8th Coast Defense Corps.
184	Ewing R. Philbin, Nov. 2, 1916	69th Infantry.
185	Hampton S. Lynch, Nov. 2, 1916	69th Infantry.
186	Samuel D. Davies, Nov. 3, 1916	23d Infantry.
187	William J. Gaskin, Nov. 12, 1916	3d Field Artillery.
188	Edward H. O'Rourke, Nov. 14, 1916	74th Infantry.
189	Van Santvoord Merle-Smith, Nov. 16, 1916	69th Infantry.
190	Martin Ambrose Ford, Nov. 21, 1916	9th Coast Defense Corps.
191	Delaney King, Nov. 25, 1916	74th Infantry.
192	Richard D. Wright, Nov. 25, 1916	74th Infantry.
193	Kenneth C. Wilson, Nov. 4, 1916	7th Infantry.
194	Edward Willis, Nov. 4, 1916	7th Infantry.
195	Thomas Joseph Brady, Nov. 6, 1916	7th Infantry.
196	John B. Howard, Nov. 12, 1916	3d Field Artillery.
197	Robert A. McAuslin, Nov. 16, 1914	2d Field Artillery.
198	Alexander Wells Peck, Nov. 24, 1916	9th Coast Defense Corps.
199	Robert H. Leake, Dec. 1, 1916	Squadron A, Cavalry.
200	Edward C. Philips, Dec. 3, 1916	3d Field Artillery.
201	James Trueman Mensie, Dec. 5, 1916	1st Cavalry.
202	Robert L. Weibesahl, Dec. 6, 1916	8th Coast Defense Corps.
203	Thomas Scofield, Dec. 6, 1916	8th Coast Defense Corps.
204	Walter D. Parlour, Dec. 16, 1916	3d Field Artillery.
205	William H. McMullen, Jr., Dec. 18, 1916	23d Infantry.
206	Harry C. Stevens, Jr., Dec. 18, 1916	23d Infantry.
207	Charles E. Toney, Dec. 20, 1916	15th Infantry.
208	John Siggelkow, Dec. 22, 1916	8th Coast Defense Corps.
209	Harold G. Mackay, Dec. 27, 1916	74th Infantry.

NAVAL MILITIA

Headquarters, U. S. S. " Granite State," foot West Ninety-seventh Street, North River, New York City

The Naval Militia was organized under the provisions of Chapter 492, Laws of 1889, as amended by Chapter 243, Laws of 1891, and was originally designated as Naval Reserve Artillery, S. N. Y. As now organised, it consists of three battalions and is commanded, under the orders of the Governor, by a Commodore.

NAME, GRADE, DATE OF RANK AND HIGHEST BREVET RANK	SERVICE		Born
	In the Army or Navy of the United States or of Foreign States	In the National Guard or Naval Militia	

COMMODORE COMMANDING THE NAVAL MILITIA

Forshew, Robert Pierpont, 24 jun. 11	graduate U. S. N. A. jun. 81, as cadet midshipman; served as such to jun. 83; lt. U. S. N....22 jun. 98 to 8 oct. 98	2 lt. 16 sep. co. N. G. N. Y.......10 may 86 to 18 may 88 lt. (4) 1 bat. N. M.23 jun. 91 lt. com'dr and ex. off. 2 naval bat.31 jul. 97 com'dr..........20 apr. 99 a. d. c. to gov.... 1 jan. 07 to 31 dec. 10 commodore, N.M., 24 jun. 11 accepted........24 jun. 11	N. Y. 1 jul. 59

STAFF OF THE COMMODORE COMMANDING THE NAVAL MILITIA

CAPTAIN

CHIEF OF STAFF

Fry, Alfred Brooks 27 mar. 16	acting asst. eng., asst. eng. and chief eng. U. S. treasury service from 1886. Still in service; passed asst. eng. (lt.) U. S. N., 30 apr. 98 to 13 sep. 98	pvt. tr. E, N. G. N. Y..........21 feb. 77 to dec. 79 pvt. 1 corps cadets seaman, acting chief machinist naval bat. Mass. V. M........21 feb. 89 to 23 mar. 93 lt. and chief eng. Mass. naval brig. 23 mar. 93 to 4 may 97 seaman, chief machinist, 1 naval bat. N. M. N. Y. 4 may 97 to 4 oct. 97 eng. lt........... 4 oct. 97 eng. lt. com'dr N. M............20 apr. 98 lt. com'dr, chief of staff of cap. com. N. M. with o. r. 5 mar. 00 a. d. c. to gov.... 9 feb. 00 to 31 dec. 04 com'dr, chief of staff of commodore, N. M.. 4 mar. 10 captain, chief of staff of commodore, N. M..27 mar.16 accepted........28 mar.16	N. Y. 3 mar. 60

NAVAL MILITIA — STAFF OF THE COMMODORE — (Concluded)

Name, Grade, Date of Rank and Highest Brevet Rank	Service		Born
	In the Army or Navy of the United States or of Foreign States	In the National Guard or Naval Militia	
NAVIGATOR AND SIGNAL OFFICER			
LIEUTENANT COMMANDER			
deKay, Eckford Craven, 25 feb. 11	U. S. N. A.....26 sep. 90 to 17 jun. 91 seaman, U. S. N. 26 apr. 98 to 2 sep. 98	seaman, gun cap. 2 class, 1 class, boatswain's mate 2 div. 1 bat....16 jun. 96 to 28 dec. 01 ensign...........28 dec. 01 lt. j. g. .... 5 may 08 lt................13 jan. 10 detailed military secretary to gov. 1 jan. 11 to 31 dec. 12 lt. com'dr, sig. off. staff of commodore, com. N. M.............25 feb. 11 accepted........25 feb. 11	N. Y. 12 jun 73
GUNNERY OFFICER			
LIEUTENANT COMMANDER			
York, Herbert Waldo, 30 sep. 11	asst. to consulting eng. U. S. Revenue Marine Service, 1882-1885, fireman and oiler, 6 months; machinist, 8 months; second asst. eng. U. S. Revenue Marine Service, 1888; returned same, 1888.	eng. lt. j. g. 1 bat.. 5 nov. 00 lt. j. g. eng. off. 1 bat. with o. r... 1 jul. 03 gunnery off. with o. r...........15 nov. 04 supn........... 7 jun. 11 assigned duty 1 bat.:......... 7 jun. 11 lt. o. o. 1 bat.....13 jul. 11 lt. com'dr o. o. staff of commodore, N. M....30 sep. 11 accepted........ 9 oct. 11	Mass. 18 feb. 64
JUDGE-ADVOCATE			
LIEUTENANT COMMANDER			
Sawyer, Warren Lockhart, 19 jun. 12	asst. paymaster, U. S. N., 20 jul. 98 to 21 feb. 99	seaman, 1 naval bat., trs. 2 naval bat...........16 jul. 95 to 8 jul. 98 asst. paymaster, ensign 2 naval bat........... 8 jul. 98 lt. j. g...........11 apr. 01 paymaster, 2 bat. lt...............26 dec. 11 j. a. N. M. lt. com'dr........19 jun. 12 accepted........20 jun. 12	N. Y. 12 sep. 71
SURGEON			
LIEUTENANT COMMANDER			
MacEvitt, John Cowell, 14 sep. 08	passed asst. surg. U. S. N. 24 may 98 to 9 sep. 98	seaman, 2 naval bat...........14 jun. 97 to 28 oct. 97 surg. lt..........28 oct. 97 surg. N. M. lt. com'dr........18 sep. 08 surg., staff of commodore, N. M., lt. com'dr.....18 feb. 10 accepted........23 feb. 10	Mo. 28 feb. 56

NAVAL MILITIA — FIRST BATTALION

Headquarters, U. S. S. "*Granite State,*" *foot West Ninety-seventh Street, North River, New York City*

This battalion was organized on June 23, 1891, as the First Battalion, Naval Reserve Artillery, which designation was changed on June 25, 1892, to First Naval Battalion. This designation was again changed on Oct. 16, 1900, to First Battalion, Naval Militia. The Seventh Division, First Battalion, Naval Militia, was mustered in on January 23, 1912, at New Rochelle. The Eighth Division was mustered in May 29, 1912, with station at Ossining. Engineer Division known as 9th Division was mustered into the service August 18, 1914. An aeronautic section was mustered into the service January 17, 1916.

The Battalion performed duty for the State during the quarantine troubles in September, 1892, and during the Spanish-American War on coast signal service, guarding mine fields at Willet's Point and on patrol duty in New York harbor.

It performed duty for the United States during the Spanish-American War in the U. S. Navy aboard the "Yankee," "Nahant," and other vessels, and in the U. S. Auxiliary Naval Force, aboard various vessels.

The battalion has received authority to place silver rings on the lance of its *National Color* engraved as follows: "Spanish-American War, 1898," "Santiago de Cuba, June 6, 1898," "Cienfuegos, June 13, 1898," "Casilda Harbor, June 20, 1898," "Guantanamo, June 7, 1898." On the lance of its *State Color*, "Spanish-American War, 1898."

NAME, GRADE, DATE OF RANK AND HIGHEST BREVET RANK	Division	SERVICE		Born
		In the Army or Navy of the United States or of Foreign States	In the National Guard or Naval Militia	
CAPTAIN				
Poor, Charles Longstreet, 27 mar. 16	....	cadet, U. S. N. A., 6 sep. 92 ensign, U. S. N. 6 may 98 lt. j. g. .... 6 may 01 lt. .... 3 mar. 03 resigned ...... 20 june 04	lt. j. g. (1) 1 bat. 16 oct. 04 lt. .... 17 nov. 09 lt. com'dr ex. off 24 june 10 lt. com'dr eng. off. N. M. .... 17 may 12 com'dr .... 30 nov. 14 capt. .... 27 mar. 16 accepted ...... 29 mar. 16	N. Y. 1 oct. 73
EXECUTIVE OFFICER **COMMANDER**				
Wait, William Bell, Jr., 1 apr. 16	....	seaman, U. S. N., 27 may 98 to 2 sep. 98	seaman, petty off. 4 class, gun cap. 2 class, 1 class, boatswain's mate 2 div. 1 bat .... 3 dec. 96 to 22 mar. 05 ensign (2) 1 bat .... 22 mar. 05 lt. j. g. .... 4 mar. 10 lt. .... 11 july 10 navigating lt. ...18 feb. 13 lt. com'dr, ex. off. .... 22 june 14 com'dr, ex. off.. 1 apr. 16 accepted ...... 3 apr. 16	N. Y. 13 july 72
NAVIGATOR LIEUTENANT COMMANDER				
Riggs, Roland Rogers, 1 apr. 16	....	midshipman, U. S. N., 29 may 00 ensign .... 2 feb. 06 lt. j. g. .... 2 feb. 09 lt. .... 2 feb. 09 lt. com'dr ..... 30 june 11 retired .... 30 june 11	ensign, 1 bat ... 1 nov. 11 lt. j. g. .... 2 feb. 12 navigating lt. ...10 nov. 14 lt. com'dr, navigator ...... 1 apr. 16 accepted .... 10 apr. 16	Conn. 16 sep. 84
ENGINEER OFFICER LIEUTENANT COMMANDER				
Boone, Charles, 1 apr. 16	eng.	cadet, U. S. N. A., 6 sep. 94 ensign, U. S. N. 4 apr. 00 to 1 dec. 02	ensign, (1) 1 bat .... 25 sep. 08 lt. j. g. .... 28 dec. 09 lt. eng. off ..... 11 july 10 lt. com'dr, eng. off. .... 1 apr. 16 accepted .... 3 apr. 16	N. H. 16 oct. 76

NAVAL MILITIA — FIRST BATTALION — (*Continued*)

Name, Grade, Date of Rank and Highest Brevet Rank	Division	Service		Born
		In the Army or Navy of the United States or of Foreign States	In the National Guard or Naval Militia	
GUNNERY OFFICER LIEUTENANT COMMANDER Farwell, Earle, 3 apr. 16	....	midshipman, U. S. N. A., 9 sep. 01 to 8 feb. 03	ensign, 1 bat...24 jan. 10 lt. j. g.........10 jan. 11 lt............ 2 feb. 12 lt. o. o........ 2 feb. 12 lt. com'dr, gun off.........15 apr. 16 accepted......21 apr. 16	Eng. 20 sep. 85
SURGEON LIEUTENANT COMMANDER Kimball, Cleveland Cady, 3 apr. 16	....	....	asst. surg. 1 bat. lt. j. g.......12 may 10 surg. lt........24 may 15 surg. lt. com'dr. 3 apr. 16 accepted......12 apr. 16	N. Y. 2 may 78
PASSED ASSISTANT SURGEON LIEUTENANT Smith, Ferdinand Montgomery, 13 dec. 16	....	....	pvt. co. I, 7 inf. 10 may 05 dropped......28 oct. 08 lt. j. g., asst. surg. 1 bat. N. M......16 june 16 p. a. surg., lt...13 dec. 16 accepted..... 5 mar. 17	N. Y. 1 june 85
ASSISTANT SURGEON LIEUTENANT, JUNIOR GRADE Fulton, Clifford Harry, 29 sep. 16	....	....	asst.surg. lt .j.g. 1 bat. N. M..29 sep. 16 accepted...... 2 oct. 16	N. Y. 2 dec. 84
PAYMASTER LIEUTENANT COMMANDER Boyd, William Henry, 3 apr. 16	....	....	landsman, seaman, 2 class, 1 class, gun cap. 1 class, chief yeoman, 4 div. 1 bat..21 aug. 02 hon. dis....... 2 dec. 07 re-enlisted.....13 dec. 07 to 26 dec. 11 asst. paymaster, 1 bat. lt. j. g.26 dec. 11 paymaster lt...24 may 15 accepted.....25 may 15 paymaster, lt. com'dr...... 3 apr. 16 accepted...... 4 apr. 16	Pa. 28 feb. 70
PASSED ASSISTANT PAYMASTER LIEUTENANT Pell, Howland Haggerty, 29 sep. 16	....	....	paymaster, lt. 1 bat........ 3 oct. 12 hon. dis.......11 may 15 res. list........28 may 15 p. a. paymaster lt...........29 sep. 16 accepted...... 2 oct. 16	N. Y. 30 may 72

NAVAL MILITIA — FIRST BATTALION — (*Continued*)

Name, Grade, Date of Rank and Highest Brevet Rank	Division	Service		Born
		In the Army or Navy of The United States or of Foreign States	In the National Guard or Naval Militia	
LIEUTENANTS Line duties only				
Bensel, Walter, 21 apr. 10	2	....	asst. surg. 1 bat. lt. j. g......13 jan. 10 surg. lt........ 5 may 10 lt.............10 feb. 15 rank from.....21 apr. 10 accepted......13 feb. 15	N. Y. 22 jan. 69
Raff, Lemuel Edson, 1 nov. 10	3	seaman, u. s. n., 28 apr. 98 to 2 sep. 98	seaman, gun cap., 1 cl. 3 div. 1 bat........15 july 97 hon. dis....... 9 feb. 04 seaman.......13 apr. 04 to 4 apr. 06 ensign, (3) 1 bat.4 apr. 06 lt. j. g........ 5 may 10 lt............. 1 nov. 10 accepted...... 9 nov. 10	N. M. 11 july 76
Mallon, William Lewis, 17 sep. 12	4	....	seaman, g u n cap. 1 class, 4 div. 1 bat.... 6 feb. 06 to 28 dec. 09 ensign, 1 bat...28 dec. 09 lt. j. g.........13 jul. 11 lt.............17 sep. 12 accepted.....20 sep. 12	N. Y. 18 jul. 84
Moore, Clarence Ambrose, 29 mar. 15	1	....	seaman, 1 div. 1 bat......... 1 dec. 02 hon. dis....... 9 dec. 07 to 21 nov. 12 seaman......13 may 12 ensign, 1 bat...21 nov. 12 lt. j. g......... 2 dec. 14 lt.............29 mar. 15 accepted...... 1 apr. 15	N. Y. 28 may 84
Condon, Richard, 5 jul. 16	6	....	seaman, qm. 1 class, sig. div. 1 bat.......13 oct. 05 to 26 may 13 ensign, 2 bat...26 may 13 lt. j. g.........21 jun. 15 lt............. 5 jul. 16 accepted...... 5 jul. 16	N. Y. 22 feb. 83
LIEUTENANTS Engineering duties only				
Willis, Walter John, 23 jun. 16	9	....	fireman,2d class.10 aug. 14 to 14 dec. 14 ensign, 1 bat...14 dec. 14 lt. j. g.........20 dec. 15 lt.............23 june 16 accepted.....26 june 16	N. Y. 31 dec. 87
Aeronautic duties only				
Harris, Lee Hurdman, 23 june 16	aer.	....	ens. eng. off. 1 bat.......26 may 13 lt. j. g......... 9 mar. 16 lt.............23 june 16 accepted...... 6 jul. 16	Pa. 14 mar. 84

NAVAL MILITIA — FIRST BATTALION — (Continued)

NAME, GRADE, DATE OF RANK AND HIGHEST BREVET RANK	Division	SERVICE		Born
		In the Army or Navy of the United States or of Foreign States	In the National Guard or Naval Militia	
LIEUTENANTS, JUNIOR GRADE				
Line duties only				
Williams, Henry Tilton, 7 feb. 12	7	....	asst. surg., lt. j. g. 1 bat..... 7 feb. 12 lt. j. g.........10 jul. 16 accepted......13 july 16	N. Y. 28 may 77
MacCollom, Augustus, Jr., 19 jun. 12	8	....	seaman, 8 div. 1 bat.........29 may 12 to 19 jun. 12 lt. j. g. 1 bat...19 jun. 12 accepted......20 jun. 12	N. Y. 3 apr. 71
Ketcham, Berkeley Searls, 24 may 15	8	....	seaman, 2 div. 1 bat.........26 may 03 to 9 dec. 07 seaman, 2 div., gunner's mate, 1 class. 6 jul. 08 to 24 may 12 ensign, 1 bat...24 may 12 lt. j. g.........24 may 15 accepted......26 may 15	N. Y. 3 sep. 83
Mason, Charles Alonzo, 21 jun. 15	5	....	seaman, 2 class, 1 class, gunner's mate. 2 class, 1 bat.. 7 jul. 07 to 2 jul. 13 ensign, 1 bat... 2 jul. 13 lt. j. g.........21 jun. 15 accepted......22 jun. 15	N. Y. 23 apr. 86
Engineering duties only				
Oatley, Henry Bigelow, 22 dec. 16	5	....	ensign, 1 bat. N. M.......22 mar. 16 lt. j. g.........22 dec. 16 accepted......27 dec. 16	N. Y. 8 sep. 76
ENSIGNS				
Line duties only				
Kenyon, Albert James, 10 jun. 12	8	....	seaman, Conn. N. M....... 7 mar. 95 to 15 mar. 98 15 apr. 98 hon. dis.......30 mar. 99 ensign, 1 bat. N. M. N. Y.....10 jun 12 accepted......12 jun. 12	Conn. 1 jul. 71
Browne, Harold Washbourne, 18 feb. 13	2	....	seaman, boatswain's mate, 1 class, 1 div. 1 bat.......16 may 10 to 18 feb. 13 ensign, 1 bat...18 feb. 13 accepted......19 feb. 13	N. J. 3 mar. 86
Russell, Frederick Arthur, 29 mar. 15	10	....	seaman, qmr. 1 class, 3 div. 1 bat......... 9 mar. 11 to 29 mar. 15 ensign.........29 mar. 15 accepted...... 2 apr. 15	N. Y. 6 mar. 90

NAVAL MILITIA — FIRST BATTALION — (Concluded)

Name, Grade, Date of Rank and Highest Brevet Rank	Division	Service		Born
		In the Army or Navy of The United States or of Foreign States	In the National Guard or Naval Militia	
Ensigns — Concluded				
Line duties only				
Dillon, Edward Joseph, Jr., 5 jun. 15	4	....	seaman, boat-swain's mate, 1 class, 1 div. 1 bat........ 6 nov. 11 to 5 jun. 15 ensign......... 5 jun. 15 accepted......10 jun. 15	N. Y. 4 feb. 91
Moore, John Robert, Jr., 5 june 15	2	....	seaman, agt., gunn. mate 1 cl. boat-swain's mate, 2 div. 1 bat.. 4 dec. 60 hon. dis.......30 oct. 11 ensign......... 5 june 15 accepted......14 june 15	N. J. 17 feb. 83
Murray, Leo Jerome 11 jul. 16	7	....	seaman, boat-swain's mate, 7 div. 1 bat. 12 nov. 13 to 11 jul. 16 ensign, 1 bat...11 jul. 16 accepted......13 jul. 16	N. Y. 27 mar. 90
Quimby, William Peet, 22 dec. 16	2	cadet U. S. N. A., — july 12 resigned....... — feb. 13 cadet U. S. N. A., — apr. 13 resigned....... — feb. 16	seaman, 1 bat..28 mar. 16 ensign, 1 bat...22 dec. 16 accepted......27 dec. 16	Wash. 17 may 94
Engineering duties only				
Moore, Robert Hartwell, 29 sep. 1916	5	....	ensign, 1 bat...14 dec. 14 res. list........16 feb. 16 ensign, 1 bat...29 sep. 16 accepted...... 9 oct. 16	Mass. 29 jul. 83
Aeronautic duties only				
Wysong, Forrest E., 30 mar. 16	aero	....	ensign, 1 bat...,30 mar. 16 accepted...... 3 apr. 16	O. 29 mar. 94
Ruttan, Charles E., 23 june 16	aero	....	ensign, 1 bat...23 june 16 accepted......23 june 16	Can. 21 aug. 84

NAVAL MILITIA — SECOND BATTALION

Headquarters, foot of Fifty-second Street, Brooklyn

This Battalion was organized and mustered in July 6, 1897, as the Second Naval Battalion. The designation was changed to Second Battalion Naval Militia, on October 16, 1900. Signal Division was mustered out December 1, 1912. Engineer Division was mustered in June 10, 1913, to be known as Sixth Division. The Seventh Division was mustered into the service March 26, 1915.

A marine company was mustered into the service May 1, 1916. An aeronautic section was mustered into the service March 9, 1916.

The Battalion performed duty for the State during the Spanish-American War on coast signal service, guarding mine fields at Willet's Point and on patrol duty in New York Harbor aboard various vessels.

It performed duty for the United States during the Spanish-American War in the U. S. Navy aboard the "Jason," and other vessels, and in the U. S. Auxiliary Naval Force aboard the "Aileen," "Elfrida," "Enquirer," "Huntress," "Kanawha," "New Hampshire," "Restless" and "Sylvia."

The Battalion has received authority to place silver rings on the lance of its *National Color*, engraved as follows: "Spanish-American War, 1898," "Havana, August 11, 1898."

Name, Grade, Date of Rank and Highest Brevet Rank	Division	Service		Born
		In the Army or Navy of the United States or of Foreign States	In the National Guard or Naval Militia	
CAPTAIN				
Fitzgerald, Edward Thomas, 11 may 16		cadet, U. S. N...13 sep. 92 asst. eng........ 8 may 96 ensign........ 3 mar. 99 lt. j. g.......... — jun. 01 lt............. 3 mar. 03 resigned........15 nov. 07	lt. 2 bat........27 nov. 09 navigating lt....17 may 12 lt. com'dr, ex. off.16 feb. 14 com'dr......... 9 feb. 16 cap.............11 may 16 accepted.......16 may 16	N. Y. 7 oct. 74.
COMMANDER EXECUTIVE OFFICER				
Perry, Arthur Irving, 10 jun. 16		qm. 2 class, U. S. N., 22 apr. 98 to 31 jul. 98	seaman. qm., chief qm. 2 naval bat.........14 jun. 97 to 19 aug. 02 lt. j. g. sig. off. 2 bat.........19 aug. 02 navigating lt....27 feb. 14 lt. com'dr......24 feb. 16 com'dr, ex. off...10 june 16 accepted......16 june 16	N. Y. 28 jul 73
LIEUTENANT COMMANDER FIRST LIEUTENANT				
Lackey, Frank Ross, 19 may, 16	1	....	seaman, gun cap. 2 class, 1 class, boatswain's mate, 1 div. 2 bat.........19 jul. 99 to 17 jul. 08 ensign (1) 2 bat..17 jul. 08 lt.............12 jul. 11 lt. com'dr, 1 lt. .19 may 16 accepted.......22 may 16	N. Y. 28 aug. 80
LIEUTENANT COMMANDER NAVIGATOR				
Nelson, Theodore, 10 jun. 16	2	cadet and cadet midshipman, U. S. N. A., 99 to 02	pvt. co. C, 7 inf. 21 dec. 10 to 5 jun. 12 lt. j. g. 2 bat. N. M............ 5 jun. 12 lt.............21 apr. 13 lt. com'dr, navigator.........10 june 16 accepted......13 june 16	Mich. 13 mar. 81

NAVAL MILITIA — SECOND BATTALION — (Continued)

NAME, GRADE, DATE OF RANK AND HIGHEST BREVET RANK	Division	SERVICE		Born
		In the Army or Navy of The United States or of Foreign States	In the National Guard or Naval Militia	
LIEUTENANT COMMANDER ENGINEER OFFICER Kane, Jasper Thomas, 1 apr. 16	eng.	chief machinist, U. S. N., 9 jun. 98 to 19 aug. 98	seaman, chief machinist, 2 naval bat.........14 jun. 97 to 19 nov. 00 eng. lt. j. g......19 nov. 00 lt. j. g. eng. off... 1 jul. 03 lt. eng. off....24 jun. 10 lt. com'dr, eng. off........... 1 apr. 16 accepted....... 4 apr. 16	N. Y. 8 may 76
LIEUTENANT COMMANDER GUNNERY OFFICER Dickinson, Leon, 28 dec. 16	....	....	seaman, gun cap., 2 div. 2 bat...11 oct. 04 to 26 jun. 11 ensign, 2 bat....26 jun. 11 lt. o. o.........25 sep. 14 lt. com'dr, gun'y off...........28 dec. 16 accepted......30 dec. 16	N. Y. 2 jul. 78
SURGEON LIEUTENANT COMMANDER Lynch, Thomas Aloysius, 10 jun. 16	....	....	hosp. apprentice, hosp. steward, 2 bat.........13 jan. 14 to 21 jun. 15 asst. surgeon, lt. j. g.........21 jun. 15 surg., lt........24 feb. 16 surg., lt. com'dr..10 june 16 accepted......13 june 16	N. Y. 7 jul. 84
PASSED ASSISTANT SURGEON LIEUTENANT Carey, John J. M., 6 july 16	....	....	asst. surg., lt. j. g., 2 bat....22 mar. 16 p. a. surg....... 6 july 16 lt..............10 july 16 accepted......10 july 16	N. Y. 11 oct. 82
ASSISTANT SURGEON LIEUTENANT, JUNIOR GRADE Nexsen, Harold, 10 july 16	....	....	asst. surg., lt. j. g., 2 bat......10 july 16 accepted......13 july 16	N. Y. 19 sep. 86
PAYMASTER LIEUTENANT COMMANDER Crissey, Charles Payne, 10 jun. 16	....	....	seaman, 3 div. 2 bat......... 6 jul. 09 to 3 apr. 12 asst. paymaster 2 bat., lt. j. g... 3 apr. 12 paymaster, 2 bat. N. M. lt......21 apr. 13 paymaster, lt. com'dr.......10 june 16 accepted......13 june 16	N. Y. 1 sep. 87

NAVAL MILITIA — SECOND BATTALION — (Continued)

Name, Grade, Date of Rank and Highest Brevet Rank	Division	Service — In the Army or Navy of the United States or of Foreign States	Service — In the National Guard or Naval Militia	Born
ASSISTANT PAYMASTER				
LIEUTENANT, JUNIOR GRADE				
Welsh, Frank John, Jr., 18 dec. 16	....	....	seaman, master at arms 2 cl. 2 bat.........21 feb. 03 to 18 dec. 16 asst. paymaster, lt. j. g........18 dec. 16 accepted.......21 dec. 16	O. 9 may 86
LIEUTENANTS Line duties only				
Finken, Charles Edwin, 16 jun. 16	4	....	seaman, gun. cap. 2 class, 1 class, 1 div. 2 bat...22 may 00 to 10 jan. 11 ensign, 2 bat....10 jan. 11 lt. j. g.......19 jun. 12 lt.............16 june 16 accepted......19 june 16	N. Y. 28 jul. 82
Holton, Luther, Hamilton, 16 jun. 16	7	....	seaman, gun. cap. 2 class, 1 class, boatswain's mate, 1 div. 2 bat.........19 feb. 00 to 10 jan. 11 ensign, 2 bat....10 jan. 11 lt. j. g....... 5 jun. 12 lt.............16 june 16 accepted......19 june 16	Can. 1 mar. 80
LIEUTENANTS Engineering duties only.				
Nexsen, Randolph Halliday, 2 jul. 13	6	....	lt. j. g. eng. off. 2 bat.........11 jul. 10 lt. eng. off...... 2 jul. 13 accepted....... 8 jul. 13	N. Y. 18 jul. 82
Bennett, Edward Russell, 10 jun. 16	5	....	seaman, chief gunner's mate, 1 div. 2 bat...14 jan. 97 hon. dis........21 jun. 00 eng. ensign, 2 bat. 3 apr. 12 lt., j. g........ 4 mar. 16 lt............10 june 16 accepted......15 june 16	N. Y. 7 aug. 74
LIEUTENANTS, JUNIOR GRADE Line duties only				
Moore, Arthur, 29 mar. 15	8	....	seaman, 1 div. 2 bat., gun cap. 2 class, boatswain's mate, boatswain's mate, 1 class...13 mar. 06 hon. dis.......10 sep. 12 seaman, 8 div. 2 bat.........20 jan. 14 to 16 feb. 14 ensign..........16 feb. 14 lt. j. g.........29 mar. 15 accepted....... 3 apr. 15	N. Y. 1 oct. 83
Ramsey, Hobart Cole, 5 july 16	4	U. S. N. A..... to... 11 13	lt., j. g., 2 bat. N. M........ 5 july 16 accepted......10 july 16	Ill. 24 july 90

NAVAL MILITIA — SECOND BATTALION — (Continued)

Name, Grade, Date of Rank and Highest Brevet Rank	Division	Service		Born
		In the Army or Navy of the United States or of Foreign States	In the National Guard or Naval Militia	
LIEUTENANT, JUNIOR GRADE				
Engineering duties only				
O'Connell, William J., 23 jun. 16	6	....	seaman, oiler, chief machinist's mate, 5 div. 2 bat.....28 may 06 to 2 jul. 13 eng. ensign, 2 bat..........2 jul. 13 lt.............23 june 16 accepted......26 june 16	N. J. 29 jun. 88
ENSIGNS				
Line duties only				
Van Auken, Frank E., 30 apr. 13	4	....	seaman, 2 bat...7 apr. 03 to 20 sep. 04 seaman, 2 bat. chief qm......6 aug. 06 to 30 apr. 13 ensign, 2 bat....30 apr. 13 accepted......30 apr. 13	N. Y. 17 feb. 86
Sesselberg, Arthur W., 26 may 13	1	....	seaman, gun cap., 2 class, boatswain's mate, 1 class, 1 div. 2 bat.........31 mar. 06 to 26 may 13 ensign, 2 bat....26 may 13 accepted......28 may 13	N. Y. 11 jul. 88
Eaton, J. Walker, 5 feb. 15	3	....	seaman, gun cap. 2 class, gun cap. 1 class, gunner's mate, 1 class, 2 bat..3 may 02 hon. dis........26 may 09 seaman, boatswain's mate, 3 div. 2 bat...21 oct. 14 to 5 feb. 15 ensign..........5 feb. 15 accepted......9 feb. 15	N. Y. 20 jan. 79
Sammis, Harold Tower, 11 feb. 15	2	....	seaman, qm. 1 class, 2 div. 2 bat., trs......22 oct. 06 to 11 feb. 15 ensign........11 feb. 15 accepted......23 feb. 15	N. Y. 22 jan. 88
Fisher, Milton Marshall, 16 june 16	3	....	seaman, gunner's mate, 2 cl. gunner's mate, 1 cl. 2 bat.........30 apr. 03 hon. dis........17 apr. 09 seaman, 1 div. 2 bat.........15 apr. 16 ensign..........16 jun. 16 accepted......19 june 16	N. Y. 2 aug. 84

15

NAVAL MILITIA — SECOND BATTALION — (Concluded)

NAME, GRADE, DATE OF RANK AND HIGHEST BREVET RANK	Division	SERVICE		Born
		In the Army or Navy of The United States or of Foreign States	In the National Guard or Naval Militia	
ENSIGNS — Continued Line duties only				
Scanlon, Philip Malone. 23 june 16	1	....	seaman, gun- ner's mate, 2 cl. boat- swain's mate, 1 cl.......... 8 apr. 09 to 23 june 16 ensign.........23 june 16 accepted......26 june 16	N. Y. 9 dec. 91
MacCullum, Clarence, 5 july 16	2	....	seaman, 2 bat...15 oct. 05 to 1 nov. 09 seaman, 2 bat... 1 dec. 15 ensign, 2 bat.... 5 july 16 accepted....... 5 july 16	N. Y. 12 may
Davoren, James Henry, 10 july 16	7	....	seaman, gun cap. 2 cl. boat- swain's mate, 1 cl. 2 bat.....17 mar. 08 to 10 july 16 ensign.........10 july 16 accepted........13 july 16	N. Y. 2 mar. 87
Sweeny, Raymond M., 10 july 16	7	....	seaman, 1 div. 2 bat., gun cap., boatswain's mate........— may 08 hon. dis........—nov. 13 ensign, 2 bat....10 july 16 accepted.......13 july 16	N. Y. 1 may 86
ENSIGNS Engineering duties only.				
Arkebauer, Jesse Oliver, 24 may 15	5	U. S. asst. insp.. 7 july 07 U. S. Marine, license.	ensign, eng. 2 bat..........24 may 15 accepted......27 may 15	Ill. Sep. 71
ENSIGNS Aeronautic duties only.				
Astor, William Vincent, 11 may 16	aero.	....	seaman, 2 bat.... 1 may 16 ensign, 2 bat....11 may 16 accepted.......13 may 16	N. Y. 15 nov. 91
Pierce, Samuel Stillman, 13 may 16	aero.	....	corp. co. I, 6 regt. inf. Mass. vol. mil., —— 12 to —— 13 seaman, 2 bat. N. M........ 1 may 16 ensign, 2 bat. N. M........13 may 16 accepted......15 may 16	Mass. 23 jan. 84
MARINE CORPS BRANCH SECOND LIEUTENANT				
Rorke, James Francis, 5 may 16	mar.	....	pvt. 13 C. D. C.— oct. 97 pvt. co. D, 23 inf., corp., sgt., 1 sgt.....20 nov. 99 hon. dis........14 dec. 14 re-enlisted......14 dec. 14 2 lieut. 2 bat. N. M........ 8 may 16 accepted....... 8 may 16	N. Y. 21 dec. 78

NAVAL MILITIA — THIRD BATTALION

State Armory, Main Street, East, Rochester; Boathouse, Charlotte

September 29, 1891, the Second Separate Battery, Naval Reserve Artillery, was mustered in the service of the State in the City of Rochester. Its designation was changed on June 25, 1892, to Second Separate Naval Division, which designation was again changed on October 16, 1900, to Second Separate Division, Naval Militia.

This Division performed duty for the United States during the Spanish-American War in the U. S. Navy, and in the U. S. Auxiliary Naval Force aboard the " Franklin " and other vessels.

July 27, 1907, the Third Separate Division, Naval Militia, was mustered in the service of the State in the City of Buffalo.

January 25, 1910, a separate signal division was organised in the city of Rochester, and on February 14, 1910, the Third Battalion, Naval Militia, was formed of the Second and Third Separate Divisions, and the separate Signal Division, above mentioned, with headquarters in the State armory in the city of Rochester. On June 1, 1912, the First Division was mustered in at Dunkirk, N. Y. The Fourth Division was mustered in at Watertown, N. Y., June 18, 1913. A separate engineer division, designated the Seventh Division, was mustered in May 12, 1914. The Signal Division is changed to a Line Division by S. O. 138, July 22, 1915. The Eighth Division was mustered into the service at Niagara Falls, N. Y., May 4, 1916. The Ninth Division was mustered into the service at Oswego, N. Y., November 15, 1916.

Name, Grade, Date of Rank and Highest Brevet Rank	Division	SERVICE		Born
		In the Army or Navy of the United States or of Foreign States	In the National Guard or Naval Militia	
CAPTAIN Walbridge, Edward Newton, 11 may 16	....	ensign, U. S. N..18 jul. 98 to 12 oct. 98	seaman, 2 sep. naval div.....21 sep. 91 to 23 nov. 91 lt..............23 nov. 91 lt. com'dr 3 bat.. 4 mar. 10 com'dr........14 oct. 12 captain.........11 may 16 accepted.......13 may 16	N. Y. 11 oct. 59
EXECUTIVE OFFICER COMMANDER Graham, William James, 15 june 16	....	pvt., sgt. co. H, 3 inf............. 1 may 98 to 17 may 98 1 lt. 201 inf....21 jul. 98 to 15 oct. 98	pvt. 1 sep. co. N. G. N. Y.....19 may 90 hon. dis........ 2 jan. 99 ensign, 2 sep. div. N. M........ 9 jul. 01 lt. j. g.........17 mar. 03 aide staff of cap. com. N. M. lt. j. g. with o. r.. 3 feb. 08 lt. aide staff of com'dr...... 4 mar. 10 lt. 3 bat........ 1 apr. 10 lt. com'dr ex. off. 9 dec. 12 com'der, ex. off..15 jun. 16 accepted.......16 jun. 16	N. Y. 22 jul. 68
FIRST LIEUTENANT LIEUTENANT COMMANDER Harris, Thomas William, 19 may 16		....	lt. j. g. 3 sep. div. 8 aug. 07 lt. 3 bat........ 7 jun. 10 navigating lt....14 oct. 12 lt. com'dr, 1 lt...19 may 16 accepted.......21 may 16	N. Y. 9 jul. 77
NAVIGATOR LIEUTENANT COMMANDER Hesselman, Leo William, 19 may 16	....	yeoman 2 class U. S. N., 30 apr. 98 to 23 nov. 98	seaman, 2 div. Chicago Crew Ill. N. M.....24 may 97 hon. dis........12 jan. 99 seaman 3 div. 1 bat. N. M. N. Y.........21 jul. 06 to 8 aug. 07 ensign, 3 sep. div. 8 aug. 07 lt. j. g. 3 bat....22 jul. 10 lt. o. o. 3 bat....26 dec. 11 lt. 3 bat........21 oct. 12 lt. o. o.........21 oct. 12 lt. com'dr nav'r..19 may 16 accepted.......22 may 16,	Ger. 27 feb. 79

NAVAL MILITIA — THIRD BATTALION — (Continued)

Name, Grade, Date of Rank and Highest Brevet Rank	Division	Service		Born
		In the Army or Navy of the United States or of Foreign States	In the National Guard or Naval Militia	
GUNNERY OFFICER				
LIEUTENANT COMMANDER				
Ulrich, Charles Francis, 15 jun. 16	3	Naval service, —, 91, re-enlisted....... 8 jun. 96 graduate gunnery school, — feb. 98 gunner, chief gunner, 11 mar. 02 to — mar. 08 retired, physical disability, — feb. 10	lt. c. o. 3 bat... 9 apr. 12 lt. com'dr, gun-nery officer... 15 jun. 16 accepted.......20 jun. 16	N. Y. 23 apr. 75
SURGEON				
LIEUTENANT COMMANDER				
Herriman, Wallace John, 15 jun. 16		....	seaman, 2 sep. naval div.....29 sep. 91 to 21 nov. 92 asst. surg. ensign 21 nov. 92 asst. surg. lt. j. g. 2 apr. 98 suspn. and reas-signed........ 7 may 08 surg., lt. com'dr..15 jun. 16 accepted......19 jun. 16	N. Y. 5 feb. 56
ASSISTANT SURGEONS				
LIEUTENANTS, JUNIOR GRADE				
Richards, Charles Howard, 5 jun. 12		....	asst. surg. 3 bat. lt. j. g........ 5 jun. 12 accepted....... 8 jun. 12	Pa. 10 feb. 68
Barnette, Maurice D., 16 dec. 15		....	asst. surg. 3 bat., lt. j. g........16 dec. 15 accepted.......21 dec. 15	N. Y. 29 aug. 87
Jayne, Luther Marshall, 15 jun. 16		....	asst. surg. 3 bat., lt. j. g........15 jun. 16 accepted.......20 jun. 16	Can. 6 jun. 83
Elder, Grover Cleveland, 23 dec. 16		....	asst. surg. 3 bat., lt. j. g........23 dec. 16 accepted.......28 dec. 16	N. Y. 15 oct. 84
PAYMASTER				
LIEUTENANT COMMANDER				
Zimmer, William Bernard, 15 jun. 16		seaman, 2 sep. naval div., 12 jul. 98 to — mar. 99	seaman, 2 sep. naval div.....30 mar. 97 to 13 jan. 08 paymaster, 3 bat. lt...........20 apr. 10 paymaster, lt. com'dr.......15 jun. 16 accepted.......21 jun. 16	N. Y. 6 apr. 78
ASSISTANT PAYMASTER				
LIEUTENANT, JUNIOR GRADE				
Plumley, Albert Walter, 9 apr. 13		....	seaman, 3 div. 3 bat..........10 jun. 12 to 9 apr. 13 asst. paymaster, 3 bat., lt. j. g. 9 apr. 13 accepted.......11 apr. 13	N. Y. 6 oct. 76

NAVAL MILITIA — THIRD BATTALION — (Continued)

Name, Grade, Date of Rank and Highest Brevet Rank	Division	Service — In the Army or Navy of the United States or of Foreign States	Service — In the National Guard or Naval Militia	Born
LIEUTENANTS Line duties only. Lyon, Harry Benjamin, 30 jun. 14	1	....	pvt. 43 sep. co. N. G. N. Y... 2 jan. 94 to 16 nov. 94 22 jun. 95 to 4 may 96 lt. j. g. 3 bat. N. M..........4 jun. 12 lt...........29 jun. 14 accepted.....30 jun. 14	N. Y. 15 mar 73
Angley, Harrison John, 28 may 15	4	....	pvt. co. C, 1 inf..24 mar. 06 to 23 sep. 98 lt. j. g. 3 bat. N. M..........27 aug. 13 lt...........28 may 15 accepted...... 1 jun. 15	N. Y. 12 dec. 74
Zimmer, Edward George, 1 dec. 15	6	....	seaman, 6 div. 3 bat..........4 aug. 11 to 3 apr. 12 ensign, 3 bat....3 apr. 12 lt...........1 dec. 15 accepted......2 dec. 15	N. Y. 18 feb. 81
LIEUTENANTS Engineering duties only Brock, Arthur Edgar, 16 feb. 16	5	....	electrician, 1 chief machinist's mate, Mich. N. M..—— 1909 to —— 1912 fireman, 2 class, acting chief electrician, 5 div. 3 bat.....29 nov. 11 to jun. 15 ensign..........4 jun. 15 lt.............16 feb. 16 accepted......17 feb. 16	Ont. 14 feb. 79
DeWolf, Roger Dennison, 16 feb. 16	7	....	pvt. tr. H, 1 cav.29 apr. 12 to 9 apr. 13 eng. ensign, 3 bat. 9 apr. 13 lt.............16 feb. 16 accepted......21 feb. 16	Ohio. 23 apr. 79
LIEUTENANTS, JUNIOR GRADE Line duties only. Maytham, Frank, 4 jun. 15	3	....	seaman, gun cap. 2 class, 3 div. 3 bat.........9 may 10 to 10 jan. 11 ensign, 3 bat....10 jan. 11 lt. j. g........4 jun. 15 accepted......7 jun. 15	N. Y. 31 mar. 73
Bailey, Frank Joel, 24 feb. 14	3	....	seaman, 3 sep. div.........27 jul. 09 to 18 sep. 09 ensign........18 sep. 09 lt. j. g........24 feb. 14 accepted......26 feb. 14	N. Y. 22 nov. 74
Johnstone, Edward James, 21 jun. 15	4	....	ensign, 3 bat....27 aug. 13 lt. j. g........21 jun. 15 accepted......23 jun. 15	N. Y. 14 jan. 84
Alexander, Henry Hermon, 23 dec. 16	9	....	lt. j. g. 3 bat., N. M........23 dec. 16 accepted......26 dec. 16	N. Y. 24 oct. 82

NAVAL MILITIA — THIRD BATTALION — (Concluded)

Name, Grade, Date of Rank and Highest Brevet Rank	Division	Service		Born
		In the Army or Navy of the United States or of Foreign States	In the National Guard or Naval Militia	
LIEUTENANTS, JUNIOR GRADE Engineering duties only.				
Howe, Henry Lawrence, Jr., 15 jun. 16	7	....	ensign as eng. off. 3 bat......... 9 apr. 13 lt. j. g., 3 bat....15 jun. 16 accepted......16 jun. 16	N. Y. 22 oct. 87
ENSIGNS Line duties only.				
Reynolds, Alfred Smith, 4 may 10	2	....	seaman, mus., gun cap. 2 class, 1 class, 2 sep. div......19 sep. 99 to 18 may 10 ensign, 3 bat....18 may 10 accepted......24 may 10	Ont. 30 dec. 77
O'Neil, Stephen Joseph, 4 may 10	2	....	seaman, gun cap. 1 class, 2 sep. div.........11 feb. 02 to 18 may 10 ensign, 3 bat....18 may 10 accepted......20 may 10	N. Y. 21 oct. 81
Dangel, Louis Henry, 27 aug. 13	4	....	pvt., corp., sgt., 89 sep. co. N. G. N. Y...... 1 dec. 96 to 30 nov. 04 2 lt............30 nov. 04 1 lt............28 sep. 05 cap............22 jul. 10 hon. dis.......12 jan. 12 ensign, 3 bat. N. M............27 aug. 13 accepted......30 aug. 13	N. Y. 9 apr. 78
Heyl, Louis, 16 feb. 15	1	....	seaman, 1 div. 3 bat.......... 1 jun. 12 to 16 feb. 15 ensign........16 feb. 15 accepted......19 feb. 15	N. Y. 22 jun. 81
Russell, Christopher Augur, 15 jun. 16	8	midshipman, U. S. N., 25 sep. 02 resigned........20 feb. 06	ensign, 3 bat., N. M........15 jun. 16 accepted......21 jun. 16	Tex. 29 jun. 83
McWhirk, Warren Ellsworth, 16 jun. 16	8	....	landsman, 8 div. 3 bat.........16 jun. 16 ensign........16 jun. 16 accepted......17 jun. 16	Mass. 17 jun. 86
Herrick, Francis Henry, 22 dec. 16	4	....	ensign.........22 dec. 16 accepted......26 dec. 16	N. Y. 21 jan. 75
Mott, Elliott Wheeler, 22 dec. 16	9	....	seaman, 9 div. 3 bat., N. M....15 nov. 16 ensign.........22 dec. 16 accepted........27 dec. 16	N. Y. 20 may 87
Walbridge, Arthur Hess, 23 dec. 16	6	....	ensign.........23 dec. 16 accepted.......26 dec. 16	N. Y. 26 aug. 89
Watson, Frank Thomas, 23 dec. 16	9	....	pvt. co. D, 3 inf. sgt............24 feb. 03 hon. dis........19 july 09 ensign.........23 dec. 16 accepted......26 dec. 16	N. Y. 15 dec. 84

RELATIVE RANK OF OFFICERS IN ACTIVE SERVICE IN THE NAVAL MILITIA

No.	NAME AND DATE OF RANK	Organization
	Commodore	
1	Robert Pierpont Forshew, June 24, 1911..........	Commanding Naval Militia.
	Captains	
1	Alfred Brooks Fry, Mar. 27, 1916................	Chief of Staff, Naval Militia.
2	Charles Longstreed Poor, Mar. 27, 1917..........	1st Battalion.
3	Edward Thomas Fitzgerald, May 11, 1916.........	2d Battalion.
4	Edward Newton Walbridge, May 11, 1916.........	3d Battalion.
	Commanders	
1	William Bell Wait, Jr., April 1, 1916.............	Executive Officer, 1st Battalion.
2	Arthur I. Perry, June 10, 1916..................	Executive Officer, 2d Battalion.
3	William James Graham, June 15, 1916...........	Executive Officer, 3d Battalion.
	Lieutenant Commanders	
1	Eckford Craven de Kay, Feb. 25, 1911.....	Navigator and Signal Officer, Naval Militia.
2	Herbert Waldo York, Sept. 20, 1911.............	Gunnery Officer, Naval Militia.
3	Warren Lockhart Sawyer, June 19, 1912..........	Judge-Advocate, Naval Militia.
4	Roland Rogers Riggs, April 1, 1916..............	Navigator, 1st Battalion.
5	Charles Boone, April 1, 1916....................	Engineer Officer, 1st Battalion.
6	Jasper Thomas Kane, April 1, 1916..............	Engineer Officer, 2d Battalion.
7	Earle Farwell, April 3, 1916....................	Gunnery Officer, 1st Battalion.
8	Thomas William Harris, May 19, 1916...........	1st Lieutenant, 3d Battalion.
9	Frank Ross Lackey, May 19, 1916...............	1st Lieutenant, 2d Battalion.
10	Leo William Hesselman, May 19, 1916...........	Navigator, 3d Battalion.
11	Theodore Nelson, June 10, 1916.................	Navigator, 2d Battalion.
12	Charles Francis Ulrich, June 15, 1916............	Gunnery Officer, 3d Battalion.
13	Leon Dickinson, Dec. 28, 1916..................	Gunnery Officer, 2d Battalion.
	Surgeons — *Lieutenant Commander*	
1	John Cowell MacEvitt, Sept. 14, 1908...........	Naval Militia.
2	Cleveland Cady Kimball, April 3, 1916...........	1st Battalion.
3	Thomas Aloysius Lynch, June 10, 1916..........	2d Battalion.
4	Wallace John Herriman, June 15, 1916..........	3d Battalion.
	Passed Assistant Surgeons — *Lieutenants*	
1	John Joseph Maria Carey, July 6, 1916..........	2d Battalion.
2	Ferdinand Montgomery Smith, Dec. 13, 1916......	1st Battalion.
	Assistant Surgeons — *Lieutenants, junior grade*	
1	Charles Howard Richards, June 5, 1912..........	3d Battalion.
2	Maurice D. Barnette, Dec. 16, 1915.............	3d Battalion.
3	Luther Marshall Jayne, June 15, 1916...........	3d Battalion.
4	Harold Nexsen, July 10, 1916..................	2d Battalion.
5	Clifford Harry Fulton, Sept. 29, 1916...........	1st Battalion.
6	Grover Cleveland Elder, Dec. 23, 1916..........	3d Battalion.
	Paymasters — *Lieutenant Commander*	
1	William Henry Boyd, April 3, 1916..............	1st Battalion.
2	Charles Payne Crissey, June 10, 1916............	2d Battalion.
3	William Bernard Zimmer, June 15, 1916..........	3d Battalion.
	Passed Assistant Paymasters — *Lieutenant*	
1	Howland Haggerty Pell, Sept. 29, 1916...........	1st Battalion.
	Assistant Paymasters — *Ensigns*	
1	Albert Walter Plumley, April 9, 1913.............	3d Battalion.
2	Frank John Welsh, Jr., Dec. 18, 1916.............	2d Battalion.

RELATIVE RANK OF OFFICERS IN ACTIVE SERVICE IN THE NAVAL MILITIA — (Concluded)

No.	NAME AND DATE OF RANK	Organization
	Lieutenants	
1	Walter Bensel, April 21, 1910....................	1st Battalion.
2	Lemuel Edson Raff, November 1, 1910............	1st Battalion.
3	William Lewis Mallon, September 17, 1912.......	1st Battalion.
4	Randolph Halliday Nexsen, July 2, 1913..........	2d Battalion.
5	Harry Benjamin Lyon, June 29, 1914............	3d Battalion.
6	Clarence Ambrose Moore, March 29, 1915.........	1st Battalion.
7	....	1st Battalion.
8	....	3d Battalion.
9	5........	3d Battalion.
10	....	3d Battalion.
11	1916......	3d Battalion.
12	....	2d Battalion.
13	Charles Edwin Finken, June 16, 1916............	2d Battalion.
14	Luther Hamilton Holton, June 16, 1916..........	2d Battalion.
15	Lee Hurdman Harris, June 23, 1916.............	1st Battalion.
16	Walter John Willis, June 23, 1916..............	1st Battalion.
17	Richard Condon, July 5, 1916...................	1st Battalion.
	Lieutenants, junior grade	
1	Henry Tilton Williams, February 7, 1912.........	1st Battalion.
2	Augustus MacCollom, Jr., June 19, 1912.........	1st Battalion.
3	Frank Joel Bailey, February 24, 1914...........	3d Battalion.
4	Arthur Moore, March 29, 1915.................	2d Battalion.
5	Berkeley Searls Ketcham, May 24, 1915.........	1st Battalion.
6	Frank Maytham, June 4, 1915.................	3d Battalion.
7	Charles Alonzo Mason, June 21, 1915...........	1st Battalion.
8	Edward James Johnstone, June 21, 1915.........	3d Battalion.
9	Henry Lawrence Howe, Jr., June 15, 1916........	3d Battalion.
10	William J. O'Connell, June 23, 1916............	2d Battalion.
11	Hobart Cole Ramsey, July 5, 1916..............	2d Battalion.
12	Henry Biglow Oatley, December 23, 1916.........	1st Battalion.
13	Henry Hermon Alexander, December 23, 1916.....	3d Battalion.
	Ensigns	
1	Alfred Smith Reynolds, May 4, 1910.............	3d Battalion.
2	Stephen Joseph O'Neil, May 4, 1910.............	3d Battalion.
3	Albert James Kenyon, June 10, 1912............	1st Battalion.
4	Harold Washburn Browne, February 18, 1913......	1st Battalion.
5	Frank E. Van Auken, April 30, 1913............	2d Battalion.
6	Arthur W. Sesselberg, May 26, 1913............	2d Battalion.
7	Louis Henry Dangel, August 27, 1913...........	3d Battalion.
8	J. Walker Eaton, February 5, 1915.............	2d Battalion.
9	Harold Tower Sammis, February 11, 1915.........	2d Battalion.
10	Louis Heyl, February 16, 1915..................	3d Battalion.
11	Frederick Arthur Russell, March 29, 1915........	1st Battalion.
12	Jesse Oliver Arkebauer, May 24, 1915	2d Battalion.
13	Edward Joseph Dillon, Jr., June 5, 1915..........	1st Battalion.
14	John Robert Moore, Jr., June 5, 1915...........	1st Battalion.
15	Forrest E. Wysong, March 30, 1916.............	1st Battalion.
16	William Vincent Astor, May 11, 1916............	2d Battalion.
17	Samuel Stillman Pierce, May 13, 1916...........	2d Battalion.
18	Christopher Augur Russell, June 15, 1916	3d Battalion.
19	Warren Ellsworth McWhirk, June 16, 1916.......	3d Battalion.
20	Milton Marshall Fisher, June 16, 1916..........	2d Battalion.
21	Philip Malone Scanlon, June 23, 1916...........	2d Battalion.
22	Charles E. Ruttan, June 23, 1916.............	1st Battalion.
23	Clarence MacCullum, July 5, 1916..............	2d Battalion.
24	James Henry Davoren, July 10, 1916............	2d Battalion.
25	Raymond M. Sweeny, July 10, 1916............	2d Battalion.
26	Leo Jerome Murray, July 11, 1916..............	1st Battalion.
27	Robert Hartwell Moore, September 29, 1916......	1st Battalion.
28	Francis Henry Herrick, December 22, 1916.......	3d Battalion.
29	Elliott Wheeler Mott, December 22, 1916........	3d Battalion.
30	William Peet Quimby, December 22, 1916........	1st Battalion.
31	Arthur Hess Walbridge, December 23, 1916.......	3d Battalion.
32	Frank Thomas Watson, December 23, 1916........	3d Battalion.
	Marine Corps Branch — *Second Lieutenants*	
1	James Francis Rorke, May 5, 1916..............	2d Battalion.

RESERVE OFFICERS

NAVAL MILITIA

Captains

Herbert L. Satterlee, Naval Militia, March 16, 1916.

Commanders

William B. Franklin, 1st Battalion, September 9, 1915.
Kingsley L. Martin, 2d Battalion, May 2, 1916.

Lieutenant Commanders

James Macfarlane, Jr., 1st Battalion, October 6, 1910.
Robert S. Sloan, Naval Militia, April 1, 1916.

Assistant Surgeons

Amos O. Squire, 1st Battalion, December 26, 1916.

Lieutenants

Telfair M. Minton, 1st Battalion, December 21, 1914.
Bertrand F. Bell, 1st Battalion, January 2, 1915.
Francis W. Perry, 2d Battalion, June 23, 1915.
Henry R. Ford, 3d Battalion, August 9, 1915.
William J. Henderson, 1st Battalion, August 29, 1916.

Lieutenants, Junior Grade

William B. Penfold, Jr., 2d Battalion, August 5, 1915.
William B. Dunning, 1st Battalion, November 69, 1915.
Alexander Duane, 1st Battalion, October 8, 1915.
Clinton E. Braine, 1st Battalion, June 14, 1916.
Earl A. Averill, 1st Battalion, June 27, 1916.
Harry O. Reeves, 1st Battalion, June 29, 1916.
Harry R. Brown, 1st Battalion, December 2, 1916.

Ensigns

Frederick O. Denecke, 1st Battalion, March 29, 1915.
William E. Dickey, Naval Militia, March 22, 1916.
Robert E. Read, 3d Battalion, June 15, 1916.
Carl T. Forsberg, 1st Battalion, July 12, 1916.

RETIRED OFFICERS

NAVAL MILITIA

Commodores

Jacob W. Miller, Naval Militia, N. Y., June 24, 1911.

Captains

Russell Raynor, 1st Battalion, November 27, 1914.

Commanders

Robert James Beach, Naval Militia, July 11, 1911.
Louis M. Josephthal, Naval Militia, July 3, 1916.

Lieutenant Commanders

Aaron Vanderbilt, Naval Militia, October 27, 1903.
John G. Agar, Naval Militia, September 15, 1911.
Starr Taintor, 1st Battalion, March 16, 1914.

Lieutenants

Robert W. Candler, 1st Battalion, December 21, 1909.
Henry N. Fletcher, 1st Battalion, January 28, 1910.

Lieutenants, Junior Grade

Courtland Avery, 3d Battalion, March 11, 1912.

Ensigns

William Lewis Tompkins, 1st Battalion, August 31, 1904.

CASUALTIES

FULL AND HONORABLE DISCHARGE

Passed Assistant Surgeon

John F. W. Meagher, 2d Battalion, January 26, 1916.

Ensigns

Louis B. Altreuter, 2d Battalion, April 3, 1916.
Ainley D. Marsh, 1st Battalion, October 21, 1916.

HONORABLE DISCHARGE

Passed Assistant Surgeon

John L. Eckel, 3d Battalion, November 27, 1916.

DIED

Commander

Charles O. Brinkerhoff, January 5, 1916.

THE MILITARY ESTABLISHMENT OF THE STATE OF NEW YORK

CONSISTS OF THE

COMMANDER-IN-CHIEF AND STAFF

THE NATIONAL GUARD

WHICH CONSTITUTES A DIVISION CONSISTING OF

1 Major General.
5 Brigadier Generals.

The several Staff Departments and Corps.

4 Field Hospitals.
4 Ambulance Companies.
1 Battalion of Signal Corps of 2 Companies.
1 Corps of Engineers of 2 Battalions.
1 Regiment of Cavalry of 12 Troops.
1 Separate Squadron of Cavalry of 4 Troops.
1 Machine Gun Troop, Cavalry.
3 Regiments of Field Artillery of 6 Batteries each.
18 Regiments of Infantry of 12 Companies each.
1 Coast Artillery Corps of 35 Companies, organized into 3 Coast Defense Commands.

THE NAVAL MILITIA

WHICH CONSISTS OF

The Commodore Commanding and his Staff,

1 Battalion of 9 Divisions and 1 Aeronautic Section.
1 Battalion of 7 Divisions, 1 Aeronautic Section and 1 Marine Company.
1 Battalion of 9 Divisions.

NOTE.— The National Guard shall not be less than 10,000 nor more than 18,000 enlisted men in time of peace; in case of war, insurrection, invasion, or imminent danger thereof the Governor has the power to increase the force beyond 18,000 and organize it as the exigencies of the service may require.

The strength of the Naval Militia in time of peace is not to exceed 2,000 men. but in time of war, invasion, insurrection, or imminent danger thereof, the Governor has power to increase it beyond 2,000 enlisted men and organize it as the exigencies of the service may require.

NAVAL MILITIA
INDEX

ILLUSTRATIONS

———

Showing Personnel, Equipment, Instruction, Sanitation and
Various Significant Phases of the Activities of the National
Guard and the Naval Militia, at Camp Whitman,
at Sea, and at the Mexican Border.

GENERAL VIEW OF HEADQUARTERS AT CAMP WHITMAN

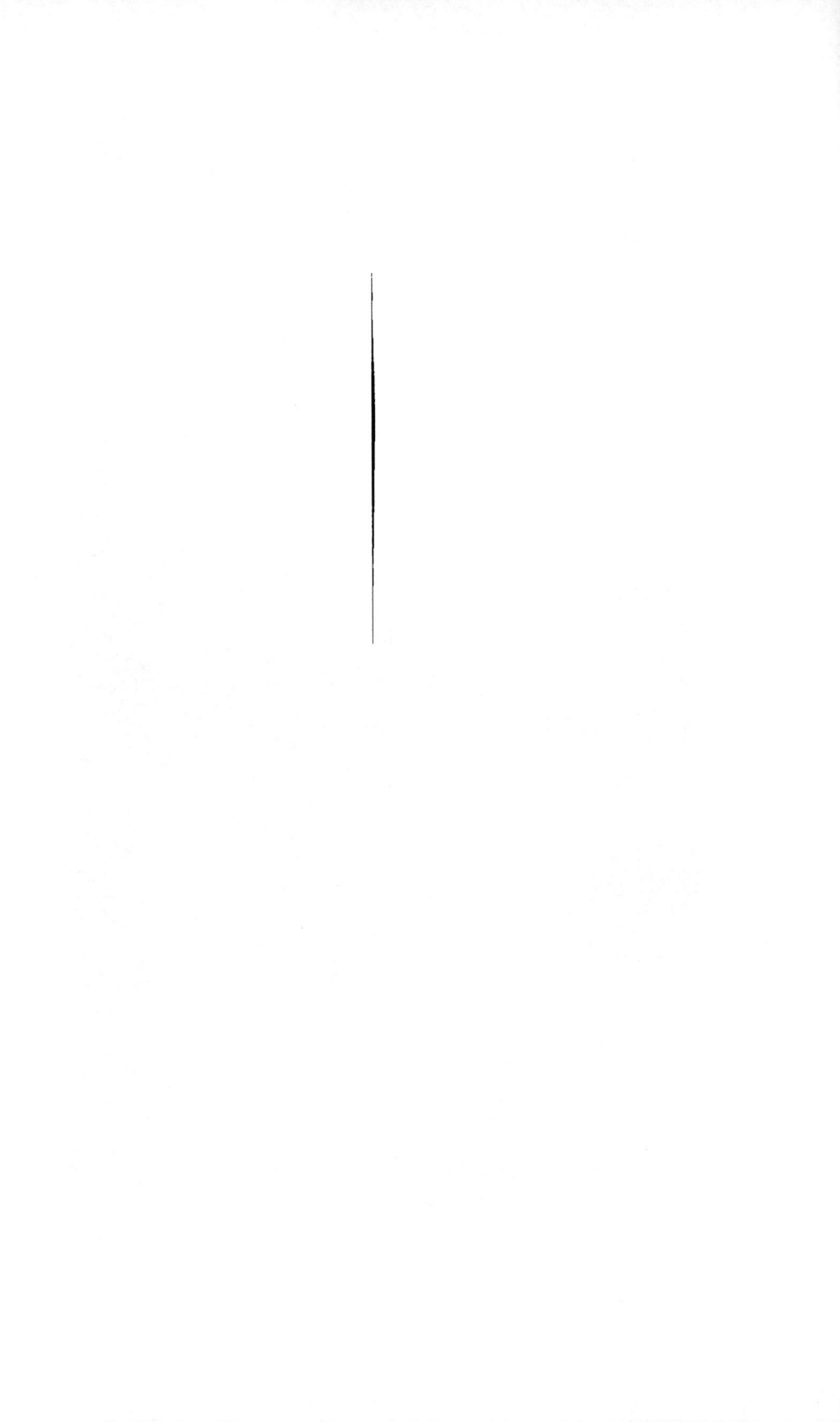

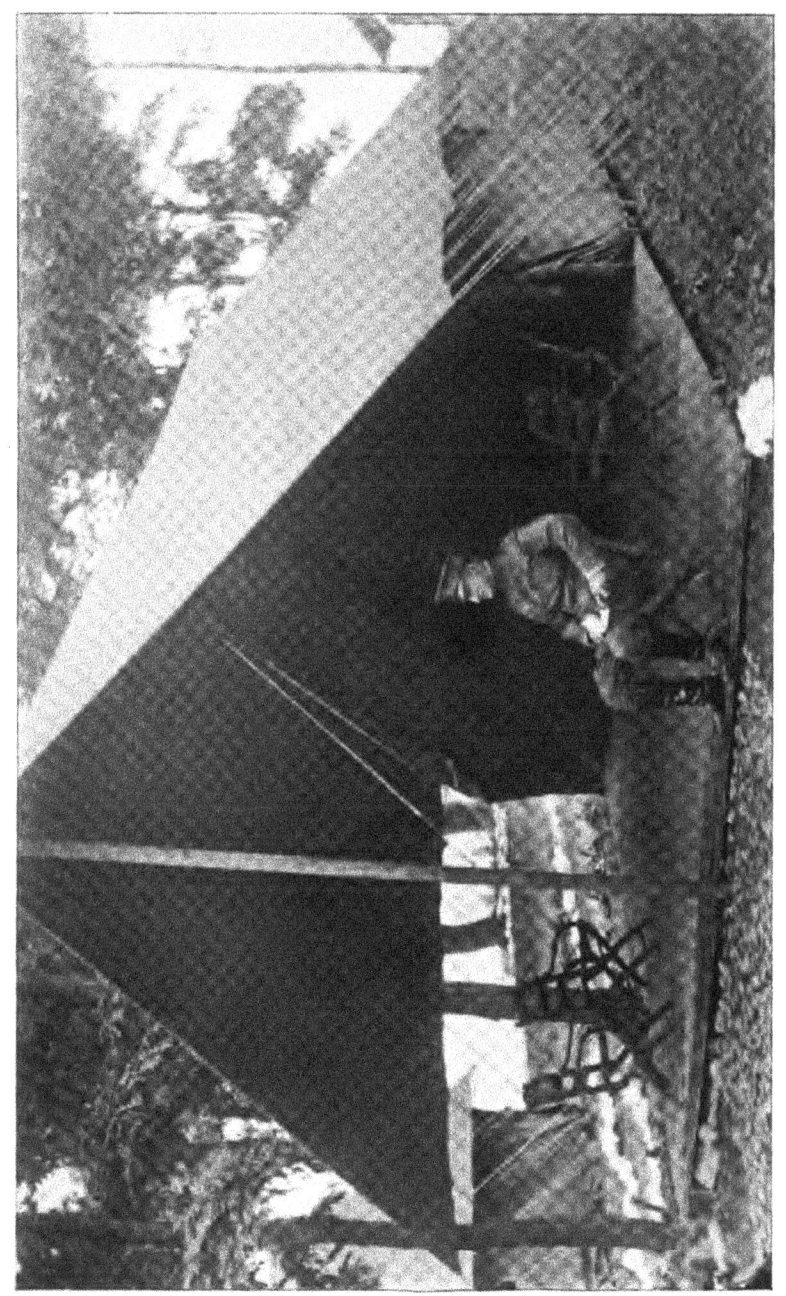

THE ADJUTANT-GENERAL AT HIS HEADQUARTERS

CAMP COMMANDER, BRIGADIER-GENERAL JOHN G. EDDY AND HIS STAFF

COLONEL DANIEL W. HAND AND OFFICERS OF THE 3D FIELD ARTILLERY

CAPT. G. V. SCHENCK, ADJUTANT, 10TH INFANTRY

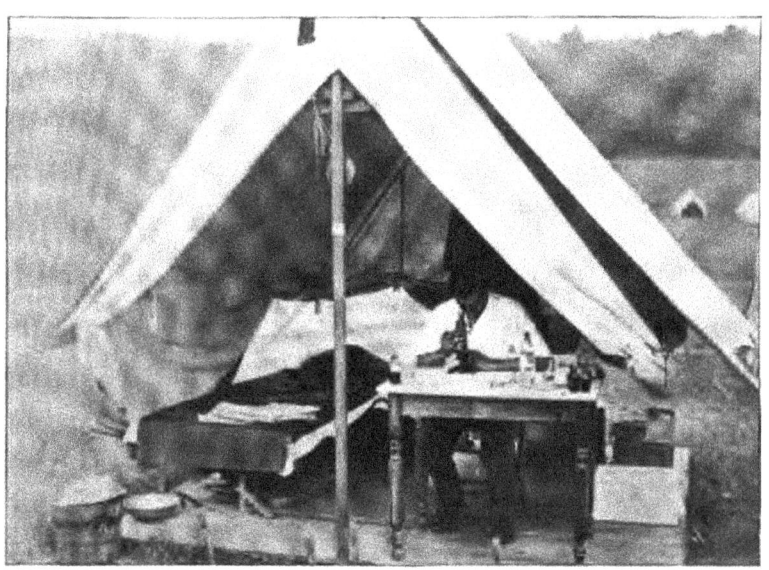

DR. HOWARD VAN WINKLE OF THE LABORATORY DIVISION, STATE BOARD
OF HEALTH, INVESTIGATING FAECES OF TROOPS

THE BAND OF THE 3D FIELD ARTILLERY, CAMP WHITMAN

The Veterinary Hospital, Camp Whitman

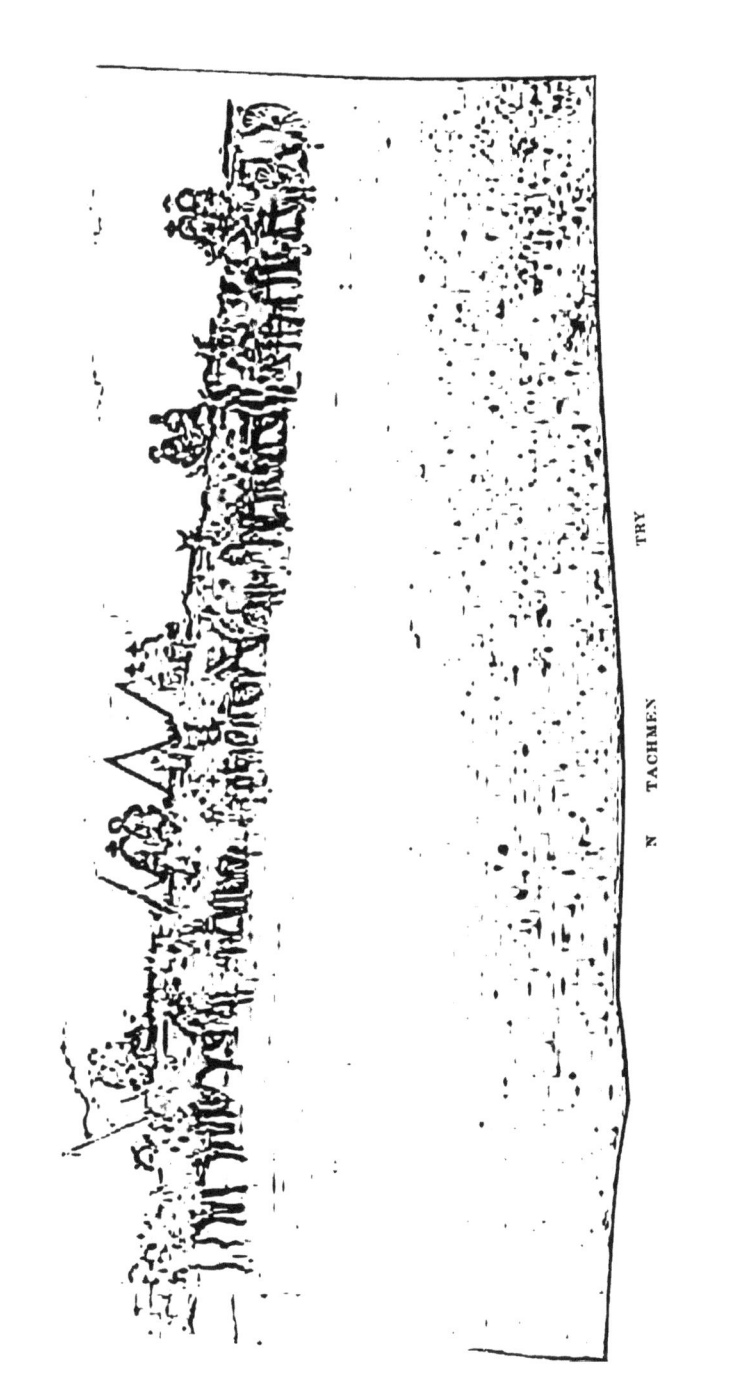

N TACHMEN   TRY

HORSES OF THE 3D FIELD ARTILLERY

HORSES OF THE 3D FIELD ARTILLERY

CAISSONS OF THE 3D FIELD ARTILLERY

ONE OF THE 4.7 HOWITZERS OF THE 3D FIELD ARTILLERY

EXAMINATION OF TROOPS FOR MUST   CAMP WHITMAN

PORTION OF THE 3D FIELD ARTILLERY CAMP, SHOWING TENTS FURLED TO EXPOSE GROUND TO THE CLEANSING EFFECT OF THE SUN'S RAYS. CAMP WHITMAN

3D FIELD HOSPITAL, CAMP WHITMAN

A MODEL COMPANY COOK TENT, WITH REST AND DINING TABLE,
CAMP WHITMAN

LATRINES EXPOSED TO THE SUN AFTER THOROUGH CLEANSING AND FILLING OF THE TRENCHES. NO ODOR OR FOULING WAS NOTED TEN DAYS AFTER THE ABANDONMENT OF THE CAMP

WINNOWING AND BURNING OF HORSE MANURE FOR THE CHEAP AND EFFECTIVE PREVENTION OF FLY-BREEDING AND THE GENERATION OF MALODOR

PRIMITIVE BUT EFFECTIVE SCREEN FOR COMPANY LATRINE, WHICH IS BEING BURNED OUT

WHITMAN INCINERATOR; ALSO A SIMPLE BUT USEFUL HOT-WATER PLANT.

A New York Naval Militia Hydroaeroplane at Bay Shore Station, L. I.

MEMBERS OF THE NAVAL MILITIA AT INSTRUCTION

The Whitman Incinerator in Operation. This was Found to be the Most Satisfactory Method for the Safe Disposal of Liquid Garbage and the Most Satisfactory from Among Many Experimental Types. It was Designed by the Machine-Gun Company, 10th Infantry, N. G., N. Y.

Hydroaeroplane Station at Bay Shore, L. I.

TYPE OF HYDROAEROPLANE IN USE BY THE N. Y. N. M.

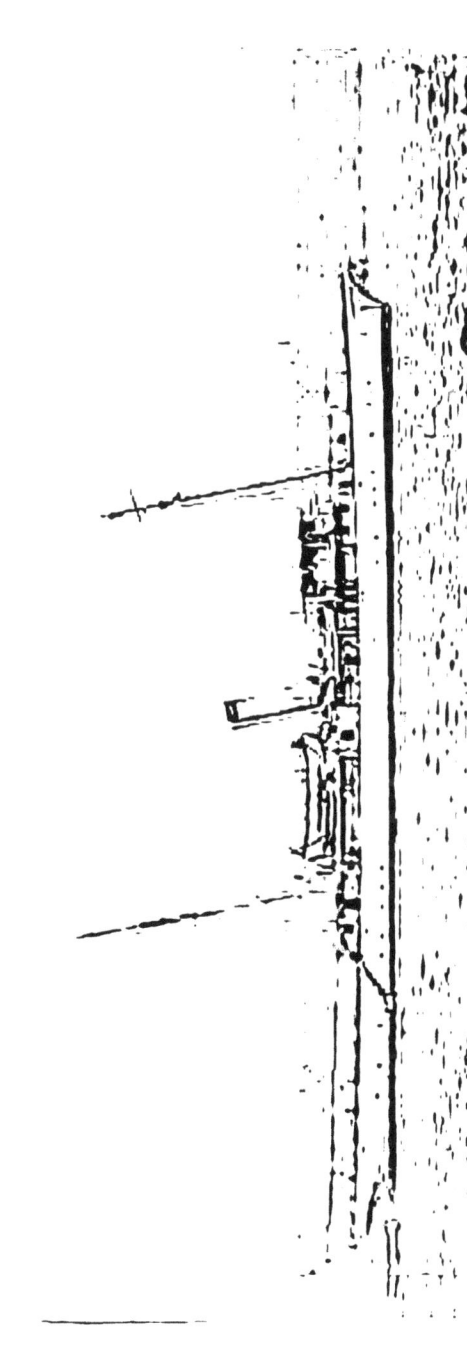

U. S. S. WASP. USED BY THE 1st BATTALION FOR CRUISING AND TARGET PRACTICE

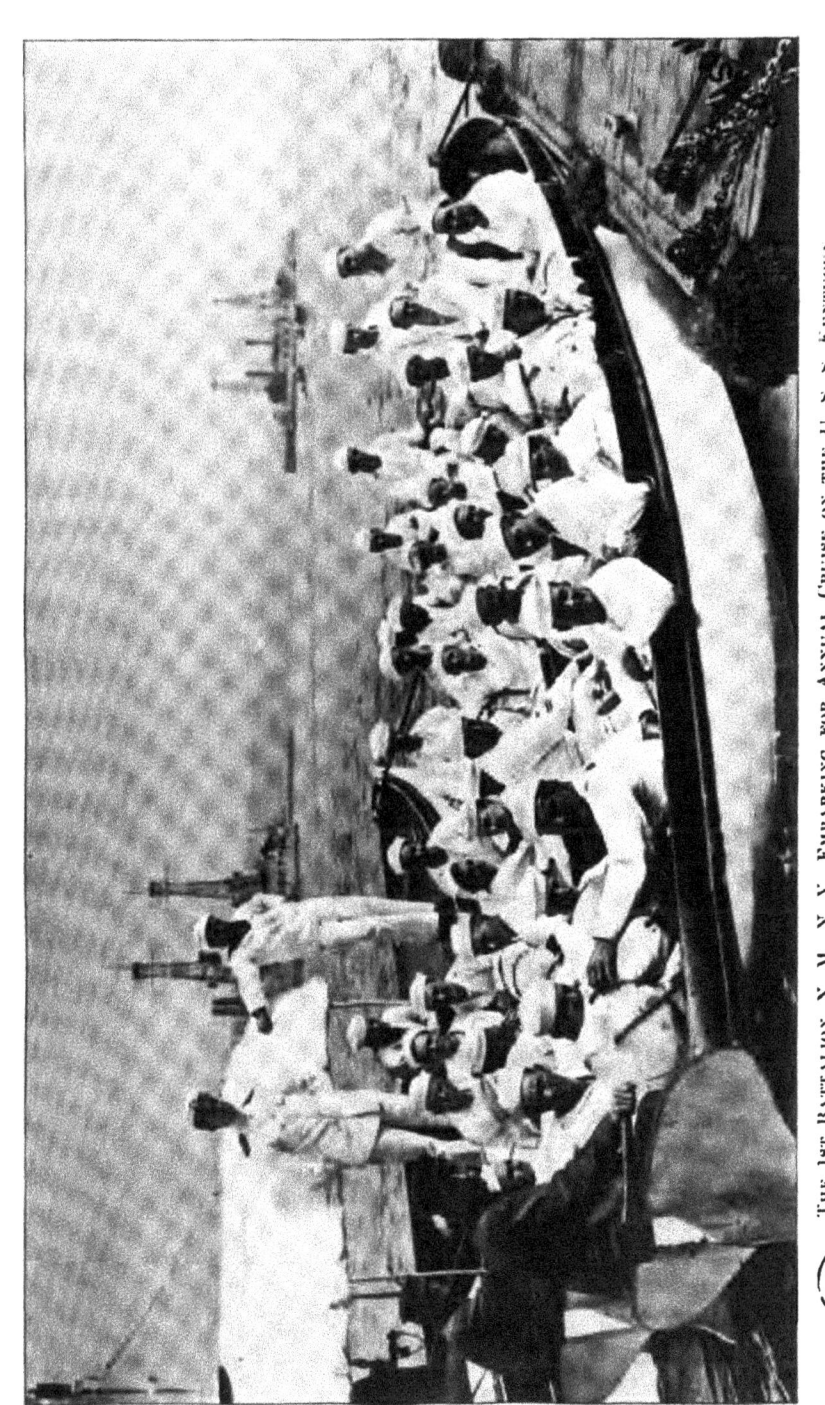

The 1st Battalion, N. M., N. Y., Embarking for Annual Cruise on the U. S. S. Kentucky

GATLING-GUN CREW, 1ST BATTALION, ON GUARD DUTY ON A PIER-HEAD

1ST BATTALION RETURNING TO ITS ARMORY, U. S. S. GRANITE STATE   :

1st Battalion Stowing Bags and Hammocks for Transportation

U. S. S. Granite State, Armory of the 1st Battalion, N. M., N. Y.

TARGET PRACTICE OF THE FIRST BATTALION   WITH 3-POUNDERS AT GARDINER'S BAY, 1916

The New 10th Division of the 1st Battalion, N. M. N. Y., at Yonkers

OFFICERS OF THE 69TH NEW YORK INFANTRY AT MCALLEN, TEXAS

A TYPICAL COMPANY OF THE 7TH NEW YORK INFANTRY AT MCALLEN, TEXAS

COMPANY OF THE 22D NEW YORK ENGINEERS AT DRILL, MCALLEN, TEXAS

A TYPICAL COMPANY, 23D NEW YORK INFANTRY, AT PHARR, TEXAS

Bridge Constructed by the 22d New York Engineers at Peñitas, Texas

3D AMBULANCE COMPANY, McALLEN, TEXAS

KITCHEN, CO. I, 69TH NEW YORK INFANTRY

OPPOSITE VIEW OF THE SAME

TYPES OF NEW YORK CAVALRYMEN IN TEXAS

BIVOUAC OF A TROOP OF SQUADRON A ON THE MARCH, TEXAS

22D New York Engineers Constructing a Ponton Bridge at Peñitas, Texas

INDEX TO SENATE DOCUMENTS, 1917

3